TATEN DES LICHTS
MACK & GOETHE

»Des echten Künstlers Lehre schließt den Sinn auf;
denn wo die Worte fehlen, spricht die That.«

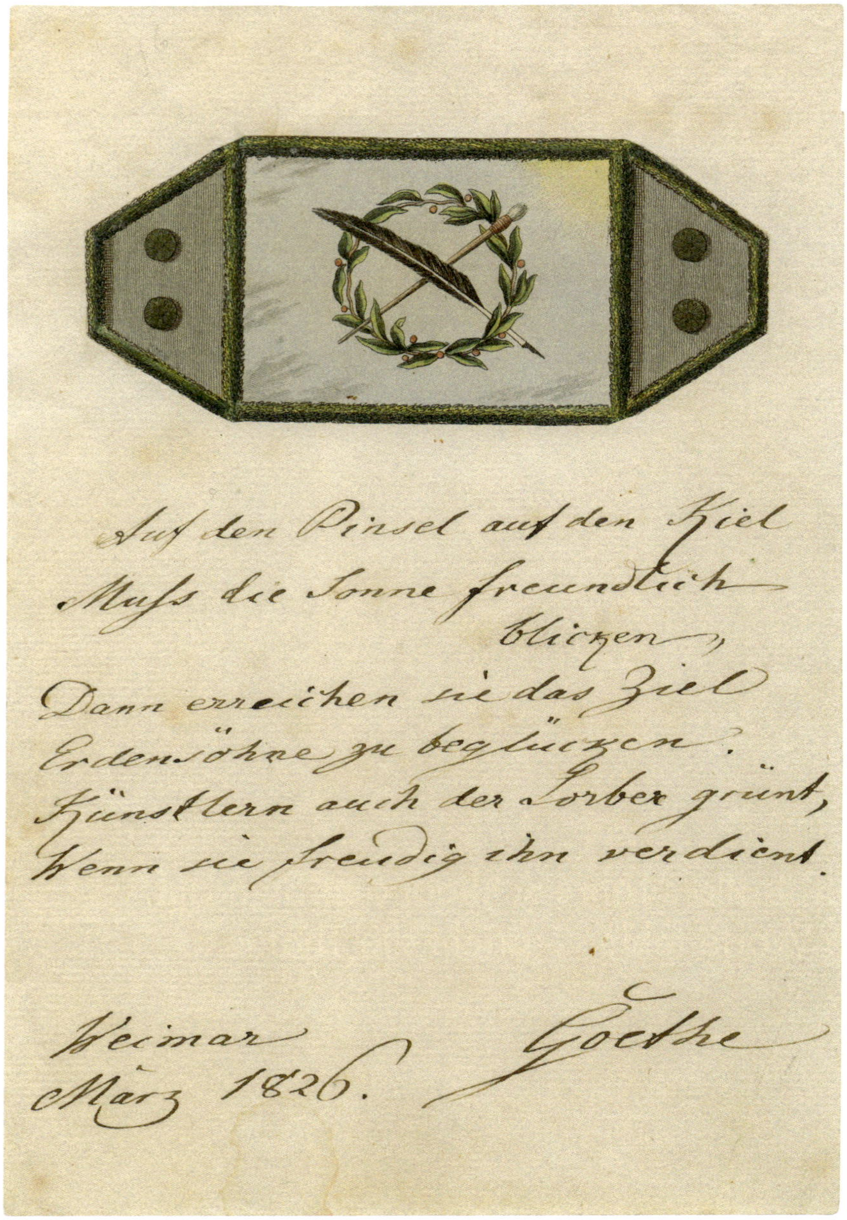
Auf den Pinsel auf den Kiel
Muss die Sonne freundlich
blicken,
Dann erreichen sie das Ziel
Erdensöhne zu beglücken.
Künstlern auch der Lorbeer grünt,
Wenn sie freudig ihn verdient.

Weimar
März 1826. Goethe

Johann Wolfgang von Goethe
Eigenhändige Reinschrift seines Gedichts:
»Auf den Pinsel auf den Kiel […]«
Signiert: »Goethe«
Datiert: »Weimar März 1826.«
Über dem Gedicht aufgeklebt ist ein
handkolorierter Kupferstich:
Pinsel und Feder im Lorbeerkranz,
von der Sonne beschienen
1 Blatt, 1 S. beschrieben
19,8 x 13,3 cm
Goethe-Museum Düsseldorf

Johann Wolfgang von Goethe
Clean copy in his own hand:
"On the brush and on the quill…"
Signed: "Goethe"
Dated: "Weimar März 1826."
Above the poem is a hand-colored
copper engraving:
Brush and quill in a laurel wreath
illuminated by the sun
1 sheet, 1 page written
19.8 x 13.3 cm
Goethe-Museum Düsseldorf

Die Vignette gehört zu einer Reihe von insgesamt acht symbolischen Motiven, die eine Serie von Gemälden en miniature wiedergeben. Die Gemälde hatte Goethe 1814 nach seinen eigenen Entwürfen von dem Zeichenschüler Alfred Heideloff (1802–1826) ausführen lassen. Damals wurden sie zur Begrüßung des Herzogs, der nach erfolgreichem Feldzug aus England zurückgekehrt war, in der Weimarer Zeichenschule ausgestellt. Nachdem sie 1825 zur 50-Jahr-Feier des Regierungsantritts von Herzog Carl August zudem die Fassade von Goethes Haus am Frauenplan geschmückt hatten, ließ Goethe sie von Carl Ermer verkleinert in Kupfer stechen, um sie zusammen mit eigens dazu verfassten, thematisch passenden Gedichten als Schmuckblätter zu verschenken. Vgl. auch die Abb. S. 81 und WA, Bd. I 4, S. 139 f.

The vignette belongs to a series of eight symbolic motifs that depict a range of paintings en miniature. In 1814, Goethe had commissioned Alfred Heideloff (1802–1826), an apprentice painter, to produce the paintings after his own sketches. At that time, the paintings were exhibited in the Art Academy in Weimar to celebrate the return of the Duke after his victorious campaign in England. After they had adorned in 1825 the façade of Goethe's house at the Frauenplan to commemorate the 50th anniversary of Karl August's reign as Duke, Goethe commissioned Ermer to fashion copper engravings in a small format that he intended to give away as decorative plates together with well-suited poems that he had composed specifically for this occasion. See ill. p. 81 and WA, vol. I 4, pp. 139–40.

TATEN DES LICHTS
MACK & GOETHE

HATJE
CANTZ

Inhalt

Contents

Der für das Goethe-Museum eigens entworfene 9 Meter hohe Farbturm steht auf dem kleinen Wiesenstück zwischen der Schlossfassade und der viel befahrenen Jacobistraße am angrenzenden Hofgarten. Er besteht aus 12 farbigen, im Wind wehenden Stoffbahnen, die in einer leiterähnlichen Edelstahlkonstruktion gefasst sind. Die Fahnen wurden für dieses Projekt speziell entwickelt, da sie einerseits wasserabweisend und andererseits so lichtecht sein müssen, dass die Sonne die Farbe der Fahnen nicht ausbleicht.

Als auffälligen Blickfang zu der ZERO-Ausstellung im Koninklijk Museum voor Schone Kunsten in Antwerpen im Jahr 1979 hat Heinz Mack erstmals eine Stele mit Farbfahnen vor einem Museumseingang aufstellen lassen. Blieben die kolorierten Stoffbahnen damals noch weitestgehend regungslos, so bewegen sie sich in Düsseldorf bei Wind, sodass die Skulptur neben der leuchtenden Farbkraft auch eine dynamische, energiegeladene Qualität erhält.

Die Farbfolge entspricht – in einem übertragenen Sinn – der Strenge des Farbspektrums und spiegelt damit das bekannte Mack'sche Farbspiel wider. Zugleich ergibt sich durch die Farbe, das Licht und die Bewegung ein weiterer verbindender Aspekt zum Ausstellungsschwerpunkt der Farbenlehre bei Mack und Goethe.

Specially created for the Goethe-Museum, Heinz Mack's nearly nine-meter-tall color tower is located on the small patch of lawn between the castle's façade and the busy Jacobistrasse, adjacent to the Hofgarten. The tower consists of twelve colored fabric panels: waving in the wind, the banners are mounted in a ladder-like stainless steel construction. They were developed specifically for this project, since they have to be water-repellent and at the same time so lightfast that they resist fading.

The first similarly striking eye-catcher Heinz Mack created was in 1979 for the ZERO exhibition held at the Koninklijk Museum voor Schone Kunsten in Antwerp, where he had a stele with colored flags placed in front of the museum entrance. Whereas the colored fabric panels were essentially motionless back then, the wind moves the ones in Düsseldorf, causing the sculpture to achieve a dynamic, energy-laden quality alongside its radiant power of color.

Figuratively speaking, the color sequence corresponds to the rigor of the color spectrum and thus mirrors Mack's well-known play of colors. At the same time, color, light, and movement constitute yet another aspect that connects Mack's and Goethe's color theories, the focus of the exhibition.

Heinz Mack
Farbturm, 2018
Edelstahl, Textilmaterial
900 x 104 x 30,5 cm
Fotomontage
(vgl. S. 194)

Heinz Mack
Color Tower, 2018
Stainless steel, fabric
900 x 104 x 30.5 cm
photo montage
(cf. p. 194)

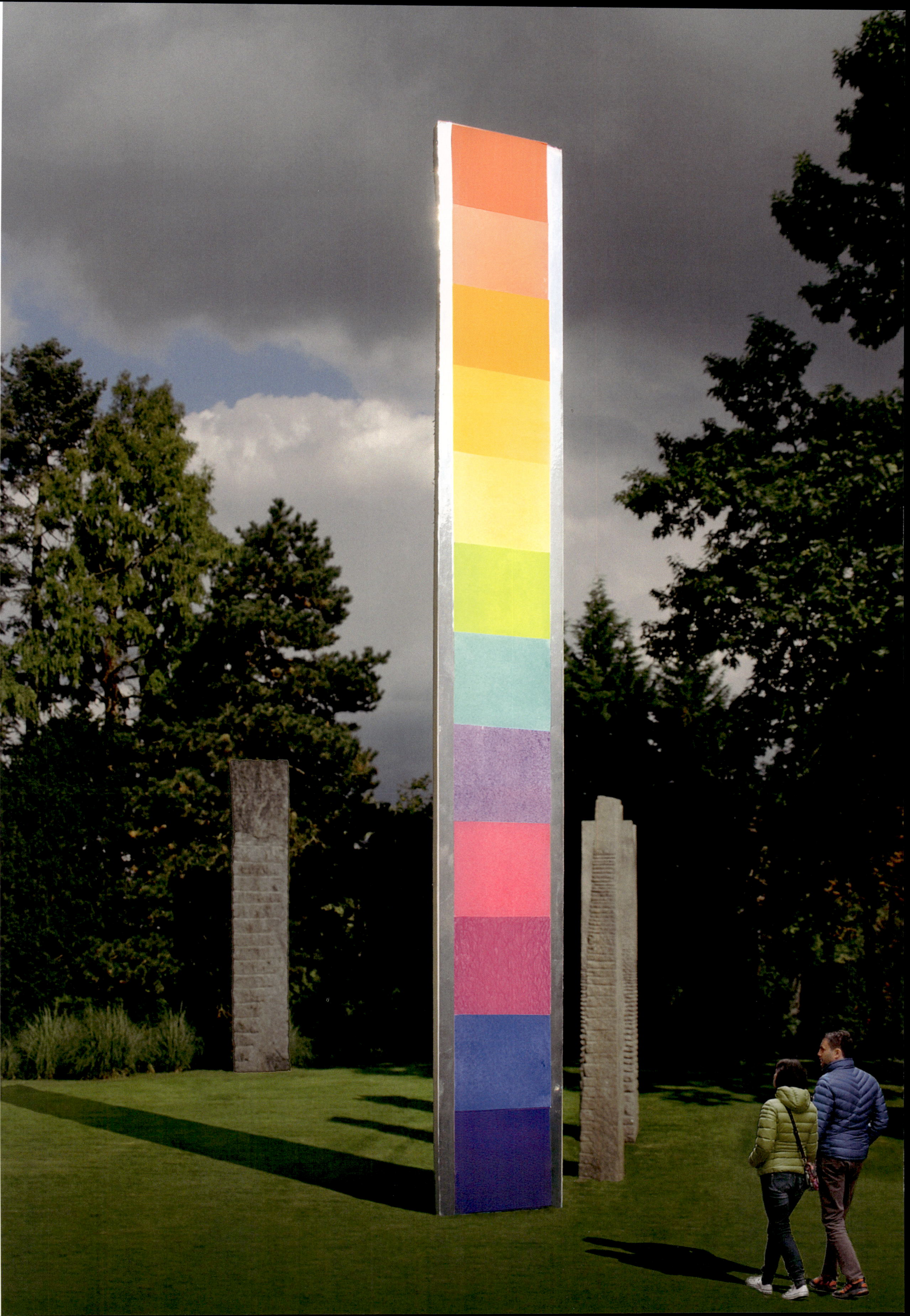

Die Ausstellung wird ermöglicht durch

NATIONAL-BANK
Mehr. Wert. Erfahren.

Geleitwort

Heinz Mack und Johann Wolfgang von Goethe in einer gemeinsamen Ausstellung! Der hoch angesehene Mitbegründer der ZERO-Gruppe und dreimalige Documenta-Teilnehmer auf der einen und der große Universalgelehrte und Dichter der deutschen Klassik auf der anderen Seite – für den unbefangenen Betrachter mag sich die Frage des »Warum?« geradezu aufdrängen. Dies vor allem auch deshalb, weil in einem engeren Sinne Mack kein Schriftsteller und Goethe kein bildender Künstler ist. Goethe war ein Kunstschaffender, einer, der sich in einer Vielzahl von Disziplinen engagierte. Als Künstler in einem weiteren Sinne war Goethe ›nur‹ in Bildkunst, Theater und Dichtung aktiv. Während Theater und Literatur ihn sein Leben lang beschäftigten, gab es mit Blick auf die Bildkunst im Februar 1788 ein abruptes Ende. Nach 18 Monaten eines Aufenthaltes in Italien, nach vertieftem Studium der alten Meister und in Selbsterkenntnis seines Könnens gab er die Malerei mit der halb ironischen Begründung auf: »Von meinem längeren Aufenthalt in Rom werde ich den Vorteil haben, dass ich auf das Ausüben der bildenden Kunst Verzicht tue.«[1]

Dennoch entstand in ihm, dem Ästheten, der Wunsch, das subjektive Erlebnis der Farben wissenschaftlich und objektiv zu ordnen. Dabei wollte er das Phänomen Farbe nicht einseitig physikalisch oder lediglich von einem ästhetischen oder praxisbezogenen Standpunkt aus beurteilen und erklären, sondern in seiner Gesamtheit erfassen und beschreiben. Er wählte deshalb den Weg über die Naturwissenschaften, indem er versuchte, erlebte Phänomene mittels physikalischer Versuche zu verifizieren. So entstanden die 1.400 Seiten umfassenden Ausführungen *Zur Farbenlehre,* die am 18. Mai 1810 in einer Auflage von 500 Stück auf weißem und 250 Stück auf grauem Papier in der Cotta'schen Verlagsbuchhandlung erschienen. Hierin stellte er sich gegen Isaac Newton und dessen Korpuskeltheorie, nach der das Licht aus kleinsten Teilchen oder Korpuskeln (Körperchen) besteht. Goethe war hingegen davon überzeugt, dass Farben aus Wechselwirkungen zwischen den nichtfarbigen Entitäten Finsternis, Trübe und Licht (»Farben sind Taten des Lichts, Taten und Leiden«) entstehen.

Schon zu seinen Lebzeiten stieß die *Farbenlehre* in Forschung und Lehre auf Widerspruch. Louis Malus oder Thomas Young und später Hermann von Helmholtz bestritten seine Behauptungen, widerlegten seine Erkenntnisse und die Richtigkeit seiner Schlussfolgerungen. Dennoch bemühte sich Goethe intensiv um die Verbreitung und Anerkennung dieses umfangreichsten seiner Werke. Bis zuletzt war er von dessen Richtigkeit überzeugt. Noch im hohen Alter sagte er zu Johann Peter Eckermann: »Auf alles, was ich als Poet geleistet habe, bilde ich mir gar nichts ein. [...] Daß ich aber in meinem Jahrhundert in der schwierigen Wissenschaft der Farbenlehre der einzige bin, der das Rechte weiß, darauf tue ich mir etwas zugute.«[2]

Anders als in der naturwissenschaftlichen Forschung fanden seine Ausführungen in der bildenden Kunst ein großes Interesse und eine bemerkenswerte Anerkennung, die bis heute von Bedeutung ist. Das gilt auch für Heinz Mack. Damit steht er in der Tradition anderer großer Künstler. Zu Lebzeiten Goethes war es vor allem der Maler und Schriftsteller

1 Sämtliche Zitate Goethes in diesem Geleitwort sind der anlässlich seines 200. Geburtstages am 28. August 1949 erschienenen Artemis-Gedenkausgabe, 24 Bde, München 1948–1971, entnommen.

2 Dabei verfügte Goethe über seinen literarischen Nachlass am 22. Januar 1831 testamentarisch, dass bei einem Nachdruck der *Farbenlehre* sowohl der zweite, polemische als auch der dritte, historische Teil weggelassen werden kann.

Philipp Otto Runge, der mit ihm in regem Austausch stand. Runge, der in kunsttheoretischer Sicht das erste dreidimensionale Farbsystem geschaffen hat, veröffentlichte 1810 seine Schrift *Farben-Kugel oder Construction des Verhältnisses aller Mischungen der Farben zu einander [...]*, die Teil dieser Ausstellung ist. Letztlich setzte Runge dadurch Goethes ›chromatische Bewegungen‹ aufs Neue in Bewegung.

Später war es etwa William Turner, der sich in seinem Spätwerk mit der Betrachtungsweise der Farben durch Goethe auseinandersetzte. Seine Arbeit *Licht und Farbe – der Morgen nach der Sintflut – Moses schreibt das Buch der Genesis* aus dem Jahre 1843 ist eine kongeniale Veranschaulichung von Goethes Verständnis von Farbe und Licht.

Zu Beginn des 20. Jahrhunderts entdecken Mitglieder der Künstlergruppe Blauer Reiter Goethe neu. Dies gilt insbesondere für Wassily Kandinsky, der sich in seiner 1911 publizierten Schrift *Über das Geistige in der Kunst, insbesondere in der Malerei* intensiv mit jenen Gedanken auseinandersetzt, auch wenn er, anders als Goethe, nicht zwischen physiologischen, physischen und chemischen Farben differenziert, sondern zur Wirkung der Farbe eine stärker wirkungsbezogene Unterscheidung zwischen »rein physischen« und »psychischen« Farben bevorzugt.[3]

Heinz Mack hat zeitlebens eine Bewunderung für Goethe empfunden. Sie hat in der Rezeption seines Werkes zwar keine wissenschaftliche Relevanz erfahren, jedoch hat insbesondere die Farbenlehre eine durchaus faszinierende Wirkung auf ihn gehabt. Mack betont zu Recht gemeinsame Interessen, denn auch für ihn sei Licht gleich Farbe und Farbe gleich Licht. Die damit verbundene Identität konstituiert den Gegenstand seiner Arbeiten, wobei er sich bewusst vom theologischen und philosophischen Bedeutungs- und Erlösungscharakter des Lichts befreit. Mack teilt Goethes Theorem der chromatischen Ästhetik, nach der unterschiedliche Farben eine unkontrollierbare Sinneswahrnehmung beim Betrachter auslösen können. Dadurch streicht der Künstler den Faktor der Wahrnehmung des Schönen und reduziert die Betrachtung des Kunstwerks auf eine allgemeine Theorie zur Empfindung und Reaktion der Sinnesorgane. So wird der Betrachter – unbeschadet konzeptioneller und struktureller Interpretationsansätze – in die Lage versetzt, die vom Maler gewählten Farben zu fühlen. Auch damit knüpft er, wenn auch unbewusst, an das Dictum des großen Dichters an, der meinte: »Ich habe nichts dagegen, wenn man die Farbe sogar zu fühlen glaubt.« Das Postulat Goethes, dass das Sehen ein denkendes Anschauen und zugleich ein anschauendes Denken ist, erfährt mithin durch den bildenden Künstler seine Bestätigung.

In einem Punkt dürften die Titelhelden dieser Ausstellung allerdings in einen leidenschaftlich geführten Disput verfallen sein: im Umgang mit den und in der Bewertung der Farben Weiß und Schwarz. So schrieb Goethe in der *Farbenlehre:* »Ein Kunstwerk schwarz und weiß kann in der Mahlerei selten vorkommen. Einige Arbeiten von Polydor[4] geben uns davon Beispiele, so wie unsre Kupferstiche und geschabten Blätter. Diese Arten, in sofern sie sich mit Formen und Haltung beschäftigen, sind schätzenswerth; allein sie haben wenig Gefälliges für's Auge, indem sie nur durch eine gewaltsame Abstraction entstehen.« Demgegenüber ist für Mack die Arbeit mit diesen Farben eine Selbstverständlichkeit und integraler Bestandteil seines Werkes. Während der Umgang mit Weiß selbsterklärend sein mag, gebrauchte Mack die Farbe Schwarz anfangs in den quälenden, traurigen Lebensphasen.

3 Wassily Kandinsky, *Über das Geistige in der Kunst, insbesondere in der Malerei. Mit acht Tafeln und zehn Originalholzschnitten*, 3. Aufl., München 1912, S. 43 ff.

4 Gemeint sind Polidoro Caldara, genannt Polidoro da Caravaggio, und die Monochromie seiner dekorativen Fassadenmalerei.

5 Die arabische Übersetzung lautet dementsprechend sehr passend: *Der östliche Divan vom westlichen Verfasser*.

6 Victoria Trunova, *Über Licht und Grenzen. Ein Interview mit Heinz Mack,* unter: http://talkingaboutart.de/über-licht-und-grenzen-ein-interview-mit-heinz-mack (Stand: 15.01.2018).

»Als junger Künstler hatte ich beim Malen meiner schwarzen Bilder auch schwarze Gedanken«, schrieb er einmal in der Reflexion seiner Ausstellung *Licht im Schwarz*. So entstand das erste schwarze Bild 1952 aus Trauer über seinen in der Kriegsgefangenschaft verstorbenen Vater. Auch in anderen sorgenvollen, teilweise depressiven Lebensabschnitten entstehen Arbeiten gleicher Farbgebung *(Schwarzes Fenster,* um 1956; *Mack 1958,* 1958; *Mein ›M‹,* 1960). Erst über die Jahre hat Mack die existenzialistische Dimension von Schwarz hinter sich gelassen, auch wenn er unverändert das Ziel verfolgt, Facetten des Wesens dieser Farbe sowohl in seiner Malerei *(Schwarz-Chromatik,* 1990; *Stunden der Nacht,* 1991; *Große Nekropolis,* 2000) als auch in seinen Skulpturen *(Meridiana,* 1999; *Schwarzes Kreuz,* 2000) an das Licht, an die Oberfläche zu holen. Sein Petitum: »Schwarz ist eine extrem schöne Farbe«, mag deshalb als partieller Widerspruch gegenüber dem großen Dichter bestehen bleiben.

Neben dem künstlerischen Faszinosum der Farbenlehre ist es aber auch die Begegnung von Abendland und Orient, die Mack und Goethe miteinander verbindet. Sie sind damit nicht allein. Über die Jahrhunderte war sowohl für Schriftsteller als auch für bildende Künstler die jeweils andere Kultur ein Gegenstand besonderer Aufmerksamkeit und interessierter Auseinandersetzung. So gelang es, die Vorstellung einer Weltliteratur beziehungsweise Weltkunst zu schaffen.

Für Goethe ist es der 1819 erschienene *West-östliche Divan,* in dem er sich erstmals ausführlich mit dem Orient und seinen prägenden Wesensmerkmalen auseinandersetzt. Es ist sowohl eine Hommage an den großen persischen Dichter Hafis als auch ein poetisches Zwiegespräch über Länder und Jahrhunderte hinweg.[5] Goethe hatte dessen *Diwan,* der 1812 von dem Orientalisten Joseph von Hammer-Purgstall ins Deutsche übersetzt wurde, 1814 gelesen. Das Werk beeindruckte ihn stark, und so begegnet das lyrische Ich dem Neuen offen und gleichberechtigt:

> Wer sich selbst und andere kennt,
> Wird auch hier erkennen:
> Orient und Okzident
> Sind nicht mehr zu trennen.

Mack hat früh ebenfalls eine Leidenschaft für den orientalischen Kulturraum erkennen lassen. 1955 reiste er erstmals in die Sahara. Wenige Jahre später folgten Marokko, Tunesien und Algerien. Aber auch Persien und Oman (Wahiba-Wüste) zählten dazu. Die Bewunderung für die kulturellen Errungenschaften dieses Teils der Welt zieht sich wie ein roter Faden durch sein Werk. In einem Interview antwortete Mack auf die Frage, wann und wie sein persönliches Interesse an den persischen und islamischen Kulturen entstanden sei: »Vielleicht war es die Lektüre von Goethes später Lyrik, deren Farbenreichtum, deren sinnliche Ausdruckskraft mich bewegte. Suleika war der Star einer leidenschaftlichen Liebe, die Goethe mit Sensibilität und Subtilität feierte, befreit von allen Problemen der Welt.«[6]

Im Umgang mit dem Orientalischen erweist sich Heinz Mack weder als Formalist noch als Kopist fremder Kulturen und ihrer formgebenden Sprachen. Er fühlt sich auch nicht als Vertreter des Westens. Selbst wenn Mack im Europäischen, im Abendländischen verwurzelt bleibt, sucht er durch gestalterische Elemente wie das Mosaik oder den thematischen Bezug auf das Ornament immer wieder Anknüpfungspunkte zum islamisch-orientalischen Kulturraum. Dabei ist es Mack durch die Wahl seiner Motive sowie durch die Verschiedenartigkeit seiner Materialien und Wirkungsebenen gelungen, die Abstraktionsleistung der islamischen Kunst noch zu übertreffen und in ihrer klaren, komplementären Farbigkeit zu vereinfachen. Besonders deutlich wurde dies in der 2001 im Teheraner Museum für Zeitgenössische Kunst präsentierten Ausstellung *Wahlverwandtschaften,* in der unterschiedliche Kelims der Ghashghai- und der Shahsavan-Nomaden aus dem 19. Jahrhundert eigenen Tusche- und Acryl-Arbeiten gegenübergestellt und Abbildungen verschiedener Moscheegewölbe mit seinen Dynamischen Strukturen und Rotoren kontrastiert wurden.

Westöstliches hat mithin vielfältig Einzug in sein Werk erhalten. Das gilt etwa für die Skulpturen aus dem Feuer, die Heinz Mack 1997 formte, brennen und glasieren ließ. Diese Keramiken zeigen dynamische Strukturen in ihrer Räumlichkeit und spielen mit Licht und Schatten auf ihrer Oberfläche. Nicht mathematisch exakt, sondern künstlerisch gestaltet zeigen sich geometrische Grundformen, die mit den Elementen der Bildsprache – Form, Farbe, Struktur, Ornament und Dekor – Schnittmengen zwischen Orient und Okzident kraftvoll zum Ausdruck bringen.

Anlässlich des 250. Geburtstags Goethes erschien 1999 das Künstlerbuch *Mack – Ein Buch der Bilder zum West-östlichen Divan von Johann Wolfgang v. Goethe.* Heinz Mack widmete es nicht allein dem deutschen Universalgelehrten, sondern ebenso Hafis, den auch er verehrt. Parallel dazu schuf er Zeichnungen, die weder darstellen noch beschreiben, sondern jene offene und menschenzugewandte Lyrik bildsprachlich begleiten.

Eine besondere Anerkennung seiner Auseinandersetzung mit dem islamisch-orientalischen Kulturraum wurde Heinz Mack durch die im Titel gegenüber Goethe mehrdeutige und schon erwähnte Ausstellung *Wahlverwandtschaften* im Teheraner Museum für Zeitgenössische Kunst sowie 2006/07 durch die von der NATIONAL-BANK mit unterstützte Werkschau *Transit zwischen Okzident und Orient* im Museum für Islamische Kunst im Pergamonmuseum in Berlin zugesprochen.

Ebenso hervorzuheben ist in diesem Zusammenhang die aus neun siebeneinhalb Meter hohen Stelen bestehende Monumentalskulptur *The Sky over Nine Columns,* die erstmals 2014 auf der Isola di San Giorgio Maggiore präsentiert worden ist. Abgesehen von der Bezugnahme auf frühere Arbeiten oder Projekte wie zum Beispiel *Vier Bronze-Pfeiler in der Wüste* (1970) besteht die Plastik aus rund 850.000 Mosaiksteinen mit 24 Karat Gold.[7] Zugleich nimmt sie sowohl in den Umrissen der Einzelkörper als auch in ihrer gestaffelten, rhythmischen Aufstellung Bezug auf das Ornament. Der orientalische Bezug wurde noch stärker akzentuiert, als die Plastik 2015/16 für knapp acht Monate im Skulpturenpark vor dem Sakıp Sabancı Museum in Istanbul gezeigt wurde und morgens die auf der Anhöhe des westlichen Ufers des Bosporus aus dem Osten kommenden Lichtstrahlen der Sonne über das Wasser bis auf die asiatische Seite reflektierte.

Wesentlich für das Verständnis der Persönlichkeit von Heinz Mack und seines Werkes ist die Tatsache, dass sein intellektueller Ausgangspunkt, auch mit Blick auf Goethe, durch die Kunst weder befangen noch begrenzt ist, denn neben dem Besuch der Staatlichen Kunst-

7 Der Produktionsprozess der Mosaiksteine lässt sich ebenfalls als ein Gleichklang von Okzident und Orient interpretieren, denn sie wurden in Venedig hergestellt, in Dubai auf eine vergleichsweise leichte Grundstruktur aufgetragen und anschließend wieder in die Lagunenstadt transportiert; siehe dazu Robert Fleck und Heinz Mack, »Das Licht zwischen Orient und Okzident«, in: *Mack – The Sky over Nine Columns,* hrsg. von Michael Beck und Ute Eggeling, Düsseldorf 2014, S. 33.

8 Das bezieht sich nicht nur auf seine Lichtreliefs, Lichtkuben, Lichtrotoren, Lichtstelen, sondern auch auf seine Malerei und seine Zeichnungen in Pastell, Tusche und Acryl, auf Druckgrafik, Fotografie, Mosaik, Keramik, die Gestaltung öffentlicher Plätze und Räume, Bühnenbilder und bibliophiler Werke.

akademie Düsseldorf hat er an der Universität zu Köln Philosophie studiert und dieses Studium mit dem Staatsexamen abgeschlossen. In einem umfassenden Sinne ist es vielmehr eine humanistische Lebenseinstellung, die beide Persönlichkeiten miteinander verbindet. Auch wenn der Humanismus seit dem 19. Jahrhundert als nur scheinbar ordnender Oberbegriff für verschiedene, teils gegensätzliche geistige Strömungen dient, steht die grundsätzlich optimistische Einschätzung der Fähigkeit, durch Menschlichkeit, Harmoniestreben, Kunstautonomie und ästhetische Lebensideale zu einer besseren Existenzform zu finden, vor der Klammer aller Interpretationsansätze. Dieser Lebensentwurf, der an das antike römische Konzept der humanitas anknüpfte, trat als normative Alternative neben das traditionell aus dem Mittelalter überkommene Menschenbild, das stark auf Gott und das Jenseits ausgerichtet gewesen war. Dabei wird ein Gesellschafts- und Bildungsideal entworfen, dessen Realisation jedem Menschen die optimale Entfaltung seiner Persönlichkeit ermöglichen soll, ein Gedanke, der uns verfassungspolitisch von der Naturrechtslehre bis in das Grundgesetz führt. Interdisziplinär ist mithin der Anknüpfungspunkt des Malers, Bildhauers und Philosophen mit dem Universalgelehrten. Vielfältig sind die damit verbundenen Dimensionen und verlockend die Versuchung, ihnen exegetisch zu erliegen. Ein Geleitwort hat jedoch die Aufgabe, sich gleich einem Kaleidoskop auf einen komprimierten Narrativ zu beschränken und wissenschaftlichen Ambitionen zu entsagen. Die Ausstellung lässt sich deshalb – kurz gesagt – als Spiegelung zweier Ausnahmekünstler beschreiben, als eine Gegenüberstellung, die nicht den Anspruch erhebt, Paarläufe und Gegenläufe des Dichters der deutschen Klassik und des bildenden Künstlers von heute herauszustellen, sondern Intellektuelles und Gestalterisches, Werkfragmente und Entwicklungslinien in ihrer Gleichheit zu zeigen und in ihrer Unterschiedlichkeit zu kontrastieren. Der Titel *Taten des Lichts* hat dabei einen doppelten Sinn: Zum einen erweist er sich für den Dichter als Referenz an seine Farbenlehre, zum anderen nimmt er Bezug auf das facettenreiche Œuvre Macks, das durch eine außerordentlich intensive Auseinandersetzung mit dem Licht geprägt ist.[8]

Mein Haus, die NATIONAL-BANK, verbindet – ebenso wie das Goethe-Museum Düsseldorf – eine lange Zusammenarbeit mit Heinz Mack. Neben der Unterstützung der schon genannten Ausstellung *Transit zwischen Okzident und Orient* im Pergamonmuseum in Berlin ist es die auf unsere Initiative zurückgehende Werkschau *Mack – Apollo in meinem Atelier,* die wir mit dem MKM Museum Küppersmühle für Moderne Kunst in Duisburg gemeinsam 2015/16 haben realisieren können. Nun ist es die Präsentation *Taten des Lichts – Mack & Goethe*. Ein besseres Beispiel für die nicht nur postulierte, sondern tatsächlich gelebte Nachhaltigkeit des kulturellen und gesellschaftlichen Engagements eines Unternehmens mag es kaum geben. Vorstand und Mitarbeiter der NATIONAL-BANK wünschen dieser Ausstellung viel Erfolg und Heinz Mack die Kraft und Unverbrüchlichkeit, sein Schaffen mit der ihm eigenen Verve lange fortzusetzen.

Dr. Thomas A. Lange
Vorsitzender des Vorstandes
NATIONAL-BANK Aktiengesellschaft

Preface

Heinz Mack and Johann Wolfgang von Goethe in a joint exhibition! On the one side, the highly respected co-founder of the artists' group ZERO who participated three times in Documenta, and on the other side the great polymath and poet of German Classicism. Viewers unfamiliar with the history might very well feel compelled to ask "why?" Especially since, strictly speaking, Mack is not a writer and Goethe was not a visual artist. Goethe produced art and was engaged in a variety of different disciplines. As an artist in a broader sense, he was 'merely' active in art, theater, and poetry. Whereas theater and literature occupied him throughout his career, his engagement with the visual arts came to an abrupt halt in February 1788. After an eighteen-month sojourn in Italy, after his in-depth study of the old masters, and cognizant of his own skills, he gave up painting with the half-ironic justification: "I shall have the benefits of my long sojourn in Rome to look back upon, even though I shall have to give up practicing the visual arts."[1]

Nevertheless, his aesthetic sensibility motivated him to organize the subjective experience of color in a scholarly, objective manner. At the same time, he did not want to evaluate and explain the phenomenon of color from a one-sided physical perspective or merely an aesthetic or practical point of view, but rather to understand and describe it in its entirety. He therefore chose a scientific approach when he decided to verify the sensory perceptions through physical experiments. Thus, on May 18, 1810, the Cotta'sche Verlagsbuchhandlung published his 1,400-page compendium *Theory of Colours* in an edition of 500 copies on white and 250 copies on gray paper. In this publication, he turned against Isaac Newton and his corpuscular theory, according to which light consists of minute parts or corpuscles. Goethe was convinced that colors develop from the interaction between the non-colored modes of darkness, turbidity, and light ("colors are acts of light; its active and passive modifications").[2]

Goethe's *Theory of Colours* already met with opposition by scientists and scholars during his lifetime. Louis Malus, Thomas Young, and later Hermann von Helmholtz contested his assertions, and discounted his findings and the validity of his conclusions. Despite the criticism, Goethe passionately pursued the dissemination and the recognition of his most comprehensive work. Until his death, he was convinced that he was right. In his late years, he said to Johann Peter Eckermann: "As for what I have done as a poet, I take no pride whatever in it. ... But that in my century I am the only person who knows the truth in the difficult science of colors—of that, I say, I am not a little proud, and here I have a consciousness of a superiority to many."[3]

Contrary to the response among scientists, his observations were met with great interest and remarkable enthusiasm in the visual arts and continue to be relevant to this day. This also holds true for Heinz Mack, who thus stands in the tradition of other major artists. During Goethe's lifetime, it was especially the painter and writer Philipp Otto Runge who participated in a lively exchange with him. In 1810, Runge, who from

1 Johann Wolfgang von Goethe, *Italian Journey [1786–1788],* trans. W. H. Auden and Elizabeth Mayer (San Francisco, 1982), p. 472.

2 Johann Wolfgang von Goethe, *Theory of Colours,* trans. Charles Lock Eastlake (London, 1840), p. xvii.

3 *Conversations of Goethe with Johann Peter Eckermann,* ed. J. K. Moorhead, trans. John Oxenford (Cambridge, MA, 1988), p. 302. With respect to his literary remains, on January 22, 1831, Goethe decreed in his will that should his *Theory of Colours* be reprinted, the second, polemical part as well as the third, historical part be omitted.

4 Wassily Kandinsky, *Concerning the Spiritual in Art,* trans. M. T. H. Sadler (New York, 1977), pp. 24ff.
5 Goethe 1840 (see note 2), p. 334. He is making reference to the monochrome, decorative façade painting by Polidoro Caldara, known as Polidoro da Caravaggio.

an art-theoretical point of view was the first to create a three-dimensional color system, published his *Farben-Kugel oder Construction des Verhältnisses aller Mischungen der Farben zu einander ...* (Color Sphere, or Construction of the Relationship between all Mixtures of Colors and in their complete Affinity ...), a book shown in this exhibition. Runge thereby ultimately set Goethe's 'chromatic movements' in motion once again.

Later, it was William Turner, who in his late work dealt with Goethe's approach to colors. His *Light and Color—the Morning after the Deluge—Moses writing the Book of Genesis* from 1843 is a kindred visualization of Goethe's understanding of color and light.

Artists of Der Blaue Reiter rediscovered Goethe in the early twentieth century. This is especially true of Wassily Kandinsky, who in his 1911 publication *Concerning the Spiritual in Art, especially in Painting* deals extensively with his ideas, although, unlike Goethe, Kandinsky does not differentiate between physiological, physical, and chemical colors but prefers a more effect-oriented distinction between "purely physical" and "psychical" colors.[4]

Heinz Mack has admired Goethe throughout his life. While not scientifically relevant for the reception of Mack's oeuvre, Goethe's theory of colors has undoubtedly always fascinated him. Mack rightly stresses shared interests, since for him, too, light equals color and color equals light. The shared identity constitutes the subject of his works, although Mack consciously liberates himself from the theological and philosophical relevance and redemptive character of light. Mack shares Goethe's theorem of chromatic aesthetics, according to which different colors can cause uncontrollable sense perceptions in the viewer. Thus the artist deletes the factor of perception of beauty and reduces the viewing of an artwork to the general theory of sensation and the reaction of the sensory organs. Hence the viewer is put into a position—regardless of conceptual or structural interpretational approaches—to feel the colors the painter chose. Here, too, Mack—even if unintentionally—connects with the great poet's dictum: "I have nothing against people who believe they can even feel colors." Consequently, the visual artist justifies Goethe's postulate that seeing is a thinking beholding and at the same time a beholding thinking.

There is one point, however, where the exhibition's eponymous heroes would most likely resort to a passionate dispute: in their handling and evaluation of the colors white and black. In his *Theory of Colors* Goethe wrote: "A picture in black and white seldom makes its appearance; some works of Polidoro are examples of this kind of art. Such works, inasmuch as they can attain form and keeping, are estimable, but they have little attraction for the eye, since their very existence supposes a violent abstraction."[5] For Mack, by contrast, it is natural to work with these colors, and they are an integral part of his oeuvre. Whereas his handling of white may be self-explanatory, Mack initially used black in the tormenting, sad phases of his life. "As a young artist, I also had black thoughts when painting my black pictures," he once wrote upon reflecting on his exhibition *Licht im Schwarz* (Light in Black). He produced his first black painting in 1952 out of grief over his father, who died as a prisoner of war. During other sorrowful, partly depressive stages of his life, he created more works with the same coloration (*Schwarzes Fenster* [Black Window], ca. 1956; *Mack 1958,* 1958; *Mein "M"* [My "M"], 1960). It was only over the years that Mack left the existentialist dimension of black behind, although it still is his unaltered goal to pursue the facets and the character of this color in his painting (*Schwarz-Chromatik* [Black Chromatics], 1990; *Stunden der Nacht* [Nocturnal Hours], 1991; *Große Nekropolis* [Big Necropolis], 2000) as well as his sculpture (*Meridiana,* 1999; *Schwarzes Kreuz* [Black Cross], 2000) and to bring them to light, to the surface. Thus his claim that "black is an extremely beautiful color" may persist as a partial contradiction vis-à-vis the great poet.

Apart from an artistic fascination with color theory, it is the encounter between Occident and Orient that also connects Mack and Goethe. And they are not alone: Over the centuries, writers and visual artists from both East and West directed their attention to the other culture and examined it with interest, enabling the creation of a notion of world literature and world art.

In Goethe's case, it was in the *West-East Divan,* published in 1819, where he dealt extensively with the Orient and its essential characteristics for the first time. It is both a tribute to the great Persian poet Háfiz as well as a poetic dialogue beyond countries and centuries.[6] Translated into German in 1812 by Orientalist Joseph von Hammer-Purgstall, Goethe read his *Diwan* in 1814. He was profoundly impressed by this opus, and hence the lyrical I encounters the unfamiliar with an open mind and on an equal footing:

> Who knows himself and others well,
> No longer may ignore:
> Orient and Occident dwell
> Separately no more.[7]

Mack likewise recognized his passion for the Oriental cultural sphere at an early age. He took his first trip to the Sahara in 1955. Several years later, he traveled to Morocco, Tunisia, and Algeria. Later he added Persia and Oman (the Wahiba desert region). His admiration for the cultural achievements of this part of the world runs like a golden thread through his oeuvre. When asked in an interview about his personal interest in Persian and Islamic cultures, Mack replied: "Maybe it was after reading Goethe's late poems, whose abundance of color and sensuous expressiveness moved me. Zuleika was the star of a passionate love that Goethe celebrated with sensitivity and subtleness, freed from all the world's problems."[8]

When dealing with Oriental aspects, Heinz Mack is neither a formalist nor a copyist of foreign cultures and their compositional languages. Neither does he consider himself a representative of the West. Even though rooted in European-Occidental culture, Mack often seeks moments of interaction with Islamic-Oriental culture, either through creative elements such as the mosaic or by making thematic reference to the

6 It is therefore quite fitting that the Arabic translation is *The Eastern Divan by a Western Author.*

7 Johann Wolfgang von Goethe, *West-East Divan,* trans. Martin Bidney (New York, 2010), p. 167.

8 Victoria Trunova, *Über Licht und Grenzen: Ein Interview mit Heinz Mack,* http://talkingaboutart.de/über-licht-und-grenzen-ein-interview-mit-heinz-mack (accessed January 15, 2018).

9 The production process of the tesserae can likewise be interpreted as a consonance of Occident and Orient: produced in Venice, they were mounted onto a relatively light basic structure in Dubai and subsequently transported back to the lagoon city; cf. Robert Fleck and Heinz Mack, "The Light Between Orient and Occident," in *Mack—The Sky over Nine Columns,* ed. Michael Beck and Ute Eggeling (Düsseldorf, 2014), p. 33.

ornament. Through his choice of motifs as well as the diversity of his materials and degrees of effect, Mack has managed to overcome the abstraction of Islamic art and to simplify it even further in its clear, complementary chromaticity. This became particularly noticeable in 2001, when he presented his art at the Tehran Museum of Contemporary Art in a show entitled *Elective Affinities:* he juxtaposed different nineteenth-century kilims of Ghashghai and Shahsavan nomads with his own pen-and-ink drawings and acrylic paintings, and contrasted images of mosque vaults with his dynamic structures and rotors.

West-eastern elements have found entry into his oeuvre in a wide variety of ways. This applies, for example, to Mack's fire sculptures that he formed, fired, and glazed in 1997. These ceramics display dynamic structures in their spatiality and play with light and shadow on their surfaces. Not mathematically exact but artistically fashioned, basic geometric forms emerge that powerfully express overlaps between Orient and Occident using the elements of pictorial language—form, color, structure, ornament, and decoration.

On the occasion of Goethe's 250th birthday in 1999, Mack published the artist's book *Mack—Ein Buch der Bilder zum West-östlichen Divan von Johann Wolfgang v. Goethe* (Mack—A Book of Pictures about the West-East Divan by Johann Wolfgang v. Goethe). Heinz Mack dedicated it to the German polymath as well as to Háfiz, whom he also admires. At the same time, he produced drawings that neither depict nor describe, but rather accompany this open, personable poetry with imagery.

Heinz Mack was awarded special recognition for his examination of the Islamic-Oriental cultural sphere through the previously mentioned exhibition *Elective Affinities*—a title that has multiple meanings with respect to Goethe—at the Tehran Museum of Contemporary Art, as well as in 2006/07 through the retrospective *Transit zwischen Okzident und Orient* (Transit between Occident and Orient) at Berlin's Museum of Islamic Art at the Pergamonmuseum, sponsored by the NATIONAL-BANK.

Likewise important to point out in this context is the monumental sculpture *The Sky over Nine Columns,* which consists of nine 7.5-meter stelae and was first presented in 2014 on the Isola di San Giorgio Maggiore, Venice. Besides making reference to previous works or projects such as *Vier Bronze-Pfeiler in der Wüste (Four Bronze Columns in the Desert,* 1970), this sculpture is comprised of some 850.000 24-karat-gold tesserae.[9] At the same time, in the outlines of the individual columns and in their staggered, rhythmic installation, it makes reference to the ornament. The Oriental connection was accentuated even more strongly when the sculpture was exhibited for eight months in the sculpture park outside Istanbul's Sakıp Sabancı Museum in 2015–16. In the mornings, the rays of light coming from the east over the water and hitting the hills on the western banks of the Bosporus were reflected all the way to the Asiatic side.

To understand the personality of Heinz Mack and his oeuvre, it is important to mention that his intellectual point of departure—also in light of Goethe—is neither self-conscious nor restricted by art, because in addition to his studies at the Staatliche Kunstakademie Düsseldorf, he also graduated from the University of Cologne with a degree in philosophy. Generally speaking, both personalities are connected through their humanist approach. Although humanism has served since the nineteenth century as an apparently collective term for different, in part contradictory intellectual currents, the principally optimistic evaluation of the ability to find a better form of existence—through humanity, striving for harmony, the autonomy of art, and aesthetic life ideals—prefaces the common elements of all interpretive approaches. Linked to the ancient Roman concept of humanitas, this philosophy of life was placed alongside the traditional notion of the medieval human being, which was strongly oriented toward God and afterlife. A social and educational ideal is created whose realization is intended to optimize the personality of each and every individual, a thought that in terms of constitutional policy takes us from the doctrine of natural law to fundamental law. Hence the connection between the painter-sculptor-philosopher and the polymath is interdisciplinary. The associated dimensions are manifold, and it is tempting to succumb to them exegetically. However, the purpose of a preface is to limit itself, like a kaleidoscope, to a compact narrative and to abstain from scholarly ambitions. In short, the exhibition can therefore be described as a mirroring of two exceptional artists, a juxtaposition that does not claim to point out parallels and discrepancies between the poet of German Classicism and the contemporary visual artist. Instead, it is the intention to point out intellectual and creative elements, work fragments, and lines of development in their similarities and to contrast dissimilarities. Of course, the title *Acts of Light* has a double meaning: on the one hand, it proves to be a testimonial to the poet's color theory, and on the other hand it is a reference to Mack's multifaceted oeuvre, which is characterized by an extraordinarily intense examination of light.[10]

Like the Goethe-Museum Düsseldorf, my institution, the NATIONAL-BANK, can look back at many years of collaborating with Heinz Mack. In addition to sponsoring the exhibition *Transit zwischen Okzident und Orient* at Berlin's Pergamonmuseum, we initiated the retrospective *Mack—Apollo in meinem Atelier* (Mack—Apollo in my Studio), which we implemented in cooperation with the MKM Museum Küppersmühle für Moderne Kunst in Duisburg in 2015–16. Now it is the presentation *Acts of Light—Mack & Goethe*. There can hardly be a better example for the not simply postulated but truly lived sustainability of a company's cultural and social commitment. The board and employees of the NATIONAL-BANK wish for this show to be a great success and for Heinz Mack to have the power and the stamina to continue his creative work with his characteristic verve for a long time to come.

Dr. Thomas A. Lange
Chairman of the Board
NATIONAL-BANK Corp.

10 This refers not only to his light reliefs, light cubes, light rotors, and light stelae but also to his paintings and drawings in pastel, pen-and-ink, and acrylic, to his prints, photography, mosaics, ceramics, his design of public squares and spaces, stage sets, and bibliophile works.

Goethe-Museum Düsseldorf
Anton-und-Katharina-Kippenberg-Stiftung
Schloss Jägerhof
2015

Goethe-Museum Düsseldorf
Anton-und-Katharina-Kippenberg-Stiftung
Schloss Jägerhof
2015

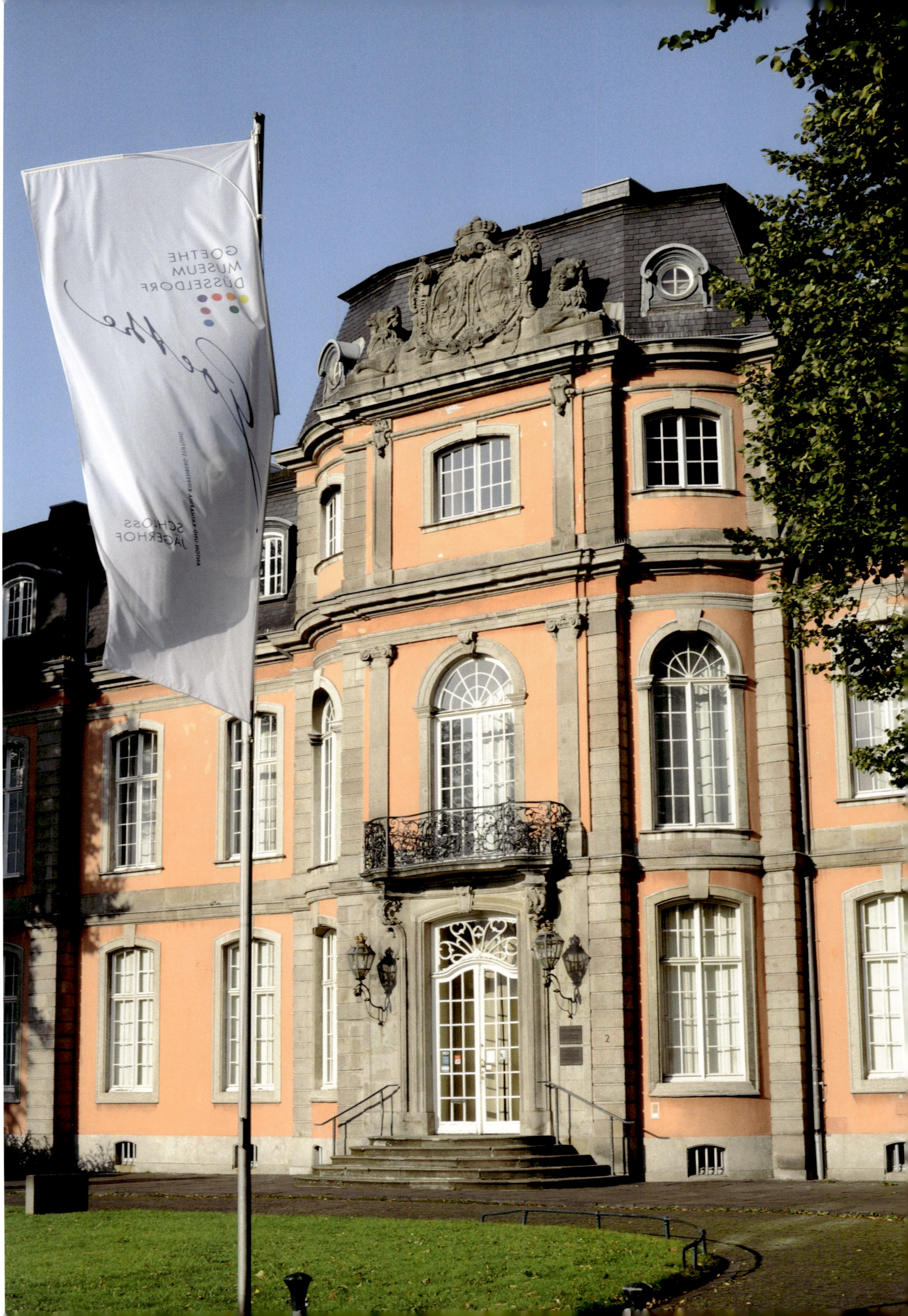
GOETHE
MUSEUM
DÜSSELDORF
SCHLOSS
JÄGERHOF

Foreword

In 1805, Goethe wrote the following in his treatise *Winckelmann and his Age:* "It is sad to have to think of anything as final and complete." He continued: "[M]useums to which nothing is added are like mausoleums haunted by ghosts. Such a limited circle of art limits our thinking. We get accustomed to regarding such collections as complete, instead of being reminded through ever-new additions that in art, as in life, we have nothing that remains finished and at rest, but rather something infinite in constant motion." The special exhibition *Acts of Light—Mack & Goethe* follows something that is this motto. It could also be the main heading of Düsseldorf's Goethe-Museum, which is identical with the Anton-und-Katharina-Kippenberg-Stiftung.

Düsseldorf is a particularly suitable place for presenting this spirit in motion, which connects the aesthetics and the natural science of the Goethe era with the works of art by Heinz Mack, one of Germany's most distinguished contemporary artists. The idea for building this bridge across time stems from the German philologist and art historian Dr. Barbara Steingiesser. As the curator of the exhibition, she displays the astonishing structural parallels between Goethe's thoughts on light, color, and morphology and Heinz Mack's thinking and creative work. In terms of content, the views of the classical German author and the contemporary visual artist feature numerous points of contact: an inquisitive, interdisciplinary spirit, insistence on scrutinizing thought, and intercultural openness.

It is not by chance that these two meet in a museum in Düsseldorf. There have already been four smaller exhibitions with works by Heinz Mack at the Goethe-Museum. The most important of them was dedicated to Mack's interpretation of Goethe's anthology *West-East Divan* (1999). Extending beyond these, this current extensive special exhibition is devoted to an overview of the two artist personalities. Whereas the structural parallels do not require a specific geographical reference, the city of Düsseldorf has been important for both Goethe and Mack. In 1950, the latter began his studies at the Kunstakademie. His appraisal of post-World War II art is well known: the young artists were literally and symbolically confronted with a gray landscape of ruins, to which Heinz Mack and Otto Piene responded by founding the avant-garde movement ZERO, giving light and motion their due.

The Goethe-Museum was founded the same year Mack graduated from the Kunstakademie. It arose out of the same spirit of optimism as modern art in Düsseldorf after World War II, and it owes its existence to the cultural-political farsightedness then prevalent in the Rhenish metropolis. It was committed to safeguarding the cultural heritage after the barbarism of the National Socialists and to linking it with a better Germany now defined by humanity and education. The city took charge of the world's largest private Goethe collection, which stemmed from the distinguished publisher and collector Anton Kippenberg (1874–1950). The Anton-und-Katharina-Kippenberg-Stiftung was founded in 1953, and the Goethe-Museum was festively inaugurated on June 30, 1956. Destroyed during the war, the Hofgärtnerhaus was reconstructed especially for the collection. Due to space, security,

Vorwort

»Traurig ist es, wenn man das Vorhandne als fertig und abgeschlossen ansehen muß«, schrieb Goethe 1805 in seiner Schrift über *Winckelmann und sein Jahrhundert* und setzte fort: »Museen, zu denen nichts hinzugefügt wird, haben etwas Grab- und Gespensterartiges; man beschränkt seinen Sinn in einem so beschränkten Kunstkreis, man gewöhnt sich solche Sammlungen als ein Ganzes anzusehen, anstatt daß man durch immer neuen Zuwachs erinnert werden sollte, daß in der Kunst, wie im Leben, kein Abgeschlossenes beharre, sondern ein Unendliches in Bewegung sei.« Die Sonderausstellung *»Taten des Lichts« – Mack & Goethe* folgt diesem Motto. Es könnte auch insgesamt über dem Goethe-Museum Düsseldorf stehen, das identisch mit der Anton-und-Katharina-Kippenberg-Stiftung ist.

Düsseldorf ist ein besonders geeigneter Ort, um diesen Geist in Bewegung zu zeigen, der die Ästhetik und Naturwissenschaft der Goethezeit mit den Kunstwerken von Heinz Mack, einem der bedeutendsten deutschen Künstler der Gegenwart, verbindet. Die Idee zu diesem Brückenschlag über die Zeiten stammt von der Germanistin und Kunsthistorikerin Dr. Barbara Steingießer, die als Kuratorin der Ausstellung die erstaunlichen Strukturparallelen von Goethes Gedanken über Licht, Farbe und Morphologie zu dem Denken und Schaffen Heinz Macks herausstellt. Der deutsche Klassiker und der bildende Künstler von heute weisen in ihren Ansichten viele inhaltliche Berührungspunkte auf: interdisziplinären Forschergeist, das Bestehen auf einem anschauenden Denken und interkulturelle Offenheit.

Dass beide in einem Düsseldorfer Museum zusammentreffen, kommt nicht von ungefähr. Im Goethe-Museum gab es schon vier kleinere Ausstellungen mit Werken von Heinz Mack. Die wichtigste galt Macks Interpretation von Goethes Gedichtsammlung *West-östlicher Divan* (1999). Die aktuelle große Sonderausstellung widmet sich darüber hinausgehend der Zusammenschau der beiden Künstlerpersönlichkeiten. Die Strukturparallelen kommen zwar ohne den Ortsbezug aus. Düsseldorf ist aber als Lokalität sowohl für Goethe als auch für Heinz Mack wichtig gewesen. Mack studierte hier ab 1950 an der Kunstakademie. Seine Bestandsaufnahme der Kunst nach dem Zweiten Weltkrieg ist bekannt: Die jungen Künstler waren buchstäblich und symbolisch konfrontiert mit einer grauen Ruinenlandschaft, gegen welche die Avantgardebewegung ZERO, die Heinz Mack mit Otto Piene begründete, Licht und Bewegung in ihr Recht setzte.

Im selben Jahr, als Mack sein Staatsexamen an der Kunstakademie machte, wurde das Goethe-Museum begründet. Es ist in derselben Aufbruchssituation wie die moderne Kunst in Düsseldorf nach dem Zweiten Weltkrieg entstanden und verdankt seine Existenz dem damaligen kulturpolitischen Weitblick der rheinischen Metropole, die sich dazu verpflichtete, das kulturelle Erbe nach der Barbarei der Nationalsozialisten zu sichern und an das bessere Deutschland der Humanität und Bildung anzuknüpfen. Die Stadt nahm die größte Goethe-Privatsammlung der Welt, die von dem bedeutenden Verleger und Sammler Anton Kippenberg (1874–1950) stammte, in ihre Obhut. 1953 wurde die Anton-und-Katharina-Kippenberg-Stiftung gegründet und am 30. Juni 1956 das Goethe-Museum feierlich eingeweiht. Für die Sammlung wurde eigens das im Krieg zerstörte Hofgärtnerhaus and conceptual reasons, the museum moved to Schloss Jägerhof in 1987 and thus into the immediate vicinity of the Jacobihaus, a place Goethe had frequented two hundred years earlier.

Attracted to Düsseldorf by the philosopher Friedrich Heinrich Jacobi, Goethe first visited the city in 1774, dropping in on Jacobi at his Pempelfort country estate, where the Weimar Court of Muses was being rehearsed. Many great minds of the day visited Jacobi's salon, among them Duchess Anna Amalia of Saxe-Weimar-Eisenach, Denis Diderot, Georg Forster, Johann Georg Hamann, Wilhelm Heinse, Johann Gottfried Herder, Wilhelm and Alexander von Humboldt, Sophie von La Roche, Johann Heinrich Merck, and Christoph Martin Wieland. Although later broken, Goethe's friendship with Jacobi was one of his most important. However, thanks to the 1774 visit and the extended sojourn in 1792, Düsseldorf became a Goethe city.

When showing Goethe's prismatic experiments in the museum today, we simply continue his lectures at the Jacobihaus around the corner. In 1792, Goethe participated in the campaign in France, the coalition war of the allied Prussian and Austrian troops against revolutionary France. He pursued his investigations on color theory during the campaign; on the retreat via the Rhine, Goethe continued his "chromatic studies," hoping to "connect the physical phenomena." Later, in Pempelfort, he attempted "to entertain [the audience] with some phenomena and experiments. I had no difficulty in producing something new, for everyone, however well educated, had been taught the doctrine of the division of light, and unfortunately wished to see that which, in itself, was full of life, and which afforded them so much enjoyment, traced back to some dead hypothesis." Although initially met with certain reservations by those listening, the demonstrations had the merit that "while conversing, I obtained some new insight into the subject, and in the flow of conversation invention came most quickly." In his letters, Goethe henceforth informed his friend Jacobi about the progress of his work regarding the 'epoptic colors' and the perception of colored shadows.

The nature of light and color are not illustrated by demonstrations alone. "Color, thou changeable one, kindly descends upon man!" as it says in the distich *Light and Color,* which Goethe and Schiller drew up together while exchanging views about the theory of colors. In Heinz Mack's creations, which are characterized by his fascination with light and pure color, we experience nature's stepping "out of its everyday indifference" (Goethe, *Beyträge zur Optik* [Contributions to Optics], § 2); they convey information about dynamic structures and yet leave a "pleasurable impression." (§ 1.)

It is a challenge to convey the theory of light in an exhibition. Like Goethe, Mack is concerned with the experience of phenomena, sensory perception. Furthermore, Goethe did not doubt that light has nearly metaphysical qualities, and Heinz Mack likewise once spoke about the emanation of light from a transcendental space. Neither the poet nor the artist assumes an inner mysticism. Rather, they are convinced that the world also explains itself in the perception of phenomena; that "every fact is already theory," as Goethe recorded in an observation in *On Science in General.* Goethe's contemporary, Achim von Arnim, intermittently in close contact with the great mind from Weimar and a graduate of wiederaufgebaut. 1987 zog das Museum dann aus Raum-, Sicherheits- und Konzeptionsgründen um in das Schloss Jägerhof und damit in direkte Nachbarschaft zum Jacobihaus, wo Goethe zweihundert Jahre zuvor ein- und ausgegangen war.

1774 hat Goethe zum ersten Mal Düsseldorf besucht, angezogen von dem Philosophen Friedrich Heinrich Jacobi, auf dessen Pempelforter Landsitz der Weimarer Musenhof geprobt wurde. Jacobis Salon besuchten viele Geistesgrößen der Zeit: Herzogin Anna Amalia von Sachsen-Weimar-Eisenach, Denis Diderot, Georg Forster, Johann Georg Hamann, Wilhelm Heinse, Johann Gottfried Herder, Wilhelm und Alexander von Humboldt, Sophie von La Roche, Johann Heinrich Merck und Christoph Martin Wieland. Die Freundschaft mit Jacobi ist eine von Goethes bedeutendsten gewesen, wenngleich sie später zerbrach. Düsseldorf aber ist durch den Besuch von 1774 und den längeren Aufenthalt im Jahr 1792 eine Goethe-Stadt geworden.

Wenn heute im Museum Goethes prismatische Experimente gezeigt werden, setzen sie Goethes Vorträge im Jacobihaus um die Ecke fort. 1792 nahm Goethe teil an der Campagne in Frankreich, dem Koalitionskrieg der alliierten preußischen und österreichischen Truppen gegen das revolutionäre Frankreich. Während des Feldzugs widmete er sich Untersuchungen zur Farbenlehre, auf dem Rückzug über den Rhein setzte Goethe seine »chromatischen Akten« fort, hoffte darauf, diese »physischen Erscheinungen in sich zu verknüpfen« und versuchte dann in Pempelfort, »die Gesellschaft mit einigen Phänomenen und Versuchen zu unterhalten, wo mir denn ganz Neues vorzubringen nicht schwer fiel: denn alle Personen, so gebildet sie auch waren, hatten das gespaltene Licht eingelernt und wollten leider das lebendige, woran sie sich erfreuten, auf jene todte Hypothese zurückgeführt wissen.« Die Demonstrationen, wenn sie auch auf gewisse Vorbehalte der Zuhörer stießen, hatten den Erfolg, dass dem Sprecher selbst »unter'm Sprechen neue Lichter« aufgingen und er »im Fluß der Rede am gewissesten« erfand. Fortan unterrichtete Goethe brieflich den Freund Jacobi vom Fortgang seiner Arbeit über die ›epoptischen Farben‹ und die Wahrnehmung farbiger Schatten.

Nicht aber nur Demonstrationen verdeutlichen das Wesen von Licht und Farbe. »Farbe, du Wechselnde, komm freundlich zum Menschen herab«, heißt es im Distichon *Licht und Farbe,* das Goethe und Schiller gemeinschaftlich entwarfen, als sie sich über die Farbenlehre austauschten. In Heinz Macks von der Faszination durch das Licht und die reine Farbe geprägten Schöpfungen erleben wir das Heraustreten der Natur »aus ihrer alltäglichen Gleichgültigkeit« (Goethe, *Beyträge zur Optik,* § 2), sie vermitteln Aufschluss über dynamische Strukturen und machen dennoch einen »vergnügenden Eindruck« (§ 1).

Die Theorie des Lichts lässt sich schwer in einer Ausstellung vermitteln. Heinz Mack geht es wie Goethe um die Erfahrung der Phänomene, die sinnliche Anschauung. Dass dem Licht darüber hinaus fast metaphysische Qualitäten zukommen, hat Goethe nicht bezweifelt, und auch Heinz Mack hat einmal von der Emanation des Lichts aus einem transzendenten Raum gesprochen. Der Dichter wie der Künstler gehen aber nicht von einer inneren Mystik aus, sondern von der Überzeugung, dass in der Wahrnehmung der Phänomene auch die Welt sich erkläre, dass »alles Factische schon Theorie ist«, wie Goethe in einer Betrachtung über *Naturwissenschaft im Allgemeinen* festhielt. Goethes Zeitgenosse Achim von Arnim, zeitweise in engem Kontakt zu dem großen Weimarer und in jungen Jahren als studierter natural science, belonged to the elite of German physicists when he was young. He used similar words: the "higher light" is "the theory of another world, just as our light, without being grasped by theory, opens up the theory of all our natural phenomena" ("Address to My Listeners" in his so-called *Novellas of 1812*). The hexameter of the aforementioned distich states: "Thou that art ever the same, with the changeless One take up thy dwelling!"

We perceive light through its reflections. Goethe and Mack share the view that nature is not spelled out but rather shaped artistically on the basis of fundamental geometric or language-related forms. Both rely on dynamic structures that manifest ambiguously: be it by virtue of the play of light and shadow on the surface of sculptures, be it by literary works of art built on the principle of the reciprocal extension of meaning. In doing so, neither the poet nor the artist simply perceives the individual as a function of structure. Both of them have a humanist aspiration.

This special exhibition was made possible by the involvement of numerous supporters. I would first of all like to thank curator Dr. Barbara Steingiesser, who provided the idea for *Acts of Light*. Without her indefatigable and proficient dedication, this project could never have been realized. It is an honor for the Goethe-Museum to be able to present the works of one of Germany's most important artists. Our heartfelt thanks go to Professor Heinz Mack for his extraordinary commitment. It was a fabulous experience to develop and discuss the concept of the presentation with the artist and his wife, Ute Mack. Heinz Mack created a nearly nine-meter-tall colored tower especially for *Acts of Light,* which has been installed on the patch of lawn in front of Schloss Jägerhof and leads visitors to the exhibition. We would like to thank Rolf Königs and AUNDE Group for the financing of this artwork. The material pertaining to Goethe in this show stems for the most part from our own exquisite holdings. In addition, the following institutions have loaned rare items: the Klassik Stiftung Weimar (Goethe- und Schiller-Archiv, Goethe-Nationalmuseum), the Österreichische Goethe-Gesellschaft, and the Technische Universität Dresden (Sammlung Farbenlehre). Our heartfelt thanks to all the lenders! We would furthermore like to express our gratitude to all of the authors for their illuminating contributions to the catalogue on the phenomenon of Mack & Goethe, as well as Prof. Dr. Roswitha Burwick (Los Angeles) for her invaluable support. Thanks are also owed to Hatje Cantz for their competent supervision and to graphic designer Saskia Kruse for her extraordinary commitment.

For the Goethe-Museum, such a large-scale exhibition could not be carried out without financial assistance. Our heartfelt appreciation goes out to the NATIONAL-BANK AG: their generous sponsorship made the project possible in the first place. In addition, the Kunststiftung NRW and the Landesverband Rheinland provided substantial financial support. We furthermore thank sponsors Prof. Dr. Dieter H. Vogel, Kötter SE & Co. KG Security Düsseldorf and the Kulturamt der Landeshauptstadt Düsseldorf.

My deputy director Dr. Heike Spies and all of the museum's staff members actively contributed to the success of this exhibition. My special gratitude goes out to them.

Prof. Dr. Christof Wingertszahn

Director of the Goethe-Museum Düsseldorf and Chairman of the Anton-und-Katharina-Kippenberg-Stiftung

Naturwissenschaftler zur Elite der deutschen Physiker gehörig, hat dies ähnlich ausgedrückt: das »höhere Licht« sei »eben so die Theorie einer andern Welt [...] wie unser Licht, ohne von einer Theorie erfaßt zu werden, die Theorie aller unsrer Naturerscheinungen aufschließt.« (»Anrede an meine Zuhörer« in der *Novellensammlung von 1812)*. Im Hexameter des schon zitierten Distichons heißt es: »Wohne du ewiglich Eines dort bei dem ewiglich Einen«.

Das Licht nehmen wir wahr in seinen Abspiegelungen. Goethe und Mack eint die Anschauung, dass Natur nicht abbuchstabiert, sondern auf der Grundlage von geometrischen oder sprachlichen Grundformen künstlerisch gestaltet wird. Beide setzen auf dynamische Strukturen, die mehrdeutig erscheinen: sei es durch das Spiel von Licht und Schatten auf der Oberfläche von Skulpturen, sei es durch nach dem Prinzip wechselseitiger Bedeutungserweiterung gebaute Wortkunstwerke. Dabei fassen der Dichter wie der Künstler das Individuum nicht einfach als Funktion der Struktur auf. Sie haben einen humanistischen Anspruch.

Die Sonderausstellung ist möglich geworden durch das Engagement vieler Förderer. An erster Stelle danke ich der Ideengeberin und Kuratorin der *Taten des Lichts,* Dr. Barbara Steingießer, ohne deren unermüdlichen und virtuosen Einsatz das Projekt nicht hätte stattfinden können. Für das Goethe-Museum ist es eine Ehre, die Werke eines der wichtigsten deutschen Künstler zeigen zu können. Wir danken Professor Heinz Mack herzlich für sein großes Engagement für das Haus. Es war ein eindrucksvolles Erlebnis, in den Gesprächen mit dem Künstler und seiner Frau Ute Mack die Konzeption der Ausstellung weiterzuspinnen und zu diskutieren. Eigens für die *Taten des Lichts* hat Heinz Mack einen neun Meter hohen Farbturm geschaffen, der auf dem Vorplatz des Schlosses Jägerhof zur Ausstellung hinführt. Für die Finanzierung dieses Kunstwerks danken wir Rolf Königs und der AUNDE Group. Die Goethe-Hälfte der Ausstellung kann das Museum zum überwiegenden Teil aus dem eigenen exquisiten Fundus bestreiten. Folgende Institutionen haben uns zusätzlich rare Stücke ausgeliehen: die Klassik Stiftung Weimar (Goethe- und Schiller-Archiv, Goethe-Nationalmuseum), die Österreichische Goethe-Gesellschaft sowie die Technische Universität Dresden (Sammlung Farbenlehre). Allen Leihgebern sei herzlich gedankt! Wir danken ferner allen Autoren des Katalogs für ihre aufschlussreichen Beiträge zum Phänomen Mack & Goethe und Prof. Dr. Roswitha Burwick (Los Angeles) für wertvolle Hilfe. Dank gebührt auch dem Verlag Hatje Cantz, der uns professionell betreut hat, sowie der Grafikerin Saskia Kruse für ihren außergewöhnlichen Einsatz.

Ohne finanzielle Ressourcen ist eine solch große Ausstellung für das Goethe-Museum nicht durchzuführen. Wir danken herzlich der NATIONAL-BANK AG, die das Projekt durch ihr großzügiges Sponsoring überhaupt erst ermöglicht hat. Die Kunststiftung NRW und der Landesverband Rheinland haben uns zusätzlich durch erhebliche Beiträge gefördert. Wir danken ferner Herrn Prof. Dr. Dieter H. Vogel, der Firma Kötter SE & Co. KG Security Düsseldorf und dem Kulturamt der Landeshauptstadt Düsseldorf als weiteren Förderern.

Meine Stellvertreterin Dr. Heike Spies und alle Mitarbeiter des Museums haben engagiert zum Gelingen der Ausstellung beigetragen; ihnen gilt mein besonderer Dank.

Prof. Dr. Christof Wingertszahn
Direktor des Goethe-Museums Düsseldorf und Vorstand der Anton-und-Katharina-Kippenberg-Stiftung

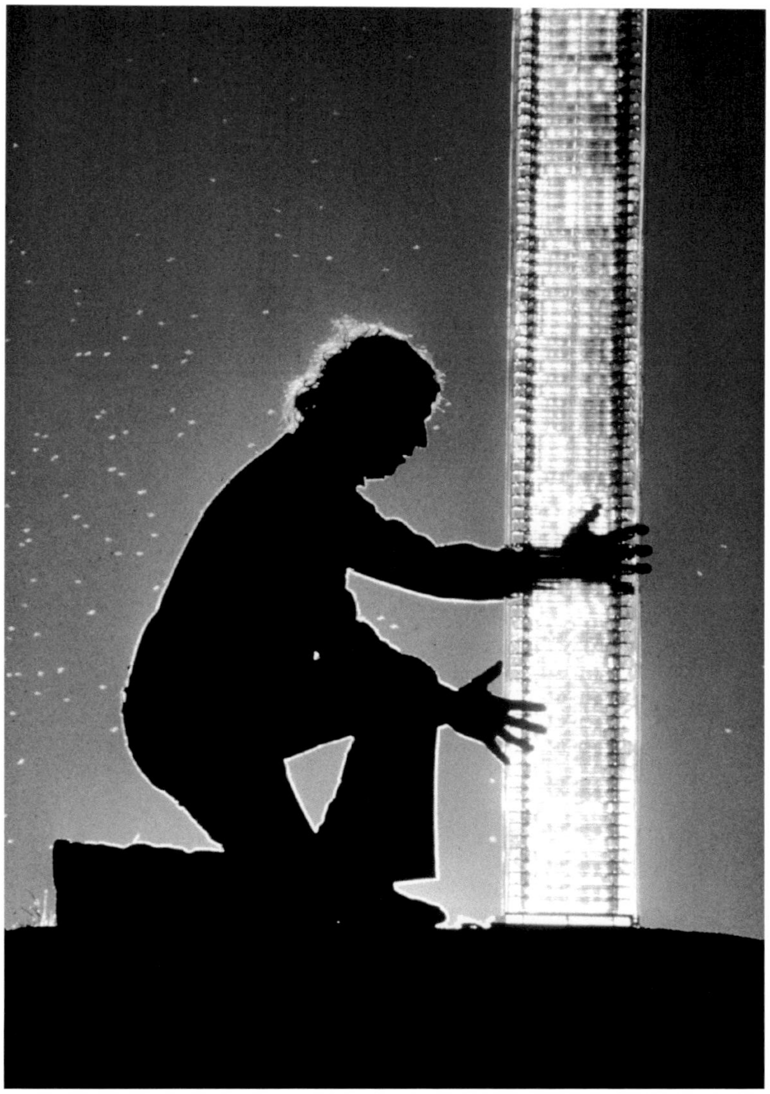

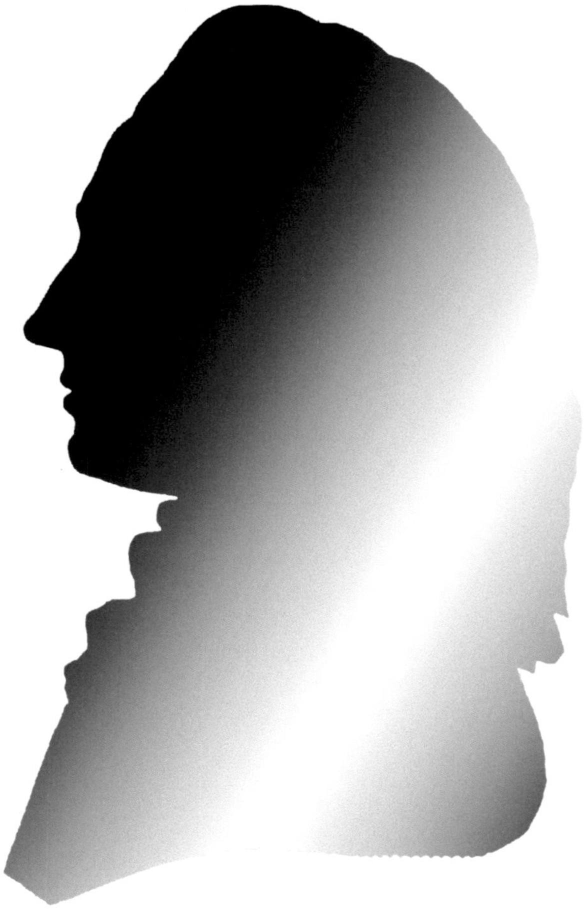

1 *Mack & Goethe – Taten des Lichts* | *Mack & Goethe – Acts of Light*

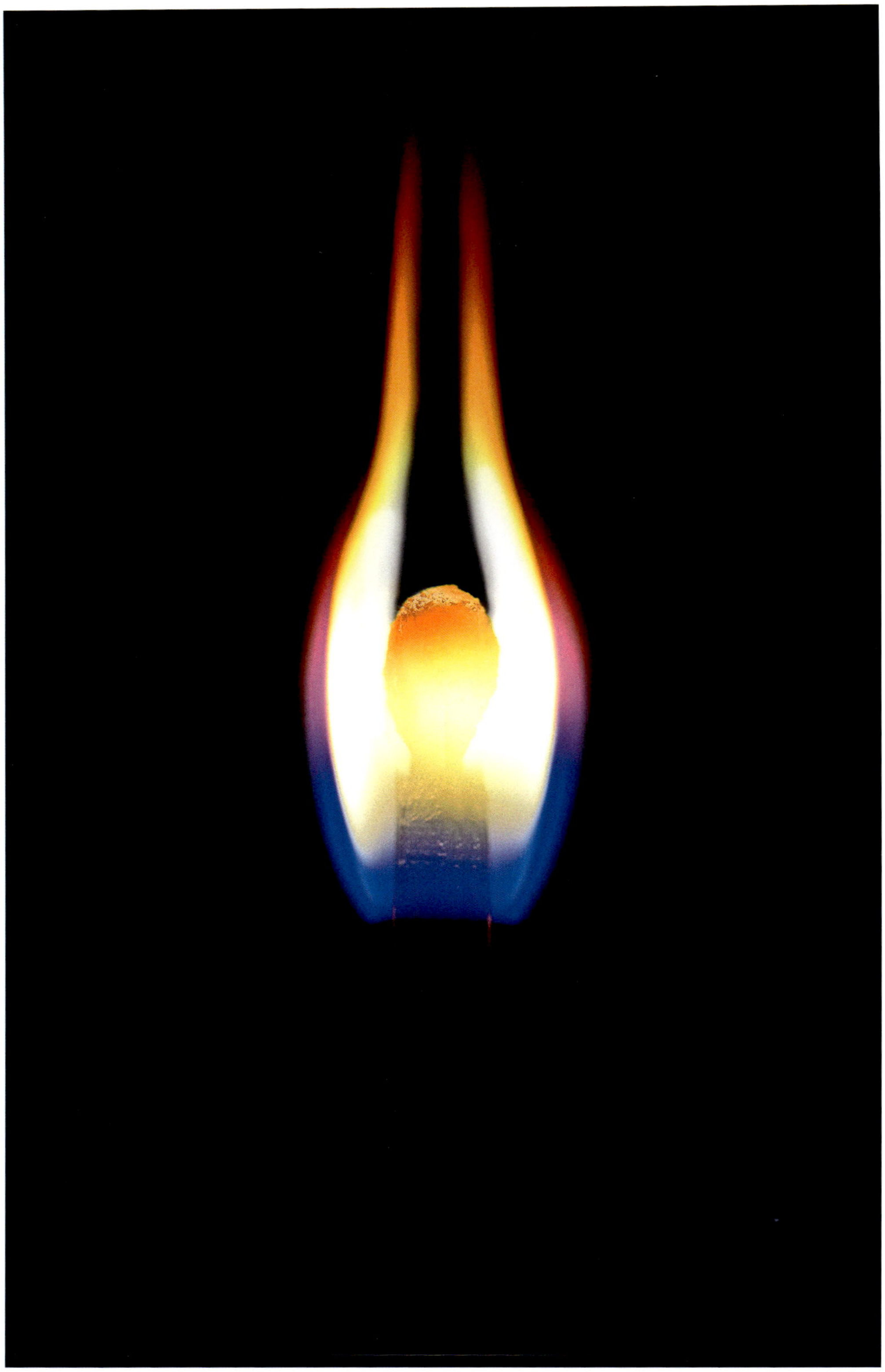

2 Heinz Mack
Engel des Bösen (Gruß an Aubertin), um 1968
Holz, Phosphor
Projektierte Höhe: ca. 10 m

2 Heinz Mack
Angel of Evil (Greetings to Aubertin), ca. 1968
Wood, phosphorus
Projected height: ca. 10 m

3 Johann Wolfgang von Goethe
Karte Nr. 15 aus dem ›Optischen Kartenspiel‹

3 Johann Wolfgang von Goethe
Card no. 15 from the 'Optical Card Game'

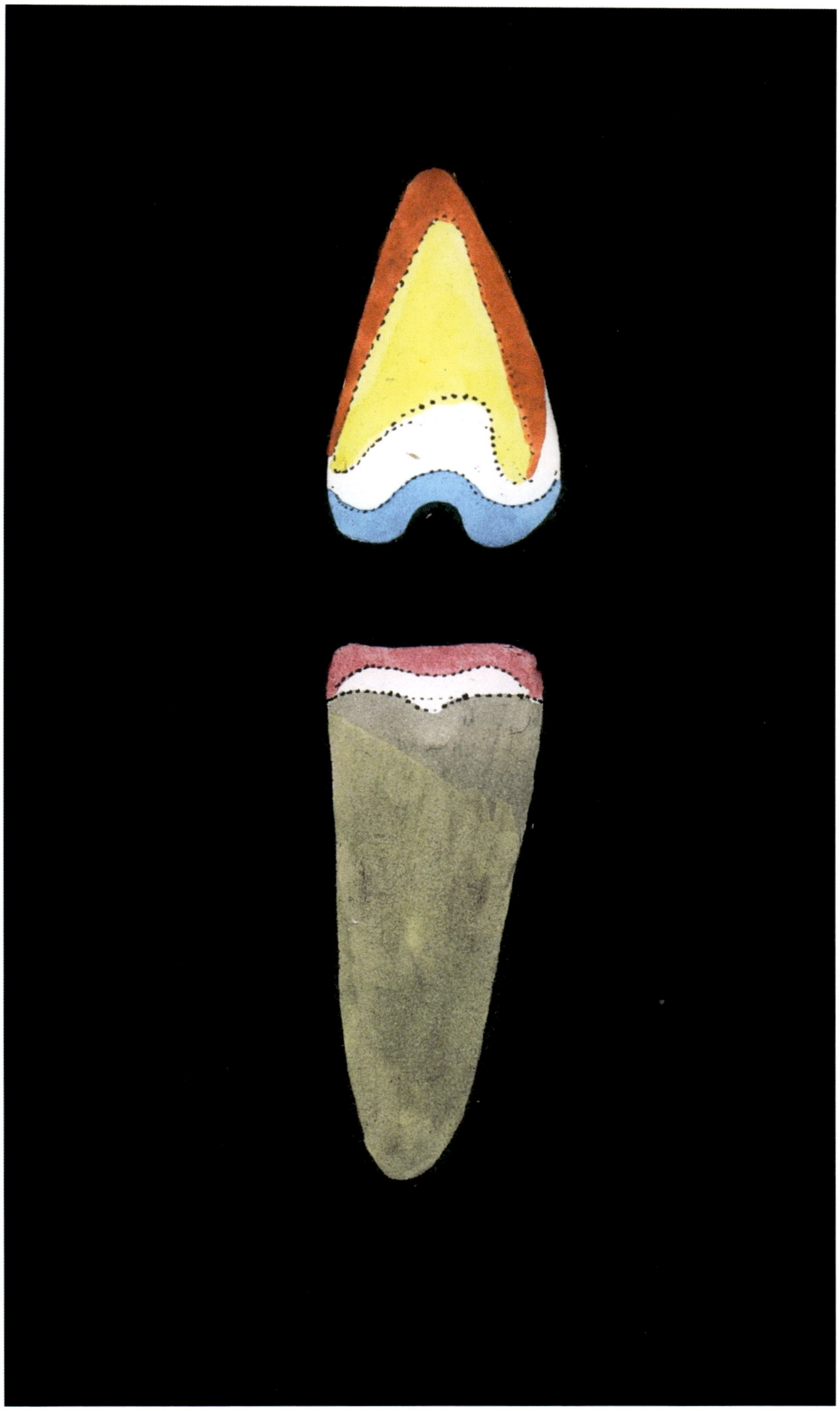

Goethe hatte als Beilage zum ersten Stück seiner *Beyträge zur Optik* von 1791 27 zum Teil handkolorierte Holzschnitttafeln in Spielkartengröße herausgegeben, anhand derer die Leser seine prismatischen Versuche im Experiment nachvollziehen konnten. Tafel Nr. 15 (erklärt in § 87 der Beyträge zur Optik) dient der Kontrolle. Sie zeigt, was man sieht, wenn man das Bild einer weißen Kerzenflamme auf schwarzem Grund durch ein gläsernes Dreikantprisma betrachtet: nämlich das ursprünglich schwarz-weiße Bild mit leuchtend farbigen Säumen dort, wo die schwarzen und weißen Flächen aneinanderstoßen.

As supplement to the first part of his *Contributions to Optics,* Goethe had issued 27 partly colored woodcuts in the size of playing cards so that the reader could reconstruct his prismatic experiments. Plate no. 15 (explained in § 87 of *Contributions to Optics)* serves as proof. It shows what you see when you look at the image of the white flame of a candle in front of a black background through a triangular glass-prism: namely, the originally black-and-white image is surrounded by colored borders where the black and white spaces intersect.

Acts of Light

"The colours are acts of light; its active and passive modifications."[1]

Barbara Steingiesser

Who's Afraid of Red, Yellow, and Blue—If you turn the title Barnett Newman chose for his key work[2] into a question, there is one very straightforward answer: "By all means, not Heinz Mack." However, that was not always the case. In remembering his youth, the artist explains:

> After 1945, for many painters the war took place again: on the canvas in the studio. Often enough, painting destroyed itself. Some paintings looked like gray ash, like dusty, cracked earth that had been furrowed and scratched open as if searching for something there without ever finding it. Other paintings were like seismographic traces of an inner shock. And yet others looked like they had been painted in a slaughterhouse. When the war was over, one color had triumphed: a dirty, dusty, lifeless gray. Even people's faces were gray. After the war, painters approached color reluctantly, as though it were an unknown quantity or life threatening.[3]

In hindsight, Heinz Mack confesses: "I was also afraid of color and kept painting my black and white pictures, my so-called vibrations."[4] Today, however, he not only says: "I am not at all afraid of color,"[5] but instead time and again admits: "I love colors and colors love me!"[6] In fact, he even notes: "The happiness I derive from colors cannot be substituted by anything else."[7]

Neither was Goethe afraid of red, yellow, and blue. While he knew that "[f]rom time immemorial it has been dangerous to treat of colour; so much so, that one of our predecessors[8] ventured on a certain occasion to say, 'The ox becomes furious if a red cloth is shown to him; but the philosopher, who speaks of colour only in a general way, begins to rave.'"[9] Still, he published his treatise *Theory of Colours,*[10] thereby putting it up for public discussion. Of the three primary colors from the subtractive color mix he initially only accepted two as basic colors in the strict sense: blue and yellow. For him, red results according to the principle of polarity and heightening by virtue of the concentration of the contrasting colors blue and yellow into their ultimate coalescence in purple.[11]

In nonrepresentational art, color serves as an energy field. It no longer has an instrumental function, but is sufficient in itself. Does one need to be afraid of strong, autonomous colors when presenting them in a museum in a castle built in 1750, which devotes itself primarily to eighteenth- and nineteenth-century literature? We say: no! Especially when visualizing that a direct line may be drawn from Goethe to the Bauhaus founded in Weimar: after all, the *Stone of Good Fortune*[12] stems from Goethe. And it consists of a sphere that rests on a cube, and thus of

1 Johann Wolfgang von Goethe, *Theory of Colours,* trans. Charles Lock Eastlake (London, 1840), p. [xvii].

2 Between 1966 and 1970 Barnett Newman (1905–1970) painted four versions of his monumental painting *Who's Afraid of Red, Yellow, and Blue* in which he placed primary colors only one beside the other; however, with regards to the format and emphasis of the color fields and stripes they varied from version to version.

3 Translated from "Zitate von Heinz Mack," in Volkmar Hansen and Heike Spies, *Die Rückkehr zur Vernunft: Klassiker zwischen 1932 und 1968,* exh. cat. Goethe Museum Düsseldorf (Düsseldorf, 1995), p. 209.

4 Ibid.

5 Karl Ruhrberg, "Realität und Utopie: Betrachtungen zum Werk von Heinz Mack," in *Utopie und Wirklichkeit im Werk von Heinz Mack,* ed. Wieland Schmied, exh. cat. Liechtensteinische Staatliche Kunstsammlung Vaduz (Cologne, 1998), pp. 315–17, esp. p. 315.

6 Most recently in a conversation with the author on October 30, 2015. On Heinz Mack's reflections on the colors red, yellow, and blue, cf. his conversation with Veit Loers in the present catalogue, pp. 436–52.

7 Ibid., pp. 446 and 448.

8 This refers to mathematician Johann Caspar Funck (1680–1729) and his book *Liber de coloribus coeli,* published in Ulm in 1716.

9 Goethe 1840 (see note 1), pp. xl–xli.

10 Cf. illustration on p. 224 in the present catalogue.

11 Cf. Goethe 1840 (see note 1), p. 352: "[T]he distinction of yellow and blue is duly comprehended, and especially the augmentation into red, by means of which the opposite qualities tend towards each other and become united in a third … ."

12 Ill. p. 37.

Taten des Lichts
»Die Farben sind Thaten des Lichts, Thaten und Leiden.«[1]

Barbara Steingießer

Wer hat Angst vor Rot, Gelb und Blau – Stellt man den Titel, den Barnett Newman für sein Hauptwerk[2] gewählt hat, als Frage, so lässt sich ohne Umschweife antworten: »Heinz Mack jedenfalls nicht.« Das war jedoch nicht immer so. In Erinnerung an seine Jugend erklärt der Künstler:

> Nach 1945 fand der Krieg für viele Maler noch einmal statt: und zwar auf der Leinwand im Atelier: dabei zerstörte sich oft genug die Malerei selbst. Einige Bilder sahen aus wie graue Asche, verstaubte, geschrundene Erde, die man zerfurcht und aufgekratzt hatte, um etwas darin zu suchen, ohne es zu finden. Andere Bilder hatten den Charakter von seismographischen Spuren einer inneren Erschütterung. Und wiederum andere sahen aus, als wären sie in einem Schlachthaus gemalt worden. Am Ende des Krieges hatte eine einzige Farbe gesiegt: ein dreckiges, staubiges, lebloses Grau. Selbst die Gesichter der Menschen waren grau. Nach dem Kriege näherten sich hierzulande die Maler den Farben mit einer Zurückhaltung, als wären diese noch gänzlich unbekannt, oder lebensgefährlich.[3]

So gesteht Heinz Mack im Rückblick: »Auch ich hatte Angst vor der Farbe und malte meine schwarzen und weißen Bilder, meine sogenannten Vibrationen.«[4] Heute jedoch sagt er nicht nur: »Ich habe überhaupt vor keiner Farbe Angst«[5], sondern bekennt immer wieder: »Ich liebe die Farben, und die Farben lieben mich!«[6] Ja, er stellt sogar fest: »Das Glück, welches mir Farben bereiten, lässt sich durch kein anderes ersetzen.«[7]

Auch Goethe fürchtete sich nicht vor Rot, Gelb und Blau. Zwar war ihm bewusst, dass es »von jeher etwas gefährliches« hatte, »von der Farbe zu handeln, dergestalt daß«, so Goethe, »einer unserer Vorgänger[8] gelegentlich gar zu äußern wagt: Hält man dem Stier ein rothes Tuch vor, so wird er wüthend; aber der Philosoph, wenn man nur überhaupt von Farbe spricht, fängt an zu rasen.«[9] Dennoch publizierte er seine Abhandlung *Zur Farbenlehre*[10] und stellte sie damit öffentlich zur Diskussion. Von den drei Primärfarben der subtraktiven Farbmischung erkennt er zunächst nur zwei als Grundfarben im eigentlichen Sinne an, das Blau und das Gelb. Das Rot entsteht bei ihm nach dem Prinzip der Polarität und Steigerung dadurch, dass sich die entgegengesetzten Farben Blau und Gelb verdichten und sich schließlich im Purpur vereinigen.[11]

In der ungegenständlichen Kunst wirkt die Farbe an sich als Energiefeld. Sie hat nicht mehr dienende Funktion, sondern genügt sich selbst. Muss man Angst vor starken, autonomen Farben haben, wenn man sie in einem Museum zeigt, das sich in einem um 1750 erbauten Schloss befindet und das sich vornehmlich der Literatur des 18. und 19. Jahrhunderts widmet? Wir meinen: Nein. Vor allem dann nicht, wenn man sich vor Augen führt, dass sich eine direkte Linie von Goethe zu dem in Weimar gegründeten Bauhaus ziehen

1 Johann Wolfgang von Goethe, *Zur Farbenlehre*, Bd. 1, Tübingen 1810 [Faksimile des didaktischen Teils, 2. Aufl., Dortmund 1982], Vorwort, S. X.
2 Von dem monumentalen Gemälde *Who's Afraid of Red, Yellow and Blue* malte Barnett Newman (1905–1970) im Zeitraum von 1966 bis 1970 vier Versionen, in denen er ausschließlich Primärfarben nebeneinandersetzte, diese jedoch im Format und in der Gewichtung der Farbfelder und -streifen von Fassung zu Fassung variierte.
3 »Zitate von Heinz Mack«, in: Volkmar Hansen und Heike Spies, *Die Rückkehr zur Vernunft. Klassiker zwischen 1932 und 1968,* Ausst.-Kat. Goethe Museum Düsseldorf, Düsseldorf 1995, S. 209.
4 Ebd.
5 Karl Ruhrberg, »Realität und Utopie. Betrachtungen zum Werk von Heinz Mack«, in: *Utopie und Wirklichkeit im Werk von Heinz Mack,* hrsg. von Wieland Schmied, Ausst.-Kat. Liechtensteinische Staatliche Kunstsammlung Vaduz, Köln 1998, S. 315 ff., hier: S. 315.
6 So zuletzt auch im Gespräch mit der Autorin am 30. Oktober 2015. – Zu Überlegungen Heinz Macks zu den Farben Rot, Gelb und Blau vgl. sein Gespräch mit Veit Loers im vorliegenden Katalog, S. 437–453.
7 Ebd., S. 447 und 449.
8 Gemeint ist der Mathematiker Johann Caspar Funck (1680–1729) mit seinem 1716 in Ulm erschienenen *Liber de coloribus coeli.*
9 Goethe 1810 (wie Anm. 1), Einleitung, S. XL.
10 Vgl. die Abb. im vorliegenden Katalog, S. 224.
11 Vgl. Goethe 1810 (wie Anm. 1), § 919, S. 337 f.: »[…] das Auseinandergehen des Gelben und Blauen […], besonders aber die Steigerung ins Rothe […], wodurch das Entgegengesetzte sich gegen einander neigt, und sich in einem Dritten vereinigt […].«

two of the three elementary Bauhaus forms Wassily Kandinsky assigned to the basic colors.[13]

On April 5, 1777, one year after moving to his Weimar garden house, Goethe had a sandstone monument placed in his garden and noted in his diary: "αγαθη τυχη gegründet!"[14] Tyche is the Greek goddess of fate, Agathé Tyche the favorable fate, comparable to the Roman goddess Fortuna. With this memorial stone, Goethe wanted to erect a monument to the good providence that had taken him to Weimar. It was a constant reminder of his personal fortune.

Concerning the formal composition, he consulted the painter and sculptor Adam Friedrich Oeser (1717–1799), his drawing teacher when he studied in Leipzig. However, Oeser showed no understanding for the memorial's modern simplicity. Although, according to Goethe's stipulation, he agreed to do without a personification of fortune, he urgently suggested that the sphere—a symbol of mutable and fleeting destiny—be at least winged and placed on a cloud. But Goethe remained firm, restricting himself to the geometric shapes of sphere and cube without allegorical attributes, and in doing so designed something very modern: the first abstract monument in Occidental art history.[15]

From a distance of 250 years, when thinking of happiness and the sphere balancing on a cube, the viewer might also call to mind something Heinz Mack once said: "Our eyes enjoy resting in restlessness."[16]

Yet this memorial only marks one of numerous connecting lines between Weimar Classicism, Bauhaus, and the art of Heinz Mack. Circular movements rotating around a central pole also have something to do with the balance between rest and restlessness. Used by Goethe—and the Bauhaus masters who succeeded him—for experiments with virtual, immaterial color mixes, Mack produces phenomena that seem like liquefied solid materials or virtual volumes. Just think of Goethe's wheel for optical color mixing,[17] the spinning top[18] that Ludwig Hirschfeld-Mack (1893–1965) developed at the Bauhaus, or Heinz Mack's dynamic rotors and light kinetic sculptures.

With the continuity of aesthetic ideas in mind, we selected *Futura* as the typeface for this exhibition catalogue. Its creator, Paul Renner (1878–1956), based it on the Roman capital letters using the basic forms circle, triangle, and square. Little wonder, then, that the Bauhaus discovered *Futura* for itself. It builds a unique bridge between art and technology,[19] between Classicism and modernity, between past and future—not only thanks to its name. It is the typeface that announces to visitors to the moon: "Here men from the planet earth first set foot upon the moon … ."[20] Thus, which letters could better match the oeuvre of Heinz Mack, who, in 1957, together with Otto Piene, started the countdown to ZERO, thereby giving the go-ahead for a rocket-like ascent. Particularly, as in the seventies, he dreamt of projecting a cross onto the moon as a marker with the aid of mirror reflectors and laser beams in order to signal all the way down to the earth: "A human being was up there."[21]

13 Cf. Hajo Düchting, *Farbe am Bauhaus: Synthese und Synästhesie (Neue Bauhausbücher)* (Berlin, 1996), p. 272, ill. 13.
14 GT, vol. 1 I, p. 40.
15 Cf., e. g, Susanne Müller-Wolff, *Ein Landschaftsgarten im Ilmtal: Die Geschichte des herzoglichen Parks in Weimar (Schriftenreihe des Freundeskreises Goethe-Nationalmuseum e. V.* 3) (Cologne et al., 2007), pp. 60–64, and Hartmut Böhme, "Goethes Skulptur *Agathé Tyche*—Figuren des Zufalls," in idem, *Natur und Figur: Goethe im Kontext* (Paderborn, 2016), pp. [213]–39.
16 Heinz Mack, "Die Ruhe der Unruhe," in *ZERO,* vol. 2, 1958, pp. 20–23, esp. p. 20; reprinted as "Resting Restlessness," in *ZERO,* ed. Otto Piene and Mack, trans. Howard Beckman (Cambridge, MA, and London, 1973), pp. 40–41, esp. p. 40.
17 Ill. p. 232.
18 Ill. p. 233.
19 *Futura* was first introduced in the 1923 Bauhaus exhibition. It was intended to characterize the typographic appearance of the Bauhaus. Walter Gropius proclaimed the motto "art and technology—a new unity."
20 On *Futura,* cf. *Futura: Die Schrift,* ed. Petra Eisele et al., exh. cat. Gutenberg-Museum Mainz (Mainz, 2016).
21 Cf. Axel Hecht: "Sahara und Arktis," in Henri Nannen, ed., *Heinz Mack: Expedition in künstliche Gärten* (Hamburg, n.d. [1976]), unpaginated.

lässt. Immerhin stammt von ihm der *Stein des guten Glücks*[12]. Und der besteht aus einer Kugel, die auf einem Würfel ruht, und damit aus zwei der drei von Wassily Kandinsky den Grundfarben zugeordneten Elementarkörpern des Bauhauses[13]. Am 5. April 1777, ein Jahr nach seinem Einzug ins Weimarer Gartenhaus, ließ Goethe das Sandsteinmonument in seinem Garten am Stern errichten und notierte im Tagebuch: »αγαθη τυχη gegründet!«[14] Tyche ist die griechische Schicksalsgöttin, Agathé Tyche das günstige Geschick, ähnlich der römischen Fortuna. Goethe wollte mit dem Gedenkstein der gütigen Vorsehung, die ihn nach Weimar geführt hatte, ein Denkmal setzen, das ihn immer wieder an sein persönliches Glück erinnern sollte. Bei der Formfindung hatte er sich mit dem Maler und Bildhauer Adam Friedrich Oeser (1717–1799) ausgetauscht, der ihn während des Studiums in Leipzig im Zeichnen unterrichtet hatte. Oeser jedoch hatte für die moderne Schlichtheit des Denkmals kein Verständnis. Zwar war er nach Goethes Vorgabe mit diesem übereingekommen, auf eine Personifikation des Glücks zu verzichten, hatte jedoch dringend dazu geraten, die Kugel als Sinnbild des wandelbaren und flüchtigen Schicksals zumindest mit Flügeln auszustatten und sie auf eine Wolke zu betten. Goethe aber ließ sich nicht beirren, beschränkte sich auf die geometrischen Formen Kugel und Kubus ohne allegorische Attribute und entwarf damit etwas sehr Modernes: das erste abstrakte Denkmal der abendländischen Kunstgeschichte. [15] Aus der Distanz von 250 Jahren mag dem Betrachter bei dem Gedanken an Glück und an die auf einem Würfel balancierende Kugel auch eine Formulierung von Heinz Mack in den Sinn kommen: »Das Glück unserer Augen ist die Ruhe der Unruhe.«[16]

Doch dieses Denkmal markiert nur eine von mehreren Verbindungslinien zwischen der Weimarer Klassik, dem Bauhaus und der Kunst von Heinz Mack. Mit der Balance zwischen Ruhe und Unruhe hat auch die um einen mittigen Pol rotierende Kreisbewegung zu tun, die Goethe – und in seiner Nachfolge die Bauhausmeister – für Experimente mit virtuellen, immateriellen Farbmischungen nutzten und mit der Mack Phänomene hervorbringt, wie scheinbare Verflüssigung fester Werkstoffe oder virtuelle Volumina. Man denke nur an Goethes Schwungrad zur optischen Farbenmischung[17], den Farbenkreisel[18], den Ludwig Hirschfeld-Mack (1893–1965) am Bauhaus entwickelte, sowie an Heinz Macks dynamische Rotoren und lichtkinetische Skulpturen.

Mit dem Gedanken an eine Kontinuität ästhetischer Ideen haben wir für den vorliegenden Ausstellungskatalog die Schrifttype *Futura* gewählt. Ihr Schöpfer Paul Renner (1878–1956) konstruierte sie nach dem Vorbild der römischen Versalien aus den Grundformen Kreis, Dreieck und Quadrat – kein Wunder, dass auch das Bauhaus die *Futura* für sich entdeckte. Sie schlägt in einzigartiger Weise eine Brücke von der Kunst zur Technik[19], von der Klassik zur Moderne, von der Vergangenheit in die Zukunft – und das nicht nur wegen ihres der Zukunft geweihten Namens. Sie ist die Schrifttype, die Besuchern auf dem Mond verkündet: »Here men from the planet earth first set foot upon the moon […]«.[20] Welche Lettern könnten also besser passen zum Werk von Heinz Mack, der 1957 gemeinsam mit Otto Piene den Countdown zählte bis ZERO und damit das Startsignal gab für einen raketenhaften Aufstieg? Zumal er in den 1970er-Jahren davon träumte, mit Spiegelreflektoren und Laserstrahlen ein Kreuz als Markierung auf den Mond zu projizieren, um bis zur Erde herab zu signalisieren: »Da oben ist ein Mensch gewesen.«[21]

12 Abb. S. 37.
13 Vgl. Hajo Düchting, *Farbe am Bauhaus. Synthese und Synästhesie (Neue Bauhausbücher)*, Berlin 1996, S. 272, Abb. 13.
14 GT, Bd. 1 I, S. 40.
15 Vgl. z. B. Susanne Müller-Wolff, *Ein Landschaftsgarten im Ilmtal. Die Geschichte des herzoglichen Parks in Weimar (Schriftenreihe des Freundeskreises Goethe-Nationalmuseum e. V.*, 3), Köln u. a. 2007, S. 60–64 und Hartmut Böhme, »Goethes Skulptur *Agathé Tyche* – Figuren des Zufalls«, in: ders., *Natur und Figur. Goethe im Kontext*, Paderborn 2016, S. [213]–239.
16 Heinz Mack, »Die Ruhe der Unruhe«, in: *ZERO*, Bd. 2, 1958, Nachdruck, 3 Bde. in 1 Bd., 1973, S. 38 f., hier: S. 38.
17 Abb. S. 232.
18 Abb. S. 233.
19 Für die Bauhausausstellung von 1923, in deren Schrifttum die *Futura*, die das typografische Erscheinungsbild des Bauhauses prägen sollte, erstmals zum Einsatz kam, hatte Walter Gropius das Motto »Kunst und Technik – eine neue Einheit« ausgerufen.
20 Zur *Futura* vgl. *Futura. Die Schrift*, hrsg. von Petra Eisele u. a., Ausst.-Kat. Gutenberg-Museum Mainz, Mainz 2016.
21 Vgl. Axel Hecht: »Sahara und Arktis«. In: *Heinz Mack. Expedition in künstliche Gärten*, fotografiert von Thomas Höpker, hrsg. von Henri Nannen. Hamburg o. J. [1976], o. S.

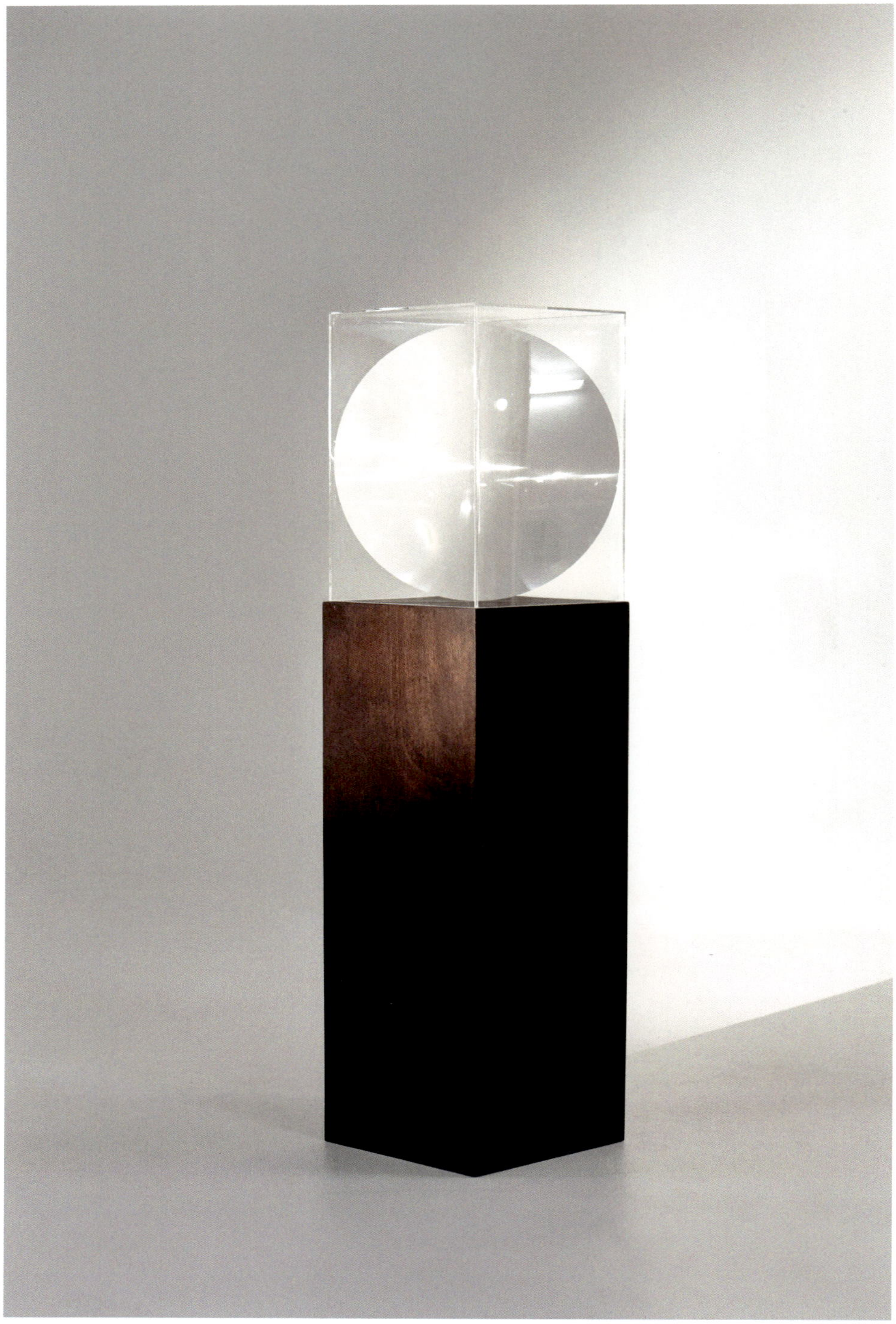

4 Heinz Mack
Transparenz und Strahlung
Signiert, datiert: »mack 9«
Plexiglas, Fresnel-Linsen, Elektrizität
63 x 44,5 x 44,5 cm

4 Heinz Mack
Transparency and Radiation
Signed, dated: "mack 9"
Plexiglass, Fresnel-lenses, electricity
63 x 44.5 x 44.5 cm

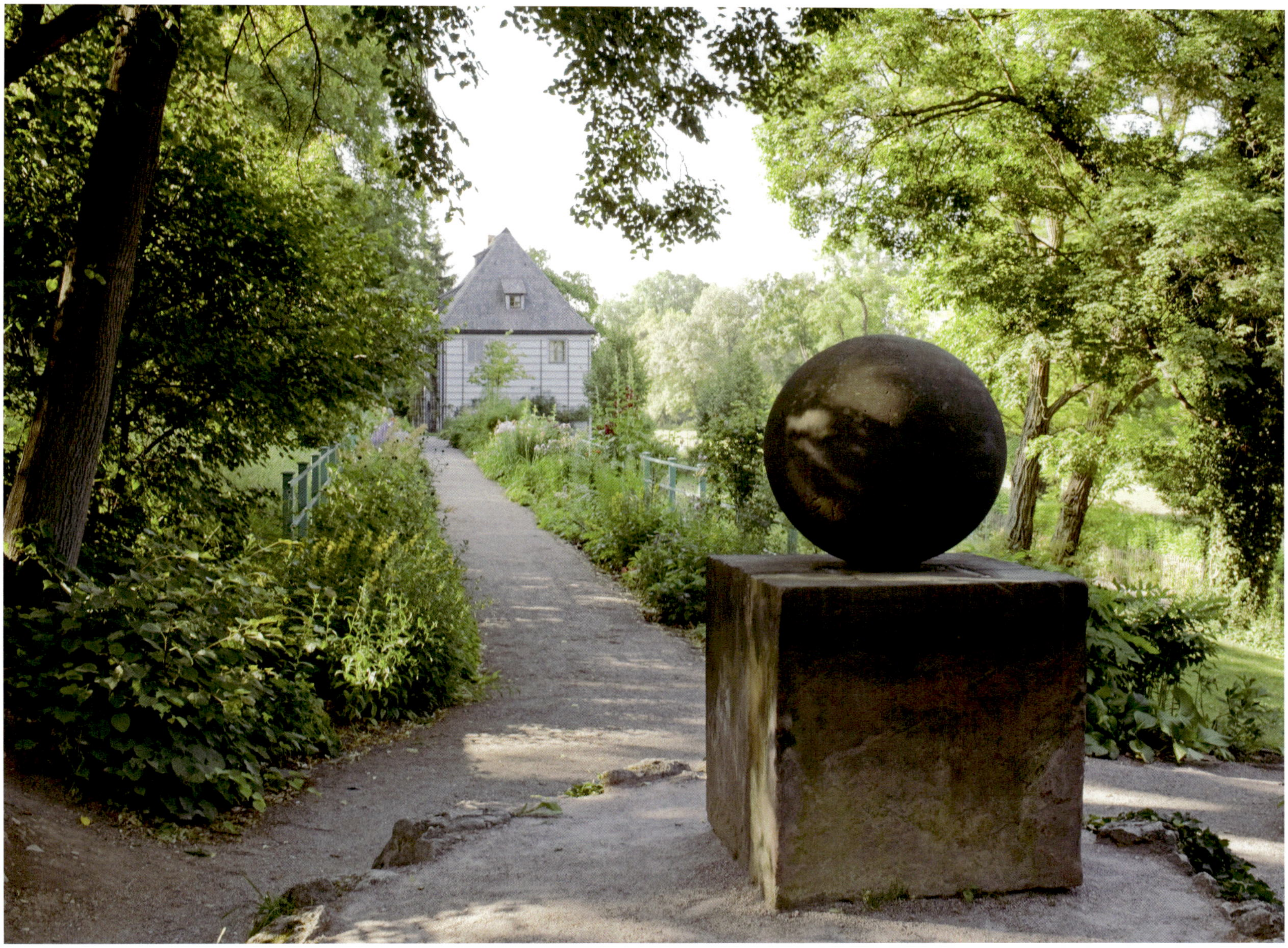

5 Johann Wolfgang von Goethe
Stein des guten Glücks in Goethes Garten am Stern in Weimar, 1777
Sandstein
160 x 89 x 89 cm

5 Johann Wolfgang von Goethe
Stone of Good Fortune in Goethe's garden at the Stern in Weimar, 1777
Sandstone
160 x 89 x 89 cm

"The Undertaking is Excused"[22]

If, as Goethe put it in his foreword to *Zur Morphologie* (On Morphology), one wanted to contradict critical remarks regarding this exhibition project, one could cite Heinz Mack, who says: "Mack and Goethe naturally do *not* meet at the same eye level!"[23] While for the painter and sculptor the poet is enthroned on Mount Parnassus, he only sees himself as "an occasional visitor in Delphi." This, on the other hand, is reminiscent of Goethe's phrase "guest on an estate not his own,"[24] which is how he felt when devoting himself to the natural sciences.

The present exhibition catalogue includes contributions by humanities scholars and natural scientists: German philologists, art historians, philosophers, and physicists, assembled like several apartments under the same roof according to the principle Goethe had originally imagined for his *Theory of Colours*. He had wished that "a group of men with quite different fields of interests might cooperate, each attacking the problem from his own point of view, in order to further such a difficult and wide-ranging undertaking."

As he later recalled, to this end he would have liked to call upon "the philosopher, the physicist, mathematician, painter, instrument maker, cloth dyer, and God knows whom else." But his brother-in-law, Johann Georg Schlosser (1739–1799), whom he informed about his plan in 1793, was unenthusiastic. Goethe states that he "laughed at me instead: he claimed that even at my age I was still just a child and a novice, that I was just dreaming if I thought anyone would take a part in anything I was interested in, or that anyone would embrace a new manner of proceeding and make it his own, or that it was at all possible for there to be any common effort or cooperation in Germany!"[25]

Since thinking in rigid categories was alien to Goethe, he noted with astonishment: "[N]owhere did anyone want to admit that science and poetry are reconcilable. They forgot that science developed out of poetry; they ignored that, after times changed, both are once again amicable, to the advantage of both sides; at a higher place they might very likely meet again."[26] Today, however—in view of increased interest in interdisciplinary research projects and multidisciplinary art concepts—such an epoch appears to be moving closer.

At any rate, the distance in terms of time is something the painter-sculptor Mack always bears in mind when thinking of Goethe. For centuries, artists attempted to paint light: directly, as a candle flame, or indirectly, when light models the arrangement of the folds of a tablecloth or is refracted through a wineglass. In contrast, Heinz Mack no longer paints light, but lets it manifest as such in his light reliefs. Light is no longer depicted. Instead, it is a performer on a stage that the artist provides (and which the light causes to become immaterial through its vibrating energy). This is why all artworks by the light artist Heinz Mack are at the same time "acts of light."

Even if Mack points out potential conformity in Goethe's and his own art concepts, he refers to this only as a "coincidence" and definitely not "coherence."[27] Nonetheless, it seems legitimate to point out some similarities. To use an aphorism

22 Translated from Johann Wolfgang von Goethe, "Das Unternehmen wird entschuldigt", in idem, *Zur Morphologie,* vol. 1 (Stuttgart and Tübingen, 1817), pp. [V]–VII.
23 Heinz Mack in a conversation with the author on September 28, 2017.
24 Goethe 1810 (see note 1), p. 353.
25 Johann Wolfgang von Goethe, *The Collected Works,* vol. 5, *Campaign in France 1792/Siege of Mainz,* ed. Thomas P. Saine and Jeffrey L. Sammons, trans. Thomas P. Saine (Princeton, 1994), pp. 775–76.
26 Translated from Goethe 1817 (see note 22), pp. 71–72.
27 Heinz Mack in conversation with the author on December 20, 2016.

»Das Unternehmen wird entschuldigt«[22]

Wollte man – wie Goethe es im Vorwort zu seinen Schriften *Zur Morphologie* tut – möglichen kritischen Äußerungen entgegenwirken, so könnte man – bezogen auf dieses Ausstellungsprojekt – Heinz Mack zitieren, der sagt: »Mack und Goethe begegnen sich selbstredend nicht auf gleicher Augenhöhe!«[23] Für den Maler und Bildhauer thront der Dichter auf dem Parnass, er selbst dagegen versteht sich nur als »gelegentlicher Besucher in Delphi«. Das wiederum erinnert an Goethes Formulierung vom »Gast in einer fremden Wohnung«[24], als der er sich empfand, wenn er sich den Naturwissenschaften widmete.

Im vorliegenden Ausstellungskatalog sind Beiträge von Geisteswissenschaftlern und Naturforschern: von Germanisten, Kunsthistorikern, Philosophen und Physikern wie mehrere Wohnungen unter einem Dach versammelt, nach dem Prinzip, das Goethe sich ursprünglich für seine Abhandlung *Zur Farbenlehre* vorgestellt hatte. Er hatte sich gewünscht, dass »eine Gesellschaft verschiedenartiger Männer zusammen arbeiten und jeder von seiner Seite mit eingreifen könnte, um ein so schwieriges und weitläufiges Unternehmen fördern zu helfen«.

Dafür hätte er gern, wie er sich später erinnert, »den Philosophen, den Physiker, Mathematiker, Mahler, Mechaniker, Färber und Gott weiß wen alles in Anspruch genommen«. Doch sein Schwager Johann Georg Schlosser (1739–1799), dem er 1793 von seinem Plan berichtet hatte, war dafür nicht zu begeistern gewesen. Er, so Goethe, »lachte mich aus: ich sei, meinte er, in meinen alten Tagen noch immer ein Kind und Neuling, daß ich mir einbilde, es werde jemand an demjenigen Theil nehmen, wofür ich Interesse zeige, es werde jemand ein fremdes Verfahren billigen und es zu dem seinigen machen, es könne in Deutschland irgendeine gemeinsame Wirkung und Mitwirkung statt finden!«[25]

Goethe, dem jegliches Denken in starren Kategorien fremd war, stellte verwundert fest: »[…] nirgends wollte man zugeben, daß Wissenschaft und Poesie vereinbar seyen. Man vergaß daß Wissenschaft sich aus Poesie entwickelt habe, man bedachte nicht daß, nach einem Umschwung von Zeiten, beyde sich wieder freundlich, zu beyderseitigem Vortheil, auf höherer Stelle, gar wohl wieder begegnen könnten.«[26] Heute dagegen scheint – angesichts des steigenden Interesses an interdisziplinären Forschungsprojekten und spartenübergreifenden Kunstkonzepten – eine solche Epoche zumindest näherzurücken.

Der zeitliche Abstand jedenfalls ist etwas, das dem Maler und Bildhauer Mack beim Gedanken an Goethe stets bewusst bleibt. Jahrhundertelang versuchten Künstler, das Licht zu malen: direkt als Kerzenflamme oder indirekt, wenn es den Faltenwurf eines Tischtuches modelliert oder sich in einem Weinglas bricht. Heinz Mack hingegen malt heute nicht mehr das Licht, sondern lässt es in seinen Lichtreliefs selbst zur Erscheinung kommen. Das Licht wird nicht mehr dargestellt, sondern es wird auf der Bühne, die der Künstler ihm bietet (und die es durch seine vibrierende Energie immaterialisiert), selbst zum Darsteller. Daher sind alle Kunstwerke des Lichtkünstlers Heinz Mack zugleich »Taten des Lichts«.

Auch wenn Mack darauf hinweist, dass es sich bei einer eventuellen Übereinstimmung zwischen seiner eigenen Kunstauffassung und derjenigen Goethes nur um eine »Koinzidenz« handeln könne, nicht jedoch um »Kohärenz«,[27] ist es gleichwohl erlaubt, die eine oder andere Gemeinsamkeit aufzudecken. Goethe selbst sagt in den unter dem Titel *Maximen und Reflexionen* bekannt gewordenen Aphorismen: »Nach Analogien denken ist nicht zu

22 Johann Wolfgang von Goethe, »Das Unternehmen wird entschuldigt«, in: ders., *Zur Morphologie*, Bd. 1, Stuttgart und Tübingen 1817, S. [V] ff.
23 Heinz Mack im Gespräch mit der Autorin am 28. September 2017.
24 Goethe 1810 (wie Anm. 1), Schlußwort, S. 350 f.
25 Johann Wolfgang von Goethe, *Belagerung von Mainz,* WA, Bd. I 33, S. 327.
26 Johann Wolfgang von Goethe, *Zur Morphologie,* Bd. 1, Stuttgart und Tübingen 1817, »Schicksal der Druckschrift«, S. 71 f.
27 Heinz Mack im Gespräch mit der Autorin am 20. Dezember 2016.

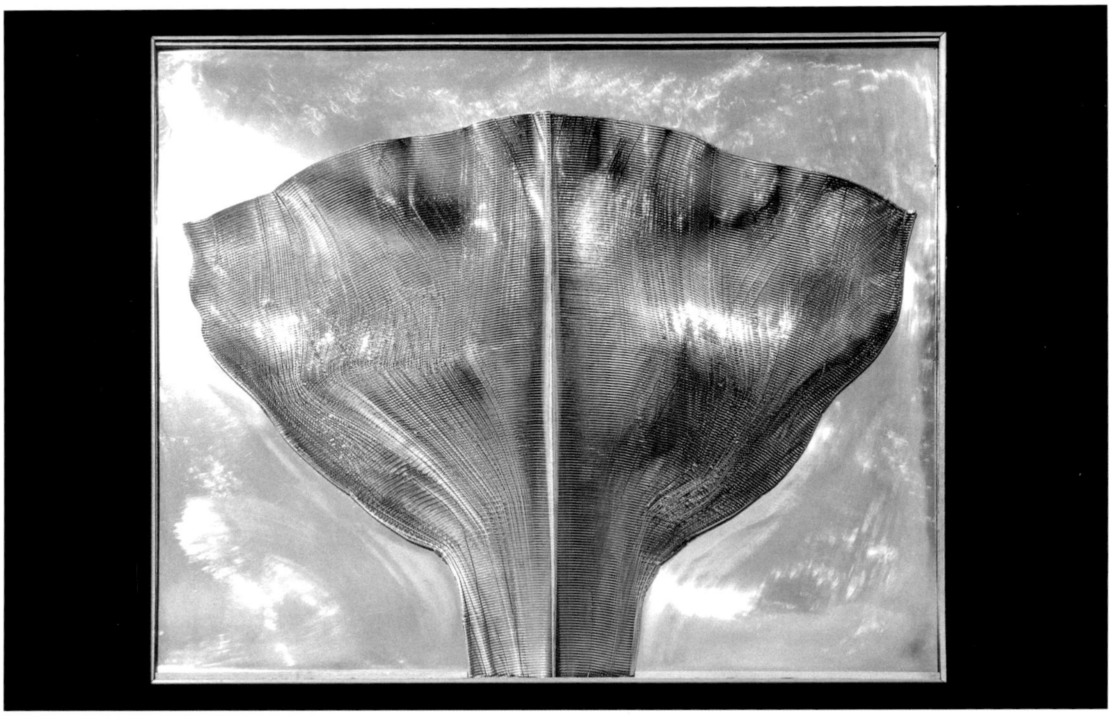

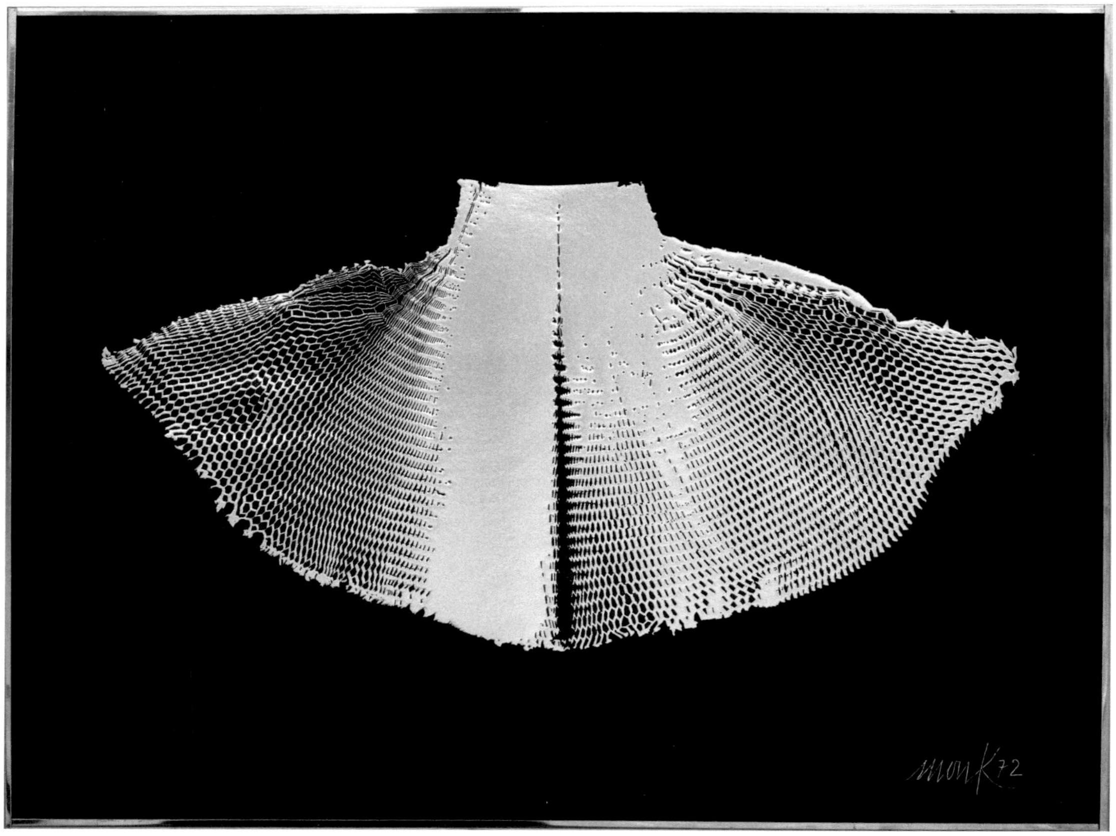

6 Heinz Mack
Ikarus, 1967
Aluminium, Edelstahl, Holz, Plexiglas
175 x 186 x 6,5 cm

Heinz Mack
Ikarus, 1967
Aluminum, stainless steel, wood, plexiglass
175 x 186 x 6.5 cm

7 Heinz Mack
Ohne Titel, signiert, datiert: »mack 72«
Silberprägung auf schwarzem Karton
43 x 55,5 cm

Heinz Mack
Untitled, signed, dated: "mack 72"
Embossed in silver on black cardboard
43 x 55.5 cm

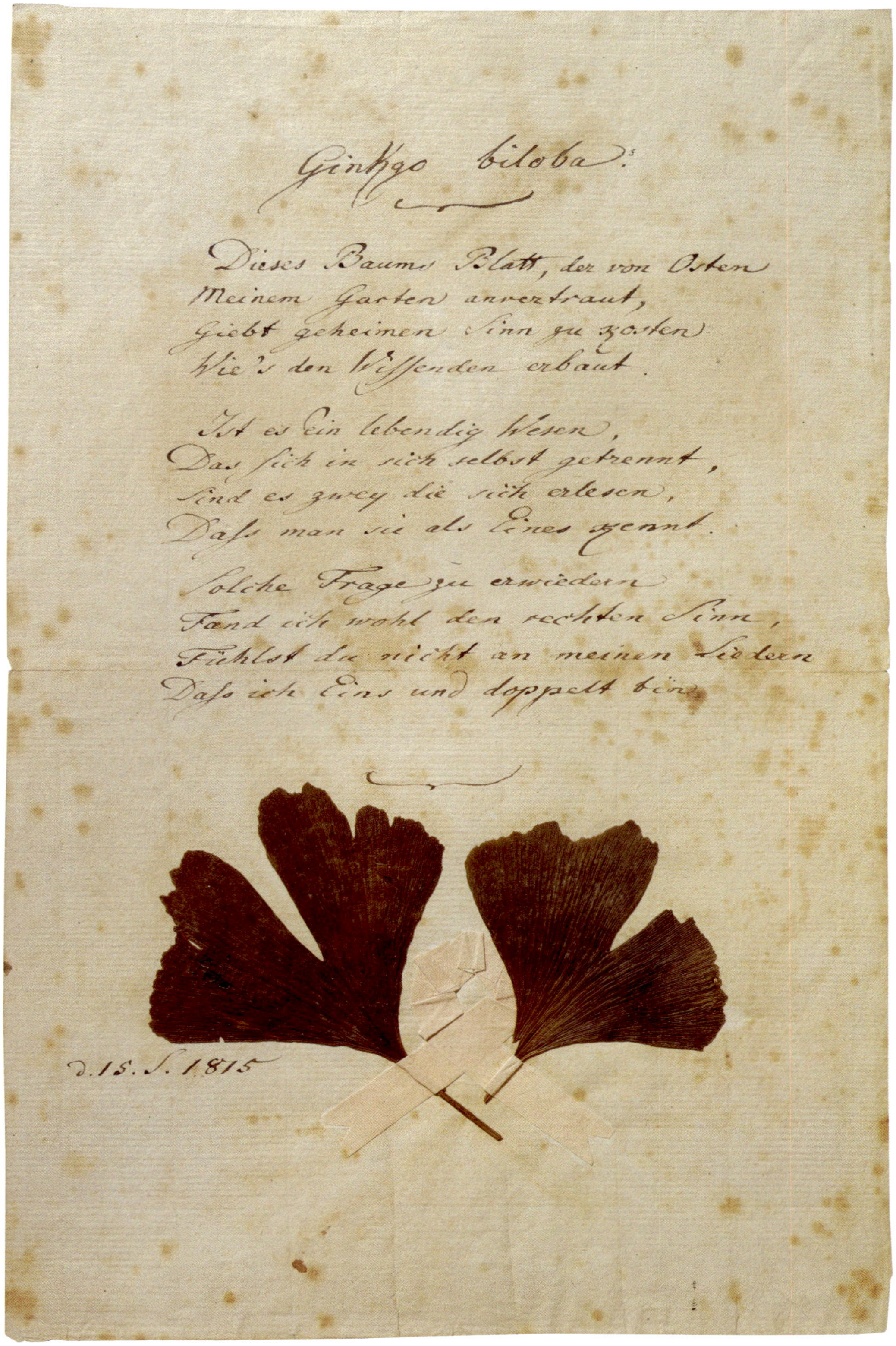
Ginkgo biloba.

Dieses Baums Blatt, der von Osten
Meinem Garten anvertraut,
Giebt geheimen Sinn zu kosten
Wie's den Wissenden erbaut.

Ist es Ein lebendig Wesen,
Das sich in sich selbst getrennt,
Sind es zwey die sich erlesen,
Daß man sie als Eines kennt.

Solche Frage zu erwiedern
Fand ich wohl den rechten Sinn,
Fühlst du nicht an meinen Liedern
Daß ich Eins und doppelt bin.

d. 15. S. 1815

8 Johann Wolfgang von Goethe
Eigenhändige Reinschrift seines Gedichtes:
Ginkgo biloba
aus dem *West-oestlichen Divan (Buch Suleika)*
Datiert: »d. 15. S[eptember]. 1815«
1 Blatt, 1 S. beschrieben, 32,8 x 21,3 cm
Mit Montierung von zwei Ginkgo-Blättern
und rosafarbenem Papierbändchen
Goethe-Museum Düsseldorf

8 Johann Wolfgang von Goethe
Clean copy of his poem in his own hand:
Ginkgo biloba
from *West-East Divan (Book of Zuleika)*
Dated: "d. 15. S[eptember]. 1815"
1 sheet, 1 page written, 32.8 x 21.3 cm
Two ginkgo leaves mounted on
pink paper ribbons
Goethe-Museum Düsseldorf

from Goethe's *Maxims and Reflections:* "We mustn't scorn thinking that proceeds by way of analogies … ."[28] Even as an octogenarian, he wrote to Zelter: "[T]here are relations everywhere and relations constitute life."[29] Associations arouse curiosity, a precondition for all creative thinking, regardless of in what area, in science or art.

Relations—this is something we learned while working on this project—exist not only between two very independent artists' personalities from two centuries, but equally between the individual segments of this exhibition, which is roughly structured into the core theme of "light and color" followed by the two secondary themes of "structure and morphology" and "Oriental inspiration."

If you begin researching Goethe's theory of colors and find a letter from the poet and physicist Thomas Seebeck (1770–1831) dealing with the influence of colored light on plant growth,[30] your gaze will wander to colors as "acts of light," to the "formation and transformation of organic nature," and hence to morphology.

Goethe's particular morphological interest was directed toward the ginkgo tree, neither a coniferous nor a deciduous wood, whose fan-like, notched leaf was a symbol of love for him. "Do we spy one living being / That had split itself in two? / Is it two things we are seeing / That we yet united view?"[31]

Goethe incorporated this poem into his *West-East Divan.*[32] Thus, the focus shifts to the Orient, independent of the tree's Chinese origin. It goes without saying that the interest in light's composition was particularly intense in regions where the sun rises. Goethe reports that the prism is "an instrument that is held in such high regard in the Orient that the Chinese emperor, as it were, reserves, as his majestic privilege, the right to be its sole owner."[33] This brings us full circle to our point of departure: to color.

28 Johann Wolfgang von Goethe, *Maxims and Reflections,* trans. Elisabeth Stopp (London 1998), p. 70.

29 Johann Wolfgang von Goethe in a letter to Carl Friedrich Zelter dated January 29, 1830. *Goethe's Letters to Zelter,* trans. A. D. Coleridge (London and New York, 1892), p. 387.

30 Letter dated February 18, 1810, WA, vol. IV 51, pp. 277–78. Cf. illustration on p. 221 in the present catalogue.

31 Johann Wolfgang von Goethe, "Ginkgo biloba," *West-East Divan,* trans. Martin Bidney (New York, 2010), pp. 92–93. Cf. illustration on p. 41 in the present catalogue.

32 Johann Wolfgang von Goethe, *West-oestlicher Divan,* Stuttgart 1819 (cf. illustration on p. 358), p. 131.

33 Translated from Johann Wolfgang von Goethe, *Beyträge zur Optik,* vol. 1 (Weimar, 1791) [facsimile, Weimar 2007], § 33, p. 19.

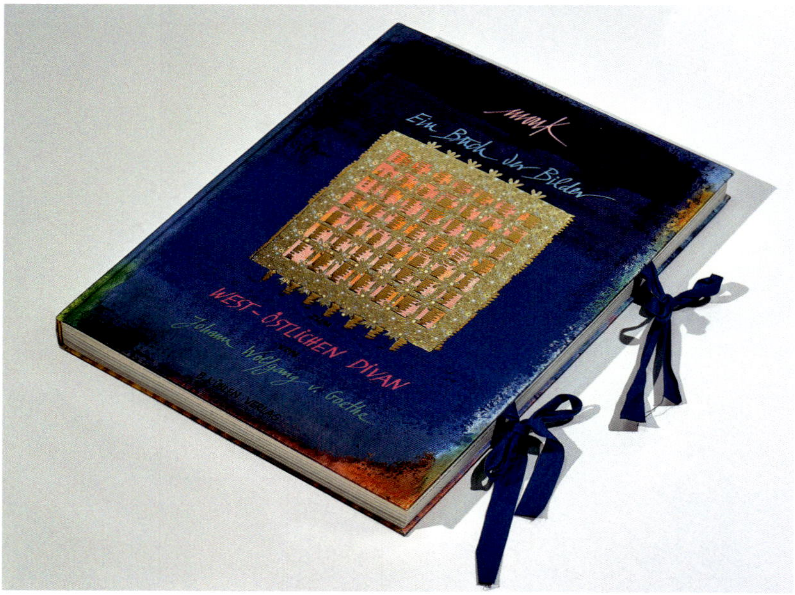

9 Heinz Mack
Ein Buch der Bilder zum West-östlichen Divan
von Johann Wolfgang v. Goethe
Mönchengladbach 1999

Heinz Mack
Ein Buch der Bilder zum West-östlichen Divan
von Johann Wolfgang v. Goethe
Mönchengladbach 1999

schelten [...].«[28] Und noch als 80-Jähriger schrieb er an Zelter: »[...] Bezüge gibt's überall und Bezüge sind das Leben.«[29] Assoziationen wecken Neugier, die Grundvoraussetzung allen schöpferischen Denkens, ganz gleich auf welchem Gebiet, in der Wissenschaft oder in der Kunst.

Bezüge – das haben wir bei der Arbeit an diesem Ausstellungsprojekt festgestellt – gibt es nicht nur zwischen zwei sehr eigenständigen Künstlerpersönlichkeiten aus zwei verschiedenen Jahrhunderten, sondern auch zwischen den einzelnen Abteilungen der Ausstellung, die sich grob in den Schwerpunkt »Licht und Farbe« sowie die beiden Nebenthemen »Struktur und Morphologie« und »Inspiration Orient« gliedern lässt.

Beginnt man bei der Recherche mit Goethes Farbenlehre und stößt dabei auf einen Brief des Dichters an den Physiker Thomas Seebeck (1770–1831), in dem es um den Einfluss farbigen Lichtes auf das Pflanzenwachstum geht[30], so wandert der Blick von den Farben als »Taten des Lichts« auf die »Bildung und Umbildung organischer Naturen« und damit zur Morphologie.

Besonderes morphologisches Interesse hatte Goethe am Ginkgo-Baum, der weder zu den Laub- noch zu den Nadelhölzern gehört und dessen fächerförmiges, in der Mitte eingekerbtes Blatt für ihn zum Symbol der Liebe wurde. »Ist es Ein lebendig Wesen, / Das sich in sich selbst getrennt«, fragt er. »Sind es zwey die sich erlesen, / Dass man sie als Eines kennt.«[31]

Goethe nahm dieses Gedicht in den *West-oestlichen Divan*[32] auf. Damit richtet sich der Fokus, auch unabhängig von der chinesischen Herkunft des Baumes, auf den Orient. Und dass dort, wo die Sonne aufgeht, das Interesse an der Zusammensetzung des Lichtes besonders groß war, versteht sich fast von selbst. Goethe weiß zu berichten, das Prisma sei »ein Instrument, welches in den Morgenländern so hoch geachtet wird, daß sich der chinesische Kayser den ausschließenden Besitz desselben, gleichsam als ein Majestätsrecht, vor behält«[33]. Damit schließt sich der Kreis zum Ausgangspunkt, zur Farbe.

Weil schon Goethe wusste: »[...] Wort und Zeichen sind nichts gegen sicheres, lebendiges Anschauen [...]«[34], haben wir alles daran gesetzt, die Bezüge zwischen Kunst und Wissenschaft und die Parallelen zwischen Goethe und Mack durch die Gegenüberstellung möglichst anschaulicher Exponate sinnlich erfahrbar zu machen, »[...] denn nur durch Zusammenstellen des Verwandten entsteht nach und nach eine Totalität, die sich selbst ausspricht und keiner weitern Erklärung bedarf.«[35]

Mack & Goethe

Was aber haben Johann Wolfgang von Goethe und Heinz Mack gemeinsam? Was verbindet den Dichter der deutschen Klassik mit dem bildenden Künstler von heute, der 1957 zusammen mit Otto Piene die internationale Avantgarde-Bewegung ZERO gegründet hat? – Dass der Farbenreichtum der Lyrik des ›Augenmenschen‹[36] Goethe den musikalisch begabten Maler Mack[37] zu einem Dialog der Rhythmen, Formen und Farben inspirierte, zeigte bereits 1999 eine Suite von Papierarbeiten, die Heinz Mack zu Goethes 250. Geburtstag dem Gedichtzyklus *West-oestlicher Divan* widmete. Die farbigen Pastelle und schwarzweißen Tuschen wurden damals im Goethe-Museum Düsseldorf präsentiert[38] und als

28 Johann Wolfgang von Goethe, *Maximen und Reflexionen über Literatur und Ethik,* WA, Bd. I 42 II, S. 180.
29 Johann Wolfgang von Goethe, Brief an Carl Friedrich Zelter vom 29. Januar 1830, WA, Bd. IV 46, S. 221–226, hier: S. 223.
30 Brief vom 18. Februar 1810, WA, Bd. IV 51, S. 277 f. Vgl. die Abb. im vorliegenden Katalog, S. 221.
31 Johann Wolfgang von Goethe, *Ginkgo biloba,* Abb. der auf den 15. September 1815 datierten Reinschrift im vorliegenden Katalog, S. 41.
32 Johann Wolfgang von Goethe, *West-oestlicher Divan,* Stuttgart 1819 (vgl. Abb. S. 358), S. 131.
33 Johann Wolfgang von Goethe, *Beyträge zur Optik,* Bd. 1, Weimar 1791 [Faksimile, Weimar 2007], § 33, S. 19.
34 Johann Wolfgang von Goethe, *Entoptische Farben, Ansprache,* LA, Bd. I 8, S. 94 f., hier: S. 94.
35 Goethe 1810 (wie Anm. 1), § 228, S. 87.
36 In *Dichtung und Wahrheit* schreibt Goethe in Erinnerung an seine Jugend: »Das Auge war vor allen anderen das Organ, womit ich die Welt faßte.« (WA, Bd. I 27, S. 16.) Und noch im Alter von 80 Jahren bekennt er mit Blick auf das »Bedürfniß nach Tönen« des Komponisten Carl Friedrich Zelter: »Bey mir ist das Auge vorwaltend [...].« (Brief an Zelter vom 27. März 1830, WA, Bd. IV 46, S. 285–288, hier: S. 285.)
37 Heinz Mack wäre vermutlich Pianist geworden, hätte nicht eine Schnittverletzung an der Hand, die ein betrunkener amerikanischer Soldat ihm kurz nach Kriegsende zugefügt hatte, das verhindert. Noch heute spielt Mack Klavier. Er sagt: »Höchsten Stellenwert hat für mich – neben Malerei und Skulptur – die Musik, ohne die ich nicht leben möchte. Wenn ich male, höre ich gerne klassische Musik oder auch ›wohltemperierten‹ Jazz.« (Heinz Mack, »Aus meinem Leben«, in: *Mack. Leben und Werk. 1931–2011. Ein Buch vom Künstler über den Künstler,* hrsg. von Heinz Mack und Ute Mack, Köln 2011, S. 8–18, hier: S. 17.)
38 Heinz Mack, *Bilder zu Goethes »West-östlichem Divan«,* Ausstellung im Goethe-Museum Düsseldorf, 15. August bis 3. Oktober 1999.

Because Goethe already knew that "word and sign are nothing compared to reliable, vivid examination, ..."[34] we did our utmost to ensure that references about art and science as well as parallels between Goethe and Mack can be sensuously experienced by juxtaposing striking, illustrative exhibits. "[F]or it is only by combining analogies that we gradually arrive at a whole which speaks for itself, and requires no further explanation."[35]

Mack & Goethe

But what do Johann Wolfgang von Goethe and Heinz Mack have in common? What connects the poet of German Classicism with the contemporary visual artist, who, in 1957, together with Otto Piene founded the international avant-garde movement ZERO? As early as 1999, a suite of works on paper by Heinz Mack dedicated to the anthology *West-East Divan* on the occasion of Goethe's 250th birthday showed that the abundance of color in the poems by the "eye person"[36] Goethe inspired the musically talented painter Mack[37] to produce a dialogue of rhythms, shapes, and colors. At the time, the Goethe-Museum in Düsseldorf presented[38] the color pastels as well as the black-and-white ink drawings, that were edited in an artist's book.[39] This was followed in 2003 by an exhibition with works by Heinz Mack dedicated to the *Song of Solomon*.[40] Goethe had translated parts of it from Hebrew in 1775 by using the Latin vulgate and several different German translations.

In 1995, Mack participated with eleven works in an exhibition at Schloss Jägerhof entitled *Die Rückkehr der Vernunft* (The Return of Reason). This was the Goethe-Museum's contribution to the program *45 ff—Kriegsende: Kontinuität und Neubeginn* (45 ff—The End of the War: Continuity and New Beginning) broaching the issue of the "historic abyss" gaping since World War II between our era and the age of Goethe. It was likewise an attempt by the postwar generation to again tie into humanist ideas in the sense of German Classicism after the atrocious crimes committed by the National Socialists.[41]

After designing the cover for the accompanying catalogue,[42] which combines a 200-year-old Goethe silhouette with Mack's own chromatology *Gruss an Goethe* (Salute to Goethe)[43] and features a jagged line symbolizing the crack through time, vertically dividing the motif in two halves—one white, the other black—Mack designed two more covers for the Goethe-Museum. For *Europa, wie Goethe es sah* (Europe as Goethe saw it)[44] the outlines of the same silhouette are filled with a satellite image of Europe from the German Center for Aerospace. For the museum's fiftieth anniversary in 2006, he had *Die Idee Goethe* light up in the form of a spectral photo experiment behind a white design drawing of the late-Baroque castle façade on a black ground.[45]

The connection between Mack and Goethe is most definitely not limited to occasional collaboration with the Goethe-Museum Düsseldorf. Since his youth, he has consistently dealt artistically with the life and work of Johann Wolfgang von Goethe. This can be deduced by references to Goethe that may be encountered throughout his

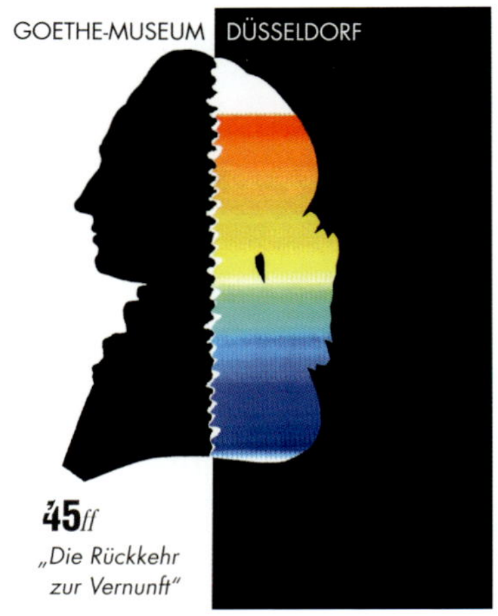

10 Heinz Mack
Cover-Entwurf zu:
Volkmar Hansen und Heike Spies
45 ff – Kriegsende: Kontinuität und Neubeginn. Die Rückkehr zur Vernunft. Klassiker zwischen 1932 und 1968
Ausst.-Kat. Goethe-Museum Düsseldorf
Düsseldorf 1995

Heinz Mack
Cover sketch for:
Volkmar Hansen and Heike Spies
45 ff – Kriegsende: Kontinuität und Neubeginn. Die Rückkehr zur Vernunft. Klassiker zwischen 1932 und 1968
Exh. cat. Goethe-Museum Düsseldorf
Düsseldorf 1995

34 Translated from Johann Wolfgang von Goethe, *Entoptische Farben, Ansprache,* LA, vol. I 8, pp. 94–95, esp. p. 94.
35 Goethe 1840 (see note 1), § 228, p. 94.
36 Recalling his youth, in *Truth and Poetry* Goethe writes: "The eye was, above all others, the organ by which I seized the world." Johann Wolfgang von Goethe, *Truth and Poetry: From My Own Life,* vol. 1, trans. John Oxenford (Cambridge, 2013), p. 187. And even at the age of eighty, with regards to the "craving for tones" he confesses to the composer Carl Friedrich Zelter: "In my case, the eye prevails ... ." Translated from a letter to Zelter dated March 27, 1830, WA, vol. IV 46, pp. 285–88, esp. p. 285.
37 It is likely that Heinz Mack would have become a pianist if he did not suffer a deep cut on his hand, inflicted upon him by a drunken US soldier shortly after the war, making this impossible. Mack still plays the piano. He says: "Alongside painting and sculpture, music has the highest priority for me. I would not like to live without it. When I paint, I like to listen to classical music or else 'well-tempered'

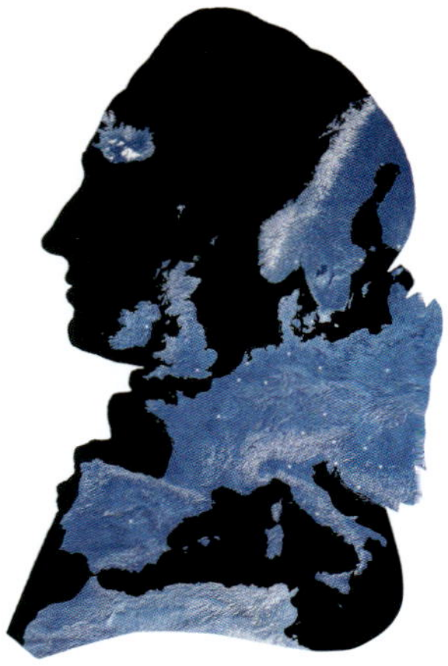

11 Heinz Mack
Motiv für den Cover-Entwurf zu:
Europa, wie Goethe es sah
hrsg. von Volkmar Hansen u. a.
Ausst.-Kat. Goethe-Museum Düsseldorf
Bologna u. a. 1999

Heinz Mack
Motif for the cover sketch:
Europa, wie Goethe es sah
ed. by Volkmar Hansen et al.
Exh. cat. Goethe-Museum Düsseldorf
Bologna et al. 1999

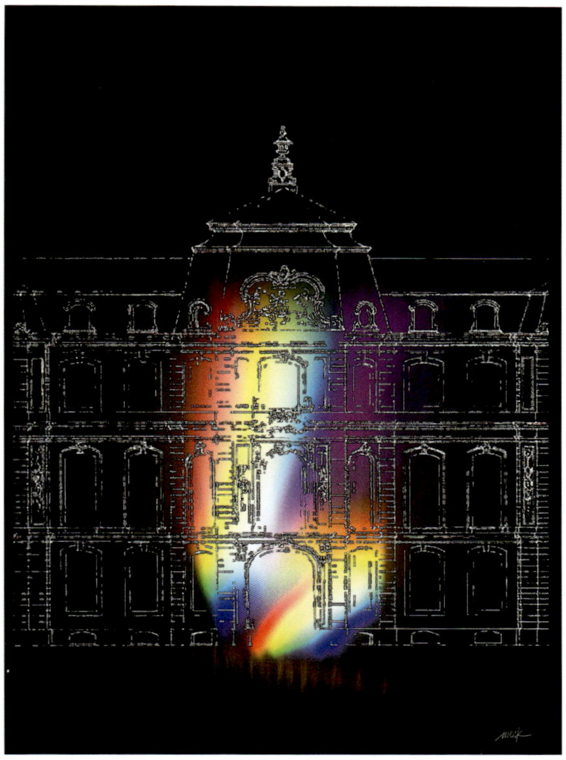

12 Heinz Mack
Cover-Entwurf zu:
Die Idee Goethe. 50 Jahre Goethe-Museum Düsseldorf
hrsg. von Volkmar Hansen u. a.
Ausst.-Kat. Goethe-Museum Düsseldorf
Düsseldorf 2006

Heinz Mack
Cover sketch for:
Die Idee Goethe. 50 Jahre Goethe-Museum Düsseldorf
ed. by Volkmar Hansen et al.
Exh. cat. Goethe-Museum Düsseldorf
Düsseldorf 2006

Künstlerbuch ediert[39]. 2003 folgte eine Ausstellung mit Arbeiten Heinz Macks zum *Hohelied Salomos*[40], das Goethe 1775 unter Verwendung der lateinischen Vulgata und mehrerer deutscher Übersetzungen auszugsweise aus dem Hebräischen übertragen hatte.

Schon 1995 hatte sich Mack im Schloss Jägerhof mit elf Werken an der Ausstellung *Die Rückkehr zur Vernunft* beteiligt. Die Schau war der Beitrag des Goethe-Museums zum Programm *45 ff – Kriegsende: Kontinuität und Neubeginn* und thematisierte den »historischen Abgrund«, der seit dem Zweiten Weltkrieg zwischen unserer Epoche und der Goethezeit klafft, sowie den Versuch der Nachkriegsgeneration, nach den unmenschlichen Verbrechen des Nationalsozialismus wieder an eine Humanitätsidee im Sinne der deutschen Klassik anzuknüpfen.[41]

Nach dem Cover-Entwurf für den Katalog zu dieser Ausstellung[42], der eine 200 Jahre alte Goethe-Silhouette mit Macks eigener Farbchromatik *Gruß an Goethe*[43] kombiniert und den Riss durch die Zeit als gezackte Linie symbolisiert, die das Motiv vertikal in zwei Hälften teilt – die eine weiß, die andere schwarz, gestaltete Heinz Mack für das Goethe-Museum noch zwei weitere Buchumschläge. Für das Cover des Katalogs zur Ausstellung *Europa, wie Goethe es sah*[44] füllte er die Umrisse der gleichen Silhouette mit einer Satellitenaufnahme Europas vom Deutschen Zentrum für Luft- und Raumfahrt. Und zum 50-jährigen Bestehen des Museums 2006 ließ er hinter der weißen Entwurfszeichnung des spätbarocken Schlossgebäudes auf schwarzem Grund *Die Idee Goethe* in Form eines spektralen Foto-Experiments aufleuchten.[45]

39 Heinz Mack, *Ein Buch der Bilder zum West-östlichen Divan von Johann Wolfgang v. Goethe*, Mönchengladbach 1999 [Faksimile als Buchhandelsausgabe des vergriffenen Künstlerbuches: Düsseldorf 2015]. Vgl. Abb. S. 359.
40 *Das Hohelied Salomos. Bilder von Heinz Mack*, Ausstellung im Goethe-Museum Düsseldorf, 16. März bis 27. April 2003.
41 *45 ff – Kriegsende: Kontinuität und Neubeginn. Die Rückkehr zur Vernunft. Klassiker zwischen 1932 und 1968*, Ausstellung im Goethe-Museum Düsseldorf, 7. Mai bis 13. August 1995.
42 Volkmar Hansen und Heike Spies, *45 ff – Kriegsende: Kontinuität und Neubeginn. Die Rückkehr zur Vernunft. Klassiker zwischen 1932 und 1968*, Ausst.-Kat. Goethe-Museum Düsseldorf, Düsseldorf 1995. Vgl. Abb. S. 44.
43 *Gruß an Goethe*, 1988, Wachskreide auf Papier, 155 x 224 cm.
44 *Europa, wie Goethe es sah*, hrsg. von Volkmar Hansen u. a., Ausst.-Kat. Goethe-Museum Düsseldorf, Bologna u. a. 1999. Vgl. Abb. 11.
45 *Die Idee Goethe. 50 Jahre Goethe-Museum Düsseldorf*, hrsg. von Volkmar Hansen u. a., Ausst.-Kat. Goethe-Museum Düsseldorf, Düsseldorf 2006. Vgl. Abb. 12.

oeuvre—ranging from the ZERO period to the present. The majority of his works are untitled or only bear the generic name of a body of work, such as *Dynamic Structures* or *Chromatic Constellations*. A dedication in the title therefore carries all the more weight. In addition to the above-mentioned *Gruss an Goethe* from 1988, in 1964, he had already produced a chromatology entitled *For Mr. Wolfgang v. Goethe*.[46] And *Hommage à Goethe* is not just the title of a three-by-four-meter color spectrum from 1981 that is reminiscent of color television's test pattern,[47] so is the *Farb-Oktett* (Color Octet), a suite of eight paintings from 1998.[48]

As soon as one deals more closely with Mack's reception of Goethe, besides concrete references such as, for example, two works on paper from 1991[49] based on color plates from Goethe's *Beyträge zur Optik* (Contributions to Optics)[50], additional content-related points of contact are revealed between the views and thoughts of two highly creative artist personalities. Almost casually, Mack cites "Ars sine scientia nihil est" (art without science is nothing), and then adds: "Neither did Goethe differentiate between art and science."[51] This hits the nail on the head and is the point of departure for all further similarities. An interdisciplinary, inquiring mind connects the painter, sculptor, and philosopher Mack with the poet, natural scientist, and politician Goethe. But this definitely does not imply the 'grey theory'[52] mentioned in *Faust*.

In his essay *Bedeutende Förderniss durch ein einziges geistreiches Wort* (Meaningful Progress by Way of a Single Witty Word), Goethe acknowledges that the psychiatrist and anthropologist Johann Christian August Heinroth (1773–1843) assessed his method of viewing nature correctly. Goethe wrote that Heinroth believed "namely that my ability to think is objectively active; he means to express: that my thinking does not sunder itself from the objects, that the elements of the objects, the intuitions, enter into my thinking and are permeated to the inmost by it, that my intuiting is itself a thinking, my thinking an intuiting … ."[53] Heinz Mack connects with this when stating: "In this sense I see Goethe as an advocate of my interests, I see his insistence on the viewing of phenomena as encouragement, because it is only through direct contemplation that something happens that transcends all physics—and hence attains metaphysical dimensions."[54]

Mack explains what he means by "metaphysical dimensions" in connection with the special light on Ibiza:

> On late summer evenings, this island is sometimes transformed into a gleaming, atmospheric, transparent, warm gold that glows in an entirely dematerialized way. The primeval substance, which Anaximander called "apeiron", the infinite from which everything comes and to which everything returns. This is a light in which the soul finds its peace—a state that artists rarely find! Everything and anything then becomes a pure, intangible apparition and the observing thinking ends in pure thinking, in wordless astonishment.[55]

jazz." Heinz Mack, "From My Life", in *Mack. Life and Work. A Book from the Artist about the Artist*, ed. Heinz Mack and Ute Mack (Cologne, 2011), pp. 19–27, esp. p. 27.

38 Heinz Mack, *Bilder zu Goethes "West-östlichem Divan,"* exhibition at the Goethe-Museum Düsseldorf, August 15–October 3, 1999.

39 Heinz Mack, *Ein Buch der Bilder zum West-östlichen Divan von Johann Wolfgang v. Goethe* (Mönchengladbach, 1999) [commercial facsimile of the out-of-print artist's book: Düsseldorf, 2015]. Cf. ill. p. 359.

40 *Das Hohelied Salomons: Bilder von Heinz Mack*, exhibition at the Goethe-Museum Düsseldorf, March 16–April 27, 2003.

41 *45 ff—Kriegsende: Kontinuität und Neubeginn. Die Rückkehr zur Vernunft. Klassiker zwischen 1932 und 1968*, exhibition at the Goethe-Museum Düsseldorf, May 7–August 13, 1995.

42 Volkmar Hansen and Heike Spies, *45 ff—Kriegsende: Kontinuität und Neubeginn. Die Rückkehr zur Vernunft. Klassiker zwischen 1932 und 1968*, exh. cat. Goethe-Museum Düsseldorf (Düsseldorf, 1995). Cf. ill. p. 44.

43 *Gruss an Goethe*, 1988, wax crayon on paper, 155 x 224 cm.

44 *Europa, wie Goethe es sah*, ed. by Volkmar Hansen et al., exh. cat. Goethe-Museum Düsseldorf (Bologna et al., 1999.) Cf. ill. p. 45.

45 *Die Idee Goethe: 50 Jahre Goethe-Museum Düsseldorf*, ed. Volkmar Hansen et al., exh. cat. Goethe-Museum Düsseldorf (Düsseldorf, 2006). Cf. ill. p. 45.

46 Ill. p. 87.

47 Ill. p. 47.

48 Cf. *Heinz Mack. Wahlverwandtschaften* (Elective Affinities), ed. Bernd Finkeldey et al., exh. cat. Tehran Museum of Contemporary Art 2001 (n. p., n. d.), ill. 15.

49 Ill. pp. 213 and 215.

50 Ill. pp. 212 and 214.

51 Mack in a conversation with the author on December 20, 2016.

52 In the second study scene of *Faust* part one Mephisto says: "Listen, my friend: the golden tree / Of life is green, all theory is grey." Johann Wolfgang von Goethe, *Faust I*, v. 2039, trans. John R. Williams (Hertfordshire, 2007), p. 61.

53 Johann Wolfgang von Goethe, quoted in Amanda Jo Goldstein, *Sweet Science: Romantic Materialism and the New Logics of Life* (Chicago and London, 2017), p. 130.

54 Translated from Heinz Mack in an unpublished letter to art historian Anette Kuhn dated April 30, 1995.

55 Marion Agthe and Heinz Mack, "Three Questions—Three Answers," in *Mack: Transit zwischen Okzident und Orient*, ed. Claus-Peter Haase, exh. cat. Museum für Islamische Kunst Berlin (Cologne, 2006), pp. 63–66, esp. p. 64.

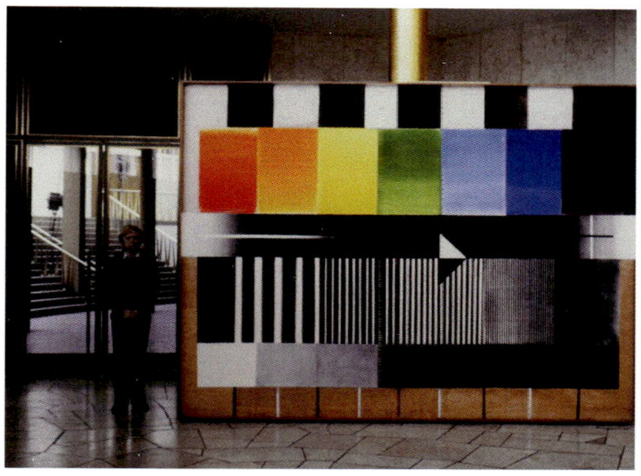

13 Heinz Mack
Hommage à Goethe
(Großes Lichtspektrum, Farbspektrum)
1981
Holz, bemalt
304 x 404 x 12 cm

Heinz Mack
Hommage à Goethe
(Big Spectrum of Light, Spectrum of Color)
1981
Painted wood
304 x 404 x 12 cm

Die Verbindung Heinz Macks zu Goethe beschränkt sich jedoch bei weitem nicht auf die gelegentliche Zusammenarbeit mit dem Goethe-Museum Düsseldorf. Seit seiner Jugend hat er sich immer wieder künstlerisch mit dem Leben und Werk Johann Wolfgang von Goethes auseinandergesetzt. Das ist an Kunstwerken mit Goethe-Bezug abzulesen, die das gesamte Œuvre durchziehen, von der ZERO-Zeit bis heute. Die meisten Arbeiten von Heinz Mack sind unbetitelt oder tragen als Bezeichnung lediglich den Oberbegriff der Werkgruppe, der sie angehören, etwa *Dynamische Strukturen* für die Bilder der ZERO-Jahre oder *Chromatische Konstellationen* für die Gemälde seit 1991. Umso mehr Gewicht erhält eine Widmung im Titel. So entstand außer dem oben erwähnten *Gruß an Goethe* von 1988 bereits 1964 eine Farbchromatik mit der Zueignung *for Mr. Wolfgang v. Goethe*[46]. Und mit *Hommage à Goethe* ist nicht nur ein 3 x 4 Meter großes Farbspektrum von 1981 betitelt, das an das Testbild des Farbfernsehens erinnert[47], sondern auch das *Farb-Oktett*, eine Suite von acht Gemälden, aus dem Jahr 1998[48].

Sobald man sich eingehender mit Macks Goethe-Rezeption befasst, offenbaren sich außer solch konkreten Bezügen wie etwa auch zwei Papierarbeiten von 1991[49], denen Farbtafeln aus Goethes genau 200 Jahre zuvor erschienenen *Beyträgen zur Optik*[50] zugrunde liegen, weitere inhaltliche Berührungspunkte zwischen den Ansichten und Gedanken zweier überaus schöpferischer Künstlerpersönlichkeiten. »Ars sine scientia nihil est« (Kunst ohne Wissenschaft ist nichts), zitiert Heinz Mack fast beiläufig und ergänzt: »Goethe hat auch nicht getrennt zwischen Kunst und Wissenschaft.«[51] Das trifft bereits den Kern, von dem alle weiteren Gemeinsamkeiten ausgehen. Es ist ein interdisziplinärer Forschergeist, der den Maler, Bildhauer und Philosophen Mack mit dem Dichter, Naturwissenschaftler und Politiker Goethe verbindet. Doch gemeint ist keineswegs die im *Faust* genannte ›graue Theorie‹[52].

In dem Aufsatz *Bedeutende Förderniß durch ein einziges geistreiches Wort* würdigt Goethe, dass der Psychiater und Anthropologe Johann Christian August Heinroth (1773–1843) sein Verfahren der Naturbetrachtung richtig eingeschätzt habe. Heinroth habe, schreibt Goethe, erkannt, »[…] daß nämlich mein Denkvermögen gegenständlich thätig sey, womit er aussprechen will: daß mein Denken sich von den Gegenständen nicht sondere, daß die Elemente der Gegenstände, die Anschauungen in dasselbe eingehen und von ihm auf das innigste durchdrungen werden, daß mein Anschauen selbst ein Denken, mein Denken ein Anschauen sey […].«[53] Heinz Mack knüpft daran an, wenn er sagt: »In diesem Sinne sehe ich in Goethe einen Anwalt meiner Interessen, sehe ich sein Beharren auf das Betrachten der Phaenomene als Ermutigung, weil sich nur in der reinen Anschauung etwas ereignet, das alle Physik übersteigt – und damit eine metaphysische Dimension erreicht.«[54]

Was er mit dieser »metaphysischen Dimension« meint, erläutert Mack im Zusammenhang mit dem besonderen Licht auf Ibiza:

> An späten Sommerabenden verwandelt sich diese Insel zuweilen in ein gleißendes, atmosphärisches, transparentes, warmes Gold, das gänzlich entstofflicht sich ausstrahlt. Der Urstoff, dass [!], was Anaximander das Apeiron nannte, das Unbegrenzte, aus dem alles hervorgeht, in das alles wieder zurückkehrt, das ist ein Licht, in dem die Seele ihren Frieden findet, – ein Zustand, den Künstler ja nur selten erreichen! Dann

46 Abb. S. 87.
47 Abb. 13.
48 Vgl. *Heinz Mack. Wahlverwandtschaften*, hrsg. von Bernd Finkeldey u. a., Ausst.-Kat. Teheraner Museum für Zeitgenössische Kunst 2001, o. O. und o. J., Abb. 15.
49 Abb. S. 213 und 215.
50 Abb. S. 212 und 214.
51 So im Gespräch mit der Autorin am 20. Dezember 2016.
52 In der zweiten Studierzimmer-Szene im ersten Teil des *Faust* sagt Mephisto: »Grau, theurer Freund, ist alle Theorie, / Und grün des Lebens goldner Baum.« (V. 2038 f., WA, Bd. I 14, S. 95.)
53 Johann Wolfgang von Goethe, *Zur Morphologie*, Bd. 2, Stuttgart und Tübingen 1823, S. 46–51, hier: S. 46.
54 Heinz Mack in einem unveröffentlichten Brief an die Kunsthistorikerin Anette Kuhn vom 30. April 1995.

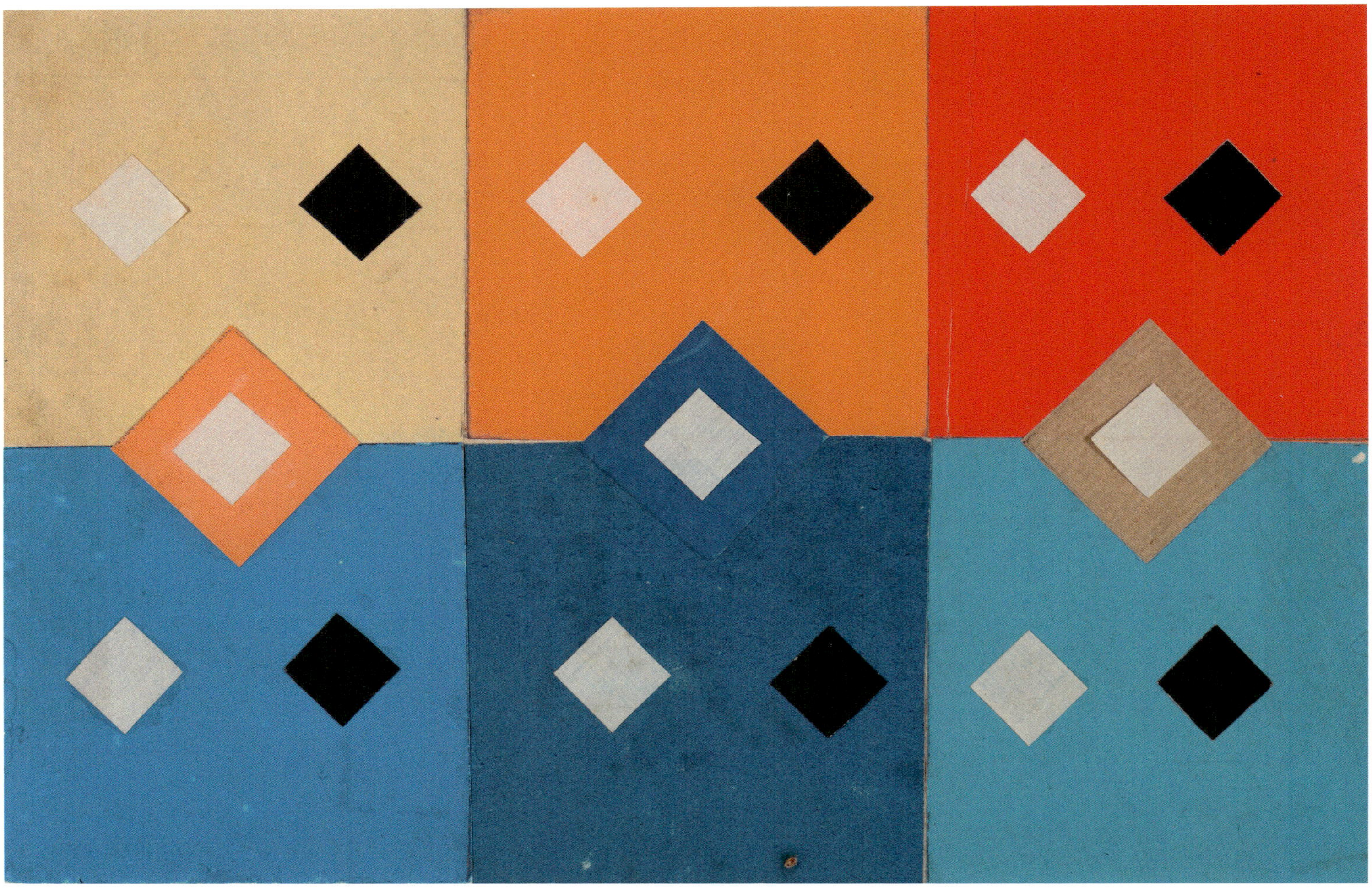

14 Johann Wolfgang von Goethe
Bunte und unbunte Flächen für prismatische Versuche, 1791/1795
Klebearbeit mit Buntpapieren; Pappe, gestrichene Papiere
15,7 x 23,6 cm
Klassik Stiftung Weimar, Museen

14 Johann Wolfgang von Goethe
Chromatic and achromatic surfaces for prismatic experiments, 1791/95
Pasted colored papers; cardboard, coated papers
15.7 x 23.6 cm
Klassik Stiftung Weimar, Museen

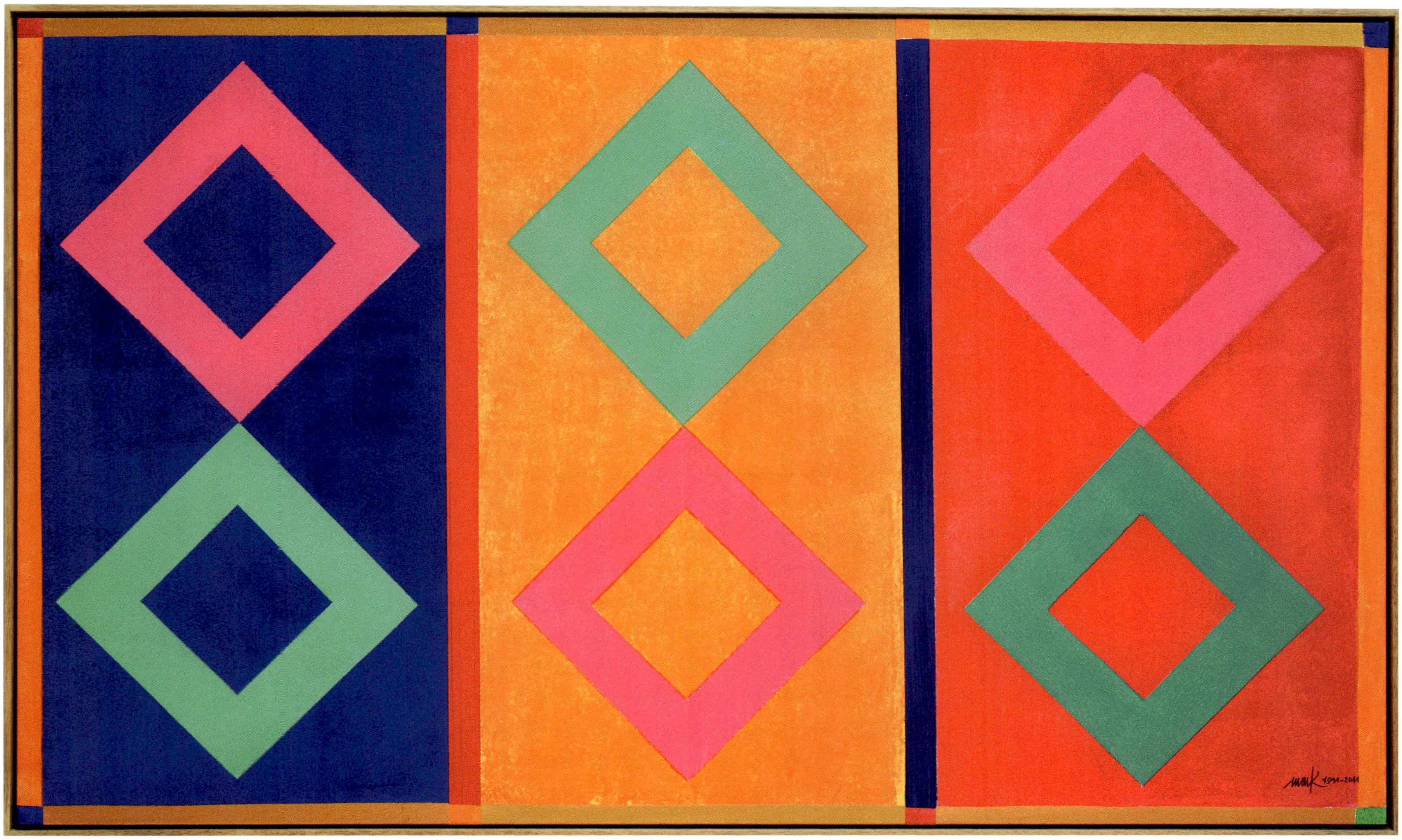

15 Heinz Mack
Chromatische Konstellation
Nach einem Experiment von Pawlik + Fessler
(zu Goethes Farbenlehre)
Signiert, datiert: »mack 1991–2011«
Acryl auf Leinwand
128 x 217 cm

15 Heinz Mack
Chromatic Constellation
According to an experiment by Pawlik + Fessler
(on the subject of Goethe's color theory)
Signed, dated: "mack 1991–2011"
Acrylic on canvas
128 x 217 cm

Goethe was also enchanted by the south. What Ibiza—which he baptized "island of light,"[56]—is to the painter-sculptor, Italy was to the poet. In his *Beyträge zur Optik,* he also described the overwhelming impression of the rising and the setting sun, albeit not solely as an apparition of light but primarily as a color phenomenon: He wrote: "[I]f we have lived for a while in fair Italy, it seems a fable to us when we remember how harmoniously there the sky is joined to the earth and spreads over it its radiance." And then:

> It usually displays to us a pure deep blue; the rising and setting sun furnishes us with notions of the most intense red to the palest yellow; light clouds drift by in manifold tints and the colors of the vault of heaven are mostly agreeable imported to the ground on which we stand. A blue distance shows us the most charming transition from heaven to earth and in a pure diffused haze a vivid sheen floats over the land in a myriad of playful gleams. Even the nearest shadows are tinted by an agreeable blue; the sun to our delight glances off leaves and branches, while the pure sky is mirrored in the water at our feet. Everything that our eye surveys is so harmoniously colored, so clear, so distinct, and we almost forget that in this picture there is also light and shade.[57]

When dealing with objects derived from nature, both artists—Goethe and Mack—are concerned with a thinking beholding and a beholding thinking. And where could this be better presented than in an exhibition? Especially since visual art inspired Goethe to time and again examine the phenomena of color, light, and shadow for four decades.

Color, Light, and Shadow

In his introduction to *Beyträge zur Optik,* Goethe writes that he "entered the circle of this science by accident, using paths other than the customary ones." He continues:

> Having dealt with artists from a young age and through my own efforts, I became aware of the important part of the art of painting, coloration, especially during the last few years when my soul welcomed a lively and joyous image of a harmoniously colored world under a clear, happy sky. If there is anyone who ought to be concerned about the effects and conditions of colors, it is the painter, who has to seek them everywhere, find them everywhere, mix, change, and gradate them … .[58]

Comprised of about 1,500 printed pages and hence his most comprehensive work, Goethe also considered *Theory of Colours* his most important,[59] ranking it before *Faust I* and *II*. Among scientists, however, the treatise was disputed for the longest time, especially because of its polemics against Newton. Goethe's color theory has recently been receiving increased attention, because, unlike its predecessors, it is not restricted exclusively to objective measuring. Goethe says:

56 Heinz Mack: "This is why I call the [sic!] Ibiza the 'Island of Light.' Strangely, the island hasn't been given this name before." (Ibid.) Cf. also Heinz Mack, *Ibiza: Insel im Licht* (Cologne, 1996).

57 Johann Wolfgang von Goethe, quoted in Nicholas Boyle, *Goethe: The Poet and the Age,* vol. 2, *Revolution and Renunciation* (Oxford, 2000), p. 102.

58 Translated from Goethe 1791 (see note 33), § 18, pp. 11–12.

59 Eckermann reports about Goethe: "'As for what I have done as a poet,' he would repeatedly say to me, 'I take no pride in it whatsoever. Excellent poets have lived at the same time with myself, poets more excellent have lived before me, and others will come after me. But that in my century I am the only person who knows the truth in the difficult science of colours—of that, I say, I am not a little proud, and here I have a consciousness of a superiority to many.'" Conversation dated February 19, 1829, in *Conversations of Goethe with Johann Peter Eckermann,* ed. J. K. Moorhead, trans. John Oxenford (Cambridge, MA, 1988), pp. 297–302, esp. p. 302.

wird alles und jedes zu einer reinen, unberührbaren Erscheinung und das anschauende Denken endet im reinen Schauen, im wortlosen Staunen.[55]

Auch Goethe ließ sich vom Süden verzaubern. Was dem Maler und Bildhauer sein Ibiza ist, das er »Insel des Lichts«[56] getauft hat, ist dem Dichter sein Italien. In den *Beyträgen zur Optik* schildert auch er den überwältigenden Eindruck der auf- oder untergehenden Sonne, jedoch nicht nur als Lichterscheinung, sondern vor allem als Farbphänomen: »[…] so wird es uns«, schreibt er, »wenn wir eine Zeitlang in dem schönen Italien gelebt, ein Mährchen, wenn wir uns erinnern, wie harmonisch dort der Himmel sich mit der Erde verbindet und seinen lebhaften Glanz über sie verbreitet.« Und weiter:

> Er zeigt uns meist ein reines, tiefes Blau; die auf und untergehende Sonne giebt uns einen Begriff vom höchsten Roth bis zum lichtesten Gelb; leichte hin und wieder ziehende Wolken färben sich mannigfaltig, und die Farben des himmlischen Gewölbes theilen sich auf die angenehmste Art dem Boden mit, auf dem wir stehen. Eine blaue Ferne zeigt uns den lieblichsten Uebergang des Himmels zur Erde, und durch einen verbreiteten reinen Duft schwebt ein lebhafter Glanz in tausendfachen Spielungen [!] über der Gegend. Ein angenehmes Blau färbt selbst die nächsten Schatten; der Abglanz der Sonne entzückt uns von Blättern und Zweigen, indeß der reine Himmel sich im Wasser zu unsern Füßen spiegelt. Alles was unser Auge übersieht, ist so harmonisch gefärbt, so klar, so deutlich, und wir vergessen fast, daß auch Licht und Schatten in diesem Bilde sey.[57]

Beiden Künstlern – Goethe und Mack – geht es bei der Beschäftigung mit Gegenständen der Natur um ein anschauendes Denken und denkendes Anschauen. Und wo wäre das besser zu präsentieren als in einer Ausstellung? Zumal es die bildende Kunst war, die Goethe dazu anregte, sich vier Jahrzehnte lang immer wieder mit den Phänomenen von Farbe, Licht und Schatten auseinanderzusetzen.

Farbe, Licht und Schatten

Goethe schreibt in der Einleitung zu den *Beyträgen zur Optik*, dass er »zufälligerweise und durch andere Wege in den Kreis dieser Wissenschaft gelangt« sei, »als diejenigen sind, durch die man sich ihr gewöhnlich nähert«. Und er fährt fort:

> Durch den Umgang mit Künstlern von Jugend auf und durch eigene Bemühungen wurde ich auf den wichtigen Theil der Mahlerkunst, auf die Farbengebung aufmerksam gemacht, besonders in den letzten Jahren, da die Seele ein lebhaftes freudiges Bild der harmonischfarbigen Welt unter einem reinen glücklichen Himmel empfing. Denn wenn jemand Ursach hat sich um die Wirkungen und Verhältnisse der Farben zu bekümmern: so ist es der Mahler, der sie überall suchen, überall finden, sie versetzen, verändern und abstufen muß […].[58]

Obwohl Goethe selbst sein mit rund 1500 Druckseiten umfangreichstes Werk *Zur Farbenlehre* auch als sein wichtigstes betrachtete[59], bedeutender noch als *Faust I* und *II*, war diese

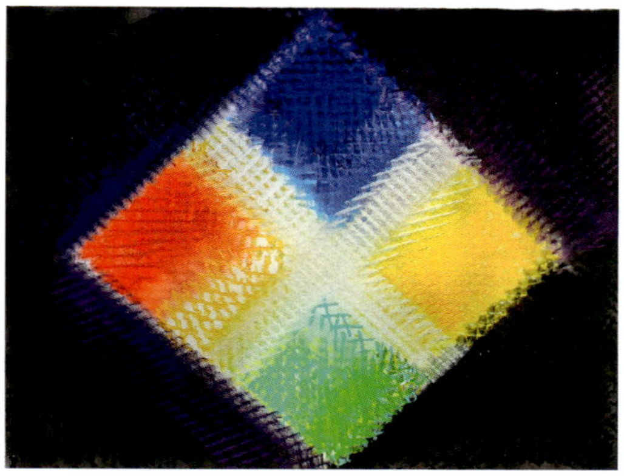

16 Heinz Mack
Taten des Lichts, 2015
Pastellkreide auf Büttenpapier
75 x 98,5 cm
Anlässlich der Ausstellung *Taten des Lichts – Mack & Goethe* erschien eine Grafik-Edition von diesem Pastell.

Heinz Mack
Taten des Lichts, 2015
Pastel on handmade paper
75 x 98.5 cm
On the occasion of the exhibition Taten des Lichts—Mack & Goethe a serigraph edition of this pastel was published.

55 Marion Agthe und Heinz Mack, »Drei Fragen – Drei Antworten«, in: *Mack. Transit zwischen Okzident und Orient. Faszination und Inspiration der islamischen Kultur. Ein Werk-Aspekt 1950–2006,* hrsg. von Claus-Peter Haase, Ausst.-Kat. Museum für Islamische Kunst Berlin, Köln 2006, S. 59–62, hier: S. 60.

56 Heinz Mack: »Ich habe Ibiza darum ›Insel des Lichts‹ genannt. Diesen Namen hatte die Insel merkwürdigerweise vorher noch nicht.« (Ebd.) Vgl. auch Heinz Mack, *Ibiza. Insel im Licht,* Köln 1996.

57 Goethe 1791 (wie Anm. 33), § 4, S. 2 f.

58 Ebd., § 18, S. 11 f.

59 So berichtet Eckermann über Goethe: »Auf Alles was ich als Poet geleistet habe, pflegte er wiederholt zu sagen, bilde ich mir gar nichts ein. Es haben treffliche Dichter mit mir gelebt, es lebten noch Trefflichere vor mir, und es werden ihrer nach mir seyn. Daß ich aber in meinem Jahrhundert in der schwierigen Wissenschaft der Farbenlehre der Einzige bin, der das Rechte weiß, darauf thue ich mir etwas zu gute, und ich habe daher ein Bewußtseyn der Superiorität über Viele.« (Gespräch vom 19. Februar 1829, in: Johann Peter Eckermann, *Gespräche mit Goethe in den letzten Jahren seines Lebens. 1823–1832,* Bd. 2, Leipzig 1836, S. 74–87, hier: S. 86 f.)

> Man in himself, in so far as he is using his sound senses, is the greatest and most exact 'physical,' i.e. scientific apparatus that can be imagined, and this, precisely, is the most disastrous aspect of modern physics: that experiments have been, as it were, segregated from the human factor and that nature is to be recognized only by the evidence of artificial instruments and in this way limits what nature wants to achieve and prove.[60]

He, on the other hand—in particular when dealing with "physiological colours" or the "effect of colour with reference to moral associations"—includes the individual with his or her subjective feelings. Daring at the time, this continues to be fascinating to this day.

However, Goethe's considerations with respect to physics, for instance, the complementarity of reverse optical spectra, show themselves—as Johannes Grebe-Ellis and Oliver Passon demonstrate in their contribution in this catalogue[61]—in a new light, as has been the case especially in recent years. Christoph Cremer even explains the path from Goethe's theory of colors to Nobel-prize-winning super-resolving fluorescence microscopy in the twenty-first century.[62]

In order to disprove Newton, Goethe assumes a "ray of darkness"[63] as the opposite pole to the ray of light; this is in keeping with Heinz Mack's conviction that both darkness and brightness contain energy. "Black is black light, white is white light,"[64] explains Mack, and: "In my black paintings, I try to make 'black light' visible. Here, black is not the absence of light but the presence of black light!"[65]

"Light is the theme of my life,"[66] says Heinz Mack, now eighty-seven years old. This applies not only to his light reliefs, light stelae, light cubes, light rotors, light wings, and light environments, but equally to his painting. He quotes the French physicist Louis de Broglie (1892–1987): "In our universe, light turns into matter and matter turns into light," he adds: "This fundamental definition of natural occurrences could equally be transferred to painting: in painting, light turns into colored matter and colored matter turns into light. The identity of light and color that is made visible in the spectrum is the subject of my painting—it is its sole subject."[67]

Regardless of which technique he employs: since 1958, that is, for sixty years, the key artistic themes of painter and sculptor Heinz Mack have been exactly these: light, shadow, and color as well as their mutual interactions. At the time, he had his "silver-bullet experience of awakening,"[68] causing him to place light into the center of his art.

An advocate of "beholding thinking" and "thinking beholding," in the context of such key experiences Goethe talks about "so-called awakenings and conversions, to which we will not deny a certain psychological value." And he further elaborates:

> They are properly what we call in scientific and poetic matters, as *'aperçu,'* the perception of a great maxim, which is always a genius-like operation of the mind; we arrive at it by pure intuition, that is, by reflection, neither by learning or tradition. … Such an *aperçu* gives the discoverer the greatest joy, because, in an original manner, it points to the infinite; it requires no length of time to work conviction; it leaps forth whole and complete in a moment.[69]

60 Goethe 1998 (see note 28), p. 143.
61 Cf. Johannes Grebe-Ellis and Oliver Passon, "Goethe's *Farbenlehre* from the Perspective of Modern Physics," in the present catalogue, pp. 124–36.
62 Cf. Christoph Cremer, "Goethe's *Farbenlehre* and Modern Optics," ibid. pp. 252–64.
63 Translated from Goethe 1791 (see note 33), § 67, p. 41.
64 Translated from Heinz Mack, "Reflexionen," in *Mack: Licht im Schwarz,* ed. Hubertus Schoeller, exh. cat. Galerie Schoeller Düsseldorf (Mönchengladbach, 2001), pp. 16–17, esp. p. 17.
65 Ibid.
66 Translated from Helga Meister, *Piene, Uecker, Mack: Zero in der Düsseldorfer Szene* (Düsseldorf, 2006), p. 66.
67 Cf. "Veit Loers in Conversation with Heinz Mack" in the present catalogue, pp. 436–52, esp. p. 452.
68 Translated from Yvonne Schwarzer, *Das Paradies auf Erden schon zu Lebzeiten betreten: Ein Gespräch mit dem Maler und Bildhauer Heinz Mack (Kunstportrait)* (Witten, 2005), p. 15.
69 Johann Wolfgang von Goethe, *Truth and Poetry: From My Own Life,* vol. 2, trans. John Oxenford (London, 1884), p. 75. On Goethe's use of the word 'aperçu,' cf. Peter Matussek, "'Es ist das Höchste, wozu es der Mensch bringt': Das Aperçu bei Goethe." in *"Wie alles sich zum Ganzen webt": Festschrift für Yoshito Takahashi zum 65. Geburtstag,* ed. Akio Ogawa et al. (Tübingen, 2010), pp. 103–15.

Schrift, vor allem wegen der darin enthaltenen Polemik gegen Newton, bei Naturwissenschaftlern lange umstritten. In jüngerer Zeit jedoch gewinnt Goethes Farbenlehre mehr und mehr Aufmerksamkeit, weil sie sich nicht – wie ihre Vorgänger – auf objektive Messungen beschränkt. Goethe sagt:

> Der Mensch an sich selbst, in so fern er sich seiner gesunden Sinne bedient, ist der größte und genauste physikalische Apparat, den es geben kann, und das ist eben das größte Unheil der neuern Physik, daß man die Experimente gleichsam vom Menschen abgesondert hat, und bloß in dem, was künstliche Instrumente zeigen, die Natur erkennen, ja was sie leisten kann dadurch beschränken und beweisen will.[60]

Er dagegen bezieht – vor allem, wenn er die »physiologischen Farben« behandelt oder die »sinnlich-sittliche Wirkung der Farbe« – den Menschen ein mit seinen subjektiven Empfindungen. Das war damals kühn und fasziniert noch heute.

Aber auch Goethes die Physik betreffenden Überlegungen, etwa zur Komplementarität umgekehrter optischer Spektren, erscheinen – wie Johannes Grebe-Ellis und Oliver Passon in ihrem Beitrag zum vorliegenden Katalog[61] zeigen – gerade seit der jüngsten Vergangenheit in neuem Licht. Christoph Cremer erläutert gar den Weg von Goethes Farbenlehre zur nobelpreisgekrönten superauflösenden Fluoreszenzmikroskopie des 21. Jahrhunderts.[62]

Wenn Goethe, um Newton zu widerlegen, als Gegenpol zum Lichtstrahl einen »Strahl der Finsterniß«[63] annimmt, dann passt dazu Heinz Macks Überzeugung von einer im Dunklen wie im Hellen enthaltenen Energie. »Schwarz ist schwarzes Licht, Weiß ist weißes Licht«[64], erklärt Mack und: »In meinen schwarzen Bildern versuche ich, ›schwarzes Licht‹ sichtbar zu machen. Schwarz ist hier nicht die Abwesenheit von Licht, sondern die Gegenwart von schwarzem Licht!«[65]

»Das Licht ist das Thema meines Lebens«[66], sagt der heute 87-jährige Heinz Mack über sich selbst. Und das gilt nicht nur für seine Lichtreliefs, die Lichtstelen, Lichtkuben, Lichtrotoren, Lichtflügel oder Licht-Environments, sondern auch für seine Malerei. Er zitiert den französischen Physiker Louis de Broglie (1892–1987): »Licht wird in unserem Universum zu Materie, und Materie wird zu Licht« und fügt hinzu: »Man könnte diese Definition allen elementaren Naturgeschehens auf die Malerei übertragen: Licht wird in der Malerei zu Farbmaterie, und die Farbmaterie wird zu Licht. Die Identität von Licht und Farbe, welche im Spektrum sichtbar wird, ist der Gegenstand meiner Malerei – sie ist ihr einziger Gegenstand.«[67] Und tatsächlich: Ganz gleich, welcher Techniken oder Werkstoffe er sich bedient: Die zentralen künstlerischen Themen des Malers und Bildhauers Heinz Mack sind seit 1958, also seit 60 Jahren, genau diese: Licht, Schatten und Farbe sowie deren Wechselwirkungen untereinander. Damals hatte er das – wie er es nennt – »alles entscheidende ›Erweckungserlebnis‹«[68], das ihn dazu brachte, das Licht ins Zentrum seiner Kunst zu stellen.

Als Verfechter des »anschauenden Denkens« und »denkenden Anschauens« spricht Goethe im Zusammenhang mit solchen Schlüsselerlebnissen von »sogenannten Erweckungen, Sinnesveränderungen, denen wir ihren psychologischen Werth nicht absprechen«. Und er führt weiter aus:

60 Johann Wolfgang von Goethe, *Über Naturwissenschaft im allgemeinen. Einzelne Betrachtungen und Aphorismen*, LA, Bd. I 11, S. 348.
61 Johannes Grebe-Ellis und Oliver Passon, »Goethes Farbenlehre aus Sicht der heutigen Physik«, im vorliegenden Katalog, S. 125–137.
62 Christoph Cremer, »Goethe und die moderne Optik«, ebd., S. 253–265.
63 Goethe 1791 (wie Anm. 33), § 67, S. 41.
64 Heinz Mack, »Reflexionen«, in: *Mack. Licht im Schwarz*, hrsg. von Hubertus Schoeller, Ausst.-Kat. Galerie Schoeller Düsseldorf, Mönchengladbach 2001, S. 16 f., hier: S. 17.
65 Ebd.
66 Helga Meister, *Piene, Uecker, Mack. Zero in der Düsseldorfer Szene*, Düsseldorf 2006, S. 66.
67 Vgl. das ›Gespräch‹ zwischen Veit Loers und Heinz Mack im vorliegenden Katalog, S. 437–453; hier: S. 453.
68 Yvonne Schwarzer, *Das Paradies auf Erden schon zu Lebzeiten betreten. Ein Gespräch mit dem Maler und Bildhauer Heinz Mack (Kunstportrait)*, Witten 2005, S. 15.

With such lightning insight—once again Goethe and Mack are in agreement—chance has to "come into play. Chance is the great secret and the great miracle."[70] When Goethe talks about "contemplation and chance"[71]—as was the case when he discovered the intermaxillary bone in humans—this touches upon what the British writer Horace Walpole (1717–1797) called 'serendipity': the gift to make joyous, unexpected discoveries. Although they do not fall from heaven, they are "discoveries, by accidents and sagacity."[72] Or, to use the words of French chemist Louis Pasteur (1822–1895): "[L]e hasard ne favorise que les esprits préparés" (chance favors only the prepared mind.)[73] Only those who examine a subject intensely will experience unexpected enlightenment.

Heinz Mack described his key experience the same year it occurred, in part two of the magazine *ZERO,* and on many occasions thereafter. A particularly graphic description followed fifteen years later:

> As chance would have it..., one day a thin piece of aluminum foil with a shiny surface lay on a sisal carpet. I accidentally stepped on the foil. Something one would usually ignore instantly became my personal magic moment, because I discovered—although only a very fine, very faint relief had formed—that this sufficed for light to articulate itself, to cause the light reflection to oscillate, to vibrate. This crucial insight came to me with the speed of light: I discovered the light relief instead of the metal relief. I have been dealing with light since that day.[74]

For Goethe, a key experience also led to his decades-long, intense study of the phenomenon of light. He had borrowed prisms for optical experiments from Jena-based natural scientist Christian Wilhelm Büttner (1716–1801). However, for the longest time he did not get around to experimenting with them; Büttner, after repeated reminders for their return, finally sent a messenger to retrieve them. In his autobiographical *Confession des Verfassers* (Confession of the Author), Goethe recalls taking a quick look through one of the prisms, something he had not done since his youth, before handing the package over to the messenger:

> I remembered well that everything appeared many-colored, but in what manner was no longer present to my mind. At that very moment I was in a room that had been painted completely white; I expected, mindful of the Newtonian theory as I placed the prism before my eyes, to see the light that comes from there to my eye split up into so many colored lights. How astonished I was, then, when the white wall, observed through the prism, remained white just as before; that only there, where darkness adjoined on it, did a more or less determinate color appear; finally, that the window bars appeared in the liveliest of colors of all, whereas no trace of coloring was to be seen in the light gray sky outside. It did not take much deliberation for me to recognize that a boundary is necessary to produce colors, and I immediately said to myself, as if by instinct, that the Newtonian teaching is false.[75]

70 Translated from Helga Meister, "Heinz Mack: Kunst mit dem Fensterwischer. Interview. Mit Werkverzeichnis zur Zero-Malerei und einer Ausstellung in Düsseldorf trumpft der 86-Jährige auf," *Westdeutsche Zeitung,* September 8, 2017.
71 Translated from Johann Wolfgang von Goethe, *Beschreibung des Zwischenkieferknochens mehrerer Tiere bezüglich auf die beliebte Einteilung und Terminologie,* LA, vol. I 10, pp. 6–22, esp. p. 6.
72 Horace Walpole, letter to Horace Mann dated January 28, 1754, in *Horace Walpole's Correspondence,* vol. 20, ed. W. S. Lewis (New Haven, 1960), pp. 407–11, esp. pp. 407–08.
73 Louis Pasteur, "Discours. Prononcé a Douai, le 7 décembre 1854, a l'occasion de l'installation solennelle de la Faculté des lettres de Douai et de la Faculté des sciences de Lille", in *Œuvres de Pasteur,* vol. 7, ed. [Louis] Pasteur Vallery-Radot (Paris, 1939), pp. [129]–32, esp. p. 131.
74 Translated from Heinz Mack, in Wulf Herzogenrath, ed., *Selbstdarstellung: Künstler über sich* (Düsseldorf, 1973), pp. 104–15, esp. p. 109.
75 Johann Wolfgang von Goethe, quoted in Dennis L. Sepper, *Goethe contra Newton: Polemics and the Project for a New Science of Color* (Cambridge et al., 1988), p. 24.

> Es sind eigentlich was wir in wissenschaftlichen und poetischen Angelegenheiten Aperçus nennen: das Gewahrwerden einer großen Maxime, welches immer eine genialische Geistesoperation ist; man kommt durch Anschauen dazu, weder durch Nachdenken noch durch Lehre oder Überlieferung. [...] Ein solches Aperçu gibt dem Entdecker die größte Freude, weil es auf originelle Weise nach dem Unendlichen hindeutet; es bedarf keiner Zeitfolge zur Überzeugung: es entspringt ganz und vollendet im Augenblick [...].[69]

Bei einer solchen blitzartigen Erkenntnis, auch darin sind Goethe und Mack sich einig, muss der Zufall »ins Spiel kommen. Er ist das große Geheimnis und das große Wunder«[70]. Wenn Goethe – wie bei seiner Entdeckung des Zwischenkieferknochens beim Menschen – von »Nachdenken und Zufall«[71] spricht, geht es um das, was der britische Schriftsteller Horace Walpole (1717–1797) ›serendipity‹ genannt hat: die Gabe, zufällig glückliche und unerwartete Entdeckungen zu machen, die jedoch nicht vom Himmel fallen, denn es handelt sich um »discoveries, by accidents and sagacity« (Entdeckungen durch Zufälle und Klugheit)[72]. Oder, um es mit den Worten des französischen Chemikers Louis Pasteur (1822–1895) zu sagen: »[...] le hasard ne favorise que les esprits préparés« (der Zufall begünstigt nur die vorbereiteten Geister)[73]. Nur, wer sich intensiv mit einer Sache auseinandersetzt, erfährt unerwartet Erleuchtung.

Heinz Mack schilderte sein Schlüsselerlebnis noch im selben Jahr, in dem es stattgefunden hatte, im zweiten Teil der Zeitschrift *ZERO* und später immer wieder. Besonders anschaulich beschreibt er dieses im doppelten Wortsinn prägende Ereignis im Abstand von 15 Jahren:

> Der Zufall wollte es [...], daß eines Tages eine dünne Aluminiumfolie mit glänzender Oberfläche auf einem Sisalteppich lag. Aus Versehen habe ich auf dieses Blech getreten. Und was man normalerweise gar nicht beachtet hätte, wurde in diesem Moment so etwas wie eine Sternstunde für mich. Ich entdeckte nämlich, obwohl sich lediglich ein sehr feines, sehr schwaches Relief abgebildet hatte, daß dieses genügte, um das Licht zu artikulieren, um die Lichtreflektion zum Schwingen, zur Vibration zu bringen. Die entscheidende, blitzschnelle Erkenntnis war erregend genug: nicht das Relief des Metalls, sondern das Relief des Lichts war meine Entdeckung. Seit diesem Tag beschäftige ich mich mit dem Licht.[74]

Auch für Goethe war ein Schlüsselerlebnis ausschlaggebend dafür, dass er sich von da an jahrzehntelang intensiv mit dem Phänomen Licht auseinandersetzte. Von dem in Jena lebenden Naturforscher Christian Wilhelm Büttner (1716–1801) hatte er sich Prismen für optische Versuche ausgeliehen, war jedoch so lange nicht dazu gekommen, damit zu experimentieren, bis Büttner nach mehreren Erinnerungen und Mahnungen an die Rückgabe schließlich einen Kurier schickte, der sie abholen sollte. Goethe erinnert sich in der autobiografischen *Confession des Verfassers:*

> Schon hatte ich den Kasten hervorgenommen, um ihn dem Boten zu übergeben, als mir einfiel, ich wolle doch noch geschwind durch ein Prisma sehen, was ich seit meiner frühsten Jugend nicht gethan hatte. [...] Eben befand ich mich in einem völlig geweiß-

69 Johann Wolfgang von Goethe, *Aus meinem Leben. Dichtung und Wahrheit,* WA, Bd. I 29, S. 28 f. Zu Goethes Verwendung des Wortes ›Aperçu‹ vgl. Peter Matussek, »›Es ist das Höchste, wozu es der Mensch bringt‹: Das Aperçu bei Goethe«, in: *»Wie alles sich zum Ganzen webt«. Festschrift für Yoshito Takahashi zum 65. Geburtstag,* hrsg. von Akio Ogawa u. a., Tübingen 2010, S. 103–115.
70 Helga Meister, »Heinz Mack: Kunst mit dem Fensterwischer. Interview. Mit Werkverzeichnis zur Zero-Malerei und einer Ausstellung in Düsseldorf trumpft der 86-Jährige auf«, in: *Westdeutsche Zeitung,* 8. September 2017.
71 Johann Wolfgang von Goethe, *Beschreibung des Zwischenkieferknochens mehrerer Tiere bezüglich auf die beliebte Einteilung und Terminologie,* LA, Bd. I 10, S. 6–22, hier: S. 6.
72 Horace Walpole, Brief an Horace Mann vom 28. Januar 1754, in: *Horace Walpole's Correspondence,* hrsg. von W. S. Lewis, Bd. 20, New Haven 1960, S. 407–411, hier: S. 407 f.
73 Louis Pasteur, »Discours. Prononcé a Douai, le 7 décembre 1854, a l'occasion de l'installation solennelle de la Faculté des lettres de Douai et de la Faculté des sciences de Lille«, in: *Œuvres de Pasteur,* hrsg. von [Louis] Pasteur Vallery-Radot, Bd. 7, Paris 1939, S. [129]–132, hier: S. 131.
74 Heinz Mack, in: *Selbstdarstellung. Künstler über sich,* hrsg. von Wulf Herzogenrath, Düsseldorf 1973, S. 104–115, hier: S. 109.

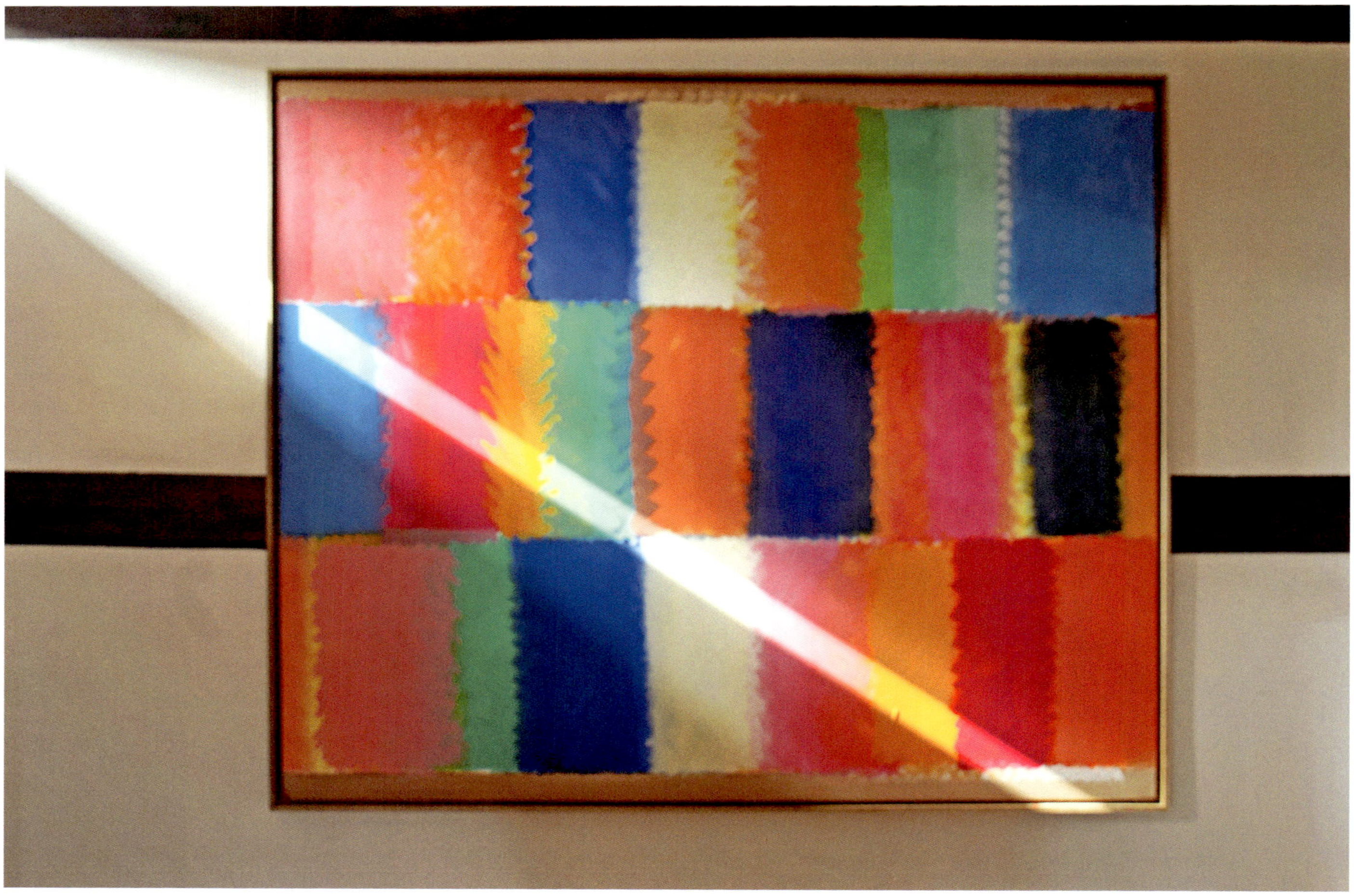

17 Heinz Mack
Ibiza-Farben
Chromatische Konstellation
Signiert, datiert: »mack 15«
Acryl auf Leinwand
130 x 160 cm
Lichtstrahl auf einer aleatorischen Reihung von Mischfarben

17 Heinz Mack
Ibiza Colors
Chromatic Constellation
Signed, dated: "mack 15"
Acrylic on canvas
130 x 160 cm
Light beam on an aleatory sequence of mixed colors

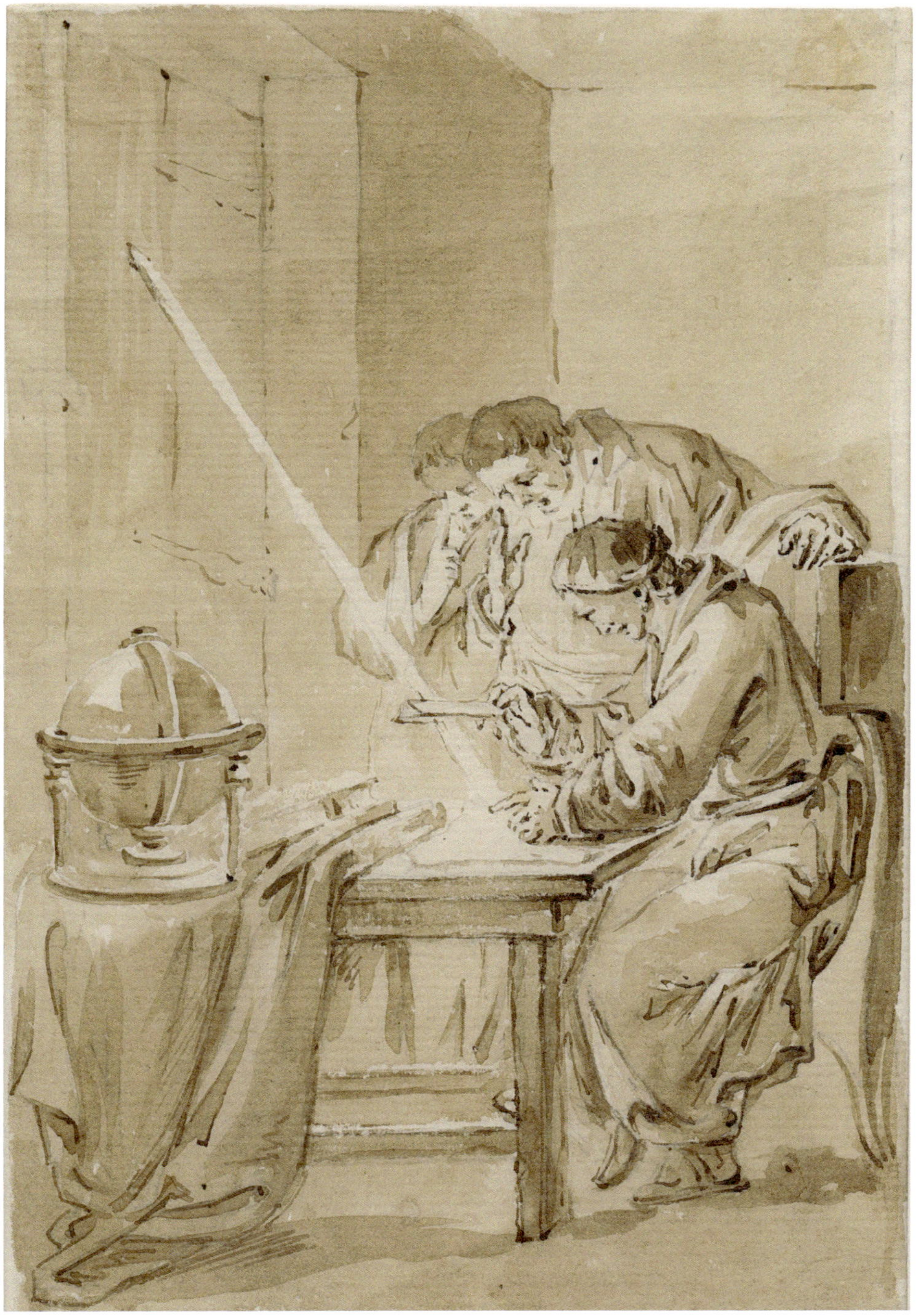

18 Christian Bernhard Rode (1727–1797)
Newton erklärt zuerst die Entstehung der Farben
1783 oder früher
Aquarell auf Papier, 13 x 8,7 cm
Goethe-Museum Düsseldorf

18 Christian Bernhard Rode (1727–1797)
Newton Explains First the Origin of Colors
In or before 1783
Watercolor on paper, 13 x 8.7 cm
Goethe-Museum Düsseldorf

Both Goethe and Mack have addressed the theory of colors bearing art in mind.[76] According to Mack: "Alongside all the 'colors of light,' I need white as the canvas, as the background, as a reflective area for light. Therefore, white always plays a crucial role in the purity and brightness of the colors. … Here color becomes an emanation of light, which occurs as both part of the spectrum and as the spectrum. This emanation affects the appearance of the color, which is itself emanating from the canvas and which fills the room."[77] What Mack writes here sounds like Goethe's assertion: "Thus every colour, in order to be seen, must have a light within or behind it. Hence the lighter and brighter the grounds are, the more brilliant the colours appear. … [N]ay, the force of the physical colours is owing principally to the circumstance that light is always acting with and behind them."[78]

What would be more appropriate than juxtaposing and more closely illuminating those two artists whose interest in light and color never ceased?[79] It will be interesting to explore what connects these apparently contrary personalities: the Classicist and the member of the avant-garde, the painting poet and the poet-painter. In addition to examining the preference for the colors of light and the radiance of colors, the show takes a look at further surprising if not literally baffling parallels between both personalities, who are separated by almost two hundred years, for instance, their shared interest in forms and structures in nature or the inspiration both derived from Oriental art.

Oriental Inspiration

Trips and working excursions to Morocco, Algeria, Egypt, and Oman; an expedition through the Ténéré desert; solo shows in Tehran, Istanbul, and at the Museum of Islamic Art in Berlin; print portfolios about the *Song of Solomon;* Goethe's *West-East Divan;* as well as texts by the Persian theologian and philosopher al-Ghazālī (1058–1111).[80] "My repeated encounters with oriental culture," says Heinz Mack, "go back half a century, and I have neither been able nor willing to resist its influence."[81]

Goethe, who encountered the "Asiatic" world—as he called it—by reading, expressed himself similarly: "The culture I thus gained therefore weaves through my entire life, and it will continue to emerge on occasion in unexpected guises … ."[82] Whereas he was already familiar with poems by the Persian poet Háfiz (ca. 1326–ca. 1390), it was not until 1814, when encountering the latter's *Diwan* in Joseph von Hammer's (1774–1856) edition[83]—the first to translate the complete collection into German—that Goethe wrote: "[T]he whole now produced all the greater impression on me, and I found myself urgently impelled to productive efforts in order to assert my own genius in conflict with this new mighty force."[84]

Goethe himself described the lyrical dialogue with Háfiz in his *West-East Divan* as "an inclination that wavers between two worlds."[85] In her essay for this catalogue, Anke Bosse calls this lyrical dialogue "oscillation" between East and West, Orient and Occident.[86] This can be compared to the aforementioned virtual movement, the swinging, vibrating, and shimmering of light on the glistening surfaces of Mack's

76 Cf. Johann Wolfgang von Goethe, *Confession des Verfassers,* in *Zur Farbenlehre,* vol. 2 (Tübingen 1810), p. 674.
77 Translated from Heinz Mack, "Mein Standort im Reich der Farbe," in *Mack: Skulpturen und Malerei,* ed. Harro Lauter, exh. cat. Galerie Lauter Mannheim (Mönchengladbach, 1992), pp. 61–65, esp. p. 63.
78 Goethe 1840 (see note 1), p. 233.
79 Even in the morning of his day of death, Goethe asked his daughter-in-law, Ottilie, to show him a folder with materials pertaining to the color theory. Cf. Manfred Wenzel, ed., *Goethe Handbuch,* vol. 2, Supplemente (Stuttgart, 2012), p. 132.
80 Published in 2003 under the title *Al Ghazali: Über die Glückseligkeit und über das Licht* in Vaduz, Liechtenstein, this is a bibliophile artist's book with serigraphs of Heinz Mack in an edition of seventy numbered and signed copies.
81 Karin Adrian von Roques, "Wahaj al Sahara: In the Light of the Desert," in idem et al., *Heinz Mack: Wahaj al Sahara. Im Licht der Wüste—In the Light of the Desert,* exh. cat. BFH Fine Art Gallery, Manama, Bahrain (Düsseldorf, 2011), pp. 8–11, esp. p. 8.
82 Translated from Johann Wolfgang von Goethe, letter to Friedrich Rochlitz dated January 30, 1812, WA, vol. IV 22, pp. 250–53, esp. p. 252.
83 Ill. p. 356.
84 Johann Wolfgang von Goethe, *Annals; or, Day and Year Papers* (London, 1884), p. 418.
85 Johann Wolfgang von Goethe in a letter to Carl Friedrich Zelter dated May 11, 1820, in London and New York 1891 (see note 29), p. 193.
86 Pp. 408–18.

ten Zimmer; ich erwartete, als ich das Prisma vor die Augen nahm, eingedenk der Newtonischen Theorie, die ganze weiße Wand nach verschiedenen Stufen gefärbt, das von da ins Auge zurückkehrende Licht in soviel farbige Lichter zersplittert zu sehen. Aber wie verwundert war ich, als die durchs Prisma angeschaute weiße Wand nach wie vor weiß blieb, daß nur da, wo ein Dunkles dran stieß, sich eine mehr oder weniger entschiedene Farbe zeigte, daß zuletzt die Fensterstäbe am allerlebhaftesten farbig erschienen, indessen am lichtgrauen Himmel draußen keine Spur von Färbung zu sehen war. Es bedurfte keiner langen Ueberlegung, so erkannte ich, daß eine Gränze nothwendig sey, um Farben hervorzubringen, und ich sprach wie durch einen Instinct sogleich vor mich laut aus, daß die Newtonische Lehre falsch sey.[75]

Beide, Goethe und Mack, haben sich »in Absicht auf Kunst«[76] mit der Farbenlehre befasst. »Bei allen ›Lichtfarben‹«, so Mack, »brauche ich das Weiß als Malfläche, als Untergrund, als Reflexionsfläche für das Licht. Das Weiß ist daher immer von wesentlicher Bedeutung für die Reinheit und Strahlkraft der Farben. [...] Hier wird Farbe zu einer Emanation des Lichts, das sich als Spektrum und im Spektrum ereignet. Diese Strahlung bewirkt die Erscheinung der Farbe, welche aus der Malfläche heraustritt und den Raum erfüllt.«[77] Wenn Heinz Mack das schreibt, klingt das wie Goethes Feststellung: »Jede Farbe also, um gesehen zu werden, muß ein Licht im Hinterhalte haben. Daher kommt es, daß je heller und glänzender die Unterlagen sind, desto schöner erscheinen die Farben. [...] Ja die Energie der physischen Farben beruht hauptsächlich darauf, daß mit und hinter ihnen das Licht immerfort wirksam ist.«[78]

Was liegt also näher, als die beiden Künstler, deren Interesse an Licht und Farbe niemals erlosch,[79] in einer Zusammenschau einander gegenüberzustellen und dabei genauer zu beleuchten, was die scheinbar gegensätzlichen Persönlichkeiten miteinander verbindet: den Klassiker und den Avantgardisten, den malenden Dichter und den dichtenden Maler? Außer der Vorliebe für die Farben des Lichts und die Leuchtkraft der Farbe untersucht die Schau weitere überraschende, ja geradezu verblüffende Parallelen zwischen den beiden Künstlerpersönlichkeiten, die fast 200 Jahre voneinander trennen, etwa das gemeinsame Interesse an Formen und Strukturen der Natur oder die Inspiration, die beide in der Kunst des Orients fanden.

Inspiration Orient

Reisen und Arbeits-Exkursionen nach Marokko, Algerien, Ägypten und Oman, Expedition durch die Ténéré-Wüste; Einzelausstellungen in Teheran, Istanbul und im Museum für Islamische Kunst in Berlin; Grafiksuiten zum Hohelied Salomos, zu Goethes *West-oestlichem Divan* sowie zu Texten des persischen Theologen und Philosophen al-Ghazālī (1058–1111)[80]. – »Meine wiederholten Begegnungen mit der orientalischen Kultur«, sagt Heinz Mack, »reichen ein halbes Jahrhundert zurück, und ich war weder in der Lage noch gewillt, mich ihrem Einfluß zu entziehen.«[81]

Bei Goethe, der die – wie er sie nennt – »asiatische« Welt durch Lektüre kennengelernt hatte, heißt es ähnlich: »Es schlingt sich die daher für mich gewonnene Cultur durch mein ganzes Leben, und wird noch manchmal in unerwarteten Erscheinungen hervortreten [...].«[82]

75 Johann Wolfgang von Goethe, *Zur Farbenlehre,* Bd. 2, Tübingen 1810, S. 666–692, hier: S. 677 f.
76 Ebd., S. 674.
77 Heinz Mack, »Mein Standort im Reich der Farbe«, in: *Mack. Skulpturen und Malerei,* hrsg. von Harro Lauter, Ausst.-Kat. Galerie Lauter Mannheim, Mönchengladbach 1992, S. 61–65, hier: S. 63.
78 Goethe 1810 (wie Anm. 1), § 583, S. 216 f.
79 Noch an seinem letzten Morgen ließ Goethe sich von seiner Schwiegertochter Ottilie eine Mappe mit Materialien zur Farbenlehre vorlegen. Vgl. *Goethe Handbuch,* Supplemente, Bd. 2, hrsg. von Manfred Wenzel, Stuttgart 2012, S. 132.
80 Unter dem Titel *Al Ghazali. Über die Glückseligkeit und über das Licht* erschien 2003 in Vaduz, Liechtenstein, ein bibliophiles Künstlerbuch mit Serigraphien von Heinz Mack in einer Auflage von 70 nummerierten und handsignierten Exemplaren.
81 Karin Adrian von Roques, »Wahaj al Sahara. Im Licht der Wüste«, in: dies. u. a., *Heinz Mack. Wahaj al Sahara. Im Licht der Wüste,* Ausst.-Kat. BFH Fine Art Gallery, Manama, Bahrein, Düsseldorf 2011, S. 12 ff., hier: S. 12.
82 Johann Wolfgang von Goethe, Brief an Friedrich Rochlitz vom 30. Januar 1812, WA, Bd. IV 22, S. 250–253, hier: S. 252.

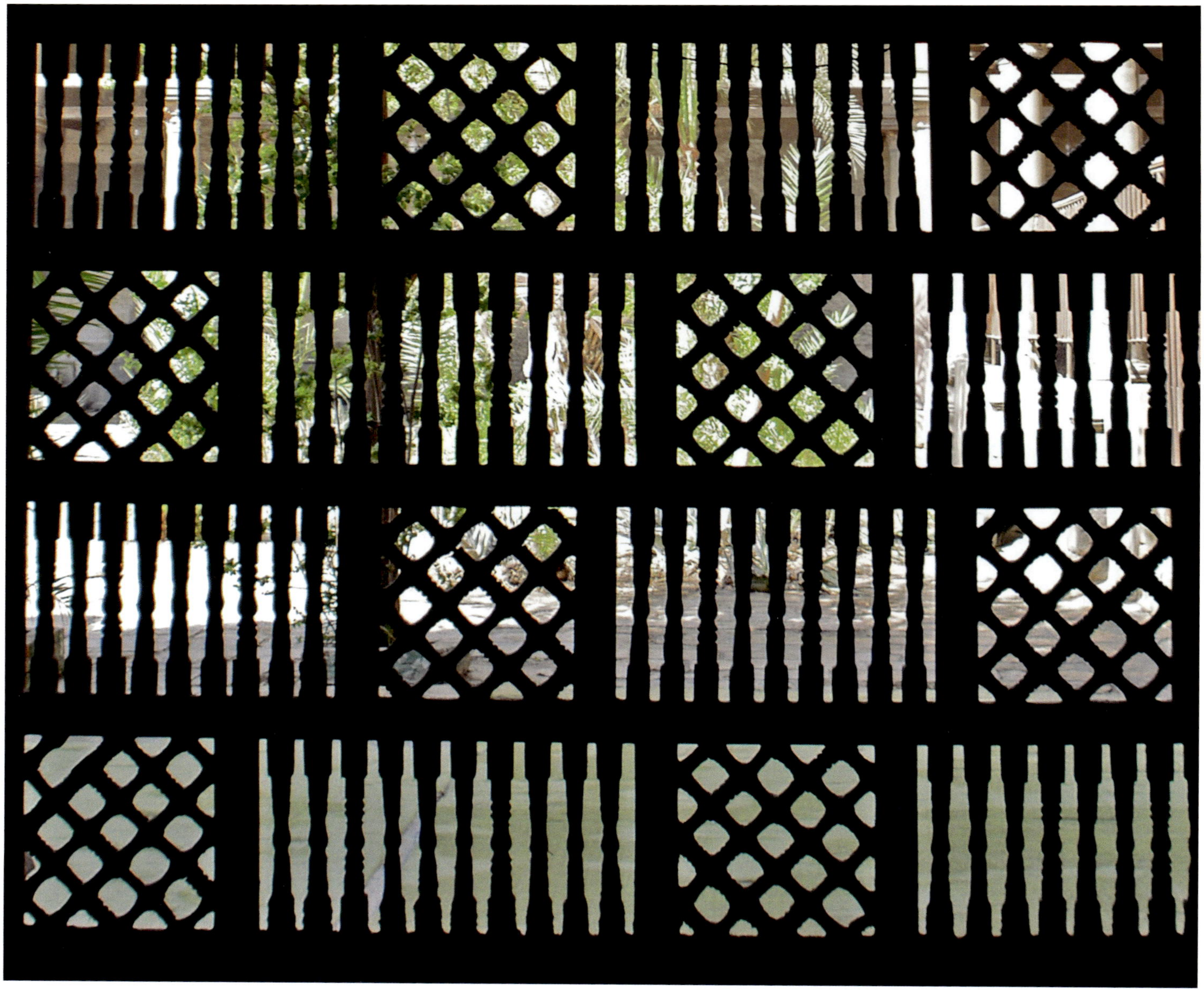

19 Maschrabiyya
Altinbugha-al-Maridani-Moschee, Kairo
1339/40

Mashrabiyya
Altinbugha al-Maridani Mosque, Cairo
1339/40

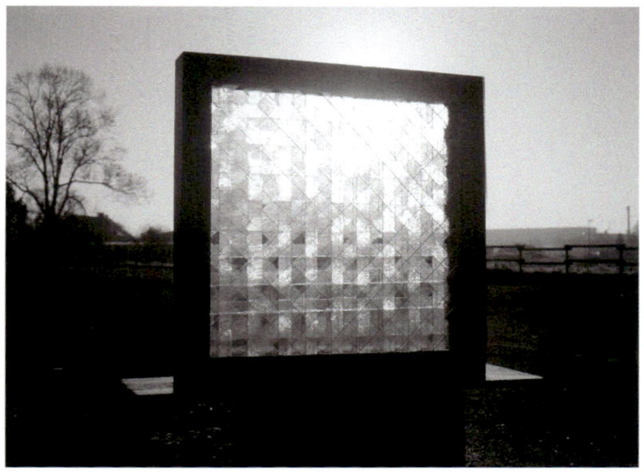

20 Heinz Mack
Licht-Gitter (Hommage à Piero Dorazio;
Modell für einen gläsernen Paravent)
Signiert, datiert: »mack 3«
Glas, Holz
62 x 62 x 9 cm
Vgl. auch die farbige Abb. S. 386.

20 Heinz Mack
Light Grid (Hommage à Piero Dorazio;
Model for a glass paravent)
Signed, dated: "mack 3"
Glass, wood
62 x 62 x 9 cm
See also the colored ill. p. 386.

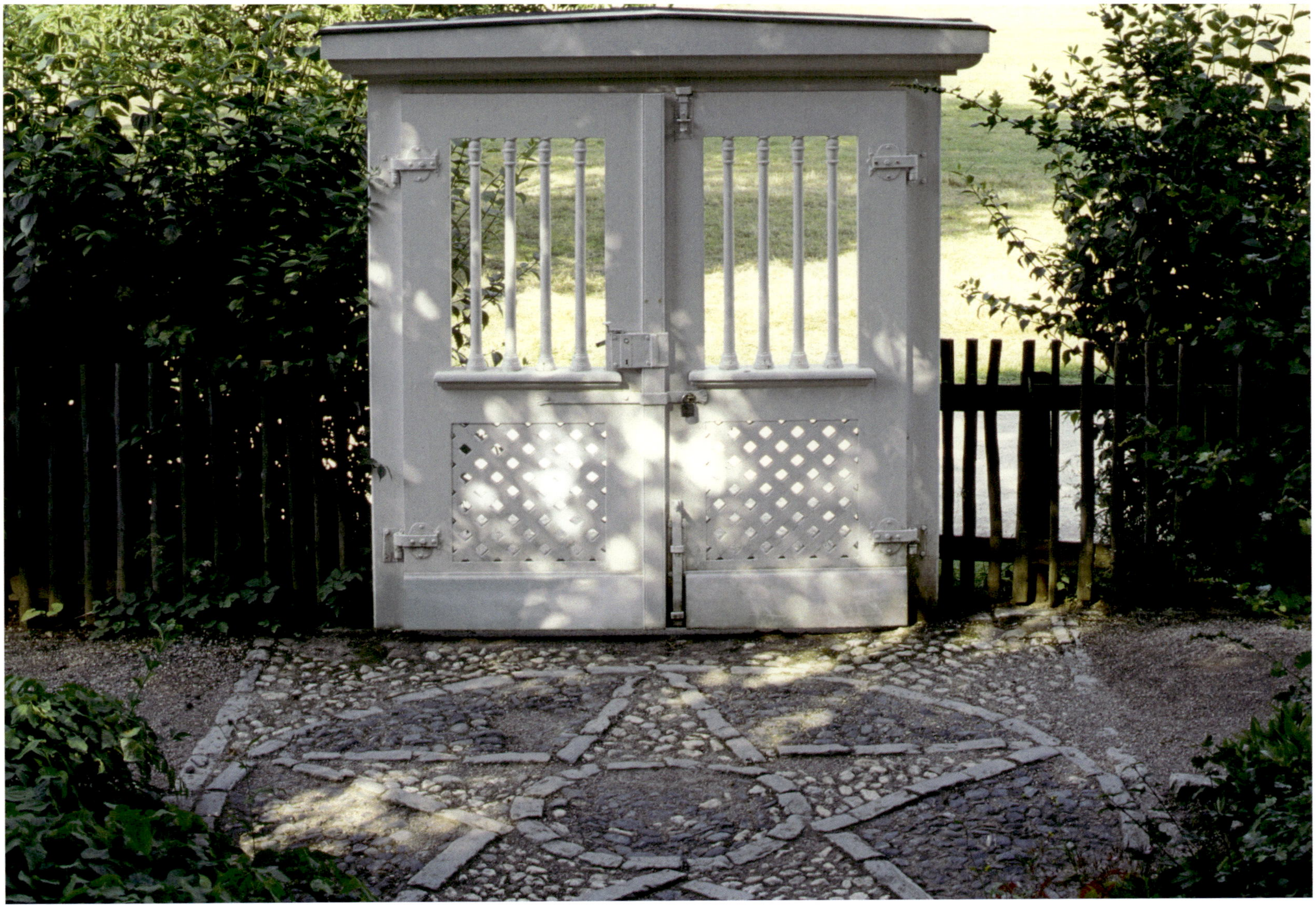

21 Tor von Goethes Garten am Stern
1830 entworfen von dem Architekten
Clemens Wenzeslaus Coudray (1775–1845)

Gate of Goethe's garden at the Stern
Designed 1830 by the architect
Clemens Wenzeslaus Coudray (1775–1845)

light sculptures. "The metallic tone values must be considered as extraordinary pictorial means," wrote Paul Klee in the notes about his Bauhaus lecture *Contributions to a Theory of Pictorial Form*. "[G]old is a vibration between saturated yellow and a dazzling white,"[87] and it makes sense that corresponding surface treatment will further enhance this effect.

Medieval Islamic architects were already familiar with such procedures. Art historian Hans Belting writes the following about thirteenth-century, gleaming gold facets decorating the walls of the Imam-Reza shrine in the Iranian city of Mashhad: "Beams of light serve as an organizing principle in interiors in the same way that patterns of lines function on the walls. Such disembodied arrangements seem to make the walls and limits of the space disappear, an effect brought about by the dominance of light and pattern over all material substance. On the shimmering walls … the reflected light almost obliterates the material substance of the structure."[88]

"Gold is the most abstract way in which the sublime can find manifestation,"[89] says Heinz Mack. It is hardly a coincidence that, especially in his works that make reference to the Orient, he occasionally uses glittering gold surfaces, for instance made of brass, polished bronze, glazed ceramics, or comprised of countless gilt tesserae.

Not a single aspect of this exhibition stands in isolation: Regardless of whether it is a matter of oscillating ideas and associations; the flickering, shimmering, and virtual fusion of colors when experimenting with Goethe's wheel for mixing colors; or the apparent liquefaction of materials in Mack's rotors. In his *Italian Journey,* Goethe wrote "I keep having new thoughts, and since there are thousands of objects around me, they awaken me now to this idea, now to that."[90] We would also like to invite our visitors to let their thoughts wander while looking at the diverse exhibits and experience one or the other flash of inspiration.

In the exhibition *Acts of Light—Mack & Goethe,* rarely or never shown works by Mack dealing with the subjects of color, light, and shadow meet with thoughts from Goethe's theory of colors. Mack's structured works encounter ideas from Goethe's morphology. Last but not least, the pictures by a Western artist, reminiscent of Oriental ornaments, find confirmation in insight derived from the periphery of the *West-East Divan:* "Orient and Occident dwell / Separately no more."[91] Overall, Mack's oeuvre reveals a surprisingly multifaceted mirror image and antithesis to Goethe's world thoughts and ideas.

Theirs is an elective affinity with regards to the universality of interests, their orientation toward the future, and in their openness vis-à-vis different cultures.—Is there anything we require more urgently today than this prudence in dealing with cultural identity?

87 Paul Klee, *Notebooks,* vol. 1, *The Thinking Eye,* trans. Charlotte Weidler and Joyce Wittenborn, (London, 1962), p. 509.
88 Hans Belting, *Florence and Baghdad: Renaissance Art and Arab Science,* trans. Deborah Lucas Schneider (Cambridge, MA, 2011), p. 116.
89 Heinz Mack, *"The Sky Over Nine Columns:* Thoughts and reflections about the project. Excerpts from the project's exposé," in *Heinz Mack: The Sky Over Nine Columns. Venice—Istanbul—Valencia—St. Moritz,* ed. Michael Beck and Ute Eggeling (Düsseldorf, 2016), pp. 20–32, esp. p. 28.
90 Johann Wolfgang von Goethe, *The Collected Works,* vol. 6, *Italian Journey,* ed. Thomas P. Saine and Jeffrey L. Sammons, trans. Robert R. Heitner (Princeton, 1989), p. 315.
91 *West-East Divan* (see note 32), p. 167.

Dichtungen des persischen Poeten Hafis (um 1326–um1390) kannte er schon länger, doch als er 1814 dessen *Diwan* in der Ausgabe von Joseph von Hammer (1774–1856)[83] in die Hände bekam, der die Gedichte der Sammlung erstmals vollständig ins Deutsche übertragen hatte, »so wirkten sie«, schreibt Goethe, »doch jetzt zusammen desto lebhafter auf mich ein, und ich mußte mich dagegen productiv verhalten, weil ich sonst vor der mächtigen Erscheinung nicht hätte bestehen können«[84].

Den lyrischen Dialog Goethes mit Hafis im *West-oestlichen Divan* – von Goethe selbst umschrieben als »zwischen zwei Welten schwebend«[85] – bezeichnet Anke Bosse in ihrem Beitrag zum vorliegenden Katalog als »Oszillieren« zwischen West und Ost, Orient und Okzident.[86] Das ist vergleichbar mit der oben erwähnten virtuellen Bewegung, dem Schwingen, Vibrieren und Flirren des Lichts auf den gleißenden Oberflächen von Macks Lichtskulpturen. »Metallwerte sind aparte bildnerische Mittel«, schreibt Paul Klee in den Notizen zu seiner Bauhaus-Vorlesung über *Bildnerische Gestaltungslehre.* »Gold ist ein hin und her vibrieren von sattem Gelb nach einem weiss von überstarker helle«[87], und es leuchtet ein, dass sich dieser Effekt durch entsprechende Oberflächenbearbeitung noch steigern lässt.

Solche Verfahren kannten bereits die islamischen Architekten des Mittelalters. So schreibt der Kunsthistoriker Hans Belting über die in goldenen Facetten erstrahlenden Wände des Imam-Reza-Schreins im iranischen Maschhad, der aus dem 13. Jahrhundert stammt: »Lichtbahnen organisieren die Innenräume ebenso wie Linienmuster die Wandflächen. In diesen körperlosen Ordnungen scheinen sich Raumgrenzen und Wände aufzulösen. Diese Wirkung kommt dadurch zustande, dass alle körperliche Substanz oder Materie hinter dem Licht und dem Dekor zurücktritt. Auf den schimmernden Wänden [...] überspielt oder überblendet das Reflexlicht die Materialität des Bauwerks.«[88]

»Gold ist die abstrakteste Ausdrucksform des Außergewöhnlichen«[89], sagt Heinz Mack. Und es scheint kein Zufall zu sein, dass er vor allem in seinen Werken mit Orientbezug außer mit leuchtenden Farben und schwarz-weißen Gitterstrukturen, die das Licht in einen funkelnden Sternenregen verwandeln, hin und wieder mit goldglänzenden Oberflächen arbeitet: aus Messing, polierter Bronze, glasierter Keramik oder aus unzähligen vergoldeten Mosaiksteinchen.

Ob es nun das Changieren von Ideen und Assoziationen ist, das Flackern, Flimmern und virtuelle Verschmelzen der Farben beim Experimentieren mit Goethes Schwungrad zur Farbenmischung oder die scheinbare Verflüssigung des Materials in Macks Rotoren: Kein Aspekt der Schau steht isoliert für sich. »Ich habe immer neue Gedanken«, schreibt Goethe in der *Italiänischen Reise,* »und da die Gegenstände um mich tausendfach sind, so wecken sie mich bald zu dieser bald zu jener Idee.«[90] Auch die Besucher sind eingeladen, beim Betrachten der vielfältigen Exponate ihre Gedanken schweifen und sich inspirieren zu lassen zu dem einen oder anderen Geistesblitz.

In der Ausstellung *Taten des Lichts – Mack & Goethe* treffen selten oder noch nie gezeigte Werke Heinz Macks zu den Themen Farbe, Licht und Schatten auf Gedanken aus Goethes Farbenlehre. Macks Struktur-Arbeiten begegnen Ideen aus Goethes Morphologie. Und die an orientalische Ornamente erinnernden Bilder eines westlichen Künstlers finden Bestätigung in der Erkenntnis aus dem Umfeld des *West-oestlichen Divans:* »Orient und

83 Abb. S. 356.
84 Johann Wolfgang von Goethe, *Tag- und Jahres-Hefte,* 1815, WA, Bd. I 36, S. 91–102, hier: S. 91.
85 Johann Wolfgang von Goethe, Brief an Carl Friedrich Zelter vom 11. Mai 1820, WA, Bd. IV 3, S. 26–29, hier: S. 27.
86 S. 409–419.
87 Paul Klees Unterrichtsnotizen sind vollständig als Faksimiles und Transkriptionen in einer Online-Datenbank publiziert, die vom Zentrum Paul Klee, Bern, erarbeitet wurde. Paul Klee, *Bildnerische Form- und Gestaltungslehre. Bildnerische Gestaltungslehre,* BG I.2/164. Abrufbar unter: http://www.kleegestaltungslehre.zpk.org/ee/ZPK/BG/2012/01/02/164/?from_search=true (Stand: 06.01.2018).
88 Hans Belting, *Florenz und Bagdad. Eine west-östliche Geschichte des Blicks,* München 2012, S. 131.
89 Heinz Mack, »*The Sky Over Nine Columns.* Gedanken und Reflexionen über das Projekt. Auszüge aus dem Projekt-Exposé«, in: *Mack. The Sky Over Nine Columns. Venedig – Instanbul – Valencia – St. Moritz,* hrsg. von Michael Beck und Ute Eggeling, Düsseldorf 2016, S. 20–32, hier: S. 28.
90 Johann Wolfgang von Goethe, *Italiänische Reise* III, 6. September 1787, WA, Bd. I 32, S. 75–78, hier: S. 75 f.

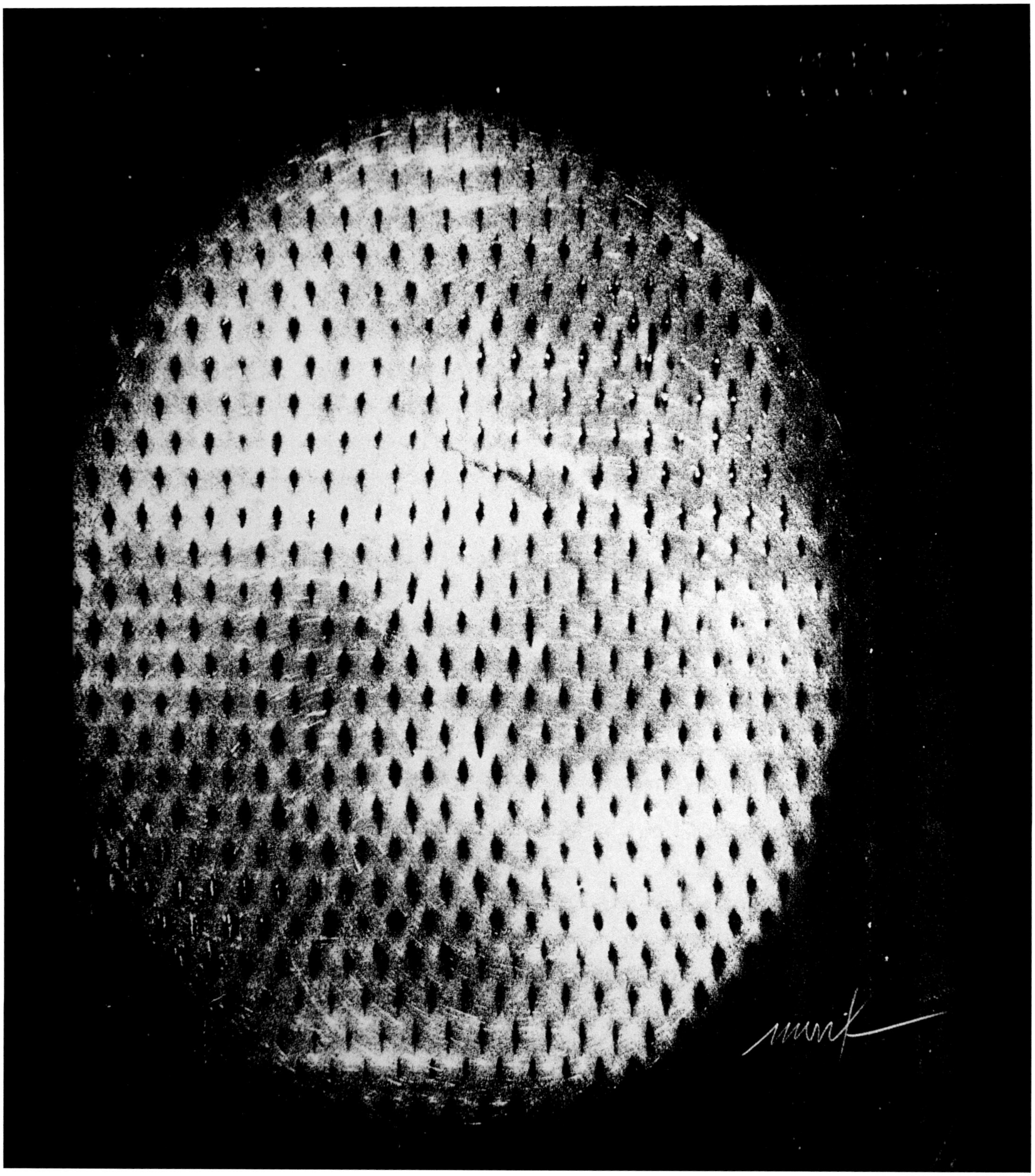

22 Heinz Mack
Ohne Titel
Signiert: »mack«, 1973
Wachspapier auf Papier; Frottage eines Metallrasters mittels hochtouriger Polierscheibe
30 x 21 cm

22 Heinz Mack
Untitled
Signed: "mack", 1973
Waxed paper on paper; frottage of a metal grid produced by a high-speed polishing wheel
30 x 21 cm

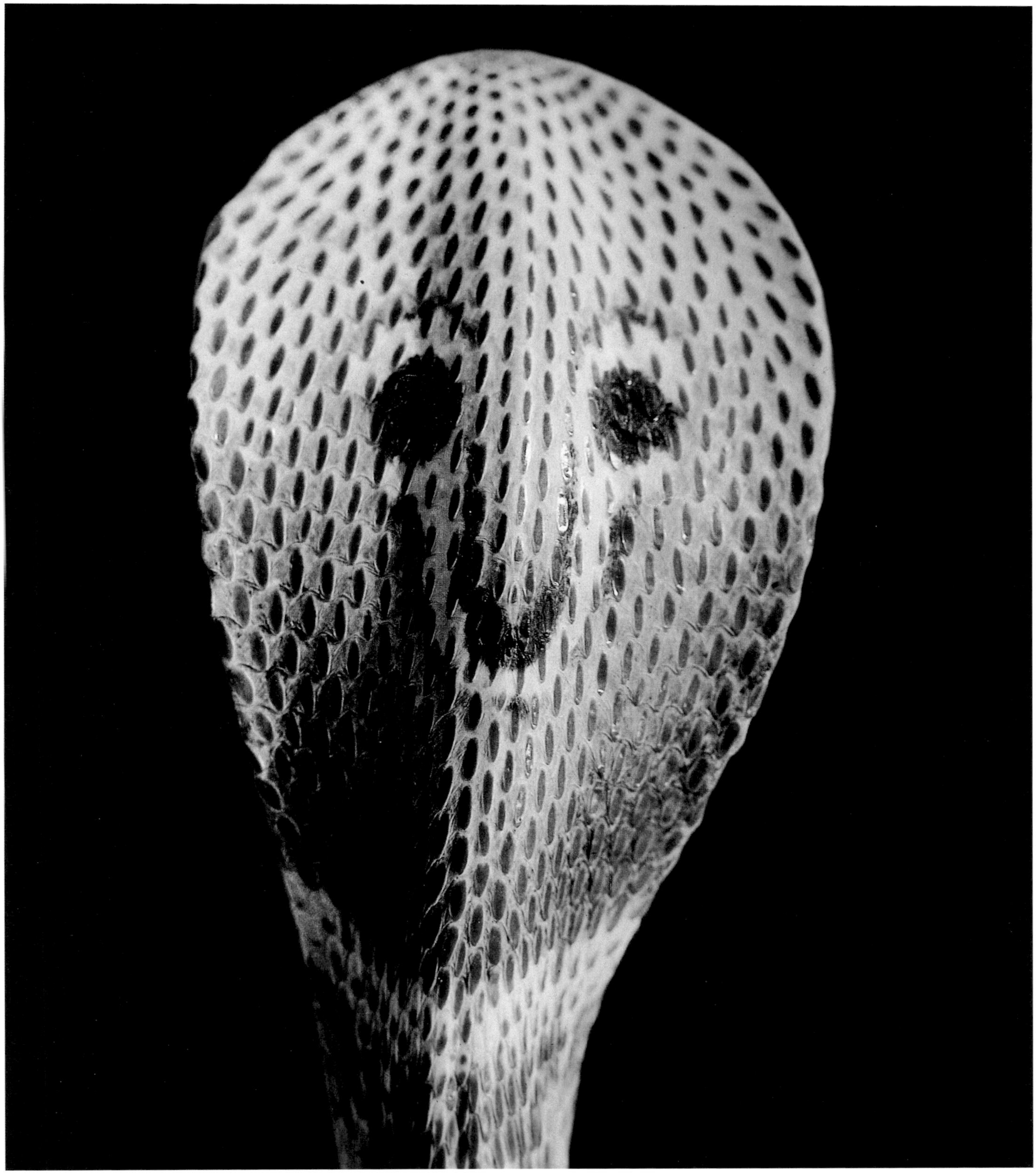

23 Hinterkopf einer Kobra | Back of a cobra's head

Structure and Morphology

"Nature and art, they go their separate ways,
It seems; yet all at once they find each other."[92]

When Goethe writes: "[S]o we must necessarily think of science as art if we expect to derive any kind of wholeness from it,"[93] this not only makes him a precursor of new interdisciplinary approaches, which make the twenty-first century such an exciting era in the history of science. Rather, in his holistic attitude, which always includes the individual in natural scientific experiments, Goethe can also be considered a progenitor of ecology.

In this context, holism not only signifies not to look at the object in question in isolation but in the greater context of nature (since in "living nature nothing happens that does not stand in a relationship to the whole"[94]), and to look at the scientist as well. Goethe writes: "[W]e must not exclude any of the human powers from scientific activity. The abysses of intuition, a sure view of the present, mathematical depth, physical precision, sublimity of reason, sharpness of intellect, agile, yearning fantasy, loving joy in the sensuous: Nothing can be foregone if there is to be a lively, fruitful seizing of the moment, through which alone a work of art, whatever its content may be, can arise."[95]

While the moment is clearly a key concept in Goethe's literary oeuvre, it plays an equally crucial role in his understanding of science as art. Heinz Mack is convinced "that fascination is everything, even if it lasts but a moment. In this sense," he says, "I make my sand drawings, which in the light of the setting sun turn into sand reliefs, spread out like artificial carpets, woven from light and shadow, impermanent like tracks in the sand."[96] His *Sahara Project*[97]—a utopia whose first design he conceived exactly sixty years ago, partially visualizing it fifty years ago with the film *Tele-Mack*[98]—points to Light Art and anticipates Land Art: neither term existed in the late fifties.

As a sculptor who works with natural stone, Mack has repeatedly studied mineralogy and travelled to the world's major quarries, from which the hidden treasures first had to be unearthed. He says:

> I will never forget an experience near Porto, in the Portuguese quarries, where massive granite monoliths, often weighing 150 tons, are cut using traditional methods. This means: only very few expansion wedges, which with intuitive knowledge are correctly placed around the fabric of the stone, and an impact hammer, hit with virility, has to suffice in order to achieve the separation of the monoliths. Something that has been resting for millennia, that has never seen light nor has been seen by a human being, suddenly becomes visible with its split-open surfaces.[99]

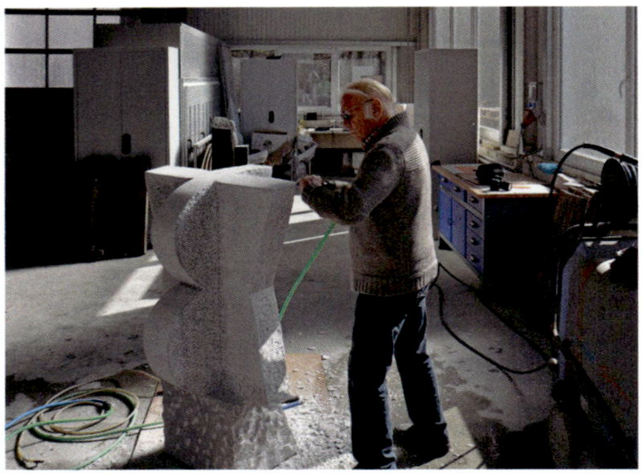

24 Heinz Mack in der Werkstatt
2016

Heinz Mack in his workshop
2016

92 Johann Wolfgang von Goethe, *Selected Poetry*, ed. and trans. David Luke (London et al., 2005), p. 125.
93 Johann Wolfgang von Goethe, quoted in Richard Wolin, *Walter Benjamin: An Aesthetic of Redemption* (Berkeley et al., 1994), p. 87.
94 Johann Wolfgang von Goethe, quoted in Sepper 1988 (see note 74), p. 69.
95 Ibid., pp. 194–95.
96 Translated from Heinz Mack, "Spuren verlieren sich im Sand", in Nannen (see note 21).
97 He conceived the thirteen stations in 1958/59 and first published them in 1961 in the third and final issue of the periodical *ZERO* (see note 16), pp. 176–79.
98 *Tele-Mack*, a film by Heinz Mack (screenplay) and Hans Emmerling (screenplay and direction). Camera: Edwin K. Braun. A coproduction of Saarländischer Rundfunk and Westdeutsches Fernsehen, 1968. In 1970, the Adolf-Grimme Award and the recognition award of the Venice Biennale Film Festival.
99 Translated from Heinz Mack, *Der Bildhauer und die Gesteinskunde: Ibiza, im Juli 2017*, unpublished text.

Occident / Sind nicht mehr zu trennen.«[91] Zusammengenommen erscheinen Macks Werke als überraschend facettenreiches Spiegel- und Gegenbild zur Gedanken- und Ideenwelt Goethes.

Mack und Goethe sind Wahlverwandte in der Universalität ihrer Interessen, in ihrer Zukunftsorientierung und in ihrer Offenheit anderen Kulturen gegenüber. – Was hätten wir heute nötiger als diese Besonnenheit im Umgang mit kultureller Identität?

Struktur und Morphologie

»Natur und Kunst sie scheinen sich zu fliehen,
Und haben sich, eh' man es denkt, gefunden [...].«[92]

Wenn Goethe schreibt: »[...] so müssen wir uns die Wissenschaft nothwendig als Kunst denken, wenn wir von ihr irgend eine Art von Ganzheit erwarten«[93], dann ist er damit nicht nur ein Vorläufer der neuen Interdisziplinarität, die das 21. Jahrhundert zu einer so spannenden Epoche der Wissenschaftsgeschichte macht. Vielmehr kann er in seiner ganzheitlichen Haltung, die bei naturwissenschaftlichen Experimenten den Menschen in seiner Umwelt immer mit einbezieht, auch als ein Urahn der Ökologie gelten.

Dabei meint Ganzheitlichkeit nicht nur den zu untersuchenden Gegenstand, der nicht isoliert, sondern im großen Zusammenhang der Natur betrachtet werden soll (denn in »der lebendigen Natur geschieht nichts, was nicht in einer Verbindung mit dem Ganzen stehe«[94]), sondern auch den Forscher selbst. Man müsste, schreibt Goethe, »[...] keine der menschlichen Kräfte bey wissenschaftlicher Thätigkeit ausschließen. Die Abgründe der Ahndung, ein sicheres Anschauen der Gegenwart, mathematische Tiefe, physische Genauigkeit, Höhe der Vernunft, Schärfe des Verstandes, bewegliche sehnsuchtsvolle Phantasie, liebevolle Freude am Sinnlichen, nichts kann entbehrt werden zum lebhaften fruchtbaren Ergreifen des Augenblicks, wodurch ganz allein ein Kunstwerk, von welchem Gehalt es auch sey, entstehen kann.«[95]

Der Augenblick ist also nicht nur ein Schlüsselbegriff in Goethes literarischem Werk, sondern spielt auch eine entscheidende Rolle für sein Verständnis von Wissenschaft als Kunst. Heinz Mack ist davon überzeugt, »daß die Faszination alles ist und wenn sie nur einen einzigen Augenblick dauert. In diesem Sinne«, sagt Mack, »mache ich meine Sandzeichnungen, die im Licht der untergehenden Sonne zu Sandreliefs werden, ausgebreitet wie künstliche Teppiche, gewebt aus Licht und Schatten, vergänglich wie Spuren im Sand.«[96] Sein *Sahara-Projekt*[97], eine Utopie, die er vor genau 60 Jahren im ersten Entwurf konzipierte und die er vor 50 Jahren mit dem Film *Tele-Mack*[98] in Teilen visualisierte, weist auf Lichtkunst und Land-Art voraus – beides Begriffe, die es Ende der 50er Jahre noch nicht einmal gab.

Als Bildhauer, der mit Naturstein arbeitet, hat Mack sich immer wieder mit Gesteinskunde befasst und ist zu den großen Steinbrüchen dieser Erde gereist, aus denen die verborgenen Schätze erst einmal gehoben werden mussten. Er sagt:

> Unvergessen bleibt ein Erlebnis unweit von Porto in den portugiesischen Steinbrüchen, wo die mächtigen Granit-Monolithe, oft 150 Tonnen schwer, mit traditionellen Mitteln

91 Johann Wolfgang von Goethe, *West-östlicher Divan. Aus dem Nachlaß*, WA, Bd. I 6, S. 276.
92 Johann Wolfgang von Goethe, *Gedichte*, WA, Bd. I 4, S. [129].
93 Goethe 1810 (wie Anm. 75), S. 120.
94 Johann Wolfgang von Goethe, »Der Versuch als Vermittler von Object und Subject«, in: ders., *Zur Naturwissenschaft überhaupt*, Bd. 2, Stuttgart und Tübingen 1823, S. 39–53, hier: S. 49.
95 Goethe 1810 (wie Anm. 75), S. 120.
96 Heinz Mack, »Spuren verlieren sich im Sand«, in: Nannen o. J. (wie Anm. 21), o. S.
97 Es wurde 1958/59 in 13 Stationen konzipiert und 1961 erstmals veröffentlicht im dritten und letzten Heft der Zeitschrift *ZERO* (wie Anm. 16), S. 176–179.
98 *Tele-Mack*. Ein Film von Heinz Mack (Buch) und Hans Emmerling (Buch und Regie). Kamera: Edwin K. Braun. Saarländischer Rundfunk in Koproduktion mit dem Westdeutschen Fernsehen 1968. Ausgezeichnet mit der Ehrenden Anerkennung der Jury des Adolf-Grimme-Preises und mit dem Anerkennungspreis der Film-Biennale Venedig.

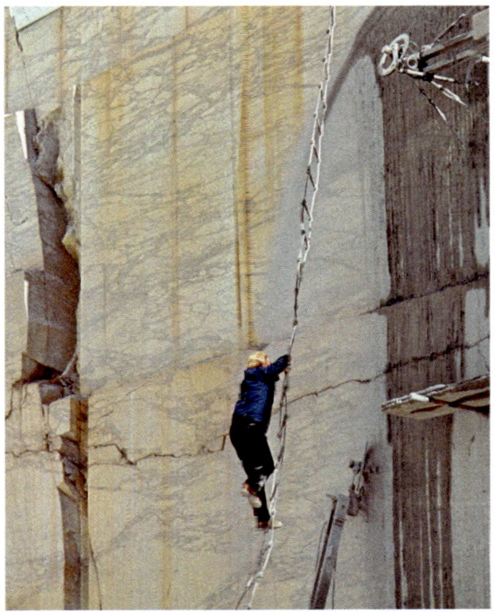

25 Heinz Mack
Carrara 1983

Heinz Mack
Carrara 1983

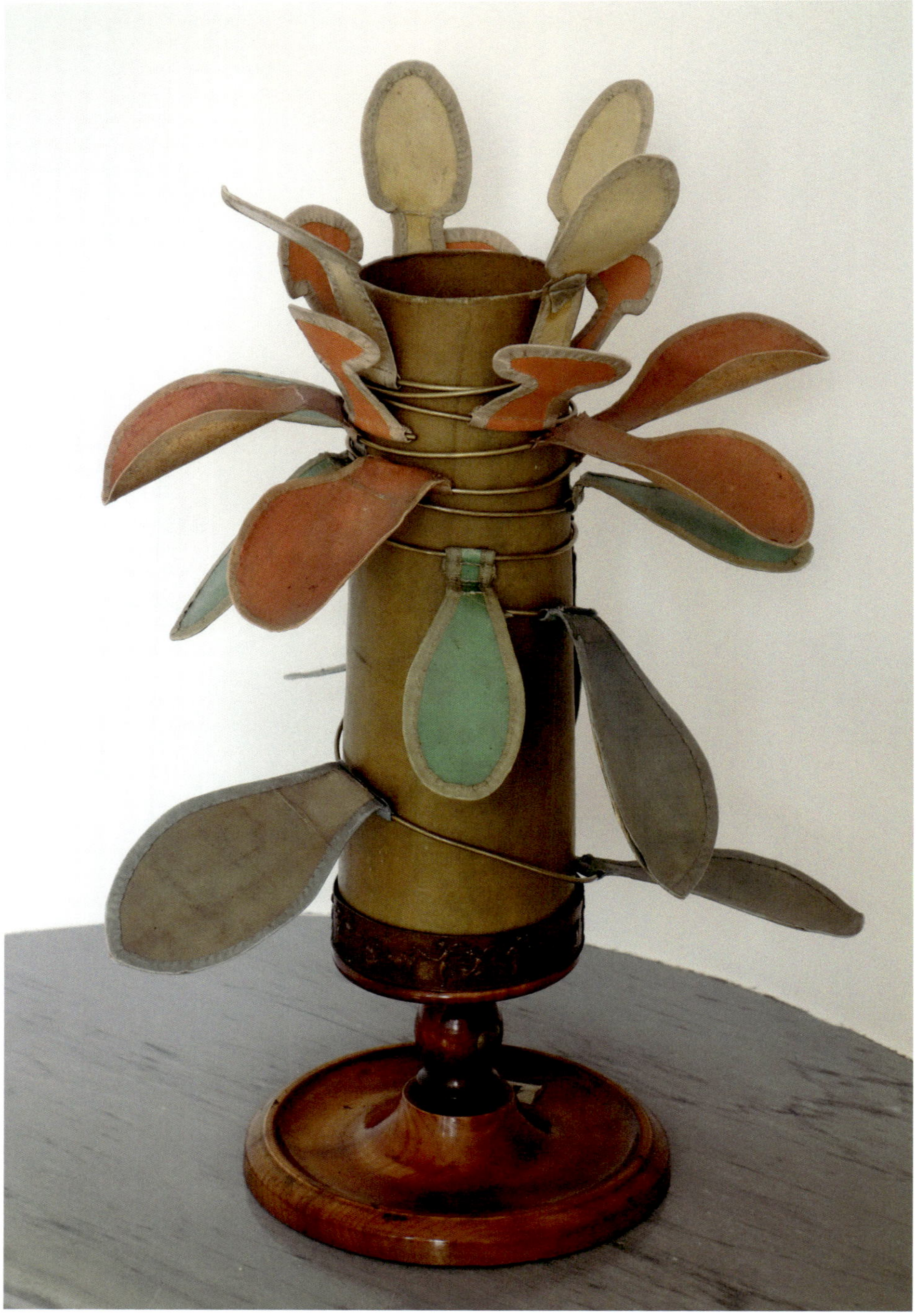

26 Heinz Mack
Trophäe des Siegers
Signiert, datiert: »mack 54«
Edelstahl
57 x 27 x 28 cm

Heinz Mack
Trophy for the Victor
Signed, dated: "mack 54"
Stainless steel
57 x 27 x 28 cm

27 Modell zur Spiraltendenz des Pflanzenwachstums nach Carl Friedrich Philipp Martius (1794–1868) aus Goethes Besitz
Österreichische Goethe-Gesellschaft

Model of spiral tendency observed in the growth of plants after Carl Friedrich Philipp Martius (1794–1868) in Goethe's possession
Österreichische Goethe-Gesellschaft

Goethe schreibt: »Nachdem ich viele Jahre nach meinen früheren Ansichten die Pflanzenwelt betrachtet und mich begnügt hatte manches Besondere ins Allgemeine zu verbinden so ward ich aufs neue kräftig angeregt durch eine gewisse neubeobachtete Spiraltendenz der Pflanzen worüber Martius 1827 in München und das folgende Jahr in Berlin Vorträge gehalten und an dem letzteren Orte zu mehrer Verdeutlichung ein Modell vorgewiesen hatte. Als dieser Werte Mann auf seiner Rückreise mich besuchte kam

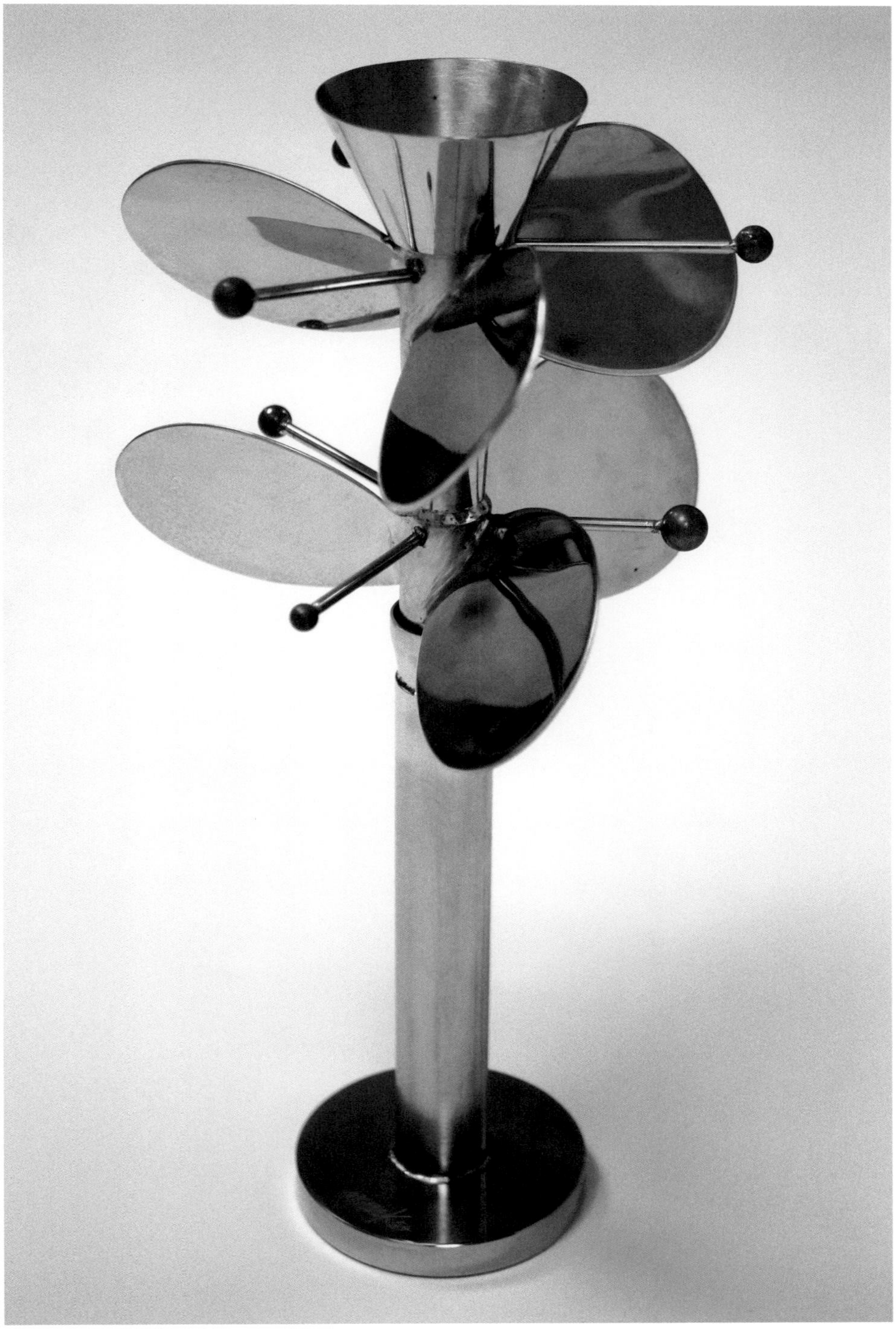

diese Angelegenheit zur Sprache, da denn derselbe durch einen gedrängten Vortrag so wie durch einige flüchtige Zeichnungen mich in diese neueröffneten Geheimnisse tief einzuführen die Gefälligkeit hatte. […] allein, da mir immer noch ein näheres Anschauen fehlte mußt ich um eine Nachbildung jenes Modells dringend ersuchen. Der nachgiebige Freund verehrte mir auch solches zu meinem Geburtstag 1829 […].« (Johann Wolfgang von Goethe, *Weitere Studien zur Spiraltendenz,* LA, Bd. I 10, S. 343–365, hier: S. 343.)

Goethe writes: "After I had observed for many years the flora according to my previous understanding, I had been content to connect some of the specific with the general; now, however, I was energized considerably by a certain newly discovered spiral tendency in plants, foremost through Martius's lectures that he had delivered in Berlin in 1827, and, a year later, in Munich, where he also provided a model. During a visit of this worthy man on his return, this topic was discussed, and, due to his generosity, he not only delivered a condensed lecture and produced some quick sketches, he also inducted me deeply into the newly discovered secrets … nevertheless, since I was still missing a clearer understanding, I had to request a copy of his model. The indulgent friend presented me with one on my birthday in 1829 … ." (Translated from Johann Wolfgang von Goethe, *Weitere Studien zur Spiraltendenz,* LA, vol. I 10, pp. 343–65, esp. p. 343.)

Out of general scientific interest and as head of the Weimar Mining Commission, Goethe also conducted geological and mineralogical studies. In old age, he recalls: "For fifty years, I have put much effort into this field: no mountain was too high, no pit too deep, no tunnel too tight, no cave labyrinthine enough … ."[100] He was full of enthusiasm when writing to Charlotte von Stein in 1780: "We climbed to the high summit and crept into the depths of the earth and wished more than anything to discover the closest tracks of the great hand of creation. Certainly another will come who sees such things clearly. We want to prepare the ground for him."[101]

It seems that Goethe not only did groundwork for succeeding generations of natural scientists or—through his (re)discovery of the intermaxillary bone in humans—in evolutionary sciences, but also in other areas. His last botanical studies, undertaken with enthusiasm in the fall of 1831, just months before his death, pertained to vegetation's 'spiral tendency.'[102] In this context, chemistry historian Otto Krätz writes: "The fact that Goethe was capable of getting closer to the true laws of plant morphology than the majority of his contemporaries was to prove itself in modern times with research on DNA, deciphering the genetic code, and the development of molecular biology or gene technology."[103]

Like Goethe two hundred years before him, in his advanced years Heinz Mack continues to be interested in the most recent scientific findings and up-to-date technical developments. In the period of emergence into a new era following World War I, the co-founder of ZERO introduced the state-of-the-art materials from aerospace technology into art, such as the so-called honeycomb, a malleable aluminum grid made of honeycomb-shaped meshes that he has been using since 1961, and today he experiments with 3D printers.[104] He is also interested in micro- and nanotechnology, looks with fascination at the hidden worlds specialists can make visible with their high-resolution scanning electron microscopes, and in hindsight recognizes structural parallels in this with his prints. Because, according to Goethe:

> And it is the One Eternal
> Multiply self-manifest:
> Small the big is, big the small.
> All things to their type arrest.
> Self-insistent, always changing,
> Near and far and far and near,
> Birth of shapes, their rearranging—
> Wonder of wonders, I am here.[105]

Heinz Mack explains:

> The purely phenomenological, purely visual affinity between the microstructures that the atomic physicist sees with his scanning electron microscope and the networks in biophysics on the one hand and the structural graphics that I create independently of these has a certain structural logic. Its ornamental quality is an

100 Translated from Johann Wolfgang von Goethe, *Bildung des Erdkörpers: Deutschland geognostisch-geologisch dargestellt von Chr. Keferstein* (Weimar, 1821), LA, vol. I 2, pp. 190–92, esp. p. 190.
101 Goethe in a letter to Charlotte von Stein dated September 7, 1780. Quoted in Katharina Mommsen, *Goethe's Art of Living*, trans. John Crosetto et al. (Victoria, 2003), p. 70.
102 Cf. Johann Wolfgang von Goethe, *Über die Spiraltendenz* und *Weitere Studien zur Spiraltendenz*, LA, vol. I 10, pp. 339–65.
103 Translated from Otto Krätz, *Goethe und die Naturwissenschaften* (Munich, 1992), p. 102.
104 Cf. ill. p. 296.
105 Johann Wolfgang von Goethe, *Parabasis*, in idem, *The Essential Goethe*, ed. Matthew Bell (Princeton and Oxford, 2016), p. 27.

gespalten werden. Das heißt: Nur wenige Sprengkeile, die mit intuitiven Kenntnissen um das Gefüge des Steins richtig gesetzt werden und ein Schlaghammer, mit Manneskraft geschlagen, müssen ausreichen, um die flächengroßen Teilungen der Monolithe zu erreichen. Was Millionen Jahre in sich ruhte, was nie das Licht und nie der Mensch gesehen hat, ist dann plötzlich in seinen aufgespaltenen Flächen sichtbar.[99]

Auch Goethe hat, aus allgemeinem naturwissenschaftlichem Interesse und als Leiter der weimarischen Bergwerkskommission, geologische und mineralogische Studien betrieben. Im Alter erinnert er sich daran: »[…] was ich mich seit funfzig Jahren in diesem Fach gemüht, wie mir kein Berg zu hoch, kein Schacht zu tief, kein Stollen zu niedrig und keine Höhle labyrinthisch genug war […].«[100] Bereits 1780 schrieb er voller Enthusiasmus an Charlotte von Stein: »Wir sind auf die hohen Gipfel gestiegen und in die Tiefen der Erde eingekrochen, und mögten gar zu gern der grosen formenden Hand nächste Spuren entdecken. Es kommt gewiss noch ein Mensch der darüber klaar sieht. Wir wollen ihm vorarbeiten.«[101]

Vorgearbeitet zu haben scheint Goethe den nachfolgenden Generationen von Naturwissenschaftlern nicht nur hier oder – durch die (Wieder-)Entdeckung des Zwischenkieferknochens beim Menschen – in der Evolutionswissenschaft, sondern auch auf anderen Gebieten. Goethes letzte botanische Studien, die er noch im Herbst 1831, wenige Monate vor seinem Tod, mit Eifer betrieb, galten der ›Spiraltendenz‹ der Vegetation.[102] Dazu schreibt der Chemiehistoriker Otto Krätz: »Daß Goethe in seinen Ansichten über die Morphologie der Pflanzen den wahren Gesetzlichkeiten näher kam als die Mehrheit seiner Zeitgenossen, sollte sich in unseren Tagen mit der Erforschung der Desoxyribonucleinsäure, der Dechiffrierung des genetischen Codes und der Entwicklung der Molekularbiologie und Gentechnologie erweisen.«[103]

Wie Goethe es vor 200 Jahren war, so ist auch Heinz Mack bis ins hohe Alter an den neuesten Forschungsergebnissen der Wissenschaft und an aktuellen technischen Entwicklungen interessiert. Der ZERO-Mitbegründer, der in der Zeit des Aufbruchs nach dem Zweiten Weltkrieg modernste Materialien aus der Luft- und Raumfahrttechnik in die Kunst einführte, etwa das sogenannte ›Honeycomb‹-Material, ein verformbares Aluminiumgitter aus wabenförmigen Maschen, das er seit 1961 verwendet, experimentiert heute mit Skulpturen aus dem 3D-Drucker.[104] Auch interessiert er sich für Mikro- und Nanotechnologie, betrachtet fasziniert die verborgenen Welten, die Spezialisten mit hochauflösenden Raster-Elektronenmikroskopen sichtbar machen können, und erkennt darin im Nachhinein strukturelle Parallelen zu seinen Grafiken. Denn, so Goethe:

[…] es ist das ewig Eine,
Das sich vielfach offenbart;
Klein das Große, groß das Kleine,
Alles nach der eignen Art.
Immer wechselnd, fest sich haltend;
Nah und fern und fern und nah;
So gestaltend, umgestaltend –
Zum Erstaunen bin ich da.[105]

99 Heinz Mack, *Der Bildhauer und die Gesteinskunde. Ibiza, im Juli 2017,* noch unpublizierter Text.
100 Johann Wolfgang von Goethe, *Bildung des Erdkörpers Deutschland geognostisch-geologisch dargestellt von Chr. Keferstein,* Weimar 1821, LA, Bd. I 2, S. 190 ff., hier: S. 190.
101 Brief vom 7. September 1780, WA, Bd. IV 4, S. 282–285, hier: S. 283.
102 Vgl. Johann Wolfgang von Goethe, *Über die Spiraltendenz* und *Weitere Studien zur Spiraltendenz,* LA, Bd. I 10, S. 339–365.
103 Otto Krätz, *Goethe und die Naturwissenschaften,* München 1992, S. 102.
104 Vgl. die Abb. S. 296.
105 Johann Wolfgang von Goethe, *Parabase,* WA, Bd. I 3, S. 84.

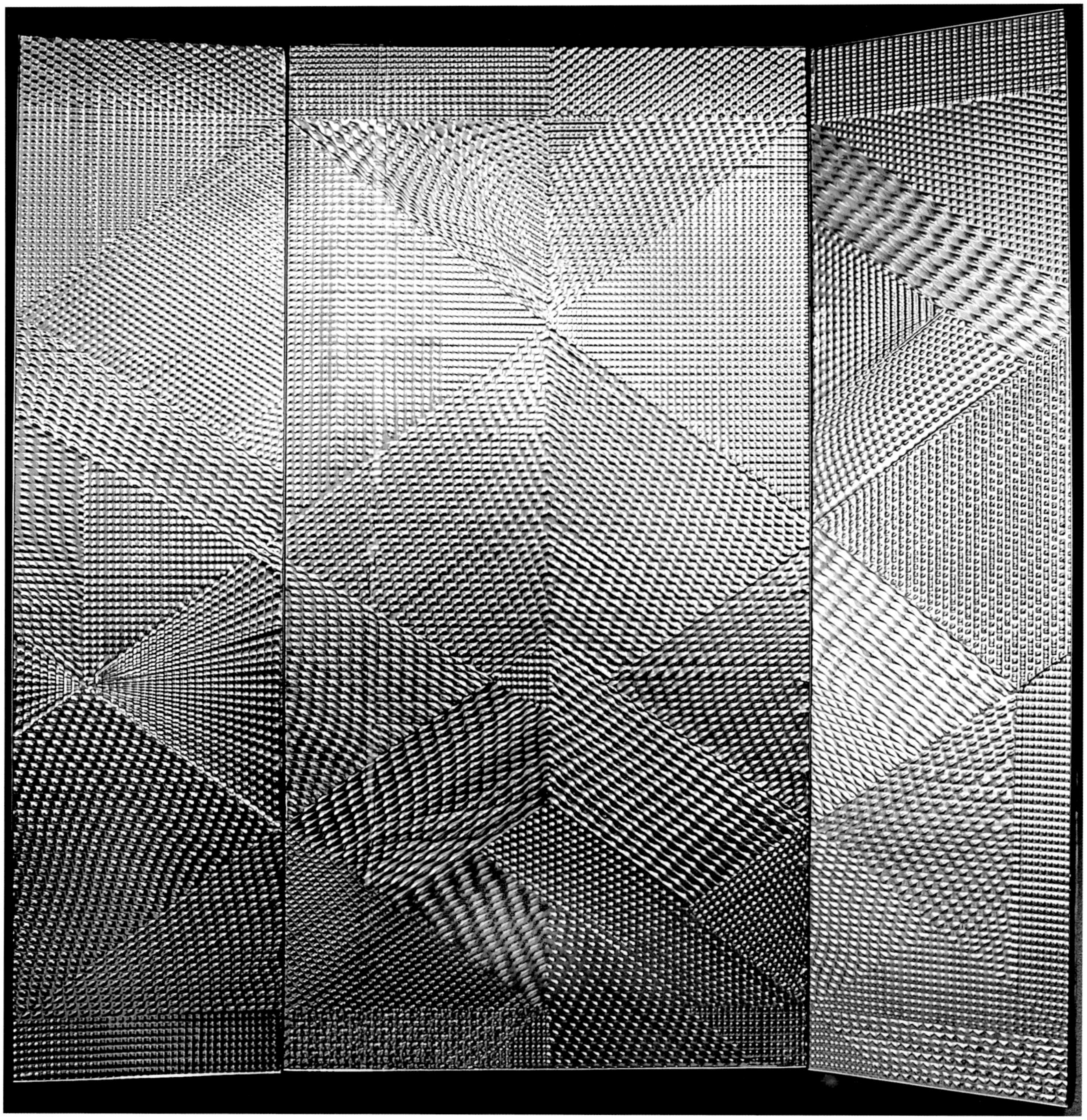

28 Heinz Mack
Mirror for an Angel, 1963/64
Aluminium auf Holz
195 x 160 x 6 cm

Heinz Mack
Mirror for an Angel, 1963/64
Aluminum on wood
195 x 160 x 6 cm

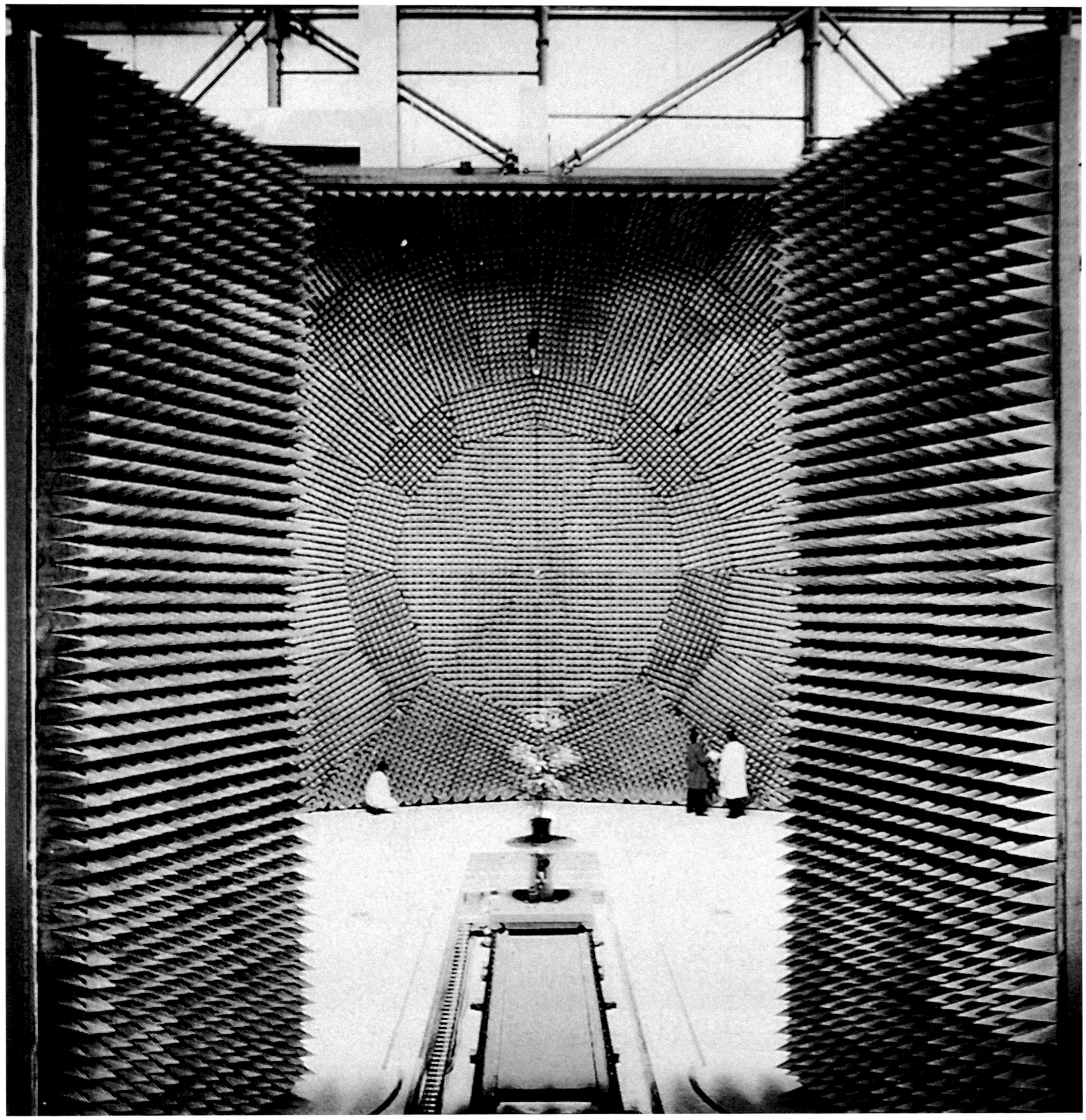

29 Forschungsprojekt Mikrowellensignatur
Forschungszentrum der Europäischen
Gemeinschaft in Ispra/Italien
FAZ, 29.04.1992

European Microwave Signature Laboratory
in Ispra/Italy
FAZ, 29.04.1992

> unexpected spin-off that seems to be just as inherent in the oriental arabesque as in my visual energy structures.[106]

Such similarities between nonrepresentational works by Heinz Mack and forms from nature and technology are purely coincidental and therefore all the more surprising. In the "Nature and Science" section of the Frankfurter Allgemeine Zeitung, Mack repeatedly finds illustrations that strikingly recall works of his from decades ago. One example is a photograph showing the European Microwave Signature Laboratory, founded in 1992 and located in Ispra, Italy:[107] It is very much alike Heinz Mack's screen *Mirror for an Angel*[108] from 1963/64. They are so similar that one catches oneself wondering if the artist may have had a vision of the future while working on the piece. This is likewise the case with *Rotor für blaue Elektrizität* (Rotor for Blue Electricity)[109] from 1968 and a look into the interior of a present-day nuclear power plant.[110]

Remarkable similarities with Mack's art are by no means limited to forms stemming from science and technology. Derived from the realms of flora and fauna, they equally extend to forms visible with the naked eye. The artist explains:

> When working in my studio, I forget all my admiration for and interest in nature. This is why it is so utterly surprising that what I have discovered, developed, and made visible all by myself often reveals shapes and structures that are strikingly similar to ones we encounter in nature. … The older I get, the better I understand that it is not art but humankind that is wonderful, as part of nature. Anyone can see this with open eyes, provided they are not merely the windows of our fantasy but mirrors of pure perception, which itself is a mirror-image of pure imagination.[111]

What this exhibition aims at is what Goethe would have called "repeated reflections," a term derived from his optical experiments. And he would have pointed out that they "not only keep the past alive but even raise it to a more exalted life," comparable to his own experiments, during which phenomena "do not grow weaker as they pass from mirror to mirror but only in doing so do they kindle into their full brilliance."[112]

106 Exh. cat. Cologne 2006 (see note 55), p. 65.
107 Ill. p. 73.
108 Ill. p. 72.
109 Ill. p. 244.
110 Ill. p. 245.
111 Translated from Dieter Honisch, *Mack: Skulpturen 1953–1986* (Düsseldorf and Vienna, 1986), p. 25.
112 Johann Wolfgang von Goethe, quoted in Richard Friedenthal, *Goethe: His Life & Times* (London and New York, 2010), p. 94.

Heinz Mack erklärt:

> Die rein phänomenologische, rein visuelle Wahlverwandtschaft zwischen den Mikrostrukturen, die der Atomphysiker mittels seines Elektronen-Raster-Mikroskops sieht, sowie den Vernetzungen in der Biophysik einerseits und den hiervon unabhängig entstandenen Strukturgraphiken von meiner Hand ist eine gewisse strukturelle Logik gemeinsam, deren ornamentale Qualität eine ungerufene Begleiterscheinung ist, welche der orientalischen Arabeske ebenso immanent zu eigen zu sein scheint wie meinen energetischen Bildstrukturen.[106]

Solche Ähnlichkeiten ungegenständlicher Arbeiten Heinz Macks zu Formen aus Natur und Technik sind rein zufällig und überraschen dadurch umso mehr. Auf den Seiten »Natur und Wissenschaft« der *Frankfurter Allgemeinen Zeitung* findet Mack immer wieder Abbildungen, die auf verblüffende Weise an eigene Werke früherer Jahrzehnte erinnern. So gleicht ein Foto vom 1992 gegründeten *European Microwave Signature Laboratory (EMSL)* im italienischen Ispra[107] Heinz Macks Paravent *Mirror for an Angel*[108] aus den Jahren 1963/64 so sehr, dass man sich dabei ertappt, darüber nachzudenken, ob der Künstler beim Arbeiten eine Zukunftsvision gehabt haben könnte. Ähnlich verhält es sich mit dem schon 1968 entstandenen *Rotor für blaue Elektrizität*[109] und einem Blick in das Innere eines Atomkraftwerks der Gegenwart[110].

Doch es sind nicht nur Formen aus Wissenschaft und Technik, zu denen sich in Macks Kunst wie von selbst Ähnlichkeiten ergeben, sondern auch Bildungen aus der mit bloßem Auge sichtbaren Flora und Fauna. Der Künstler erklärt:

> Alle Bewunderung und mein Interesse an der Natur vergesse ich aber, wenn ich in meiner Werkstatt arbeite. Um so mehr erstaunt es mich, daß das, was ich ganz allein und für mich und aus mir heraus entdeckt, entwickelt und sichtbar gemacht habe, einer oft frappierend verwandten Form und Struktur entspricht, welche wir in der Natur vorfinden. […] Je älter ich werde, desto besser begreife ich, wie nicht die Kunst das Wunderbare ist, sondern der Mensch, als Teil der Natur. Das kann jeder mit offenen Augen sehen, wenn diese nicht nur die Fenster seiner Phantasie sind, sondern auch Spiegel der reinen Anschauung, welche selbst ein Spiegelbild der reinen Vorstellung ist.[111]

Das, worauf die Ausstellung abzielt, hätte Goethe mit einem Begriff seiner optischen Experimente wohl »wiederholte Spiegelungen« genannt. Und er hätte darauf hingewiesen, dass sie »das Vergangene nicht allein lebendig erhalten, sondern sogar zu einem höheren Leben empor steigern«, wie bei den von ihm selbst durchgeführten Versuchen, bei denen die Erscheinungen »von Spiegel zu Spiegel nicht etwa verbleichen, sondern sich erst recht entzünden«[112].

106 Marion Agthe und Heinz Mack 2006 (wie Anm. 55), S. 61.
107 Abb. S. 73.
108 Abb. S. 72.
109 Abb. S. 244.
110 Abb. S. 245.
111 Dieter Honisch, *Mack. Skulpturen 1953–1986*, Düsseldorf und Wien 1986, S. 25.
112 Johann Wolfgang von Goethe, *[Wiederholte Spiegelungen]*. WA, Bd. 42 II, S. [56] f.

GOETHE
MUSEUM
DÜSSELDORF

Goethe

ANTON-UND-KATHARINA-KIPPENBERG-STIFTUNG

SCHLOSS
JÄGERHOF

30 Logo des Goethe-Museums Düsseldorf
2013 entworfen von Dietrich Rünger (*1939)

Unter Verwendung einer Signatur Goethes und eines Ausschnitts aus der ersten Tafel zu Goethes *Farbenlehre*

30 Logo of the Goethe-Museum Düsseldorf
Designed by Dietrich Rünger (*1939) in 2013

With the use of Goethe's signature and a section of the first table of Goethe's *Theory of Colours*

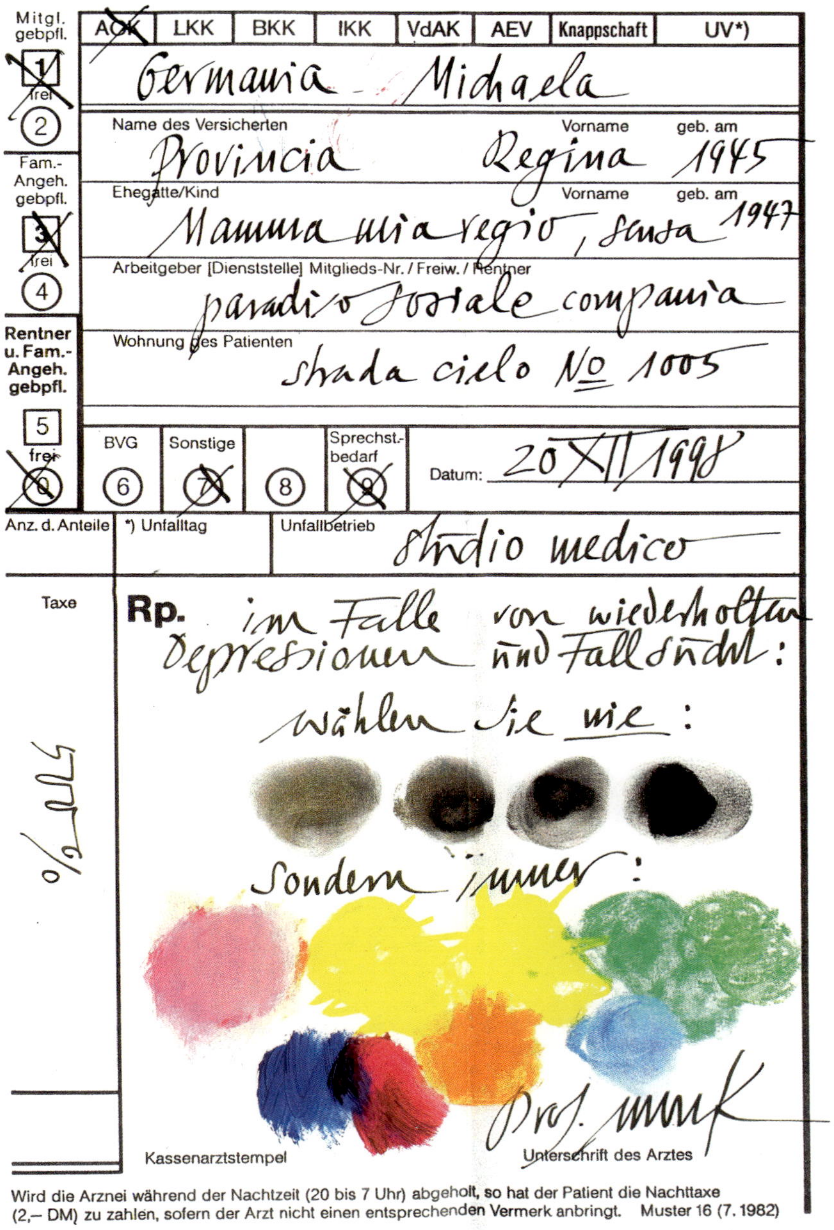

31 Heinz Mack
Kunst auf Rezept
Signiert: »Prof. mack«, datiert: »20 XII 1998«
Tusche, Acryl und mehrfarbige Pastellkreide
auf vergrößerter Kopie eines Rezeptes
42,5 x 30 cm

Heinz Mack
Kunst auf Rezept (Art on Prescription)
Signed: "Prof. mack", dated: "20 XII 1998"
Ink, acrylic and multicolored pastel chalk
on an enlarged copy of a prescription
42.5 x 30 cm

Als in den 1980er-Jahren in Deutschland die alten schwarz-weißen Vordrucke für kassenärztliche Rezepte durch neue Formulare ersetzt wurden, warf der Kölner Psychoanalytiker und Kunstsammler Hartmut Kraft (*1949) seinen ungültigen Rezeptblock nicht einfach weg. Unter dem Titel *Kunst auf Rezept* sandte er an 240 Künstler jeweils ein Blankorezept mit der Bitte, sich darauf künstlerisch zu äußern. 162 Künstler beteiligten sich an der Aktion, unter ihnen Heinz Mack, der starke Farben gegen »Depressionen und Fallsucht« verordnete.

When in the 1980s the old black-and-white preprinted forms issued by the Association for Physicians were replaced by new forms, the psychoanalyst and art collector Hartmut Kraft (*1949) who lived in Cologne, did not simply discard his invalid pad of prescriptions. Under the title *Kunst auf Rezept* (Art on Prescription), he mailed a blank prescription to 240 artists asking them to express themselves through their art. 162 artists participated in the action, among others Heinz Mack, who prescribed powerful colors against "depression and epilepsy."

LICHT ALS FARBE

LIGHT AS COLOR

»Jede Farbe also, um gesehen zu werden, muß ein Licht im Hinterhalte haben. Daher kommt es, daß je heller und glänzender die Unterlagen sind, desto schöner erscheinen die Farben. […] Ja die Energie der physischen Farben beruht hauptsächlich darauf, daß mit und hinter ihnen das Licht immerfort wirksam ist.«

"Thus every colour, in order to be seen, must have a light within or behind it. Hence the lighter and brighter the grounds are, the more brilliant the colours appear. … nay, the force of the physical colours is owing principally to the circumstance that light is always acting with and behind them."

GOETHE

»Bei allen ›Lichtfarben‹ brauche ich das Weiß als Malfläche, als Untergrund, als Reflexionsfläche für das Licht. Das Weiß ist daher immer von wesentlicher Bedeutung für die Reinheit und Strahlkraft der Farben. […] Hier wird Farbe zu einer Emanation des Lichts, das sich als Spektrum und im Spektrum ereignet. Diese Strahlung bewirkt die Erscheinung der Farbe, welche aus der Malfläche heraustritt und den Raum erfüllt.«

"Alongside all the 'colors of light', I need white as the canvas, as the background, as a reflective area for light. Therefore, white always plays a crucial role in the purity and brightness of the colors. … Here color becomes an emanation of light, which occurs as both part of the spectrum and as the spectrum. This emanation effects the appearance of the color, which is itself emanating from the canvas and which fills the room."

MACK

1+2 Johann Wolfgang von Goethe
Eigenhändige Reinschrift seines Gedichtes:
»Aus des Regens düstrer Trübe
Glänzt das Bild das immer neue
Aus den Thränen zarter Liebe
Spiegelt sich der Engel – Treue«
Signiert: »JWGoethe«
Datiert: »Weimar d. 21 August 1827.«
1 Blatt, 1 S. beschrieben
6,7 x 11,9 cm
Beiliegend ein handkolorierter Kupferstich, ausgeschnitten und auf Papier aufgeklebt:
Regenbogen über grünendem Gebirg, in grauen Wolken
6,4 x 11,9 cm
Goethe-Museum Düsseldorf
Vgl. auch die Erläuterung zur Abb. auf S. [2] und WA, Bd. I 4, S. 136.

Anders als in den meisten Darstellungen zeigt dieser Regenbogen nicht sieben Farben, sondern nur drei, und diese auch in anderer Anordnung. Es sind die drei wichtigsten Farben aus Goethes Lehre: als entgegengesetzte Pole das der Finsternis am nächsten gelegene Blau und das Gelb als die dem Licht benachbarte Farbe sowie dazwischen die Farbe Purpur, die entsteht, wenn Blau und Gelb sich nach dem Prinzip der Steigerung verdichten.

1+2 Johann Wolfgang von Goethe
Clean copy of Goethe's poem in his own hand:
"From the rain's gloomy haze
The image shines forever new
On the tears of tender love
A reflection of an angel—Faithfulness"
Signed: "JWGoethe"
Dated: "Weimar d. 21 August 1827."
1 sheet, 1 page written
6.7 x 11.9 cm
Enclosed a hand-colored copper engraving, cut out and pasted on paper:
Rainbow over green Mountains, in gray Clouds
6.4 x 11.9 cm
Goethe-Museum Düsseldorf
See also the commentary to the illustration on p. [2] and WA, vol. I 4, p. 136.

Different from most depictions, this rainbow does not show seven colors but three, which are also placed in a different order. These are the three most important colors from Goethe's theory of colors: as opposite poles, the blue is the color closest to darkness while yellow is the color closest to light; in between is purple, that is created when blue and yellow intensify according to the principle of progression.

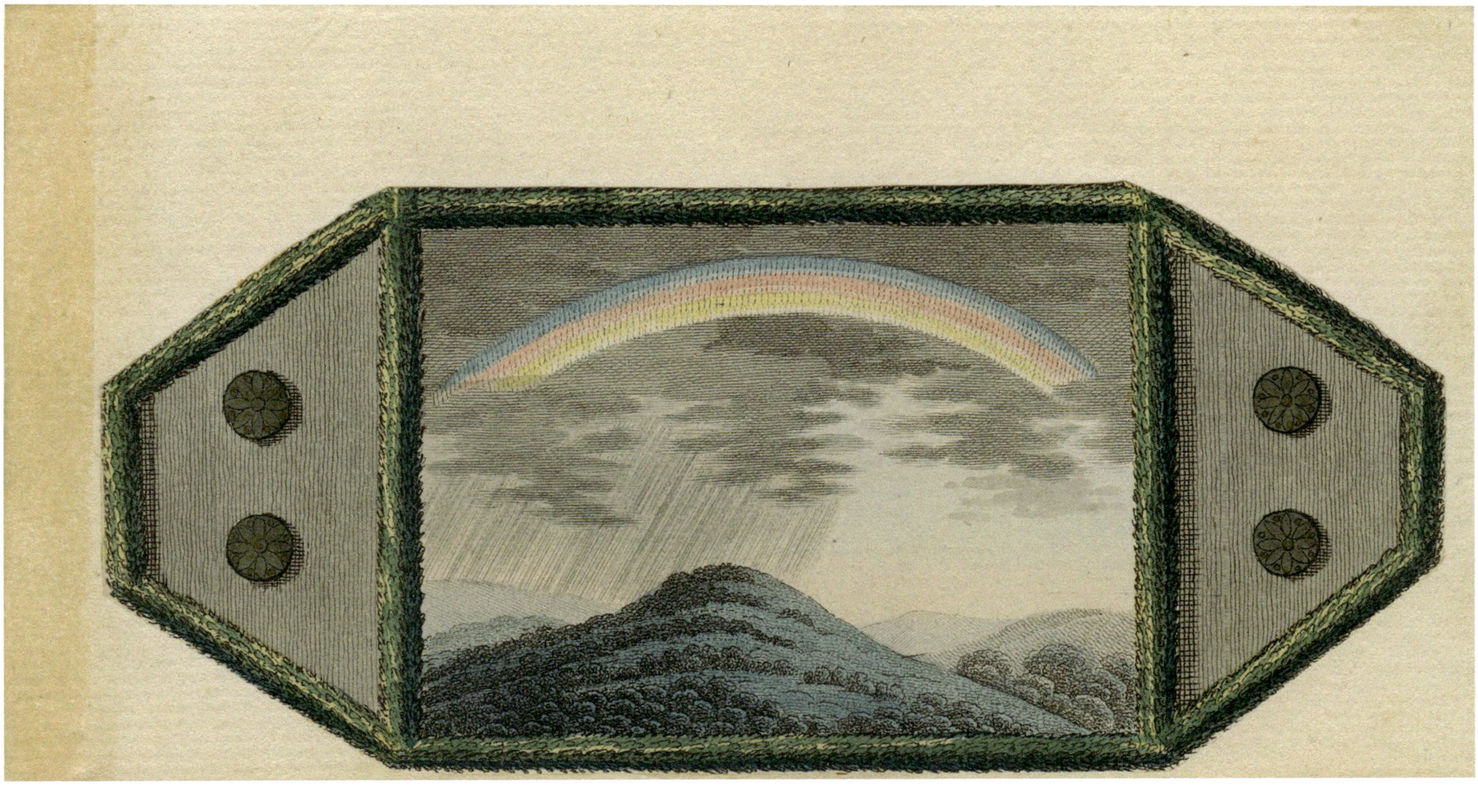

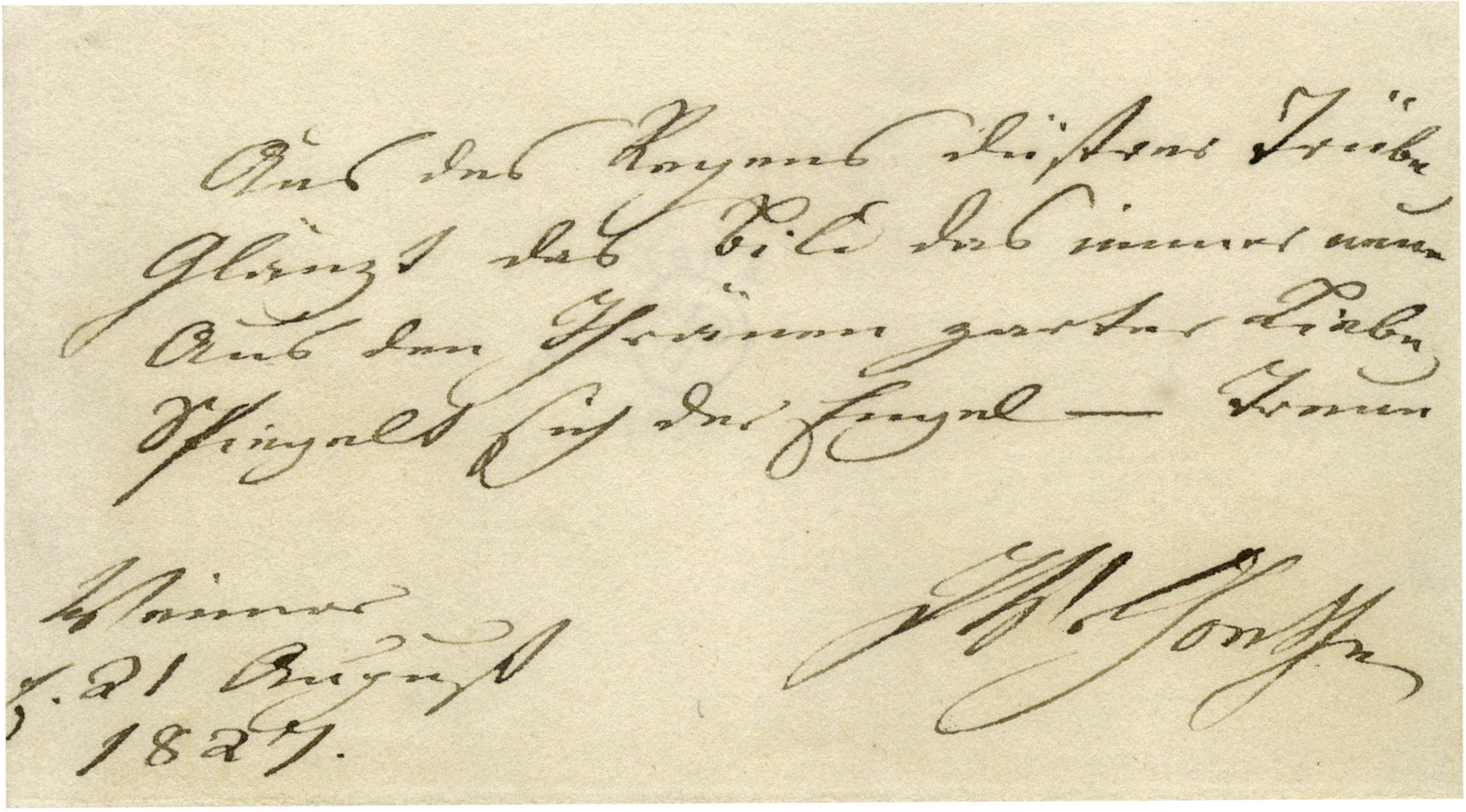

Auf des Regens düstrer Trübe
Glänzt das Bild das immer neu
Aus den Thränen zarter Liebe
Spiegelt sich der Himmel — Treue

Weimar
d. 21 August
1827.

J W v Goethe

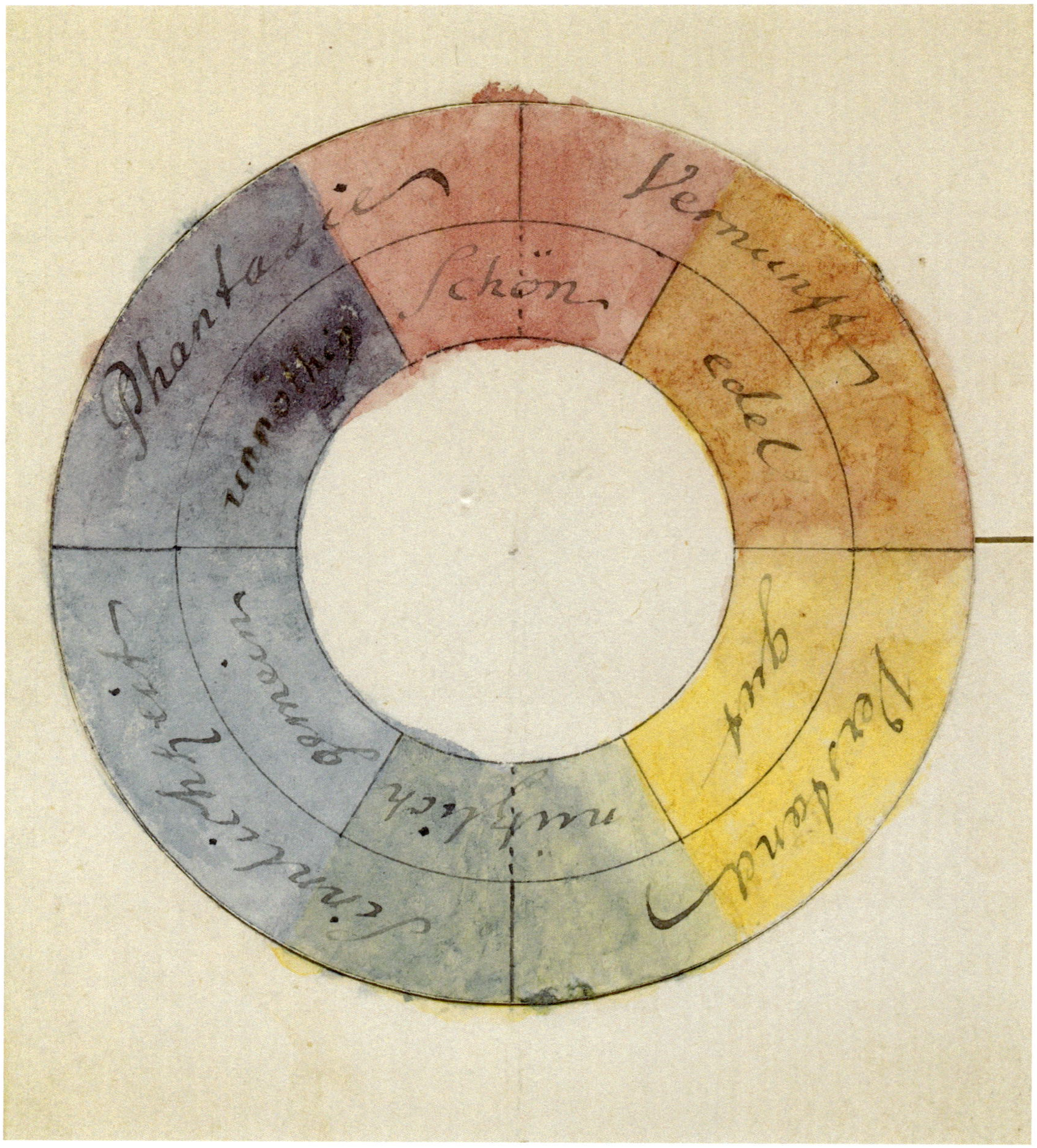

3 Johann Wolfgang von Goethe
Farbenkreis zur Symbolisierung des menschlichen Geistes- und Seelenlebens
November 1809
Eigenhändige Federzeichnung mit schwarzer Tinte, aquarelliert auf gelblichem Papier, auf Karton montiert, 11,6 x 7,8 cm
Freies Deutsches Hochstift – Frankfurter Goethe-Museum

Der innere Ring ordnet jeder Farbe des sechsteiligen Farbenkreises eine Eigenschaft zu: »nützlich« dem Grün, »gut« dem Gelb, »edel« dem Gelbrot, »schön« dem Purpur, »unnöthig« dem Violett und »gemein« dem Blau. Für die vier Seelenkräfte »Verstand«, »Vernunft«, »Phantasie« und »Sinnlichkeit« dagegen stehen im äußeren Ring jeweils zwei Farben. Vgl. LA, Bd. II 1 A, S. 264–269 sowie ferner die Farbenkreise im vorliegenden Katalog, S. 142 und S. 237.

3 Johann Wolfgang von Goethe
Color wheel for the symbolization of the life of the human mind and soul
November 1809
Pen-drawing in black ink in Goethe's hand; water-colored on yellowish paper and mounted on cardboard.
11.6 x 7.8 cm
Freies Deutsches Hochstift – Frankfurter Goethe-Museum

The inner circle assigns a specific quality to each color: green is "useful," yellow is "good," yellow-red is "noble," purple is "beautiful," violet is "unnecessary," and blue is "mean." For each of the four spiritual forces "reason," "understanding," "imagination," and "sensibility" there are two colors assigned in the outer circle. See LA, vol. II 1 A, pp. 264–69 and also the color wheels in this catalogue, p. 142 and p. 237.

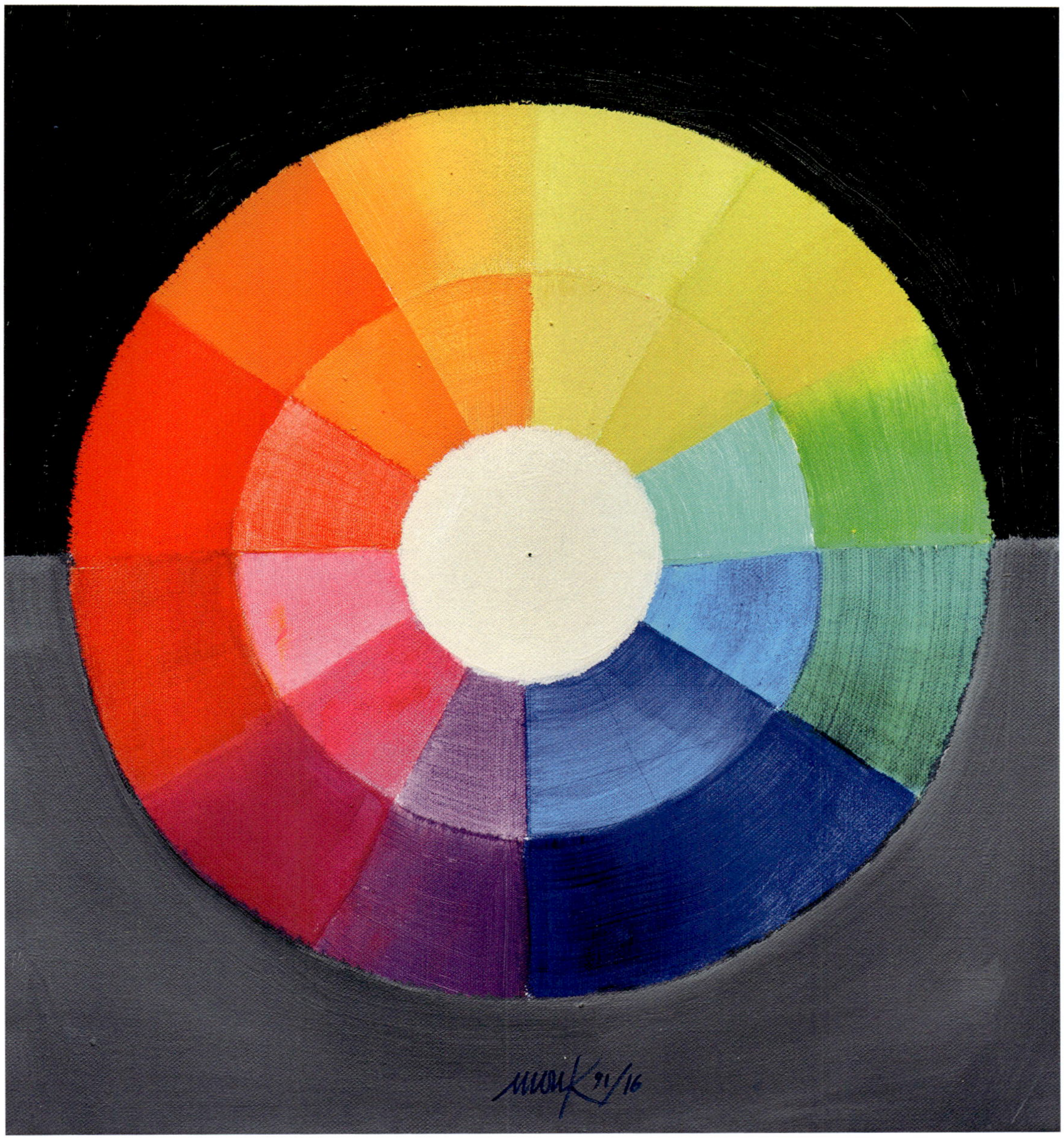

4 Heinz Mack
Ohne Titel *(Chromatische Konstellation)*
Signiert, datiert: »mack 91/16«
(Entwurf 1991, Ausführung 2016)
Acryl auf Leinwand
77 x 70 cm

4 Heinz Mack
Untitled *(Chromatic Constellation)*
Signed, dated: "mack 91/16"
(draft 1991, completion 2016)
Acrylic on canvas
77 x 70 cm

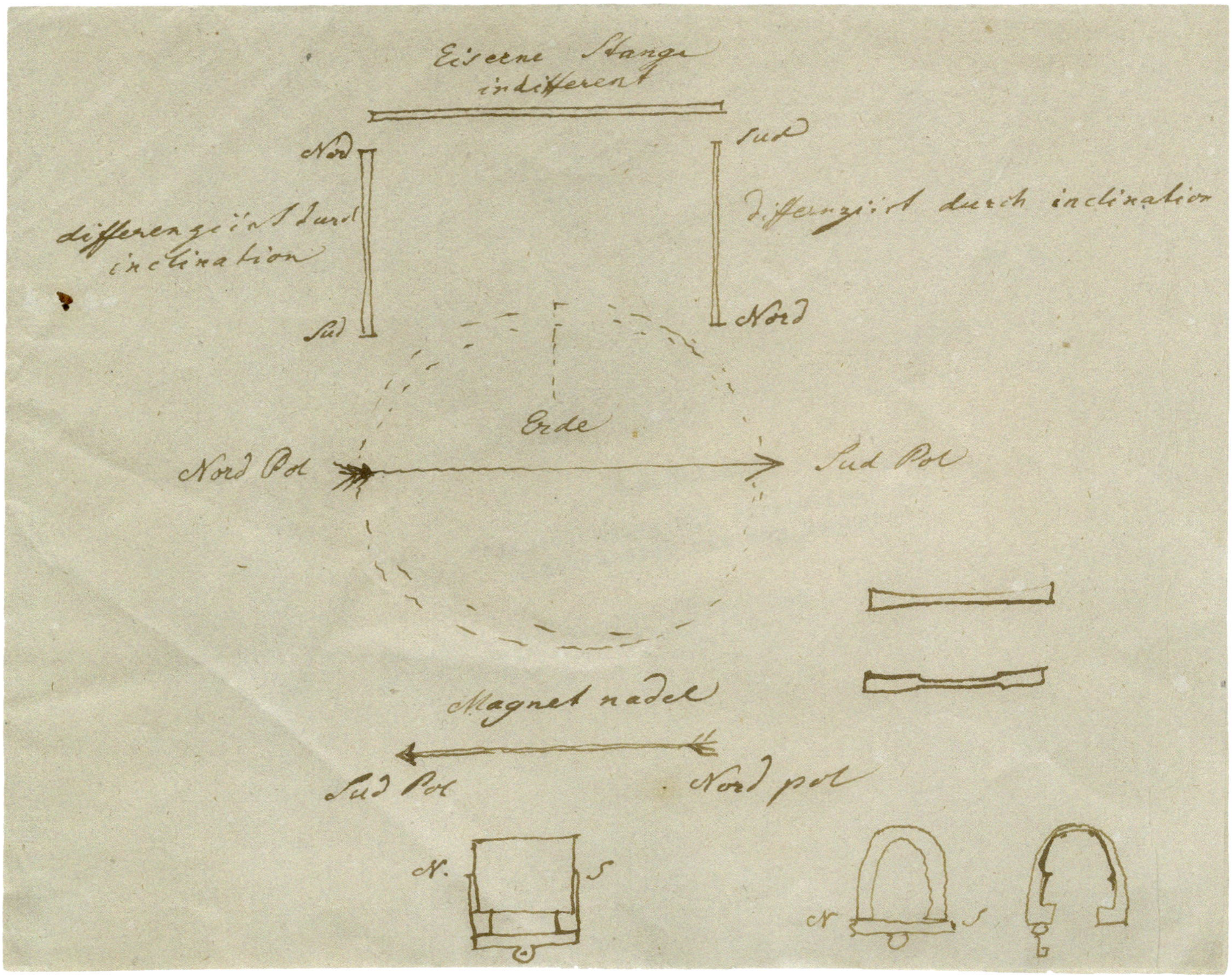

5 Johann Wolfgang von Goethe
Erläuterungen zum Magnetismus
Eigenhändige Federzeichnung
16,7 x 20,1 cm
Goethe-Museum Düsseldorf

In seinem Brief an Thomas Seebeck vom 15. Januar 1813 schreibt Goethe: »Der Hoffnung, den Magnetismus an die electrischchemischen und folglich auch an die Farbenwirkungen anzuschließen, kann ich nicht ganz entsagen. Ich sehne mich nach einem hellen Tage, um gewiße Versuche durchzuführen.« (Handschrift: Goethe-Museum Düsseldorf.)

5 Johann Wolfgang von Goethe
Explanations of Magnetism
Pen-drawing in Goethe's hand
16.7 x 20.1 cm
Goethe-Museum Düsseldorf

In his letter to Thomas Seebeck from January 15, 1813, Goethe writes: "I cannot renounce the hope to be able to connect magnetism with the electro-chemical and necessarily the effects of color. I am yearning for a bright day to conduct certain experiments." (Manuscript: Goethe-Museum Düsseldorf.)

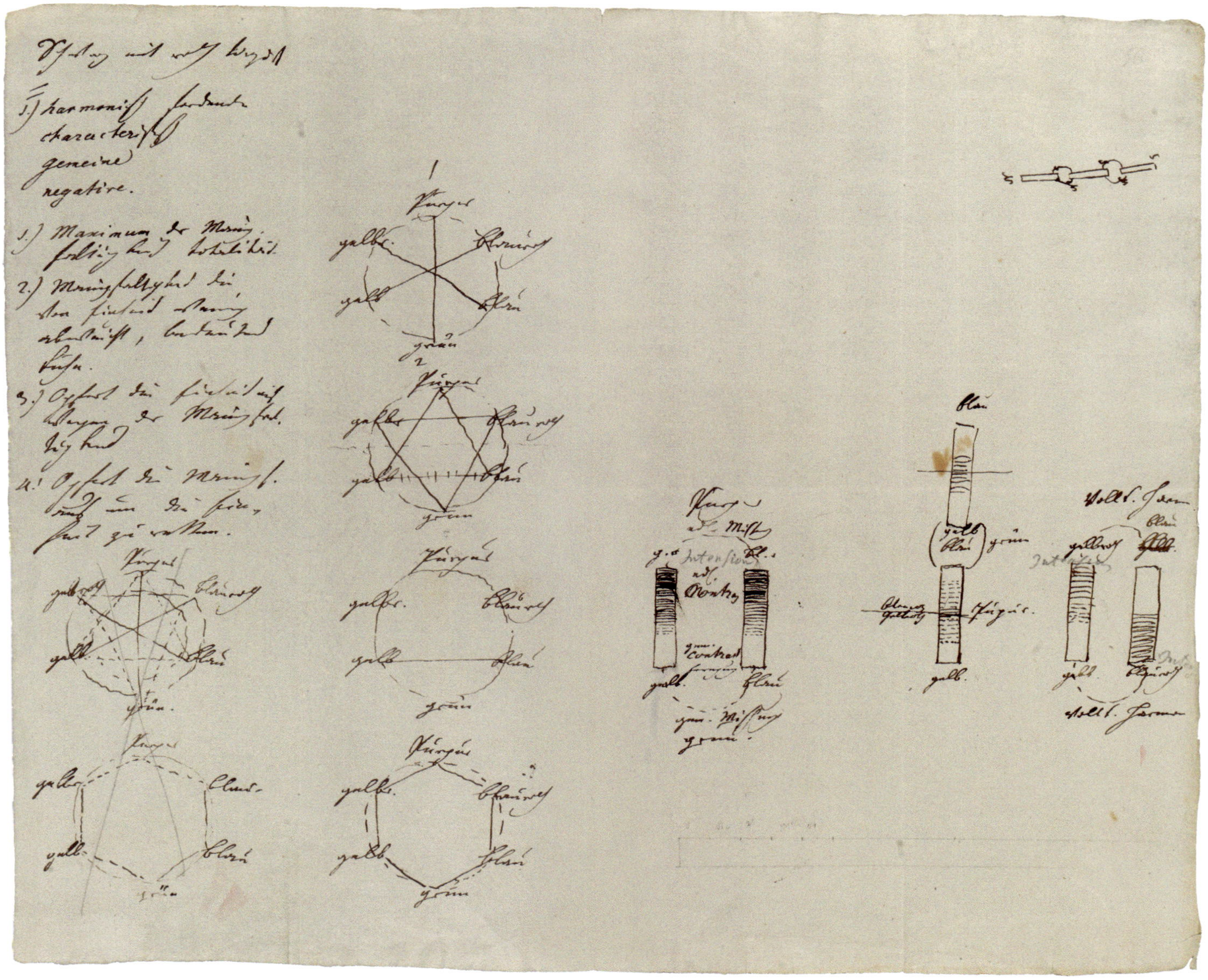

6 Johann Wolfgang von Goethe
Eigenhändige Notizen zu Goethes Harmonielehre der Farben und eigenhändiger Entwurf mit Ergänzungen von Schillers Hand zu der von Goethe nicht veröffentlichten Farbtafel *Symbolische Annäherung zum Magneten* (vgl. die Abb. S. 86).
14. November 1798
Doppelblatt blassblauen gerippten Papiers, 2 S. mit Tinte und Bleistift beschrieben
34,3 x 41,4 cm (aufgeklappt)
Klassik Stiftung Weimar, Goethe- und Schiller-Archiv
Signatur: GSA 26/L, 9
Vgl. LA, Bd. I 3, S. 386 und Bd. II 3, S. 359–362.

6 Johann Wolfgang von Goethe
Notes in Goethe's own hand to his doctrine of the harmony of colors and a draft in his own hand with additions in Schiller's hand to Goethe's unpublished color plate *Symbolic Convergence with the Magnet* (see ill. p. 86).
November 14, 1798
Double sheet pale blue ribbed paper, 2 pages written in ink and pencil
34.3 x 41.4 cm (unfolded)
Klassik Stiftung Weimar, Goethe- und Schiller-Archiv
Shelf mark: GSA 26/L, 9
See LA, vol. I 3, p. 386 and vol. II 3, pp. 359–62.

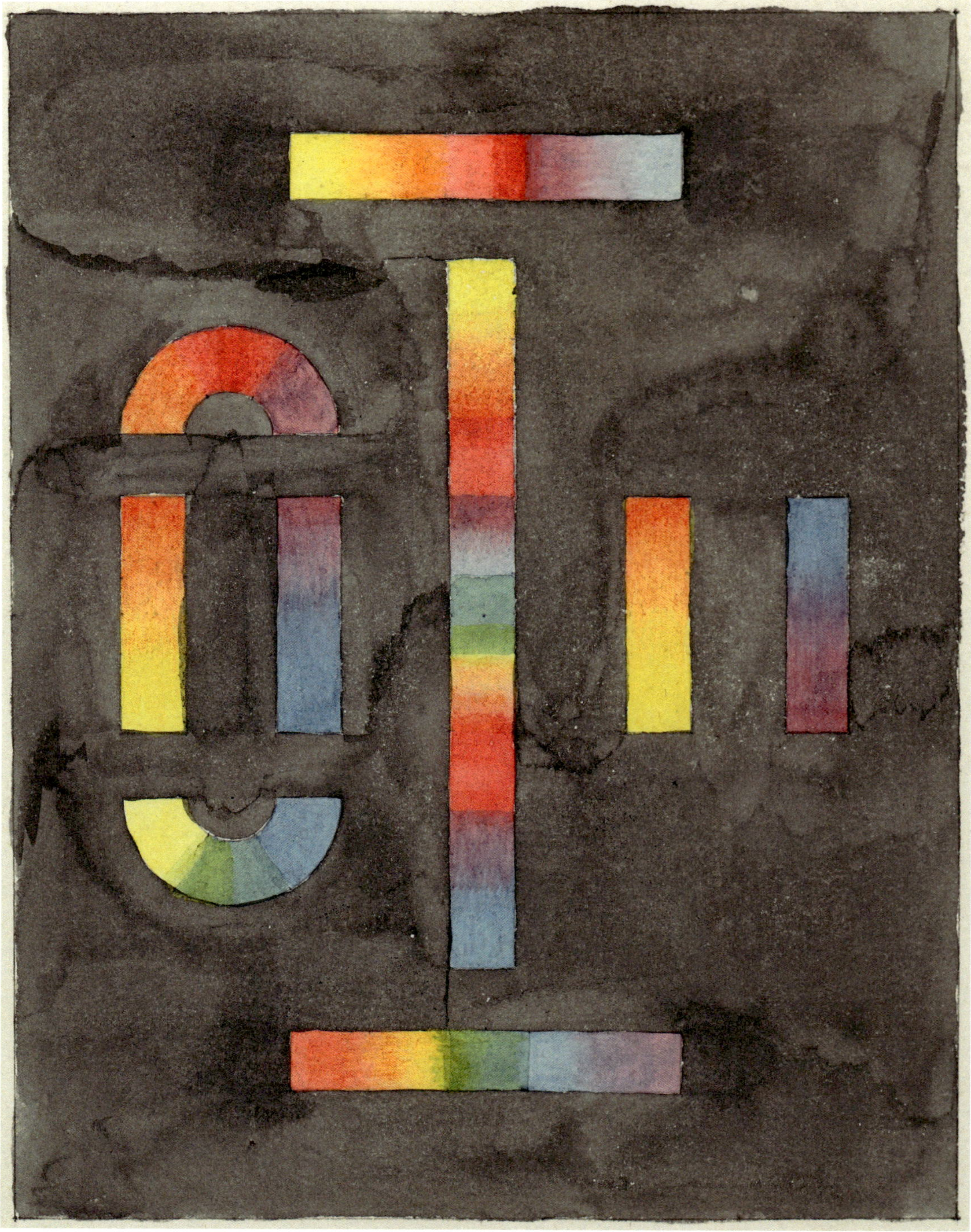

7 Johann Wolfgang von Goethe
Symbolische Annäherung zum Magneten
15. November 1798
Aquarell auf weißem, geripptem Karton
19,7 x 16,1 cm
Klassik Stiftung Weimar, Museen

Diese Tafel ist zum Verständnis von Goethes Farbenlehre besonders aufschlussreich, weil sie zeigt, dass Goethes sechsteiliger Farbenkreis über die Kantenspektren aus seinen prismatischen Versuchen abgeleitet wurde. Der Magnet galt Goethe als Symbol für die Polarität aller Naturkräfte. Vgl. LA, Bd. I 3, S. 387 und Bd. II 3, S. 362–365.

7 Johann Wolfgang von Goethe
Symbolic Convergence with the Magnet
November 15, 1798
Water-color on white ribbed cardboard
19.7 x 16.1 cm
Klassik Stiftung Weimar, Museen

This plate is especially informative for the understanding of Goethe's theory of colors because it shows that Goethe's six-part color wheel had been derived from the edge spectra in his prismatic experiments. For Goethe, the magnet signified the symbol for the polarity of natural forces. See LA, vol. I 3, p. 387 and vol. II 3, pp. 362–65.

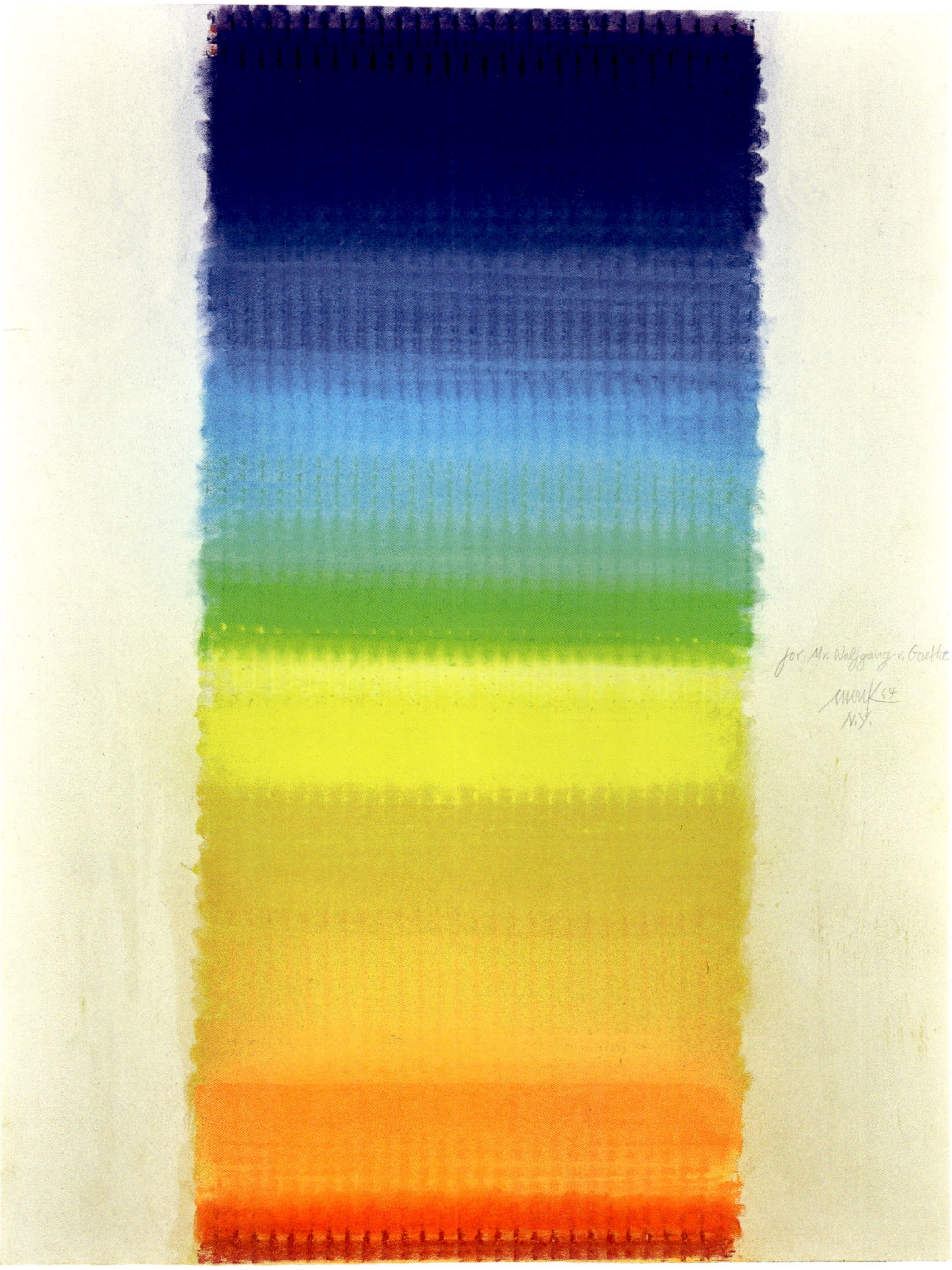

8 Heinz Mack
For Mr. Wolfgang v. Goethe
Signiert, datiert: »mack 64 N. Y.«
Pastellkreide auf Büttenpapier
105 x 78 cm

Eine ähnlich große Farbchromatik aus demselben Jahr trägt den Titel *for Mr. Newton.*

8 Heinz Mack
For Mr. Wolfgang v. Goethe
Signed, dated: "mack 64 N. Y."
Pastel on handmade paper
105 x 78 cm

Another color chromatic of similar measurements is entitled *for Mr. Newton.*

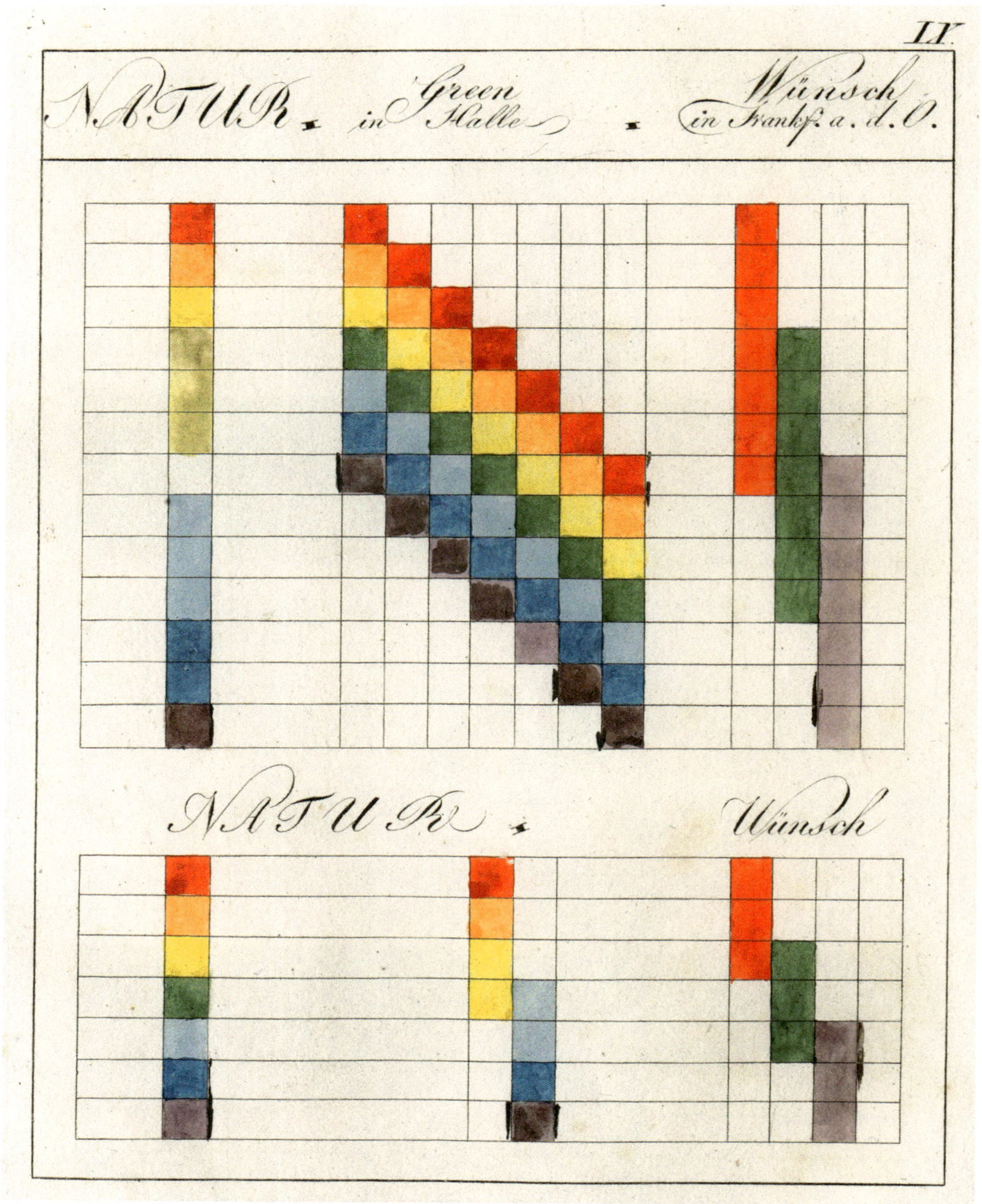

9 Johann Wolfgang von Goethe
Tafel Nr. IX aus dem Supplementband zu seiner *Farbenlehre* von 1810
Handkolorierter Kupferstich

Mit dieser Tafel versuchte er, die Theorien seiner Zeitgenossen Friedrich Albert Karl Gren (Green) (1760–1798) und Christian Ernst Wünsch (1744–1828) zu widerlegen.

9 Johann Wolfgang von Goethe
Plate no. IX from the supplement to his *Farbenlehre (Theory of Colours)* of 1810
Hand-colored copper engraving

With this plate, Goethe attempted to refute the theories of his contemporaries Friedrich Albert Karl Gren (Green) (1760–1798) and Chistian Ernst Wünsch (1744–1828).

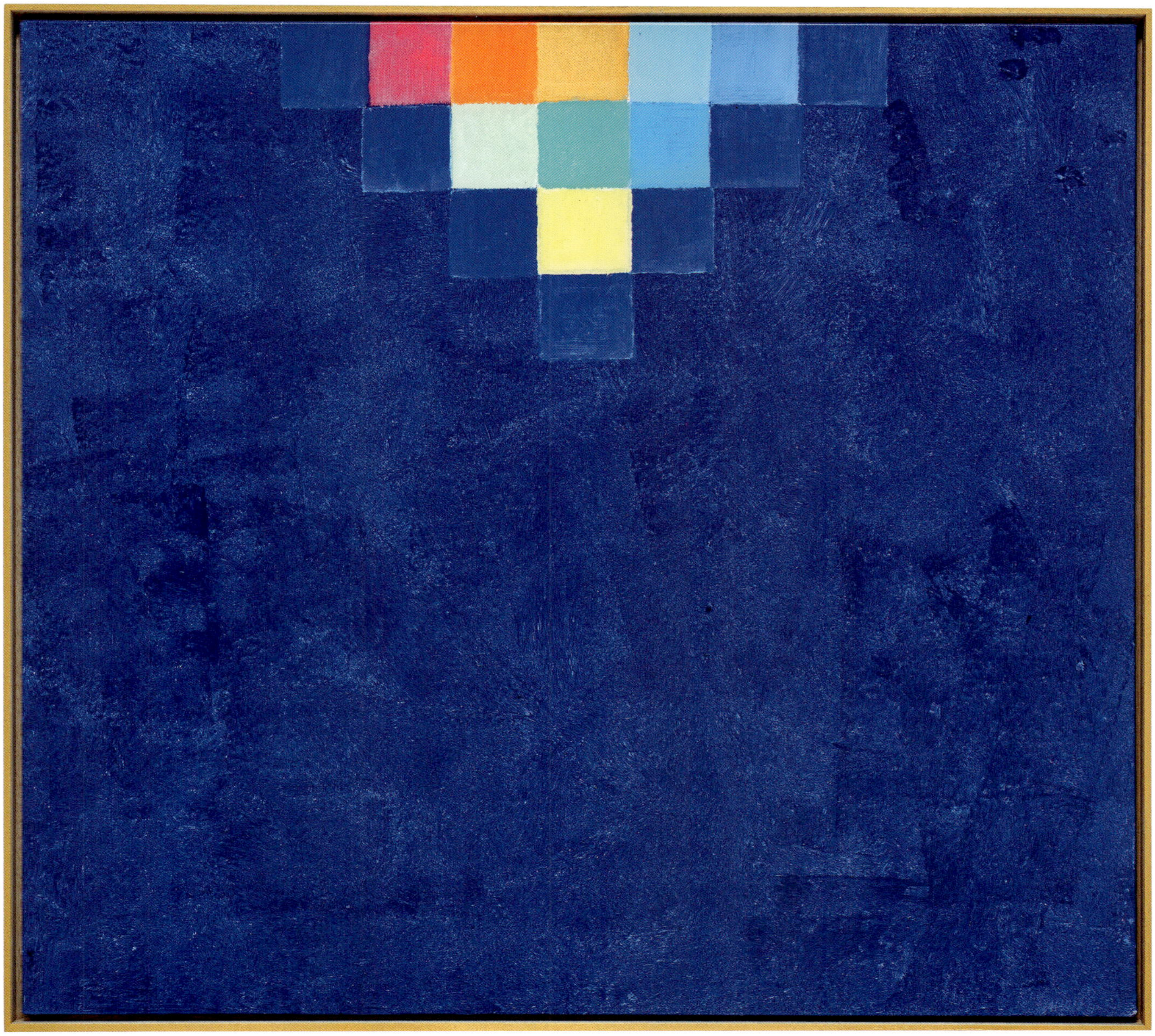

10 Heinz Mack
Ohne Titel *(Chromatische Konstellation)*
Signiert, datiert: »mack 17«
Acryl auf Leinwand
146 x 160 cm

10 Heinz Mack
Untitled *(Chromatic Constellation)*
Signed, dated: "mack 17"
Acrylic on canvas
146 x 160 cm

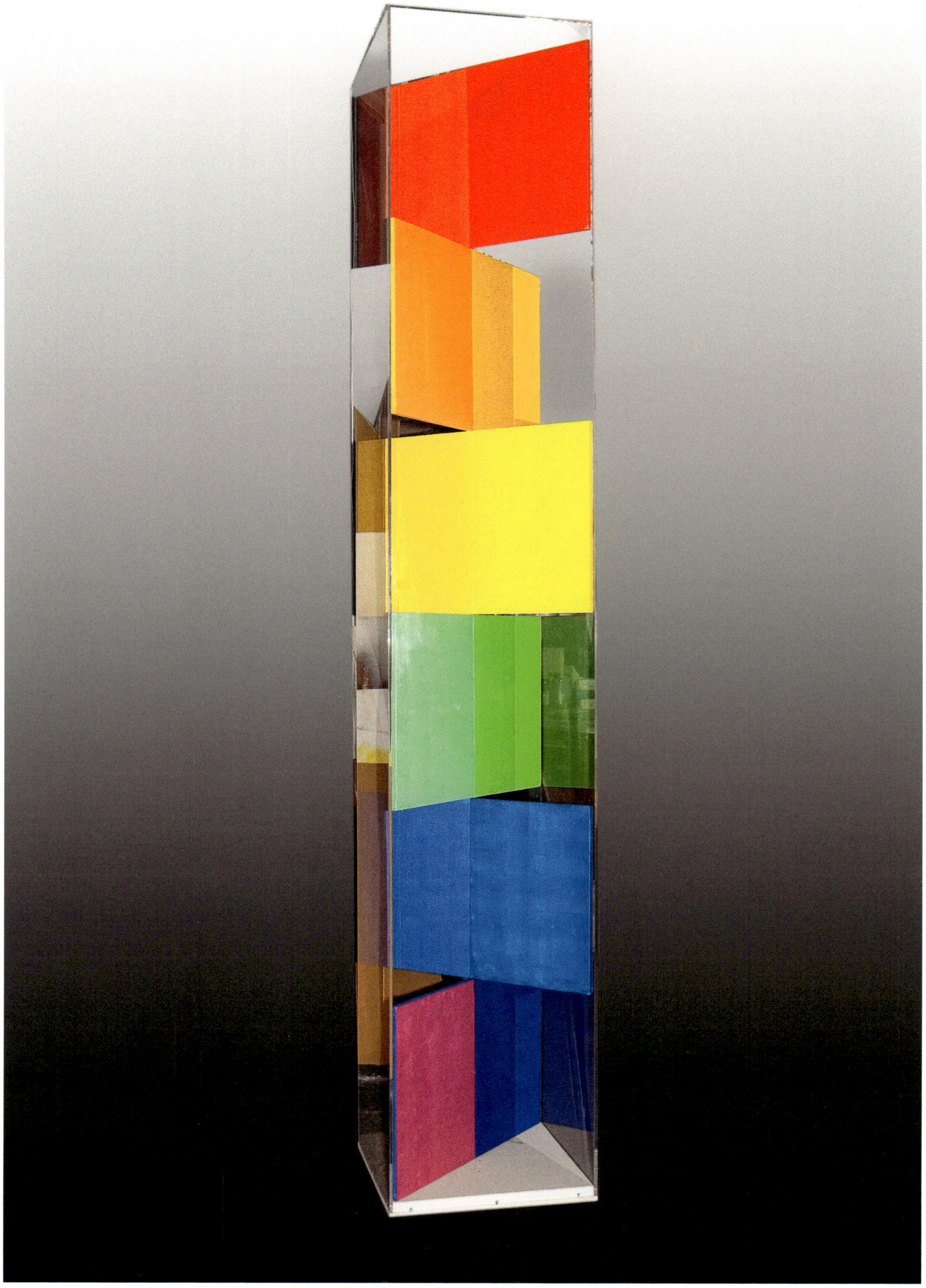

11 Heinz Mack
Ohne Titel
Signiert, datiert: »mack 95«
Karton, bemalt, Plexiglas, Holz
222 x 39 x 39 cm

11 Heinz Mack
Untitled
Signed, dated: "mack 95"
Cardboard, painted, plexiglass, wood
222 x 39 x 39 cm

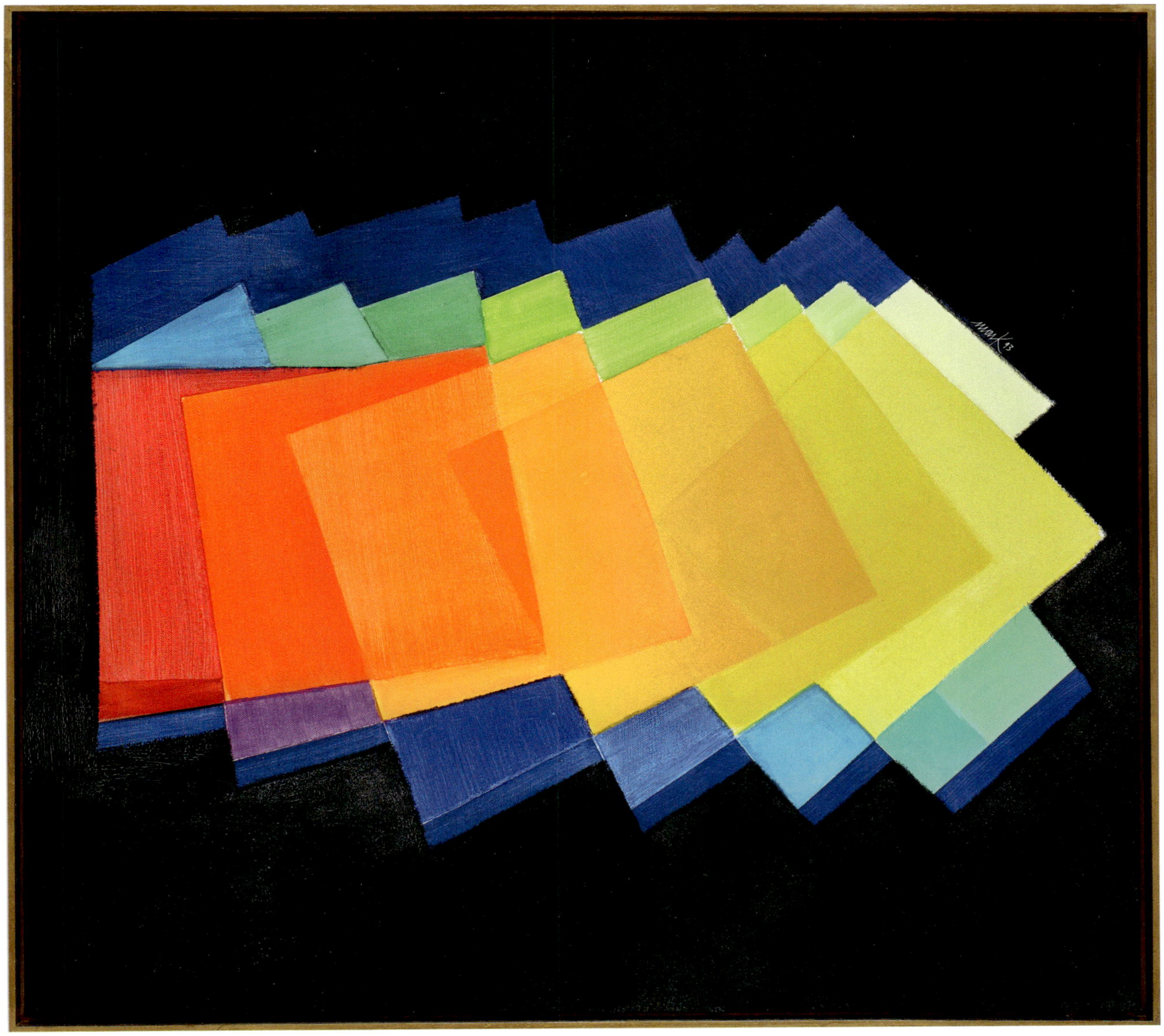

12 Heinz Mack
Ohne Titel *(Chromatische Konstellation)*
Signiert, datiert: »mack 93«
Acryl auf Leinwand
130 x 142 cm

12 Heinz Mack
Untitled *(Chromatic Constellation)*
Signed, dated: "mack 93"
Acrylic on canvas
130 x 142 cm

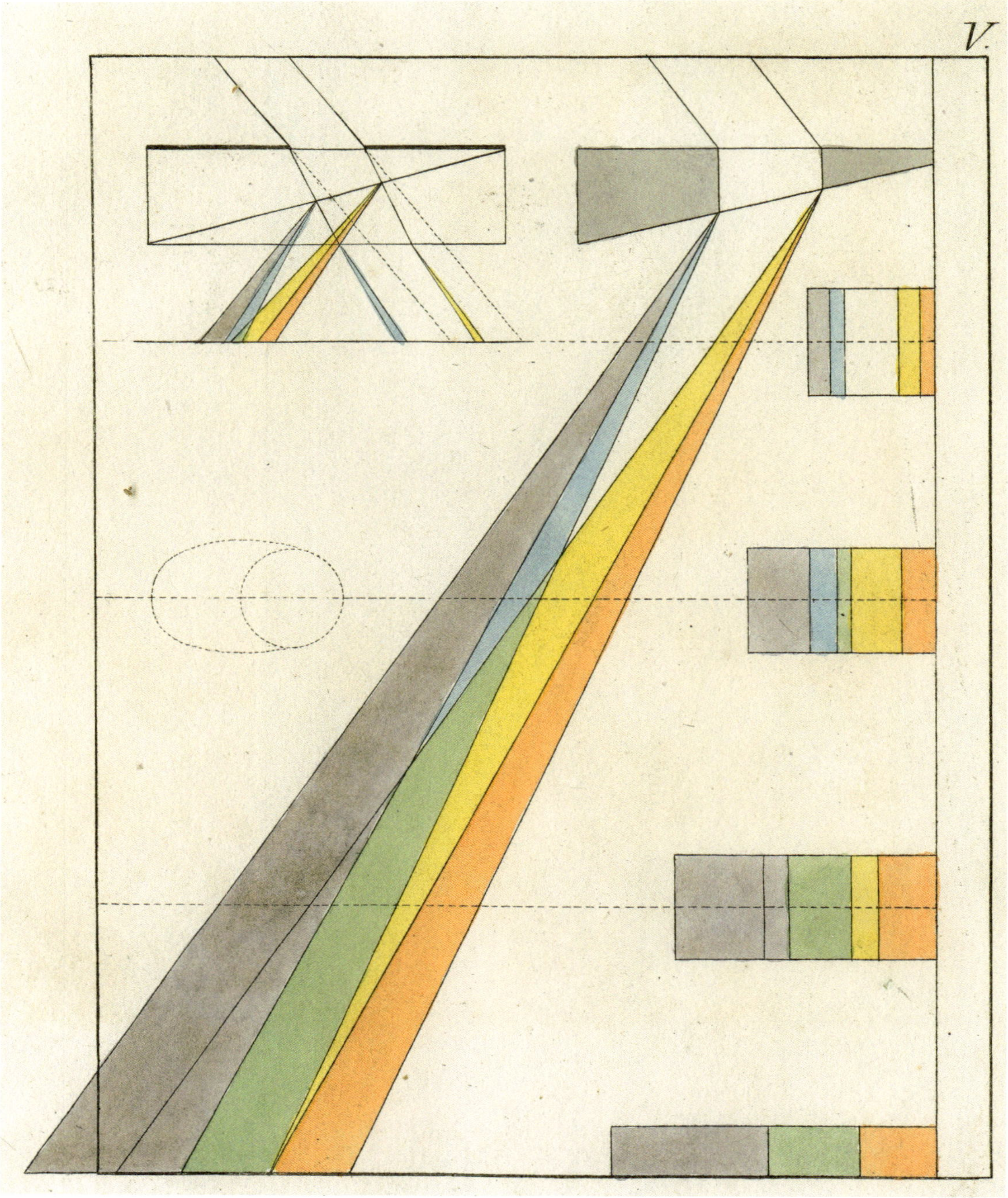

13 Johann Wolfgang von Goethe
Tafel Nr. V aus dem Supplementband zu seiner *Farbenlehre* von 1810
Handkolorierter Kupferstich

In der Erklärung zu dieser Tafel empfiehlt Goethe, das Blatt zum besseren Verständnis um 90 Grad (nach rechts) zu drehen. Es zeigt die Veränderung des Newton-Spektrums in Abhängigkeit vom Abstand zum Prisma. Anders als Newton betrachtet Goethe als Ursache für die Farbentstehung nicht die Spaltbarkeit des Sonnenlichtes, sondern die durch die Brechung am Prisma hervorgerufene optische Verschiebung des Sonnenbildes. Vgl. auch S. 132, Abb. 2.

13 Johann Wolfgang von Goethe
Plate no. V from the supplement to his *Theory of Colours* of 1810
Hand-colored copper engraving

According to the commentary for this plate, Goethe recommends turning the page 90 degrees (to the right) to better understand the image. It shows that the change of Newton's spectrum depended on its distance from the prisma. In contrast to Newton, Goethe understood the creation of color not by its ability to separate sunlight but by its prismatic refraction generated by the optical shift of the image of the sun. See also p. 132, fig. 2.

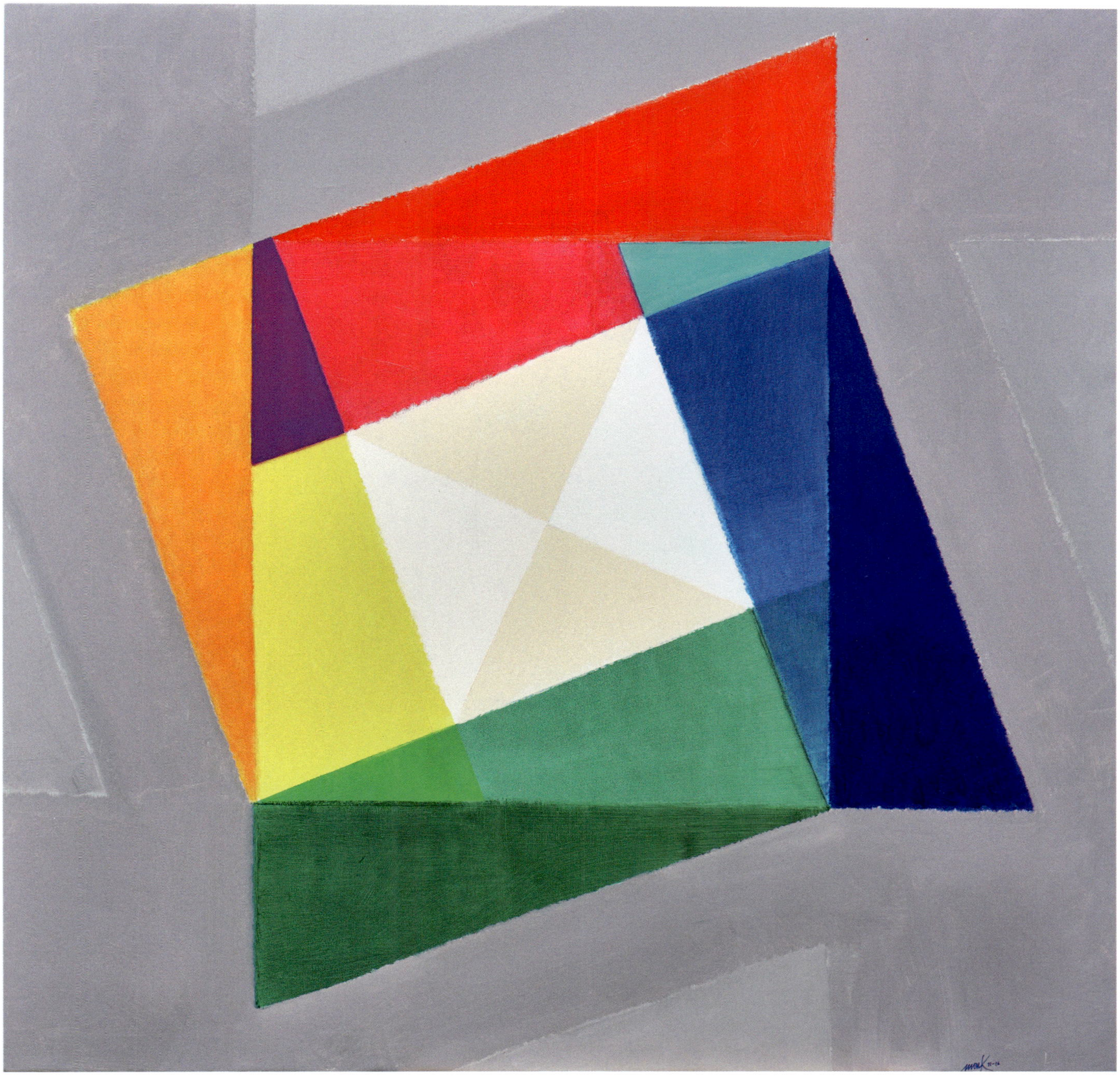

14 Heinz Mack
Ohne Titel *(Chromatische Konstellation)*
Signiert, datiert: »mack 91–16«
Acryl auf Leinwand
210 x 214 cm

14 Heinz Mack
Untitled *(Chromatic Constellation)*
Signed, dated: "mack 91–16"
Acrylic on canvas
210 x 214 cm

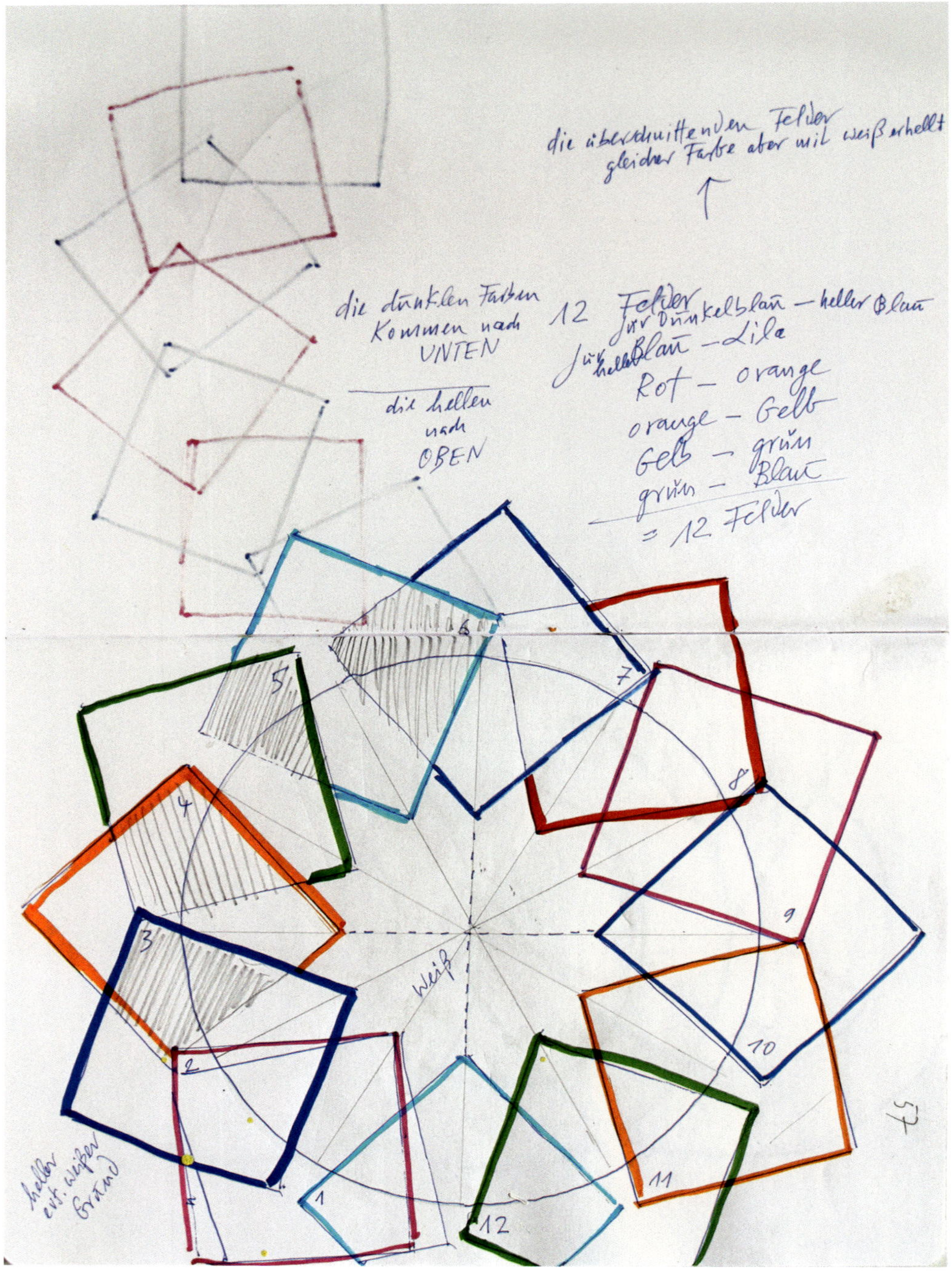

15 Heinz Mack
Skizze zur *Chromatischen Konstellation*
auf der gegenüberliegenden Seite
29,7 x 21 cm

15 Heinz Mack
Sketch for *Chromatic Constellation*
on the opposite page
29.7 x 21 cm

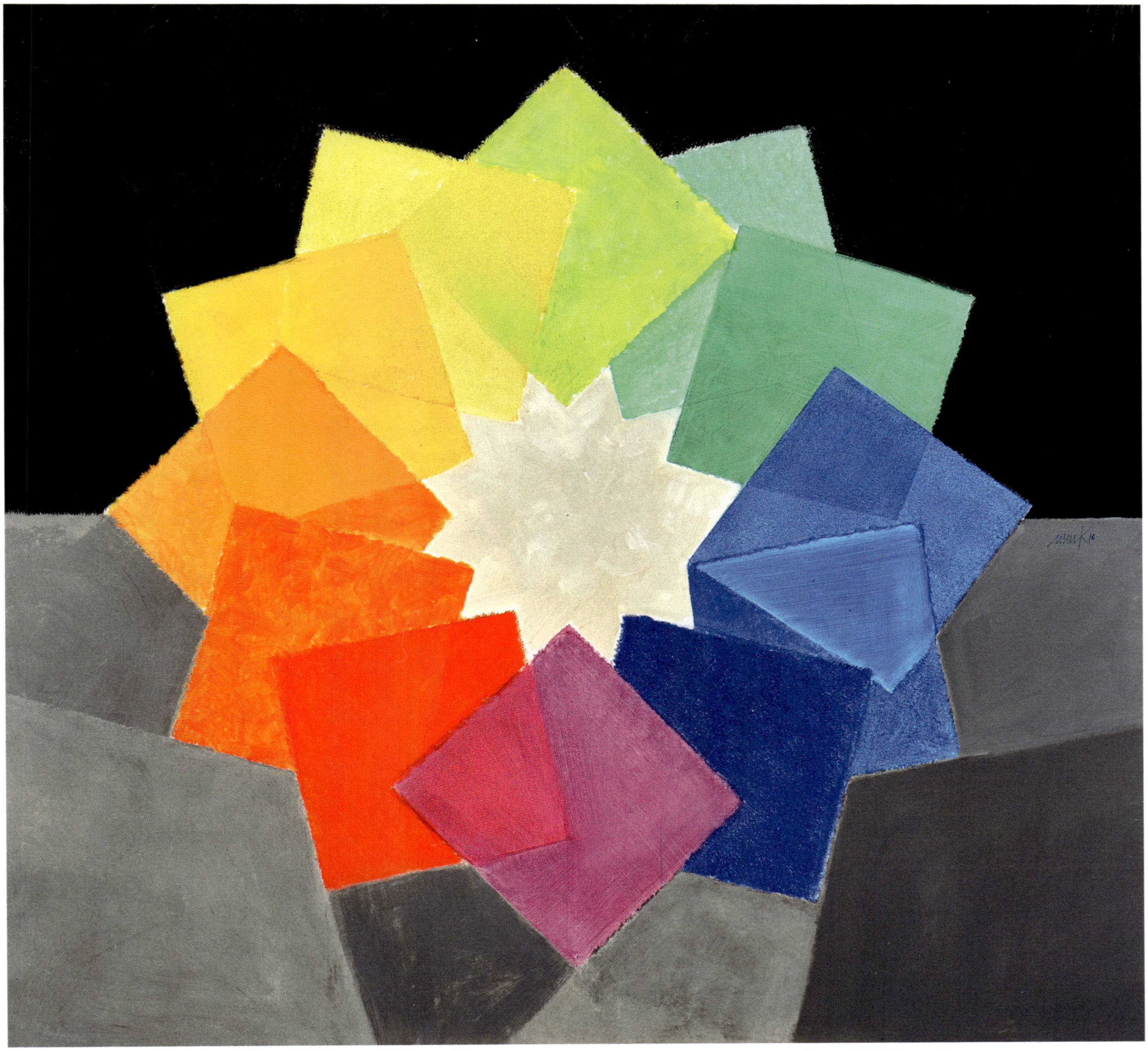

16 Heinz Mack
Ohne Titel *(Chromatische Konstellation)*
Signiert, datiert: »mack 16«
Acryl auf Leinwand
210 x 223 cm

16 Heinz Mack
Untitled *(Chromatic Constellation)*
Signed, dated: "mack 16"
Acrylic on canvas
210 x 223 cm

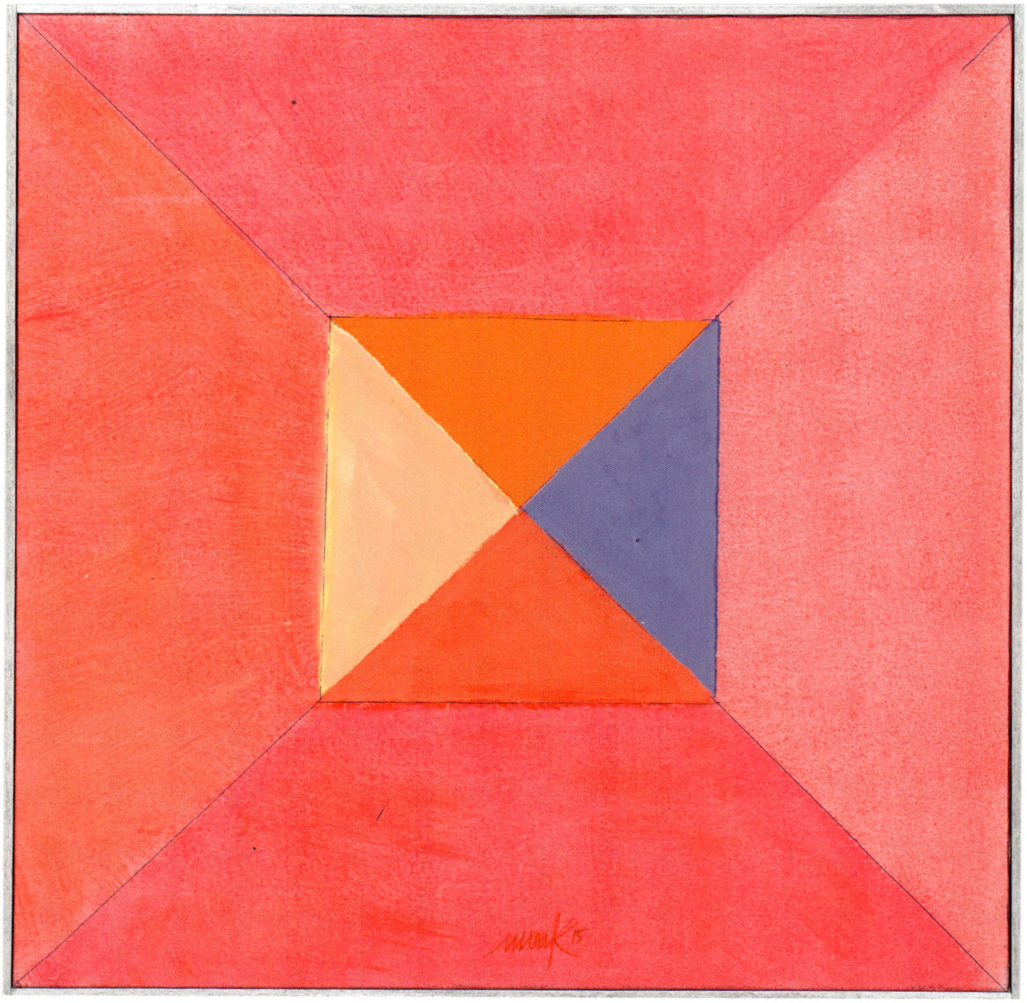

17 Heinz Mack
Sea Flag II (Chromatische Konstellation)
Signiert, datiert: »mack 15«
Acryl auf Leinwand
77 x 77 cm

17 Heinz Mack
Sea Flag II (Chromatic Constellation)
Signed, dated: "mack 15"
Acrylic on canvas
77 x 77 cm

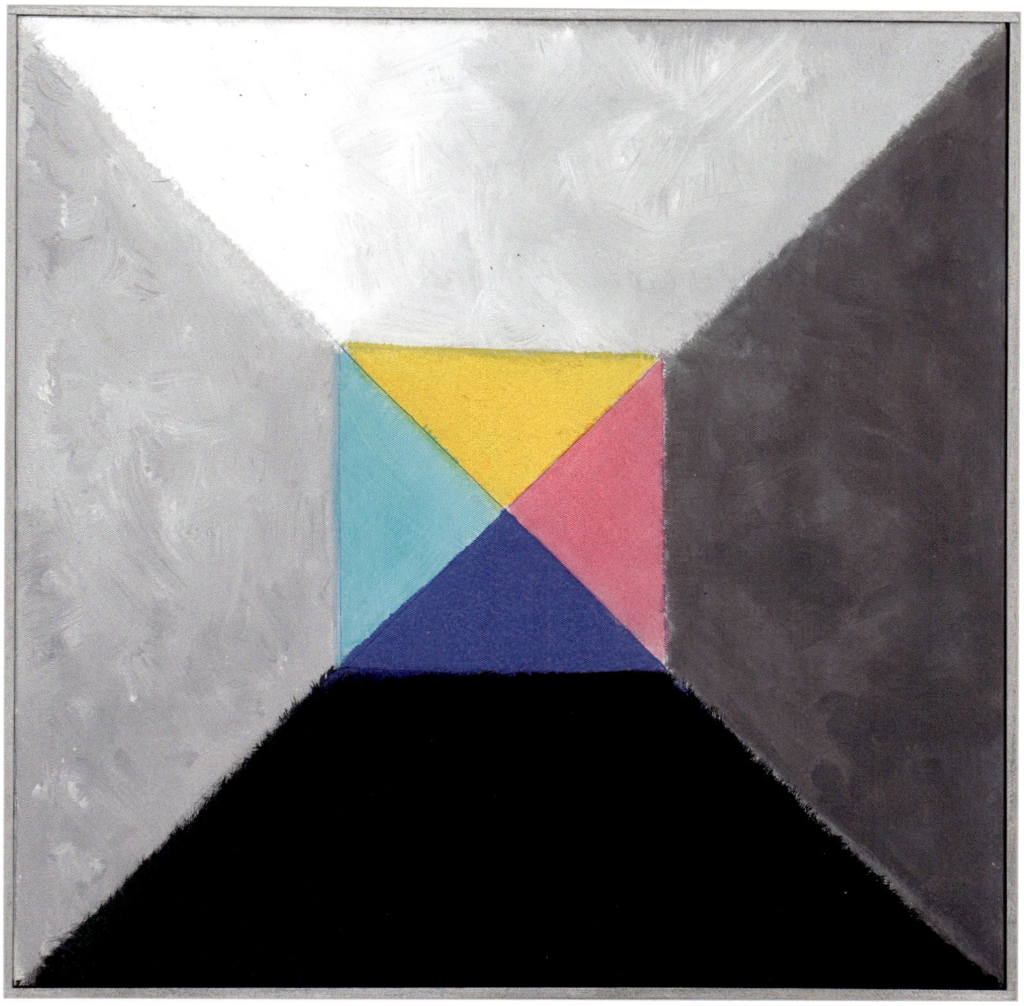

18 Heinz Mack
Sea Flag I (Chromatische Konstellation)
Signiert, datiert: »mack 15«
Acryl auf Leinwand
77 x 77 cm

18 Heinz Mack
Sea Flag I (Chromatic Constellation)
Signed, dated: "mack 15"
Acrylic on canvas
77 x 77 cm

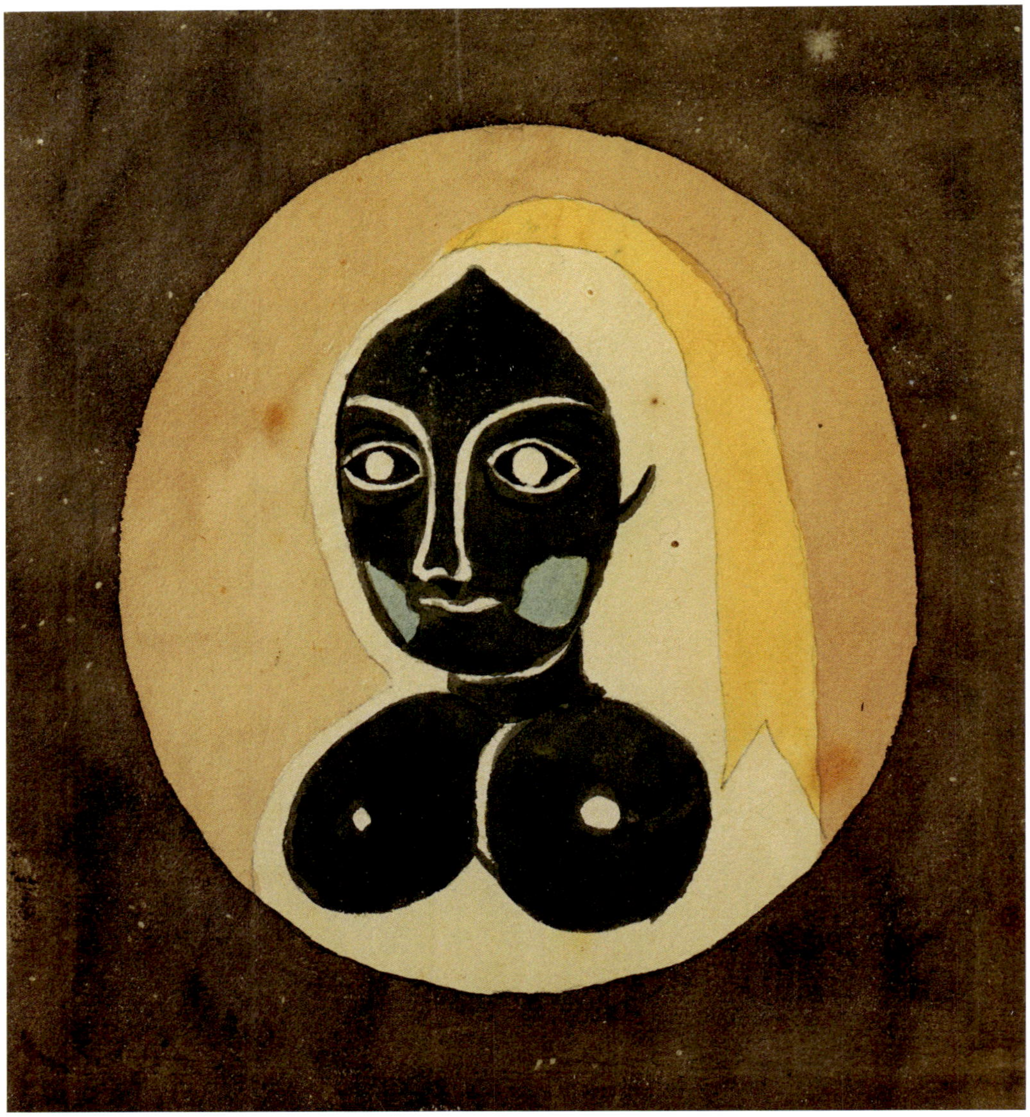

19+20 Johann Wolfgang von Goethe
Mädchen in umgekehrten Farben, 1795/1805
Aquarell mit Bleistiftumrissen
15,8 x 14,6 cm
Klassik Stiftung Weimar, Museen
Die Ausstellung zeigt eine Reproduktion.

Goethe schreibt in der *Farbenlehre* zur Erläuterung des Sukzessivkontrasts: »Als ich gegen Abend in ein Wirthshaus eintrat und ein wohlgewachsenes Mädchen mit blendendweißem Gesicht, schwarzen Haaren und einem scharlachrothen Mieder zu mir ins Zimmer trat, blickte ich sie, die in einiger Entfernung vor mir stand, in der Halbdämmerung scharf an. Indem sie sich nun darauf hinwegbewegte, sah ich auf der mir entgegenstehenden weißen Wand ein schwarzes Gesicht, mit einem hellen Schein umgeben, und die übrige Bekleidung der völlig deutlichen Figur erschien von einem schönen Meergrün.« *(Zur Farbenlehre,* Bd. 1, Tübingen 1810, § 52, S. 20.) Das Nachbild, wie es ihm auf der weißen Wand erschienen ist, hat Goethe in diesem Aquarell festgehalten. Fixiert man nun wiederum dieses dem ursprünglichen Sinneseindruck komplementäre Bild für eine Weile und blickt dann auf eine weiße Wand, so erscheint dem Betrachter wieder ein Mädchen mit hellem Teint, roten Wangen und schwarzem Haar, wie es die mit dem Computer hergestellte invertierte Version (s. Abb. S. 99) des Goethe'schen Aquarells zeigt.

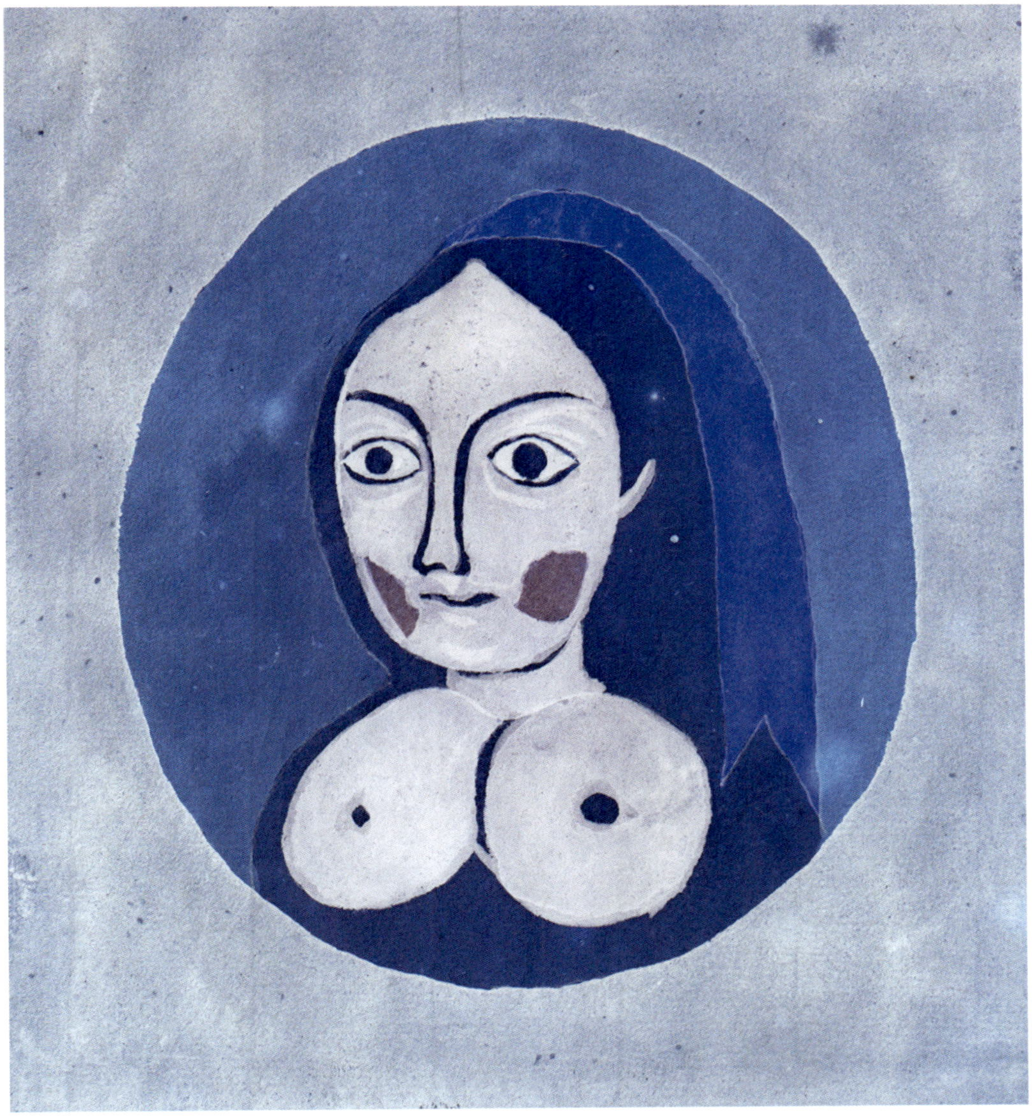

19+20 Johann Wolfgang von Goethe
Girl in Reverse Colors, 1795/1805
Watercolor and pencil
15.8 x 14.6 cm
Klassik Stiftung Weimar, Museen
The exhibition is displaying a reproduction.

Goethe offers in his *Theory of Colours* an explanation of the successive contrast: "I had entered an inn towards evening, and, as a well-favoured girl, with a brilliantly fair complexion, black hair, and a scarlet bodice, came into the room, I looked attentively at her as she stood before me at some distance in half shadow. As she presently afterwards turned away, I saw on the white wall, which was now before me, a black face surrounded with a bright light, while the dress of the perfectly distinct figure appeared of a beautiful sea-green." (Theory of Colours, trans. Charles Lock Eastlake [London, 1840], § 52, p. 22.)

Goethe has captured the after image as it appeared on the white wall in this watercolor (see ill. p. 98). If the viewer fixates for a while the image that is complementary with the original sensory perception and then looks again at the white wall, they see again a girl with fair complexion and black hair, exactly as the inverted version of Goethe's watercolor is represented in the computer image above.

Goethe's Theory of Colors – Claim and Discourse

Eckhard Bendin

I.

According to an old prejudice, accuracy, sensuousness, and fantasy are incompatible and must therefore be assigned different frames of reference. Even today, we consider logically defined and quantitative-mathematical branches of science to be exact only if they block out the associative-descriptive elements of fantasy so their system is not endangered. Yet, we ought to remember that Goethe's *Theory of Colours*—published more than two hundred years ago and in part intended as a critique of science—called for an "exact sensuous fantasy" for the reason of its frequent manifestation in art.[1] Goethe's wish to organically connect the seemingly incompatible corresponds to his phenomenological focus on the reality of life and his ideal of "science as art." In his own time, Goethe was far from isolated with this inclusive concept. Among those who considered art as a model for science was Johann Wilhelm Ritter (1776–1810). A physicist who discovered UV rays and founded electrochemistry, he maintained a lively exchange with Goethe. Based on its history, he interpreted natural science as life science, consolidating his vision in the 1806 article "Physics as Art," which posited that "Art is what we speak of in the first place: at one point, it will be infinite—universal in every sense."[2]

In order to understand Goethe's claim, it suffices to glance at the first section of *Materials on the History of Color Theory,* where he presents "science as art" and states that no human abilities should be excluded:

> Neither knowledge nor reflection can produce the whole, since the one lacks essence and the other lacks appearance; we necessarily have to imagine science as art if we expect any kind of wholeness from it. To approach such a challenge, however, we must not exclude any of the human powers in our scientific activity. The abyss of intuition, a confident look at the present, mathematical depth, physical accuracy, the heights of reason, acuity of intellect, moving and longing imagination, affectionate joy for the sensuous, nothing can lack for a lively, fruitful seizing of the moment, where single-handedly a work of art—whatever form it may be—can be created.[3]

Goethe showed the exceedingly close connection between the dimensions of cultural-intellectual and natural-technical history in his *Materials on the History of Color Theory*. Our present knowledge on the nature of light and color phenomena has equally led to a gradual increase of information and the promotion of new fields of application. Innovative artistic ideas and artifacts have advanced scientific and technical developments as well. By accelerating the development of science-based conceptual dimensions, art

1 Johann Wolfgang von Goethe, review of Ernst Stiedenroth, *Psychologie zur Erklärung der Seelenerscheinungen,* (Berlin, 1824), LA, vol. 110, p. 226.
2 Johann Wilhelm Ritter, "Die Physik als Kunst," *Fragmente aus dem Nachlasse eines jungen Physikers,* eds. Steffen and Birgit Dietzsch (Leipzig, 1984).
3 Johann Wolfgang von Goethe, *Zur Farbenlehre,* vol. 2, (Tübingen, 1810), pp. 119–20.

Goethes Farbenlehre – Anspruch und Diskurs

Eckhard Bendin

I.

Es ist ein altes Vorurteil, dass Exaktheit, Sinnlichkeit und Phantasie unvereinbare Größen seien, die man unterschiedlichen Bezugssystemen zuzuordnen habe. Auch heute noch gelten die logisch definierten und quantitativ-mathematisch begründeten Wissenschaftszweige allgemein als exakt, wenn sie das Assoziativ-Anschauliche der Fantasie ausblenden, um ihr System nicht zu gefährden. Doch ist heute daran zu erinnern, dass Goethe mit seiner auch als Wissenschaftskritik angelegten *Farbenlehre* vor über 200 Jahren eine »exakte sinnliche Phantasie« einforderte, wie sie vielfach in der Kunst wirke.[1] Goethes Anspruch, das scheinbar Unvereinbare organisch zu verbinden, entsprach seiner phänomenologischen Ausrichtung auf die Lebenswirklichkeit und seinem Ideal von »Wissenschaft als Kunst«. Mit jener integrativen Auffassung stand Goethe in seiner Zeit nicht allein. So wissen wir von Johann Wilhelm Ritter (1776–1810), Physiker und Begründer der Elektrochemie, mit dem Goethe eng im Austausch stand und dem unter anderem die Entdeckung der UV-Strahlen zu danken ist, dass er ebenfalls die Kunst als Vorbild für die Wissenschaft achtete und die Naturwissenschaft aus ihrer Geschichte heraus als Lebenswissenschaft deutete. Seine Vision verdichtet er 1806 im Aufsatz »Die Physik als Kunst« in der Formel: »[…] Kunst überhaupt erst, ist, wovon wir sprechen: in jedem Sinn unendlich – allgemein – wird sie einst sein.«[2]

Um uns Goethes Anspruch zu vergegenwärtigen, genügt schon ein Blick in die erste Abteilung seiner *Materialien zur Geschichte der Farbenlehre,* in der er »Wissenschaft als Kunst« vorstellt, bei der keine der menschlichen Kräfte ausgeschlossen werden sollte:

> Da im Wissen sowohl als in der Reflexion kein Ganzes zusammengebracht werden kann, weil jenem das Innre, dieser das Aeußere fehlt; so müssen wir uns die Wissenschaft nothwendig als Kunst denken, wenn wir von ihr irgend eine Art von Ganzheit erwarten. […] Um aber einer solchen Forderung sich zu nähern, so müßte man keine der menschlichen Kräfte bey wissenschaftlicher Thätigkeit ausschließen. Die Abgründe der Ahndung, ein sicheres Anschauen der Gegenwart, mathematische Tiefe, physische Genauigkeit, Höhe der Vernunft, Schärfe des Verstandes, bewegliche sehnsuchtsvolle Phantasie, liebevolle Freude am Sinnlichen, nichts kann entbehrt werden zum lebhaften fruchtbaren Ergreifen des Augenblicks, wodurch ganz allein ein Kunstwerk, von welchem Gehalt es auch sey, entstehen kann.[3]

Bereits in seinen *Materialien zur Geschichte der Farbenlehre* zeigte Goethe, dass die geistes- und kulturgeschichtlichen Dimensionen mit den wissenschafts- und technikgeschichtlichen in engster Verbindung stehen. Auch unser heutiges Wissen über die Natur des Lichtes und der mit ihm verbundenen Farbphänomene hat stufenartig zu Erkenntnisgewinn und Beförderung neuer Anwendungsfelder und -techniken geführt. Ebenso haben vorauseilende künstlerische

1 Johann Wolfgang von Goethe, Besprechung zu: Ernst Stiedenroth, *Psychologie zur Erklärung der Seelenerscheinungen,* Berlin 1824, LA, Bd. I 10, S. 226.

2 Johann Wilhelm Ritter, »Die Physik als Kunst«, Rede, München 1806, in: ders., *Fragmente aus dem Nachlasse eines jungen Physikers (Gustav Kiepenheuer Bücherei,* 42), hrsg. von Steffen und Birgit Dietzsch, Leipzig, Weimar 1984.

3 Johann Wolfgang von Goethe, *Zur Farbenlehre,* Bd. 2, Tübingen 1810, Historischer Theil, S. 119 f.

has gained value, acting increasingly as a model for scientists. In the scholarly interplay between originality and relevance, innovative and surprising elements have turned out to be progressively useful and practically applicable. The development of abstract, serial and conceptual art has also inspired creative techniques and sensuously refined methods in the scientific terrain. This includes, for instance—in the interest of a better perception of reality and an improved communicability of scientific contents—simulation and virtual reality. It is with good reason that Goethe valued the investigative ideas and modeling fantasies of his contemporary, the young painter Philipp Otto Runge. He considered the latter's differentiation of the appearance of 'translucent' and 'opaque' colors and his modeling of a *Color Sphere* as the first three-dimensional representation of the genesis of color and its plurality.[4]

Then again, the secrets that could be scientifically extracted from the mysteries of light and color have had reflexive effects on art. Accordingly, Maxwell's experimental studies on additive mixing of color and the resulting trichromatic theory of vision of Young and Helmholtz, as well as Chevreul's studies on concurrent contrasts and Brücke's and Bezold's exploration of appearances of contrasts, affected art theory and the development of art in the late nineteenth century rather significantly.

As part of the early twentieth-century spiritual departure, new tendencies seeking an affinity between art, science, and technology began to take shape. This is apparent by physiologically and psychologically motivated color theories of artists and theoreticians from the Russian avant-garde, the Dutch De Stijl movement, the Werkbund, and the Bauhaus. Among the concepts that fascinated the artistic avant-garde were Gustav Theodor Fechner's psychophysics and his "aesthetics from below," Ernst Mach's optical-acoustic tests, Wilhelm Wundt's experimental psychology, and the natural philosophy of Wilhelm Ostwald, "energetics," with its unitarian postulate, "Everything that happens in the world is nothing but a conversion of energy."[5] The concept of radiating energy provoked, for instance, the artistic imagination of Mikhail Matyushin, influencing his seemingly post-impressionist, dynamic paint structures. In the beginning, the new theories primarily offered artists impulses for metaphoric empathy, expressive-symbolic processing, or, more rarely, for methodically exploiting visual phenomena.

In the early twentieth century, aspects of these changes manifested themselves and became more general. For 'new design'—especially the De Stijl movement—the phenomenon of color attained unprecedented autonomy as an independent factor of awareness and design. 'Determination,' as postulated by Mondrian, became a declared concern, specifically in concrete art, and continued to be effective in the realm of consciousness. Yet, increased psychologizing also put an ever more articulate emphasis on an immanent metaphoric diversity and the ambivalence of color and its emotional potential. Gestalt psychology and psychoanalysis promoted the formation of expressionist and surrealist tendencies. In fields that perceived and experienced color, a plethora of new insights and findings emerged that began to influence art and design.

On the brink of the twentieth century, increasing industrialization brought not only technical but also regulatory scientific and serial factors more and more to attention.

4 Philipp Otto Runge, *Farben-Kugel oder Construction des Verhältnisses aller Mischungen der Farben zu einander, und ihre vollständige Affinität, mit angehängtem Versuch einer Ableitung der Harmonie in den Zusammenstellungen der Farben* (Hamburg, 1810). See the illustration in this catalogue on p. 230.

5 See Wilhelm Ostwald, "Grundriß der Naturphilosophie," *Bücher der Naturwissenschaft 1* (1908) and Ostwald, "Die Energie," *Wissen und Können 1* (1908).

Ideen und Artefakte wissenschaftlich-technische Entwicklungen befördert. Indem die Kunst zunehmend wissenschaftsorientierte, konzeptionelle Dimensionen entwickelte, gewann sie auch für den Wissenschaftler an Modellcharakter und Wert. Im wissenschaftlichen Spannungsfeld zwischen Originalität und Relevanz erwies sich Neuartiges und Überraschendes zunehmend als nützlich und praktisch relevant. Die Entwicklung konstruktiv-abstrakter, serieller und konzeptioneller Kunst- und Anschauungsformen hat auch auf wissenschaftlichem Terrain kreative Techniken und sinnlich verfeinerte Praktiken evoziert, zum Beispiel im Interesse einer besseren Realitätswahrnehmung und Kommunizierbarkeit wissenschaftlicher Inhalte durch Simulation und Virtualität. Nicht von ungefähr schätzte Goethe in seiner Zeit die forschende Anschauung und modellierende Fantasie des jungen Malers Philipp Otto Runge, dessen Unterscheidung der Erscheinungsweisen ›durchsichtiger‹ und ›undurchsichtiger‹ Farben sowie dessen Modellierung einer *Farbenkugel* als erste dreidimensionale Repräsentation der Genese und Mannigfaltigkeit der Farben.[4]

Andererseits wirkten auch die Geheimnisse, die den Mysterien Licht und Farbe wissenschaftlich zu entlocken waren, reflexartig in der Kunst. So hatten beispielsweise Maxwells experimentelle Studien zur additiven Farbmischung und die daraus folgende trichromatische Theorie des Sehens nach Young und Helmholtz, ebenso Chevreuls Studien zum Simultankontrast und die durch Brücke und Bezold untersuchten Kontrasterscheinungen große Auswirkungen auf Kunsttheorie und Kunstentwicklung im ausgehenden 19. Jahrhundert.

Im geistigen Aufbruch zu Beginn des 20. Jahrhunderts bildeten sich neue Tendenzen einer Affinität zwischen Kunst, Wissenschaft und Technik heraus. Ausdruck hierfür war auch eine Hinwendung der Künstler und Theoretiker der russischen Avantgarde, der holländischen Stijl-Bewegung, des Werkbundes und des Bauhauses zu Farbtheorien, die physiologisch und psychologisch begründet waren. Gustav Theodor Fechners Psychophysik und seine »Ästhetik von unten«, Ernst Machs optisch-akustische Versuche oder Wilhelm Wundts experimentelle Psychologie übten – ebenso wie die Naturphilosophie Wilhelm Ostwalds als »Energetik« mit dem unitaristischen Postulat »Alles, was in der Welt geschieht, ist nichts als ein Energiewandel«[5] – große Faszination auf die künstlerische Avantgarde aus. Der Begriff der strahlenden Energie forderte zu künstlerischer Imagination heraus, zum Bespiel in der postimpressionistisch anmutenden dynamischen Malstruktur Michail Matjuschins. Die neuen Theorien boten für das Verständnis der Künstler anfangs vor allem Impulse für ein metaphorisches Einfühlen und expressiv-symbolisches Verarbeiten, seltener noch für eine methodische Ausbeute der visuellen Phänomene.

Der Aspektewandel manifestierte und verallgemeinerte sich zu Beginn des 20. Jahrhunderts. Das Phänomen Farbe erlangte in der ›Neuen Gestaltung‹ vor allem der holländischen Stijl-Bewegung eine vorher nie gekannte Autonomie als eigenständige Bewusstseins- und Gestaltungsgröße. Die durch Mondrian postulierte ›Bestimmtheit‹ wurde nicht nur zum erklärten Anliegen vor allem in der konkreten Kunst, sondern wirkte auch auf der Bewusstseinsebene weiter. Die zunehmende Psychologisierung hob allerdings auch die immanente metaphorische Vielfalt und Ambivalenz der Farbe und deren emotionale Potenz immer deutlicher hervor. Gestaltpsychologie und Psychoanalyse beförderten die Herausbildung expressionistischer und surrealistischer Strömungen. Auf dem Feld des Wahrnehmens und Erlebens

4 Philipp Otto Runge, *Farben-Kugel oder Construction des Verhältnisses aller Mischungen der Farben zu einander, und ihre vollständige Affinität, mit angehängtem Versuch einer Ableitung der Harmonie in den Zusammenstellungen der Farben*, Hamburg 1810. Siehe die Abbildung im vorliegenden Katalog auf S. 230.

5 Vgl. z. B. Wilhelm Ostwald, *Grundriß der Naturphilosophie (Bücher der Naturwissenschaft, 1)*, Leipzig 1908 und ders., *Die Energie (Wissen und Können, 1)*, Leipzig 1908.

It was in the interests of quality assurance and control to inquire after the possible rules and systematizations regarding color variety and its reproducibility. Although, thanks to the discovery of spectral lines (Fraunhofer, 1814) and spectral analysis (Kirchhoff and Bunsen, 1859), the fundamentals for spectrometry and spectroscopy had been established; with regards to methods for measuring colors, much groundwork was yet required. This mammoth task was mainly pursued by the polymath Wilhelm Ostwald. One hundred years ago, his subsequent concept of a 'new color art' also provoked a rethinking of traditional positions in art and art education.

The rapid development of the visual media of photography, print, film, and TV offered new opportunities, increasingly placing technical queries in an artistic domain. Photographic, typographic, and scenographic elements gained influence in this field of experimentation, furthering a purely optical interplay of light and shadow that produced fascinating modulations in time and space. Examples of this trend from the 1920s include Naum Gabo's kinetic pendulum sculpture *Standing Wave* and László Moholy-Nagy's *Light-Space Modulator,* early focal points that experimentally visualized light's design potential as dark and bright, transparent and turbid, soft and hard, and stationary and moving. It was only a minor step, then, for the phenomenon of color and its diversity to express effects in time and space. In his *Theory of Colours,* Goethe refers to the "acts of light; its active and passive modifications."[6] Just decades later, artists like Richard Paul Lohse, Hans Hinterreiter, Josef Albers, Max Bill, and Victor Vasarely—with the aid of serial experiments—referred to color's ability to change and reproduce, and to its relativity. Their works were fundamental stimulants. In particular, Heinz Mack—whose oeuvre of the 1950s and 60s is characterized by permanent experimentation with material, light, and movement—gave voice to the most experimental parts of light's vibrant energy and visual power. Proof of this can be found in the *Dynamic Structures* of his paintings and numerous sculptural works, which include light reliefs, kinetic rotors, monumental light stelae, and light-reflecting cubes. In keeping with Goethe, Mack sought advancement and enlightenment in nature and imagined its visible structures as 'visual networks.'

The late twentieth-century digital revolution was accompanied by the development of electronic, digital, and interactive media in conjunction with modern light technologies (laser, LED, OLED), giving our daily culture, and hence the visual arts, an enormous boost, and thereby opening up further fields of exploration, such as the forays in information aesthetics in the 1980s. Computer art in Max Bense's sense of 'generative aesthetics' exploited the possibilities of predictability and algorithms, following from the generative principles that are based on programming codes. Ultimately, the new digitally controllable light technology enabled Light Art to gain a new momentum and a growing audience.

Goethe definitely recognized technology's revolutionary and formative power, acknowledging it in the figure of Faust and his activities as a creative mind. However, mainly thanks to his *Theory of Colours,* Goethe initiated a critical discourse, which continues to this day, that forces us to rethink traditional views. Based on the experience of

6 Johann Wolfgang von Goethe, *Theory of Colours,* trans. Charles Lock Eastlake (London, 1840), p. xvii.

von Farbe kam es zu einer Fülle neuer Einblicke und Erkenntnisse, die ihren Einfluss auf Kunst und Gestaltung nahmen.

Mit zunehmender Industrialisierung an der Schwelle des 20. Jahrhunderts rückte nicht nur der technische, sondern auch der ordnungswissenschaftliche und serielle Aspekt mehr und mehr ins Zentrum der Aufmerksamkeit. Im Interesse von Qualitätssicherung und -kontrolle stellte sich die Frage nach einer möglichen Bestimmung und Systematisierung der Farbenmannigfaltigkeit sowie nach deren Reproduzierbarkeit. Obwohl durch die Entdeckung der Spektrallinien (Fraunhofer 1814) sowie mit der Spektralanalyse (Kirchhoff/Bunsen 1859) bereits wesentliche Grundlagen für Spektrometrie und Spektroskopie gelegt waren, bedurfte es hinsichtlich der Farbmessmethoden noch grundlegender Arbeiten. Dieser Mammutaufgabe widmete sich vor allem der Universalgelehrte Wilhelm Ostwald. Seine daraus auch folgenden Ansätze zu einer ›Neuen Farbkunst‹ forderten vor 100 Jahren ebenfalls zum Überdenken tradierter künstlerischer und kunstpädagogischer Positionen heraus.

Die rasante Entwicklung der visuellen Medien Fotografie, Druck, Film und Fernsehen eröffnete neue Möglichkeiten und rückte zunehmend wieder auch technische Fragen in den künstlerischen Fokus. Nicht nur foto-, typo- und szenografische Elemente nahmen mehr und mehr Einfluss auf das Experimentieren, sondern schlechthin auch das optische Spiel von Licht und Schatten als faszinierende Modulationen in Raum und Zeit. In den 1920er-Jahren stand dafür neben Naum Gabos kinetischer Pendelskulptur *Standing Wave* auch der *Licht-Raum-Modulator* von László Moholy-Nagy als ein früher Kristallisationspunkt experimenteller Visualisierung des lichtgestalterischen Potenzials als Helles und Dunkles, Transparentes und Trübes, Hartes und Weiches oder Ruhendes und Bewegtes. Zum Phänomen Farbe und dessen Mannigfaltig- und Wandelbarkeit als Ausdruck der Wirkungen in Raum und Zeit – beziehungsweise als Ausdruck der »Taten und Leiden« des Lichts, wie Goethe es in seiner *Farbenlehre* charakterisiert[6] – war hier nur ein kleiner Schritt. Nur Jahrzehnte später verwiesen Künstler wie Richard Paul Lohse, Hans Hinterreiter, Josef Albers, Max Bill oder Victor Vasarely durch ihr serielles Experimentieren explizit auch auf die Wandel- und Reproduzierbarkeit beziehungsweise die Relativität der Farbe und gaben mit ihrem Werk wegweisende Anstöße. Insbesondere aber Heinz Mack, dessen Schaffen in den 1950er- und 1960er-Jahren durch permanentes Experimentieren mit Material, Licht und Bewegung geprägt war, lotete sowohl in den *Dynamischen Strukturen* seiner Malerei als auch in zahlreichen skulpturalen Werken – Lichtreliefs, kinetisch arbeitenden Rotoren, monumentalen Lichtstelen oder lichtreflektierenden Kuben – die vibrierende Energie und visuelle Kraft des Lichts experimentell aus. Dazu suchte er durchaus im Goethe'schen Sinne Beförderung und Aufklärung in der Natur und deren sichtbaren Strukturen als ›visuellen Netzwerken‹.

Die mit der digitalen Revolution gegen Ende des 20. Jahrhunderts einhergehende Entwicklung elektronischer, digitaler und interaktiver Medien im Verbund mit moderner Lichttechnik (Laser, LED, OLED) verliehen unserer Alltagskultur und damit auch den visuellen Künsten einen enormen Schub und eröffneten weitere Spielräume, zum Beispiel in den Exkursen der Informationsästhetiker der 1980er-Jahre. Die Computerkunst im Sinne der ›Generativen Ästhetik‹ Max Benses nutzte die Möglichkeiten der Berechenbarkeit und Algorithmik der aus den Programmcodes folgenden generativen Prinzipien. Die neue, digital

6 Johann Wolfgang von Goethe, *Zur Farbenlehre*, Bd. 1, Tübingen 1810, Vorwort, S. X: »Die Farben sind Thaten des Lichts, Thaten und Leiden.«

'light and darkness,' this is especially true in light of the ubiquitously apparent genesis of the variety of colored phenomena.

Even before Goethe's polemics against Newton's 'division of white light' were published, Huygens, Young, and Fresnel had already developed positions vis-à-vis the justification of the nature of light waves. But it was not until the mid-twentieth century that Goethe's claim began to be taken more seriously—as a critique of the ever increasingly independent 'exact' sciences. Grounded in phenomenology, his *Theory of Colours* was conceived as a counter-project to the dilemma of our knowledge of the 'nature of things,' that is still relevant today. In the meantime, however, "the comprehensive and obviously increasingly profound discussion of Goethe's scientific studies has led to certain insights concerning potentials and limitations of science in general."[7]

Furthermore, thanks to the insight—promoted by Planck and Einstein—that light is double natured, and hence that particles and waves are equally justifiable, the polemics are now less severe. Additionally, the understanding of the incomparability of Newton's and Goethe's methods and points of departure has grown, although there is still no shortage of misconstrued interpretations in both camps. Whereas for Goethe, 'seeing,' as the subject's phenomenal act, took center stage, Newton removed the subject in his approach entirely. This is where two truths meet that really complement each other. Goethe mobilized the direct truth of clear thinking against the indirect truth of experimental reduction. The historic impact of Goethe's *Theory of Colours* clarifies how vital a synopsis is. Time and again, major scholars have taken interdisciplinary approaches and positions on the interrelationship of light and color, among them the Nobel laureates Ostwald, Born, Schrödinger, and Heisenberg. In his 1941 lecture *Goethe's and Newton's Theories of Color in the Light of Modern Physics,* the latter concluded with the insight that the scholar "only fully comprehends science where—at the outer borders of its previous research methods—he discovers relationships to life itself."[8]

After Heisenberg's attempt to mediate between 'scientific truth'—sought by virtue of analysis and reduction—and 'truth based in reality'—i.e. on phenomenology, subjective reflection, and synthesis—a bridge of coexistence emerged: both positions could meet without either side losing face. Rather, they profited from the encounter: particularly during the last century, scholarly and artistic disputes have borne witness to this by demonstrating that insights into the supposed other world are now essential.

II.

While the continuing discourse provokes philosophical conclusions in the field of theoretical science,[9] previous positions on the physical relation between light, dark, and color genesis are also being reassessed.[10] Especially since—beside the polarity preferred by Goethe—there have long been sufficient indications about the effect of formative morphogenetic principles, such as symmetry, iteration, 'complication,' and

7 See Rainer Mausfeld, "'Wär' nicht das Auge sonnenhaft…,' Goethes Farbenlehre: Nur eine Poesie des Chromatischen oder Beitrag zu einer naturwissenschaftlichen Psychologie?," *ZiF Mitteilungen 4* (1996).

8 Werner Heisenberg, "Die Goethesche und die Newtonsche Farbenlehre im Lichte der modernen Physik," *Geist der Zeit 19* (1941), pp. 261–75.

9 See Theda Rehbock, *Goethe und die 'Rettung der Phänomene': Philosophische Kritik des naturwissenschaftlichen Weltbilds am Beispiel der Farbenlehre* (Konstanz, 1995), and Olaf L. Müller, *Mehr Licht: Goethe mit Newton im Streit um die Farben* (Frankfurt am Main, 2015).

10 See August Kirschmann, "Das umgekehrte Spektrum und seine Farben sowie seine Bedeutung für die optische Wissenschaft," *Neue psychologische Studien,* vol. 2: Licht und Farbe, ed. Felix Krueger (Munich, 1926), pp. 411–42; Eckart Heimendahl, *Licht und Farbe: Ordnung und Funktion der Farbwelt* (Berlin, 1961); Ingo Nussbaumer, *Zur Farbenlehre: Entdeckung der unordentlichen Spektren* (Vienna, 2008); Johannes Grebe-Ellis and Matthias Rang, *Experimentum lucis,* exh. cat. Humboldt Universität Berlin and Kunsthochschule Burg Giebichenstein Halle an der Saale (Lüneburg, 2010).

steuerbare Lichttechnik schließlich verlieh insbesondere der Lichtkunst eigendynamischen Auftrieb und zunehmende Öffentlichkeit.

Goethe hatte den umwälzenden, gestaltenden Faktor Technik durchaus erkannt und gewürdigt in der Gestalt seines Faust und dessen Tätigsein als schaffender Geist. Insbesondere aber durch seine *Farbenlehre* eröffnete Goethe einen bis heute anhaltenden kritischen Diskurs, der uns mehr und mehr zum Überdenken tradierter Anschauungen zwingt. Auf dem Erfahrungshintergrund von ›Licht und Finsternis‹ gilt dies insbesondere hinsichtlich einer allgegenwärtig sich uns offenbarenden Genese der Mannigfaltigkeit farbiger Erscheinungen.

Bereits vor Goethes Polemik gegen die Newtonsche ›Zerlegung des weißen Lichtes‹ hatten sich aus der Begründung der Wellennatur des Lichtes durch Huygens, Young und Fresnel bereits streitbare Positionen entwickelt. Aber erst Mitte des 20. Jahrhunderts begann man zunehmend, Goethes Anspruch auch als Wissenschaftskritik an den immer mehr sich verselbstständigenden ›exakten‹ Wissenschaften ernster zu nehmen. Seine *Farbenlehre* wird als phänomenologisch begründeter, exemplarischer Gegenentwurf zu dem heute sogar noch schärfer hervortretenden Dilemma unseres Wissens von der ›Natur der Dinge‹ aufgefasst. Inzwischen hat immerhin die umfangreiche und offensichtlich an Tiefe gewinnende Auseinandersetzung mit Goethes naturwissenschaftlichen Studien zu Erkenntnissen hinsichtlich der Möglichkeiten und Grenzen von Wissenschaft überhaupt geführt.[7]

Auch vermochte die durch Planck und Einstein geförderte Erkenntnis der Doppelnatur des Lichtes, in der Teilchen- und Wellencharakter gleichermaßen Berechtigung haben, die Polemiken zu entschärfen. Zudem ist die Einsicht in die Unvergleichbarkeit der Ausgangspunkte und Methoden Newtons und Goethes inzwischen gewachsen, obwohl es auch heute nicht an missverstandenen Interpretationen in beiden Lagern fehlt. Während Goethe das ›Schauen‹ als phänomenalen Akt des Subjekts in den Mittelpunkt rückte, nahm Newton das Subjekt ganz aus seiner Betrachtung heraus. Hier treffen zwei Wahrheiten aufeinander, die einander im Grunde ergänzen. Goethe bietet die unmittelbare Wahrheit des anschaulichen Denkens auf gegen die mittelbare Wahrheit experimenteller Reduktion. Die Wirkungsgeschichte der Goethe'schen *Farbenlehre* legt Zeugnis ab von der Notwendigkeit einer Zusammenschau. Immer wieder haben sich bedeutende Wissenschaftler dem Verhältnis von Licht und Farbe transdisziplinär zugewandt und positioniert, unter ihnen die Nobelpreisträger Ostwald, Born und Schrödinger sowie Heisenberg, der 1941 in seinem Vortrag über *Die Goethesche und die Newtonsche Farbenlehre im Lichte der modernen Physik* mit der Einsicht schließt, dass dem Wissenschaftler nur »dort, wo diese Wissenschaft an den äußersten Grenzen ihrer bisherigen Forschungsweise Beziehungen zum Leben selbst entdeckt, [...] ihr Sinn verständlich« wird.[8]

Spätestens aber seit jenem Vermittlungsversuch Heisenbergs zwischen der mittels Analyse und Reduktion gesuchten ›wissenschaftlichen Wahrheit‹ und einer auf phänomenaler Grundlage, subjektiver Reflexion und Synthese beruhenden ›lebensweltlichen Wahrheit‹ besteht eine Brücke der Koexistenz, auf der sich beide Positionen begegnen konnten, ohne die jeweils andere zu blockieren. Im Gegenteil, sie profitierten sogar, wovon gerade im letzten Jahrhundert wissenschaftliche wie auch künstlerische Auseinandersetzungen zeugen, denen Einsichten aus der vermeintlich anderen Welt wesenseigen geworden sind.

7 Vgl. Rainer Mausfeld, »›Wär' nicht das Auge sonnenhaft.. ‹ Goethes Farbenlehre: Nur eine Poesie des Chromatischen oder Beitrag zu einer naturwissenschaftlichen Psychologie?, in: *ZiF Mitteilungen*, 4, 1996.

8 Werner Heisenberg, »Die Goethesche und die Newtonsche Farbenlehre im Lichte der modernen Physik«, in: *Geist der Zeit, 19, 1941, S. 261–275.*

'combination,' in scientific and humanistic contexts that can be closely connected to the perception of light and color.[11] Particularly in light of Viktor Goldschmidt's mathematically-based 'complication theory,' an extension of the 'mathematical method' favored by Goethe to investigations of non-quantitative and non-geometric objects would be desirable: "The circumspect and pure nature of the mathematical method manifests itself in every phase as assertion ..."[12]

Initially, Goethe approached the task as an artist in order to discover something about colors "with the intention of art in mind,"[13] but he hoped that, with the aid of the *Theory of Colours* and his understanding of 'nature's language,' he would also attain a more complete unity of knowledge. Goethe hoped that, with the aid of his *Materials on the History of Color Theory,* he would be able to provide a "small-scale history of the human spirit,"[14] as he stated in a letter to Wilhelm von Humboldt.

Goethe placed the 'physiological colors' at the top of his work because he believed: "They are the foundation of the whole doctrine ..."[15] This was the first attempt to gather and order things that are difficult to grasp by the living eye. It was to Goethe's merit that he classified the eye's achievements in gradual adaptation as regular visual functions instead of the previously held view of 'deception of the eye.'

Introduced by Goethe to the theory of colors in 1814, Schopenhauer, who later supported it actively, discerned that a special key had to be located in the physiology of the visual process. In his 1816 treatise *On Vision and Colors,* Schopenhauer accentuated the connection of the physiologically complementary colors through a specially modified activity of the retina: "The basic conception of the true color theory consists of complementary color pairs, color always appears as duality since it is the retina's qualitatively bipartition activity ..."[16] Earlier than all subsequent sensory physiologists, Schopenhauer attributed significance to this connection.

Ultimately, Goethe addressed the question of the vital relation between the human eye and light as well as the 'sensuous, moral effect' of color on humans ("effect of colour with reference to moral associations"). To reach his 'ultimate aim,' his method of orientation meant for the artist to immerse himself in everything that we have stated.[17] He tried to make it easier by summarizing the innumerable occurrences of phenomena under specific main categories, assigning, especially in sections four and six, generative and aesthetic terms like origin, choice, excitement, mixture, increase, polarity, totality, unity, variety, conduct, coloring, and mode.

Here, too, Goethe focused on polarity as the generative aspect: "Considered in a general point of view, colour is determined towards one of two sides. It thus presents a contrast which we call a polarity, and which we may fitly designate by the expressions plus and minus."[18] After Huygens discovered double refraction, the polarization of light was increasingly resolved by Fresnel, Biot, and Malus. Bearing in mind its double nature—as electromagnetic radiation with its triple determination through frequency, amplitude, and vibration level—light offers, in the form of vertical oscillating electric and magnetic fields, polar conditions, that can be associated with color occurrences. Additionally, Goethe continued to study the color phenomena connected

11 See Viktor Goldschmidt, *Ueber Harmonie und Complication* (Berlin and Heidelberg, 1901); Hans Kayser, *Lehrbuch der Harmonik* (Zürich, 1950); Rudolf Haase, "Harmonikale Synthese," *Grundlagenforschung 12* (Vienna, 1980); Eckhard Bendin, *Zur Farbenlehre: Studien, Modelle, Texte* (Dresden, 2010).

12 Johann Wolfgang von Goethe, *The Experiment as Mediator of Object and Subject,* 1792, LA, vol. I 3, p. 293.

13 Goethe 1810 (see note 3), p. 674.

14 Johann Wolfgang von Goethe to Wilhelm von Humboldt, February 7, 1798, in WA, vol. IV 13, pp. 55–58.

15 Goethe 1840 (see note 6), p. 1.

16 Arthur Schopenhauer, *Ueber das Sehn und die Farben,* (Leipzig, 1816), p. 43.

17 Goethe 1840 (see note 6), p. 345.

18 Goethe 1840 (see note 6), p. 276.

II.

Der anhaltende Diskurs fordert nicht nur dazu heraus, philosophische Schlussfolgerungen auf dem Feld der Wissenschaftstheorie zu ziehen,[9] sondern auch bisherige Positionen zum physikalischen Verhältnis von Licht, Finsternis und Farbgenese zu überdenken.[10] Dies umso mehr, als es lange auch schon neben der von Goethe ins Feld geführten Polarität hinreichende Indizien für das Wirken morphogenetischer Bildungsprinzipien wie Symmetrie, Iteration, ›Complication‹ und ›Combination‹ in natur- und geisteswissenschaftlichen Sachverhalten gibt, die mit der Wahrnehmung des Lichtes und der Farbe eng verknüpft werden können.[11] Insbesondere angesichts der mathematisch begründeten ›Complicationstheorie‹ Viktor Goldschmidts wäre eine Ausweitung der auch von Goethe präferierten ›mathematischen Methode‹ auf die Betrachtung nicht-quantitativer und nicht-geometrischer Gegenstände wünschenswert. »Denn eigentlich ist es die mathematische Methode, welche wegen ihrer Bedächtlichkeit und Reinheit gleich jeden Sprung in der Assertion [Behauptung] offenbart […].«[12]

Goethe ging die Aufgabe zunächst jedoch als Künstler an, um »in Absicht auf Kunst«[13] etwas über die Farben zu gewinnen, obwohl er hoffte, mit der Farbenlehre aus seinem Verständnis der ›Sprache der Natur‹ heraus auch eine vollkommene Einheit des Wissens zu erreichen. Mit seinen *Materialien zur Geschichte der Farbenlehre* hoffte Goethe, auch eine »Geschichte des menschlichen Geistes im kleinen«[14] liefern zu können, wie einem Brief an Wilhelm von Humboldt zu entnehmen ist.

Die ›Physiologischen Farben‹ stellte Goethe an die Spitze seines Werkes, weil sie »das Fundament der ganzen Lehre«[15] ausmachen. Es ist der erstmalige Versuch, die schwer zu fassenden Erscheinungen des lebendigen Auges zu sammeln und zu ordnen, wobei ihm das Verdienst gebührt, auch dessen Anpassungsleistungen nicht wie vordem üblich als ›Augentäuschung‹, sondern als normale Sehfunktionen gewertet zu haben.

Auch Schopenhauer erkannte – durch Goethe 1814 in dessen Farbenlehre eingewiesen und sie später durchaus unterstützend begleitend – ein besonderer Schlüssel müsse in der Physiologie des Sehvorganges liegen. In seiner Schrift *Über das Sehn und die Farben* hob Schopenhauer 1816 den in einer qualitativ geteilten Retinatätigkeit begründeten paarigen Zusammenhang der physiologischen Gegenfarben hervor: »[…] die Farbe erscheint immer als Dualität, da sie die qualitative Bipartition der Thätigkeit des Auges ist. Man muß daher gar nicht von einzelnen Farben reden, sondern von Farbenpaaren […].«[16] Schopenhauer maß diesem Zusammenhang früher als alle nachfolgenden Sinnesphysiologen Bedeutung zu.

Goethes Interesse war letztlich auf die Frage nach der lebendigen Beziehung zwischen dem menschlichen Auge und dem Licht sowie nach der ›sinnlich-sittlichen Wirkung‹ der Farbe auf den Menschen gerichtet. Zum Erreichen des ›letzten Zweckes‹ orientierte er methodisch auf ein Durchdrungensein des Künstlers von der Übersicht des Ganzen.[17] Dies suchte Goethe zu erleichtern, indem er die unzähligen Fälle der Erscheinungen unter gewisse Hauptphänomene zusammenfasste und vor allem in der vierten sowie sechsten Abteilung generativen und ästhetischen Termini zuordnete wie Entstehung, Entscheidung, Erregung, Mischung, Steigerung, Polarität, Totalität, Einheit, Mannigfaltigkeit, Haltung, Kolorit oder Tonart.

9 Vgl. Theda Rehbock, *Goethe und die ›Rettung der Phänomene‹. Philosophische Kritik des naturwissenschaftlichen Weltbilds am Beispiel der Farbenlehre,* Konstanz 1995 und Olaf L. Müller, *Mehr Licht. Goethe mit Newton im Streit um die Farben,* Frankfurt am Main 2015.

10 Vgl. August Kirschmann, »Das umgekehrte Spektrum und seine Farben sowie seine Bedeutung für die optische Wissenschaft«, in: *Neue psychologische Studien,* hrsg. von Felix Krueger, Bd. 2: Licht und Farbe, München 1926, S. 411–442; Eckart Heimendahl, *Licht und Farbe. Ordnung und Funktion der Farbwelt,* mit einem Geleitwort von Carl Friedrich von Weizsäcker, Berlin 1961; Ingo Nussbaumer, *Zur Farbenlehre. Entdeckung der unordentlichen Spektren,* Wien 2008 und Johannes Grebe-Ellis und Matthias Rang, *Experimentum lucis,* Ausst.-Kat. Humboldt Universität Berlin und Kunsthochschule Burg Giebichenstein Halle an der Saale, Lüneburg 2010.

11 V. Goldschmidt, *Ueber Harmonie und Complication,* Berlin und Heidelberg 1901; Hans Kayser, *Lehrbuch der Harmonik,* Zürich 1950; Rudolf Haase, *Harmonikale Synthese (Beiträge zur harmonikalen Grundlagenforschung, 12),* Wien 1980; Eckhard Bendin, *Zur Farbenlehre. Studien – Modelle – Texte. Dresden 2010.*

12 Johann Wolfgang von Goethe, *Der Versuch als Vermittler von Objekt und Subjekt,* 1792, LA, Bd. I 3, S. 293.

13 Goethe 1810 (wie Anm. 3), S. 674.

14 Johann Wolfgang von Goethe, Brief an Wilhelm von Humboldt vom 7. Februar 1798, WA, Bd. IV 13, S. 55–58.

15 Goethe 1810 (wie Anm. 6), didaktischer Theil, § 1, S. 1.

16 Arthur Schopenhauer, *Ueber das Sehn und die Farben,* Leipzig 1816, S. 43.

17 Vgl. Goethe 1810 (wie Anm. 6), didaktischer Theil, § 901, S. 331.

to double refraction and the interference on crystals. In the case of optically anisotropic media, connections between vibration level and color occurrence are evident. In this context, Goethe utilized various polarization apparatuses with filters, causing the light to polarize and produce counter-colored occurrences as observable symmetries.

As Goethe pointed out in the 'polemical part' of his *Theory of Colours*—especially with regards to Newton's gradual color differentiation—in the emergence of difference, either a contrast can develop that manifests itself artificially on two sides, or a gradual and constant linear development can occur.[19] In the field of color, we find a differentiation in the artificially divergent that brings about different qualities. Like the color tones in the color wheel, these materialize beside each other. On the other hand, there is a differentiation in the gradually divergent that demonstrates an ongoing gradation of the similar, for example, in an equal hue triangle. A difficulty in understanding arises because of the fact that color differentiation—whether in a continuous line or closed circle—is obviously composed of a combination of artificial and gradual differentiation. The more differentiated a color wheel (over 24 tones, for example), the more the gradual differentiation comes into play; whereas with the simplest differentiation (6 to 12 tones, for example), the artificial wins out.

The main argument against an artificial differentiation of color tones, from the physical standpoint, is that it is the gradual continuum of electromagnetic waves that first emerges in the visual field. However, based on Goldschmidt's 'complication theory' mentioned above, this is not a contradiction since the 'light organ'—originating from the spectrum's two 'end nodes'—learned its evolutionary form and differentiation, according to the mathematical 'complication' laws, thanks to inserting 'intermediate nodes.' It is striking that the eye's receiving range encompasses exactly one octave, that is, the wavelength of the deepest red is twice as big as the outermost blue violet.

Apparently, first of all a middle-sized 'intermediate node' we call dominant $p = 1$ inserted itself on the seemingly dark ground for the uptake of light stimuli and their processing into emotions. Then, from both sides of $p = 1$, a medium level, further 'intermediate nodes' will have developed as different, seemingly artificial emotions.

The basic issue about polarity and symmetry appearing in color phenomena is currently relevant again from another perspective. Basing his early findings on a reversal of Newton's spectrum, experimental psychologist August Kirschmann published his conclusions in 1926. Other physicists like Torger Holtsmark and Pehr Sällström then began physical experiments during the second half of the twentieth century. Their work recently experienced a significant revival by Nussbaumer, Rang, and Grebe-Ellis, who inspired a philosophical discourse about a generalization of Newton's 'experimentum crucis.' Thus, strengthened through ideas and discourse, Goethe's concept of the polarity of light and darkness as a color-generating principle is once again in the public focus.

19 Goethe 1810 (see note 6), pp. 371–72.

Als generierenden Aspekt rückte Goethe hier auch die Polarität in den Fokus: »Entstehen der Farbe und sich entscheiden ist eins. [...] Im Allgemeinen betrachtet entscheidet sie sich nach zwey Seiten. Sie stellt einen Gegensatz dar, den wir eine Polarität nennen und durch ein + und - recht gut bezeichnen können.«[18] Seit der Entdeckung der Doppelbrechung durch Huygens wurde insbesondere durch Fresnel, Biot und Malus die Polarisation des Lichtes mehr und mehr aufgeklärt. Angesichts seiner Doppelnatur bietet das Licht als elektromagnetische Strahlung mit seiner dreifachen Bestimmung durch Frequenz, Amplitude und Schwingungsebenen schon in Gestalt der senkrecht zueinander schwingenden elektrischen und magnetischen Felder polare Verhältnisse, die man mit farbigen Erscheinungen in Verbindung bringen kann. Auch Goethe studierte zunehmend die farbigen Phänomene, die mit Doppelbrechung und Interferenz an Kristallen zusammenhängen. Bei optisch anisotropen Medien werden Zusammenhänge zwischen Schwingungsebene und Farberscheinung augenfällig. Goethe benutzte bereits verschiedene Polarisationsapparate mit Filtern, um das Licht zu polarisieren und gegenfarbige Erscheinungen als Symmetrien hervorzurufen.

Wie Goethe im ›polemischen Teil‹ seiner Farbenlehre mit Blick auf Newtons graduelle Farbdifferenzierung prinzipiell hervorhob, kann zum Entstehen einer Differenz entweder ein Gegensatz hervortreten, der sich artifiziell nach zwei Seiten manifestiert, oder eine Entwicklung stetig in einer Reihe vor sich gehen.[19] Wir finden auf dem Feld der Farbe sowohl eine Differenzierung ins artifiziell Verschiedene, die verschiedenartige Qualitäten hervorbringt und sie wie bei den Farbtönen im Kreis nebeneinander erscheinen lässt, andererseits eine Differenzierung ins graduell Verschiedene, die eine Stufung des Gleichartigen zeigt, zum Beispiel in einem farbtongleichen Dreieck. Eine Schwierigkeit des Verständnisses liegt darin, dass die Farbton-Differenzierung, ob im kontinuierlichen Band oder geschlossenen Kreis, offensichtlich eine Kombination artifizieller mit gradueller Differenzierung bietet. Je stärker ein Farbtonkreis differenziert ist (zum Beispiel mehr als 24 Töne), umso stärker kommt eine graduelle Differenzierung ins Spiel, wohingegen bei einfachster Differenzierung (zum Beispiel bei 6 bis 12 Tönen) die artifizielle vorherrscht.

Als Hauptargument gegen eine artifizielle Differenzierung der Farbtöne erscheint zunächst aus physikalischer Sicht das graduelle Kontinuum der elektromagnetischen Wellen im sichtbaren Bereich. Auf dem Boden der schon erwähnten ›Complikationstheorie‹ Goldschmidts erscheint dies jedoch nicht als Widerspruch, weil das ›Lichtorgan‹ seine evolutionäre Ausprägung und Differenzierung ausgehend von den beiden ›Endknoten‹ des Spektrums nach dem mathematischen Gesetz der ›Complikation‹ durch Einschiebung von ›Zwischenknoten‹ erfahren hat. Auffällig hierbei ist, dass der Aufnahmebereich des Auges genau eine Oktave umfasst, das heißt die Wellenlänge des tiefsten Rot ist doppelt so groß wie die des äußersten Blauviolett.

Offensichtlich hat sich auf dem uns finster erscheinenden Grund zur Aufnahme der Lichtreize und deren Verarbeitung zu Empfindungen zunächst ein mittlerer ›Zwischenknoten‹ als Dominante p = 1 eingeschoben, ein mittleres Niveau, von dem aus sich dann beidseits weitere ›Zwischenknoten‹ als artifiziell verschieden erscheinende Empfindungen ausgebildet haben.

Die Grundfrage nach einer in den Farberscheinungen wirkenden Polarität und Symmetrie erhielt auch aus anderer Perspektive neue Aktualität. Analog zu den frühen Erkennt-

18 Goethe 1810 (wie Anm. 6), didaktischer Theil, § 695 f., S. 258 f.
19 Vgl. Goethe 1810 (wie Anm. 6), polemischer Theil, § 27, S. 371 f.

III.

In comparison with the history of humankind, a timespan of two hundred years is minute and insignificant. Yet, this period seems to be of utmost importance, not simply because of its still tangible historic proximity and continuing relevance, but also due to the breathtakingly fast scientific, technical, and cultural development that presented new impulses for our ideas in a short span of time, leaving numerous new imprints on the zeitgeist. Over comparatively short time periods, our range of experience has expanded enormously. This is especially apparent in the elemental field of visual perception, which is indeed fundamentally determined by color.

What is most remarkable, however, is that the farther humankind has penetrated the micro and macro areas of existence and the more our ideas and knowledge branch out and differentiate, the more our desire and opportunity for a connecting purview becomes apparent. Images generated by space telescopes, geo-satellites, sonographs, computer tomographs, and electro-microscopes have entered the collective memory. The way we perceive and imagine the world has become aligned with the new worlds of images; our traditional visual experience was developed and sharpened in such a way that structural similarities became more clearly visible. This applies both to micro and macro structures, as well as to those images that determine our daily lives and everyday experiences in the 'normal perspective.'

Evidently, at the base of the different levels of perception we find generative principles that give rise to analogies. Ultimately, they create a confounding multiplicity of appearances. Furthermore, biological energetics has revealed—as have new systematic, theoretical models of fractal geometry and self-organization—that the behavior of the dynamics of a complex system is determined by very few regulatory parameters. Thus, only a few equations suffice to describe it. At the same time, both symmetry and polarity in particular are fundamental modes of action for the emergence of multiple phenomena. For example, we owe an infinite multiplicity of shapes to a finite number of symmetry operations. Today we know—on the basis of chaos theory and fractal geometry—that the simplest symmetry or polarity-based algorithms are able to generate highly complex amounts of information.

Concerning the number of appearances and perceptions of color, today, these findings seem like a late rehabilitation of Goethe's past endeavors. We presently assume that simple, fundamental parameters form the basis of the complexity and multiplicity of color. Computers dominate our present world. In the end, its plurality originates from the binary code of 1 (true/yes) and 0 (wrong/no), so it is immediately clear to everyone that the combinatorial linking of opposite parameters can produce a multiplicity of states and situations. Therefore, it is hardly surprising that two old traditions of thought have resurfaced again. Thanks to a renewed doctrine of harmonics, there has been a revival of the Pythagorean view of the cosmos as a harmoniously ordered entity, while the *I Ching*—a binary code-based combinatorial analysis—has received growing attention in the Western world.

nissen des Experimentalpsychologen August Kirschmann, der eine Umkehrung des Newton-Spektrums erzeugte und 1926 entsprechende Schlussfolgerungen veröffentlichte, hatten in der zweiten Hälfte des 20. Jahrhunderts die Physiker Torger Holtsmark und Pehr Sällström ebenfalls physikalische Experimente begonnen, die jüngst erst durch Nussbaumer, Rang und Grebe-Ellis – vorher namentlich bereits erwähnt – wesentliche Erweiterungen erfahren und zum philosophischen Diskurs über eine Verallgemeinerung von Newtons ›Experimentum Crucis‹ angeregt haben. Derart durch Anschauung und Diskurs bestärkt, rückte Goethes Auffassung der Polarität von Licht und Finsternis als farbgenerierendes Prinzip erneut in den Fokus der Öffentlichkeit.

III.

Gemessen an der Menschheitsgeschichte ist der Zeitraum von 200 Jahren verschwindend klein. Und doch scheint er uns von besonderer Bedeutung nicht nur wegen seiner noch spürbaren, historischen Nähe und fortwirkenden Aktualität, sondern auch wegen jener atemberaubenden Beschleunigung wissenschaftlich-technischer und kultureller Entwicklung, die unserer Anschauung in kürzestem Zeitraum neue Impulse verliehen und dem Zeitgeist manch neuen Stempel aufgedrückt hat. In vergleichsweise kurzen Zeiträumen hat sich unser Erfahrungshorizont enorm erweitert. Dies zeigt sich besonders auch auf dem elementaren Feld der visuellen Wahrnehmung, das wesentlich ja durch Farbe bestimmt wird.

Höchst bemerkenswert dabei ist aber, dass, je weiter der Mensch in die Mikro- und Makrobereiche seines Seins vordringen konnte und sich Anschauung und Wissen zunehmend verzweigt und differenziert haben, für ihn die Notwendigkeit und Möglichkeit einer verbindenden Überschau deutlicher geworden sind. Die von Weltraumteleskopen und Geosatelliten beziehungsweise Sonografen, Computertomografen oder Elektronenmikroskopen erzeugten Bilder haben Eingang ins kollektive Gedächtnis gefunden. Die Wahrnehmungs- und Vorstellungswelt wurde durch den Abgleich jener neuen Bildwelten mit den überkommenen Seherfahrungen dahingehend entwickelt und geschärft, dass strukturelle Übereinstimmungen deutlicher sichtbar wurden nicht nur zwischen den Mikro- und Makrostrukturen, sondern auch zu jenen Bildstrukturen, die das tägliche Leben und Erleben des Menschen in der ›Normalperspektive‹ bestimmen.

Offensichtlich liegen den verschiedenen Wahrnehmungsebenen übereinstimmende generative Prinzipien zugrunde, die jene Analogien bewirken und letztlich eine verblüffende Erscheinungsmannigfaltigkeit hervorbringen. Zudem zeigte sich in der biologischen Energetik wie auch bei den neuen systemtheoretischen Modellen der fraktalen Geometrie und Selbstorganisation, dass das Verhalten, also die Dynamik der Teile eines komplexen Systems nur durch wenige Ordnungsparameter bestimmt wird und sich ebenso durch nur wenige Gleichungen beschreiben lässt. Dabei gelten insbesondere Symmetrie und Polarität als grundlegende Wirkprinzipien für das Entstehen mannigfaltiger Erscheinungen. Wir verdanken zum Beispiel einer überschaubaren Anzahl von Symmetrieoperationen eine unübersehbare Vielfalt an Gestalten und wissen heute auf der Grundlage der Chaostheorie und fraktalen Geometrie, dass einfachste Algorithmen, die auf Symmetrie beziehungsweise Polarität beruhen, hochkomplexe Informationsmengen erzeugen können.

The harmonics doctrine was already known at the beginning of the European exact sciences. To this day, its concern is the relationship between measure and value, expressed in quantity and quality or number and sensation (for example, in music, string length and sensed pitch). Contemporary teaching harmonics is supported by 'experimental aesthetics,' an established discipline of psychophysics founded by Fechner. Twentieth-century surveys by authors such as Albert von Thimus, Hans Kayser, and Rudolf Haase provided a new impetus and demonstrated that an apparent 'psychophysical disposition' determines the relationship between measure and value, that is, a disposition for the integrality of intervals, the differentiation of consonance and dissonance, and diatonicism and chromatics.

Already in 1901, crystallographer Victor Goldschmidt deduced a generally valid principle concerning the appearance and formation of crystal shapes. He substantiated the 'complication' law mathematically, transferring it onto other areas in science, including color theory. In his survey of Fraunhofer's solar spectrum lines, Goldschmidt could also show that the predominantly constitutional reciprocal relationships in the 'complications'—between 0 and 1 and 1 and ∞— correspond to the matrix of the 'Lambdoma,' a harmonic measure going back to Pythagoras. A more recent investigation of the gradation of the twelve most incisive color shade sensations within the spectral color band confirmed the generative 'complication' principle Goldschmidt had found. The detected chromatic gradation of the 'dominant wave-lengths' corresponds exactly to the major shade levels of the Ancient Greek Pythagorean system. Hence, the spectrum of visible light bears the character of a harmonic structure in itself.[20]

Although in all these cases mathematics contributed the assertive, explaining input, those connections would not have been detected without the creative impulse of intuition. It appears that, thanks to intuition, humankind possesses the special gift of introspection, enabling us to unfold and survey the spheres of our existence and experiences. In this sense, the phenomenon of color is an object of intuition and fantasy just as much as one of scientific and harmonic purpose.

The lifework of Goldschmidt's student Siegfried Rösch also gives testimony to this gift. As a mineralogist, crystallographer, number theorist, and genealogist, he is considered a doyen of scientific color theory and color metrics in Germany. Always distinguished by intuition and ideas, Rösch's trans-boundary oeuvre seems exemplary in view of Goethe's spirit: in an exchange with the important Goethe scholar Rupprecht Matthaei, Rösch undertook analyses of Goethe's 1810 color circle, which Matthaei reconstructed in 1932. A few years later, he also mediated the acquisition of Matthaei's private collection by the Goethe-Museum in Düsseldorf for a permanent exhibition on color theory.

The progression of history has definitely promoted Goethe's and Ritter's desire to intimately connect scientific and aesthetic ideas. But Runge's vision for an art renewal wherein "science was supposed to widen the scope for the artist's emotion" has also become a reality.[21] Notably, Ostwald's turning to general solutions one

20 See Eckhard Bendin, "Strukturuntersuchung im Spektralfarbenband: Zur Harmonik der Farbton-Struktur," [Querschnittsanalyse 1996], in *Zur Farbenlehre: Studien, Modelle, Texte* (Dresden, 2010), pp. 50–53.

21 Philipp Otto Runge to Johann Wolfgang von Goethe, February 1, 1810, in *Schriften der Goethe-Gesellschaft 51*, eds. Hellmuth Freiherrn von Maltzahn (Weimar, 1940); see Jörg Traeger, *Philipp Otto Runge oder Die Geburt einer neuen Kunst* (Munich, 1977).

In Bezug auf die Erscheinungs- und Wahrnehmungsgröße Farbe müssen jene Erkenntnisse heute wie eine späte Rehabilitation der einstigen Bemühungen Goethes anmuten, auch für die Komplexität und Mannigfaltigkeit der Farbe einfache grundlegende Parameter anzunehmen. In unserer heute durch Computertechnik bestimmten Welt, deren Mannigfaltigkeit letztlich aus dem binären Code von 1 (wahr/ja) und 0 (falsch/nein) erwächst, leuchtet jedem sofort ein, dass die kombinatorische Verknüpfung gegensätzlicher Parameter eine Vielfalt an Zuständen beziehungsweise Situationen hervorzubringen vermag. Im neuzeitlichen Bewusstsein haben sich deshalb auch nicht von ungefähr zwei alte Denktraditionen erneut Bahn gebrochen. Neben einer Wiederbelebung der pythagoräischen Sicht auf den Kosmos als harmonisch geordnetes Ganzes durch eine erneuerte Lehre der Harmonik hat in der westlichen Welt inzwischen auch die auf binärem Code basierende Kombinatorik des *I Ging* größere Aufmerksamkeit gefunden.

Die Lehre der Harmonik stand bereits am Anfang des europäisch-exaktwissenschaftlichen Denkens. Deren Anliegen ist bis heute, das Verhältnis von Maß und Wert, ausgedrückt in Quantität und Qualität beziehungsweise Zahl und Empfindung, zu untersuchen (zum Beispiel in der Musik: Saitenlänge und empfundene Tonhöhe). Die heutige Lehre der Harmonik wird unterstützt von der ›experimentellen Ästhetik‹, einer inzwischen etablierten Disziplin der von Fechner einst begründeten Psychophysik. Sie erhielt im 20. Jahrhundert insbesondere durch Untersuchungen von Albert von Thimus, Hans Kayser und Rudolf Haase neuen Auftrieb und konnte zeigen, dass es offenbar ›psychophysische Disponiertheiten‹ gibt, die das Verhältnis von Maß und Wert bestimmen, zum Beispiel eine Disponiertheit für Ganzzahligkeit von Intervallen, Konsonanz-Dissonanz-Unterscheidung, Diatonik und Chromatik.

Auch leitete der Kristallograf Victor Goldschmidt bereits 1901 ein allgemeingültiges Erscheinungs- und Bildungsprinzip aus den Kristallformen ab. Er begründete das Gesetz der ›Complikation‹ mathematisch und übertrug es auf andere Wissensbereiche einschließlich der Farbenlehre. Auch in seiner Untersuchung der Fraunhofer'schen Linien des Sonnenspektrums konnte Goldschmidt zeigen, daß die in ›Complikationen‹ vorherrschenden gesetzmäßig reziproken Beziehungen zwischen 0 und 1 sowie 1 und ∞ der Matrix des ›Lambdoma‹ entsprechen, einer auf Pythagoras zurückgehenden harmonikalen Maßbeziehung. Eine neuere Untersuchung zur Stufung der zwölf prägnantesten Farbton-Empfindungen im Spektralfarbenband konnte das von Goldschmidt gefundene generative Prinzip der ›Complikation‹ bestätigen. Die gefundene chromatische Stufung der ›dominanten Wellenlängen‹ entspricht exakt den Haupttonstufen des altgriechischen pythagoreischen Stimmungssystems. Das Spektrum des sichtbaren Lichtes trägt also den Charakter einer harmonikalen Struktur in sich.[20]

Obwohl in all jenen Fällen die Mathematik den sichernden, aufklärenden Beitrag geleistet hat, wären jene Zusammenhänge ohne den schöpferischen Impuls der Intuition wohl nicht aufgedeckt worden. Der Mensch verfügt offensichtlich mit seiner Intuition über eine besondere Gabe der Wesensschau, die es ihm ermöglicht, die Ebenen seines Seins und Erlebens zu entfalten und zu überschauen. In diesem Sinne bietet sich auch das Phänomen Farbe sowohl als Gegenstand der Intuition und Fantasie als auch wissenschaftlicher und harmonikaler Bestimmung an.

20 Vgl. Eckhard Bendin, »Strukturuntersuchung im Spektralfarbenband. Zur Harmonik der Farbton-Struktur« [Querschrittsanalyse 1996], in: ders, *Zur Farbenlehre. Studien – Modelle – Texte. Dresden 2010.* S. 50–53.

hundred years ago, profoundly inspired that technical-instrumental and artistic development.

The general awareness of color's autonomy as an elemental phenomenon of life is valuable to our relationship vis-à-vis color in the twentieth century. In the realms of relativity, information, chaos theory, biopsychology, genetic and brain research, electronics and new media, the impressive demonstrations of new color and Light Art have above all promoted, enriched, and permeated—in the subtlest ways—public awareness, resulting in new attitudes.

Introduced by Kazimir Malevich, who established the supremacy of color, and continued by, among others, Piet Mondrian's and Theo van Doesburg's demonstrations of the boldness of color, Richard Paul Lohse's structural dynamics, Josef Albers's demonstration of relativity and interaction of color, the suggestive materiality of color in the oeuvre of Yves Klein, the color vibrations of Heinz Mack and Bridget Riley, and not to forget Mark Rothko's atmospheric differentiations and the indifference of Gerhard Richter's grey paintings—all artists, who saw concrete light as an orientation, ultimately carried color in an avant-garde manner towards its transcendence and liberation.

The range of artistic discourses on light is manifold. Whether we turn to the creations of Adolf Luther, Francois Morellet, Heinz Mack, Dan Flavin, Keith Sonnier, or James Turrell, or if we look at more recent works by Ulrich Bachmann or Carsten Nicolai—they can all be seen as sensuously experienced artifacts with the embedded claim of experience and intuition. This is what Goethe intended to introduce us to with his theory of colors. At the same time, these works are witnesses of an unbroken, continuing scientific and artistic discourse.

Nevertheless, even today we should not comprehend color as a solely generative or autonomous phenomenon on physical or aesthetic grounds. Instead, we ought to take into consideration the biological dimension of color as an evolutionary, physiological, biopsychological, and perpetually dynamic factor in our perception of the life and the world surrounding us. On the basis of self-organized processes, color not only determines our aesthetic judgments and creative attitudes—quite existentially, color determines our being.

Von dieser Gabe zeugt auch das Lebenswerk des Goldschmidt-Schülers Siegfried Rösch, der als Mineraloge, Kristallograf, Zahlentheoretiker und Genealoge auch als ein Nestor der wissenschaftlichen Farbenlehre und Farbmetrik in Deutschland galt. Röschs grenzüberschreitendes Werk, das stets auch von Intuition und Anschauung bestimmt war, erscheint im Hinblick auf den Goethe'schen Geist beispielhaft. Im Austausch mit dem bedeutenden Goethe-Forscher Rupprecht Matthaei nahm Rösch zum Beispiel Analysen an Goethes Farbenkreis von 1810 sowie dessen Rekonstruktion durch Matthaei von 1932 vor. Rösch war es auch, der wenige Jahre später die Übernahme der Privatsammlung von Matthaei für eine ständige Ausstellung zur Farbenlehre im Düsseldorfer Goethe-Museum vermittelte.

Der Gang der Geschichte hat Goethes und Ritters einstiges Anliegen durchaus befördert, die naturwissenschaftlichen und ästhetischen Ideen innig zu verbinden. Aber auch Runges Vision einer Erneuerung der Kunst, bei der »die Wissenschaft den Spielraum für das Gefühl des Künstlers« erweitern sollte, wurde Realität.[21] Insbesondere Ostwalds Hinwendung zu allgemeingültigen Lösungen vor 100 Jahren beflügelte die technisch-instrumentale und künstlerische Entwicklung nachhaltig.

Das allgemeine Bewusstwerden der Autonomie der Farbe als elementares Lebensphänomen wurde zudem ein wertvolles Entwicklungsgut unseres Verhältnisses zur Farbe im 20. Jahrhundert. Auf dem Boden der Relativitäts-, Informations- und Chaostheorie, der Biopsychologie, Gen- und Hirnforschung, der Elektronik und neuen Medien sind es vor allem aber die eindrucksvollen Demonstrationen der neuen Farb- und Lichtkunst, die auf subtile Weise in das öffentliche Bewusstsein gedrungen sind, es bereichert und neue Einstellungen befördert haben.

Eingeleitet durch die Supremation der Farbe durch Kasimir Malewitsch – fortgeführt unter anderem in den Demonstrationen der Bestimmtheit der Farbe durch Piet Mondrian und Theo van Doesburg, in Richard Paul Lohses struktureller Dynamik, in der von Josef Albers demonstrierten Relativität und Interaktion der Farbe, der suggestiven Materialität der Farbe bei Yves Klein, den Farbvibrationen bei Heinz Mack oder Bridget Riley sowie den atmosphärischen Differenzierungen eines Mark Rothko bis zur Indifferenz der grauen Bilder von Gerhard Richter – haben letztlich die am konkreten Licht orientierten Künstler avantgardistisch die Farbe zu Transzendenz und Befreiung geführt.

Die Spannweite der lichtkünstlerischen Diskurse ist mannigfaltig. Ob nun die Kreationen von Adolf Luther, François Morellet oder Heinz Mack, von Dan Flavin, Keith Sonnier oder James Turrell beziehungsweise jüngere Arbeiten von Ulrich Bachmann oder Carsten Nicolai – sie alle können sinnlich erfahrbare Artefakte jenes Anspruchs an Erfahrung und Intuition sein, den Goethe uns mit seiner Farbenlehre eröffnen wollte, aber zugleich auch beredte Zeugnisse eines ungebrochen fortgesetzten Diskurses in Wissenschaft und Kunst.

Wir sollten jedoch auch heute Farbe nicht nur begreifen als ein generatives Phänomen auf physikalischem oder ästhetischem Hintergrund, sondern vor allem auch als biologische Größe, das heißt als eine evolutionär gewachsene, physiologisch und biopsychologisch begründete, stets dynamische Größe lebensweltlicher Wahrnehmung, die auf dem Hintergrund selbstorganisatorischer Prozesse nicht nur unsere ästhetischen Wertungen und gestalterischen Haltungen wesentlich bestimmt, sondern existenziell auch unser Sein.

21 Philipp Otto Runge, Brief an Goethe vom 1. Februar 1810, in: *Philipp Otto Runges Briefwechsel mit Goethe (Schriften der Goethe-Gesellschaft, 51)*, hrsg. von Hellmuth Freiherrn von Maltzahn, Weimar 1940; vgl. Jörg Traeger, *Philipp Otto Runge oder Die Geburt einer neuen Kunst*, München 1977.

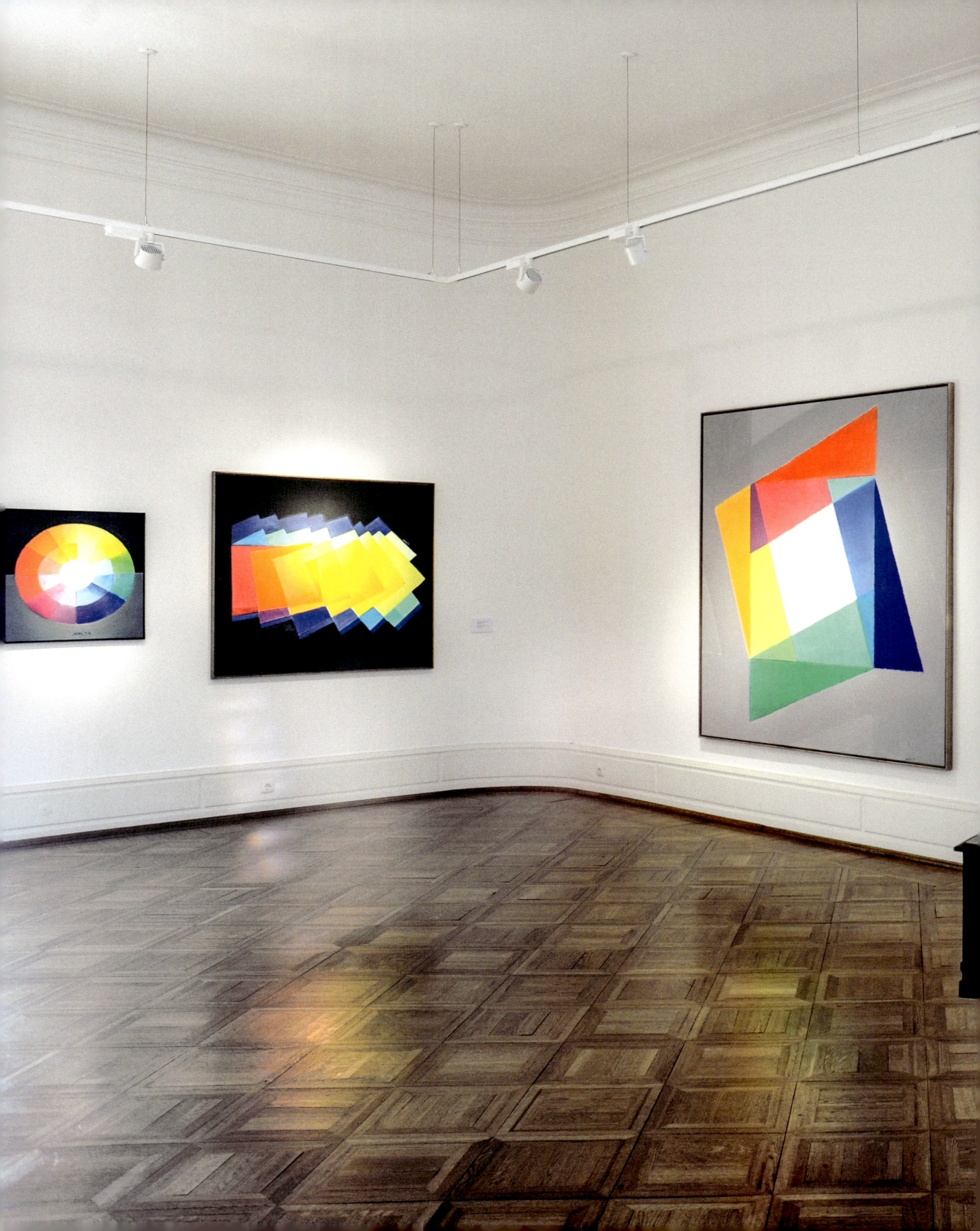

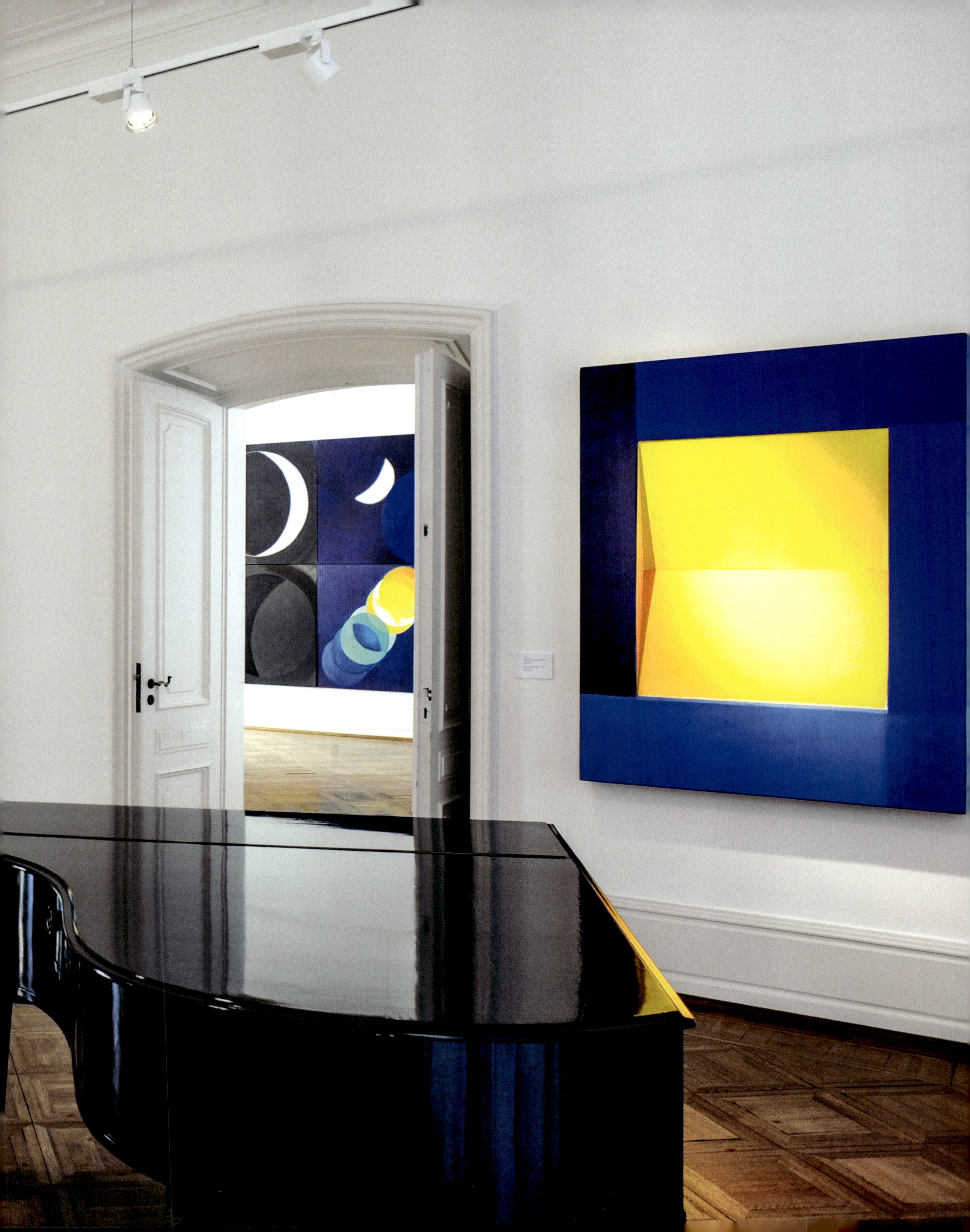

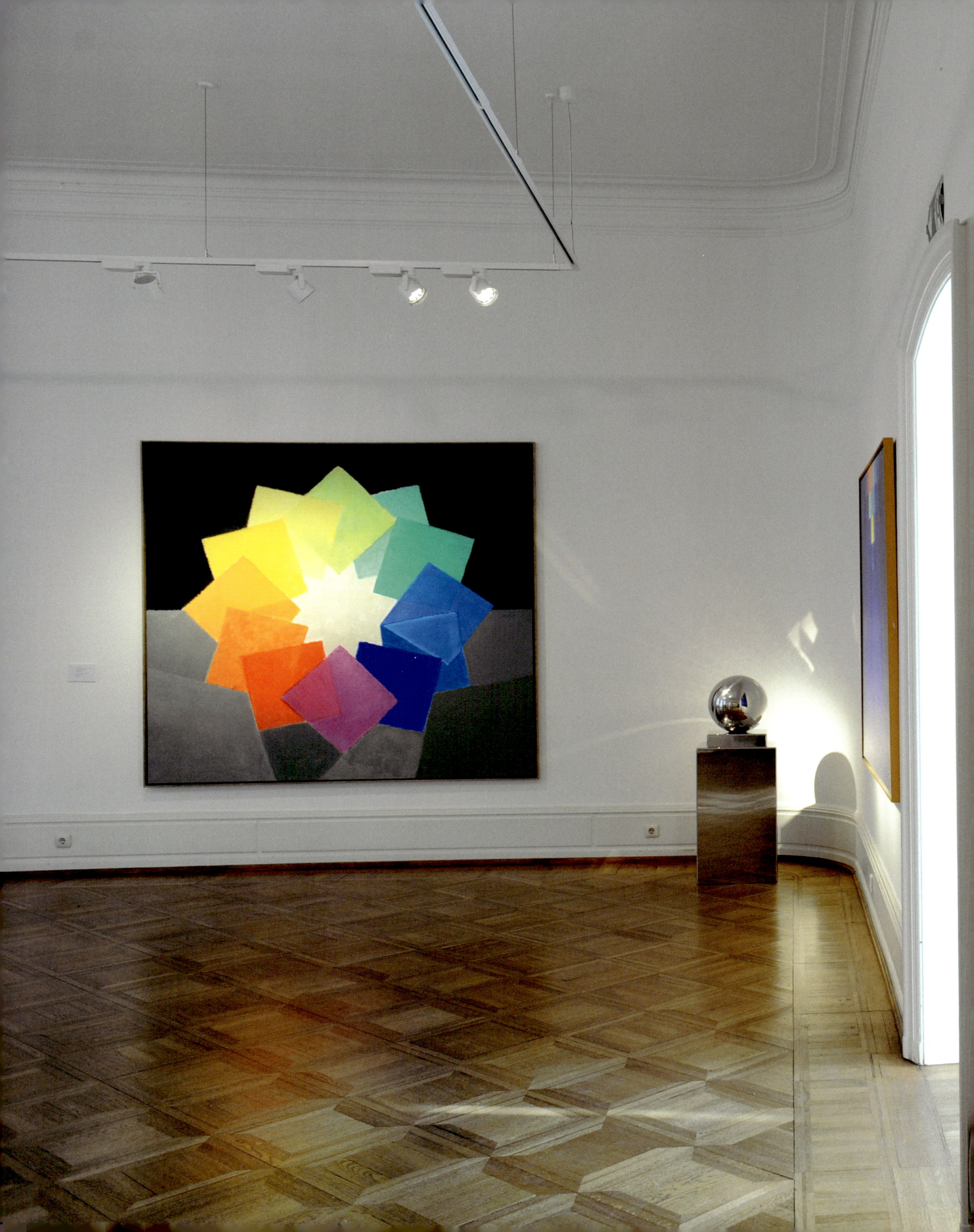

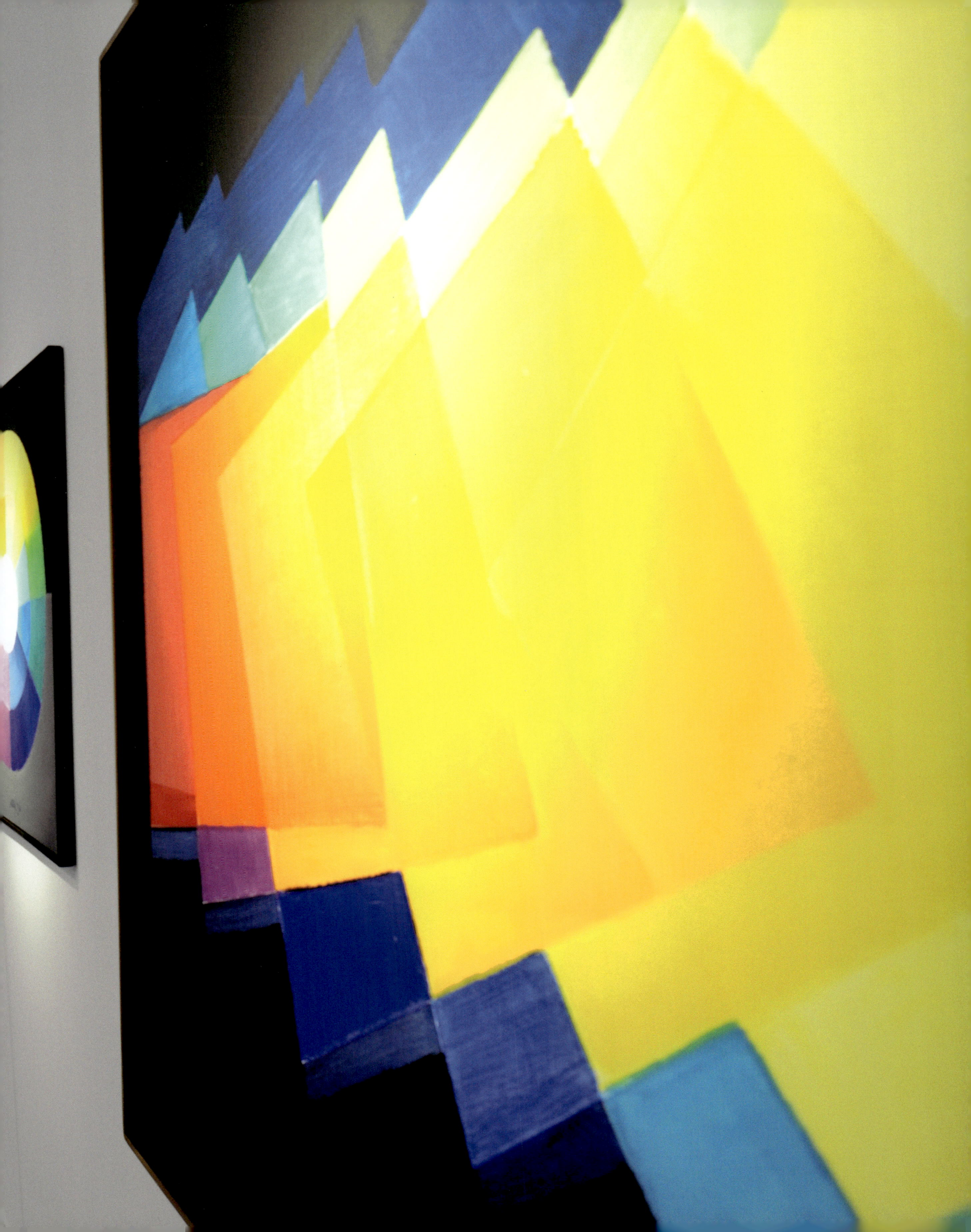

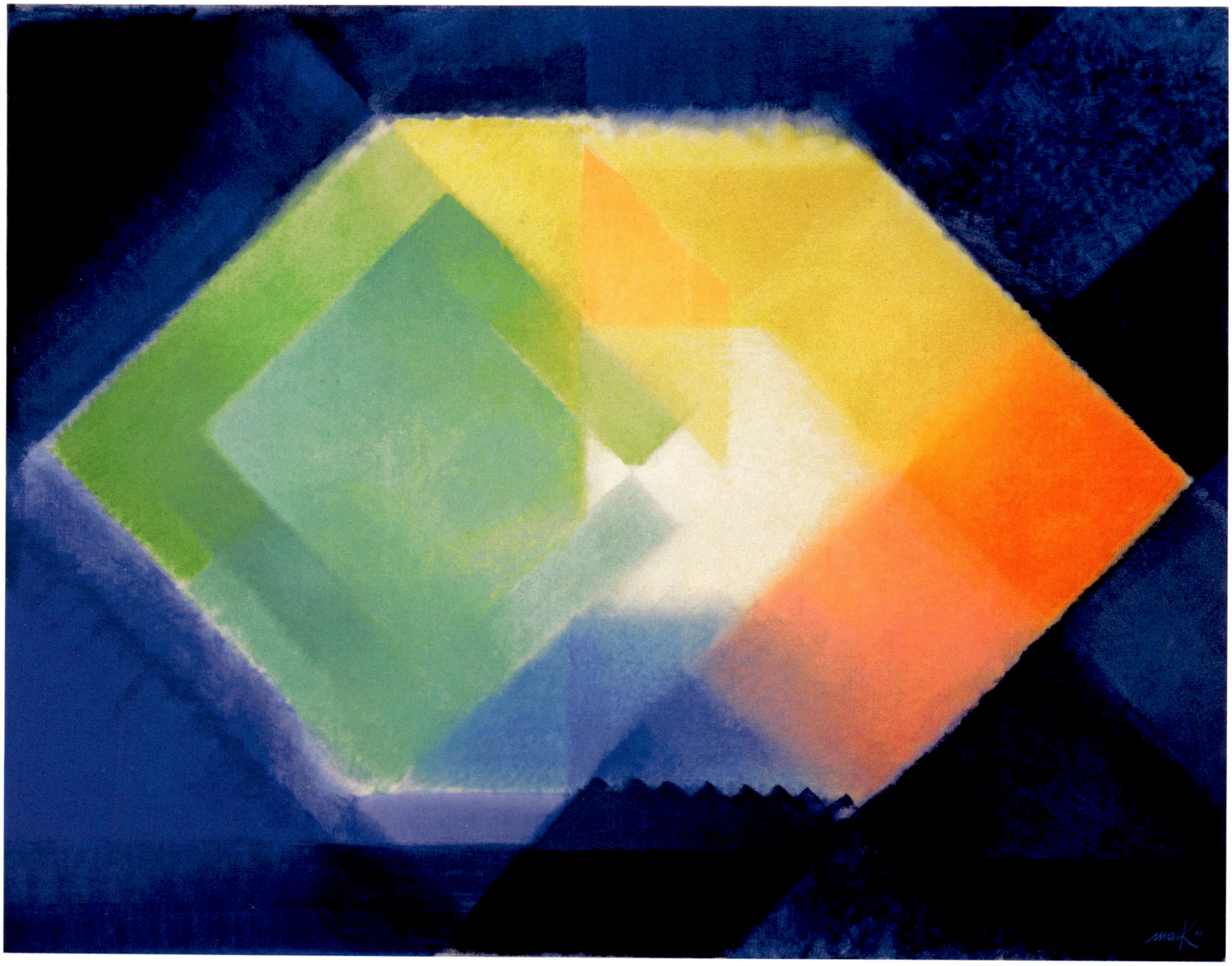

Heinz Mack
Le jardin artificiel (Chromatische Konstellation)
Signiert, datiert: »mack 97«
Acryl auf Leinwand
225 x 280 cm

Heinz Mack
Le jardin artificiel (Chromatic Constellation)
Signed, dated: "mack 97"
Acrylic on canvas
225 x 280 cm

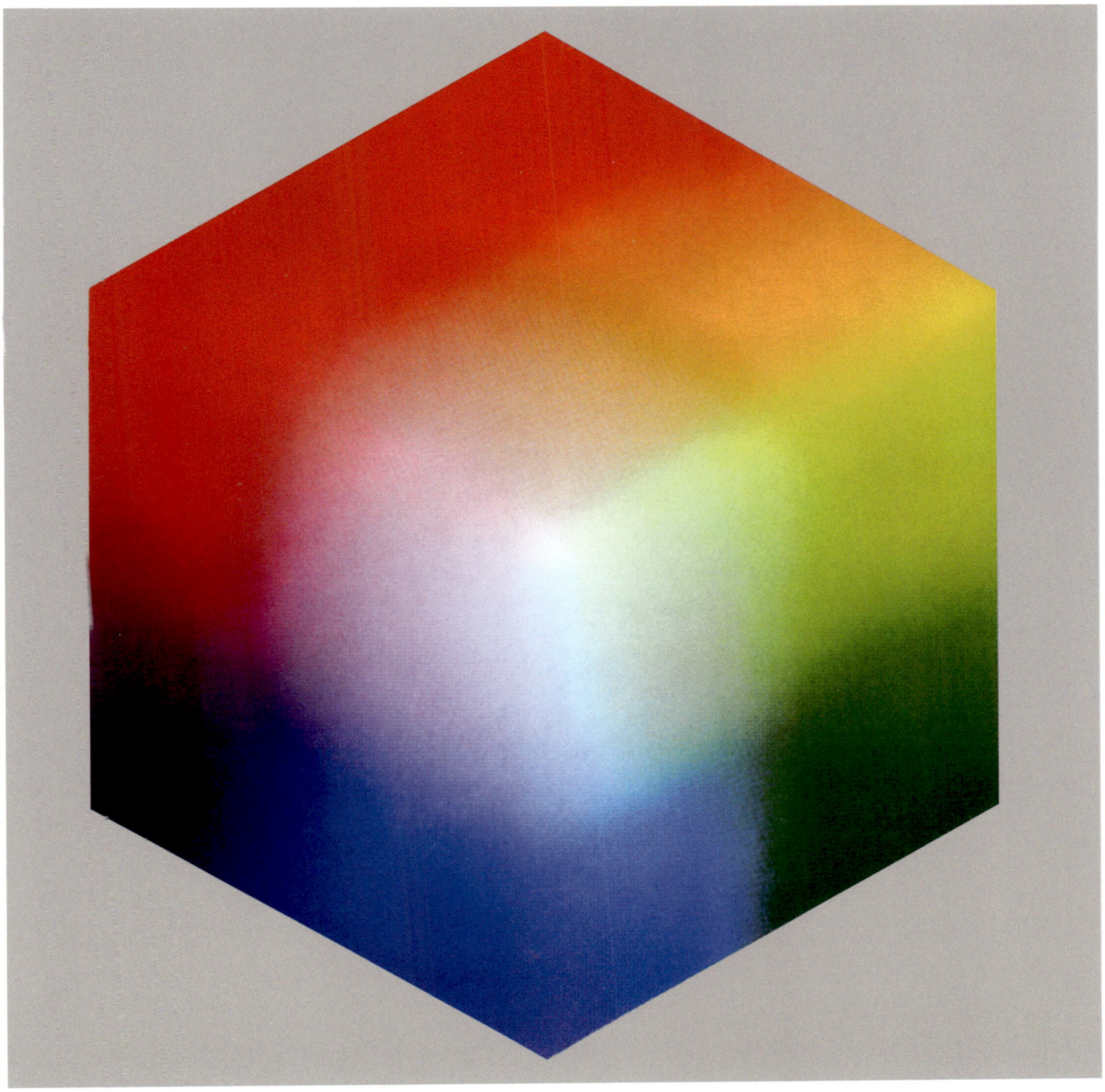

Das Farbensechseck mit der logischen quantitativen Ordnung der bunten Farben

The color hexagon with the logical quantitative ordering of the various colors

Goethe's Theory of Colors from the Perspective of Modern Physics

Johannes Grebe-Ellis and Oliver Passon

"Of mine they can destroy nothing," writes Goethe in his *Scientific Notebooks* (Hefte *Zur Naturwissenschaft)* of the opponents to his *Farbenlehre,* "for I have built nothing; rather I have sown, and so wide in the world that they cannot taint the seeds."[1] What is the situation today—roughly 200 years later—regarding Goethe's 'optical seeds'? The influence of his color studies on the development of technical, artistic, and scientific aspects of color research up to the present day is undeniable. But what about his physical contributions to color research? Here, the shift in the assessment of Goethe's scientific studies—brought about by Hermann von Helmholtz in the second half of the nineteenth century—and the 'seeds of thought' sown within them are instructive. In his 1892 lecture *Goethe's Premonitions Concerning Coming Natural Scientific Ideas,* Helmholtz revised his judgment from 1853 that claimed the *Farbenlehre* was a 'failure,' and, with a comparison with Faraday and Kirchhoff, gave Goethe a place in the community of physicists.[2] The case of 'Goethe contra Newton' has since stirred up many minds; there is hardly a scientific controversy about which more has been written.[3] The efforts of notable twentieth-century physicists to recognize Goethe as a pioneer of a holistic view of nature do not, however, change the fact that, from the perspective of physics, the *Farbenlehre* was considered to be a settled matter.[4]

This consensus has been called into question in the last few years by new historical, philosophical, and experimental investigations. Against the background of a few remarks on the problematic reception of the *Farbenlehre,* along with an outline of the status of historical and philosophical research, this essay presents the results of experimental research done over the last decade that has led to a new assessment of Goethe's contributions to physics through his *Farbenlehre.*[5]

Newton or Goethe—Who Is Right?

Whoever takes up the topic of Goethe's *Farbenlehre* comes to experience that it is nearly impossible to speak on the strictly physical part of it without at the same time taking a position on the 'Goethe contra Newton' controversy. The question "Who is right?" is valid. This has a long tradition that ultimately goes back to Goethe himself, who, even though he later came to regret it, initiated the debate with his polemic against Newton's *Opticks*. However, the history of the reception of the *Farbenlehre* has shown that an undue emphasis on this question leads to an impasse. From a modern perspective, the suspicion arises that the debate on the *Farbenlehre,* together with its relevance for physical optics, has gone astray because it has remained limited to three positions: 1) "pro Newton," mainly advocated by physi-

1 Anterior introduction (probably early 1815), in LA, Bd. I 8, pp. 182–83.

2 See for example Hermann von Helmholtz, "Über Goethes naturwissenschaftliche Arbeiten" (On Goethe's Scientific Works), in *Vorträge und Reden,* vol. 1 (Braunschweig, 1896), pp. 1–40; "Goethes Vorahnungen kommender naturwissenschaftlicher Ideen" (Goethe's Premonitions Concerning Coming Natural Scientific Ideas), in *Vorträge und Reden,* vol. 2 (Braunschweig, 1896), pp. 335–61; for the shift in Helmholtz's opinion, see Friedrich Steinle, "'Das Nächste ans Nächste reihen': Goethe, Newton und das Experiment," *Philosophia Naturalis* 39 (2002), pp. 141–72.

3 For the history of the reception of Goethe's *Farbenlehre,* see the relevant commentary in the LA. For further information, see Manfred Wenzel, *Goethe Handbuch:* Supplemente 2: Naturwissenschaften (Stuttgart, 2012). A useful overview is also given in Volkmar Schüller, "Goethe versus Newton. Zum 250. Geburtstag von Johann Wolfgang von Goethe," *Physikalische Blätter* 55 (1999), pp. 62–66.

4 See for example Max Born, "Betrachtungen zur Farbenlehre," *Die Naturwissenschaften* 50 (1963), pp. 29–39; Werner Heisenberg, "Die Goethesche und die Newtonsche Farbenlehre im Lichte der modernen Physik," in *Wandlungen in den Grundlagen der Naturwissenschaft* (Stuttgart, 1959), pp. 85–106; "Das Naturbild Goethes und die technisch-naturwissenschaftliche Welt," *Goethe-Jahrbuch* 29 (1967), pp. 27–42; Arnold Sommerfeld, "Goethes Farbenlehre im Urteile der Zeit," *Deutsche Revue* 42 (1917), pp. 100–06; Carl Friedrich von Weizsäcker, "Einige Begriffe aus Goethes Naturwissenschaft," in *Gesammelte Werke,* vol. 13 (1989), pp. 539–55.

5 Sections of this article have already been published in Johannes Grebe-Ellis "Goethes Farbenlehre im Lichte neuer Experimente zur Symmetrie spektraler Phänomene," in Gernot Böhme, *Goethes Naturwissenschaft: Schriften der Darmstädter Goethe-Gesellschaft,* vol. 7 (2017) pp. 39–58; Matthias Rang et al., "Optische Komplementarität: Experimente zur Symmetrie spektraler Phänomene," *Physik Journal* 16 (2017), pp. 43–49; idem and Matthias Rang, "Power Area Density in Inverse Spectra," *Journal for General Philosophy of Science,* March 2018, https://doi.org/10.1007/s10838-017-9394-8 (accessed July 20, 2018).

6 Olaf Müller, *Mehr Licht! Goethe mit Newton im Streit um die Farben* (Munich, 2015).

Goethes Farbenlehre aus Sicht der heutigen Physik

Johannes Grebe-Ellis und Oliver Passon

»Mir aber können sie nichts zerstören«, schreibt Goethe in den Heften *Zur Naturwissenschaft* über die Gegner seiner *Farbenlehre* und fährt fort: »denn ich habe nicht gebaut; aber gesäet habe ich und so weit in die Welt hinaus, dass sie die Saat nicht verderben können [...].«[1] Wie ist es heute – rund 200 Jahre später – um die ›optische Saat‹ Goethes bestellt? Der Einfluss, den seine Farbforschungen auf die Entwicklung technischer, künstlerischer und wissenschaftlicher Aspekte der Farbenlehre bis heute gehabt haben, ist unstrittig. Wie steht es aber um die physikalischen Beiträge zur Farbenlehre? Aufschlussreich ist der Wandel, den die Beurteilung der naturwissenschaftlichen Arbeiten Goethes und der in ihnen gesäten ›Gedankenkeime‹ durch Hermann von Helmholtz in der zweiten Hälfte des 19. Jahrhunderts erfahren hat. In seiner Rede von 1892 über *Goethes Vorahnungen kommender naturwissenschaftlicher Ideen* revidierte Helmholtz sein Urteil von 1853 über das ›Scheitern‹ der *Farbenlehre* und nahm Goethe durch den Vergleich mit Faraday und Kirchhoff in die Gemeinschaft der Physiker auf.[2] Der Fall ›Goethe contra Newton‹ hat seither viele Gemüter erregt; über kaum eine wissenschaftliche Kontroverse ist mehr geschrieben worden.[3] Die Bemühungen namhafter Physiker des 20. Jahrhunderts um eine Würdigung Goethes als Wegbereiter einer ganzheitlichen Naturanschauung änderten indessen nichts daran, dass die *Farbenlehre* aus physikalischer Sicht als erledigt gilt.[4]

Dieser Konsens wird seit einigen Jahren durch neuere historische, wissenschaftsphilosophische und experimentelle Untersuchungen infrage gestellt. Vor dem Hintergrund einiger Anmerkungen zur Rezeptionsproblematik und zum Stand der historischen und wissenschaftsphilosophischen Forschung zur *Farbenlehre* werden im Folgenden die Ergebnisse experimenteller Untersuchungen vorgestellt, die in den letzten Jahren zu einer Neubewertung der physikalischen Beiträge Goethes in der *Farbenlehre* geführt haben.[5]

Goethe, Newton – wer hat Recht?

Wer zum Thema ›Goethes Farbenlehre‹ das Wort ergreift, macht die Erfahrung, dass es nahezu unmöglich ist, über die im engeren Sinne physikalischen Teile seiner *Farbenlehre* zu sprechen, ohne sich gleichzeitig auf eine Position in der ›Goethe contra Newton‹-Kontroverse festlegen zu lassen. Die Frage »Wer hat Recht?« ist berechtigt. Sie hat eine lange Tradition, und schließlich war es Goethe selbst, der sie mit seiner Polemik gegen die *Opticks* Newtons einführte, auch wenn er dies später bedauerte. Andererseits zeigt die Rezeptionsgeschichte der *Farbenlehre*, dass diese Frage in eine Sackgasse geführt hat. Es entsteht der Eindruck, dass die Debatte über die *Farbenlehre* und ihre Bedeutung für die physikalische Optik deshalb weitgehend unfruchtbar verlaufen ist, weil sie auf drei Positionen beschränkt geblieben ist: 1. »Pro Newton«, zumeist vertreten von Physikern; 2. »Pro Goethe«, zumeist vertreten von Philosophen und 3. »Beide haben Recht«, vertreten von philosophierenden

1 Ältere Einleitung (vermutl. Anfang 1815), veröffentlicht in den Naturwissenschaftlichen Heften, 4. Heft des ersten Bandes (1817–1822), in: LA, Bd. I 8, S. 182 f.

2 Hermann von Helmholtz (1853), »Über Goethes naturwissenschaftliche Arbeiten«, Vortrag vor der Deutschen Gesellschaft in Königsberg, in: *Vorträge und Reden*, Braunschweig 1896. Bd. 1, S. 1–40; ders., »Goethes Vorahnungen kommender naturwissenschaftlicher Ideen«, Rede, gehalten in der Generalversammlung der Goethe-Gesellschaft in Weimar, 11. Juni 1892, in: ebd., Bd. 2, S. 335–361. Vgl. auch die Nachzeichnung des Wandels im Urteil von Helmholtz in: Friedrich Steinle, »›Das Nächste ans Nächste reihen‹: Goethe, Newton und das Experiment«, in: *Philosophia Naturalis*, 39, 2002, S. 141–172.

3 Zur Rezeptionsgeschichte der *Farbenlehre* Goethes vgl. die entsprechenden Kommentare in der LA. Vgl. ferner *Goethe Handbuch*, Supplemente 2: Naturwissenschaften, hrsg. von Manfred Wenzel, Stuttgart und Weimar 2012. Einen lesenswerten Überblick gibt Volkmar Schüller: »Goethe versus Newton. Zum 250. Geburtstag von Johann Wolfgang von Goethe«, in: *Physikalische Blätter*, 55, 12, Dezember 1999, S. 62–66.

4 Vgl. z. B. Max Born, »Betrachtungen zur Farbenlehre«, in: *Die Naturwissenschaften*, 50, 2, Januar 1963, S. 29–39; Werner Heisenberg (1941), »Die Goethesche und die Newtonsche Farbenlehre im Lichte der modernen Physik«, in: ders, *Wandlungen in den Grundlagen der Naturwissenschaft*, Stuttgart 1959, S. 85–106; ders., »Das Naturbild Goethes und die technisch-naturwissenschaftliche Welt«, Vortrag auf der Hauptversammlung der Goethe-Gesellschaft in Weimar am 21. Mai 1967, in: *Goethe-Jahrbuch*, 29, 1967, S. 27–42; Arnold Sommerfeld, »Goethes Farbenlehre im Urteile der Zeit«, in: *Deutsche Revue*, 42, 3, 1917, S. 100–106; Carl Friedrich von Weizsäcker, »Einige Begriffe aus Goethes Naturwissenschaft«, in: HA, Bd. 13, S. 539–555.

5 Einige Teile des vorliegenden Aufsatzes wurden bereits veröffentlicht in: Johannes Grebe-Ellis, »Goethes Farbenlehre im Lichte neuer Experimente zur Symmetrie spektraler Phänomene«, in: Gernot Böhme (Hrsg.), *Goethes Naturwissenschaft (Schriften der Darmstädter Goethe-Gesellschaft, 7)*, Bielefeld 2017, S. 39–58; Johannes Grebe-Ellis u. a., »Optische Komplementarität. Experimente zur Symmetrie spektraler Phänomene«, in: *Physik Journal*,

cists; 2) "pro Goethe," mainly advocated by philosophers; and 3) "both are right," advocated by philosophical physicists such as Werner Heisenberg and Carl Friedrich von Weizsäcker, who attempted to 'save' Goethe by advocating the thesis that the *Farbenlehre* presents a purely subjective, aesthetic view of reality, which can be granted its own domain of validity that is independent of the objective, physical reality described in Newton's *Opticks*.

If one studies the argumentation of the positions mentioned above, one comes to the surprising conclusion that Olaf Müller, a Berlin-based philosopher of science, emphasizes in the following claim:[6] Goethe's *Farbenlehre*[7] has only been thoroughly studied by a few people, his discovery of the symmetry of spectral phenomena[8] has been overlooked, and serious experimentation to investigate the complementarity of inverse optical spectra has not been carried out. "It [the *Farbenlehre]* is very hard to communicate, ... for, as you know, it requires not only to be read and studied, but to be done, and this is difficult." Goethe informed Eckermann a few months before his death.[9] None of the mentioned physicists have heeded Goethe's request to not only study the *Farbenlehre* theoretically, but also to test it experimentally—a request that Goethe was justified in making, as he himself had done with respect to Newton's *Opticks* by carrying out countless experiments over his forty years of color research.

The question of the results that can be obtained by attempting to physically refine Goethe's argument for symmetry and investigate it experimentally not only provides an escape from the impasse described above; it also leads into an area of research which, by drawing on Goethe's research method, has led to a series of investigations in the last decade that can be understood as contributions to an image-based or phenomenological exploration of optical phenomena.[10] Experimental developments are also part of this area of research and will be described below.

Goethe's Method in the Context of His Time

"Goethe's color research can hardly be understood from the perspective of the history of science if it is not taken seriously as a whole and placed in the context of its time." In the 2016 study[11] *Goethe and the Color Research of his Time (Goethe und die Farbenforschung seiner Zeit)*, Friedrich Steinle, a historian of science in Berlin, points out the astonishing fact that so far hardly anyone has taken Goethe's aspiration seriously to contribute to the science of his time with his theory of colors. "To this day," remarks Steinle, "we are lacking a picture of how Goethe's *Farbenlehre* from 1810 is to be evaluated in the context of contemporary color research."

On the basis of an investigation spanning many years into the status of color research at the end of the eighteenth century, Steinle comes to the conclusion that Goethe's work in the field of color appears "in no way as an exotic undertaking"; rather it "is situated squarely within the research questions of its time." Steinle shows that Goethe had taken up the most important strands of contemporary research and had convincingly and successfully further developed a number of them. It would

7 The work consists of three parts: the *Didactic Part* comprises 920 paragraphs in which Goethe undertakes a systematic arrangement of diverse classes of chromatic phenomena. The *Polemic Part* is dedicated to a critique of Newton's *Opticks;* in 680 paragraphs Goethe presents his critical commentary and documents the results of his analysis of Newton's experiments. The *Historical Part* is still the most comprehensive history of thought and research on color since 1800.

8 From his research on 'colored after-images' (successive contrast) and the phenomenon of 'colored shadows' (chromatic adaptation), Goethe was already aware of the relation of complementary color pairs. In this context, he spoke of "opposing" (entgegengesetzt) and "mutually demanding" colors (wechselweise sich fordernd), and characterized the relationship between a color and its opposite color (Gegenfarbe) as a "totality" *(Didactic Part,* §§ 48–80). In connection with a key insight ("prismatic aperçu") in May 1791, described at the end of the *Historical Part* of the *Farbenlehre* under the title *Confession of the Author,* Goethe discovered that the principle of 'complementary color' could also be found in the context of 'prismatic colors' (ibid., §§ 195–247, 309–40). See the system of Goethe's subjective and objective experiments with optical contrasts in the second section of the *Didactic Part (Physical Colors)* and their summary in the fourth section *(General Introspective Observations)*. LA I, vol. 4. In a supplement to the *Farbenlehre* in the first notebook of the fourth volume of the *Scientific Notebooks* (1817–22), under the title *Complementary Colors (Komplementare Farben),* Goethe notes that "just as with light and darkness, so too do colors immediately demand their opposite, so that, namely in thesis and antithesis, all are always contained. Therefore, the demanded color has been called complementary ..." LA I, vol. 8, p. 190. In modern colorimetry, pairs of visual color sensations are named 'compensative' when they lie on a line that passes through the achromatic point of the CIE chromaticity diagram and their additive mixture is achromatic. On the other hand, color pairs are named 'complementary' when their color stimulus functions can be added to yield white. Complementary colors are therefore always compensative, but that does not hold for the reverse. Moreover, complementary colors must be distinguished from contrast colors, which, as color and opposite color, appear in the context of optical contrast perception and chromatic adaptation, and whose relation depends on the fact that they mutually 'demand' each other in the act of perception. There are, nevertheless, indications that additive-mixing complementary colors become more like contrast colors when desaturated (such as with the Abney effect and Bezold-Brücke effect). See for example Sebastian Hümbert-Schnurr, *Farbe im Spannungsfeld zwischen Wahrnehmung und Messung* (Berlin, 2018).

Physikern wie zum Beispiel Werner Heisenberg oder Carl Friedrich von Weizsäcker, die Goethe zu ›retten‹ versuchten, indem sie die These vertraten, die *Farbenlehre* handele von einer rein subjektiven, ästhetischen Schicht der Wirklichkeit, der unabhängig von der objektiven, in Newtons *Opticks* beschriebenen physikalischen Realität ein eigener, subjektbezogener Geltungsanspruch zugestanden werden könne.

Studiert man die Begründungen der genannten Positionen, gelangt man zu einem überraschenden Ergebnis, das der Berliner Wissenschaftsphilosoph Olaf Müller auf die Feststellung[6] zuspitzt: Die *Farbenlehre*[7] Goethes wurde nur von wenigen gründlich studiert, Goethes Entdeckung[8] der Symmetrie spektraler Phänomene blieb unbeachtet, und ernst zu nehmende Versuche, die Komplementarität inverser optischer Spektren experimentell zu untersuchen, haben nicht stattgefunden. »Sie [die *Farbenlehre]* ist sehr schwer zu überliefern […], denn sie will, wie Sie wissen, nicht bloß gelesen und studiert, sondern sie will getan sein, und das hat seine Schwierigkeit«, so Goethe zu Eckermann wenige Monate vor seinem Tod.[9] Keiner der genannten Physiker ist der Aufforderung Goethes gefolgt, die physikalischen Teile seiner *Farbenlehre* nicht nur theoretisch zu studieren, sondern sie im Experiment zu prüfen – eine Forderung, die Goethe zu Recht stellen konnte, nachdem er sie gegenüber der *Opticks* Newtons in seiner über 40 Jahre währenden Beschäftigung mit der Farbenlehre in zahllosen Experimenten selbst erfüllt hatte.

Die Frage, zu welchen Ergebnissen man kommt, wenn man versucht, Goethes Symmetrieargument physikalisch zu präzisieren und experimentell zu untersuchen, eröffnet vor diesem Hintergrund nicht nur einen Ausweg aus der oben beschriebenen Sackgasse. Sie führt darüber hinaus in ein Forschungsfeld, in dem die Anknüpfung an die Forschungsmethode Goethes in den letzten Jahrzehnten zu einer Reihe von Arbeiten geführt hat, die sich als Beiträge zu einer bildoptischen beziehungsweise phänomenologischen Erschließung optischer Phänomene verstehen.[10] Diesem Forschungsfeld sind auch die experimentellen Entwicklungen zuzurechnen, von denen weiter unten berichtet wird.

Goethes Arbeitsweise im Kontext seiner Zeit

»Goethes Farbenforschung kann wissenschaftshistorisch nicht verstanden werden, ohne dass sie in ihrer Breite ernst genommen und in den Kontext ihrer Zeit gesetzt wird.« In einer Studie[11] von 2016 über *Goethe und die Farbenforschung seiner Zeit* verweist der Berliner Wissenschaftshistoriker Friedrich Steinle auf die erstaunliche Tatsache, dass in der umfangreichen Forschungsliteratur zu Goethes Farbenlehre bisher kaum jemand Goethes Anspruch ernst genommen hat, mit seiner Farbenlehre einen Beitrag zur Wissenschaft seiner Zeit zu liefern. »Bis heute«, so Steinle, »fehlt uns ein Bild davon, wie Goethes *Farbenlehre* von 1810 in der zeitgenössischen Farbenforschung einzuschätzen ist«.

Auf der Grundlage langjähriger Untersuchungen zur Situation der Farbenforschung am Ende des 18. Jahrhunderts kommt Steinle zu dem Ergebnis, dass sich Goethes Arbeit auf dem Feld der Farbenlehre »keinesfalls als exotische Unternehmung, sondern als mitten in den Forschungsfragen seiner Zeit befindlich darstellt«. Steinle kann zeigen, dass Goethe die wichtigsten Stränge der zeitgenössischen Forschung aufgegriffen und in mehreren Bereichen überzeugend und erfolgreich weitergeführt hat. Offenbar ging es Goethe bei der Konzep-

16, 3, März 2017, S. 43–49; ders. und Matthias Rang, »Power Area Density in Inverse Spectra«, *Journal for General Philosophy of Science*, März 2018, https://doi.org/10.1007/s10838-017-9394-8 (Stand: 20.07.2018).

6 Olaf L. Müller, *Mehr Licht. Goethe mit Newton im Streit um die Farben*, München 2015.

7 Das Werk besteht aus drei Teilen: Der *Didaktische Teil* umfasst 920 Paragraphen, in denen Goethe eine systematische Anordnung verschiedener Klassen von Farbphänomenen unternimmt. Der *Polemische Teil* ist der Kritik an Newtons *Opticks* gewidmet; Goethe legt in 680 Paragraphen seine kritische Lektüre vor und dokumentiert die Ergebnisse seiner Analyse der Experimente Newtons. Der *Historische Teil* stellt die bis heute umfassendste Geschichte der Farbenlehre bis 1800 dar.

8 Aus seinen Untersuchungen zu ›farbigen Nachbildern‹ (Sukzessivkontrast) und zum Phänomen des ›farbigen Schattens‹ (chromatische Adaption) war Goethe die Beziehung sich ergänzender Farbpaare bereits bekannt. Er spricht in diesem Zusammenhang von »entgegengesetzten« bzw. sich »wechselweise fordernden« Farben und charakterisiert die Beziehung zwischen Farbe und Gegenfarbe als »Totalität« (*Didaktischer Teil*, §§ 48–80). Dass sich das Prinzip der ›Gegenfarbigkeit‹ auch im Kontext der ›prismatischen Farben‹ auffinden lässt (ebd., §§ 195–247, 309–340), entdeckte Goethe in Anknüpfung an ein Schlüsselerlebnis (»Prismenaperçu«) im Mai 1791, das er am Ende der *Geschichte der Farbenlehre* unter dem Titel *Konfession des Verfassers* beschreibt. Vgl. die Systematik der subjektiven und objektiven Experimente Goethes an entgegengesetzten optischen Kontrasten in der 2. Abteilung des *Didaktischen Teils (Physische Farben)* sowie deren Zusammenfassung in der 4. Abteilung *(Allgemeine Ansichten nach innen)*, LA, Bd. I 4. In einem *Komplementare Farben* überschriebenen Nachtrag zur *Farbenlehre* im ersten Heft des 4. Bandes der *Naturwissenschaftlichen Hefte* (1817–1822) fasst Goethe zusammen, »dass ebenso wie Hell und Dunkel auch die Farben sich ihrem Gegensatze nach unmittelbar fordern, so dass, nämlich im Satz und Gegensatz, alle immer zugleich enthalten sind. Deswegen hat man auch die geforderten Farben komplementare [sic!] genannt […].« LA, Bd. I 8, S. 190. – In der heutigen Farbmetrik werden Paare visueller Farbempfindungen als ›kompensativ‹ bezeichnet, die sich in der CIE-Normtafel auf einer Geraden durch den Unbuntpunkt gegenüber liegen und aus denen man additiv Unbunt ermischen kann. Im Unterschied dazu bezeichnet man Farbpaare als ›komplementär‹, wenn sich ihre Farbreizfunktionen additiv zu Weiß ergänzen. Komplementärfarben sind also stets auch kompensativ, aber nicht umgekehrt. Ferner sind Komplementärfarben von Kontrastfarben zu unterscheiden, die als Farben und Gegenfarben im Kontext der optischen Kontrastwahrnehmung und chromatischen Adaption auftre-

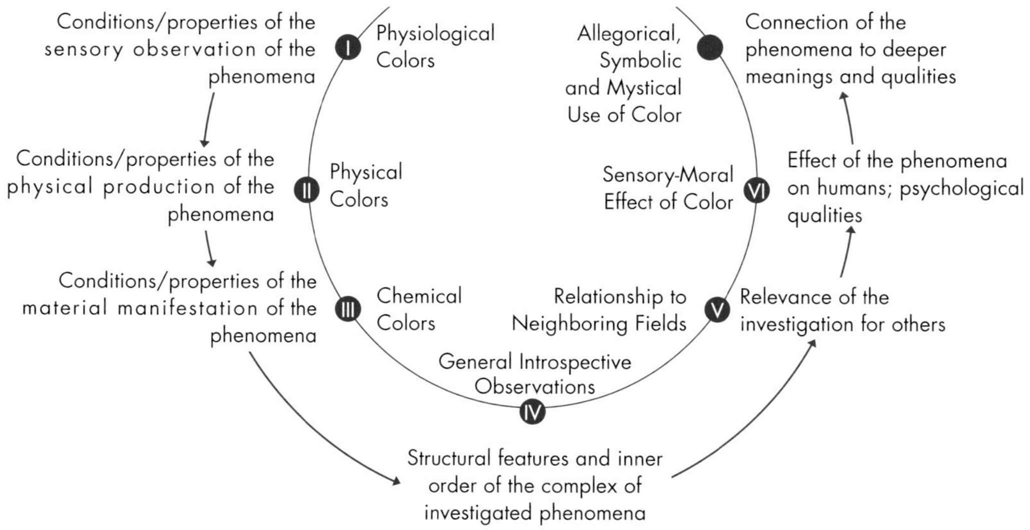

1 The structure of the *Didactic Part* of the *Farbenlehre* as an outline of a genetic, multiperspective approach to research. Inner part: The six sections of the *Didactic Part* with the addition of Rang and Kühl's suggested section *Allegorical, Symbolic and Mystical Use of Color*. Outer part: Generalized formulation of the respective research perspective based on Rang and Kühl (2014, pp. 162–63).

appear that Goethe, in conceiving his *Farbenlehre,* was attempting nothing less than to bring the technical and artistic practical knowledge and the extensive scientific color research of his time "under an encompassing approach that unified all the individual areas under a single principle."[12] In view of this primary goal, "the polemical dispute with the dominant physical theories of light and color" was of secondary importance, a means to an end. To bring color in its relation to the eye, as the result of physical conditions and a property of bodies, "under a common principle, which is most prominently expressed in the color circle, was his central intention[13]—far more important than the polemic" (see figure 1).

A further aspect of Goethe's scientific research that, even though it has been partly investigated, has so far scarcely been viewed in a historical context: it is his own research method. In connection with his chromatic studies, Goethe develops his own reflections on phenomena, theories, and experimentation, i.e., the way that theoretical conclusions are drawn from observations and experiments. The methodological writings that appear in this context show that he had greater concerns than just critically reflecting on his own methodology and demarcating it from Newton's. They present an outline of a general method of experimental research, which contains considerations that are still relevant today on the conditions and possibilities for acquiring knowledge based on experimental data.[14]

How Goethe's philosophical reflections relate to his own scientific practice and fit into the historical context of the French Enlightenment has been investigated by Steinle in the comprehensive study *"Experience of a Higher Kind": Goethe, Experimental Method and the French Enlightenment ("Erfahrung der höhern Art": Goethe, die experimentelle Methode und die französische Aufklärung).*[15] On the basis of Goethe's key methodological text *The Experiment as Mediator between Object and Subject,* Steinle reconstructs Goethe's epistemological critique of stand-

9 *Conversations of Goethe with Eckermann and Soret,* trans. John Oxenford (London, 1850), vol. 2, p. 410.

10 See for example the contributions to phenomenological optics in the book series *Phänomenologie in der Naturwissenschaft* (Berlin). This draws upon, among others, Gernot Böhme's concept of the "phenomenology of nature" as found in "Ist Goethes Farbenlehre Wissenschaft?" *Studia Leibnitiana* 9 (1977), pp. 27–54; Böhme and Gregor Schiemann, *Phänomenologie der Natur* (Berlin, 1997); see also the 'image optical' writings of Georg Maier, who explicitly builds on Rudolf Steiner's studies of Goethe in Maier, *Optik der Bilder* (Dürnau, 1986); Maier, *blicken – sehen – schauen,* ed. Johannes Grebe-Ellis (Dürnau 2004).

11 Friedrich Steinle, "Goethe und die Farbenforschung seiner Zeit," in *Die Farben der Klassik,* ed. Martin Dönike et al. (Göttingen, 2016), pp. 255–89.

12 In an investigation of the structure of the *Didactic Part* of the *Farbenlehre,* Rang und Kühl have shown that the order of its six sections is not arbitrarily chosen, but rather follows a compositional principle that was called a "model for physical research" by Schiller in a letter to Goethe, and can be understood as a generalizable program of an interdisciplinary, multi-perspective approach to research. See Johannes Kühl and Matthias Rang, "ein Muster…, wie man physikalische Forschung behandeln soll…," *Elemente der Naturwissenschaft* 100 (2014), pp. 152–71. In this connection, it is interesting that, as a text from 1793 with the title *A Few General Propositions (Einige allgemeine Sätze)* demonstrates, Goethe originally had the idea of involving "a community of diverse men" in his *Farbenlehre* by working with various specific areas of research—

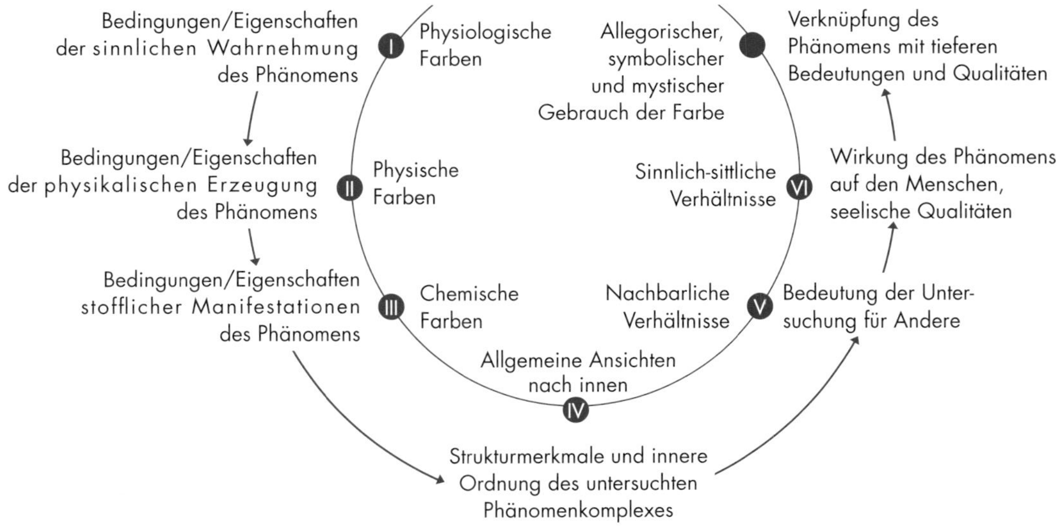

1 Der Aufbau des *Didaktischen Teils der Farbenlehre* als Entwurf eines genetisch angelegten, multiperspektivischen Forschungsansatzes. Innen: Die sechs Abteilungen des Didaktischen Teils, ergänzt nach einem Vorschlag von Rang und Kühl durch den Abschnitt *Allegorischer, symbolischer und mystischer Gebrauch der Farbe*. Außen: Verallgemeinerte Formulierung der jeweiligen Forschungsperspektive, angelehnt an Rang und Kühl (2014, S. 162 f.).

tion der *Farbenlehre* um nichts Geringeres als den Versuch, das technische und künstlerische Praxiswissen sowie die weitverzweigten naturwissenschaftlichen Farbforschungen seiner Zeit »zu einem umfassenden, alle einzelnen Bereiche unter einem gemeinsamen Prinzip vereinenden Ansatz[12] zusammenzubinden«. In Hinblick auf dieses übergeordnete Ziel war »die polemische Auseinandersetzung mit der vorherrschenden physikalischen Licht- und Farbentheorie« von untergeordneter Bedeutung, nur Mittel zum Zweck. Farbe in ihrer Beziehung zum Auge, als Folge physikalischer Bedingungen und als Eigenschaft von Körpern »unter ein gemeinsames Prinzip zu stellen, das im Farbenkreis seinen markantesten Ausdruck fand, war ihm das zentrale Anliegen[13] – weit wichtiger als die Polemik« (vgl. Abb. 1).

Ein weiterer Aspekt der naturwissenschaftlichen Forschung Goethes, der zwar punktuell untersucht, bisher aber kaum im historischen Kontext betrachtet wurde, betrifft seine eigene Forschungsmethode. Im Zusammenhang mit seinen Farbstudien entwickelte Goethe eigene Überlegungen zum Verhältnis von Phänomen, Theorie und Experiment, das heißt zu der Art und Weise, wie aus Beobachtungen und Experimenten theoretische Schlussfolgerungen gezogen werden. Die methodischen Schriften, die in diesem Zusammenhang entstanden, zeigen, dass es ihm dabei um mehr ging, als nur die eigene Arbeitspraxis kritisch zu reflektieren und gegen das Vorgehen Newtons abzugrenzen. Sie stellen den Entwurf einer allgemeinen Methodik der Experimentalforschung dar, die auch heute noch gültige Überlegungen zu den Bedingungen und Möglichkeiten der Erkenntnisgewinnung auf der Basis experimentell gewonnener Daten enthält.[14]

Wie sich diese wissenschaftstheoretischen Überlegungen Goethes zu seiner eigenen Forschungspraxis verhalten und sich in den historischen Kontext der französischen Aufklärung einfügen, ist von Steinle in einer umfassenden Studie von 2014 über *»Erfahrung der höhern Art« – Goethe, die experimentelle Methode und die französische Aufklärung* untersucht worden.[15] Auf der Grundlage des methodischen Schlüsseltextes *Der Versuch als Vermittler von Objekt und Subjekt* rekonstruiert Steinle Goethes epistemologische Kritik am

ten und deren Beziehung darauf beruht, dass sie sich im Sehakt gegenseitig ›fordern‹. Es gibt allerdings Hinweise darauf, dass die additiv mischenden Komplementärfarben unter Entsättigung den Kontrastfarben ähnlicher werden (Abney-Effekt und Bezold-Brücke-Effekt), vgl. Sebastian Hümbert-Schnurr, *Farbe im Spannungsfeld zwischen Wahrnehmung und Messung*, Berlin 2018.

9 Johann Peter Eckermann, *Gespräche mit Goethe in den letzten Jahren seines Lebens 1823-1832*, Gespräch vom 21. Dezember 1831, FA, Bd. 39, S. 490 ff.

10 Vgl. z. B. die Beiträge zur Phänomenologischen Optik in der Buchreihe *Phänomenologie in der Naturwissenschaft*, die ihr programmatisches Selbstverständnis u. a. auf Gernot Böhmes Konzept der »Phänomenologie der Natur« bezieht: Gernot Böhme, »Ist Goethes Farbenlehre Wissenschaft?«, in: *Studia Leibnitiana*, 9, 1, 1977, S. 27–54; ders. und Gregor Schiemann (Hrsg.), *Phänomenologie der Natur*, Berlin 1997. Vgl. ferner die bildoptischen Schriften Georg Maiers, der explizit an Rudolf Steiners Goethe-Arbeiten anknüpft: Georg Maier, *Optik der Bilder*, Dürnau 1986; ders., *blicken – sehen – schauen*, hrsg. von Johannes Grebe-Ellis, Dürnau 2004.

11 Friedrich Steinle, »Goethe und die Farbenforschung seiner Zeit«, in: *Die Farben der Klassik (Schriftenreihe des Zentrums für Klassikforschung, 3)*, hrsg. von Martin Dönike u. a., Göttingen 2016, S. 255–289.

12 Rang und Kühl haben in einer strukturellen Untersuchung zum Aufbau des *Didaktischen Teils* der *Farbenlehre* gezeigt, dass die Anordnung der sechs Abteilungen nicht willkürlich gewählt ist, sondern einem Kompositionsprinzip folgt, das von Schiller in einem Brief an Goethe als »Muster physikalischer

alone experiments and sketches a method of "manifolding" them through the systematic variation of the parameters in the experimental setup: "According to Goethe's general thesis, the basis for theorizing first appears in the form of a series of experiments adjacent to one another." For it is only in varying the individual observations that the functional relations of an observational context can become visible. This leads, following the example of the "mathematical method,"[16] to a kind of experience composed of many others, which Goethe therefore called "an experience of a higher kind." Only this "experience of a higher kind," which Goethe also sometimes referred to as "pure phenomenon" or "archetypal phenomenon," can present the basis of empirical rules and generalizing conclusions. By drawing a connection[17] to the French encyclopedists d'Alembert and Diderot, Steinle was able to show that Goethe's methodological considerations are "in no way as exotic as sometimes presented." Regarding considerations of this kind, the question of whether there were, in addition to the editors of the *Encyclopédie,* other parallels or possible exemplars cannot be conclusively answered at present. However, it is already "clear that Goethe, with his reflections on experimental practice and reasoning, was employing a practice that is encountered far more widely in science than has been assumed so far, and therefore deserves a prominent place in a yet to be written history of the philosophy of experiment."

New Experiments Confirming the Symmetry of Spectral Phenomena

In view of new historical and philosophical investigations on Goethe's *Farbenlehre,* let us return to the initial question of how the 'optical seeds' fare today from the perspective of modern physics. The answer is given by experimental developments that have been elaborated in the last ten years by the physicist Matthias Rang.[18] These developments relate to Goethe's investigations in the third section of the *Didactic Part,*—the more strictly physical part of the *Farbenlehre*—which was the most important part for Goethe, and which also suffered the harshest rejection by physicists. Using technical optics, Rang shows how the unity of complementary spectral phenomena, which was discovered by Goethe but remained neglected in optics, can be framed in terms of physics and demonstrated to be a fundamental condition of these phenomena.

The results of Rang's experiments can be summarized as follows: Goethe discovered complementarity as a symmetric property of spectral phenomena. According to modern physics, complementary and inverse spectral states result from the conservation of energy of the optical system. Complementary spectra arise simultaneously from a mirrored slit aperture and are functionally dependent on each other, like with the transmission and reflection of a filter. The experiments represent symmetrical extensions and generalizations of Newton's experiments.

How did Goethe arrive at the idea of the symmetry of spectral phenomena? He searched for the observable conditions for the appearance of color. For him, the most fundamental of these conditions seemed to be that color only appears at

today one would say, forming a scientific research cooperation. He had in mind a chemist, physicist, mathematician, engineer, natural historian, painter, historian, critic, anatomist, and philosopher (LA I, vol. 3, pp. 130–36).

13 This enumeration refers to the first four sections of the *Didactic Part:* 1) *Psychological Colors,* 2) *Physical Colors,* 3) *Chemical Colors,* 4) *General Introspective Observations.*

14 Beside dispersed methodological remarks in *Contributions to Optics (Beiträge zur Optik)* from 1791–92 and in the *Farbenlehre* from 1810, two articles in particular are worth mentioning as key philosophical texts: first, *The Experiment as Mediator between Object and Subject (Der Versuch als Vermittler von Objekt und Subjekt), Naturwissenschaftliche Hefte* (1792), LA, vol. I 8, pp. 305–15; second, *The Pure Phenomenon (Das reine Phänomen)* (1798), LA, vol. I 3, pp. 306–08, or LA, vol. I 11, pp. 39–40. For Goethe's understanding of science, see also Rudolf Steiner, *Nature's Open Secret: Introductions to Goethe's Scientific Writings* (New York, 1910). This volume contains introductions and commentary on Goethe's scientific writings, as edited by Steiner 1884–97, in the context of the Kürschner-Ausgabe. See especially Chapter XVI: "Goethe As Thinker and Researcher." See Michael Mandelartz, "Goethe, Newton und die Wissenschaftstheorie: Zur Wissenschaftskritik und zur Methodologie der Farbenlehre," in *Goethe, Kleist* (Berlin, 2011), pp. 240–81.

15 Friedrich Steinle, "'Erfahrung der höhern Art': Goethe, die experimentelle Methode und die französische Aufklärung," in *Heikle Balancen: Die Weimarer Klassik im Prozess der Moderne,* ed. Thorsten Valk (Göttingen, 2014), pp. 221–49; see also Friedrich Steinle, "'Das Nächste ans Nächste reihen': Goethe, Newton und das Experiment," *Philosophia Naturalis* 39 (2002), pp. 141–72.

16 In the aforementioned article *The Experiment as Mediator between Object and Subject,* one finds, "From the mathematician we must learn the meticulous care required to connect things in unbroken succession, or rather, to derive things step by step. Even where we do not venture to apply mathematics we must always work as though we had to satisfy the strictest of geometricians. In the mathematical method (emphasis added by Johannes Grebe-Ellis) we find an approach which by its deliberate and pure nature instantly exposes every leap in an assertion": Douglas Miller, *Scientific Studies* (New York, 1988), p. 16. See also "Relationship to Mathematics," Didactic Part §§ 722–29; Wolfgang Krohn, "Goethes Versuch über den Versuch," in *Goethe und die Verzeitlichung der Natur,* ed. Peter Matussek (Munich, 1998), pp. 399–413.

17 In an 1826 text from the archive, *On Mathematics and its Abuse,* Goethe cites d'Alembert from the *Encyclopédie,* and thus he himself gives an indication of the methodical parallels between his

Einzelexperiment und skizziert seine Methode der »Vermannigfaltigung« von Experimenten durch systematische Variation der Parameter im experimentellen Aufbau. »Erst in Form einer Reihe von aneinander grenzenden Versuchen, so Goethes Generalthese, tauge die Erfahrung als Grundlage des Theoretisierens.« Denn erst die »Vermannigfaltigung« einzelner Beobachtungen lasse die funktionalen Verknüpfungen eines Beobachtungszusammenhangs sichtbar werden. Sie führe nach dem Vorbild der »mathematischen Methode«[16] zu einer Art von Erfahrung, die aus mehreren anderen besteht und die Goethe deshalb »Erfahrungen der höhern Art« genannt hat. Erst diese »Erfahrungen der höhern Art«, von Goethe gelegentlich auch als »reine Phänomene« oder »Urphänomene« bezeichnet, können den Ausgangspunkt empirischer Regeln und verallgemeinernder Schlussfolgerungen darstellen. – Durch den Bezug[17] auf die französischen Enzyklopädisten d'Alembert und Diderot gelingt es Steinle, zu zeigen, dass Goethes methodologische Überlegungen »keineswegs so exotisch waren wie bisweilen dargestellt«. Die Frage, ob es zu dieser Art von Überlegungen neben den Herausgebern der *Encyclopédie* weitere Parallelen oder mögliche Vorbilder gibt, kann heute nicht abschließend beantwortet werden. Schon jetzt ist aber »deutlich, dass Goethe mit seinen Reflexionen zum experimentellen Arbeiten und Schließen eine in der Naturwissenschaft viel breiter anzutreffende Arbeitsweise erfasst hat als bislang angenommen und damit in einer (erst noch zu schreibenden) Geschichte der Philosophie des Experiments einen markanten Platz verdient«.

Neue Experimente bestätigen die Symmetrie spektraler Phänomene

Vor dem Hintergrund der Ausblicke auf neuere historische und wissenschaftsphilosophische Untersuchungen zu Goethes *Farbenlehre* kommen wir zurück auf die eingangs gestellte Frage, wie es heute aus der Sicht der Physik um die ›optische Saat‹ Goethes bestellt ist? Die Antwort darauf geben experimentelle Entwicklungen, die in den letzten zehn Jahren von dem Physiker Matthias Rang ausgearbeitet wurden.[18] Sie beziehen sich auf Goethes Untersuchungen in der dritten Abteilung des *Didaktischen Teils,* das heißt auf den im engeren Sinne physikalischen Teil der *Farbenlehre,* der Goethe am wichtigsten war – und der zugleich von den Physikern die schärfste Ablehnung erfuhr. Rang zeigt mit den Mitteln der technischen Optik, wie sich die von Goethe entdeckte, aber in der Optik bisher vernachlässigte Eigenschaft der Zusammengehörigkeit komplementärer Spektralphänomene in eine physikalische Problemstellung übersetzen und als fundamentale Bedingung solcher Phänomene nachweisen lässt.

Die Ergebnisse der Experimente Rangs lassen sich folgendermaßen zusammenfassen: Goethe entdeckte die Komplementarität als Symmetrieeigenschaft spektraler Phänomene. Komplementäre und inverse spektrale Zustände folgen nach heutigem Verständnis aus der Energieerhaltung des optischen Systems. Komplementäre Spektren entstehen simultan an einer verspiegelten Spaltblende und bedingen sich funktionell wie Transmission und Reflexion an einem Filter. Die entsprechenden Experimente stellen symmetrisierte Erweiterungen und Verallgemeinerungen der Experimente Newtons dar.

Auf welchem Weg gelangte Goethe zu der Auffassung von der Symmetrie spektraler Farbphänomene? Er suchte nach den beobachtbaren Bedingungen der Farbentstehung.

Forschung« bezeichnet wurde und das sich als verallgemeinerbares Programm eines interdisziplinären und multiperspektiven Forschungsansatzes lesen lässt. Vgl. Johannes Kühl und Matthias Rang, »›ein Muster ..., wie man physikalische Forschung behandeln soll ...‹ Eine Betrachtung zum ›goetheanistischen Vorgehen in der Physik am Beispiel von Goethes Farbenlehre«, in: *Elemente der Naturwissenschaft,* 100, 2014, S. 152–172. Interessant ist in diesem Zusammenhang, dass Goethe, wie ein mit *Einige allgemeine Sätze* überschriebener Text von 1793 belegt, ursprünglich die Idee hatte, »eine Gesellschaft verschiedenartiger Männer« an seiner *Farbenlehre* durch Übertragung einzelner Fachgebiete zu beteiligen – heute würde man sagen: eine wissenschaftliche Forschungskooperation zu bilden. Er dachte dabei an Chemiker, Physiker, Mathematiker, Mechaniker, Naturhistoriker, Maler, Historiker, Kritiker, Anatom, Philosoph (LA, Bd. I 3, S. 130–136).

13 Gemeint sind mit dieser Aufzählung die ersten vier Abteilungen des *Didaktischen Teils:* 1. *Physiologische Farben,* 2. *Physische Farben,* 3. *Chemische Farben,* 4. *Allgemeine Ansichten nach innen.*

14 Neben verstreuten methodischen Anmerkungen in den *Beiträgen zur Optik* von 1791/92 und in dem *Entwurf einer Farbenlehre* von 1810 sind als wissenschaftsphilosophische Schlüsseltexte Goethes insbesondere zwei Aufsätze zu nennen: 1. *Der Versuch als Vermittler von Objekt und Subjekt* (1792), *Naturwissenschaftliche Hefte.* LA, Bd. I 8, S. 305–315; 2. *Das reine Phänomen* (1798), LA, Bd. I 3, S. 306–308 oder LA, Bd. I 11, S. 39–40. Vgl. zum Wissenschaftsverständnis Goethes auch Rudolf Steiner, *Einleitungen zu Goethes Naturwissenschaftlichen Schriften* (Einleitungen und Kommentare zu den 1884–1897 von Steiner herausgegebenen naturwissenschaftlichen Schriften Goethes im Rahmen der Kürschner-Ausgabe), Dornach 1987, insbes. Kap. XVI: »Goethe als Denker und Forscher«, S. 258–301. Vgl. ferner Michael Mandelartz, »Goethe, Newton und die Wissenschaftstheorie. Zur Wissenschaftskritik und zur Methodologie der Farbenlehre«, in: ders., *Goethe, Kleist. Literatur, Politik und Wissenschaft um 1800,* Berlin 2011, S. 240–281.

15 Friedrich Steinle, »›Erfahrung der höhern Art‹. Goethe, die experimentelle Methode und die französische Aufklärung«, in: *Heikle Balancen. Die Weimarer Klassik im Prozess der Moderne,* hrsg. von Thorsten Valk Göttingen 2014, S. 221–249; vgl. auch ders., »›Das Nächste ans Nächste reihen‹: Goethe, Newton und das Experiment«, in: *Philosophia Naturalis,* 39, 1, 2002, S. 141–172.

16 In dem o. g. Aufsatz *Der Versuch als Vermittler von Objekt und Subjekt* heißt es u. a. »Diese Bedächtlichkeit nur das Nächste ans Nächste zu reihen, oder vielmehr das Nächste aus dem Nächsten zu folgern, haben wir von den Mathematikern zu lernen, und selbst da, wo wir uns keiner Rechnung

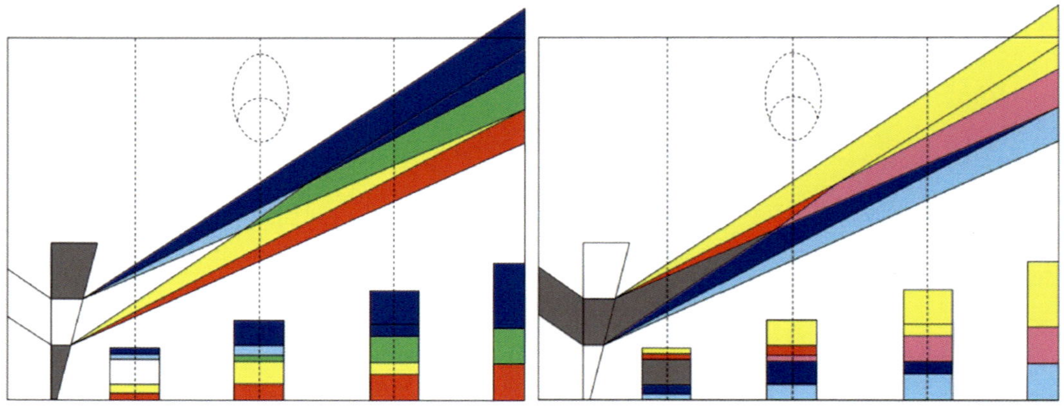

2 Goethes Darstellung zur Entstehung komplementärer Vollspektren durch sukzessive Überlagerung komplementärer Kantenspektren als Funktion des Abstands vom Prisma. Links: Spaltspektrum, rechts der symmetrische Fall des Stegspektrums, bei dem der Spalt durch einen Steg bzw. das Lichtbündel in dunkler Umgebung durch ein Schattenbündel in heller Umgebung ersetzt ist. | Goethe's representation of the formation of complementary complete spectra by successive overlapping of complementary edge spectra as a function of the distance from prism. Left: slit spectrum. Right: the complementary case of the bar spectrum in which the slit is replaced by a bar, i.e., the light rays in a dark environment are replaced by a shadow in a light environment.

optical contrasts, i.e., at the limits of light and darkness. By systematically varying and inverting these contrast conditions, Goethe arrived at the realization that producing images by passing inverse optical contrasts through a prism always results in isomorphic, complementary spectra. Against the background of the representation he had found in Newton's *Opticks,* this was an unexpected discovery. In light of the symmetrical conditions of appearance, it seemed consistent to Goethe to view the complementary spectrum as the equal counterpart to Newton's spectrum, and to emphasize that the spectra belong together (see figure 2). It is therefore immediately understandable why Goethe could also see, in the organizational schema of the color circle, an adequate representation of the lawfulness he found with respect to the complementarity and mixing of color.

It seemed obvious to Goethe to expect a theory of spectral phenomena to take into account the symmetry that the phenomena show. Because of this, he insisted on the observation that, for color to arise, an interaction of light and darkness is always necessary. Newton's limitation by the slit spectrum awoke in him the impression of an arbitrary interference with empirical data, an interference that resulted in the suppression of a whole class of phenomena and with it a structural feature of spectral phenomena, which could be observed in other areas such as atmospheric and polarized colors and therefore seemed of general significance.

Goethe could only provide qualitative and rudimentary experimental verifications of optical complementarity as a symmetrical property of spectral phenomena. Nevertheless, with his experimentation and representation of the formation of color at inverse optical contrasts, Goethe sketched the methodological path that should, in principle, lead to such verification. It was the Norwegian André Bjerke who, in the 1950s, symmetrized spectral phenomena through systematic inversion, i.e., turned the interchange of light and darkness in Newton's most important experiments into a research program.[19] The decisive breakthrough that led to the success of this program was first made by Matthias Rang, who built on Torger Holtsmark's work with the introduction of a mirrored slit aperture and the concept of an optical light room (see figures 3, 4, and 5).

method of "manifolding" (Vermannigfaltigung) and mathematics. See Steiner's footnote to the d'Alembert quote: "The first proposition in mathematics is for Goethe an experience of a higher kind in science. The way that d'Alembert also thinks of this manifolding of the proposition is completely analogous to what Goethe says about the relation between experience of a higher kind and normal empirical experience." Goethe, *Naturwissenschaftliche Schriften,* vol. 2 (1982), ed. Rudolf Steiner. Photomechanical reproduction of the first edition (1884–97). 4th Edition (Dornach, 1982), p. 47.

18 Matthias Rang, *Phänomenologie komplementärer Spektren* (Berlin, 2015); Johannes Grebe-Ellis and Matthias Rang, "Komplementäre Spektren – Experimente mit einer Spiegel-Spalt-Blende," *Mathematisch Naturwissenschaftlicher Unterricht (MNU)* 62 (2009), pp. 227–31; Johannes Grebe-Ellis et al., "Optische Komplementarität: Experimente zur Symmetrie spektraler Phänomene," *Physik Journal* 16 (2017), pp. 43–49.

19 With his suggestion of constructing a mechanical inversion of Newton's fundamental experiment, Goethe was able to give a perspicuous presentation of his discovery of the symmetry of complementary spectra. From a modern perspective, however, the impression arises that with this example of inversion, Goethe also helped foster an incomplete, mechanical understanding of inversion. In the twentieth century, this resulted in a tradition of attempts at inversion that were to remain ineffective so long as it was not recognized that the inversion problem is in principle not mechanically but optically soluble. It is nevertheless worth mentioning the work of Kirschmann, who in 1917 was the first to show that the inverted spectrum can in principle be used spectroscopically in the same way as the slit spectrum. See August Kirschmann, "Das umgekehrte Spektrum und seine Komplementärverhältnisse," *Physikalische*

bedienen, müssen wir immer so zu Werke gehen, als wenn wir dem strengsten Geometer Rechenschaft zu geben schuldig wären. Denn eigentlich ist es die mathematische Methode [Hervorhebung J. G-E], welche wegen ihrer Bedächtlichkeit und Reinheit gleich jeden Sprung in der Assertion offenbart [..].« S. ferner *Verhältnis zur Mathematik, Didaktischer Teil* § 722–729. Vgl. dazu Wolfgang Krohn, »Goethes Versuch über den Versuch«, in: *Goethe und die Verzeitlichung der Natur,* hrsg. von Peter Matussek, München 1998, S. 399–413.

17 In dem Nachlasstext *Über Mathematik und deren Missbrauch* (1826) zitiert Goethe d'Alembert aus der *Encyclopédie* und liefert auf diese Weise selbst den Hinweis auf die methodische Parallele seines Verfahrens der »Vermannigfaltigung« zur Mathematik. Vgl. die Fußnote Steiners zu Goethes d'Alembert-Zitat: »Die erste Proposition ist in der Mathematik das, was für Goethe in der Naturwissenschaft eine Erfahrung der höhern Art ist. Auch die Art, wie d'Alembert sich die Vermannichfaltigung dieser Proposition denkt, ist vollkommen dem analog, was Goethe über den Zusammenhang der Erfahrung der höhern Art und der gewöhnlichen empirischen sagt.« Johann Wolfgang von Goethe, *Naturwissenschaftliche Schriften,* hrsg. und eingeleitet von Rudolf Steiner, fotomechanischer Nachdruck der Erstauflage (1884–1897), Bd. 2, 4. Aufl., Dornach 1982, S. 47.

18 Matthias Rang, *Phänomenologie komplementärer Spektren (Phänomenologie in der Naturwissenschaft, 9),* Berlin 2015; Johannes Grebe-Ellis und Matthias Rang, »Komplementäre Spektren – Experimente mit einer Spiegel-Spalt-Blende«, in: *Mathematisch Naturwissenschaftlicher Unterricht (MNU),* 62, 4 2009, S. 227–231; Johannes Grebe-Ellis u. a., »Optische Komplementarität. Experimente zur Symmetrie spektraler Phänomene«, In: *Physik Journal,* 16, 3, 2017, S. 43–49.

Die grundlegendste dieser Bedingungen zeigte sich ihm darin, dass Farben stets an optischen Kontrasten, das heißt an Hell-Dunkel-Grenzen entstehen. Durch die systematische Variation und Umkehrung dieser Kontrastbedingung gelangte Goethe zu der Feststellung, dass die Abbildung zueinander inverser optischer Kontraste durch ein Prisma stets zu isomorphen und komplementären Spektren führt. Vor dem Hintergrund der Darstellung, die er in Newtons *Opticks* gefunden hatte, war dies eine unerwartete Entdeckung. Angesichts der symmetrischen Entstehungsbedingungen erschien es ihm nur folgerichtig, das komplementäre Spektrum als gleichwertiges Gegenstück zu Newtons Spektrum anzusehen und die Zusammengehörigkeit der Spektren hervorzuheben (Abb. 2). Und es ist unmittelbar nachvollziehbar, weshalb Goethe in dem Ordnungsschema des Farbkreises auch für die Entstehung der ›prismatischen Farben‹ eine angemessene Darstellung der gefundenen Regelmäßigkeiten hinsichtlich der Ergänzungs- und Mischungsverhältnisse der Farben sehen konnte.

Es erschien Goethe selbstverständlich, von einer Theorie spektraler Phänomene eine Berücksichtigung der Symmetrieverhältnisse zu erwarten, die die Phänomene zeigten. Aus diesem Grunde beharrte er auf der Beobachtung, dass es zur Entstehung von Farbe stets des Zusammenwirkens von Hell und Dunkel bedürfe. Newtons Beschränkung auf das Spaltspektrum weckte bei ihm den Eindruck eines willkürlichen Eingriffs in die Empirie, der die Unterdrückung einer ganzen Klasse von Phänomenen und damit eines Strukturmerkmals spektraler Phänomene zufolge hatte, das auch in anderen Bereichen wie zum Beispiel bei den atmosphärischen Farben oder den Polarisationsfarben zu beobachten war und insofern von allgemeinerer Bedeutung zu sein schien.

Den experimentellen Nachweis der optischen Komplementarität als Symmetrieeigenschaft spektraler Farbphänomene konnte Goethe nur qualitativ und ansatzweise liefern. Mit seinen Experimenten und Darstellungen zur Farbentstehung an inversen optischen Kontrasten skizzierte er immerhin den methodischen Weg, auf dem sich dieser Nachweis im Prinzip führen lassen sollte. Es war der Norweger André Bjerke, der in den 50er-Jahren des 20. Jahrhunderts die Symmetrisierung der spektralen Farbphänomene durch systematisches Invertie-

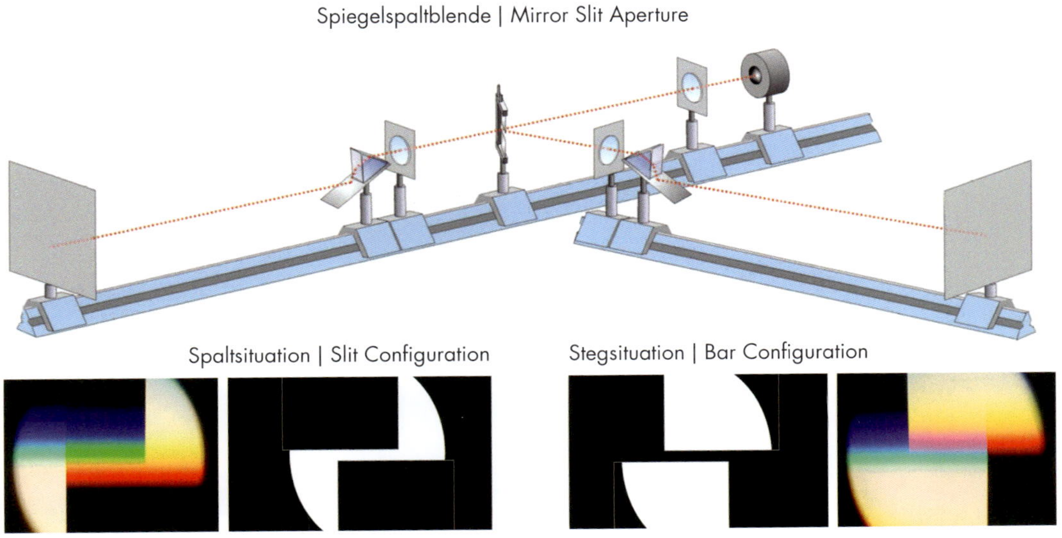

3 Simultane Erzeugung komplementärer Spektren durch Verwendung einer verspiegelten Spaltblende. Transmissions- (links) und Reflexionsstrahlengang (rechts) sind, bezogen auf die Ebene der Spiegelblende, spiegelsymmetrisch zueinander aufgebaut. Ohne Prismen erscheint die Blende in Transmission als Spalt, in Reflexion als Steg abgebildet. Fotos: M. Rang.
The simultaneous production of complementary spectra using a mirror slit aperture. The optical transmission path (left) and reflection path (right) are constructed to be reflectionally symmetrical with respect to the plane of the mirror aperture. Without the prism, the mirrored aperture appears as a slit in the transmission path and as a bar in the reflection path. Photos: M. Rang.

Within this framework, Rang has been able to show in the last few years that, in principle, all of Newton's experiments can be inverted in the sense of Goethe's idea of polarity. Optical complementarity, as a property of chromatic phenomena that are produced by a strictly inverse setup, is obtained when energy is preserved in the observed optical system. This is especially valid for the various versions of the *experimentum crucis,* an experiment that Newton conceived to prove the purity of spectral colors, which essentially consists of two consecutively placed prisms (figure 5 shows a variant of this experiment). Rang concluded that this results in a generalization of the concept of monochromaticity, which relates the behavior of a selected spectral area when tested for spectral purity in the context of its production: whether a color behaves in a spectrally pure manner depends on whether it is investigated in the environment in which it was produced.

Zeitschrift, XVIII (1917), pp. 195–205; "Das umgekehrte Spektrum und die Spektralanalyse," *Zeitschrift für Instrumentenkunde,* XLIV (1924), pp. 173–75. Significant preliminary work on overcoming the mechanical image of inversion was carried out towards the end of the 1950s by Bjerke and his group in Olso. See André Bjerke, *Neue Beiträge zu Goethes Farbenlehre* (Stuttgart, 1961). This led to Holtsmark's suggestion on the generalization of the *experimentum crucis,* which was realized experimentally by Sällström at the end of the 1970s. See Torger Holtsmark, "Newton's Experimentum Crucis Reconsidered," *American Journal of Physics* 38 (1970), pp. 1229–35; *Colour and Image: Phenomenology of Visual Experience,* ed. Johannes Grebe-Ellis (Berlin, 2012); Pehr Sällström, *Monochromatic Shadow Rays,* experimental film, ed. Johannes Grebe-Ellis (Gerlingen, 2010).

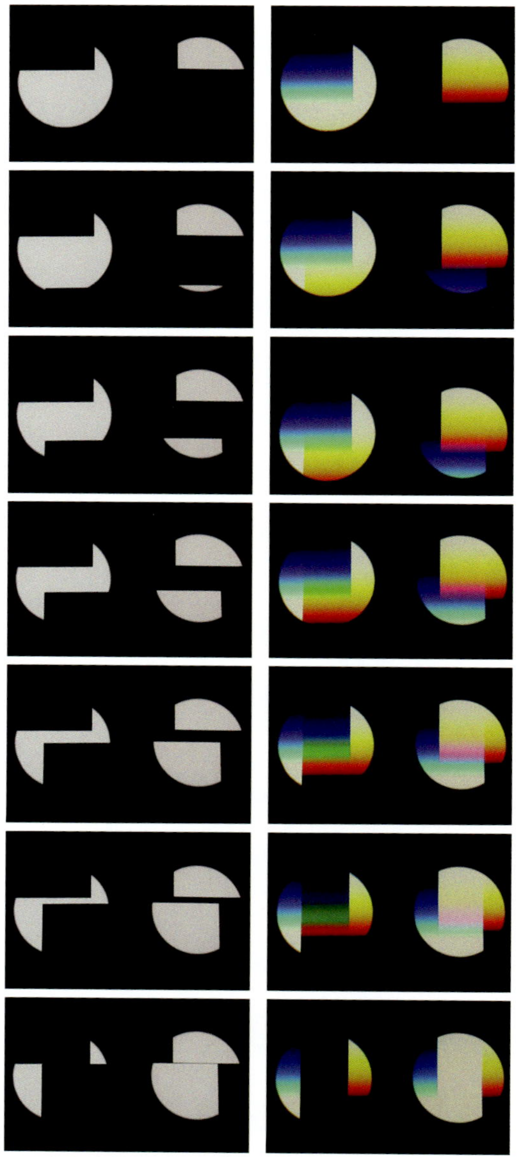

4 Phasen simultan erzeugter komplementärer Spektren einer Xenon-Höchstdrucklampe bei schrittweisem Schließen der Spiegelspaltblende. In der linken Spalte ist die Blendensituation gezeigt, rechts die jeweiligen Spektren. Fotos: J. Grebe-Ellis & Sebastian Hümbert-Schnurr.
Phases of the simultaneously produced complementary spectra of a high pressure xenon lamp with decreasing aperture. The left column shows the aperture and the right the corresponding spectra. Photos: J. Grebe-Ellis and S. Hümbert-Schnurr.

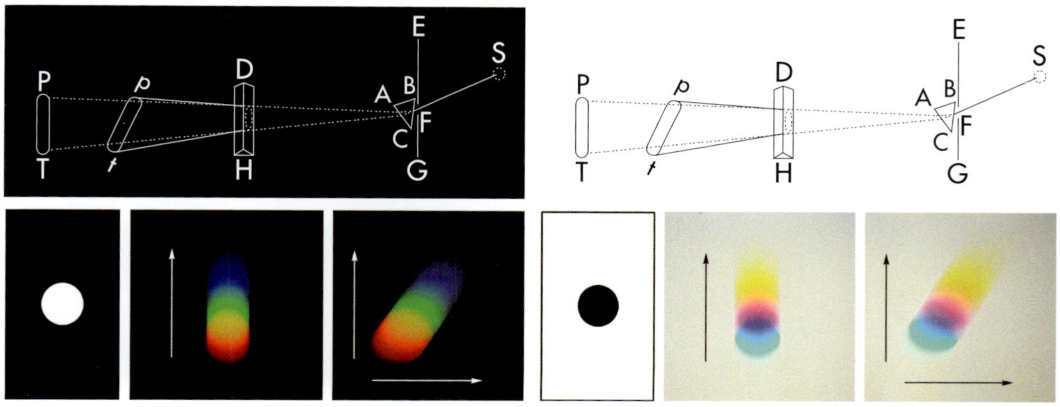

5 Newtons *Experimentum Crucis* mit gekreuzten Prismen (links) und invertierte Version (rechts). Untere Zeile: Erzeugung (Mitte) und Analyse (rechts) des Spektrums einer sonnenähnlichen Lichtquelle in dunkler Umgebung (links) bzw. des komplementären Spektrums einer ›schwarzen Sonne‹ in heller Umgebung. Die Pfeile geben die jeweilige Brechungsrichtung der Prismen an. Fotos: M. Rang. | Newton's *experimentum crucis* with crossed prisms (left) and the inverted version (right). Bottom row: The production (center) and analysis (right) of the spectrum of a light source similar to the sun with a dark background (left), together with the complementary spectrum of a 'dark sun' with a light background. The arrows indicate the prisms' direction of refraction. Photos: M. Rang.

ren, das heißt Vertauschen von Hell und Dunkel in den wichtigsten Experimenten Newtons zum Programm erhob.[19] Der entscheidende Durchbruch zur erfolgreichen Ausführung dieses Programms gelang allerdings erst Matthias Rang in Anknüpfung an Torger Holtsmark durch die Einführung verspiegelter Spaltblenden und das Konzept des optischen Hellraums (Abb. 3, 4 und 5).

Auf dieser Grundlage konnte Rang in den letzten Jahren zeigen, dass im Prinzip alle Experimente Newtons im Sinne der Polaritätsidee Goethes invertiert werden können: Die optische Komplementarität als Eigenschaft von Farbphänomenen, die mit streng inversen experimentellen Aufbauten erzeugt werden, ist erhalten, wenn die Energie in dem betrachteten optischen System erhalten ist. Dies gilt insbesondere auch für die verschiedenen Varianten des *Experimentum Crucis,* ein Experiment, das Newton zum Nachweis der Reinheit der Spektralfarben entwarf und das im Wesentlichen aus zwei hintereinander geschalteten Prismen besteht (Abb. 5 zeigt eine Variante dieses Experiments). Für Rang ergab sich daraus eine Verallgemeinerung des Monochromatizitätsbegriffs, die das Verhalten eines ausgewählten Spektralbereichs gegenüber dem Test auf spektrale Reinheit auf den Kontext seiner Erzeugung bezieht: Ob sich eine Farbe spektral rein verhält oder nicht, hängt davon ab, ob sie in dem Umfeld untersucht wird, in dem sie erzeugt wurde.

Diese Ergebnisse gehen weit über den historischen Kontext der *Farbenlehre* Goethes hinaus. Sie ergeben sich aus erweiterten, modifizierten und verallgemeinerten Varianten der Experimente Newtons und bestätigen Goethes Beobachtungen hinsichtlich der Bedeutung der Komplementarität spektraler Phänomene. Dass sich die Symmetrie komplementärer Spektralphänomene nicht auf den Bereich des im engeren Sinne optischen Teils des elektromagnetischen Spektrums beschränkt, sondern allgemein als Eigenschaft der Strahlungsenergie auch für die angrenzenden Spektralbereiche des Ultraviolett (UV) und Infrarot (IR) nachgewiesen werden kann, haben Rang und Grebe-Ellis durch die Vermessung komplementärer Spektren einer Xenon-Höchstdrucklampe gezeigt (Abb. 6).[20] Vor diesem Hintergrund kann von den UV- und IR-Bereichen im gewöhnlichen Spektrum korrespondierenden Bereichen Ultra-Yellow (UY) und Infra-Cyan (IC) im komplementären Spektrum gesprochen werden. Ob

19 Goethe konnte mit seinem Vorschlag, die Invertierung des Newtonschen Grundversuchs mechanisch zu realisieren, zwar eine anschauliche Darstellung seiner Entdeckung der Symmetrie komplementärer Spektren geben. Aus heutiger Sicht entsteht jedoch der Eindruck, dass er mit diesem Invertierungsvorbild gleichzeitig einem unvollständigen, mechanischen Invertierungsverständnis Vorschub geleistet hat. Dies hat im 20. Jahrhundert zu einer Tradition von Invertierungsversuchen geführt, die so lange wirkungslos bleiben musste, als nicht erkannt wurde, dass das Invertierungsproblem prinzipiell nicht mechanisch, sondern nur optisch lösbar ist. Erwähnenswert sind allerdings die Arbeiten Kirschmanns, der 1917 als Erster gezeigt hat, dass sich das umgekehrte Spektrum im Prinzip ebenso spektroskopisch nutzen lässt, wie das Spaltspektrum. Vgl. August Kirschmann, »Das umgekehrte Spektrum und seine Komplementärverhältnisse«, in: *Physikalische Zeitschrift,* 18, 1917, S. 195–205; ders., »Das umgekehrte Spektrum und die Spektralanalyse«, in: *Zeitschrift für Instrumentenkunde,* 44, 1924, S. 173–175. Maßgebliche Vorarbeiten zur Überwindung der mechanischen Invertierungsvorstellung wurden Ende der 50er-Jahre des 20. Jahrhunderts in der Osloer Arbeitsgruppe um Bjerke geleistet, vgl. André Bjerke, *Neue Beiträge zu Goethes Farbenlehre,* Stuttgart 1961. Sie führten zu einem Vorschlag zur Verallgemeinerung des *Experimentum Crucis* von Holtsmark, der Ende der 70er-Jahre erstmals von Sällström experimentell realisiert wurde, s. Torger Holtsmark, »Newton's Experimentum Crucis reconsidered«, in: *American Journal of Physics,* 38, 10, 1970, S. 1229–1235 und *Colour and Image. Phenomenology of Visual Experience,* Hrsg. von Johannes Grebe-Ellis, Berlin 2012; Pehr Sällström, *Monochromatic Shadow Rays,* Experimentalfilm, Hrsg. von Johannes Grebe-Ellis, Gerlingen 2010.

These results go far beyond the historical context of Goethe's *Farbenlehre*. They result from extended, modified, and generalized variants of Newton's experiments and confirm Goethe's observations regarding the importance of the complementarity of spectral phenomena. The symmetry of complementary spectral phenomena is not limited to the strictly optical part of the electromagnetic spectrum. Being a general property of radiation energy, it can also be demonstrated in the neighboring ultraviolet (UV) and infrared (IR) spectral regions. This has been done by Rang and Grebe-Ellis in their measuring of the complementary spectra of a high-pressure xenon lamp (see figure 6).[20] In light of this research, one can speak of ultra-yellow (UY) and infra-cyan (IC) regions of the complementary spectrum that correspond to the UV and IR regions of the normal spectrum. It remains to be seen whether, on the basis of Rang's techniques, spectroscopic applications can be developed that have advantages in specific cases over established methods.

This presentation of recent historical, philosophical, and physical investigations of Goethe's theory of colors shows that the image of Goethe as a scientist and color researcher has been reanimated in recent years. Research on the *Farbenlehre* is in no way finished. On the contrary, the studies presented above clearly show that we are in many ways at the beginning—and that this beginning is promising.

20 Johannes Grebe-Ellis and Matthias Rang, "Power Area Density in Inverse Spectra", *Journal for General Philosophy of Science,* March 2018, https://doi.org/10.1007/s10838-017-9394-8 (accessed July 20, 2018).

6 Bestrahlungsstärke im Spaltspektrum (oben) und im komplementären Stegspektrum (unten) einer Xenon-Höchstdrucklampe. Fotos: M. Rang und J. Grebe-Ellis.
The Intensity of irradiation in the slit spectrum (top) and the complementary bar spectrum (below) of a high-pressure xenon lamp. Photos: M. Rang and J. Grebe-Ellis.

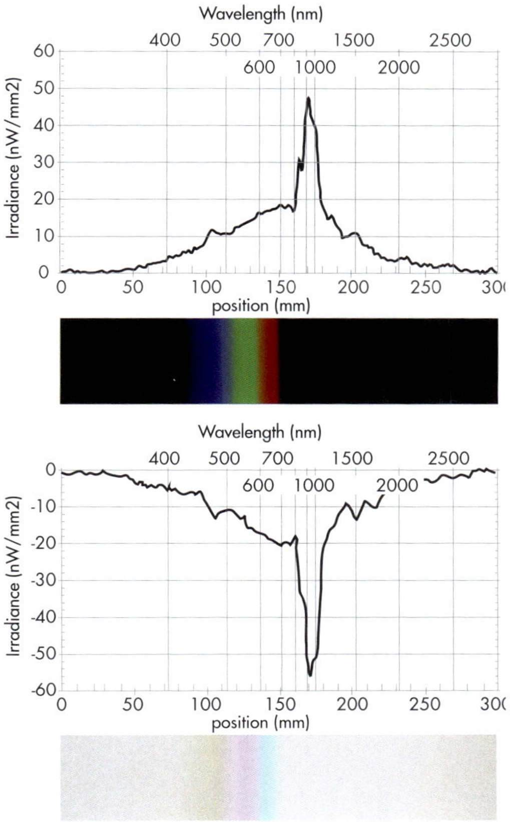

sich auf der Grundlage von Rangs Techniken spektroskopische Anwendungen realisieren lassen, die in speziellen Fällen Vorteile gegenüber etablierten Verfahren haben, bleibt abzuwarten.

Der hiermit vorgestellte Blick auf neuere historische, wissenschaftsphilosophische und physikalische Untersuchungen zu Goethes Farbenlehre zeigt, dass das Bild Goethes als Naturwissenschaftler und Farbenforscher in den letzten Jahren neu in Bewegung gekommen ist. Die Forschung zur *Farbenlehre* ist keineswegs abgeschlossen, im Gegenteil. Die vorgestellten Arbeiten machen deutlich, dass man noch vielfach am Anfang steht – und sie zeigen, dass dieser Anfang ein vielversprechender ist.

20 Johannes Grebe-Ellis und Matthias Rang, »Power Area Density in Inverse Spectra«, *Journal for General Philosophy of Science*, März 2018, https://doi.org/10.1007/s10838-017-9394-8 (Stand: 20.07.2018).

LICHT UND SCHATTEN

LIGHT AND SHADOW

»Wie wir nun auf diese Weise farbige Körper und Pigmente theils finden, theils bereiten und mischen können, welche die prismatischen Farben so ziemlich repräsentiren: so ist das reine Weiß dagegen ein Repräsentant des Lichts, das reine Schwarz ein Repräsentant der Finsterniß […].«

"In much the same way that we can either find or prepare and mix colored solids and pigments so that they give a fair representation of the colors of the prism: in contrast, pure white is representative of light, and pure black representative of darkness."

GOETHE

»So sehr auch dem Schwarz wie dem Weiß die Eigenschaft zukommt, eine Lichtfarbe zu sein, so ist das Weiß doch nicht die Farbe, welche dem Schwarz am nächsten steht, denn die Chromatik aller Graustufen verbindet und trennt zugleich das Schwarz vom Weiß.«

"The ability to be a color of light is equally ascribed to both black and white, however, white is not the color which is the most similar to black, because all the monochromatic shades of gray both bind and separate black from white."

MACK

1 Johann Wolfgang von Goethe
Eigenhändige Reinschrift seines Gedichtes:
»Wär' nicht das Auge sonnenhaft […]«
Signiert, datiert: »Lauchstedt d. 1 Sept 1805.
Goethe«
1 Blatt mit Zierrand und Goldschnitt,
1 S. beschrieben
9,5 x 15,5 cm
Goethe-Museum Düsseldorf

Goethe nahm diese Verse in leicht veränderter Form in die Einleitung zum didaktischen Teil seiner *Farbenlehre* auf, wo sie lauten:
»Wär' nicht das Auge sonnenhaft,
Wie könnten wir das Licht erblicken?
Lebt' nicht in uns des Gottes eigne Kraft,
Wie könnt' uns Göttliches entzücken?«
Goethe bezieht sich mit diesem Gedicht auf den griechischen Philosophen Plotin (205–270), bei dem es heißt: »Nie hätte das Auge jemals die Sonne gesehen, wenn es nicht selber sonnenhaft wäre; so kann auch eine Seele das Schöne nicht sehen, wenn sie nicht selbst schön ist. Darum werde jeder zuerst gottähnlich und schön, wenn er das Gute und Schöne sehen will.« (Plotin, *Enneaden,* übersetzt von Friedrich Müller, Bd. 1, Berlin 1878, Enneade 1, Buch 6, Kap. 9, S. 53.) Vgl. LA, Bd. II 3, S. [389]–393 und Bd. II 4, S. 286 ff. Vgl. auch folgende Gedanken Goethes über das Auge:
»Das Auge ist das letzte, höchste Resultat des Lichtes auf den organischen Körper.
Das Auge als ein Geschöpf des Lichtes leistet alles, was das Licht selbst leisten kann.
Das Licht überliefert das Sichtbare dem Auge; das Auge überliefert's dem ganzen Menschen.
Das Ohr ist stumm, der Mund ist taub; aber das Auge vernimmt und spricht.
In ihm spiegelt sich von außen die Welt, von innen der Mensch.
Die Totalität des Innern und Äußern wird durchs Auge vollendet.« (LA, Bd. I 3, S. 437.)

1 Johann Wolfgang von Goethe
Clean copy of Goethes poem in his own hand:
"Wär' nicht das Auge sonnenhaft …"
(If the eye were not sunny …)
Signed, dated: "Lauchstedt d. 1 Sept 1805.
Goethe"
1 sheet with decorative border and gilt edging,
1 page written
9.5 x 15.5 cm
Goethe-Museum Düsseldorf

Goethe included the verses in slightly altered form in his Introduction to the didactic part of his *Theory of Colours:*
"If the eye were not sunny,
how could we perceive light?
If God's own strength lived not in us,
how could we delight in Divine things?"
In these lines, Goethe refers to the Greek philosopher Plotinus (205–270), who wrote: "Never did eye see the sun unless it had first become sunlike, and never can the soul have vision of the First Beauty unless itself be beautiful. Therefore, first let each become godlike and each beautiful who cares to see God and Beauty." (Plotinus, *The Enneads I*, 6, 9, trans. Stephen MacKenna, rev. B. S. Page [London, 1956], p. 64). See LA, vol. II 3, pp. [389]–93 and vol. II 4, pp. 286–88. See also the following idea of Goethe's about the eye:
"The eye is the last and highest result of light on the organism. The eye as a creation of light achieves everything that light itself can achieve. Light conveys the visible to the eye; the eye conveys it to the whole human being. The ear is deaf, the mouth is mute; but the eye hears and speaks. It reflects from the outside the world, from the inside the human being. The totality of the interior and the exterior is perfected in the eye." (LA, vol. I 3, p. 437.)

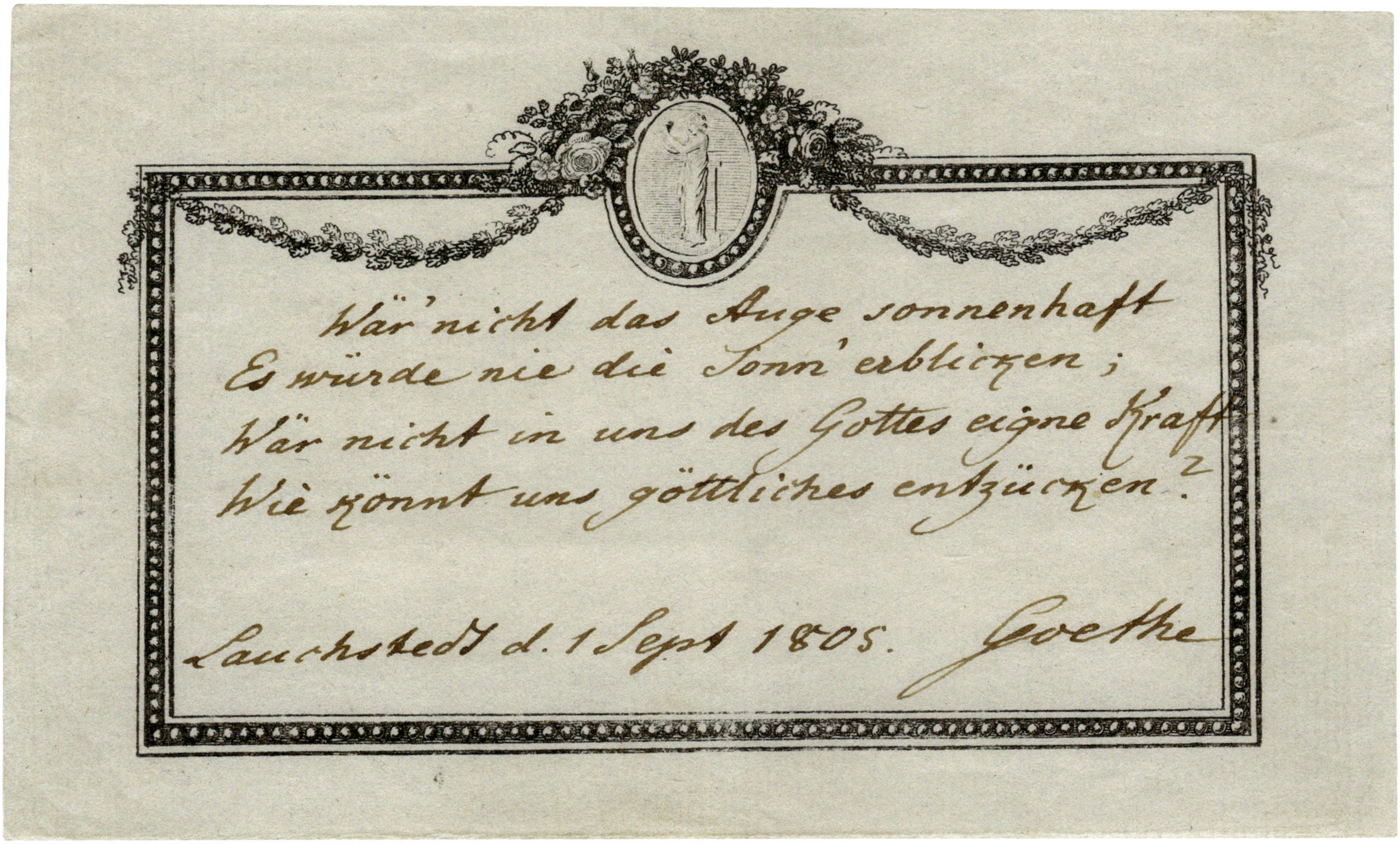

Wär' nicht das Auge sonnenhaft
Es würde nie die Sonn' erblicken;
Wär nicht in uns des Gottes eigne Kraft
Wie könnt uns göttliches entzücken?

Lauchstedt d. 1 Sept 1805. Goethe

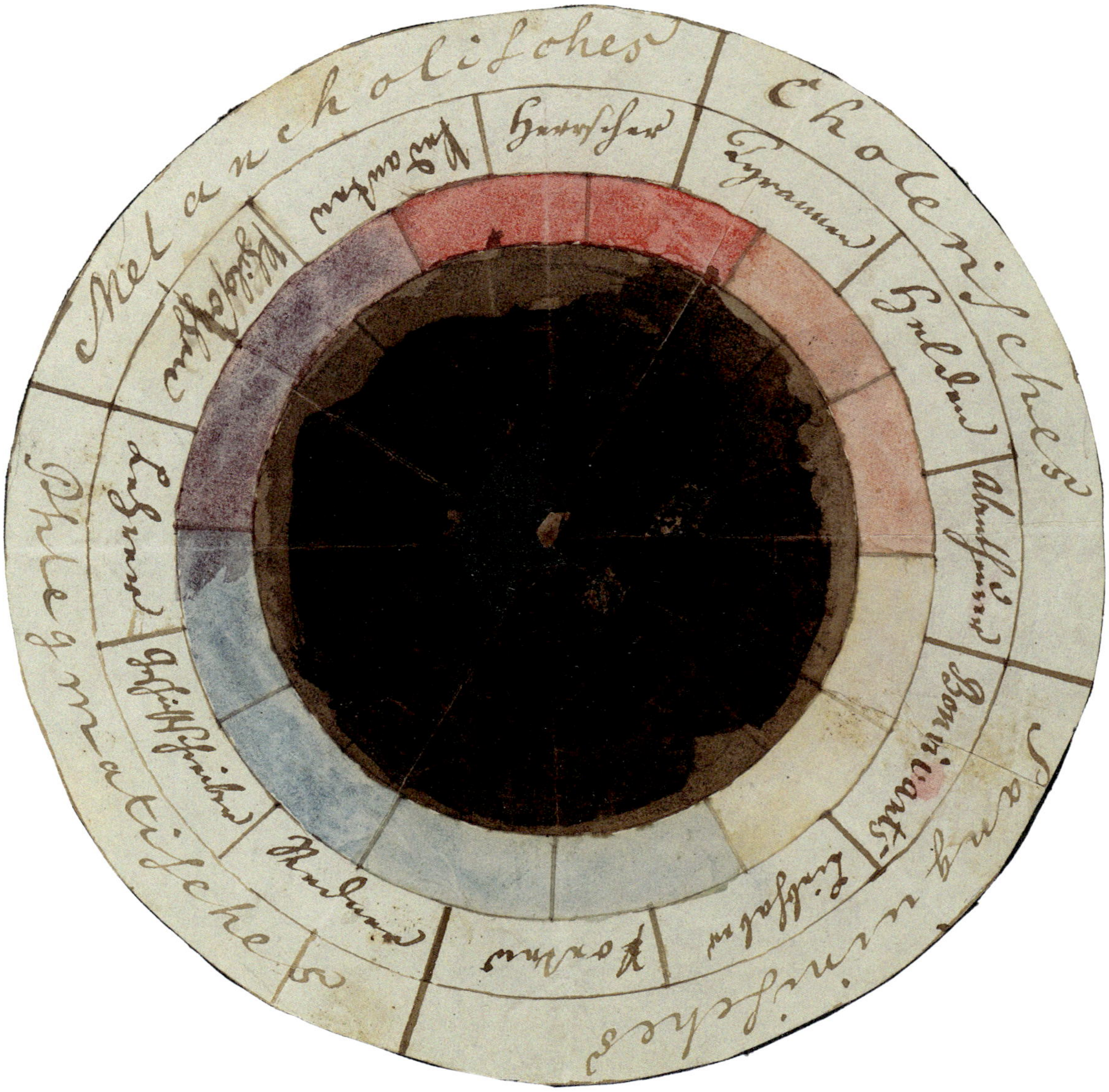

2 Friedrich Schiller und
Johann Wolfgang von Goethe
Temperamentenrose, 1798/99
Feder und Aquarell, Beschriftung von Schillers Hand
Kreisförmige Scheibe aus dünnem Papier, auf Kaliko aufgezogen
Ø 15,3 cm
Klassik Stiftung Weimar, Museen
Die Ausstellung zeigt ein Faksimile.

Goethe und Schiller entwickelten in gemeinsamen Gesprächen die sogenannte *Temperamentenrose,* die eine Beziehung zwischen Farben, Temperamenten und charakteristischen Personengruppen herstellt. Dafür umgaben sie einen Farbenkreis aus sechs Farben mit zwei weiteren Kreisen. Der mittlere Kreis, in dessen Felder Schiller die Bezeichnung für die Personengruppen eintrug, ist zwölfteilig und so um den inneren verschoben, dass den Personen- oder Berufsgruppen jeweils eine oder zwei Farben zugeordnet werden und jeder Farbe drei Personengruppen. Den äußeren Kreis bilden die vier Temperamente, zu denen jeweils drei Personengruppen und zwei oder drei Farben gehören. Auf der aktiven Seite des Farbenkreises finden sich – entsprechend dem cholerischen und dem sanguinischen Temperament – Tyrannen, Helden, Abenteurer, Bonvivants, Liebhaber und Poeten. Auf der passiven dagegen – dem melancholischen und dem phlegmatischen Temperament zugeordnet – Herrscher, Pedanten, Philosophen, Lehrer, Geschichtsschreiber und Redner. An der *Temperamentenrose* lassen sich jedoch nicht nur Entsprechungen, sondern auch Gegensätze ablesen. So stehen sich nicht nur Farben wie Purpur und Grün als Pole gegenüber, die einander harmonisch zur Totalität ergänzen, sondern auch Herrscher und Poeten. Vgl. LA, Bd. II 1 B, S. [1194]–1203.

2 Friedrich Schiller and
Johann Wolfgang von Goethe
Rose of Temperaments, 1798/99
Pen and watercolor, inscription in Schiller's hand
Round disc made from thin paper, mounted on calico
Ø 15.3 cm
Klassik Stiftung Weimar, Museen
The exhibition is displaying a facsimile.

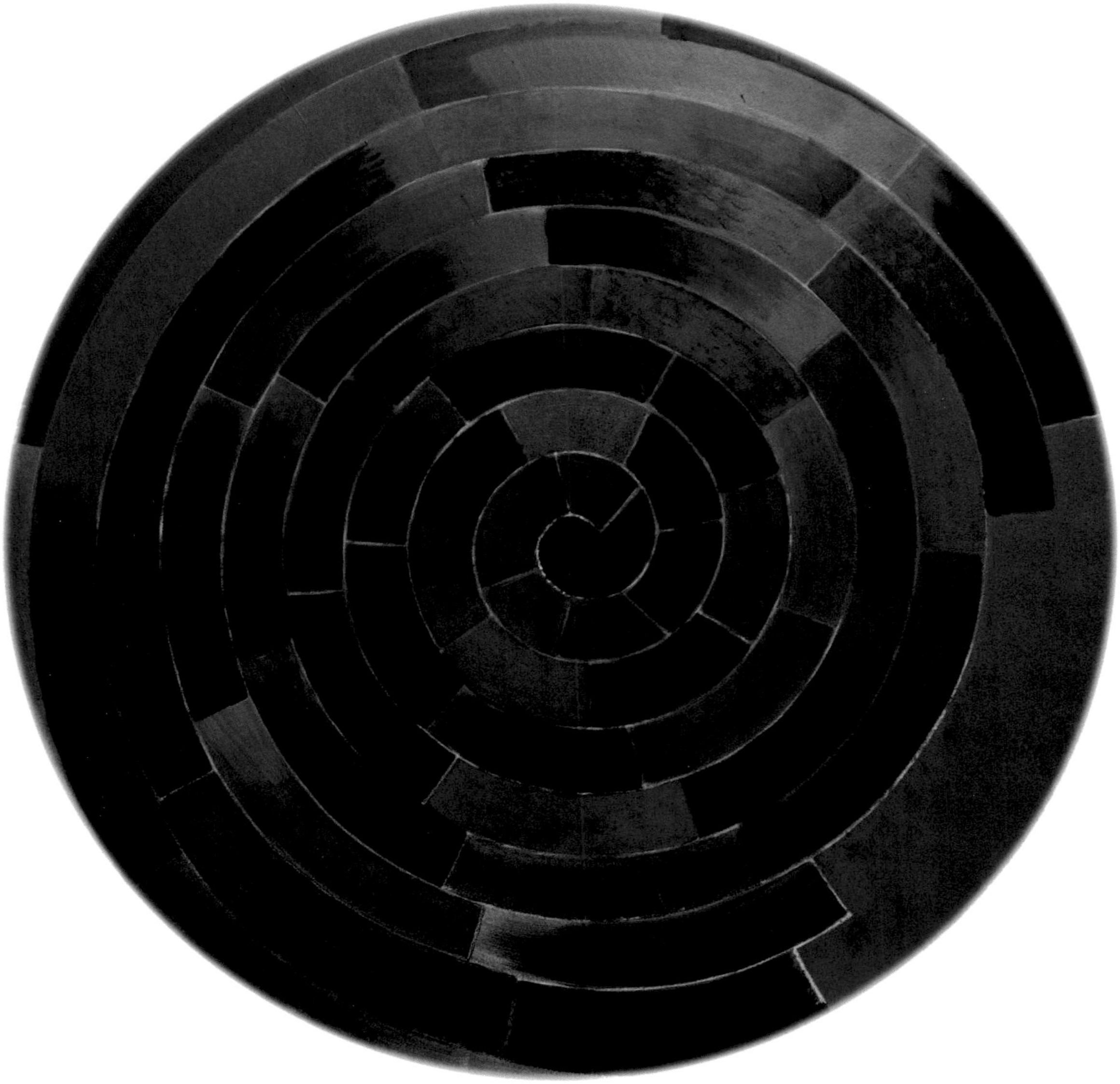

In their conversations, Goethe and Schiller developed the so-called *Rose of Temperaments* that establishes a close connection between colors, temperaments and character traits. A color circle with six colors is surrounded with two additional circles. The middle circle, in which Schiller entered the description of groups of people, consists of twelve parts and is aligned in such a manner with the inner circle that the groups or professions are lined up with one or two colors and each color is designated to three groups. The outer circle is marked with the four temperaments that are linked with three groups and two or three colors. On the active side of the color wheel are — according to the choleric and sanguine temperaments — tyrants, heroes, adventurers, hedonists, lovers, and poets. On the passive side are — according to the melancholic and phlegmatic temperaments — rulers, pedants, philosophers, teachers, historians, and orators. However, the *Rose of Temperaments* not only shows congruencies but also opposites. Therefore, not only colors, such as purple and green, are polar opposites that complement each other in harmony to form totality, but also rulers and poets. See LA, vol. II 1 B, pp. [1194]–1203.

3 Heinz Mack
Black Rotation
Signiert, datiert: »mack 56–57,
2008 von mir als neue Fassung restauriert«
Acryl auf Holz
Ø 180 cm

3 Heinz Mack
Black Rotation
Signed, dated: "mack 56–57,
2008 von mir als neue Fassung restauriert"
Acrylic on wood
Ø 180 cm

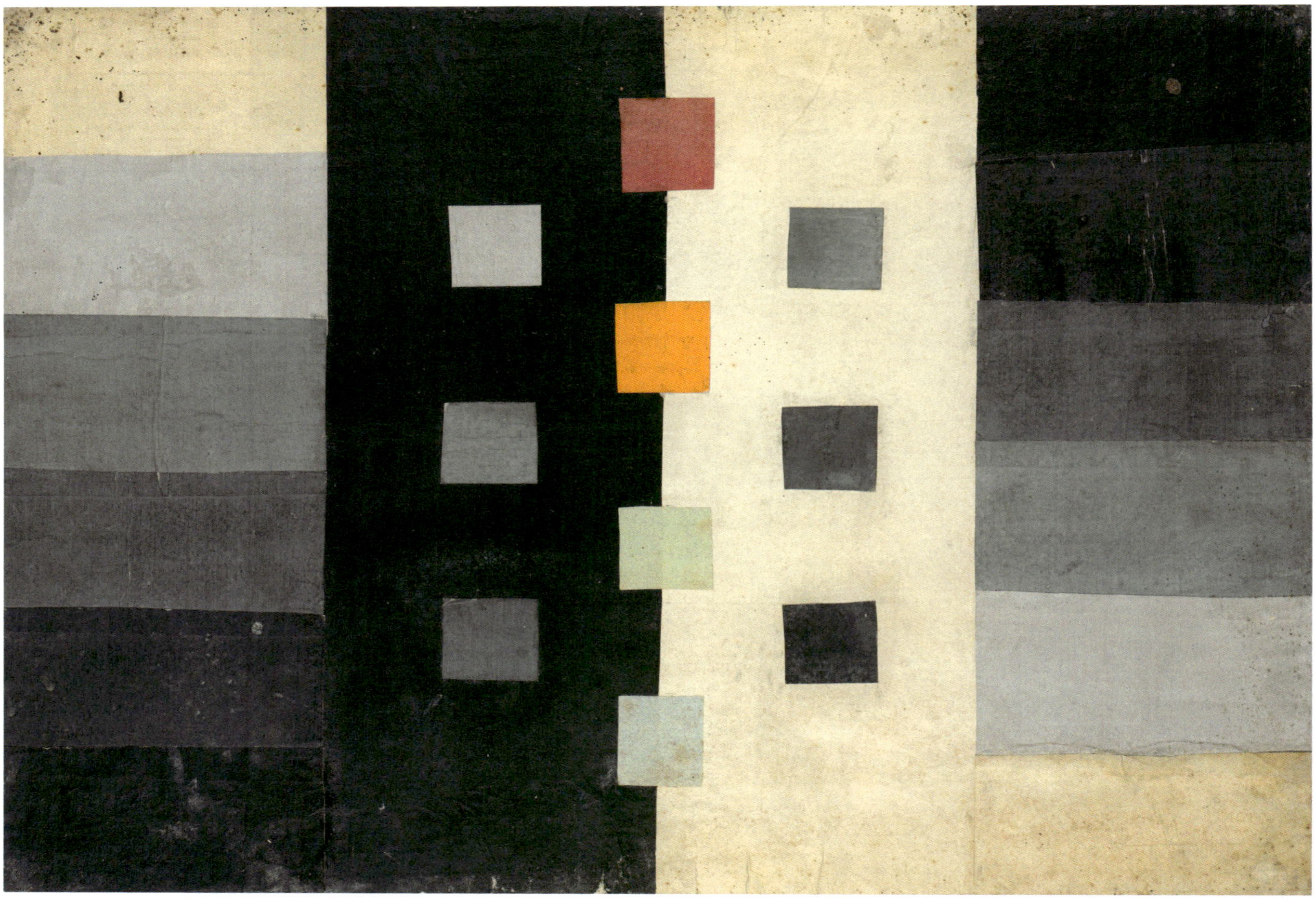

4 Johann Wolfgang von Goethe
Große Farbtafel als Beilage zum zweiten Stück der *Beyträge zur Optik* von 1792
55,2 x 38,3 cm
Württembergische Landesbibliothek Stuttgart
Signatur: Ra 18 Goe 1
Vgl. LA, Bd. II 3, S. 191 ff.

4 Johann Wolfgang von Goethe
Large color plate as supplement to the second part of *Contributions to Optics,* 1792
55.2 x 38.3 cm
Württembergische Landesbibliothek Stuttgart
Shelf mark: Ra 18 Goe 1
See LA, vol. II 3, pp. 191–93.

5 Heinz Mack
Chromatik des Lichts
Signiert, datiert: »mack 63«
Acryl auf Leinwand
200 x 130 cm

5 Heinz Mack
Chromatic of Light
Signed, dated: "mack 63"
Acrylic on canvas
200 x 130 cm

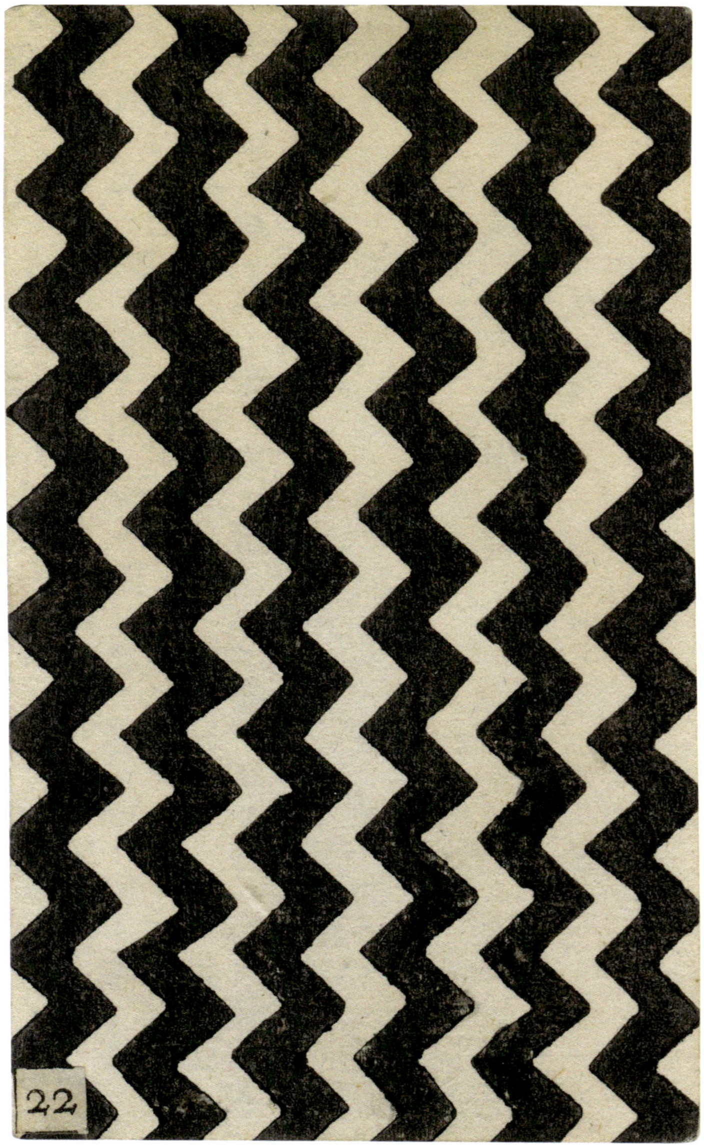

6 Johann Wolfgang von Goethe
Karte Nr. 22 aus dem ›Optischen Kartenspiel‹

Goethe hatte als Beilage zum ersten Stück seiner *Beyträge zur Optik* (1791) 27 zum Teil kolorierte Holzschnitttafeln in Spielkartengröße herausgegeben, anhand derer die Leser seine prismatischen Versuche im Experiment nachvollziehen konnten. Tafel Nr. 22 (erklärt in § 44 der *Beyträge zur Optik)* zeigt bei der Betrachtung durch ein Prisma, dass sich die Farberscheinungen verändern, wenn man die Karte dreht.

6 Johann Wolfgang von Goethe
Card no. 22 from the 'Optical Card Game'

Goethe had added as supplement to the first part of his *Contributions to Optics* (1791) 27 partly colored woodcuts in the size of playing cards, so that readers could reconstruct his prismatic experiments. Plate no. 22 (explained in § 44 of his *Contributions to Optics)* shows that colors, when viewed through a prism, change when the cards are shifted.

7 Heinz Mack
Ohne Titel *(Chromatische Konstellation)*
Signiert, datiert: »mack 16«
Acryl auf Leinwand
144 x 172 cm

7 Heinz Mack
Untitled *(Chromatic Constellation)*
Signed, dated: "mack 16"
Acrylic on canvas
144 x 172 cm

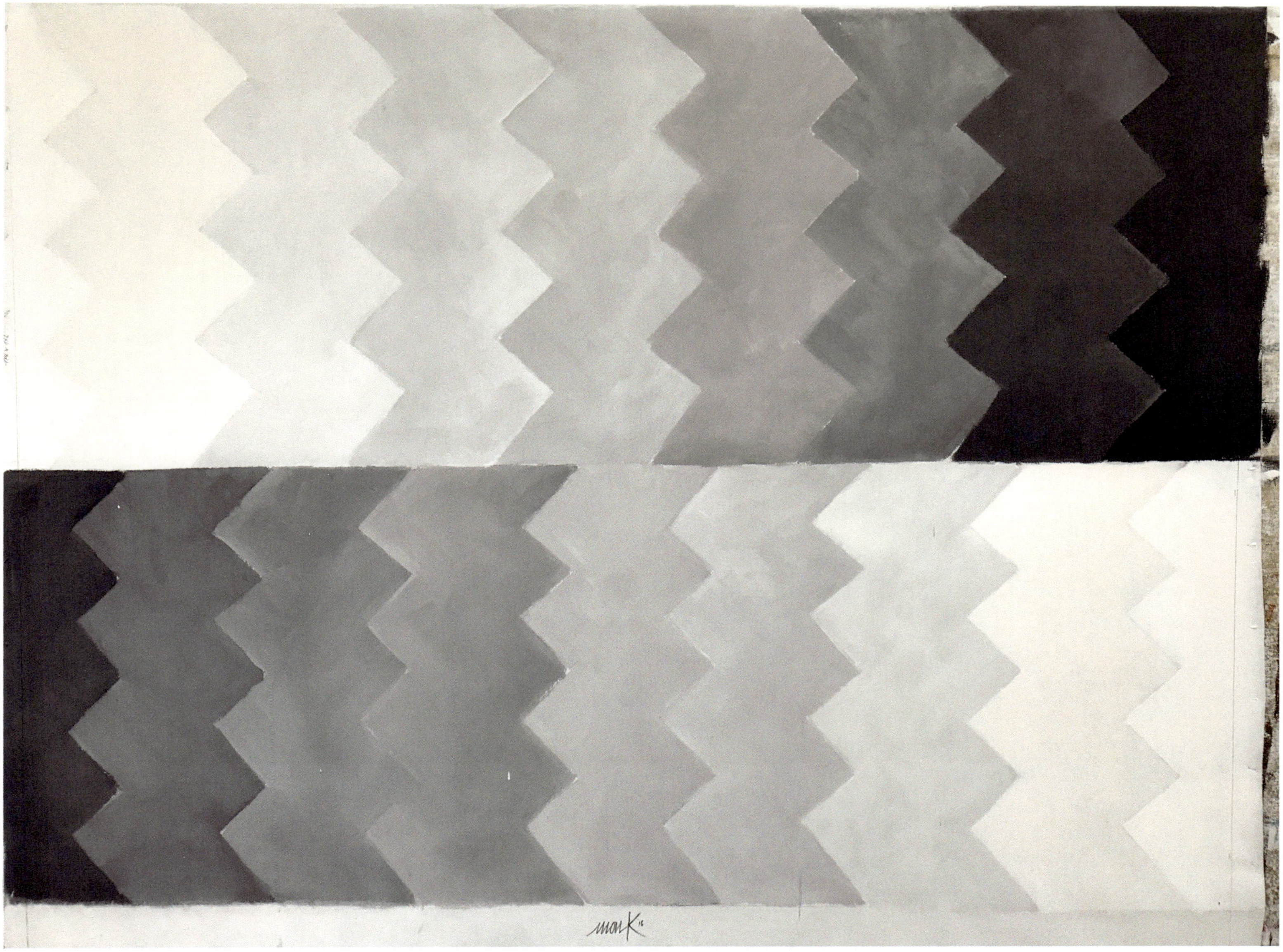

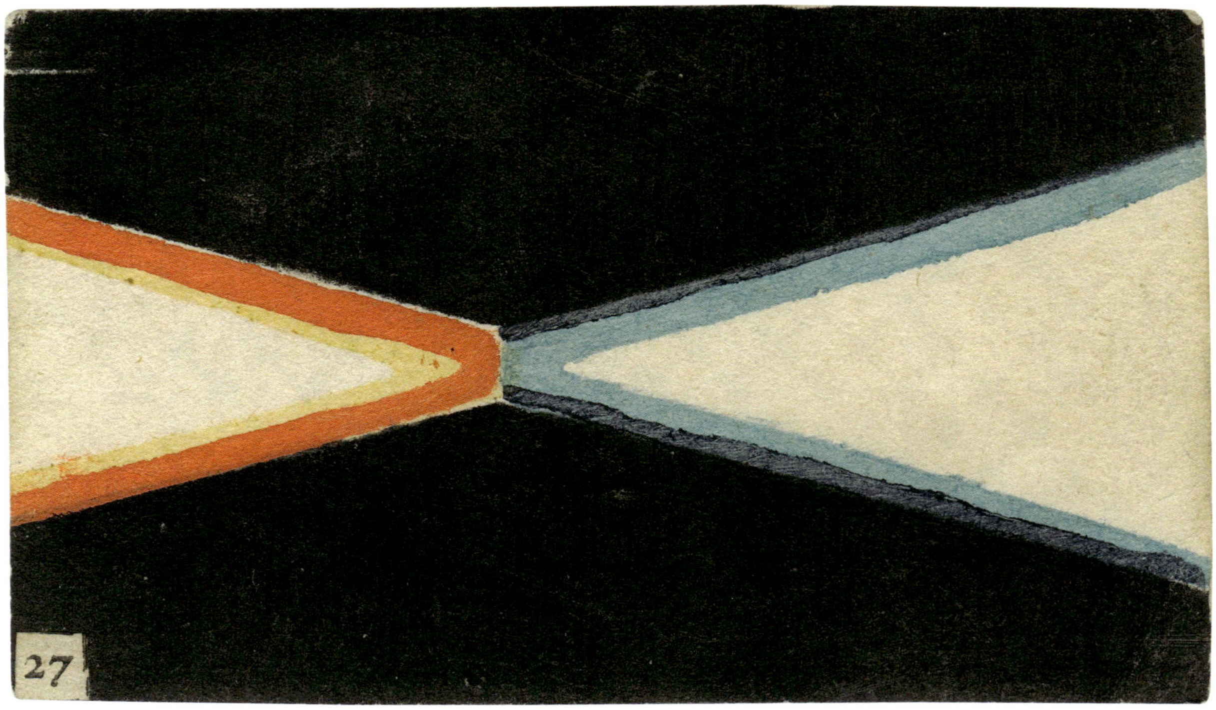

8 Johann Wolfgang von Goethe
Karte Nr. 27 aus dem ›Optischen Kartenspiel‹

Goethe hatte als Beilage zum ersten Stück seiner *Beyträge zur Optik* (1791) 27 zum Teil kolorierte Holzschnitttafeln in Spielkartengröße herausgegeben, anhand derer die Leser seine prismatischen Versuche im Experiment nachvollziehen konnten.

8 Johann Wolfgang von Goethe
Card no. 27 from the 'Optical Card Game'

As supplement to the first part of his *Contributions to Optics* (1791), Goethe had issued 27 partly colored woodcuts in the size of playing cards so that the reader could reconstruct his prismatic experiments.

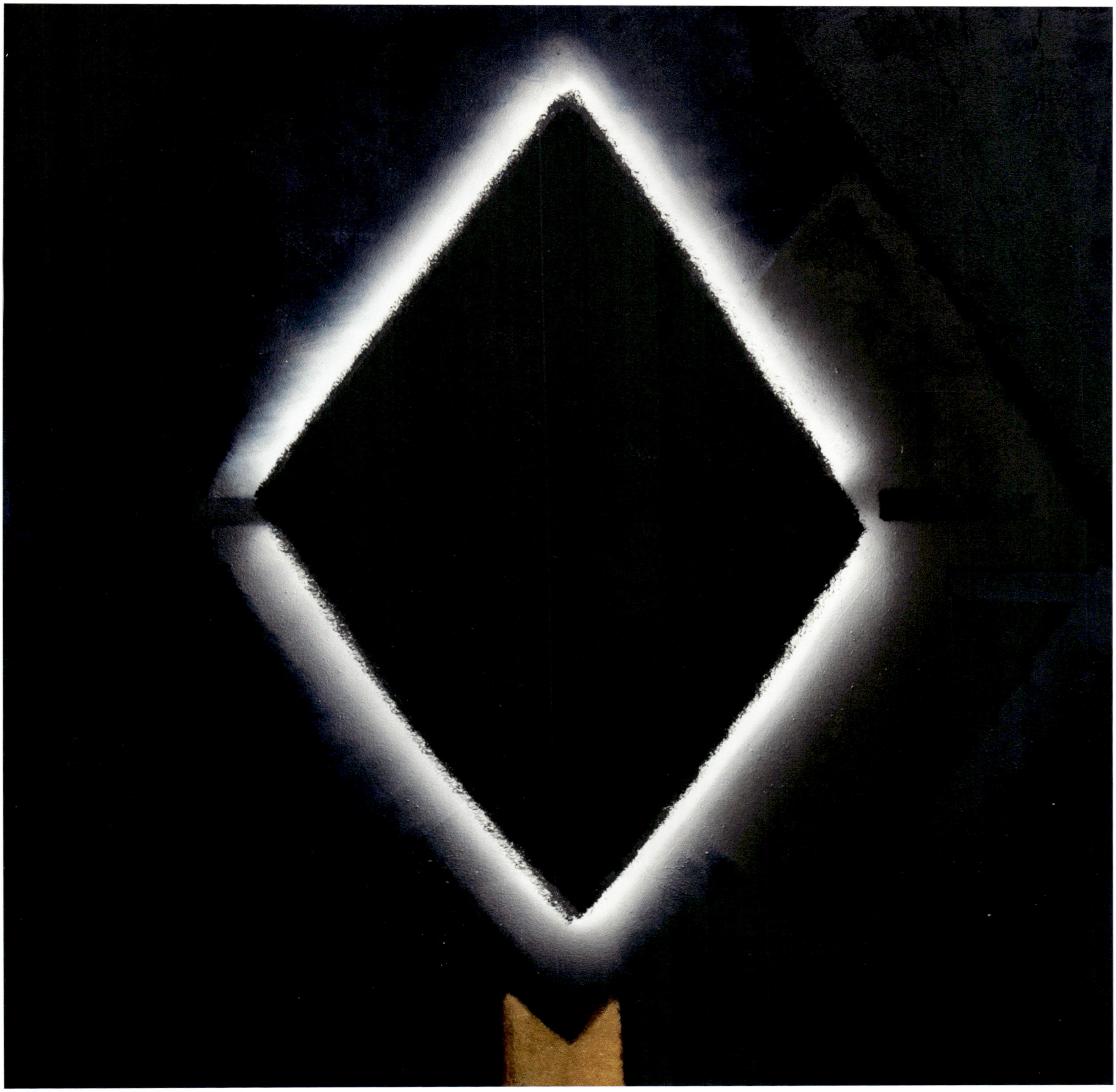

9 Heinz Mack
Upside-Down (Chromatische Konstellation)
Signiert, datiert, betitelt: »mack 08, upside-down«
Acryl auf Leinwand
200 x 200 cm

9 Heinz Mack
Upside-Down (Chromatic Constellation)
Signed, dated, entitled: "mack 08, upside-down"
Acrylic on canvas
200 x 200 cm

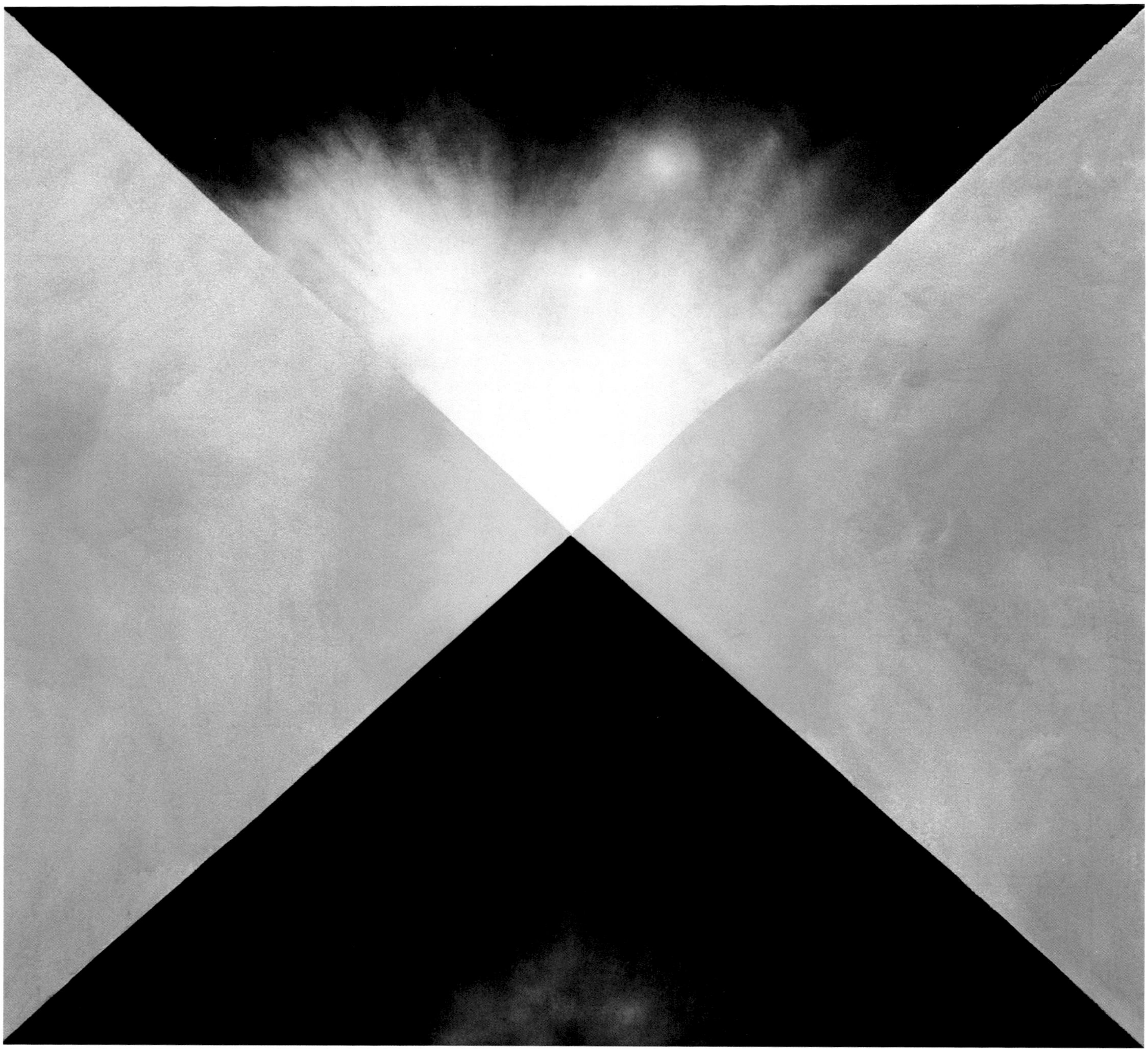

10 Heinz Mack
The Time of Light (Chromatische Konstellation)
Signiert, datiert: »mack 71–08«
Acryl auf Leinwand
183 x 196 cm

10 Heinz Mack
The Time of Light (Chromatic Constellation)
Signed, dated: "mack 71–08"
Acrylic on canvas
183 x 196 cm

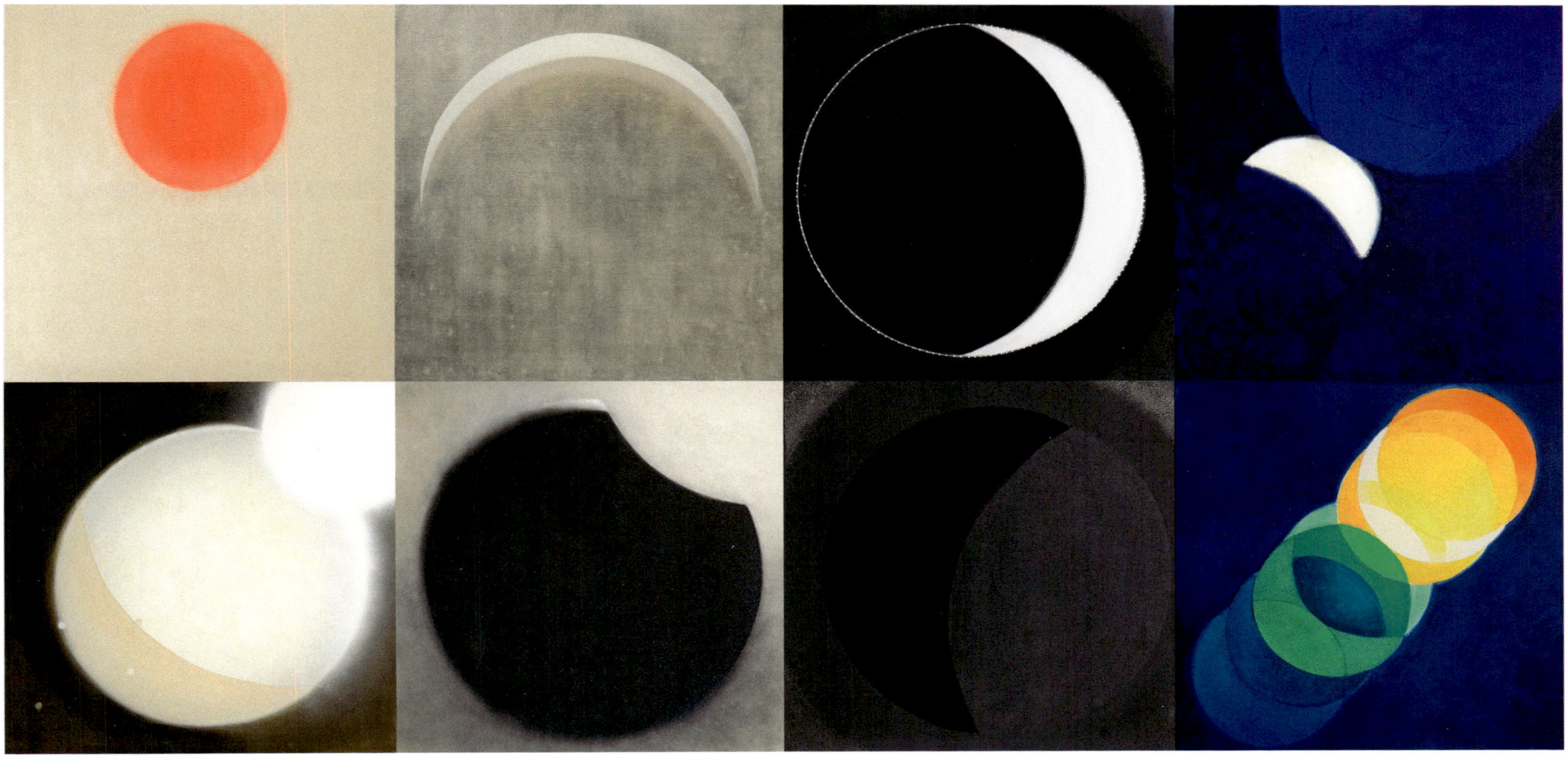

and 18 (see §§ 65–66 and 85 in his *Contributions to Optics)* show the colored borders one can see when viewing a card through a three-edged glass prism, that is divided in the middle, with a white circle on a black background and a black circle on a white background.

15 Heinz Mack
Deklination des Mondes
(Chromatische Konstellation)
Signiert, datiert: »mack 5«
Acryl auf Leinwand
250 x 500 cm (8-teiliges Ensemble, je 125 x 125 cm)

15 Heinz Mack
Declination of the Moon
(Chromatic Constellation)
Signed, dated: "mack 5"
Acrylic on canvas
250 x 500 cm (8-piece ensemble, each 125 x 125 cm)

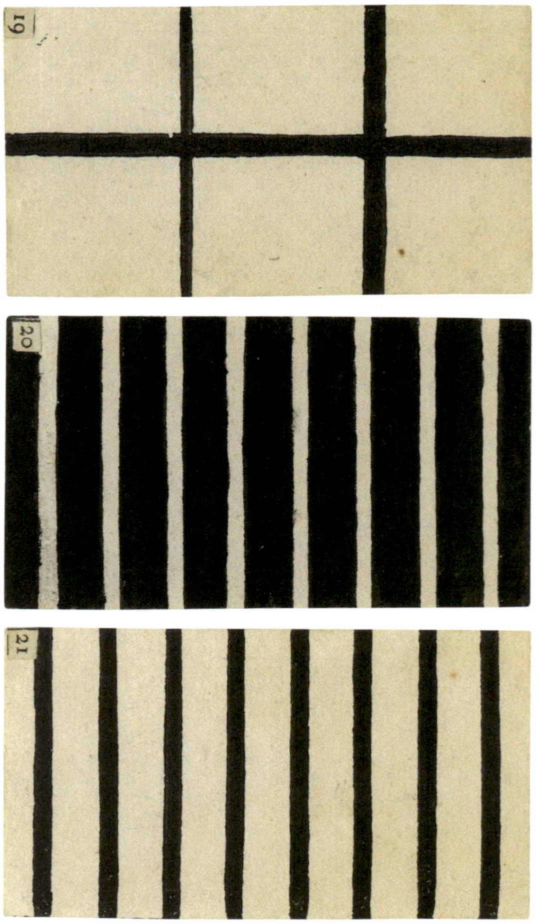

16–18 Johann Wolfgang von Goethe
Karten Nr. 19–21 aus dem ›Optischen Kartenspiel‹

Goethe hatte als Beilage zum ersten Stück seiner *Beyträge zur Optik* (1791) 27 zum Teil kolorierte Holzschnitttafeln in Spielkartengröße herausgegeben, anhand derer die Leser seine prismatischen Versuche im Experiment nachvollziehen konnten. Die abgebildeten Karten (vgl. §§ 44, 61 f. und 65 der *Beyträge zur Optik)* zeigen bei der Betrachtung durch ein Prisma, dass sich die Farberscheinungen verändern, wenn man die Richtung oder die Entfernung zum Prisma variiert.

16–18 Johann Wolfgang von Goethe
Card nos. 19–21 from the 'Optical Card Game'

As supplement to the first part of his *Contributions to Optics* (1791), Goethe had issued 27 partly colored woodcuts in the size of playing cards so that the reader could reconstruct his experiments with the three-edged prism and lenses. These plates serve as proof. The plates 19–21 (see §§ 44, 61–62 and 65 in his *Contributions to Optics)* show, when viewed through a prism, changes of colors when direction to and distance from the prism vary.

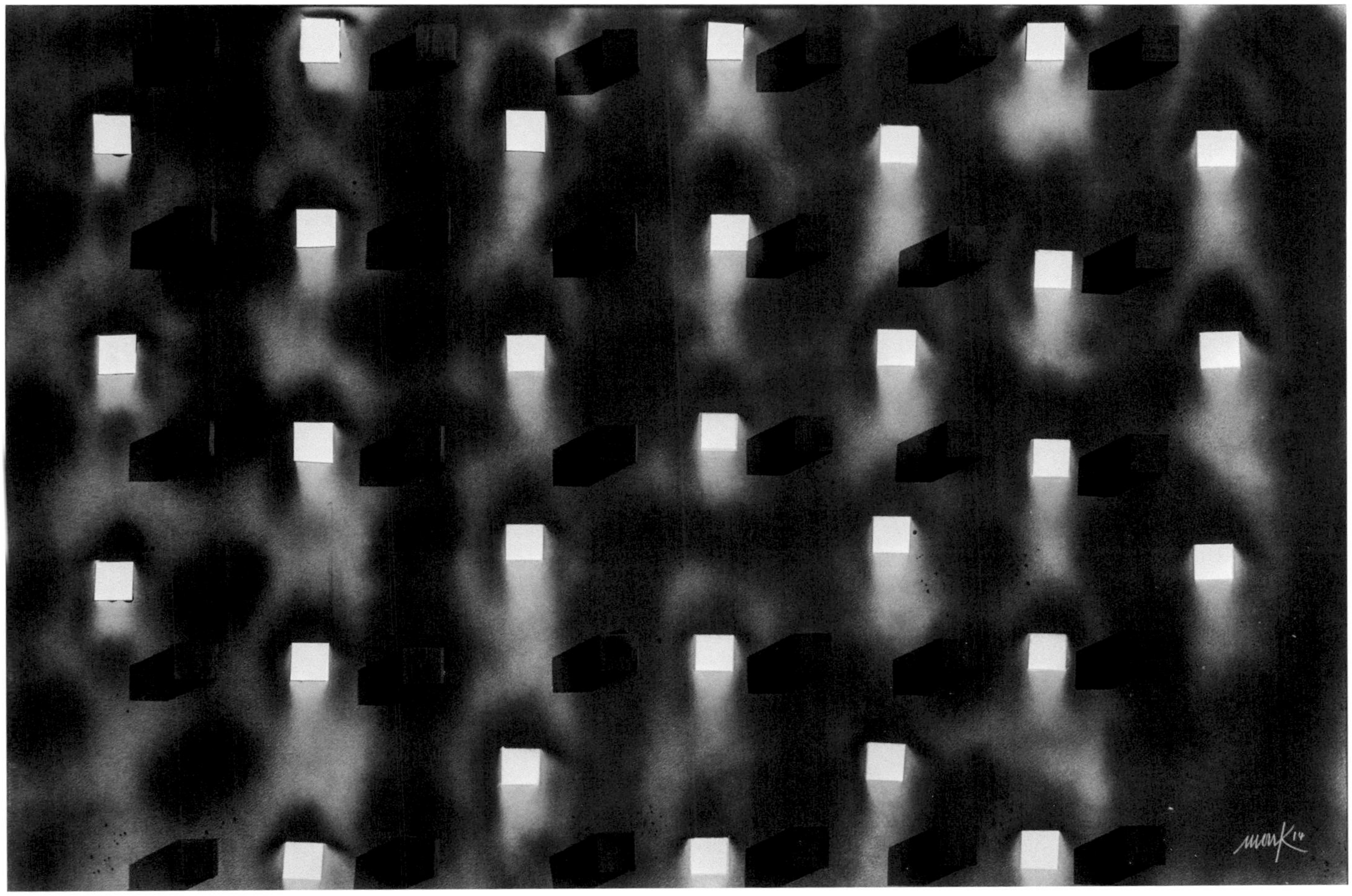

19 Heinz Mack
Licht und Schatten
Signiert, datiert: »mack 14«
75 x 115 x 5,5 cm

19 Heinz Mack
Light and Shadow
Signed, dated: "mack 14"
75 x 115 x 5.5 cm

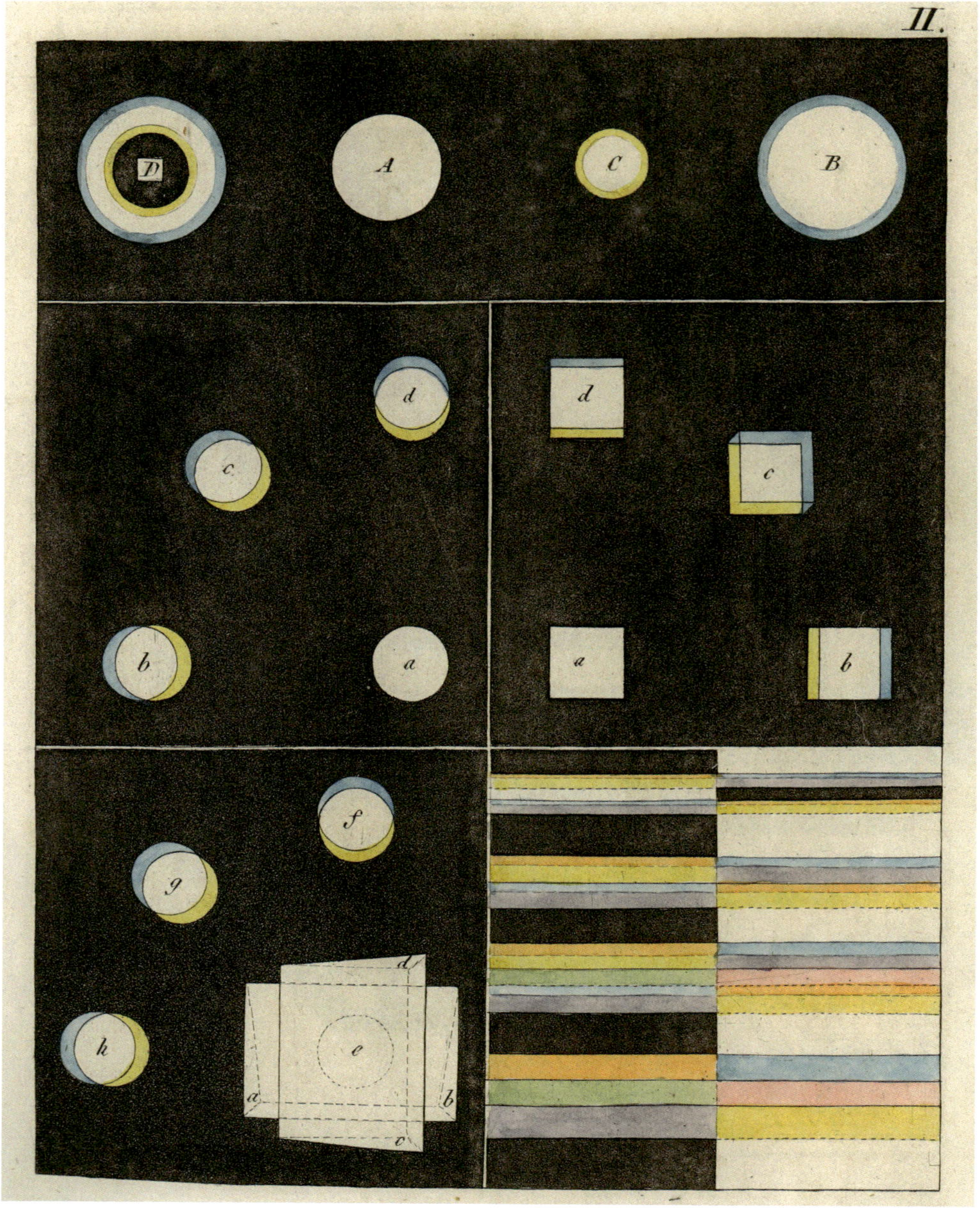

20 Johann Wolfgang von Goethe
Tafel Nr. II aus dem Supplementband zu seiner *Farbenlehre* von 1810
Handkolorierter Kupferstich

20 Johann Wolfgang von Goethe
Plate no. II from the supplement to his *Farbenlehre (Theory of Colours)* of 1810
Hand-colored copper engraving

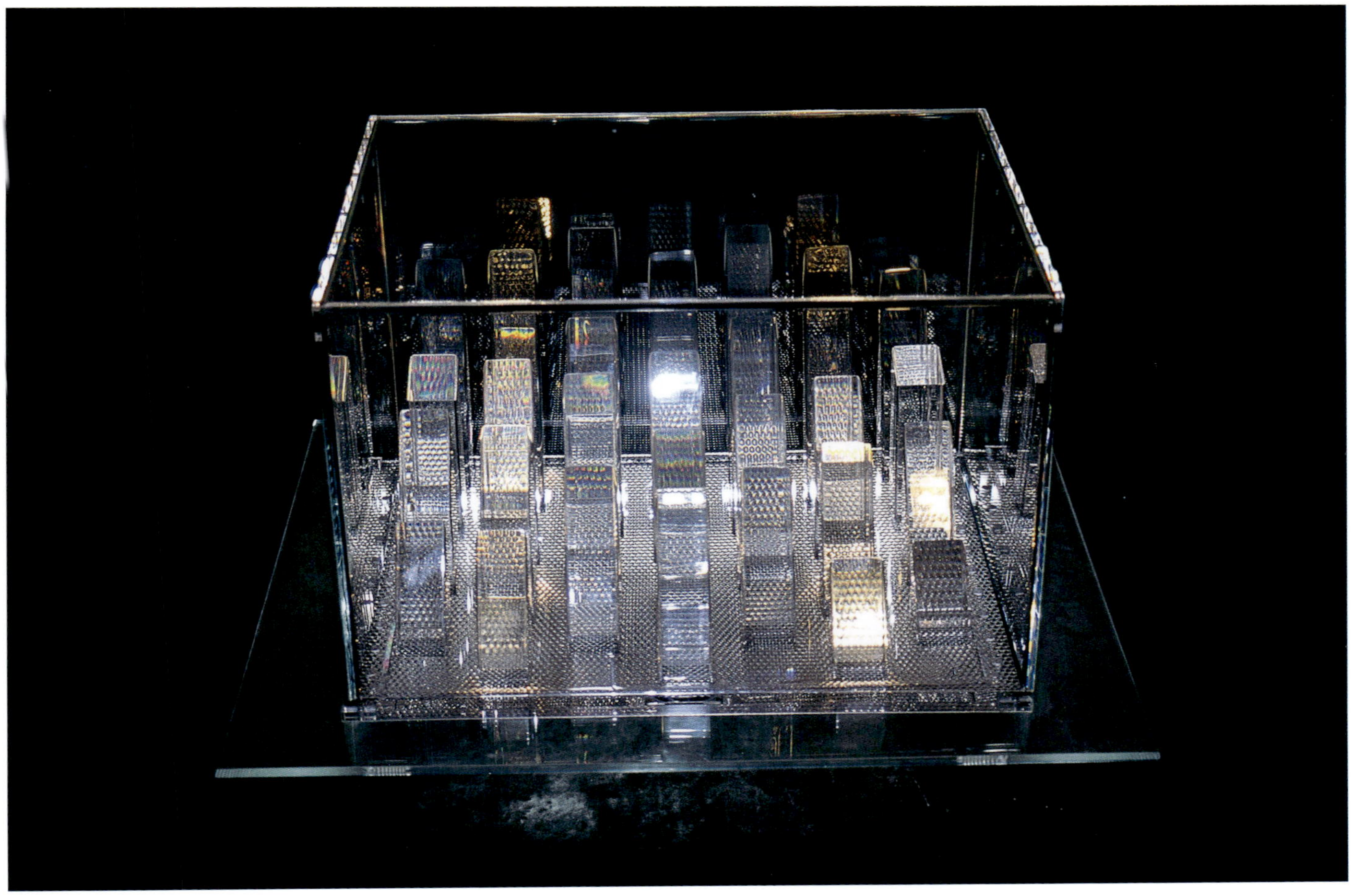

21 Heinz Mack
Licht-Kristalle
Signiert, datiert: »mack 4«
(Replik einer verschollenen Arbeit von 1964)
3-teilige Skulptur
Plexiglas, Holz, Edelstahl,
Halogenlampen, Ventilatoren
63 x 82 x 68 cm

21 Heinz Mack
Light Crystals
Signed, dated: "mack 4"
(replica of lost 1964 original)
3-part sculpture
Plexiglass, wood, stainless steel,
halogen lamps, fans
63 x 82 x 68 cm

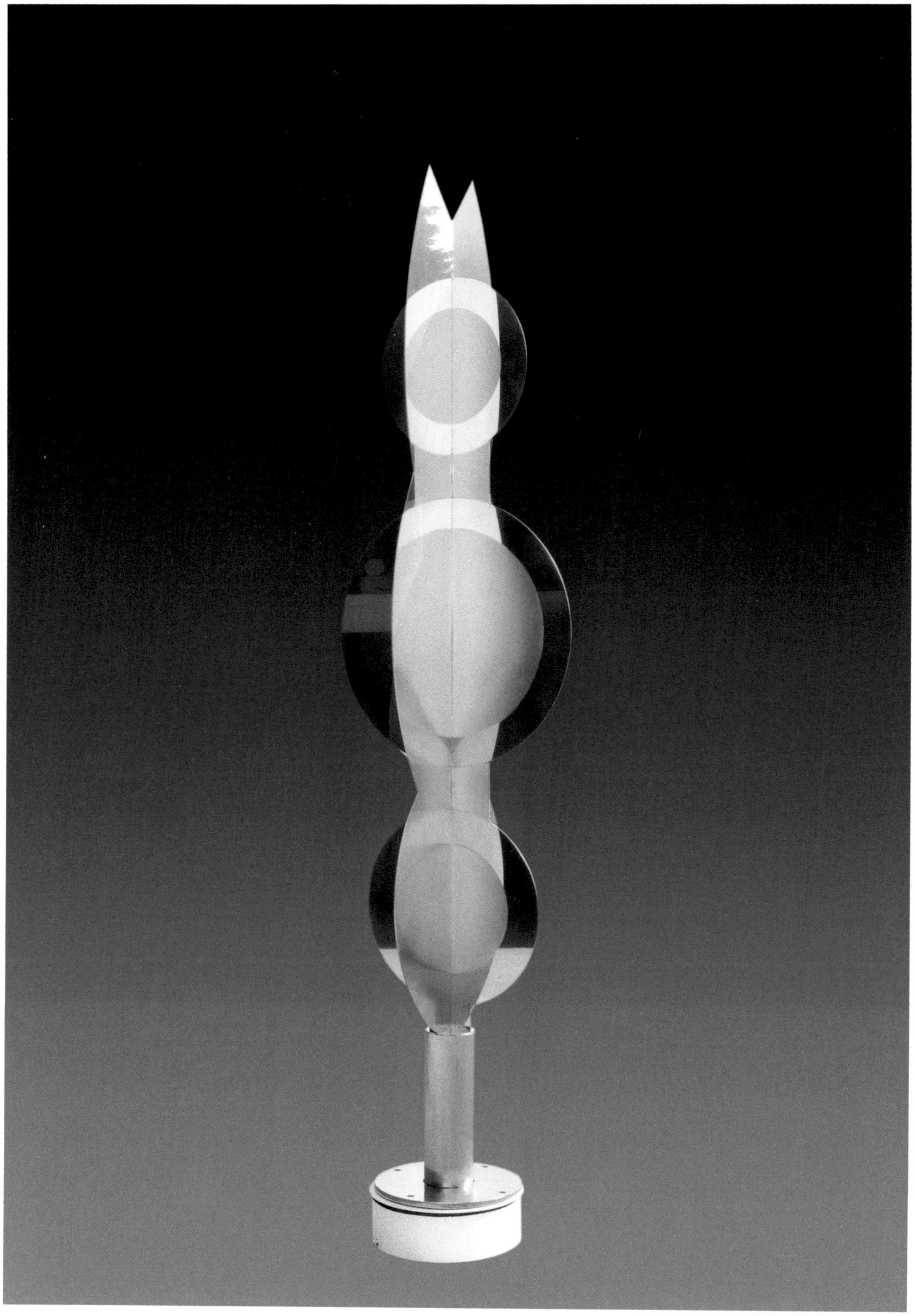

22+23 Heinz Mack
Ohne Titel
Signiert, datiert: »mack 13«
Edelstahl (poliert und geschliffen), Motor
212 x 56,5 x 42,5 cm

22+23 Heinz Mack
Untitled
Signed, dated: "mack 13"
Stainless steel (polished and sanded), motor
212 x 56.5 x 42.5 cm

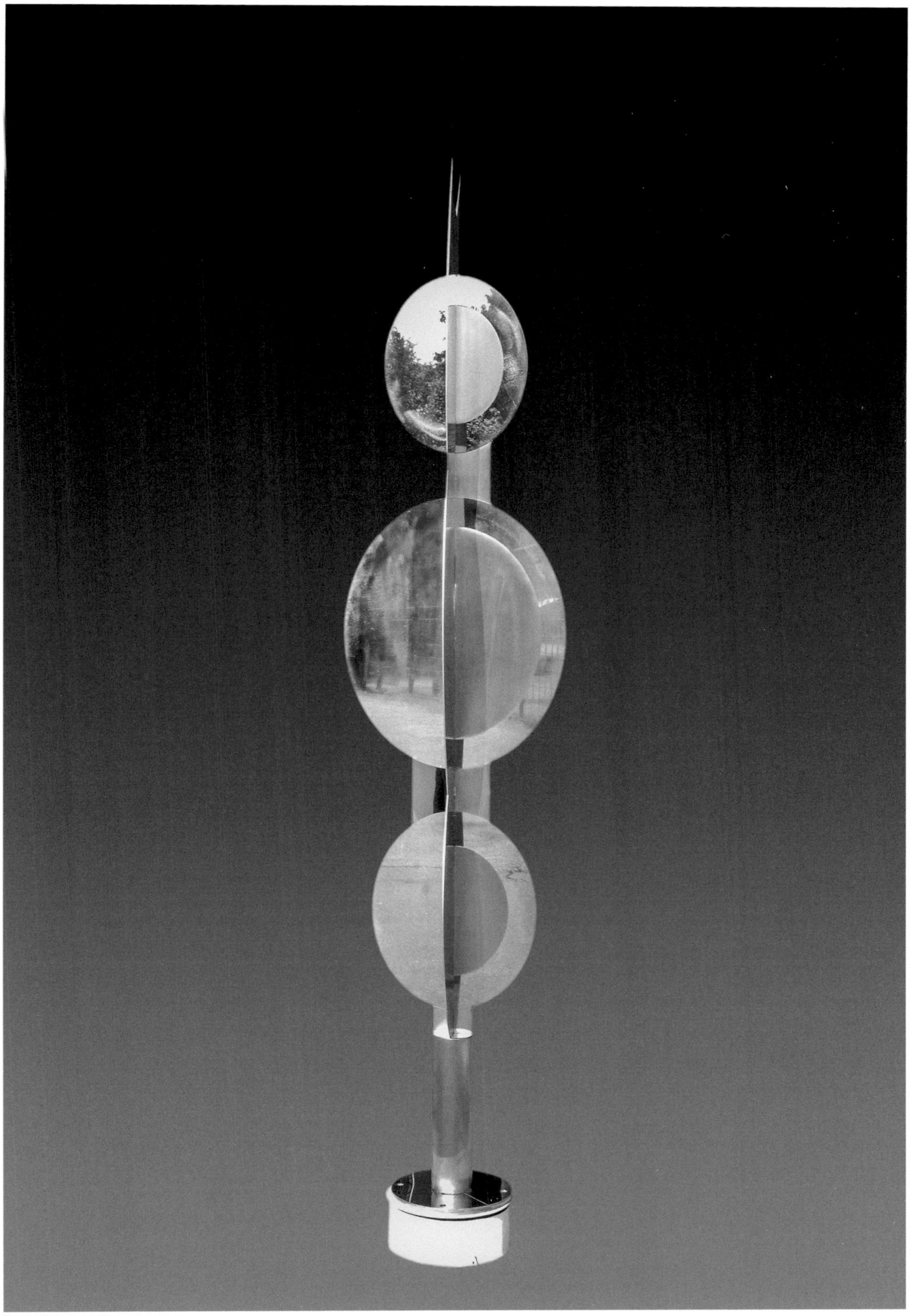

Light at Work
Light Aesthetics in the Works of Goethe and Mack

Gernot Böhme

> I am part of that part that at the first was one,
> Part of the darkness from which light has sprung,
> Proud light, that now competes with Mother Night
> For room and status, and disputes her ancient right.
> But it will not succeed, because it clings
> To sullen matter, to corporeal things.
> Matter reflects its beauty to the eye,
> But matter hinders its triumphant course;
> It cannot last for ever, and perforce
> When matter perishes, then light must die.
> (*Faust I,* v. 1349–58, trans. John R. Williams, Hertfordshire, 2007, pp. 42–43)

This is what Mephistopheles says in the first study scene when he introduces himself to Faust; we can therefore assume that it is not the entire truth. Yet it is one of the few places where Goethe talks about 'illumination,' and what he says is important. In his own way, Mephistopheles articulates the interrelation between light and matter: light depends on matter in order to even appear in the first place. It only appeares, as he and many others believe,[1] through what it causes in matter—without it, it would "die." And what is the effect of light on it? It "reflects its beauty." Beauty is, according to Plato and neo-Platonism, which Goethe follows, that which 'shines forth the most.' 'To beautify something' is tantamount causing it to emerge in its contours, indeed, to make it appear in the first place.

This already suggests Goethe's fundamental thesis regarding the aesthetics of light—in particular as it relates to works of visual art: It is the light that, due to illumination, gives them contour; it is the atmosphere of the light in which they 'live.'

After the startling discovery with the prism, Goethe was so fixated on the deeds of light as color that he paid very little attention to light as such: Within the context of color theory, it is only one out of three conditions under which colors appear, namely light, darkness, and turbidity. This is why we find only two places in his comprehensive *Theory of Colours* where he talks about illumination. One pertains to colored shadows (paragraphs 62–80), in the part that addresses physiological colors. A shadow is not colored 'per se.' This is why a second source of light is required in order for the colored shadow to appear that illuminates the surrounding area in color: then the complementary color of this light appears in the shadow area. The second place at which Goethe talks about the effect of colored illumination deals with phosphorescent minerals, thus substances that turn themselves into light sources through to colored illumination.

1 For objections to this, see my essay "Seeing Light" in Gernot Böhme, *The Aesthetics of Atmospheres* (London and New York, 2017), pp. 193–204.

Licht am Werk
Licht-Ästhetik bei Goethe und Mack

Gernot Böhme

> Ich bin ein Teil des Teils, der Anfangs alles war,
> Ein Teil der Finsternis, die sich das Licht gebar,
> Das stolze Licht, das nun der Mutter Nacht
> Den alten Rang, den Raum ihr streitig macht,
> Und doch gelingt's ihm nicht, da es, so viel es strebt,
> Verhaftet an den Körpern klebt.
> Von Körpern strömt's, die Körper macht es schön,
> Ein Körper hemmt's auf seinem Gange,
> So, hoff' ich, dauert es nicht lange
> Und mit den Körpern wird's zu Grunde gehn.
> (*Faust I*, V. 1349–1358)

Das sagt Mephisto in der Studierzimmer-Szene I, als er sich Faust vorstellt – und so können wir davon ausgehen, dass es nicht die ganze Wahrheit ist. Doch diese Stelle ist eine der wenigen, an denen Goethe etwas zum Thema ›Beleuchtung‹ sagt. Doch was er sagt, ist wichtig. Mephisto artikuliert hier auf seine Weise die Wechselbeziehung von Licht und Körper: Das Licht ist, um überhaupt in Erscheinung zu treten, auf die Körper angewiesen. Es erscheint nur, wie er und viele meinen[1], durch das, was es an den Körpern bewirkt – ohne sie würde es »zu Grunde gehn«. Und was bewirkt es an ihnen? »Die Körper macht es schön«. Schönheit ist nach Platon und dem Neuplatonismus, dem Goethe folgt, das ›Hervorscheinendste‹. ›Etwas schön machen‹ heißt so viel wie, es in seinen Konturen hervortreten zu lassen, ja, es überhaupt zur Erscheinung zu bringen.

Damit deutet sich schon Goethes Grundthese zur Lichtästhetik an, wie sie sich vor allem auf Werke der bildenden Kunst bezieht: Es ist das Licht qua Beleuchtung, das ihnen Kontur gibt, es ist die Atmosphäre des Lichtes, in der sie ›leben‹.

Goethe war durch sein Initiationserlebnis am Prisma derartig auf die Taten des Lichtes als Farbe fixiert, dass er dem Licht als solchem kaum Aufmerksamkeit zugewandt hat: Im Rahmen der Farbenlehre ist es nur eine von drei Bedingungen, unter denen Farben erscheinen, nämlich Licht, Finsternis und Trübe. Deshalb finden sich in seinen umfangreichen Studien *Zur Farbenlehre* nur zwei Stellen, an denen er über Beleuchtung spricht. Die eine betrifft die farbigen Schatten, die Paragraphen 62–80 im Teil, der sich den physiologischen Farben zuwendet. Ein Schatten ist ›an sich‹ nicht farbig. Man bedarf deshalb für die Erscheinung des farbigen Schattens einer zweiten Lichtquelle, die das Umfeld farbig beleuchtet: Dann erscheint im Schattenbereich die zu diesem Licht komplementäre Farbe. – Die zweite Stelle, an der Goethe auf die »Wirkung farbiger Beleuchtung« eingeht, handelt von phosphoreszierenden Mineralien, also solchen Stoffen, die aufgrund farbiger Beleuchtung selbst zu Lichtquellen werden.

1 Einwände dagegen in meinem Aufsatz »Licht sehen«, in: Gernot Böhme, *Atmosphäre. Essays zur Neuen Ästhetik*, Frankfurt am Main, 7. erweiterte und überarbeitete Aufl. 2013, S. 143–158.

The crucial place at which Goethe acknowledges the aesthetic meaning of light is found in a different context: it is his essay *On the Laocoon Group*. Goethe saw a replica of this sculpture at the Mannheim Castle during his travels to and from Strasbourg. The essay is an account of his experiences and—as it turns out on closer perusal—a first attempt at an aesthetic of reception. It contains advice on how works of visual art ought to be viewed. In this context, illumination plays an important role: it is only due to light that they turn into what they actually are. With this phrase Goethe already participates in the particularly heated art-historical debate on this sculpture that is carried out at the time and that dealt primarily with its origin and its meaning. According to Goethe, it is a question of the experience one has in the physical presence of the artwork. And this is largely dependent on lighting. Goethe makes two remarks in this context, of which the first is not so important, namely that within the general forest of figures in the gallery it is not until it is appropriately illuminated that one can adequately value this work individually. His second remark is much more important: One ought to vary the illumination. Alternating lighting would animate the otherwise static figure—an effect that manifests itself especially during a visit with nighttime torchlight.

In this description or, rather, this practice of reception, Goethe refers to Lessing's publication *Laocoon,* in which he states that the visual artist—naturally limited to items standing side by side—can only show movement by depicting his figures at a 'productive' or 'incisive' instant. It is the moment in which we sense, in the sculpture's posture, the tendency of motion of what is depicted. In order to appreciate this productive moment as such, Goethe gives the following advice with respect to reception aesthetics: one should close one's eyes for a moment and then look at the sculpture again—then one would expect to find it in a different posture.

Let us note: According to Goethe, one must be physically present in order to experience a work of visual art. But then the lighting in which it appears plays a crucial role. It is the light that causes it to appear as what it is in the first place. And it is the ephemeral play of light surrounding the work that lends it its striking vitality.

Goethe's remarks on aesthetic reception in *On the Laocoon Group* are seminal for the question of the effect of light as illumination. Otherwise, his remarks regarding the topic of light are sparse. One of the reasons is that lighting was still almost impossible to 'handle' at his time. One only needs to read about the effort with which the architect in Goethe's *Elective Affinities* stages an illumination for the 'tableaux vivants.'[2] Today, however, specific illumination research is developing that is not only motivated by an incredible development of light fixtures and their technical control, but also by the respective expansion of the area of application—from the aesthetics of merchandise to the light design of entire cities and the staging of major sports and art events. The Farblichtlabor in Zurich in particular has again taken up research that Josef Albers originally began in his book *Interaction of Color* at the Bauhaus. The key question is in which color products—ranging from fruit to clothing—appear under specific lighting conditions.[3]

2 Johann Wolfgang von Goethe, Goethe, *Elective Affinities* (London, 1978), pp. 203ff.

3 Josef Albers, *Interaction of Color* (New Haven, 2013); Ulrich Bachmann, ed., *Colours between Light and Darkness* (Sulgen and Zurich, 2005).

Die entscheidende Stelle, an der Goethe die ästhetische Bedeutung des Lichtes würdigt, findet sich in anderem Zusammenhang. Es ist seine kleine Schrift *Über Laokoon*. Goethe hat diese Skulptur im Mannheimer Schloss (als Replik) bei seinen Reisen von und nach Straßburg gesehen. Die Schrift *Über Laokoon* ist der Bericht über seine Erfahrungen und, wie sich nach genauerer Lektüre herausstellt, der erste Versuch einer Rezeptionsästhetik. Sie enthält Ratschläge, wie man Werke der bildenden Kunst betrachten soll, und dabei spielt die Beleuchtung eine entscheidende Rolle: Erst im Licht werden sie zu dem, was sie eigentlich sind. Schon durch diese Wendung bezieht Goethe Stellung gegenüber der damaligen, gerade bei diesem Werk besonders erregten kunstgeschichtlichen Debatte, die sich vornehmlich mit der Herkunft und der Bedeutung des Werkes beschäftigte. Nach Goethe kommt es auf die Erfahrung an, die man in leiblicher Anwesenheit bei dem Kunstwerk macht. Und die hängt wesentlich von der Beleuchtung ab. Dazu macht Goethe zwei Bemerkungen, von denen die erste nicht so wichtig ist, nämlich dass im allgemeinen Figurenwald des Saales man erst durch entsprechende Beleuchtung dieses Werk als Einzelnes würdigen könne. Die zweite ist viel wichtiger: Man solle die Beleuchtung wechseln lassen. Durch diese wechselnde Beleuchtung würde die an sich statische Figur belebt – eine Wirkung, die sich besonders bei einem Besuch mit nächtlichem Fackelschein zeige.

Mit dieser Beschreibung und, besser gesagt, dieser Rezeptionspraxis bezieht sich Goethe auf Lessings Schrift *Laokoon,* in der dieser sagt, der bildende Künstler, der naturgemäß auf ein Nebeneinander eingeschränkt sei, könne Bewegung nur darstellen, indem er seine Figuren im ›fruchtbaren‹ oder ›prägnanten‹ Augenblick darstelle. Nämlich dem Moment, in dem man in der Haltung der Skulptur die Bewegungstendenz des Dargestellten spüre. Um diesen fruchtbaren Augenblick als solchen zu würdigen, gibt Goethe noch folgenden rezeptionsästhetischen Ratschlag: Man schließe für einen Moment die Augen und blicke dann wieder auf die Skulptur – dann werde man erwarten, sie in einer anderen Haltung wiederzufinden.

Halten wir fest: Nach Goethe muss ein Werk der bildenden Kunst in leiblicher Anwesenheit erfahren werden. Dann aber spielt die Beleuchtung, in der es erscheint, eine entscheidende Rolle. Es ist das Licht am Werk, das erst, was es ist, zur Erscheinung bringt. Und es ist das ephemere Spiel des Lichtes am Werk, das diesem seine eindrucksvolle Lebendigkeit verleiht.

Goethes rezeptionsästhetische Bemerkungen in *Über Laokoon* sind für die Frage, was Licht qua Beleuchtung bewirkt, bahnbrechend. Sonst sind seine Bemerkungen zum Thema Beleuchtung spärlich. Das liegt aber auch daran, dass man zu seiner Zeit Beleuchtungen noch kaum ›handhaben‹ konnte – man lese nur nach, mit welchem Aufwand der Architekt in Goethes *Wahlverwandtschaften* für die ›stehenden Bilder‹ eine Beleuchtung inszeniert.[2] Heute dagegen entwickelt sich eine regelrechte Beleuchtungsforschung, die nicht nur durch die ungeheure Entwicklung von Leuchten und ihrer technischen Steuerung motiviert ist, sondern auch durch die entsprechende Ausweitung des Anwendungsfeldes – von der Warenästhetik bis hin zum Lichtdesign ganzer Städte und der Inszenierung von sportlichen und künstlerischen Großereignissen. Insbesondere das Farblichtlabor in Zürich hat Forschungen wieder aufgenommen, die ursprünglich Josef Albers in seinem Buch *Interaction of Color*

2 Johann Wolfgang Goethe, *Die Wahlverwandtschaften,* Teil 2, Kap. 5, HA, Bd. 6, S. 392.

Of course, illumination entails an entire spectrum of further topics that no longer have anything to do with the interaction of colors, including luster, gleam, and glooming, but rather concentrate on the interaction of light with surfaces structured in a specific way. Newton already incorporated the latter theme under the keyword "colours of transparent bodies" in his *Opticks*.[4] These color phenomena, as they are produced under specific surface conditions, also play a part in nature, for example, in bird feathers or in the coloring of certain amphibians.[5] And of course once you get interested in the effect of light on bodies, one can also reverse and ask what effect bodies have that shine themselves.

Heinz Mack has become involved in this illumination research in all of its facets as his artistic project. His light design installations, his sculptures that cause light itself to emerge, or his sculptures in which light is at work are convincing examples for something that is talked about so much but hardly ever realized, namely 'art as research.' Admittedly, it is research of the Baconian type, like we used to call it at the time,[6] meaning explorative, investigative, yet not explanatory. This attitude already reveals Mack as akin to Goethe, who, in his maxims and reflections wrote: "Better not to search behind the phenomena. They themselves are the teaching." For Goethe it was therefore not a question of an *experimentum crucis* through which a decision was to be made between two competing hypotheses. Rather, he developed entire series of experiments for specific phenomena by varying the conditions for the appearance of the phenomenon in question. Thus we also have entire series of works by Mack that in terms of aesthetics take us through specific areas of light phenomena by varying arrangements of light fixtures in space, of grid structures on whose surfaces light plays, and of the surface designs of illuminated bodies, as well as of their arrangement in space. These variations are also brought about by movement, be it the movement of illuminated or illuminating bodies, or be it by the illuminations' ephemeral character, for instance, the changing daylight or position of the sun. Light technology has played a role from the beginning, and this means the potential of light design that has been developing since the early twentieth century.

It is a lucky coincidence that in Mack's case—as with Goethe's account regarding his first experiences with the prism—testimony of his original experience has also survived: In World War II, the young Heinz Mack used a concertina camera to record a light spectacle that was visible due to the anti-aircraft searchlights during the bombing of the city of Krefeld.[7] The urban silhouette, comprised of smokestacks and towers, is still discernible in front of the almost explosive cluster of searchlights, as are the stars and several scattered clouds of light in the sky. It is amazing how, in all the confusion and horror of a bombardment, a boy was capable of aesthetically capturing the sublime of this night of bombing.

Later, he himself became the maître de plaisir of such light spectacles. Perhaps we should proceed straight to the end of the series, where he staged light and water festivals and ultimately became a pyrotechnician himself.[8] Yes, 'maître de plaisir' is the correct term insofar as Mack wanted to celebrate the playfulness, the ease of Light Art

4 Sir Isaac Newton, *Opticks* (New York, 1952); cf. book 2, parts 1–3, where Newton comes close to the interpretations of colors of transparent bodies as interference phenomena.

5 Cf. Adolf Portmann, *Die Tiergestalt: Studien über die Bedeutung tierischer Erscheinung* (Basel, n.d.), pp. 17f. "The iridescence (of the hummingbird's feathers) is brought about according to the same optical law as soap bubbles: the feather also contains interference phenomena."

6 Gernot Böhme et al., *Experimentelle Philosophie: Ursprünge autonomer Wissenschaftsentwicklung* (Frankfurt am Main, 1977).

7 Helmut Friedel, *Mack, Light Experiments, 1957–2017* (Munich, 2017), no. 122.

8 Ibid., esp. nos. 186–203.

bereits am Bauhaus begonnen hatte. Dabei geht es vor allem um die Frage, wie Waren – vom Obst bis zum Kleidungsstück – wie, das heißt, in welcher Farbe sie bei bestimmter Beleuchtung erscheinen.[3]

Doch es geht bei der Beleuchtung noch um ein ganzes Spektrum weiterer Themen, die nicht mehr mit der Interaktion von Farben zu tun haben. So um Glanz, Schimmer, um Strahlen, aber auch um die Wechselwirkung von Licht mit in bestimmter Weise strukturierten Oberflächen. Letzteres Thema ist unter dem Stichwort »Farben dünner Blättchen« bereits von Newton in seine *Opticks* aufgenommen worden.[4] Und natürlich spielen diese Farberscheinungen, wie sie durch bestimmte Oberflächenbeschaffenheiten erzeugt werden, auch im Naturreich eine Rolle, beispielsweise bei Vogelfedern und bei der Färbung gewisser Amphibien.[5] Und natürlich, wenn man sich schon dafür interessiert, was Licht an Körpern bewirkt, dann kann man auch die Frage umdrehen, nämlich wie Körper, die selbst leuchten, wirken.

Auf diese Beleuchtungsforschung in ihrer ganzen Vielfältigkeit hat sich Heinz Mack eingelassen, und zwar als künstlerisches Projekt. Wir haben in seinen Lichtdesigninstallationen, in seinen Skulpturen, die das Licht selbst zur Erscheinung bringen, beziehungsweise seinen Skulpturen, an denen das Licht am Werk ist, ein überzeugendes Beispiel für das, was immer wieder behauptet, aber kaum realisiert wird, nämlich ›Kunst als Forschung‹. Freilich, das ist eine Forschung vom baconischen Typ – wie wir sie seinerzeit genannt haben[6], nämlich explorativ, erkundend, nicht aber erklärend. Schon in dieser Haltung ist Mack Goethe verwandt, der ja in seinen Maximen und Reflektionen formuliert: »Man suche nur nichts hinter den Phänomenen. Sie selbst sind die Lehre.« Deshalb kam es bei Goethe auch nicht auf ein *experimentum crucis* an, durch das zwischen konkurrierenden Hypothesen entschieden werden soll. Vielmehr entwickelte er für bestimmte Phänomenbereiche ganze Versuchsreihen, indem er die Bedingungen für das Erscheinen des betreffenden Phänomens variierte. So haben wir auch von Mack ganze Reihen von Werken, die ästhetisch durch bestimmte Bereiche der Lichtphänomene führen, indem die Anordnung von Beleuchtungskörpern im Raum, von Gitterstrukturen, an denen das Licht spielt, von Oberflächengestaltungen beleuchteter Körper, aber auch von deren Anordnung im Raum variiert werden. Diese Variationen kommen aber auch durch Bewegung zustande, sei es durch die Bewegung der beleuchteten oder leuchtenden Körper selbst, sei es durch den ephemeren Charakter der Beleuchtungen, etwa des wechselnden Tageslichtes oder des Sonnenstandes. Dabei spielt von Anfang an die Lichttechnik eine Rolle, das heißt, die seit Anfang des 20. Jahrhunderts sich entwickelnde Möglichkeit des Lichtdesigns.

Es ist ein glücklicher Zufall, dass sich, wie bei Goethe durch seinen Bericht über seine ersten Erfahrungen mit dem Prisma, auch für Mack das Zeugnis eines Initiationserlebnisses erhalten hat: Noch während des Zweiten Weltkrieges hat der junge Heinz Mack mit einer Ziehharmonika-Kamera ein Lichtspektakel festgehalten, das durch die Flak-Scheinwerfer während eines Bombardements der Stadt Krefeld zu sehen war.[7] Vor dem geradezu explosiven Bündel der Scheinwerfer ist vorne noch die von Schornsteinen und Türmen gebildete Stadtsilhouette zu sehen und oben am Himmel die Sterne und einzelne verstreute Lichtwolken. Es ist erstaunlich, wie hier ein Junge in all den Wirrnissen und Schrecken einer Bombennacht ästhetisch das Erhabene einer Lichtszenerie hat erfassen können.

3 Josef Albers, *Interaction of Color*. Grundlegung einer Didaktik des Sehens, Köln 1997; Ulrich Bachmann (Hrsg.), *Farben zwischen Licht und Dunkelheit*, Sulgen und Zürich 2005.

4 Sir Isaac Newton, *Opticks*, New York 1952, vgl. dazu das 2. Buch der Opticks, Teil 1–3. Newton kommt hier der Deutung der Farben dünner Blättchen (bei ihm: »Colours of transparent Bodies«) als Interferenzerscheinungen nahe.

5 Vgl. dazu Adolf Portmann, *Die Tiergestalt. Studien über die Bedeutung tierischer Erscheinung*, Basel o. J., S. 17 f.: »Dieses Schillern [der Kolibri-Federn] kommt hier wie in Seifenblasen nach den gleichen optischen Gesetzen zustande: auch in der Feder sind es Interferenzerscheinungen […].«

6 Gernot Böhme u. a., *Experimentelle Philosophie. Ursprünge autonomer Wissensentwicklung*, Frankfurt am Main 1977.

7 Nr. 122 in: Helmut Friedel (Hrsg.), *Mack, Licht Experimente. 1957–2017*, München 2017.

in these works in a very special way. Far from wanting to create a work for eternity, they were events for the spectators who were present. This is the moment where we must quote Adorno: he speaks (with Ernst Schoen) about the "unsurpassable noblesse of fireworks as the only art that aspires not to duration but only to glow for an instant and fade away."[9] Indeed, Heinz Mack's Light Art is ephemeral art.[10] Since light as illumination is always an event, the event character also belongs to Mack's works. They are intended as objects on which light is at work, even in instances where they still have the materiality that Mack lends them as a sculptor. One actually needs to be present and wait to see what happens in order to be able to adequately estimate the work. The same holds true for the massive granite pillar on Cologne's Cathedral Square, whose lithic force definitely establishes a relationship with the filigree cathedral building. Yet this applies even more so to metal stelae such as *Die fortwährende Wiederkehr* (The perpetual Return) on Mathildenhöhe in Darmstadt or the *Große Stele* (Large Stele) in front of the Mercedes-Benz Museum in Stuttgart.[11] In its sculptural simplicity, the latter work—as such a simple triangular pillar made of steel with an equilateral plinth that in six phases tapers from the bottom upwards to transform from a triangle to a concave hexagon to ultimately terminate in the Mercedes star—in particular demonstrates how much depends on the play of light: the sun, whose position always causes different areas of the pillar to shine forth, right up to an incredible blaze that dazzles the visitor like a second sun.

Even as objects, Mack's artworks have an ephemeral character. This is not only because they age or fall victim to building or sales measures, but also due to the fact that their surfaces undergo weather-related changes, so that the light occasionally no longer falls on structures on which it can and should develop a fascinating effect. Mack's material works are sometimes not intended to be works in a classic sense—with a claim to eternity. Instead, they have more the character of props used for a staging. This is especially the case when they are taken to remote regions such as the Arctic near Greenland or the Sahara. The work of art is then an event in the way it manifests itself in the light or how light manifests itself on it.

Due to this ephemeral character of Light Art, photographs gain increasing importance. This was also the case with Beuys, who was a true performance artist. Much like what survives of his stagings now spreads out in museums as his works are actually documents, so do Mack's photographs have documentary character. They are testimony of light events and will remain with us as works by the photographic artist Heinz Mack. It is no surprise that a fair number of his pieces are considered photo experiments from the very beginning.[12] Heinz Mack, painter, sculptor: as a light artist, he is necessarily also a photographer. What remains are the images. For the viewer, they also contain what Mack's event-like art conveyed to the attendant spectators: delight in being there.

9 Theodor W. Adorno, *Aesthetic Theory*, ed. and trans. Robert Hullot-Kentor (London, 1997), p. 28.

10 Cf. Gernot Böhme. *Die sanfte Kunst des Ephemeren* (Essen, 2008). Also in Mira Fliescher et al., eds., *Sichtbarkeiten I: Erscheinen—Zur Praxis des Präsentiven* (Berlin, 2013), pp. 87–108.

11 Cf. Heinz Mack, ed., *Mack: Ars urbana. Kunst für die Stadt, 1952–2008* (Munich 2007) in the sequence nos. 28, 21, 44–72.

12 Friedel 2017 (see note 7), nos. 160–69.

Später wurde er dann selbst zum Maître de Plaisir solcher Lichtspektakel. Vielleicht sollte man gleich ans Ende der Reihe gehen, nämlich dorthin, wo er Lichtfeste oder Licht- und Wasserfeste inszenierte oder schließlich gar selbst zum Pyrotechniker wurde.[8] Ja, ›Maître de Plaisir‹ ist der richtige Ausdruck, insofern Mack in diesen Arbeiten in besonderer Weise das Spielerische, das Leichte der Lichtkunst zelebrieren, alles andere als ein Werk für die Ewigkeit schaffen wollte, sondern ein Ereignis für die anwesenden Zuschauer. Das ist der Moment, in dem Adorno zitiert werden muss: Er spricht (mit Ernst Schoen) von der »unübertrefflichen Noblesse des Feuerwerks […], das als einzige Kunst nicht dauern wolle, sondern einen Augenblick lang strahlen und verpuffen«.[9] Ja, es ist ephemere Kunst[10], die Lichtkunst von Heinz Mack. Da Licht als Beleuchtung immer ein Geschehen ist, gehört zu den Werken von Mack auch ihr Ereignischarakter. Selbst dort, wo sie noch eine handfeste Dinglichkeit haben, die ihnen Mack als Bildhauer verleiht, sind sie gemeint als Objekte, an denen das Licht am Werk ist. Man muss schon da sein und abwarten, was geschieht, will man dem Werk entsprechen. Das gilt auch für den massiven Granitpfeiler auf dem Domplatz zu Köln, der ja durch seine steinerne Wucht durchaus in Beziehung zum filigranen Dombau tritt, aber es gilt vielmehr noch für Metallstelen wie für *Die fortwährende Wiederkehr* auf der Mathildenhöhe in Darmstadt und die *Große Stele* vor dem Benz-Museum in Stuttgart.[11] Gerade das letzte Werk – an sich ein schlichter Dreikantpfeiler aus Stahl, der in seiner Form lediglich dadurch, dass von der gleichseitigen Basis sich die Seiten mehr und mehr in der Mitte einknicken, um schließlich ganz oben den Mercedes-Stern zu bilden – also gerade dieses Werk demonstriert in seiner skulpturalen Schlichtheit, wie sehr alles auf das Spiel des Lichtes daran ankommt: die Sonne, deren Stand dann jeweils andere Bereiche der Stele aufleuchten lässt, bis hin zu einem ungeheuren Strahlen, das den Besucher quasi wie eine zweite Sonne blendet.

Macks Kunstwerke haben auch als Gegenstände einen ephemeren Charakter. Das liegt nicht nur daran, dass sie altern oder gar Bau- und Verkaufsmaßnahmen zum Opfer fallen, sondern vielmehr auch an der Tatsache, dass ihre Oberflächen witterungsbedingt sich verändern und deshalb manchmal dem Licht nicht mehr jene Strukturen entgegenhalten, an denen es sein faszinierendes Werk tun kann und sollte. Manchmal aber sind die dinglichen Werke von Mack auch gar nicht im klassischen Sinne als Werk gemeint – mit Anspruch auf Ewigkeit, sondern haben eher den Charakter von Utensilien zu einer Inszenierung. Das ist insbesondere dann der Fall, wenn sie in entlegene Gegenden, wie die Arktis bei Grönland, oder in die Sahara gebracht werden. Das Kunstwerk ist dann das Ereignis, wie sie dort im Licht erscheinen beziehungsweise wie das Licht an ihnen erscheint.

Durch diesen ephemeren Charakter der Lichtkunst wird das Foto in zunehmendem Maße wichtig. So wie auch bei Beuys, der ja eigentlich ein Performancekünstler war. Wie, was von seinen Inszenierungen bleibt und sich nun in Museen als sein Werk aufspreizt, eigentlich Dokumente sind, so haben die Fotos von Heinz Mack einen ähnlichen Charakter. Sie sind Zeugnisse für ein Lichtereignis und bleiben uns als Werke des Fotokünstlers Mack. Kein Wunder, dass nicht wenige seiner Werke von vorneherein als Fotoexperimente gelten.[12] Heinz Mack, Maler, Bildhauer: Als Lichtkünstler ist er notwendig auch Fotograf. Was uns bleibt, sind die Bilder. Auch sie noch enthalten für den Betrachter, was die ereignishafte Kunst von Mack den anwesenden Zuschauern vermittelte: die Freude, da zu sein.

8 Vgl. ebd., besonders Nr. 186–203.

9 Theodor W. Adorno, *Ästhetische Theorie*, 7. Aufl., Frankfurt am Main 1985, S. 49; vgl. auch ebd., S. 125 f.

10 Vgl. Gernot Böhme, *Die sanfte Kunst des Ephemeren*, Essen 2008; auch in: Sichtbarkeiten 1. Erscheinen. Zur Praxis des Präsentativen, hrsg. von Mira Fliescher u. a., Berlin 2013, S. 87–108.

11 Vgl. Heinz Mack (Hrsg.): *Mack. Ars urbana. Kunst für die Stadt. 1952–2008*, München 2007, der Reihe nach Nr. 28, 21 und 44–72.

12 Friedel 2017 (wie Anm. 7), Nr. 160–169.

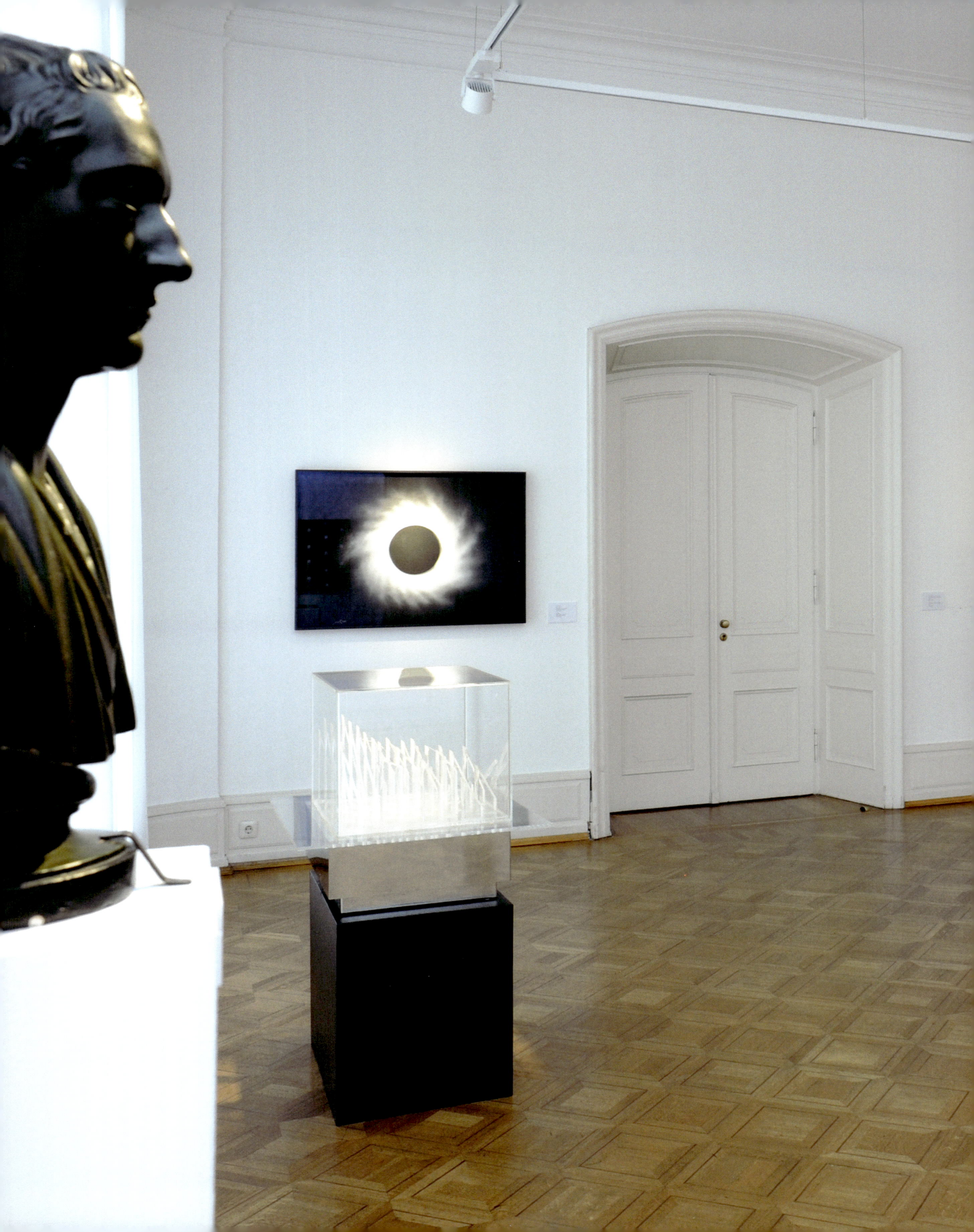

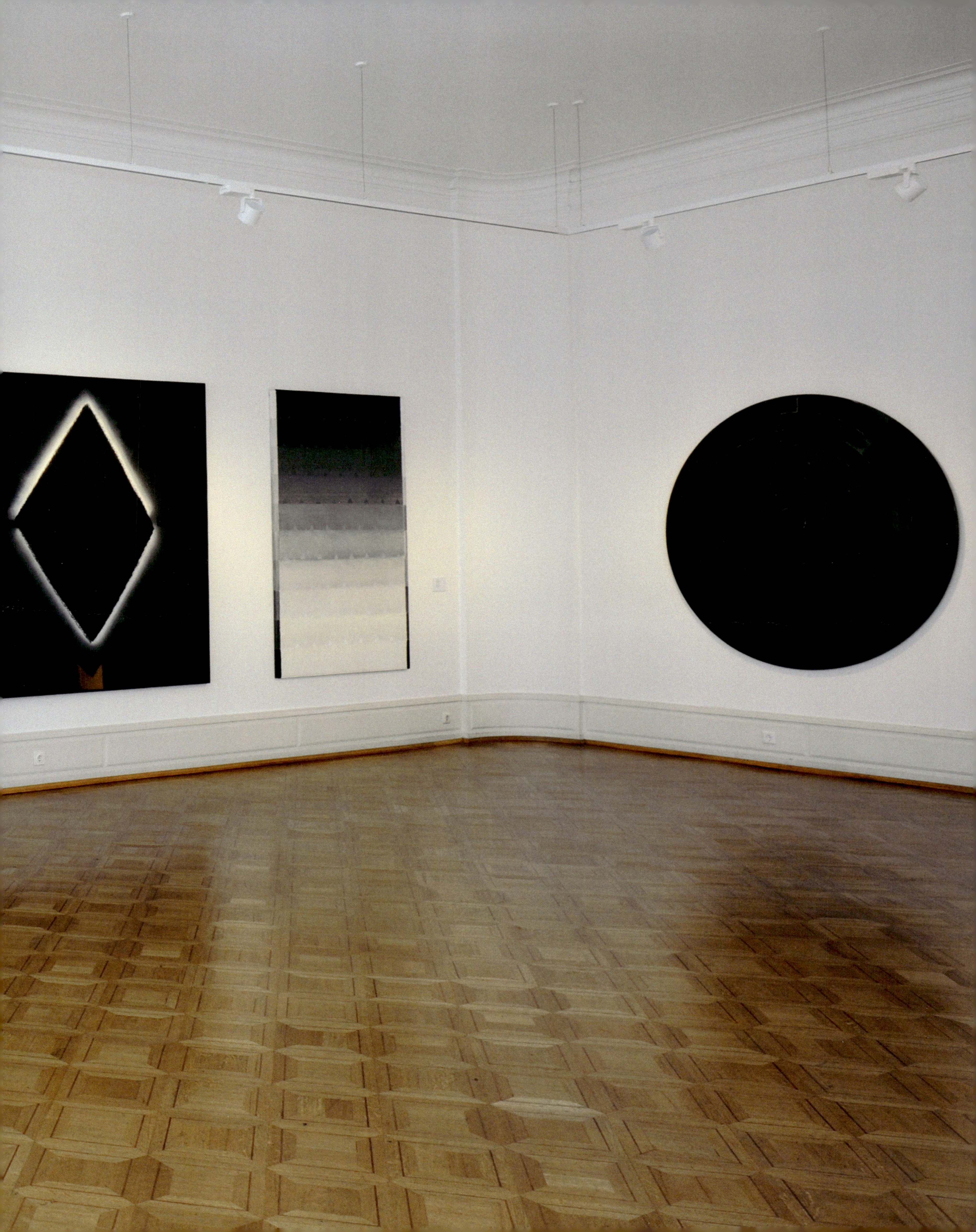

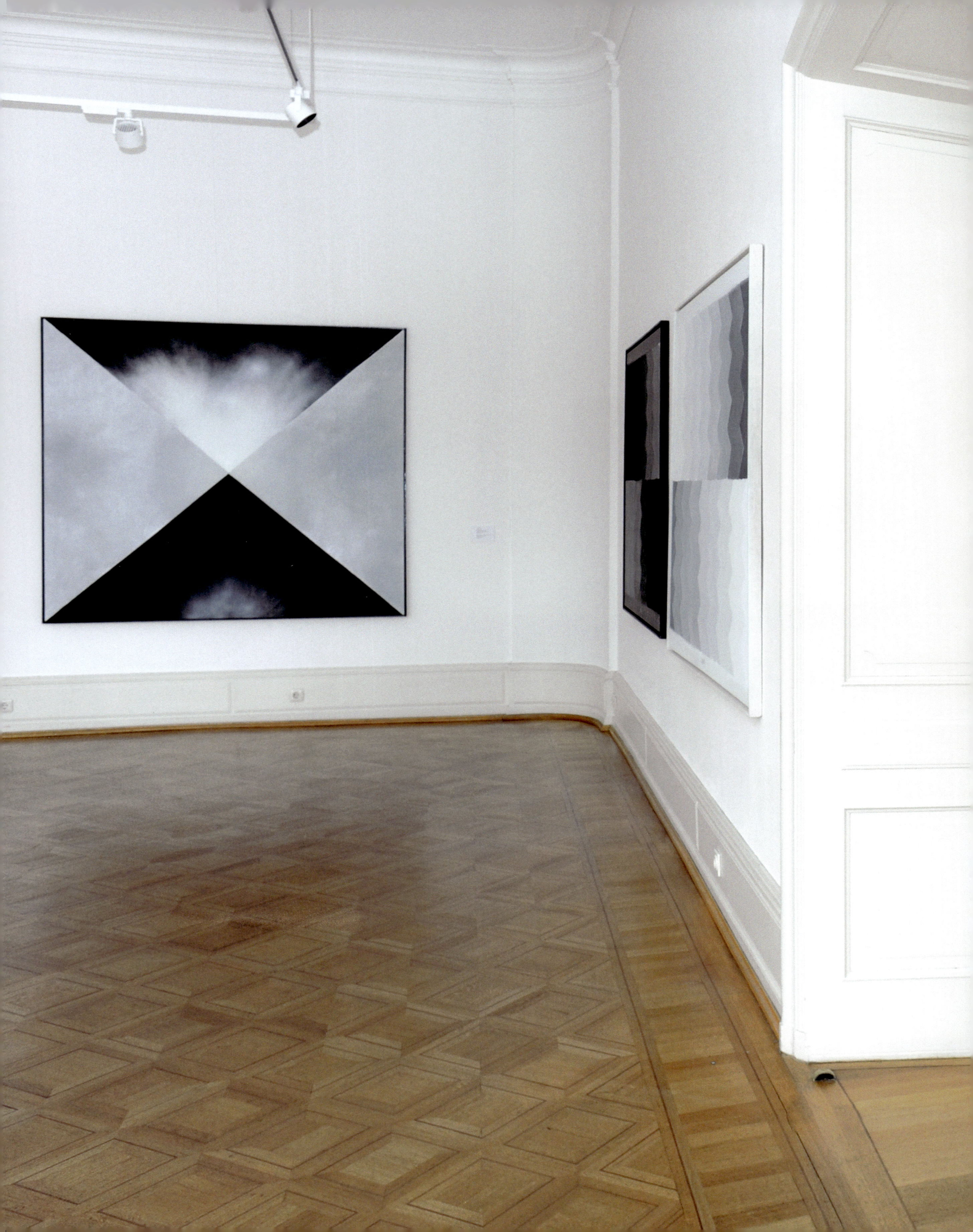

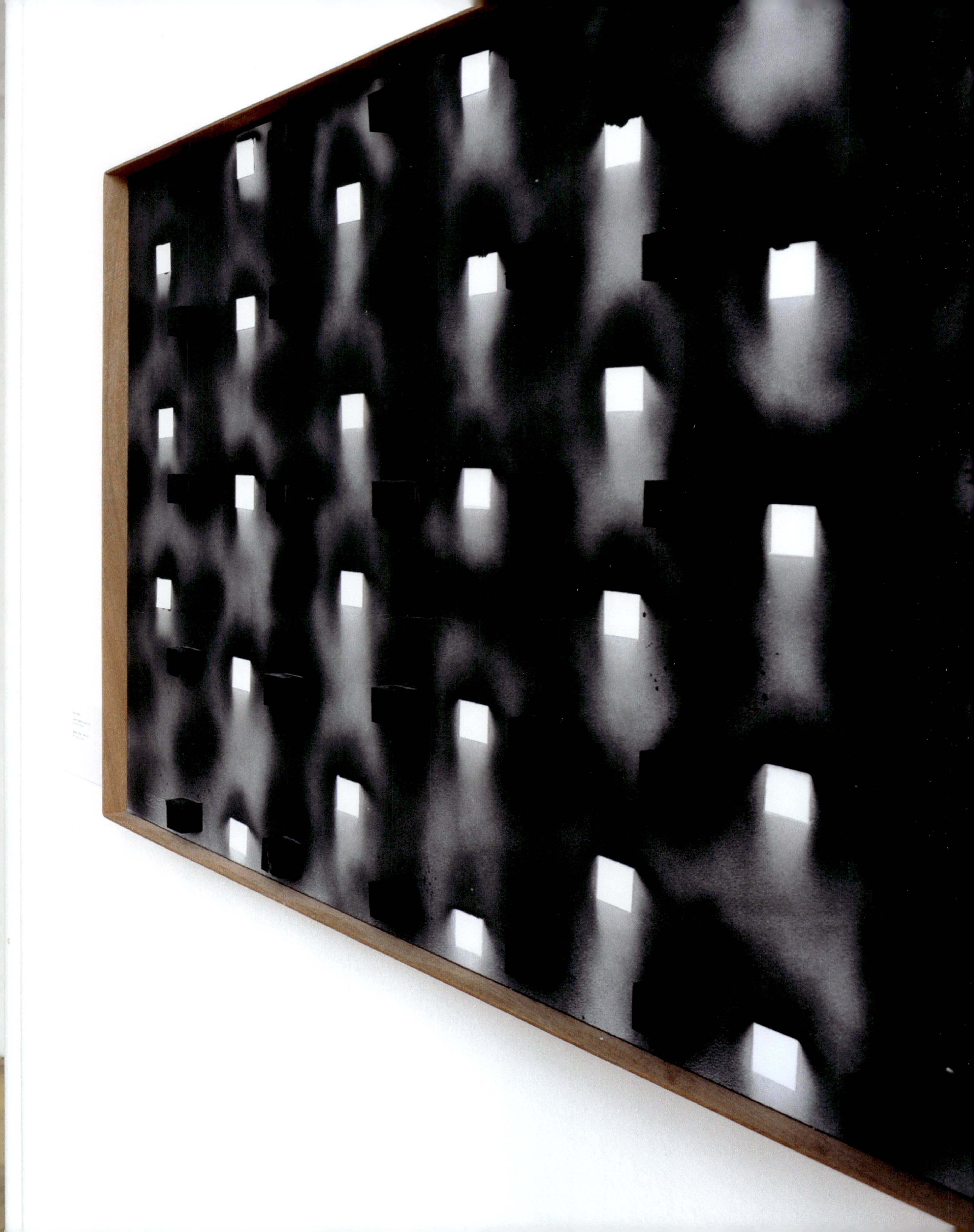

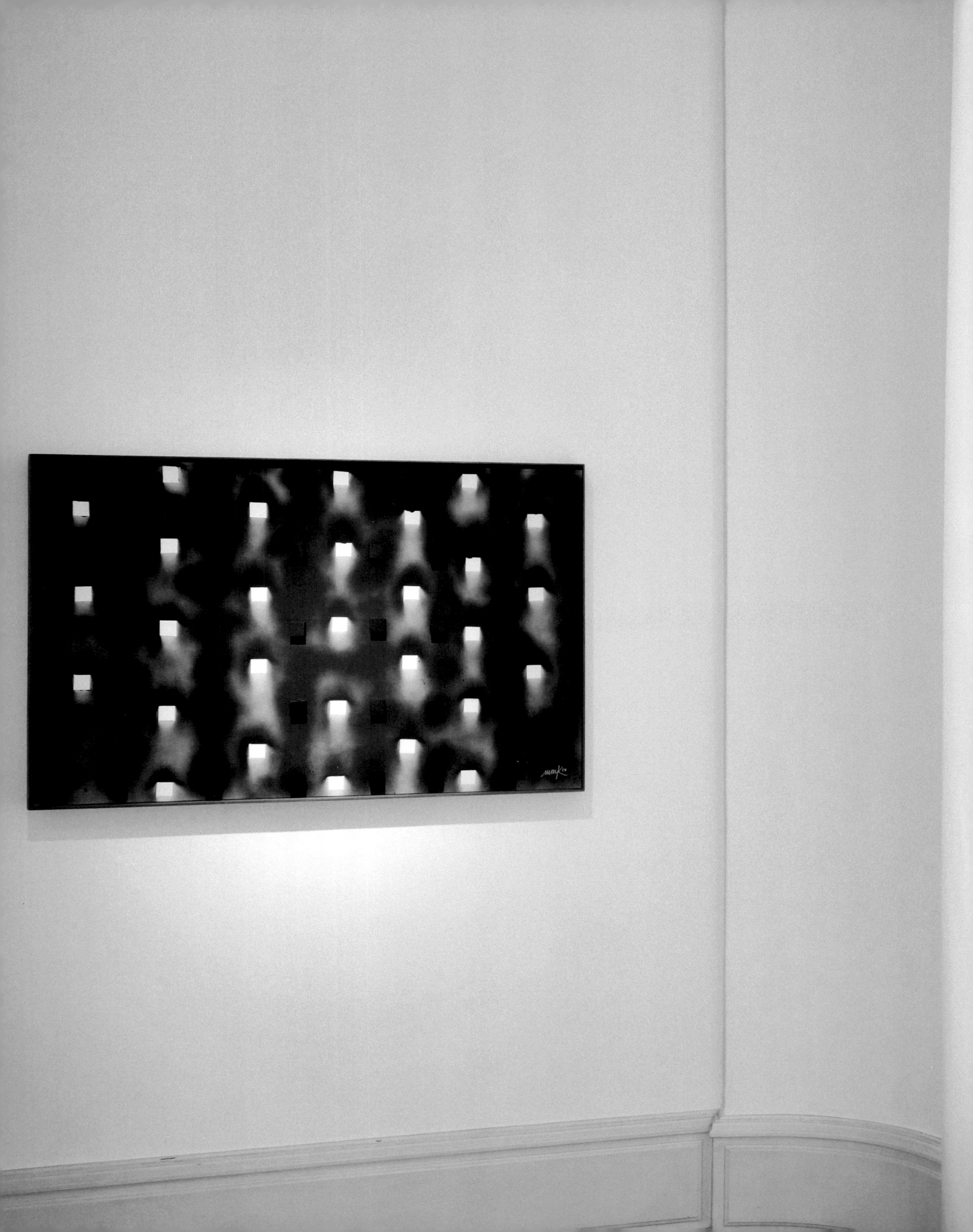

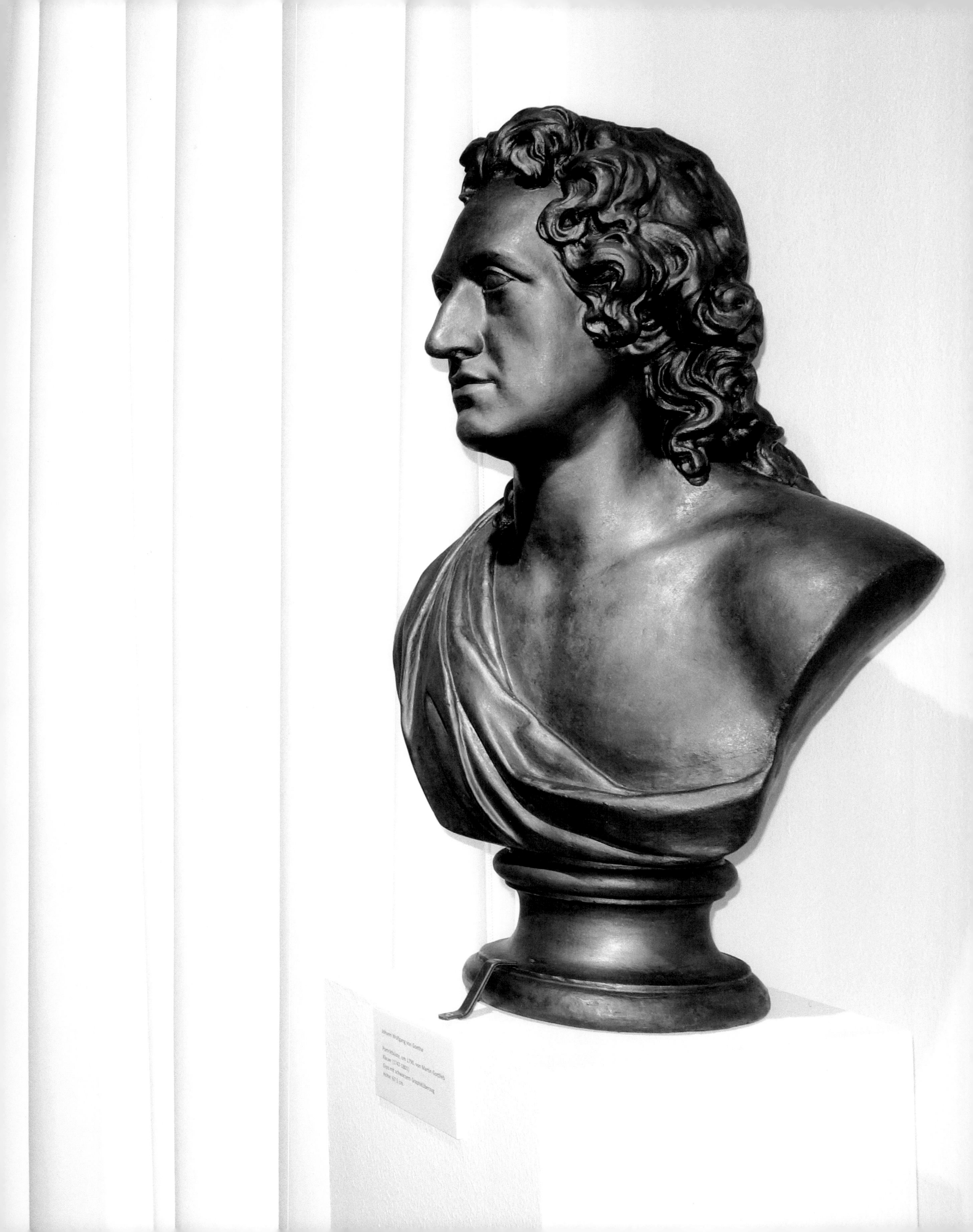
Johann Wolfgang von Goethe
Porträtbüste, um 1790, von Martin Gottlieb
Klauer (1742-1801)
Gips mit schwarzem Graphitüberzug
Höhe: 67,5 cm

Images and Creations of Light in Goethe's and Heinz Mack's Works

Hartmut Böhme

1. Deep Night and Paradisial Light

At the beginning of *Faust II,* the audience is confronted with powerful scenes of light and darkness. In the midst of an Alpine landscape—a "pleasant landscape," or 'locus amoenus'—and tormented by guilt (three casualties burden his conscience), Faust awakens from a healing sleep. As he is bathed "with dew from Lethe's stream" (v. 4629), he is freed from the nightmares of guilt. Benevolent 'spirits' speak to him while he sleeps: "Recover, wholly: / Trust the sight of breaking day" (v. 4652–53). Just as "the new day is appearing" (v. 4668) after the night, Faust will be returned to the "holy light." Goethe's fundamental belief is that the rhythm of night and day, of darkness and light, is the rhythm of life par excellence. Death-like absence and rebirth are poles of archaic transitional rites. In this case, they also signify, morally and physically, recreation and metamorphosis. This is not Faust's achievement, but more of a passive experience of the very power of life; it reveals itself in the pendulum's movement between darkness and light, or in the rhythms of breathing of the systole and diastole, where it is also a perpetual physical presence.

> Thus, inspiration already presupposes expiration; thus every systole its diastole. It is the universal formula of life which manifests itself in this as in all other cases. When darkness is presented to the eye it demands brightness, and vice versâ: it shows its vital energy, its fitness to receive the impression of the object, precisely by spontaneously tending to an opposite state. (Goethe, *Theory of Colours,* p. 15.)[1]

In its need for contrasts and polarities, the eye does not act any differently. Thus, Faust, after the night's darkness, also takes delight in greeting the day's brightness, the shadow, and the contrasts of color. Out of the blackness of night, things increasingly elevate themselves into more light, until a sudden gaze at the risen sun's light becomes unbearable, which prompts Faust to mitigate the eyes' physiological need for contrasts: with the sun at his back, he can enjoy the waterfall's colorful haze as a rainbow plays over the falling water. What he 'sees in the world' as dynamically organized light reflects, at the same time, the process of his inner self: the spiritual (the liberating refreshment), the moral (the healing of guilt), and the cognitive (the comprehension of his own position in life, v. 4626–27). The light's appearance during sunrise is an early artwork of light—in the eye of the beholder, subjectively, and objectively in the natural cosmic play of light.

1 "The eye after sleep exhibits its vital elasticity more especially by its tendency to alternate its impressions, which in the simplest form change from dark to light, and from light to dark. The eye cannot for a moment remain in a particular state determined by the object it looks upon. On the contrary, it is forced to a sort of opposition, which, in contrasting extreme with extreme, intermediate degree with intermediate degree, at the same time combines these opposite impressions, and thus ever tends to a whole, whether the impressions are successive, or simultaneous and confined to one image." (Goethe, *Theory of Colours,* trans. Charles Lock Eastlake [London, 1840], p. 13.)

Bilder und Bildungen des Lichts bei Goethe und Heinz Mack

Hartmut Böhme

Vorhergehende Doppelseite/
Previous double page:
Heinz Mack
Licht und Schatten, s. S. 155
und Martin Gottlieb Klauer (1742–1801)
Goethe, Porträtbüste, um 1790
Gips mit schwarzem Grafitüberzug
67,5 x 40 x 26 cm
Goethe-Museum Düsseldorf

Heinz Mack
Light and Shadow, see p. 155
and Martin Gottlieb Klauer (1742–1801)
Goethe, Portrait bust, um 1790
Plaster of Paris with black graphite coating
67.5 x 40 x 26 cm
Goethe-Museum Düsseldorf

1. Tiefe Nacht und Paradieseshelle

Zu Beginn von *Faust II* wird der Zuschauer mit gewaltigen Dunkel- und Licht-Szenerien konfrontiert. In einer alpinen Landschaft, gebettet in eine »anmutige Gegend«, einen ›locus amoenus‹, erwacht Faust, von inneren Schuldgefühlen gepeinigt (drei Tote beschweren sein Gewissen), aus einem Heilschlaf. Er wird »im Tau aus Lethes Flut« gebadet (V. 4629), nämlich von den Albträumen der Schuld befreit. Die wohltätigen ›Geister‹ sprechen dem Schlafenden zu: »[...] du wirst gesunden; / Traue neuem Tagesblick.« (V. 4652 f.) Wie nach der Nacht »der neue Tag geboren« wird (V. 4668), so wird Faust »dem heiligen Licht« zurückgegeben. Goethes Grundüberzeugung ist: Der Rhythmus von Nacht und Tag, von Dunkel und Licht ist der Rhythmus des Lebens schlechthin. Todesähnliche Absenz und Wiedergeburt sind die Pole uralter Übergangsriten. Hier aber bedeuten sie auch moralisch wie medizinisch eine Rekreation und Metamorphose. Dies ist nicht Fausts Verdienst, sondern die passive Erfahrung eben jener Macht des Lebens, die sich im Pendelschlag von Finsternis und Licht zeigt oder die im Atmen als Systole und Diastole auch leiblich ständig präsent ist.

> So setzt das Einatmen schon das Ausatmen voraus und umgekehrt; so jede Systole ihre Diastole. Es ist die ewige Formel des Lebens, die sich auch hier äußert. Wie dem Auge das Dunkle geboten wird, so fordert es das Helle; es fordert Dunkel, wenn man ihm Hell entgegenbringt und zeigt eben dadurch seine Lebendigkeit, sein Recht das Objekt zu fassen, indem es etwas, das dem Objekt entgegengesetzt ist, aus sich selbst hervorbringt. (FA, Bd. I 23 I, S. 41.)[1]

Nicht anders, nämlich im Bedürfnis nach Kontrasten und Polaritäten, agiert das Auge. Und so auch begrüßt Faust nach dem Dunkel der Nacht beglückt die Tageshelle, die Schattierungen und Farbkontraste. Aus der Schwärze der Nacht heben sich die Dinge ins Lichte und immer Lichtere, bis im unvermittelten Blick auf die aufgegangene Sonne das Licht unerträglich wird und Faust dem augenphysiologischen Bedürfnis nach Kontrasten folgt: Die Sonne im Rücken vermag er im Gischtschleier des Wasserfalls das lebhafte Spiel der Farben des stehenden Regenbogens über den stürzenden Wassern genießen. Was er ›in der Welt‹ als dynamische Organisiertheit des Lichts ›sieht‹, das spiegelt zugleich den Prozess seines Inneren, im Seelischen (die befreiende Erquickung), im Moralischen (die Heilung von der Schuld) und im Kognitiven (im Begreifen der eigenen Position im Leben, V. 4626 f.). Die Lichterscheinungen während des Sonnenaufgangs sind ein erstes Lichtkunstwerk – im Auge des Betrachters, subjektiv also, und objektiv im kosmischen Lichtspiel freier Natur.

1 »Das Auge eines Wachenden äußert seine Lebendigkeit besonders darin, daß es durchaus in seinen Zuständen abzuwechseln verlangt, die sich am einfachsten vom Dunkeln zum Hellen und umgekehrt bewegen. Das Auge kann und mag nicht einen Moment in einem besondern, in einem durch das Objekt spezifizierten Zustande identisch verharren. Es ist vielmehr zu einer Art von Opposition genötigt, die, indem sie das Extrem dem Extreme, das Mittlere dem Mittleren entgegensetzt, sogleich das Entgegengesetzte verbindet, und in der Sukzession sowohl als in der Gleichzeitigkeit und Gleichörtlichkeit nach einem Ganzen strebt.« (FA, Bd. I 23 I, S. 39.)

2. Sounds of Light

Let us remember that *Faust I* (v. 243–54) also begins with a cosmic spectacle of light: the path of the sun makes us perceive a change from "paradisial light" to "night's awesome profound," i.e. the cosmic rhythm. Causing the change from light and darkness, the revolution of the sphere is not only seen here as an overwhelming theater of light, like in antiquity, but it is also heard as a spherical sound (v. 243–66). In *Faust II,* the "din the daylight's bringing" is also acoustically announced as a "trombone- and trumpeting": Ariel says, "Listen!" as if we could hear the rising sun with 'spiritual ears' even before seeing it—a type of synesthetic imagination.

From here, perspectives emerge on the work of the musically talented Heinz Mack. His aesthetic principles—the formal structure, energetic dynamics, rhythm of space-time, and the combination of light phenomena in an ensemble—are all, despite their technical translation into visual shapes, unmistakably inspired by classical and modern music. They are sounds of light developing in time and space. The design of musical and visual art both share the following: the processes of rasterization and symmetry, variation and repetition, geometric construction, ornamentation, and seriality. When inspecting Mack's work, it is helpful to perceive it in a synesthetic way, particularly when contemplating what a given artwork of light is associated with, such as pieces of music by John Cage or György Ligeti, for example.

The scenes in *Faust* of light and darkness correspond quite clearly to the pre-Socratic philosopher Parmenides: he lets his world order emerge from the polarity and mixture of brightness and darkness, which is also Goethe's approach in his theory of colors. Parmenides prepares his own initiation into philosophy by following the audible light heard at sunrise, when Helios's wagon leaves "the house of the night." This is not only a description of the ritual work of the cosmic creation of light, but at the same time it is also an outline of the philosopher's path. He will search for the undying, light-filled truth that is far removed from "humankind's usual path" (Diels/Kranz 28A, B 10; 28 B 1). One might recall Plato's *Allegory of the Cave* here *(Politeia* 514 a–518 b), an account of the crowd's sensory fascination with the play of disembodied shadows, and of the paradigmatic ascent of a youngster who is eager to discover knowledge when he emerges from a gloomy cave into the initially blinding sunlight, and advances to reason.

Furthermore, let us not forget that after Act III, the Helena Act, Faust, in a 'translatio,' moves on a cloud from the south of Greece to a high northern mountain range, from where he observes and classifies the fleeting development of clouds in the sunlight, like an expert of the Howard-Goethe meteorology. More importantly, however, he identifies his erotic icons in the clouds, from Gretchen to Helena, as if the clouds were the cinema of his phantasies. In an act of simultaneity, the eye perceives at once objects of outer and inner nature, such as clouds and the phantasms of one's beloved. With the ultimate cloud, the cirrus—ascending towards the ether—"the best of what I am" is also carried away (v. 10,039–66). This congruence of high and low—macro and micro constellations and processes, objective conditions and subjective perceptions—also defines Goethe's theory of colors and Mack's art of light.

2. Tönendes Licht

Vergessen wir nicht, dass auch *Faust I* (V. 243–254) mit einem kosmischen Lichtspektakel beginnt: Am Gang der Sonne wird der Wechsel von »Paradieses-Helle« und »tiefer schauervoller Nacht«, mithin der Rhythmik des Kosmos wahrgenommen. Die Revolutionen der Sphären, die den Wechsel von Licht und Dunkel bedingen, werden hier, wie schon in der Antike, nicht nur als ein gewaltiges Lichttheater gesehen, sondern auch als Sphärenklang (V. 243–266) gehört. Auch zu Beginn von *Faust II* kündigt sich das »Herannahen der Sonne« akustisch an, als »Ungeheures Getöse«: »Horchet!« heißt es, als könne man die aufgehende Sonne mit »Geistes-Ohren« vernehmen, noch bevor man sie sieht: eine Art synästhetische Imagination.

Von hier aus ergeben sich Perspektiven auf das Werk des musikalisch hochtalentierten Heinz Mack. Seine ästhetischen Prinzipien – die formale Struktur, die energetische Dynamik, der Rhythmus in der Raumzeit und die Zusammenstimmung der Licht-Phänomene zu einem Ensemble –, sie alle sind, wiewohl in visuelle Gestalten technisch übersetzt, unverkennbar von der klassischen wie vor allem von der modernen Musik inspiriert. Es sind Lichtklänge, die sich in Raum und Zeit entwickeln. Und auch die Verfahren der Rasterung und der Symmetrie, der Wiederholung und der Variation, der geometrischen Konstruktion, des Ornaments und des Seriellen gelten sowohl für die musikalische wie die bildkünstlerische Gestaltung. Stets ist es angemessen, bei der Betrachtung von Macks Werken synästhetisch zu empfinden und angesichts dessen, was als Lichtkunstwerk vor Augen steht, Musikstücke etwa von John Cage oder György Ligeti zu assoziieren.

Die Dunkel-Licht-Szenen im *Faust* entsprechen durchaus dem Vorsokratiker Parmenides, der die Weltordnung aus der Polarität und Mischung des Hellen und des Dunklen hervorgehen lässt. Das ist auch der Ansatz der Goethe'schen Farbenlehre. Die eigene Initiation in die Philosophie entwickelt Parmenides im Modus einer ebenfalls tönenden Lichtwerdung während des Sonnenaufgangs, wenn der Helioswagen »das Haus der Nacht« verlässt. Nicht nur wird hier das rituelle Werk der kosmischen Lichtwerdung geschildert, sondern zugleich der Weg des Philosophen vorgezeichnet: Er wird die unsterbliche, lichtvolle Wahrheit weitab vom »üblichen Pfad der Menschen« (Diels / Kranz 28 A 10; 28 B 1) suchen. Man darf auch an Platons *Höhlengleichnis* denken (*Politeia* 514a–518b), worin die sinnliche Faszination der Menge durch das Spiel der wesenlosen Schatten sowie der paradigmatische Aufstieg des erkenntnisbegierigen Jünglings aus der düsteren Höhle in das zunächst blendende Licht der Sonne und der Vernunft geschildert wird.

Und vergessen wir nicht, dass nach dem dritten, dem Helena-Akt, Faust von einer Wolke aus dem griechischen Süden ins nordische Hochgebirge translationiert wird. Von dort oben, wie ein Experte der Howard-Goethe'schen Witterungslehre, beobachtet und klassifiziert er die flüchtigen Bildungen der Wolken im Sonnenlicht. Wichtiger aber ist, dass er in den Wolkengebilden seine erotischen Ikonen – von Gretchen bis Helena – identifiziert, als wären die Wolken das Kino seiner Fantasien. Das Auge sieht zugleich Objekte der äußeren Natur, die Wolken, und der inneren Natur, nämlich die Fantasmata der Geliebten. Mit der letzten Wolke, dem Cirrus, die sich zum »Äther hin« erhebt, zieht auch »das Beste meines Innern« fort (V. 10039–10066). Diese Korrespondenz von Oben und Unten, von makro- und mikro-

3. New Radiance and Clarity

But let us return to the "pleasant landscape" scene at the beginning of *Faust II.* Upon awakening, Faust does indeed feel relaxed. "Life's pulses beating now," his "breath is quickening," and he feels surrounded by the joy to "stir the strengthening resolution" in him—one of Goethe's basic impulses. It is with great sensitivity that Faust recognizes the changes occurring in the landscape in relationship to light, which takes place during the transition from dawn to the sun's perfect appearance:

> Now the world unfolds, in half-light's gleam,
> The wood's alive, its thousand harmonies singing,
> While through the valleys, misted ribbons stream:
> And heavenly light now penetrates the deep:
> Twigs, branches shoot, with fresher life it seems,
> From fragrant gulfs, where they were sunk in sleep:
> Colour on colour lifts now from the ground,
> As leaf and flower with trembling dewdrops weep —
> And a paradise reveals itself, all round.
>
> Gaze upwards! — The vast mountain heights
> Already with the solemn hour resound:
> They are the first to enjoy the eternal light
> That later, for us, will work its way below.
> Now, to the sloping Alpine meadows bright,
> It gives a fresh clarity, a newer glow,
> And step by step it reaches us down here: —
> It blazes out! — Ah, already blinded, though
> I turn away, my eyesight wounded, pierced.
> (V. 4686–4703.)

We realize that for Goethe, the art of light begins with natural light. It is inextricably bound to the viewer's eye. What would light be if it were not perceived? What would the eye be if there was no light? In the world of objects, the viewer—and this applies both to Goethe and Mack—comprehends light's physical optical and its chemically effective force ἐνέργεια (energeia). Similar to that which is manifest to the eye as embodied and obvious: this is evidence, the ενάργεια (enargeia).[2] Both artists are concerned with the aesthetic 'rescue of phenomena' in distinction from (but not in opposition to) their natural scientific and technical objectification. At the same time, we do not experience pure phenomenological differentiation. But thanks to the latter, light does permit things to enter into visibility and thoughts into their truth. But we also endure blindness. Eye and light are indeed interrelated—the eye even "owe[s] its existence to light" *(Theory of Colours,* p. xxxix)—revealing a "sense that is akin to itself."[3] Nevertheless—and this has been known since ancient philosophy and religion—there is a disproportionality, an over-brightness of light that may expose something overwhelming.

2 For a differentiation between energeia and enargeia in light and other important issues pertaining to the aesthetics of nature, see Hartmut Böhme, *Aussichten der Natur: Naturästhetik in Wechselwirkung von Natur und Kultur* (Berlin, 2017), pp. 17–27.

3 "We are here reminded of a significant adage in constant use with the ancient Ionian school—'Like is not only known by Like;' and again, of the words of an old mystic writer, which may be thus rendered, 'If the eye were not sunny, how could we perceive light? If God's own strength lived not in us, how could we delight in Divine things?'" *(Theory of Colours,* p. xxxix.)—We know that this is a free lyrical translation from Plotinus. *The Enneads,* 1st Ennead, 6th section, no. 9, vol. 1 (Berlin, 1878), p. 53.

kosmischen Konstellationen und Prozessen, von objektiven Bedingungen und subjektiven Wahrnehmungen, bestimmt auch die Farbenlehre Goethes – und die Lichtkunst von Mack.

3. Neuer Glanz und Deutlichkeit

Doch zurück zur Szene »Anmutige Gegend« zu Beginn von *Faust II*. Tatsächlich fühlt sich der erwachende Faust rekreiert. »Des Lebens Pulse schlagen«, er atmet »neu erquickt« und fühlt sich von Lust umgeben, »Zum höchsten Dasein immerfort zu streben« – ein Grundimpuls Goethes. Mit großer ästhetischer Sensibilität nimmt Faust die Veränderungen wahr, die sich im landschaftlichen Gefüge des Lichts während des Übergangs vom Dämmern zum vollendeten Erscheinen der Sonne vollziehen:

> In Dämmerschein liegt schon die Welt erschlossen,
> Der Wald ertönt von tausendstimmigem Leben
> Tal aus, Tal ein ist Nebelstreif ergossen,
> Doch senkt sich Himmelsklarheit in die Tiefen,
> Und Zweig und Äste, frisch erquickt, entsprossen
> Dem duft'gen Abgrund wo versenkt sie schliefen;
> Auch Farb' an Farbe klärt sich los vom Grunde,
> Wo Blum' und Blatt von Zitterperle triefen,
> Ein Paradies wird um mich her die Runde.
>
> Hinaufgeschaut! – Der Berge Gipfelriesen
> Verkünden schon die feierlichste Stunde,
> Sie dürfen früh des ewigen Lichts genießen
> Das später sich zu uns hernieder wendet.
> Jetzt zu der Alpe grüngesenkten Wiesen
> Wird neuer Glanz und Deutlichkeit gespendet,
> Und stufenweis herab ist es gelungen; –
> Sie tritt hervor! – und, leider schon geblendet,
> Kehr' ich mich weg, vom Augenschmerz durchdrungen.
> (V. 4686–4703.)

Man erkennt, dass bei Goethe die Lichtkunst mit dem natürlichen Licht beginnt, in unauflöslicher Koppelung mit dem Auge des Betrachters. Was wäre das Licht, wenn es nicht wahrgenommen würde? Was wäre das Auge, wenn es Licht nicht gäbe? Der Betrachter – und das gilt für Goethe wie Mack – begreift in der gegenständlichen Welt sowohl die optisch-physikalische und chemische Wirkkraft (energeia, ἐνέργεια) wie auch das vor uns verkörperte Augenscheinliche und Augenfällige: das ist die Evidenz, die ἐνάργεια (enargeia) des Lichts.[2] Für beide Künstler geht es um die ästhetische ›Rettung der Phänomene‹ im Unterschied (aber nicht im Gegensatz) zu ihrer naturwissenschaftlichen und technischen Vergegenständlichung. Dabei wird nicht nur die Erfahrung phänomenologischer Differenzierung gemacht, durch die das Licht die Dinge erst in ihre Sichtbarkeit und die Gedanken erst in ihre Wahrheit treten lässt. Sondern erlitten wird auch eine Blendung. Zwar sind Auge und

2 Zur Unterscheidung von Energeia und Enargeia, die für naturästhetische Fragen wichtig ist, vgl. Hartmut Böhme, *Aussichten der Natur. Naturästhetik in Wechselwirkung von Natur und Kultur*, Berlin 2017, S. 17–27.

This overwhelming brightness—the desert is a place where it can be experienced particularly well—can also be a kind of enlightenment. Thus, the desert and other remote and empty spaces have turned into the preferred spots for the visionary. In his 1959 text on the *Sahara Project,* Heinz Mack talks about "reserves of nature" and the "serenity of their untiring expanse." In the desert, space is "deep and open, unbounded even by the horizons." Therefore, the "clarity of light and the fullness of stillness steadily spread out." In such "reserves of nature," the "reservation of art" can be realized. Light Art develops beyond narrative and symbolic sense, beyond the "graveyards" of the museums and "the disordered contents of this world," devoid of religion and metaphysics.[4]

4. Colored Reflection

"And darkness overspread his eyes in the midst of so much light" (suntque oculis tenebrae per tantum lumen obortae, Ovid, Met. II, 181).[5] The sun god's hybrid son, Phaeton, experiences the above upon attempting to ride along the sky in Helios's extraordinary carriage. But as he gazes down from the heights of the ether (which is comparable to Faust in the high mountains), vertigo and fear besiege him—and he crashes. Faust, on the other hand, attempting to preserve himself, turns his back on the source of light. On the earth's stable surface (v. 4681), he wishes not just to identify objects, powers, and movements, but also light phenomena: only the latter allow him to position himself appropriately, within the human scale in the world of the visible, i.e. the 'mundus sensibilis.' This concerns "refracted colour" (v. 4727), the world of reflections and mixtures, not the religious metaphysics of light or the sensual directness of the sun's pure light.

> So it is, when to the thing we yearn for
> The highest wish so intimately rehearsed,
> We find fulfilment opening wide the door:
> And then, from eternal space, there breaks
> A flood of flame, we stand amazed before:
> We wished to set the torch of life ablaze,
> A sea of fire consumes us, and such fire!
> Love, is it, then? Or hate? This fierce embrace,
> The joy and pain of alternating pyres,
> So that, gazing back to earth again,
> We seek to veil ourselves in youth's desire.
>
> Let the sun shine on, behind me, then!
> (V. 4705–15.)

Turning his back on this "flood of flame," Faust sets his sights on earth: "We live our life amongst refracted colour," which indicates the colors of the rainbow (v. 4715–27). In Goethe's view, the rainbow is an archetypal light phenomenon created through turbidity (the means, the medium)—in this case, the haze of water in the air—which,

4 Heinz Mack, "The Sahara-Project", in *Transit zwischen Okzident und Orient,* ed. Claus-Peter Haase, exh. cat. Pergamon Museum, Berlin (Cologne, 2006), pp. 75–79.
5 A nuanced analysis of such a 'black light' may be found in: Heinz Mack, *Mack – Licht im Schwarz,* ed. Hubertus Schoeller, exh. cat. (Mönchengladbach, 2001).

Licht aufeinander bezogen, ja, das Auge hat »sein Dasein dem Licht zu danken« (FA, Bd. I 23 I, S. 24), sodass sich eine »unmittelbare Verwandtschaft des Lichtes und des Auges« zeigt.[3] Gleichwohl gibt es – das ist seit alters in Philosophie und Religion bekannt – eine Übermaßstäblichkeit, eine Überhelle des Lichts, die etwas Niederschlagendes aufweisen kann.

Diese überwältigende Helle, die besonders in der Wüste zu erfahren ist, kann auch der Modus der Erleuchtung sein. Darum ist die Wüste, wie überhaupt Räume des Abgelegenen und Leeren, zu bevorzugten Räumen des Visionären geworden. Heinz Mack spricht schon 1959 im Text zum *Sahara-Projekt* von »Reservaten der Natur« und von der »Gelassenheit ihrer unermüdlichen Ausdehnung«: In der Wüste findet der Raum »noch im Horizont nicht seine Begrenzung« und gerade darum breiten sich »die Klarheit des Lichtes und die Fülle der Ruhe beständig aus«. In den »Reservaten der Natur« lässt sich die »Reservation der Kunst« realisieren: Lichtkunst, die sich jenseits von Erzählung und symbolischem Sinn, von Metaphysik und Religion, jenseits von den »Friedhöfen« der Museen und dem »konfusen Inventar der Welt« entwickelt.[4]

4. Farbiger Abglanz

»Und schwarz vor die Augen tritt durch so viel Licht ihm das Dunkel« (suntque oculis tenebrae per tantum lumen obortae, Ovid, Met. II, 181).[5] So heißt es von Phaëton, dem hybriden Sohn des Sonnengottes, als er den ungeheuren Wagen des Helios über den Himmel zu fahren versucht. Doch von den Höhen des Äthers (wie Faust vom Hochgebirge) herabblickend wird er von Schwindel und Angst erfasst – und stürzt ab. Faust hingegen, sich selbst erhaltend, wendet der Urquelle des Lichts den Rücken zu. Auf der beständigen Erde (V. 4681) will er nicht nur die Gegenstände, Kräfte und Bewegungen, sondern auch die Lichtphänomene erkennen. Denn sie erst erlauben ihm, sich in der Welt des Sichtbaren, dem ›mundus sensibilis‹, angemessen und menschenmaßstäblich zu positionieren: Es geht gerade nicht um eine religiöse Metaphysik des Lichts und auch nicht um eine sinnliche Unmittelbarkeit zum reinen Licht der Sonne, sondern um die Welt der Brechungen und Mischungen, um den »farbigen Abglanz«.

> So ist es also, wenn ein sehnend Hoffen
> Dem höchsten Wunsch sich traulich zugerungen,
> Erfüllungspforten findet flügeloffen,
> Nun aber bricht aus jenen ewigen Gründen
> Ein Flammen-Übermaß, wir stehn betroffen;
> Des Lebens Fackel wollten wir entzünden,
> Ein Feuermeer umschlingt uns, welch ein Feuer!
> Ist's Lieb'? ist's Haß? die glühend uns umwinden?
> Mit Schmerz und Freuden wechselnd ungeheuer,
> So daß wir wieder nach der Erde blicken,
> Zu bergen uns in jugendlichstem Schleier.
>
> So bleibe denn die Sonne mir im Rücken!
> (V. 4704–4715.)

3 »Hierbei erinnern wir uns der alten ionischen Schule, welche mit so großer Bedeutsamkeit immer wiederholte: nur von Gleichem werde Gleiches erkannt; wie auch der Worte eines alten Mystikers, die wir in deutschen Reimen folgendermaßen ausdrücken möchten:
Wär' nicht das Auge sonnenhaft,
Wie könnten wir das Licht erblicken?
Lebt' nicht in uns des Gottes eigne Kraft,
Wie könnt' uns Göttliches entzücken?« (FA, Bd. I 23 I, S. 24.) – Es ist bekannt, dass dies eine freie lyrische Übersetzung ist aus Plotin: *Die Enneaden*, 1. Enneade, Buch 6, Nr. 9.)

4 Heinz Mack, »Das Sahara-Projekt«, in: *Utopie und Wirklichkeit im Werk von Heinz Mack*, hrsg. von Wieland Schmied, Ausst.-Kat. Liechtensteinische Staatliche Kunstsammlung Vaduz, Köln 1998, S. 17–21, hier: S. 17. Der Sahara-Text ist auch nachzulesen in: *Heinz Mack. Licht Schatten*, hrsg. von Helmut Friedel, Ausst.-Kat. Museum Frieder Burda Baden-Baden, München 2015, S. 129–135.

5 Eine differenzierte Auseinandersetzung mit einem solchen ›Schwarzlicht‹ findet man auch in dem von Heinz Mack gestalteten und von Hubertus Schoeller herausgegebenen Ausstellungskatalog: *Mack. Licht im Schwarz*, Mönchengladbach 2001.

shifting between light and darkness brings about colors (cf. Goethe, *Theory of Colours,* pp. 59–76, 335–36 and more often).

> Such an original phenomenon is that which has lately engaged our attention. We see on the one side light, brightness; on the other darkness, obscurity: we bring the semi-transparent medium between the two, and from these contrasts and this medium the colours develop themselves, contrasted, in like manner, but soon, through a reciprocal relation, directly tending again to a point of union.
> (Goethe, *Theory of Colours,* p. 72.)

In a symbolic sense, however, "the rainbow's arch of colour" *(Faust II,* v. 4722) invokes the biblical arch as a sign of reconciliation and peace between god and humankind after the deluge (Gen 9, 13–16). To Goethe, the light phenomenon represents "life" beyond catastrophe.

> The waterfall that splits the cliffs' broad edge,
> I gaze at with a growing pleasure, when
> A thousand torrents plunge from ledge to ledge,
> And still a thousand more pour down that stair,
> Spraying the bright foam skywards from their beds.
> And in lone splendour, through the tumult there,
> The rainbow's arch of colour, bending brightly,
> Is clearly marked, and then dissolved in air,
> Around it the cool showers, falling lightly.
> There the efforts of mankind they mirror.
> Reflect on it, you'll understand precisely:
> We live our life amongst refracted colour.
> *(Faust II,* v. 4716–27.)

In reference to the *Theory of Colours,* this means that the framing of all colors by pure white, which itself includes all colors but does not make them visible, and black, which rejects all colors and is pure absence of light, et sic in infinitum, creates the two modes of a full-scale, exceeding its boundaries. It is through these two modes, emanating from the poles or fringes, that representation is initially made possible. Immersed in light, the colored world of appearance emerges. At the same time, this light forms the limits of our perception, of our practice, and of the visual arts. In the world of color, we encounter "life": its dynamics and kinetics, its polarity as attraction and repulsion, and the "active and passive modifications" of light, whose "lively alternating action" (Goethe, *Theory of Colours,* p. 2) is also revealed in the eye and the human body.

In the introduction to *Theory of Colours,* we learn that "colour is an elementary phenomenon in nature adapted to the sense of vision; a phenomenon which, like all others, exhibits itself by separation and contrast, by commixture and union, by augmentation and neutralization, by communication and dissolution: under these general terms its nature may be best comprehended." (Goethe, *Theory of Colours,* p. xl.)

Von diesem »Flammen-Übermaß« wendet Faust sich ab und kehrt sich der Erde zu: »Am farbigen Abglanz haben wir das Leben«, will sagen: an den Farben des Regenbogens (V. 4715–4727). Für Goethe ist der Regenbogen ein Urphänomen des Lichts, hervorgebracht durch jene Trübe (das Mittel, das Medium) – hier: der Wasserschleier in der Luft –, die, zwischen das Dunkle und das Helle gebracht, die Farben hervorbringt (vgl. FA, Bd. I 23 I, S. 72–83, 271 f. u. ö.).

> Ein solches Urphänomen ist dasjenige, das wir bisher dargestellt haben. Wir sehen auf der einen Seite das Licht, das Helle, auf der andern die Finsternis, das Dunkle, wir bringen die Trübe zwischen beide, und aus diesen Gegensätzen, mit Hülfe gedachter Vermittlung, entwickeln sich, gleichfalls in einem Gegensatz, die Farben, deuten aber alsbald, durch einen Wechselbezug unmittelbar auf ein Gemeinsames wieder zurück.
> (FA, Bd. I 23 I, S. 81.)

Im symbolischen Sinn aber zitiert »des bunten Bogens Wechsel-Dauer« *(Faust II,* V. 4722) den biblischen Bogen als Zeichen der Versöhnung und des Friedens zwischen Gott und Menschen nach der Sintflut (Gen 9,13–16). So auch repräsentiert das Lichtphänomen für Goethe »das Leben« jenseits der Katastrophe.

> Der Wassersturz, das Felsenriff durchbrausend,
> Ihn schau' ich an mit wachsendem Entzücken.
> Von Sturz zu Sturzen wälzt er jetzt in tausend
> Dann abertausend Strömen sich ergießend,
> Hoch in die Lüfte Schaum an Schäume sausend.
> Allein wie herrlich diesem Sturm entsprießend
> Wölbt sich des bunten Bogens Wechsel-Dauer
> Bald rein gezeichnet, bald in Luft zerfließend,
> Umher verbreitend duftig kühle Schauer.
> Der spiegelt ab das menschliche Bestreben.
> Ihm sinne nach und du begreifst genauer:
> Am farbigen Abglanz haben wir das Leben.
> *(Faust II,* V. 4716–4727.)

Von der *Farbenlehre* her heißt dies: Die Flankierung der Farben durch das reine Weiß, das alle Farben, alle Bestimmungen inkludiert, aber nicht erscheinen lässt, und durch das Schwarz, das alle Bestimmungen abweist und die reine Abwesenheit ist – et sic in infinitum –, dies erzeugt die beiden Modi des Übermaßstäblichen, durch die, von den Polen oder Rändern her, allererst Darstellung ermöglicht wird. So entsteht die ins Licht getauchte und also farbige Welt der Erscheinungen. Dieses Licht schließt zugleich die Grenzen unserer Wahrnehmung, unserer Praxis und der bildenden Kunst ein. In der Welt der Farben begegnet das »Leben«: seine Dynamik und Kinetik, seine Polarität in Attraktion und Repulsion, die »Taten und Leiden« des Lichts, dessen »lebendiges Wechselwirken« (FA, Bd. I 23 I, S. 12 und S. 31) sich auch am Auge und am menschlichen Leib zeigen.

Here we definitely encounter a move against the traditional metaphysics and religiosity of light. Yet, within the framework of art and aesthetic experience, Goethe continues to accept light's divineness. This also applies to Mack. He understands his objects of light as facilitators of an experience of the immaterial, namely pure light. Nonetheless, this is not an indicator of spiritualization. The non-negotiable prerequisites, which enable the visual presentation of light by means of experiments and aesthetic manifestations, are the same for Goethe and Mack. They are technical apparatuses and natural light phenomena as bound to things, atmospheres, and celestial objects. In the first place, light is a natural phenomenon and as such it is an occurrence of the material, sensual world. The 'immaterial' of pure light that Mack talks about is nothing spiritual. Rather, it refers to light as the transcendental requirement of the sensual world. However, conditional light itself is still an appearance, an archetypal phenomenon, as Goethe puts it, or an "absolute metaphor," as Hans Blumenberg says. In this sense, Goethe can even talk about the "metaphysics of phenomena," thereby finding formulations that cover both 'pure light' and the 'immaterial,' as in Mack's case.

> Out of both the greatest and the smallest (and only presentable to man through the most artificial means) emerge the metaphysics of phenomena. In the middle lies the particular, what befits our senses, what I rely on. Thus, bless from the heart those talented individuals who bring this region nearer to me.
> (MA, vol. 17, p. 922.)
> The highest is to understand that all fact is really theory. The blue of the sky reveals to us the basic law of color. Search nothing beyond the phenomena, they themselves are the theory. (MA, vol. 17, p. 533.)

This direct presence did not prevent Goethe from conducting endless experiments with light. These were technical arrangements. The same goes for Mack, who pursues a technical constructivism in his Light Art, and whose only intention is to transform light into an aistheton, i.e. to transform it so that nature can be subjectively experienced, even in instances where an absolute cultural and technical dominance prevails, like in cities, industries, laboratories, and museums.

5. Desert Art

We do not need to point out that Heinz Mack is one of the world's most important light artists. He can be considered a founding father of Light Art and Land Art.

He works outdoors, in the studio, in galleries and museums, in public spaces and on the street, in urban and rural places, in dense architectural contexts, and in far-removed "reserves of nature."[6] The latter can be parks or gardens, but the term predominantly refers to the primeval landscape of the desert, which finds an aesthetic counterpoint and counterpart in the Arctic Sea and Greenland's bare ice landscapes. In his artistic expeditions to these places, Mack strives for the greatest conceivable purity of space and light (just like many writers, such as Alfred Andersch, for example, and artists like Gerhard Richter). Only in these places can one experience natural

6 Mack, "The Sahara-Project" (see note four). This text clearly predates the documents and works of other Light and Land Artists, like those of Robert Smithson, Walter De Maria, James Turrell, and Michael Heizer. — Here, the references to light objects by Mack refer to pages 14–89 in: *Utopie und Wirklichkeit im Werk von Heinz Mack,* ed. Wieland Schmied, exh. cat. Kunstsammlung Vaduz (Cologne, 1998). There is a plethora of beautiful books and catalogues about and by Mack, among them: *Mack: Skulpturen im Raum der Natur,* fotografiert vom Künstler (Cologne, 1991).

»Die Farbe«, so heißt es schon in der Einleitung, »sei ein elementares Naturphänomen für den Sinn des Auges, das sich, wie die übrigen alle, durch Trennung und Gegensatz, durch Mischung und Vereinigung, durch Erhöhung und Neutralisation, durch Mitteilung und Verteilung und so weiter manifestiert und unter diesen allgemeinen Naturformeln am besten angeschaut und begriffen werden kann.« (FA, Bd. I 23 I, S. 25.)

Dies ist durchaus eine Wendung gegen die Metaphysik und Religiosität des Lichts, wie sie in der Tradition üblich sind. Doch im Rahmen der Kunst und der ästhetischen Erfahrung akzeptiert Goethe die Göttlichkeit des Lichtes weiterhin. Das trifft auch auf Mack zu, der seine Licht-Objekte als Ermöglichung einer Erfahrung des Immateriellen, nämlich des reinen Lichts versteht. Nun sollte man dies nicht als Indiz für eine Spiritualisierung verstehen. Die technischen Apparate wie aber auch die natürlichen Lichtphänomene, die an Dinge, Atmosphären oder Himmelskörper gebunden sind: Sie sind bei Goethe wie Mack unhintergehbare Bedingungen, um überhaupt Experimente und ästhetische Manifestationen des Lichts ›vor Augen zu stellen‹. Licht ist zuerst ein Naturphänomen und als ein solches eine Erscheinung der materiell-sinnlichen Welt. Das ›Immaterielle‹ des reinen Lichts, von dem Mack spricht, ist nichts Geistiges, sondern meint das Licht als transzendentale Bedingung der sinnlichen Welt. Das bedingende Licht ist aber selbst wieder eine Erscheinung, ein Urphänomen, wie Goethe sagt, oder eine »absolute Metapher«, wie Hans Blumenberg bemerkt. In diesem Sinn kann Goethe sogar von »Metaphysik der Erscheinungen« sprechen und findet damit zu Formulierungen, die auch das Immaterielle des reinen Lichts bei Mack abdecken.

> Aus dem Größten wie aus dem Kleinsten (nur durch künstlichste Mittel dem Menschen zu vergegenwärtigen) geht die Metaphysik der Erscheinungen hervor; in der Mitte liegt das Besondere unsern Sinnen angemessene worauf ich angewiesen bin, deshalb aber die Begabten von Herzen segne die jene Regionen zu mir heranbringen. (MA, Bd. 17, S. 922.)
>
> Das Höchste wäre, zu begreifen, daß alles Faktische schon Theorie ist. Die Bläue des Himmels offenbart uns das Grundgesetz der Chromatik. Man suche nur nichts hinter den Phänomenen; sie selbst sind die Lehre. (MA, Bd. 17, S. 533.)

Diese unmittelbare Präsenz hinderte Goethe nicht daran, endlose Versuchsreihen mit dem Licht anzustellen. Sie sind technische Arrangements – so wie Mack in seiner Lichtkunst einem technischen Konstruktivismus folgt, der dennoch kein anderes Ziel hat, als eben das Licht zu einem Aistheton, zu einem subjektiv Erfahrbaren von Natur zu verwandeln – auch dort, wo eine absolut kulturelle und technische Dominanz besteht wie in den Städten, den Industrien, den Laboren, den Museen.

5. Wüsten-Kunst

Heinz Mack, so muss nicht mehr betont werden, gehört zu den weltweit bedeutendsten Lichtkünstlern, ja, er kann als ein Gründungsvater der Lichtkunst und der Land-Art gelten.

Er arbeitet in Pleinair, im Studio, in Galerien und Museen, auf öffentlichen Plätzen und Straßen, in Städten und auf dem Land, in hochverdichteten baulichen Kontexten oder in zivilisationsfernen »Reservaten der Natur«[6]. Das können Parks oder Gärten sein, vor allem aber

6 Vgl. Heinz Mack, *Das Sahara-Projekt*. Der Text (1959) ist deutlich früher als die Texte und Werke von Licht- oder Land-Art-Künstlern wie Robert Smithson, Walter De Maria, James Turrell, Michael Heizer u. a., in: Schmied 1998 (wie Anm. 4). Meine folgenden Referenzen auf Lichtobjekte von Mack beziehen sich auf die Seiten 14–89 des genannten Buches. Es gibt sehr viele und schöne Bücher und Kataloge von und zu Mack. Ich nenne hier nur noch: *Mack. Skulpturen im Raum der Natur,* fotografiert vom Künstler, Köln 1991 und: *Mack. Licht der Wüste – Licht des Eismeeres,* hrsg. von Uwe Rüth. Ausst.-Kat. Glaskasten Marl, Ostfildern 2001.

light and empty space. Mack establishes a primordial and even existentialist relationship to them, enabling him to continue the path he began during the ZERO years: discovering the aesthetic values of technical light. This entails experiments not only with artificial light and lens techniques, but also the exploration of the properties of reflection, mirroring, and refraction in any number of materials, including water, air, aluminum, glass,[7] plexiglass, ceramics, wood, synthetic resin, stone, sand, stainless steel, bronze, and copper—in countless processed types and states of aggregation.

In his art, Mack has developed absolutely unique surfaces. These designs are crucial for stelae, cubes, sculptures, and even paintings, which, depending on their materiality, become distinctive reagents of light. For this reason, Mack labors on grids, flutings, creases, frottage, patterns, reliefs, slats, chemically treated metal surfaces, serial ornaments, and arabesques (which also testifies to his dealings with the non-mimetic art of the Orient). In short, he experiments with the dynamic structuring of surfaces. Incidentally, Goethe's *Theory of Colours* reveals that he, similarly to Mack, was well informed about the chemical and mechanical alterations of metallic surfaces, which lead to altered types of light reflection and color refraction (pp. 157–58, 199–200). The elaborately treated surfaces turn into sensitive, multi-variant, shimmering responses to light, refracting and reflecting differently in each instance, as light hits the objects from the exterior or penetrates them from the interior through their diaphanous lines. Just as there is resonance in the acoustic, I would like to talk here about relucence[8] in reference to these surfaces. It is, however, also possible to call this "refracted colour."

First, we have the early desert expeditions, where Mack placed trails and space markers of polished aluminum, crosses and arrows—mirroring the blue desert-sky above them—into the gentle yet merciless Sahara dunes. But for whom could they provide orientation in this empty space? And who but Mack himself was marked by the eight-meter-long acetate foil he let flutter in the Tunisian desert wind while dressed in silver, light-reflecting overalls like a Martian? The artist as a light stele? What does it mean when he erects light columns, mirror cubes, and entire mirror colonies in the sand? And yet, does it have to signify anything at all? These works frequently create images within the image, often in such a way that heaven and earth exchange places. Mirrored stainless steel and aluminum panels form a desert 'light city' made up from nothing but light, or they conjure up a phantasmagoric palace on a distant horizon. Is this the anchoretic art of a utopia with particular affinity for technology?[9] Are these markers of an aesthetic expedition that is at the same time a pilgrimage to the end of the world—not into the *Heart of Darkness* but the heart of light?

Mack places a linearly arranged series of slender aluminum stelae into the desert sand, making them scaffold the light. He implants the anodized, honeycomb aluminum sculptures like inorganic plants that change their looks day and night, depending on the position of the sun. The result is a Fata Morgana of a *Jardin artificiel* that is no less fantastic and artificial than *Les paradis artificiels* of Charles Baudelaire, but rather much more equilibrated. In the Tunisian desert, Mack uses a round anodized-

7 Glass is a pivotal means of design for Mack's Light Art. See Iris Nestler and Heinz Mack, *Licht im Glas: Ein Werk-Aspekt 1955–2005,* exh. cat. Glasmalerei-Museum Linnich (Mönchengladbach, 2005).

8 Derived from the Latin relucere, meaning reflect or flash. If Mack assigns the function of flashing to his objects, even though they are often enough self-reflective—and if he thereby ascribes a type of ontological subordination to them—this is due to the fact that ultimately all his works have the one task: to enable us to experience pure light, whose 'primordial phenomenon' is the desert light.

9 Mack is unlike the many Land Artists who try to escape city life and computerized society. Clearly, the idea of light stelae and rastered surfaces, and the use of modern industrial materials and the latest light technology, originates in the *Sahara Project* (this is part of art mythology). His subsequent works also reveal that stelae, especially when in an ensemble, are reminiscent of skyscraper landscapes. Surface structures recall industrial design. His silver foil suit and the honeycomb aluminum grids remind us of space travel. The glass sculptures bring futurist architecture to mind, and so forth. It is not by coincidence that Mack not only places his sculptures in parks, gardens, and natural landscapes, but also in the hearts of pulsating cities and traffic hubs, in front of banks, on boulevards, and in malls and squares. While Mack cannot be won over by a romanticization of nature, he is for a utopian reconciliation of nature and technology.

ist es seine Urlandschaft, die Wüste. Sie findet ihren ästhetischen Kontrapunkt und ihre Entsprechung im arktischen Meer und den leeren Eislandschaften Grönlands. Die künstlerischen Expeditionen dorthin gelten der größtmöglichen Reinheit des Raumes und dem Licht (viele Literaten, wie Alfred Andersch, und Künstler, wie Gerhard Richter, werden folgen). Nirgends kann man so wie dort erfahren, was natürliches Licht und leerer Raum sind. Zu ihnen entwickelt Mack eine primordiale, ja existentielle Beziehung, die ihn befähigt, jene Linie fortzusetzen, die in den ZERO-Jahren begonnen wurde: die Entdeckung der ästhetischen Valenzen auch des technischen Lichts. Dazu gehörte das Experimentieren nicht nur mit den Kunstlicht- und Linsentechniken, sondern auch die Erkundung der Reflexions-, Spiegel- und Brechungseigenschaften aller möglichen Materialien, wie Wasser, Luft, Aluminium, Glas[7], Plexiglas, Keramik, Holz, Kunstharz, Stein, Sand, Edelstahl, Bronze, Kupfer et cetera in zahllosen Verarbeitungsformen und Aggregaten.

Mack entwickelt dabei eine absolut einmalige Oberflächenkunst. Denn entscheidend für die Reaktionen der Stelen, Kuben, Skulpturen, ja auch der Gemälde ist die Gestaltung ihrer Oberflächen, die je nach ihrer materiellen Beschaffenheit zu charakteristischen Reagenzien des Lichts werden. Darum arbeitet Mack an Gittern, Riffelungen, Knitterungen, Frottagen, Mustern, Reliefs, Lamellen, chemisch bearbeiteten Metallflächen, an seriellen Ornamenten und Arabesken (die auch eine Auseinandersetzung mit der nicht-mimetischen Kunst des Orients darstellen). Kurzum, er experimentiert mit der dynamischen Strukturierung von Oberflächen. Übrigens kann man in der *Farbenlehre* sehen, dass Goethe, ganz ähnlich wie Mack, gut unterrichtet war über chemische und mechanische Veränderungen metallener Oberflächen, die zu veränderten Formen der Licht-Reflexion und der Farbbrechung führen (FA, Bd. I 23 I, S. 140, und S. 170 f.). Die aufwändig bearbeiteten Oberflächen werden zu sensiblen, variantenreichen, changierenden, an jedem Punkt anders brechenden oder reflektierenden Antworten auf das Licht, das von außen auf die Objekte fällt oder von innen her durch ihre diaphanen Grenzen dringt. Wie es im Akustischen eine Resonanz gibt, so möchte man hier von der Reluzenz[8] der Oberflächen sprechen. Man kann es aber auch den »farbigen Abglanz« nennen.

Dies beginnt schon in den frühen Wüsten-Expeditionen. So setzt Mack in die sanften, doch auch gnadenlosen Dünungen der Sahara Spuren oder Raummarker aus poliertem Aluminium, Kreuze und Pfeile, durch Spiegelung so blau wie der Wüstenhimmel über ihnen. Für wen aber sollten sie im leeren Raum Orientierungen bieten? Und wen als nur den Künstler selbst markiert die acht Meter lange Ultraphanfolie, die Mack in der Tunesischen Wüste im Wind flattern lässt, während er wie ein Bewohner eines anderen Sterns in einen silbernen, lichtreflektierenden Overall gehüllt ist, selbst eine Lichtstele? Was bedeutet es – aber muss es überhaupt etwas bedeuten? –, wenn er Lichtsäulen, Spiegelkuben und ganze Kolonien von Spiegeln im Sand aufstellt? Sie erzeugen Bilder im Bild, oft so, dass Himmel und Erde ihre Lokale vertauschen, upside down. Spiegelnde Edelstahl- und Aluminium-Platten bilden eine Wüsten-›Lichtstadt‹ aus nichts als Licht oder sie zaubern einen phantasmagorischen Palast an einen fernen Horizont. Ist dies die anachoretische Kunst eines technikaffinen Utopisten?[9] Sind es Marker einer ästhetischen Expedition, die auch eine Pilgerreise ans Ende der Welt ist – nicht ins *Heart of Darkness,* sondern ins Herz des Lichtes?

7 Das Glas ist ein außerordentlich wichtiges Gestaltungsmittel der Lichtkunst von Mack, vgl. dazu: *Mack. Licht im Glas. Ein Werk-Aspekt 1955–2005,* hrsg. von Iris Nestler, Ausst.-Kat. Deutsches Glasmalerei-Museum Linnich, Mönchengladbach 2005.

8 Abgeleitet von lat. relucere = zurückleuchten. Wenn Mack seinen Objekten die Funktion der Reluzenz zuschreibt, obwohl sie oft genug selbstleuchtend sind, und wenn er ihnen dadurch eine Art ontologische Nachrangigkeit zuweist, so liegt das daran, dass alle seine Arbeiten letztlich die eine Aufgabe haben, Erfahrungen des reinen Lichts zu ermöglichen. Dessen ›Urphänomen‹ ist das Wüstenlicht.

9 Mack ist nicht einer der vielen Land-Art-Künstler, die der Großstadt und der technisierten Gesellschaft entfliehen wollten. Es ist nicht zu übersehen, dass die Idee der Licht-Stele, der gerasterten Oberflächen, die Verwendung modernen Industrie-Materials und neuester Licht-Techniken zwar ihren Ursprung im Sahara-Projekt haben (das gehört zur Kunst-Mythologie). Doch in den nachfolgenden Werken erkennt man, dass die Stelen, insbesondere als Ensemble, an Wolkenkratzer-Landschaften, die Oberflächen-Strukturen an Industriedesign, der Silberfolien-Overall des Künstlers und die Honeycomb-Aluminium-Netze an Raumfahrt, Glas-Skulpturen an futuristische Architekturen erinnern – und so immer weiter fort. Es ist kein Zufall, dass Mack seine Skulpturen nicht nur stadtfern in Parks, Gärten und Landschaften, sondern ins Herz pulsierender Städte und Verkehrsknoten implantiert, von Banken, Boulevards, Malls, Squares. Mack ist nicht für eine Romantisierung von Natur zu gewinnen, wohl aber für eine utopische Versöhnung von Natur und Technik.

aluminum disk as a rotor: an artificial sun that produces an endless flood of broken reflections from its oxidized and porous surface.

What does it mean when Mack marks the surfaces of windswept dunes with rigorous, geometric grids and reliefs: are they unmistakable yet fleeting signs of human rather than natural work?[10] With his geometric shapes, Mack leaves behind striking traces and light signs. Bound to disappear, they are codes and 'attestations of cultural presence' in the nowhere of a prehistoric landscape, away from the art aficionados of big cities.

What does it mean when Mack lets fanned-out, wing- or plant-like glass structures grow from sand dunes, when grids consisting of thousands of prisms and aluminum cells with countless light refractions bring forth, in dwindling sunlight, bizarre dark yet transparent shadows, which endow the light on the surfaces with a silvery shimmer? It does not have to signify anything. A liberation from meaning. ZERO. Just a phenomenon, an appearance of light.

The desert's natural light was a great and strict teacher. Without it, Mack's art would be inconceivable. We are unable to see the light spectacles in *Faust I* and *II,* just as we are unable to see the light installations in the deserts Mack visited unless we consult photographs or films. But taken in relation to the immediacy of the light-based epiphanies Mack created or maybe only experienced in the desert, these are posterior media documents. This is the same in Goethe's case: he attempted to depict the phenomenality of light in the equally posterior medium of language. He was never capable of making its immediacy evident, which for him manifested itself in the primordial phenomenon of light.

> We never sufficiently reflect that a language, strictly speaking, can only be symbolical and figurative, that it can never express things directly, but only, as it were, reflectedly. ... Yet, how difficult it is to avoid substituting the sign for the thing; how difficult to keep the essential quality still living before us, and not to kill it with the word. (Goethe, *Theory of Colours,* pp. 300–02.)

This formulation is close to the aesthetic problems Mack addresses. In his concept of light, Goethe only manages to provisionally articulate the unity of light in the term 'primordial phenomenon,' as this only expresses the 'matter' indirectly. In hundreds of experiments and observations, Goethe multiplies the phenomenality of light and color. And yet, the unity of the concept he appears to have found in the 'primordial phenomenon' gets lost. Similarly, Mack's aesthetic epiphanies in the African deserts or on the Arabian Peninsula turned into media reminiscences. They are indirect testimonies of pure light, unable to manifest themselves in museums, urban spaces, galleries, or lounges, no matter how technically, materially, or formally developed Mack's primordial experience of the desert light becomes.

10 In his study *Traces on the Rhodian Shore,* Clarence J. Glacken used as a title motif an anecdote handed down by the architectural theoretician Vitruvius about the shipwrecked Aristippus: stranded on Rhodes, he noticed geometric figures in the sand. To his relief he found that this was a place where, instead of wild nature, culture left its markings. Clarence J. Glacken, *Traces on the Rhodian Shore: Nature and Culture in Western Thought from Ancient Times to the End of the Eighteenth Century* (Berkeley et al., 1967).

Mack lässt eine linear ausgerichtete Serie von schlanken Aluminium-Stelen das Licht deklinieren und implantiert in den Wüstensand eloxierte, feinwabige Aluminium-Skulpturen wie anorganische Pflanzen, die Tag und Nacht ihr Aussehen in Abhängigkeit zum Stand der Sonne ändern. Es entsteht die Fata Morgana eines *Jardin artificiel,* nicht weniger fantastisch und künstlich, doch ungleich äquilibrierter als *Les paradis artificiels* von Charles Baudelaire. In der tunesischen Wüste montiert Mack eine kreisrunde eloxierte Aluminiumscheibe als Rotor: eine künstliche Sonne, deren oxidischer und poriger Oberfläche er eine endlose Flut von gebrochenen Reflexionen abgewinnt.

Was bedeutet es, wenn Mack die vom Wind geriffelte Oberfläche der Dünen mit strengen geometrischen Rastern und Reliefs markiert: Sind es untrügliche, wenn auch flüchtige Zeichen, die anzeigen, dass hier ein Mensch und nicht Natur am Werke war?[10] Mit den geometrischen Formen hinterlässt Mack auffällige, doch dem Verschwinden anheimgegebene Spuren und Lichtzeichen. Es sind Chiffren und ›Testate kultureller Präsenz‹ im Nirgendwo einer vorzivilisatorischen Landschaft – ohne das Kunst-Publikum der großen Städte.

Was bedeutet es, wenn Mack flügel- oder pflanzenartig aufgefächerte Gebilde aus Glas aus den Sanddünen wachsen lässt, Gitter aus tausenden von Prismen und Aluminiumzellen mit unendlichen Licht-Refraktionen, bis sie im letzten Licht der Sonne eigentümlich dunkel-transparente Schatten hervorbringen und das Licht auf ihrer Oberfläche silbern changieren lassen? Es muss nichts bedeuten. Es ist Befreiung vom Sinn. ZERO. Es ist nichts als Phänomen, Erscheinung des Lichts.

Das natürliche Licht der Wüste war der große und strenge Lehrer, ohne den die Kunst Macks nicht zu denken ist. So wenig wie wir die Lichtspektakel in *Faust I* und *II* sehen können, so wenig könnten wir die Lichtinstallationen in den von Mack besuchten Wüsten sehen, wenn wir nicht Fotografien und Film hätten. Doch sie sind im Verhältnis zur Unmittelbarkeit jener Licht-Epiphanien, die Mack in der Wüste herstellte oder auch nur erlebte, ein nachzeitiges Mediendokument. Das ist nicht anders bei Goethe, wenn er die Phänomenalität des Lichts im ebenfalls nachzeitigen Sprachmedium darzustellen suchte und niemals jene Unmittelbarkeit zur Evidenz bringen konnte, die für ihn im Urphänomen Licht anschaulich wurde.

> Man bedenkt niemals genug, daß eine Sprache eigentlich nur symbolisch, nur bildlich sei und die Gegenstände niemals unmittelbar, sondern nur im Widerscheine ausdrücke. [...] Jedoch wie schwer ist es, das Zeichen nicht an die Stelle der Sache zu setzen, das Wesen immer lebendig vor sich zu haben und es nicht durch das Wort zu töten. (FA, Bd. I 23 I, S. 244 f.)

Diese Formulierungen liegen ganz nah an dem ästhetischen Problem, das auch Mack umtreibt. Goethe kann die Einheit seiner Lichtkonzeption, das ›Urphänomen‹, nur behelfsmäßig in ein Wort fassen. Das Wort ›Urphänomen‹ drückt die ›Sache‹ nur indirekt aus. In hunderten von Beobachtungen und Experimenten vermannigfaltigt Goethe die Phänomenalität von Licht und Farbe, doch geht ihm die Einheit der Anschauung, die im ›Urphänomen‹ gefunden zu sein scheint, wieder verloren. Ganz ähnlich sind die ästhetischen Epiphanien Macks in den Wüsten Afrikas oder der arabischen Halbinsel zu medialen Reminiszenzen

10 Clarence J. Glacken nutzte in seiner klassischen Studie *Traces on the Rhodian Shore* als Titelmotiv die vom Architekturtheoretiker Vitruv überlieferte Anekdote vom schiffbrüchigen Aristipp: Gestrandet auf Rhodos, fand er im Sand geometrische Figuren vor – zu seiner Erleichterung: Hier herrscht nicht wilde Natur, sondern Kultur hat ihre Prägespuren hinterlassen (Clarence J. Glacken, *Traces on the Rhodian Shore. Nature and Culture in Western Thought from Ancient Times to the End of the Eighteenth Century,* Berkeley u. a. 1967).

6. Art as Second Nature

However, maybe we are simply looking at a peaceful paragon between art and nature. In his relation to the logic of domination and hostility, Mack strives for an equally dynamic and equilibristic interplay of art and nature. Regardless of how nonrepresentational, geometric, and technically engineered his light installations may be, he wrote in 1969:

> Immeasurable and abundantly shaped, nature, which does not obey any tradition of seeing, does not constitute a contrast to art when it is totally artificial, including in its inherent dynamic and thought-free qualities; i.e. art must give nature a chance to manifest itself as nature, because only then will art for its part get a chance to manifest itself in nature... My art is not an abstraction of nature, and nor does it strive to be the winner; nature is not my enemy.[11]

Here, Mack and Goethe are very close. It was Goethe's concept—in his art and his theory of colors, in anatomy and geology—to bring more closely together again the poles of art and nature that scholars of the Enlightenment had torn apart. Nature was to be considered the other "art," to become "second nature."[12] If, as we read in the Tobler fragment, nature is the "sole artist,"[13] it does not mean that art must imitate nature. Rather, art ought to go back to the technical and formative processes immanent in nature, "to recognize the measure by which, and up to which, our inward nature has been shaped by culture."[14] The artist understands that "art is called art exactly because it is not nature,"[15] although, at the same time, "it pursues nature's trail."[16] This corresponds to how Mack outlined his art 200 years later.

Something we are barely capable of fathoming today is that "Beauty is a manifestation of secret laws of nature; without their appearance, they would have been forever hidden from us."[17]

Immanuel Kant, too, talks about the "technic of nature" (KdU B 56, 77). Nature is not only an object of reason and a causal mechanism, but also a "purposiveness" that appears "to belong to art as an analogy" (KdU B 77). Thus, Kant keeps open the possibility of a "fit" between nature and art, technology and aesthetics. This is the gate through which Goethe's theory of colors—despite its stubborn hostility toward Newton—and Mack's Light Art can proceed to explore the nature of light.

7. From out of the Void – the Light

In the *Sahara Project,* Mack combined ancient desert anchoret traditions and divine inspirations with ornamental Islamic patterns and calligraphy. This early encounter of Orient and Occident in Mack's art again connects him with Goethe, whose *West-East Divan* inspired Mack and served as a model for his book *Ein Buch der Bilder* (1999, see ill. p. 359). Beyond numerous works on paper, it includes handwritten renderings of Goethe's poems. Here, we perceive a passionate encounter between Mack's own arsenal of geometric structures and patterns and the Oriental world of ornament and design. We enter his richly organized world of color between the black and white

11 *Utopie und Wirklichkeit im Werk von Heinz Mack,* see note 6, p. 55.
12 Goethe, MA, vol. 15, p. 464 *(Italian Journey).*
13 Goethe, MA, vol. 2 II, p. 477 *(Nature).* In his reaction to Goethe, zoologist and monist Ernst Haeckel dedicates his natural science to the program of proving art in nature. Ernst Haeckel, *Die Natur als Künstlerin* (Berlin, 1913); and *Kunstformen der Natur.* Zweite Sammlung.
14 Goethe, MA, vol. 17, p. 835 *(Wilhelm Meister's Apprenticeship, From Makarien's Archive).*
15 Goethe, MA, vol. 17, p. 480 *(Wilhelm Meister's Apprenticeship).*
16 Goethe, MA, vol. 4 I, p. 701 *(Xenia).*
17 Goethe, MA, vol. 17, p. 749 *(Maxims and Reflections* no. 183, from: *About Art and Antiquity,* vol. 3, issue 1, 1821).

geworden. Es sind indirekte Zeugnisse des reinen Lichts, das in keinem Museum, auf keinem urbanen Platz, in keiner Galerie oder Lounge manifest werden kann, so inständig Mack eben diese Urerfahrung des Wüstenlichts technisch, material, formal vervielfältigt.

6. Kunst als zweite Natur

Vielleicht aber handelt es sich auch um einen friedlichen Paragone zwischen Kunst und Natur. Mack strebt gegenüber der Herrschaftslogik und Feindseligkeit im Verhältnis von Kultur und Natur ein wechselwirkendes, ebenso dynamisches wie äquilibriertes Verhältnis zwischen beiden Seiten an. So gegenstandslos, geometrisch und technisch konstruiert seine Licht-Installationen sein mögen, so schreibt er schon 1969:

> Die unermeßliche und formenreiche Natur, die keiner Tradition des Sehens gehorchen muß, steht nicht im Gegensatz zur Kunst, wenn diese vollkommen artizifiell ist und eine dynamische und gedankenfreie Qualität hat; d. h. Kunst muß der Natur eine Chance lassen, sich als Natur in ihr zu manifestieren; denn nur dann gewinnt die Kunst ihrerseits eine Chance, sich in der Natur zu manifestieren. [...] Meine Kunst ist keine Abstraktion der Natur, und sie möchte nicht den Sieg über die Natur davontragen; die Natur ist nicht mein Feind.[11]

Hier kommt Mack Goethe sehr nahe. Goethes Konzept – in der Kunst wie in der Farbenlehre, in der Anatomie wie in der Geologie – war es, die in der wissenschaftlichen Aufklärung auseinandergerissenen Pole von Natur und Kunst einander wieder anzunähern. Natur soll als andere Kunst betrachtet werden und »Kunst [...] wie eine zweite Natur«[12] erscheinen. Ist die Natur »die einzige Künstlerin«, wie es im Tobler-Fragment heißt[13], so bedeutet dies nicht, dass Kunst im äußerlichen Sinn Natur nachzuahmen habe. Vielmehr soll die Kunst auf das der Natur selbst immanente technische und formgebende Verfahren, also »auf jenes Vernünftige zurückgehen aus welchem die Natur bestehet und wornach sie handelt«[14]. Der Künstler begreift, »daß Kunst eben darum Kunst heiße, weil sie nicht Natur ist«[15], aber gleichwohl »auf der Spur der Natur«[16] bleibt. Das ist so gedacht, wie auch Mack zweihundert Jahre später seine Kunst entwirft.

»Das Schöne«, so heißt es und wir Heutigen vermögen dies kaum zu glauben, »ist eine Manifestation geheimer Natur-Gesetze, die uns ohne dessen Erscheinung ewig wären verborgen geblieben.«[17]

Immerhin spricht sogar Immanuel Kant von einer »Technik der Natur« (KdU B 56, 77). Natur ist nicht nur ein Objekt des Verstandes und ein Kausalmechanismus, sondern auch eine »Zweckmäßigkeit«, die »als zur Analogie mit der Kunst gehörig« erscheint (KdU B 77). Damit hält Kant die Möglichkeit einer »Passung« von Natur und Kunst, von Technik und Ästhetik offen. Dies ist das Tor, durch das die Goethe'sche Farbenlehre, trotz ihrer verbissenen Feindschaft zu Newton, und durch das die Lichtkunst Macks gehen können, um der Natur des Lichts auf die Spur zu kommen.

11 Heinz Mack, »Zwischen Tag und Traum«, in: Schmied 1998 (wie Anm. 4), S. 55.
12 Goethe, *Italienische Reise*, MA, Bd. 15, S. 464.
13 Goethe, *Die Natur*, MA, Bd. 2 II, S. 477. – In Reaktion auf Goethe widmet der Zoologe und Monist Ernst Haeckel seine Naturforschung dem Programm, die Kunst in der Natur nachzuweisen (Ernst Haeckel, *Die Natur als Künstlerin*, Berlin 1913; ders., *Kunstformen der Natur*. Zweite Sammlung, o. O., o. J.).
14 Goethe, *Wilhelm Meisters Wanderjahre. Aus Makariens Archiv*, MA, Bd. 17, S. 835.
15 Goethe, *Wilhelm Meisters Wanderjahre*, MA, Bd. 17, S. 480.
16 Goethe, *Xenien*, MA, Bd. 4 I, S. 701.
17 Goethe, *Maximen und Reflexionen*, Nr. 183, aus: *Über Kunst und Altertum*, Bd. 3, H. 1, 1821, MA, Bd. 17, S. 749.

poles and through a 'collection' of lyrical texts, an ornamental carpet—a metamorphosis of Goethe's chromatics and his *Divan*.[18]

Just as decisive for Mack are the typical features of modern art, such as technical arrangements, geometric constructions, and abstract-serial systems. Media and material technologies are indispensable for installation and Light Art. All but technophobic, Mack utilizes them intensely. At the same time, we recognize Mack's modern yearning for a radical evacuation of the cluttered, aesthetically trashy spaces of the big cities, as he yearns to encounter beauty, sublimity, uninhabited places, and the epiphany of the eternal present. This is the aesthetically fulfilled moment par excellence after which Faust kept yearning in vain throughout his life. Perhaps this artistic momentum is only capable of showing itself if—with the aid of minimal representational interventions in the void of the desert or the polar ice—the first moment of all media manifests itself—light, in all its varieties, colors, shades, and nuances, with its radiant ascent and its nocturnal fade into nothingness.

This is the yearning toward ZERO. Mack's expeditions into the Arctic Sea and the ice also served this zero. Since then, both have been associated with the desert. Spaces devoid of objects, where silence and emptiness prevail, offer uniquely intense and overwhelming experiences of light as an elementary phenomenon. Equally capable of being life-threatening locations of loneliness and death, these places of sublime beauty can become locations of fear and possible doom. Nowhere else do we find such monochromatic expanses that lend themselves to Mack's light and color experiments, which clearly predate American Light and Land Art.

An anodized, colored aluminum stele on a salt lake in Formentera sums up the principle: the requirements are for an object-free and abstract yet supporting ground, as well as a structure without meaning, message, or narrative—free of thought, as Mack says—i.e. the light column captures, modulates, refracts, and transforms light. In brief, we need that which makes the phenomenon visible and places it in front of our eyes. This is evidentia—visualization. The point of departure for art is the white sheet, the tabula rasa. The blank and unmarked, the beneficial emptiness. There is never a horror vacui in Mack's oeuvre. On the contrary, he seeks out empty space in order to construct his works from that emptiness, and then to bring them to (self-)radiance. Thus, light columns rise—ideally on evacuated squares—from ground to sky, like the 'axis mundi,' the world pillar of cosmogonic myths, wherein heaven and earth are held equally bound and unbound, like Constantin Brâncuși's *Endless Column*.

Regardless of how passionately Mack, like Goethe before him, experiments with technical procedures that make nothing but light and color evident, light remains a primordial phenomenon, which, beyond all terrestrial manifestations, first and foremost enables us to grasp what cosmos means. At its core, the art of Mack is an aesthetics of the cosmos. This also applies to Goethe's *Theory of Colours* and his literary works, which have the ultimate intention of rendering a natural philosophy that at the same time intends to be a cosmology—the teachings of nature's 'ornamented order.'

18 Heinz Mack, *Ein Buch der Bilder zum West-Östlichen Divan von Johann Wolfgang v. Goethe* (Mönchengladbach, 1999) [commercial facsimile of the out-of-print artist's book: Düsseldorf, 2015]. This book includes essays by Volkmar Hansen and Amir Abdolhosseini. Note, Goethe liked the fact that his grandfather took the name 'Textor,' which means a text-maker who is an author. He often traveled anonymously under the name 'Weber' or 'Weaver.' The metaphor of weaving may be encountered repeatedly in his writings.

7. Aus dem Leeren – das Licht

In seinem *Sahara-Projekt* verbindet Mack uralte Überlieferungen von Wüsten-Anachoreten und Gotteserleuchtungen mit Formmustern der islamischen Ornamentik und Kalligrafie. Diese schon früh angelegte Begegnung von Orient und Okzident in der Kunst von Mack verbindet ihn mit Goethe, dessen *West-östlicher Divan* die Anregung und Vorlage für das Künstlerbuch *Ein Buch der Bilder* (1999, s. Abb. S. 359) lieferte, das zahlreiche Papierarbeiten Macks sowie handschriftliche Wiedergaben der Goethe-Gedichte enthält. Hier begegnet uns eine verdichtete Auseinandersetzung Macks mit der Formenwelt der orientalischen Ornamentik und seinem eigenen geometrisierten Struktur- und Musterarsenal. Es begegnet die reich gegliederte Farbenwelt zwischen den Polen Schwarz und Weiß, eine Metamorphose der Goethe'schen Chromatik und seines *Divans,* der eine ›Sammlung‹ ist von lyrischen Texturen, ein ornamentaler Teppich aus Worten.[18]

Nicht weniger bestimmend aber sind bei Mack die technischen Arrangements, geometrischen Konstruktionen und abstrakt-seriellen Ordnungen, wie sie für die Kunst der Moderne charakteristisch sind. In der Installations- und Lichtkunst sind Medien- und Materialtechniken unverzichtbar und sie werden von Mack, der keinerlei technophobe Motive kennt, intensiv genutzt. Zugleich erkennen wir die moderne Sehnsucht des Künstlers nach einer radikalen Evakuierung der zugestellten und ästhetisch vermüllten Räume der großen Städte, Sehnsucht nach der Begegnung von Schönheit und Erhabenheit, nach Menschenleere und der Epiphanie der ewigen Gegenwart. Diese ist der ästhetisch erfüllte Augenblick par excellence, nach dem sich auch Faust lebenslang vergeblich sehnt. Vielleicht kann sich dieses künstlerische Momentum nur zeigen, wenn im Leerraum der Wüste oder des Polar-Eises sich durch minimale gegenständliche Interventionen das erste aller Medien manifestiert: das Licht – in allen seinen Spielarten, Farben, Schattierungen, Nuancen, in seinem strahlenden Aufgehen und seinem Verlöschen in Nacht und Nichts.

Das ist die Sehnsucht nach ZERO. Dem Zero dienen auch die Mack'schen Expeditionen ins arktische Meer und Eis. Beide sind seit jeher mit der Wüste assoziiert. Nirgends kann das Elementarphänomen Licht so intensiv und überwältigend erfahren werden wie in Räumen der Objektlosigkeit, der Stille und der Leere. Diese können sich indes auch als lebensgefährliche Orte der Einsamkeit und des Todes erweisen. Dann werden die Räume des Schönen und Erhabenen zu solchen der Angst und womöglich des Untergangs. Nirgends auch findet man derart gedehnte Flächen der Monochromie, welche den ›Grund‹ hergeben für die Licht- und Farbexperimente Macks – deutlich vor den amerikanischen Lichtkünstlern und Land-Artisten.

Eine Stele aus farbig eloxiertem Aluminium auf einem Salzsee von Formentera resümiert das Prinzip: Es bedarf eines objektlosen, abstrakten, aber tragenden Grundes, ferner eines von Bedeutung, Botschaft oder Narration befreiten, wie Mack sagt, gedankenfreien Formgebildes – eben der Lichtsäule, die das Licht einfängt, moduliert, bricht, verwandelt, kurzum: die das Erscheinende zur Erscheinung bringt und vor Augen stellt. Das ist Evidentia. Kunst geht gewissermaßen vom ›white sheet‹, von der tabula rasa aus. Dies ist das Unbeschriebene, Unbezeichnete, das heilsam Leere. Es gibt bei Mack niemals einen horror vacui. Im Gegenteil sucht er die Leere, um aus dieser Leere heraus seine Werke

18 Heinz Mack, *Ein Buch der Bilder zum West-Östlichen Divan von Johann Wolfgang v. Goethe,* Buchhandelsausgabe des Künstlerbuches von 1999: Düsseldorf 2015. Vgl. dort auch die Aufsätze von Volkmar Hansen und Amir Abdolhosseini. – Goethe war es willkommen, dass sein Großvater ›Textor‹ hieß; er selbst reiste anonym unter dem Namen ›Weber‹ = ein ›Textor‹, der Autor ist. Vielfach findet sich im Werk die Metaphorik des Webens.

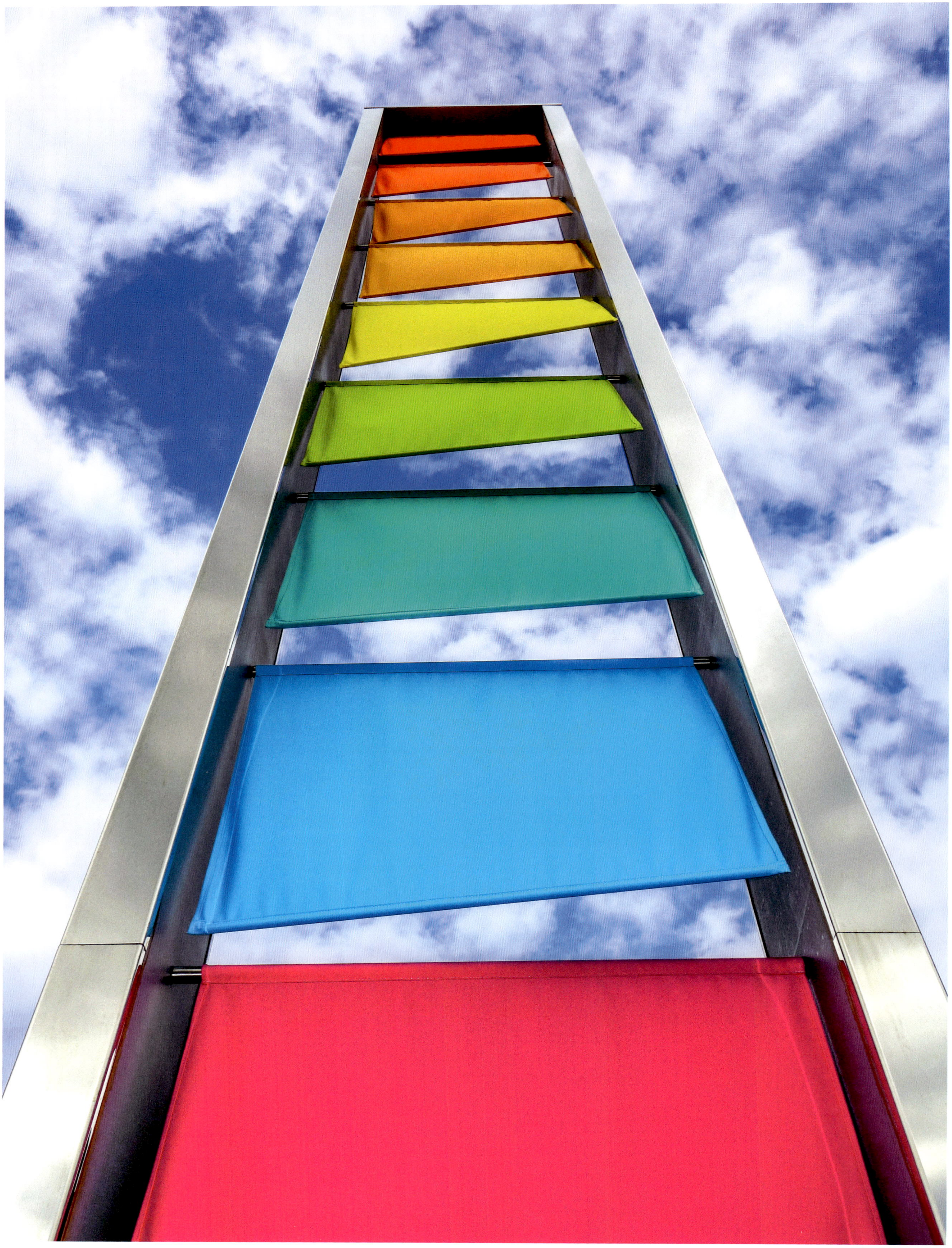

konstruieren zu können und sie dadurch ins (Selbst-)Leuchten zu bringen. So erheben sich auf den idealiter evakuierten Plätzen die Säulen des Lichts, vom Grund aufragend in den Himmel, wie die ›axis mundi‹, die Weltsäule der kosmogonischen Mythen, in denen Himmel und Erde verbunden wie auch getrennt gehalten werden, oder die *Endlose Säule* von Constantin Brâncuși.

Denn wie bei Goethe ist auch bei Mack, so leidenschaftlich beide experimentieren und nach technischen Verfahren suchen, nichts als Licht und Farbe zur Evidenz zu bringen, bei beiden also ist das Licht ein primordiales Phänomen, das über alle terrestrischen Manifestationen hinaus uns allererst einen Begriff des Kosmos bilden lässt. Im Kern ist die Kunst Macks eine Kosmoästhetik. Und dies gilt auch für die *Farbenlehre* und die Sprachkunstwerke Goethes, die zuerst und zuletzt Darstellungen einer Naturphilosophie sein wollen, die zugleich Kosmologie ist: die Lehre von der ›geschmückten Ordnung‹ der Natur.

Heinz Mack
Farbturm, 2018
Edelstahl, Textilmaterial
900 x 104 x 30,5 cm

Heinz Mack
Color Tower, 2018
Stainless steel, fabric
900 x 104 x 30.5 cm

LICHT UND BEWEGUNG

LIGHT AND MOTION

»Mit leisem Gewicht und Gegengewicht wägt sich die Natur hin und her, und so entsteht ein Hüben und Drüben, ein Oben und Unten, ein Zuvor und Hernach, wodurch alle die Erscheinungen bedingt werden, die uns im Raum und in der Zeit entgegentreten. Diese […] Bewegungen […] werden wir auf die verschiedenste Weise gewahr, bald als ein einfaches Abstoßen und Anziehen, bald als ein aufblickendes und verschwindendes Licht […].«

"With light poise and counterpoise, Nature oscillates within her prescribed limits, yet thus arise all the varieties and conditions of the phenomena which are presented to us in space and time. Infinitely various are the means by which we become acquainted with these … movements … now as a simple repulsion and attraction, now as an upsparkling and vanishing light."

GOETHE

»[…] ich als Künstler [bin] auf die sinnliche Erfahrung von Raum, Zeit, Licht und Bewegung angewiesen […], wenn ich meine Ideen sichtbar machen möchte. […] Mich fasziniert […] das wunderbare Phänomen der körperlosen, virtuellen Volumen, die ich mit Licht erscheinen lassen kann; mich interessieren […] Bewegungsabläufe, die Raum artikulieren […], und nicht zuletzt interessieren mich die Grenzbereiche, wenn ein Stillstand in Bewegung übergeht und umgekehrt, Statik und Dynamik sich bedingen und relativieren.«

"As an artist I depend upon the sensory perception of space, time, light, and movement if I want to make my ideas visible. I am fascinated by the wonderful phenomenon of the non-corporeal, virtual volumes that I can reveal with light. I am interested in the sequence of motions that give expression to space and, last but not least, I am interested in the border zones where motionlessness flows into motion and vice versa, where static and dynamic condition and relativize each other."

MACK

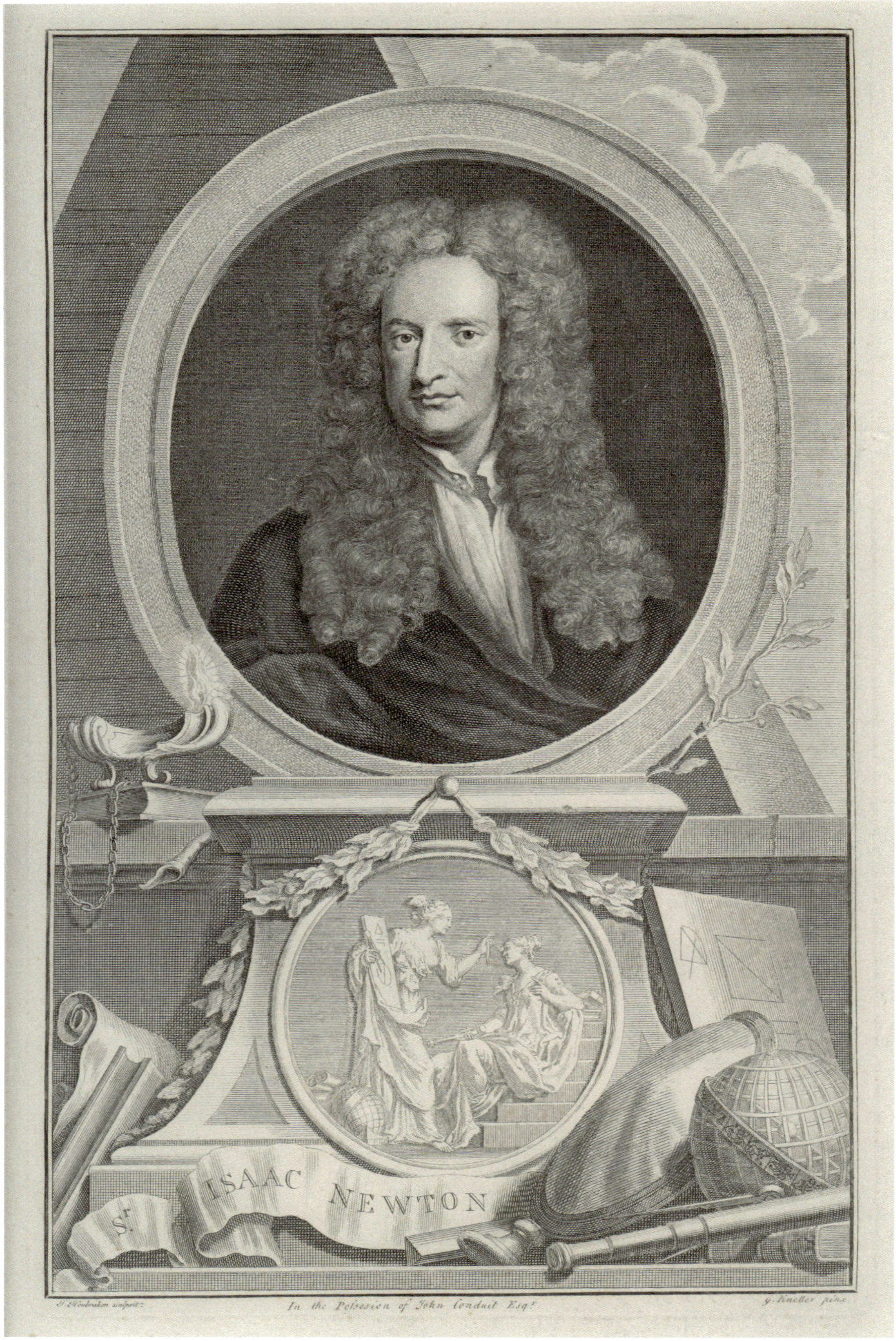

1 Sir Isaac Newton (1643–1727)
Kupferstich von Jacobus Houbraken (1660–1719) nach Godfrey Kneller (1646–1723)
1743
37 x 23,4 cm

Die Gegenstände im Vordergrund – darunter, neben Büchern, geometrischen Zeichnungen, Zirkel und Weltkugel, auch ein Fernrohr, eine große Linse und ein Dreikantprisma – verweisen auf Newtons Forschungsgebiete.

1 Sir Isaac Newton (1643–1727)
Copperplate engraving by Jacobus Houbraken (1660–1719) after a portrait by Godfrey Kneller (1646–1723)
1743
37 x 23.4 cm

The items in the foreground – including books, geometric drawings, a compass and a globe, as well as a telescope, a large lens and triangular prism – make reference to Newton's scientific research.

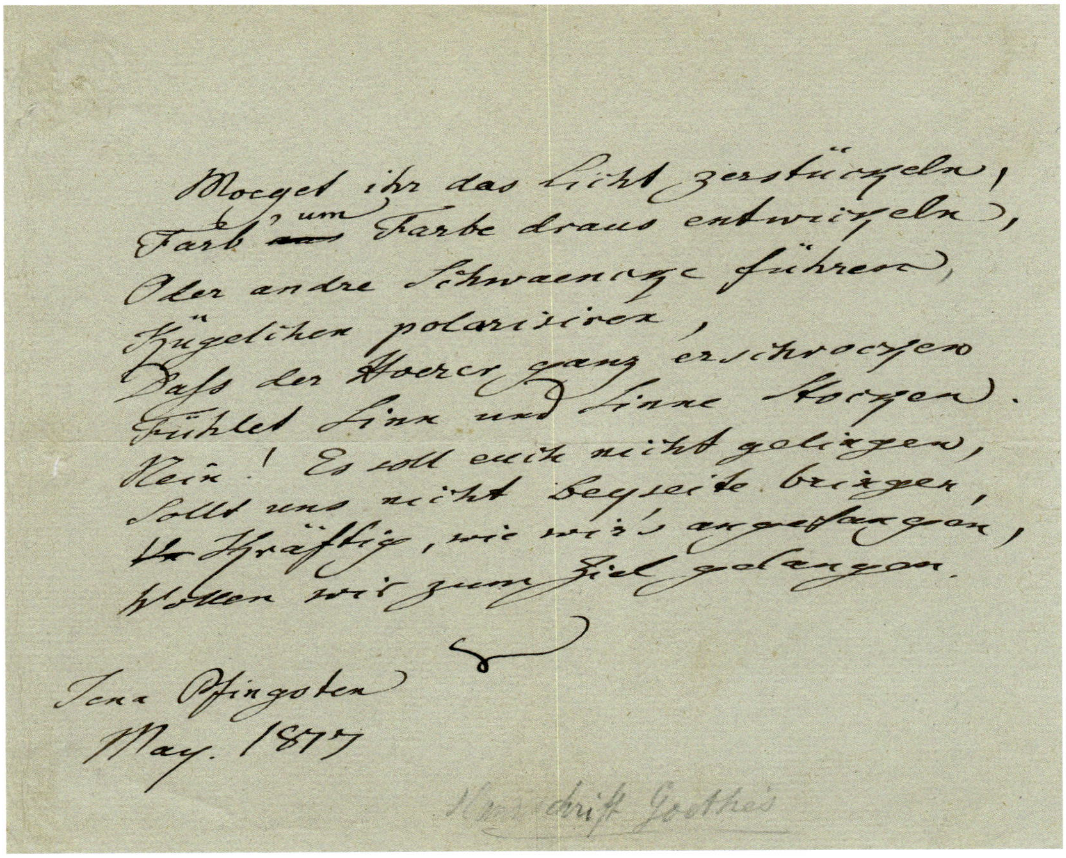

Moeget ihr das Licht zerstückeln,
Farb' um Farbe draus entwickeln,
Oder andre Schwaenke führen,
Kügelchen polarisiren,
Dass der Hoerer ganz erschrocken
Fühlet Sinn und Sinne stocken.
Nein! Es soll euch nicht gelingen,
Sollt uns nicht beyseite bringen,
Kräftig, wie wir's angefangen,
Wollen wir zum Ziel gelangen.

Jena Pfingsten
May. 1817

Handschrift Goethes

2 Johann Wolfgang von Goethe
Eigenhändige Reinschrift seines Gedichtes:
»Moeget ihr das Licht zerstückeln […]«
Datiert: »Jena Pfingsten May. 1817«
1 Blatt, 1 S. beschrieben
16,6 x 20 cm
Goethe-Museum Düsseldorf

Das polemische Gedicht erschien erstmals 1817 im ersten Band von Goethes Schriften *Zur Naturwissenschaft überhaupt.* Dort ist es als eines von zwei Motti dem Kapitel *Zur Farbenlehre* vorangestellt, das den Beitrag *Geschichte der entoptischen Farben* enthält. Der Vers »Moeget ihr das Licht zerstückeln« wendet sich gegen Newtons Aufspaltung des Lichts in sieben farbige Bestandteile, während die Formulierung »Kügelchen polarisiren« auf Louis Malus (1775–1812) anspielt. Malus nahm an, dass im Sonnenlicht zunächst ungeordnete Lichtteilchen enthalten seien, die sich beim Durchgang durch einen Kalkspatkristall orientieren. Vgl. LA, Bd. II 5 B/2, S. [1439] f.

2 Johann Wolfgang von Goethe
Clean copy of Goethe's poem in his own hand:
"Moeget ihr das Licht zerstückeln …"
Dated: "Jena Pfingsten [Pentecost] May. 1817"
1 sheet, 1 page written
16.6 x 20 cm
Goethe-Museum Düsseldorf

This polemical poem was first published in 1817 in the first volume of Goethe's writings *Zur Naturwissenschaft überhaupt.* Within this volume the poem is one of two mottos preceding the chapter *Zur Farbenlehre,* which also contains the contribution known as *Geschichte der entoptischen Farben.* The line "Moeget ihr das Licht zerstükkeln …" (May ye chop the light in pieces …) positions itself against Newton's separation of light into seven constituent colors, while the phrase "Kügelchen polarisiren" (Polarize the tiny sliver) alludes to Louis Malus (1775–1812). Malus hypothesized that sunlight was initially comprised of disordered light particles which subsequently orient themselves as they pass through calcite crystal. See. LA, vol. II 5 B/2, pp. [1439]–40.

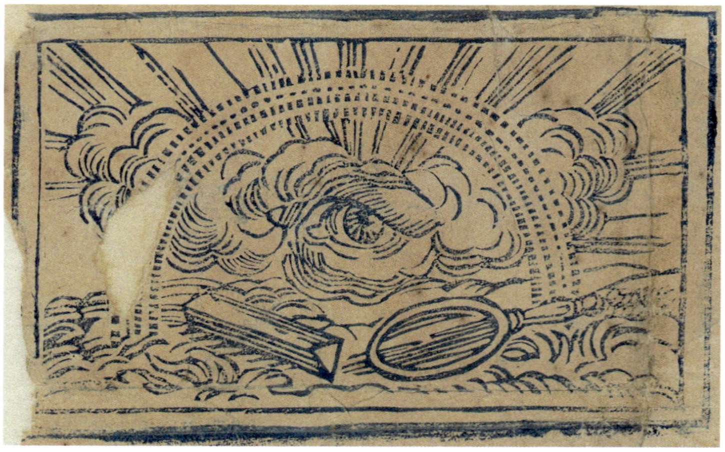

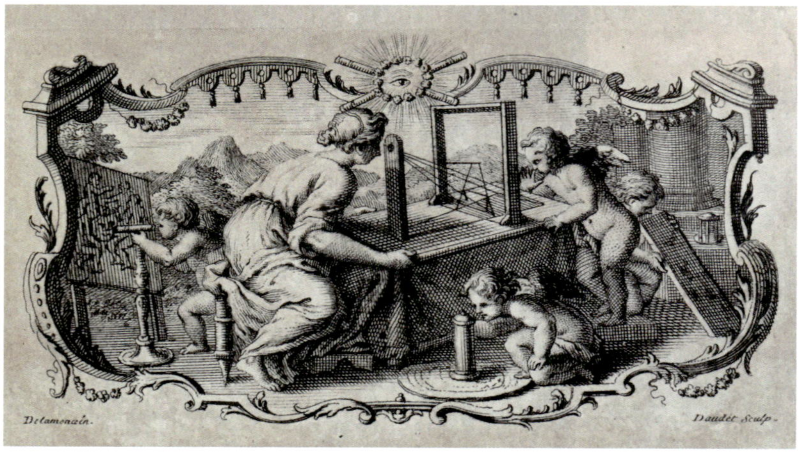

3 Johann Wolfgang von Goethe
Augenvignette
Holzschnitt von Unbekannt nach Goethes Entwurf
6,1 x 10,4 cm
Klassik Stiftung Weimar, Museen

Die *Beyträge zur Optik*, erschienen in zwei Bänden 1791 und 1792, waren Goethes erste Veröffentlichung zum Thema der Farbenlehre. Als Beilage zum ersten Stück hatte er 27 zum Teil kolorierte Holzschnitttafeln in Spielkartengröße herausgegeben, anhand derer die Leser seine prismatischen Versuche im Experiment nachvollziehen konnten. Eingewickelt war das ›Optische Kartenspiel‹ in ein mit Siegellack zum Umschlag geschlossenes Blatt Papier, bedruckt mit einer Holzschnittvignette. Die Vignette zeigt eine Landschaft mit bewölktem Himmel und Regenbogen, dessen Zentrum – umgeben von Sonnenstrahlen – ein mächtiges Auge bildet (vgl. das Gedicht »Wär' nicht das Auge sonnenhaft […]« auf S. 141). Im Vordergrund sind ein Dreikantprisma und eine Lupe dargestellt, die einfachen Hilfsmittel, die man braucht, um Goethes Versuche experimentell zu überprüfen.

3 Johann Wolfgang von Goethe
Eye vignette
Woodcut by unknown according to Goethe's design
6.1 cm x 10.4 cm
Klassik Stiftung Weimar, Museen

The *Contributions to Optics*, published in two volumes in 1791 and 1792, were Goethe's first publication on the subject of color theory. As an appendix to the first volume, he had included 27 partly colored woodcut boards the size of playing cards, which his readers could then use as an aid in order to understand his prismatic experiments. This 'Optical Card Game' was wrapped in paper, folded to form an envelope and sealed with wax. The paper comprising the envelope was printed with a woodcut vignette. This shows a landscape with a cloudy sky and a rainbow, the center of which – surrounded by rays of sunshine – forms a powerful eye (see the poem "If the eye were not sunny …" on p. 141). In the foreground a triangular prism and a magnifying glass are depicted, the simple tools that one requires to recreate Goethe's experiments.

4 Jean Louis Daudet nach Delamoncein
Titelvignette der lateinischen Ausgabe von Newtons *Opticks* aus dem Jahr 1740. Sie zeigt eine weibliche Gestalt, umgeben von vier Putti, allesamt beschäftigt mit optischen Instrumenten. Besonderes Augenmerk verdient im Zusammenhang mit Goethes *Beyträgen zur Optik* die obere Mitte der barock geschwungenen Einfassung der Szene. Bei genauem Hinschauen erkennt man dort am Himmel als winziges Detail ein Auge vor gekreuzten Fernrohren, umgeben von einem (an bauschige Wölkchen erinnernden) Blütenkranz, von dem wiederum Sonnenstrahlen ringsum in alle Richtungen ausgehen. Möglicherweise spielt Goethe mit seiner (oben links abgebildeten) Augenvignette auf Newton an und rückt damit zugleich statt der komplizierten Apparaturen das Auge selbst in den Mittelpunkt. »Der Mensch an sich selbst«, sagt Goethe, »insofern er sich seiner gesunden Sinne bedient, ist der größte und genauste physikalische Apparat, den es geben kann; und das ist eben das größte Unheil der neuern Physik, daß man die Experimente gleichsam vom Menschen abgesondert hat, und bloß in dem, was künstliche Instrumente zeigen, die Natur erkennen, ja was sie leisten kann dadurch beschränken und beweisen will.« (WA, Bd. II 11, S. 118.)

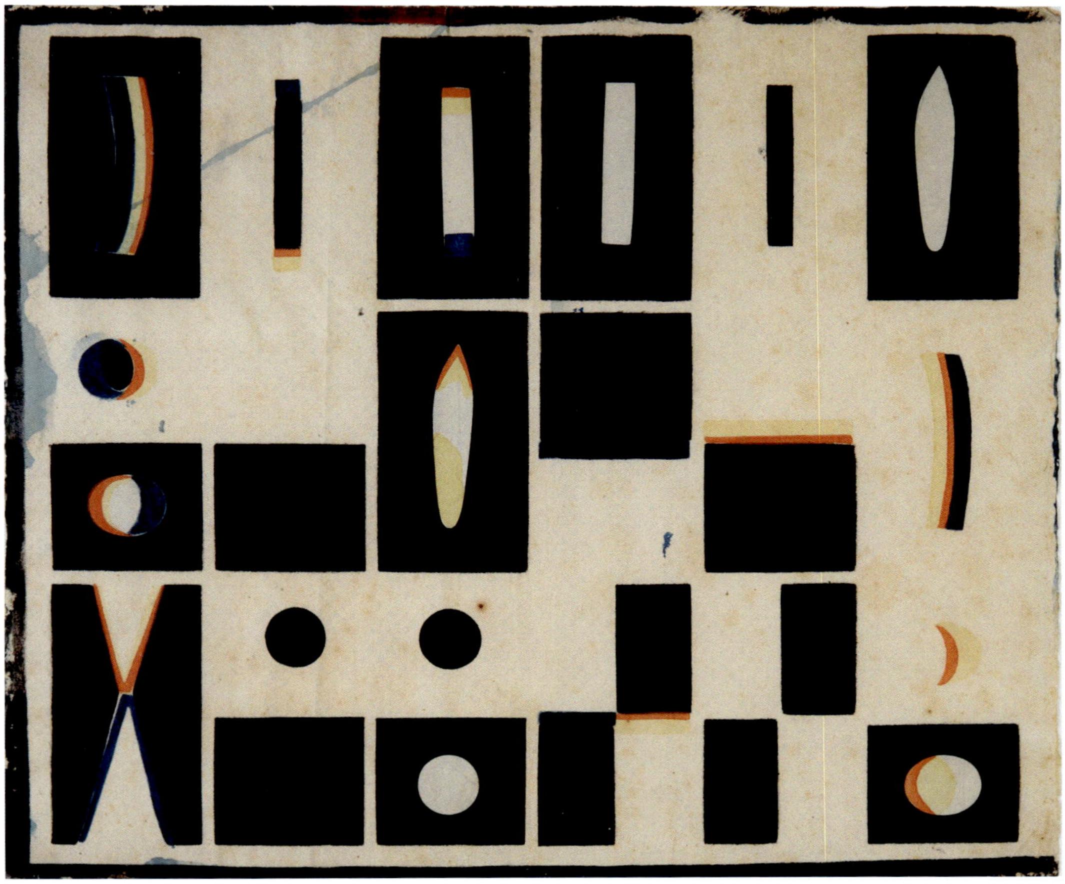

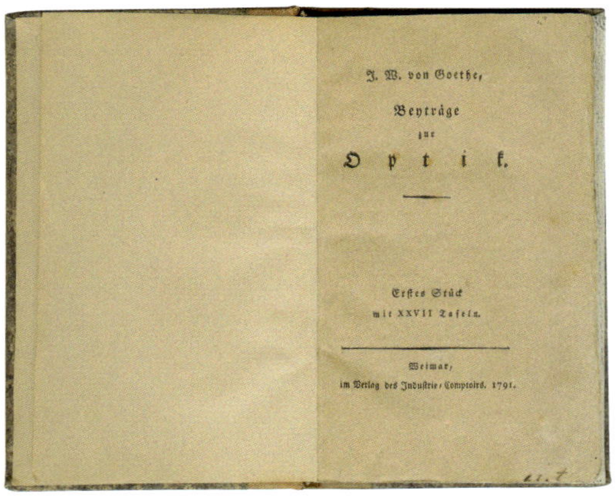

4 Jean Louis Daudet after Delamoncein
Title vignette from the Latin edition of Newton's *Opticks* from 1740. It shows a female figure who is surrounded by four cherubs, all of whom are occupied with optical instruments. With reference to Goethe's *Contributions to Optics*, particular attention should be drawn to the upper middle of the scene's curved Baroque border. If one looks closely it's possible to discern that in the sky there is a tiny detail, an eye in front of crossed telescopes, surrounded by a wreath of flowers (reminiscent of fluffy clouds). This in turn is surrounded by rays of sunshine emanating in all directions. It is therefore conceivable that Goethe's eye vignette (above left) refers back to Newton whilst simultaneously moving the focus of the piece away from the complicated scientific apparatus and onto the eye itself. "Man in and of himself", said Goethe "insofar as he makes use of his sound senses, is the greatest and most exact physical apparatus that can exist, and the greatest evil of modern physics is that experiments have been separated from man so that we can only understand nature through what can be proved with the limitations of artificial instruments and experiments." (WA, vol. II 11, p. 118.)

5 Johann Wolfgang von Goethe
Kolorierter Druckbogen für das
›Optische Kartenspiel‹
1791
Holzschnitt auf starkem weißem Papier
34,8 x 41,8 cm
Klassik Stiftung Weimar, Museen

Goethe ließ die 27 kleinen Tafeln, die als Experimentiergrundlage für seine *Beyträge zur Optik* dienen sollten, in einer sehr aufwendigen Kombination aus Holzschnitt- und Schabloniertechnik herstellen. Produziert wurden sie in Weimar in der Spielkartenfabrik seines ehemaligen Dieners und Schreibers Christoph Erhard Sutor (1754–1838). Vgl. LA, Bd. II 3, S. 166–171.

5 Johann Wolfgang von Goethe
Colored Print for the 'Optical Card Game'
1791
Woodcut on strong white paper
34.8 x 41.8 cm
Klassik Stiftung Weimar, Museen

Goethe had the 27 small boards produced, using an elaborate combination of woodcut and stencilling, so that they would then serve as the experimental basis for his *Contributions to Optics*. The cards were produced in Weimar at the playing card factory of his former servant and scribe, Christoph Erhard Sutor (1754–1838). See LA, vol. II 3, pp. 166–71.

6 Johann Wolfgang von Goethe
Beyträge zur Optik, Bd. 1
1791

Das zweibändige Experimentierbuch erschien 1791/92 im Verlag des Weimarer Unternehmers Friedrich Justin Bertuch (1747–1822).

6 Johann Wolfgang von Goethe
Contribution on Optics, vol. 1
1791

The two-volume experiment book was published in 1791/92 by the publishing house of Weimar businessman Friedrich Justin Bertuch (1747–1822).

7 Johann Wolfgang von Goethe
Brief an Georg Christoph Lichtenberg
(1742–1799)
vom 11. Mai 1792
Schreiberhand mit eigenhändiger
Schlussformel und Unterschrift
Doppelblatt, 2 1/2 S. beschrieben
29,1 x 17,7 cm (zugeklappt)
Goethe-Museum Düsseldorf

Mit diesem Brief eröffnete Goethe seine Korrespondenz mit dem Göttinger Professor der Physik, mit dem er sich wissenschaftlich austauschen und den er für seine Farbenlehre gewinnen wollte. Er sandte Lichtenberg seine *Beyträge zur Optik* deren zweiter Band gerade erschienen war, und schickte ihm auch Wandschirme (wie auf S. 209 abgebildet), die ein besonders komfortables Nachexperimentieren der in den *Beyträgen* beschriebenen Versuche ermöglichen sollten. Goethe schreibt:

Wohlgebohrner!
Hochgeehrtester Herr!
Könnte es Ew. Wohlgeb. bekannt seyn, wieviel ich Denenselben in dem Studio der Naturlehre schuldig geworden, so müßten Sie es ganz natürlich finden, daß ich eine Gelegenheit ergreife Ihnen dafür Dank zu sagen.
Die Achtung die ich für Dieselben hege, läßt mich zugleich den lebhaften Wunsch empfinden, daß meine Beyträge zur Optik Ihnen nicht uninteressant scheinen mögen.
Ew. Wohlgeb. erhalten durch einen Fuhrmann ein Kästchen, dessen Inhalt auf dem beyliegenden Blatte bezeignet ist, und ich wünsche demselben eine gütige Aufnahme.
Da die Versuche, welche ich in meinem ersten und zweyten Stücke der optischen Beyträge den Liebhabern der Naturlehre empfehle, sich alle auf einen einzigen Hauptversuch zurückführen lassen und in einer Reihe betrachtet lehrreich sind, wenn sie einzeln genommen den Beobachter mehr verwirren können, so sind die kleinen überzogenen Gestelle bequem sie im Ganzen zu übersehen, und die mannigfaltigen Verhältnisse und Verbindungen mit Einem Blicke zu beobachten.
Wenn Ew. Wohlgeb. sie in Ihrem Musäo aufzustellen für werth halten, so wird es mir zum größten Vergnügen gereichen. Sie erlauben mir, daß ich Denenselben, so wie ich fortfahre, weiter von meinen Arbeiten Rechenschaft gebe.
Es ist meine Absicht, daß diese Kleinigkeiten Ihnen auf keine Weise lästig seyn mögen. Es hat daher der Fuhrmann, wie sein Frachtbrief besagt, Ihnen dieselben völlig frey zu überliefern.
Ich empfehle mich Ew. Wohlgeb. geneigtem Andenken und wünsche zu hören, daß Sie sich recht wohl befinden.
Weimar / den 11t May / 1792.
Ew Wohlgeb. / ergebenster / Goethe.

In der autobiografischen *Confession des Verfassers* im zweiten Band seiner Schrift *Zur Farbenlehre* blickt Goethe auf seinen vergeblichen Versuch zurück, den Newton-Anhänger umzustimmen: »Mit Lichtenberg correspondirte ich eine Zeit lang und sendete ihm ein paar auf Gestellen bewegliche Schirme, woran die sämmtlichen subjectiven Erscheinungen auf eine bequeme Weise dargestellt werden konnten [...]. Eine Zeit lang antwortete er mir; als ich aber zuletzt dringender ward und das ekelhafte Newtonische Weiß mit Gewalt verfolgte, brach er ab über diese Dinge zu scheiben und zu antworten; ja er hatte nicht einmal die Freundlichkeit, ungeachtet eines so guten Verhältnisses, meiner Beyträge in der letzten Ausgabe seines Erxlebens zu erwähnen. So war ich denn wieder auf meinen eigenen Weg gewiesen.« (Johann Wolfgang von Goethe, *Zur Farbenlehre,* Bd. 2, Tübingen 1810, S. 683–684.)

7 Johann Wolfgang von Goethe
Letter to Georg Christoph Lichtenberg
(1742–1799)
May 11, 1792
Written by a scribe but with a valediction
and signature by Goethe personally
Double sheet, 2 1/2 pages written
29.1 x 17.7 cm (closed)
Goethe-Museum Düsseldorf

With this letter Goethe opens his correspondence with the professor of physics at the University of Göttingen, with whom he exchanged scientific knowledge and whom he wished to win over with his theory of colors. He sent Lichtenberg a copy of his *Contributions to Optics* whose second volume had been published recently. He also sent him screens (pictured on p. 209). These would allow for a particularly convenient way to repeat the experiments described in the book. Goethe wrote:

Your Excellency!
Could it be known to your excellency how much I have become indebted to you in the studies of natural sciences, you would consider it to be most natural then that I seize this opportunity with which to thank you.
The esteem I hold you in allows me to express my vigorous desire that my Contributions to Optics will not appear uninteresting to you.
Excellency, you will obtain from a courier a small box, whose contents are described on the accompanying sheet which I hope you will gratefully recieve.
The experiments that I recommend to lovers of natural science in the first and second parts of my Contributions to Optics can all be traced back to a single main experiment, but are most instructive when conducted one after the other so as not to cause confusion to the observer. The small stands make it easier to observe the experiments as a whole, which allows for the observation of the varied relationships and connections with a single look.
If your Excellency would consider it worthwhile to install them in your Musée, it would afford me the greatest pleasure. You will allow me to give you a more comprehensive account of my work as I continue.
It is not my intention to inconvenience you with these things. Therefore the courier, as indicated by his waybill, is completely without charge.
I commend myself to your kind remembrance, Excellency, and hope to hear that you are indeed well.
Weimar / 11th May / 1792
Your exellency / most loyal / Goethe.

In the autobiographical *Confession of the Author* contained within the second volume of his *Theory of Colours,* Goethe looks back at his futile attempts to convert the Newtonians: "I corresponded with Lichtenberg for a time and sent him moveable screens on stands, so that my subjective results could be demonstrated in a convenient manner. ... For a while he answered me but, finally, as my letters became more urgent, and I persecuted the disgusting Newtonian white with such terrible force, he broke off the correspondence. Indeed, he didn't even have the courtesy, despite our good relationship, to mention my contributions in the last edition of his Erxleben. So, I was back to forging my own path." (Johann Wolfgang von Goethe, *Zur Farbenlehre,* vol. 2, Tübingen 1810, pp. 683–84.)

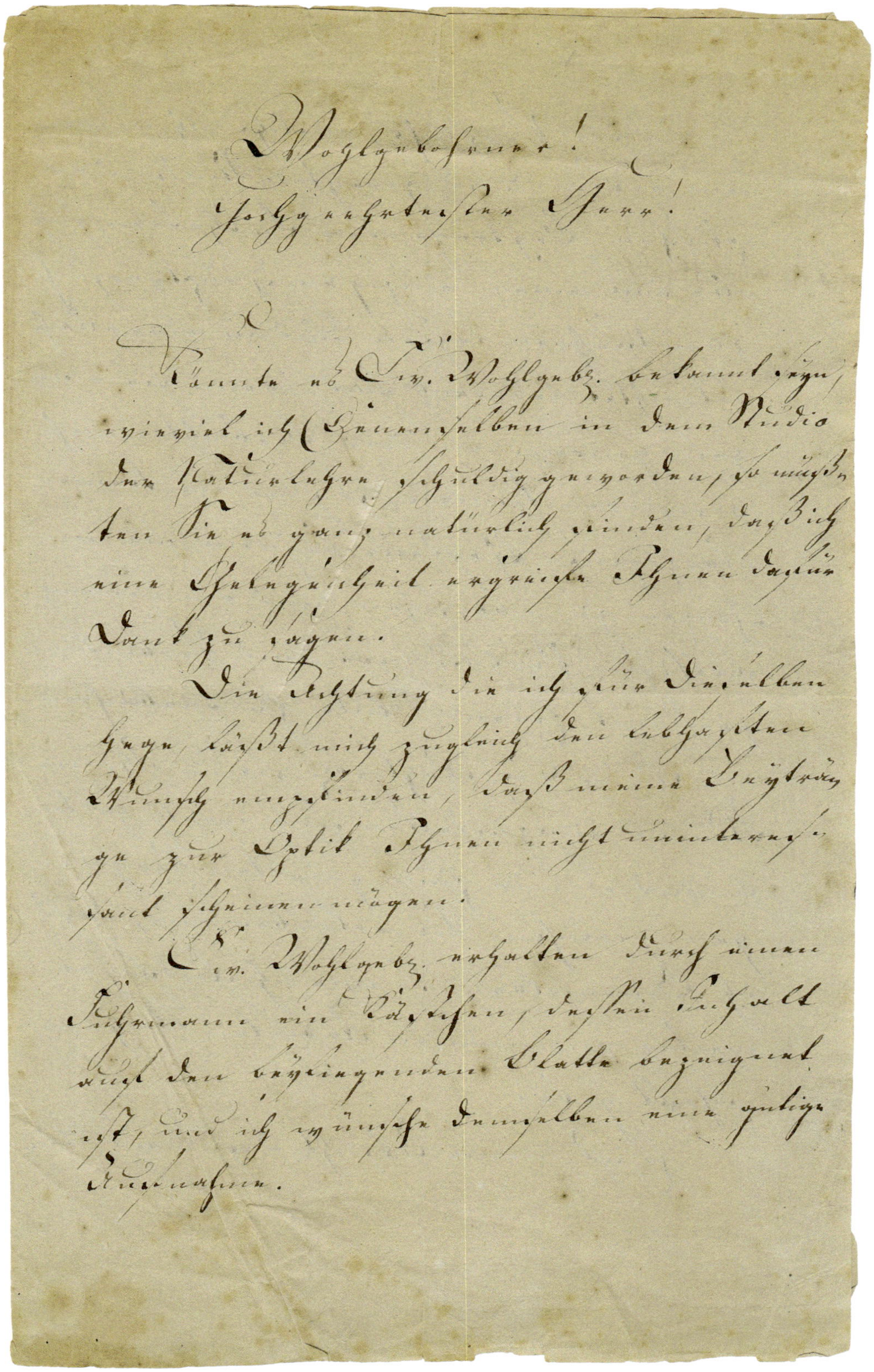
Wohlgeborner!

Hochzuachtender Herr!

Könnte es Ew. Wohlgeb. bekannt seyn, wieviel ich Denenselben in dem Studio der Naturlehre schuldig geworden, so möchten Sie es ganz natürlich finden, daß ich eine Gelegenheit ergreife Ihnen dafür Dank zu sagen.

Die Achtung die ich für Dieselben hege, läßt mich zugleich den lebhaften Wunsch empfinden, daß meine Beyträge zur Optik Ihnen nicht uninteressant scheinen mögen.

Ew. Wohlgeb. erhalten durch einen Fuhrmann ein Kästchen, dessen Inhalt auf dem beyliegenden Blatte bezeichnet ist, und ich wünsche denenselben eine gütige Aufnahme.

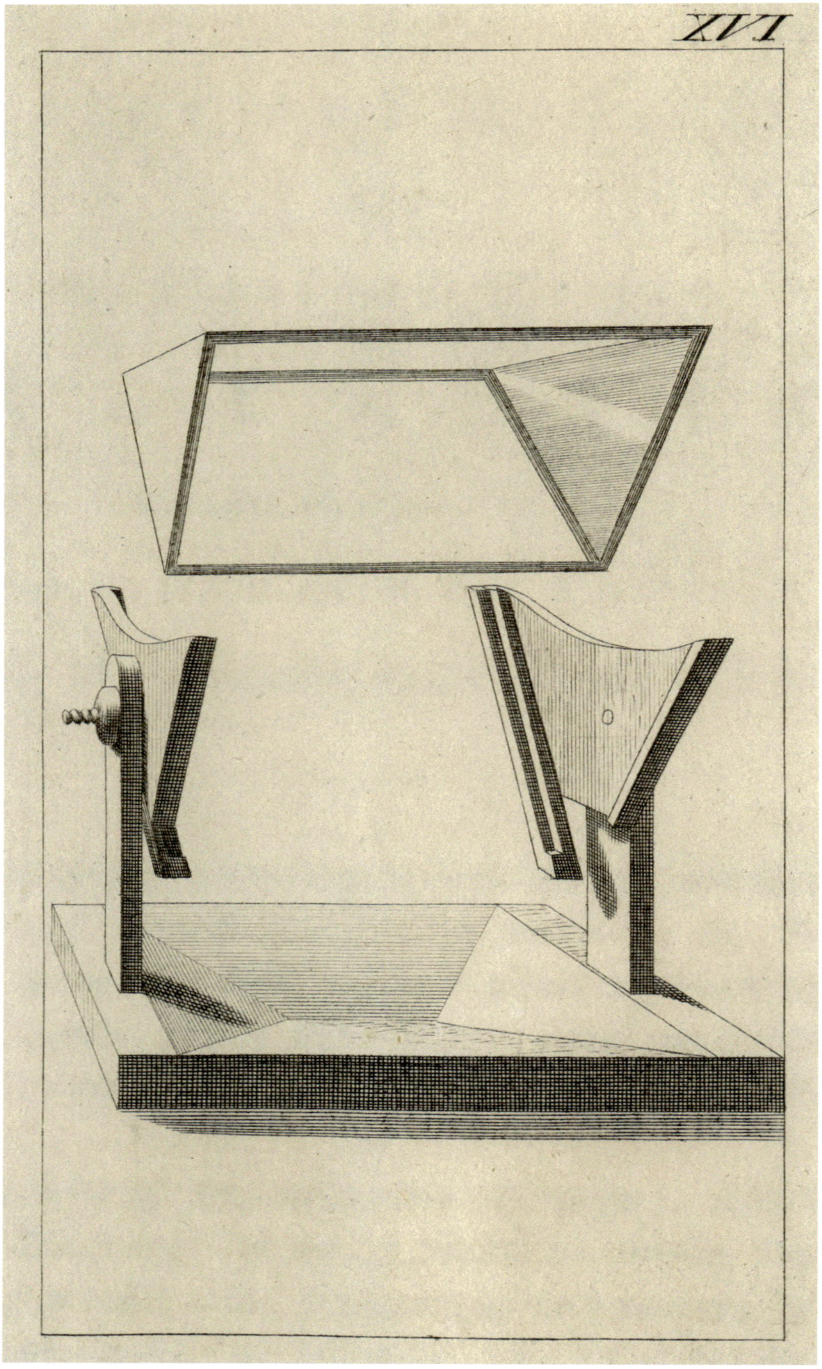

8 Johann Wolfgang von Goethe
Tafel Nr. XVI aus dem Supplementband
zu seiner *Farbenlehre* von 1810
Kupferstich

Die Tafel, die bereits 1792 im zweiten Stück von Goethes *Beyträgen zur Optik* erschienen war, zeigt die Konstruktionszeichnung für den Bau eines von Goethe entworfenen großen Wasserprismas, das sich besonders gut zur Durchführung der von ihm beschriebenen prismatischen Versuche eignete. Dafür füllte man das Gefäß, das aus zwei keilförmig gegeneinandergesetzten Glasscheiben in einem Gestell aus Holz und Blei bestand, mit Wasser. Goethe schreibt dazu: »Als ich die schwarzen und weißen kleinen Tafeln, mit dem ersten Stücke dieser Beyträge, dem Publiko vorlegte, hatte ich die Absicht meinen Lesern dadurch die anzustellenden Beobachtungen bequem zu machen. Ich hoffte sie würden sich ein Prisma leicht anschaffen, und alsdann die Erfahrungen, die ich beschrieb, ohne weitere Umstände wiederholen können. Allein es hat sich gezeigt, daß die Prismen beynahe gänzlich aus dem Handel verschwunden sind, und daß viele Liebhaber, dieses sonst so gemeine Instrument, wenigstens für den Augenblick, nicht finden können.« (Johann Wolfgang von Goethe, *Beyträge zur Optik*, Bd. 2, Weimar 1792 [Faksimile, Weimar 2007], S. [1.])

8 Johann Wolfgang von Goethe
Illustration no. XVI from the supplemental volume of his *Farbenlehre* (Theory of Colours) of 1810
Copper engraving

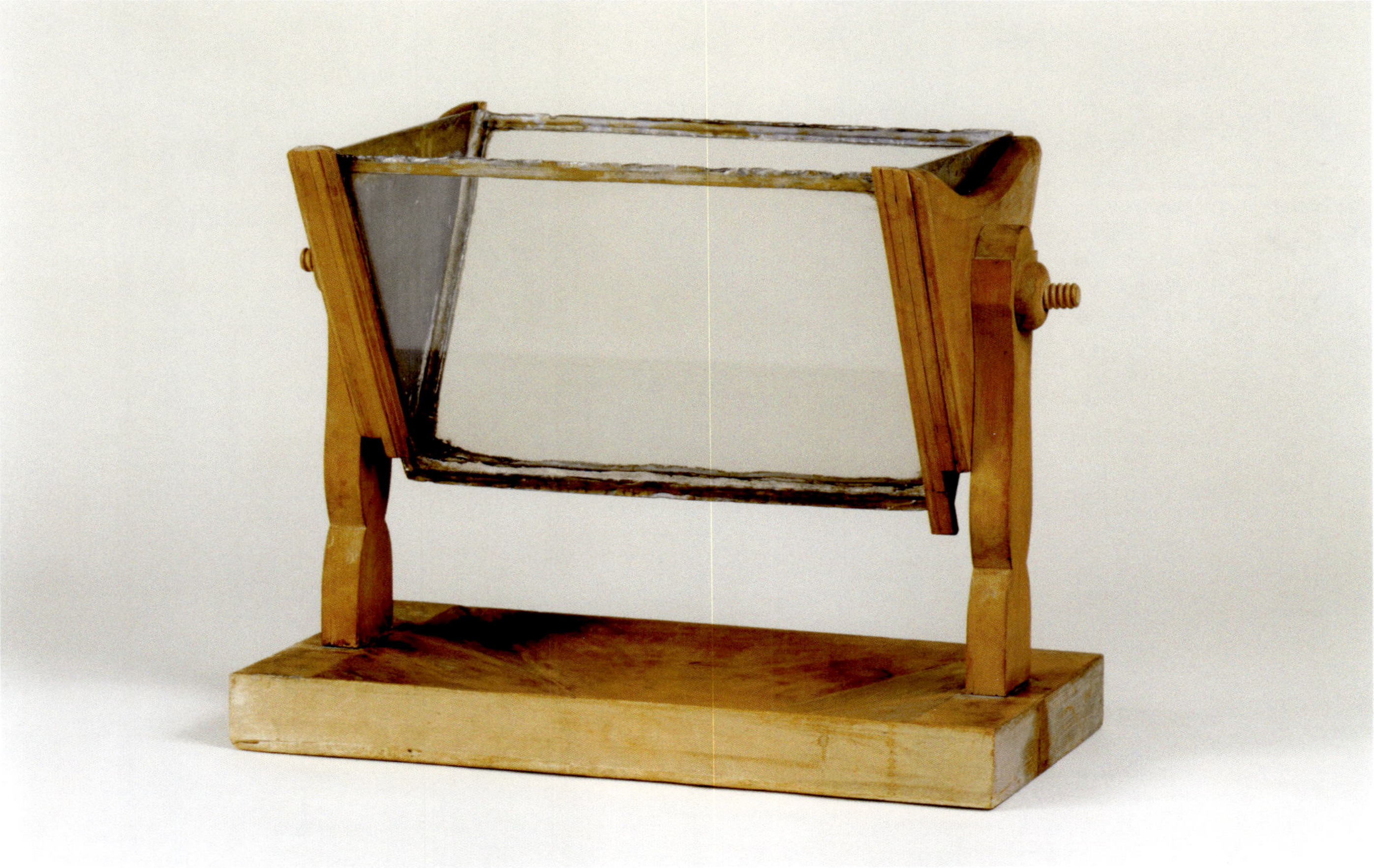

This illustration, which appeared in the second part of Goethe's *Contributions to Optics* as early as 1792, shows a blueprint for the construction of a large water prism designed by Goethe, which was particularly well suited to carrying out the prismatic experiments described by him. The wedge shaped prism was made from two panes of glass in a frame made of wood and lead which would then be filled with water. Goethe wrote: "When I presented the public with the first part of my Contributions, the black and white cards, I intended to make my readers comfortable with the observations. I had hoped that they would be able to acquire a prism easily, and then with little fuss repeat my experiments. However it has been shown that such prisms have almost completely disappeared from commerce, so that at least for the time being enthusiasts cannot find them." (Johann Wolfgang von Goethe, *Beyträge zur Optik,* vol. 2, Weimar 1792 [Facsimile, Weimar 2007], p. [1.]

9 Wasserprisma aus Goethes Besitz,
nach seiner Anleitung gefertigt
Vermutlich 1791
Holz, Blei, Glas
Höhe: 34 cm, brechender Winkel: 60°
Klassik Stiftung Weimar, Museen
Die Ausstellung zeigt einen Nachbau von
Eckhard Bendin aus der Sammlung Farbenlehre
der Technischen Universität Dresden.

9 Water prism from Goethe's estate,
made in accordance with his instructions
Probably 1791
Wood, lead, glass
Height: 34 cm, refracting angle: 60°
Klassik Stiftung Weimar, Museen
The exhibition is displaying a replica by
Eckhard Bendin from the Sammlung Farbenlehre, Technische Universität Dresden.

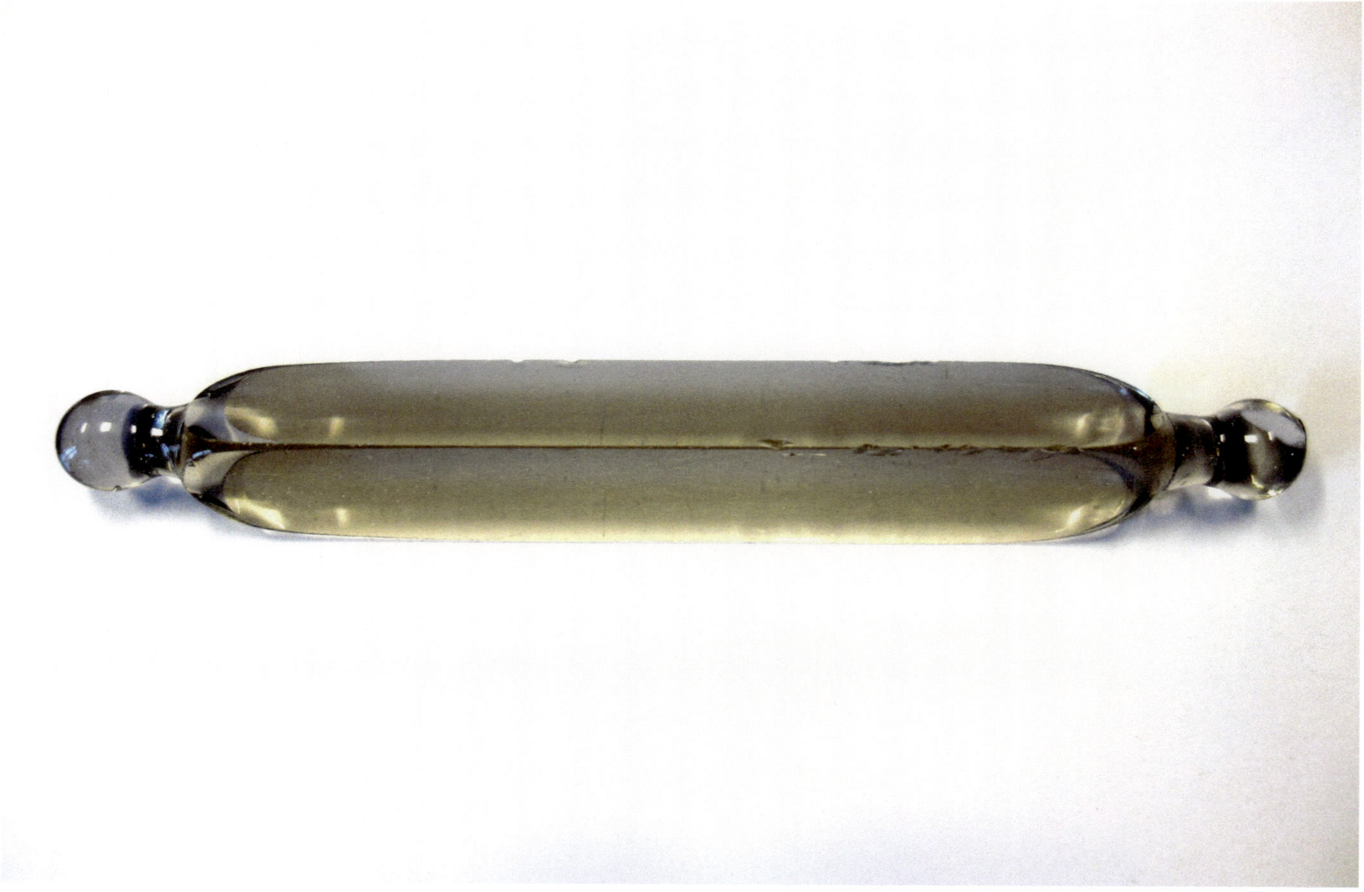

10 Dreikantprisma mit seitlichen Kugelknöpfen
18./19. Jahrhundert
Glas
Länge: 23,5 cm
Goethe-Museum Düsseldorf

10 Triangular prism with lateral ball knobs
18th/19th Century
Glass
Length: 23.5 cm
Goethe-Museum Düsseldorf

Das Prisma stammt aus dem Besitz des Erlanger Professors für Physik und Chemie Johann Salomo Christoph Schweigger (1779–1857), der mit Goethe im wissenschaftlichen Austausch stand. In Goethes Nachlass befinden sich Prismen von ähnlicher Form und Größe. Die Länge des Prismas erlaubt es, mit beiden Augen zugleich hindurchzuschauen, während man es an den Knöpfen so hält, dass die brechende Kante nach unten zeigt.

The prism originates from the collection of Johann Salomo Christoph Schweigger (1779–1857), professor of physics and chemistry at the University of Erlangen, who was engaged in scientific exchange with Goethe. Goethe's estate contains prisms of a similar size and shape. The length of the prism allows for looking through it with both eyes at the same time, whilst holding it by the buttons so that the refractive edge points downwards.

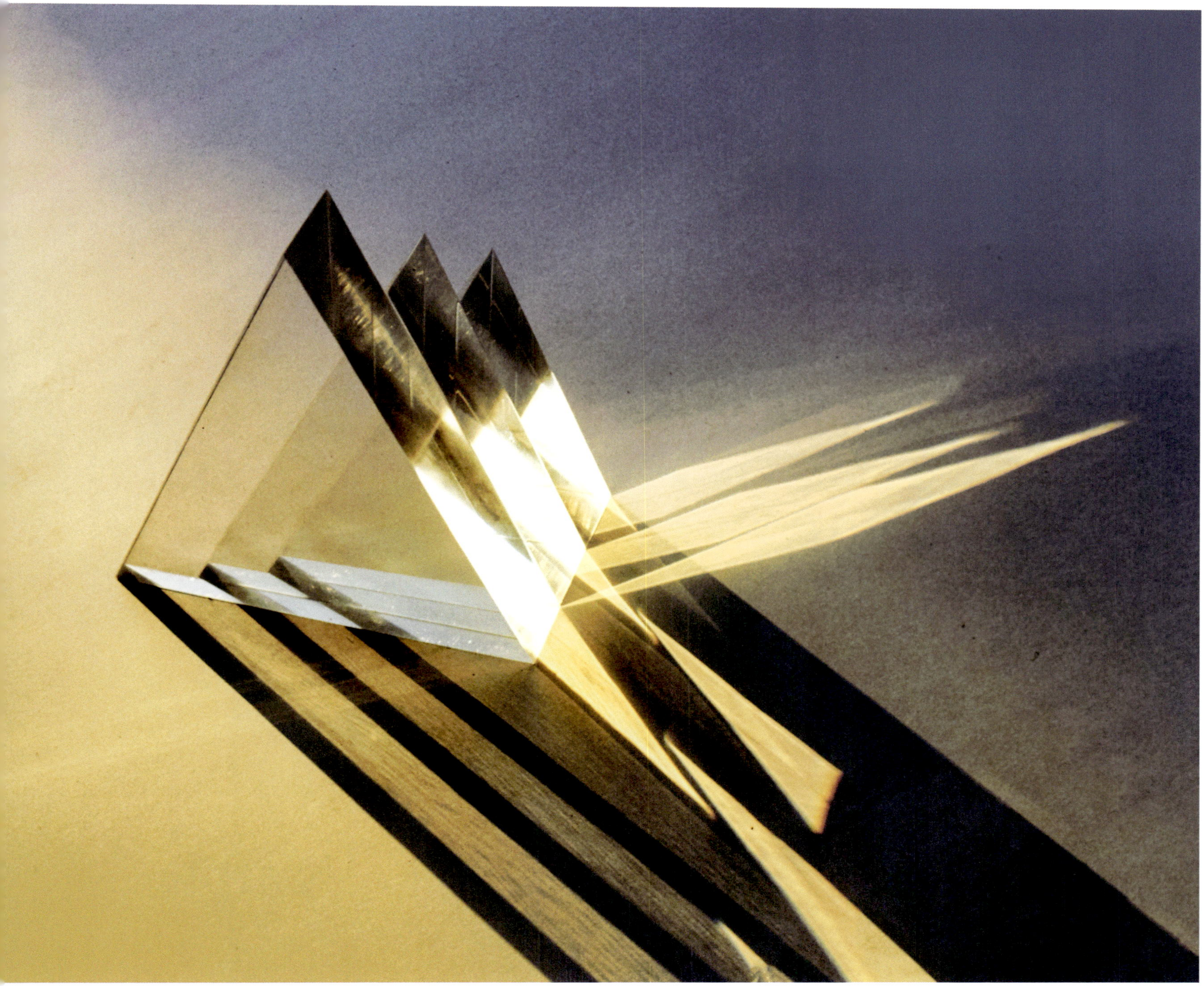

11 Heinz Mack
Modell für eine Glasskulptur
(zu Ehren von Falcon Scott)
1970
Plexiglas
30 x 30 x 20 cm

11 Heinz Mack
Model for a glass sculpture
(in honor of Falcon Scott)
1970
Plexiglass
30 x 30 x 20 cm

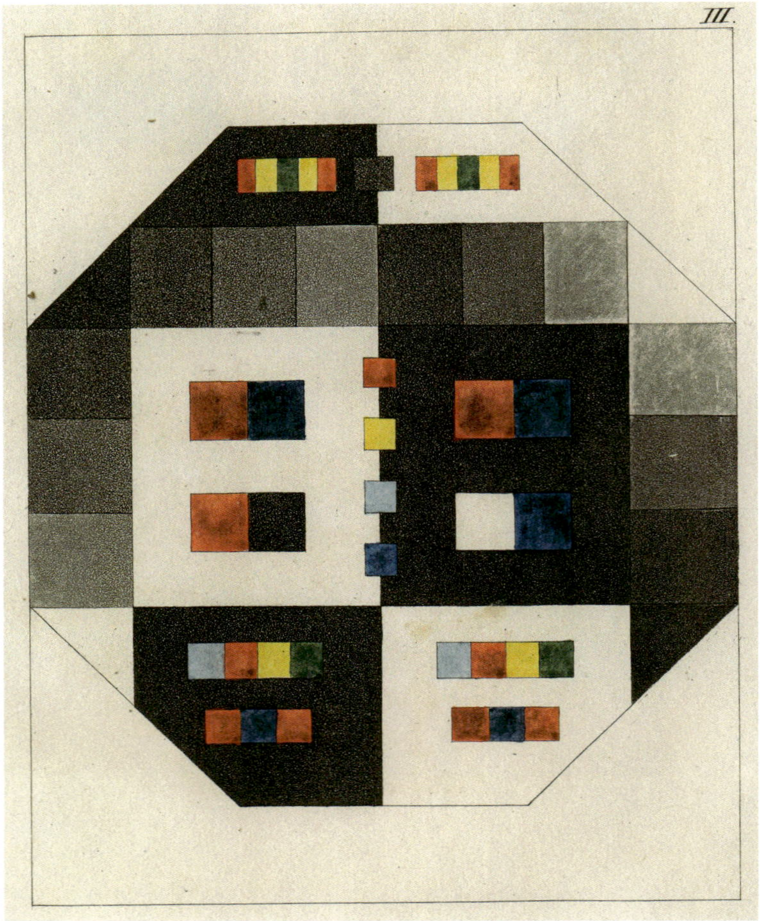

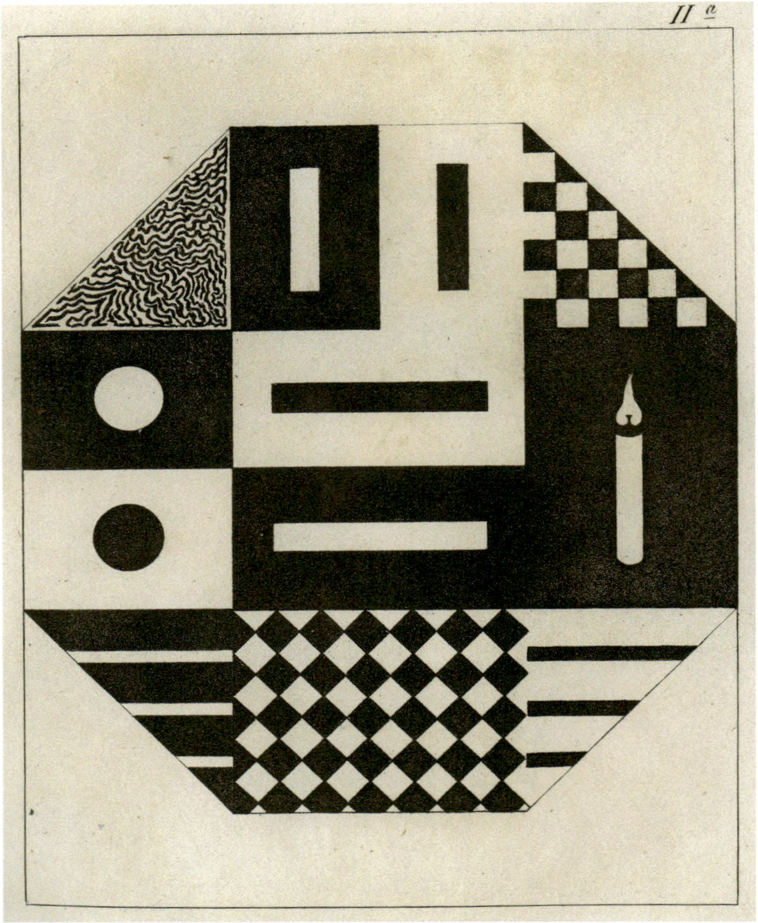

12 Johann Wolfgang von Goethe
Tafel Nr. III aus dem Supplementband
zu seiner *Farbenlehre* von 1810
Kupferstich und Aquatinta, handkoloriert

12 Johann Wolfgang von Goethe
Table no. III from the supplementary volume
of his *Farbenlehre* (Theory of Colours) of 1810
Copper engraving and aquatint, hand-painted

13 Johann Wolfgang von Goethe
Tafel Nr. II a aus dem Supplementband
zu seiner *Farbenlehre* von 1810
Kupferstich

In dieser Tafel kombiniert Goethe die wichtigsten Motive, die er bereits für das ›Optische Kartenspiel‹ entwickelt hatte, das 1791 als Beilage zum ersten Stück seiner *Beyträge zur Optik* erschienen war. Anhand der Vielfalt der Formen und Muster kann der Betrachter mit einem Blick überschauen, welche Farberscheinungen auftreten, wenn die durchs Prisma betrachtete Schwarz-Weiß-Grenze waagerecht, senkrecht oder diagonal zur Achse des Prismas steht.

13 Johann Wolfgang von Goethe
Table no. II a from the supplementary volume
of his *Farbenlehre* (Theory of Colours) of 1810
Copper engraving

In this table Goethe combines the most important motifs that he had developed for his 'Optical Card Game' included in volume one of his *Contributions to Optics*, published in 1791. By means of the variety of shapes and patterns, the observer can see at a glance what color phenomena occur when the black-and-white border is viewed through the prism horizontally, perpendicularly, or diagonally.

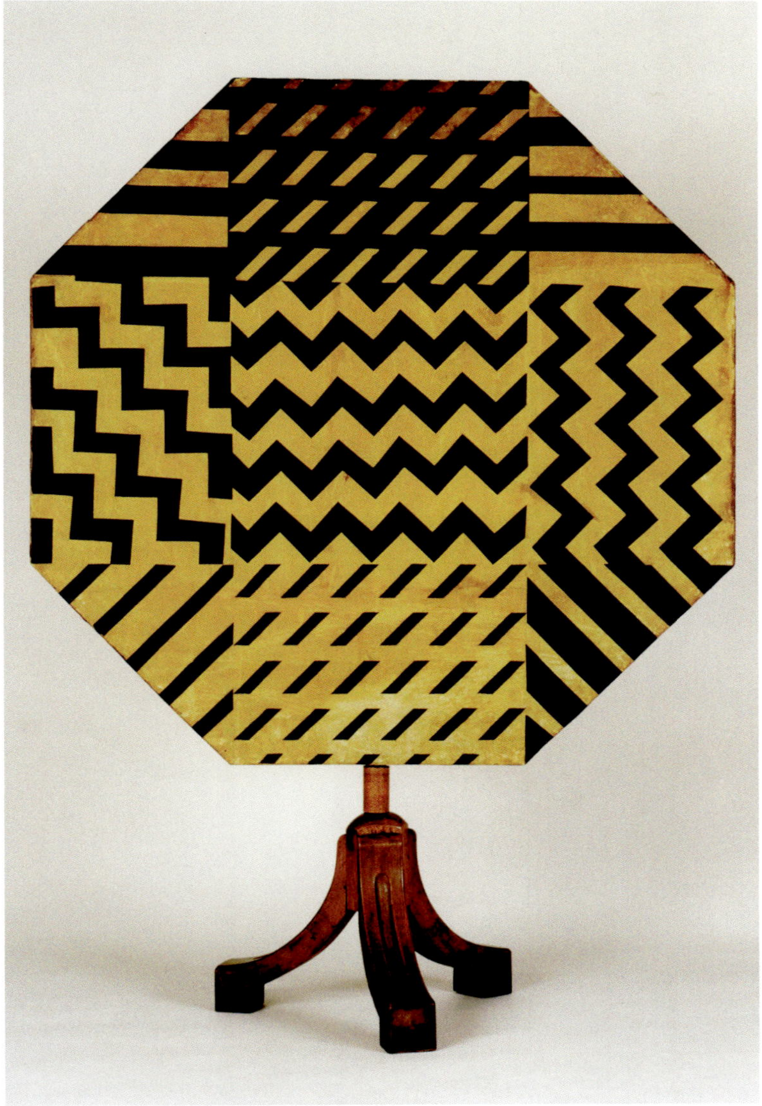

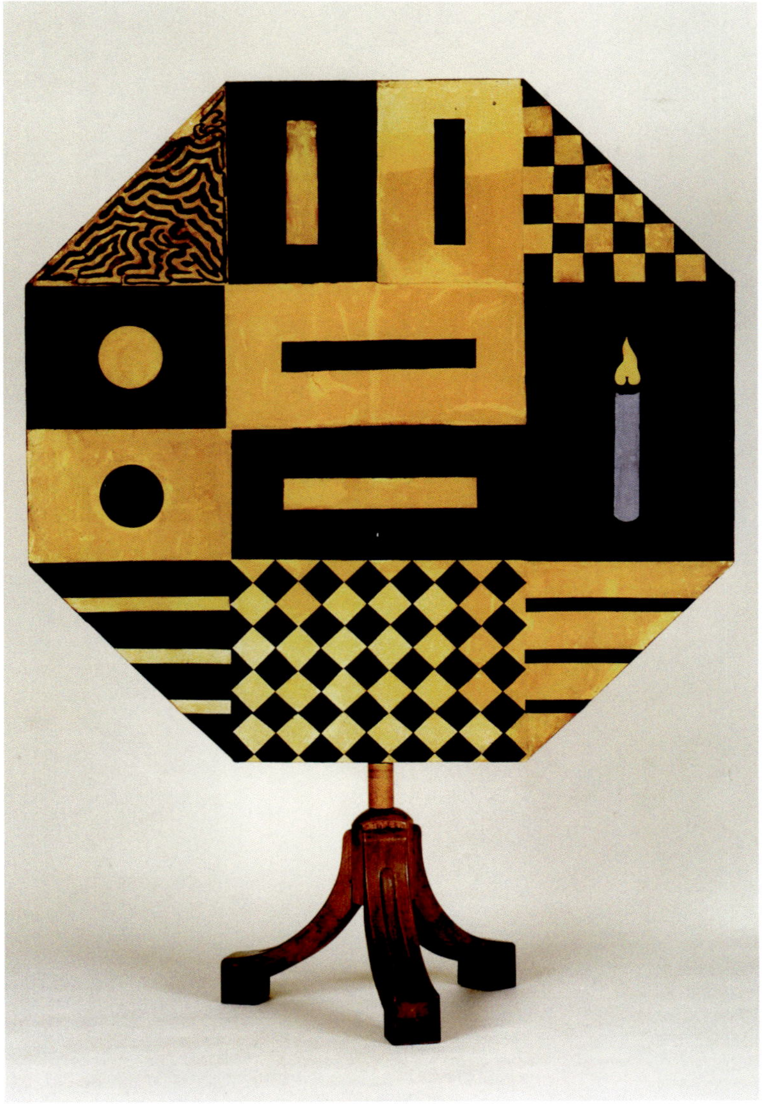

14+15 Johann Wolfgang von Goethe
Schirm zur Farbenlehre auf Holzfuß,
Rückseite und Vorderseite
1791/92 oder 1805/06
Holz, Leinwand, Papier
93,7 x 73,5 x 21,5 cm
Klassik Stiftung Weimar, Museen
Die Ausstellung zeigt Nachbauten aus der Sammlung Farbenlehre der Technischen Universität Dresden.

Zur Demonstration subjektiver prismatischer Versuche vor Publikum ließ Goethe vergrößerte Versionen seiner ›Spielkarten‹ zu den *Beyträgen zur Optik* auf große achteckige Schirme ziehen, die er bei Vorträgen am Veranstaltungsort aufstellen konnte.

14+15 Johann Wolfgang von Goethe
Screen for color theory on wooden base,
reverse side and front side
1791/92 or 1805/06
Wood, canvas, paper
93.7 x 73.5 x 21.5 cm
Klassik Stiftung Weimar, Museen
The exhibition is displaying a replica by Eckhard Bendin from the Sammlung Farbenlehre, Technische Universität Dresden.

For the demonstration of subjective prismatic experiments in front of an audience, Goethe had larger versions of his cards from *Contributions to Optics* drawn on octagonal screens which he was then able to set up in the lecture hall.

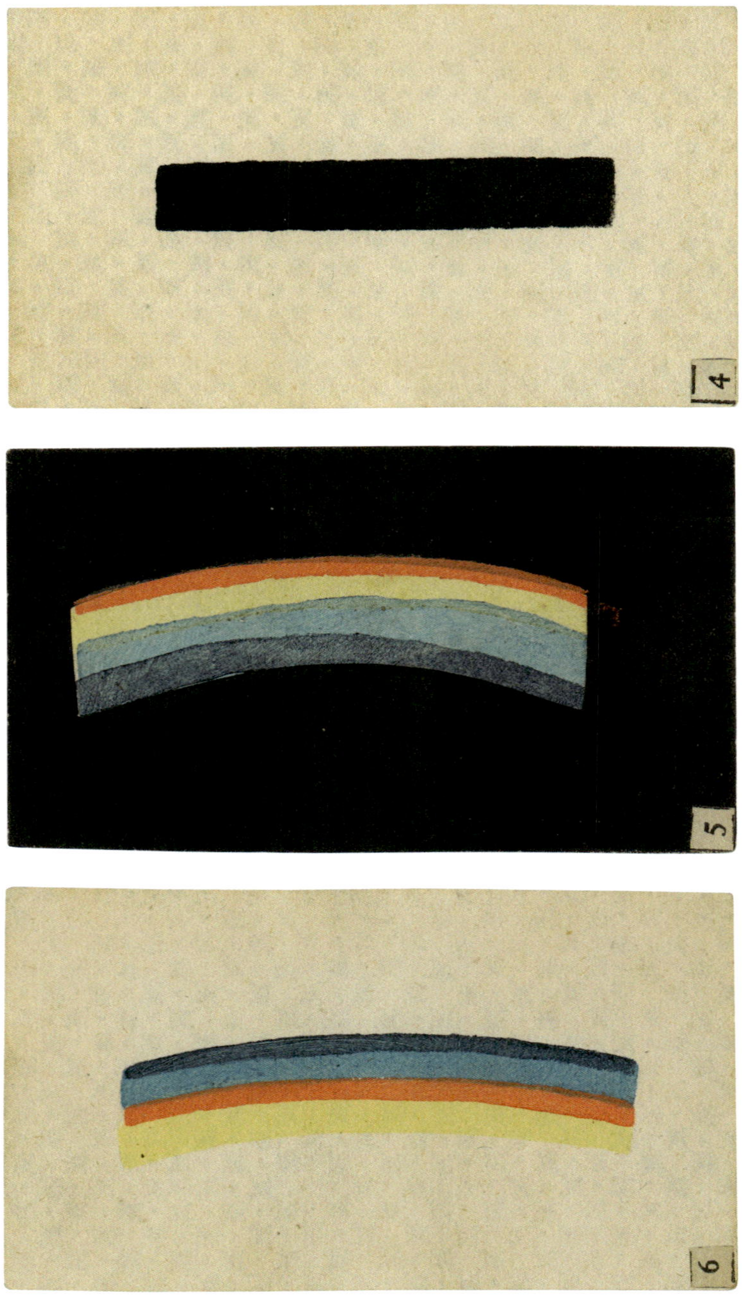

16–18 Johann Wolfgang von Goethe
Karte Nr. 4–6 aus dem ›Optischen Kartenspiel‹

Goethe hatte als Beilage zum ersten Stück seiner *Beyträge zur Optik* von 1791 27 zum Teil kolorierte Holzschnitttafeln in Spielkartengröße herausgegeben, anhand derer die Leser seine prismatischen Versuche im Experiment nachvollziehen konnten. Karte Nr. 6 (erklärt in § 46 der *Beyträge zur Optik)* zeigt, was man sieht, wenn man durchs Prisma auf Karte Nr. 4 schaut. Hätte man dort statt eines schwarzen Balkens auf weißem einen weißen Balken auf schwarzem Grund (vgl. § 45), so zeigte sich beim Blick durchs Prisma das mittlere Bild: auch wieder ein ›Regenbogenstreif‹, die Abfolge der Farben jedoch differiert bei den beiden Versuchen.

16–18 Johann Wolfgang von Goethe
Card nos. 4–6 from the 'Optical Card Game'

As a supplement to the first volume of his *Contributions to Optics* (1791), Goethe had an appendix published comprising 27 partly colored woodcuts the size of playing cards. These then enabled the reader to better understand his prism experiments. Card no. 6 (explained in § 46 of *Contributions to Optics)* shows what you see when you gaze at card no. 4 through a prism. If you had a white stripe on a black background instead of a black stripe on a white background (see § 45), the result of a gaze through the prism would be the middle picture: also again a rainbow whose colors appear in a different order.

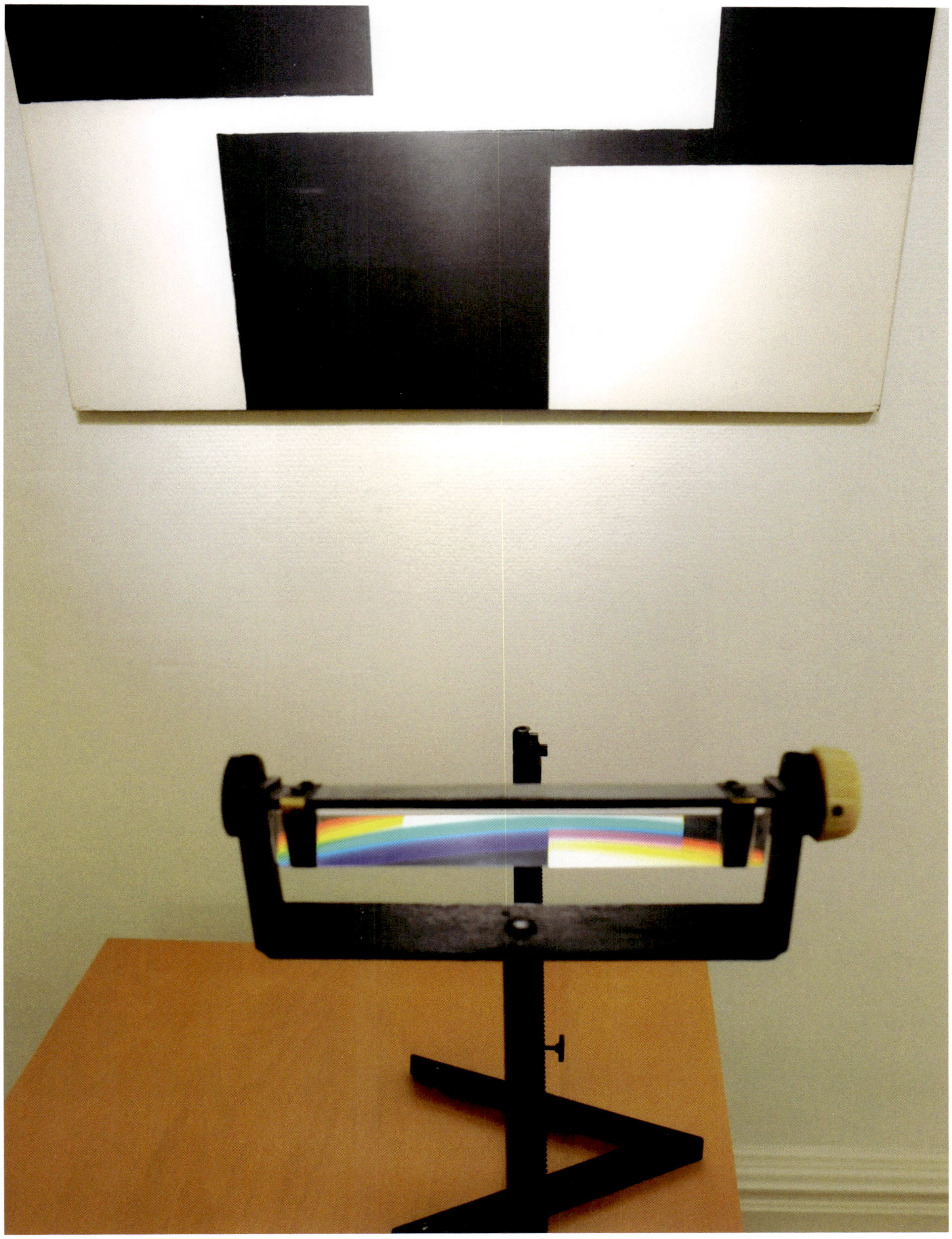

19 Stativ mit Dreikantprisma und Versuchstafel mit schwarzen und weißen Flächen
65,3 x 41,2 x 24 cm (Stativ mit Prisma)
Goethe-Museum Düsseldorf

Ähnlich wie bei den großen Wandschirmen Goethes lassen sich an dieser Tafel verschiedene prismatische Farberscheinungen beobachten. Im Foto festgehalten ist der Blick durch das Prisma auf die beiden schmalen Stege, den weißen links und den schwarzen rechts im Bild.

Im Prisma zeigt sich eine Kombination der beiden von Goethe auf den Kärtchen Nr. 5 und 6 (vgl. links gegenüber) festgehaltenen Versuchsergebnissen.

19 Stand with three-sided prism and black-and-white-patterned experiment screen
65.3 x 41.2 x 24 cm (stand with prism)
Goethe-Museum Düsseldorf

Similar to Goethe's large wall screens this screen allows for the observation of a variety of prismatic color phenomena. The photo captures the view through the prism of two narrow strips, the white strip on the left and black on the right of the photo. The prism shows a combination of both of Goethe's experimental results from cards 5 and 6. (See opposite left.)

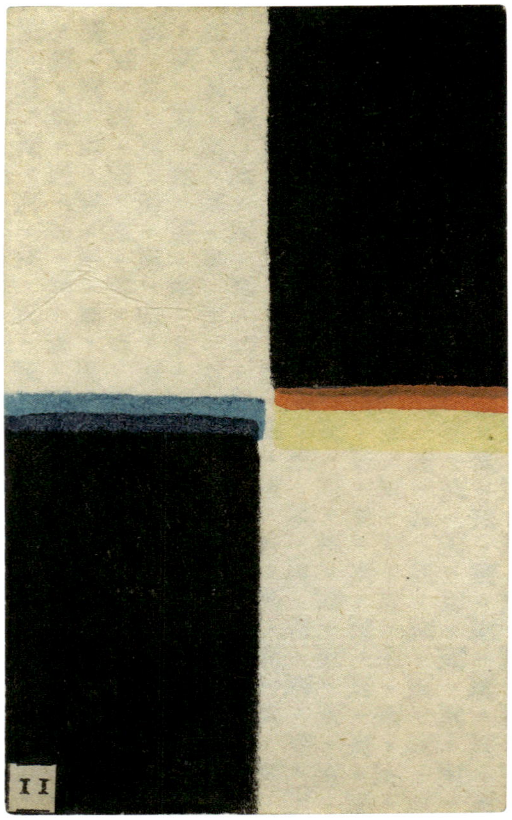

20 Johann Wolfgang von Goethe
Karte Nr. 11 aus dem ›Optischen Kartenspiel‹

Goethe hatte als Beilage zum ersten Stück seiner *Beyträge zur Optik* von 1791 27 zum Teil kolorierte Holzschnitttafeln in Spielkartengröße herausgegeben, anhand derer die Leser seine prismatischen Versuche im Experiment nachvollziehen konnten. Tafel Nr. 11 (erklärt in § 50 der *Beyträge zur Optik)* dient der Kontrolle. Sie zeigt, was man sieht, wenn man Tafel Nr. 10 (zwei weiße und zwei schwarze Rechtecke wechselweise übereck gegenübergestellt) durch ein gläsernes Dreikantprisma betrachtet: nämlich das ursprünglich schwarz-weiße Bild mit leuchtend farbigen Säumen dort, wo die schwarzen und weißen Flächen aneinanderstoßen.

20 Johann Wolfgang von Goethe
Card no. 11 from the 'Optical Card Game'

As a supplement to the first volume of his *Contributions to Optics* (1791), Goethe had an appendix published comprising 27 partly colored woodcuts the size of playing cards. These then enabled the reader to better understand his prism experiments. Card no. 11 (explained in § 50 of *Contributions to Optics)* serves as control. It shows what you can observe with card no. 10 (two black and two white squares arranged alternately opposite each other) when you look through a glass three-sided prism: namely the original black and white image with brightly colored seams where the black and white sections meet.

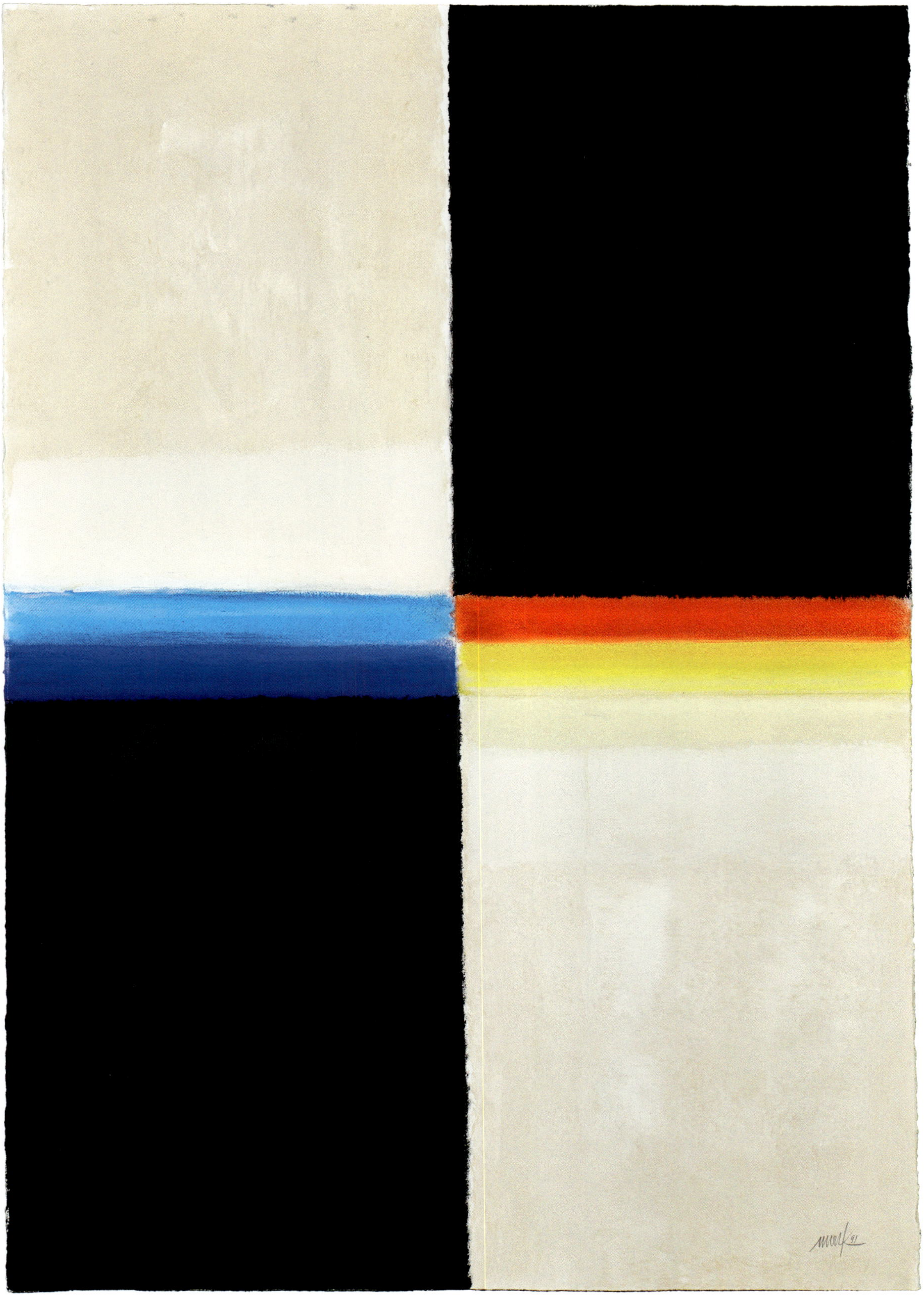

21 Heinz Mack
Ohne Titel, nach einer Vorlage von Goethe
Signiert, datiert: »mack 91«
Pastell auf Bütten
111 x 76,5 cm

21 Heinz Mack
Untitled, after a model by Goethe
Signed, dated: "mack 91"
Pastel on handmade paper
111 x 76.5 cm

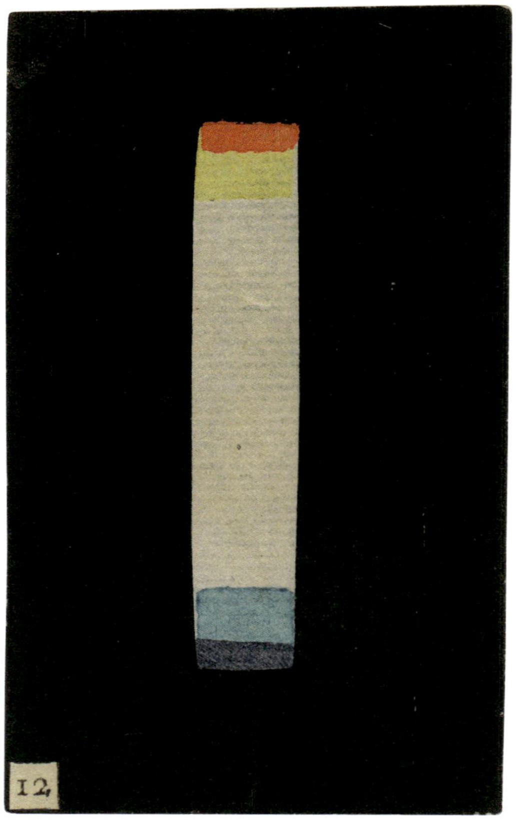

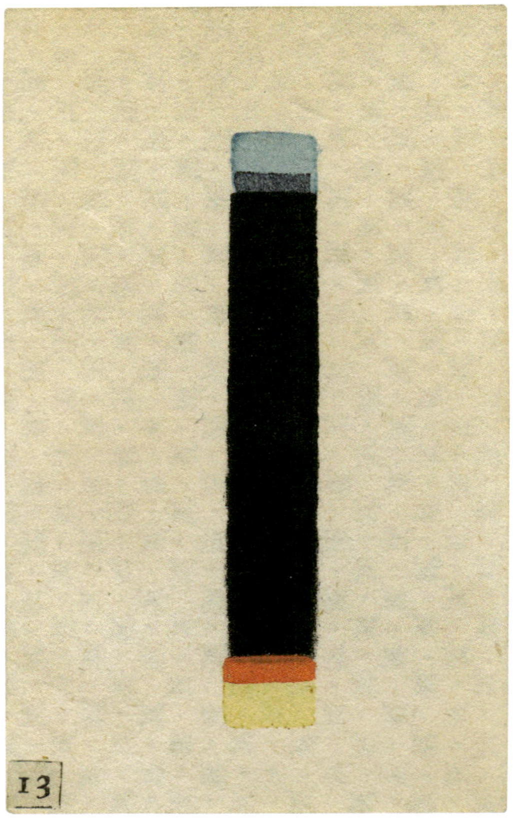

22+23 Johann Wolfgang von Goethe
Karten Nr. 13 und 12 aus dem
›Optischen Kartenspiel‹

Goethe hatte als Beilage zum ersten Stück seiner *Beyträge zur Optik* von 1791 27 zum Teil kolorierte Holzschnitttafeln in Spielkartengröße herausgegeben, anhand derer die Leser seine prismatischen Versuche im Experiment nachvollziehen konnten. Die Karten Nr. 13 und 12 (erklärt in §§ 51 und 52 der *Beyträge zur Optik)* zeigen, was man sieht, wenn man durchs Prisma auf die vertikal gehaltenen Tafeln Nr. 3 und 4 schaut. Bei horizontaler Ausrichtung dagegen erhält man das in den Karten Nr. 5 und 6 festgehaltene Versuchsergebnis. Vgl. S. 210.

22+23 Johann Wolfgang von Goethe
Cards 13 and 12 from the
'Optical Card Game'

As a supplement to the first volume of his *Contributions to Optics* (1791), Goethe had an appendix published comprising 27 partly colored woodcuts the size of playing cards. Cards 13 and 12 (explained in §§ 51 and 52 of *Contributions to Optics)* show what you see when you look through a prism at cards 3 and 4 if you orient them vertically. If the cards are oriented horizontally instead, you get the same results as cards 5 and 6 show. See p. 210.

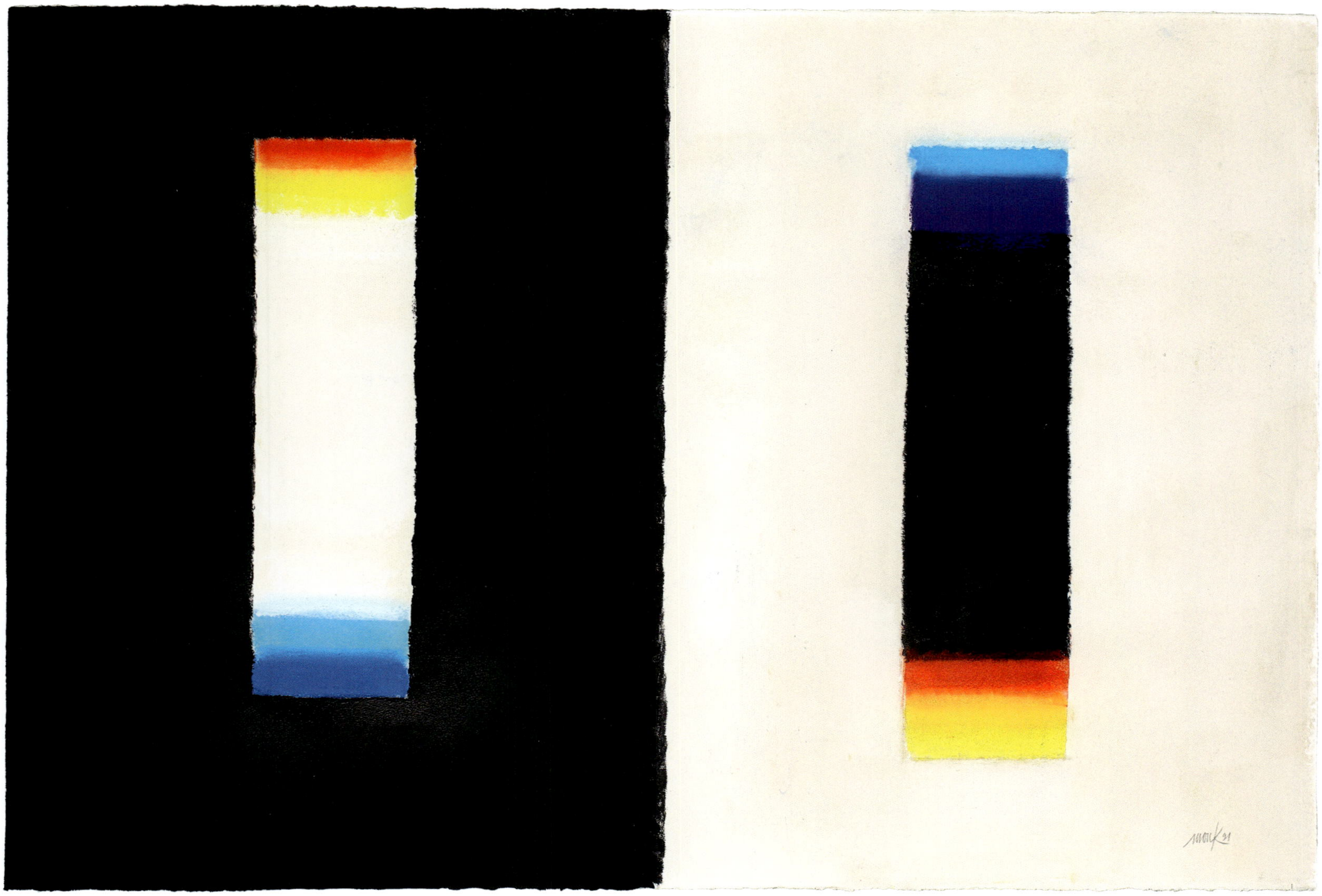

24 Heinz Mack
Ohne Titel, nach einer Vorlage von Goethe
Signiert, datiert: »mack 91«
Pastell auf Bütten
76,5 x 111 cm

24 Heinz Mack
Untitled, after a model by Goethe
Signed, dated: "mack 91"
Pastel on handmade paper
76.5 x 111 cm

25 Heinz Mack
Ohne Titel (Farbige Lichtkette)
Signiert, datiert: »mack 7«
Plexiglas, programmiertes LED-Licht
303 x 21,5 x 21 cm

25 Heinz Mack
Untitled (Coloured Light String)
Signed, dated: "mack 7"
Plexiglass, programmed LED Light
303 x 21.5 x 21 cm

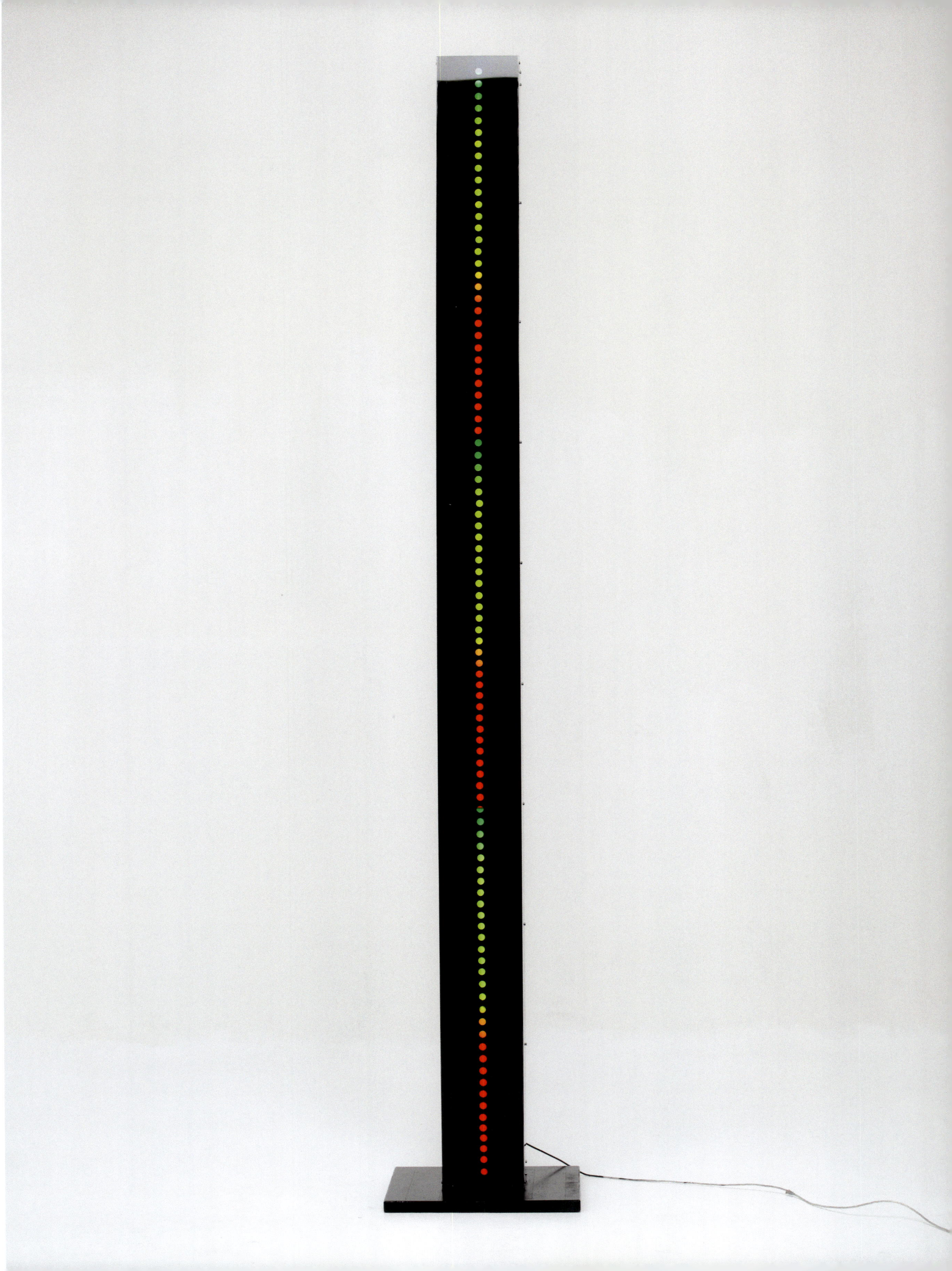

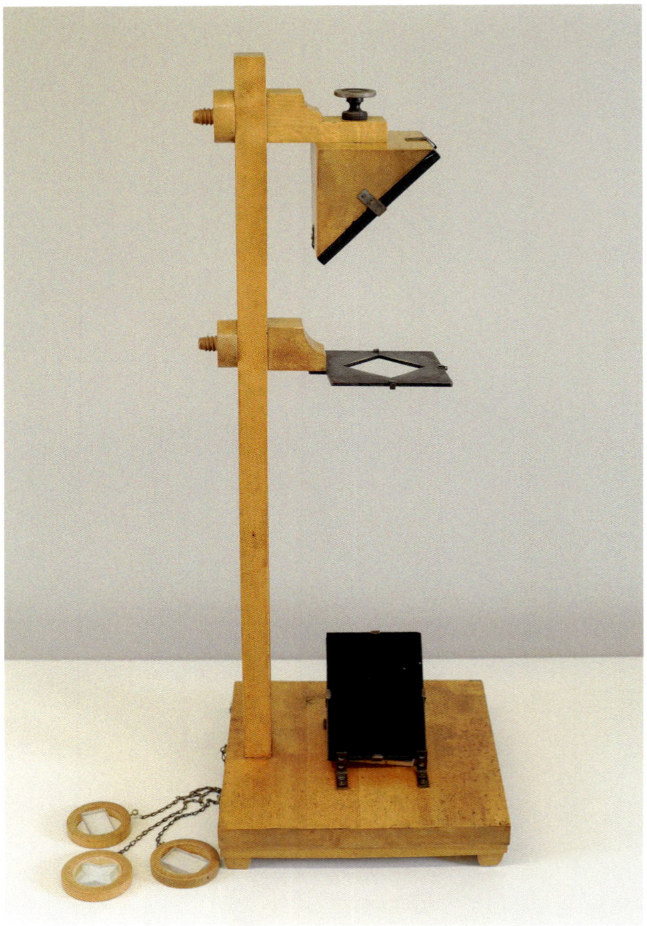

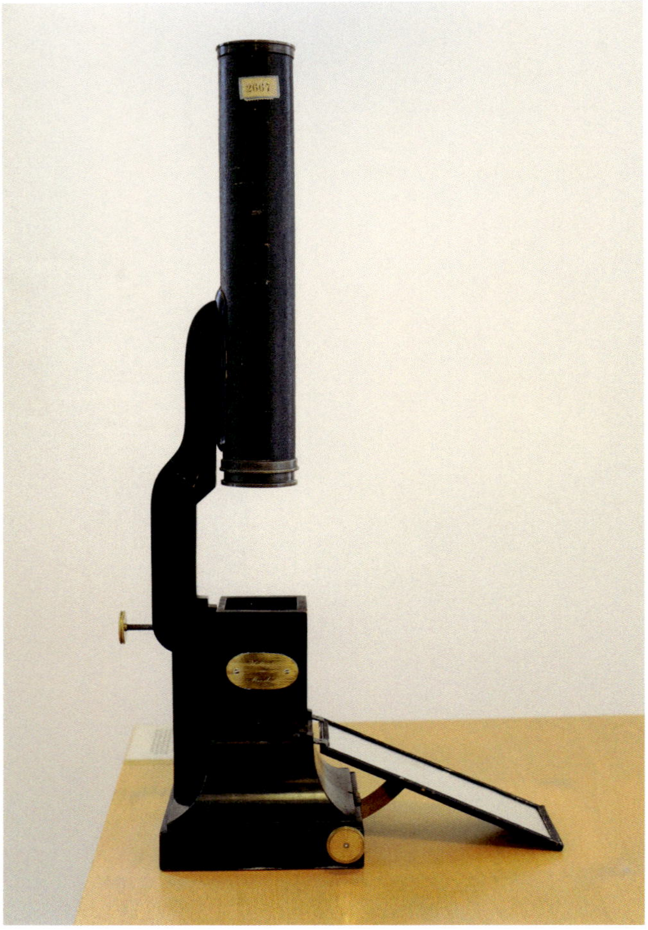

26 *Entoptisches Gestell*
75 x 27 x 27 cm
Goethe-Museum Düsseldorf

Diese Apparatur ist eine originalgetreue Nachbildung des von dem Physiker und Chemiker Thomas Johann Seebeck (1770–1831) entwickelten *Entoptischen Gestells,* das Goethe von diesem als Geschenk erhalten hatte. Mit Seebeck führte er eine umfangreiche, im Goethe-Museum Düsseldorf aufbewahrte Korrespondenz über die Farbenlehre (vgl. zum Beispiel den Brief auf S. 220 f.). Am 22. März 1816 schreibt Goethe an den Physiker: »Ihr werther unterrichtender Brief war mir höchst erfreulich, da schon seit mehreren Wochen der entoptische Apparat nicht von meinem Fenstertische kommt, auch alle Freunde und Fremde in die Spiegel sehen müssen [...]. Es ist die schönste Entdeckung, die seit langer Zeit gemacht worden, ja diesem Phänomen ist kein anderes optisches zu vergleichen." (WA, Bd. IV 26, S. 300.)

Seebeck forschte zunächst in Jena, später in Berlin zur Farbenphysik. Er knüpfte an den französischen Physiker Louis Malus (1775–1812) an, der 1808 die Polarisation des Lichts entdeckt hatte, und experimentierte dazu an einer Versuchsapparatur, die er als ›entoptisches Gestell‹ bezeichnete. ›Entoptisch‹ nannte Seebeck Farben, die durch Reflexion innerhalb von Glaskörpern und Kristallen entstehen. Goethe untersuchte einige Jahre lang diese bei der Polarisation des Lichts entstehenden Farbphänomene und veröffentlichte 1820 seine gesammelten Erkenntnisse als bedeutenden Nachtrag zur *Farbenlehre* in der Zeitschrift *Zur Naturwissenschaft überhaupt*. Vgl. LA, Bd. I 8, S. 105 f. und Bd. II 5/2, S. 1508–1511.

26 *Entoptic Stand*
75 x 27 x 27 cm
Goethe-Museum, Düsseldorf

This apparatus is an exact replica of the mounted entoptic device developed by the physicist and chemist Thomas Johann Seebeck (1770–1831) which he gifted to Goethe. Seebeck and Goethe conducted an extensive correspondence with each other on the topic of color theory. These letters are held here at the Goethe-Museum, Düsseldorf (see the letter on pp. 220–21). On the 22nd March 1816 Goethe wrote the following to Seebeck: "Your valuable and informative letter was most pleasing to me, since for several weeks the entopic device has not left my window table—all friends and strangers have to look in the mirrors as well. ... This is the most beautiful discovery to have been made for a long time; indeed, this optical phenomenon cannot be compared to anything else." (WA, Bd. IV 26, p. 300.)

Initially, Seebeck conducted his research on color theory in Jena, and later on in Berlin. He referenced the French physicist Louis Malus (1775–1812), who had discovered the polarity of light in 1808, and conducted his experiments with an apparatus that he named 'entoptic frame.' Seebeck called 'entoptic colors' those that develop through reflexion within bodies of glass and crystals. Goethe examined for a few years these color phenomena that are formed with the polarization of light and published his collected findings as significant appendix to his *Theory of Colours* in the journal *Zur Naturwissenschaft überhaupt*. See LA, vol. I 8, pp. 105–06 and vol. II 5/2, pp. 1508–11.

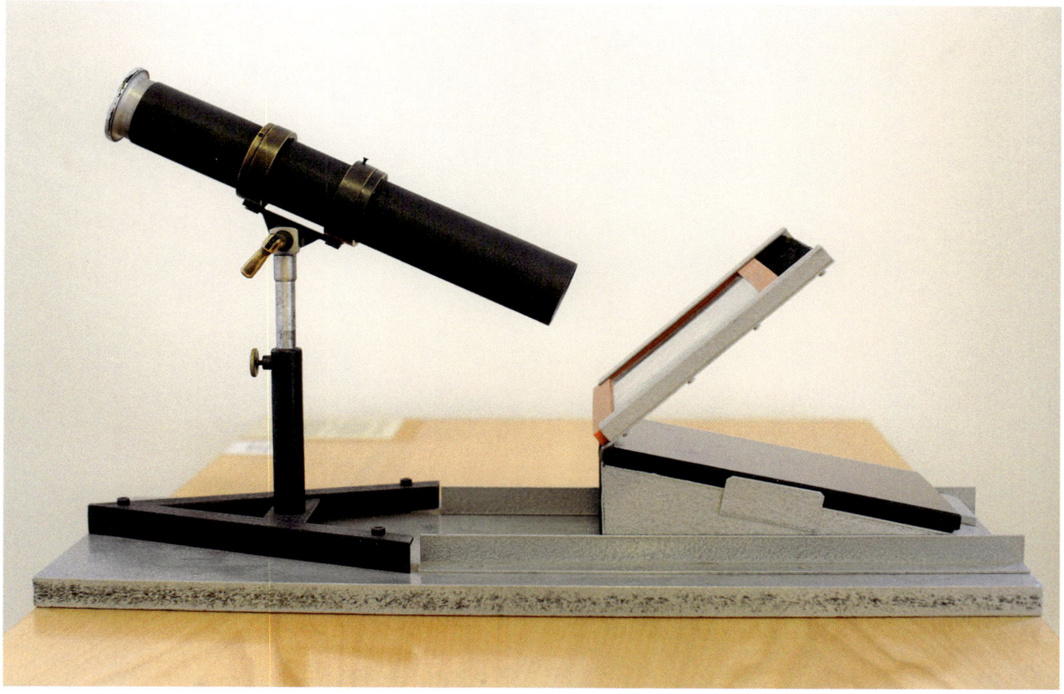

27 *Entoptischer Apparat*
58 x 14 x 28 cm
Dauerleihgabe des Deutschen Museums, München

Das nach den Angaben des Erlanger Professors der Physik und Chemie Johann Salomo Christoph Schweigger (1779–1857) in ein Mikroskopstativ eingebaute Lichtpolarisationsgerät wurde von dem Optiker Raimund Hellauer angefertigt, dem Nachfolger des Münchner Glasschleifers und Brillenmachers Josef Niggl, der die Exemplare aus Goethes Besitz hergestellt hatte. Im Okular des ausgestellten Gerätes befindet sich ein Kalkspat (Doppelspat). Goethe besaß mehrere Varianten solcher Polarisationsapparate; der erste war ein Geschenk Schweiggers zu Goethes Geburtstag am 28. August 1818.

27 *Entoptic Apparatus*
58 x 14 x 28 cm
On permanent loan from the Deutsches Museum, Munich

This light polarisation device, built into a microscope stand, was produced according to the specifications of the professor of physics and chemistry at the University of Erlangen, Johann Salomo Christoph Schweigger (1779–1857) by the optician Raimund Hellauer, the successor of Munich glasses maker and glass cutter, Josef Niggl, who had manufactured other such devices found in Goethe's estate. In the eyepiece of the display example there is a calcite (calc spar). Goethe owned several kinds of these polarisation devices, the first of which was a birthday present given to him on 28th August 1818 by Prof. Schweigger.

28 *Entoptischer Apparat*
Gebaut nach Angaben von Rupprecht Matthaei
27,5 x 60 x 24 cm
Goethe-Museum Düsseldorf

Der Physiologe Rupprecht Matthaei (1895–1976), der die Farbenlehre-Sammlung des Goethe-Museums Düsseldorf aufbaute, schreibt zu den hier abgebildeten Experimentiergeräten: »Allen drei Apparaten gemeinsam sind zwei Schwarzspiegel. Der französische Physiker Etienne Louis Malus machte 1810 die zufällige Beobachtung, daß Licht, wenn es von einem Spiegel zurückgeworfen wurde, von einem zweiten Spiegel nur dann optimal reflektiert wird, wenn die Flächen der Spiegel parallel verlaufen. Und er schloß daraus, das Licht werde durch Reflexion ausgerichtet oder ›polarisiert‹. Der mit Goethe befreundete Thomas Johann Seebeck wiederholte die Versuche des Franzosen und entdeckte, wie im polarisierten Licht in Glasflüssen farbige Figuren entstehen. Die Erscheinungen waren besonders lebhaft, wenn er das Licht von einem Schwarzspiegel unter 45° reflektierte und es durch ein Stück Glastafel schickte, das er vorher bis zur Glut erhitzt hatte und dann rasch abkühlte. Da die Erscheinungen im Glase auftreten, nannte sie Seebeck ›entoptische Farben‹, indem er sich an die Nomenklatur der Goetheschen Farbenlehre anschloß.« (Rupprecht Matthaei, *Die Farbenlehre im Goethe-Museum Düsseldorf,* Düsseldorf 1973, o. S.)

28 *Entoptic Apparatus*
Built to the specifications of Rupprecht Matthaei
27.5 x 60 x 24cm
Goethe-Museum Düsseldorf

The physiologist Ruprecht Matthei (1895–1976), who assembled the Goethe-Museum Düsseldorf's color theory collection, wrote the following about the pictured apparatus: "What all three devices have in common are two black mirrors. In 1810 the French physicist Etienne Louis Malus made the chance observation that light when reflected in a mirror is only optimally reflected in a second mirror when the reflective surfaces of the mirrors are arranged parallel to each other. He concluded from this that the light was, through reflection, being ordered or 'polarised.' A friend of Goethe, Thomas Johann Seebeck repeated the experiments of the Frenchman and discovered that with polarised light in vitrification colored figures emerge. These were most vivid when he reflected light from a black mirror at a 45° angle and passed the light through a pane of glass which he had heated to the point of glowing, and then quickly cooled. Since the phenomena appear in glass, Seebeck named them 'entoptic colors' using nomenclature from Goethe's color theory." (Rupprecht Matthaei, *Die Farbenlehre im Goethe-Museum Düsseldorf* [Düsseldorf, 1973], n. p.)

29 Johann Wolfgang von Goethe
Brief an Thomas Seebeck (1770–1831)
vom 18. Februar 1810
Schreiberhand mit eigenhändiger Unterschrift: »Goethe«
1 Blatt, 2 S. beschrieben
23,3 x 19,2 cm
Goethe-Museum Düsseldorf

Ew. Wohlgebornen
Haben mir durch den letzten Brief und das zugleich gesendete, ein ganz außerordentliches Vergnügen gemacht. Sie erlauben, daß ich jenen in meiner Geschichte der Farbenlehre mit abdrucken lasse. Er ist wieder ein neuer Beleg, wie die Newtonische Schule, von ewigen Vorurtheilen umnebelt, sich selbst und andern jedes wahrhaft Entdeckte verbarg und verkümmerte, wenn es ihr nicht gelegen kam.
Möchten Sie wohl, wenn es nicht vielleicht schon geschehen, sich nach demjenigen umthun, was Senebier über den Einfluß der sogenannten farbigen Lichter auf Pflanzenwachsthum geleistet hat. Ich habe darüber etwas in meinen Collectaneen, erinnere mich auch wohl einiger Versuche, die ich selbst gemacht, indem ich in einem Beet, das durch verschiedene Wände abgetheilt und mit einem mehrfarbigen Glasfenster bedeckt war, leicht wachsende Pflanzen erzog. Wenn ich nicht irre, so schienen mir damals die Resultate blos daher zu entspringen, daß Eine Scheibe mehr Hellung als die andre durchließ. Ob man bey genauerer Beobachtung etwas Specifisches finden möchte, würde wohl von Ew. Wohlgebornen am ersten zu entdecken seyn.
Zu Anfang März hoffe ich hinüber zu kommen und mich einige Zeit in Ihrer Nähe aufzuhalten, um mein langwieriges Opus endlich zu Stande zu bringen, mit dem ich hier in Weimar wohl niemals fertig werde. Haben Sie die Güte zu überdenken was wir etwa in der Zeit für Versuche zusammen anstellen könnten, die zu dem bekannten Zweck führen, und was ich etwa von Instrumenten und Vorbereitungen mitbringen sollte.
Die zwey Hefte des Journal de Physique habe mit Vergnügen und Belehrung durchlaufen; auch der Aufsatz über die achromatischen Gläser, war mir in dem Augenblicke sehr willkommen. Mich bestens empfehlend.
Weimar den 18 Februar 1810.
Goethe

Der Genfer Naturforscher Jean Senebier (1742–1809) hatte wichtige Arbeiten zur Pflanzenphysiologie publiziert. Die erwähnten Versuche zum Einfluss farbigen Lichts auf das Wachstum von Kressesamen und Bohnen hatte Goethe im Sommer 1796 durchgeführt (»Versuche über die Einwirkung des Lichts auf das Wachstum der Pflanzen«, LA, Bd. I 3, S. 249 f. und Bd. I 10, S. 145–167). Im zweiten Band der *Farbenlehre* veröffentlichte Goethe Seebecks Aufsatz über die »Wirkung farbiger Beleuchtung« (LA, Bd. I 7, S. 25–39).

29 Johann Wolfgang von Goethe
Letter to Thomas Seebeck (1770–1831)
Februrary 18, 1810
Written by a scribe but signed by Goethe
1 sheet, 2 pages written
23.3 x 19.2 cm
Goethe-Museum Düsseldorf

Your excellency!
Through your last letter, and the enclosure, you have afforded me extraordinary pleasure. You allow me to print that in my history of color theory. It is a further proof of the way in which the Newtonian school, enveloped in its own eternal prejudices, stunted itself by concealing true discoveries that were inconvenient for them.
Would you please, if you haven't already done it, look around for what Senebier has been doing with the influence of colored light on plant growth? I have something about it in my collectanea, and I also remember a few of the experiments that I made myself by cultivating easily growing plants in a bed split up by several walls and covered with a multicolored pane of glass. If I am not mistaken, at that time the results seemed to originate from the fact that one pane let more brightness through than the other. Whether you wanted to find something through more precise observations, you'd be likely, your excellency, the first to make a discovery.
At the beginning of March, I hope to be able to come over and spend some time in your company so that I can finally finish my opus, which I'll never manage to finish here in Weimar. I'd be most grateful if you could give some thought to the experiments we could conduct, and their presumed outcomes, so that I can bring the necessary instruments and make preparations.
I've very much enjoyed going through the two volumes of the Journal de Physique. The essay on achromatic filter glasses was most welcome at the moment. I heartily recommend it.
Weimar 18th Feb, 1810
Goethe

The Genevan natural philosopher Jean Senebier (1742–1809) had published important contributions to the physiology of plants. Goethe had also conducted the aforementioned experiments on the effect of light on the growth of cress seeds and beans in the summer of 1796 ("Experiments on the Effect of Light on the Growth of Plants," LA, vol. I 3, pp. 249–50 and vol. I 10, pp. 145–67). In the second volume of the *Theory of Colours,* Goethe published Seebeck's essay on the "Effect of Colored Light" (LA, vol. I 7, pp. 25–39).

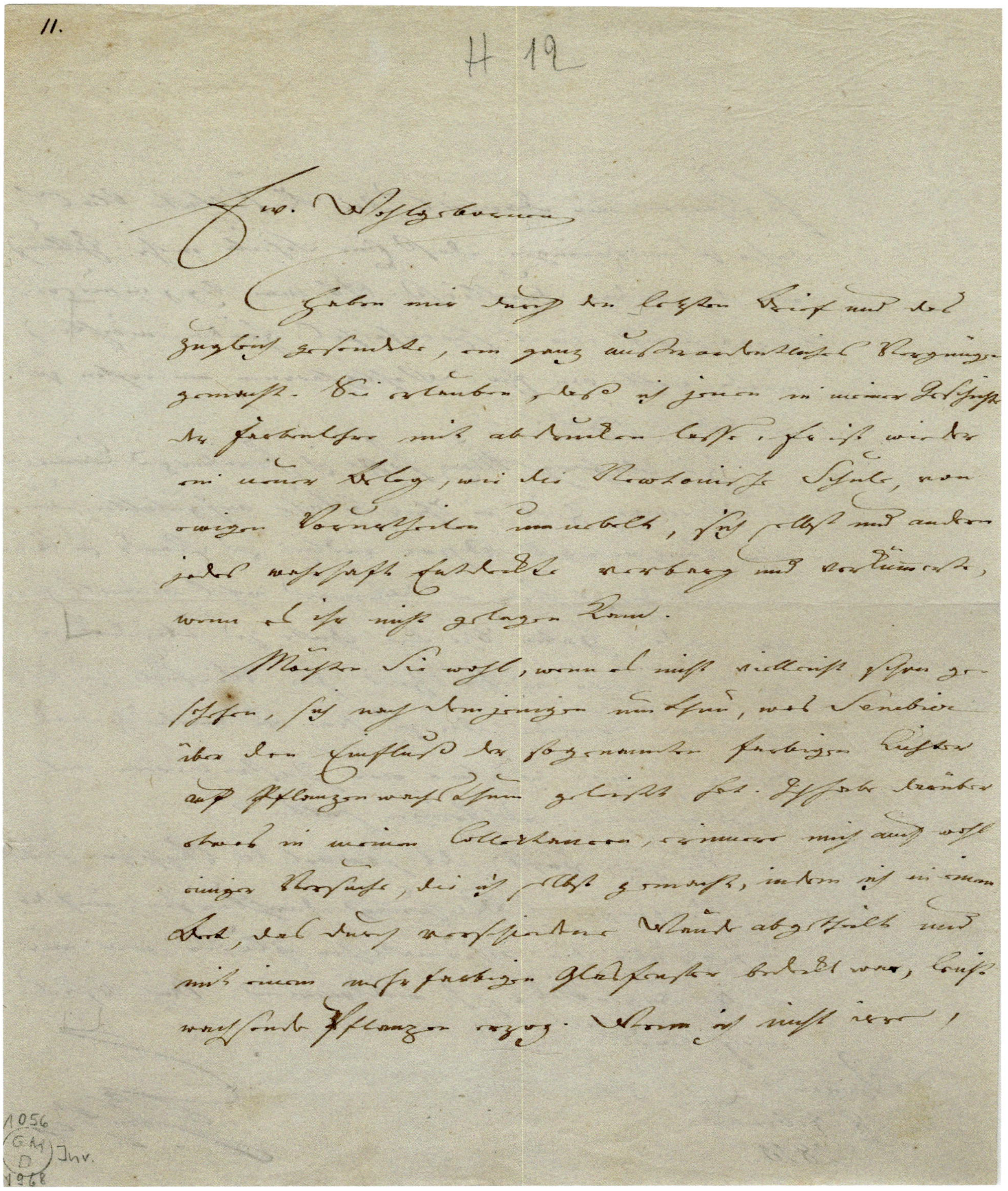

11.

H 12

Ew. Wohlgeboren

haben mir durch den letzten Brief und das
Zugleich gesendete, ein ganz außerordentliches Vergnügen
gemacht. Sie erlauben, daß ich jenen in meiner Geschichte
der Farbenlehre mit abdrucken lasse; es ist wieder
ein neuer Beleg, wie die Newtonische Schule, von
ewigen Vorurtheilen umnebelt, sich selbst und andern
jedes wahrhaft Entdeckte verbarg und verkümmerte,
wenn es ihr nicht behagen konnte.

Möchten Sie wohl, wenn es nicht vielleicht schon ge-
schehen, sich nach demjenigen umthun, was Senebier
über den Einfluß der sogenannten farbigen Lichter
auf Pflanzenwachsthum geleistet hat. Ich habe darüber
etwas in meinen Collectaneen, erinnere mich auch wohl
einiger Versuche, die ich selbst gemacht, indem ich in einem
Beet, das durch verschiedene Wände abgetheilt und
mit einem mehrfarbigen Glasfenster bedeckt war, keim-[?]
wachsende Pflanzen erzog. Wenn ich nicht irre[?],

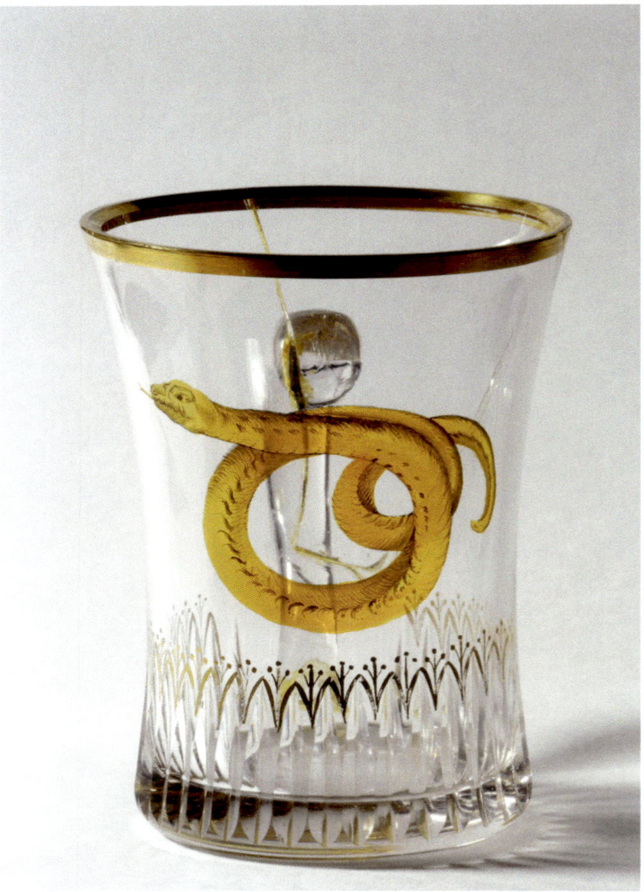

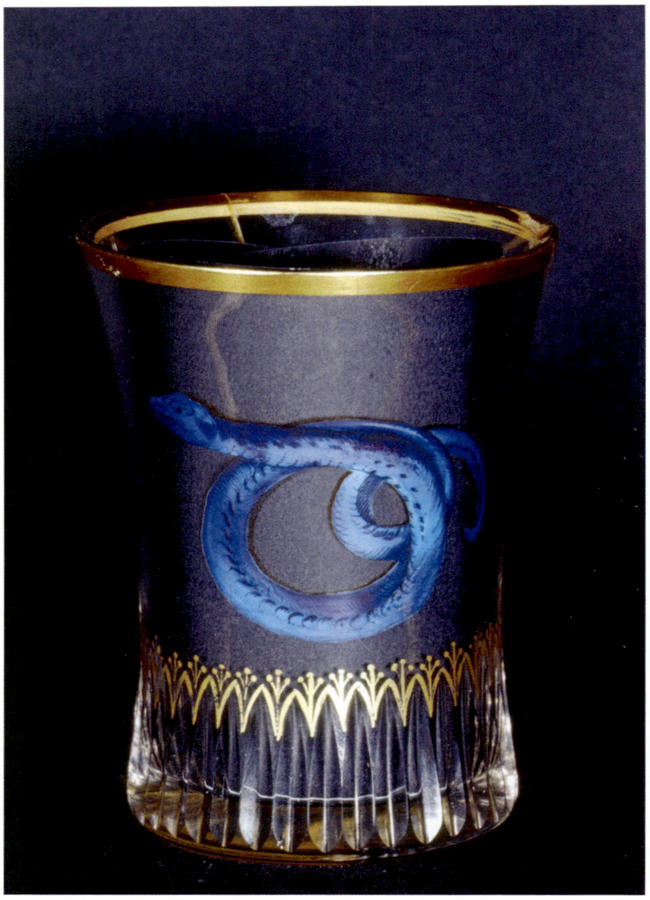

30+31 Andreas Vincenz Peter Mattoni (1779–1864)
Karlsbader Glas
Um 1820
Glas mit Goldrand und Farblasur ›Ätzgelb‹ (bestehend aus aufgeschmolzenem schwefelsaurem Silberoxyd)
10 x 8 x 8 cm
Klassik Stiftung Weimar, Museen

Goethe schreibt dazu: »In der neuern Zeit, wo die Glasmalerei wieder sehr löblich geübt wird, habe ich auf Wiener und Karlsbader Trinkgläsern dieses herrliche Phänomen in seiner größten Vollkommenheit gesehen. Am letztern Orte hat der Glasarbeiter Mattoni den guten Gedanken gehabt auf einem Glasbecher eine geringelte Schlange mit einer solchen Lasur zu überziehen, welche, bei durchscheinendem Licht, oder auf einen weißen Grund gehalten, hochgelb; bei aufscheinendem Licht und dunklem Grunde aber das schönste Blau sehen läßt.« (LA, Bd. I 8, S. 195 f., vgl. auch LA, Bd. II 5 B/2, S. 1586 ff.) Solche Kurgläser nutzte Goethe, um zu erklären, warum der Himmel blau ist und die untergehende Sonne gelb. Diese alltäglich in der Natur zu beobachtende Erscheinung war für ihn das ›Urphänomen‹ der Farbentstehung aus Licht und Finsternis unter Beteiligung eines trüben Mittels. Die Rolle des leicht durchscheinenden Schmelzes der Bemalung auf dem Glas spielt in der Natur die trübe Atmosphäre. Wenn sie die weiße Sonne verhüllt, wird deren Farbe verdunkelt, verdichtet und gesteigert zu Gelb, Orange und Gelbrot. Wenn aber Dunst vor weit entfernte, bewaldete Berge zieht, wird das Schwarz der Tannen aufgehellt und gesteigert zu Blau.

30+31 Andreas Vincenz Peter Mattoni (1779–1864)
Carlsbad Glass
Ca. 1820
Glass with gold rim and colored glaze 'etch yellow' (made from molten sulphur silver oxide)
10 x 8 x 8cm
Klassik Stiftung Weimar, Museen

Goethe wrote about this object: "In the modern era, where glass painting of a commendable standard is once again practiced, I've seen this wonderful phenomenon of the highest standard on drinking glasses from both Vienna and Carlsbad. At Carlsbad the glass-worker Mattoni had the good idea to apply such a glaze to create a curled serpent, which, when placed in translucent light or against a white background looks bright yellow, but with light on dark background looks to be the most beautiful blue." (LA, vol. I 8, pp. 195–96; see LA, vol. II 5 B/2, pp. 1586–88.) Goethe used painted glass like this to explain why the sky is blue and the setting sun is yellow. For him the observation of this everyday natural phenomenon was an 'archetypal phenomenon' of color formation made from light and darkness with the involvement of blurry agent. The role of the slightly translucent enamel of the paint on the glass is played in nature by the blurry atmosphere. When it covers the white sun, its color is darkened, condensed and enhanced to yellow, orange and yellow/red. But when the haze reaches the distant, wooded mountains, the black of the firs is brightened up and enhanced to blue.

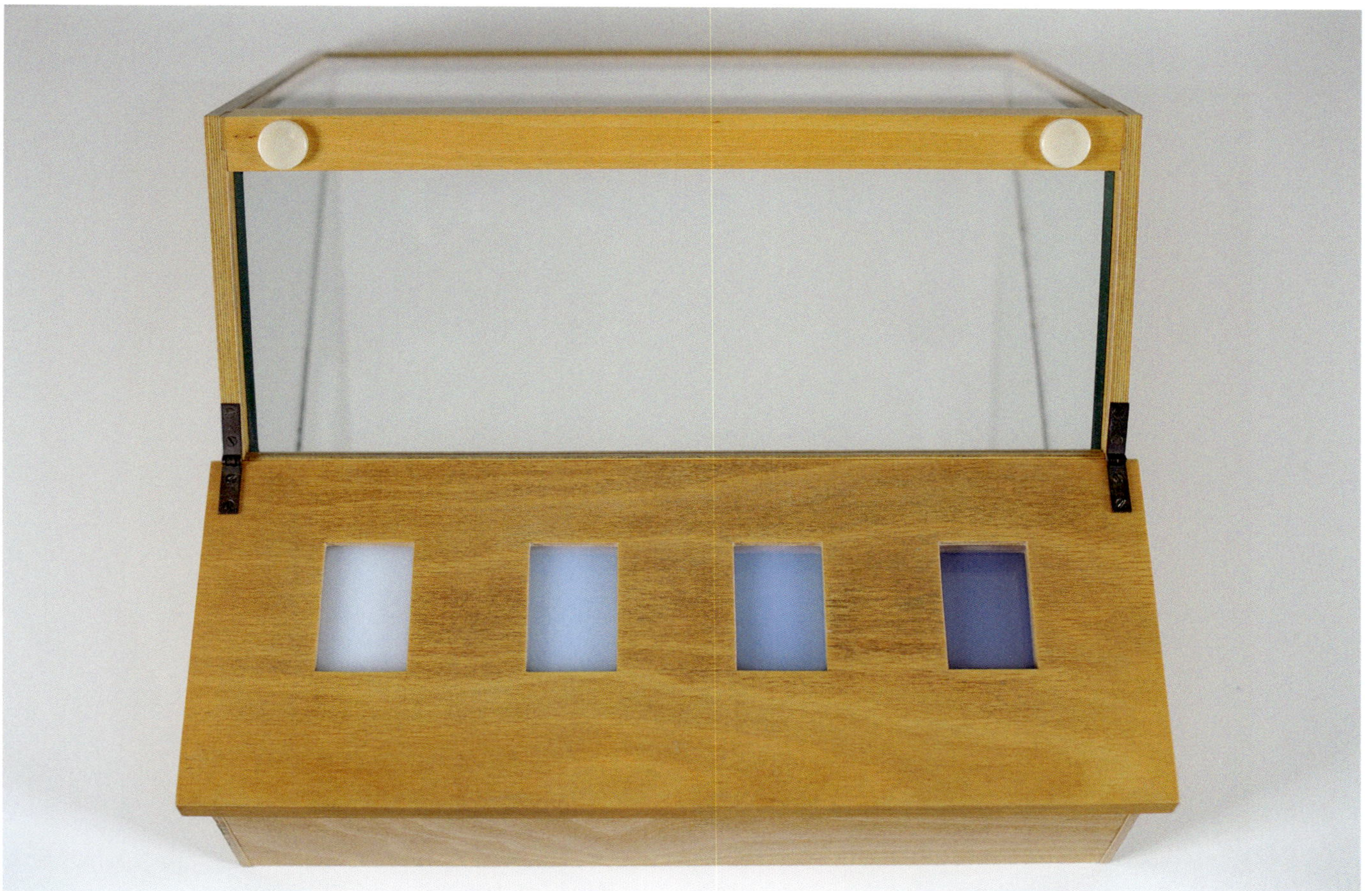

32 Spiegelkasten zur Demonstration
der Polarität bei Verwendung trüber Mittel
20,6 x 36 x 43,4 cm
Goethe-Museum Düsseldorf
Die trüben Gläser, die eigens angefertigt wurden, sind ein Geschenk der Firma Zeiss, Jena.

Einen solchen Kasten ließ Goethe sich bauen mit Gläsern, die der junge Chemiker Friedrich Christian (Fritz) Fikentscher (1799–1864) 1822 in Marktredwitz in Goethes Anwesenheit hergestellt hatte.
Der mit schwarzem Samt ausgekleidete Kasten hat in seinem Klappdeckel vier Fensterchen mit verschieden stark eingetrübten Gläsern. Sie erscheinen vor dem Dunkel des Kasten-Inneren in Abstufungen von milchig weiß bis über himmel- und mittel- bis dunkelblau. Klappt man den Deckel auf und lehnt ihn gegen einen das Sonnenlicht reflektierenden Spiegel, so werden die Gläser orangerot bis hellgelb.

32 Mirror box for the demonstration of polarity
through the use of semi-transparent filters
20.6 x 36 x 43.4 cm
Goethe-Museum Düsseldorf
The semi-transparent filters were specially made and a gift from the Zeiss lens company of Jena.

Goethe had such a box built with panes of filter glass made by the young chemist Friedrich Christian (Fritz) Fikentscher (1799–1864) in 1822 during one of Goethe's visits to Marktredwitz.
The box, lined with black velvet, has four little windows in its hinged lid and these have varying degrees of opacity. With the darkness of the box behind them they appear in gradations from milky white to various blues from sky blue through to navy blue. If you open the lid and lean it against a reflecting sunlight mirror, the panes become orange-red to bright yellow.

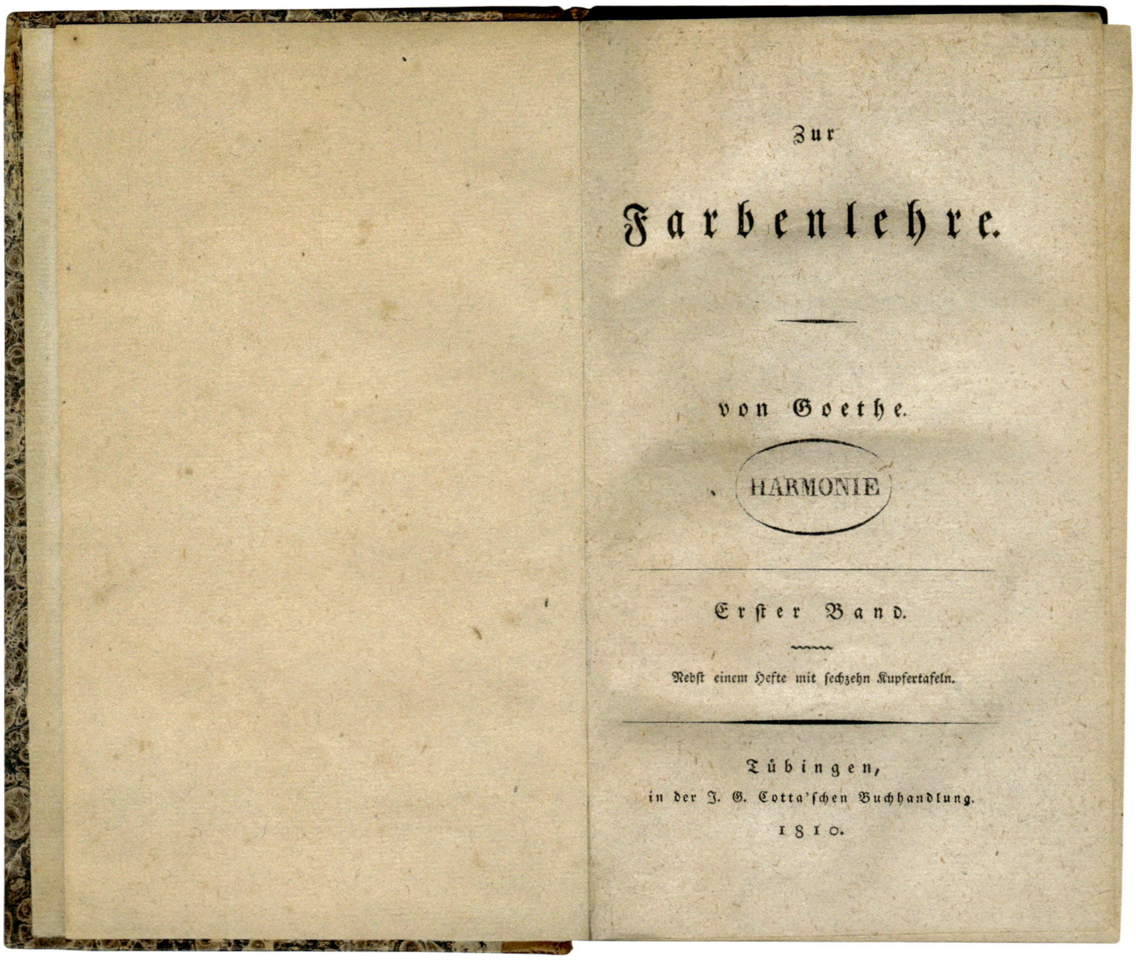

33 Johann Wolfgang von Goethe
Zur Farbenlehre. Von Goethe. Nebst einem Hefte mit sechzehn Kupfertafeln. Tübingen, in der J. G. Cotta'schen Buchhandlung. 1810.

Der erste Band enthält den didaktischen und den polemischen, der zweite den historischen Teil der *Farbenlehre*. Ergänzt werden die beiden Textbände durch einen Tafelband, der auch Erläuterungen zu den Abbildungen enthält.

33 Johann Wolfgang von Goethe
Zur Farbenlehre. Von Goethe. Nebst einem Hefte mit sechzehn Kupfertafeln. Tübingen, in der J. G. Cotta'schen Buchhandlung. 1810.

The first volume of *Theory of Colours* contains the didactic and polemical sections of the book, whilst the second volume contains the historical section. Both text volumes are complemented by a volume of plates, which also comprises annotations to accompany the illustrations.

34 Johann Wolfgang von Goethe
Tafel Nr. I aus dem Supplementband zu seiner *Farbenlehre* von 1810
Handkolorierter Kupferstich

Die erste Tafel ist den physiologischen Farben gewidmet. Abb. 1 darauf zeigt Goethes Farbenkreis, Abb. 2, 8 und 11 behandeln verschiedene Ausprägungen von Farbenblindheit, Abb. 3 und 4 stellen das Phänomen subjektiver Höfe vor, Abb. 5 und 6 zeigen Versuche mit farbigen Schatten, Abb. 7 behandelt Farberscheinungen von Flammen, Abb. 9 eine komplementärfarbige Doppelspiegelung und Abb. 10 abklingende Nachbilder nach einer Blendung.

34 Johann Wolfgang von Goethe
Illustration no. 1 from the supplemental volume of his 1810 *Theory of Colours*
Hand-colored copper engraving

The first illustration is dedicated to physiological colors. Fig. 1 shows Goethe's color wheel, figs. 2, 8 and 11 are concerned with different manifestations of color blindness, figs. 3 and 4 present the phenomenon of subjective halos, figs. 5 and 6 show experiments with colored shadows, fig. 7 deals with the color phenomena of flames, fig. 9 is a complementary colored double mirroring, and fig. 10 shows fading afterimages following a glare.

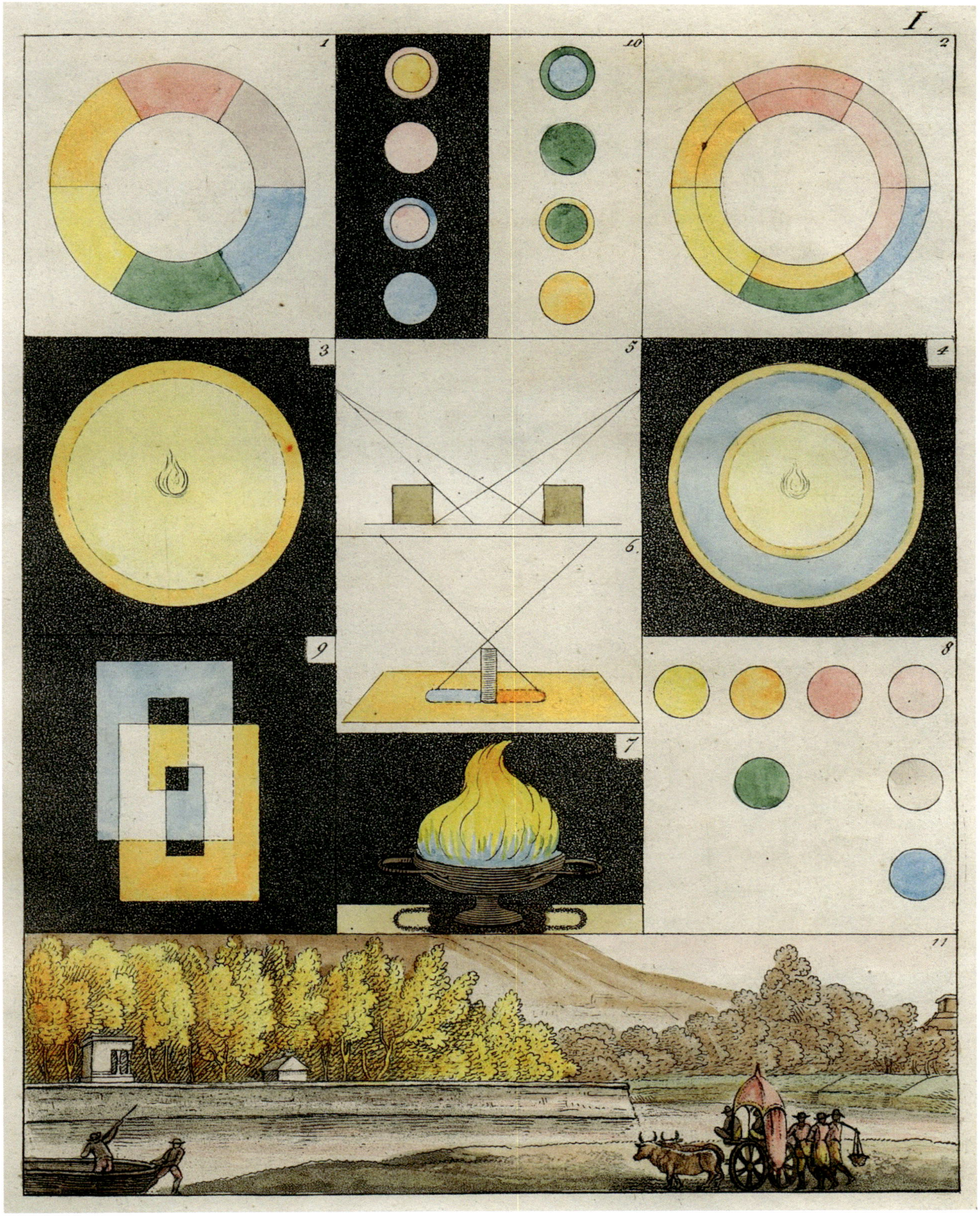
I.
1
10
2
3
5
4
6.
9
8
7
11

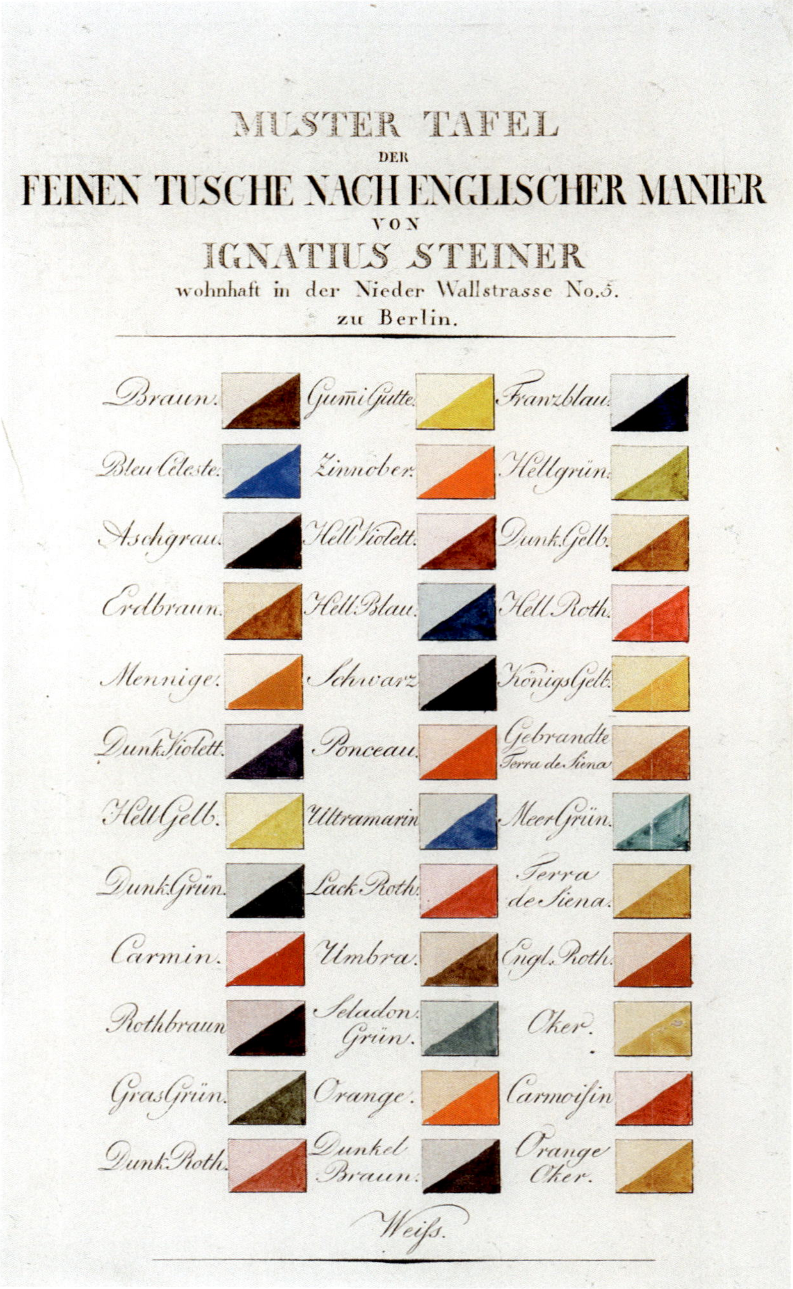

35 Ignatius Steiner
Muster Tafel der feinen Tusche nach englischer Manier
Um 1803

Diese Mustertafel enthält die von Hand aufgetragenen Aufstriche 36 verschiedener Farbtöne, jeweils einmal nahezu deckend und einmal in stark verdünnter Lasur. Im Augustheft 1803 des *Journals für Fabrik, Manufaktur, Handlung und Mode* liest man: »Welche Vortheile und Bequemlichkeit den mit Wasserfarben mahlenden Künstlern und mit Miniatur-Mahlerei sich beschäftigenden Personen die Erfindung der kouleurten so genannten bunten Tuschen gewähret, ist jedem, der sich derselben bedient hat, bekannt […]. Denn wer das unangenehme, schmutzige und mühsame des Farbenreibens und der Gebrauchszubereitung der Farben überhaupt kennt, wird sich gewiß gern desselben überheben, wenn er ohne dieses seinen Zweck erreichen kann.« (S. 122.)

35 Ignatius Steiner
Sample of fine Indian Ink in the English Style
Ca. 1803

This hand-crafted sample board is made up of 36 ink applications in different colors, each almost opaque, as well as highly diluted. In the August 1803 edition of the *Journal für Fabrik, Manufaktur, Handlung und Mode* (Journal of Fabrication, Manufacture, Trade and Fashion) it says: "What advantages and convenience the artists of watercolor painting and people engaged in miniature painting enjoy, with the invention of these so-called multicolored inks. This convenience is well known to anyone who has used them. … For those who know the unpleasant, dirty, and laborious work of grinding paint and preparing paint for use, will certainly be glad of it, if they can achieve their purpose without such preparations." (p. 122.)

36 Johann Wolfgang von Goethe
Tafel Nr. XII aus dem Supplementband zu seiner *Farbenlehre* von 1810
Handkolorierter Kupferstich

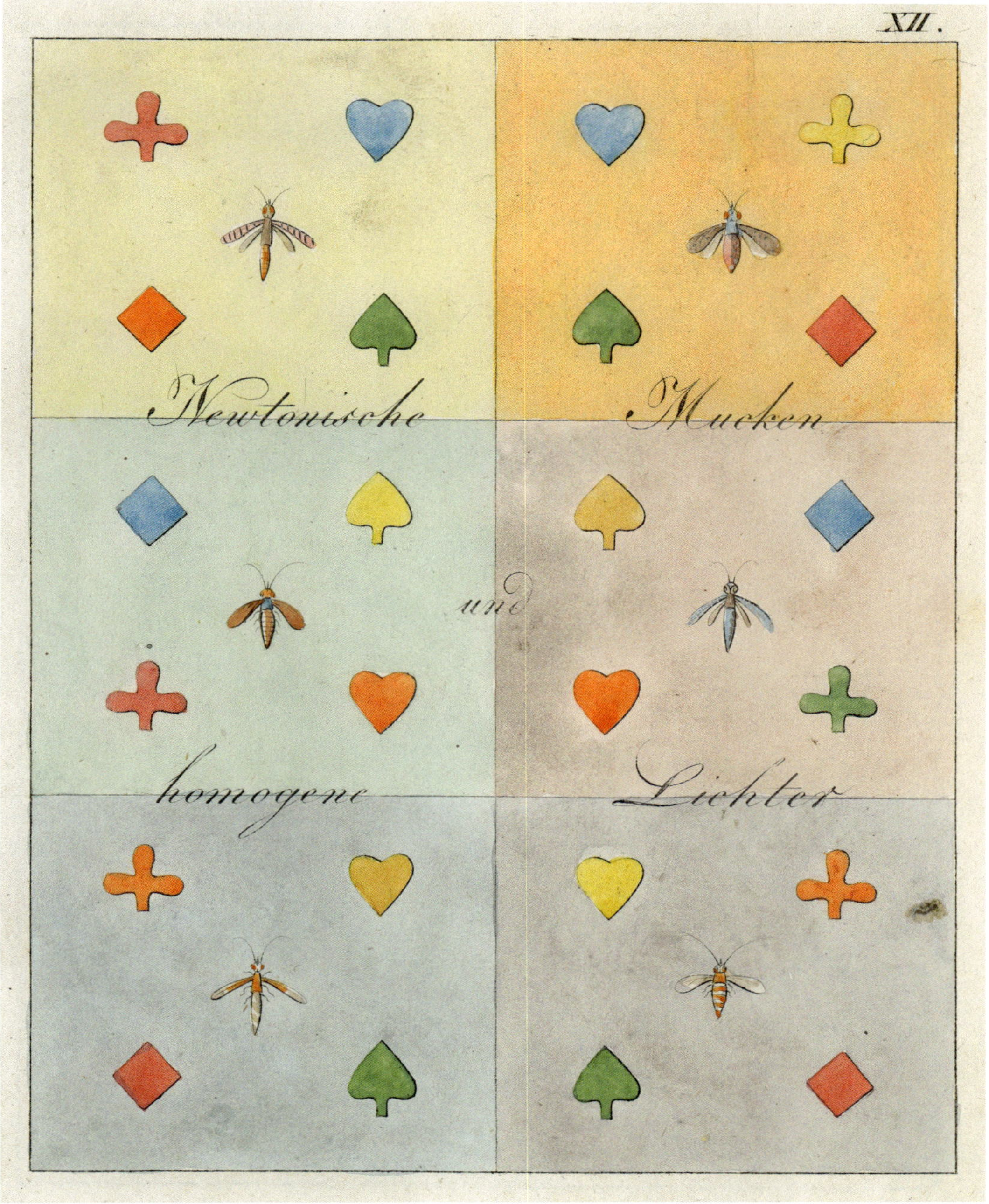

Goethe schreibt in der Erläuterung zu dieser Tafel: »Der wegen seiner Versuche so berühmte Newton läßt während seiner Untersuchungen und Beobachtungen, welche so scharf und genau seyn sollen, immer wieder, ehe man sich's versieht, mancherley Zufälligkeiten obwalten. Eine Fliege die ihm über die Wand läuft, die Lettern eines aufgeschlagenen Buches […] und was ihm sonst in die Quere kommt, wird mit herein gezogen, und die dabey eintretenden Erscheinungen müssen dann gelten was sie können." (*Anzeige und Uebersicht des Goethischen Werkes zur Farbenlehre.* Ein Heft mit XVI. illuminirten Kupfertafeln und deren Erklärung. Tübingen, in der J. G. Cotta'schen Buchhandlung. 1810. S. 20.) Newtons These, dass sich in farbigem Licht bei der Betrachtung durch ein Prisma keine Farbsäume zeigen, versucht Goethe zu widerlegen und zugleich zu verspotten, indem er auf der Farbtafel, mit der im Experiment das Gegenteil bewiesen werden soll, genau das abbildet, was Newton in seinen Ausführungen nennt: Fliegen, kleine Gegenstände und Buchstaben. Und bei ›Mucken‹ denkt man freilich nicht nur an Insekten.

36 Johann Wolfgang von Goethe
Illustration no. XII from the supplemental volume of the *Theory of Colours* (1810)
Hand-colored copper engraving

In his commentary to this illustration Goethe writes: "Newton who is so famous for his experiments allowed during his investigations and observations, which ought to be completely sharp and precise, again and again for some coincidences, and then before you know it, it is those very coincidences which prevail. A fly wandering across the wall, the lettering of an open book … or whatever else gets in his way is pulled into the experiment, so you just have to make what you can from the resulting phenomena." (*Anzeige und Uebersicht des Goethischen Werkes zur Farbenlehre,* Tübingen, 1810, p. 20.) Newton's theory that when colored light is viewed through a prism the fringes are color free is one which Goethe both mocked and tried to refute by depicting on a color chart, with which he intended to prove the opposite, exactly what Newton cites in his findings: flies, small objects, and letters.

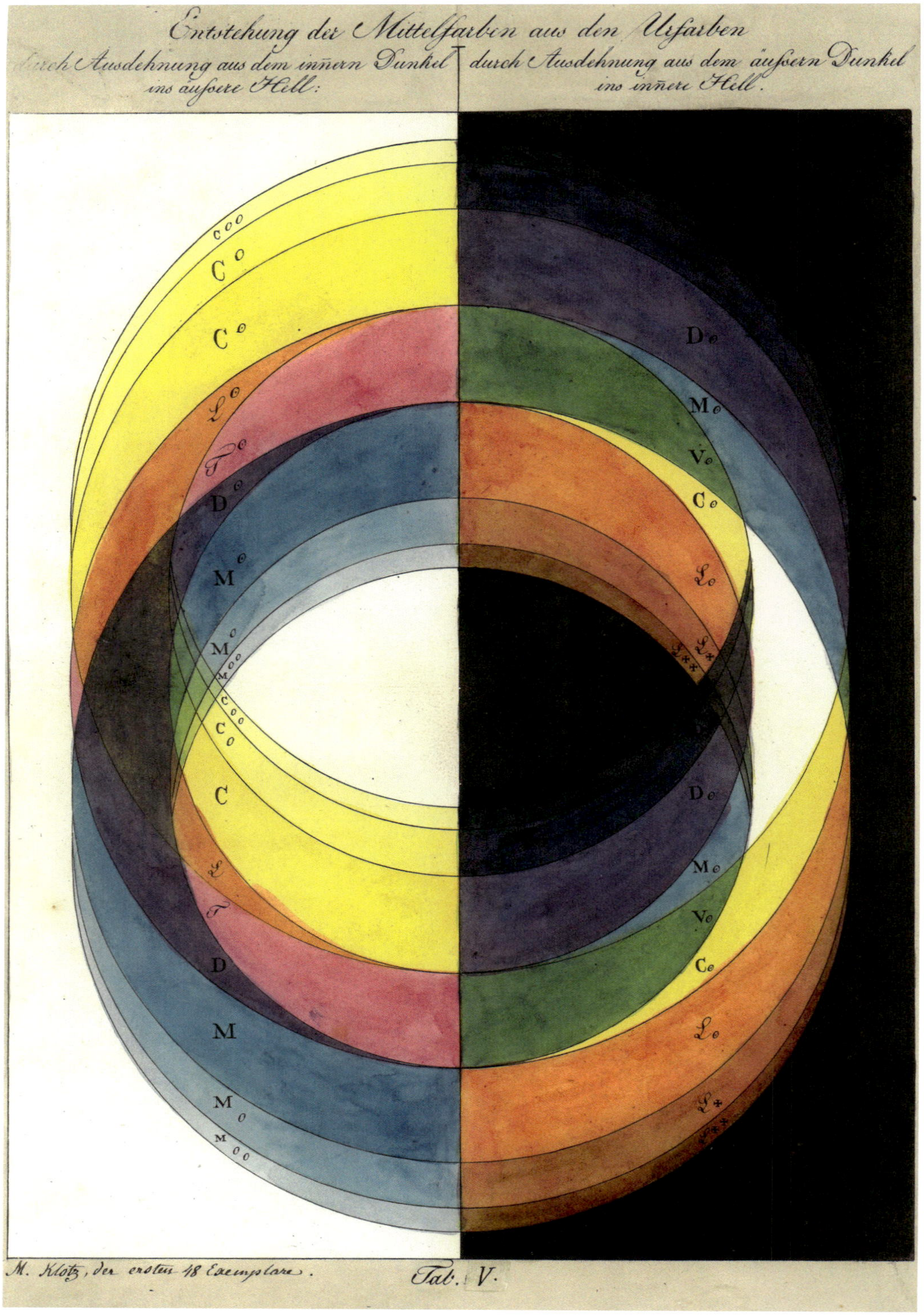

37+38 Zwei der handkolorierten Tafeln aus: Mathias Klotz
Gründliche Farbenlehre / mit / vier vom Verfasser selbst gemalten Tafeln, sammt einer schematischen Erklärungsscheibe des in Kreisform (Tab. VI) vorgetragenen chromatisch-absoluten Farbkanons, und zwei unfärbig gezeichneten zum Prismatisiren. / Erster Abschnitt. / Allgemeine Chromatologie als Farbkunstlehre. / Zweyter Abschnitt. / Reine Prismatologie als Farbnaturlehre. / Von / Mathias Klotz, / königlich bayrischem Hofmaler. / In Kommission in der Lindauer'schen Buchhandlung / München 1816. / Gedruckt mit Zängl'schen Schriften.

Der Münchner Hofmaler Mathias Klotz (1748–1821) hatte mehrfach versucht, Kontakt mit Goethe aufzunehmen und mit diesem in einen fachlichen Dialog zu treten, jedoch mit wenig Erfolg. In seiner *Gründlichen Farbenlehre,* einem der ersten Bücher zum Thema, das nach Goethes umfangreichem Werk *Zur Farbenlehre* erschien, geht er zwar sowohl auf Newton als auch auf Goethe ein, schließt sich jedoch keinem der beiden an.

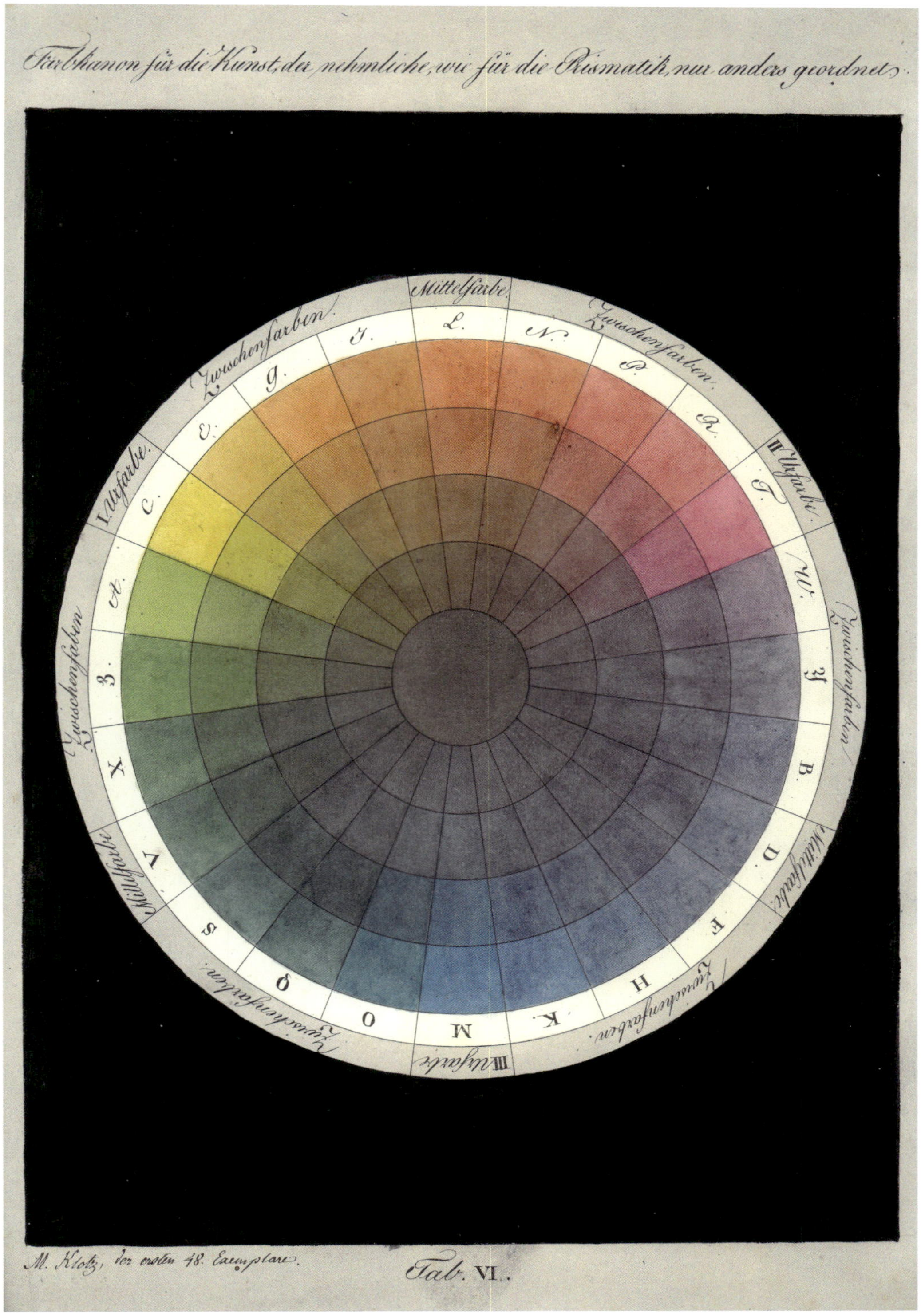

37+38 Two of the hand-colored plates from:
Mathias Klotz
Gründliche Farbenlehre
Munich, 1816

Mathias Klotz, court painter in Munich (1748–1821), had made several attempts to contact Goethe to discuss with him the subject of color, but to no avail. In his *Gründliche Farbenlehre* (The Fundamentals of Color Theory), one of the first treatises of the topic that was published after Goethe's voluminous work *Zur Farbenlehre,* he talks about both Newton and Goethe, yet he does not agree with either one.

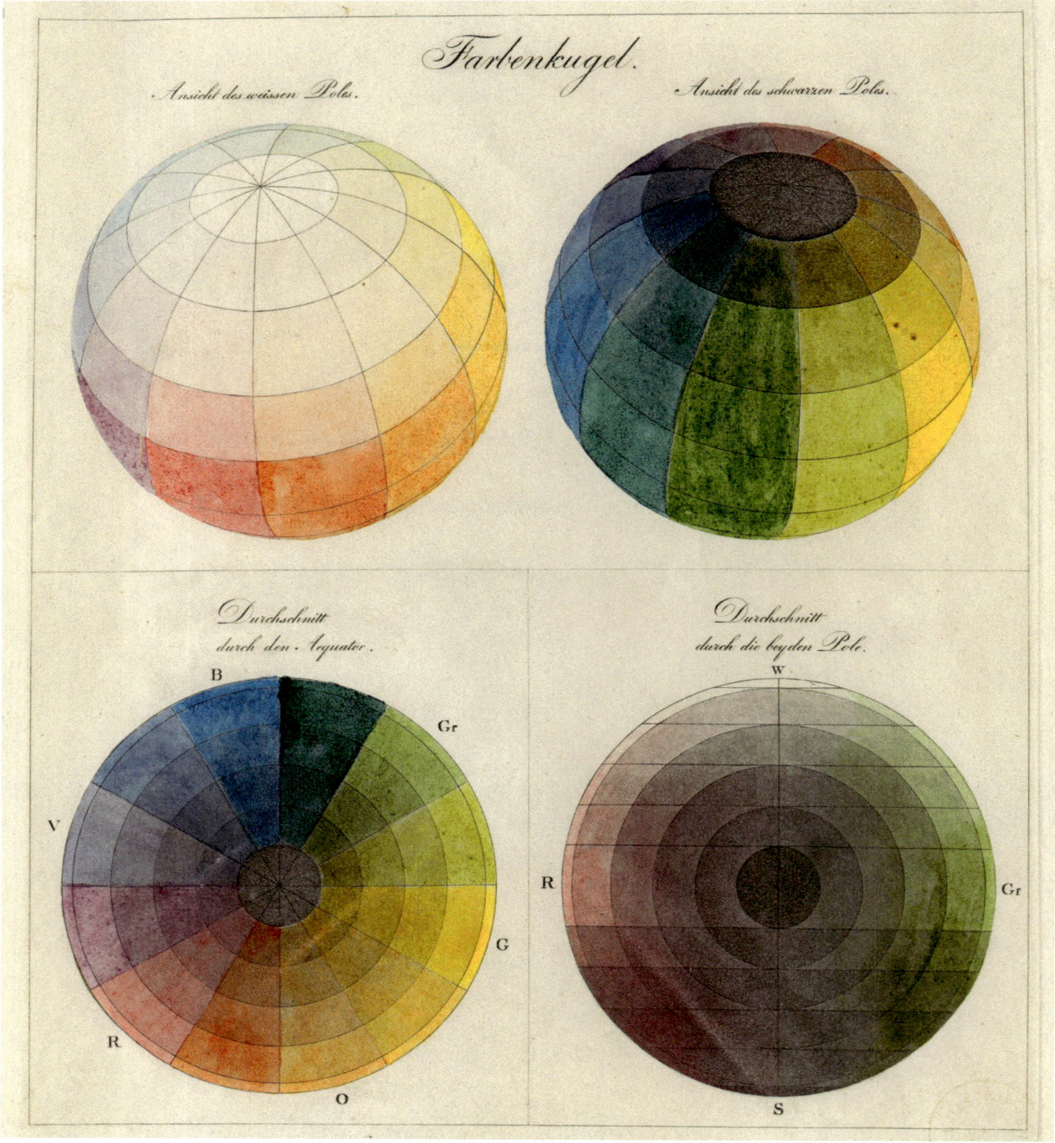

39 Philipp Otto Runge
Farben-Kugel / oder / Construction des Verhältnisses aller Mischungen der Farben zu / einander, und ihrer vollständigen Affinität, / mit angehängtem / Versuch einer Ableitung der Harmonie in den Zusammenstellungen / der Farben. / Von / Philipp Otto Runge, Mahler. / Nebst einer Abhandlung / über die Bedeutung der Farben in der Natur, / Von Hrn. Prof. Henrik Steffens in Halle. / Mit einem Kupfer, und einer beygelegten Farbentafel. / Hamburg, / bey Friedrich Perthes. / 1810.

Im selben Jahr wie Goethes *Farbenlehre* erschien die *Farben-Kugel*, eine Schrift des Malers Philipp Otto Runge (1777–1810). Ausgehend von einem zwölfteiligen Farbenkreis als Äquator hatte Runge durch Einbindung von Weiß und Schwarz als Nord- und Südpol einen Farbglobus entwikkelt – die erste vollständige dreidimensionale Darstellung eines Farbsystems. Nach der persönlichen Begegnung und Gesprächen in Weimar 1803 wechselten Goethe und Runge Briefe, um sich zum Thema Farbe auszutauschen. Runges Schreiben vom 3. Juli 1806, in dem der junge Maler die Grundzüge seiner Theorie darlegte, nahm Goethe als ›Zugabe‹ in den didaktischen Teil seiner Farbenlehre auf (S. 339–349).

39 Philipp Otto Runge
Farben-Kugel (Color Sphere)
Hamburg, 1810

In the same year as Goethe's publication of *Theory of Colours*, Philipp Otto Runge (1777–1810) published his work, *Farben-Kugel*. Proceeding from a twelve-part color wheel acting as an equator, Runge developed a color globe by integrating white and black and using them to represent the North and South poles – the first entirely three-dimensional representation of a color system. After a meeting with Goethe in person and having discussions with him in Weimar in 1803, the two began to correspond regularly to discuss color theory. Runge's letter from 3rd July 1806 in which the young painter set out the basis of his theories, was published by Goethe as an add-on to the didactic part of his *Farbenlehre*.

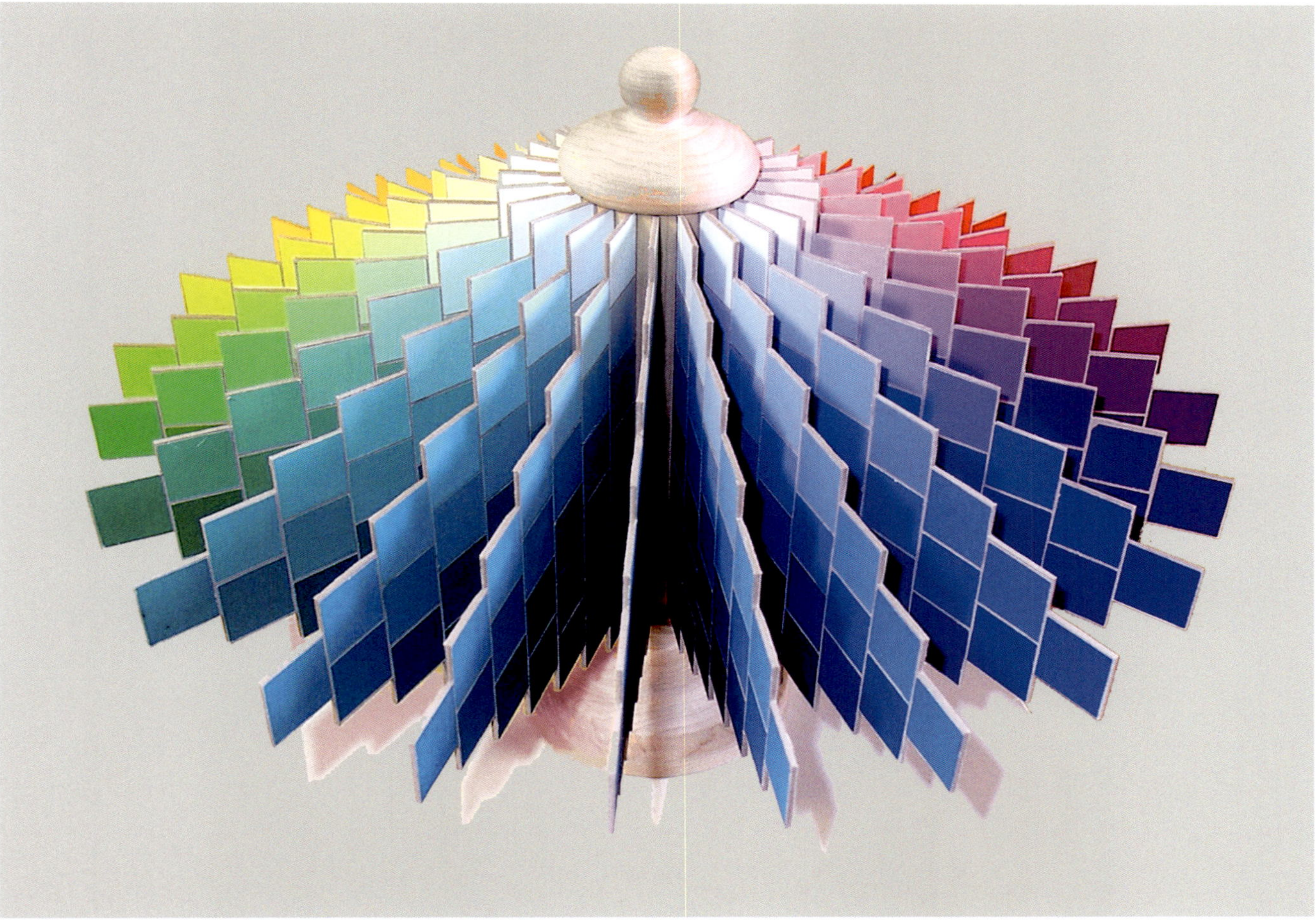

40 Wilhelm Ostwald
Farbkörpermodell *(Doppelkegel),* 680-teilig
Rekonstruktion von Eckhard Bendin, Nachbau des *Doppelkegels* von 1921 unter Verwendung von originalen Farbmustern der ›Londoner Ausgabe‹ aus dem Nachlass Manfred Adam
2003
Holzkern, Leimfarbenaufstriche auf Karton
Sammlung Farbenlehre der Technischen Universität Dresden

Im 20. Jahrhundert entwickelte der Physikochemiker und Nobelpreisträger Wilhelm Ostwald (1853–1932) mit seinem *Doppelkegel* ein anderes dreidimensionales Modell. Für jede Farbe seines 24-teiligen Farbenkreises konstruierte er ein, wie er es nannte, ›farbtongleiches Dreieck‹. Dieses gleichseitige Dreieck spannt sich auf zwischen den drei Ecken Vollfarbe (außen), Weiß (oben) und Schwarz (unten) und enthält alle gleichabständig gestuften Abkömmlinge einer Farbe. Fügt man nun alle 24 ›farbtongleichen Dreiecke‹ an der Grauachse zwischen den beiden Polen Weiß und Schwarz zusammen, so erhält man den Farbraum in einem *Doppelkegel*.

40 Wilhelm Ostwald
Color Solid *(Double Cone)*
680 colored squares
Reconstruction by Eckhard Bendin of an Ostwald *Double Cone* from 1921 using original color samples from the ›London Edition‹ from the estate of Manfred Adam
2003
Wooden core, distemper on cardboard
Sammlung Farbenlehre, Technische Universität Dresden

In the 20th Century the physical chemist and Nobel Prize winner Wilhelm Ostwald (1853–1932) developed his *Double Cone* – a different three dimensional color model. For each section of his 24 part color wheel he built, what he called, an 'equal hue' triangle. These equilateral triangles have colors on the outside faces, arranged in equidistantly graded hues, with a white top edge and black bottom edge. When all of the 24 equivalent-hue triangles are joined together on the grey axis between both of the white and black poles the result is a *Double Cone*.

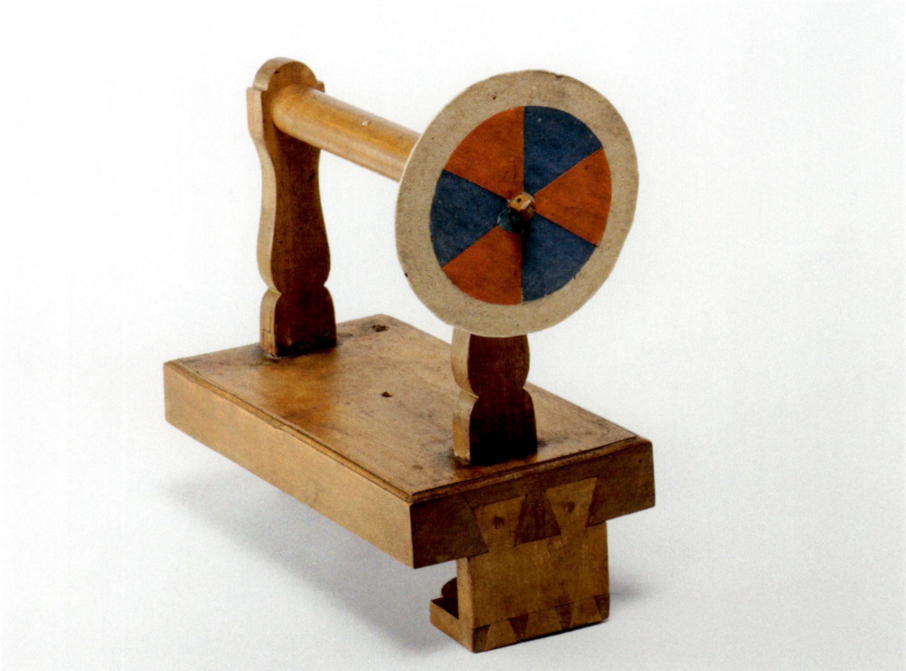

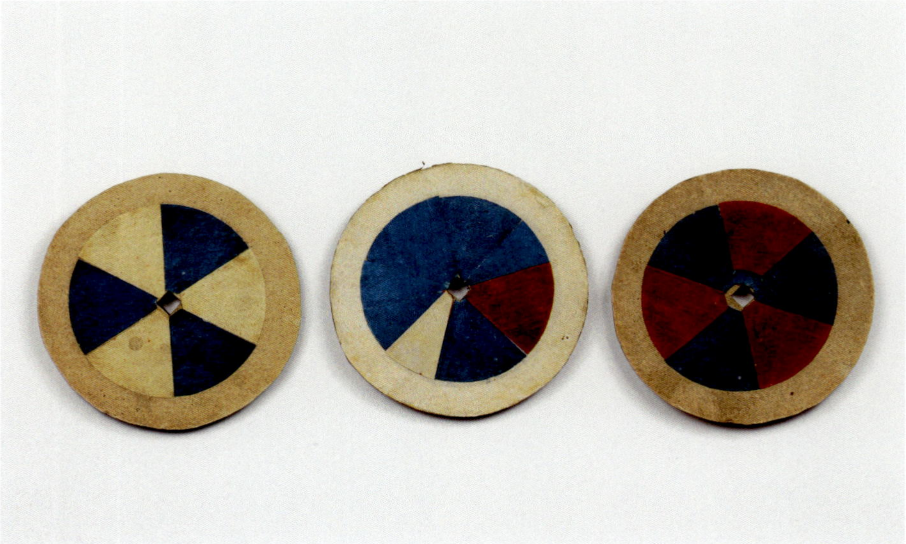

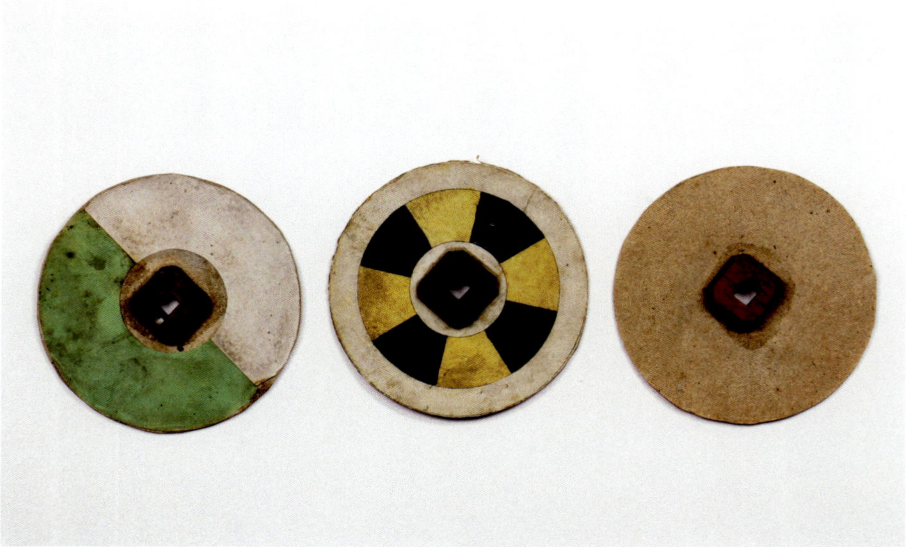

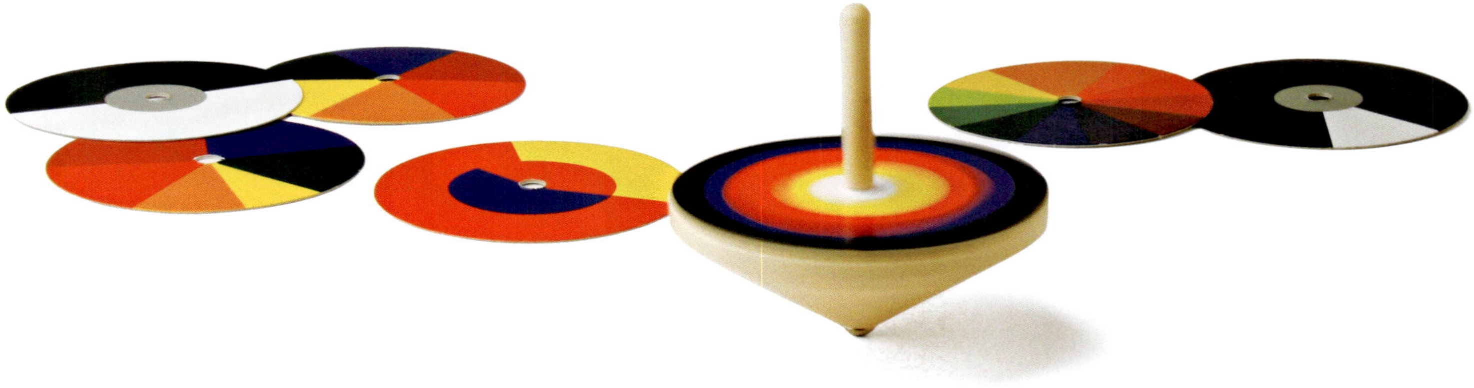

41–43 Johann Wolfgang von Goethe
Schwungrad (Dorl) zur Farbenmischung und verschiedene Kreiselscheiben
Um 1810
Holz, mit farbigem Papier beklebte Pappe, Schnur
30,2 x 30,8 x 16,4 cm
Klassik Stiftung Weimar, Museen
Die Ausstellung zeigt einen Nachbau von Eckhard Bendin aus der Sammlung Farbenlehre der Technischen Universität Dresden.

Auf einem Brett, das an einer Tischplatte festgeschraubt werden kann, sind zwei Stützen mit einer drehbaren Welle befestigt, auf deren eines Ende eine runde Pappscheibe gesteckt ist. Der äußere Rand der Pappscheibe ist grau, während der innere Kreis in sechs gleich große Sektoren aufgeteilt ist, die abwechselnd mit blauem und orangefarbenem Papier beklebt sind. Wenn die Kreiselscheibe mit einer Schnur, die an der Welle befestigt ist, in Rotation versetzt wird, erscheint das Innere der Scheibe so grau wie der Rand. Unter dem Stichwort »Mischung. Scheinbare« schreibt Goethe im didaktischen Teil der *Farbenlehre:* »Unter dem Apparat wird künftig auch das Schwungrad abgehandelt werden, auf welchem die scheinbare Mischung durch Schnelligkeit hervorgebracht wird. Auf einer Scheibe bringt man verschiedene Farben im Kreise nebeneinander an, dreht dieselben durch die Gewalt des Schwunges mit größter Schnelligkeit herum, und kann so, wenn man mehrere Scheiben zubereitet, alle möglichen Mischungen vor Augen stellen, so wie zuletzt auch die Mischung aller Farben zum Grau naturgemäß auf oben angezeigte Weise.« (§ 561, S. 210 f.)

41–43 Johann Wolfgang von Goethe
Flywheel for the mixing of paint and assorted centrifuge wheels
Around 1810
Wood, cardboard lined with colored paper, string
30.2 x 30.8 x 16.4 cm
Klassik Stiftung Weimar, Museen
The exhibition is displaying a replica by Eckhard Bendin from the Sammlung Farbenlehre, Technische Universität Dresden.

On a board that can be screwed to a table top, two supports are fixed to a rotatable shaft, at one end of which a round cardboard disc can be inserted. The outer edge of the cardboard disc is grey, while the inner circle is divided into six equal sections which are alternately covered with blue and orange paper. When the gyroscope is rotated with the string cord attached to the shaft, the interior of the disc appears to be as grey as the rim. Referred to by the keyword "intermixture, apparent," Goethe wrote in the didactic section of his *Theory of Colours:* "In the description of our apparatus we shall have occasion to mention the wheel by means of which the apparent intermixture is produced by rapid movement. Various colours are arranged near each other round the edge of a disc, which is made to revolve with velocity, and thus by having several such disks ready, every possible intermixture can be presented to the eye, as well as the mixture of all colours to grey, darker or lighter, according to the depth of the tints as above explained." (Johann Wolfgang von Goethe, *Theory of Colours,* trans. Charles Lock Eastlake London, 1840, pp. 226–27.)

44 Ludwig Hirschfeld-Mack
Optischer Farbenmischer
1924
Ahornholz, Metall, bedruckter Karton
Nachbau, Naef Spiele AG

Der *Optische Farbenmischer* ist von Ludwig Hirschfeld-Mack (1893–1965) als didaktisches Spielzeug am Bauhaus entworfen und in der Tischlerei des Bauhauses seit etwa 1924 vervielfältigt worden. Hirschfeld-Mack führt dem Betrachter vor Augen, wie das Rotieren des Kreisels eine optische Mischung der (auf den auflegbaren Scheiben aufgedruckten) Farben zur Folge hat. Einige Aspekte der Farbentheorien – von Goethe und Schopenhauer bis hin zu Hölzel – werden demonstriert.

44 Ludwig Hirschfeld-Mack
Optical Color Mixer
1924
Maple wood, metal, printed cardboard
Replica, Naef Spiele AG

The *Optical Color Mixer* had been designed by Ludwig Hirschfeld-Mack (1893–1965) as a didactic toy at the Bauhaus and has been reproduced in the joinery workshop of the Bauhaus since about 1924. Hirschfeld-Mack demonstrates how the rotation of the gyrating top produces the optical mixing of the colors printed upon the laid-on plates. Some aspects of the color theories – from Goethe and Schopenhauer right up to Hölzel – are being demonstrated.

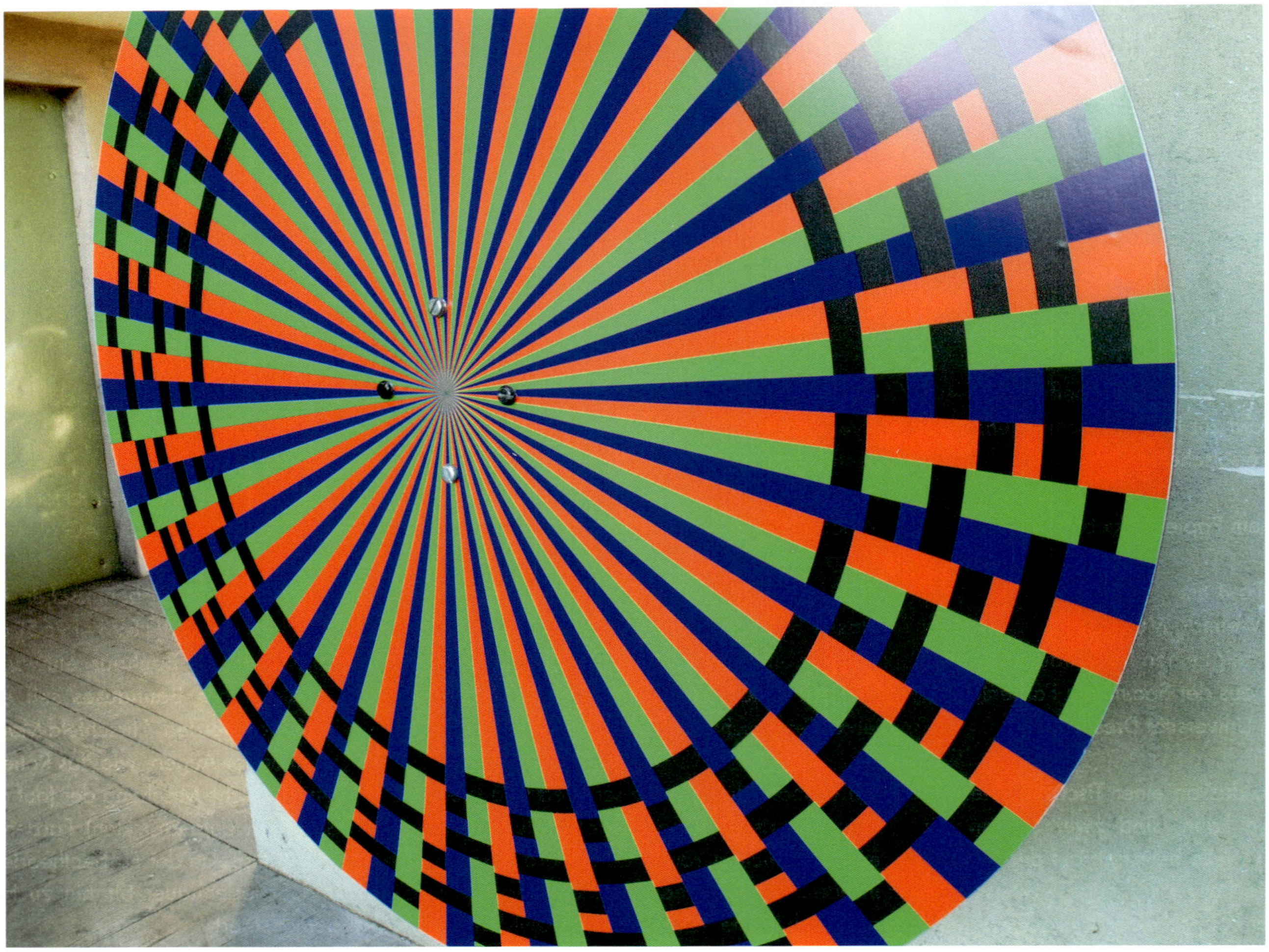

45+46 Andreas Hofer
RGB-Drehscheibe
2005
Bedruckte Pappe
Sammlung Farbenlehre der Technischen Universität Dresden

Der Schweizer Künstler Andreas Hofer (*1956) entwickelte eine Drehscheibe, bei der die Grundfarben der additiven Farbmischung Rot, Grün und Blau so angeordnet sind, dass sie sich während der Drehung anders ausrichten und zusammen mit den durch die Rotation zusätzlich erzeugten Druck-Ausgangsfarben Cyan, Magenta und Gelb einen ›Regenbogen‹ bilden, der alle sechs Hauptfarben der modernen Farbenlehre enthält.

45+46 Andreas Hofer
RGB-Spinning Disc
2005
Printed cardboard
Sammlung Farbenlehre, Technische Universität Dresden

The Swiss artist Andreas Hofer (*1956) developed a spinning disc, upon which the base colors of red, green, and blue are applied and organized in such a way that when the disc is spun, the colors become differently aligned, resulting in the output of new colors not printed on the disc: cyan, magenta and yellow. When spinning, the output of these new colors creates a 'rainbow' comprising the six main colors of modern color theory.

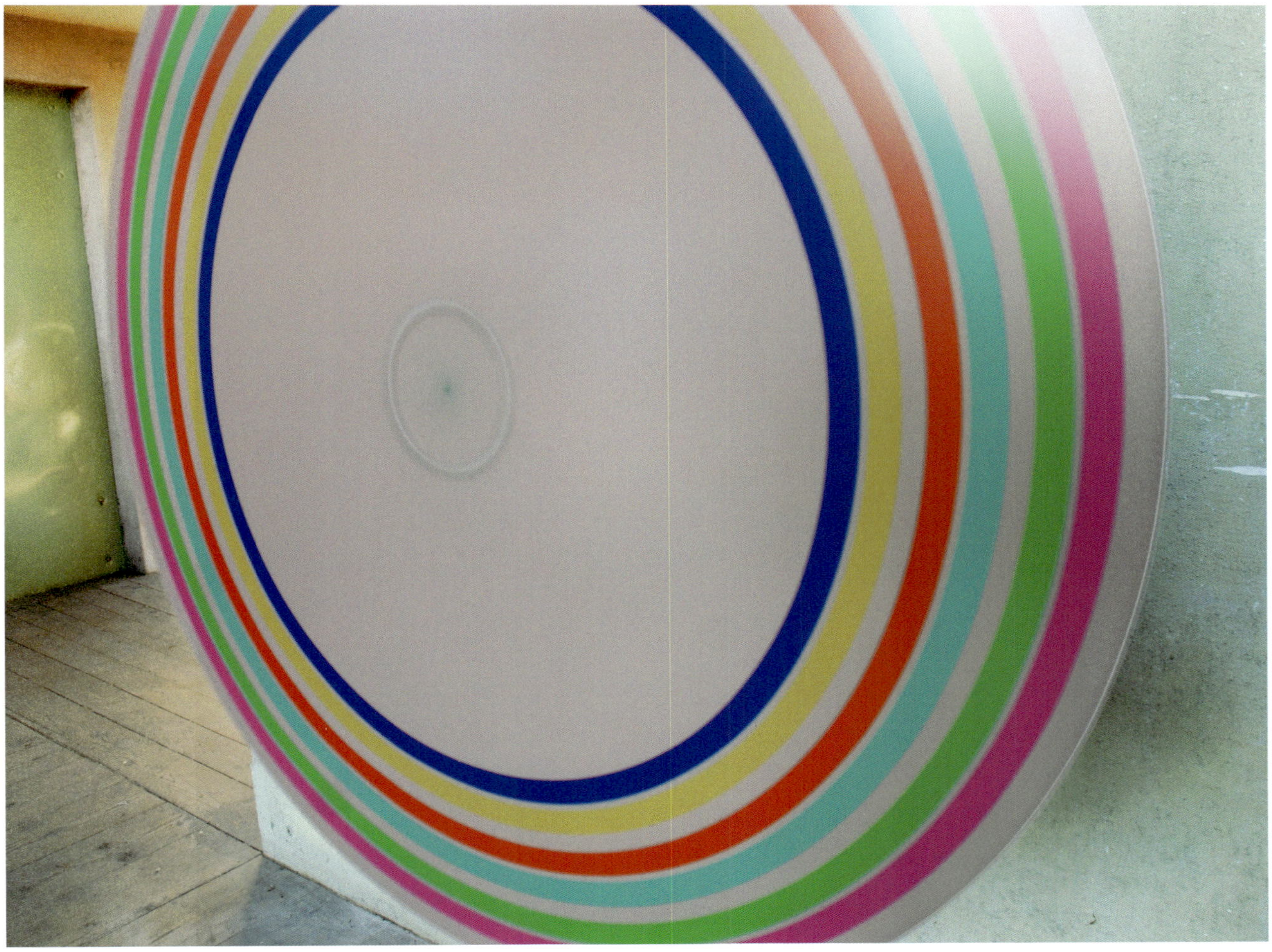

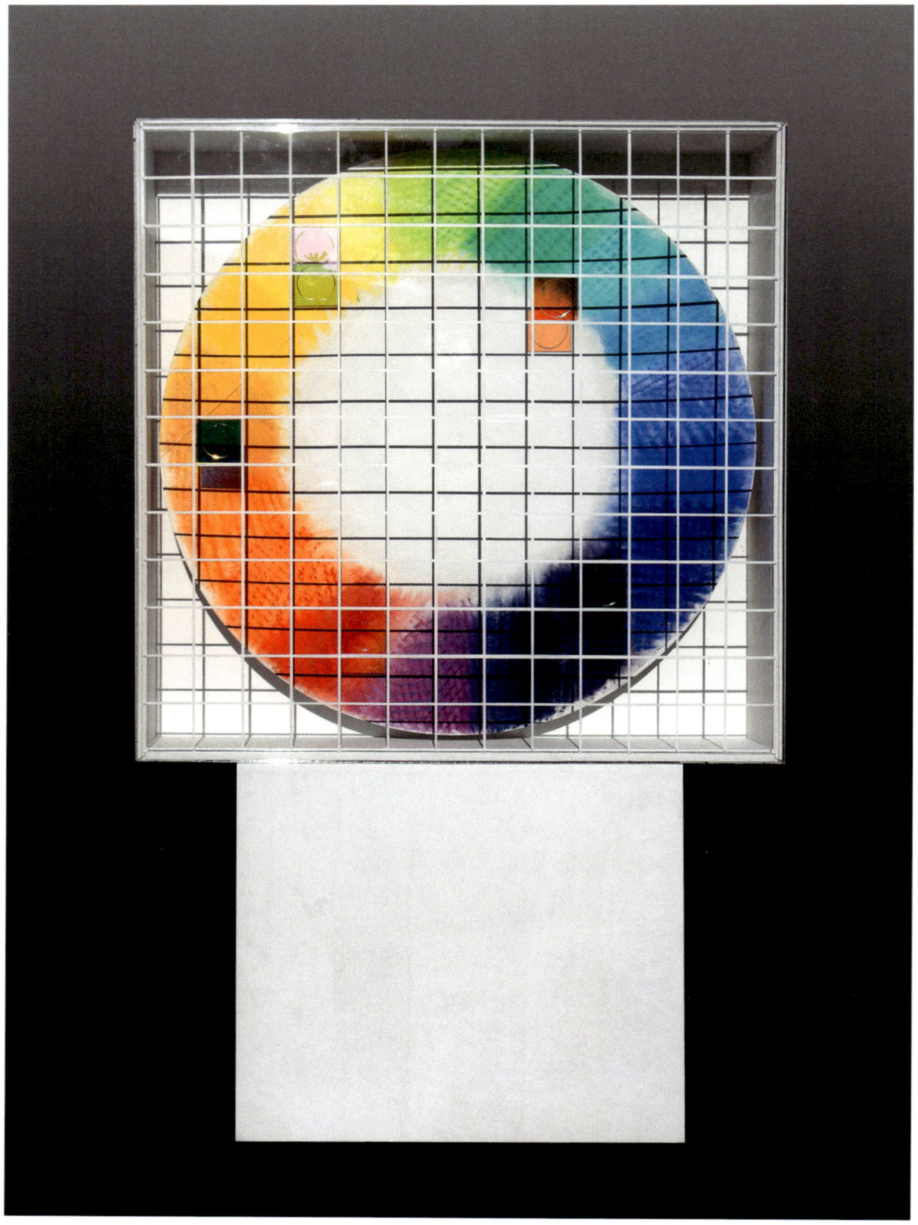

47 Heinz Mack
Colour-Rotor
Signiert, datiert: »colour-rotor 2010, mack«
Holz, Acrylfarbe, Pastellkreide, Plexiglas, Motor
101 x 101 x 34 cm

47 Heinz Mack
Colour-Rotor
Signed, dated: "colour-rotor 2010, mack"
Wood, acrylic color, pastel, plexiglass, motor
101 x 101 x 34 cm

48 Johann Wolfgang von Goethe
Farbenkreis in 12 Stufen zur Veranschaulichung französischer, deutscher und griechischer Farbnamen
Tinte und Bleistift auf weißem Papier, koloriert
21,4 x 17 cm
Klassik Stiftung Weimar, Museen
Die Ausstellung zeigt ein Faksimile.

Diesen Farbenkreis müsste man um 180 Grad drehen, um die Anordnung von Goethes regulären Farbenkreis zu erhalten. Dass es ihm hier jedoch weniger auf diese Ausrichtung und auf die perfekte Mischung der Zwischenstufen ankam als auf die sprachlichen Bezeichnungen, unterstreicht auch Goethes Bemerkung am Fuß des Blattes: »ist nicht gut ausgeführt. Dient nur zur allgemeinen Idee.« Vgl. LA, Bd. II 6, S. 16–21.

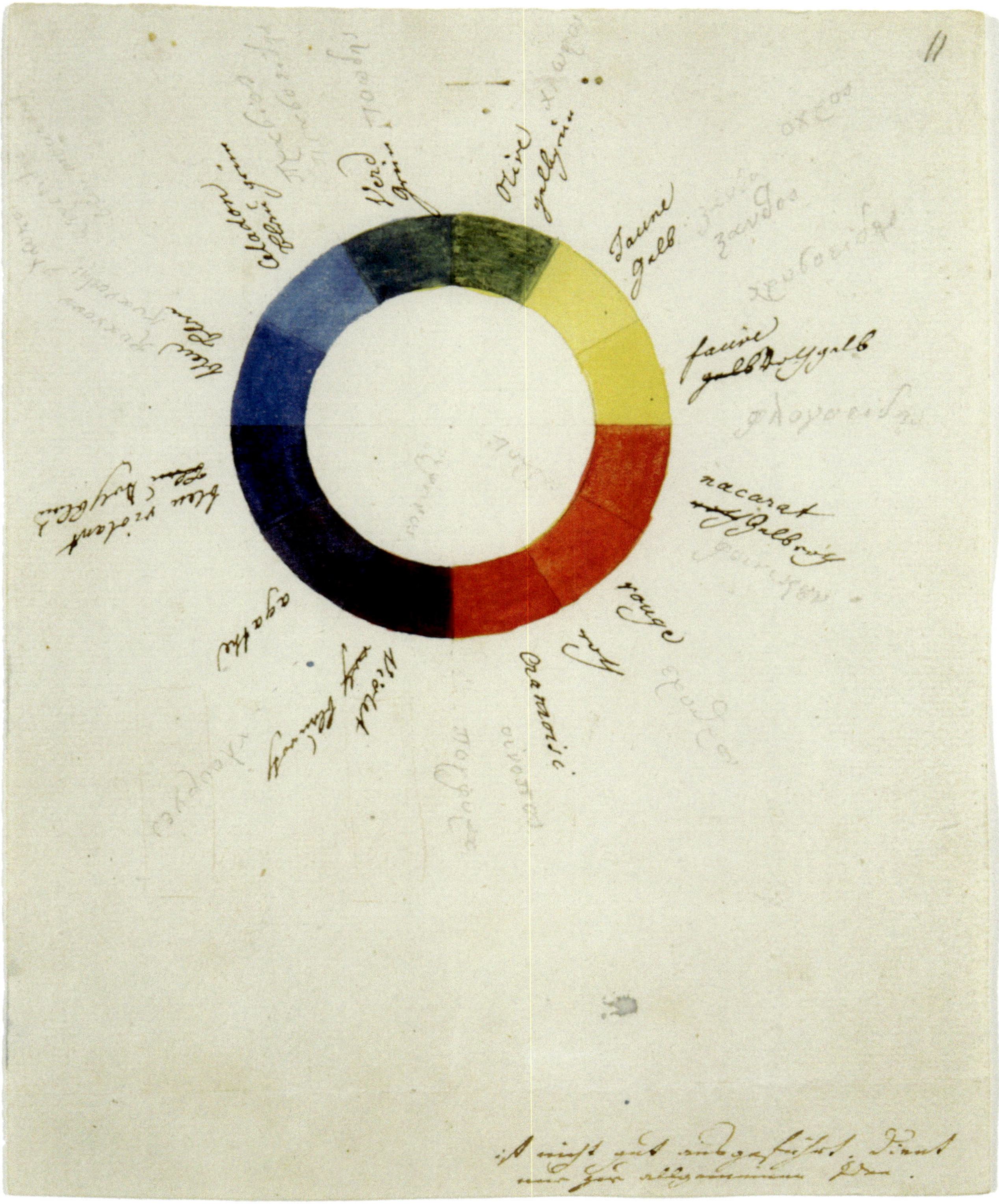

48 Johann Wolfgang von Goethe
12 step color wheel to illustrate French, German and Greek color names
Ink and pencil on white paper, colored
21.4 x 17 cm
Klassik Stiftung Weimar, Museen
The exhibition is displaying a facsimile.

This color wheel needs to be rotated by 180° for it to be ordered the same way as Goethe's usual color wheel. He was, however, less concerned with the perfect ordering of the colors and more with the linguistic labelling. This is further underlined by Goethe's comment at the foot of the page: "It's not well made, but it demonstrates the general idea." See LA, vol. II 6, pp. 16–21.

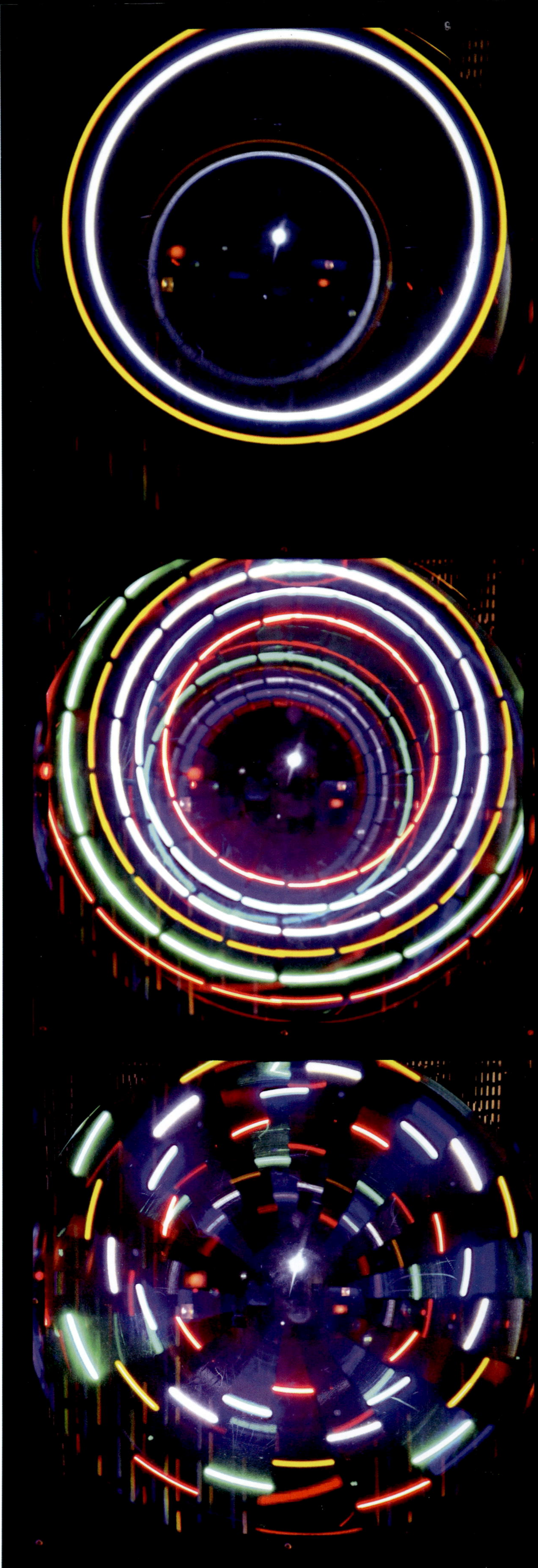

49–57 Heinz Mack
Lichtventilator
2009
Holz, Motor, elektrisches Zubehör
53 x 40 x 40 cm

49–57 Heinz Mack
Light Fan
2009
Wood, motor, electrical equipment
53 x 40 x 40 cm

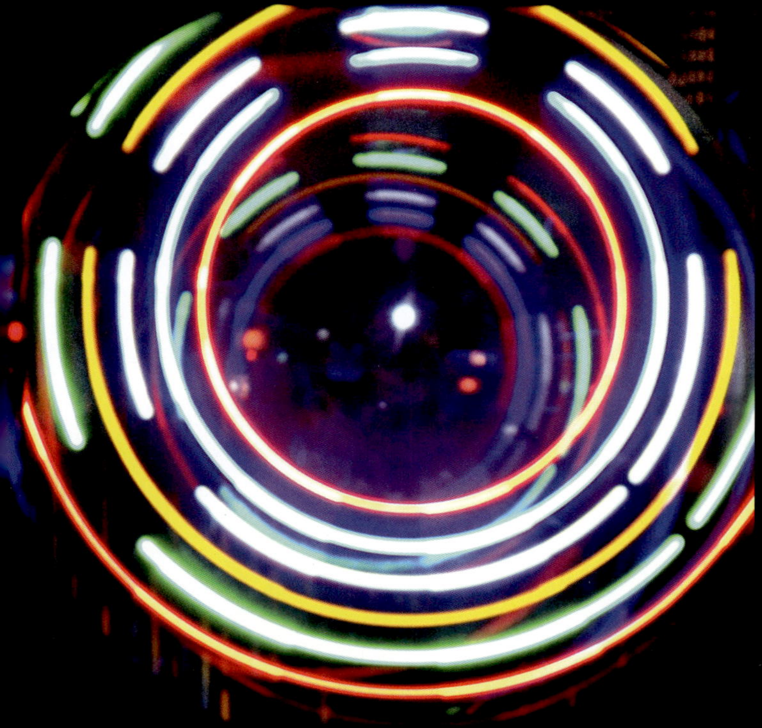
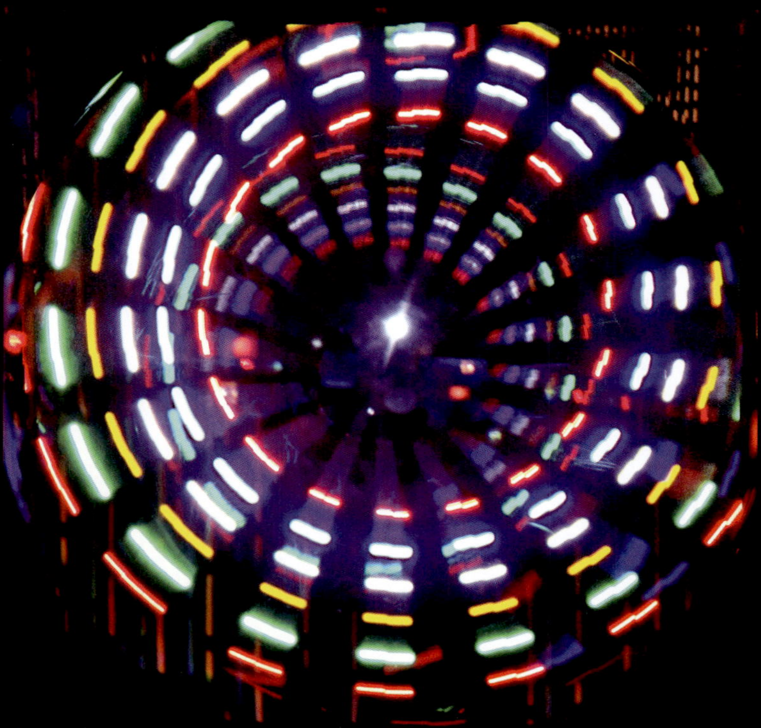
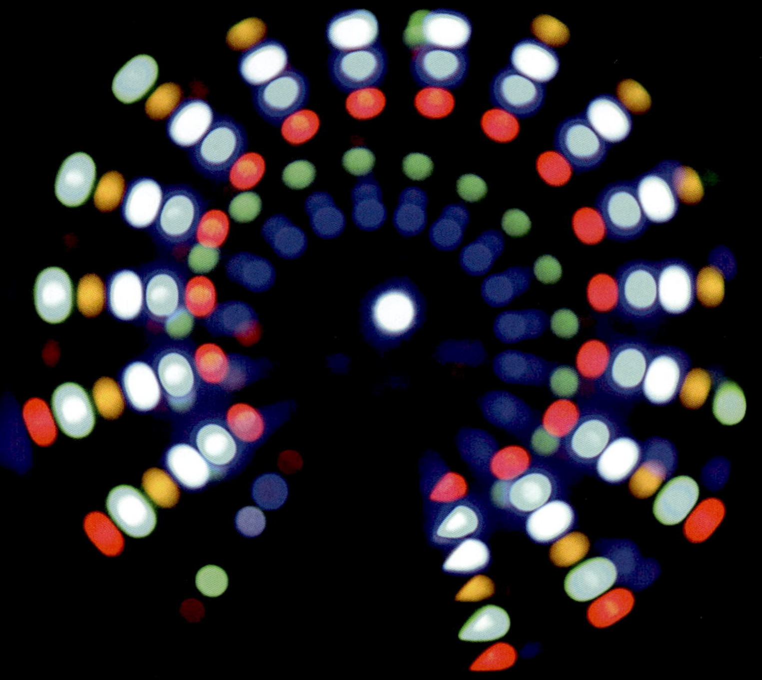
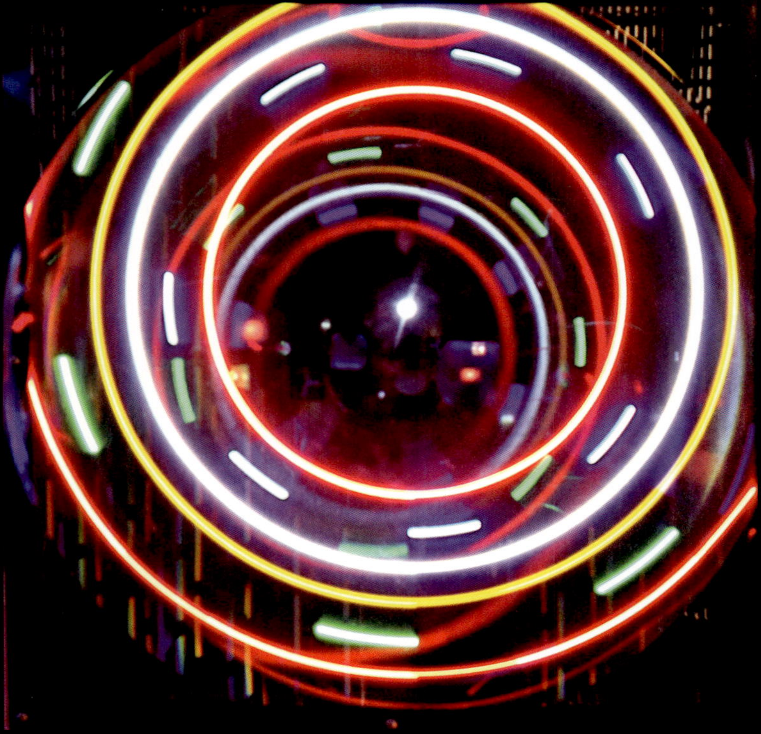
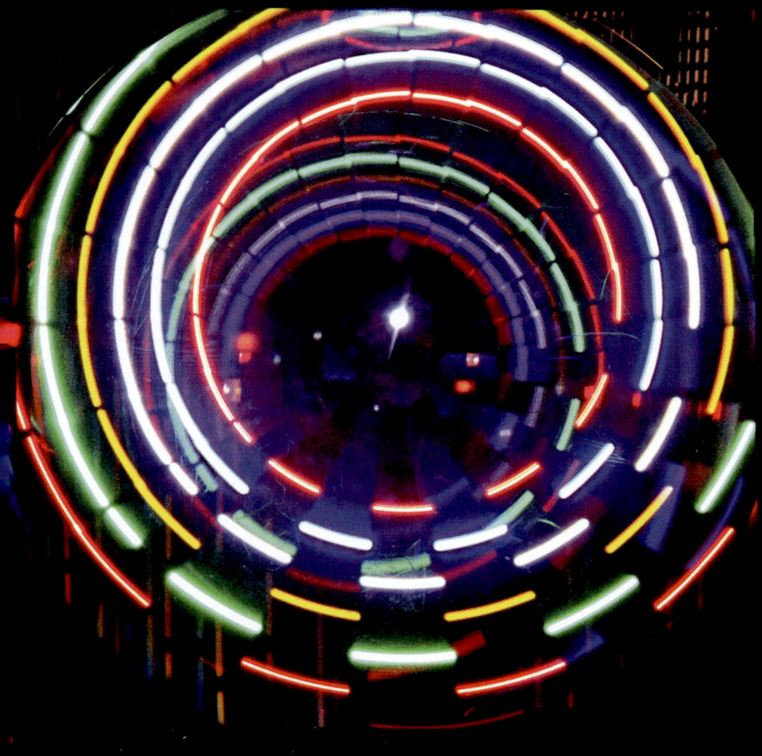
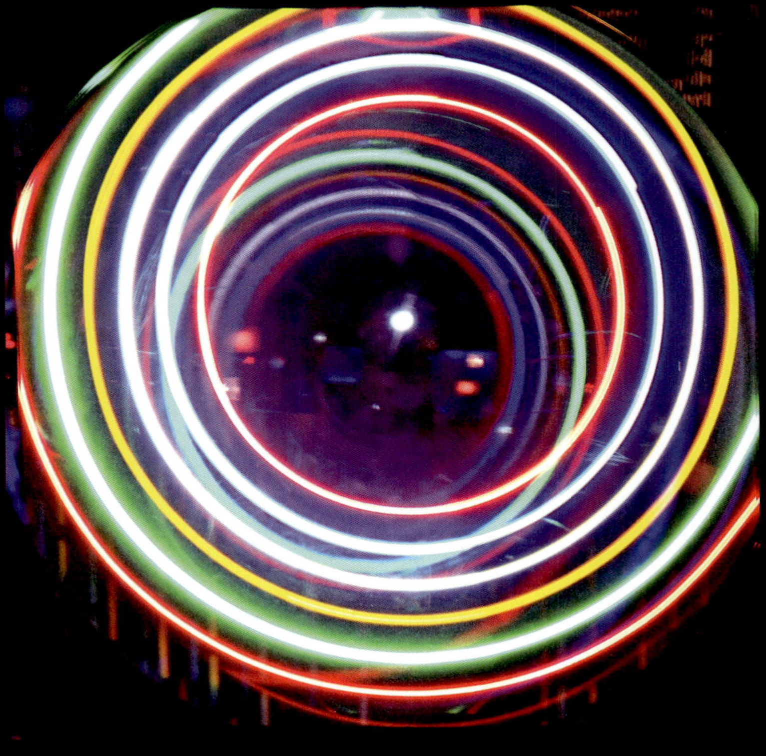

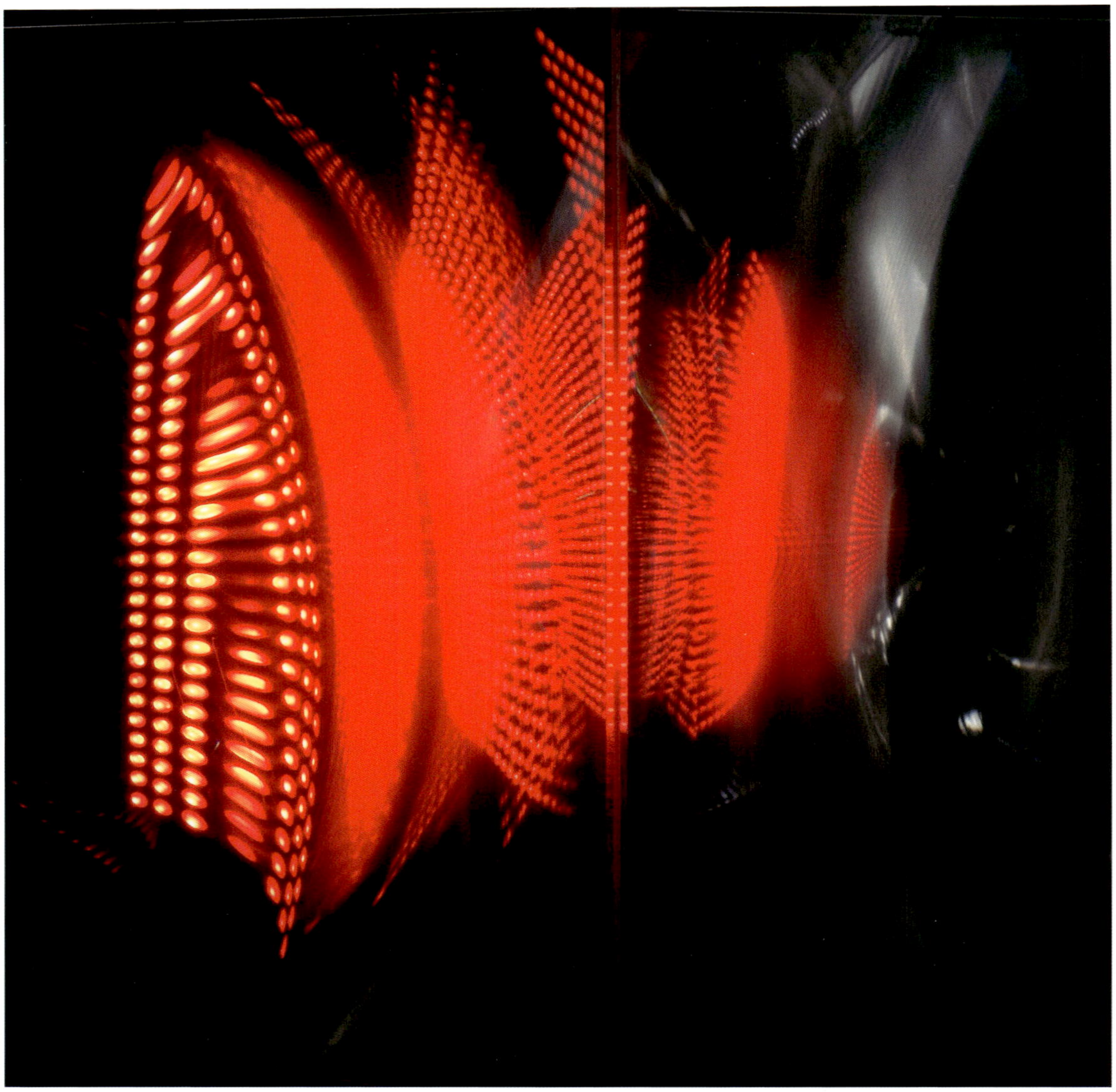

58+59 Heinz Mack
Space-Corner (4 Phasen)
Signiert, datiert: »mack 1980–92 und 2004«
Fresnel-Linsen, Elektronik, Holz
49 x 54 x 54 cm

58+59 Heinz Mack
Space-Corner (4 phases)
Signed, dated: "mack 1980–92 und 2004"
Fresnel lenses, electronics, wood
49 x 54 x 54 cm

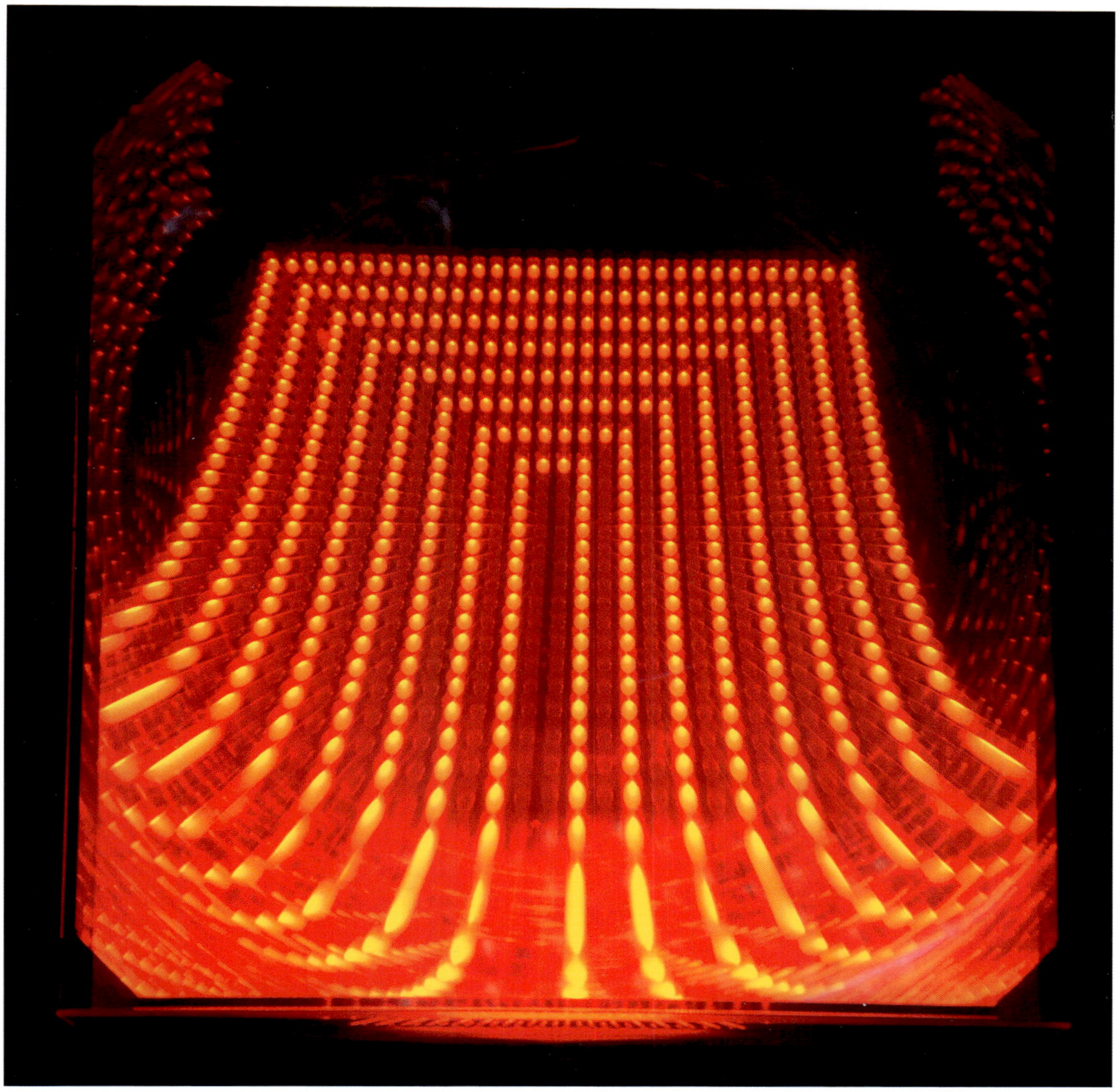

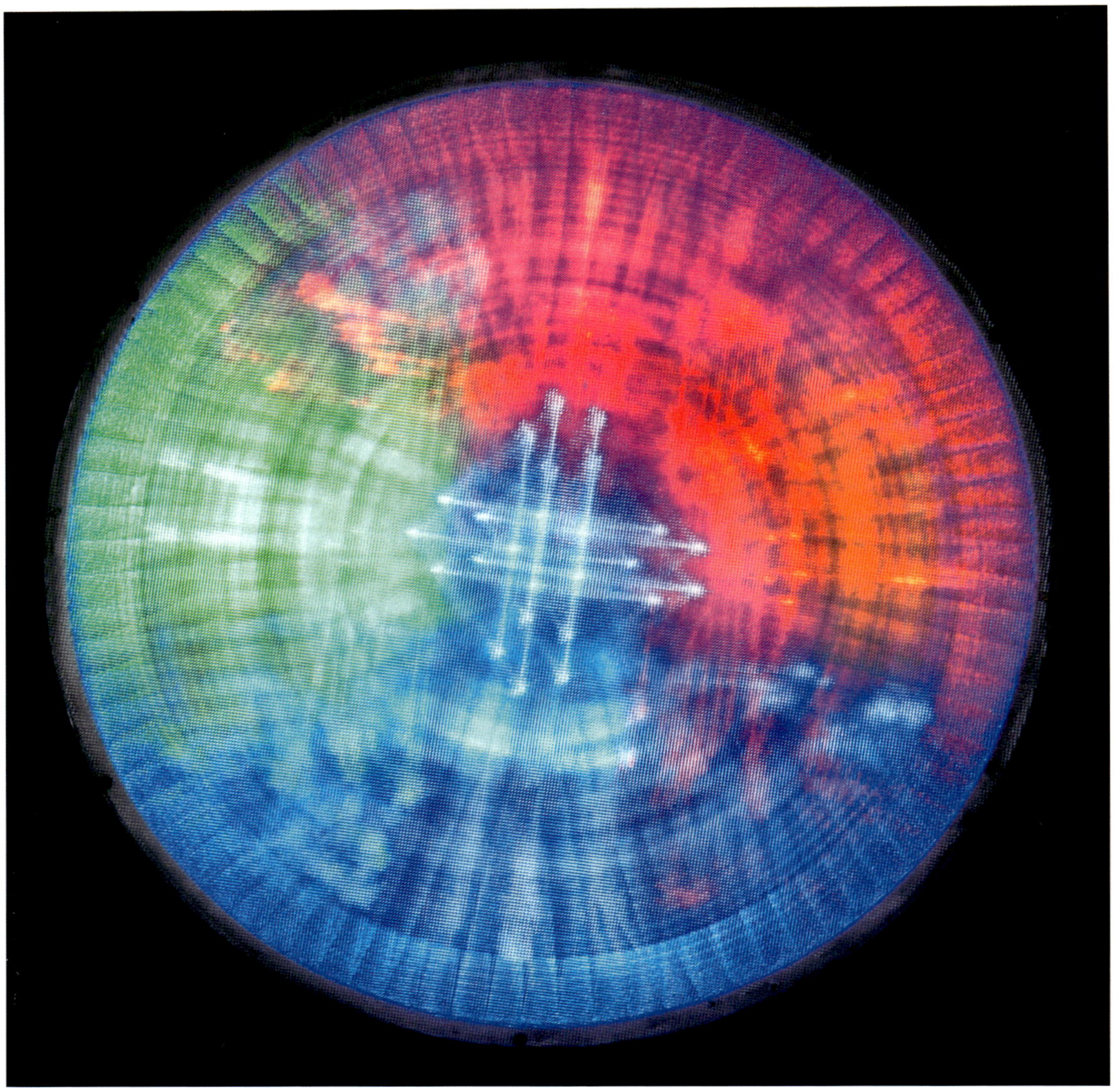

60 Heinz Mack
Electrical Sun
Signiert, datiert: »mack 10«
Facettenreflektor, Plexiglas, Holz, elektronisches Zubehör
70 x 70 x 37 cm

60 Heinz Mack
Electrical Sun
Signed, dated: "mack 10"
Facetted reflector, plexiglass, wood, electronic accessories
70 x 70 x 37 cm

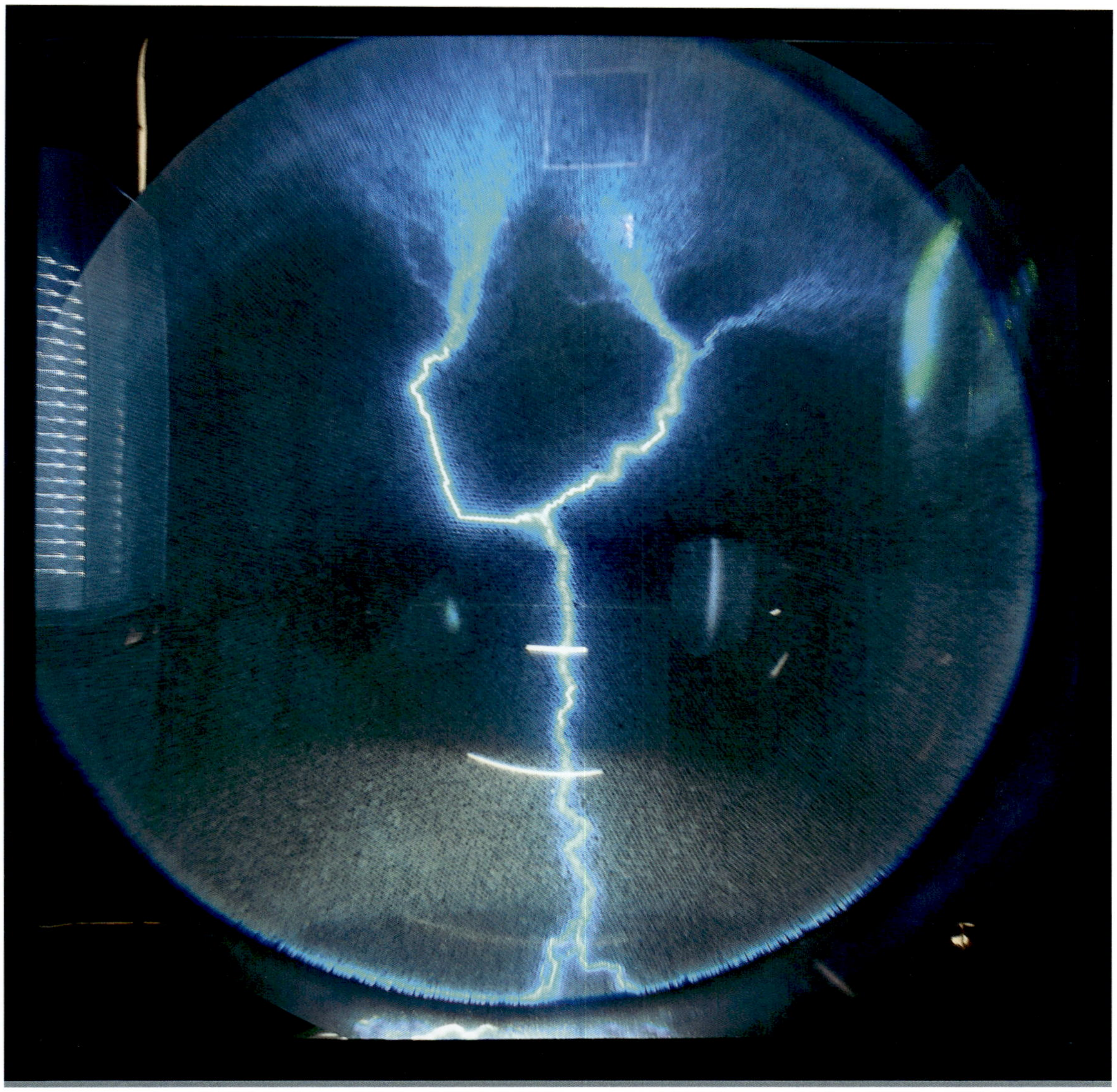

61 Heinz Mack
Natur und Artefakt
Signiert, datiert: »mack 80«
Aluminium, Holz, elektrisches Zubehör, Filter, Fresnel-Linse
62 x 60 x 51 cm

61 Heinz Mack
Nature and Artifact
Signed, dated: "mack 80"
Aluminum, wood, electrical accessories, filter, Fresnel lense
62 x 60 x 51 cm

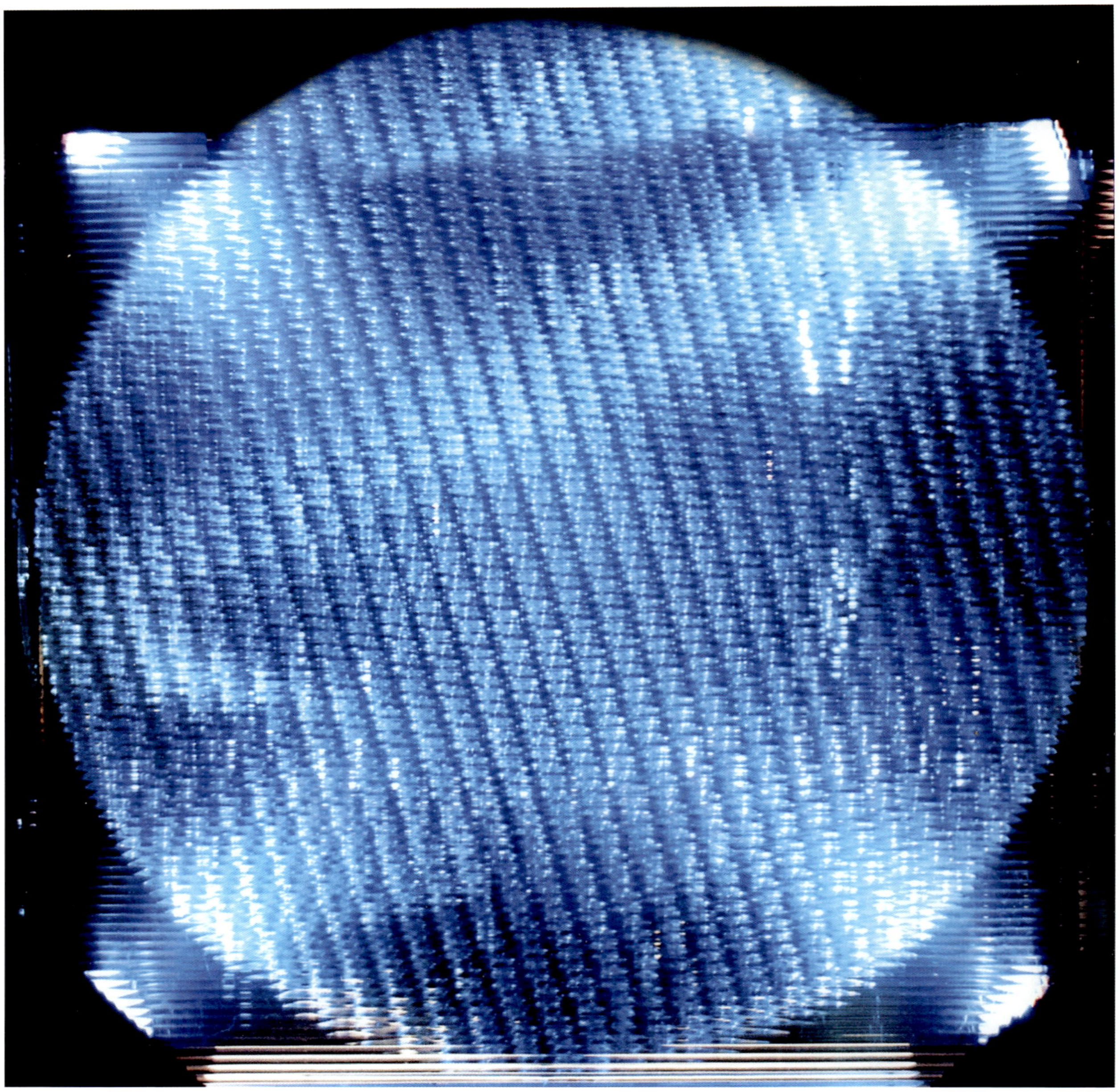

62 Heinz Mack
Rotor für blaue Elektrizität
Signiert, datiert: »mack 1968«
Aluminium, Kunststoff, Glas, Holz,
elektrisches Zubehör
143 x 143 x 27 cm

62 Heinz Mack
Rotor for Blue Electricity
Signed, dated: "mack 1968"
Aluminum, plastic, glass, wood,
electrical accessories
143 x 143 x 27 cm

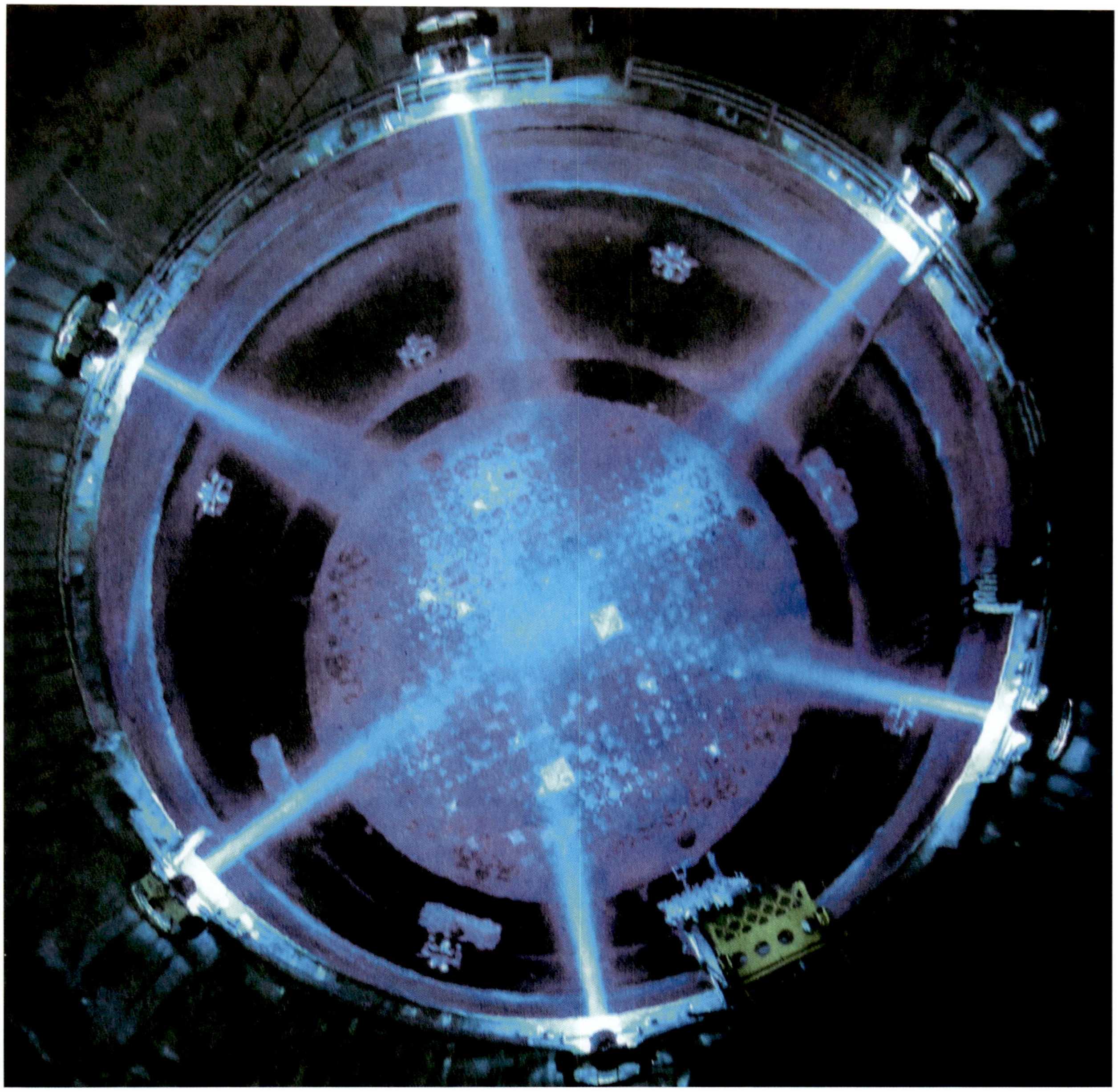

63 Blick in den geöffneten Reaktor eines Kernkraftwerks

63 View into the open reactor of a nuclear power station

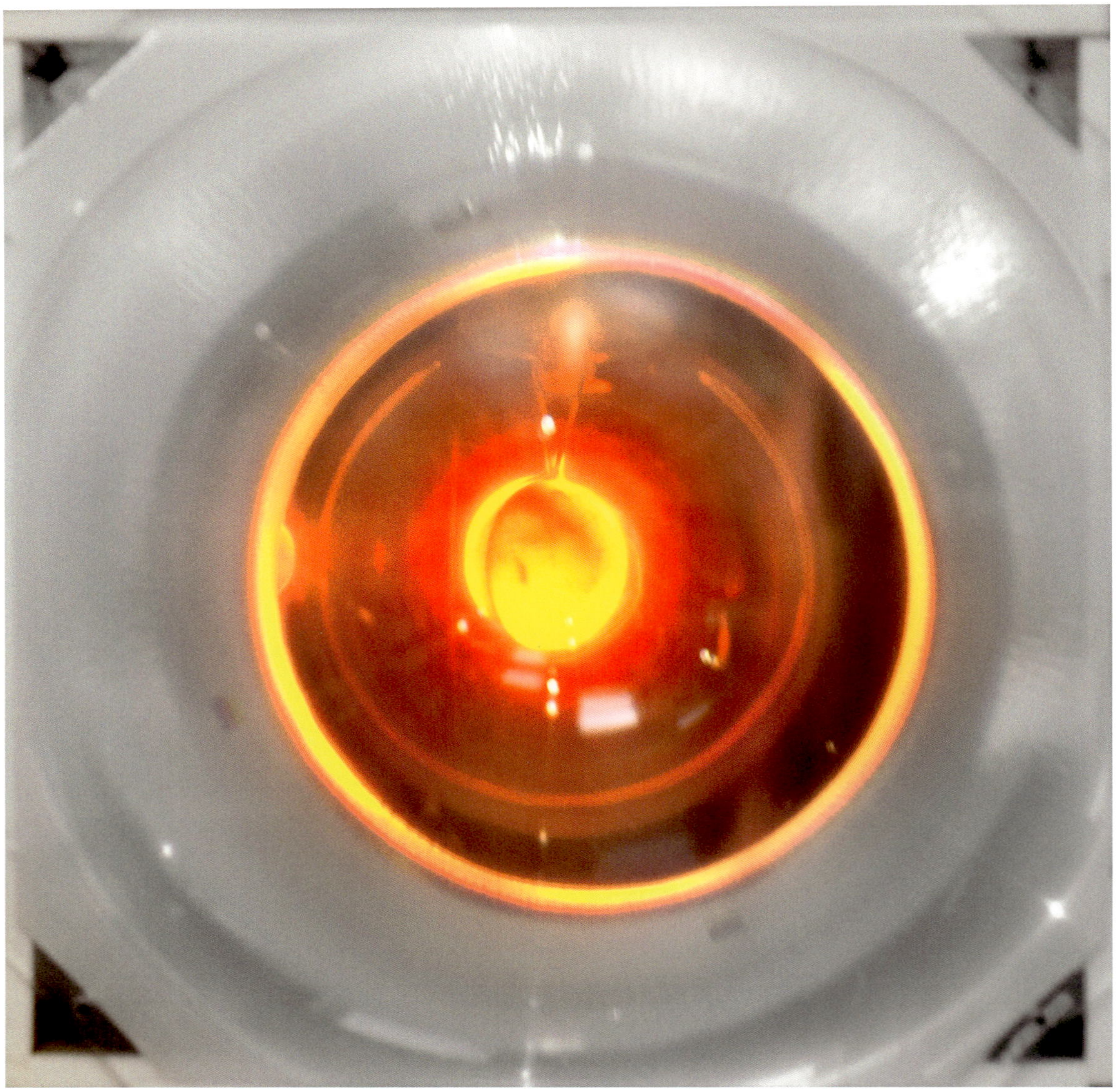

64 Heinz Mack
Fire Ring
1960
Plexiglas, elektrisches Zubehör
31,3 x 31,3 x 27 cm

64 Heinz Mack
Fire Ring
1960
Plexiglass, electrical accessories
31.3 x 31.3 x 27 cm

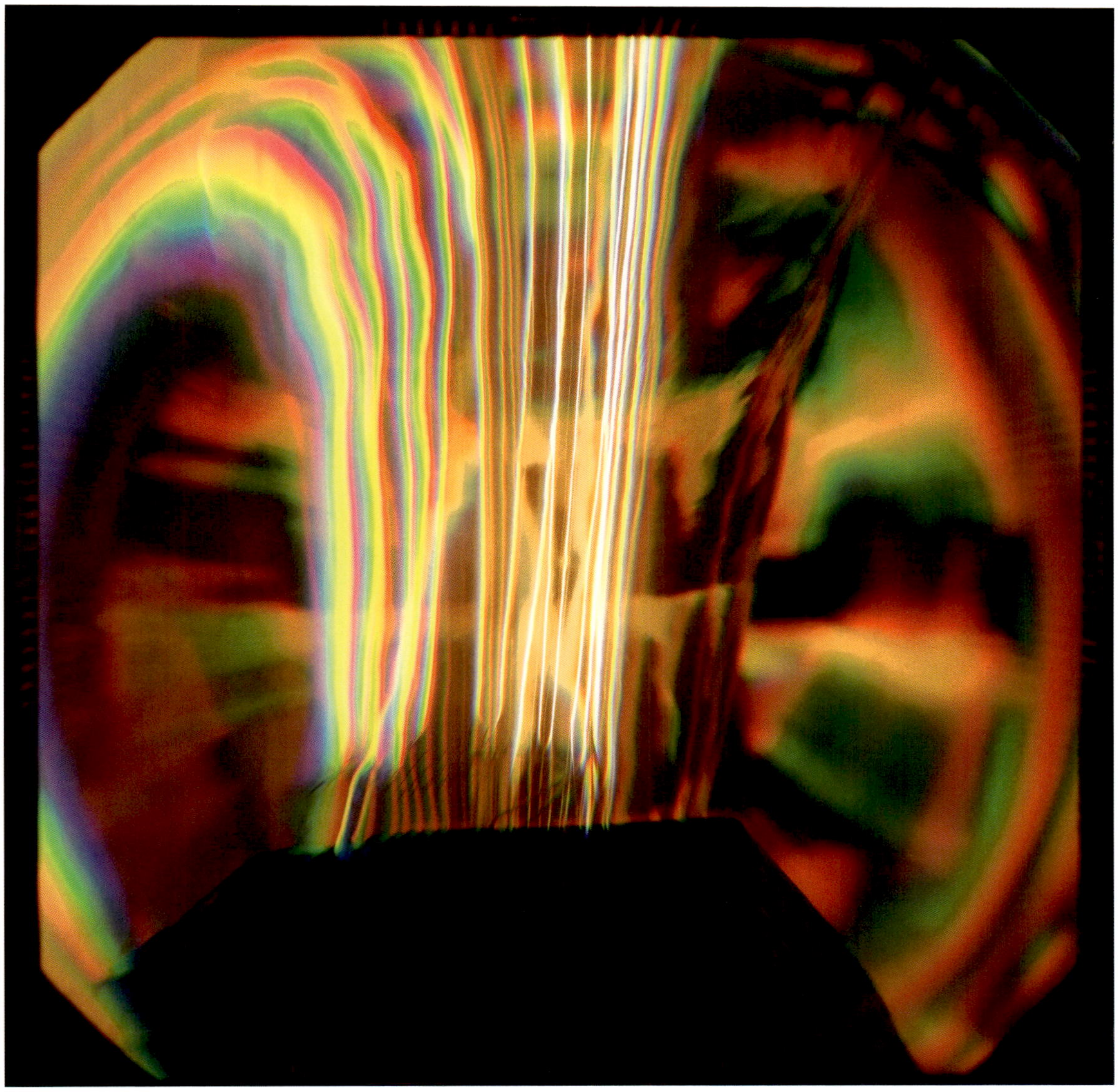

65 Heinz Mack
Virtuelles Volumen II
Signiert, datiert: »mack 64«
Plexiglas, Aluminium, Holz,
elektrisches Zubehör
41 x 41 x 33,3 cm

65 Heinz Mack
Virtual Volume II
Signed, dated: "mack 64"
Plexiglass, aluminum, wood,
electrical accessories
41 x 41 x 33.3 cm

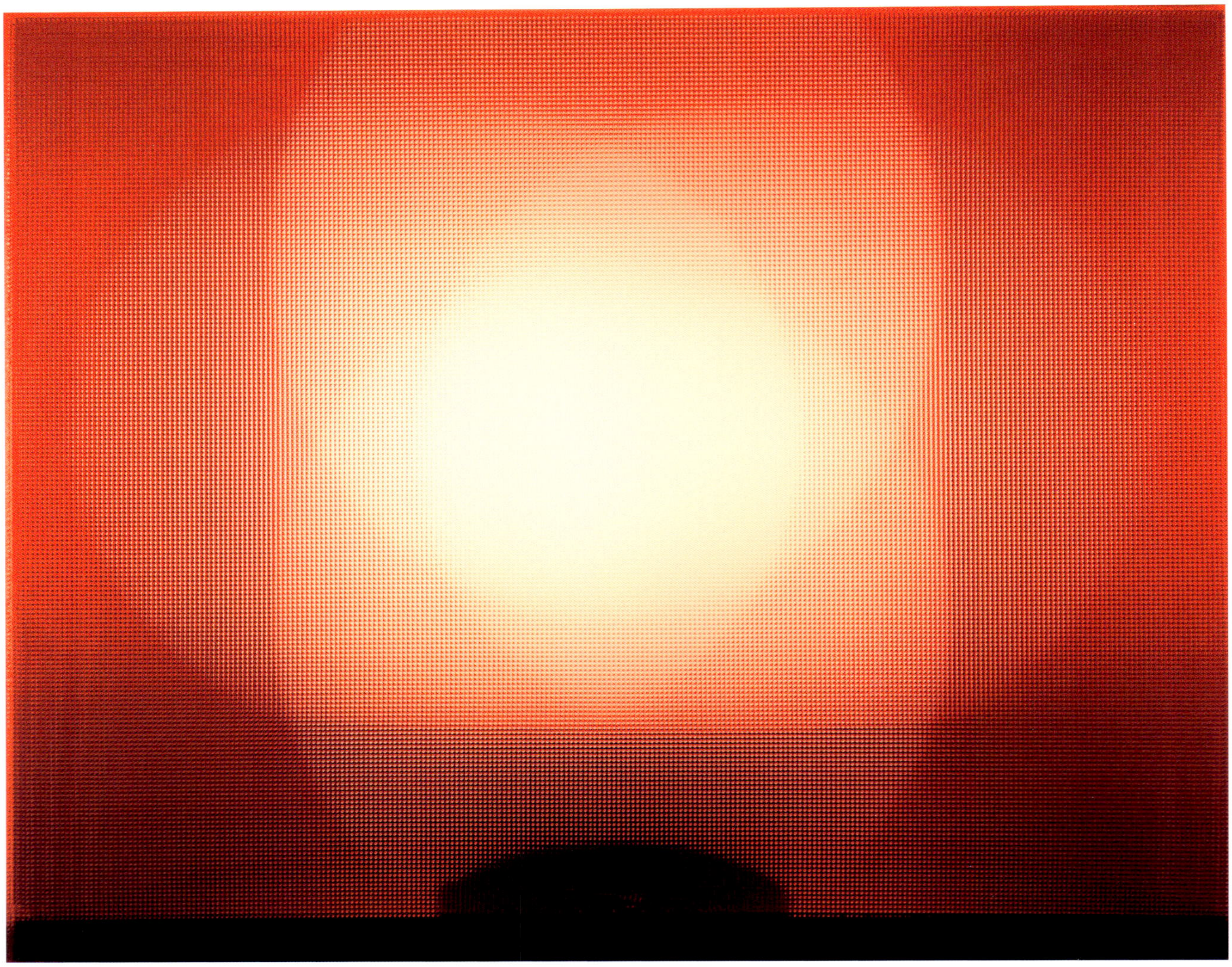

66 Heinz Mack
Ohne Titel
Signiert, datiert: »mack 69«
Plexiglas, elektrisches Zubehör
40 x 51 x 36 cm

66 Heinz Mack
Untitled
Signed, dated: "mack 69"
Plexiglass, electrical accessories
40 x 51 x 36 cm

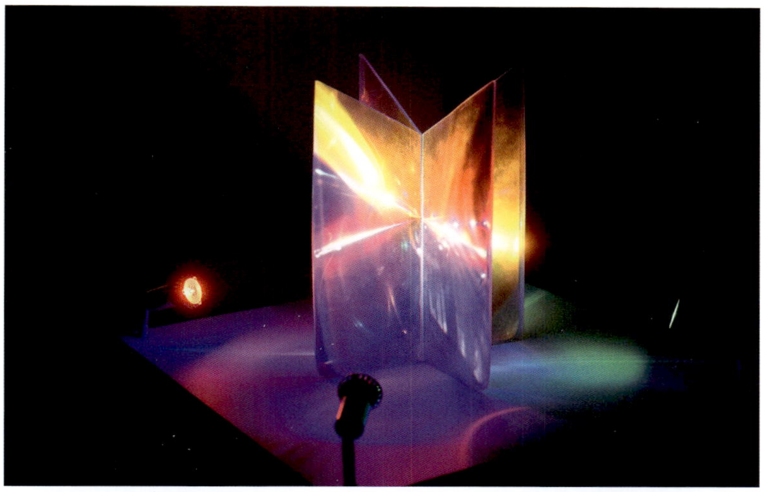

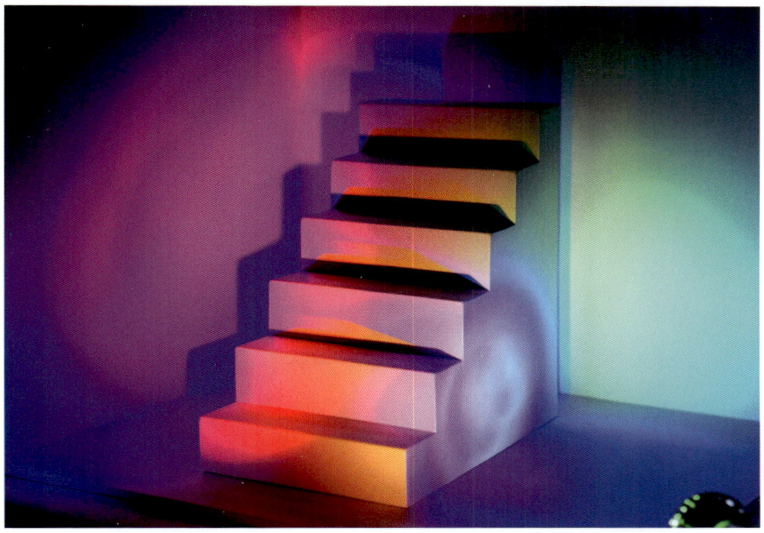

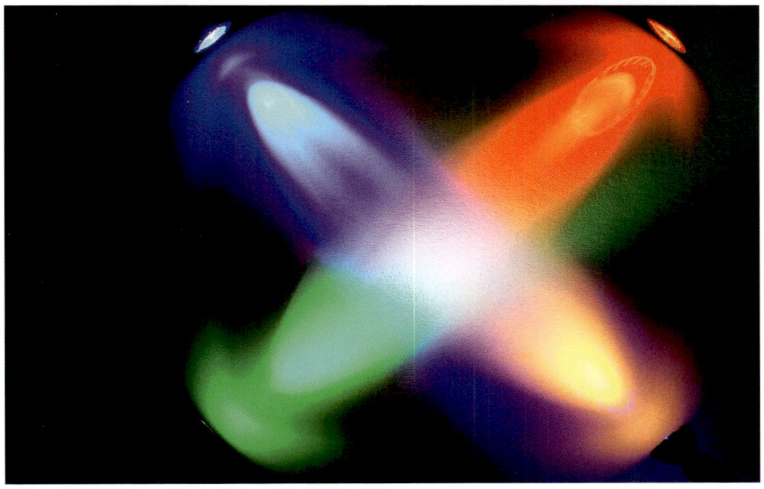

67–69 Heinz Mack
Lichtexperimente
2017
Leuchtkästen
34 x 51 cm

67–69 Heinz Mack
Light experiments
2017
Light boxes
34 x 51 cm

70 Florian Bachmann (*1975)
und Marcus Pericin (*1968)
Farb-Licht-Box
2010/11
Aluminiumgehäuse mit LED-Installation
Sammlung Farbenlehre der Technischen
Universität Dresden

Die Farb-Licht-Box wurde am Farb-Licht-Zentrum der Zürcher Hochschule der Künste (ZHdK) entwickelt. Sie ermöglicht einen spielerisch-experimentellen Zugang zu grundlegenden Wahrnehmungsphänomenen rund um Farbe und Licht. Der einfache Aufbau mit zwei dynamisch steuerbaren RGB-LED-Lichtquellen und einer Zwischenwand mit Fenster ermöglicht die räumliche Inszenierung verschiedenster Farbkombinationen durch farbiges Licht. Anhand vorprogrammierter Kontrastprogramme können Phänomene wie farbige Schatten, Nachbilder, Simultankontrast oder Hell-Dunkel-Kontrast im Experiment erprobt werden.

70 Florian Bachmann (*1975)
and Marcus Pericin (*1968)
Colour-Light-Box
2010/11
Aluminum casing with LED installation
Sammlung Farbenlehre der Technischen
Universität Dresden

The *Colour-Light-Box* was developed at the Colour-Light-Centre of the Zurich University of the Arts. It enables playful experimentation with the basic concepts and scientific phenomena surrounding color and light. The simple construction with two dynamic, steerable RGB LED light sources and a central windowed partition allows spatial staging of various combinations of colored light. Using pre-programmed contrast programs, phenomena such as colored shadows, afterimages, simultaneous contrast or light-dark contrasting can be experimentally investigated.

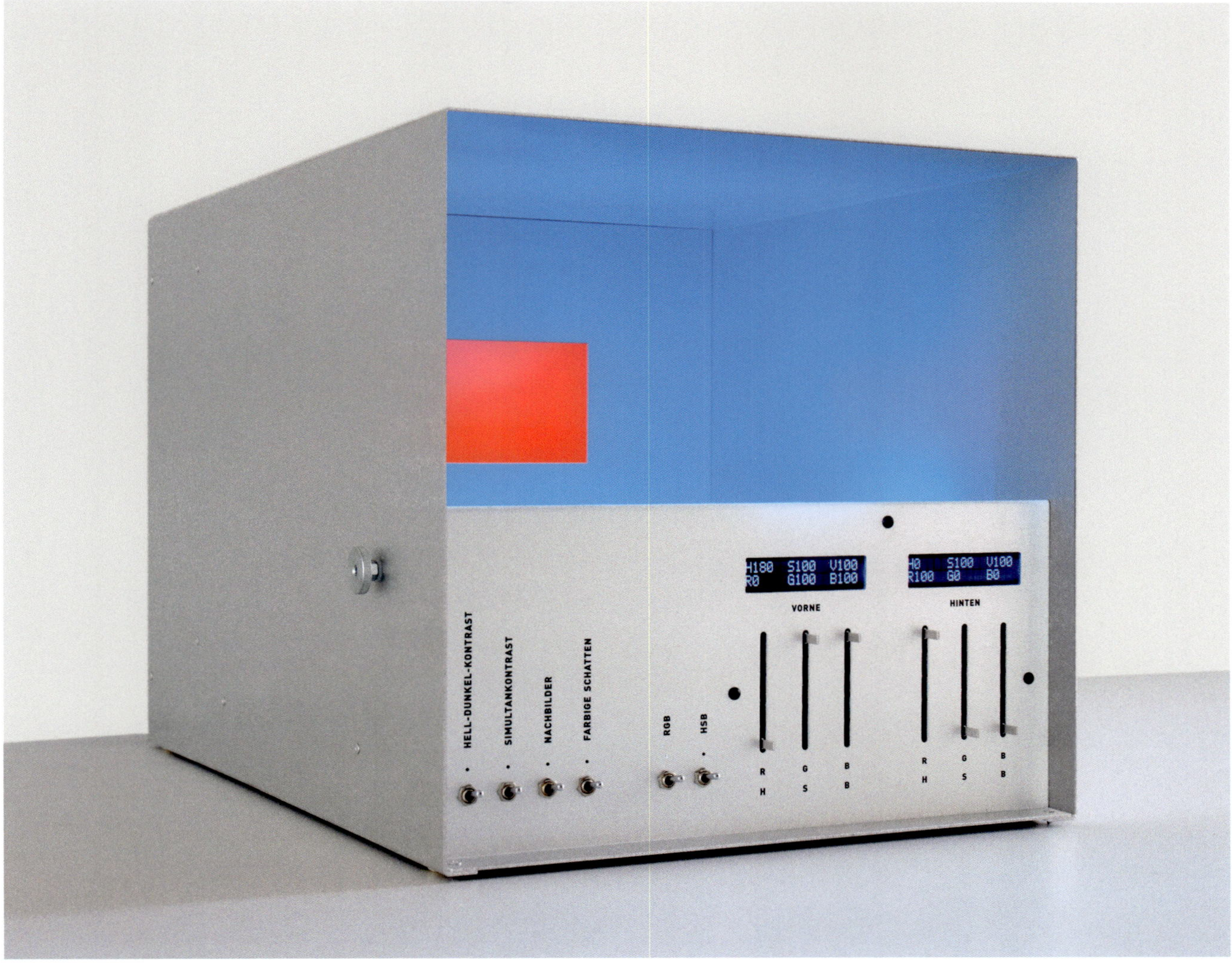
HELL-DUNKEL-KONTRAST
SIMULTANKONTRAST
NACHBILDER
FARBIGE SCHATTEN
RGB
HSB
H180 S100 V100
R0 G100 B100
VORNE
H0 S100 V100
R100 G0 B0
HINTEN
R G B
H S B
R G B
H S B

Goethe's Theory of Colors and Modern Optics[1]

Christoph Cremer

What does Goethe's theory of colors have to do with modern optics? The question seems to be a contradiction in itself. On the one side are world renowned physicists such as Isaac Newton, Gustav Kirchhoff, James Clerk Maxwell, Max Planck, Albert Einstein, Niels Bohr, Erwin Schrödinger, Werner Heisenberg, and many others who, with their experimental and theoretical work, have erected the immense edifice of modern optics, along with its applications that have permeated all areas of life, from electric lights to the optical fiber cables of digital networks and the diverse optical systems of the life sciences. On the other side is Goethe, whose literary and artistic descriptions of observations of light phenomena reflect, according to widespread opinion, the worldview of a poetically talented dilettante, whose opposition to Newton's pioneering optical investigations is incomprehensible from a modern perspective.

Was Goethe really a dilettante in the field of color and light? When one surveys the usual characteristics that are nowadays considered to demonstrate professional scientific activity—perseverance, sustained engagement, knowledge of scientific literature, one's own experimentation and its rational interpretation, procurement and management of research funds, and lastly, the oral and written presentation of the obtained results in a form that invites critical assessment—then Goethe fulfills these criteria of genuine scientific engagement in the field of optical phenomena. Goethe occupied himself his entire life with the fundamental question of nature and its relation to other areas of human activity. He not only corresponded with leading scientists of his time who are still famous today, such as Johann Wilhelm Ritter, Johann Wolfgang Döbereiner, Thomas Johann Seebeck, and Alexander von Humboldt, but also experimented with them.

Although it is typical to picture Goethe sitting at his writing desk and Newton standing in his laboratory, in reality it was the other way around. During his life, Goethe conducted far more optical experiments in total than Newton. Nevertheless, Goethe's color investigations are still often seen as the pastime of an optical enthusiast and lacking scientific relevance. Goethe was, furthermore, not a 'tinkerer,' but a very exact observer. In 1810, he laid down the results of his studies on the phenomenology of light in *Zur Farbenlehre,* a work whose scope corresponds to around 200 scientific publications of typical length in optics, or the life's work of a modern scientist.

However, Goethe did not make many friends among the experts with this work. His approach to the archetypal phenomena of light; his refusal to reduce light to polarized corpuscles or vibrations in a thinly dispersed ether, according to the

1 This contribution is a revised and shortened version of the article "Vom Farbenkreis zum Supermikroskop: Goethe – Dilettant oder Fachmann?", published in *Bayerische Akademie der Schönen Künste, Jahrbuch,* 25, 2011, pp. 74–96.

Goethes Farbenlehre und die moderne Optik[1]

Christoph Cremer

Was hat Goethes Farbenlehre mit der Entwicklung der modernen Optik zu tun? Schon die Frage scheint ein Widerspruch in sich selbst zu sein: Auf der einen Seite stehen weltberühmte Physiker wie Isaac Newton, Gustav Kirchhoff, Clerk Maxwell, Max Planck, Albert Einstein, Niels Bohr, Erwin Schrödinger, Werner Heisenberg und viele andere, die mit ihren theoretischen und experimentellen Arbeiten das himmelragende Gebäude der heutigen Optik und ihrer alle Lebensbereiche durchdringenden Anwendungen errichtet haben, vom elektrischen Licht bis zu den Glasfaserkabeln der digitalen Vernetzung und den vielfältigen optischen Systemen der Lebenswissenschaften. Auf der anderen Seite steht Goethe, dessen literarisch-künstlerisch beschriebene Erfahrungen mit Lichterscheinungen – so eine vielfach verbreitete Meinung – die Weltsicht eines dichterisch begabten Dilettanten widerspiegeln, dessen Widerspruch zu Newtons bahnbrechenden optischen Untersuchungen aus heutiger Sicht unverständlich sei.

War Goethe wirklich nur ein Dilettant im Reich der Farben und des Lichts? Wenn man die heute zum Nachweis einer professionell naturwissenschaftlichen Tätigkeit üblichen Merkmale heranzieht: Dauer, Nachhaltigkeit der Beschäftigung, Kenntnis der Fachliteratur, eigene experimentelle Untersuchungen und deren vernunftgeleitete Interpretation, Einwerbung und Einsatz von Forschungsmitteln und schließlich die mündliche und schriftliche Darstellung der erzielten Ergebnisse in einer zur kritischen Würdigung einladenden Form: so erfüllt Goethe diese Kriterien für eine genuin wissenschaftliche Beschäftigung im Bereich der Erforschung optischer Phänomene. Sein ganzes Leben lang hat sich Goethe mit diesem Grundthema der Naturerkenntnis und seinen Relationen zu anderen Feldern menschlicher Tätigkeit befasst; mit führenden, noch heute berühmten Naturwissenschaftlern seiner Zeit wie Johann Wilhelm Ritter, Johann Wolfgang Döbereiner, Thomas Johann Seebeck oder Alexander von Humboldt hat er nicht nur korrespondiert, sondern auch experimentiert.

Während man sich typischerweise Goethe am Schreibtisch sitzend vorstellt und Newton im Labor stehend, war es in Wirklichkeit umgekehrt: Goethe hat in seinem Leben insgesamt viel mehr optische Versuche durchgeführt als Newton. Dennoch werden Goethes Farbenforschungen vielfach noch als Freizeitbeschäftigung eines Optik-Liebhabers ohne besondere Folgewirkung für Wissenschaft und Technik angesehen. Goethe war aber nicht ein ›Tüftler und Bastler‹, sondern ein sehr genauer Beobachter. Die Resultate seiner Studien zur Phänomenologie des Lichtes hat er 1810 in seinem Werk *Zur Farbenlehre* niedergelegt, einem Werk, dessen Ausmaß rund 200 Fachpublikationen üblicher Länge oder dem Lebenswerk eines heutigen Wissenschaftlers entspricht.

Allerdings hat Goethe sich mit diesem Werk bei den Fachgelehrten nicht viele Freunde gemacht: Goethes Herangehensweise an das Urphänomen des Lichtes, seine Weigerung, das Licht der damaligen mechanistischen Sichtweise gemäß auf polarisierte

1 Der vorliegende Beitrag ist eine überarbeitete und gekürzte Fassung des Artikels »Vom Farbenkreis zum Supermikroskop. Goethe – Dilettant oder Fachmann?«, in: *Bayerische Akademie der Schönen Künste, Jahrbuch*, 25, 2011, S. 74–96.

contemporary mechanical conception; his skepticism of the explanatory power of a pure mathematical treatment; and his crude polemic against Isaac Newton can only have had a polarizing effect. Newton (1643–1727) was for many not only an Olympian, as was Goethe; he was the ruler of scientific Olympus and revered as such. As early as the first half of the eighteenth century, a life-size marble statue in honor of the archangel of modern physics and optics was erected in the center of the entrance halls of Trinity College Chapel in Cambridge, where Newton had taught. He holds a prism in his hand as his chief divine attribute.

Nevertheless, what remained elusive to Goethe during his lifetime—the recognition of leading scientists—was later acknowledged in his work. Hermann von Helmholtz, for example, one of the most important physicists of the nineteenth century who was honored during his lifetime with monuments in the United States, studied Goethe's *Farbenlehre* intensively and, in particular, thought very highly of Goethe's observations on the physiology of perception. A few of the twentieth century's most important physicists developed the work on Goethe's theory of colors further. To be mentioned here are Max Planck (1858–1947), Werner Heisenberg (1901–1976), and Carl Friedrich von Weizsäcker (1912–2007), all of whom, despite their individual criticisms of the *Farbenlehre,* nevertheless drew inspiration from its deeper meaning. In the words of Carl Friedrich von Weizsäcker, Goethe's "light is not that of a lighthouse … which indicates the port, but rather that of a star, which will accompany us on every journey." The following exposition will trace this maxim from the personal view of an experimental physicist who works in the field of applied optics. It will not, however, attempt to justify Goethe's rejection of Newtonian optics or defend the absence of quantification and mathematization, which is seen today as the essential character of optical investigations; rather, it will address the inspirational effect that Goethe, in his efforts to gain knowledge of light, had on the development of modern applied optics.

Basically, in the world of science all theories are allowed in principle as long as they do not contradict experimental observations. Additionally, modern theories of science demand that theories can be experimentally 'rebutted': they must lead to predictions that can be refuted by observation. Goethe wanted to apply this modern scientific principle to the great 'false teacher,' namely, Newton. Newton had claimed that the production of imaging optical systems (e.g. telescopes) without chromatic aberration, so-called 'achromat' systems, was not possible using glass lenses. Should it have been possible to build such an achromat then—so Goethe thought—an important consequence of Newton's theory would have been 'rebutted.' A few decades after Newton's death, it was indeed demonstrated that this dilemma could be significantly reduced using specific types of glass. Goethe was therefore very keen to confront his opponents in the field of applied optics, i.e., to facilitate the production of achromatic optical systems.

Yet, this required the production of optical glass with highly specific refractive properties. This presented Goethe with a series of difficult problems, which exist in

Kügelchen oder Schwingungen in einem feinverteilten Ätherstoff zurückzuführen, seine Skepsis gegenüber der Aussagekraft einer rein mathematischen Behandlung, seine derbe Polemik gegenüber Isaak Newton – das musste stark polarisierend wirken. Newton (1643–1727) war vielen nicht nur einer der Olympier, wie Goethe; er war der Herr des wissenschaftlichen Olymps und wurde wie ein solcher verehrt. Bereits in der ersten Hälfte des 18. Jahrhunderts wurde in der Eingangshalle der Kirche des Trinity College in Cambridge, wo Newton gelehrt hatte, diesem Erzengel der modernen Physik und Optik eine in der Mitte des Saales stehende, lebensgroße Marmorstatue errichtet, die als himmlisches Hauptattribut ein Prisma in der Hand hält.

Dennoch: Was Goethe zu Lebzeiten versagt blieb, das anerkennende Interesse von führenden Naturforschern, das wurde seinem Werk später zuteil. So hat sich Herrmann von Helmholtz, einer der bedeutendsten Physiker des 19. Jahrhunderts, dem bereits zu Lebzeiten in den Vereinigten Staaten Denkmäler gesetzt wurden, intensiv mit Goethes *Farbenlehre* auseinandergesetzt und insbesondere dessen Beobachtungen zur Physiologie des Sehens sehr positiv beurteilt. Im vergangenen 20. Jahrhundert haben einige der bedeutendsten Physiker die Beschäftigung mit Goethes Farbenlehre weitergeführt. Zu nennen sind hier Max Planck (1858–1947), Werner Heisenberg (1901–1976) und Carl Friedrich von Weizsäcker (1912–2007), die bei aller Kritik an der *Farbenlehre* im Einzelnen sich doch von ihrer tiefen Bedeutung inspirieren ließen. So ist – mit einem Wort von Carl Friedrich von Weizsäcker – Goethes »Licht nicht das des Leuchtturms [...], der den Hafen anzeigt, sondern das eines Sterns, der uns auf jeder Reise begleiten wird«. Die vorliegenden Ausführungen folgen dieser Maxime aus der persönlichen Sicht eines experimentell auf dem Gebiete der Angewandten Optik und ihrer Anwendungen arbeitenden Physikers. Hier soll nicht der Versuch gemacht werden, Goethes Ablehnung der Newtonschen Optik zu rechtfertigen oder das Fehlen der heute als Wesensmerkmal optischer Untersuchungen angesehenen Quantifizierung und Mathematisierung zu verteidigen, sondern auf die Anregungen einzugehen, die Goethes Mühen um die Erkenntnis des Lichts für die Entwicklung der modernen angewandten Optik hatten.

Grundsätzlich sind in der Welt der Naturwissenschaften im Prinzip alle Theorien erlaubt, die nicht in Widerspruch mit experimentellen Beobachtungen stehen. Moderne Wissenschaftstheorien verlangen darüber hinaus, dass Theorien experimentell ›falsifizierbar‹ sein müssen: Sie müssen zu Voraussagen führen, die durch Beobachtungen widerlegt werden können. Dieses moderne Wissenschaftsprinzip wollte auch Goethe zur Anwendung gegen den großen ›Irrlehrer‹ Newton bringen: Dieser hatte behauptet, die Herstellung von abbildenden optischen Systemen (zum Beispiel Fernrohren) ohne Farbfehler, sogenannte Achromate, mit Hilfe von Glaslinsen sei physikalisch unmöglich. Könnten solche Achromate doch realisiert werden, wäre – so glaubte Goethe – eine wichtige Folgerung von Newtons Theorie ›falsifiziert‹ worden. In der Tat konnte einige Jahrzehnte nach Newtons Tod nachgewiesen werden, dass dieses Dilemma mit ganz bestimmten Glassorten wesentlich reduziert werden konnte. So war Goethe sehr interessiert, seinem Kontrahenten auch auf der Ebene der angewandten Optik die Stirne zu bieten, also die Herstellung achromatischer optischer Systeme zu fördern.

an analogous form today, just like 200 years ago. The first problem was the acquisition of the requisite financial means for research and production. The funds available from public coffers (in this case, the coffers of the Grand Duke) were far too insufficient for establishing the specialist glassworks required for obtaining the desired optical materials. Goethe found a solution in seeking private sponsors for his ambitious plans. He was able to win an affluent participant in his seminar on color as a sponsor: Grand Duchess Maria Pavlovna (1786–1859), wife of Grand Duke Charles Frederick and sister of tsars Alexander I and Nicholas I.

Goethe's coffers, which had been filled by Maria Pavlovna, provided a sound basis for solving the second fundamental problem: acquiring the necessary information for the production of special optical glass. Here—so the story goes—Goethe engaged in a bit of industrial espionage. During a visit to Weimar in 1822 from Georg von Reichenbach, a partner of the Fraunhofer glassworks in Benediktbeuern in Upper Bavaria, the old privy councilor engaged him in such a friendly manner that Reichenbach revealed the fundamental secret of Fraunhofer glass production. Then Goethe began to overcome the third, and today still significant, fundamental problem: the appointment of a suitable scientist to oversee the project. For this Goethe won Friedrich Körner (1778–1847) as his color assistant. Although he was lacking a nice-sounding doctorate, in Goethe's time a little help from the minister of state was not a crime. It was also not a crime to apply a little pressure in order to promote the doctor of philosophy to the position of lecturer at the University of Jena.

Goethe's help, which would be politically incorrect today, did not, however, end up going to anyone undeserving. Körner, the director of the glassworks, had a student, whose name still has an almost mythical ring throughout the whole world of science and technology: Carl Zeiss (1816–1888). Carl Zeiss was from Weimar and a godson of Grand Duke Carl Friedrich, the husband of Maria Pavlovna, the sponsor of Goethe's optics. Carl Zeiss worked for Friedrich Körner for four years, from 1834 to 1838, before founding a workshop for precision engineering and optics in 1846. Today, the Carl-Zeiss company, with its headquarters once again in Jena, belongs to the global market leaders in the optics industry, as does its sister company, which was also founded by Carl Zeiss, known today as Schott AG. It is highly improbable that this small university town in Thuringia would have achieved its fame without Goethe's support of optical science.

Carl Zeiss was the first to recognize the significance of the theory for the construction of high-performance microscopes. That is why, in 1866, he employed a physicist from Jena who later became the director of the university's observatory, Ernst Abbe (1840–1905). The goal was to enable the development of significantly improved microscope systems with the help of quantitative numerical calculations (today this would be called optical simulations). With this basis, the microscopes built by Zeiss in Jena around 1880 were the best in the world.

The new microscopes from Zeiss and other leading manufacturers of optics enabled the foundation of modern cell biology, modern pathology, and microbiology.

Dazu wurde jedoch die Herstellung optischer Gläser mit hochspezifischen Brechungseigenschaften benötigt. Dies stellte Goethe vor eine Reihe schwieriger Probleme, die in analoger Form heute noch genauso existieren wie vor 200 Jahren. Das erste Problem war die Beschaffung der zu Forschung und Produktion erforderlichen Finanzmittel. Das aus öffentlichen Kassen (hier die großherzogliche Schatulle) erhältliche Geld reichte bei weitem nicht zur Gründung der zur Gewinnung des gewünschten optischen Materials benötigten Spezialglashütte aus. Hier fand Goethe eine Lösung, indem er zur Unterstützung seiner ambitionierten Pläne private Sponsoren auftrieb. Es gelang ihm, eine betuchte Teilnehmerin seines Farbenseminars als Sponsorin seiner Glashütte zu gewinnen: Maria Pawlowna (1786–1859), Kaiserliche Hoheit, die Gemahlin von Großherzog Carl Friedrich und Schwester der Zaren Alexander I. und Nikolaus I.

Die dank Maria Pawlowna gefüllte Drittmittelkasse Goethes war eine gute Grundlage für die Lösung des zweiten Fundamentalproblems: der Beschaffung der zur Herstellung von optischen Spezialgläsern erforderlichen Information. Hierzu betrieb Goethe – so wird behauptet – ein bisschen Industriespionage: Bei einem Besuch von Georg von Reichenbach, dem Teilhaber von Fraunhofers Glashütte im oberbayrischen Bendediktbeuren, in Weimar (1822), wickelte der alte Geheimrat diesen so freundlich ein, dass Reichenbach ihm das Grundgeheimnis der Fraunhoferschen Glasproduktion verriet. Nun machte sich Goethe an die Bewältigung des dritten, auch heute noch wesentlichen Hauptproblems: der Berufung eines geeigneten Wissenschaftlers als Leiter des Unternehmens. Hierzu gewann Goethe Friedrich Körner (1778–1847), seinen Farbenassistenten. Diesem fehlte zwar noch ein wohlklingender Doktortitel; aber zu Zeiten Goethes war ein wenig Nachhilfe durch den Einfluss des Herrn Staatsministers keine Sünde. Ebenso wenig sündhaft war es, den Herrn Dr. phil. dann mit etwas Nachdruck zum Dozenten an der Universität Jena zu ernennen.

Goethes heute politisch inkorrekte Hilfe traf jedoch keinen Unwürdigen. So hatte der Glashüttendirektor Körner einen Studenten, dessen Name heute noch in der gesamten Welt von Wissenschaft und Technik einen fast mythischen Klang hat: Es war Carl Zeiss (1816—1888). Der Weimarer Carl Zeiss war ein Patensohn von Großherzog Carl Friedrich, dem Gemahl von Maria Pawlowna, der Sponsorin von Goethes Optik. Vier Jahre lang, von 1834 bis 1838, arbeitete Carl Zeiss bei Friedrich Körner, bevor er im Jahre 1846 eine Werkstatt für Feinmechanik und Optik gründete. Heute zählt der Carl-Zeiss-Konzern, wieder mit einem Hauptsitz im angestammten Jena, zusammen mit seinem schon von Carl Zeiss selbst gegründeten Schwesterunternehmen zur Glasherstellung, der heutigen Schott AG, zu den Weltmarktführern der optischen Industrie. Es ist sehr unwahrscheinlich, dass diese kleine Universitätsstadt in Thüringen ohne die Förderung der optischen Wissenschaften durch Goethe zu diesem Ruhm gelangt wäre.

Zeiss war der Erste, der die Bedeutung der Theorie für den Bau von Hochleistungsmikroskopen erkannte. Daher engagierte er 1866 den Jenaer Physiker und späteren Direktor der dortigen Universitätssternwarte Ernst Abbe (1840–1905). Das Ziel war, auf der Basis quantitativer numerischer Rechnungen (heute würde man das Optik-Simulationen nennen) die Entwicklung wesentlich verbesserter Mikroskopsysteme zu ermöglichen. Um 1880 waren die von Zeiss in Jena auf dieser Grundlage gebauten Mikroskope die besten der Welt.

As good as the high-performance microscopes were, they had a serious problem: structural details of cells, microbes, and their often-deadly interactions with cells of the body could only be discerned when they were bigger than approximately 0.2 microns (1 micron [μm] is 1/1000 millimeter). Below this resolution limit, the image was as blurry as a newspaper at a great distance from the naked eye. Despite all the attempts at improvement, this limit of conventional light microscopy could not be overcome. Even the best microscopes from Zeiss, Leitz, and others did not allow the detection of structural details beyond this magical limit of 0.2 microns.

Ernst Abbe, the physicist at Jena and main partner of Carl Zeiss, occupied himself intensively with this astonishing and disconcerting phenomenon and found a solution. It became clear that this was no longer a technical hurdle, but rather a fundamental limit to obtaining knowledge of nature using light. In 1873, he summarized his findings in one of the most famous works of modern optics. This contained as many mathematical formulae as Goethe's *Farbenlehre,* namely, not a single one. Nevertheless, the knowledge of physics was so radical that he is mentioned in every introductory lecture on physics.

Fundamental new discoveries in physics, optoelectronics, information technology, and molecular biology have allowed the 'Abbe limit' of the light-optical knowledge of nature to be practically overcome. On the basis of these previously unforeseeable new developments, an array of techniques has been developed in the last two decades to dramatically overcome, or, more precisely, circumvent the limits of the optical resolution of light microscopes, which had previously been considered absolute.

One of the methods of 'superresolution' light microscopy rests on the use of different colored molecules. For example, one can (to use the words of Goethe's *Farbenlehre)* use "chemical colours," whose characteristic is "duration"; another possibility is to use molecules whose luminosity depends on where they are located or change over time as it does with lighthouses and supernova explosions in astronomy. Using suitable light irradiation and environmental conditions, such molecules can be made to emit light in a determinate way during a determinate short interval, i.e. be in a 'light' state. At other times, they do not emit light and are therefore in a 'dark' state. Light, dark, and color refer in this way to the registration (light state) and non-registration (dark state) of light emission with a specific color. A high-resolution image can be formed from such light and dark states of different dye molecules in different locations, according to a fundamental idea that was already expressed by Goethe 200 years ago:

> We now assert, extraordinary as it may in some degree appear, that the eye sees no form, inasmuch as light, shade, and colour together constitute that which to our vision distinguishes object from object, and the parts of an object from each other. From these three, light, shade, and colour, we construct the visible world … .
> (J.W. Goethe, *Theory of Colours.)*

Die neuen Mikroskope von Zeiss und anderen führenden Optikherstellern ermöglichten die Begründung der modernen Zellbiologie, aber auch der heutigen Pathologie und Mikrobiologie. So gut die neuen Hochleistungsmikroskope aber auch waren, sie hatten ein gravierendes Problem: Struktureinzelheiten von Zellen, Mikroben und ihren oft todbringenden Wechselwirkungen mit den Zellen des Körpers konnten nur erkannt werden, wenn diese größer waren als ungefähr 0,2 Mikrometer. 1 Mikrometer (μm) ist 1/1000 Millimeter. Unterhalb dieser Auflösungsgrenze war das Bild so verschwommen wie eine Zeitung aus großer Entfernung für das bloße Auge. Allen Verbesserungsversuchen zum Trotz konnte diese Grenze der konventionellen Lichtmikroskopie nicht überwunden werden. Auch die besten Mikroskope von Zeiss, Leitz und anderen erlaubten keine Erkennung von Struktureinzelheiten unterhalb dieser magischen Grenze von 0,2 μm.

Ernst Abbe hat sich intensiv mit diesem erstaunlichen und beunruhigenden Phänomen befasst und die Lösung gefunden. Offenbar handelte es sich hier nicht mehr um ein technisches Problem, sondern um eine fundamentale Grenze der mit Licht möglichen Naturerkenntnis. Im Jahre 1873 fasste er seine Erkenntnisse in einer der berühmtesten Arbeiten der modernen Optik zusammen. Diese enthielt so viele mathematische Formeln wie die *Farbenlehre* Goethes, nämlich keine einzige; dennoch war der physikalische Gehalt so brisant, dass er seitdem in jeder Physik-Grundvorlesung zur Sprache kommt.

Fundamentale neue Entdeckungen in Physik, Optoelektronik, Informationstechnologie und Molekularbiologie ermöglichen heute die praktische Überwindung der ›Abbe-Grenze‹ der lichtoptischen Naturerkenntnis. Auf der Grundlage dieser neuen, damals nicht vorhersehbaren Entwicklungen sind in den letzten beiden Jahrzehnten eine Reihe von Verfahren realisiert worden, die es erlaubten, die bislang für absolut gehaltene Grenze der optischen Auflösung in der Lichtmikroskopie in dramatischer Weise zu überwinden, genauer gesagt zu umgehen.

Eine dieser Methoden der ›superauflösenden‹ Lichtmikroskopieverfahren beruht auf der Verwendung verschiedenfarbiger Moleküle. Zum Beispiel kann man (um mit Goethes *Farbenlehre* zu sprechen) »chemische Farben« nutzen, deren »Kennzeichen« die »Dauer« ist; eine andere Möglichkeit besteht darin, Moleküle zu verwenden, deren Leuchtkraft vom Ort abhängt, an dem sie sich befinden, oder die auf andere Weise ihre Leuchtkraft zeitlich verändern, wie das bei Leuchttürmen geschieht, oder in der Astronomie bei Supernova-Ausbrüchen. Solche Moleküle können durch geeignete Lichteinstrahlung und Umweltbedingungen dazu gebracht werden, dass sie während einer bestimmten kurzen Zeitspanne in bestimmter Weise leuchten, also sich in einem ›Hell‹-Zustand befinden; außerhalb dieser Zeiten leuchten sie nicht, sie sind in einem ›Dunkel‹-Zustand. Hell, Dunkel und Farbe beziehen sich dabei auf die Registrierung (Hell-Zustand) oder Nicht-Registrierung (Dunkel-Zustand) der Lichtemission mit einer bestimmten Farbe. Aus solchen Hell- und Dunkel-Zuständen von vielen verschiedenen Farbstoffmolekülen an verschiedenen Orten kann dann ein hochaufgelöstes Bild aufgebaut werden, gemäß einer schon vor 200 Jahren von Goethe ausgesprochenen Leitidee:

Thus, an optical superresolution is possible that is significantly better than the limits that were detailed by Abbe and considered insurmountable for over 100 years. Figure one shows one of many examples.

While conventional microscopy permits only a completely washed-out image of the 'landscape' of genetic information (DNA), it is as if this 'fog' is blown away by 'light, dark, and color' localization microscopy, as the highly complex nanostructure of DNA distribution becomes visible. In this way, the positions of hundreds of thousands of individual molecules are determined according to the 'light, dark, and color' principle, and the image is composed from these, similar to what is done on a screen. Incidentally, this case is a cardiac muscle cell under conditions of infarction (lack of oxygen); with normal oxygen supply the 'nuclear landscape' looks very different. This opens up new possibilities for investigations of molecular superresolution of the effects of pharmaceuticals against infarction at the level of individual cardiac muscle cells.

In view of this idea, it would have been conceivable 100 years ago to demonstrate the basic principle of optical imaging, which far exceeds the classical resolution limit, using the principle of 'light, dark, and color.' For at least the last thirty years, its experimental realization would also have been possible. However, no one had the idea until around twenty years ago when the first concepts of "chemical colours" were developed, whose characteristic is "duration." Then another decade passed before, in 2006, a group from King's College London and the United States' University of Maine and the Howard Hughes Institute experimentally achieved superresolution based on the 'lighthouse principle' of the alteration of 'light, dark, and color.' The first person to achieve this with a biological application was the physicist Eric Betzig, who left academic science for many years and worked in the field of engineering. With his return to optical research in 2005, he brought a 'clear view' that had been sharpened by his long absence, and at the beginning of 2006, he realized the method of superresolution microscopy sketched above in his living room (at least according to legend).

From the perspective of official science, one could have called this, in view of Goethe's method, 'dilettantism.' The Swedish Academy of Sciences rightly saw it differently. In 2014, Betzig was awarded the Nobel Prize in Chemistry for his pioneering achievements in the development of superresolution microscopy. In the justification for the award, it was pointed out that such methods would lead to a revolution of scientific knowledge in biology and medicine.

The development of superresolution light microscopy is an example of Goethe's statement in *The Green Snake and the Beautiful Lily:* "What is the most important [secret]? ... The open one." With respect to scientific knowledge, this aphorism could be reformulated in the following way: "What is the most difficult to know? ... That which is evident."

Goethe's suggestions also appear in other areas of the development of modern optics and atomic physics. While Newton and Huygens attempted to reduce

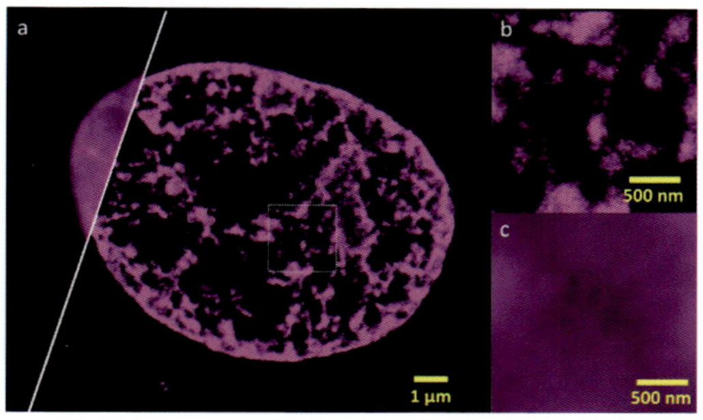

1 Räumliche Verteilung der Erbinformation (DNA) im Kern einer Herzmuskelzelle der Maus. a) Links von der weißen schrägen Trennungslinie ist das Ergebnis bei konventioneller Mikroskopie zu sehen, rechts davon das Bild, das mit der auf dem ›Hell, Dunkel und Farbe‹-Prinzip beruhenden superauflösenden Lokalisationsmikroskopie erzielt wurde. b) Vergrößerung des in a) rechts Mitte gezeigten kleinen, blau umrandeten Ausschnitts; c) derselbe Ausschnitt wie in b), aber bei konventioneller Auflösung. Aus: Jahresbericht 2016 des Institute of Molecular Biology (IMB), Mainz (www.imb-mainz.de).
Spatial distribution of genetic information (DNA) in the nucleus of a cardiac muscle cell of a mouse: a) left of the inclined white dividing line shows the result of conventional microscopy, right of it the superresolution localization microscopy, which is based on the principle of "light, dark, and color"; b) magnification of the small, blue-bordered section shown in a); c) the same section but shown in conventional resolution. From the 2016 yearly report of the Institute of Molecular Biology (IMB), Mainz (www.imb-mainz.de).

> Nunmehr behaupten wir, wenn es auch einigermaßen sonderbar klingen mag, daß das Auge keine Form sehe, indem Hell, Dunkel und Farbe zusammen allein dasjenige ausmachen, was den Gegenstand vom Gegenstand, die Teile des Gegenstandes voneinander fürs Auge unterscheidet. Und so erbauen wir aus diesen dreien die sichtbare Welt […]. (Johann Wolfgang Goethe, *Entwurf einer Farbenlehre,* 1808.)

Damit wurde eine optische Superauflösung möglich, die um ein Vielfaches besser ist als die von Abbe aufgezeigten, über hundert Jahre lang für unüberwindlich gehaltenen Grenzen. Abbildung 1 zeigt eines von vielen Beispielen.

Während die konventionelle Mikroskopie nur ein vollständig verwaschenes Bild der ›Landschaft‹ der Erbinformation (DNA) zulässt, ist dieser ›Nebel‹ bei der auf ›Hell, Dunkel und Farbe‹ beruhenden Lokalisationsmikroskopie wie weggeblasen, und die hoch komplexen Nanostrukturen der DNA Verteilung werden sichtbar; dabei wurden die Positionen von Hunderttausenden einzelner Moleküle nach dem ›Hell, Dunkel und Farbe‹-Prinzip bestimmt und daraus das Bild zusammengesetzt, ähnlich wie dies bei einem Bildschirm gemacht wird. Übrigens handelt es sich hier um eine Herzmuskelzelle unter Infarktbedingungen (Sauerstoffmangel); bei normaler Sauerstoffzufuhr sieht die ›Kernlandschaft‹ ganz anders aus. Dies eröffnet neue Möglichkeiten, die Wirkung von Pharmaka gegen Infarkt auf der Ebene einzelner Herzmuskelzellen mit molekularer Superauflösung zu untersuchen.

Von der Idee her gesehen, wäre es bereits vor 100 Jahren denkbar gewesen, das Grundprinzip einer die klassische Auflösungsgrenze weit überschreitenden, auf ›Hell, Dunkel und Farbe‹ beruhenden optischen Bildgebung darzustellen; seit mindestens 30 Jahren wäre auch seine experimentelle Realisierung möglich gewesen. Doch niemand kam auf diese Idee, bis vor rund 20 Jahren erste konkrete Konzepte mit »chemischen Farben« entwickelt wurden, deren »Kennzeichen« die »Dauer« war; dann verging noch einmal ein weiteres Jahrzehnt, bis im Jahre 2006 Gruppen am King's College in London, an der University of Maine und am Howard Hughes Institute in den USA eine auf dem ›Leuchtturmprinzip‹ des Wechsels von ›Hell, Dunkel und Farbe‹ beruhende Superauflösung erstmals auch experimentell realisierten. Der Erste, der dies im Kontext einer biologischen Anwendung verwirklichte, war der Physiker Eric Betzig, der für viele Jahre aus der Wissenschaft ausgeschieden war und im Bereich Maschinenbau arbeitete. Bei der Rückkehr in die optische Forschung (2005) brachte er einen durch die lange Abwesenheit geschärften ›klaren Blick‹ mit und realisierte Anfang 2006 die oben skizzierte Methode der superauflösenden Lichtmikroskopie in seinem Wohnzimmer (so will es zumindest die Legende).

Von Seiten der offiziellen Wissenschaft her gesehen hätte man dies im Hinblick auf Goethes Tätigkeit als naturforschender ›Privatgelehrter‹ auch als ›Dilettantismus‹ bezeichnen können. Die schwedische Akademie der Wissenschaften sah dies zu Recht anders: Im Jahre 2014 wurde ihm für seine bahnbrechenden Leistungen bei der Entwicklung superauflösender Mikroskopiemethoden der Nobelpreis für Chemie verliehen. In der Begründung wurde darauf hingewiesen, dass derartige Methoden zu einer Revolution der wissenschaftlichen Erkenntnis in Biologie und Medizin führen werden.

light to small material particles, Goethe rejected this vehemently. In Goethe's credo, light is a fundamental phenomenon of nature, an archetypal phenomenon that absolutely cannot be explained with polarized corpuscles/cubes or vibrations of a mechanical ether. Rather, he adheres to the basic postulate that "light is the most simple, most undecomposable, most homogenous essence that we know. It is not composite" (J.W. Goethe, Encampment by Marienborn, July 15, 1793). This conception of light as an elementary, irreducible natural phenomenon comes much closer to the modern theory of light than a naïve particle theory. In the modern quantum theory of light, which was established by Max Planck in 1900 and developed further by Albert Einstein, the photon can also be conceived of as "the most simple, most undecomposable, most homogenous essence that we know."

What do these fascinating developments of modern optics have to do with Goethe's *Farbenlehre?* Is this not 'reading into' it things of which the author would have never thought? Of course one can see it that way. But Newtonian physics also led to diverse discoveries and technical developments, from the discovery of the planet Uranus to the Mars rockets, of which Newton certainly also never thought. Nevertheless, he is rightfully honored as a significant pioneer of modern physics and optics, without whose fundamental insights further development would not have been possible.

A commonly held opinion regarding the significance of contributions in the past could be called the 'Berlin Wall Model' of scientific knowledge. In this model, individual disciplines exist in which theories (special ideas) and practice (special areas of experience) are interconnected. Scientists in theoretical optics speak with those in applied optics (at least sometimes); poets speak with professors of literary criticism; internists speak with microbiologists. However, significant exchange between more distant disciplines (e.g. scientists in optics on one side and literary critics on the other) generally does not occur. In the 'Berlin Wall Model,' it is quite unthinkable that Goethe's theory of colors could have had a significant influence of some kind on the scientific thinking of a physicist. According to this idea, Hermann von Helmholtz, Max Planck, Werner Heisenberg, Niels Bohr, Erwin Schrödinger, and Albert Einstein could well have known of Goethe's theory of colors, but it could never have had a stimulating influence on their scientific thinking.

There is also the opposing view, which is, however, generally only held by relatively 'unsuccessful' scientists, for example, many Nobel Prize holders. One could call it the 'Limes Model,' borrowing from the fortifications that formed the borders of the Roman Empire for hundreds of years. In the 'Limes Model,' the individual scientific areas mentioned above still exist. Again, there is normally little contact between distant disciplines. Yet, between their territories there exist individual gateways, like with the Limes, through which in times of peace active trading took place between Romans over here and Germanic people on the other side. In this 'Limes Model,' it is possible that experiences in one area can be useful for another discipline when suitably metamorphosed.

Die Entwicklung der superauflösenden Lichtmikroskopie ist ein aktuelles Beispiel für die Feststellung Goethes im *Märchen:* »Welches ist das wichtigste [Geheimnis]?« – »Das offenbare [...].« Diesen Aphorismus könnte man im Hinblick auf wissenschaftliche Erkenntnis auch so umschreiben: »Was ist am Schwersten zu erkennen? – Das Offenbare.«

Goethes Anregungen finden sich auch auf anderen Gebieten der Entwicklung der modernen Optik und Atomphysik wieder. Während Newton und Huygens versuchten, das Licht auf kleine materielle Teilchen zurückzuführen, wird dies von Goethe vehement abgelehnt. In Goethes Credo ist Licht eine grundlegende Erscheinung der Natur, ein Urphänomen, das grundsätzlich nicht durch kleine polarisierte Kügelchen/Würfel oder mechanische Ätherschwingungen erklärt werden kann, sondern es gilt ihm das Grundpostulat: »Das Licht ist das einfachste, unzerlegteste, homogenste Wesen, das wir kennen. Es ist nicht zusammengesetzt.« (Johann Wolfgang Goethe, Lager bei Marienborn, den 15. Juli 1793.) Diese Auffassung des Lichtes als eines elementaren, nichtreduzierbaren Naturphänomens kommt der modernen Theorie des Lichts sehr viel näher als eine naive Teilchentheorie oder als mechanische Ätherschwingungen. Auch in der modernen, im Jahre 1900 von Max Planck begründeten und von Albert Einstein weitergeführten Quantentheorie des Lichts kann das Photon aufgefasst werden als »das einfachste, unzerlegteste, homogenste Wesen, das wir kennen«.

Was haben diese faszinierenden Entwicklungen der modernen Optik mit Goethes *Farbenlehre* zu tun? Ist das nicht ein ›Hinein-Interpretieren‹ von Dingen, an die der Autor nie im Leben gedacht hat? Natürlich kann man das so sehen. Aber auch die Newton'sche Physik hat zu vielfältigen Entdeckungen und technischen Fortschritten geführt, von der Entdeckung des Planeten Uranos bis zu den Mars-Raketen, an die Newton sicher ebenfalls niemals dachte. Dennoch wird er mit Recht als wesentlicher Pionier der modernen Physik und Optik gewürdigt, ohne dessen grundlegende Erkenntnisse die weitere Entwicklung nicht möglich gewesen wäre.

Eine vielfach vertretene Meinung zur Bedeutung von Beiträgen der Vergangenheit könnte man als das ›Berlin-Wall-Modell‹ der wissenschaftlichen Erkenntnis bezeichnen. Darin gibt es einzelne Fachdisziplinen, in denen Theorie (spezielle Ideen) und Praxis (spezielle Erfahrungsgebiete) jeweils miteinander verbunden sind: Experten der Theoretischen reden mit solchen der Angewandten Optik (zumindest manchmal), Dichter mit Germanistik-Professoren, Internisten mit Mikrobiologen. Ein relevanter Austausch zwischen weiter entfernten Disziplinen (zum Beispiel Optik auf der einen, Germanistik auf der anderen Seite) kommt jedoch meist nicht zustande. Im ›Berlin-Wall-Modell‹ ist es ziemlich undenkbar, dass die Farbenlehre Goethes irgendeinen bedeutsamen Einfluss auf das wissenschaftliche Denken eines Physikers oder das technische Handeln eines Industriepioniers gehabt haben könnte. Hermann von Helmholtz, Max Planck, Werner Heisenberg, Niels Bohr, Erwin Schrödinger und Albert Einstein mögen die Farbenlehre Goethes gut gekannt haben, einen anregenden Einfluss auf ihr wissenschaftliches Denken kann sie nicht gehabt haben, so diese Meinung.

Es gibt jedoch auch die gegenteilige Ansicht, die aber oftmals nur von relativ ›erfolglosen‹ Wissenschaftlern vertreten wird, wie zum Beispiel von vielen Nobelpreisträgern. Man könnte sie als das ›Limes-Modell‹ bezeichnen, in Anlehnung an die Befestigungen, die

Goethe was probably a believer in the 'Limes Model.' He was a great advocate of interdisciplinary research. In the theory of colors it was his great desire to establish a color academy in which all the individual disciplines could work together: "I would have made use of a philosopher, a physicist, a mathematician, a painter, an engineer, a dyer, and God knows whom else" (J.W. Goethe, *Poetry and Truth)*. This vision of Goethe's is more relevant today than ever before. The motto of such an institution that would continue Goethe's intentions with the means of modern science could be: "The colours are acts of light; its active and passive modifications."[2]

2 Further reading: Christoph Cremer, "Vorstoß in den Nanokosmos: Neue Mikroskope überschreiten für bislang unüberwindlich gehaltene Grenzen;" *Ruperto Carola Forschungsmagazin der Universität Heidelberg* 3 (2008), pp. 4–12; idem, "Lokalisationsmikroskopie – Lichtmikroskopie unterhalb des Abbe-Limits," *Physik in unserer Zeit* 42 (2011), pp. 21–29; idem, "Mikroskope und Mikroben," in *Viren und andere Mikroben: Heil oder Plage? Zum 100. Todestag von Robert Koch,* ed. Karlheinz Sonntag. Heidelberg, 2011, pp. 99–135; idem et al., "Superresolution Imaging of Biological Nanostructures by Spectral Precision Distance Microscopy." *Biotechnology* 6 (2011), pp. 1037–51; idem and B. R. Masters, "Resolution Enhancement Techniques in Microscopy," *The European Physical Journal,* no. 38 (2013), pp. 281–344; idem et al., "Superresolution Microscopy Approaches to Nuclear Nanostructure Imaging," *Methods,* 123 (2017), pp. 11–32; Thomas Cremer, et al. "Chromosomenterritorien und Chromatindomänen," *Biologie in unserer Zeit* 5 (2016), 290–99; Otto Krätz, *Goethe und die Naturwissenschaften*. Munich, 1998. Katharina Mommsen, ed., *Die Entstehung von Goethes Werken in Dokumenten, Bd. IV: Entstehen – Farbenlehre*. Berlin, 2010. For further information see *www.optics.imb-mainz.de.*

jahrhundertelang die Grenze des Imperium Romanum bildeten. Normalerweise gibt es auch hier nur wenige Kontakte zwischen weiter entfernten Disziplinen. Dennoch existieren zwischen ihren Territorien einzelne Tore, wie beim Limes, wo in Friedenszeiten reger Handel zwischen römischem Hüben und germanischem Drüben betrieben wurde. In diesem ›Limes-Modell‹ kann es vorkommen, dass Erfahrungen auf dem einen Gebiet in geeigneter Metamorphose auch für die andere Disziplin nutzbar werden.

Goethe dürfte ein Anhänger des ›Limes-Modells‹ gewesen sein. Er war ein großer Befürworter von Interdisziplinarität. In der Farbenlehre war es sein großer Wunsch, eine Farbenakademie zu errichten, in der alle Einzeldisziplinen zusammenarbeiten sollten: »Ich hatte den Philosophen, den Physiker, Mathematiker, Maler, Mechaniker, Färber und Gott weiß wen alles in Anspruch genommen [...].« (Johann Wolfgang Goethe, *Dichtung und Wahrheit).* Diese Vision Goethes ist heute aktueller denn je. Motto einer solchen, Goethes Intentionen mit den Mitteln der modernen Wissenschaft fortsetzenden Institution könnte die immer noch lebendig wirksame Erkenntnis des Dichters und Naturforschers Goethe sein: »Die Farben sind Taten des Lichts, Taten und Leiden«.[2]

2 Weiterführende Literatur: Christoph Cremer, »Vorstoß in den Nanokosmos: Neue Mikroskope überschreiten für unüberwindlich gehaltene Grenzen", in: *Ruperto Carola,* Forschungsmagazin Universität Heidelberg, 3, 2008, S. 4–21; ders.: »Lokalisationsmikroskopie. Lichtmikroskopie unterhalb des Abbe-Limits«, in: *Physik in unserer Zeit,* 42, 1, Januar 2011, S. 21–29; ders.: »Mikroskope und Mikroben«, in: Karlheinz Sonntag (Hrsg.): *Viren und andere Mikroben: Heil oder Plage? Zum 100. Todestag von Robert Koch,* Heidelberg 2011, S. 99–135; ders. u. a., »Superresolution Imaging of Biological Nanostructures by Spectral Precision Distance Microscopy«, in: *Biotechnology Journal,* 6, 9, September 2011, S. 1037–1051; ders. und Barry R. Masters, »Resolution Enhancement Techniques in Microscopy«, in: *The European Physical Journal H,* 38, 3, April 2013, S. 281–244; Udo J. Birk u. a., »Super-Resolution Microscopy approaches to Nuclear Nanostructure Imaging«, in: *Methods,* 123, Juli 2017, S. 11-32; Christoph Cremer u. a., »Der Zellkern – eine Stadt in der Zelle, Teil 1: Chromosomenterritorien und Chromatindomänen«, in: *Biologie in unserer Zeit,* 46, 5, Oktober 2016, S. 290–299; Otto Krätz, *Goethe und die Naturwissenschaften,* München 1998; Katharina Mommsen (Hrsg.): *Die Entstehung von Goethes Werken in Dokumenten,* Bd. 4: Entstehen – Farbenlehre, Berlin 2008; für weitere Informationen s. www.optics.imb-mainz.de

STRUKTUR UND MORPHOLOGIE

STRUCTURE AND MORPHOLOGY

»Bedeutend hab' ich immer die Betrachtung gefunden, die uns das makro-mikromegische Verfahren der Natur einzusehen fähig macht: denn diese thut nichts im Großen was sie nicht auch im Kleinen thäte, bewirkt nichts im Verborgenen was sie nicht auch am Tageslicht offenbarte.«

"I have always found it meaningful to reflect upon the insights which result from contemplating how natural processes occur on both micro and macro levels, because nature does not do anything on a large scale that it would not do on a small scale, and does nothing in secret that it would not reveal in daylight."
GOETHE

»Das korrespondiert mit der Naturwissenschaft, die ja heute auch nicht mehr die Natur beschreibt, die man draußen vor der Haustür fotografieren kann, sondern alles durch das Elektronenrastermikroskop sieht und den Nanobereich erforscht. Diese Dialektik der Struktur, in der das einzelne Element nur das Gesamte vertritt, finde ich unglaublich aufregend. Das Eine vertritt das Ganze, aber auch das Ganze ist im Einen schon präsent.«

"This corresponds with the natural sciences, which nowadays, of course, no longer describe nature that you can photograph from your front door, but rather that which can be seen through an electron microscope and which can only be discovered in the nano-realm. I find this dialectic of structure incredibly exciting. The one element represents the whole, but the whole is already present in the one."
MACK

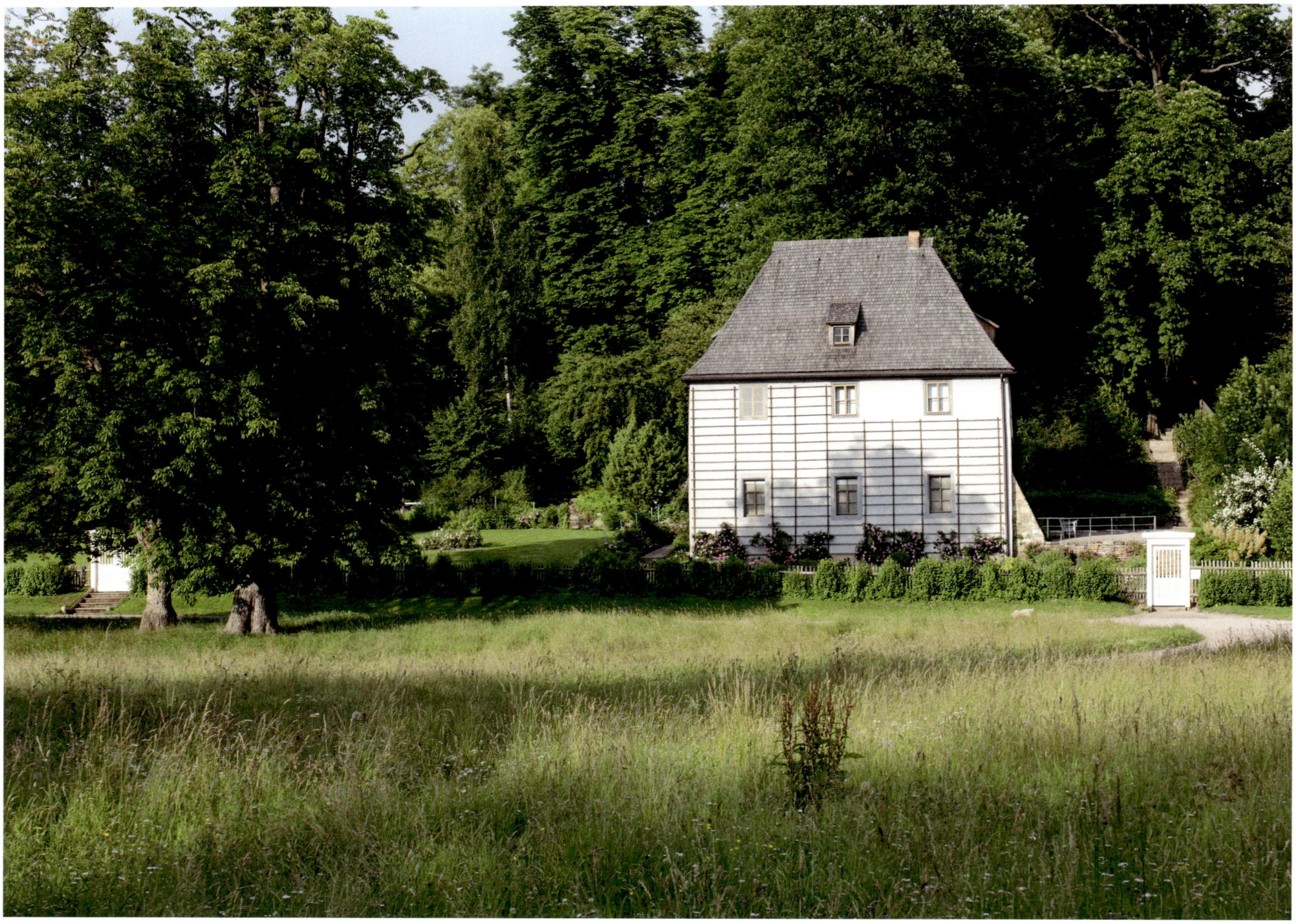

1 Goethes Gartenhaus am Stern (Wegekreuz) im Park an der Ilm in Weimar
Wenige Monate nach Goethes Eintreffen in Weimar schenkte Herzog Carl August ihm das vermutlich gegen Ende des 16. Jahrhunderts als Weinberghaus erbaute Gebäude und den dazugehörigen 9.700 m² großen Garten, den der Dichter nach seinen Vorstellungen umgestaltete. Bis zum Umzug an den Frauenplan 1782 war das Gartenhaus sein ständiger Wohnsitz. Später diente es ihm als Rückzugsort.

1 Goethe's Garden House in the Park an der Ilm (a large, landscaped park situated on the river Ilm) in Weimar.
A few months after Goethe's arrival in Weimar, Duke Carl August gifted him the building and the associated 9,700 m² garden which Goethe redesigned. The house was probably built toward the end of the 16th century as a vineyard house. Until his 1782 move to Frauenplan Square in Weimar, the Garden House was Goethe's permanent residence. Later, it served as a retreat.

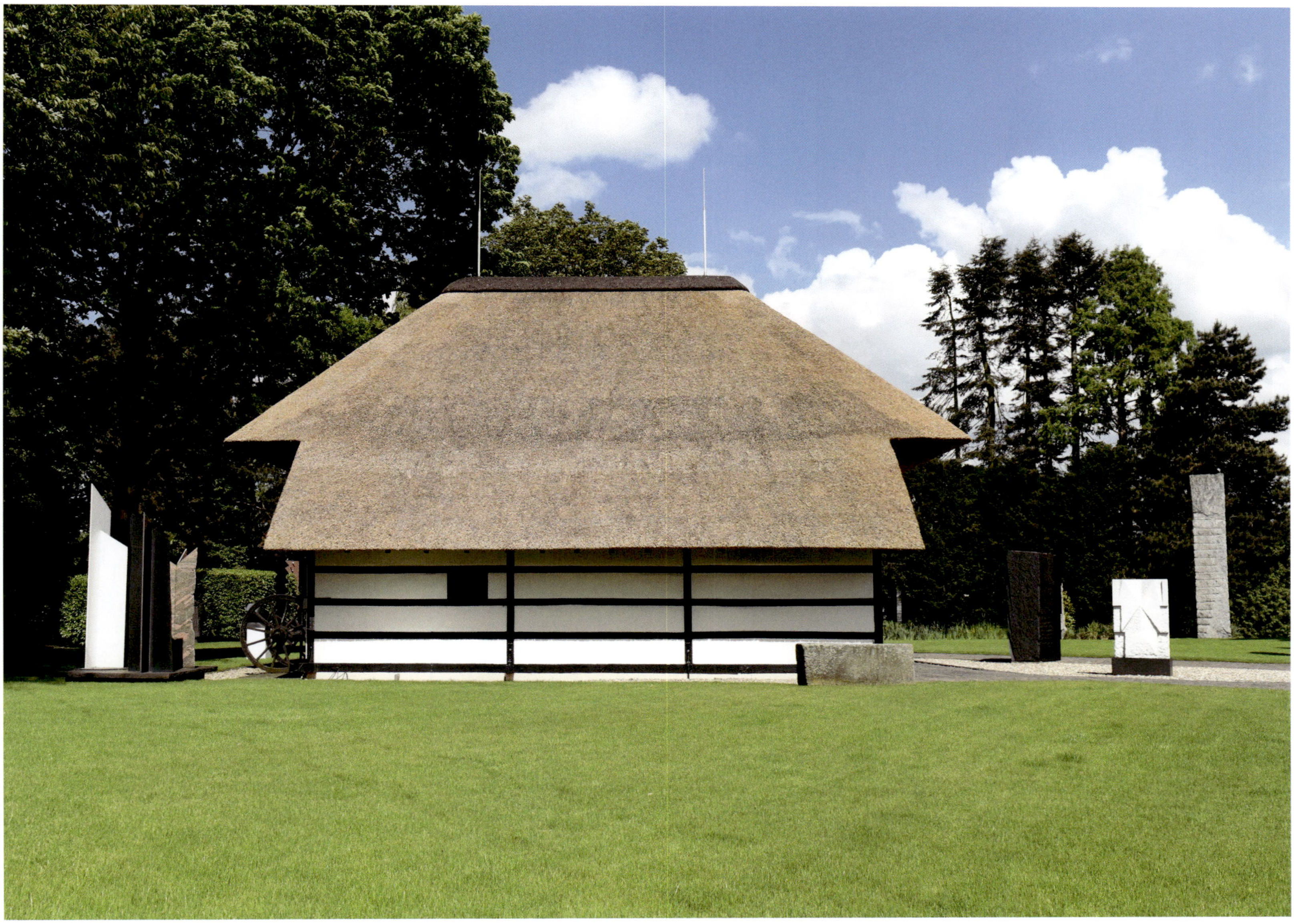

2 Heinz Macks Huppertzhof in Mönchengladbach, Nebengebäude
Das Haupthaus der aus drei Gebäuden bestehenden offenen Hofanlage stammt – wie Goethes Gartenhaus aus dem 16. Jahrhundert, der umgebende Garten, der vom Künstler in einen Skulpturenpark umgewandelt wurde, ist mit 10.000 m^2 ungefähr so groß wie Goethes Garten am Stern. Hier lebt und arbeitet Heinz Mack seit 1967, wenn er nicht gerade auf Ibiza weilt.

2 Heinz Mack's Huppertzhof in Mönchengladbach, outbuilding
The main building of three which surround an open courtyard is like Goethe's Garden House from the 16th Century. The surrounding garden was redesigned by the artist. At 10,000 m^2 around, it is roughly the same size as Goethe's garden and has been transformed by the artist into a sculpture park. Since 1967, this has been Heinz Mack's domicile where he has lived and worked, when he's not on Ibiza.

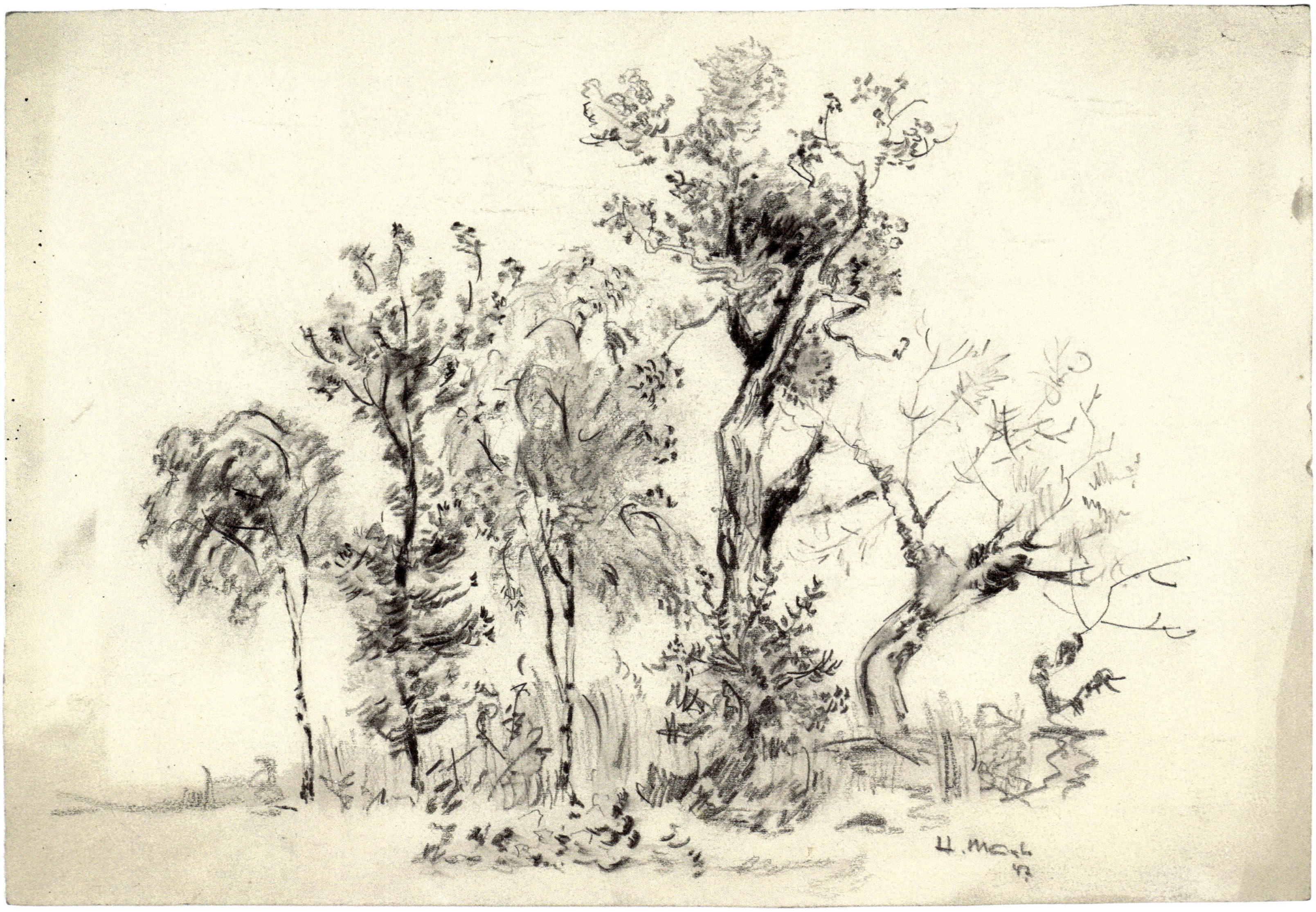

3 Heinz Mack
Ohne Titel
Signiert, datiert: »H. Mack 47«
Grafit auf Papier
22,5 x 32,5 cm

3 Heinz Mack
Untitled
Signed, dated: "H. Mack 47"
Graphite on paper
22.5 x 32.5 cm

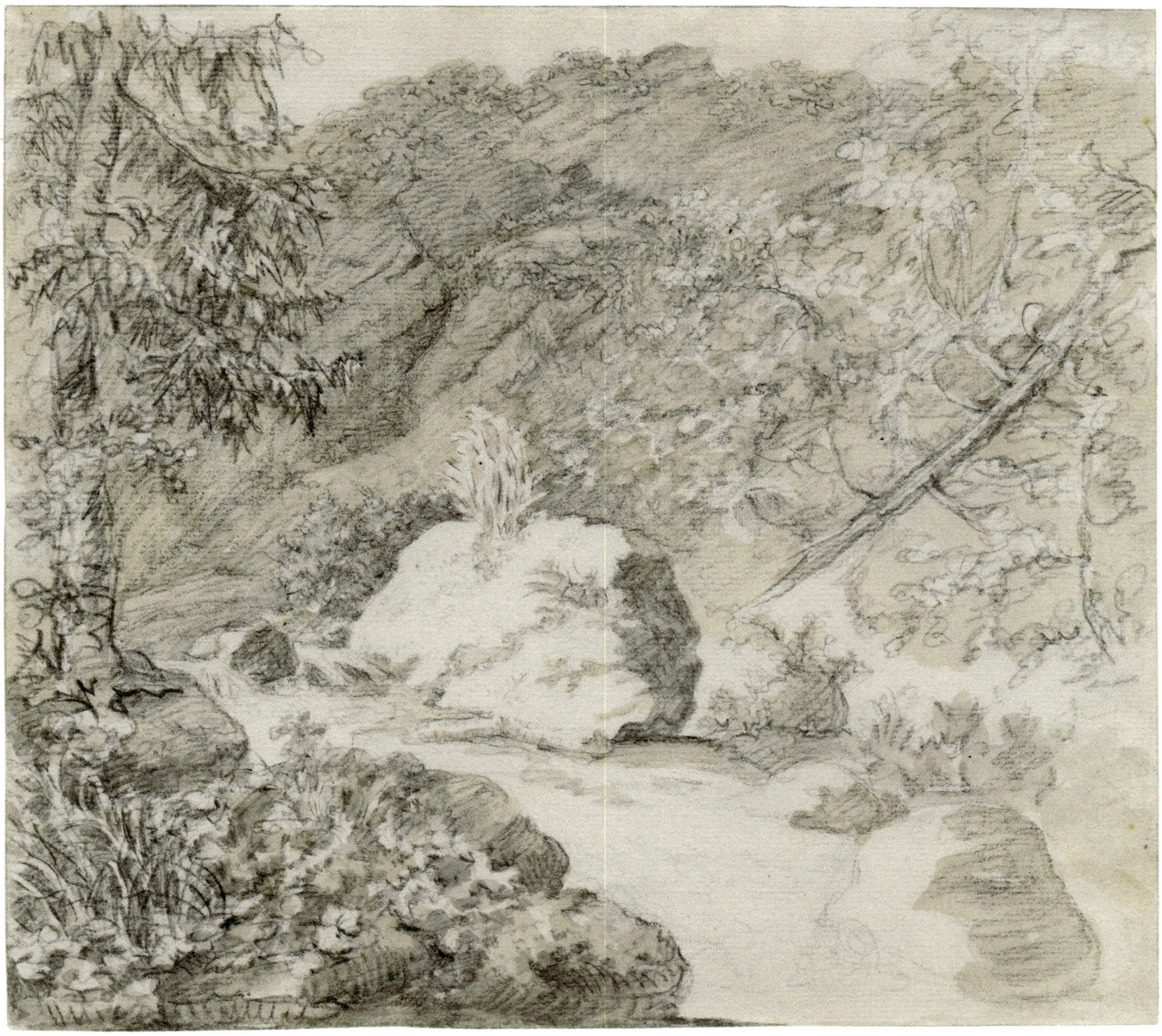

4 Johann Wolfgang von Goethe
Harzlandschaft am Oberlauf der Oker oder Bode
September 1784
Bleistift- und schwarze Kreide auf Papier, laviert und mit Weiß gehöht
24,8 x 27,5 cm
Goethe-Museum Düsseldorf

4 Johann Wolfgang von Goethe
Landscape of the Harz on the upper reaches of the Oker or Bode Rivers
September 1784
Pencil and black chalk on paper, washed and heightened with white
24.8 x 27.5 cm
Goethe-Museum Düsseldorf

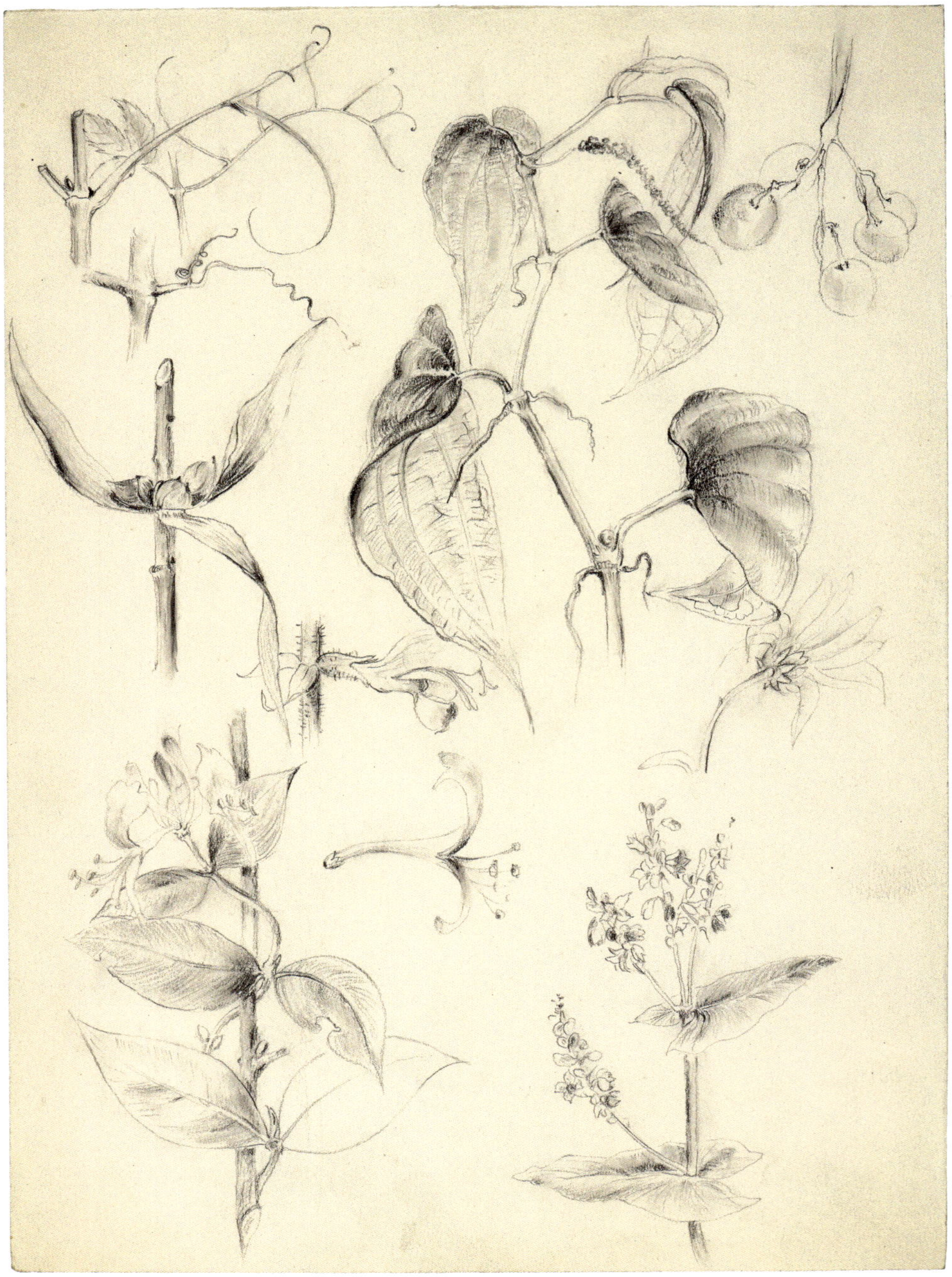

5 Heinz Mack
Ohne Titel
Um 1950
Grafit auf Papier
31 x 22,5 cm

5 Heinz Mack
Untitled
Ca. 1950
Graphite on paper
31 x 22.5 cm

6–8 Johann Wolfgang von Goethe
Weinreben
Datiert: »1828«
Feder in Schwarz auf graubräunlichem Papier
Doppelblatt, 3 S. mit Zeichnungen versehen
Auf einer Seite am Falz außerdem u. a. die Verse: »Schmerzlich trat ich hinein, getrost entfern ich mich wieder / Gönne dem Herren der Burg alles Erfreuliche Gott. 1828.«
33 x 20,3 cm (zugeklappt)
Klassik Stiftung Weimar, Goethe- und Schiller-Archiv
Signatur: GSA 26 / LV, 8
Die Ausstellung zeigt ein Faksimile.

Nachdem am 14. Juni 1828 Großherzog Carl August von Sachsen-Weimar-Eisenach gestorben war, zog sich Goethe von Juli bis September nach Dornburg zurück, um seine Trauer zu überwinden. Dort wohnte er im Renaissance-Schloss, einem der drei auf steilem Felsen mit Blick auf das Saaletal gelegenen kleinen Schlösser, und widmete sich morphologischen Zeichnungen von Weinreben und dem Studium des Weinbaus. »Die Aussicht ist herrlich und fröhlich«, schrieb er am 10. Juli 1828 an Zelter, »die Blumen blühen in den wohlunterhaltenen Gärten, die Traubengeländer sind reichlich behangen, und unter meinem Fenster seh ich einen wohlgediehenen

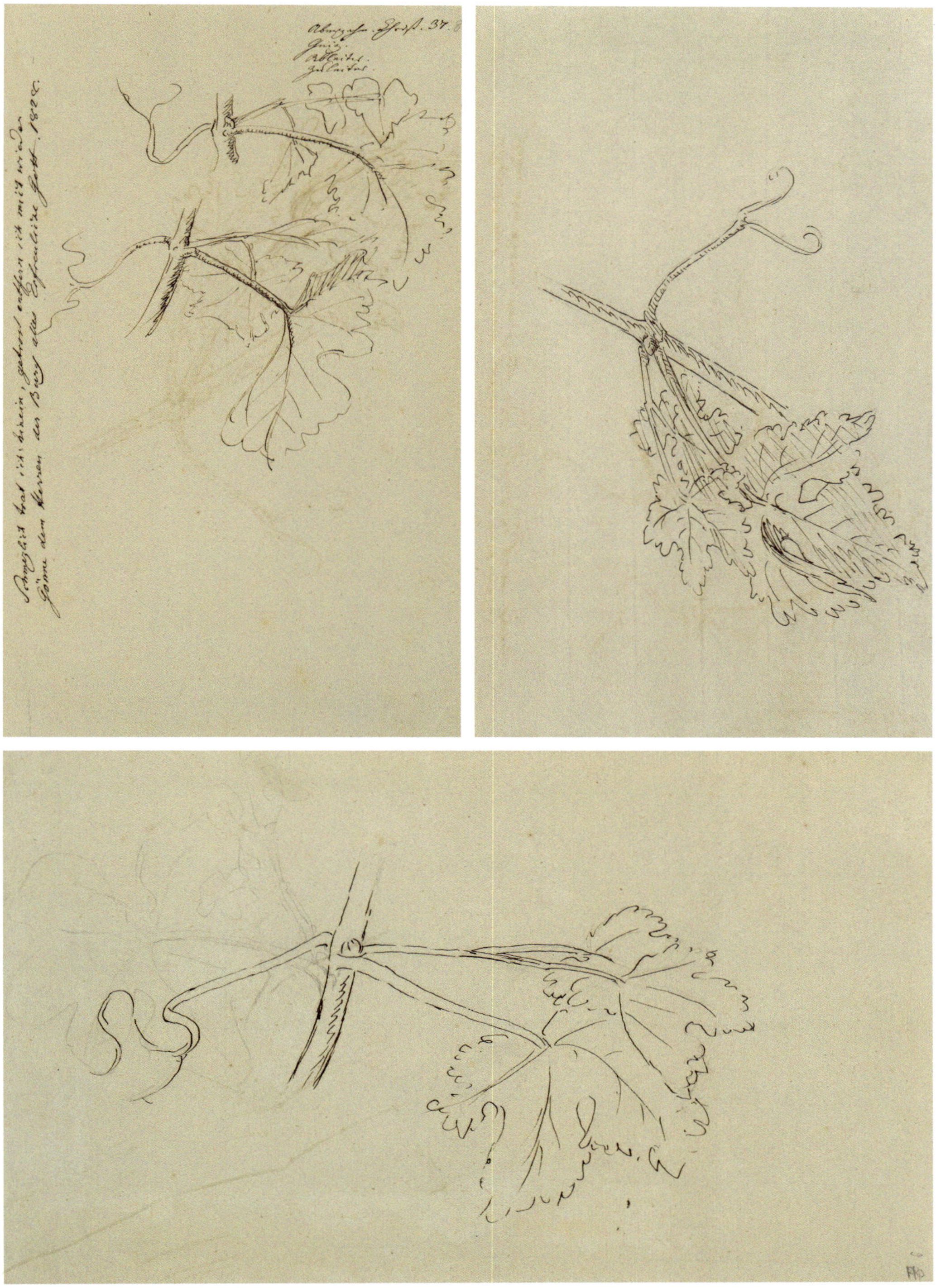

Weinberg, den der Verblichene [...] noch vor drey Jahren anlegen ließ [...] und mir erscheint das alles in erhöhteren Farben wie der Regenbogen auf schwarzgrauem Grunde«. Die lateinische Inschrift des Schlossportals: »Gaudeat ingrediens, laetetur et aede recedens, / His qui praeter eunt det bona cuncta Deus, 1608«, die Goethe übersetzt mit: »Freudig trete herein und froh entferne dich wieder! / Ziehst du als Wandrer vorbei, segne die Pfade dir Gott.« (WA, Bd. I 4, S. 338), inspirierte ihn zu den eigenen, seine Selbstheilung reflektierenden Versen. Vgl. Corpus, Bd. V B, S. 48.

6–8 Johann Wolfgang von Goethe
Grape vine
Dated: "1828"
Quill pen in black on gray-brown paper
Double sheet, 3 pages with drawings
On one page at the fold, amongst other things, the verse: "Painfully, I stepped inside, confidently I leave again / God grant the Lords of the Castle with all that is pleasing. 1828."
33 x 20.3 cm (closed)
Klassik Stiftung Weimar, Goethe- und Schiller-Archiv
Shelf mark: GSA 26 / LV, 8

After the death of Grand Duke Carl August of Saxe-Weimar-Eisenach on the 14th of June, 1828, Goethe retired to Dornburg where he remained from July until September in order to overcome his grief. There, he lived in the Renaissance era castle, one of three small castles on the steep cliffs overlooking the Saale Valley, devoting himself to studying viticulture and drawing morphological sketches of grape vines. "The view is glorious and joyful", he wrote on July 10, 1828, in a letter to Zelter, "the flowers bloom in the well-kept gardens, the vineyards are richly laden, and under my window I see a well-to-do vineyard laid

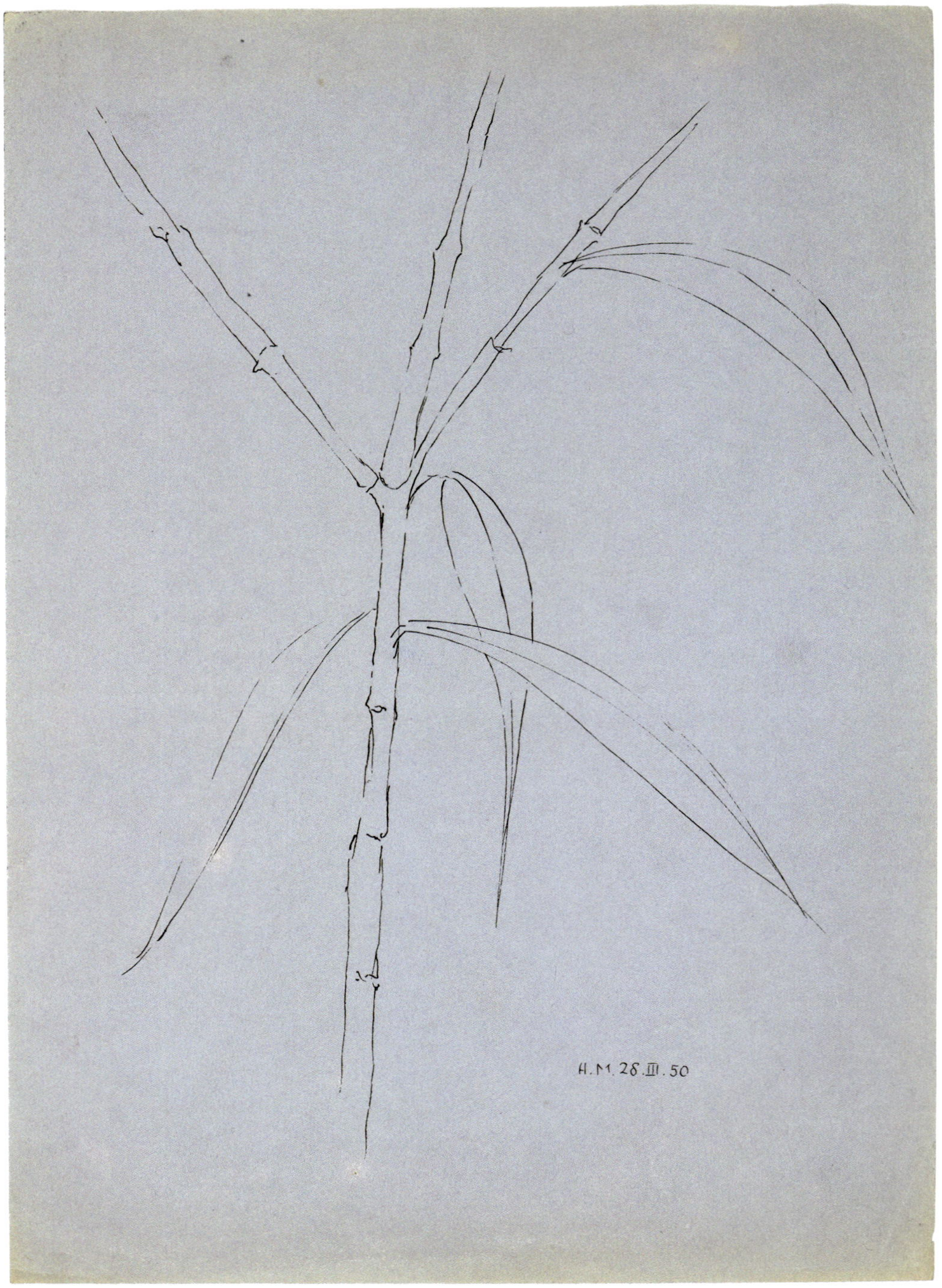

down by the deceased … just three years ago …, all of which seem to me to have colors as intense as a rainbow on a gray-black background." The Latin inscription above the castle portal: "Gaudeat ingrediens, laetetur et aede recedens / His qui praeter eunt det bona cuncta Deus, 1608." Goethe translated this as: "Step inside with joy and leave again happy! If you are passing by as a wanderer God bless your path", inspiring him to his own verses of self-healing. See Corpus, vol. V B, p. 48.

9 Heinz Mack
Ohne Titel
Signiert, datiert: »H. M. 28.III.50«
Tusche mit Rohrfeder auf Papier
29,5 x 21 cm

9 Heinz Mack
Untitled
Signed, dated: "H. M. 28.III.50"
Indian ink applied to paper with reed pen
29.5 x 21 cm

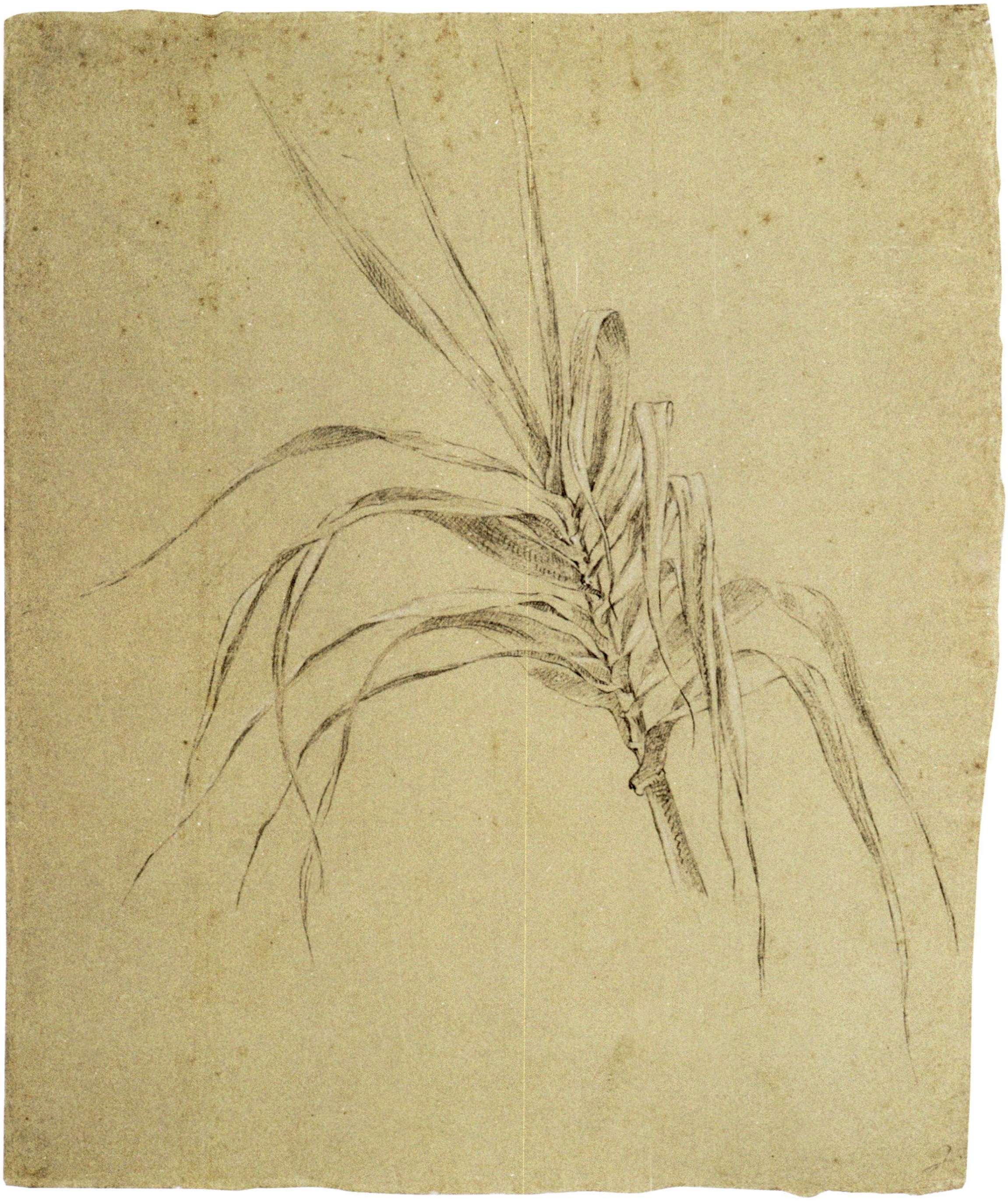

10 Johann Wolfgang von Goethe
Pflanzenskizze
Signiert: »G.«
Bleistift auf bräunlichem Zeichenpapier,
mit Kreide gehöht
43,2 x 35,8 cm
Klassik Stiftung Weimar, Museen
Die Ausstellung zeigt ein Faksimile.

Goethe hat sich zeitlebens für das Sammeln, die Beschreibung und die Erforschung von Pflanzen interessiert, auch im Zusammenhang mit seiner amtlichen Tätigkeit bei der Forst- und Gartenverwaltung. Die vorliegende Zeichnung ist wahrscheinlich 1787/88 in Italien entstanden.

10 Johann Wolfgang von Goethe
Plant sketch
Signed: "G."
Pencil on brownish drawing paper,
heightened with chalk
43.2 x 35.8 cm
Klassik Stiftung Weimar, Museen
The exhibition is displaying a facsimile.

Throughout his life, and in connection with his work as a civil servant in the Forestry and Garden Department, Goethe was interested in collecting, describing and conducting research of plants. This drawing was probably made in 1787/88 in Italy.

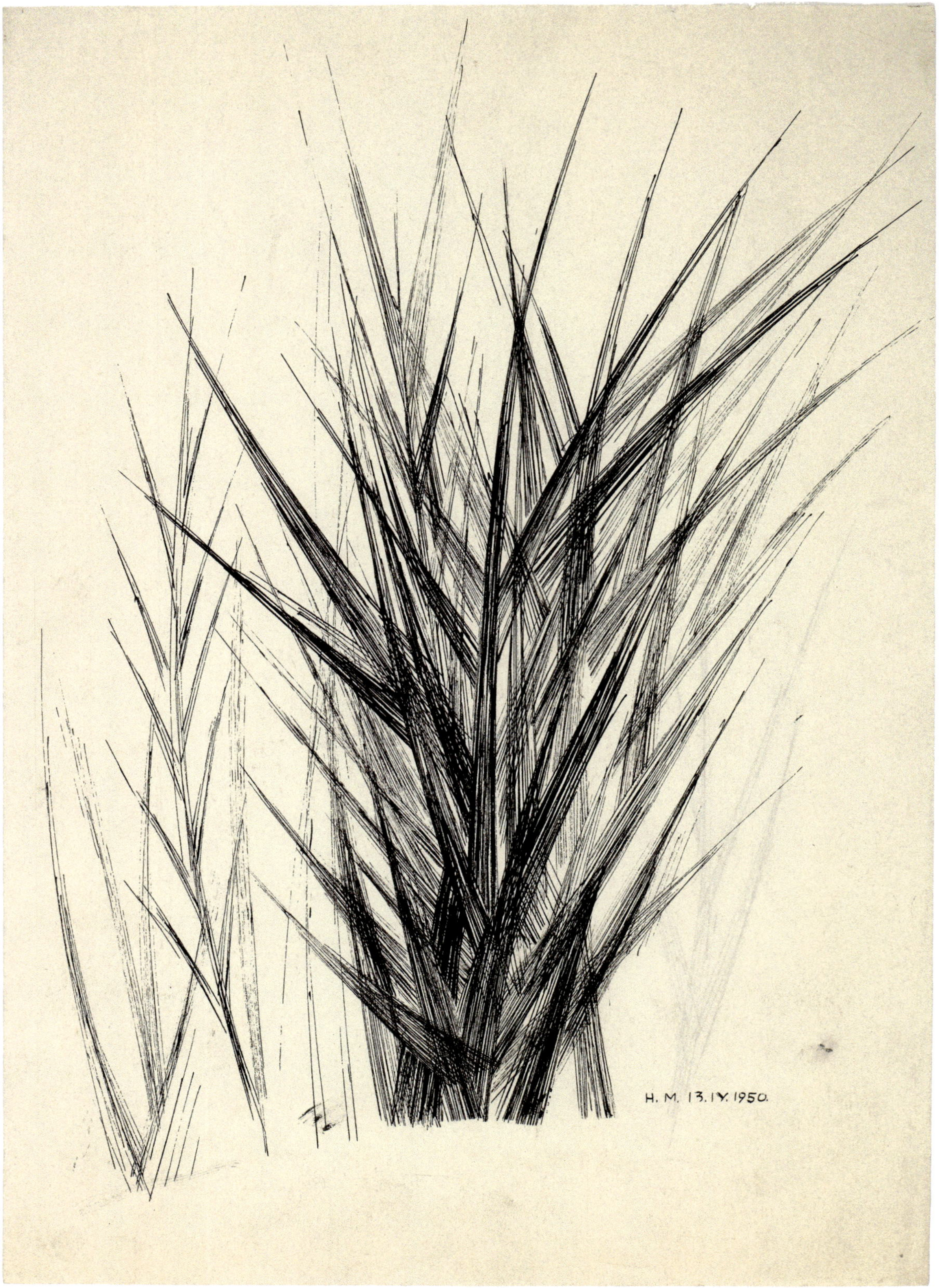

11 Heinz Mack
Ohne Titel
Signiert, datiert: »H. M. 13.IV.50.«
Tusche mit Rohrfeder auf Papier
29,5 x 21 cm

11 Heinz Mack
Untitled
Signed, dated: "H. M. 13.IV.50."
Indian ink applied to paper with reed pen
29.5 x 21 cm

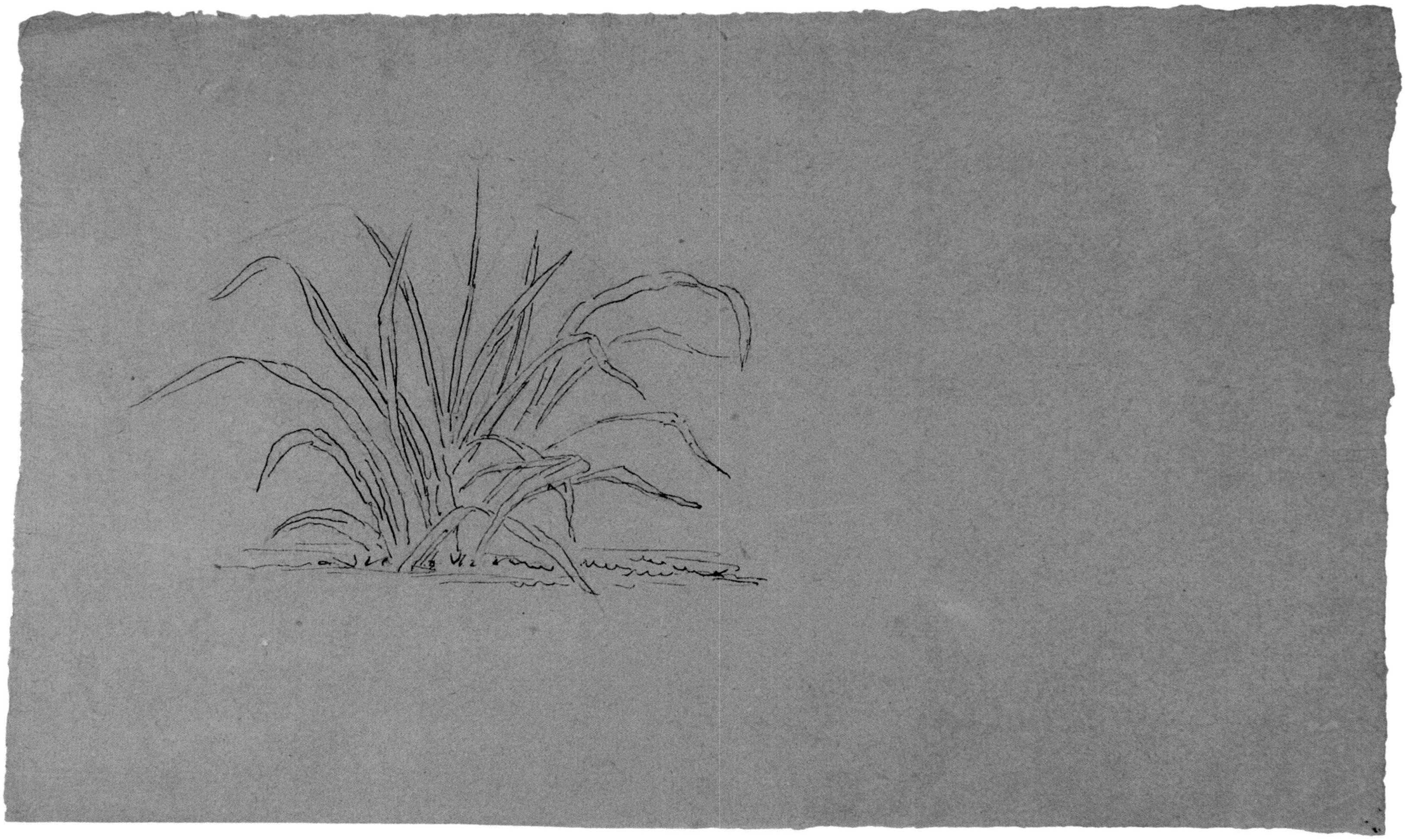

12 Johann Wolfgang von Goethe
Einkeimblättrige Pflanze
1812
Bleistift, Feder mit Tinte auf blauem Papier
20,9 x 34 cm
Klassik Stiftung Weimar, Museen

12 Johann Wolfgang von Goethe
Monocotyledonous plant
1812
Pencil, quill pen and ink on blue paper
20.9 x 34 cm
Klassik Stiftung Weimar, Museen

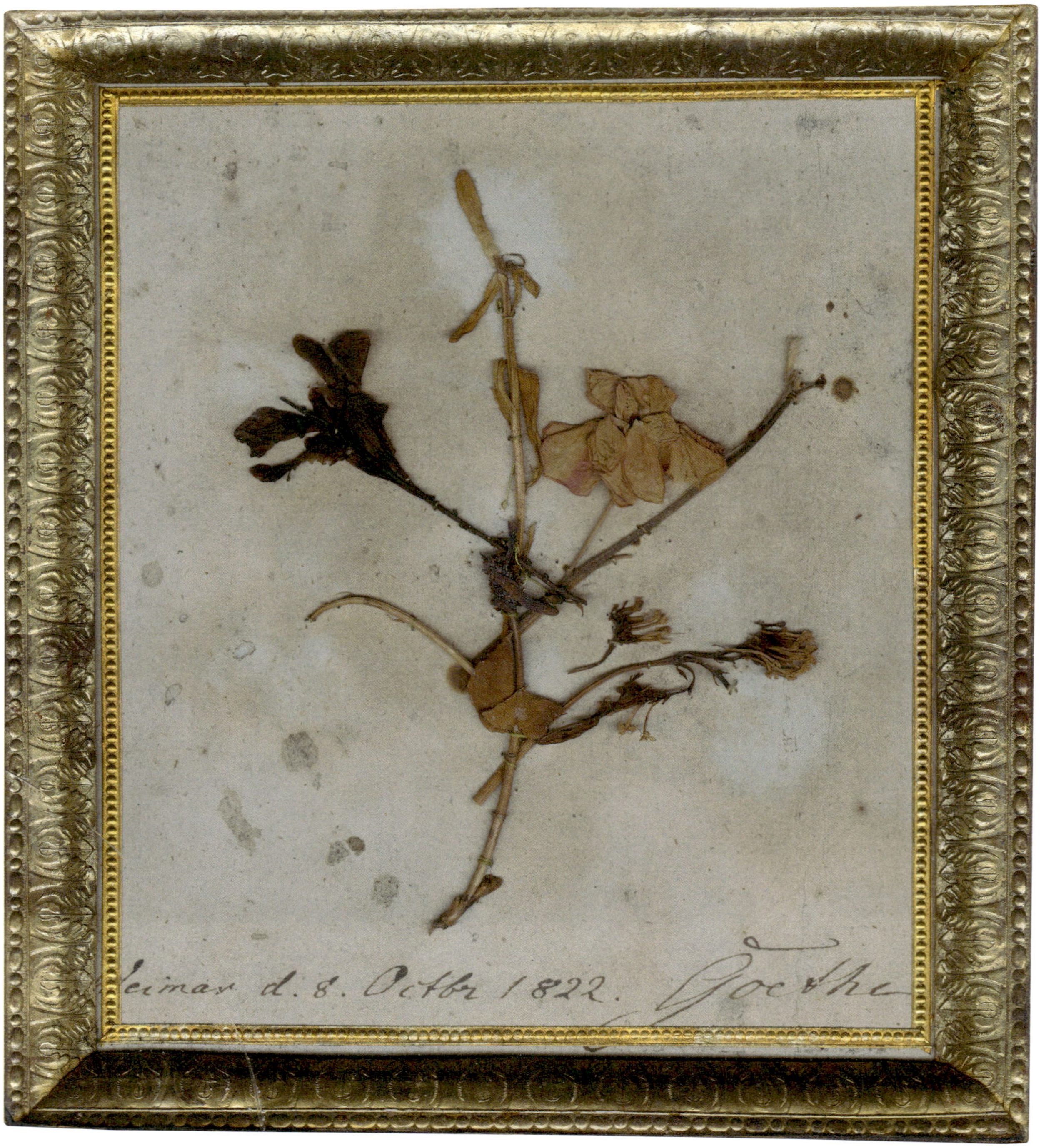

13 Johann Wolfgang von Goethe
Getrocknete Blumen auf Pappe
Signiert, datiert: »Weimar d. 8. Octbr 1822. Goethe«
21,2 x 19,7 cm
Goethe-Museum Düsseldorf

13 Johann Wolfgang von Goethe
Dried flowers on cardboard
Signed and dated: "Weimar d. 8. Octbr 1822. Goethe"
21.2 x 19.7 cm
Goethe-Museum Düsseldorf

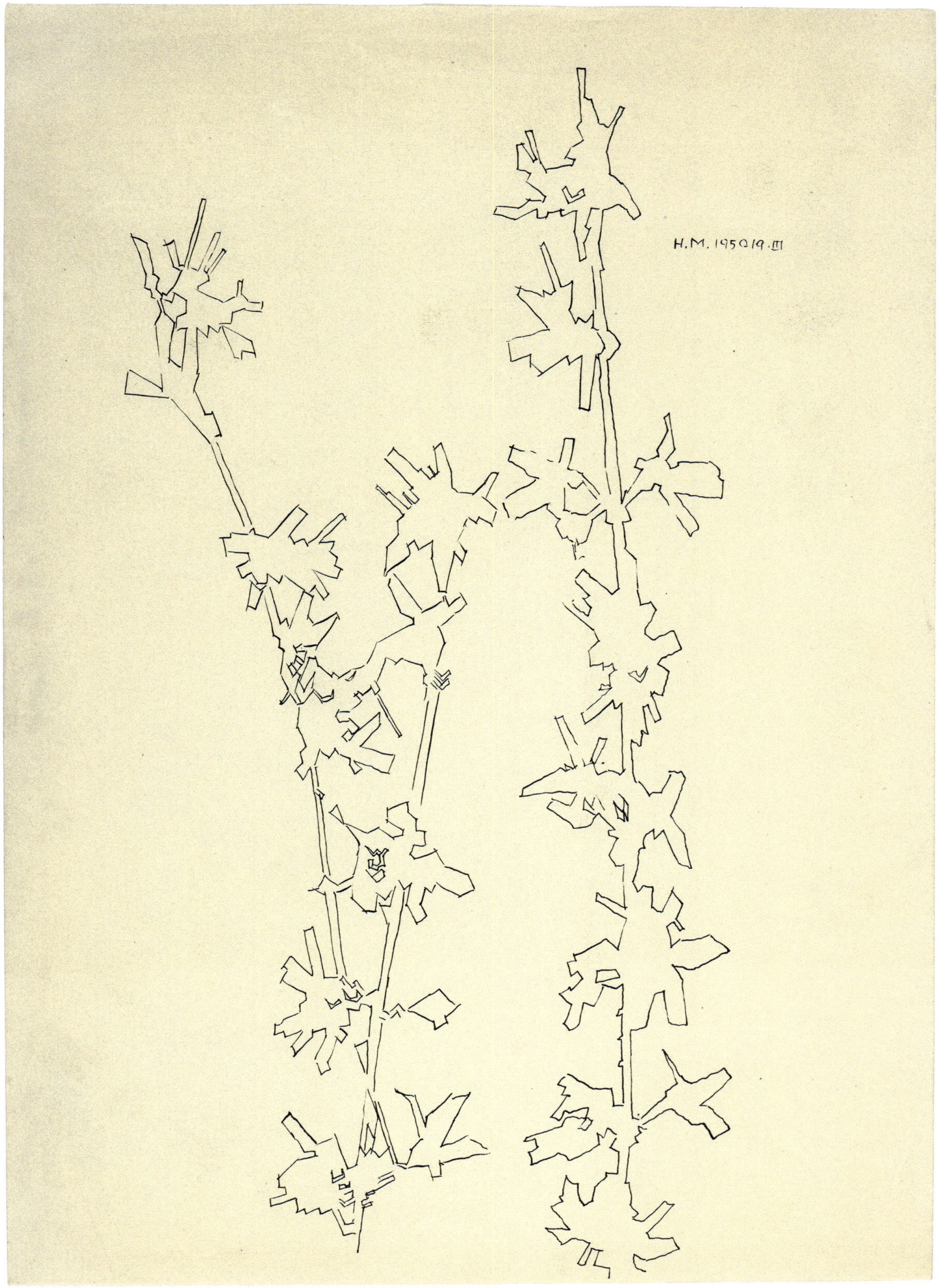

14 Heinz Mack
Ohne Titel
Signiert, datiert: »H. M. 1950 19.III«
Tusche mit Rohrfeder auf Papier
29,5 x 21 cm

14 Heinz Mack
Untitled
Signed, dated: "H. M. 1950 19.III"
Indian ink applied to paper with reed pen
29.5 x 21 cm

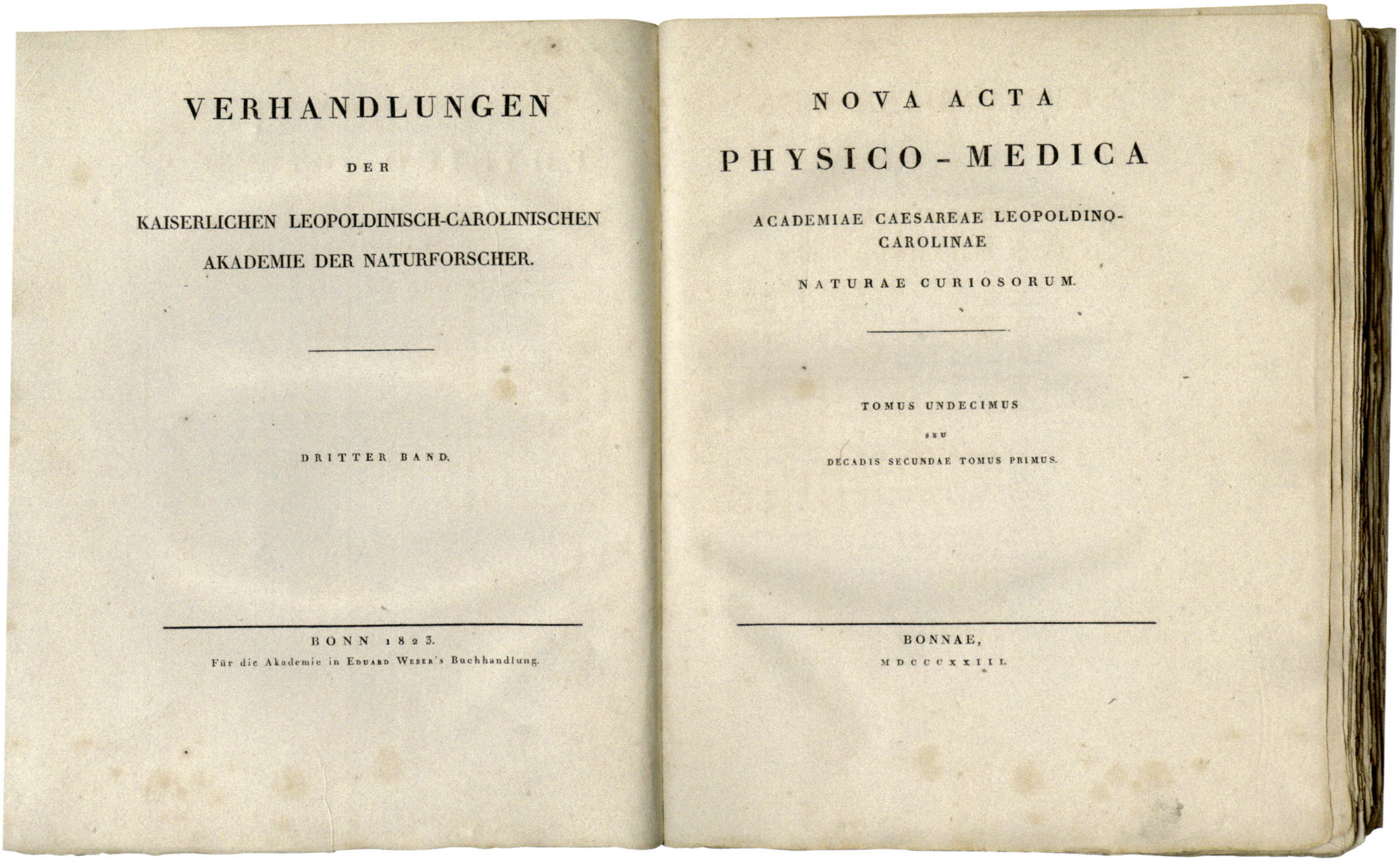

VERHANDLUNGEN

DER

KAISERLICHEN LEOPOLDINISCH-CAROLINISCHEN

AKADEMIE DER NATURFORSCHER.

DRITTER BAND.

BONN 1823.

Für die Akademie in Eduard Weber's Buchhandlung.

NOVA ACTA

PHYSICO-MEDICA

ACADEMIAE CAESAREAE LEOPOLDINO-CAROLINAE

NATURAE CURIOSORUM.

TOMUS UNDECIMUS

SEU

DECADIS SECUNDAE TOMUS PRIMUS.

BONNAE,

MDCCCXXIII.

15+16 *Göthea cauliflora N. et M.*
Kupferstich von Eduard Joseph d'Alton (1772–1840) nach Th. Wild
Tafel VIII in: *Verhandlungen der kaiserlichen Leopoldinisch-Carolinischen Akademie der Naturforscher,* Bd. 3, Bonn 1823.

1817 entdeckte Maximilian Prinz zu Wied-Neuwied (1782–1867) in Brasilien ein bislang unbekanntes Malvengewächs, das der Botaniker und Forschungsreisende Carl Friedrich Philipp von Martius (1794–1868) nach Deutschland brachte. Der mit Goethe bekannte Bonner Botaniker Christian Gottfried Daniel Nees von Esenbeck (1776–1858) nannte diese Pflanze *Goethea.* Martius und Nees von Esenbeck beschrieben die Neuentdeckung 1823 in den *Verhandlungen der kaiserlichen Leopoldinisch-Carolinischen Akademie der Naturforscher* unter dem Titel »Goethea, novum plantarum genus« (S. 89–103). Sie unterschieden die Arten ›semperflorens‹ (immerblühend) und ›cauliflora‹ (stammblütig). Goethe dankte Nees von Esenbeck in einem Brief vom 24. April 1823 dafür, dass »Sie mich bey so einer herrlich ausgezeichneten Pflanze zum Gevattersmann berufen und meinem Namen dadurch eine so schöne Stelle unter den wissenschaftlichen Gegenständen anweisen« (WA, Bd. IV 37, S. 27). Heute gibt es die Gattungsbezeichnung *Goethea* nicht mehr. Die beiden *Goethea*-Arten werden inzwischen der Gattung *Pavonia* zugeordnet. Vgl. LA, Bd. II 10 A, S. 454 f. und S. 606 f.

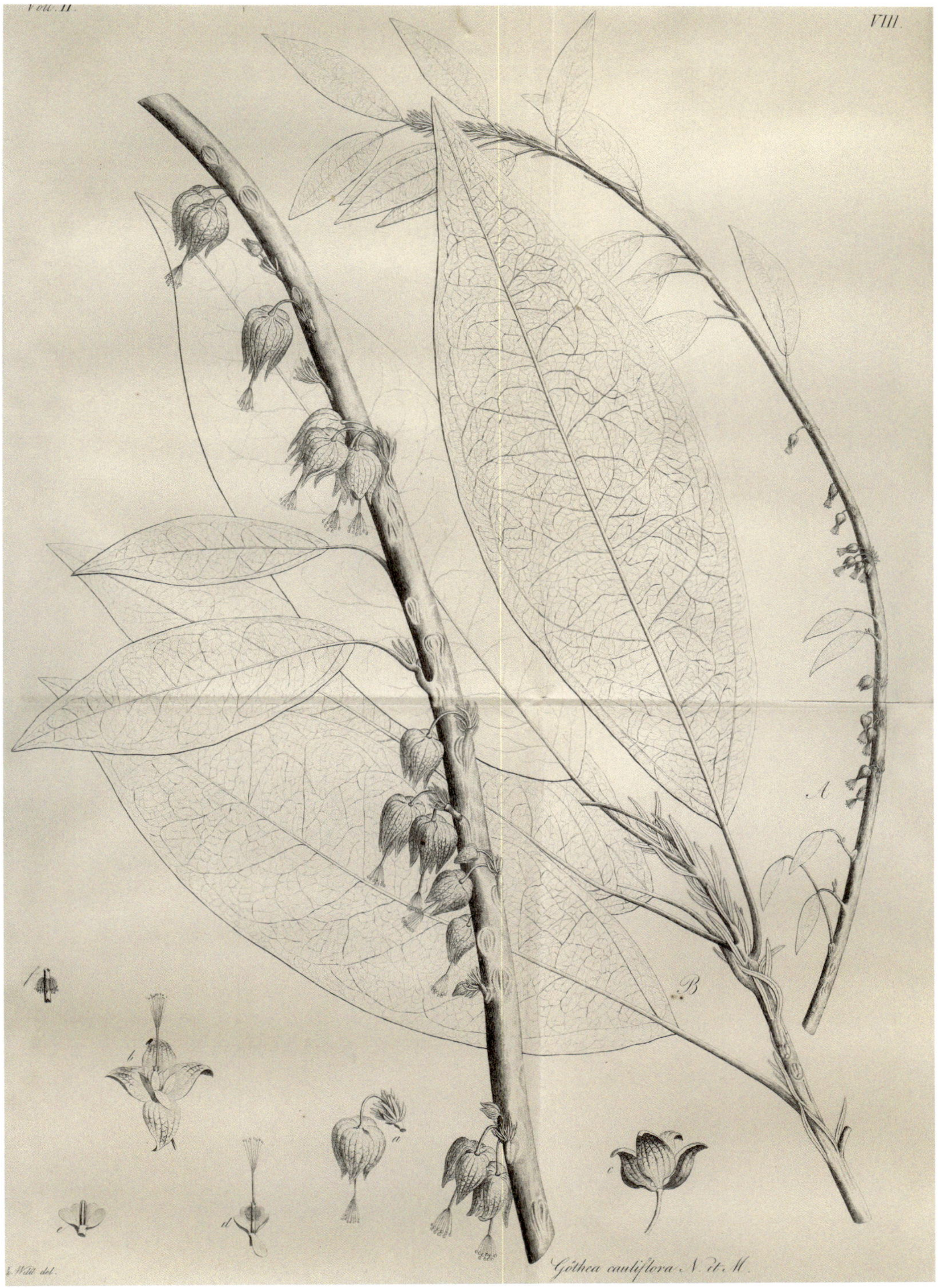

15+16 *Göthea cauliflora N. et M.*
Copper engraving by Eduard Joseph d'Alton (1772–1840) after Th. Wild
Fig. VIII in: *Verhandlungen der kaiserlichen Leopoldinisch-Carolinischen Akademie der Naturforscher,* vol. 3, Bonn, 1823.

In 1817 Maximilian, Prince of Wied-Neuwied (1782–1867) discovered a hitherto unknown type of mallow plant in Brazil, which was then transported Germany by the botanist and explorer Carl Friedrich Philipp von Martius (1794–1868). The botanist Christian Gottfried Daniel Nees von Esenbeck (1776–1858), who was acquainted with Goethe, then named the plant after him and introduced it under the title "Goethea, novum plantarum genus" (pp. 89–103). Martius and Nees von Esenbeck divided the species in two, 'semperflorens' (evergreen) and 'cauliflora' (stem-flowered). In a letter dated April 24th 1823 Goethe thanked Nees von Esenbeck for "making me the godfather of such a splendidly distinguished plant and thereby placing my name in a beautiful position amongst scientific objects." (WA, vol. IV 37, p. 27). Both of these species of *Goethea* are now assigned to the genus *Pavonia*. See LA, vol. II 10 A, pp. 454–55 and 606–07.

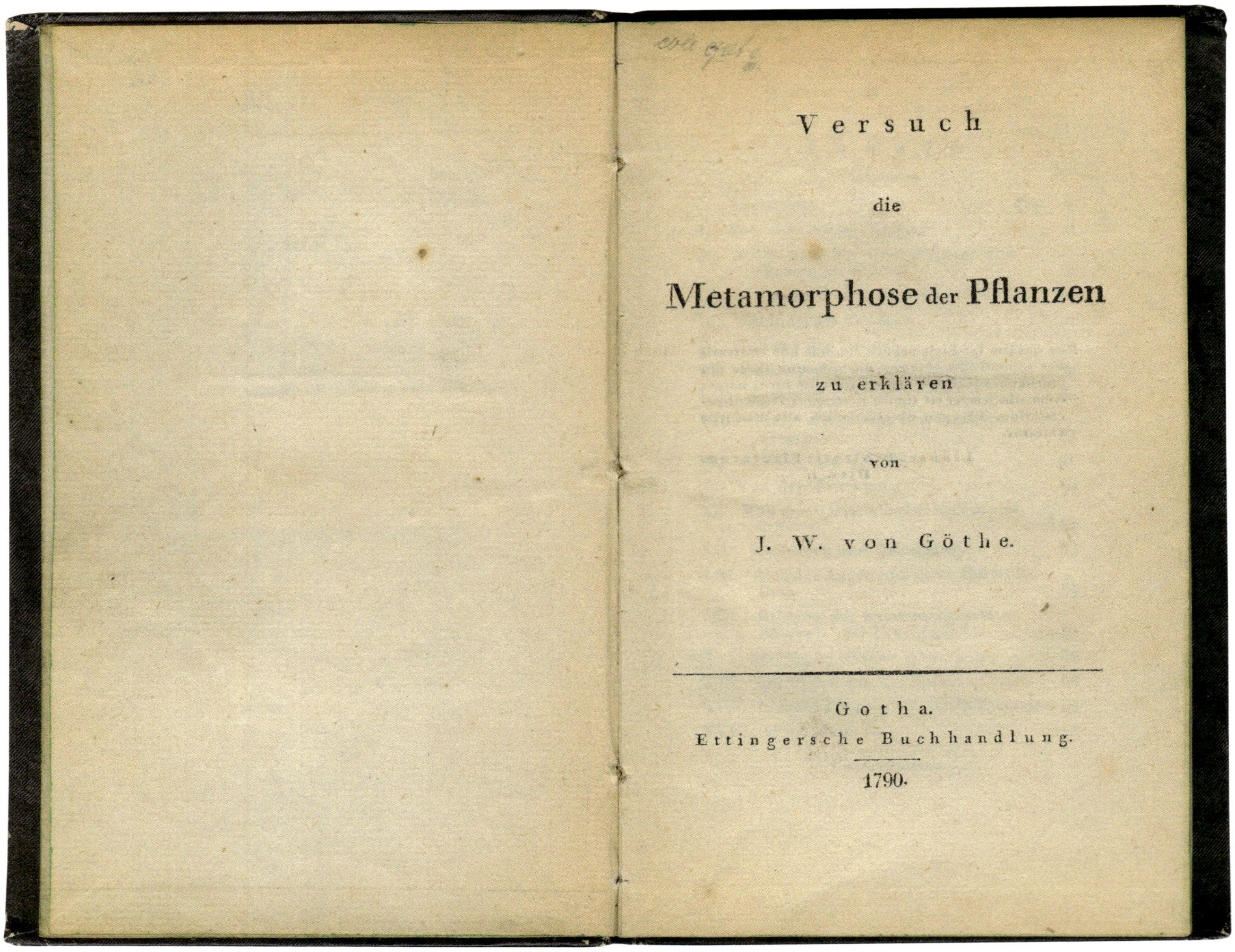

17 Johann Wolfgang von Goethe
J. W. von Goethe Herzoglich Sachsen-Weimarischen Geheimenraths
Versuch die Metamorphose der Pflanzen zu erklären. Gotha, bey Carl Wilhelm Ettinger. 1790.

17 Johann Wolfgang von Goethe
J. W. von Goethe Herzoglich Sachsen-Weimarischen Geheimenraths
Versuch die Metamorphose der Pflanzen zu erklären. Gotha, bey Carl Wilhelm Ettinger. 1790.

18 Johann Wolfgang von Goethe
Eigenhändige Notizen in lateinischer Sprache: »Metam[orphosis] radicis […]«
1 Blatt, 1 S. beschrieben; darunter und auf der Rückseite handschriftliche Echtheitsbestätigungen von Frédéric Soret
16,5 x 10,5 cm
Goethe-Museum Düsseldorf

In späteren Jahren hat sich Goethe mit der wissenschaftlichen Wirkung seiner Abhandlung *Versuch die Metamorphose der Pflanzen zu erklären* befasst. Er veröffentlichte dazu den Aufsatz »Wirkung dieser Schrift und weitere Entfaltung der darin vorgetragenen Idee« innerhalb einer deutsch-französischen Parallelausgabe seiner Abhandlung, die 1831 bei Cotta erschien und zu der Goethes Mitarbeiter Frédéric Jacob Soret (1795–1865) die Übertragung beisteuerte *(Versuch über die Metamorphose der Pflanzen / Essai sur la métamorphose des plantes)*. Goethes Notizen beziehen sich mit Seitenzahlen auf die Schrift *Elementa philosophiae botanicae* (Berlin 1824) des Universalgelehrten Heinrich Friedrich Link (1767–1851), der ab 1815 eine ordentliche Professur für Botanik an der Berliner Universität innehatte und zugleich Direktor des Botanischen Gartens war. (Link hatte schon 1813 zusammen mit Carl Joseph Hieronymus Windischmann Goethes Farbenlehre rezensiert.) Die Notizen sind eine Vorarbeit zu Goethes Aufsatz über die »Wirkung«, worin Goethe Links falsche »Belobung« der Goethe'schen Metamorphosenlehre verurteilte. Er kritisierte scharf Links Anlehnung an den Systematiker Carl von Linné (1707–1778) und dessen Konzept der Antizipation

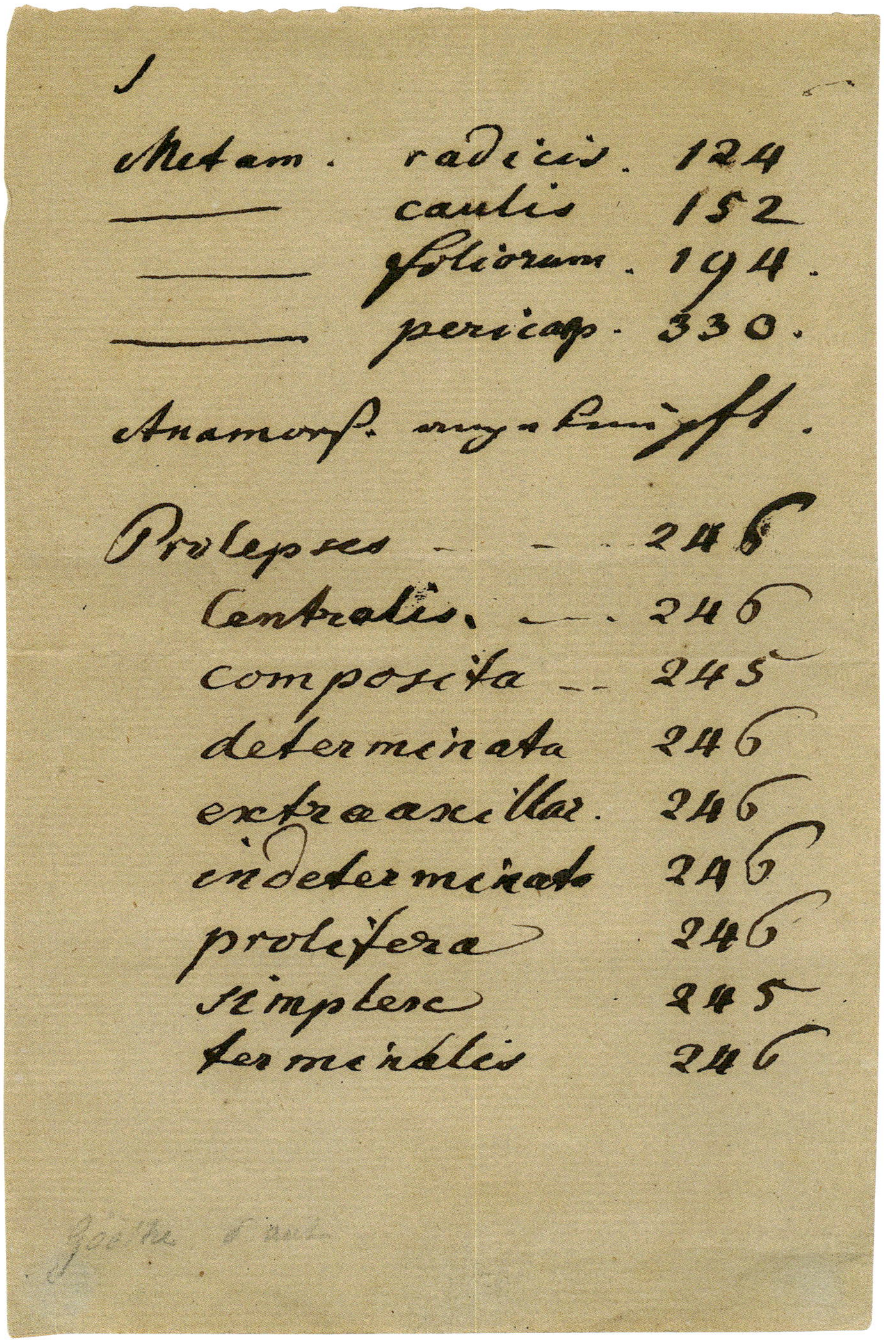

1

Metam. radicis. 124
——— caulis 152
——— foliorum. 194.
——— pericarp. 330.

Anamorph. [illegible]

Prolepses 246
Centralis. .. 246
composita .. 245
determinata 246
extraaxillar. 246
indeterminata 246
prolifera 246
simplex 245
terminalis 246

oder »prolepsis« (Vorwegnahme), der in der Botanik ein frühzeitiges Austreiben von Sprossen meint: »Genug! ja zuviel! Mit dem Irrtum sollte man nicht streiten, ihn anzudeuten möge hinreichen.« (LA, Bd. I 10, S. 308; vgl. LA, Bd. II 10 B/2, S. 950.)

18 Johann Wolfgang von Goethe
Notes in his own hand in Latin:
"Metam[orphosis] radicis …"
1 sheet, 1 page written; here below and on the reverse side, handwritten statements of authenticity by Frédéric Soret
16.5 x 10.5 cm
Goethe-Museum Düsseldorf

In his later years Goethe occupied himself with the impact of his scientific treatise *The Metamorphosis of Plants*. He published an essay in connection with this called "Wirkung dieser Schrift und weitere Entfaltung der darin vorgetragenen Idee" (The Effect of These Writings and Further Development of the Ideas Presented Therein) within an 1831 parallel German-French version of the treatise *(Versuch über die Metamorphose der Pflanzen / Essai sur la métamorphose des plantes)*, translated by Frédéric Jacob Soret (1795–1865). Goethe's notes refer to page numbers of *Elementa philosophiae botanicae* (Berlin 1824) by Heinrich Friedrich Link (1767–1851), a polymath, who from 1815 held a professorship in botany at the University of Berlin and was also director of the botanical garden. (Link had already reviewed Goethe's *Theory of Colours* in 1813 together with Carl Joseph Hieronymus Windischmann.) The notes are part of the preliminary work to Goethe's essay on the "effect" in which he condemned Links false "praise" of Goethe's theory of metamorphosis. He sharply criticized dependence on the taxonomist Carl von Linné (1707–1778) and his concept of anticipation or "prolepsis" (pre-emption), which in botany means an early expulsion of sprouts: "Enough! too much! One should not argue with the error, it should suffice to let it be known." (LA, vol. I 10, p. 308; see LA, vol. II 10 B/2, p. 950.)

19+20 Johann Wolfgang von Goethe
Zwei Schemata (Vorder- und Rückseite) zur Spiraltendenz der Vegetation; auf der einen Seite auch durchgestrichene Notizen von fremder Hand (zum Teil mit Tinte)
Bleistift
Vermutlich Oktober 1828
17 x 14 cm
Klassik Stiftung Weimar, Goethe- und Schiller-Archiv
Signatur: GSA 26 / LXI, 3, 7
Die Ausstellung zeigt ein Faksimile.

In den letzten Jahren seines Lebens hat sich Goethe, angeregt durch den Naturforscher Carl Friedrich Philipp von Martius, mit der spiralförmigen Wuchsrichtung von Pflanzen befasst. Als Frucht seiner Überlegungen entstand der Aufsatz »Über die Spiraltendenz der Vegetation«, der 1831 in der deutsch-französischen Ausgabe des *Versuchs über die Metamorphose der Pflanzen* veröffentlicht wurde. Im Nachlass befinden sich zahlreiche Entwürfe und Notizen zum Thema. ›Spiraltendenz‹ meint den »spiraligen Umlauf der Blätter in der Blumenbildung« (Martius an Goethe, 10. November 1827, LA, Bd. II 10 B/1, S. 341). Goethe erkannte in der äußeren Ausbildung der Pflanze eine spiralförmige Anordnung der Blätter und versuchte dieses Gestaltprinzip auch auf die Sprossen- und Fasernbildung im Inneren zu beziehen.
Die Skizzen entstanden vermutlich während des Besuchs von Martius bei Goethe im Oktober 1828. Eine Seite des Blattes zeigt die »Grundbildung der Blumen« nach Martius, die andere eine Skizze des Spiralsystems mit fünf Kelchblättern und der Anlagelinie der Kronblätter (cor. = Corolla). Vgl. LA, Bd. II 10 B/1, S. 111 f.

19+20 Johann Wolfgang von Goethe
Two schematic diagrams (front and back sides) on the spiral tendency of vegetation; on one of the pages crossed out notes, not by Goethe (partly in ink)
Pencil
Probably October 1828
17 x 14 cm
Klassik Stiftung Weimar, Goethe- und Schiller-Archiv
Shelf mark: GSA 26 / LXI, 3, 7
The exhibition is displaying a facsimile.

In the final years of his life, Goethe, inspired by the natural scientist Carl Friedrich Philipp von Martius, concerned himself with the spiral growth of plants. As a result of these reflections, the essay "The Spiral Tendency in Vegetation" was published in the 1831 Franco-German edition of *The Metamorphosis of Plants*. His estate contains numerous drafts and notes on the subject of 'Spiral tendency,' which is defined as the "spiralling circulation of leaves and petals in flower formation" (Martius to Goethe, 10th November 1827, LA, vol. II 10 B/1, p. 341). Goethe recognized in the outer formation of the plant a spiral arrangement of the leaves and tried to apply this Gestalt principle to the sprout and fiber formation of the interior as well.
The sketches were probably made during Martius's visit to Goethe in October 1828. One side of the sheet shows Martius's "basic formation of flowers," the other a sketch of the spiral system with five sepals and the arrangement of the petals (cor. = Corolla). See LA, vol. II 10 B/1, pp. 111–12.

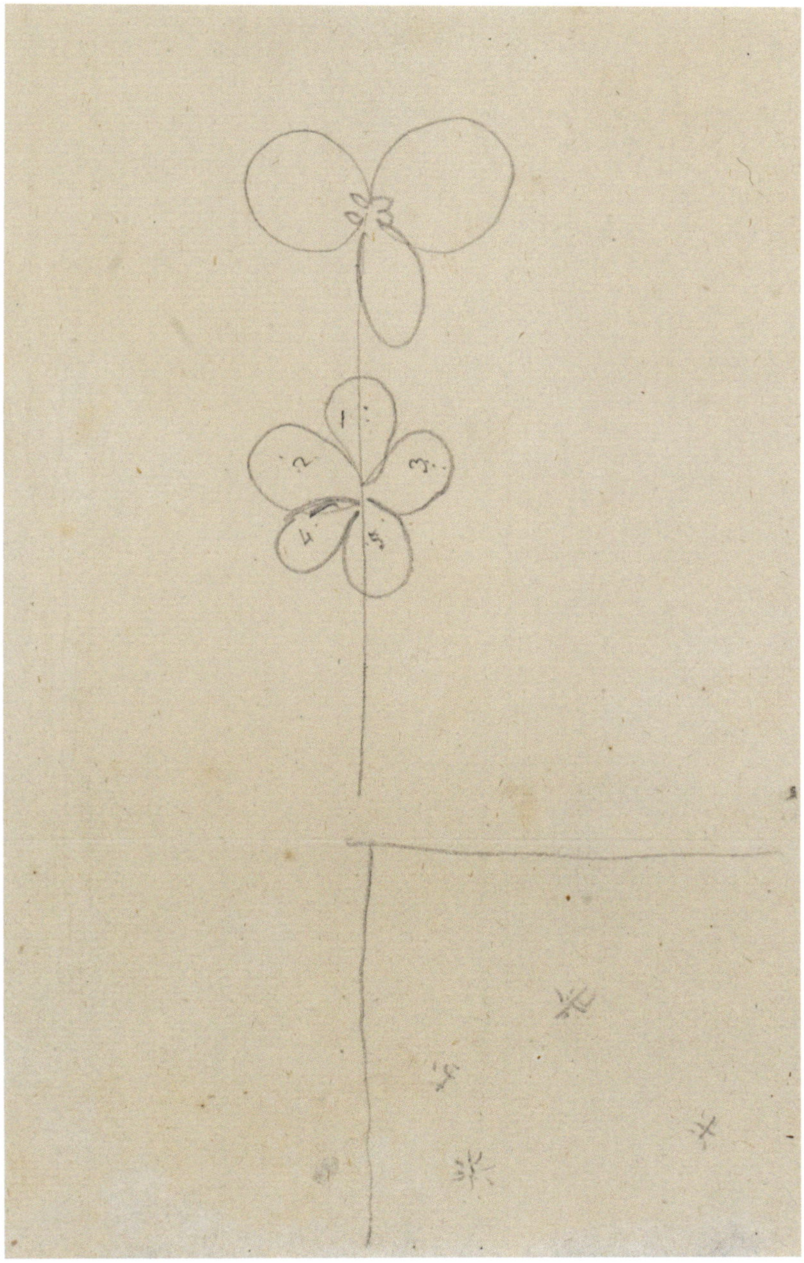

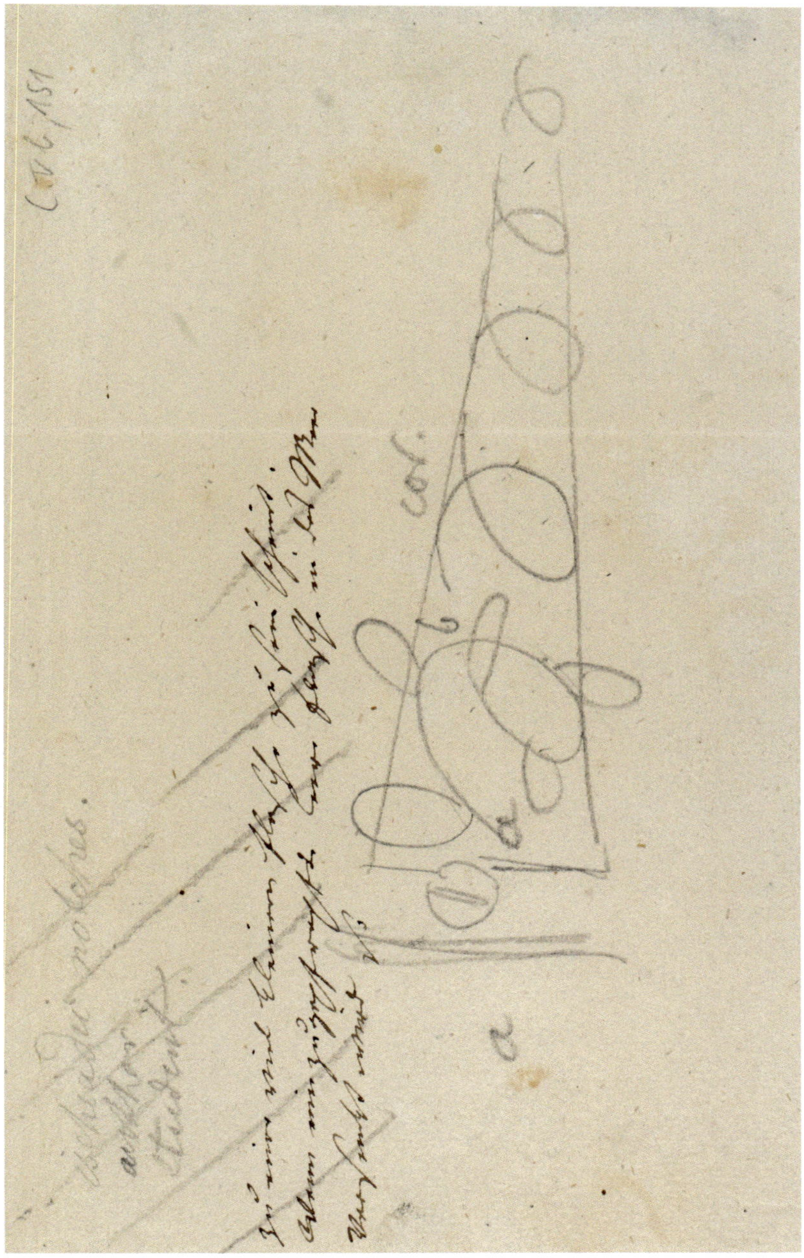

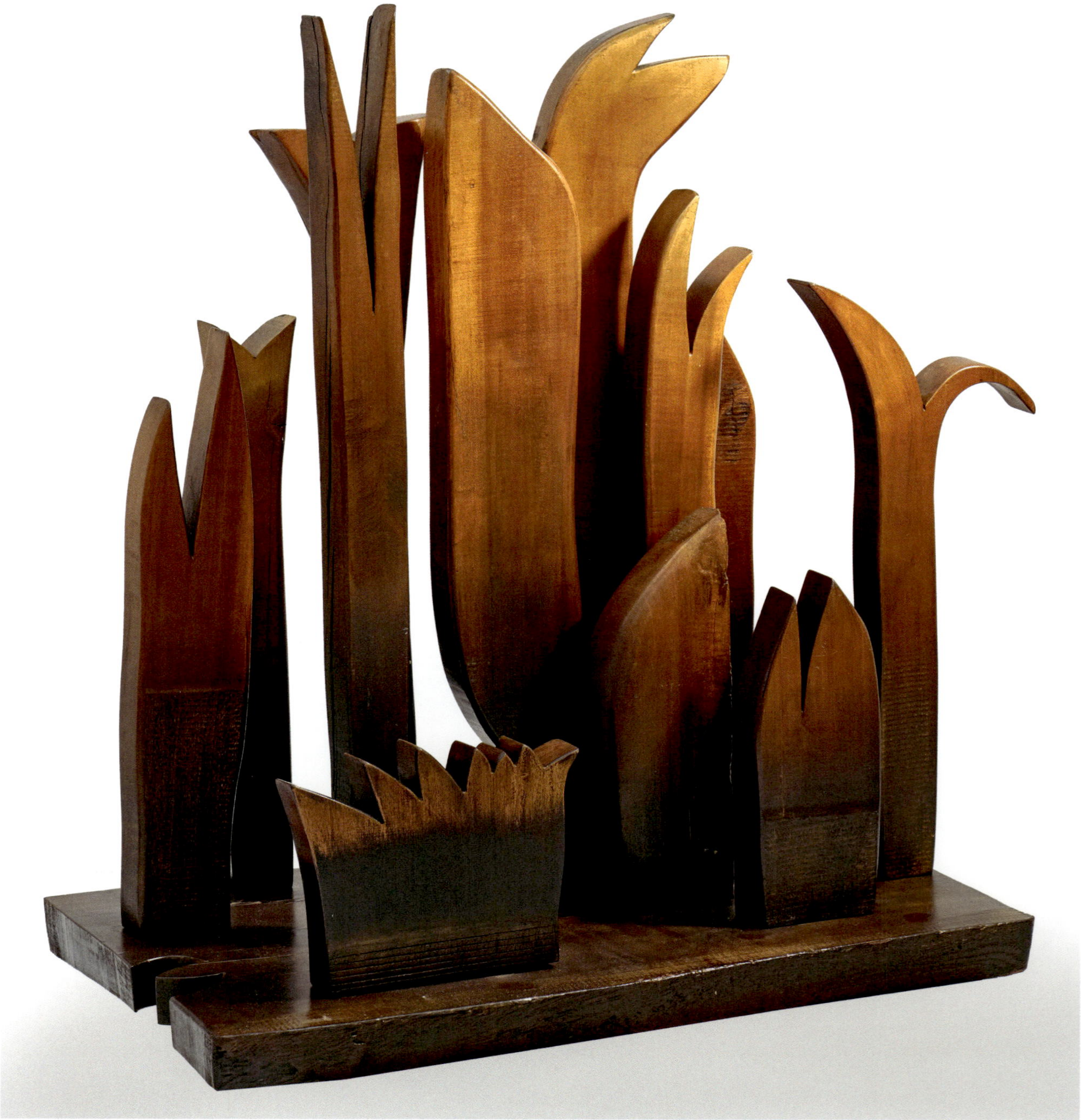

21 Heinz Mack
Großes Wiesenstück
1954
Holz
106,5 x 93 x 58 cm

21 Heinz Mack
Large Patch of Meadow
1954
Wood
106.5 x 93 x 58 cm

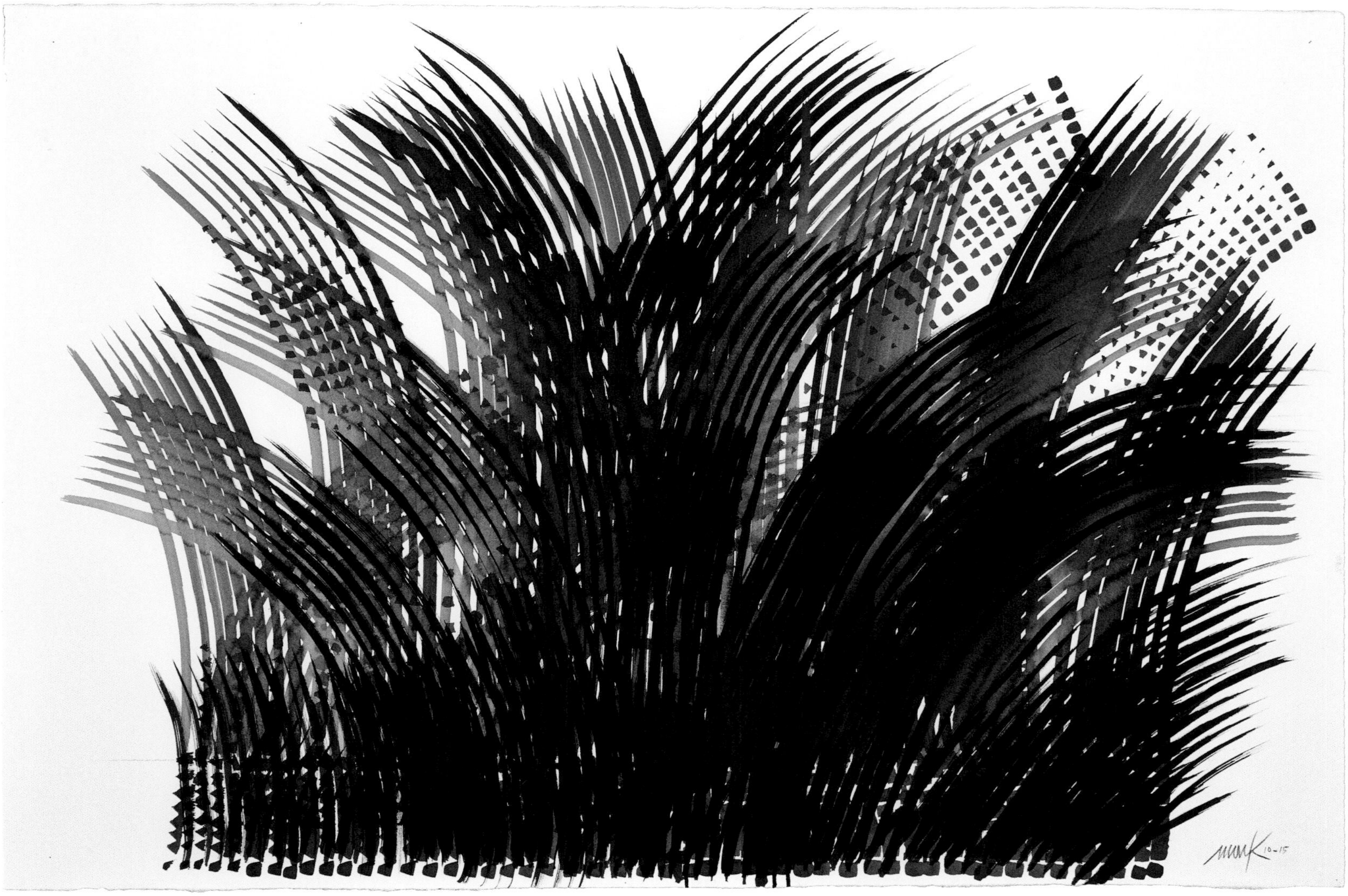

22 Heinz Mack
Ohne Titel
Signiert, datiert: »mack 10–15«
Tusche auf Büttenpapier
76 x 112 cm

22 Heinz Mack
Untitled
Signed, dated: "mack 10–15"
Indian ink on handmade paper
76 x 112 cm

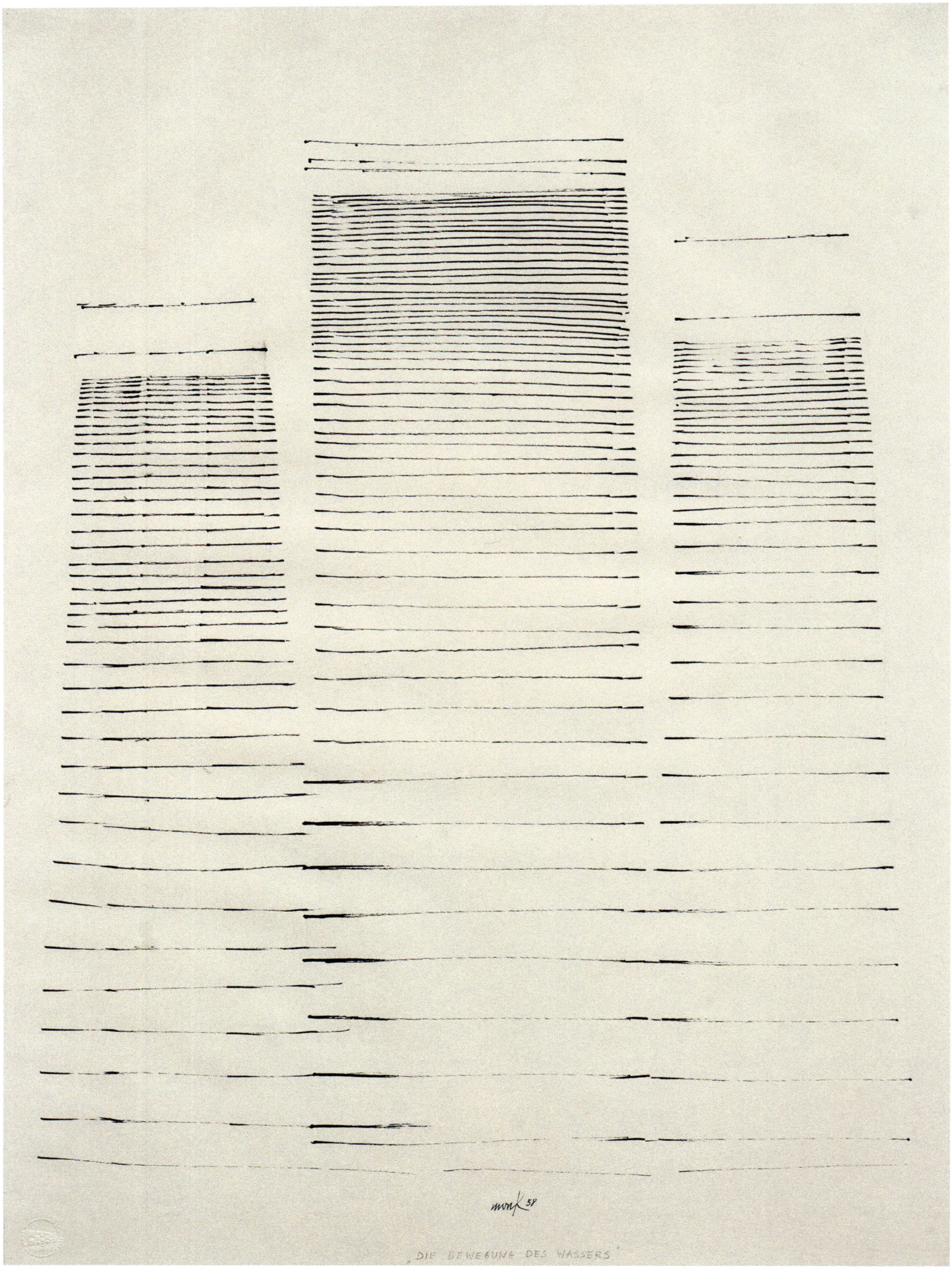

23 Heinz Mack
Die Bewegung des Wassers
Signiert, datiert: »mack 58«
Stahlfeder, schwarze Tinte auf
weißem Schoeller-Papier
63 x 45 cm

23 Heinz Mack
The Movement of Water
Signed, dated: "mack 58"
Black ink applied to white Schoeller
paper with steel nib
63 x 45 cm

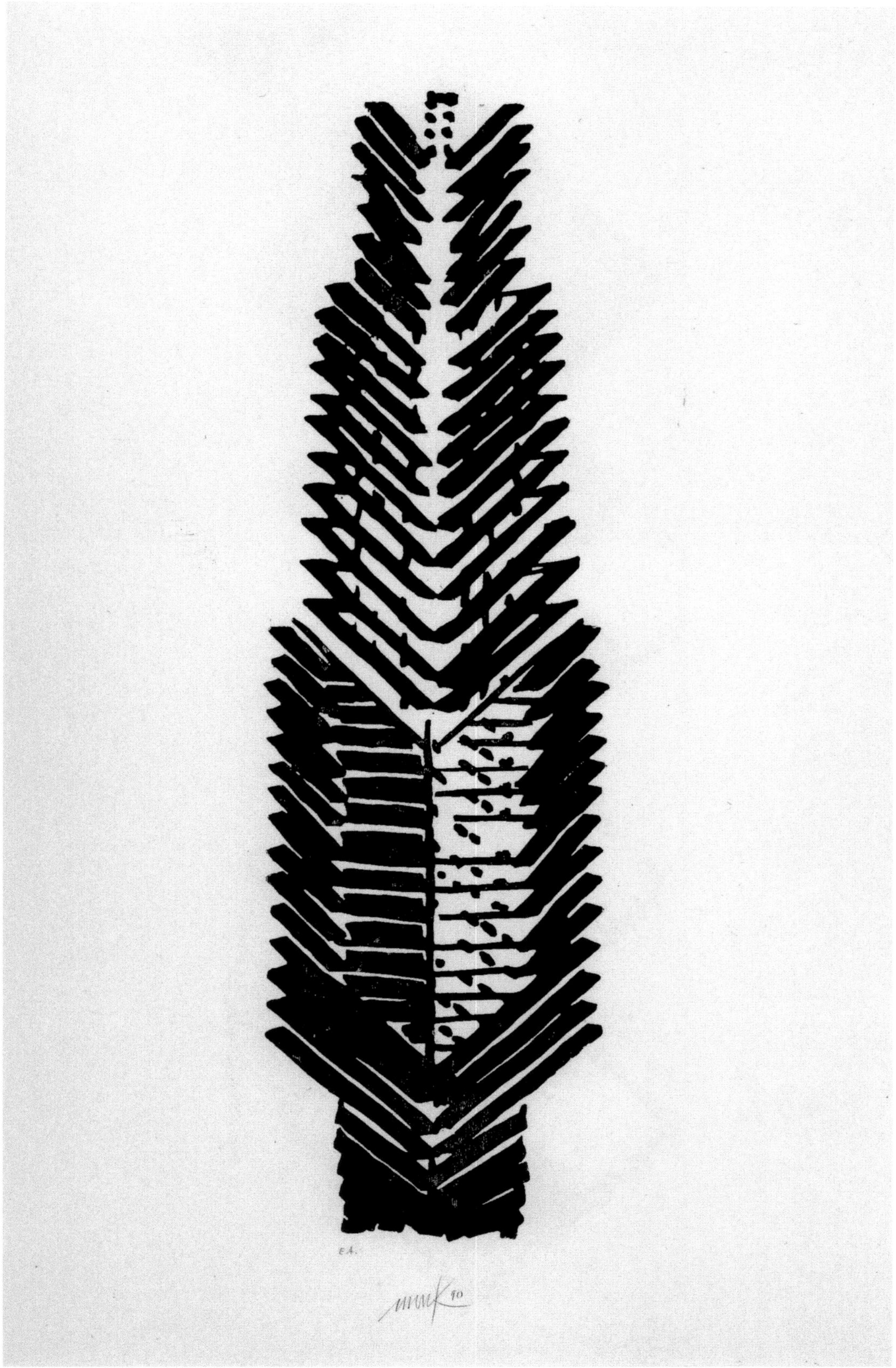

24 Heinz Mack
Ohne Titel
Signiert, datiert: »mack 90«
Holzschnitt
20 nummerierte, signierte Handabzüge
auf Hahnemühle-Büttenpapier
113 x 63,5 cm

24 Heinz Mack
Untitled
Signed, dated: “mack 90”
Woodcut
20 numbered, signed manual prints
on Hahnemühle handmade paper
113 x 63.5 cm

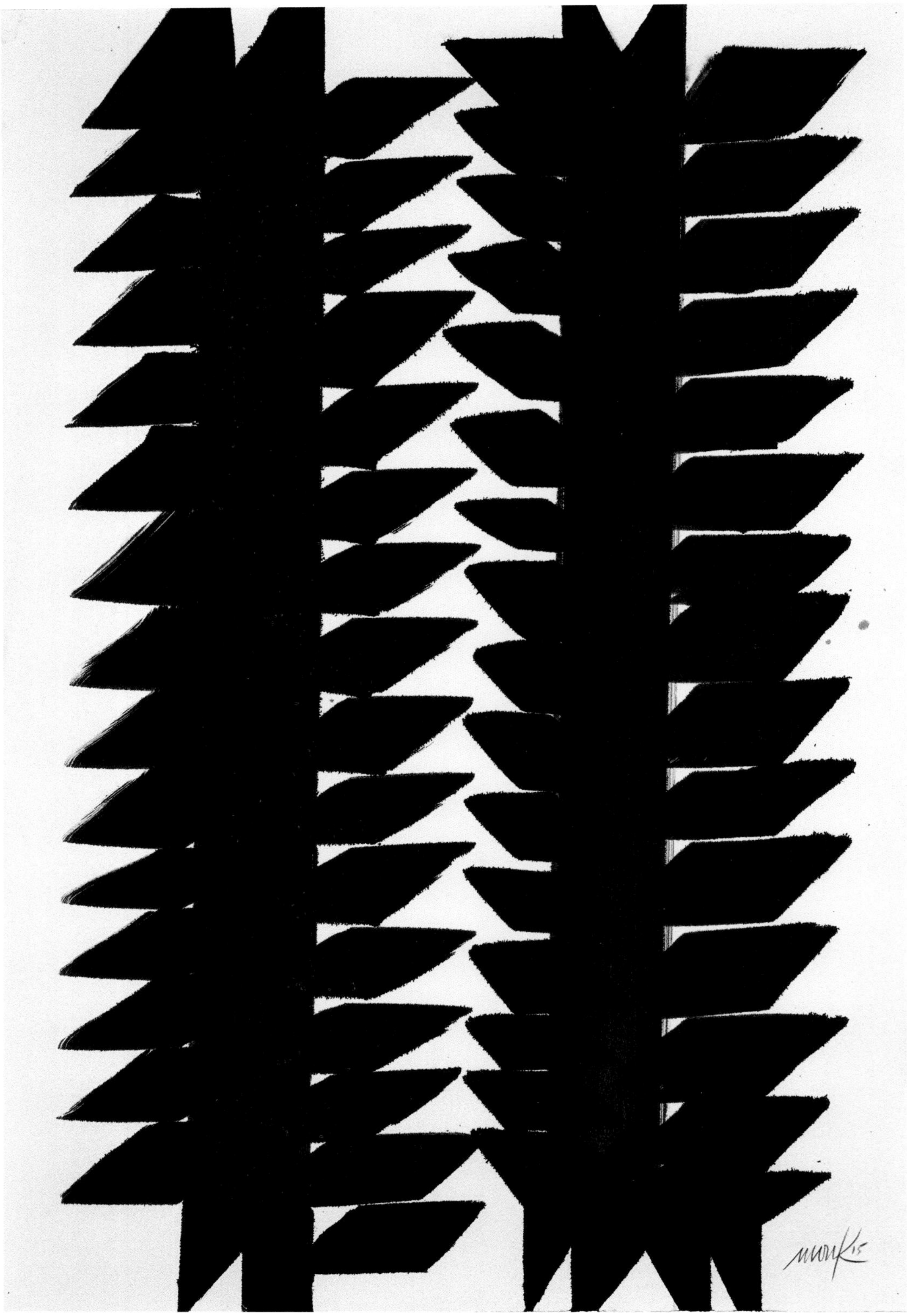

25 Heinz Mack
Ohne Titel
Signiert, datiert: »mack 15«
Tusche auf Büttenpapier
112 x 76 cm

25 Heinz Mack
Untitled
Signed, dated: "mack 15"
Indian ink on handmade paper
112 x 76 cm

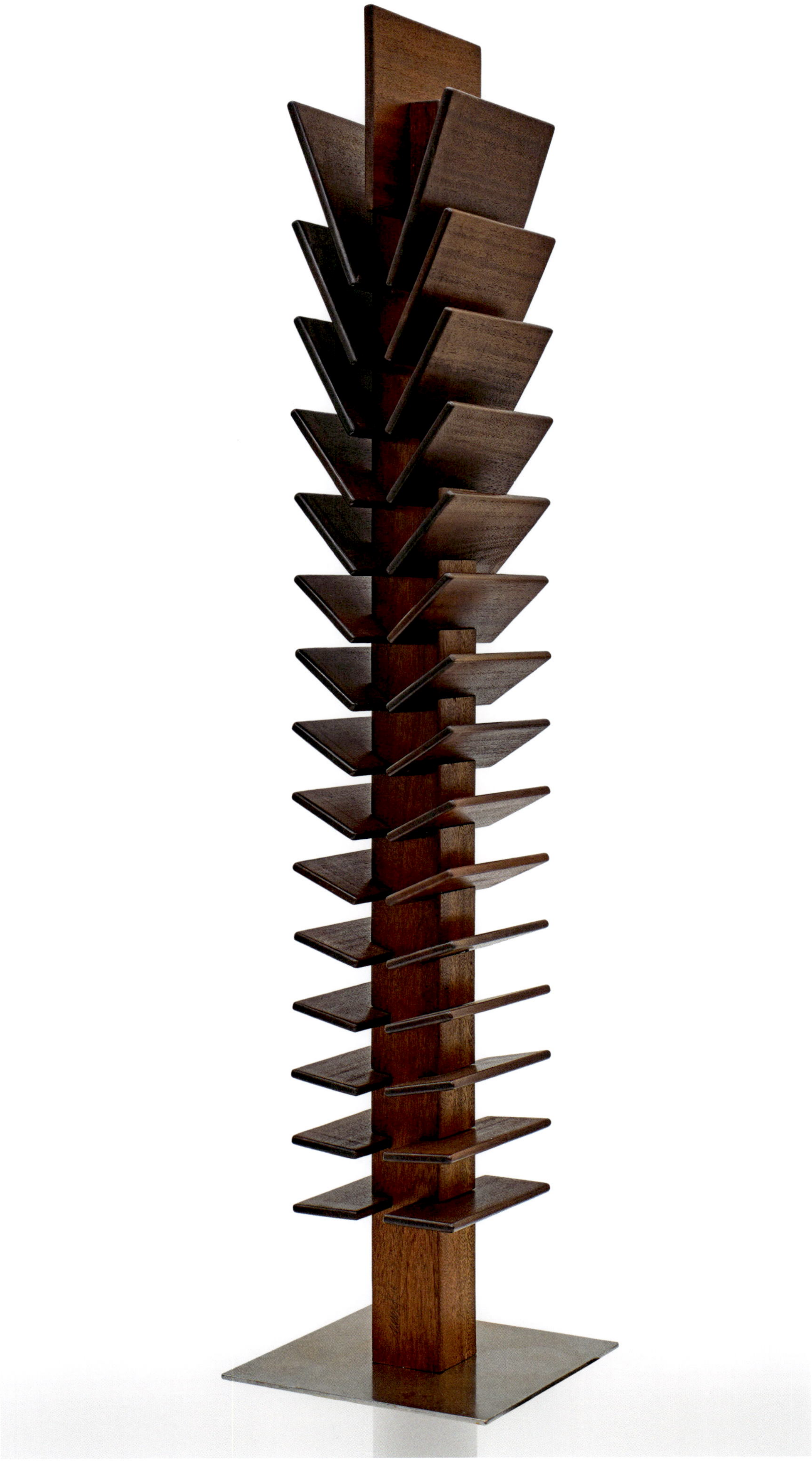

26 Heinz Mack
Ohne Titel
Signiert, datiert: »mack 16«
Holz
252 x 34 x 40 cm

26 Heinz Mack
Untitled
Signed, dated: "mack 16"
Wood
252 x 34 x 40 cm

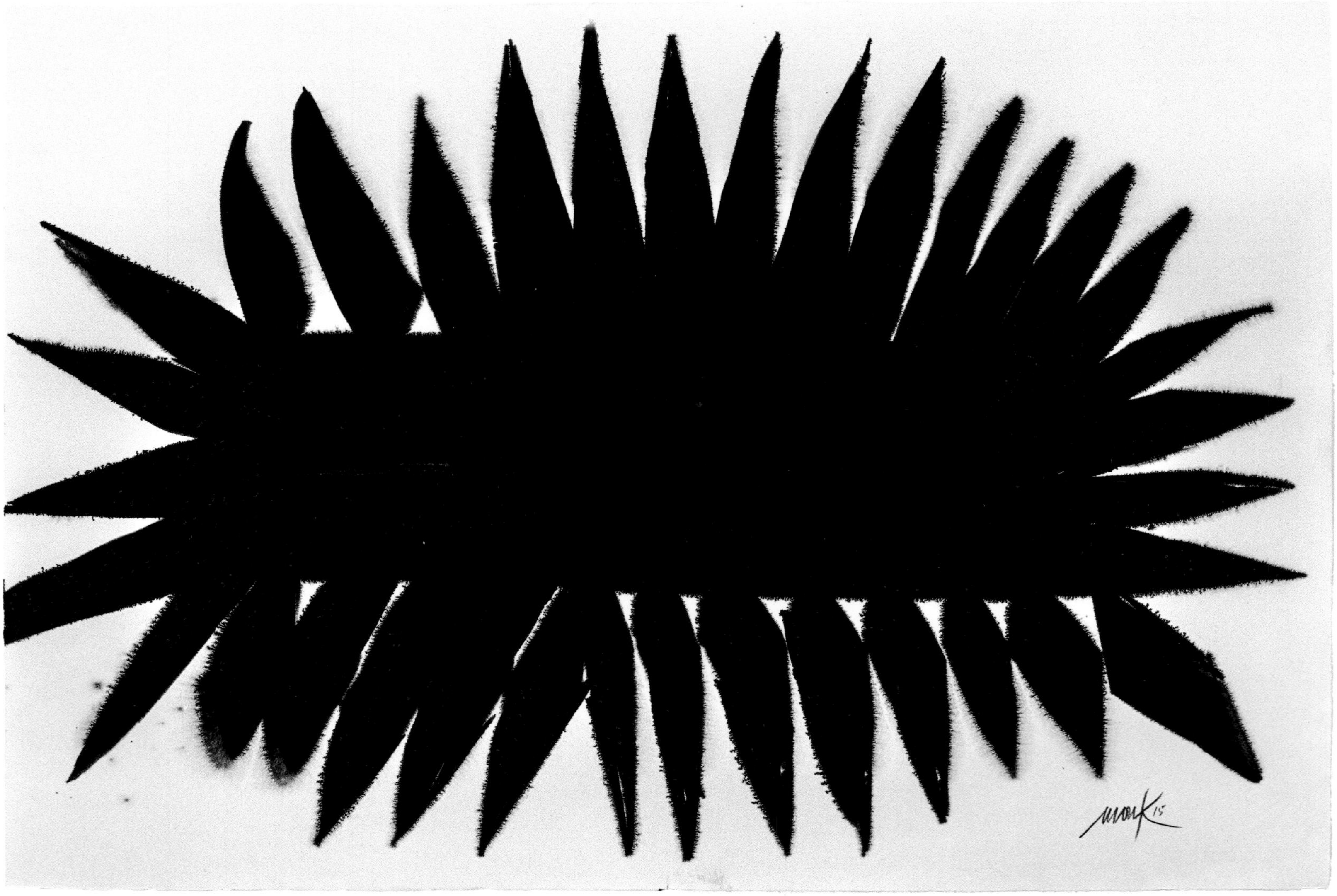

27 Heinz Mack
Ohne Titel
Signiert, datiert: »mack 15«
Tusche auf Büttenpapier
76 x 112 cm

27 Heinz Mack
Untitled
Signed, dated: "mack 15"
Indian ink on handmade paper
76 x 112 cm

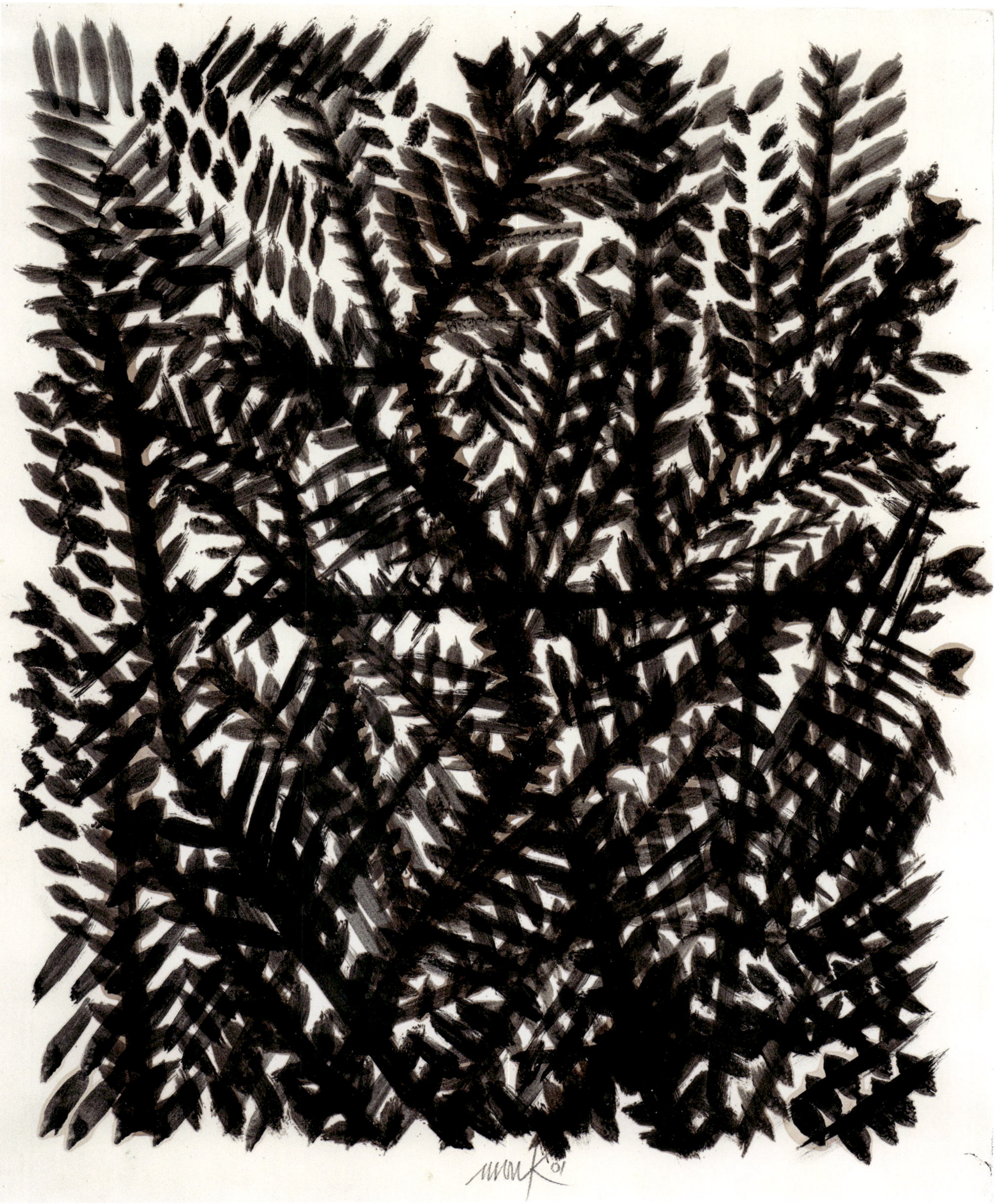

28 Heinz Mack
Ohne Titel
Signiert, datiert: »mack 01«
Tusche mit Pinsel auf Büttenpapier
64,5 x 53 cm

28 Heinz Mack
Untitled
Signed, dated: "mack 01"
Indian ink with brush on handmade paper
64.5 x 53 cm

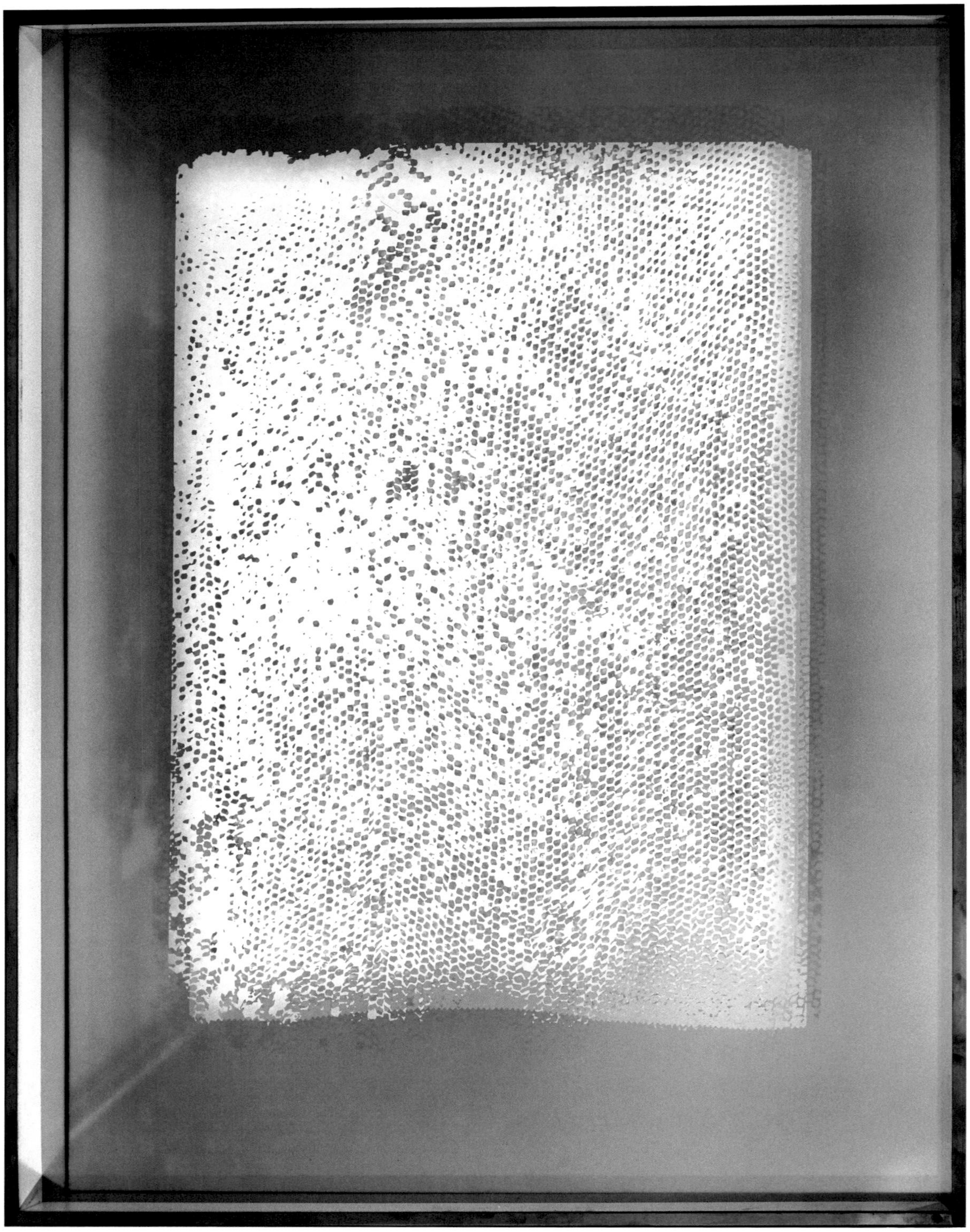

29 Heinz Mack
Haus der Bienen
1986 (Entwurf 1967)
Weißer Siebdruck auf transparentem Plexiglas in 5 cm Abstand vor Aluminiumtafel, die im Siebdruckverfahren auf unterschiedlichem Fond bedruckt ist.

Die Auflage umfasst 4 x 10 arabisch nummerierte und signierte Exemplare.
100 x 85 x 5,5 cm

29 Heinz Mack
House of Bees
1986 (sketch 1967)
White screen print on transparent plexiglass placed 5 cm in front of an aluminum panel with a screen print on different backgrounds.

The print run consists of 4 x 10 copies, which are numbered with Arabic numerals and signed.
100 x 85 x 5.5 cm

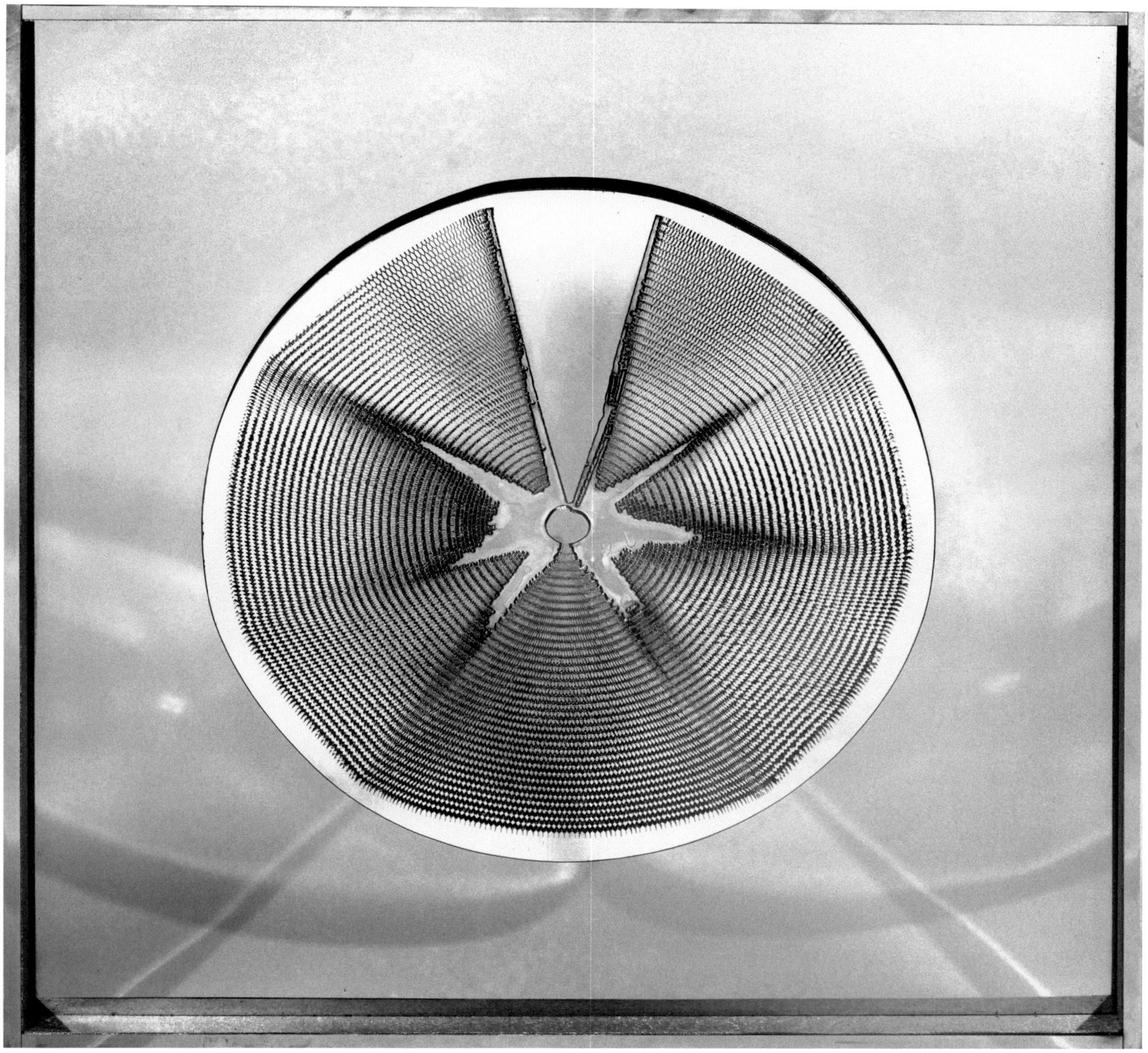

30 Heinz Mack
Ohne Titel
Signiert, datiert: »mack 66«
Zink, verkupfert und verchromt,
Edelstahl, Holz
75 x 75 x 4,8 cm

30 Heinz Mack
Untitled
Signed, dated: "mack 66"
Zinc, coppered and chromed,
stainless steel, wood
75 x 75 x 4.8 cm

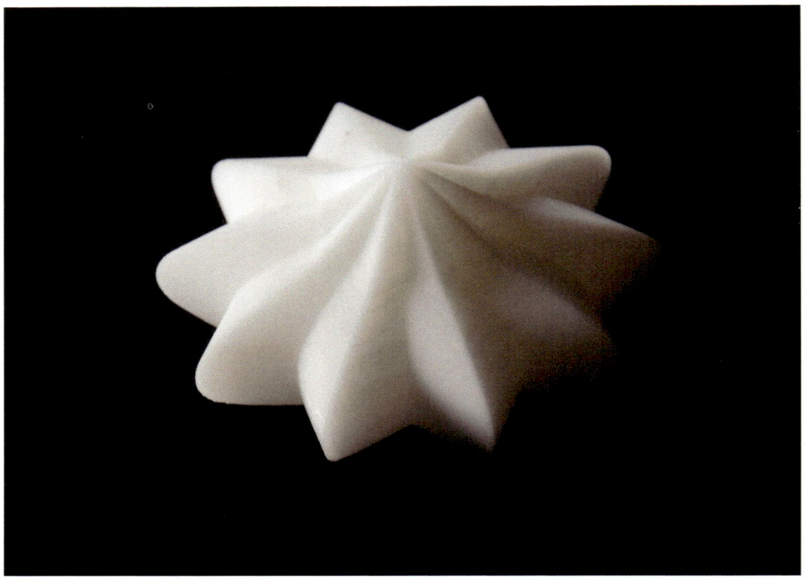

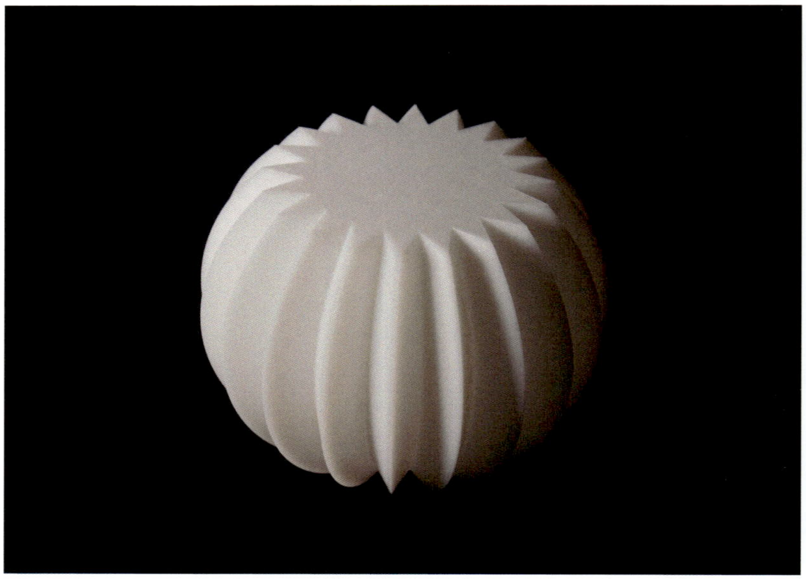

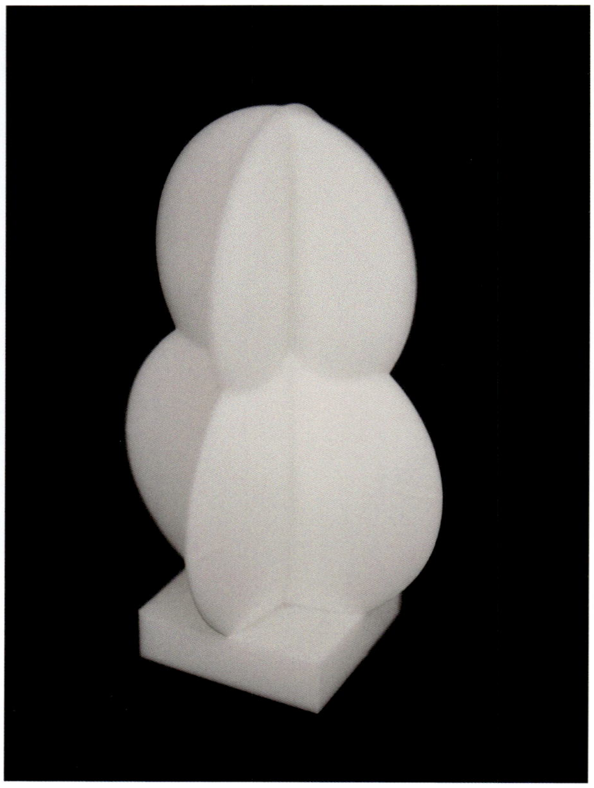

31 Heinz Mack
Kleiner Pavillon
Signiert, datiert: »mack 17«
3D-Druck (1/1), Kunststoff
5,8 x 10 x 10 cm

31 Heinz Mack
Little Pavillon
Signed, dated: "mack 17"
3D print (1/1), synthetic material
5.8 x 10 x 10 cm

32 Heinz Mack
Star Arena
Signiert, datiert: »mack 17«
3D-Druck (1/1), Kunststoff
14 x 15 x 15 cm

32 Heinz Mack
Star Arena
Signed, dated: "mack 17"
3D print (1/1), synthetic material
14 x 15 x 15 cm

33 Heinz Mack
Kleines Idol
Signiert, datiert: »mack 17«
3D-Druck (1/1), Kunststoff
16,3 x 10 x 10 cm

33 Heinz Mack
Little Idol
Signed, dated: "mack 17"
3D print (1/1), synthetic material
16.3 x 10 x 10 cm

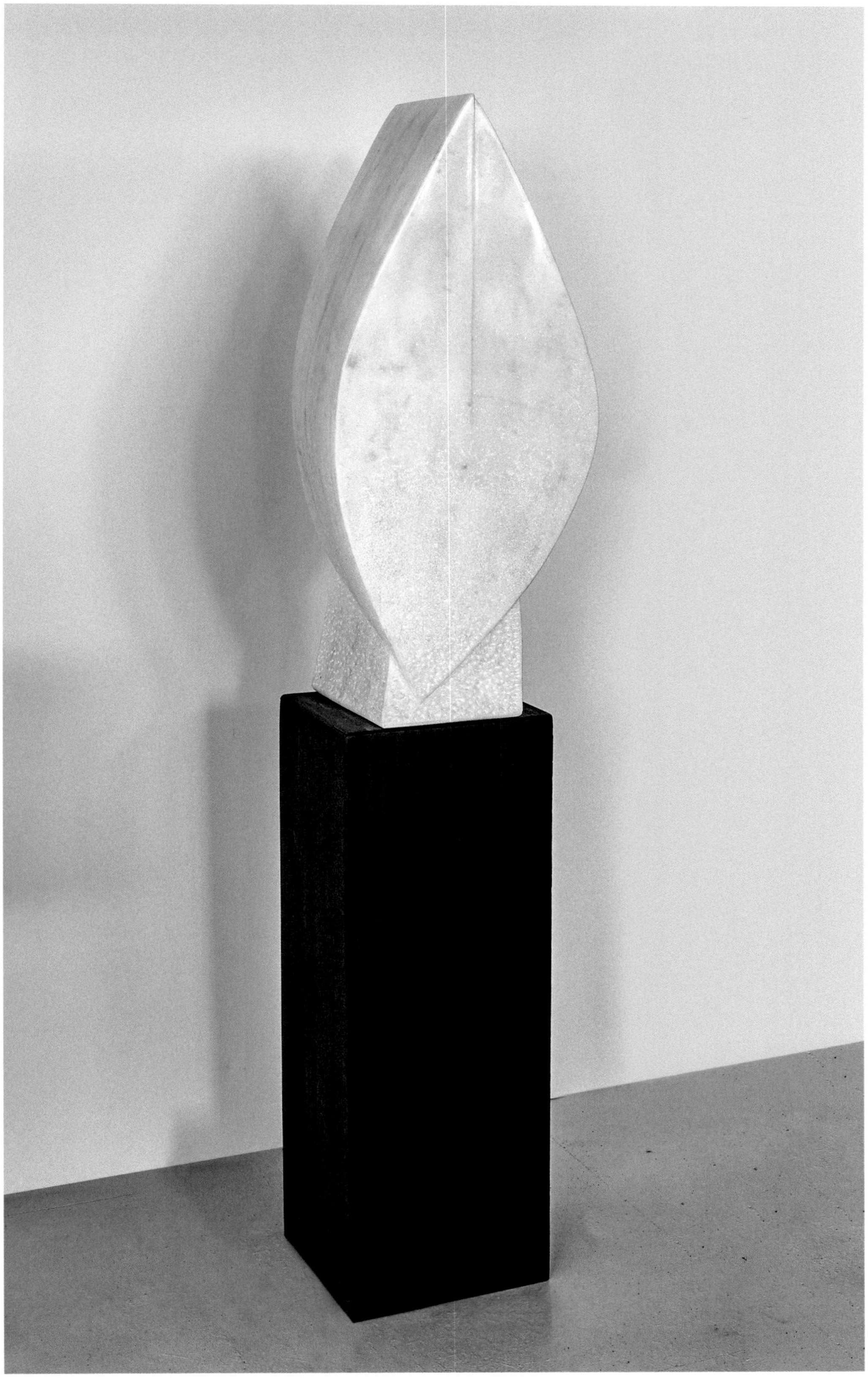

34 Heinz Mack
Regina
Signiert: »mack«
1996
Marmor (cremefarben, aus Portugal), poliert, teils bossiert
89,5 x 37,5 x 31 cm

34 Heinz Mack
Regina
Signed: "mack"
1996
Marble (cream colored, from Portugal), polished, in part dressed
89.5 x 37.5 x 31 cm

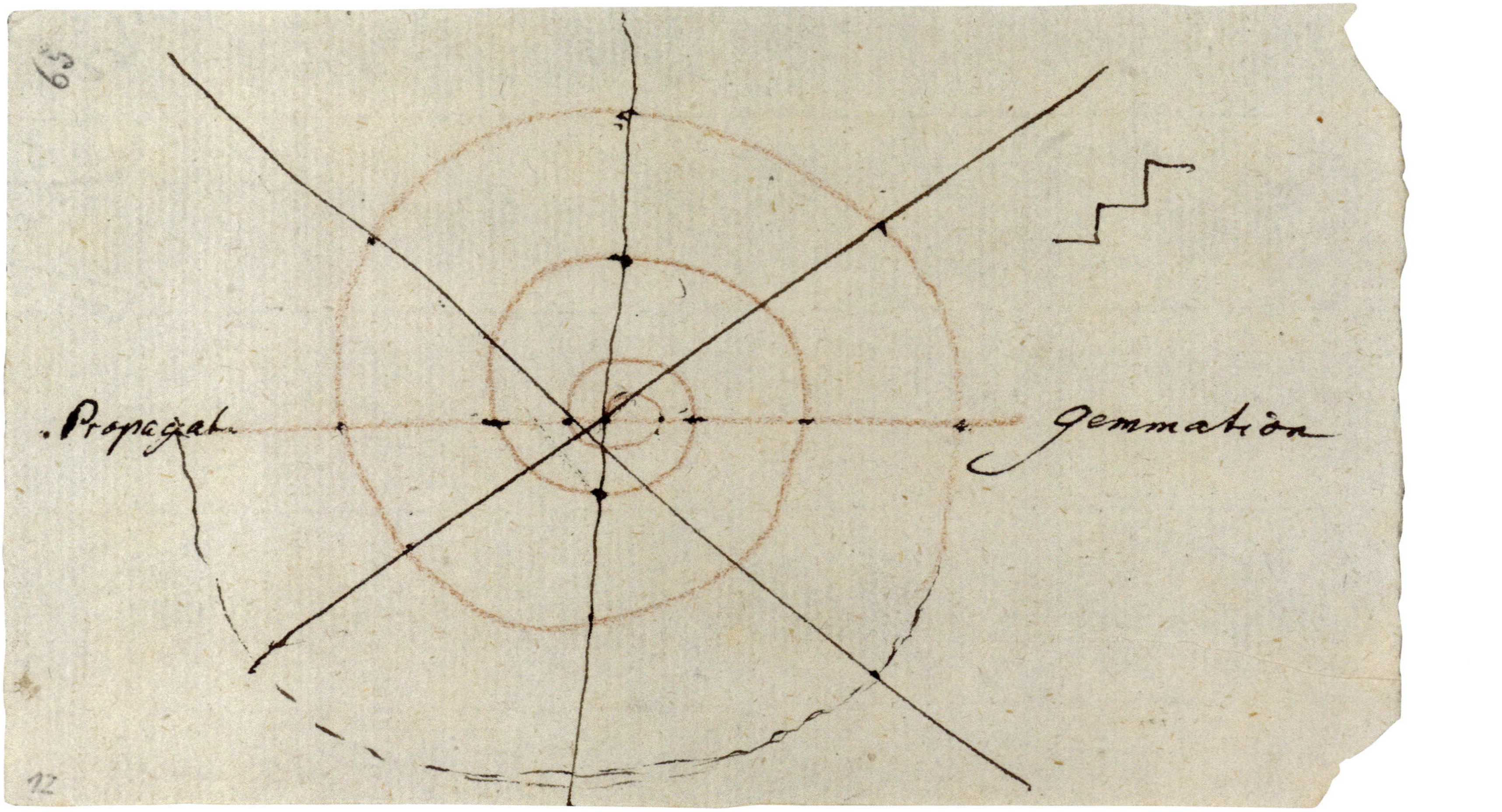

35 Johann Wolfgang von Goethe
Schema zur Spiraltendenz der Vegetation
Um 1829
Rötel und Feder mit Tinte
10,2 x 17,3 cm
Klassik Stiftung Weimar, Goethe- und Schiller-Archiv
Signatur: GSA 26 / LXI, 7

»Propagat[ion]« meint das Streben der Pflanze nach Wachstum, »gemmation« bezeichnet die Tendenz zur Knospung beziehungsweise Samenbildung. Vgl. LA, Bd. II 10 B/1, S. 116 f.

35 Johann Wolfgang von Goethe
Schematic diagram of the spiral tendency in vegetation
Ca. 1829
Red chalk, and quill with ink
10.2 x 17.3 cm
Klassik Stiftung Weimar, Goethe- und Schiller-Archiv
Shelf mark: GSA 26 / LXI, 7

"Propagat[ion]" means the striving of the plant for growth, "gemmation" denotes the tendency to bud or seed. See LA, Vol. II 10 B/1 pp. 116–17.

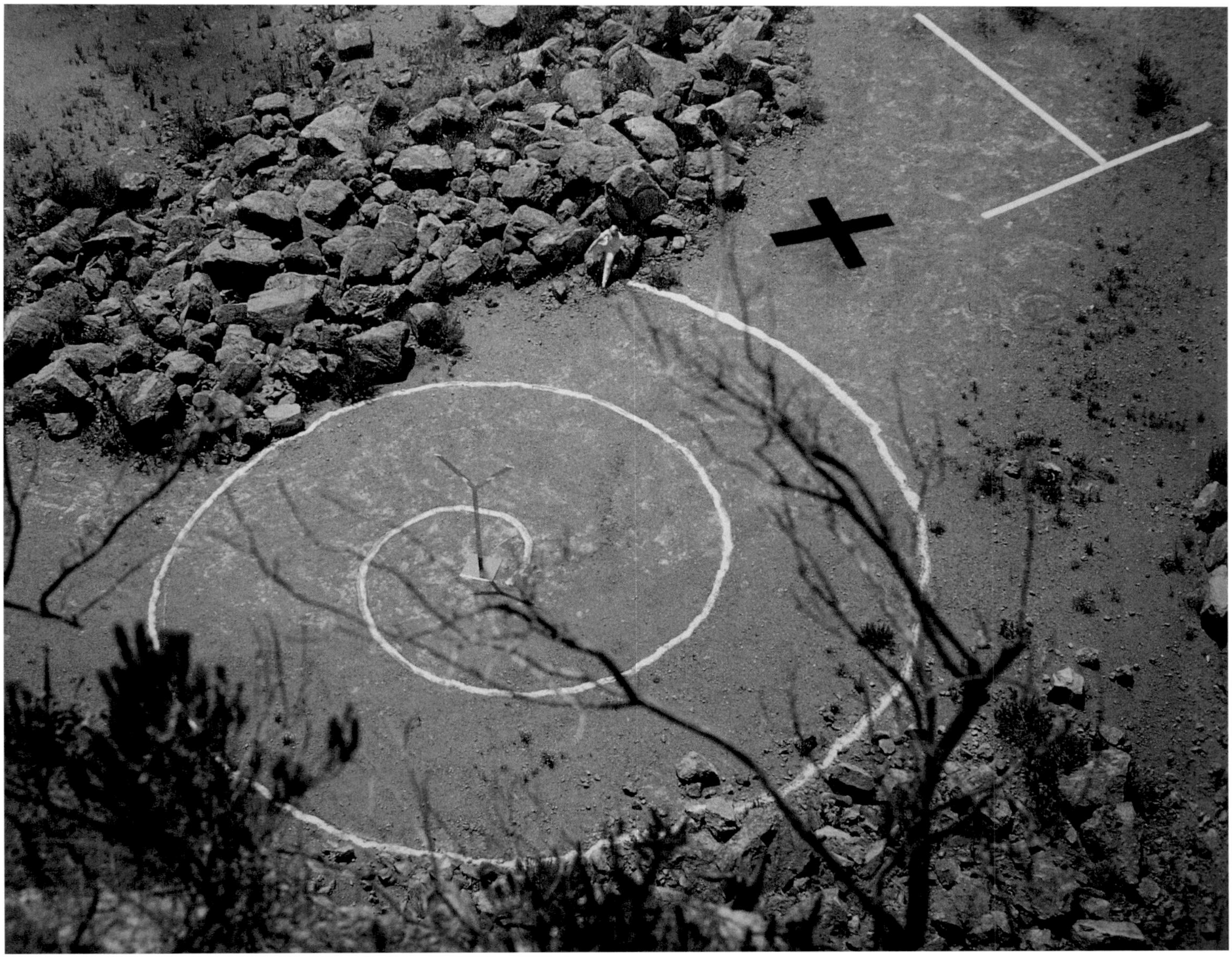

36 Heinz Mack
Ausdehnung – Standort – Ausrichtung
1990
Kalk, Zement, schwarzes Pigment
in einem Steinbruch, Ibiza

36 Heinz Mack
Expansion — Location — Orientation
1990
Limestone, cement and black pigment
in a quarry, Ibiza

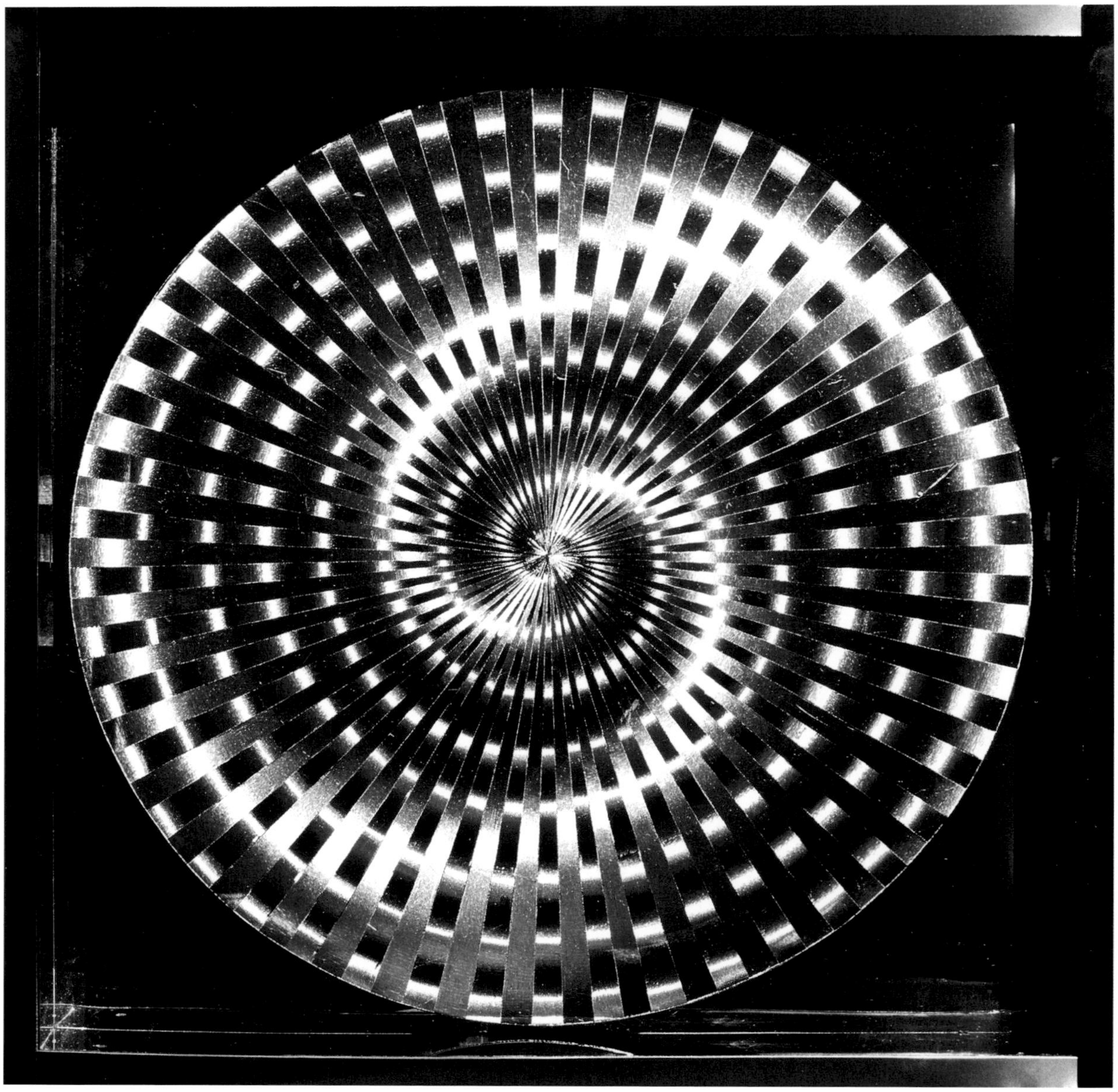

37 Heinz Mack
Ohne Titel
Signiert, datiert: »mack 68, Replik 2004«
Edelstahl, Aluminium, Glas, Holz,
elektrisches Zubehör
34,2 x 34,2 x 10,2 cm

37 Heinz Mack
Untitled
Signed, dated: "mack 68, Replik 2004"
Stainless steel, aluminum, glass, wood,
electric accessories
34.2 x 34.2 x 10.2 cm

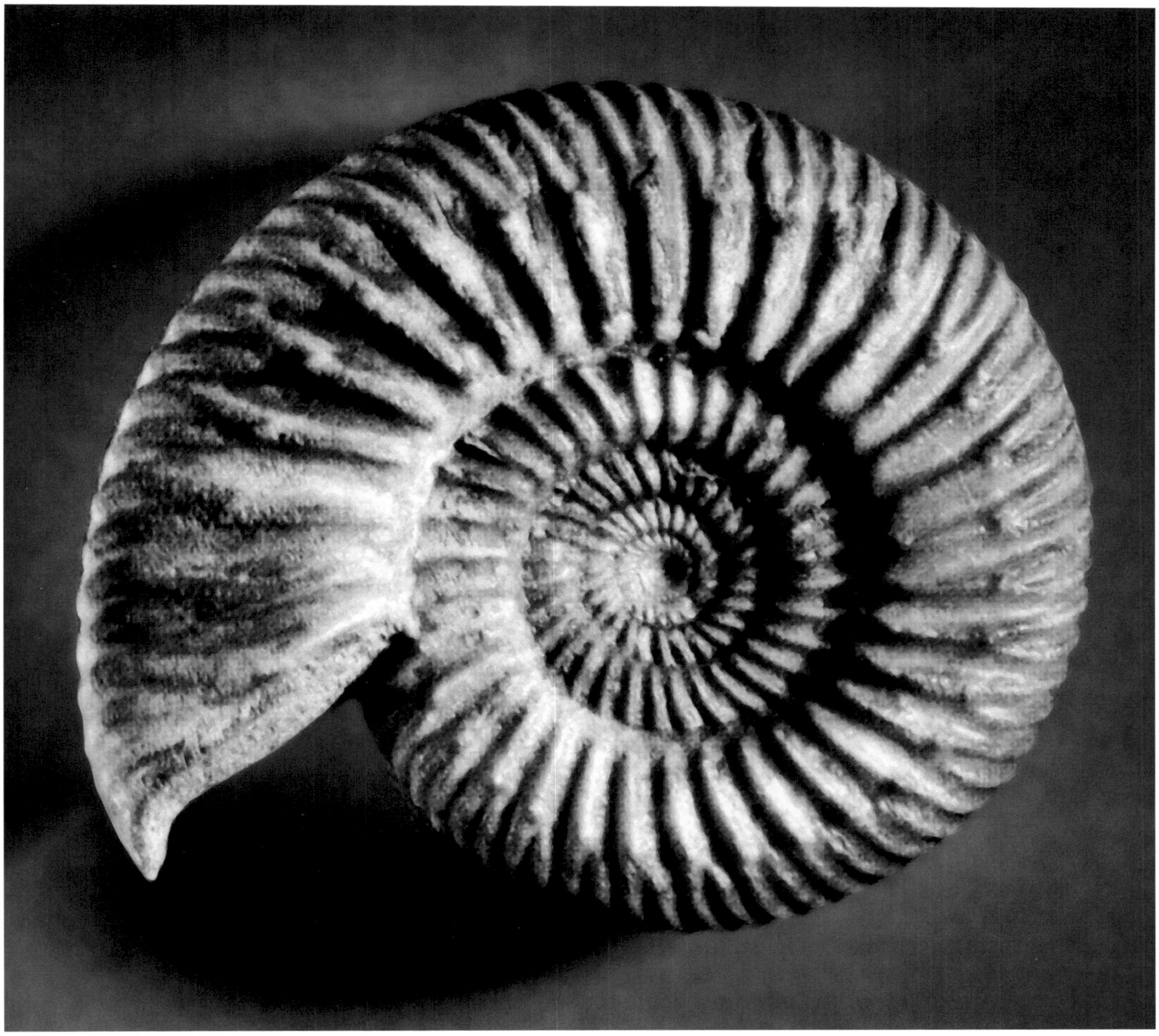

38 Ammonit Parkinsonia depressa
Mitteljura
Fundort: Sengenthal

38 Ammonite Parkinsonia depressa
Middle Jurassic period
Location found: Sengenthal, Bavaria

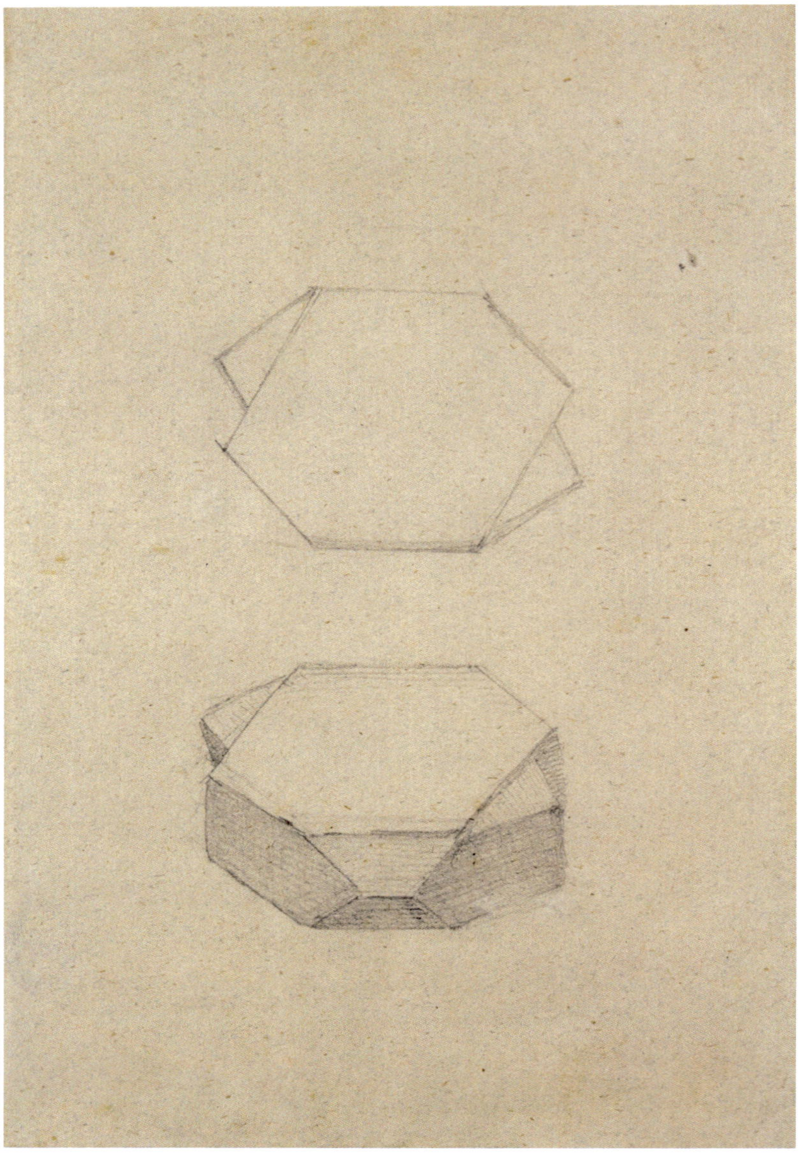

39 Johann Wolfgang von Goethe
Karlsbader Zwillinge
20. Juli 1807
Bleistift
20,8 x 14 cm
Klassik Stiftung Weimar, Museen

Zwei verschiedene Ansichten von Feldspat-Zwillingen, das heißt Feldspaten, bei denen sich zwei tafelförmige Kristalle durchdringen. Granit setzt sich aus Feldspat, Quarz und Glimmer zusammen. Der von diesem ›Urgestein‹ faszinierte Goethe entdeckte bei seinen geologischen Studien in der Karlsbader Gegend auch große Feldspate in den Graniten und stellte sie 1807 in seiner Beschreibung der Mineraliensammlung des Steinschneiders Joseph Müller (1727–1817) als Zwillingskristalle vor: »[…] es gibt große Massen des Karlsbader Granits, worin man vollkommene Kristalle und zwar von sehr komplizierter Bildung antrifft. Es sind Doppelkristalle, welche aus zwei in- und übereinandergreifenden Kristallen zu bestehen scheinen, ohne daß man jedoch den einen ohne den andern einzeln denken könnte. Ihre Form ist durch Beschreibung nicht wohl vor die Einbildungskraft zu bringen, man kann sich solche aber im ganzen als zwei ineinandergefügte rhombische Tafeln vorstellen […].« (»Sammlung zur Kenntnis der Gebirge von und um Karlsbad angezeigt und erläutert«, in: LA, Bd. I 1, S. 331; vgl. LA, Bd. I 8, S. 29 und Bd. II 8 A, S. [648]–658.)

39 Johann Wolfgang von Goethe
Carlsbad Twins
July, 20, 1807
Pencil
20.8 x 14 cm
Klassik Stiftung Weimar, Museen

Two different views of feldspar twins, that is, feldspars, in which two tabular crystals interfuse. Granite is composed of feldspar, quartz and mica. Goethe, who was fascinated by this 'primeval stone,' also discovered large feldspars in the granites of the Carlsbad area during his geological studies there and presented them as 'twin crystals' in his description of the mineral collection of the stone cutter Joseph Mueller (1727–1817): "… there are large masses of Carlsbad granite, in which one finds perfect crystals and that of a very complicated formation. These are double crystals, which seem to consist of two intertwined and overlapping crystals, without, however, being able to think of one existing without the other. Their form is through description difficult to conceive, but one can imagine them as a whole as two intertwined rhombic tablets." ("Sammlung zur Kenntnis der Gebirge von und um Karlsbad angezeigt und erläutert," in LA, vol. I 1, p. 331; cf. LA, vol. I 8, p. 29 and vol. II 8 A, pp. [648]–58.)

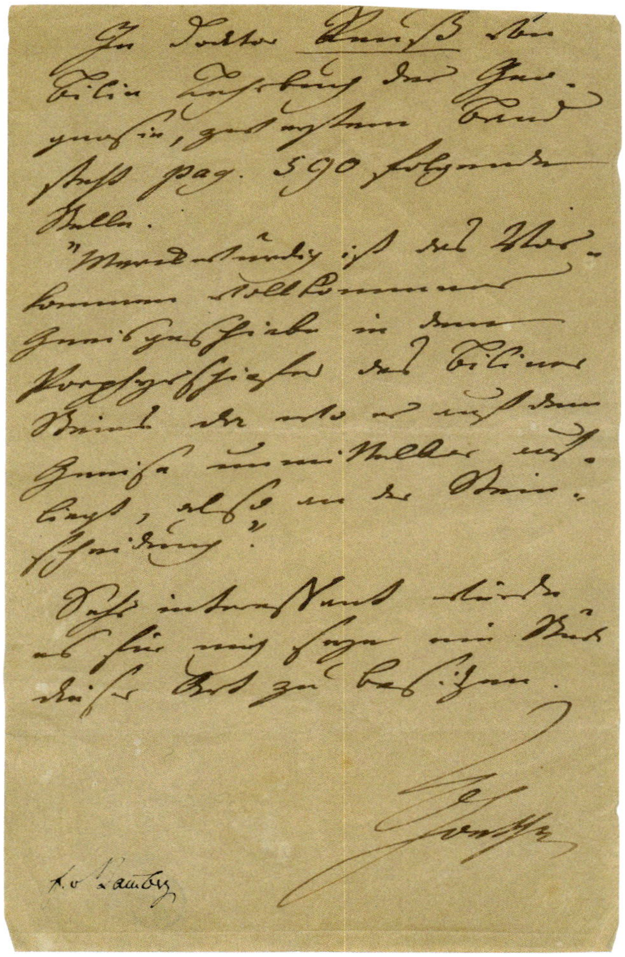

40 Johann Wolfgang von Goethe
Eigenhändiges Billett:
»In Docktor Reuß von Bilin Lehrbuch […]«
1807
1 Blatt, 1 S. beschrieben
17 x 10,5 cm
Goethe-Museum Düsseldorf

»In Docktor Reuß von Bilin Lehrbuch der Geognosie, zweytem Band steht pag. 590 folgende Stelle. ›Merckwürdig ist das Vorkommen vollkommener Gneisgeschiebe in dem Porphyrschiefer des Biliner Steins da wo er auf dem Gneise unmittelbar aufliegt, also an der Steinscheidung‹. Sehr interessant würde es für mich seyn ein Stück dieser Art zu besitzen. Goethe«
Während seiner Kuraufenthalte in Böhmen untersuchte Goethe auch die Geologie der Gegend. Er besuchte mehrfach den Geologen Franz Ambrosius Reuß (1761–1830), der als Badearzt in der böhmischen Stadt Bilin bei Teplitz wirkte. Die handschriftliche Notiz bezieht sich auf Reuß' *Lehrbuch der Geognosie* (Leipzig 1805) und dokumentiert Goethes morphologisches Interesse an Gesteinsformationen. Der Granit galt ihm als ältestes Gestein der Erde, das als Sediment aus dem Urmeer entstanden sei. Den kristallinen Gneis betrachtete Goethe als Ablagerung des älteren Granits und statuierte fälschlich, dass eine Gneisschicht stets über dem Granit liegen müsse. Ein Stück des Porphyrschiefers erwarb Goethe tatsächlich. Das geht aus seinem Brief vom 25. November 1807 an den Hanauer Geologen und Mineralogen Carl Caesar Leonhard (1779–1862) hervor, den Goethe (nach der Publikation 1808 durch Leonhard selbst) 1824 in der Zeitschrift *Zur Naturwissenschaft überhaupt* wiederveröffentlichte und in dem er die hier wiedergegebene Passage aus dem Lehrbuch von Reuß erneut zitiert. Vgl. LA, Bd. I 1, S. 347–353, Bd. I 8, S. 380–386 und Bd. II 8 A, S. [659]–666.

40 Johann Wolfgang von Goethe
Card in his own hand:
"In Doctor Reuss von Bilin's textbook …"
1807
1 sheet, 1 page written
17 x 10.5 cm
Goethe-Museum Düsseldorf

"In Doctor Reuss von Bilin's textbook of Geognosy, second volume p. 590 is the following passage: 'Strange is the occurrence of perfect gneiss shingle in the porphyry shale of stone from Bilin where it rests directly on the gneiss, so at the stone separation'. It would be very interesting for me to acquire a piece of this. Goethe"
During his spa stays in Bohemia, Goethe also examined the geology of the area. On multiple occasions he visited the geologist Franz Ambrosius Reuss (1761–1830), who worked as a bath doctor in the Bohemian town of Bilin near Teplitz. The handwritten note refers to Reuss' Textbook of Geognosy (Leipzig 1805) and documents Goethe's interest in morphological rock formations. Granite was for him as Earth's oldest rock type, which originated as sediment from the primeval sea. Goethe regarded the crystalline gneiss as a deposit of the older granite and falsely stated that a gneiss layer must always lie above the granite. Goethe actually acquired a piece of porphyry shale. This is evident from his letter of November 25, 1807, to the Hanau geologist and mineralogist Carl Caesar Leonhard (1779–1862), which (after Leonhard had printed it in 1808) Goethe re-published in 1824 in the journal *Zur Naturwissenschaft überhaupt* and in which he reproduced the above passage from Reuss' textbook. (See LA, vol. I 1, pp. 347–53, vol. I 8, pp. 380–86, and vol. II 8 A, pp. [659]–66.)

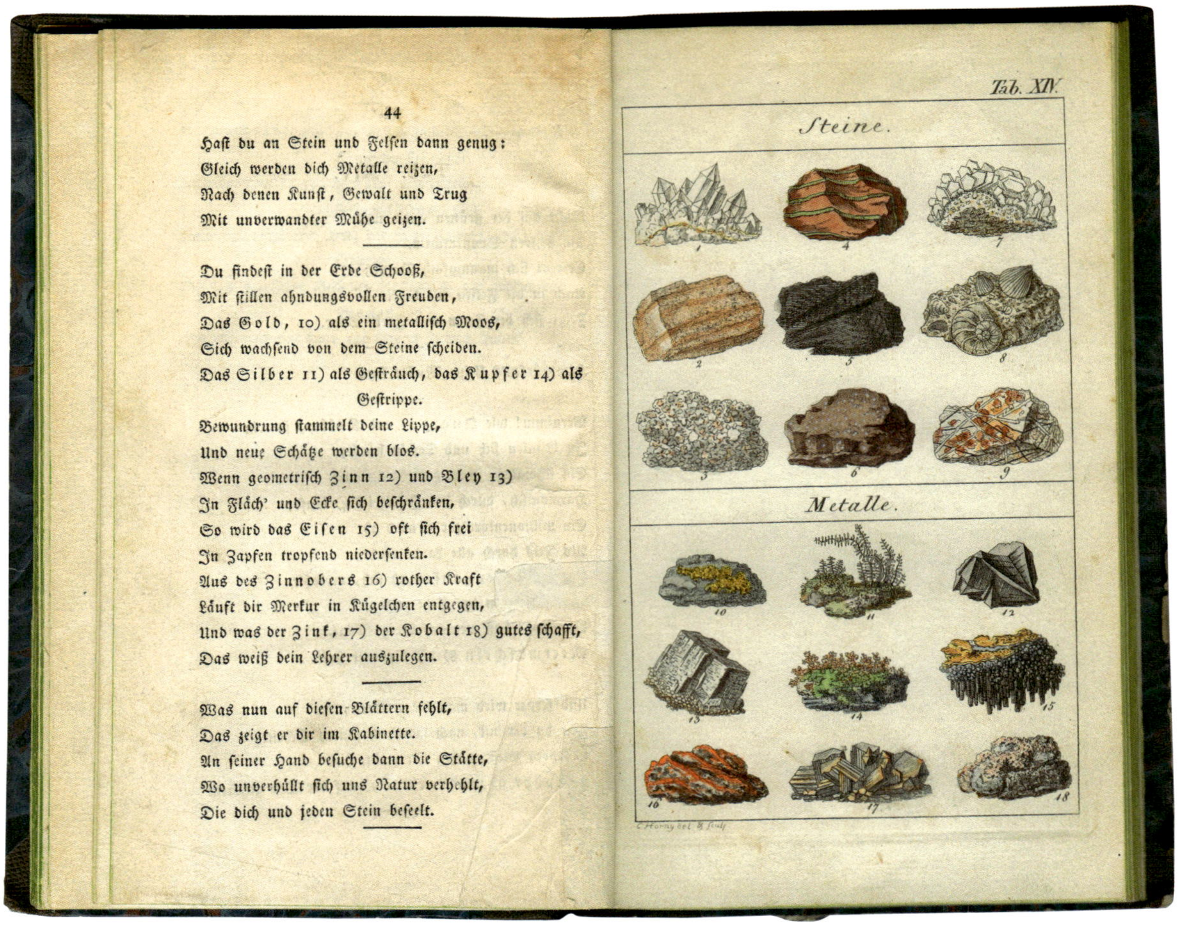

41 Jakob Glatz
Naturhistorisches / Bilder- und Lese-Buch / oder / Erzählungen / über Gegenstände / aus den drei Reichen der Natur. / Von / Jakob Glatz, / Mitarbeiter an der Erziehungsanstalt zu Schnepfenthal. / Nebst 300 illuminirten Abbildungen von Horny / und einer kurzen Erklärung derselben in Versen. / Jena, bei Friedrich Frommann.
Aufgeschlagen: Tafel XIV (Steine und Metalle) mit dem erläuternden Gedicht Goethes

Der spätaufklärerische Pädagoge und Theologe Jakob Glatz (1776–1831) unterrichtete in der philanthropischen Erziehungsanstalt in Schnepfenthal und veröffentlichte 1803 sein *Naturhistorisches Bilder- und Lese-Buch oder Erzählungen über Gegenstände aus den drei Reichen der Natur* [Tiere, Pflanzen und Steine]. Das Buch erschien mit 14 Kupfertafeln des Malers und Kupferstechers Konrad Horny (1764–1807) und dazugehörigen Erläuterungen in Versen.
Goethe interessierte sich zeitlebens für Geologie, aus persönlicher Neigung und beruflichem Interesse als Zuständiger für den Bergbau im Fürstentum Sachsen-Weimar-Eisenach. Er war davon überzeugt, dass ohne das »Steinreich [...] die berühmte Morphologie nicht vollständig werden würde« (an Schiller, 12. November 1796, WA, Bd. IV 11, S. 260). Auch über etliche eigene Schriften hinaus war es ihm ein Anliegen, auf populäre Weise naturgeschichtliches Wissen zu vermitteln. So regte Goethe den Medizinstudenten Nikolaus Meyer (1775–1855) dazu an, zu einigen Kupfertafeln für das naturhistorische Bilderbuch von Glatz versifizierte Erklärungen zu schreiben. Das erläuternde Gedicht zur Tafel XIV (Steine und Metalle) verfasste Goethe selbst und empfahl darin den Kindern, an der Hand des Lehrers die Stätte zu besuchen, »wo unverhüllt sich uns Natur verhehlt, / Die dich und jeden Stein beseelt.« (LA, Bd. I 1, S. 281 f.; vgl. LA, Bd. II 7, S. 489 f. und 518 f.)

41 Jakob Glatz
Naturhistorisches Bilder- und Lese-Buch oder Erzählungen über Gegenstände aus den drei Reichen der Natur
Jena, 1803
Opened at: plate XIV (stones and metals) with an explanatory poem by Goethe

The late Enlightenment educator and theologian Jakob Glatz (1776–1831) taught at the philanthropic educational institution in Schnepfenthal and in 1803 published his natural history picture and reading book. The book about the three realms of nature (animals, plants and stones) was published with 14 copper plates by the painter and engraver Konrad Horny (1764–1807) with related explanations in verse.
Throughout his life, Goethe was interested in geology, through both personal inclination and professional interest as a civil servant responsible for mining in the principality of "Saxe-Weimar-Eisenach. He was convinced that without the "Empire of the Stone ... the famous morphology would not be completed" (letter to Schiller, 12 November 1796, WA, vol. IV 11, p. 260). Beyond several of his own writings, he also wanted to impart knowledge of natural history to the general public. Thus, Goethe encouraged the medical student Nikolaus Meyer (1775–1855) to write versified explanations for some copper plates for the natural history picture book by Glatz. The explanatory poem for plate XIV (stones and metals) was written by Goethe himself, who recommended that the children visit places at their teacher's side, "where nature hides and is unveiled to us, which animates you and every stone." (LA, vol. I 1, pp. 281–82; cf. LA, vol. II 7, pp. 489–90 and 518–19.)

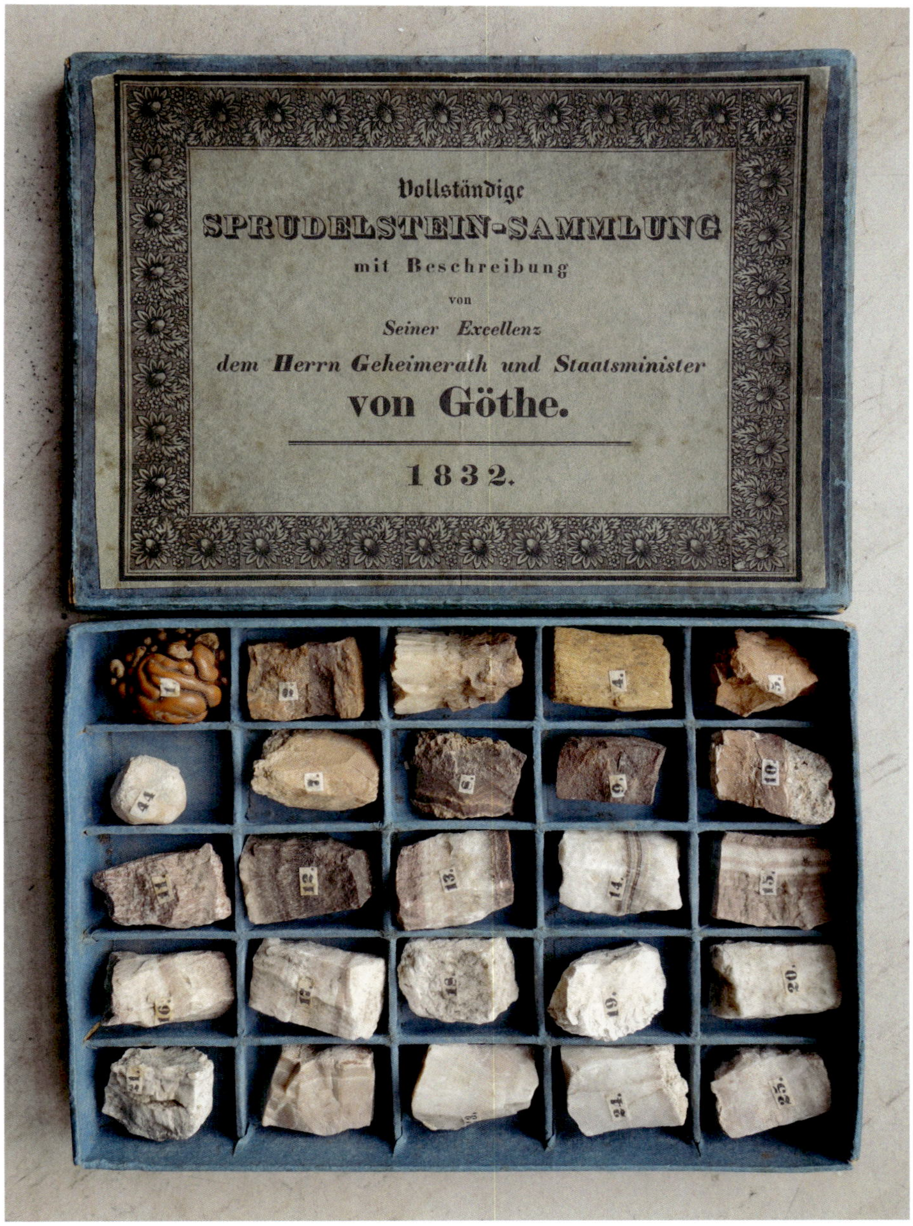

42 Vollständige Sprudelstein-Sammlung mit Beschreibung von Seiner Excellenz dem Herrn Geheimerath und Staatsminister von Göthe. 1832.
Flaches Pappkästchen, mit blauem Papier beklebt, 12 x 15,4 x 2,5 cm, das 25 nummerierte Proben von Karlsbader Sintersteinen enthält. Ein gedrucktes Verzeichnis liegt bei.
Goethe-Museum Düsseldorf

Goethe erforschte nicht nur auf Exkursionen das Steinreich, sondern interessierte sich zeitlebens für mineralogische Sammlungen, förderte deren Aufbau und stellte selbst Verzeichnisse dazu her. Insbesondere in der Gegend von Karlsbad, wohin er regelmäßig zur Badekur fuhr, untersuchte er die dortigen Mineralien. Er stand in engem Kontakt zu dem Steinschneider und Mineralienhändler Joseph Müller (1727–1817), der vor allem sogenannte ›Sprudelsteine‹ (Aragonite), die aus Kalkablagerungen im Wasser entstehen, an Kurgäste verkaufte. Goethe beschrieb dessen Steinsammlung und erneuerte 1831 sein Verzeichnis für den Karlsbader Kaufmann David Knoll, der die Müller'sche Sammlung übernommen hatte. Musterkollektionen dieser Steinsammlung wurden mit dem werbewirksamen Verzeichnis zum Verkauf angeboten.

42 Complete peastone collection with description from His Excellency the Privy Councilor and Minister of State Göthe. 1832.
Flat cardboard box, covered with blue paper, 12 x 15.4 x 2.5 cm, containing 25 numbered samples of Carlsbad sintered stone. A printed directory is enclosed.
Goethe-Museum Düsseldorf

Goethe not only explored the 'stone realm' on excursions, but was interested in mineralogical collections throughout his life, promoting their establishment and even producing directories on the subject. Especially in the area surrounding Carlsbad he examined the local minerals, where he regularly took the waters. He was in close contact with the stone cutter and mineral merchant Joseph Müller (1727–1817), who mainly sold so-called 'peastones' (Aragonites), which arise from calcium carbonate deposits in the water, to spa guests. Goethe described Müller's collection of stones and in 1831 revised his catalogue for the Carlsbad merchant David Knoll, who had taken over the Mueller collection. Sample collections of this stone collection were offered for sale with the promotional directory.

Goethe, Ovid, and Heinz Mack
On Forms and the Change of Forms

Hartmut Böhme

1. A Summary of Goethe's Morphology

The first mention of the term 'morphology' in Goethe's diary is dated September 25, 1796. However, this theory on the characteristics and organization of living creatures is at least six years older. Goethe developed it on a broad scale—in botany, osteology, and in the anatomy of humankind and animals. Time and again, almost until his death in 1832, Goethe worked on this and related topics, including the concepts of metamorphosis, organization, formation, the primordial phenomenon, and typology. Without ever having spelled out his concept of morphology in theory, it can nevertheless be considered his core view of nature for the following reasons:

(1) Almost all of his nature studies are centered on the question of how natural processes, from the smallest to largest, manifest themselves in stable, recognizable, and also generative forms or shapes.

(2) And yet, to Goethe, 'shape' is not a static term, but rather indicates that each formation or model is a moment within a continuum of re-formation or re-modeling. Each shaping finds its antithesis in de-shaping; each presupposed whole or synthesis finds its opposite in fragmentation or mediation. 'Shape' is thus characterized by the principle of polarity, which is inherent to nature. That which is stable in a specimen permits the identification and recognizability of it as belonging to its species or generic group ('This is a cat'). What is variable in it permits innumerable variations within the limitations of its pattern, and, within a lifecycle or measure of time, formal modifications up to the point of metamorphosis.

(3) 'Shape' is not an abstract term that can only be thought. Rather, it has had an aesthetic dimension from the outset. Not only can shapes be perceived, they must be. They are part, albeit not exclusively so, of the sensory world. Although the general term 'shape' is not a category of pure reason, it is a category of the power of judgment, which proves itself in intuition. This leads to the formation of concepts that hold transcendental status. If this were not the case, Goethe would not talk about morphology, i.e. shape (morphé) is a science to itself. As an empirical entity or contingent formation, 'shape' is not only to be understood in its individualizing phenomenality—it is also applicable on the preceding plane of the general condition of phenomena. The special shape of 'this individual rose' is thus to be differentiated from the overall pattern of 'roses in general.' But both are part of morphology, in which Goethe clearly separates specimen and type.

(4) 'Shape' is a formative ability inherent in nature (Schiller calls it 'formal drive'). For Goethe, this formative ability expresses a type of art, a subject-less technique of nature, in contrast to human art. It presupposes that subjects are 'creating' (artist,

Goethe, Ovid und Heinz Mack
Über Formen und Formwandel

Hartmut Böhme

1. Goethes Morphologie im Überblick

Im Tagebuch vom 25. September 1796 verwendet Goethe den Ausdruck ›Morphologie‹ zum ersten Mal. Der Sache nach ist die Lehre von den Gestalten organisierter Lebewesen wenigstens sechs Jahre älter. Sie wurde von Goethe auf breiter Front entwickelt – in der Botanik, in der Osteologie, in der Anatomie von Tieren und Menschen. Immer wieder, bis kurz vor seinem Tod 1832, arbeitete Goethe an diesem und verwandten Thematiken, also etwa zum Konzept der Metamorphose, der Organisation, der Bildung, des Urphänomens, des Typus et cetera. Ohne dass Goethe sein Konzept je theoretisch ausformuliert hätte, kann die Morphologie doch als das Kernstück seiner Naturauffassung gelten. Und dies aus mehreren Gründen:

(1) Fast alle seine Naturstudien kreisen um die Frage, wie natürliche Prozesse, im Großen wie im Kleinsten, sich in stabilen, wiedererkennbaren, ja auch generativen Formen beziehungsweise Gestalten manifestieren.

(2) Dabei ist ›Gestalt‹ für Goethe kein statischer Begriff, sondern jede Bildung ist ein Moment im Kontinuum der Umbildungen. Jede Gestaltung findet ihren Gegenpol in Entstaltung, jede vorausgesetzte Ganzheit/Synthese hat in der Fragmentierung/Analyse ihr Gegenteil. ›Gestalt‹ ist also durch das der Natur selbst immanente Prinzip der Polarität gekennzeichnet. Was an ihr stabil ist, erlaubt die Identifizierung und Wiedererkennbarkeit eines Exemplars als zu einer Spezies oder Gattung gehörig (›Dies da ist eine Katze.‹); was an ihr variabel ist, erlaubt innerhalb der Grenzen eines Musters zahllose Variationen und innerhalb eines Lebenszyklus oder einer Zeiteinheit Formmodifikationen bis hin zur Metamorphose.

(3) ›Gestalt‹ ist kein abstrakter Begriff, der nur zu denken ist, sondern er hat eine von vornherein ästhetische Dimension: Gestalten können nicht nur, sondern sie müssen wahrgenommen werden. Sie gehören der sinnlichen Welt an – doch nicht dieser allein. Zwar ist der allgemeine Begriff ›Gestalt‹ keine Kategorie der reinen Vernunft, sondern der in Anschauungen sich bewährenden Urteilskraft. Diese findet zu Begriffsbildungen, die einen transzendentalen Status haben. Wenn dies nicht so wäre, würde Goethe nicht von Morphologie sprechen, das heißt von der Wissenschaftsförmigkeit der Gestalt (morphé). Als empirische Größe oder kontingente Bildung ist ›Gestalt‹ nicht nur in ihrer individuierenden Phänomenalität zu verstehen, sondern sie ist auch auf der vorgängigen Ebene der Bedingung von Phänomenen wirksam. Die besondere Gestalt ›dieser einzelnen Rose‹ ist also vom allgemeinen Muster ›Rosen überhaupt‹ zu unterscheiden. Beides gehört zur Morphologie, in der Goethe sauber zwischen Exemplar und Typus trennt.

(4) ›Gestalt‹ ist ein der Natur innewohnendes Formvermögen (Schiller nennt es ›Formtrieb‹). Dieses Bildungsvermögen weist für Goethe eine Art Kunst auf, eine subjektlose

author, genius). Art and nature are mutually interdependent. In nature, we discover the inventive power (inventio, vis plastica) characteristic of the artist in the human world. Conversely, we discover in art, in its procreative power, a parallel movement of 'natura naturans.' This means that art is not art insofar as it imitates products or things of nature but by proceeding like nature.

'Shape' is something 'substantial' (Greek: hypokeimenon, Latin: substantia). This is one side of a guiding difference in effect since antiquity. Its antithesis is the 'byplay,' synbebekós, or accidens—an action occurring at the side. This guiding difference reminds us that morphé (Latin: forma), too, belongs to the Occident's guiding differences. Its antithesis is hyle, or materia. Considered to be chaotic, disorderly, unstructured, and yet dynamic, hyle is equipped with the potential to attain morphé, forma, or shape. Dynamis is itself effective in matter. According to Goethe, 'shape' is the law that brings the metamorphosis of unstructured matter to a state of high (self-)organization, which means to obtain a shape. While art—"born—like Minerva, out of Jupiter's head—out of the heads of the greatest men"[1]—is thus a manifestation of poiesis, it is also close to the effective force of nature (a beautiful dream of immediacy). The 2,000-year-old maxim "ars imitatur naturam"[2] does not necessarily signify a copying of the factual. In Goethe's case, it does, however, refer to those shaping processes that objectify or manifest themselves in nature.

Modeling and remodeling do not make up a normative set of cognitive, moral, or cultural values. The terms also do not refer to the habitus of a species, for example. In our context, modeling refers to a relatively stable or transient metamorphic modeling of plants, animals, and humans, but also of artworks, which are manually 'modeled,' or of rock formations or landscapes representing formations of earth.

Shape is not to be understood teleologically, even though 'modeling' represents a type of "regulation of nature" (FA, vol. I 24, p. 149) that may form the groundwork leading towards "great purposes" (FA, vol. I 24, p. 111), namely procreation (as well as other functions such as nourishment, etc.) Surely, each part of an organized body has a function. Yet, this is not the realization of an intentional design. The shape is rather an assembly of all functions and body parts in a holistic configuration.

Therefore, as a substitute for 'shape,' we can likewise talk about 'model' or 'type.' This refers to the "rule" that ensures the recognition of that which is 'underlying,' i.e. the 'rose-like' quality in many roses. Considering the plethora of flower types, we identify them in turn as plants in contrast to animals or stones. Perceiving a thing 'as a plant' means we have a scheme of 'plants in general.' Goethe is able to perceive a confusing multitude of objects as elements of a type because we have blueprints. In the case of plants, this is what makes a plant a plant. Goethe calls this underlying blueprint the 'primordial plant.' It floats peculiarly between a vivid image, a general pattern of plants, and the many plants in front of our eyes. Each plant represents in and of itself a variation of the primordial plant. We could also refer to the primordial plant as 'idéa' (shape, archetype) or 'eîdos,' given that in doing so we realize, at the same time, the ideational structure and graphic clarity—and generative power, too,

1 Johann Wolfgang von Goethe, *Italienische Reise,* MA vol. XV, p. 464.

2 Kurt Flasch, "Ars imitatur naturam. Platonischer Naturbegriff und mittelalterliche Philosophie der Kunst," in *Parusia: Studien zur Philosophie Platons und zur Problemgeschichte des Platonismus,* ed. Kurt Flasch (Frankfurt am Main, 1965), pp. 265–306.

Technik der Natur, im Gegensatz zur Menschenkunst, die stets Subjekte des ›Machens‹ voraussetzt (Künstler, Autor, Genie). Kunst und Natur verweisen aufeinander: in der Natur entdecken wir eine erfinderische Kraft (inventio, vis plastica), die in der Menschenwelt für den Künstler charakteristisch ist. Umgekehrt entdecken wir in der Kunst, in ihrer prokreativen Kraft eine Parallelbewegung zur ›Natura naturans‹. Kunst ist also nicht Kunst, insofern sie Produkte oder Dinge der Natur nachahmt, sondern indem sie verfährt wie Natur.

›Gestalt‹ ist ein ›Zugrundeliegendes‹, griechisch: hypokeimenon, lateinisch: substantia. Dies ist die eine Seite einer seit der Antike wirksamen Leitdifferenz, deren Gegenpol das ›Beiherspielende‹, synbebekós oder accidens ist; dies ist eine zufällige Bestimmung. Diese Leitdifferenz erinnert daran, dass auch griechisch: morphé, lateinisch: forma, zu den abendländischen Leitdifferenzen gehört: Sie ist der Gegenpol zu hyle/materia. Diese gilt als chaotisch, ordnungslos, strukturlos, aber doch als dynamisch, das heißt mit dem Vermögen (potentia) ausgestattet, zur morphé/forma/Gestalt zu werden. Die in der Materie selbst wirksame dynamis findet bei Goethe die Wendung, dass ›Gestalt‹ dasjenige Gesetz ist, das die Metamorphose der strukturlosen Materie zur (Selbst-)Organisiertheit bewirkt. Das aber heißt: zur Gestalt werden. Indem nun Kunst »gleich der Minerva aus dem Haupte Jupiters, so aus dem Haupte der größten Menschen geboren«[1] und mithin zur Manifestation einer Poiesis wird, ist Kunst der Wirkkraft der Natur nahe (ein schöner Traum von Unmittelbarkeit). Der zweitausendjährige Grundsatz »ars imitatur naturam«[2] muss keineswegs ein Nachäffen des Faktischen heißen. Sondern er verweist bei Goethe auf eben jene Gestaltprozesse, die in der Natur sich objektivieren beziehungsweise manifestieren.

Bildung und Umbildung sind kein normatives Set von kognitiven, moralischen oder kulturellen Werten. Sie meinen auch nicht den Habitus zum Beispiel einer Spezies. In unserem Zusammenhang meint Bildung die relativ stabile beziehungsweise die übergängliche, metamorphisierende Gestalt von Pflanzen, Tieren und Menschen, aber auch von Kunstwerken (die handwerklich ›gebildet‹ werden) oder von Fels- oder Landschaftsformationen, die Erdbildungen darstellen.

Auf keinen Fall ist Gestalt teleologisch zu verstehen, auch wenn die ›Gestalt‹ eine Art »Vorschrift der Natur« (FA, Bd. I 24, S. 149) darstellt oder sogar einem »großen Zwecke« (FA, Bd. I 24, S. 111) zuarbeitet, nämlich der Fortpflanzung (und anderen Funktionen wie der Ernährung et cetera). Gewiss hat jeder Teil eines organisierten Körpers eine Funktion, aber diese ist nicht die Realisierung eines absichtsvollen Designs. Die Gestalt ist eher die Versammlung aller Funktionen und Körperteile zu einer ganzheitlichen Figuration.

Darum kann man ersatzweise für ›Gestalt‹ auch von ›Modell‹ oder ›Typus‹ reden. Damit ist jene »Vorschrift« gemeint, die das ›Zugrundeliegende‹ erkennen lässt, nämlich unter vielen Rosen ›das Rosenhafte‹. Bei einer Vielzahl von Blumensorten identifizieren wir diese wiederum als Pflanzen, im Unterschied zu Tieren oder Steinen. Ein Ding ›als Pflanze‹ wahrzunehmen, heißt, dass wir über ein Schema von ›Pflanzen überhaupt‹ verfügen. Eine verwirrende Vielfalt von Objekten als Elemente einer Einheit wahrzunehmen, ist für Goethe möglich, weil wir über einen Bauplan dessen verfügen, was eine Pflanze zur Pflanze macht. Diesen zugrundeliegenden Bauplan nennt Goethe die ›Urpflanze‹. Sie schwebt eigenartig zwischen einem anschaulichen Bild, einem Muster von Pflanzen überhaupt, und den vielen

1 Goethe, *Italienische Reise,* MA Bd. XV, S. 464.
2 Kurt Flasch, »Ars imitatur naturam. Platonischer Naturbegriff und mittelalterliche Philosophie der Kunst«, in: ders. (Hrsg.): *Parusia. Studien zur Philosophie Platons und zur Problemgeschichte des Platonismus. Festgabe für Johannes Hirschberger,* Frankfurt am Main 1965, S. 265–306.

because 'shape' and 'type' incorporate the genesis and decay, for example, of roses or wolves (in Goethe's case, this also applies to clouds). 'Shape,' or 'primordial phenomenon,' is the blueprint of creation.

Whereas this sounds like teleology, as if Goethe takes an intentional design to the basis of the three kingdoms of nature, the opposite is the case. He does not believe in the preformation theory that claims the later individual is already 'nested' in semen or the egg and only unfolds thanks to consequent growth. This would mean the later shape would be 'there' from the beginning as a material a priori, as preexistence—the homunculus in semen. The development Goethe talks about is not an 'unwrapping' but rather a perpetual development, a metamorphosis. According to epigeneticist Caspar Friedrich Wolff—Goethe was an appreciative follower of his—we should accept rather a "vim essentialem, conjoining everything that intended to produce itself." For this "incomprehensible point" of self-organizing matter, Johann Friedrich Blumenbach coined the term "nisus formativus" *(Bildungstrieb,* 1810, FA, vol. I 24, p. 451). This drive causes a creature to attain a shape. The 'formative drive' is therefore the power that enables unformed matter to take a reproducible shape. Thus, the creative principle is placed into nature. It knows no author. Goethe turns quite decisively against physico-theological, teleological, and creationist assumptions. *(Versuch einer allgemeinen Vergleichungslehre,* ca. 1790, FA, vol. I 24, pp. 209–14). He considers such hypotheses to be projections through which we refer to ourselves as everything that is:

> Because he needs the things and can use them, one could argue that they have been created so that he can use them. … Why should he not call an herb that he cannot use a weed? Because it really should not exist for him at this particular moment. He would rather attribute the appearance of the thistle that renders his work in the fields cumbersome to the curse of an angry good spirit and not to the malice of a spiteful evil one; he should actually consider this thistle as the child of a great universal nature who cares as much for it as she does for the carefully tended and much valued wheat. (FA, vol. I 24, pp. 210–11.)

Clearly, Goethe's notion of nature follows neither 'intentions' nor 'motifs.' Rather, it is a purpose-free, subjectless process where the old stoic argument "mundus propter nos conditus" (the world was created for us) no longer applies. Nature is not a service company created for humankind, according to which we may assume, "since everything that exists should exist for his sake, and everything exists only as a tool and resource for his existence, the natural consequence is: that nature would work equally intentionally and purposefully to supply him with the same tools that he manufactures himself." (FA, vol. I 24, p. 211.)

By no means does nature function in an anthropocentric way. Science must take this into account by keeping humankind's utilitarian measures of value out of science.

Pflanzen da vor meinem Auge, von denen jede für sich die Urpflanze variierend darstellt. Man könnte die Urpflanze auch als ›idéa‹ (Gestalt, Urbild) oder ›eîdos‹ fassen, wenn wir dabei ideelle Struktur und Anschaulichkeit zugleich realisieren. Und generative Kraft: Denn die ›Gestalt‹ oder der ›Typus‹ realisieren das Werden und Vergehen zum Beispiel von Rosen oder Wölfen (bei Goethe aber auch von Wolken). ›Gestalt‹ oder ›Urphänomen‹ meint den Bauplan des Werdens.

Dieses klingt nach Teleologie, als würde Goethe den drei Naturreichen ein absichtsvolles Design zugrunde legen. Das Gegenteil ist der Fall. Goethe hängt nicht der Präformationsthese an, wonach das spätere Individuum bereits im Samen oder Ei ›eingeschachtelt‹ ist und durch Wachstum sich nur ausfaltet. Hiernach wäre die spätere Gestalt von Anfang an ›da‹, als materielles Apriori, als Präexistenz: der Homunculus im Samen. Die Entwicklung, von der Goethe spricht, ist kein ›Sich-Auseinanderwickeln‹, sondern ein ständiges Umwandeln, eine Metamorphose. Nach dem Epigenetiker Caspar Friedrich Wolff, dem Goethe dankbar folgt, muss man eher »eine vim essentialem« annehmen, »die sich zu allem fügt, was sich selbst hervorbringen wollte«. Johann Friedrich Blumenbach wiederum prägt für diesen »unbegreiflichen Punkt« der sich selbst organisierenden Materie den Begriff des »nisus formativus« *(Bildungstrieb,* 1810, FA, Bd. I 24, S. 451). Dies ist ein Trieb, der die Gestaltwerdung eines Lebewesens bewirkt. Der ›Bildungstrieb‹ ist mithin jene Kraft, die aus formlosem Stoff eine reproduktionsfähige Gestalt werden lässt. Damit ist das gestaltende Prinzip in die Natur hineinverlegt und kennt keinen Autor. Gegen physikotheologische, teleologische oder kreationistische Annahmen wendet sich Goethe entschieden *(Versuch einer allgemeinen Vergleichungslehre,* um 1790, FA, Bd. I 24, S. 209–214). Er hält solche Hypothesen für Projektionen, durch die der Mensch alles, was ist, auf sich selbst bezieht:

> Weil er die Sachen braucht und brauchen kann, so folget daraus; sie sein hervorgebracht daß er sie brauche. […] Warum sollte er ein Kraut das er nicht nutzen kann nicht Unkraut nennen? da es wirklich nicht an dieser Stelle für ihn existieren sollte. Eher wird er die Entstehung [der] Distel die ihm die Arbeit auf seinem Acker sauer macht dem Fluch eines erzürnten guten Wesens, der Tücke eines schadenfrohen bösen Wesens zuschreiben; als eben diese Distel für ein Kind der großen allgemeinen Natur zu halten das ihr ebenso nahe am Herzen liegt, als der sorgfältig gebauete und so sehr geschätzte Weizen. (FA, Bd. I 24, S. 210 f.)

Es ist hier deutlich, dass Goethes Natur nicht ›Absichten‹ und ›Motiven‹ folgt, sondern ein sinnfreier, subjektloser Prozess ist, in dem das alte stoische Argument »mundus propter nos conditus« (die Welt ist unsretwegen geschaffen) nicht mehr gilt. Natur ist kein für den Menschen eingerichteter Dienstleistungsbetrieb, wonach man annehmen dürfe, »[…] daß alles was existiert um seinetwillen existiere, alles nur als Werkzeug als Hülfsmittel seines Daseins existiere, so folgt wie natürlich daraus: daß die Natur auch eben so absichtlich und zweckmäßig verfahren habe, ihm Werkzeuge zu verschaffen, wie er sie sich selbst verschafft.« (FA, Bd. I 24, S. 211.)

> How much a natural philosopher, who wants to continue to reflect about universal questions, has cause to distance himself from this belief we can see in the example of botany. To botany as science, the most colorful and splendid flowers, the most edible and beautiful fruits are in a certain sense no more than the despised weed in its natural habitat or the dried out useless seed pod. (FA, vol. I 24, p. 211.)

The "organized world," its "fabric of form," originates from an indecipherable "primordial power of nature" (FA, vol. I 24, pp. 213–14). While this is definitely not a wish come true, it is also not an enemy we have any reason to eliminate. It is only upon disregarding ourselves—and at most considering ourselves part of natural history—that morphology begins to make sense.

The interaction between intrinsic form construction and epigenetic influences, to which each individual process of formation is subjected, offers space for a non-anthropocentric exploration of nature, including in botany, comparative anatomy, zoology, and even in the formation of mountains and clouds. However, this does not preclude understanding humans as the tightest knot within nature's network, which turns us into a microcosm. But this is not to say we rank highest within the cosmos—humans as the crown of creation. Rather, the reverse is true. Within their own makeup, humans recognize the survival of simpler animals:

> The final understanding that the human being is built in such a way that he unites so many characteristics and natures and therefore in his physical being represents a small universe and exists as a representative of all the species of animals, all this can only become absolutely clear and beautiful, when we do not—which unfortunately happens too often—look at things from above and seek human nature in the animals; we rather have to start from below and discover the simple animal again in the complexity of the human body. (*Vorträge über die drei ersten Kapitel des Entwurfs einer Allgemeinen Einleitung in die Vergleichende Anatomie …*, 1796, FA, vol. I 24, p. 266.)

We note that such an insight is the clearest and the prettiest. 'Clarity' corresponds to the Cartesian ideal of cognition. Combining beauty with cognition and science corresponds to the aestheticization of non-artistic domains and practices that occurred around 1800, where Novalis was able to talk about "beautiful mining." When introducing 'shape' to science, Goethe utilizes a direct aesthetic term. This is also true for metamorphosis, the mythic-poetic concept Ovid implanted in occidental thought.

2. Ovid's Metamorphoses

Metamorphoses are not simply alterations, not just genesis and decay or vanitas ("tempus edax rerum," Met. XV, 234–36), not only instability and flow. That would mean its dynamics were within the continuum of one time, within one space, one cosmos. However, Ovid teaches the disruption of the continuum and thus a complete change of

Mitnichten verfährt Natur auf diese anthropozentrische Weise. Und dem müsse die Wissenschaft Rechnung tragen, indem sie utilitaristische Wertmaßstäbe des Menschen aus der Wissenschaft heraushält.

> Wie sehr aber ein Naturforscher, derjenige der über die allgemeinen Dinge weiter denken will, Ursache habe sich von dieser Vorstellungsart zu entfernen, können wir an dem bloßen Beispiel der Botanik sehen. Der Botanik als Wissenschaft, sind die buntesten und gefülltesten Blumen, die eßbarsten und schönsten Früchte nicht mehr, ja im gewissen Sinne nicht einmal so viel wert als ein verachtetes Unkraut im natürlichen Zustande, als eine trockne unbrauchbare Samenkapsel. (FA, Bd. I 24, S. 211.)

Die »organisierte Welt«, ihr »Bau der Bildung« erwächst einer unenträtselten »Urkraft der Natur« (FA, Bd. I 24, S. 213 f.). Aber ganz gewiss ist diese kein Wünsch-dir-Was. Doch sie ist auch kein Feind, den niederzuringen wir allen Anlass haben. Von uns absehend, allenfalls uns als Teil der Naturgeschichte begreifend, gewinnt die Morphologie erst ihren Sinn.

Die Wechselwirkung zwischen intrinsischer Formbildung und epigenetischen Einflüssen, denen jeder einzelne Bildungsvorgang unterliegt, gibt Raum für eine nicht-anthropozentrische Erforschung der Natur, sei es in der Botanik, der vergleichenden Anatomie, der Tierkunde oder gar der Gebirgs- oder Wolkenbildung. Das schließt nicht aus, den Menschen als den dichtesten Knoten im Netzwerk der Natur zu verstehen, was ihn zum Mikrokosmos werden lässt. Das meint nicht den höchsten Rang im Kosmos – der Mensch als Krone der Schöpfung. Sondern es ist umgekehrt: In der eigenen Komposition erkennt der Mensch die Survivals der einfacheren Tiere:

> […] die Einsicht zuletzt, wie der Mensch dergestalt gebaut sei, daß er so viele Eigenschaften und Naturen in sich vereinige und dadurch auch schon physisch als eine kleine Weit, als ein Repräsentant der übrigen Tiergattungen existiere, alles dieses kann nur dann am deutlichsten und schönsten eingesehen werden, wenn wir, nicht wie bisher leider nur zu oft geschehen, unsere Betrachtungen von oben herab anstellen und den Menschen im Tiere suchen, sondern wenn wir von unten herauf anfangen und das einfachere Tier im zusammengesetzten Menschen endlich wieder entdecken. *(Vorträge über die drei ersten Kapitel des Entwurfs einer Allgemeinen Einleitung in die Vergleichende Anatomie […],* 1796, FA, Bd. I 24, S. 266.)

Wir halten fest, dass eine solche Einsicht die deutlichste u n d die schönste sei. ›Deutlichkeit‹ entspricht dem cartesianischen Erkenntnisideal. Schönheit aber mit Erkenntnis und Wissenschaft zu verbinden, entspricht der Ästhetisierung außerkünstlerischer Bereiche und Praktiken um 1800, sodass Novalis vom »schönen Bergbau« sprechen kann oder Goethe mit der ›Gestalt‹ einen unmittelbar ästhetischen Begriff in die Wissenschaft einführt. Das gilt auch für die Metamorphose, die ein mythopoetisches Konzept ist, wie es von Ovid ins abendländische Denken implantiert wurde.

shape: from one genus to another, the transgression of species' boundaries (according to Aristotle, this cannot exist), jumps from one realm of nature to another (into the fields of minerals, animals, or plants), from the organic to inorganic, terrestrial to astral, from one element to the next, and the transformation from old to young, living to dead (but not vice versa). In the process, partial identities are kept. Therefore, disruption and continuity are not contradictory. (For example, Actaeon, after his transformation into a stag, held on to his internal language, but he could only utter animal sounds to the outside world.) Metamorphosis is usually a change in shape (like when Daphne, fleeing from rape, turns into a laurel tree), but often a change of material can occur while the form remains (as with Pygmalion, the ivory sculpture that turns into a woman of flesh and blood). Frequently, metamorphosis also reduces a person to a characteristic that will determine them from then on (for example, Niobe, in total mourning, dissolves into watery marble; the tears of satyrs and nymphs turn into the Marsyas river; and Cyane dissolves into water and is incapable of telling Ceres where her daughter Proserpina is; Met. III, 428–31, 466–67, cf. Arethusa, V, 632–41).

This is evidently not based on Ovid's view of historia. Rather, his epic poem fluctuates between natural philosophy, the turning of myths into literature, and history. So, what is the basic principle? An atomistic dynamism. It is the principle of the lively powers of nature, which penetrate into and weave their way through everything. History and histories are but ephemeral embodiments of nature's dynamic processes.

Ovid's dynamism is not peaceful. He lets ubiquitous violence gain power beside erotic dynamics to reveal nature's two faces. While nature exhibits no unambiguous quality, it also shows no clear goal, no teleology. In Ovid's world, these do not exist. If people read teleology in what they observe, it is due to misunderstandings or the projections of humans. It would be equally erroneous to say that history follows intentions, no matter how much it may have been intentionally invested in the world. In the case of Ovid, the unpredictable (chance, game, disaster, or fate—these are all nature's game types) prevails, even if the metamorphosis appears to be the consequence of an action. That is exactly the illusion.

Ovid's metamorphic worldview is not mythical or religious. Metamorphosis is the world's meta-process, and the various metamorphoses are the mythic-poetic consequences Ovid derives from atomism and the philosophy of elements. The metamorphic principle allows one to underpin the formerly mythical narratives with a philosophy of nature, where even the gods are only fellow players in nature's changing shape.

This does not contradict the fact that art is the capability Ovid values most—because nature, by its very essence, is a maker of shapes and thus an artist. Art can be nature and vice versa, and nature hides that it is art. On the other hand, an artwork can be so perfect that it is considered nature. Goethe is very close to this formulation, but he does not share the limitless and at times wild elements of Ovid's *Metamorphoses*. To Goethe, a metamorphosis is an especially orderly process of self-organization. It is hardly surprising that in this sense he shows greater proximity to modern biology than to Ovid's *Metamorphoses*.

2. Ovids Metamorphosen

Metamorphosen sind nicht einfach Veränderungen, nicht nur Werden und Vergehen oder vanitas (»tempus edax rerum«, Met. XV, 234 ff.), nicht nur Unbeständigkeit und Fluss. Das wäre Dynamik im Kontinuum der einen Zeit, in dem einen Raum, dem einen Kosmos. Ovid aber lehrt die Disruption des Kontinuums und damit einen oft kompletten Gestaltwechsel: von einem Genus ins andere, Sprünge über die Speziesgrenzen hinweg (die es nach Aristoteles nicht geben kann), Sprünge von einem Naturreich ins andere (ins Mineralische, Tierische, Pflanzliche), vom Organischen ins Anorganische, vom Terrestrischen ins Astrale, vom Element zum anderen Element, Wandlung vom Alten zum Jungen, vom Lebenden zum Toten (aber nicht umgekehrt). Dabei werden oft Teil-Identitäten beibehalten, sodass Disruption und Kontinuität sich nicht widersprechen (so behält der in einen Hirsch verwandelte Aktaeon seine innere Sprache, während er nach außen hin nur Tierlaute von sich geben kann). Meist ist die Metamorphose ein Gestaltwechsel (Daphne, die, auf der Flucht vor Vergewaltigung, zu einem Lorbeerstrauch wird), öfters aber auch ein Stoff-Wechsel bei Erhaltung der Form (die Elfenbeinplastik Pygmalions wird zu einer Frau aus Fleisch und Blut). Öfters auch ist die Metamorphose die Reduktion auf eine Eigenschaft, die fortan die Person bestimmt (Niobe ist ganz Trauer und löst sich in tränenden Marmor auf; die Tränen der Satyrn und Nymphen, die zum Fluss Marsyas verwandelt werden; Cyane löst sich in Wasser auf und kann Ceres nicht mehr sagen, wo ihre Tochter Proserpina ist; Met. III, 428–431, 466 f., vgl. Arethusa, Met. V, 632–641).

Dahinter steht nicht etwa eine Auffassung von Historia, sondern Ovids Epos schwankt eigenartig zwischen Naturphilosophie, Literarisierung des Mythos und Geschichte. Was also ist das Grundlegende? Ein atomistischer Dynamismus. Er ist das Prinzip der lebendigen Kräfte der Natur, die in alles hinein- und durch alles hindurchwirken. Geschichte und Geschichten sind nur ephemere Verkörperungen dynamischer Prozesse der Natur.

Der Dynamismus Ovids ist nicht friedfertig. Die ubiquitäre Gewalt, die Ovid neben den erotischen Dynamiken mächtig werden lässt, zeigt das Zwiegesicht der Natur, die keine eindeutige Qualität aufweist, ebenso wenig wie ein eindeutiges Ziel, eine Teleologie. Sie gibt es in der Welt Ovids nicht. Es sind Missverständnisse und Projektionen der Menschen, wenn sie Teleologie aus dem, was sie beobachten, herauszulesen glauben. Ebenso irrig wäre es zu meinen, Geschichte würde Intentionen folgen, so viel auch intentional in die Welt investiert werden mag. Bei Ovid herrscht das Unvorhersehbare (Zufall, Spiel, Verhängnis, Fatum: Spielformen der Natur), auch dann, wenn die Metamorphose die Konsequenz einer Handlung zu sein scheint. Aber eben dies ist Schein.

Das metamorphotische Weltbild Ovids ist nicht mehr mythisch, nicht mehr religiös. Das Metamorphotische ist der Metaprozess der Welt. Die Metamorphose ist die mythopoetische Konsequenz, die Ovid aus dem Atomismus und der Elementenphilosophie zieht. Das metamorphotische Prinzip erlaubt es, die ehemals mythischen Narrative zu unterlegen mit einer Philosophie der Natur, in der auch die Götter nur Mitspieler im Gestaltwandel der Natur sind.

Dem widerspricht nicht, dass Kunst dasjenige Vermögen ist, das Ovid am höchsten schätzt. Denn Natur ist ihrem Wesen nach Formbildnerin, also Künstlerin. Kunst kann Natur

There is another aspect that reveals a surprising closeness between Ovid, Goethe, and modernity. Disruptions invariably result in something new while destroying something else. This is closely related to the "creative destruction" that Joseph A. Schumpeter considers a principle of modern economics and art.[3] For Ovid and Goethe, creative destruction is a basic mechanism of nature, hence the omnipresence of eros and violence, which both embody disruptive and procreative elements. Both sides belong to nature. They are poles between which human actions oscillate. In the *Metamorphoses*—especially in the erotic domain—truly horrendous abysses of violence open up, making it a challenge to accept this dimension as belonging to homo sapiens (the carnage between Phineus and his entourage, for example, or between Perseus and his followers, Met. V, 1–243).

This is why Ovid and Goethe are far removed from harmonic visions of nature and, consequently, a law-shaped cosmos, or 'nous.' Nature is not only double-faced in its principles, but also instable vis-à-vis its formal arsenal. Accordingly, Ovid does not develop a 'systema naturae,' but a confusing, powerful, and mobile texture, which, for its part, does not represent an eternal order, but a perpetual state of dissolution and new creation.

One example that elucidates Ovid's view of art is the myth of Arachne, a 'story of weaving,' as well as the myth of Philomela. Of course, Ovid already knew of its reversal—'weaving a story.' The 'textor' is the weaver—and Goethe was delighted to pick up on the fact that one of his ancestors, Wolfgang Weber, latinized his name to Textor. Goethe absolutely saw himself as a weaver of texts. 'Textum / textus' means fabric, or structure, and the formation of speech. These metaphoric transfers gave rise to poetics, the doctrine on the creation of artful fabrics made of words. Ovid knew this. His *Metamorphoses* is an enormous narrative carpet made of countless woven images.

It is no surprise that Goethe, in the prose piece *Bedenken und Ergebung* in the first volume of his 1817 *Hefte zur Morphologie*, sheds light on his verses that describe nature as "a master-weaver's fabric," a fabric that unfolds itself dynamically. This is reminiscent of Mephistopheles's famous weaving verse in *Faust I* (v. 1922–41). Goethe differs from Ovid in that to him nature has a 'structure,' pattern, and an order, which is a clear contrast to the artful chaos Ovid develops in his narrative carpet.

Arachne, whose name means 'spider,' has a grandiose reputation as a weaver. As reckless as she is proud, she challenges Athena, the patroness of the art of weaving, to a contest. She is Hybris, a Goethean, Promethean rebel in female form.

The goddess and the country girl, Arachne, then create two picture stories, artworks of picture weaving, in tapestries and carpets. Athena depicts how she settled her conflict with Poseidon over which of the two should give their name to the city. In this story, Nike grants Athena the victory, and she becomes the eponym of the city of Athens.

Yet, Arachne weaves her work. By depicting the affairs of Jupiter and other gods with mortal women, she demonstrates the gods' violence and their libido. The verism of her tapestry weaving is extraordinary. The spectator thinks they 'really' (verum) see the

3 Cf. Hartmut Böhme, "Das Schumpetersche Paradox und die späte Triebtheorie Freuds," in *Kreative Zerstörung: Über Macht und Ohnmacht des Destruktiven in den Künsten*, ed. Wolfram Bergande (Vienna, 2017), pp. 18–56.

sein und Natur Kunst; oder aber die Natur verbirgt, dass sie Kunst ist; wie umgekehrt in einem Werk die Kunst so perfekt ist, dass man sie für Natur hält. Das ist sehr nahe bei Goethe. Doch das Schrankenlose, ja bisweilen Wüste der Metamorphose teilt er mit Ovid nicht, weil für Goethe die Metamorphose gerade ein geregelter Prozess der Selbstorganisation ist. Darin steht er, was nicht überrascht, der modernen Biologie näher als den Ovidschen *Metamorphosen*.

In einem anderen Aspekt sind Goethe wie Ovid der Moderne überraschend nah. Disruptionen schaffen etwas Neues und zugleich zerstören sie anderes. Dies ist nahe verwandt der »kreativen Zerstörung«, die Joseph A. Schumpeter für ein Prinzip der modernen Wirtschaft und der Kunst hält.[3] Bei Ovid und Goethe ist kreative Zerstörung ein basaler Mechanismus der Natur. Darum die Omnipräsenz von Eros und Gewalt. In ihnen verkörpert sich das Disruptive zugleich mit dem Prokreativen. Beide Seiten gehören zur Natur. Es sind die Pole, zwischen denen das menschliche Handeln pendelt. In den *Metamorphosen* öffnen sich, gerade im erotischen Feld, derart horrende Abgründe der Gewalt, dass es bis heute schwer fällt, diese Dimension als zum homo sapiens gehörig zu akzeptieren (zum Beispiel das Gemetzel zwischen Phineus und seinem Gefolge und Perseus und den Seinen, Met. V, 1–243).

Darum ist Ovid, wie auch Goethe, weit entfernt von harmonikalen Vorstellungen über Natur, also einem gesetzesförmigen Kosmos, der ›Nous‹ ist. Natur ist nicht nur doppelgesichtig in ihren Prinzipien, sondern auch instabil in ihrem Formenarsenal. Darum entwickelt sie bei Ovid auch keine ›systema naturae‹, sondern ein unübersichtliches, gewaltiges und mobiles Gewebe, das seinerseits nicht eine ewige Ordnung repräsentiert, sondern sich ständig auflöst und neu schöpft.

Ein Beispiel soll Ovids Auffassung von der Kunst verdeutlichen. Es ist die Mythe von Arachne, eine ›Erzählung des Webens‹, wie auch die von Philomela. Natürlich wusste Ovid schon von der Umkehrung: dem ›Weben der Erzählungen‹. Der ›textor‹ ist der Weber – und Goethe hat es gerne aufgenommen, dass sein Vorfahr seinen Namen Wolfgang Weber zu Textor latinisierte. Denn als Weber von Texten verstand sich Goethe unbedingt. ›Textum / textus‹ meint sowohl das Gewebe, als auch das Gefüge, den Bau der Rede. Aus diesen metaphorischen Transfers entstand eine Poetik, die Lehre vom Herstellen kunstvoller Gewebe aus Wörtern. Das ist Ovid bewusst. Die *Metamorphosen* sind ein gewaltiger Erzählteppich aus zahllosen Wirk-Bildern.

Es ist kein Wunder, dass Goethe im ersten Band der *Hefte zur Morphologie* von 1817 ins Prosastück *Bedenken und Ergebung* Verse einflicht, in denen er die Natur als »der ewigen Weberin Meisterstück«, als dynamisch sich entwickelndes Gewebe entwirft. Dies erinnert an die berühmten Web-Verse von Mephisto in *Faust I* (V. 1922–1941). Von Ovid unterscheidet sich Goethe dadurch, dass die Natur, so gewaltig und gewaltsam sie sich immer wieder zeigt, doch im Ganzen eine ›Textur‹, ein Muster und eine Ordnung aufweist, durchaus im Unterschied zu dem kunstvollen Chaos, das Ovid in seinem Erzählteppich entwickelt.

Arachne nun, deren Name ›Spinne‹ bedeutet, hat einen grandiosen Ruhm als Weberin. Ebenso leichtsinnig wie stolz fordert sie Athene, Patronin der Webkunst, zum Wettstreit. Das ist Hybris (sie ist ein Goethe'scher Prometheus-Rebell in weiblicher Gestalt).

3 Vgl. Hartmut Böhme, »Das Schumpetersche Paradox und die späte Triebtheorie Freuds«, in: *Kreative Zerstörung. Über Macht und Ohnmacht des Destruktiven in den Künsten,* hrsg. von Wolfram Bergande, Berlin und Wien 2017, S. 18–56.

bull and sea and even the abduction of Europa 'herself' (ipsa). Arachne 'creates' (fecit) a 'work' (opus) of unmatched illusionism with warp and weft. Everything attains a living shape. Her stories are framed by a border of flowers and ivy vines, a classic feature of ornamental art. Athena sees nothing to criticize in Arachne's art. For that exact reason, she tears apart the woven picture of the "divine crimes" and hits Arachne on the forehead. Humiliated, Arachne hangs herself. Athena then transforms her into a spider, which, in Virgil's work, is "Minerva's enemy."

Weaving is one of the skills that make it possible to separate humans and the gods. Athena, Arachne, and spider; goddess, human and animal. In the space between animal and god, autonomous human art emerges. As Arachne's work shows, human art serves to criticize the gods. If, following Gottfried Semper, weaving is in fact a basic technique of our culture,[4] then, located on the threshold between myth and Enlightenment, Arachne is both a heroine and a victim. We will soon see that even Heinz Mack has developed his aesthetics out of this tradition.

Even though metamorphoses are often divine punishments, Ovid shows that the principle of changing shape is a dynamic that is situated within nature itself. Nothing in nature keeps its shape, which means that anything can take the shape of something else. Precisely for the reason that, for Ovid, nature is a limitless site for the creation of malleable forms, natural history must be open to the fabled and the curious, the miracles and secret signs, and to narratives that appear to transcend the boundaries of the kingdoms of nature.

Ovid obviously permits art to participate in the type of metamorphosis that generally applies to bodies: "nostra quoque ipsorum semper requieque sine ulla / corpora vertuntur" (our bodies also, always change, Met. XV, 214–15). This is because "artifices natura manus admovit" (nature changed us with her skillful touch / put on artist's hands, Met. XV, 218). What Ovid attests to here, by the authority of Pythagoras, is generally true for his *Metamorphoses.* Goethe could have referred to it. Ovid's art corresponds to the art of nature itself, just like we know it as 'sollertia naturae' from Cicero and as 'daedala tellus' from Lucretius. There is, however, one significant difference to note in the Pygmalion myth. Pygmalion is only capable of giving the statue a living shape but not the living spark (this anticipates the contrast of 'vivacitá' and 'viva,' a central issue in contemporary art debates). The statue is not a woman but is rather undead, simply a work of art. Wherever such creatures appear, the gods are near, and so is madness and art.

3. "Vis superba formae"—An Interlude

"Vis superba formae. A beautiful expression by Johannes Secundus," quotes Goethe in *Maxims and Reflections* (No. 362; MA, vol. 17, p. 782). This is the last line of the poem *Basium VIII* from a collection entitled *Basia* by the Dutchman Jan Nicolai Everaerts (1511–1536), who called himself Johannes Secundus. Goethe was quite familiar with his slim body of work.

4 Gottfried Semper, *Der Stil in den technischen und tektonischen Künsten oder Praktische Ästhetik: Ein Handbuch für Techniker, Künstler und Kunstfreunde,* vol. 1 (Frankfurt am Main, 1860) pp. 13–525.

Die Göttin und das Provinzmädel Arachne schaffen nun zwei Bild-Erzählungen, Inkunabeln der Bild-Wirkerei, der Tapisserien und Teppiche. Athene schildert, wie sie den Streit mit Poseidon austrägt, wer denn von beiden der Stadt seinen Namen geben dürfe. Nike teilt Athene den Sieg zu, die damit Eponyme der Stadt Athen wird.

Arachne aber webt ihr Werk: die Affären Jupiters (und anderer Götter) mit sterblichen Frauen. Sie demonstriert die Gewalt und Triebhaftigkeit der Götter. Der Verismus ihrer Bildwirkerei ist stupend: Der Betrachter glaubt, den Stier ›wirklich‹ und das Meer ›wirklich‹ (verum) zu sehen, und auch die Europa ›selbst‹ (ipsa), wie sie entführt wird. Arachne ›malt‹ (fecit) mit Kett- und Schussfäden ein ›Werk‹ (opus) von unübertrefflichem Illusionismus. Alles wird zur lebendigen Gestalt. Gerahmt werden die Bild-Erzählungen von einer Bordüre aus Blumen und Efeugerank. Ein Klassiker der Ornamentkunst. Athene hat an der Kunst Arachnes nichts zu kritisieren. Doch eben darum zerreißt sie das Web-Bild der »göttlichen Verbrechen« und sticht Arachne in die Stirn. Gedemütigt hängt sich Arachne auf. Athene verwandelt Arachne in eine Spinne, die bei Vergil die »Feindin Minervas« ist.

Die Webkunst gehört zu jenen Kompetenzen, mittels derer die Loslösung der Menschen von den Göttern möglich wird. Athene – Arachne – Spinne, Göttin – Mensch – Tier: Im Zwischenraum zwischen Tier und Gott entsteht die menschliche Kunst in ihrer Eigenständigkeit. Sie wird, wie das Bildwerk Arachnes zeigt, zur Kritik der Götter. Wenn Webkunst, nach Gottfried Semper, eine basale Technik menschlicher Kultur ist,[4] dann ist, auf der Schwelle zwischen Mythos und Aufklärung, Arachne ihre Heroine und ihr Opfer zugleich. Wir werden sehen, dass noch Heinz Mack seine Ästhetik in dieser Tradition entwickelt.

Auch wenn die Metamorphosen oft Strafen der Götter sind, so zeigt doch Ovid, dass das Prinzip des Gestaltwandels eine ins Innere der Natur selbst gehörende Dynamik ist. Nichts in der Natur behält seine Form – und das heißt: Alles kann die Form von anderem annehmen. Gerade weil die Natur bei Ovid eine gewaltige Zeugungsstätte von plastischen Formen ist, muss die Naturgeschichte offen sein für Fabulae und Curiosa, für Wunder und geheimnisvolle Zeichen, für Narrative, welche die Grenzen zwischen den Naturreichen zu überspielen scheinen.

Deutlich ist, dass Ovid die Kunst teilhaben lässt an jener Verwandlung, die für Körper prinzipiell gilt: »nostra quoque ipsorum semper requieque sine ulla / corpora vertuntur« (ruhelos wird auch unser Leib immerzu verwandelt, Met. XV, 214 f.). Denn: »artifices natura manus admovit« (die Natur legte Künstlerhände an, Met. XV, 218). Was Ovid hier durch die Autorität des Pythagoras beglaubigt, gilt für die *Metamorphosen* überhaupt. Goethe hätte sich darauf berufen können. Ovids Kunst entspricht der Kunst der Natur selbst, wie wir sie auch als ›sollertia naturae‹ bei Cicero, als ›daedala tellus‹ bei Lukrez kennen. Mit einem wesentlichen Unterschied, den wir im Pygmalion-Mythos erkennen: Pygmalion vermag der Statue nur die Form des Lebendigen zu geben, nicht aber den lebendigen Funken (das nimmt den Gegensatz von ›vivacitá‹ und ›viva‹ vorweg, wie er in der Kunstdiskussion der Neuzeit zentral wird). Die Statue ist keine Frau, sondern eine Untote, ein Kunstwerk eben. Wo immer derartige Wesen erscheinen, sind die Götter nah, der Wahn oder die Kunst.

4 Gottfried Semper, *Der Stil in den technischen und tektonischen Künsten oder Praktische Aesthetik. Ein Handbuch für Techniker, Künstler und Kunstfreunde*, Bd. 1, Frankfurt am Main 1860, Textile Kunst: S. 13–525.

"Vis superba formae." This could be the self-confident attitude of an artist-genius whose autonomous work considers the world primarily from a formal, aesthetic point of view—nature as a form aggregate analogous to art. Goethe is interested in the natural dynamis that is realized in nature's formal configurations, which he calls entelechy. Under the direction of regulation and organization, entelechy determines the shape of objects and living creatures (and in the case of living creatures, this also entails reproduction). It is not governed by a determining causality, but rather the interplay of contingency and order permeated with surprising multiple bifurcations and non-linear developments. It requires power to generate form and form itself is a power—it has an impact. One can say it has 'virtus' and 'vis' in the multiple senses of the words: vigor, merit, morality, value, and healing power, and also strength, power, effectiveness, meaning, and violence. Yes, even violence. Goethe's aesthetics are based on these kinds of characteristics and dynamics. "Vis superba formae."

The foundation of the universe of objects consists of basic substances like water, stone, soil, and flesh. They must always represent themselves to become perceivable. To this end, light is the first and last prerequisite. Consequently, substances are the material carriers and agents of shape, the 'morphé' of bodies and world. They are the requirements that underpin the real and the possible. Substances are the material a priori of shapes. The "powers behind the shapes"[5] are to be differentiated from substances and objects. Without this interplay of powers there would be no kinetics, the movement of and in the world. The artistic part of Goethe is fascinated by shape and movement more than anything else (and this applies to Mack, too). For Goethe, however, everything is in motion. Not just living creatures—plants, animals, humans—but even the most rigid thing, the lithosphere, which therefore has a relationship to even the most flexible thing, humans. It is only due to the interplay of substances and shapes, powers and matter, that the world becomes the living world, which Goethe calls "farbigen Abglanz" *(Faust II,* v. 4727).

4. Primeval Forms in Mack's Work

In the following, I will attempt to identify those characteristic primeval forms in Mack's art that harmonize with Goethe. Following Ovid and Semper, we are dealing with the textures of art, i.e. those generative structures that, like in Goethean morphology, permit the creation of an infinite diversity of variants and series. A finite formal alphabet generates infinite potential realizations, a fact that helps explain the overwhelming creative abundance of Mack's oeuvre. When reading Semper's statements about Textile Art, one cannot help but note his astonishing proximity to Heinz Mack. Semper analyzes garments, blankets, and other articles close to the periphery of human vestments. But these merely represent the core from which all object types can be accounted for, or at least any article whose shell, surface, skin, or cover offers free space for geometric ornamentation—all the way to the artistic decor of buildings. Ornament, rhythm, relief, pattern—in brief, stylistic forms do not serve functionality (utility). Rather, they serve the depiction, the performance, and ultimately the object's aesthetics.

5 Beate Ermarcora et al., ed., *Die Kräfte hinter den Formen: Erdgeschichte, Materie, Prozess in der zeitgenössischen Kunst,* exh. cat. Galerie im Taxispalais, Kunstmuseum Krefeld, Kunstmuseum Thun (Cologne, 2016).

3. »Vis superba formae« – Ein Zwischenspiel

»Vis superba formae. Ein schönes Wort von Johannes Secundus«, zitiert Goethe in den *Maximen und Reflexionen* (Nr. 362, MA, Bd. 17, S. 782). Es handelt sich um den letzten Vers des Gedichts *Basium VIII* aus der Sammlung *Basia* des Niederländers Jan Nicolai Everaerts (1511–1536), der sich Johannes Secundus nannte. Goethe kannte sein schmales Werk gut.

»Vis superba formae« – das könnte auch die selbstbewusste Attitüde eines Künstlergenies sein, dessen Werk autonome Formerzeugung ist und der die Welt zuallererst unter formästhetischen Aspekten betrachtet: die Natur als kunstanaloges Formaggregat. Goethe ist es um jene natürliche Dynamis zu tun, die sich in den Formgestalten der Natur verwirklicht. Das nennt er Entelechie, welche die Gestaltungen der Dinge und Lebewesen in der Regie von Regulation und Organisation bestimmt (bei Lebewesen auch von Reproduktion). Darin herrscht keine determinierende Kausalität, sondern ein Zusammenspiel von Kontingenz und Ordnung. In diese sind überraschende Verzweigungen und nicht-lineare Entwicklungen eingeschlossen. Form bedarf einer Kraft zu ihrer Hervorbringung und Form ist selbst eine Kraft; sie hat Wirkung. Man darf auch sagen: Sie hat ›virtus‹ und ›vis‹, im mehrfachen Sinn der Wörter: Tatkraft, Vorzug, Sittlichkeit, Wert, Heilkraft sowie Stärke, Macht, Wirksamkeit, Bedeutung, Gewalt; ja, auch Gewalt. Auf solchen Eigenschaften und Dynamiken beruht Goethes Ästhetik. »Vis superba formae.«

Es sind die basalen Stoffe wie Wasser, Stein, Erde oder Fleisch, die dem Universum der Dinge zu Grunde liegen und sich stets im Besonderen verkörpern müssen, um zur Anschauung zu werden – wozu das Licht die erste und letzte Bedingung ist. Die Stoffe sind folglich die materialen Träger und die Agenten der Gestalten, der ›morphé‹ von Körpern und Welt. Sie sind das Notwendige, das dem Wirklichen und dem Möglichen zugrunde liegt. Stoffe sind das materiale Apriori der Formen. Von den Stoffen und Dingen zu unterscheiden sind die »Kräfte hinter den Formen«[5]. Gäbe es dieses Zusammenspiel der Kräfte nicht, dann gäbe es auch nicht die Kinetik, die Bewegung der Welt und in der Welt. Gestalt und Bewegung faszinieren den Künstler Goethe vor allem (und das gilt auch für Mack). Doch für Goethe sind nicht nur Lebewesen – Pflanzen, Tiere, Menschen –, sondern alles ist in Bewegung, auch das Starrste, die Lithosphäre, die deswegen Verwandtschaft sogar zum Beweglichsten, dem Menschen zeigt. Erst im Zusammenspiel also von Stoffen und Formen, Kräften und Grund wird die Welt zur lebendigen Welt, die Goethe den »farbigen Abglanz« nennt (*Faust II*, V. 4727).

4. Urformen bei Mack

Im Folgenden wird versucht, im Sinne Goethes die für Mack charakteristischen Urformen seiner Kunst zu identifizieren. Ovid und Semper folgend, handelt es sich dabei um Texturen seiner Kunst, also um jene generativen Strukturen, die, wie die Goethe'sche Morphologie, eine schier unbegrenzte Mannigfaltigkeit von Varianten und Serien zu schaffen erlauben. Ein begrenztes Alphabet der Formen generiert eine unbegrenzte Möglichkeit von Realisationen. Das erklärt auch die schier überwältigend kreative Fülle des Mack'schen Werkes.

5 *Die Kräfte hinter den Formen. Erdgeschichte, Materie, Prozess in der zeitgenössischen Kunst*, hrsg. von Beate Ermarcora u. a., Ausst.-Kat. Galerie im Taxispalais Innsbruck; Kunstmusenm Krefeld, Museen Haus Lange Haus Esters; Kunstmuseum Thun, Köln 2016.

The materials and techniques from which articles are made therefore play a formative role. Examples of these include arrangements, bands, seams, meshes, fabrics, knots, and threads, as well as, among others, cloth, rubber, varnish, cotton, silk, ceramics, glass, and stone. The typical basic forms are generated by combining patterns, structures, and materials—thanks to the interplay of hyle, or materia, and morphé, or forma—for tents, carpets, and clothes, and for homes, temples, and palaces. The utilitarian functions are finite while the ornamental aesthetics are innumerable. This becomes clear with Semper's world trip through all cultures. With this action, he turns his structural approach into an empirical-material and historical study. For both Goethe and Semper, structure is not a static factor but rather a power-generating abundance of pattern. Semper starts out with "destruction and restructuring." This is the formula for both the dynamics of the universe and the arts, which merges into the 'shapeless,' the initiating 'restructuring.' Analyzing Mack, we detect this type of extension in his art, one that draws its aesthetic energies from Europe, Africa, the Orient, or Japan. After centuries marked by an abundance of forms, ZERO was the basic evacuating gesture toward the void, zero, the 'shapeless,' and then, with that as the point of departure, toward the creation of a new world.

Mack's geometric shapes include rectangles, squares, triangles, circles, spirals, scales, rhombuses, grates, fans, grids, flutings, wedges, and radials. On the one-dimensional level, we encounter lines, vectors, diagonals, stripes, dotting, waves, parabolas, ellipses, and transversals. When expanding into three dimensions, we find cubes, cylinders, spheres, prisms, and, above all, stelae, which one could describe as Mack's archetypal object. All his surfaces undergo varying chemical and mechanical processes. The surfaces of the objects attain a delicate, mostly geometrically arranged relief that is suited to being a sensitive respondent to light.

Almost all planes and bodies are constructed "more geometrico," as Spinoza says. Mack's god is "deus geometra."[6] We should remember that during antiquity, geometry formed the basis for understanding the world (and its 'hypokeimenon'). This was thanks to its measurements, proportions, symmetries, transformations, mathematical conditions, and its closeness to technologies like architecture. Geometry stands close to the divine demiurge that, during an earlier Christian period, could be considered a geometer or architect. Geometry is the creative spirit's first objectification, its translation into forms and figures. The second divine objectification is light—*Chromatic Constellations,* as Mack entitles his acrylic paintings—which, refracted into color, may equally be considered emanations of the spirit.

Regardless of how immaterial form may be (as a light artist, Mack's particular focus is on the immaterial), it is always tied to matter. Consequently, the elements fundamental to his art—water, earth, fire, air, and the divine medium of 'quinta essentia,' or ether—follow geometric archetypes. In their polar and transformative circular form, the elements constitute the sensual world, the whole of nature. They encode the qualities of pairs, such as warm and cold (and thus the extremes of the desert and the Arctic—Mack's crucial primeval landscapes) and the dry and humid. All elements play a role in

6 Friedrich Ohly, "Deus Geometra: Skizzen zur Geschichte einer Vorstellung von Gott," in *Tradition als historische Kraft: Interdisziplinäre Forschungen zur Geschichte des frühen Mittelalters,* eds., Norbert Kamp and Joachim Wollasch (Berlin, 1982), pp. 1–42.

Wenn man die Ausführungen Gottfried Sempers zur Textilen Kunst liest, erstaunt die Nähe zu Heinz Mack. Semper analysiert zwar auch Bekleidung, Decken und ähnliche zur vestimentären Peripherie des Menschen gehörige Artefakte. Doch diese sind nur der Kern, von dem aus alle Objekttypen erfasst werden, deren Hülle, Oberfläche, Haut oder Bedeckung freien Raum schenken für geometrisierte Ornamentiken – bis hin zur künstlerischen Ausstattung (= ›Bekleidung‹) von Bauwerken. Ornament, Rhythmus, Relief, Muster, kurz: die Stilformen dienen nicht der Funktionalität (Nützlichkeit), sondern der Darstellung, der Performance, mithin der Ästhetik des Objekts.

Dabei spielen die Stoffe und die Techniken, aus denen Artefakte gefertigt werden, eine formgebende Rolle, etwa Reihungen, Bänder, Nähte, Geflechte, Gewebe, Knoten, Fäden sowie Stoffe, Kautschuk, Lacke, Baumwolle, Seide, Keramiken, Glas, Stein et cetera. Aus dem Zusammenwirken von Mustern, Strukturen und Stoffen – aus der Wechselwirkung von hyle / materia und morphé / forma – werden die charakteristischen Grundformen und ihre Variationen generiert – für Zelte, Teppiche oder Kleider, für Wohnhäuser, Tempel oder Paläste. Die Gebrauchsfunktionen sind endlich, die ornamentalen Ästhetiken zahllos. Dies wird deutlich, wenn Semper eine Weltreise durch alle Kulturräume unternimmt. Sein strukturalistischer Ansatz wird dadurch empirisch-material und historisch. Wie bei Goethe ist auch bei Semper die Struktur nicht eine statische Größe, sondern eine Kraft, die Mustervielfalt hervortreibt. Semper beginnt mit der Formel »Zerstörung und Neugestaltung«. Es ist die Formel für Dynamiken des Weltalls … und der Künste, die ins ›Gestaltlose‹ übergehen und ›Neugestaltung‹ initiieren. Auch bei Mack findet sich eine solche Erweiterung seiner Kunst, die ihre ästhetischen Energien aus Europa, Afrika, dem Orient oder Japan bezieht. ZERO war die evakuierende Grundgeste, nach jahrhundertelanger Abundanz der Formen die Leere, die Null, das ›Gestaltlose‹ zu erreichen und von ihm ausgehend eine neue Welt zu kreieren.

Geometrische Grundformen bei Mack sind Rechteck, Quadrat, Dreieck, Kreis, Spirale, Skalen, Rhomben, Gitter, Fächer, Raster, Riffelungen, Keile, Radiale. Ins Eindimensionale zurückgehend gewinnt man die Linie, den Vektor, die Diagonale, den Streifen, die Punktierung, die Welle, die Parabel, die Ellipse, die Transversale. Ins Dreidimensionale sich erweiternd finden sich Quader und Kuben, Zylinder und Kugeln, Prismen und vor allem Stelen, die man den Mack'schen Urkörper nennen kann. Die Oberflächen der Körper und der Reliefs werden durchweg bearbeitet, chemisch oder mechanisch: Die Haut der Körper erhält eine zarte, zumeist geometrisch geordnete Reliefstruktur, die geeignet ist, zu einer sensiblen Respondenz des Lichtes zu werden. Fast alle Flächen und Körper sind »more geometrico« (Spinoza) konstruiert. Der Gott Macks ist der »deus geometra«[6]. Wir dürfen erinnern, dass es in der Antike die Geometrie war, die der Welt zugrunde liegt (sie ist ihr ›hypokeimenon‹) – mit ihren Maßen und Proportionen, Symmetrien und Transformationen, mit ihren mathematischen Verhältnissen und ihrer Nähe zur Technik, wie etwa der Architektur. Geometrie steht dem göttlichen Demiurgen nahe, der noch im Christentum als Geometer oder Architekt gelten konnte. Geometrie ist die erste Objektivierung des schöpferischen Geistes, in Formen und Figuren übersetzt. Und die zweite Objektivation des Göttlichen ist das Licht, das zur Farbe, zu *Chromatischen Konstellationen* gebrochen wird, wie Mack seine Gemälde in Acryl betitelt, die ebenfalls als Emanationen des Geistes gelten können.

6 Friedrich Ohly, »Deus Geometra. Skizzen zur Geschichte einer Vorstellung von Gott«, in: *Tradition als historische Kraft. Interdisziplinäre Forschungen zur Geschichte des früheren Mittelalters,* hrsg. von Norbert Kamp und Joachim Wollasch, Berlin und New York 1982, S. 1–42.

his work. For example, in light and water installations, with light rain and water houses, in stone, metal, or earthy sculptures; in transparent, diaphanous building elements, and in glass forests. Cosmological constellations are frequently touched upon, as with *Time of the Stars, Spiral Star, Star Path,* and *Stellar Declination*. Fluid and solid, mobile and static, and kinetic and sculptural aspects characterize his oeuvre.

But primordial elements would not be phenomena if they were not reborn in light, or at least brought into appearance. Light is for Mack, before making his experiments with artificial light, the light of the sun and the stars, the skylight, a light that holds messages of the cosmos. An archetype of his art is the circular sun-rotor, formed as an aluminum relief, plexiglass panel, or mirror disk, which makes the sunlight's new reflections shine every second. Like in the case of the light stelae, these reflections are a cosmic communication. In accordance with their shape and light reflections, the communication is to be understood as a dialogue with heaven. Ultimately, all communication takes place with the medium light, the quintessence.

This even applies to *Black Sun* (2008). In this work, Mack refers to 'sol niger,' the black sun of hermetic alchemy, and 'nigredo,' which represents the abyss of time, the black universe's depth. He also invokes the 'soleil noir de la mélancolie.' Invented by alchemists and rediscovered by nineteenth-century French symbolists, this served as the title for a book on melancholy by Julia Kristeva.[7] While Mack is doubtlessly an enthusiastic messenger of a light-flooded future, we cannot ignore the major role that black plays in the formal language of his Light Art. Simply think of the paintings *Black Continent* (1993) and *Black Light* (1966/2008), or shows like *Licht im Schwarz* (2001) and *Licht Schatten* (2015).

For Mack, the four main elements are also interconnected in their material manifestations via cycles of metamorphoses, for example, in sand, ice, glass, ceramics, aluminum, and stainless steel. The art of transformation is further intensified by formation and reformation, distortion and focusing, and through transparence, mirroring, and the refraction of light: the fastest, most versatile, ethereal, and all-encompassing medium. Almost all of Mack's imaging and formation processes are *Acts of Light*. Anything can change instantly, from moment to moment, causing it to shine in a new light or in a chromatic variation. Or it can vanish in the stream of matter, the desert sand, the Arctic Sea, the devouring fire, or the cosmic night. If formative light has become the archetype of any artist, it would be Heinz Mack, for whom morphology is no longer tied to living organisms, as in the case of Goethe. Light and matter, inorganic media, drive the metamorphoses.

In conclusion, let us turn to the sculpture *The Garden in the Garden* (1979/80). The garden invokes a cultivated natural space. It was a place where Goethe pursued his studies that aimed at revealing the secret creation of shapes and the metamorphosis. Mack, too, works in gardens, parks, and other natural outdoor spaces. He is thus always utilizing materials and methods that stem from contemporary technologies. In *Garden in the Garden,* Mack formed various shapes from fine, flexible aluminum netting. They all conformed to his preferred shapes: plant, wing, star, wedge, disk, curve.

7 Cf. Hartmut Böhme, "La ricezione letteraria dell'incisione di Albrecht Dürer *Melencolia I.*" In: *Annali dell'Istituto storico italo-germanico in Trento,* 40, 2014/1, pp. 9–33.

Doch Form, so immateriell sie auch sein mag (Mack strebt gerade als Lichtkünstler das Immaterielle an), ist stets an Stoff gebunden. So folgen auf die geometrischen Urformen die Elemente, die in seiner Kunst fundamental sind: Wasser, Erde, Feuer, Luft und als ›quinta essentia‹ der Äther, das göttliche Medium. In ihrer polaren und transformativen Kreisform bilden die Elemente die sinnliche Welt, das Ganze der Natur. Sie codieren die Qualitätenpaare, das Warme und das Kalte (und damit an den Extremen die Wüste und die Arktis, die wichtigsten Urlandschaften Macks) sowie das Trockene und das Feuchte. Alle Elemente spielen in Macks Werk eine Rolle, etwa als Licht / Wasser-Installationen, als Lichtregen, Wasserhaus, als steinerne, metallene oder erdige Skulptur, als gläserner, diaphaner Baukörper, als Glaswald, als Steinskulptur et cetera. Oft genug werden kosmologische Konstellationen assoziiert, etwa *Die Zeit der Sterne, Spiral-Stern, Bahn der Sterne, Stellare Deklination*. Das Fluidale und das Feste, das Mobile und das Statische, das Kinetische und das Skulpturale charakterisieren die Werke.

Doch die Urelemente wären nicht Phänomene, wenn sie nicht im Licht noch einmal geboren, wenigstens zur Erscheinung gebracht würden. Licht ist für Mack, bevor er die Welt des künstlichen Lichts durchexperimentiert, das Licht der Sonne und der Sterne, Himmelslicht – Botschaften des Kosmos. Eine Urform der Mack'schen Kunst ist der kreisrunde Sonnenrotor als Aluminiumrelief, Plexiglas- oder Spiegelscheibe, der sekündlich neue Reflexionen des Sonnenlichts aufscheinen lässt. Hier geht es ebenso um eine Kommunikation mit dem Kosmos wie in den Lichtstelen, die von ihrer Form wie von ihren Lichtreflexen her als Dialog mit dem Himmel zu verstehen sind. Alle Kommunikation erfolgt zuletzt im Medium des Lichts, der Quintessenz.

Dies gilt sogar für die *Black Sun* (2008). Mit ihr zitiert Mack ›sol niger‹, die schwarze Sonne der hermetistischen Alchemie, die ›nigredo‹, die den Abgrund der Zeit darstellt, die Tiefe des schwarzen Universums, aber auch ›soleil noir de la mélancolie‹, wie sie von den Alchemisten erfunden, von den französischen Symbolisten des 19. Jahrhunderts wiederentdeckt und noch bei Julia Kristeva zum Titel eines Buches über die Melancholie wurde.[7] Ganz gewiss ist Mack der enthusiastische Bote einer gelichteten Zukunft – doch kann man nicht übersehen, welche Rolle das Schwarze für die Formensprache seiner Lichtkunst spielt. Man denke zum Beispiel an die Gemälde *Schwarzer Kontinent* (1993) und *Black Light* (1966/2008), an Ausstellungen wie *Licht im Schwarz* (2001) und *Licht Schatten* (2015).

Die vier Elemente sind bei Mack auch in ihren stofflichen Manifestationen, also etwa im Sand, im Eis, in Glas und Keramik, in Aluminium und Edelstahl miteinander verbunden im Kreislauf der Metamorphosen. Doch gesteigert wird diese Verwandlungskunst in der Bildung und Umbildung, Verzerrung und Fokussierung, in der Transparenz, Spiegelung und Refraktion des schnellsten, wandlungsfähigsten, feinststofflichen und alles einhüllenden Mediums des Lichts. Fast alle Bild- und Bildungsprozesse bei Mack sind *Taten des Lichts*. Instantiell, von Augenblick zu Augenblick kann alles verwandelt sein und in neuem Licht oder chromatischer Variation erstrahlen oder im Strom der Stoffe versinken – im Sand der Wüste, im arktischen Meer, im verzehrenden Feuer, in der kosmischen Nacht. Wenn irgendwo, dann ist im Mack'schen Werk das formgebende Licht zur Urform der Kunst geworden. Morphologie ist

7 Vgl. Hartmut Böhme, »La ricezione letteraria dell'incisione di Albrecht Dürer *Melencolia I*«, in: *Annali dell'Istituto storico italo-germanico in Trento*, 40, 1, Januar–Juni 2014, S. 9–33.

Once applied to the finely woven aluminum background, the netting was placed between large-size plexiglass panels. The plexiglass panels offered support to the filigree structures. Mounted in three parts, the sculpture is a triptych. Illuminated from the verso, the light produces and emphasizes the graphic structures, its compression, and its diaphanousness. At the same time, this work is an homage to the material of aluminum and the morphological possibilities it holds. When looking at the triptych, it is like standing in front of a cabinet from Mack's 'Kunstkammer' that features the archetypes of form he favored at the time. The title lets us infer that the garden, as an archetype of the synthesis between nature and culture, has become a model of the nature of art. It is tempting to suggest that Mack's occupation with the garden as art form is perpetual, regardless of whether that garden is in cities, parks, deserts, oceans, ice, squares, museums, or galleries. A criterion of our contemporary culture is 'acute artification.' In this setting, Mack turns the artificial into art that reflects nature.

nicht mehr an lebende Organismen gebunden wie bei Goethe. Licht und Stoffe – anorganische Medien – treiben die Metamorphose voran.

Nehmen wir zum Abschluss die Skulptur *Der Garten im Garten* von 1979/80: Aufgerufen wird mit dem Garten jener kultivierte Naturraum, in dem Goethe seinen morphologischen Studien nachging, um das Geheimnis der Gestaltbildung und Metamorphose zu lüften. Auch Mack arbeitet in Gärten und Parks und anderen Räumen freier Natur, doch stets mit Materialien und Verfahren, die der technischen Moderne entstammen. Im *Garten im Garten* legt Mack zwischen großformatige Plexiglasscheiben feine, elastische Aluminiumnetze, die er zu einer Vielzahl von Formen verfaltet. Sie alle gehören zu seinen bevorzugten Gestalten: Pflanze, Flügel, Stern, Keil, Kreisscheibe, Bogen et cetera. Diese Formgebilde werden auf einen feinmaschigen Aluminiumhintergrund appliziert. Die Plexiglasscheiben geben den filigranen Gebilden Halt. Dreiteilig aufgestellt bildet die Skulptur ein Triptychon. Wenn es den *Garten im Garten* von hinten beleuchtet, erzeugt und betont das Licht die grafischen Strukturen, ihre Verdichtungen und ihre Diaphanie. Es ist auch eine Hommage an das Material, das Aluminium, und die morphologischen Möglichkeiten, die es birgt. Man steht vor dem Triptychon wie vor einem Mack'schen Kunstkammer-Schrank mit den Archetypen der Form, die er seinerzeit favorisierte. Der Titel assoziiert den Garten als Urform der Synthese von Natur und Kultur, die zum Modell der Kunstnatur geworden ist. Immer, möchte man vermuten, arbeitet Mack am Garten, der zur Kunst werden soll, in den Großstädten genauso wie im Park, in der Wüste wie in Meer und Eis, auf Plätzen, in Museen und Galerien. In der äußersten Artifizierung, die zum Merkmal unserer Kultur geworden ist, wird bei Mack das Künstliche zur Kunst, die Natur reflektiert.

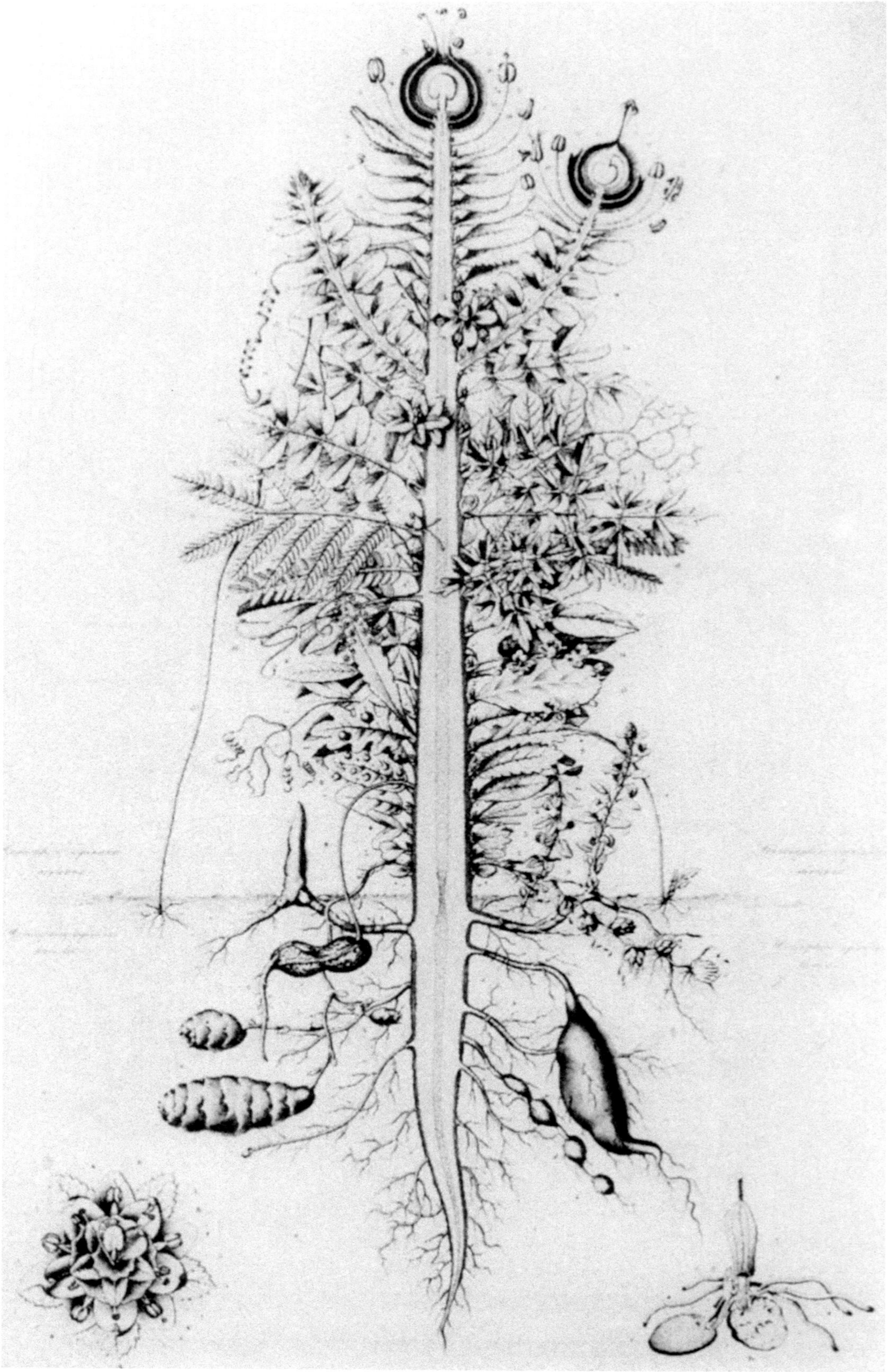

Pierre Jean François Turpin (1775–1840)
Urpflanze, nach Goethe, 1804/1837
Holzschnitt

Pierre Jean François Turpin (1775–1840)
Primordial plant, after Goethe, 1804/37
Woodcut

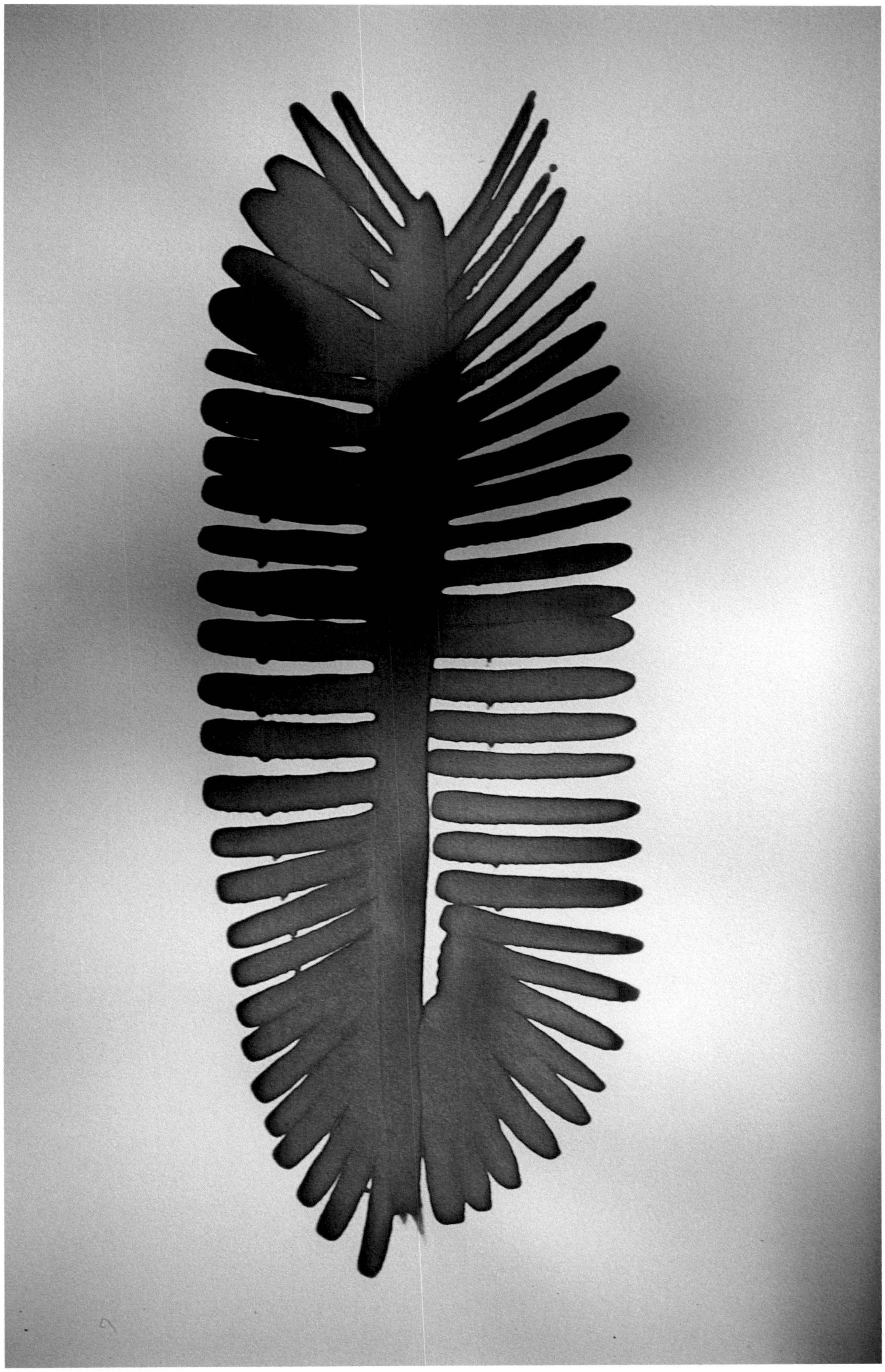

Heinz Mack
Ohne Titel
Signiert, datiert: »mack 01«
Tusche mit Pinsel auf Kupfertiefdruckpapier
106 x 78,5 cm

Heinz Mack
Untitled
Signed, dated: "mack 01"
Indian ink applied to photogravure paper
with brush, 106 x 78.5 cm

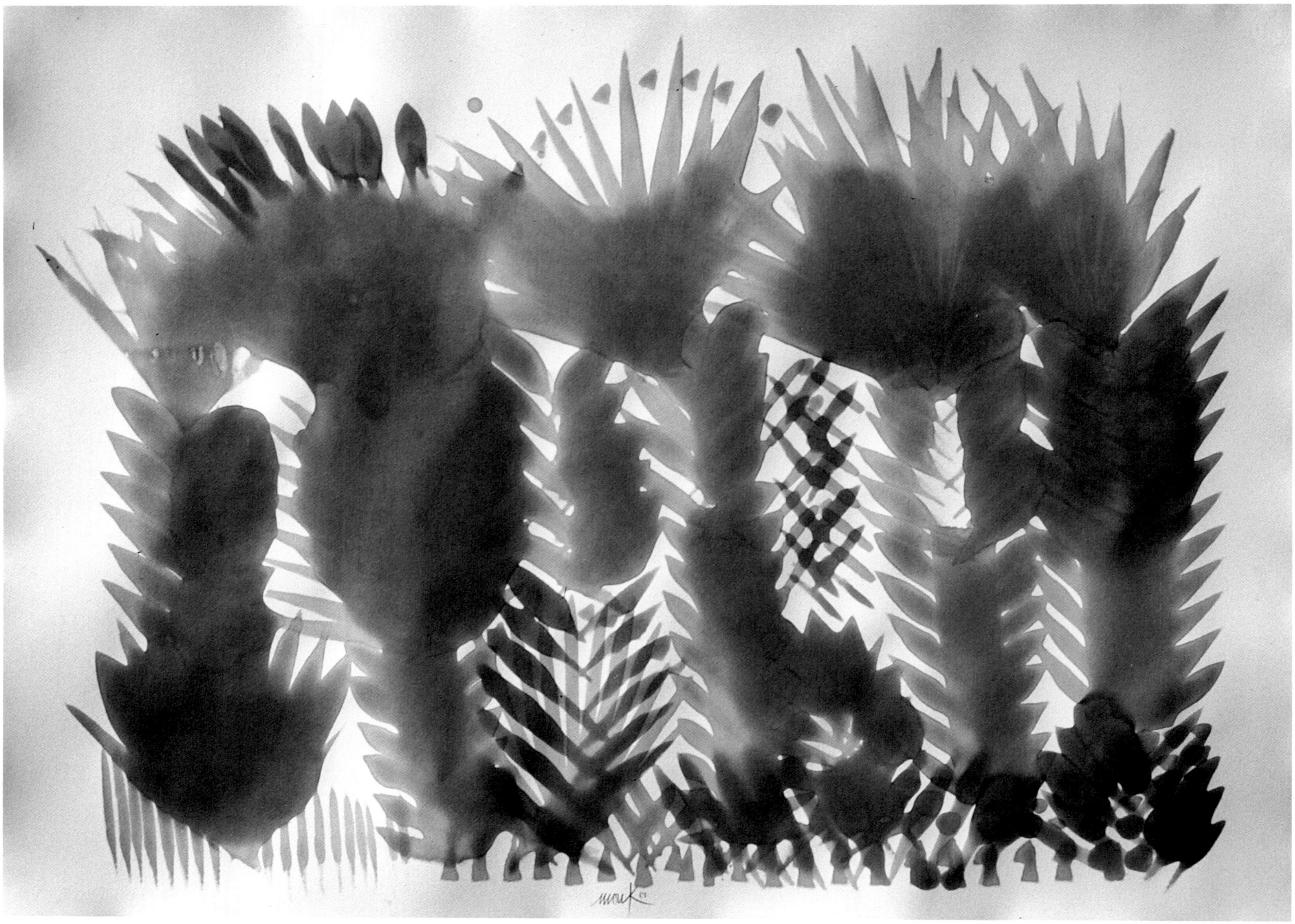

Heinz Mack
Ohne Titel
Signiert, datiert: »mack 01«
Tusche mit Pinsel auf Kupfertiefdruckpapier
78 x 106 cm

Heinz Mack
Untitled
Signed, dated: "mack 01"
Indian ink applied to photogravure paper
with brush, 78 x 106 cm

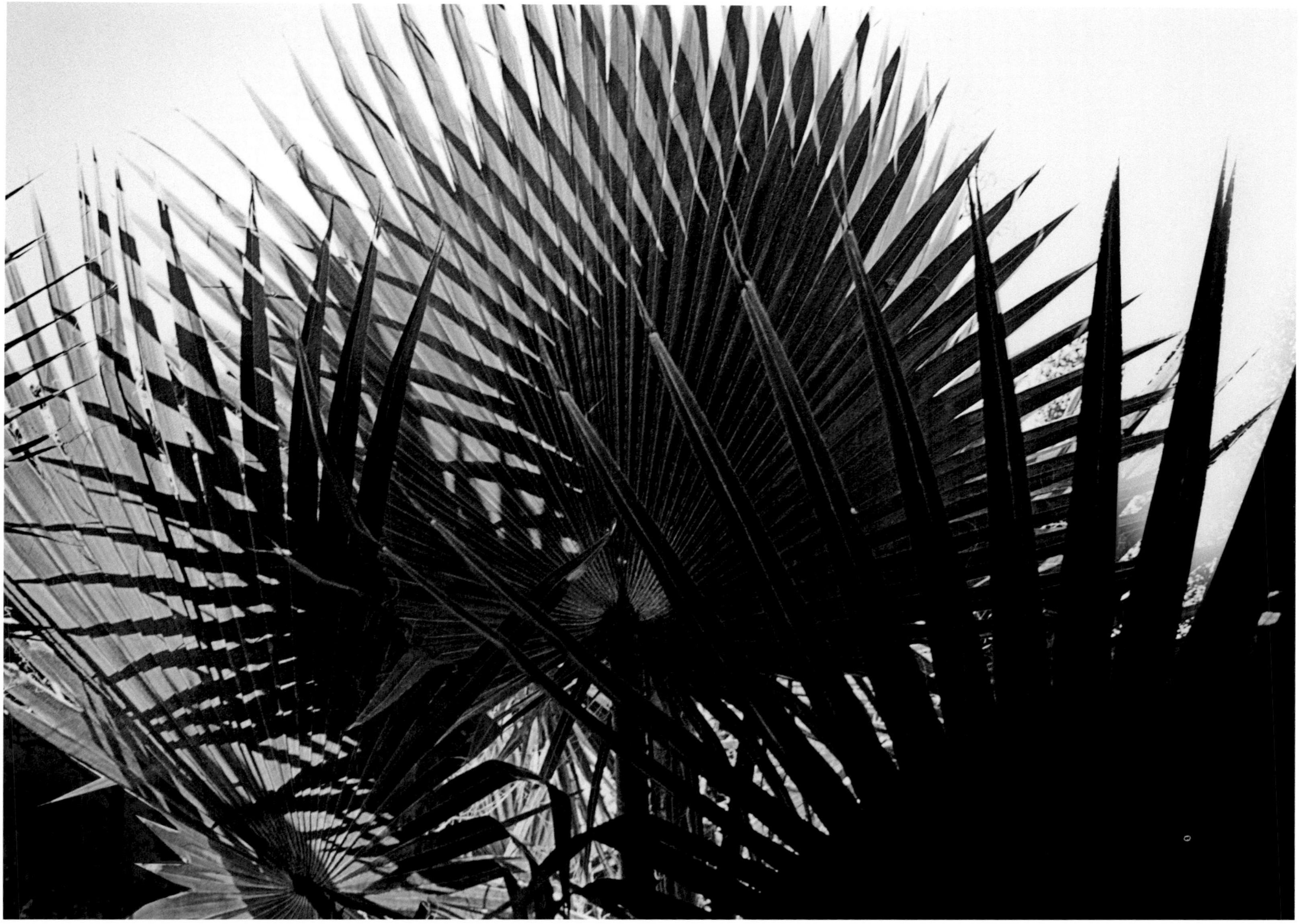

Heinz Mack
Palmen im Garten des Künstlers, Ibiza
2009
Fotografie

Heinz Mack
Palm trees in the artist's garden, Ibiza
2009
Photograph

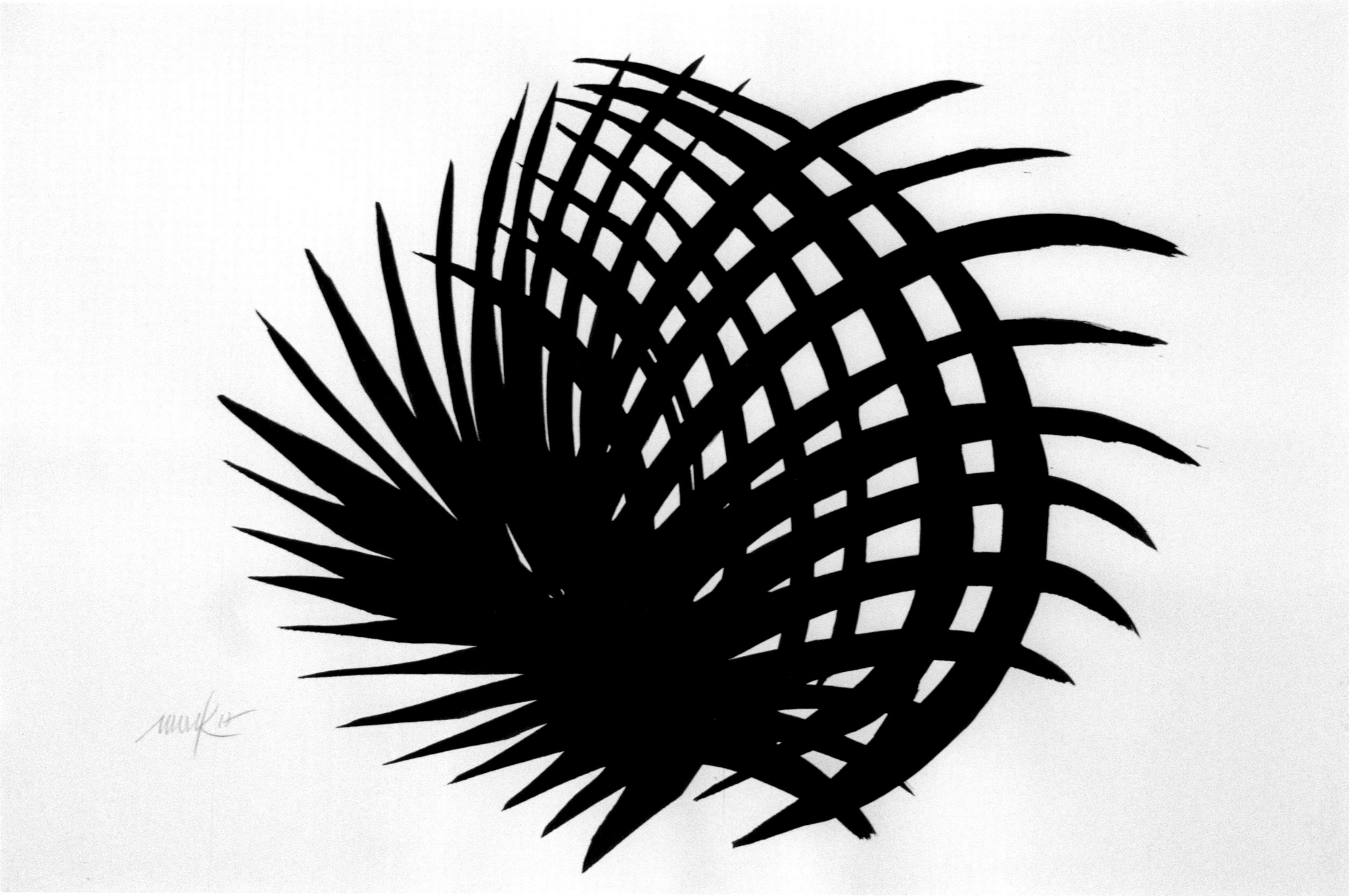

Heinz Mack
Ohne Titel, 2017
Tusche auf Büttenpapier
56,5 x 110,5 cm

Heinz Mack
Untitled, 2017
Indian ink on handmade paper
56.5 x 110.5 cm

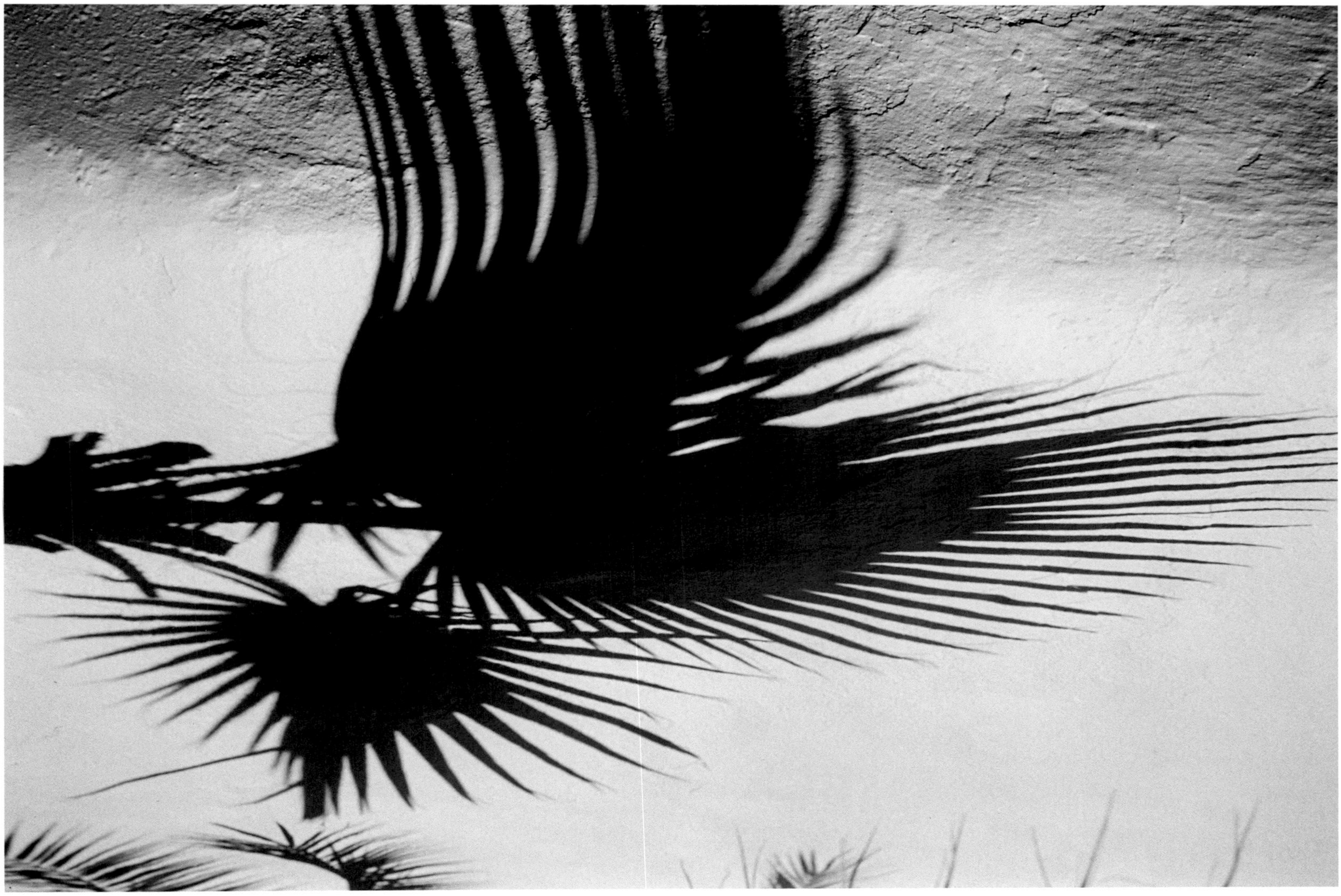

Heinz Mack
Schattenspiel mit Palmenblättern im Garten
des Künstlers auf Ibiza, 2017
Fotografie

Heinz Mack
Shadow play with palm leaves in the garden
of the artist on Ibiza, 2017
Photograph

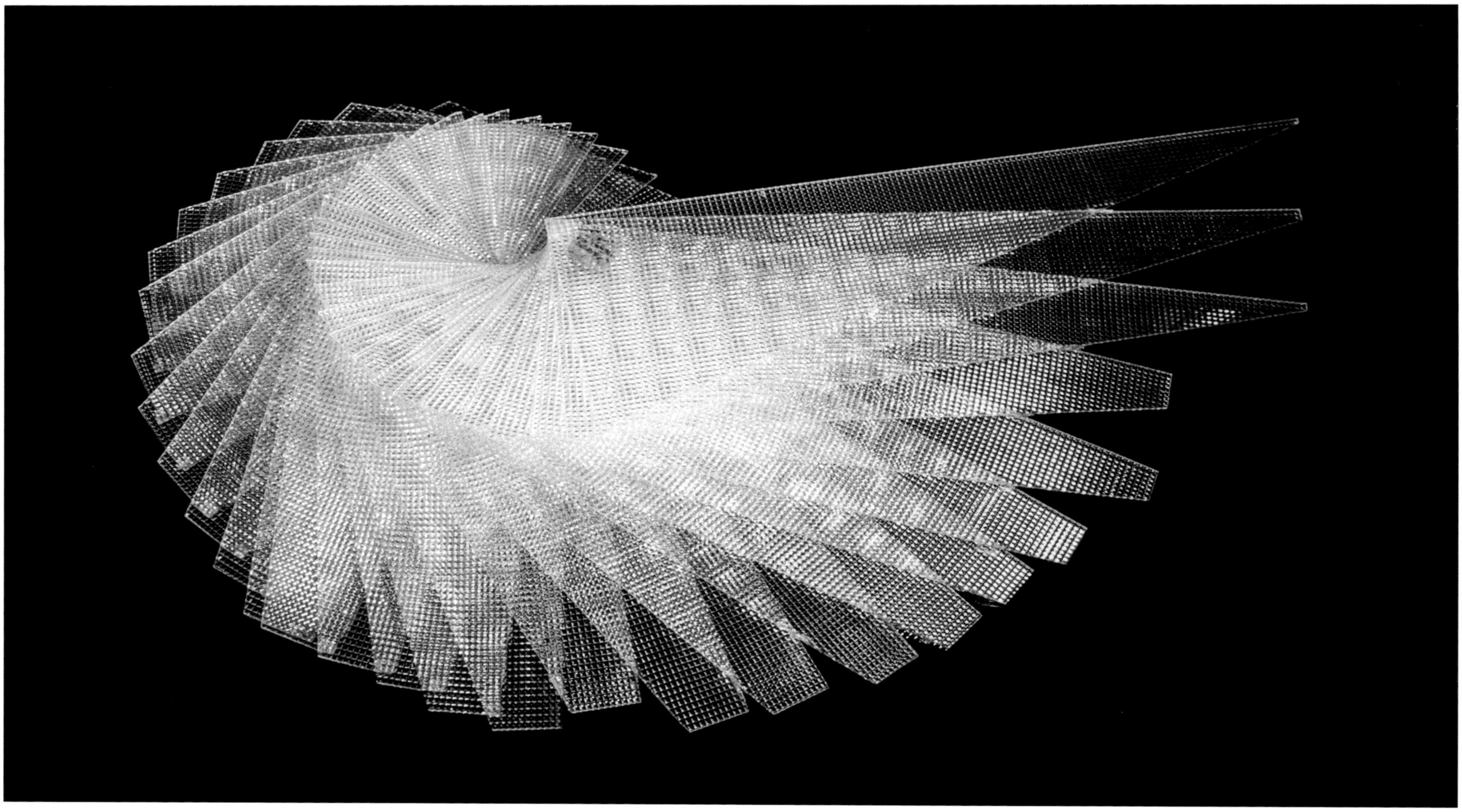

Heinz Mack
Light-Bird
Signiert, datiert: »mack 82«
Plexiglas
45 x 75 x 10 cm

Heinz Mack
Light-Bird
Signed, dated: "mack 82"
Plexiglass
45 x 75 x 10 cm

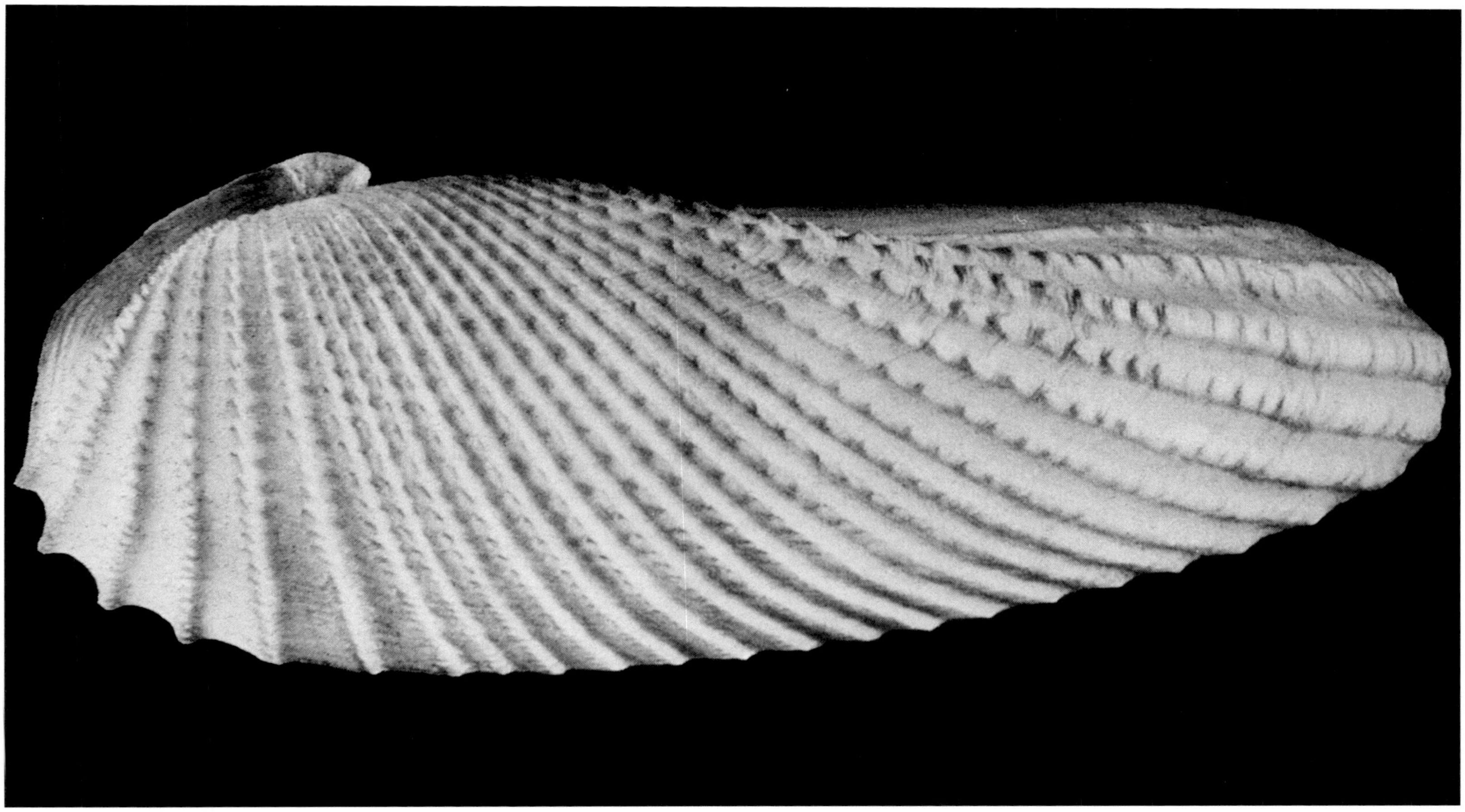

Fossile Muschel | Fossil shell

Structure

Heinz Mack

In 1958, I wrote a text for the catalogue that accompanied our ZERO exhibition in which I bid farewell to the principle of composition and of central perspective that had dominated Occidental art since the Renaissance.

The title of my text manifested a concept that was eminently important for the ZERO movement: *The New Dynamic Structure*.

I soon came to realize that I was not alone in this matter—all of my artist friends from the ZERO period created structures instead of traditional compositions; a true novum after six hundred years. However, the grand art-historical preludes and discoveries of the modern era were similarly driven by the urge to question composition as well as central perspective. Ultimately, among those who lived up to this expectation were Rothko and Barnett Newman. Olga Rozanova and Ivan Kliun had already in part preceded them—in the sense of anticipation. And what came before them? Who and what questioned the old formal principle of composition? In his last works, the extremely bold *Boogie Woogie* paintings, Mondrian achieved something that appeared altogether novel: I call it a kind of structural grid. Yet even Monet's cathedral paintings or Cézanne's landscapes no longer feature a compositional background. Instead, an even and rigorous brushstroke flows across the entire surface. Picasso follows suit as he pursues his analytical Cubism with unerring revolutionary consistency. Finally, three of Rodchenko's monochrome panels from 1921 must be named before Yves Klein laid claim to the monochrome. In this context, Strzemiński's Unistic works from around 1930 ought to be remembered, as they make use of the entire painted surface.

It was not until later that I began to realize that a nonfigurative and completely nonrepresentational art was created in the Orient and the Far East. In it, ornamental structures define two-dimensional spaces, thereby developing an independent aesthetics. Ornaments are the soul of book art, lettering, mosaics, and mashrabiyyas; only the muqarnas—that stalactite vaulting with elaborate, multicolored honeycomb patterns—as well as the finely chiseled capitals on top of the column shafts reveal a three-dimensionality, thus counteracting the dominance of planes. Thanks to their continuous expansion, the arabesques—frequently intertwined like complicated networks—are reminiscent of Pollock, who also had no need for either compositions or linear perspectives.

Modernity had discovered a completely new pictorial space!

Matisse travelled to the Maghreb in 1913, before Paul Klee and August Macke. Towards the end of his life, he intensified his relationship with the Orient once again: filling the entire wall, his gouache cutouts, some of them larger than four by eight meters, are two-dimensional, and he referred to them as 'decorations.'

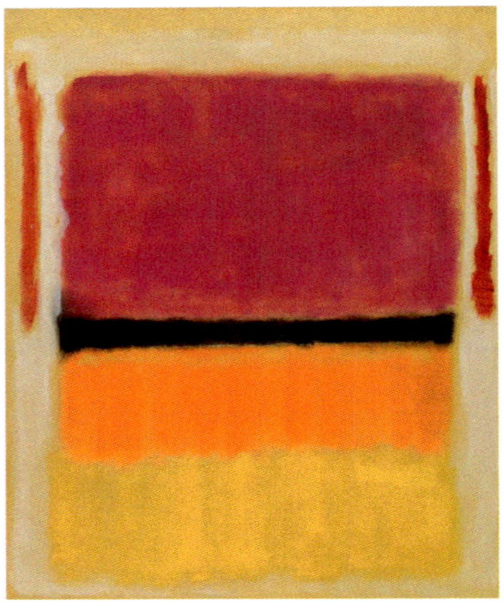

1 Mark Rothko
Ohne Titel *(Violet, Schwarz, Orange, Gelb auf Weiß und Rot)* /
Untitled *(Violet, Black, Orange, Yellow on White and Red)*, 1949
Öl auf Leinwand / oil on canvas
207 x 167,6 cm
Solomon R. Guggenheim Museum, New York
Foto: bpk / The Solomon R. Guggenheim Foundation / Art Resource, NY

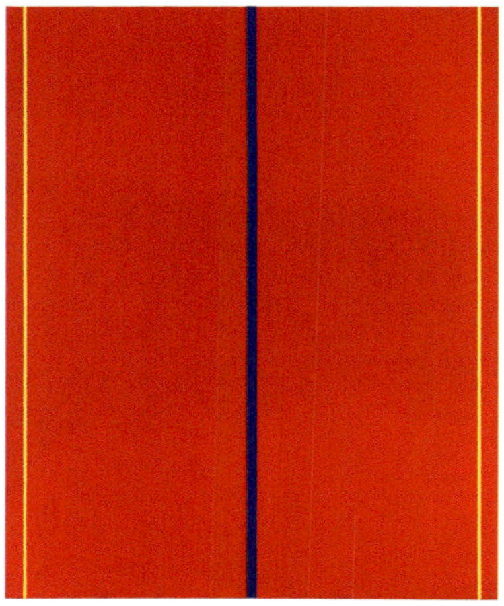

2 Barnett Newman
Wer hat Angst vor Rot, Gelb und Blau II /
Who's Afraid of Red, Yellow and Blue II
1967
Acryl auf Leinwand / acrylic on canvas
305 x 257 cm
Staatsgalerie Stuttgart
Foto: Bruce White

Struktur

Heinz Mack

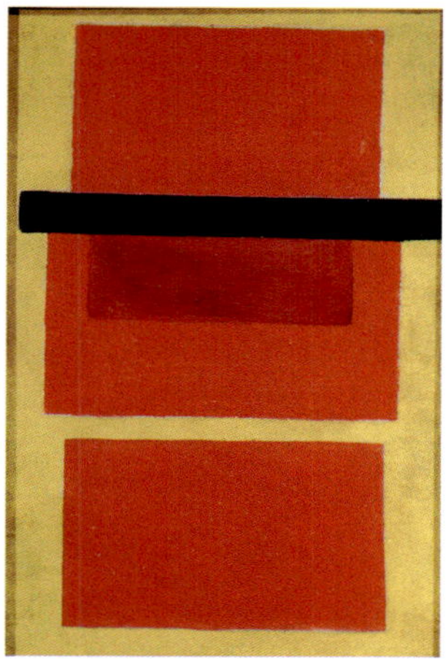

3 Olga Rosanowa
Gegenstandslose Komposition / Abstract composition, 1918
Öl auf Leinwand / oil on canvas
62,5 x 40,5 cm
The State Russian Museum, St. Petersburg
Foto: State Russian Museum, St. Petersburg

1958 habe ich für den Katalog unserer ZERO-Ausstellung einen Text formuliert, um das Prinzip der Komposition und der Zentralperspektive zu verabschieden, das seit der Renaissance die Kunst des Abendlandes dominierte.

Im Titel manifestierte ich einen für die ZERO-Bewegung so wichtigen Begriff: *Die neue dynamische Struktur.*

Bald musste ich erkennen, dass ich hier nicht alleine war; alle Künstlerfreunde der ZERO-Zeit haben Strukturen anstelle der traditionellen Komposition geschaffen, ein Novum nach 600 Jahren. Aber da waren auch die großen kunsthistorischen Vorspiele und Entdeckungen der Neuzeit, von dem Drang beseelt, die Komposition und die Zentralperspektive infrage zu stellen. Endgültig erfüllten sich diese Erwartungen zum Beispiel bei Rothko und Barnett Newman, und diesen waren schon partiell vorausgegangen Olga Rosanowa und Iwan Kljun im Sinne der Antizipation. Und was ging diesen voraus? Wer und was stellte das alte Gestaltungsprinzip der Komposition infrage? Bei den letzten Werken Mondrians, den überaus kühnen Boogie-Woogie-Bildern, kommt etwas zustande, was gänzlich neu erschien: Ich nenne es eine Art Strukturgitter. Aber schon die Kathedralbilder Monets oder die Landschaften Cézannes zeigen keinen kompositorischen Hintergrund mehr, stattdessen durchströmt ein gleichmäßiger stringenter Pinselduktus die gesamte Malfläche. Dem folgt Picasso mit seinem analytischen Kubismus in einer unbeirrbar revolutionären Konsequenz. Und schließlich müssen noch Rodtschenkos drei monochrome Tafelbilder von 1921 genannt werden, bevor Yves Klein die Monochromie für sich reklamierte. Aber nicht vergessen werden sollten auch Strzemińskis unistische Werke um 1930, welche die gesamte Malfläche in Anspruch nehmen.

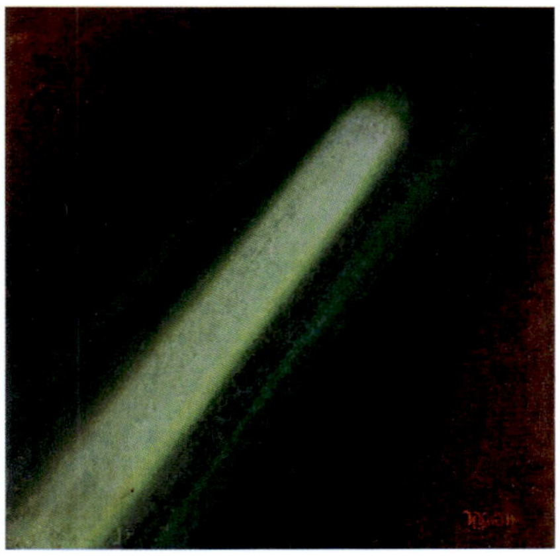

4 Iwan Kljun
Sphärische Komposition / Spherical composition, 1923
Öl auf Leinwand / oil on canvas
64,5 x 64,5 cm
Museum Ludwig, Köln / Cologne
Foto: Rheinisches Bildarchiv Köln

Erst später wurde mir bewusst, dass im Orient sowie im Fernen Osten eine nicht figurative und vollkommen gegenstandslose Kunst gestaltet wurde, in der ornamentale Strukturen einen zweidimensionalen Raum bestimmten und damit eine eigenständige Ästhetik entwickelten. Die Ornamente waren die Seele der Buchkunst, der Schrift, der Mosaiken, der Maschrabiyyas, und lediglich die Muqarnas, jene Stalaktitengewölbe mit ihren raffinierten, multikolorierten Wabenmustern, zeigen ebenso wie die differenziert ziselierten Kapitelle der Säulen eine Dreidimensionalität, welche die Dominanz der Flächen konterkariert. Die oft wie komplizierte Netzwerke verflochtenen Arabesken erinnern in ihrer fortlaufenden Ausdehnung an Pollock, der ebenso keine Kompositionen oder Linearperspektiven brauchte.

Die Moderne hatte einen vollkommen neuen Bildraum entdeckt!

Matisse, der 1913 schon vor Paul Klee und August Macke in den Maghreb reiste, steigerte am Ende seines Lebens noch einmal sein Verhältnis zum Orient: Seine Gouache-Scherenschnitte, zum Teil vier mal acht Meter groß, waren zweidimensional und wandfüllend und wurden von ihm ›Dekorationen‹ genannt.

To the best of my knowledge, there has not yet been an art-historical analysis or an interpretation that has made this eminent change in Occidental European art the subject of current and relevant consideration or research.

Even Malevich's Suprematist paintings still feature—albeit in a somewhat downscaled way—the principles of traditional composition. And while Matisse's quasi-ultimate canvas *The Snail* from 1953, which displays clear primary colors as geometric cutouts on a white ground, is not far away from Malevich on the one hand, we recognize in it on the other hand an ornamental, spiraled sequence and hence, paradoxically, a structure.

Naturally, one must bear in mind that as a universal empire, nature is not concerned with composition but exhibits creative structures. The microscope enabled microbiologists to identify the immanent logic of ornamental structures. This process began in the early twentieth century with Ernst Haeckel's discovery of fine silicate crystals and diatoms, presenting a fascinating abundance of patterns and perpetually repeating symmetries that reach far into the nanoscale. Thanks to their multiple symmetries, ice crystals produce mesmerizing structures. Yet we do not fully comprehend how their shapes and facets multiply so creatively. Mineralogy is a type of crystallography wherein atoms develop a particular structure that may lead to ornamental arrangements. In instances where light leads to phenomena of interference, the result is a surprising sequence of colors. Without these patterns and their symmetries physicists might hardly be able, if not even be unable, to explain the universal design of our world!

Moreover, we ought to remember bilateral mirror symmetries, which may be observed in almost all animals; for instance in butterflies, zebras, starfish, fishes, on tiger's fur, the bumpy skin of the chameleon, peacock feathers, and so on and so forth.

One ought to likewise call to mind the microscopic-sized spirals and the enormous dimensions of hurricanes and in cosmic galaxies. Or let us recall cacti, pinecones, roses, and the oft-cited kernels in the blossoms of large sunflowers. The latter move in spirals in opposite directions, thereby creating their distinctive pattern (actually comparable to Uecker's radial nail reliefs). The astonishing honeycombs are also worth remembering. Often employed in aircraft construction, honeycomb aluminum grids are frequently used in modern technology. In addition, they appear in my so-called *Light Reliefs,* in whose cell structures light is caught and emitted.

Last but not least, as a sculptor, I am enthusiastic about prism-shaped basaltic columns. Consisting of six sides, their cross-sections are almost perfectly hexagonal in shape and stand up vertically like petrified organ pipes. And as a painter I find the colored patterns of birds' feathers especially beautiful, because their choicest structures reflect the colored light waves. But the scaled skin of snakes or chameleons also features fantastic ornamental structures. This is common to all of them in nature: a motif repeats itself in strict sequences.

Finally, one can assert that nature is predominated by harmonious forms and varying normative structures that delight us aesthetically and are, miraculously, in part self-

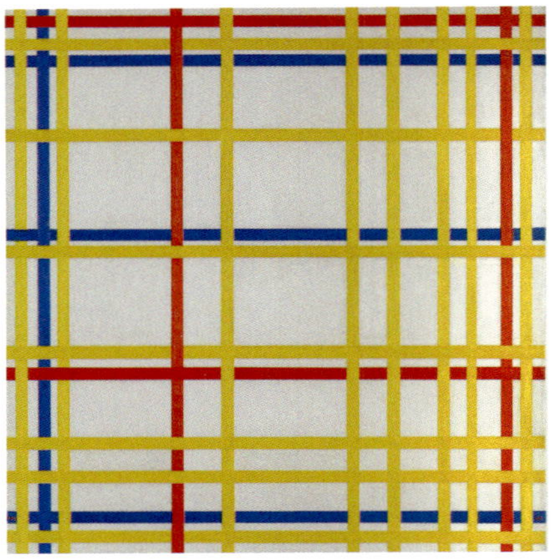

5 Piet Mondrian
New York City I, 1942
Öl auf Leinwand / oil on canvas
119,3 x 114,2 cm
Centre Pompidou MNAM, Paris
Foto: bpk / CNAC-MNAM / Philippe Migeat

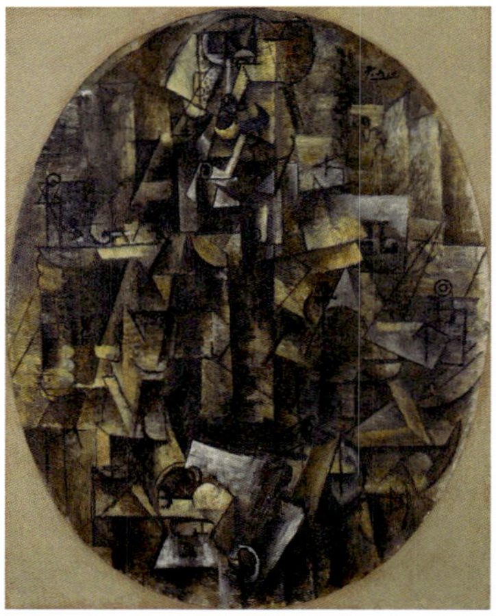

6 Pablo Picasso
Der Mann mit der Pfeife / Man with a Pipe, 1906
Öl auf Leinwand / oil on canvas
90,7 x 71 cm
Kimbell Art Museum, Fort Worth, Texas
Foto: Kimbell Art Museum, Fort Worth, Texas

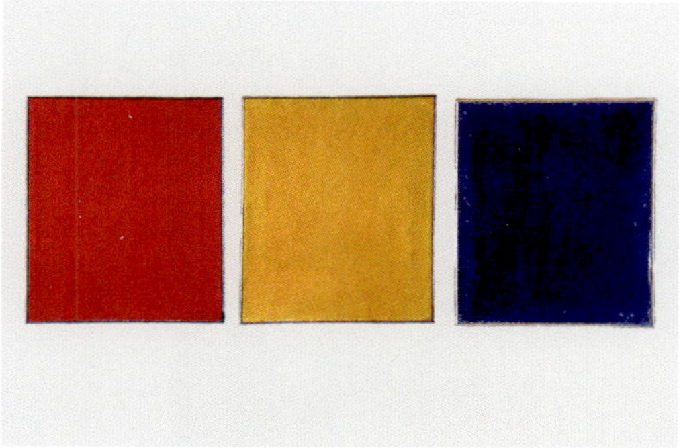

7 Alexander Rodtschenko
Reine Farbe Rot, Reine Farbe Gelb, Reine Farbe Blau / Pure Red Color, Pure Yellow Color, Pure Blue Color, 1921
Öl auf Leinwand / oil on canvas
je 62 x 52,5 cm
Rodtschenko-Archiv, Moskau

8 Władysław Strzemiński
Struktur (Unistische Komposition) / Structure (Unistic Composition), 1932
Öl auf Leinwand / oil on canvas
50,7 x 30,1 cm
Sammlung / Collection Kröller-Müller Museum, Otterlo
Foto: Sammlung / Collection Kröller-Müller Museum, Otterlo

Meines Wissens hat bislang keine kunsthistorische Untersuchung und Interpretation diesen eminenten Wechsel der abendländisch-europäischen Kunst zum Gegenstand aktueller und relevanter Betrachtung sowie Forschung gemacht.

Auch die suprematistischen Bilder Malewitschs zeigen noch, wenn auch reduziert, die Prinzipien traditioneller Komposition – das reicht bis zur Ikone. Selbst das quasi letzte Leinwandbild von Matisse, *Die Schnecke* von 1953, wo auf einem weißen Bildgrund klare Primärfarben als geometrische Scherenschnitte erscheinen, ist einerseits nicht weit von Malewitsch entfernt, andererseits erkennt man hier die ornamentale, spiralförmige Reihung und damit paradoxerweise eine Struktur.

Nun muss natürlich auch in Betracht gezogen werden, dass die Natur in ihrem universalen Imperium keine Komposition, sondern kreative Strukturen zeigt. Dank des Mikroskops konnte die Mikrobiologie die immanente Logik der ornamentalen Strukturen erkennen. Das beginnt Anfang des 20. Jahrhunderts mit den Entdeckungen feiner Silicatkristalle und Kieselalgen durch Ernst Haeckel und zeigt eine faszinierende Fülle von Mustern und immer wiederkehrenden Symmetrien bis tief in den Nanobereich. Eiskristalle und ihre vielfachen Symmetrien ergeben faszinierende Strukturen, und noch immer ist nicht erklärlich, auf welche Weise ihre Formen und Facetten sich kreativ multiplizieren. Die Mineralogie ist eine Kristallografie, in der die Atome eine besondere Struktur entwickeln und eine ornamentale Anordnung bewirken können. Wenn Licht hier Interferenzeffekte bewirkt, entstehen überraschende Farbsequenzen. Ohne diese Muster und deren Symmetrien könnte die Physik die universelle Gestaltung unserer Welt kaum oder gar nicht erklären!

Ferner denke man an die Spiegelsymmetrien, welche bilateral bei fast allen Tieren zu beobachten sind, zum Beispiel bei Schmetterlingen, Zebras, Seesternen, Fischen, an dem Fell der Tiger, der Noppenhaut des Chamäleons, den Federn eines Pfaus et cetera, et cetera.

Man denke ebenso an die Spiralen in mikroskopischer Größe und ebenso an die gewaltigen Dimensionen bei einem Hurrikan oder in kosmischen Galaxien. Oder man denke wiederum an Kakteen, Tannenzapfen, Rosen und die vielmals zitierten Samenkerne in den Blüten der großen Sonnenblumen, welche sich in zwei Spiralen gegeneinander bewegen, um das so einprägsame Muster zu bilden (vergleichbar mit den radialen Nagelreliefs von Uecker). Auch die erstaunlichen Bienenwaben, welche in der modernen Technik als Honeycomb-Aluminiumnetze auftreten, vielfach genutzt zum Beispiel im Flugzeugbau und in meinen sogenannten *Lichtreliefs,* in deren Zellstrukturen das Licht sich fängt und ausstrahlt.

Als Bildhauer begeistern mich nicht zuletzt die prismenförmigen Basaltsäulen, welche sechs Seiten haben und deren Querschnitte annähernd exakt hexagonal sind und die wie steinerne Orgelpfeifen aufrecht stehen. Und als Maler empfinde ich die farbigen Muster der Vogelfedern als besonders schön, wenn deren allerfeinste Strukturen die Lichtwellen farbig reflektieren. Aber auch die Schuppen der Schlangen oder des Chamäleons zeigen fantastische ornamentale Strukturen; dies ist ihnen allen in der Natur gemeinsam: Ein Motiv wiederholt sich in strenger Reihung.

Schließlich kann man behaupten, dass in der gesamten Natur harmonische Formen und variationsreiche Ordnungsstrukturen herrschen, die uns ästhetisch beglücken und die organized, mysteriously including aleatoric irregularities, by which means the patterns become even more interesting. In such cases, perfect structure and symmetry are not necessarily a given at all times, one example being the spider web, a masterpiece of nature. Its inner logic has not yet been fully understood and still causes mathematicians headaches. When looking at a defoliated tree in winter, one realizes that all the branches reveal how they became increasingly intertwined during the growth process. Even the tiny, outermost twigs are emblematic of the entire tree. This is a case where the entire structure still represents the individual parts and vice versa, where all of the branches make up the entirety, the tree. One might call to mind Goethe's morphology and his analogous reflections, in which the spiral motif—accompanying vertically rising energy—lends expression to overall growth. In this context, current science uses the term algorithm, in which the growth process is quasi-pre-assigned. Thus one approaches fractal structures that nature employs in each leaf with its system of finely ramified veins. This also holds true vis-à-vis multibranched rivers or striated deserts with their regular, parallel structures shaped by the wind.

Immanuel Kant already saw structure as a combination of the parts, whose intent and purpose it is to facilitate the unity of the entirety, and thus to be immanent to the unity, so to speak. All parts are themselves in turn unities acting simultaneously and striving to create integral orders and fill them with synergy.[1]

In the context of my ZERO paintings I created optically vibrating energy fields that display a type of kinetic visuality, an essential ingredient of Op Art. Important Op artists include Vasarely, Bridget Riley, and the American Anuszkiewicz. Repeating a simple element with discernible form and in a balanced alongside- and with-one-another, thus integrating it into a serial network, produces a suggestive impression of rhythm and hence of time. The process of repeating the repetition tends to result in a harmonious unison that has to be confined gradually in order not to run idle and thus paralyze the latent tensions in the desired energy field.

This is accompanied by the proportionality between the size and formal character of the individual part on the one hand, and the size or expanse of the structure field on the other. The same applies to my sculptures, in which constructive structures and their spatial expanses are also comparable to those in painting in that serial elements are set into motion and in doing so demonstrate movement, as it were.

It is hence fair to call structure a holistic framework in the sense of a strict order! Structure is moreover a term in digital programming that refers to the overall structure of a frame of reference into which all parts are equally integrated. Their purpose is to bear and sustain the structural order and to make the aesthetic unity visible. This is both a sensuous as well as a mental event.

Another word for structure field is 'pattern' or 'grid.' Physicists use scanning electron microscopes to research the microworld, making advances into the atomic realm. Digital computer calculations facilitate visual diagrams and make aspects of nature visible to our eyes that we are otherwise unable to discern.

1 Reto Luzius Fetz, "Struktur," in Christian Bermes and Ulrich Diese, eds., *Schlüsselbegriffe der Philosophie des 20. Jahrhunderts* (Hamburg, 2010), pp. 355–69.

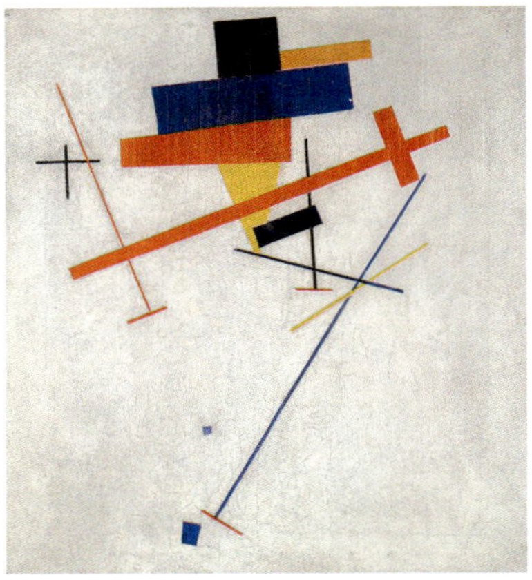

9 Kasimir Malewitsch
Suprematistische Komposition / Suprematist Composition, ca. 1915/16
Öl auf Leinwand / oil on canvas
49,5 x 44,7 cm
Wilhelm Hack Museum, Ludwigshafen
Foto: Wilhelm Hack Museum, Ludwigshafen

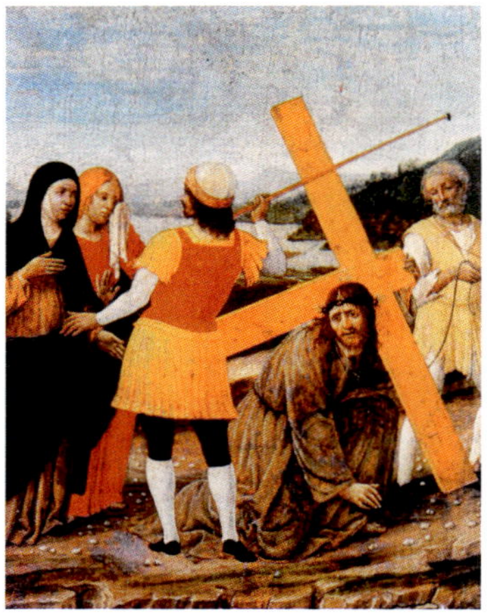

10 Giovanni Ambrogio Bevilacqua
(ca. 1474–1516, Mailand)
Andata al Calvario / Weg nach Golgotha / Road to Calvary
undatiert / year unknown
Tempera auf Tafel / tempera on board
34 x 27,5 cm

1 Reto Luzius Fetz, »Struktur«, in: *Schlüsselbegriffe der Philosophie des 20. Jahrhunderts,* hrsg. von Christian Bermes und Ulrich Dierse, Hamburg 2010, S. 355–369.

sich phänomenalerweise partiell selbst organisieren, aleatorische Unregelmäßigkeiten rätselhafterweise einbegriffen, wodurch die Muster eher noch interessanter werden. In solchen Fällen ist eine perfekte Struktur und Symmetrie nicht immer mehr gegeben: beim Spinnennetz zum Beispiel, einem Meisterwerk der Natur, das eine noch nicht erkennbare innere logische Ordnung hat, welche den Mathematikern Kopfzerbrechen bereitet. Betrachtet man ferner einen blätterlosen Baum im Winter, erkennt man, dass alle Zweige sichtbar machen, wie sie sich wachsend immer mehr verzweigt haben; ja selbst die äußersten kleinen Äste sind quasi ein Sinnbild des ganzen Baumes. Hier wird die Struktur des Ganzen von den Einzelteilen noch vertreten, und vice versa ergeben alle Verzweigungen zusammen das Ganze, den Baum. Man denke auch an die Morphologie Goethes mit seinen analogen Betrachtungen, in denen das Spiralmotiv als Begleitung der vertikal aufsteigenden Energie das gesamte Wachstum zum Ausdruck bringt. In der gegenwärtigen Wissenschaft spricht man hier von einem Algorithmus, welcher den Wachstumsprozess quasi vorprogrammiert. Damit nähert man sich dem Fraktalen, wie es sich in der Natur auch in jedem Baumblatt mit seinem System von sich verzweigenden Adern zeigt. So auch in der Makrostruktur sich verzweigender Flüsse oder geriffelter Wüsten mit vom Wind geformten regelmäßigen parallelen Strukturen.

Schon Immanuel Kant sah in der Struktur eine Verbindung der Teile, deren Zweck und Bestimmung es sei, die Einheit des Ganzen zu ermöglichen und damit der Einheit immanent zu sein. Alle Teile selbst sind wieder Einheiten, die simultan agieren, um ganzheitliche Ordnungen zu schaffen und diese mit Synergie zu erfüllen.[1]

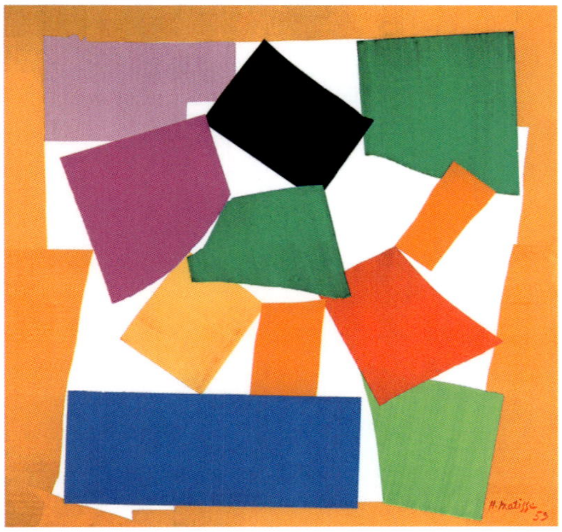

11 Henri Matisse
Die Schnecke / The Snail, 1953
Gouache auf Papier, geschnitten und eingeklebt auf Papier montiert auf Leinwand montiert / Gouache on paper, cut and pasted on paper mounted on canvas
286,4 x 287 cm
Tate Gallery of Modern Art, London
Foto: Tate, London 2017

In meiner Malerei aus der ZERO-Zeit entstanden hierzu Energiefelder, die optisch vibrieren und damit eine Art kinetische Visualität zeigen, wie sie in der Optical Art eine essenzielle Bedeutung fand. Wichtige Künstler waren hier Vasarely, Bridget Riley und der Amerikaner Anuszkiewicz. Indem man ein einfaches Element mit erkennbarer Form in einem gleichgewichtigen Neben- und Miteinander wiederholt, also in ein serielles Netzwerk integriert, entsteht ein suggestiver Eindruck von Rhythmus und damit von Zeit. Dieser Prozess der Wiederholung der Wiederholung tendiert zu einem Gleichklang, der im Verlauf begrenzt werden muss, um nicht in einen Leerlauf zu geraten und die latenten Spannungen des gewünschten Energiefeldes zu paralysieren.

Damit geht einher die Verhältnismäßigkeit zwischen der Größe und dem Formcharakter des einzelnen Teils einerseits und der Größe oder Ausdehnung des Strukturfeldes andererseits. Das gilt auch für meine Skulpturen, in denen eine konstruktive Struktur und deren Ausdehnung im Raum mit denen der Malerei vergleichbar sind, indem serielle Elemente in Bewegung geraten und quasi das Movens zeigen.

Struktur ist also ein ganzheitliches Gefüge im Sinne einer strengen Ordnung! Struktur ist auch der Begriff einer digitalen Programmierung, die den Gesamtaufbau eines Bezugssystems meint, in dem alle Teile gleichwertig integriert sind und die Funktion haben, das Ordnungsgefüge zu tragen und als ästhetischen Gleichklang sichtbar zu machen. Dies ist ein sowohl sinnliches als auch mentales Ereignis.

Das Strukturfeld wird auch ›Muster‹ oder ›Raster‹ genannt. In der Physik dient das Rasterelektronenmikroskop der Erforschung der Mikrowelt, die bis in den atomaren Bereich

I find that what biochemistry investigates regarding cell structures or what surfaces in neurology as a highly complex system of synapses, vibrations, impulses, interferences, and control functions has a phenomenal parallel with aesthetic digressions. They, too, appear to be subject to a code whose entity enables a digital logic. Mysteriously, the enigmatic latter determines the creative artistic processes. Let me suggest a daring explanation: seen from this vantage point, the artist himself becomes the medium of a creative process.

A Johann Sebastian Bach fugue with a terminal serial cadenza is the epitome of a complex musical structure and possesses the same harmonic beauty we encounter in nature. To mention another prime example: Ravel's *Boléro* not only has an Oriental, ornamental atmosphere, it is equally characterized by the utmost stringent sequencing of a motif that is repeated until it reaches its energetic climax. Other composers 'composing' serially structured music include Stravinsky, Schönberg, Stockhausen, my friend Ligeti, Steve Reich, and Philip Glass—and it was Bach who had already anticipated much of this.

Let me conclude my thoughts about the nature of structure and the structure of nature with a question I asked myself: Is it a contradiction or is it comprehensible that an artist like myself—who has worked nonfiguratively throughout his career and who is still suspected to be a follower of 'l'art pour l'art'—is capable of finding a deep connection to nature? Or, to put it differently: What is the nature of a contemporary artist's relationship to the visible natural world that has been photographed millions of times over the past one hundred years? And are micro- as well as macrocosm exclusively the subject of science or—at this point—also of art? Thus we touch upon the query: what type of space emanates from paintings with all their colors if the structures the artist creates take the place of traditional composition and central perspective?

vordringt. Mit digitalen Computerrechnungen werden visuelle Diagramme geschaffen und es wird etwas sichtbar gemacht, was jenseits der für unsere Augen sichtbaren Natur liegt.

Was in der Biochemie hinsichtlich der Zellstrukturen erforscht wird oder in der Neurologie als ein hochkomplexes System von Synapsen, Schwingungen, Impulsen, Interferenzen und Steuerfunktionen erscheint, hat für mich eine phänomenale Parallelität zu den ästhetischen Exkursen. Auch sie scheinen einem Code zu unterliegen, dessen Entität eine digitale Logik ermöglicht, welche rätselhaft die kreativen künstlerischen Prozesse determiniert. Eine gewagte Erklärung: Der Künstler wird unter diesem Aspekt selbst zum Medium eines kreativen Prozesses.

Eine Fuge von Johann Sebastian Bach mit abschließender serieller Kadenz hat die höchste Form einer komplexen musikalischen Struktur und die gleiche harmonische Schönheit, die wir in der Natur finden. Oder um ein Paradebeispiel zu nennen: Ravels *Boléro* hat nicht nur eine orientalisch-ornamentale Atmosphäre, sondern eine denkbar stringente Reihung eines Motivs, das so lange wiederholt wird, bis eine energetische Hochspannung erreicht ist. Und auch Komponisten wie Strawinsky, Schönberg, Stockhausen, der mir befreundete Ligeti, Steve Reich oder Philip Glass ›komponierten‹ oder ›komponieren‹ seriell strukturierte Musik; das alles wurde weitgehend bereits von Bach vorausgenommen.

Ich beende meine Gedanken über die Natur der Struktur und über die Struktur in der Natur mit einer mir selbst gestellten Frage: Ist es ein Widerspruch oder ist es nachvollziehbar, dass ein Künstler wie ich, der lebenslang nonfigurativ gearbeitet hat und immer noch im Verdacht steht, Nachfolger des ›L'art pour l'art‹ zu sein, einen tieferen Bezug zur Natur finden kann? Oder anders gefragt: Welche Beziehung hat heute der Künstler zur sichtbaren Natur, die man seit hundert Jahren millionenfach fotografiert hat? Und sind der Mikro- sowie der Makrokosmos allein Gegenstände der Wissenschaft oder nun auch der Kunst? Damit berühren wir auch die Frage, welchen Raum die Malerei mit ihren Farben ausstrahlt, wenn die vom Künstler geschaffenen Strukturen an die Stelle der traditionellen Komposition und Zentralperspektive treten.

Morphology

Heinz Mack

It is a mystery to me that plants defy the law of gravity and grow vertically, whereas their roots obey the law of gravity and grow downward. What mystifies me even more is the point at which plants leave the soil. This is where both forces come into play at the same place and where the decision regarding 'upwards' and 'downwards' is made simultaneously, as it were; here, the surface of the earth is the interface of these opposing forces.

Furthermore: If, for instance, I cut through a cactus column horizontally and place the upper part moderately into the soil, then roots now begin to grow downwards at the very place where growth previously occurred vertically. To me, this is difficult to explain.

Something I repeatedly observe is the law that predetermines the overall shape of many trees and tree-like plants—not a single branch leaves the outer contour of the treetop. Gardeners take this as an inspiration and enhance the often seemingly geometric form by pruning. Just think of the Baroque or the Japanese art of gardening.

Something else I notice is how, for example, the willow lets its branches grow until they reach the ground and lets them hang, only to terminate its urge to grow. On the other hand, there is another willow that makes a very rare exception: its branches continue to grow until they lie flat on the ground more than three feet in length. To me, this is also enigmatic.

In my Mediterranean garden, I grow palms and cypresses, as well as dragon-fruit agaves, Araucaria acacias, and cycas palms. They are prototypical examples of clear, three-dimensional tree silhouettes. In contrast to the lovely Aleppo pines, stone pines have the tendency to let their branches 'accidentally' grow into space. The tamarisk then appears to be almost wild.

Some seeds or fruits as well as shapes of leaves appear to be 'male' or 'female' if looked at anthropomorphically, which means that they can be related to human forms.

In the case of Melianthus leaves, it is striking with how much fantasy they absorb the light while at the same time partially protecting themselves from the shade.

Morphologie

Heinz Mack

Ein Rätsel ist für mich, dass die Pflanzen die Erdanziehung überwinden und senkrecht hochwachsen, wogegen deren Wurzeln der Gravität folgen und abwärts wachsen. Besonders rätselhaft erscheint mir der Bereich, wo die Pflanzen die Erde verlassen: Dort kommen beide Kräfte am gleichen Ort ins Spiel, in dem das Aufwärts und das Abwärts quasi gleichzeitig entschieden werden; die Erdoberfläche ist hier der Grenzbereich dieser entgegengesetzten Kräfte.

Ferner: Schneide ich zum Beispiel eine Kaktussäule horizontal durch und setze den oberen Teil moderat in die Erde, dann wachsen an der Stelle, wo vorher das Wachstum nach oben gerichtet war, nun Wurzeln, die nach unten wachsen. Das erscheint mir schwer erklärbar.

Was ich immer wieder sehend erkenne, ist die Gesetzmäßigkeit, die quasi die Gesamtform vieler Bäume und baumähnlicher Pflanzen vorprogrammiert – da ist kein Zweig, der die äußere Kontur der Baumkrone verlässt. Gärtner lassen sich hiervon anregen und steigern durch entsprechende Schnitte die oft geometrisch erscheinende Form; man denke an die barocke oder an die japanische Gartenkunst.

Ebenso fällt auf, wie zum Beispiel die Weide ihre Zweige bis zur Erdoberfläche wachsen und hängen lässt, um dann hier den Wachstumsdrang zu beenden. Andererseits macht eine andere Weide eine Ausnahme, was sehr selten ist: Ihre Zweige wachsen weiter, bis sie mit einer Länge von mehr als einem Meter sich flach auf den Boden legen. Das erscheint mir ebenfalls rätselhaft.

In meinem mediterranen Garten sind die Palmen und die Zypressen sowie die Drachenbaum-Agaven oder die Araucaria-Akazien und Cycas-Palmen Musterbeispiele für klare, dreidimensionale Baumsilhouetten. Im Gegensatz zu den schönen Aleppo-Kiefern sind die Pinien geneigt, ihre Zweige ›zufällig‹ in den Raum wachsen zu lassen – fast wild erscheint dann die Tamariske.

Manche Samen und Früchte sowie Blattformen erscheinen ›männlich‹ oder ›weiblich‹, also anthropomorphisch gesehen, das heißt, man kann sie auf die menschlichen Gestalten beziehen.

Bei den Melianthus-Blättern fällt auf, wie fantasiereich sie das Licht aufnehmen und partiell sich zugleich gegenüber dem Schatten schützen.

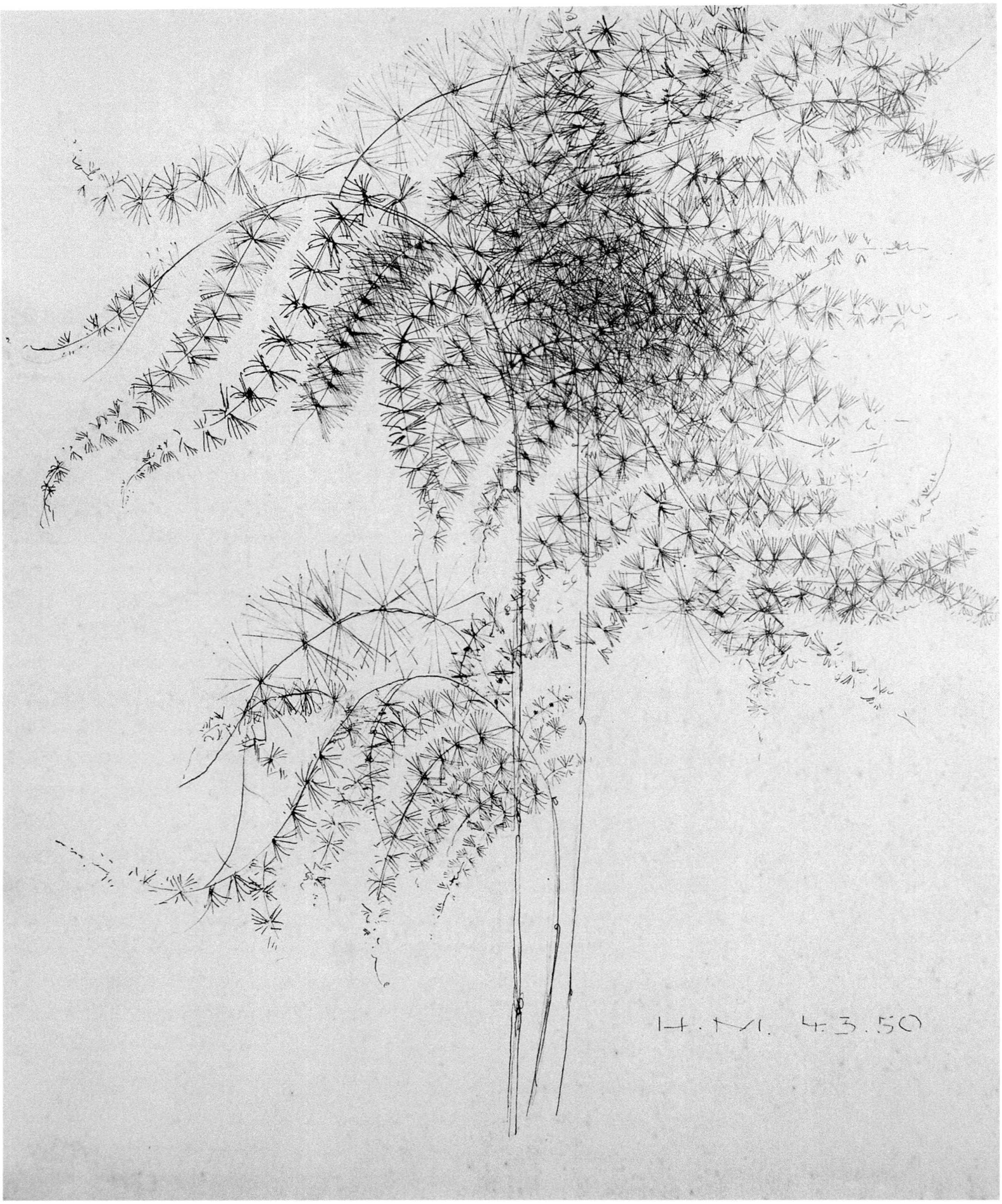

Heinz Mack
Pflanzenstudie
Signiert, datiert: »H. M. 4.3.50«
Schwarze Tusche mit Feder auf Papier
22 x 27 cm

Heinz Mack
Plant study
Signed, dated: "H. M. 4.3.50"
Black ink applied to paper with steel nib
22 x 27 cm

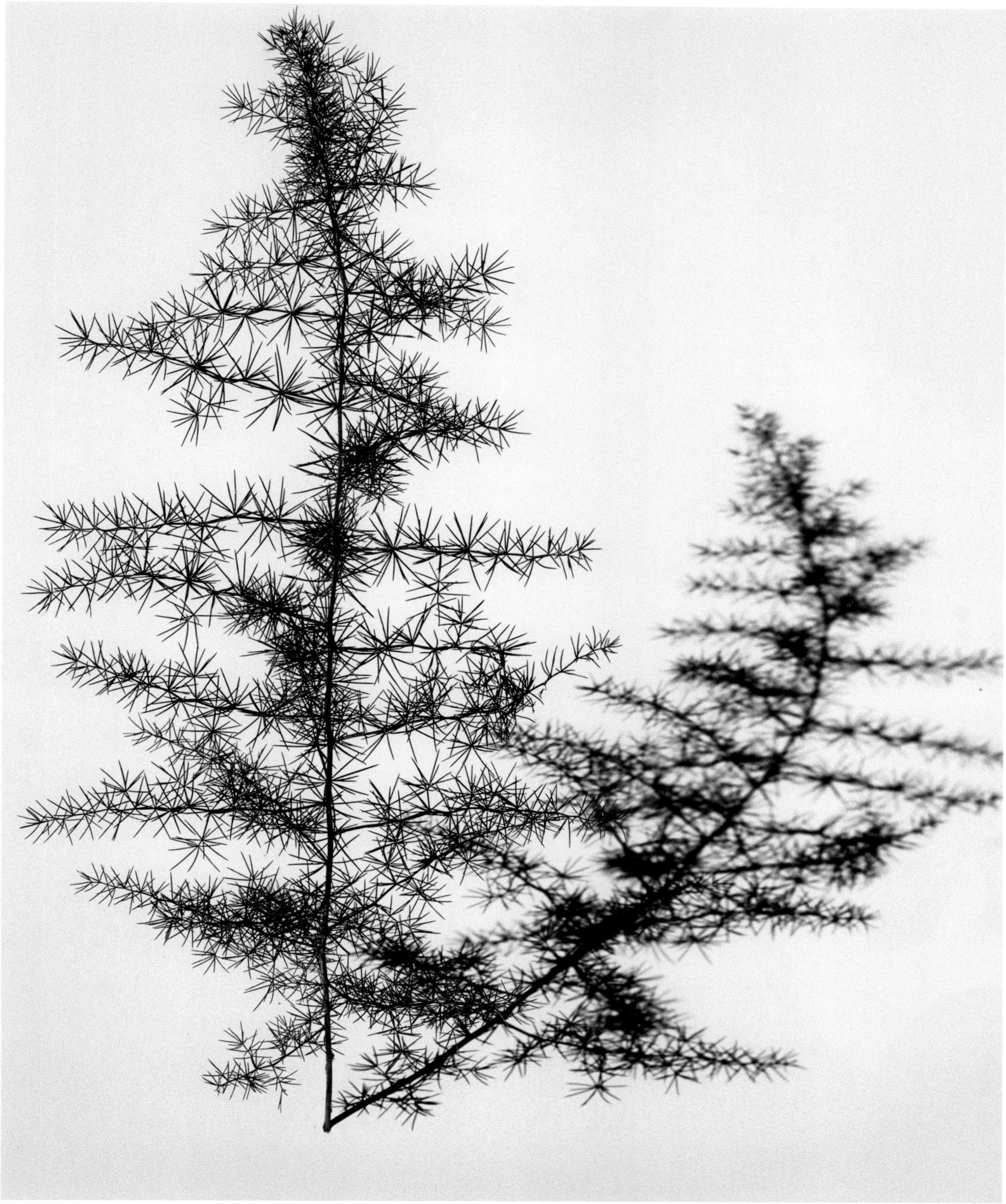

Heinz Mack
Schattenexperiment mit Pflanzenzweig, 2016
Fotografie

Heinz Mack
Shadow experiment with plant sprig, 2016
Photograph

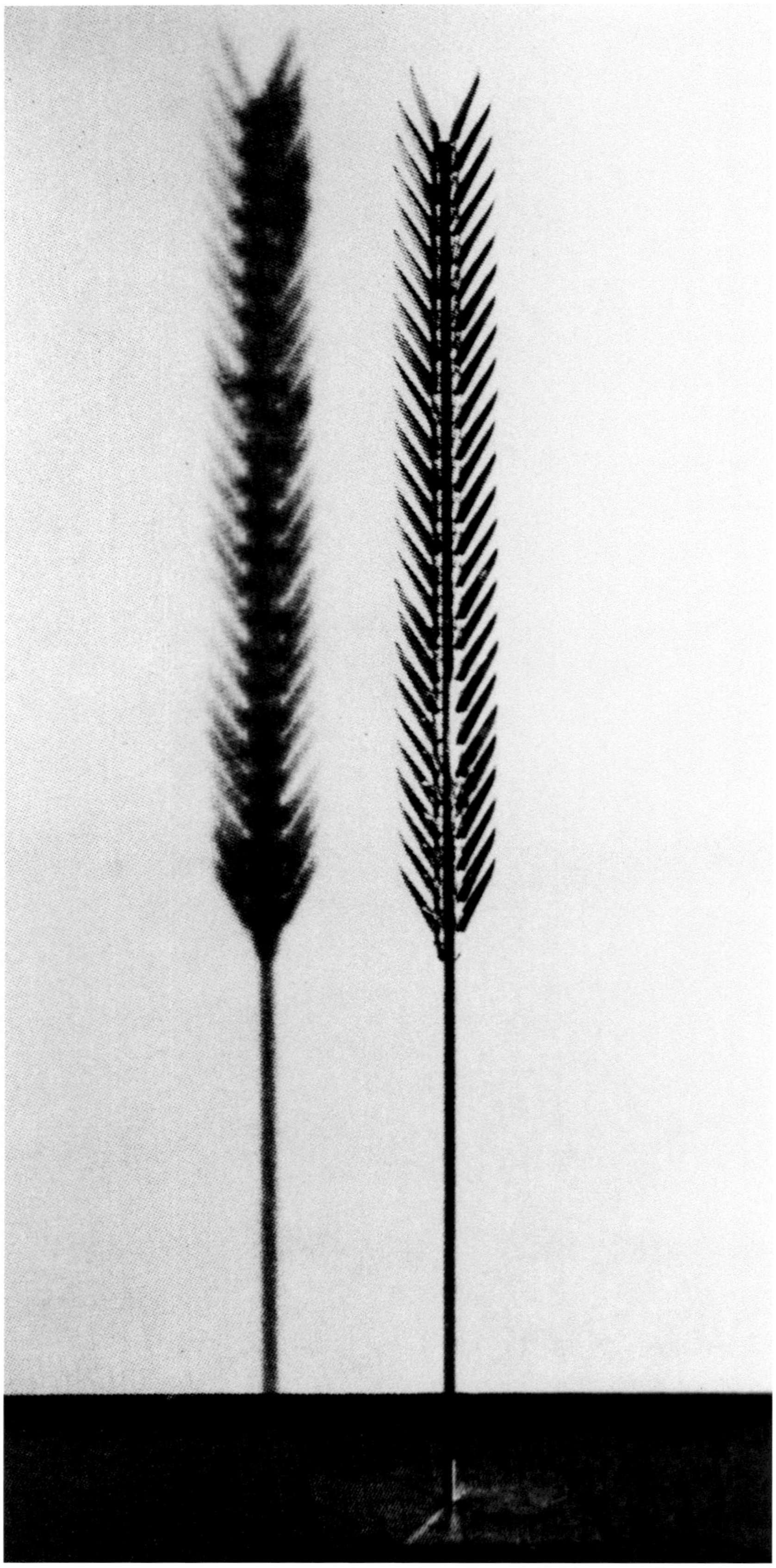

Heinz Mack
Joy, 1964
Verchromter Stahl
265 x 18 x 10 cm

Heinz Mack
Joy, 1964
Chromed steel
265 x 18 x 10 cm

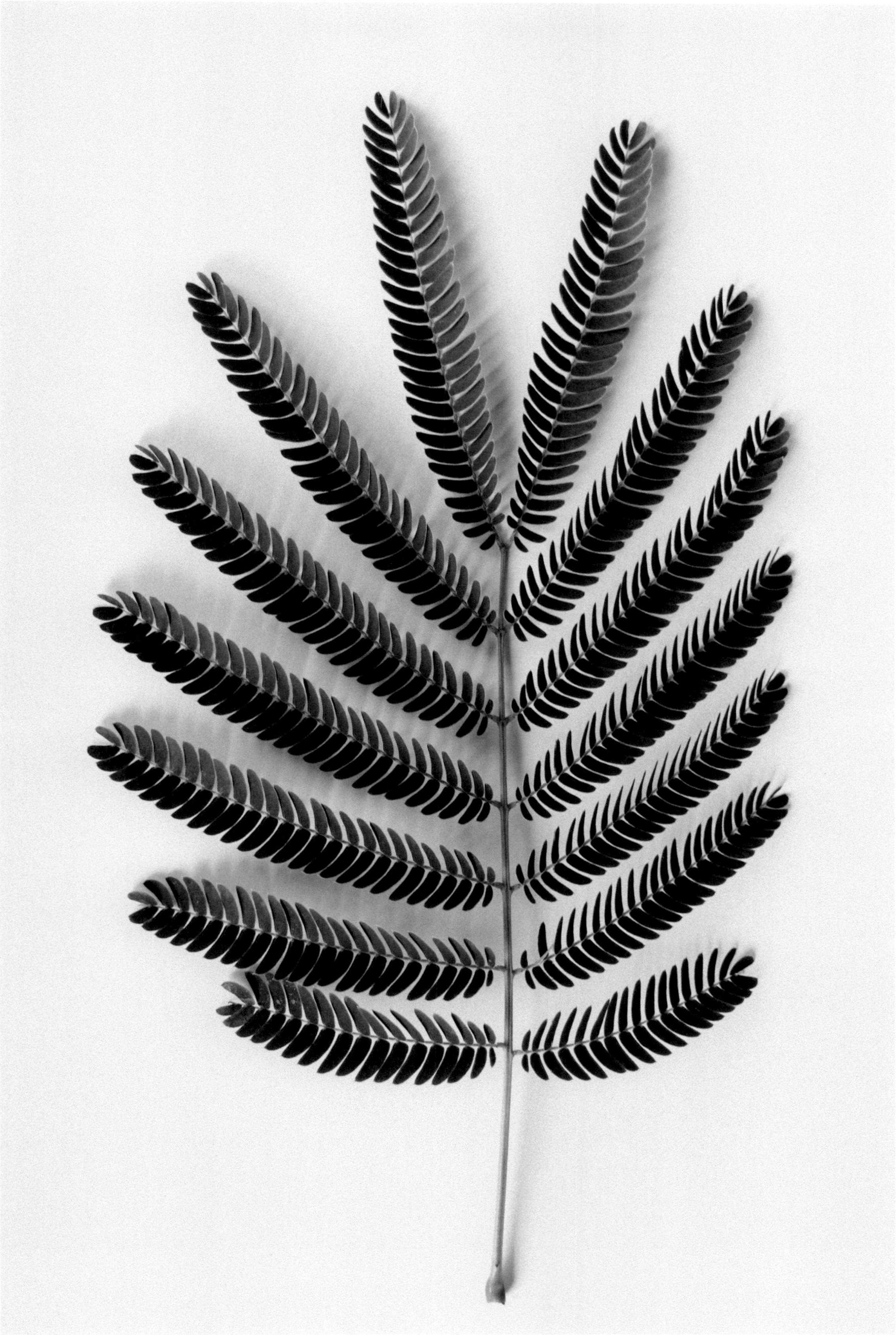

Heinz Mack
Mimosenblatt, 2016
Fotografie

Heinz Mack
Mimosa leave, 2016
Photograph

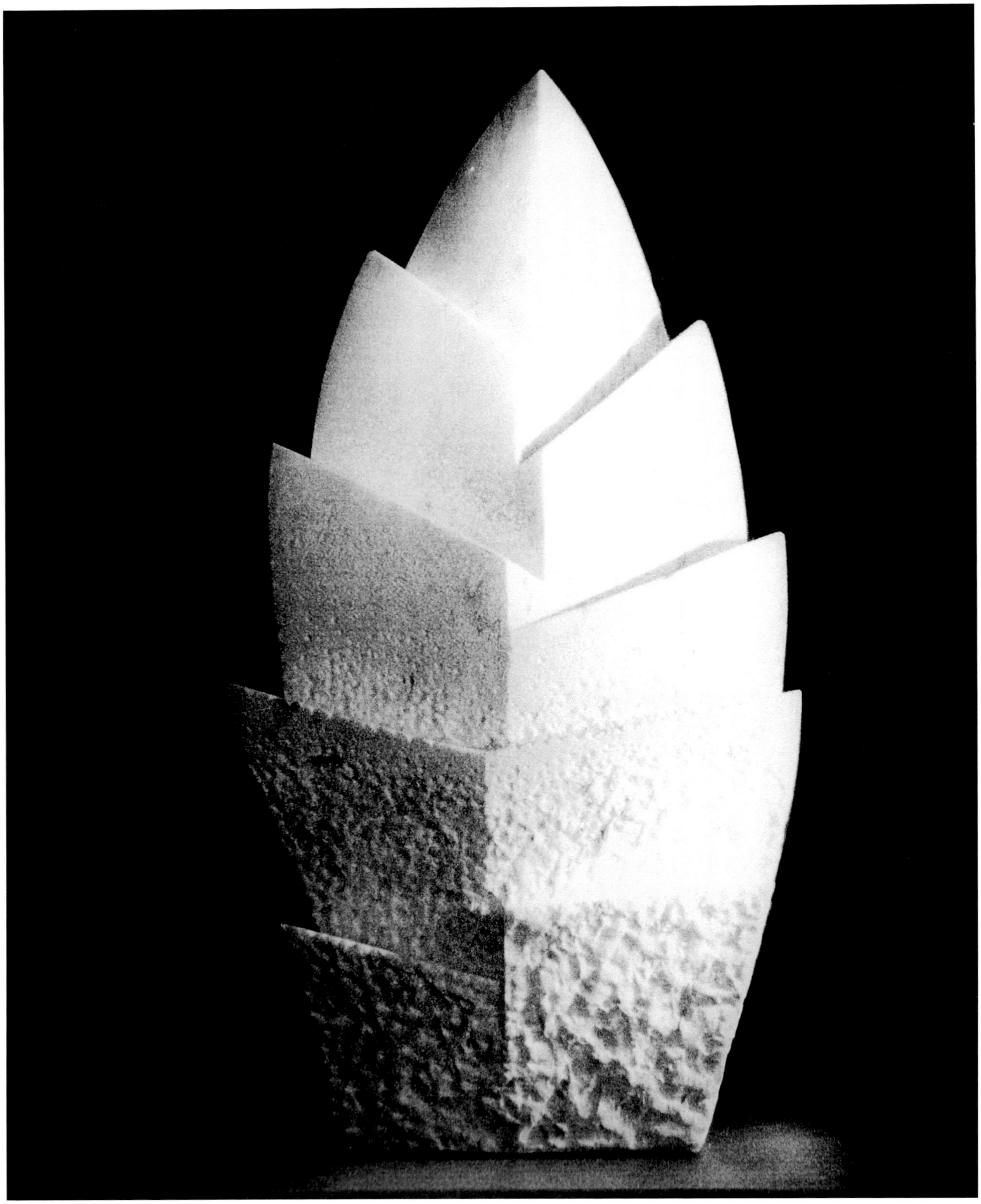

Heinz Mack
Flora
Signiert, datiert: »mack 96«
Marmor (cremefarben, aus Portugal),
teils poliert, teils geschliffen, teils bossiert
102 x 57 x 21 cm

Heinz Mack
Flora
Signed, datiert: "mack 96"
Marble (cream colored, from Portugal),
part polished, part burnished, part dressed
102 x 57 x 21 cm

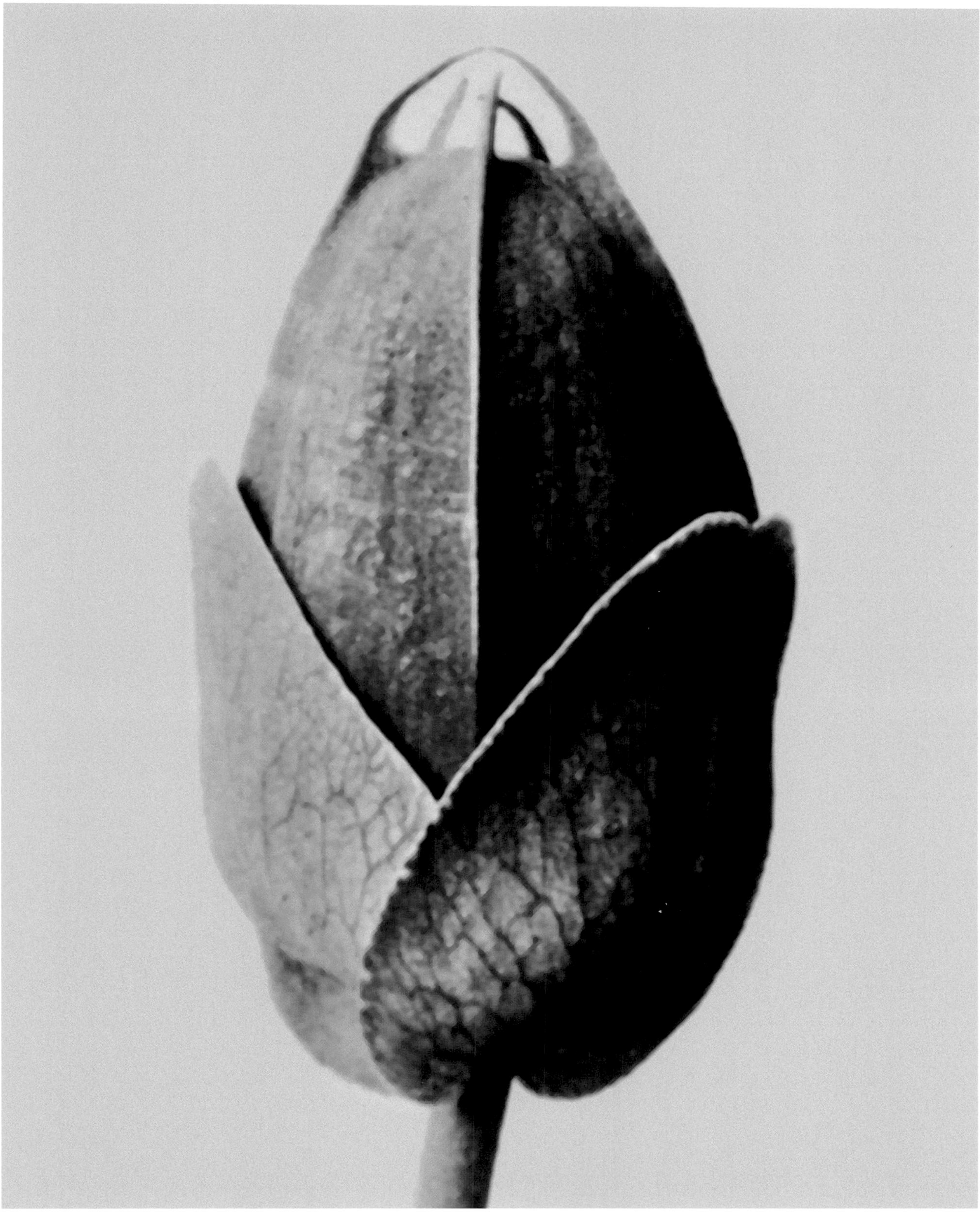

Karl Blossfeldt
Passionsblume
Fotografie

Karl Blossfeldt
Passion Flower
Photograph

INSPIRATION ORIENT

INSPIRATION ORIENT

»Schon im vorigen Jahre waren mir die sämmtlichen Gedichte Hafis in der von Hammer'schen Übersetzung zugekommen [...], und ich mußte mich dagegen productiv verhalten, weil ich sonst vor der mächtigen Erscheinung nicht hätte bestehen können.«

"Last year the collected poems of Háfiz translated by von Hammer were sent to me... and I had to react productively towards them or I would have been unable to survive in the face of this powerful manifestation."

GOETHE

»Meine wiederholten Begegnungen mit der orientalischen Kultur reichen ein halbes Jahrhundert zurück, und ich war weder in der Lage noch gewillt, mich ihrem Einfluß zu entziehen.«

"My repeated encounters with oriental culture go back half a century, and I have neither been able nor willing to resist its influence."

MACK

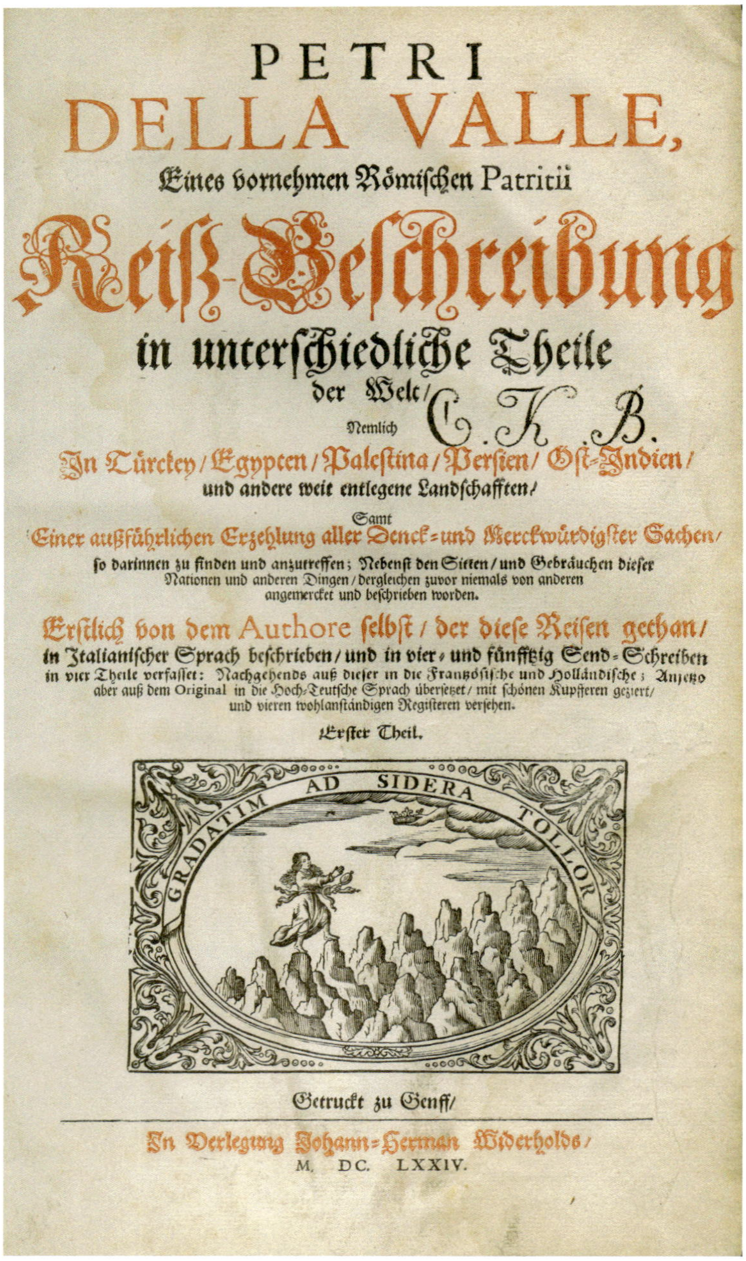

PETRI
DELLA VALLE,
Eines vornehmen Römischen Patricii
Reiß-Beschreibung
in unterschiedliche Theile
der Welt /
Nemlich
In Türckey / Egypten / Palestina / Persien / Ost-Indien /
und andere weit entlegene Landschafften /
Samt
Einer außführlichen Erzehlung aller Denck- und Merckwürdigster Sachen /
so darinnen zu finden und anzutreffen; Nebenst den Sitten / und Gebräuchen dieser Nationen und anderen Dingen / dergleichen zuvor niemals von anderen angemercket und beschrieben worden.
Erstlich von dem Authore selbst / der diese Reisen gethan / in Italianischer Sprach beschrieben / und in vier- und fünfftzig Send-Schreiben in vier Theile verfasset: Nachgehends auß dieser in die Frantzösische und Holländische; Anjetzo aber auß dem Original in die Hoch-Teutsche Sprach übersetzet / mit schönen Kupfferen geziert / und vieren wohlanständigen Registeren versehen.
Erster Theil.

Getruckt zu Genff /
In Verlegung Johann-Herman Widerholds /
M. DC. LXXIV.

1 Pietro della Valle
Reiß-Beschreibung
Genf 1674:

Petri della Valle, Eines vornehmen Römischen Patritii Reiß-Beschreibung in unterschiedliche Theile der Welt / Nemlich In Türckey / Egypten / Palestina / Persien / Ost-Indien / und andere weit entlegene Landschafften / Samt Einer außführlichen Erzehlung aller Denck- und Merckwürdigster Sachen / so darinnen zu finden und anzutreffen; Nebenst den Sitten / und Gebräuchen dieser Nationen und anderen Dingen / dergleichen zuvor niemals von anderen angemercket und beschrieben worden. [...] Erster Theil, Getruckt zu Genff / In Verlegung Johann-Herman Widerholds / M. DC. LXXIV.

Die Erstausgabe der Reisebeschreibung des italienischen Orientreisenden Pietro della Valle (1586–1652) war unter dem Titel *Viaggi di Pietro della Valle il Pellegrino Con minuto ragguaglio Di tutte le cose notabili osseruate in essi, Descritti da lui medesimo in 54. Lettere familiari* erschienen (3 Bde., Rom 1650–1663). Der Bericht über seine Reise nach Persien in den Jahren 1617 bis 1619 befindet sich im zweiten Teil der deutschen Übersetzung. Goethe las die Reisebeschreibung 1815 und 1819 und kommentierte das Werk in den *Noten und Abhandlungen zu besserem Verständniß des West-östlichen Divans* (WA, Bd. 17, S. 189–210).

1 Pietro della Valle
Travelogue
Geneva 1674

The first edition of the travelogue of the Italian Orient traveler Pietro della Valle (1586–1652) was published as three volumes in 1650–63 in Rome with the Title: *Viaggi di Pietro della Valle il Pellegrino Con minuto ragguaglio Di tutte le cose notabili osseruate in essi, Descritti da lui medesimo in 54. Lettere familiari*. The report of his journey to Persia in the years 1617 to 1619 is part of the second volume of the German translation. Goethe read the travelogue 1815 and 1819 and commented on the work in *Notes and Essays for a Better Understanding of the West-East Divan* (Johann Wolfgang von Goethe, *West-East Divan*, trans. Martin Bidney, New York, 2010, pp. 259–69).

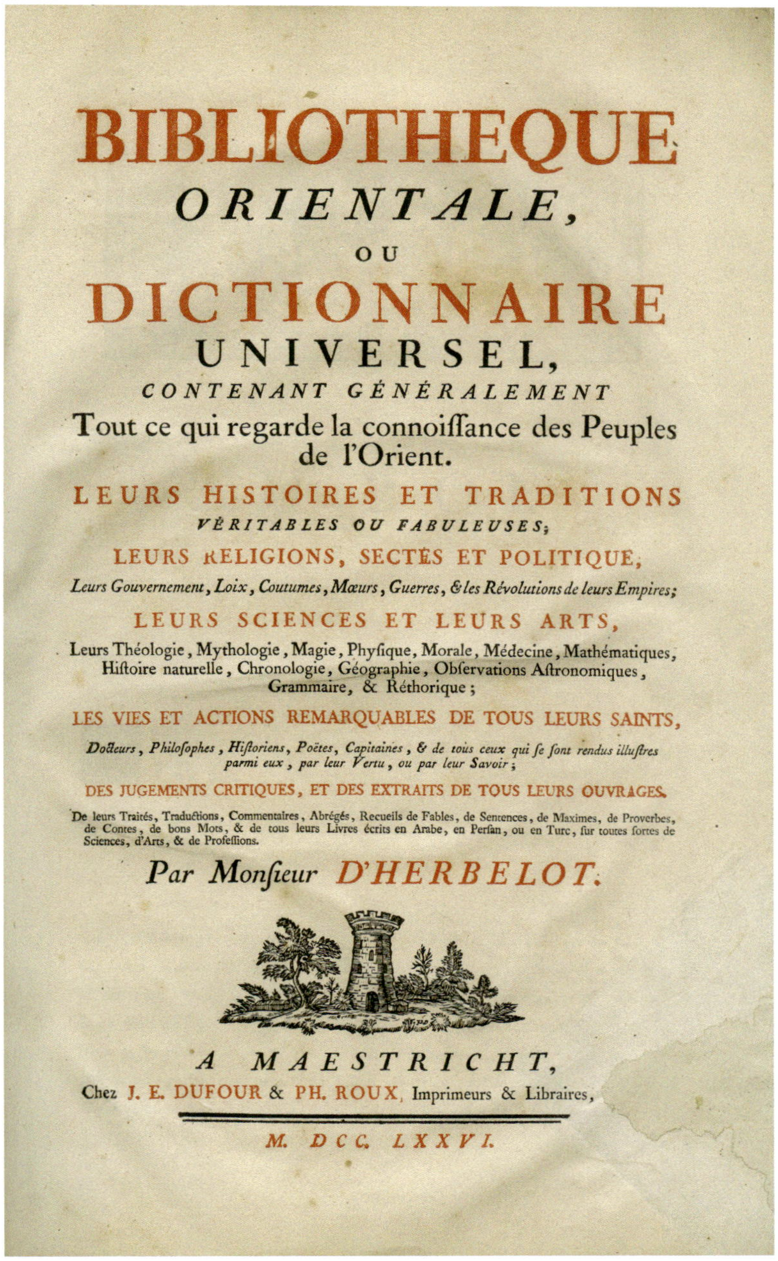

BIBLIOTHEQUE
ORIENTALE,
OU
DICTIONNAIRE
UNIVERSEL,
CONTENANT GÉNÉRALEMENT
Tout ce qui regarde la connoissance des Peuples de l'Orient.
LEURS HISTOIRES ET TRADITIONS
VÉRITABLES OU FABULEUSES;
LEURS RELIGIONS, SECTES ET POLITIQUE,
Leurs Gouvernement, Loix, Coutumes, Mœurs, Guerres, & les Révolutions de leurs Empires;
LEURS SCIENCES ET LEURS ARTS,
Leurs Théologie, Mythologie, Magie, Physique, Morale, Médecine, Mathématiques, Histoire naturelle, Chronologie, Géographie, Observations Astronomiques, Grammaire, & Réthorique;
LES VIES ET ACTIONS REMARQUABLES DE TOUS LEURS SAINTS,
Docteurs, Philosophes, Historiens, Poëtes, Capitaines, & de tous ceux qui se sont rendus illustres parmi eux, par leur Vertu, ou par leur Savoir;
DES JUGEMENTS CRITIQUES, ET DES EXTRAITS DE TOUS LEURS OUVRAGES.
De leurs Traités, Traductions, Commentaires, Abrégés, Recueils de Fables, de Sentences, de Maximes, de Proverbes, de Contes, de bons Mots, & de tous leurs Livres écrits en Arabe, en Persan, ou en Turc, sur toutes sortes de Sciences, d'Arts, & de Professions.
Par Monsieur D'HERBELOT.
A MAESTRICHT,
Chez J. E. DUFOUR & PH. ROUX, Imprimeurs & Libraires,
M. DCC. LXXVI.

2 Barthélemy d'Herbelot de Molainville
Bibliotheque orientale
Maastricht 1776

Das erstmals 1697 in Paris erschienene Lexikon des französischen Orientalisten Barthélemy d'Herbelot de Molainville (1625–1695) las Goethe 1814/15 und 1818/19, dazu auch die deutsche Übersetzung von Johann Christoph Friedrich Schulz: *Orientalische Bibliothek,* 4 Bde., Halle 1785–1790.
In den *Noten und Abhandlungen zu besserem Verständniß des West-östlichen Divans* (WA, Bd. 17, S. 253) schreibt Goethe: »Unter französischem Geleit sind wir hauptsächlich in jene Gegenden eingeführt worden. Herbelots Wörterbuch kam unsern Wünschen zu Hülfe. Nun mußte der französische Gelehrte orientalische Worte und Namen der nationellen Aussprache und Hörweise aneignen und gefällig machen, welches denn auch in deutsche Cultur nach und nach herüberging. So sagen wir noch Hegire lieber als Hedschra, des angenehmen Klanges und der alten Bekanntschaft wegen.«

2 Barthélemy d'Herbelot de Molainville
Bibliotheque orientale
Maastricht 1776

The encyclopaedia of the French Orientalist Barthélemy d'Herbelot de Molainville (1625–1695), first published in Paris in 1697, was read by Goethe in 1814–15 and 1818–19, along with the German translation by Johann Christoph Friedrich Schulz: *Orientalische Bibliothek,* 4 vols., Halle 1785–90.
In *Notes and Essays for a Better Understanding of the West-East Divan* Goethe writes:
"It is under French escort that I was chiefly led into those areas. The dictionary of Herbelot assisted me in my desires. But the French scholar had to adapt Oriental words and names to French pronunciation and phonic expectations; and these versions eventually entered Germany. So even today we prefer to say Hegire, rather than Hejra, as more pleasant and more familiar." (Johann Wolfgang von Goethe, *West-East Divan,* trans. Martin Bidney, New York, 2010, p. 287.)

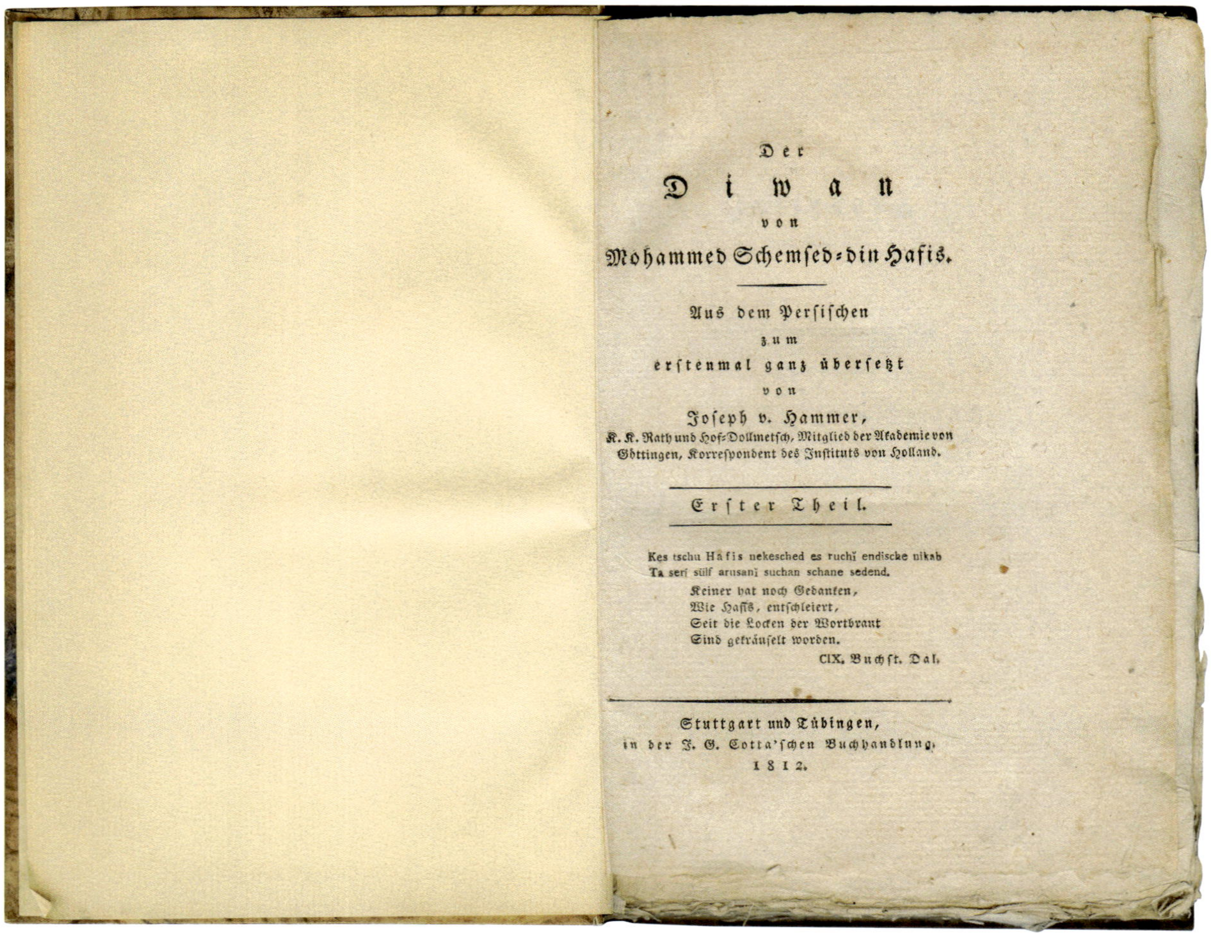
Der
Diwan
von
Mohammed Schemsed-din Hafis.

Aus dem Persischen
zum
erstenmal ganz übersetzt
von
Joseph v. Hammer,
K. K. Rath und Hof-Dollmetsch, Mitglied der Akademie von Göttingen, Korrespondent des Instituts von Holland.

Erster Theil.

Kes tschu Hâfis nekesched es ruchî endische nikab
Ta serî sülf arusanî suchan schane sedend.
Keiner hat noch Gedanken,
Wie Hafis, entschleiert,
Seit die Locken der Wortbraut
Sind gekräuselt worden.
CIX. Buchst. Dal.

Stuttgart und Tübingen,
in der J. G. Cotta'schen Buchhandlung.
1812.

3 Hafis
Der Diwan
Stuttgart und Tübingen 1812–1813 [recte: 1814]:
Der Diwan von Mohammed Schemsed-din Hafis. Aus dem Persischen zum erstenmal ganz übersetzt von Joseph v. Hammer […]. Erster Theil. […] Stuttgart und Tübingen, in der J. G. Cotta'schen Buchhandlung. 1812

Im Frühsommer 1814 studierte Goethe die Lyrik des Orients. Er las begeistert die Gedichte des bedeutendsten persischen Dichters Mohammed Schemsed-din Hafis (um 1326–um 1390) in der zweibändigen deutschen Übersetzung des österreichischen Diplomaten und Dolmetschers Joseph von Hammer (1774–1856). ›Diwan‹ meint ›(Ver)-sammlung‹. In Hafis erkannte Goethe einen formvollendeten geistesverwandten Dichter, ja einen Zwillingsbruder im Geiste, und ließ sich durch dessen Trink-, Liebes- und mystische Lieder zu seiner eigenen Gedichtsammlung *West-oestlicher Divan* inspirieren.

3 Hafis
Der Diwan
Stuttgart and Tübingen 1812–13
[recte: 1814]

In the early summer of 1814, Goethe studied the poetry of the Orient. He enthusiastically read the poems of the most important Persian poet, Mohammed Schemsed-din Háfiz (ca. 1326–ca. 1390) in the two-volume German translation by the Austrian diplomat and interpreter Joseph von Hammer (1774–1856). The word 'diwan' means 'collection'. In Háfiz, Goethe recognized a poet, a master of form and a kindred spirit. Goethe was inspired by Háfiz's songs on love, drinking and mysticism which lead him to create his own collection of poems entitled *West-East Divan*.

4 Heinz Mack
Ohne Titel, aus der Bildersuite zum *West-oestlichen Divan* von Johann Wolfgang von Goethe
Signiert, datiert: »mack 98«
Öl, Tusche, Pastell
86 x 61 cm

4 Heinz Mack
Untitled, from the suite of pictures of the *West-East Divan* by Johann Wolfgang von Goethe
Signed, dated: "mack 98"
Oil, Indian ink, pastel
86 x 61 cm

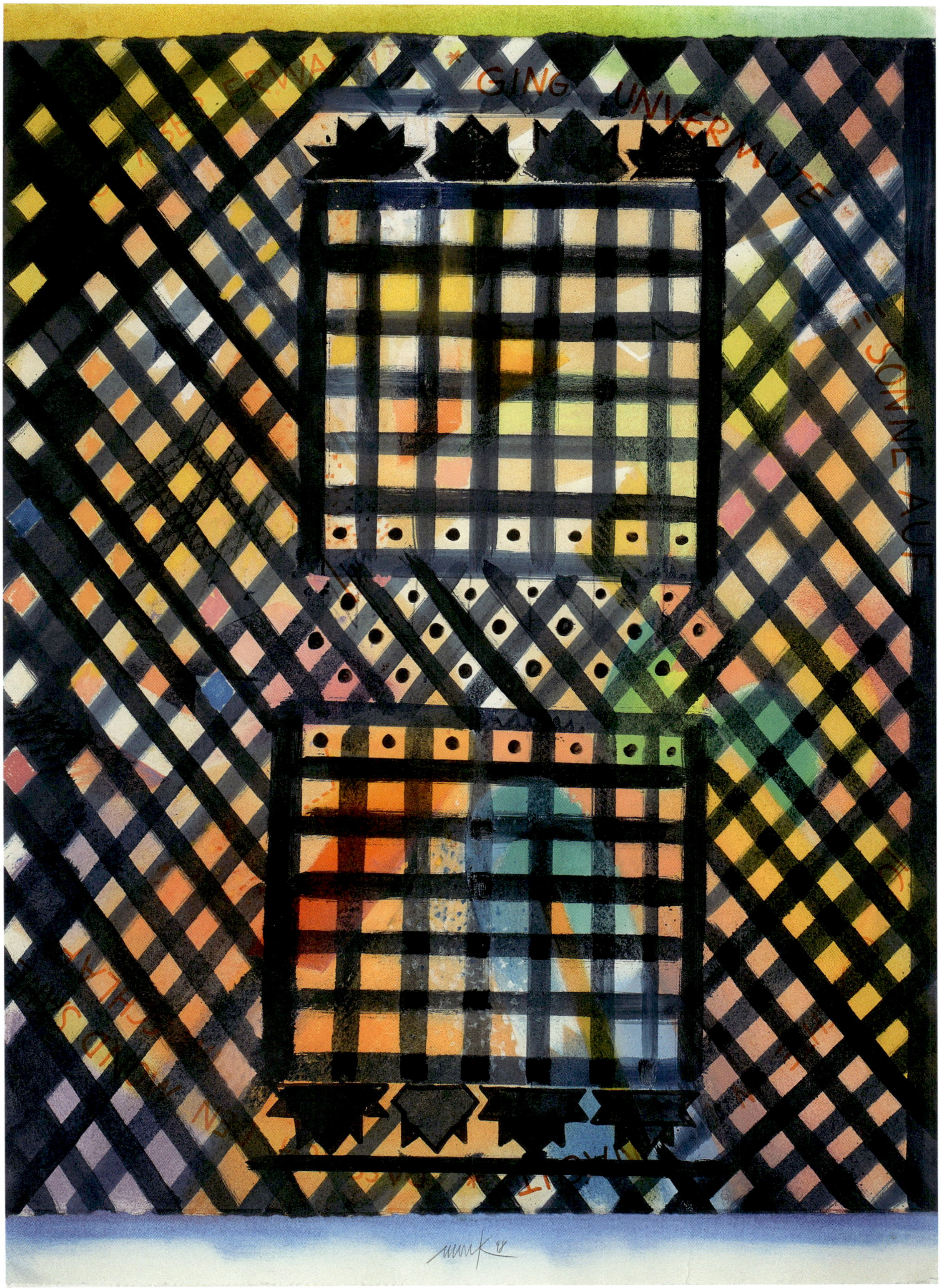
GING UNVERMUTE
SONNE AU

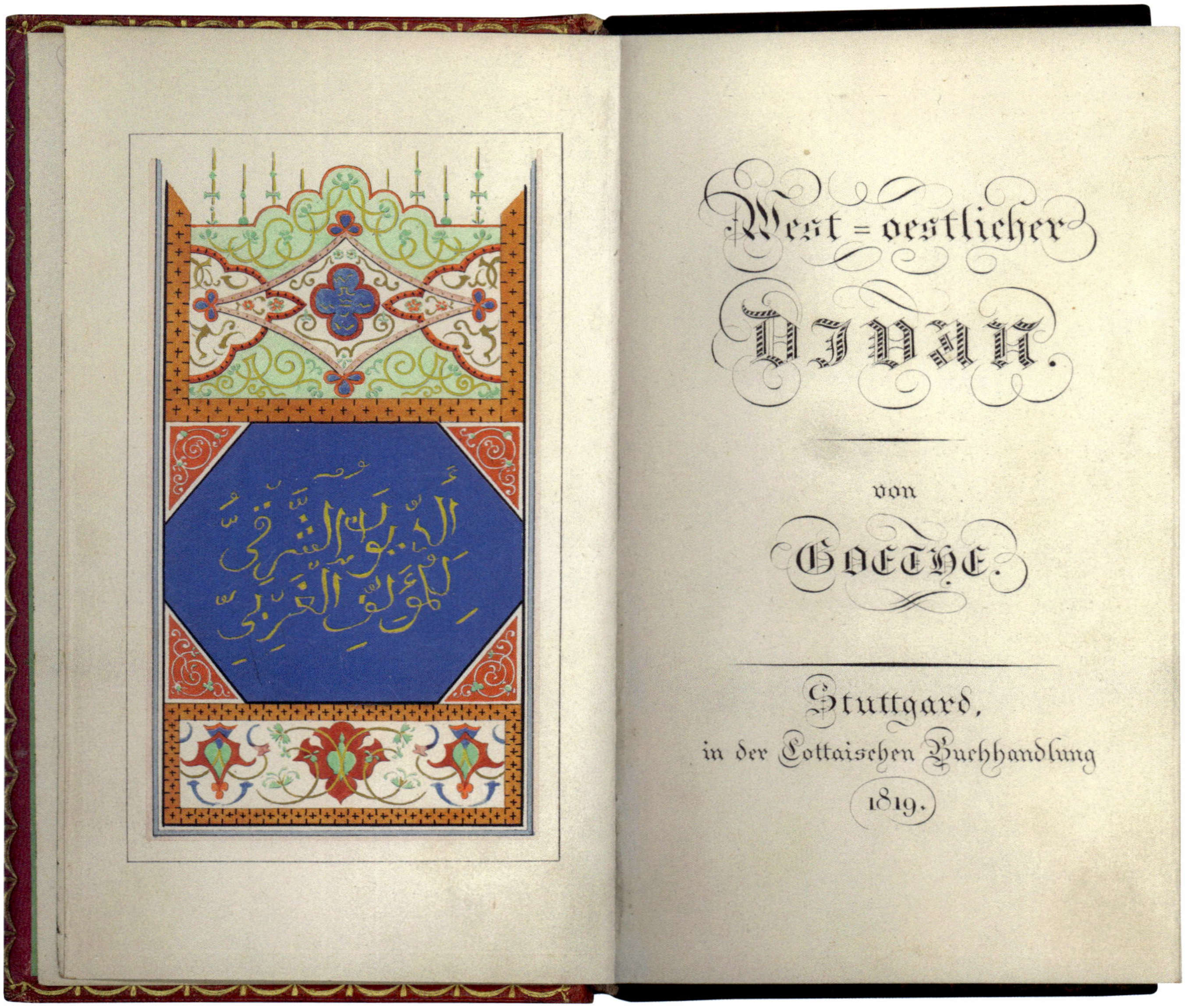

5 Johann Wolfgang von Goethe
West-oestlicher Divan:
West-oestlicher Divan. von Goethe. Stuttgard, in der Cottaischen Buchhandlung 1819.
Goethe-Museum Düsseldorf

Geschenk-Exemplar für den mit Goethe befreundeten Kölner Kaufmann und Kunstsammler Sulpiz Boisserée (1783–1854). Das Titelblatt in deutscher Frakturschrift ist mit einem Titelkupfer kombiniert, das der Zeichner Carl Lieber (1791–1861) im Auftrag Goethes nach Handschriften in der Weimarer Hofbibliothek gestaltet hat und das von dem Kupferstecher Ermer ausgeführt wurde. Die arabischen Schriftzeichen bilden die Rückübersetzung des Titels *West-oestlicher Divan* und meinen »Der östliche Diwan des westlichen Verfassers«. Das Titelkupfer wurde ausgemalt von Goethes Hausfreund und Kunstberater Heinrich Meyer (1760–1832).

5 Johann Wolfgang von Goethe
West-oestlicher Divan:
West-oestlicher Divan. von Goethe. Stuttgard, in der Cottaischen Buchhandlung 1819.
Goethe-Museum Düsseldorf

Gift copy for the Cologne merchant and art collector Sulpiz Boisserée (1783–1854), a friend of Goethe. The title page in German Fraktur script is combined with a title copper plate engraving designed by the illustrator Carl Lieber (1791–1861), commissioned by Goethe from manuscripts in the Weimar Court Library and executed by the engraver Ermer. The Arabic characters form the retranslation of the title *West-East Divan* and read "The Eastern Divan of the Western Author." The title copper plate was then coloured by Goethe's friend and art consultant Heinrich Meyer (1760–1832).

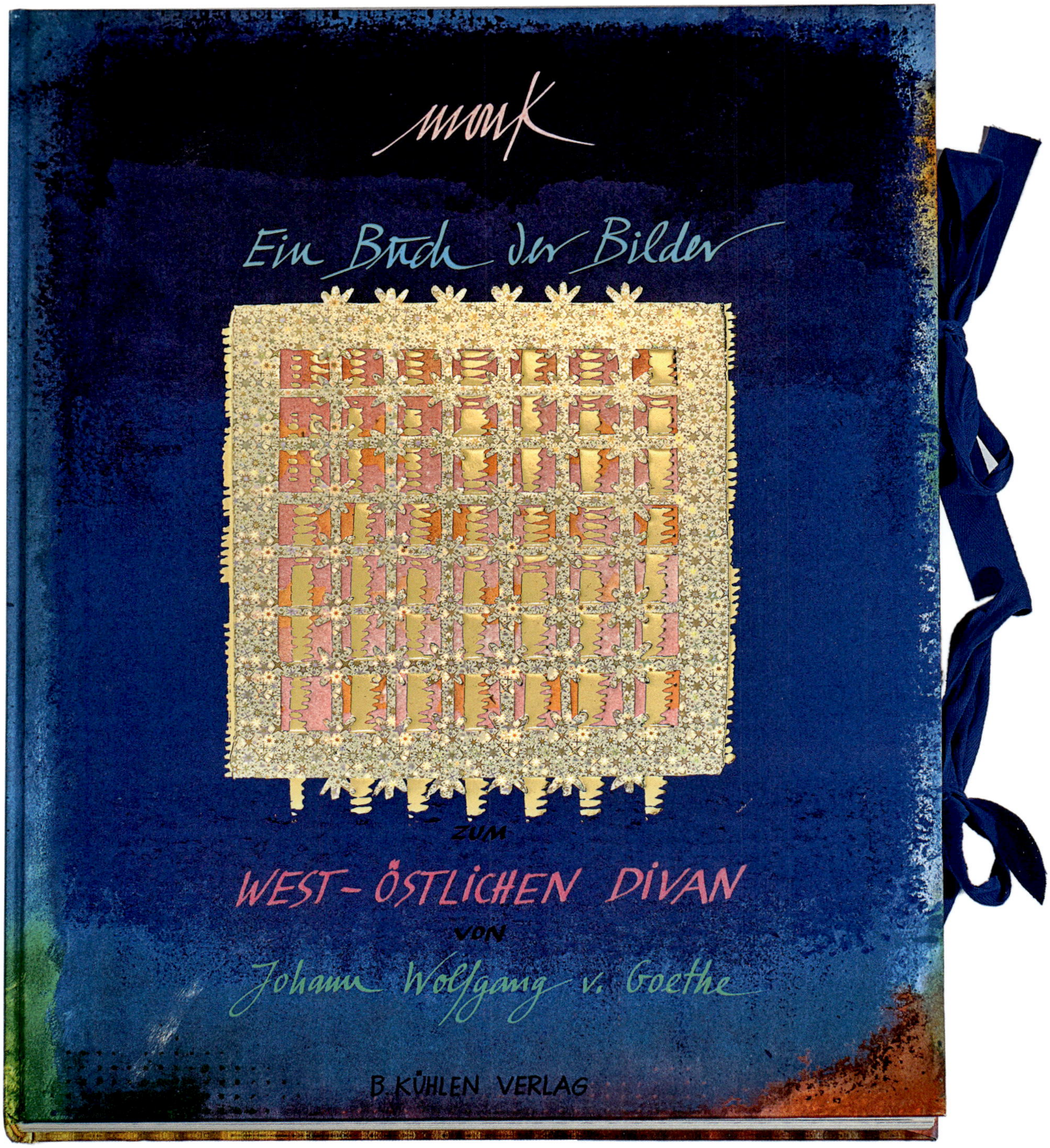

6 Heinz Mack
Ein Buch der Bilder zum West-östlichen Divan von Johann Wolfgang v. Goethe
Mönchengladbach 1999

6 Heinz Mack
Ein Buch der Bilder zum West-östlichen Divan von Johann Wolfgang v. Goethe
(A book of pictures for the West-East Divan by Johann Wolfgang v. Goethe)
Mönchengladbach 1999

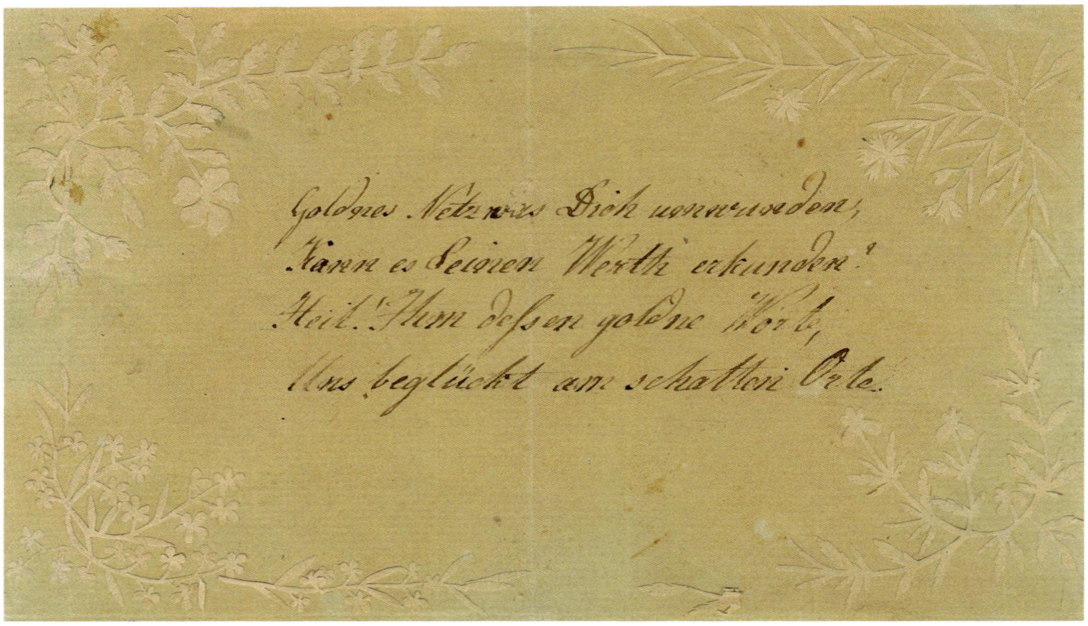

Goldnes Netz was Dich umwunden,
Kann es Deinen Werth erkunden?
Heil! Ihm dessen goldne Worte,
Uns beglückt am schattgen Orte.

7 Marianne von Willemer
Eigenhändige Reinschrift ihres Gedichtes:
»Goldnes Netz was Dich umwunden […]«
Ende April 1815
1 Blatt, 1 S. beschrieben
Ringsum mit weißen Scherenschnittblumen verziert
8,4 x 14,3 cm
Goethe-Museum Düsseldorf

Goethe lernte die 35 Jahre jüngere Schauspielerin Marianne Jung (1784–1860) im August 1814 bei dem Bankier Johann Jacob von Willemer kennen. Willemer hatte sie 1800 als 15-jährige Pflegetochter in sein Haus aufgenommen und heiratete sie im September 1814. Zwischen der hochbegabten jungen Frau und Goethe entwickelte sich eine leidenschaftliche (nicht sinnlich ausgelebte) Liebe. Marianne von Willemer inspirierte Goethe zu den Liebesgedichten des *West-oestlichen Divans* und ging als Vorbild der Suleika in die Sammlung ein. Umgekehrt wurde auch Sie von dem Dichter zu kongenialen Versen begeistert, die Goethe zum Teil anonym in den *Divan* aufgenommen hat.

Der Vierzeiler antwortet auf das von Goethe am 26. April an Johann Jacob von Willemer geschickte Gedicht *Reicher Blumen goldne Rancken,* das Goethe von dem Weimarer Zeichner Carl Lieber mit ebensolchen hatte verzieren lassen und worin es heißt: »Goldnes Netz das euch umwunden! / Wer will dessen Werth erkunden? / Wie dem heil'gen Stein der Alten / Muß sich Golde Gold entfalten.« (WA, Bd. I 4, S. 20.) Marianne von Willemer legte ihr mit Scherenschnittranken geschmücktes Billett ihrem und Willemers Brief an Goethe vom 1. Mai 1815 bei. Mit diesen gewechselten Gedichten begann der Hatem-Suleika-Dialog.

7 Marianne von Willemer
Clean copy in her own hand:
"Goldnes Netz was Dich umwunden …"
End of April 1815
1 sheet, 1 page written
Encircled by decorative white silhouette flowers
8.4 x 14.3 cm
Goethe-Museum Düsseldorf

Goethe was introduced to the actress Marianne Jung (1784–1860), who was thirty-five years his junior, in August 1814 by the banker Johann Jacob von Willemer. Willemer took her into his home as a fifteen-year-old foster daughter in 1800 and subsequently married her in September 1814. Shortly after they had met, a passionate (but not carnal) love developed between the highly gifted young woman and Goethe. Marianne von Willemer inspired Goethe to write the love poems of the *West-East Divan* and became a model for Suleika in the collection. In return, she too was inspired by the poet to write congenial verses, which Goethe partly included anonymously in the *Divan.*

The quatrain answers to the flower-decorated sheet with a poem that Goethe had sent to Johann Jacob von Willemer on April 26, *Reicher Blumen goldene Rancken:* "Goldnes Netz das euch umwunden! / Wer will dessen Werth erkunden? / Wie dem heil'gen Stein der Alten / Muß sich Golde Gold entfalten." (WA, Vol. I 4, p. 20.) Marianne von Willemer enclosed her answering verses with the letter that she and her husband sent to Goethe on May 1, 1815. The Hatem-Suleika dialogue began with these exchanged poems.

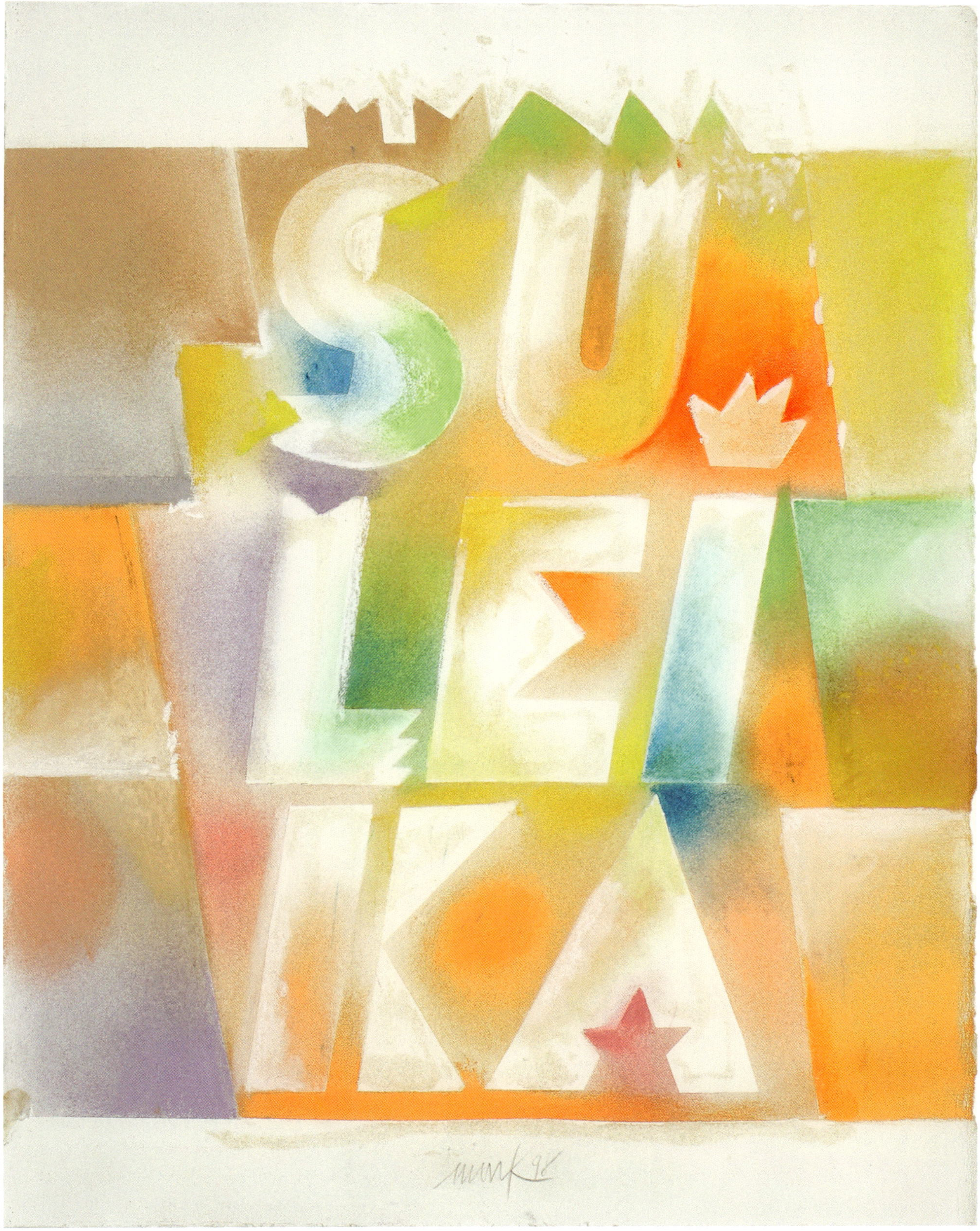

8 Heinz Mack
Ohne Titel, aus der Bildersuite zum *West-oestlichen Divan* von Johann Wolfgang von Goethe
Signiert, datiert: »mack 98«
Pastell und Öl
51 x 40 cm

8 Heinz Mack
Untitled, from the suite of pictures for the *West-East Divan* by Johann Wolfgang von Goethe
Signed, dated: "mack 98"
Pastel and oil
51 x 40 cm

9+10 Johann Wolfgang von Goethe
Zwei eigenhändige Chiffrenbriefe an
Marianne von Willemer

1
Wahrscheinlich 21. September 1815
Visitenkarte mit Goldschnitt, 1 S. beschrieben,
mit arabisch geschriebener Überschrift:
»Suleika«
8,5 x 5,8 cm
Goethe-Museum Düsseldorf

2
Datiert: »10. O[ktober]. 1815.«
1 Blatt, 1 S. beschrieben; auf der Rückseite
die Widmung: »Mariannen«
12,4 x 10,3 cm
Goethe-Museum Düsseldorf

Die Ziffern in diesen Briefen Goethes an Marianne von Willemer sind verschlüsselte Liebesbekundungen, die sich auf Verszeilen in Joseph von Hammers zweibändiger deutscher Übersetzung der Gedichtsammlung *Diwan* des persischen Dichters Hafis beziehen, die Goethe der Adressatin geschenkt hatte. Die Visitenkarte ist der erste Brief in der Reihe. Mit der arabischen Überschrift spielt Goethe auf den Namen der Liebenden Suleika in seinem *West-oestlichen Divan* an, die mit dem Geliebten Hatem in einen lyrischen Dialog tritt. (Dabei hat er wohl irrtümlich »Sulaiha« geschrieben statt »Suleika«.) Die linke Zahlenreihe bezieht sich auf die Seiten-, die rechte auf die Verszahlen im ersten Band von Hammers Übersetzung. Die erste Ziffernreihe lautet aufgelöst: »Leicht' ist die Lieb' im Anfang / Es folgen aber Schwierigkeiten.«
Goethes zweiter Chiffrenbrief entstand auf der Rückreise vom Rhein zwischen Meiningen und Gotha. Die römischen Zahlen bezeichnen den Band, die arabischen die Seiten und Verse der Übersetzung. (Vgl. Marianne von Willemers Auflösung der beiden Chiffrenbriefe im vorliegenden Katalog, S. 366–69.)

9+10 Johann Wolfgang von Goethe
Two cipher letters to Marianne von Willemer
in Goethe's own hand

1
Probably 21st September 1815
Calling card with gilt edge. 1 page written,
headed "Suleika" in Arabic script
8.5 x 5.8 cm
Goethe-Museum Düsseldorf

2
Dated: "10. O[ctober]. 1815."
1 sheet, 1 page written. On the reverse
the dedication: "Mariannen"
12.4 x 10.3 cm
Goethe-Museum Düsseldorf

The numbers in these letters of Goethe to Marianne von Willemer are encoded expressions of love. They refer to lines of verse in Joseph von Hammers two-volume German translation of the collection of poems *Diwan* by the Persian poet Háfiz that Goethe had gifted to Marianne. The calling card is the first letter in the series. In the Arabic title Goethe alludes to the name of Suleika in his *West-East Divan,* who enters into a lyrical dialogue with her lover Hatem. (Goethe probably mistakenly wrote "Sulaiha" instead of "Suleika.") The left series of numbers refers to the page numbers, the right to the verse numbers in the first volume of Hammer's translation.
Goethe's second cipher letter was written on the return journey from the Rhine between Meiningen and Gotha. The Roman numbers denote the volume, the Arabic the pages and verses of the translation. (See Marianne von Willemer's resolution of the two cipher letters in this catalogue, pp. 366–69.)

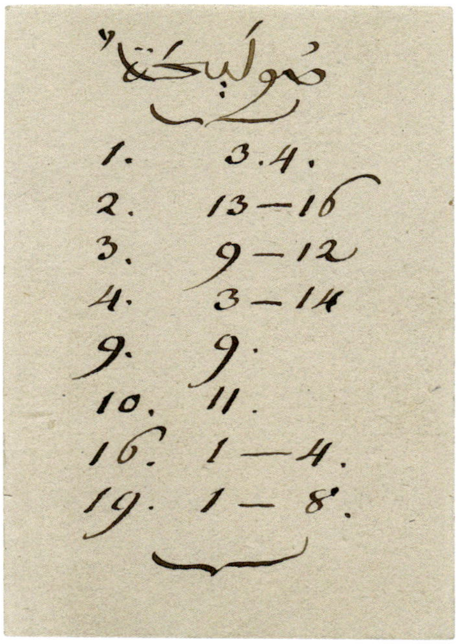
صُولَيكَة
1. 3.4.
2. 13–16
3. 9–12
4. 3–14
9. 9.
10. 11.
16. 1–4.
19. 1–8.

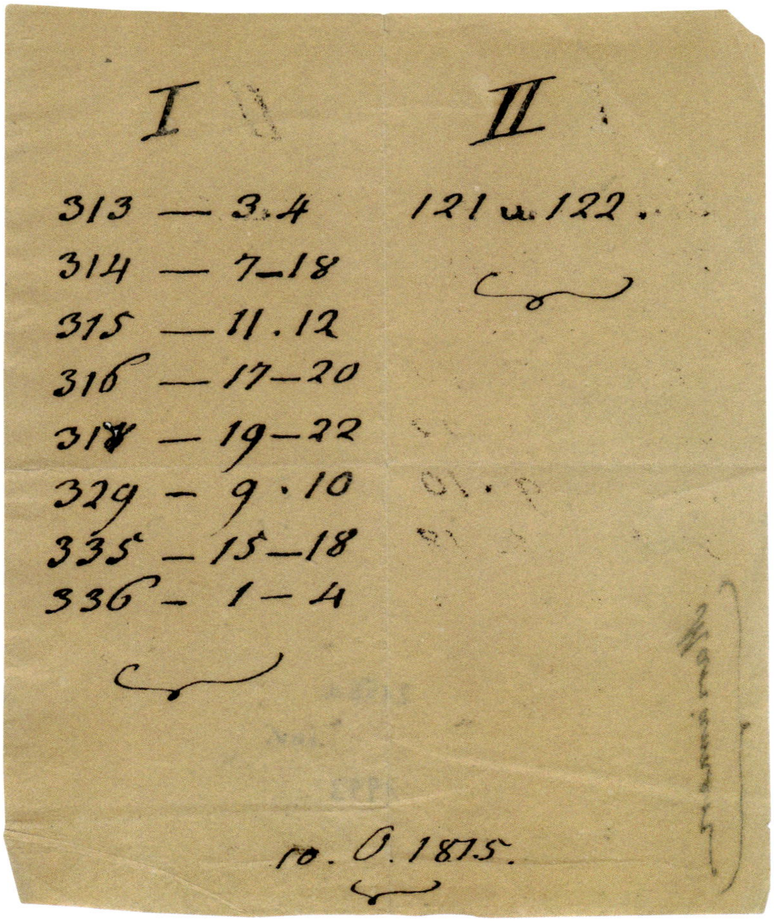
I
II
313 — 3.4
314 — 7–18
315 — 11.12
316 — 17–20
317 — 19–22
329 — 9.10
335 — 15–18
336 — 1–4
121 u. 122.
10. 6. 1815.

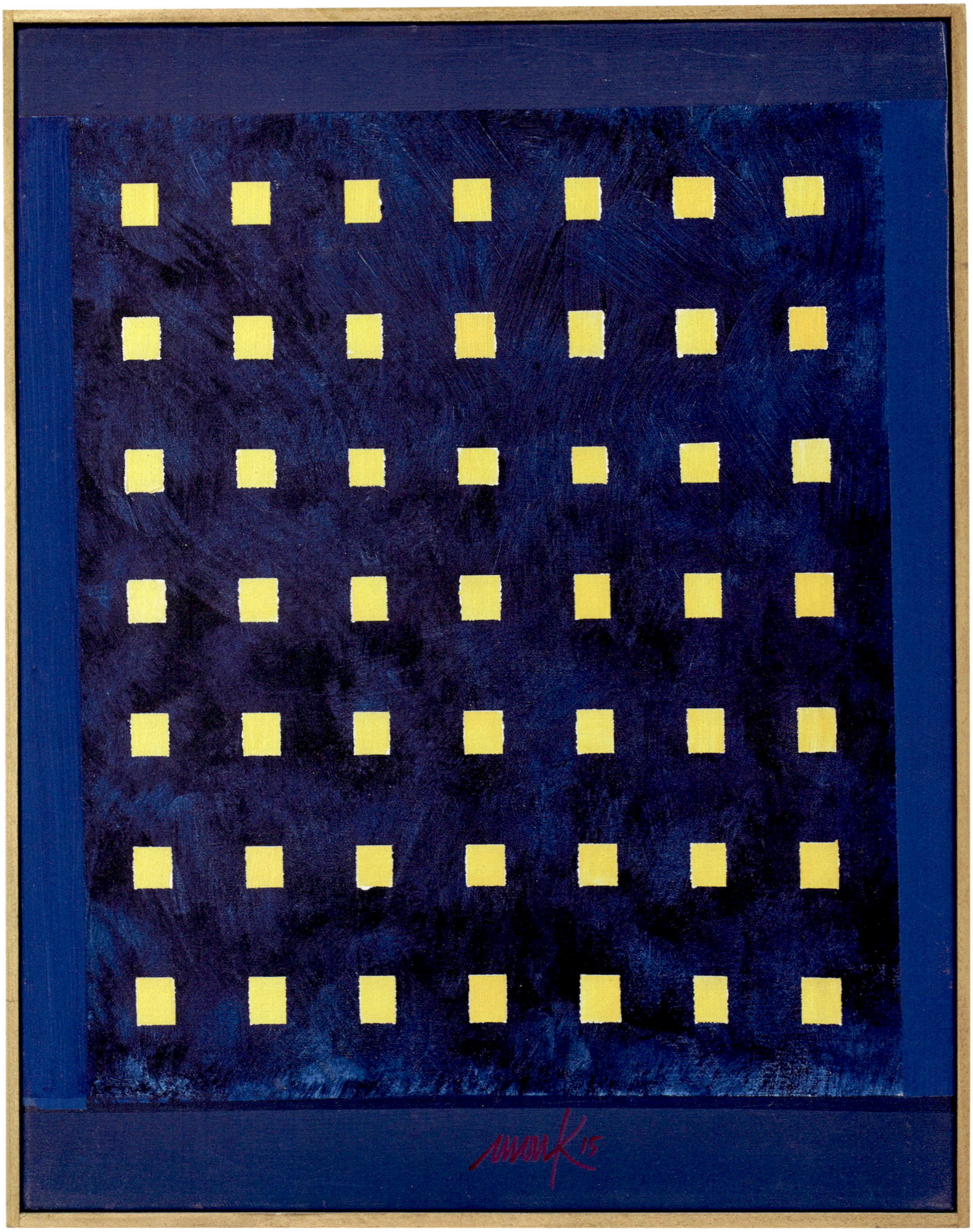

11 Heinz Mack
Ohne Titel *(Chromatische Konstellation)*
Datiert, signiert: »mack 15«
Acryl auf Leinwand
63 x 48 cm

11 Heinz Mack
Untitled *(Chromatic Constellation)*
Dated, signed: "mack 15"
Acrylic on canvas
63 x 48 cm

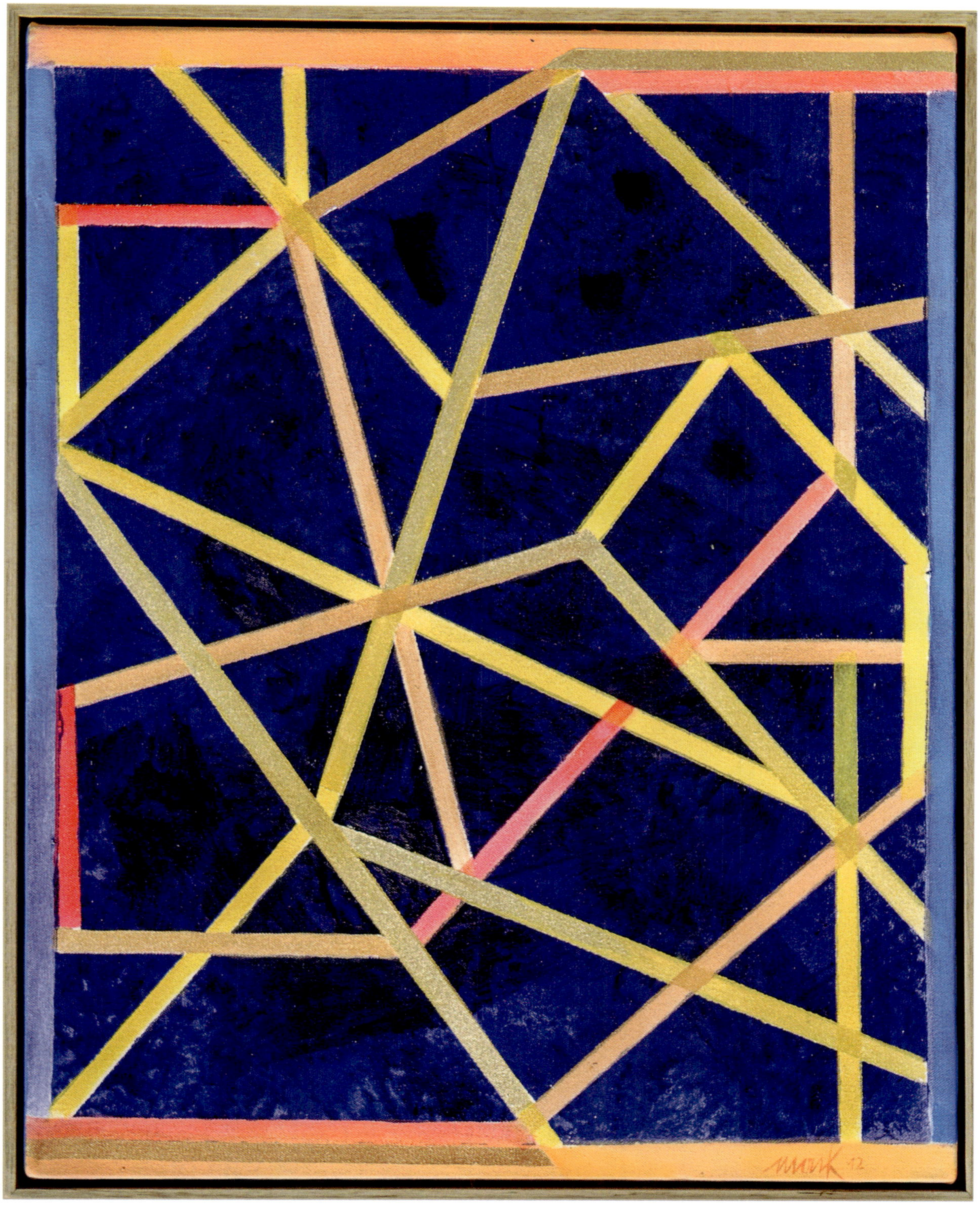

12 Heinz Mack
Map for Light-Beams
(Chromatische Constellation)
Signiert, datiert: »mack 12«
Acryl on Leinwand
100 x 79 cm

12 Heinz Mack
Map for Light-Beams
(Chromatic Constellation)
Signed, dated: "mack 12"
Acrylic on canvas
100 x 79 cm

13+14 Marianne von Willemer
Auflösung von zwei Chiffrenbriefen Goethes
(vgl. S. 362–363)
Vermutlich 1857
1 Blatt, 2 S. beschrieben
20,8 x 17,7 cm (aufgeklappt)
Goethe-Museum Düsseldorf

Marianne von Willemers Anteil am *West-oestlichen Divan* ist erst 1869 durch den Literarhistoriker Herman Grimm (1828–1901) aufgedeckt worden. Dem Sohn des Philologen und Märchensammlers Wilhelm Grimm hatte die Schreiberin ihre Auflösung von Goethes Chiffrenbriefen in einer späteren Abschrift übermittelt, ebenso wie die Niederschrift ihrer Gedichte *Ostwind* und *Westwind*. Die auf den zweiten Band bezogenen Chiffren wurden von Marianne von Willemer nicht aufgelöst. Die unter dem Text vermerkten Verweise auf Goethes *Divan* beziehen sich auf das Gedicht *Geheimschrift* (WA, Bd. I 6, S. 191 f.) und auf das Stichwort »Chiffer« in den *Noten und Abhandlungen zu besserem Verständniß des West-östlichen Divans,* wo Goethe »eine, zwar wohlbekannte, aber doch immer geheimnißvolle Weise, sich in Chiffern mitzutheilen«, erläutert, »wenn nämlich zwei Personen, die ein Buch verabreden und, indem sie Seiten- und Zeilenzahl zu einem Briefe verbinden, gewiß sind, daß der Empfänger mit geringem Bemühen den Sinn zusammen finden werde. [...] Liebende werden einig Hafisens Gedichte zum Werkzeug ihres Gefühlwechsels zu legen; sie bezeichnen Seite und Zeile die ihrem gegenwärtigen Zustand ausdrückt, und so entstehen zusammengeschriebene Lieder vom schönsten Ausdruck; herrliche zerstreute Stellen des unschätzbaren Dichters werden durch Leidenschaft und Gefühl verbunden, Neigung und Wahl verleihen dem Ganzen eine inneres Leben, und die Entfernten finden ein tröstliches Ergeben, indem sie ihre Trauer mit Perlen seiner Worte schmücken.« (WA, Bd. I 7, S. 130 f.)

[Chiffrenbrief 2]
Die Einsamkeit ist schön,
Sobald die Freundin meine Freundin ist
—
Aus meinem Kopfe gehet
Die Sehnsucht deines Aufenthaltes nicht
weil dort das irre Herz.
Des armen Fremdlings wie zu Hause ist
—
Was brauchet es noch mehr.
Vom Herzensbrande einen Comentar
Er wird ja leicht erkannt
Am Feuer das in meinen Worten ist
Und hätte auch Hafis
Zehn Zungen wie die Lilien er schwieg.
Den Rosenknospen gleich
Weil durch die Lieb sein Mund versiegelt ist.
—
Liebe ist ein Zustand
Dem die Leitung nöthig ist
—
Von allen Seiten flogen Pfeile
Von meinem Gebete ab.
Vieleicht das einer von denselben
Doch etwas erziehlen wird.
—
Mein Herz betrübe dich nicht
Geduldig trage alles weil doch
Zulezt aus diesem Abend Morgen
Und Licht aus diesem Schatten wird
—
Was mich traf von den Leiden
der Liebe, das hat mich getroffen
Vor dem Bösen des Augs schütze
die Geliebte O Herr!

Welch ein seltner Pfad.
Der Liebe Pfad.
Wo der Liebende selbst.
Verirrt ist.

Hör mich! bringe dein Herz.
Der Schönen dar,
Welche ohne Geschmeid
Die Schönste ist.
—
[Chiffrenbrief 1]
Leicht ist die Liebe im Anfang
aber es folgen Schwierigkeiten.
—
Wünschest du Ruhe Hafis
Folge dem köstlichen Rath.
Wilst du das Liebchen finden
Verlaß die Welt und laß sie gehen
—
Des Sinnes dich zu schauen kam
Mein Geist auf meine Lippen
Soll er entfliehen? Soll er zurück
Was ist dein Herrscherwille.
—
Was nützet die Enthaltsamkeit
Dem der dein Auge sah.
Viel besser ist's dein Nüchternheit
Dem Trunknen nicht verkaufen
—
Mein träges Glük das lange schlief
ist endlich aufgewacht.
Der Schimmer deines Angesichts
hat ihm ins Aug geblitzet.

bezügliche Stellen im Divan
Seite 173 und
– – – 393 bis 396

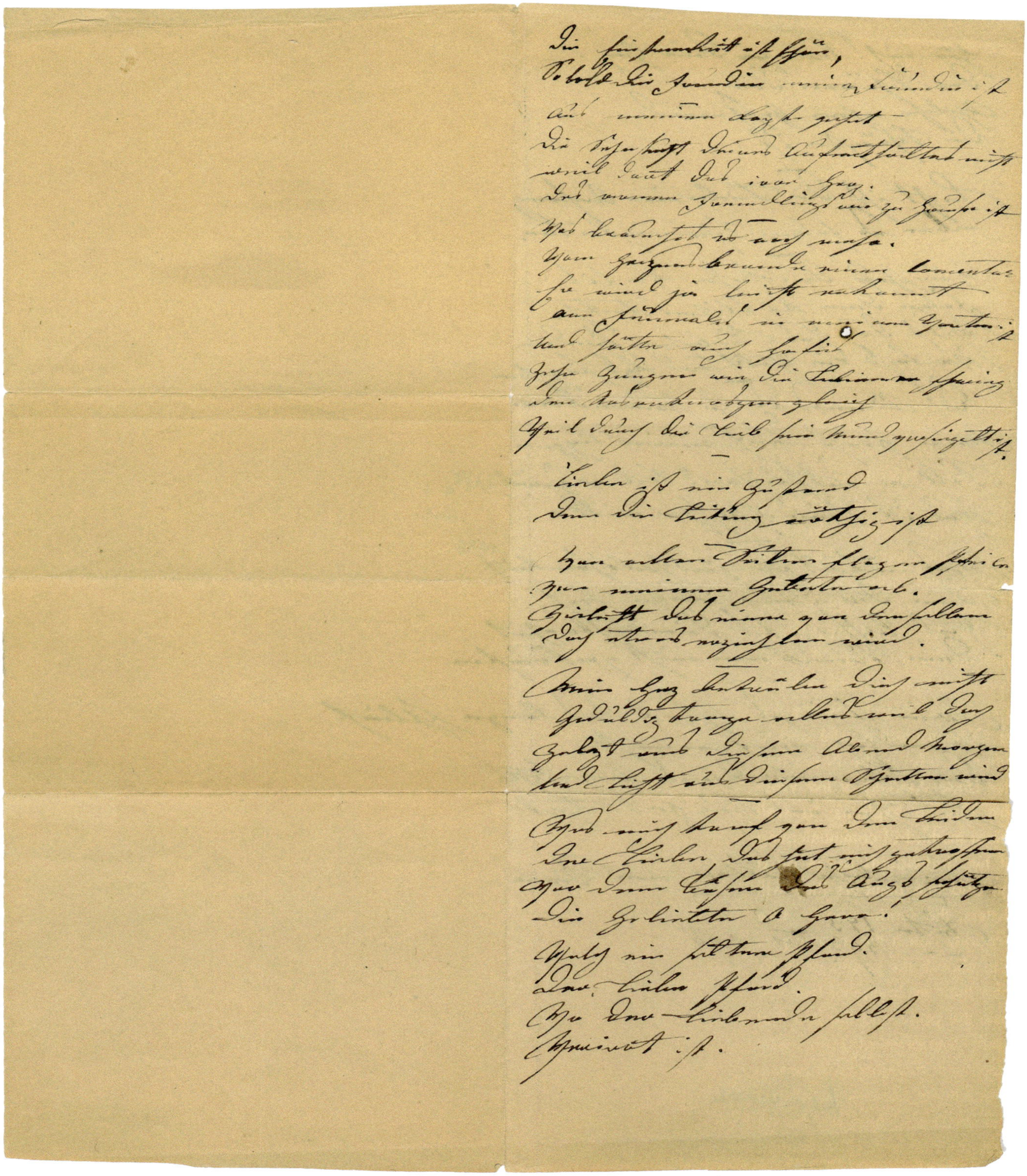

13+14 Marianne von Willemer
Decoding of two cipher letters of Goethe
(see pp. 362–63)
Probably 1857
1 sheet, 2 pages written
20.8 x 17.7 cm (unfolded)
Goethe-Museum Düsseldorf

Marianne von Willemer's contribution to the *West-East Divan* was first discovered in 1869 by the literary historian Herman Grimm. Marianne had sent later copies of decoded cipher letters of Goethe to the son of the philologist and fairytale collector, Wilhelm Grimm, along with a transcript of her poems *East Wind* and *West Wind*. Marianne von Willemer did not release the solution to the ciphers related to the second volume. The references to Goethe's *Divan* below the text refer to the poem *Geheimschrift* (Code) and to the keyword "Chiffer" (Code) in the *Notes and Essays for a Better Understanding of the West-East Divan* where Goethe explains "a well known, yet still secret method of communicating through codes: if two individuals agree on a book whose page and line numbers they will refer to in their letters, the sender can be sure the recipient will readily detect the meaning. … Two lovers agree to choose the poems of Háfiz as the instrument for their exchange of feelings; they each designate the page and the line that embody their present state of mind. In this way songs are composed, with thoughts most beautifully expressed. Magnificent passages scattered in the pages of the invaluable poet are bound together through passion and feeling. Inclination and choice lend the whole an inner life. And, though separated, the lovers find themselves comforted in their resignation as they adorn their grief with the pearls of his words." (Johann Wolfgang von Goethe, *West-East Divan,* trans. Martin Bidney, New York, 2010, pp. 117–18 and 231–33.)

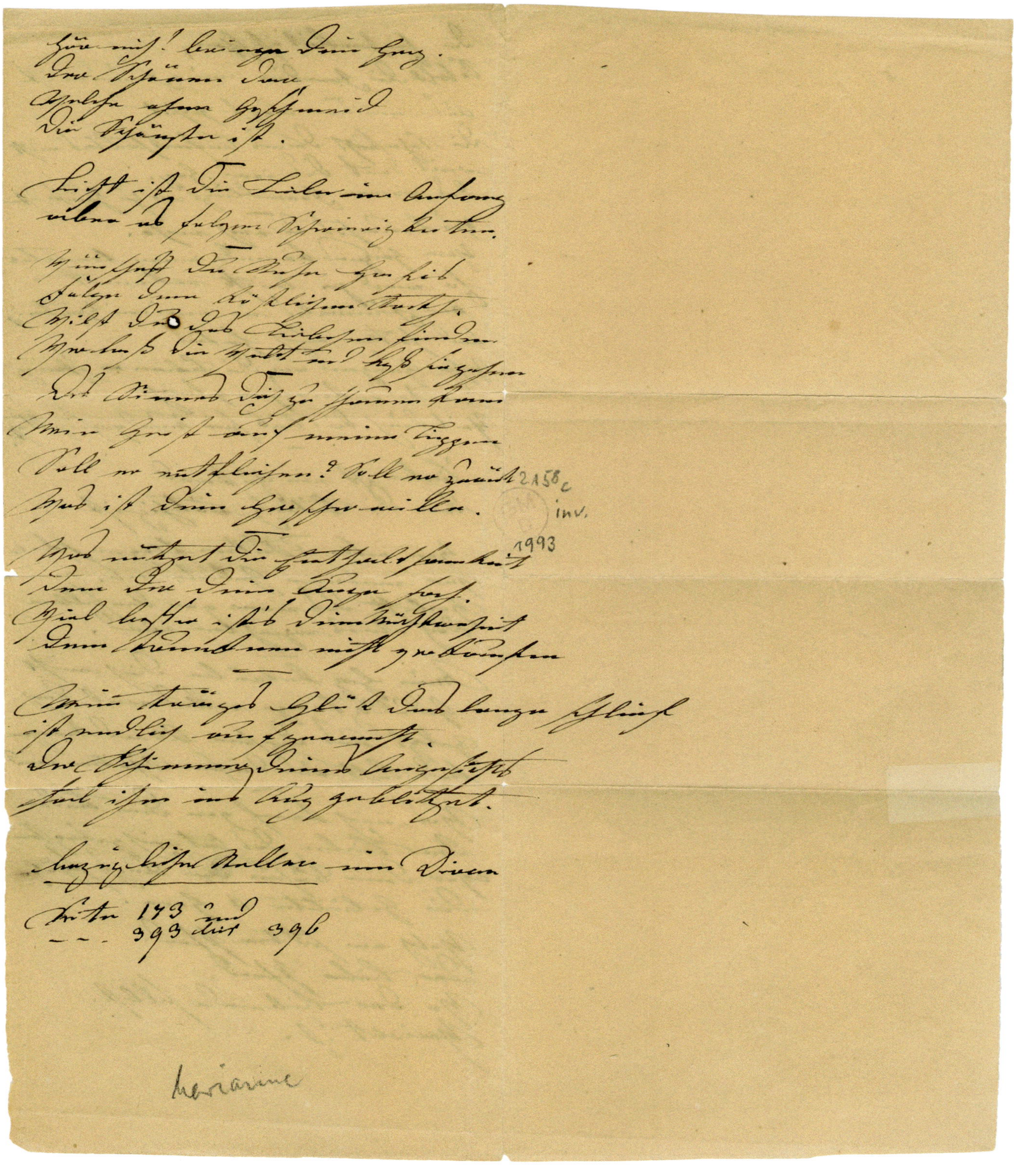
2158c
inv.
1993
Marianne

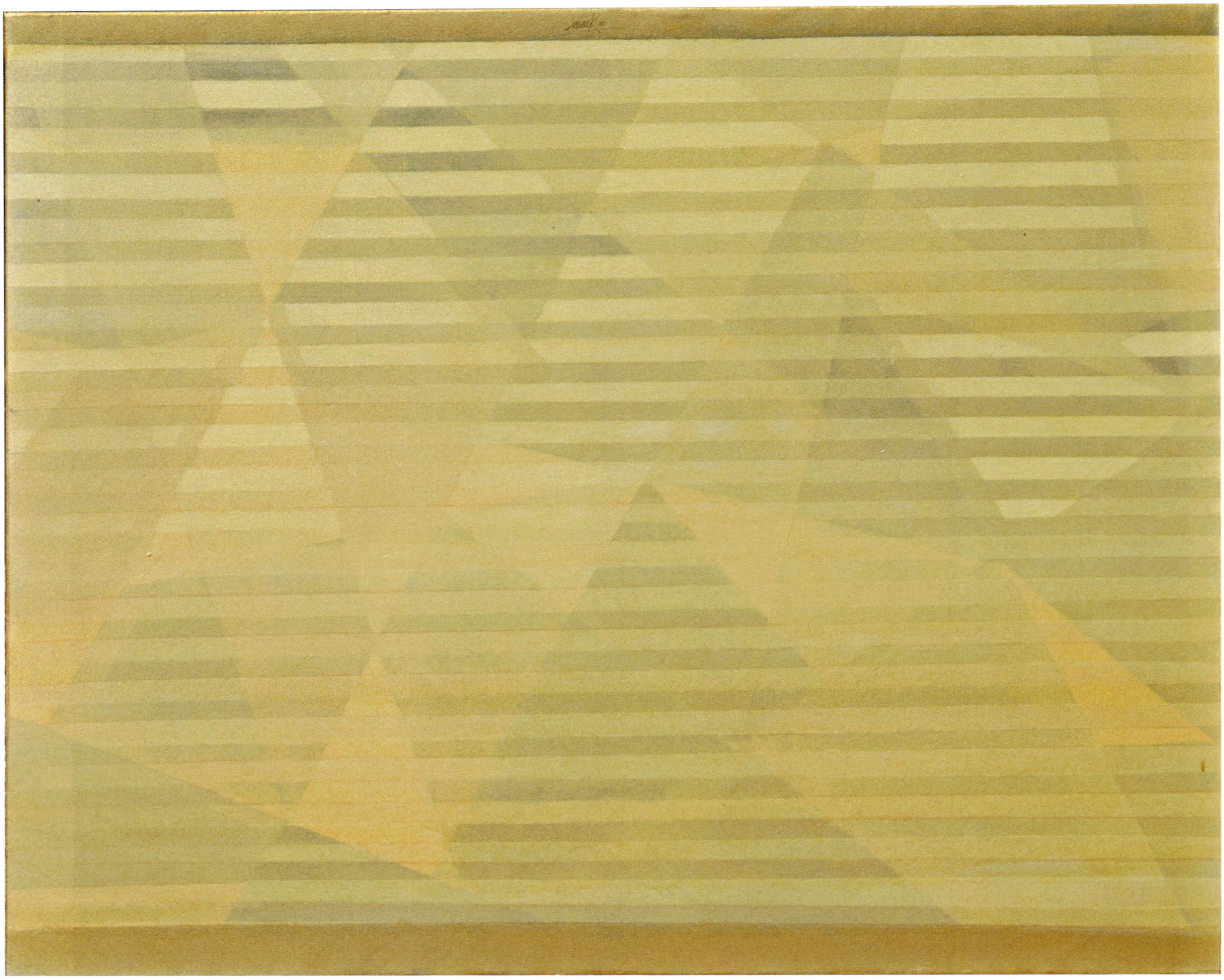

15 Heinz Mack
Ohne Titel *(Chromatische Konstellation)*
Signiert, datiert: »mack 11«
Acryl und Goldbronze auf Leinwand
130 x 160 cm

15 Heinz Mack
Untitled *(Chromatic Constellation)*
Signed, dated: "mack 11"
Acrylic and gold bronze on canvas
130 x 160 cm

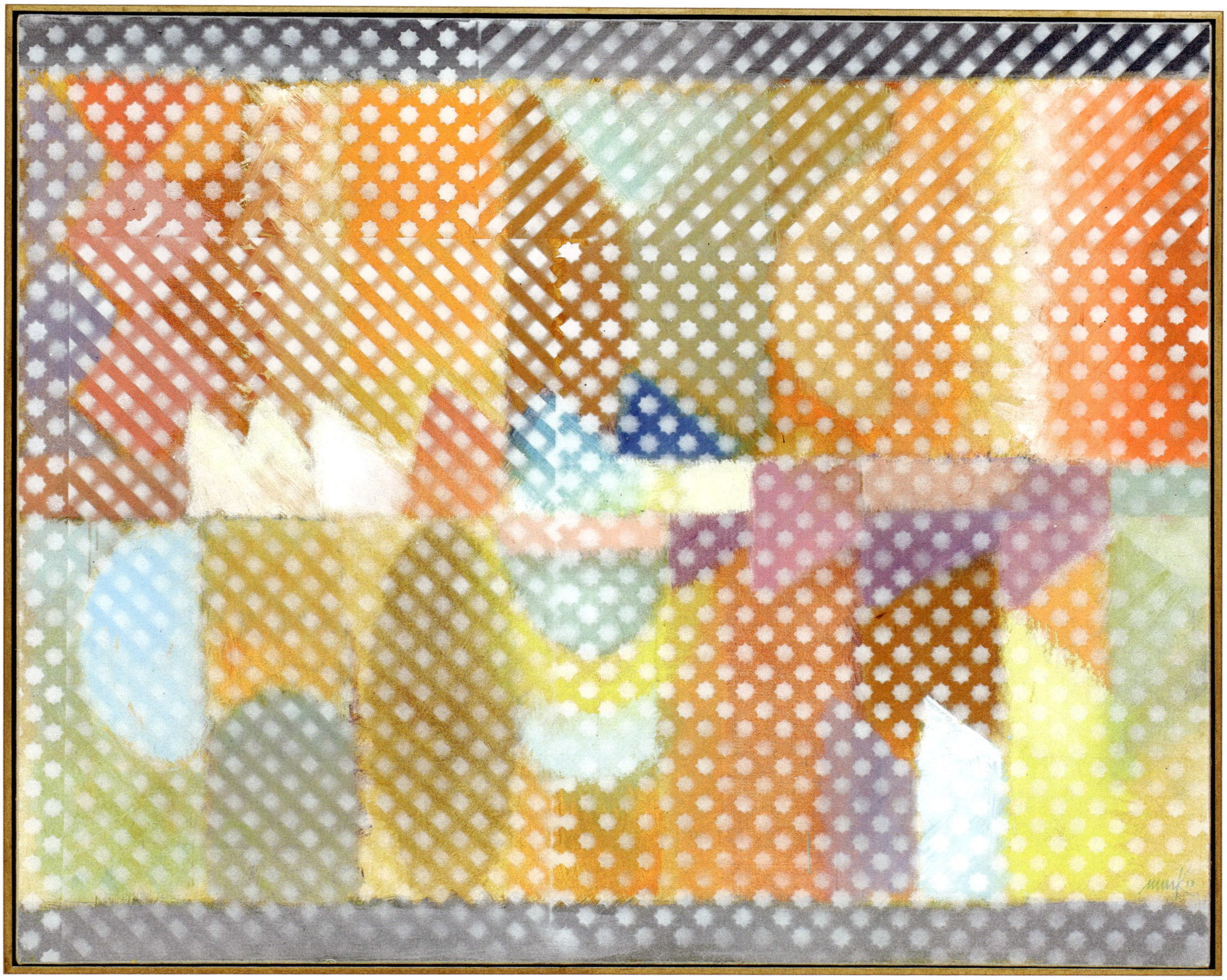

16 Heinz Mack
Ohne Titel *(Chromatische Konstellation)*
Signiert, datiert: »mack 13«
Acryl auf Leinwand
130 x 160 cm

16 Heinz Mack
Untitled *(Chromatic Constellation)*
Signed, dated: "mack 13"
Acrylic on canvas
130 x 160 cm

17 Johann Wolfgang von Goethe
Eigenhändige arabische Schreibübung
1815 oder 1817
1 Blatt, 1 S. beschrieben
20,2 x 23,4 cm
Klassik Stiftung Weimar, Goethe- und Schiller-Archiv
Signatur: GSA 25 / W 1151

Fasziniert von der orientalischen Kalligraphie, übte Goethe 1815 arabische Schriftzeichen: »[…] wenigstens soviel will ich mich in den Schreibezügen üben, daß ich die Amulette, Talismane, Abraxas und Siegel in der Urschrift nachbilden kann. In keiner Sprache ist vielleicht Geist, Wort und Schrift so uranfänglich zusammengekörpert.« (Brief an Christian Heinrich Schlosser vom 23. Januar 1815, WA, Bd. IV 25, S. 165.) Die vorliegende Schreibübung zeigt die sogenannte »Basmala«-Formel. Damit ist die Einleitungsformel der Suren des Korans gemeint: »Bismi llāḥi r-raḥmāni r-raḥīmi.« (Im Namen des gnädigen, des barmherzigen Gottes.) Vermutlich hatte Goethe Anschauungsmaterial in einem Blatt aus einem arabischen Korankodex, das Weimarer Soldaten 1813 aus dem Krieg in Spanien mitgebracht hatten.

17 Johann Wolfgang von Goethe
Arabic writings in his own hand
1815 or 1817
1 sheet, 1 page written
20.2 x 23.4 cm
Klassik Stiftung Weimar, Goethe- und Schiller-Archiv
Shelf mark: GSA 25 / W 1151

Fascinated by oriental calligraphy, Goethe practiced Arabic characters in 1815: "… I want to practice at least the writing strokes enough that I can copy the amulets, talismans, abraxas and seals in the original. Perhaps in no language are spirit, word and writing so primordially embodied." (Letter to Christian Heinrich Schlosser of January 23, 1815, WA, vol. IV 25, p. 165.) This writing exercise shows the so-called "Basmala" formula. This is the opening formula of the Suras of the Qur'an: "Bismi llāḥi r-raḥmāni r-raḥīmi." (In the name of God, the Merciful, the Compassionate.) Presumably Goethe had visual material on a sheet from an Arabic Qur'an codex, which Weimar soldiers had brought back from the war in Spain in 1813.

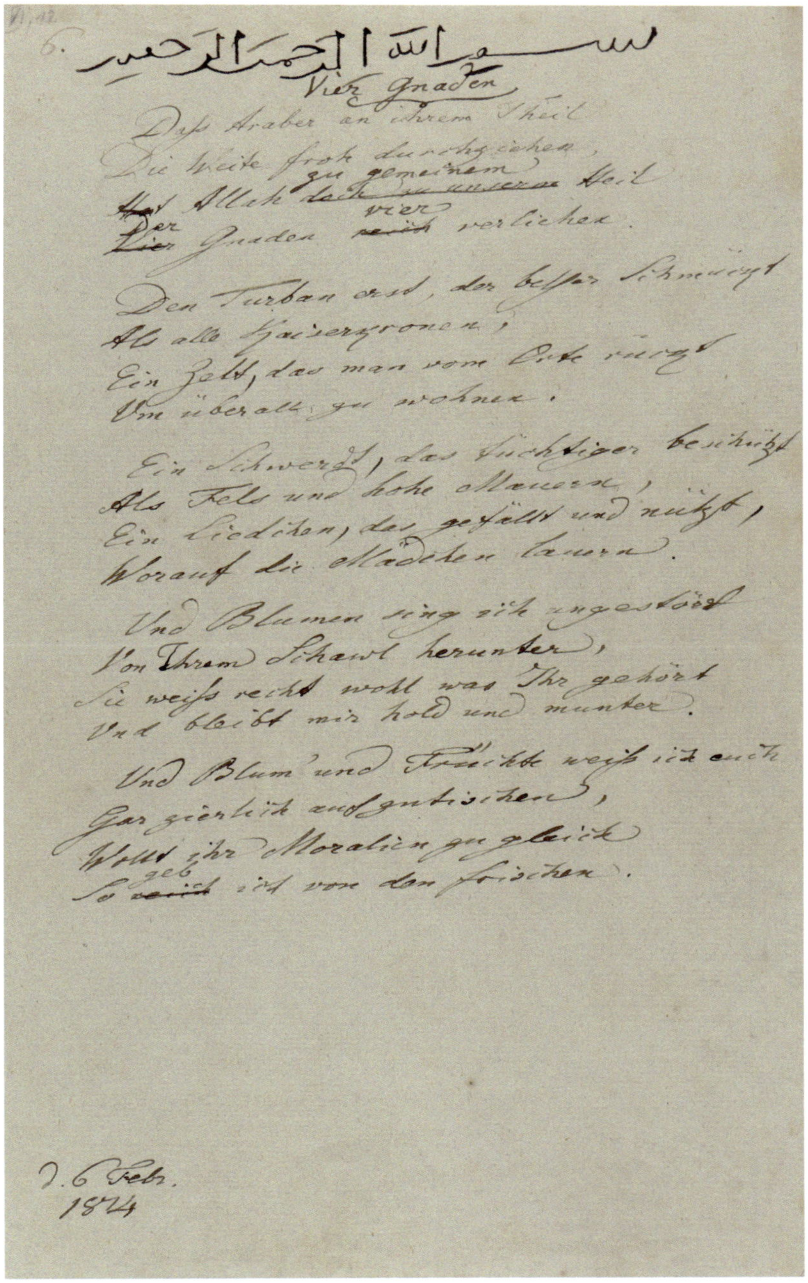

6.

بسم الله الرحمن الرحيم

Vier Gnaden

Daß Araber an ihrem Theil
Die Weite froh durchziehen,
Hat Allah ~~sich zu unserm~~ zu gemeinem Heil
~~Vier~~ Der Gnaden ~~sich~~ vier verliehen.

Den Turban erst, der besser schmückt
Als alle Kaiserkronen;
Ein Zelt, das man vom Orte rückt
Um überall zu wohnen.

Ein Schwerdt, das tüchtiger beschützt
Als Fels und hohe Mauern,
Ein Liedchen, das gefällt und nützt,
Worauf die Mädchen lauern.

Und Blumen sing ich ungestört
Von Ihrem Schawl herunter,
Sie weiß recht wohl was Ihr gehört
Und bleibt mir hold und munter.

Und Blum und Früchte weiß ich euch
Gar zierlich aufzutischen,
Wollt ihr Moralien zugleich
So ~~reich~~ geb ich von den frischen.

d. 6 Febr.
1814

18 Johann Wolfgang von Goethe
Eigenhändige Reinschrift seines Gedichtes:
Vier Gnaden
(mit arabischer Schreibübung)
Datiert: »d. 6 Febr. 1814 [recte: 1815]«
1 Blatt, 1 S. beschrieben
33,7 x 20,6 cm
Klassik Stiftung Weimar, Goethe- und Schiller-Archiv
Signatur: GSA 25 / W 798

Eines der einleitenden Programmgedichte im ersten Buch des *West-oestlichen Divans*. Über die »vier Gnaden der Araber« – Turban, Zelt, Schwert und Dichtung – hat sich Goethe aus der Reisebeschreibung *Voyages du chevalier Chardin, en Perse, et autres lieux de l'Orient* von Jean Chardin (Amsterdam 1735) unterrichtet. Über dem Gedichttitel steht in arabischer Schrift die »Basmala«, die Einleitungsformel zu den Suren des Korans.

18 Johann Wolfgang von Goethe
Clean copy in his own hand:
Vier Gnaden (Four Gifts of Grace)
(with Arabic writing)
Dated: "d. 6 Febr. 1814 [recte: 1815]"
1 sheet, 1 page written
33.7 x 20.6 cm
Klassik Stiftung Weimar, Goethe- und Schiller-Archiv
Shelf mark: GSA 25 / W 798

One of the introductory poems in the first book of the *West-East Divan*. Goethe taught himself about "the Arabs' four gifts of grace" – turban, tent, sword and poetry – from the travelogue *Voyages du chevalier Chardin, en Perse, et autres lieux de l'Orient* by Jean Chardin (Amsterdam 1735). Above the title of the poem is the "Basmala" in Arabic script, the introduction to the Suras of the Qur'an.

19 Johann Wolfgang von Goethe
Eigenhändig beschriebener und getuschter Umschlag
Vermutlich März 1819
1 S. beschrieben, mit zusätzlich aufgeklebtem Papierstreifen
23,2 x 36,5 cm
Klassik Stiftung Weimar, Goethe- und Schiller-Archiv
Signatur: GSA 25 / W 788

Goethe hat wahrscheinlich im März 1819 diesen Umschlag aus Papier angelegt, als er das Kapitel »Künftiger Divan« für die *Noten und Abhandlungen zu besserem Verständniß des West-östlichen Divans* entwarf. Das im Nachlass enthaltene Kuvert ist heute leer; es enthielt vermutlich weitere, nach der Drucklegung der Erstausgabe des *Divans* entstandene Gedichte. »Zum künftigen Divan.« schrieb er unter die Ornamentzeichnung mit den arabischen Schriftzeichen »Ali walī Allāh« (Ali ist der Freund Gottes). Gemeint ist der Schwiegersohn Mohammeds. Die Schreibweise dieser schiitischen Zusatzformel zum islamischen Glaubensbekenntnis ist allerdings nicht ganz korrekt. Oben auf dem Umschlag ist ein Zettel von der Hand des Goethe beratenden Jenaer Orientalisten Johann Gottfried Ludwig Kosegarten (1792–1860) aufgeklebt, der den arabischen Titel des *West-oestlichen* Divans in persischer Transkription und zugleich in lateinischer Übersetzung enthält: »Der östliche Divan eines westlichen Autors.«

19 Johann Wolfgang von Goethe
Written and Indian-inked envelope in his own hand
Probably March 1819
1 page written with additional glued on paper strip
23.2 x 36.5 cm
Klassik Stiftung Weimar, Goethe- und Schiller-Archiv
Shelf mark: GSA 25 / 788

Goethe probably created this paper envelope in March 1819 when he designed the chapter "A Future Divan" for *Notes and Essays for a Better Understanding of the West-East Divan*. The envelope from Goethe's estate is empty today; but it probably contained further poems written after the first edition of the *Divan* went to press. "To the future Divan" he wrote under the ornamental drawing with the Arabic characters "Ali walī Allāh" (Ali is the friend of God). It means Muhammad's son-in-law. However, the spelling of this additional Shiite formulation to the Islamic creed is not entirely correct. On top of the cover is a piece of paper by Johann Gottfried Ludwig Kosegarten (1792–1860), an Orientalist from Jena who advised Goethe. The paper contains the Arabic title of the *West-East Divan* in Persian transcription and in Latin. The translation for both is: "The Eastern Divan of a Western Author."

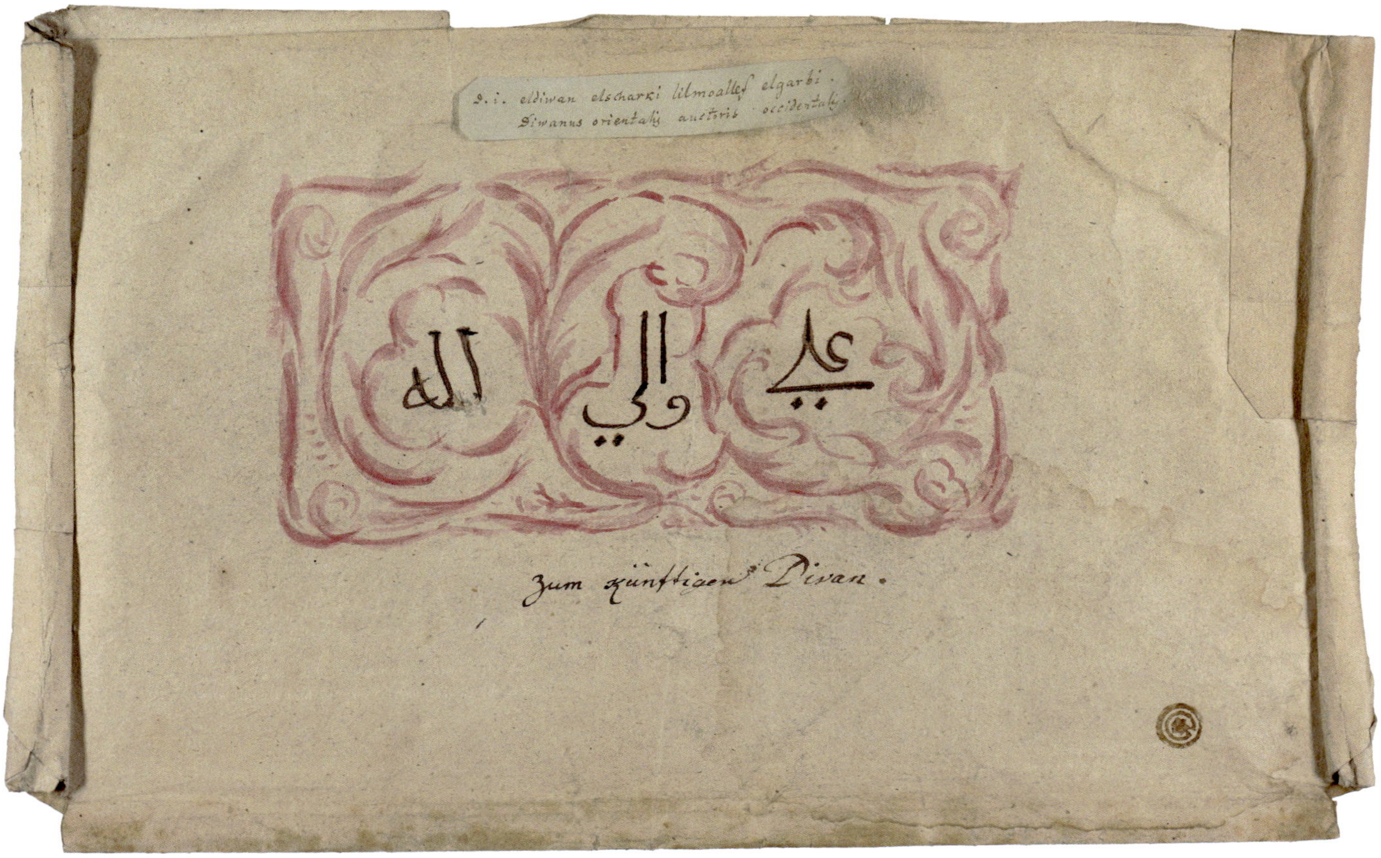
d. i. eldiwan elscharki lilmoallef elgarbi.
Diwanus orientalis auctoris occidentalis.
علي ولي الله
Zum künftigen Divan.

20 Johann Wolfgang von Goethe
Eigenhändige kalligrafische Reinschrift des ersten Vierzeilers der *Talismane*
Vermutlich zwischen Mitte Dezember 1814 und Anfang Januar 1815
1 Doppelblatt, 1 S. montiert mit 2 Kalligrafien desselben Vierzeilers
34,4 x 21,3 cm (zugeklappt)
Klassik Stiftung Weimar, Goethe- und Schiller-Archiv
Signatur: GSA 25 / W 797

Das Schmuckblatt enthält zwei Reinschriften des ersten von insgesamt fünf unter der Überschrift *Talismane* zusammengefassten Spruchgedichten aus dem ersten Buch des *West-oestlichen Divans*. Talisman meint ein ›Segenspfand‹, einen Spruch, der Allahs Wort rein verkörpert. Die Verse sind inspiriert durch Joseph von Hammers Übersetzung des 142. Verses der zweiten Sure des Korans, die als Motto auf dem Titel von allen sechs Bänden der Zeitschrift *Fundgruben des Orients* (1809–1818) steht: »Sag: Gottes ist der Orient, und Gottes ist der Occident; / Er leitet, wen er will, den wahren Pfad«. Der Zeichner Goethe hat die Wörter mit wolkenartigen Umrisslinien im Stil von Koran-Kalligrafien und persischen Gedichthandschriften hervorgehoben.

20 Johann Wolfgang von Goethe
Calligraphic clean copy in his own hand of the first quatrain of the *Talismans*
Probably from between mid-December 1814 and early January 1815
1 double page, 1 page mounted with 2 calligraphies of the same quatrain
34.4 x 21.3 cm (closed)
Klassik Stiftung Weimar, Goethe- und Schiller-Archiv
Shelf mark: GSA 25 / W 797

This decorative sheet of paper contains two clean copies of the first of a total of five poems from the first book of the *West-East Divan* summarised under the heading *Talismans*. Talisman means to 'pledge a blessing,' a saying that embodies the pure word of Allah. The verses are inspired by Joseph von Hammer's translation of the 142nd verse of the second Sura of the Qur'an, which is the motto of all six volumes of his publication, *Fundgruben des Orients* (Treasure Troves of the Orient, 1809–18): "Say: God is the Orient, and God is the Occident; / He guides whom he will, along the true path." Goethe the illustrator accentuated the words with cloud-like outlines in the style of Qur'an calligraphies and poetic Persian manuscripts.

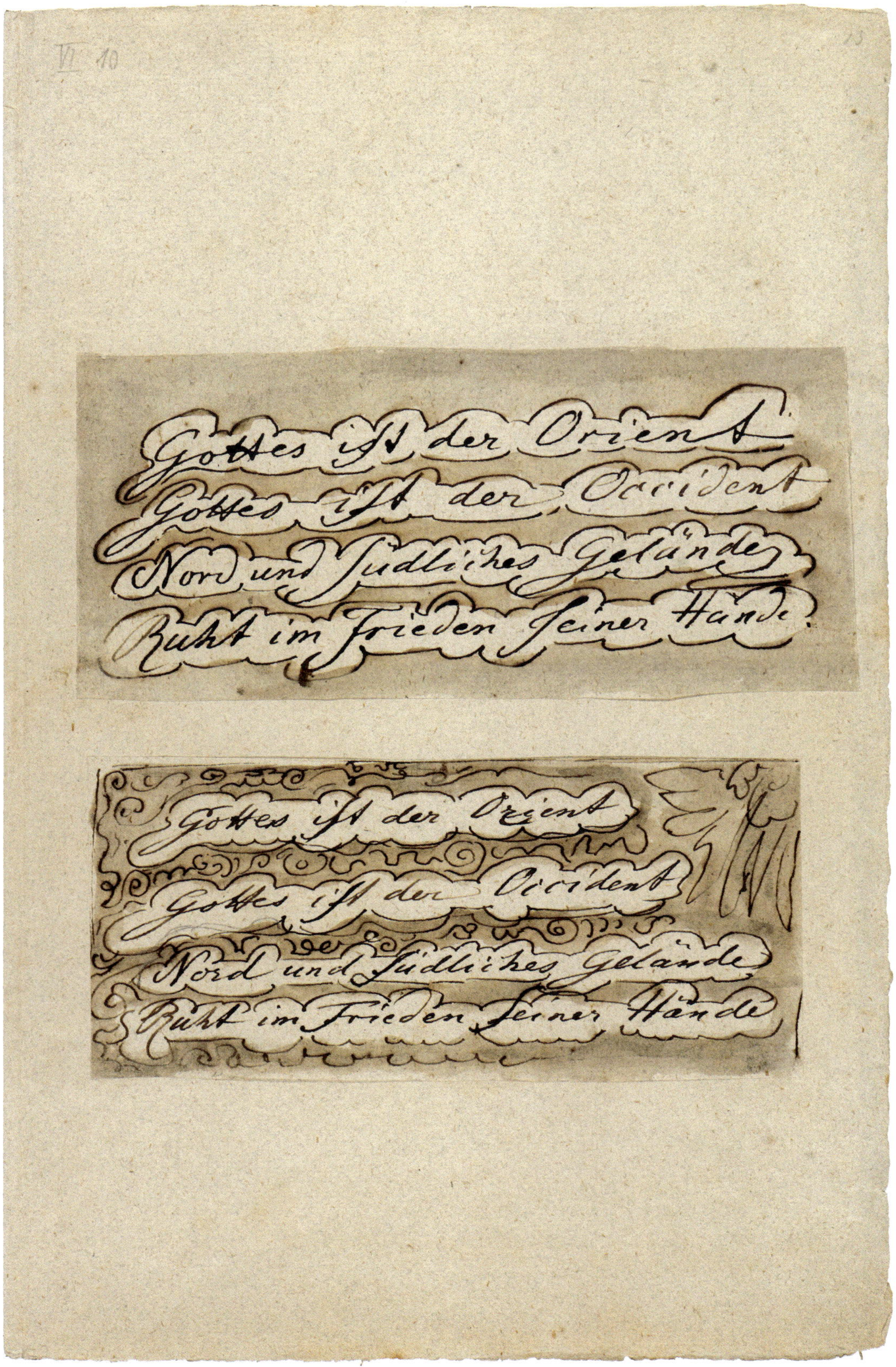
Gottes ist der Orient
Gottes ist der Occident
Nord und Südliches Gelände
Ruht im Frieden seiner Hände.

Gottes ist der Orient
Gottes ist der Occident
Nord und Südliches Gelände
Ruht im Frieden seiner Hände

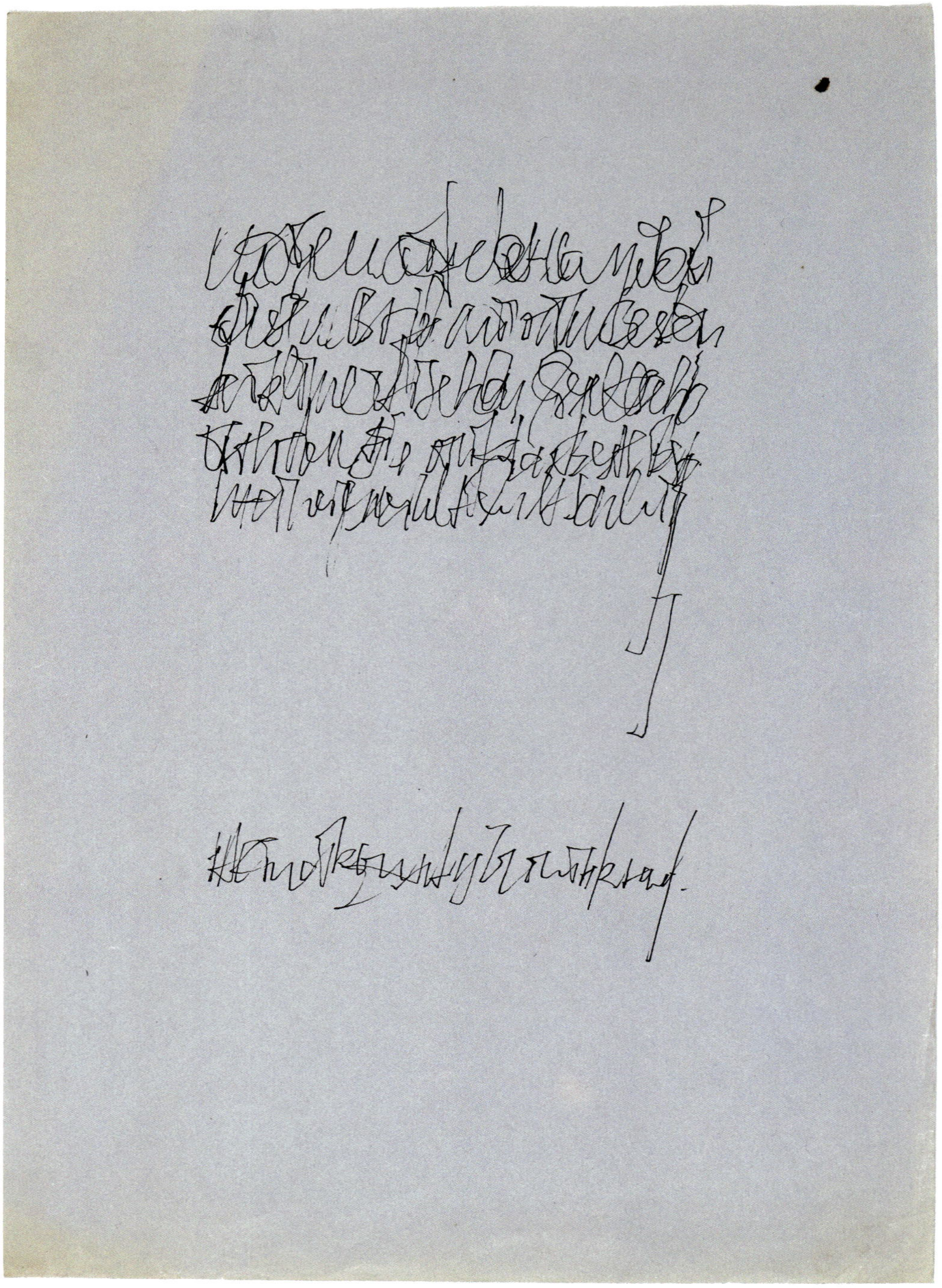

21 Heinz Mack
Ohne Titel (Fantasieschrift)
Datiert: »28.III.1950«
Tusche mit Rohrfeder auf Papier
29,5 x 21 cm

21 Heinz Mack
Untitled (fantasy writing)
Dated: "28.III.1950"
Indian ink applied to paper with reed pen
29.5 x 21 cm

22 Johann Wolfgang von Goethe
Eigenhändige Reinschrift seines Gedichtes:
»Schreibt er in Nessky […]«
Vermutlich Ende Januar 1816
1 Blatt, 1 S. beschrieben
34,6 x 21 cm
Klassik Stiftung Weimar, Goethe- und
Schiller-Archiv
Signatur: GSA 25 / W 943

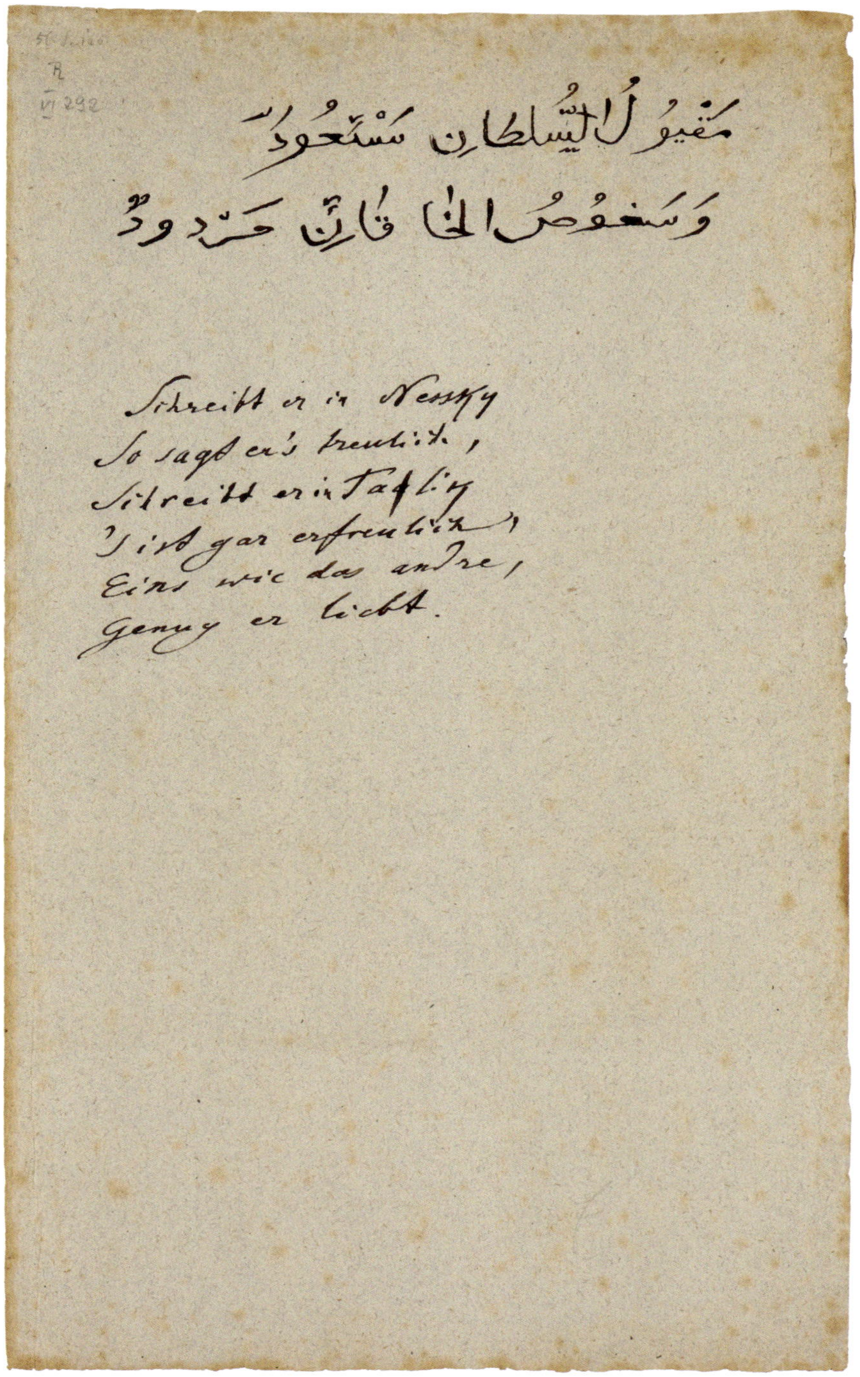

مقبول السلطان مسعود
ومبغوض الخاقان مردود

Schreibt er in Nessky
So sagt er's treulich,
Schreibt er in Talik
's ist gar erfreulich,
Eins wie das andre,
Genug er liebt.

Das Gedicht ist Ende Januar 1816 wohl von dem letzten Chiffrenbrief Marianne von Willemers an Goethe aus demselben Monat angeregt worden. Es wurde 1836 von Goethes Nachlassverwaltern im *Divan* unter dem Titel *Die Liebende abermals* abgedruckt. ›Nessky‹ (= Nasqī) und ›Talik‹ bezeichnen verschiedene arabische Schriften: die arabische Standardkursive und die Kurrentschrift. In ›Nessky‹ geschrieben ist das einleitende arabische Verspaar unbekannter Herkunft, das übersetzt heißt: »Wer beim Sultan gut angesehen ist, ist glücklich, / Und wer dem Kaiser verhasst ist, ist ausgestoßen.« (Übersetzung von Hendrik Birus.)

22 Johann Wolfgang von Goethe
Clean copy of Goethe's poem in his own hand: "Schreibt er in Nessky …"
Probably end of January 1816
1 sheet, 1 page written
34.6 x 21 cm
Klassik Stiftung Weimar, Goethe- und Schiller-Archiv
Shelf mark: GSA 25 / W 943

The poem was probably inspired by Marianne von Willemer's last cipher letter to Goethe of the same month. It was published in 1836 by the administrators of Goethe's estate in the *Divan* under the title *Die Liebende abermals* (The Lover Once Again). 'Nessky' (= Nasqī) and 'Talik' denote different Arabic scripts: the standard Arabic script and the cursive. Written in 'Nessky' is the introductory Arabic couplet of unknown origin, which translated means: "He who is well regarded by the Sultan is happy / And he who is hated by the Emperor is outcast."

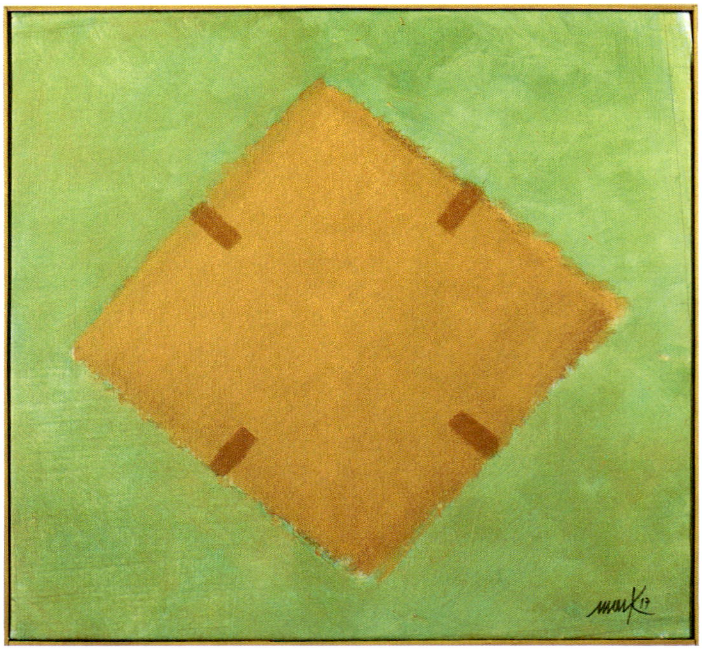

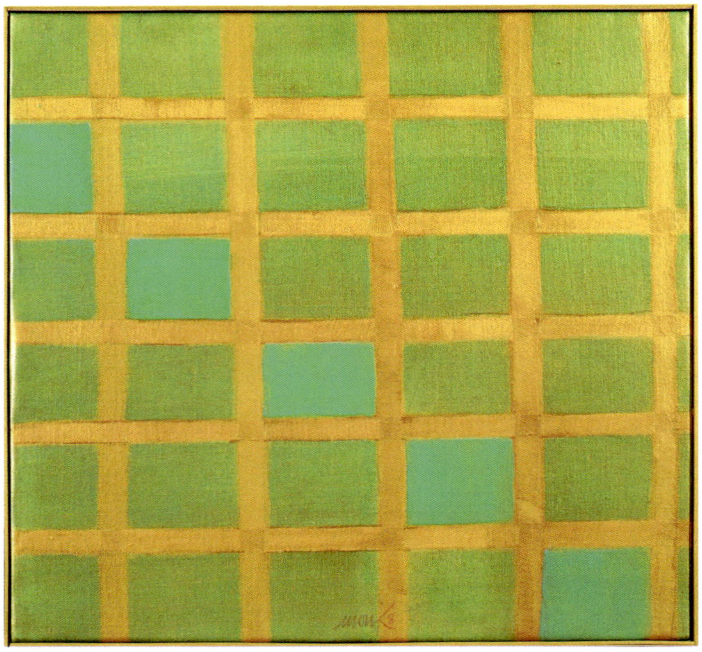

23 Heinz Mack
Ohne Titel *(Chromatische Konstellation)*
Signiert, datiert: »mack 17«
Acryl auf Leinwand
60 x 64 cm

23 Heinz Mack
Untitled *(Chromatic Constellation)*
Signed, dated: "mack 17"
Acrylic on canvas
60 x 64 cm

24 Heinz Mack
Ohne Titel *(Chromatische Konstellation)*
Signiert, datiert: »mack 8«
Acryl auf Leinwand
60 x 64 cm

24 Heinz Mack
Untitled *(Chromatic Constellation)*
Signed, dated: "mack 8"
Acrylic on canvas
60 x 64 cm

25 Heinz Mack
Little Secret (Chromatische Konstellation)
Signiert, datiert: »mack 8«
Acryl auf Leinwand
48 x 43 cm

25 Heinz Mack
Little Secret (Chromatic Constellation)
Signed, dated: "mack 8"
Acrylic on canvas
48 x 43 cm

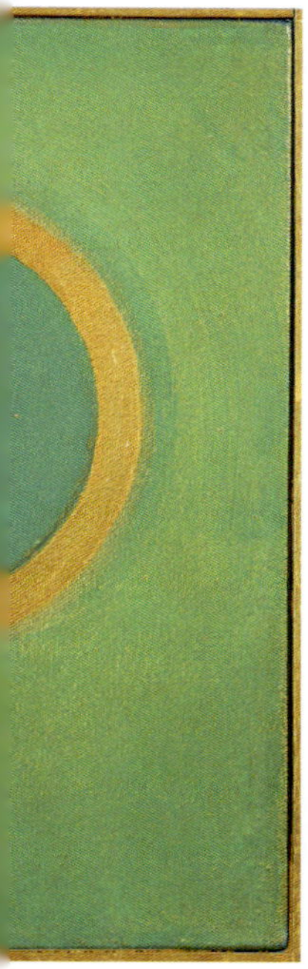

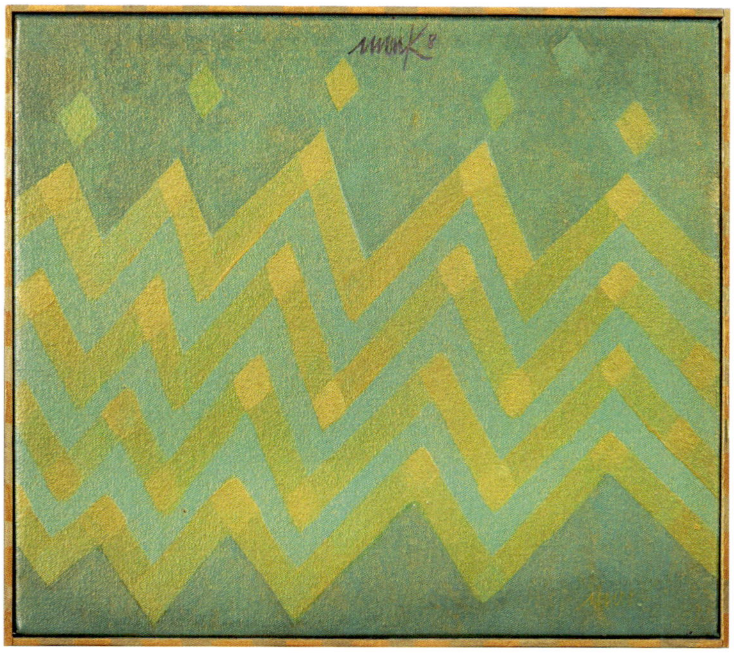

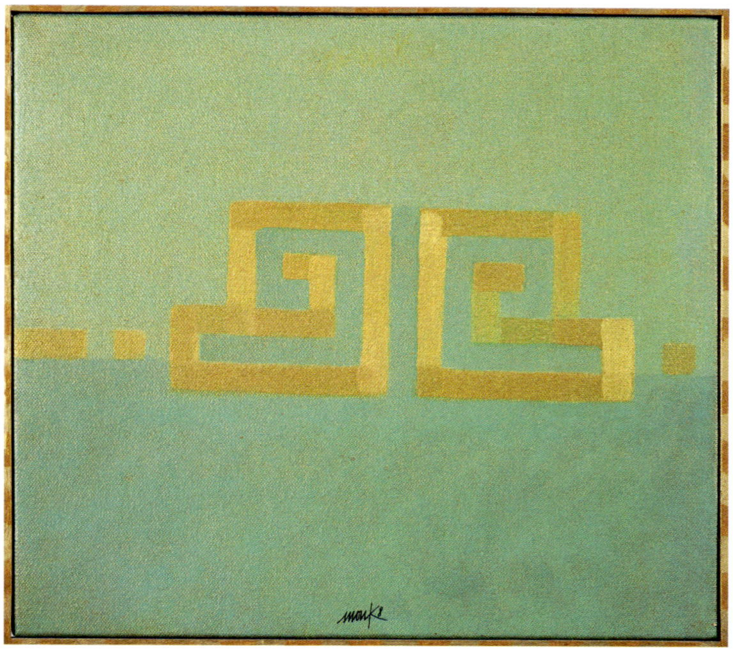

26 Heinz Mack
Oriental Curtain (Chromatische Konstellation)
Signiert, datiert: »mack 8«
Acryl auf Leinwand
38 x 43 cm

26 Heinz Mack
Oriental Curtain (Chromatic Constellation)
Signed, dated: "mack 8"
Acrylic on canvas
38 x 43 cm

27 Heinz Mack
Ornament (Chromatische Konstellation)
Signiert, datiert: »mack 8«
Acryl auf Leinwand
43 x 48 cm

27 Heinz Mack
Ornament (Chromatic Constellation)
Signed, dated: "mack 8"
Acrylic on canvas
43 x 48 cm

28+29 Marianne von Willemer
Eigenhändige Abschriften ihrer Gedichte:
Ostwind Wiedersehen und
Westwind Rückkehr von Heidelberg
Datiert: »d. 6. 8ber [18]15.« und
»Oktober 1815.«
1 Blatt, 2 S. beschrieben
15,6 x 9,5 cm
Goethe-Museum Düsseldorf

Marianne von Willemers Gedichte *Ostwind* und *Westwind* nahm Goethe ohne Titel und ohne Nennung der Verfasserin in seine eigene Sammlung *West-oestlicher Divan* auf, wobei er die Verse für den Druck nur leicht veränderte. Die einzig überlieferte eigenhändige Originalhandschrift der beiden Gedichte ist diese spätere Abschrift, die Marianne von Willemer 1857 für den Literarhistoriker Herman Grimm anfertigte. Er wiederum machte 1869 Marianne von Willemers Urheberschaft der Öffentlichkeit bekannt. Das Blatt ist erst 1993 aus Privatbesitz wieder aufgetaucht und seither im Besitz des Goethe-Museums Düsseldorf:

Ostwind Wiedersehen

Was bedeutet die Bewegung?
Bringt der Ostwind frohe Kunde?
Seiner Schwingen frische Regung
Kühlt des Herzens tiefe Wunde.

Kosend spielt er mit dem Staube
Jagt ihn auf in leichten Wölkchen
Treibt zur sichern Rebenlaube,
Der Insekten frohes Völkchen

Lindert sanft der Sonne Glühen
Kühlt auch mir die heißen Wangen
Küßt die Reben noch im Fliehen
Die auf Feld und Hügel prangen

Und mich soll sein leises Flüstern
Von dem Freunde lieblich grüßen
Eh noch diese Hügel düstern
Sitz ich still zu seinen Füßen

Und du magst nun weiter ziehen
Diene Frohen und betrübten
Dort wo hohe Mauern glühen
Finde ich den Vielgeliebten

Ach die wahre Herzenskunde
Liebeshauch erfrischtes Leben
Wird mir nur aus seinem Munde
Kann mir nur sein Athem geben

28+29 Marianne von Willemer
Copy in her own hand of her poems:
Ostwind Wiedersehen and
Westwind Rückkehr von Heidelberg
Dated: "d. 6. 8ber [18]15." and
"Oktober 1815."
1 sheet, 2 pages written
15.6 x 9.5 cm
Goethe-Museum Düsseldorf

The only surviving original manuscript of these poems in Marianne von Willemer's hand is this later copy, made for the literary historian Herman Grimm in 1857, who publicized her authorship in 1869. The autograph did not re-emerge from private ownership until 1993 and has been in the possession of the Goethe-Museum Düsseldorf since then.
Goethe took these poems without title and without naming Marianne von Willemer as the author and inserted them into his own collection *West-East Divan,* only slightly changing the verses for their publication:

What's the meaning of the stirring?
What's the east wind heralding? –
With its wings refreshing, whirring,
Cooling, soothing heart-wounds' sting.

With the dust it plays, caressing,
Whirls it up in lightsome cloud,
Driving, safe, to vineyard-blessing
Newly vital insect-crowd.

Mildens lightened solar glowing
While it cools my heated cheek,
Kissing vines while fleeing, flowing
Fieldward to the season-peak.

To a whisper soft I hearken,
Myriad greetings from a friend;
And before the hillocks darken,
Myriad kisses will it send.

Forward, onward well you wander!
Serve your friends and those that grieve.
Near the glowing mountains yonder
Soon I'll find him. I believe.

Ah, the heart-borne tidings true,
Breath of love, new-freshened from
Longed-for lips will come to you,
Only from his breath can come.

(Johann Wolfgang von Goethe, *West-East Divan,* trans. Martin Bidney, New York, 2010, pp. 111–12.)

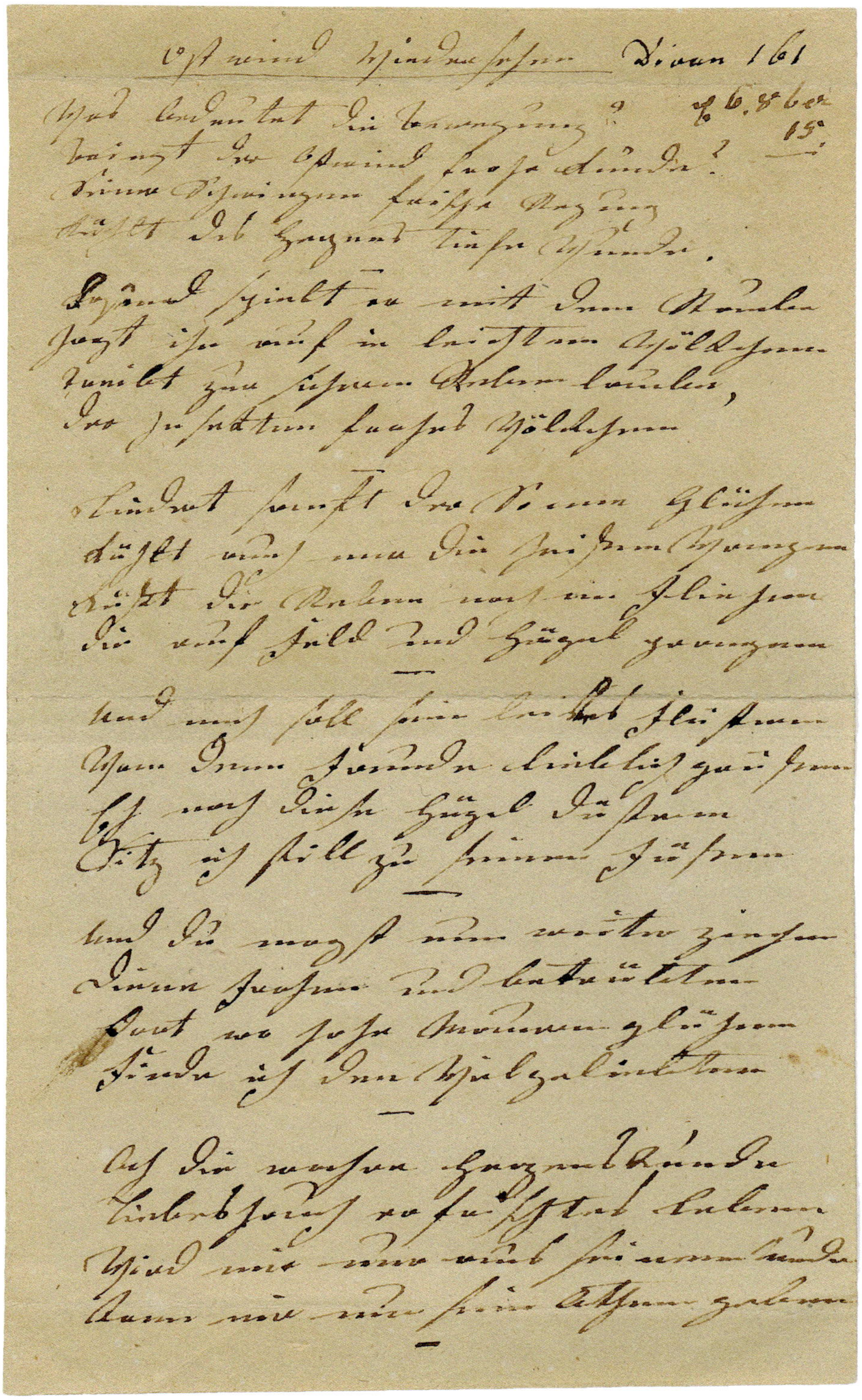
Ostwind Wiedersehen Divan 161

Was bedeutet die Bewegung? d. 6. 8ber 15
Bringt der Ostwind frohe Kunde?
Seiner Schwingen frische Regung
Kühlt des Herzens tiefe Wunde.

Kosend spielt er mit dem Staube,
Jagt ihn auf in leichten Wölkchen,
Treibt zur sichern Rebenlaube
Der Insekten frohes Völkchen,

Lindert sanft der Sonne Glühen
Kühlt auch mir die heißen Wangen
Küßt die Reben noch im Fliehen
Die auf Feld und Hügel prangen

Und mich soll sein leises Flüstern
Von dem Freunde lieblich grüßen
Eh noch diese Hügel düstern
Sitz ich still zu seinen Füßen

Und du magst nun weiter ziehen
Diene Frohen und Betrübten
Dort wo hohe Mauern glühen
Finde ich den Vielgeliebten

Ach die wahre Herzenskunde
Liebeshauch erfrischtes Leben
Wird mir nur aus seinem Munde
Kann mir nur sein Athem geben

Westwind Rückkehr von Heidelberg

Ach! um deine feuchten Schwingen
West wie sehr ich dich beneide
Denn du kannst ihm Kunde bringen
Was ich durch die Trennung leide.

Die Bewegung deiner Flügel
Weckt im Busen stilles Sehnen;
Blumen, Augen, Wald und Hügel.
Stehn bei deinem Hauch in Thränen

Doch dein mildes sanftes Wehen
Kühlt die wunden Augenlieder
Ach für Leid müßt ich vergehen
Hoft ich nicht: wir sehn uns wieder

Geh denn hin zu meinem Lieben
Spreche sanft zu seinem Herzen
Doch vermeid ihn zu betrüben
Und verschweig ihm meine Schmerzen

Sag ihm nur, doch sags bescheiden
Seine Liebe sey mein Leben
Freudiges Gefühl von beiden
Wird mir seine Nähe geben«

Oh how, West Wind, those rain-wet wings
I envy you, in desolation –
Messenger who the missive brings
Of how I pine, in separation.

The moving of your wing appears,
Wakes in the breast a longing, still;
Flower and eye and wood and hill
Are by your breathing bathed in tears.

And yet – your wafting, mild and soft –
Cooling my hurt and fevered eyes!
I'd long have died of woe, did oft
My hope to see him not arise.

To my beloved hasten, graced:
Calmingly speaking to his heart,
Conceal the grief that I have faced,
And hide my pain, the searing smart.

Say to him only, quietly,
That in his love alone I live,
That life and love will both, for me,
With bliss again his nearness give.

(Johann Wolfgang von Goethe, *West-East Divan,* trans. Martin Bidney, New York, 2010, p. 114.)

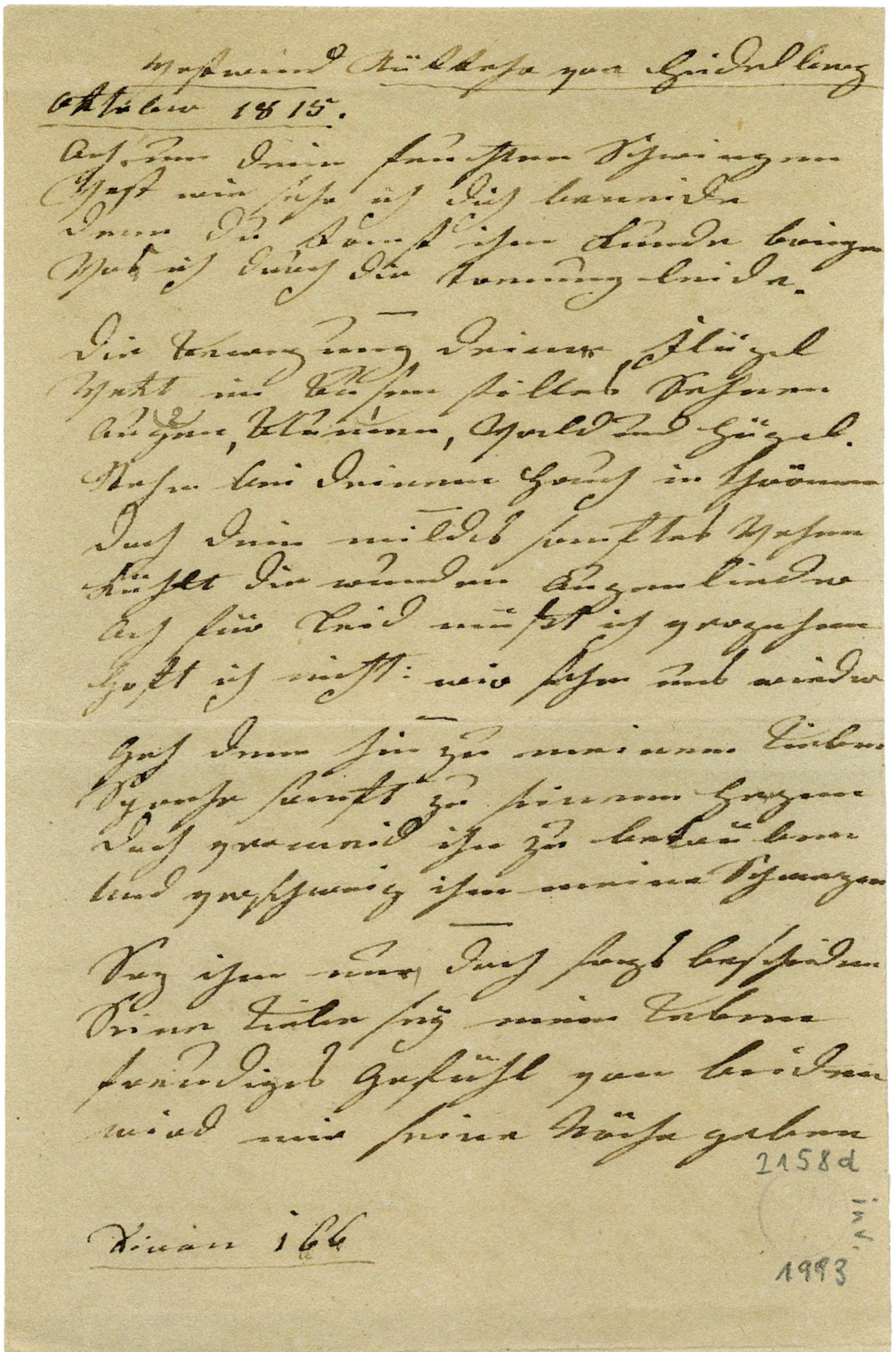

Westwind Rückreise von Heidelberg
Oktober 1815.

Ach um deine feuchten Schwingen
West wie sehr ich dich beneide
Denn du kannst ihm Kunde bringen
Was ich durch die Trennung leide.

Die Bewegung deiner Flügel
Weckt im Busen stilles Sehnen
Augen, Blumen, Wald und Hügel.
Stehn bei deinem Hauch in Thränen
Doch dein mildes sanftes Wehen
Kühlt die wunden Augenlieder
Ach für Leid müßt ich vergehen
Hofft ich nicht: wir sehn uns wieder

Geh denn hin zu meinem Lieben
Spreche sanft zu seinem Herzen
Doch vermeid ihn zu betrüben
Und verschweig ihm meine Schmerzen

Sag ihm nur, doch sags bescheiden
Seine Liebe sey mein Leben
Freudiges Gefühl von beiden
Wird mir seine Nähe geben

Divan 166

2158d
Inv. 1993

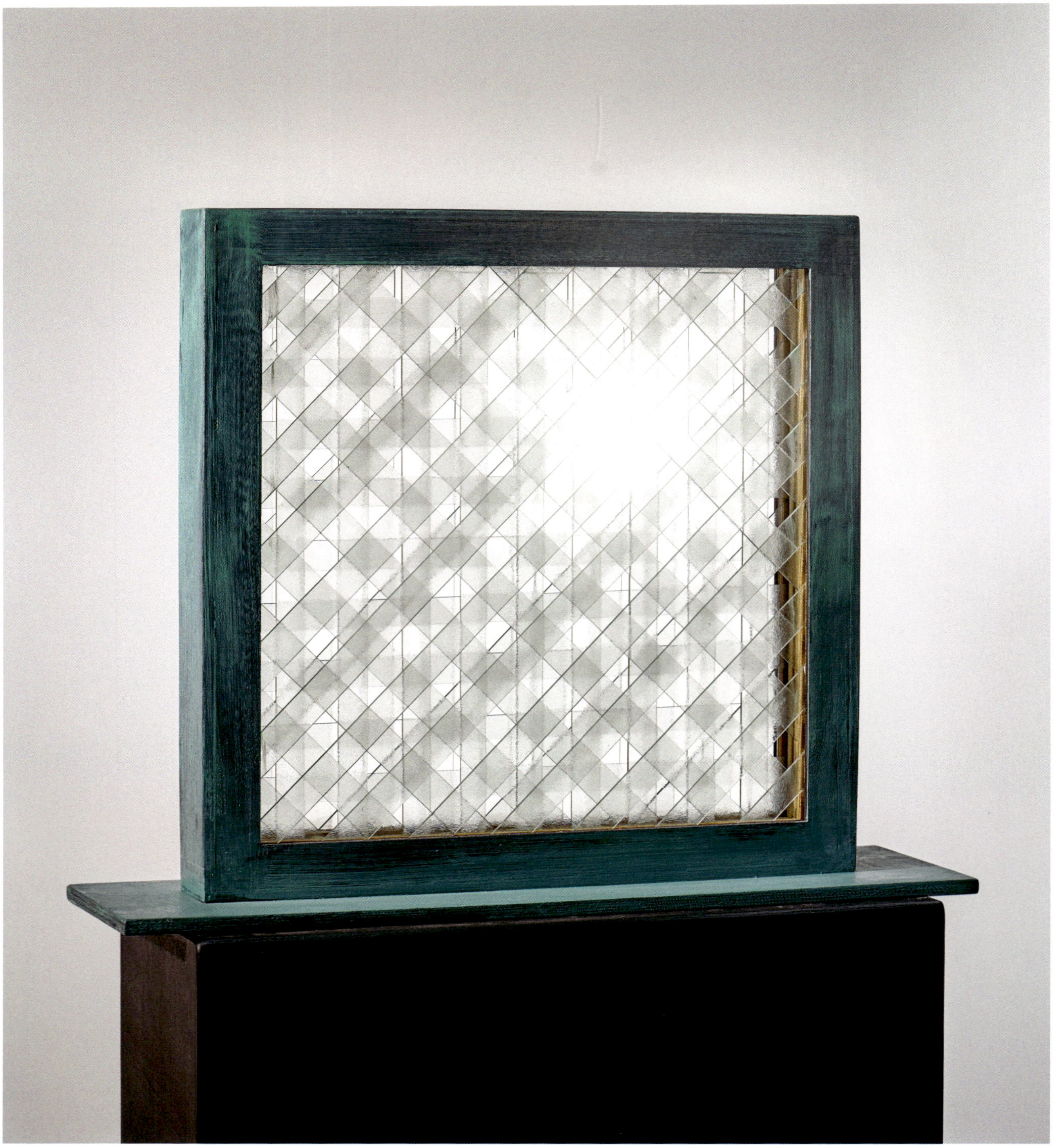

30 Heinz Mack
Licht-Gitter (Hommage à Piero Dorazio; Modell für einen gläsernen Paravent)
Signiert, datiert: »mack 3«
Glas, Holz
62 x 62 x 9 cm
Vgl. auch S. 61.

30 Heinz Mack
Light Grid (Hommage à Piero Dorazio; Model for a Glass Paravent)
Signed, dated: "mack 3"
Glass, wood
62 x 62 x 9 cm
See also p. 61.

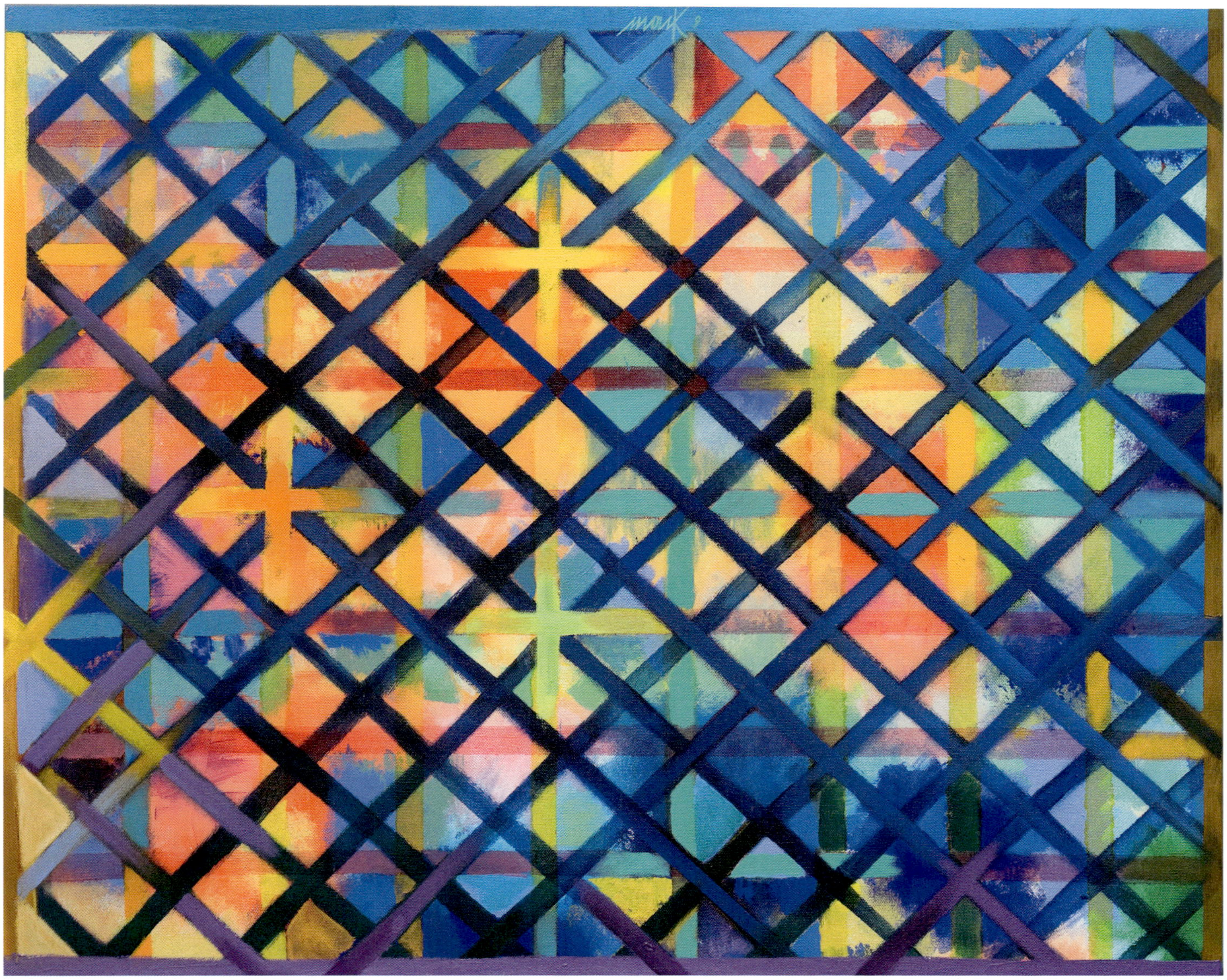

31 Heinz Mack
Ohne Titel
Signiert, datiert: »mack 9«
Acryl auf Leinwand
85 x 104 cm

31 Heinz Mack
Untitled
Signed, dated: "mack 9"
Acrylic on canvas
85 x 104 cm

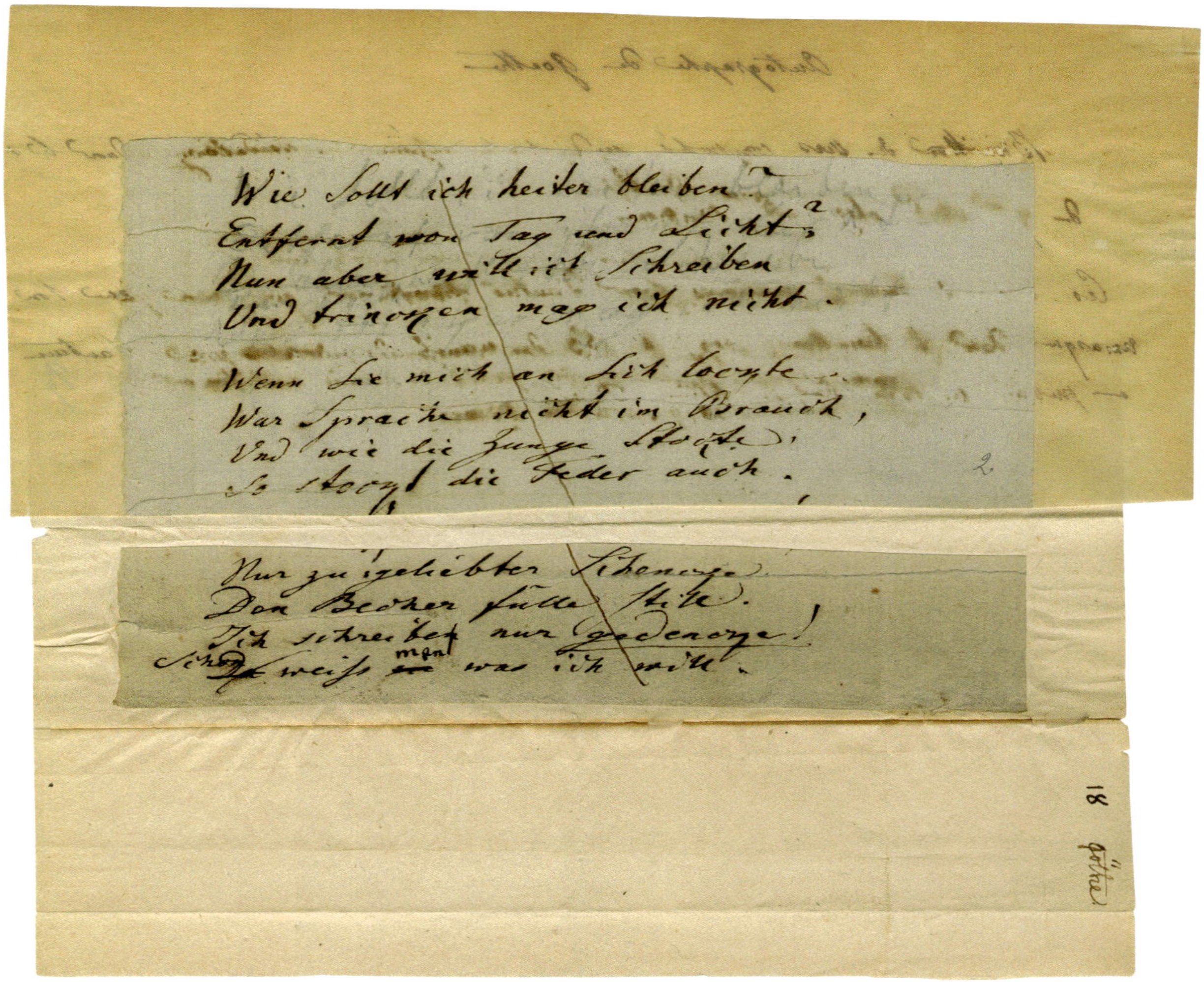

Wie sollt ich heiter bleiben?
Entfernt von Tag und Licht?
Nun aber will ich schreiben
Und trinken mag ich nicht.

Wenn sie mich an sich lockte
War Sprache nicht im Brauch,
Und wie die Zunge stockte,
So stockt die Feder auch.

Nur zu geliebter Schenke
Den Becher fülle still.
Ich schreibe nur Gedenke!
Schon weiss man was ich will.

2.

18
Göthe

32 Johann Wolfgang von Goethe
Eigenhändiger Entwurf zu seinem Gedicht:
»Wie sollt ich heiter bleiben? […]«
aus dem *West-oestlichen Divan (Buch Suleika)*
2 Fragmente eines Blattes, beschrieben mit
Bleistift und Tinte
6,9–7,6 x 18 cm und 3–3,5 x 18 cm
jeweils auf ein größeres Blatt montiert,
auf dem ersten davon rückseitig Echtheitsbestätigung in französischer Sprache
Goethe-Museum Düsseldorf

Goethes Gedicht entstand am 1. Oktober 1815 oder kurz davor, nach dem letzten Abschied von Marianne von Willemer. Die beiden Fragmente wurden 1974 beziehungsweise 1980 von verschiedenen Besitzern erworben und liegen seither wiedervereinigt im Goethe-Museum vor.

32 Johann Wolfgang von Goethe
Draft of Goethe's poem in his own hand:
"Wie sollt ich heiter bleiben? …"
(How am I supposed to remain cheerful? …)
from the *West-East Divan (Book of Zuleika)*
2 fragments of a sheet, written in pencil and ink
6.9–7.6 x 18 cm and 3–3.5 x 18 cm
Goethe-Museum Düsseldorf

The poem was written on October 1, 1815, or shortly before – after Goethe's and Marianne von Willemer's last farewell. The two fragments were acquired by various owners in 1974 and 1980, respectively, and have since been reunited in the Goethe-Museum.

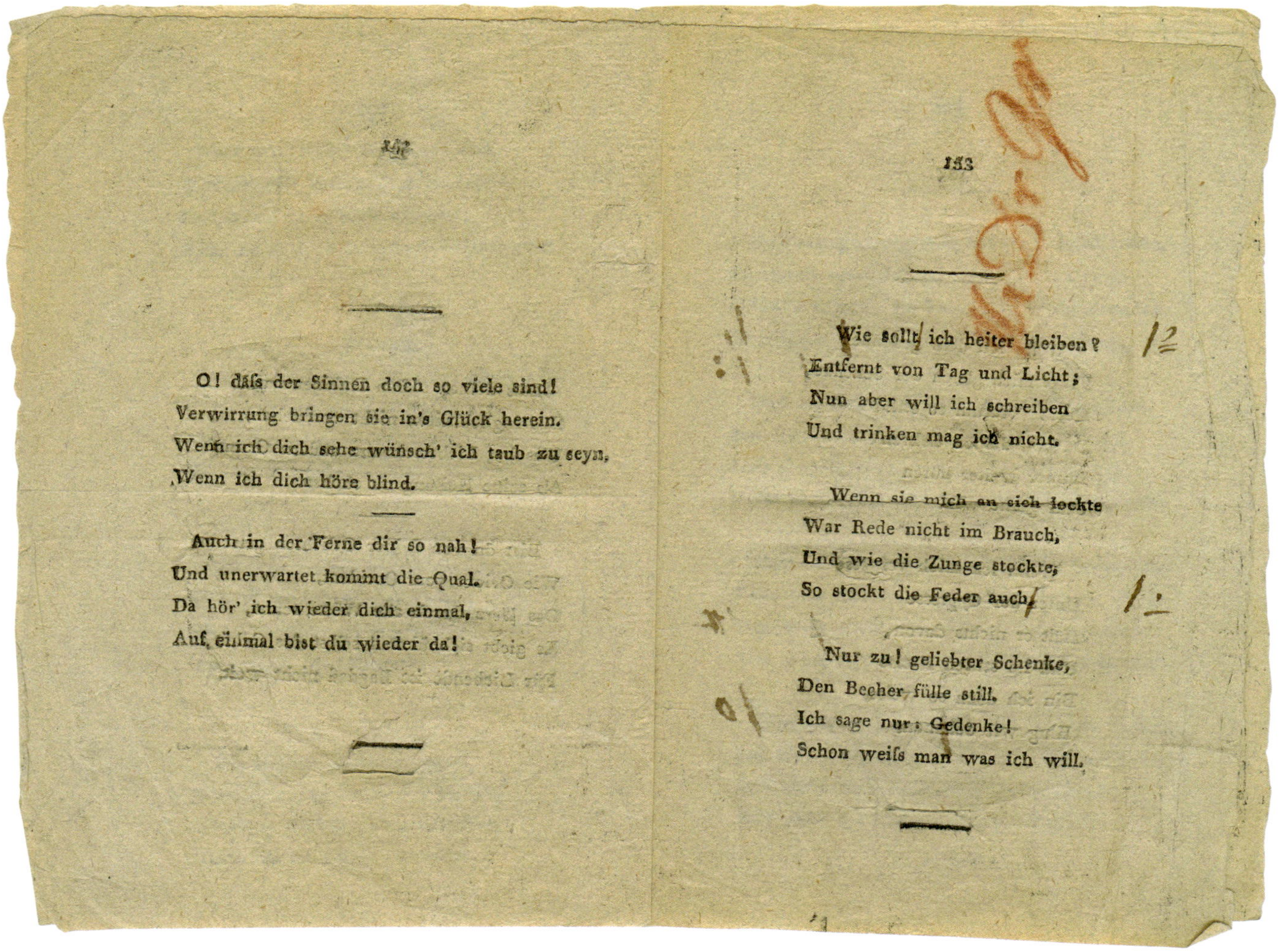

O! daſs der Sinnen doch so viele sind!
Verwirrung bringen sie in's Glück herein.
Wenn ich dich sehe wünsch' ich taub zu seyn,
Wenn ich dich höre blind.

Auch in der Ferne dir so nah!
Und unerwartet kommt die Qual.
Da hör' ich wieder dich einmal,
Auf einmal bist du wieder da!

153

Wie sollt ich heiter bleiben?
Entfernt von Tag und Licht;
Nun aber will ich schreiben
Und trinken mag ich nicht.

Wenn sie mich an sich lockte
War Rede nicht im Brauch,
Und wie die Zunge stockte,
So stockt die Feder auch.

Nur zu! geliebter Schenke,
Den Becher fülle still.
Ich sage nur: Gedenke!
Schon weiſs man was ich will.

33 Johann Wolfgang von Goethe
»Wie sollt ich heiter bleiben? […]«
Korrekturbogen zum *West-oestlichen Divan*
16,5 x 22,6 cm
Goethe-Museum Düsseldorf

33 Johann Wolfgang von Goethe
"Wie sollt ich heiter bleiben? …"
(How am I supposed to remain cheerful? …)
Correction sheet for *West-East Divan*
16.5 x 22.6 cm
Goethe-Museum Düsseldorf

34 Johann Wolfgang von Goethe
Eigenhändige Reinschrift seines Gedichtes:
Erwiederung
Datiert: »am 7 Nov. [1825]«
1 Blatt, 1 S. beschrieben; zweite Seite
eines Briefes an Marianne von Willemer,
dessen erste Seite fehlt
20,2 x 16,8 cm
Goethe-Museum Düsseldorf

Erwiederung ist die Antwort auf Marianne von Willemers Gedicht »Zarter Blumen reich Gewinde […]«, das sie zu Goethes Geburtstag am 28. August 1825 auf ein mit getrockneten Blütenblättern verziertes Blatt geschrieben hatte. Da sich zunächst keine Gelegenheit zur sicheren Beförderung ergab, wurde das Gedicht erst Ende Oktober überbracht, als von allen Seiten Glückwünsche zum 50. Jahrestag von Goethes Ankunft in Weimar eintrafen. Goethe überarbeitete ihr Gedicht und stellte es mit seiner poetischen Antwort als Wechselgesang zwischen »Sie« und »Er« zusammen. Schließlich datierte er es auf den Tag seines Weimarer Jubiläums. Vgl. WA, Bd. I 4, S. 268 f.

34 Johann Wolfgang von Goethe
Clean copy of Goethe's poem in his own hand:
Erwiederung (Reply)
Dated: "am 7 Nov. [1825]"
1 sheet, 1 page written; second page
of a letter to Marianne von Willemer,
the first page of which is missing
20.2 x 16.8 cm
Goethe-Museum Düsseldorf

Erwiederung is the answer to Marianne von Willemer's poem "Zarter Blumen reich Gewinde …" (Tender Flowers rich Thread …), which she sent to Goethe on the occasion of his birthday on 28 August 1825 on a page decorated with dried petals. Since there was no immediate opportunity to send it in a secure conveyance, the poem was delivered at the end of October, when congratulations to Goethe's 50th anniversary of his residence in Weimar arrived from all sides. Goethe revised her poem and combined it with his poetic answer as an exchange between "She" and "He." In the end, he dated it on the day of his Weimar anniversary. Cf. WA, vol. I 4, pp. 268–69.

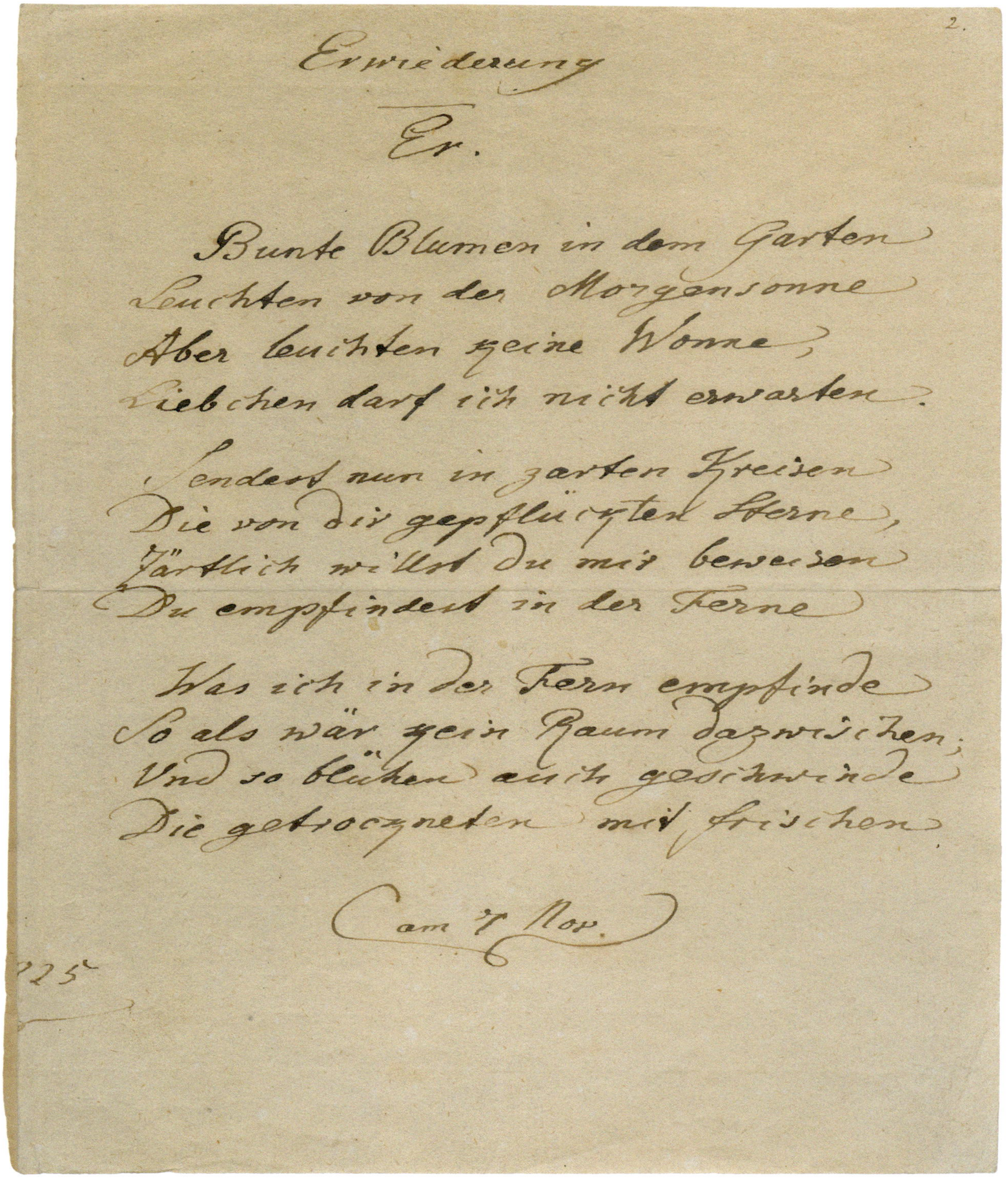

2.

Erwiederung

Er.

Bunte Blumen in dem Garten
Leuchten von der Morgensonne
Aber leuchten keine Wonne,
Liebchen darf ich nicht erwarten.

Sendest nun in zarten Kreisen
Die von dir gepflückten Sterne,
Zärtlich willst du mir beweisen
Du empfindest in der Ferne

Was ich in der Fern empfinde
So als wär kein Raum dazwischen,
Und so blühen auch geschwinde
Die getrockneten mit frischen.

am 7 Nov.

225

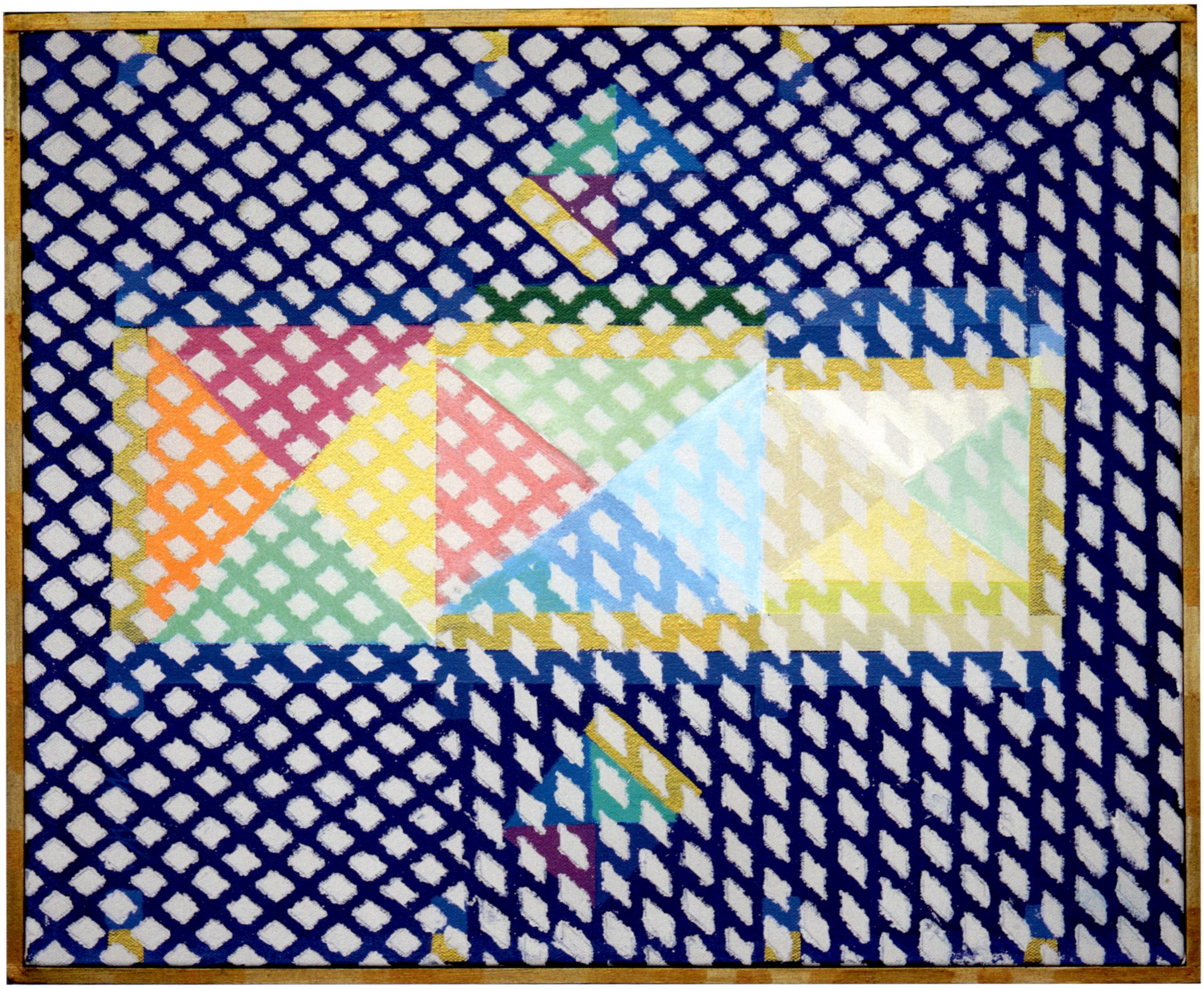

35 Heinz Mack
For an Oriental Mirror
(Chromatische Konstellation)
Signiert, datiert: »mack 8«
Acryl auf Leinwand
60 x 72 cm

35 Heinz Mack
For an Oriental Mirror
(Chromatic Constellation)
Signed, dated: "mack 8"
Acrylic on canvas
60 x 72 cm

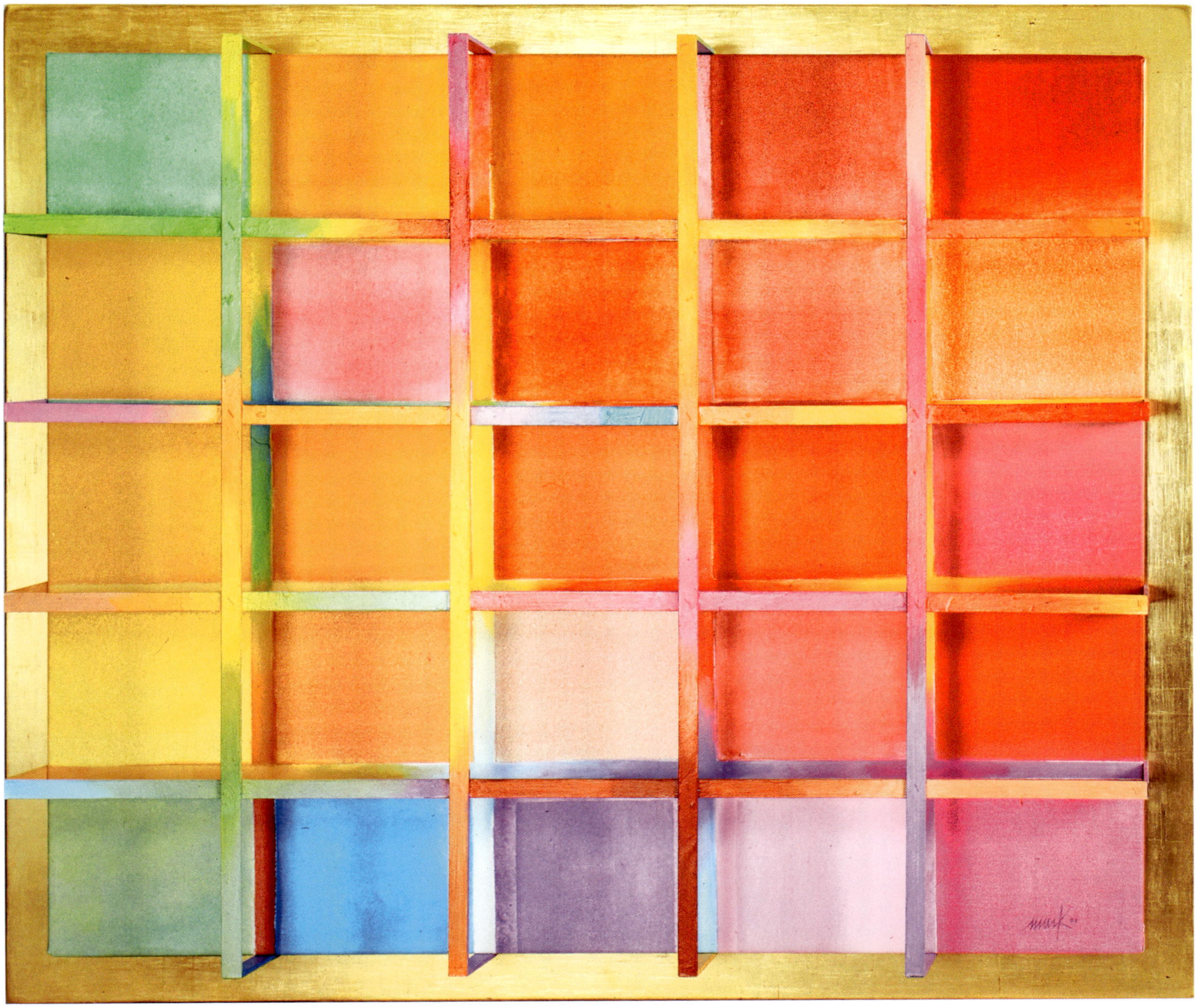

36 Heinz Mack
Gitterbild (Chromatische Konstellation)
Signiert, datiert: »mack 00«
Acryl, Leinwand, Holz, Goldplattierung
120 x 139 x 17 cm

36 Heinz Mack
Grid Pattern (Chromatic Constellation)
Signed, dated: "mack 00"
Acrylic, canvas, wood, gold plating
120 x 139 x 17 cm

37 Johann Wolfgang von Goethe
Eigenhändige Reinschrift seines Gedichtes:
»Was ist schwer zu verbergen? [...]«
Datiert: »Frfurt d. 27 May 1815.«
1 Blatt, 1/2 S. beschrieben
34,5 x 21,4 cm
Goethe-Museum Düsseldorf

Goethe schrieb das Gedicht auf der Reise von Frankfurt nach Wiesbaden. Unter dem Titel *Geständniss* wurde es im ersten Teil des *West-oestlichen Divans* gedruckt.

37 Johann Wolfgang von Goethe
Clean copy of Goethe's poem in his own hand:
"Was ist schwer zu verbergen? ..."
(What will resist being hid? ...)
Dated: "Frfurt d. 27 May 1815."
1 sheet, 1/2 page written
34.5 x 21.4 cm
Goethe Museum-Düsseldorf

Goethe wrote this poem while travelling from Frankfurt to Wiesbaden. It was printed under the title *Geständniss* (Confession) in the first part of the *West-East Divan*.

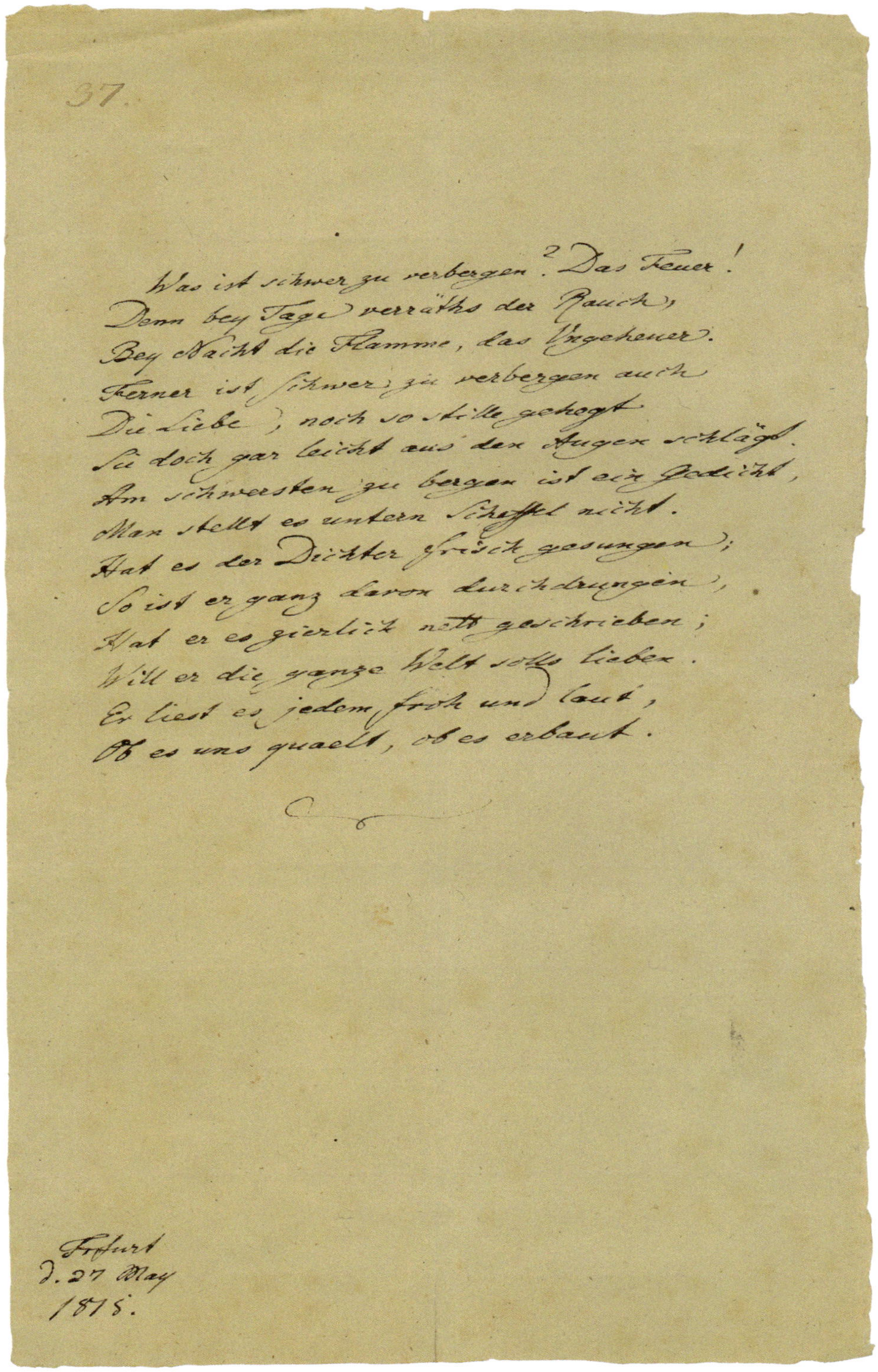

37.

Was ist schwer zu verbergen? Das Feuer!
Denn bey Tage verräths der Rauch,
Bey Nacht die Flamme, das Ungeheuer.
Ferner ist schwer zu verbergen auch
Die Liebe, noch so stille gehegt
Sie doch gar leicht aus den Augen schlägt.
Am schwersten zu bergen ist ein Gedicht,
Man stellt es untern Scheffel nicht.
Hat es der Dichter frisch gesungen;
So ist er ganz davon durchdrungen,
Hat er es zierlich nett geschrieben;
Will er die ganze Welt solls lieben.
Er liest es jedem froh und laut,
Ob es uns quaelt, ob es erbaut.

Erfurt
d. 27 May
1818.

38 Johann Wolfgang von Goethe
Eigenhändige Reinschrift seines Gedichtes:
»Herrinn! sag was heisst das Flüstern? [...]«
Datiert: »d. 24. Octbr 1815.«
1 Blatt, 1 S. mit Tinte beschrieben, Bleistiftkorrekturen; mit einer aufgeklebten Variante der zweiten Strophe; der aufgeklebte Zettel verdeckt die darunter liegende, mehrfach korrigierte erste Fassung dieser Strophe
33,4 x 20,6 cm
Goethe-Museum Düsseldorf

Das Wechselgedicht zwischen der Herrin Suleika und ihrer Dienerin entstand nach Goethes Rückkehr vom Rhein und Main nach Weimar und knüpft an einen Chiffrenbrief Marianne von Willemers vom 18. Oktober 1815 an, worin sie den Dichter Hafis zitiert: »Immer sehnt sich mein Herz nach deinen Lippen« *(Diwan,* Bd. 1, S. 424). Die Replik der Herrin entlehnte Goethe ebenfalls aus einem Ghasel von Hafis' *Diwan:* »Ich will küßen, küßen, sprach ich« (Bd. 1, S. 434). Im *West-oestlichen Divan (Buch Suleika)* erschien das Gedicht unter dem Titel *Vollmondnacht.*

38 Johann Wolfgang von Goethe
Clean copy of Goethe's poem in his own hand:
"Herrinn! sag was heisst das Flüstern? ..."
(Mistress, tell me, why the whispers? ...)
Dated: "d. 24. Octbr 1815."
1 sheet, 1 page written in ink, pencil corrections, with a glued-on variant of the second verse. The glued-on piece covers over the first version of the verse which is underneath and has been corrected several times.
33.4 x 20.6 cm
Goethe-Museum Düsseldorf

The exchange of poems between Mistress Zuleika and her servant was written after Goethe's return from the Rhine and Main to Weimar and ties in with a cipher letter by Marianne von Willemers from 18 October 1815, in which she quotes the poet Háfiz: "Immer sehnt sich mein Herz nach deinen Lippen" (My heart always longs for your lips; *Diwan,* trans. Joseph v. Hammer, vol. 1, p. 424). Goethe also borrowed the mistress's replica from a ghazel of Háfiz's *Diwan:* "Ich will küßen, küßen, sprach ich" (I want to kiss, kiss, I said; vol. 1, p. 434). In the *West-East Divan (Book of Zuleika)* the poem was published under the title *Full-Moon Night.*

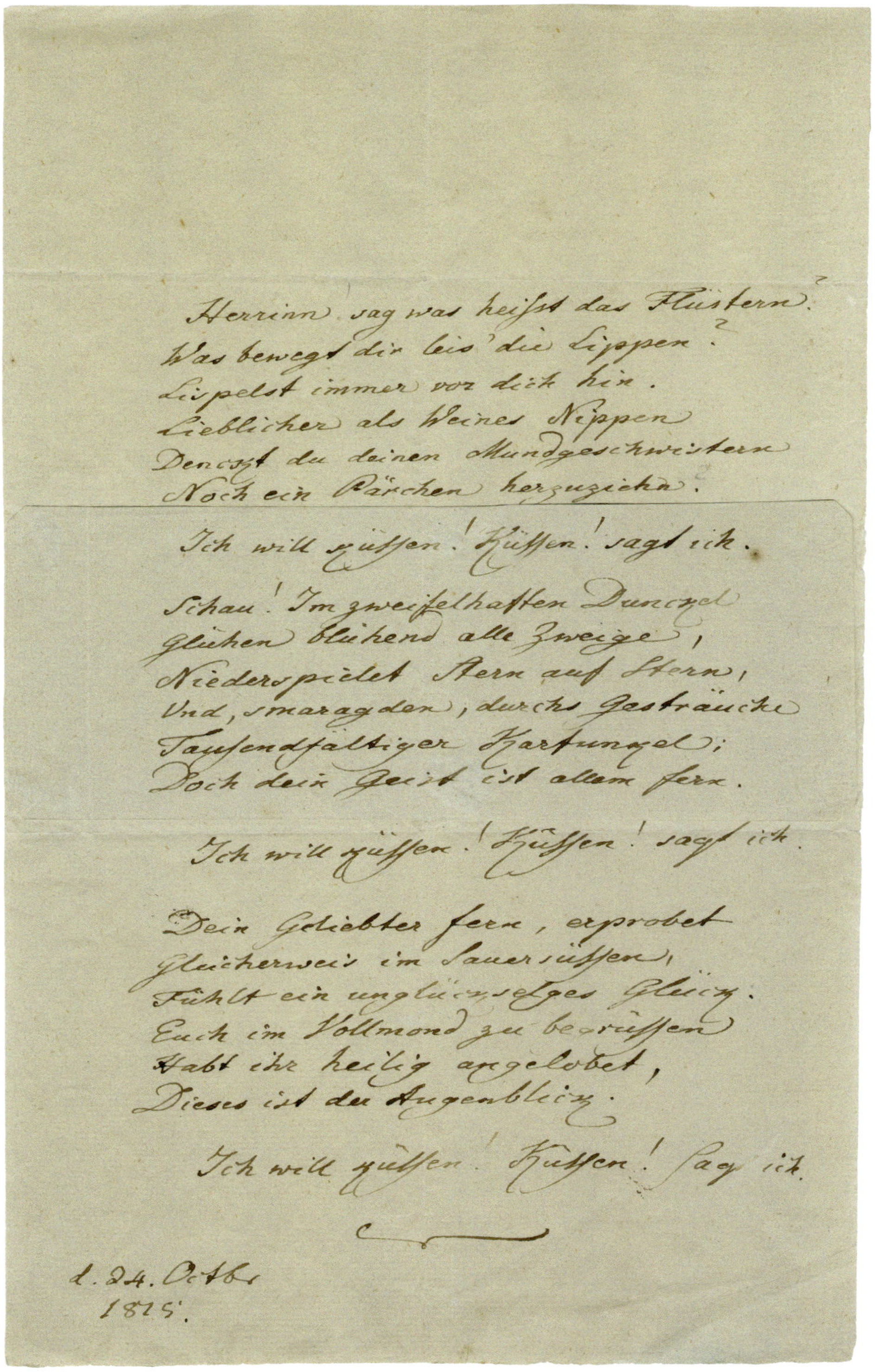

Herrinn sag was heißt das Flüstern?
Was bewegt dir leis die Lippen?
Lispelst immer vor dich hin.
Lieblicher als Weines Nippen
Denckst du deinen Mundgeschwistern
Noch ein Pärchen herzuziehn.

Ich will küssen! Küssen! sagt ich.

Schau! Im zweifelhaften Dunckel
Glühen blühend alle Zweige,
Niederspielet Stern auf Stern,
Und, smaragden, durchs Gesträuche
Tausendfältiger Karfunckel;
Doch dein Geist ist allem fern.

Ich will küssen! Küssen! sagt ich.

Dein Geliebter fern, erprobet
Gleicherweis im Sauersüssen,
Fühlt ein unglückselges Glück.
Euch im Vollmond zu begrüssen
Habt ihr heilig angelobet,
Dieses ist der Augenblick.

Ich will küssen! Küssen! sag ich.

d. 24. Octbr
1815.

39 Eigenhändige Reinschrift seines Gedichtes:
»Was wird mir jede Stunde so bang? […]«
Datiert: »22 Jul. 1818«
1 Blatt, 1 S. beschrieben
19,8 x 16,4 cm
Aufgezogen auf Untersatzkarton
(24, 8 x 20,1 cm), den Goethe, bevor er
das Autograf verschenkte, mit dem Vermerk
versah: »d. 3. Apr 1824. Goethes Handschrift«
Goethe-Museum Düsseldorf

Gedruckt erschien das Gedicht zunächst 1821 in der Erstausgabe von *Wilhelm Meisters Wanderjahren* und 1827 im *Divan* der Ausgabe letzter Hand.

39 Johann Wolfgang von Goethe
Clean copy of Goethe’s poem in his own hand:
“Was wird mir jede Stunde so bang? …”
(Something, I fear, each hour is wrong, …)
Dated: “22 Jul. 1818”
1 sheet, 1 page written
19.8 x 16.4 cm
Mounted on a card to which he added the note:
“d. 3. Apr 1824. Goethes Handschrift”
Goethe-Museum Düsseldorf

The poem was first published in 1821 in the first edition of *Wilhelm Meister’s Years of Travel,* and then again in 1827 in Goethe's final edition of the *Divan*.

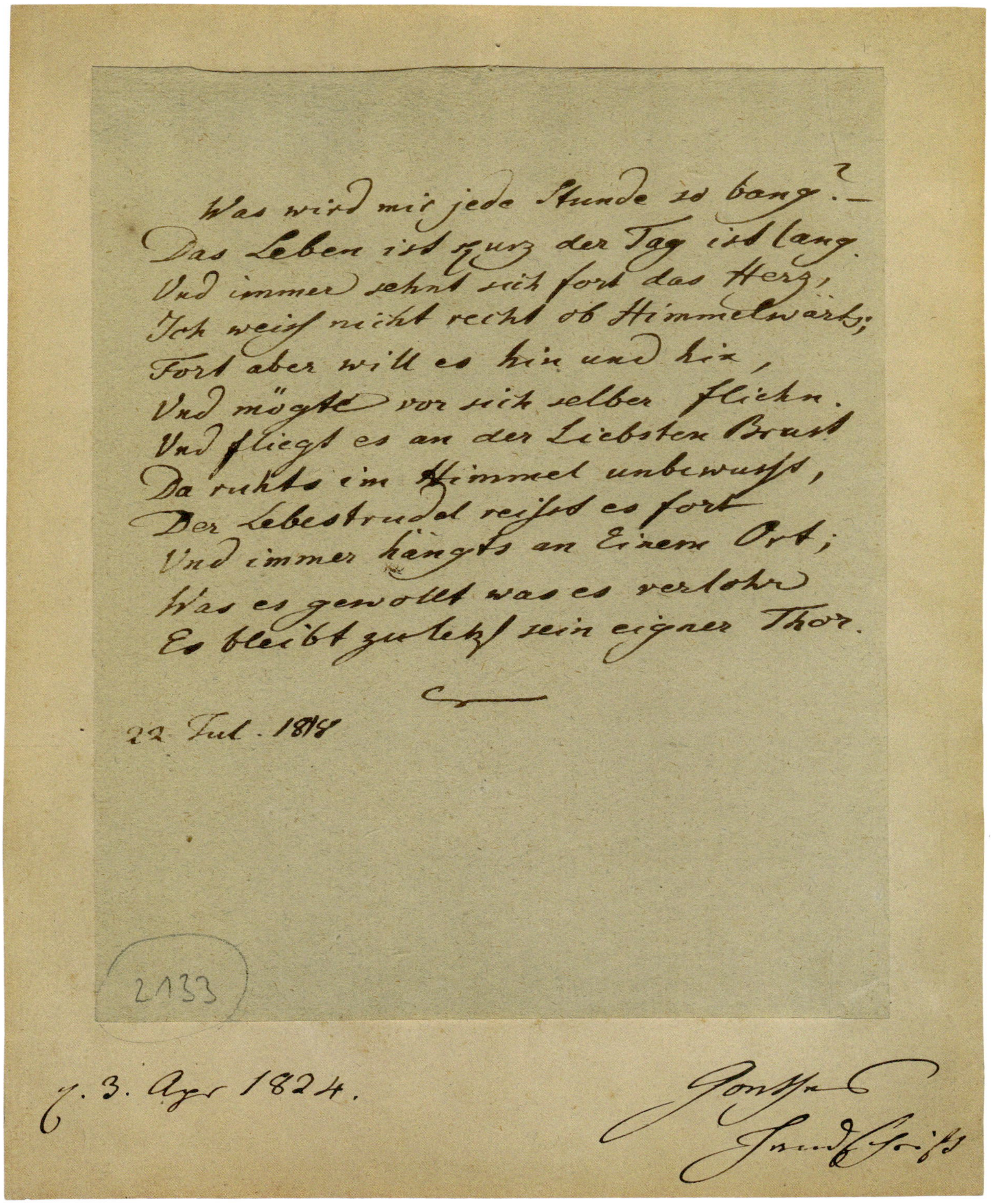
Was wird mir jede Stunde so bang? —
Das Leben ist kurz der Tag ist lang.
Und immer sehnt sich fort das Herz,
Ich weiß nicht recht ob Himmelwärts;
Fort aber will es hin und hin,
Und möchte vor sich selber fliehn.
Und fliegt es an der Liebsten Brust
Da ruhts im Himmel unbewußt,
Der Lebestrudel reißt es fort
Und immer hängts an Einem Ort;
Was es gewollt was es verlohr
Es bleibt zuletzt sein eigner Thor.

22 Jul. 1818

2133

d. 3. Apr 1824.

Goethe
Handschrift

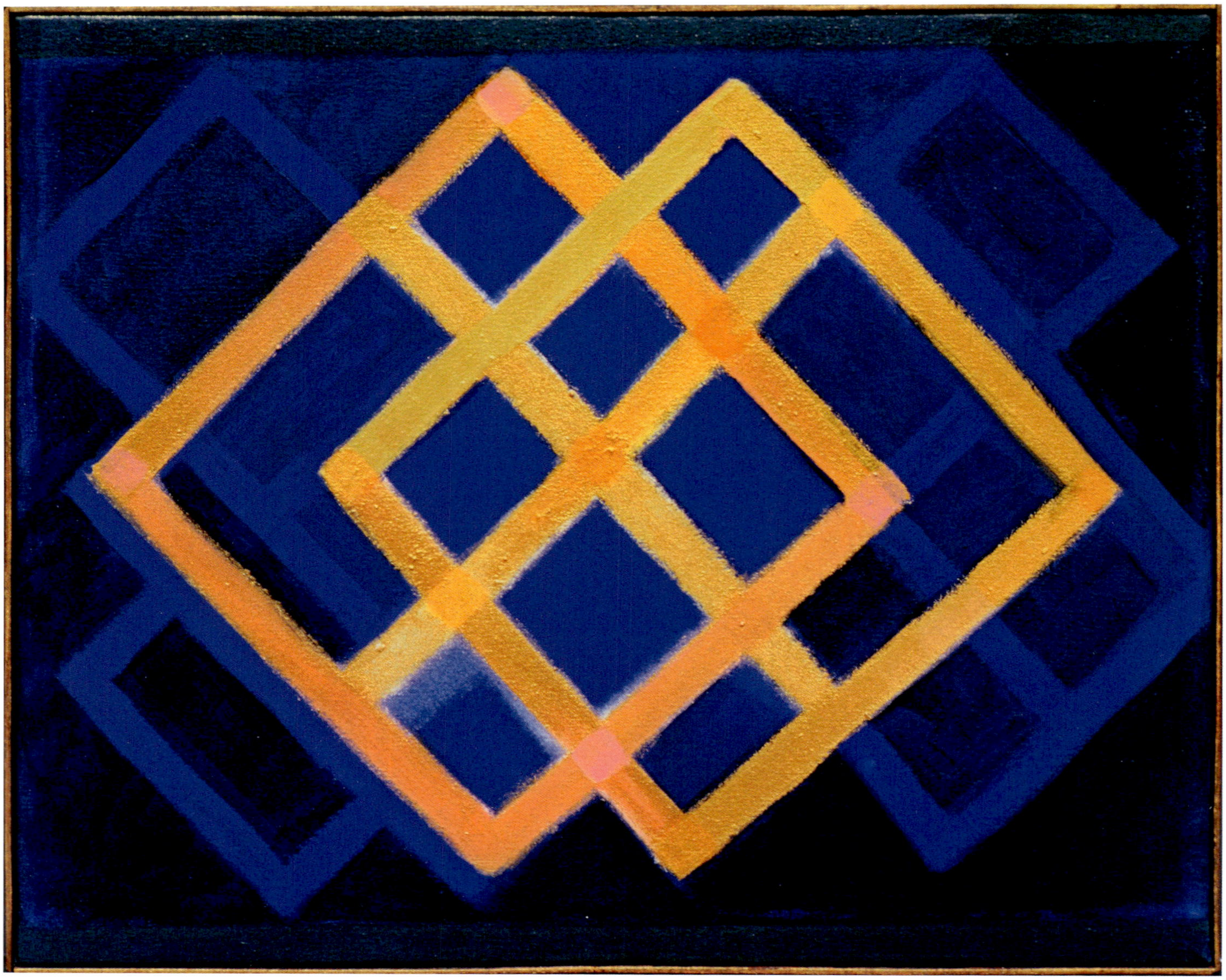

40 Heinz Mack
Ornament und Spiel
(Chromatische Konstellation)
Signiert, datiert: »mack 5«
Acryl auf Leinwand
52 x 63 cm

40 Heinz Mack
Ornament and Game
(Chromatic Constellation)
Signed, dated: "mack 5"
Acrylic on canvas
52 x 63 cm

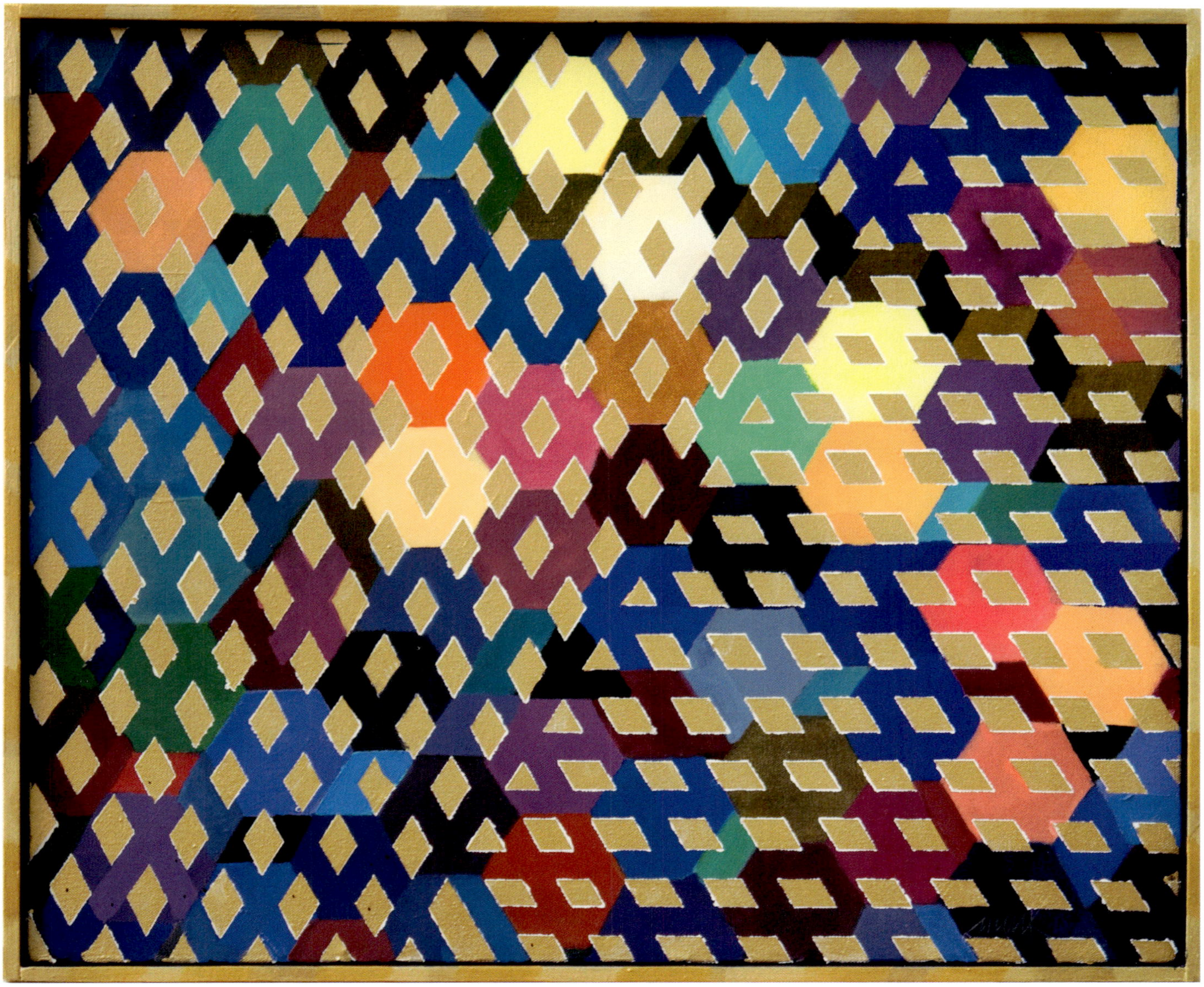

41 Heinz Mack
Ohne Titel *(Chromatische Konstellation)*
Signiert, datiert: »mack 10«
Acryl auf Leinwand
78 x 92 cm

41 Heinz Mack
Untitled *(Chromatic Constellation)*
Signed, dated: "mack 10"
Acrylic on canvas
78 x 92 cm

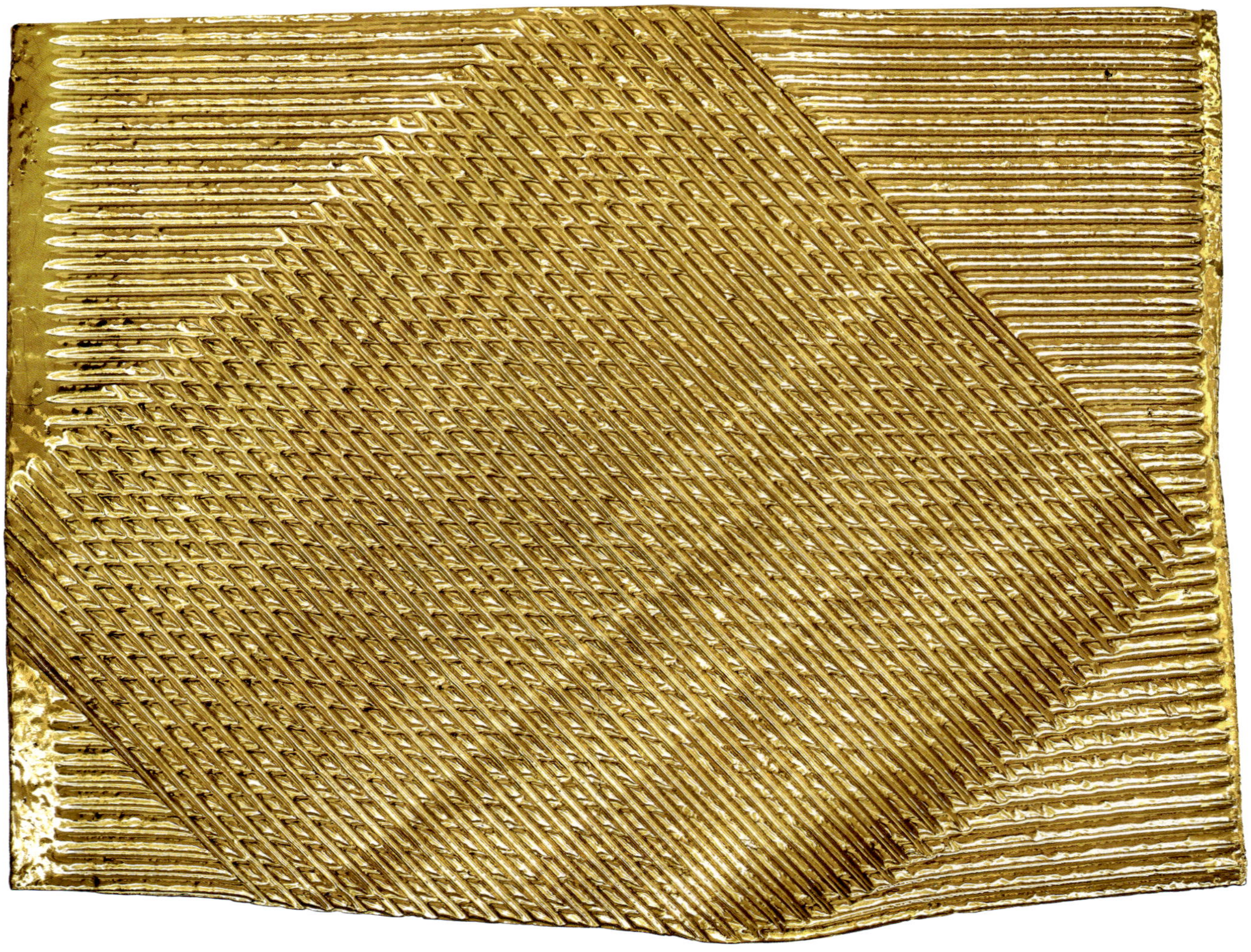

42 Heinz Mack
Ohne Titel
Signiert, datiert: »mack 17«
Keramik, glasiert, Poliergold
40 x 50 x 5 cm

42 Heinz Mack
Untitled
Signed, dated: "mack 17"
Ceramic, glazed, burnished gold
40 x 50 x 5 cm

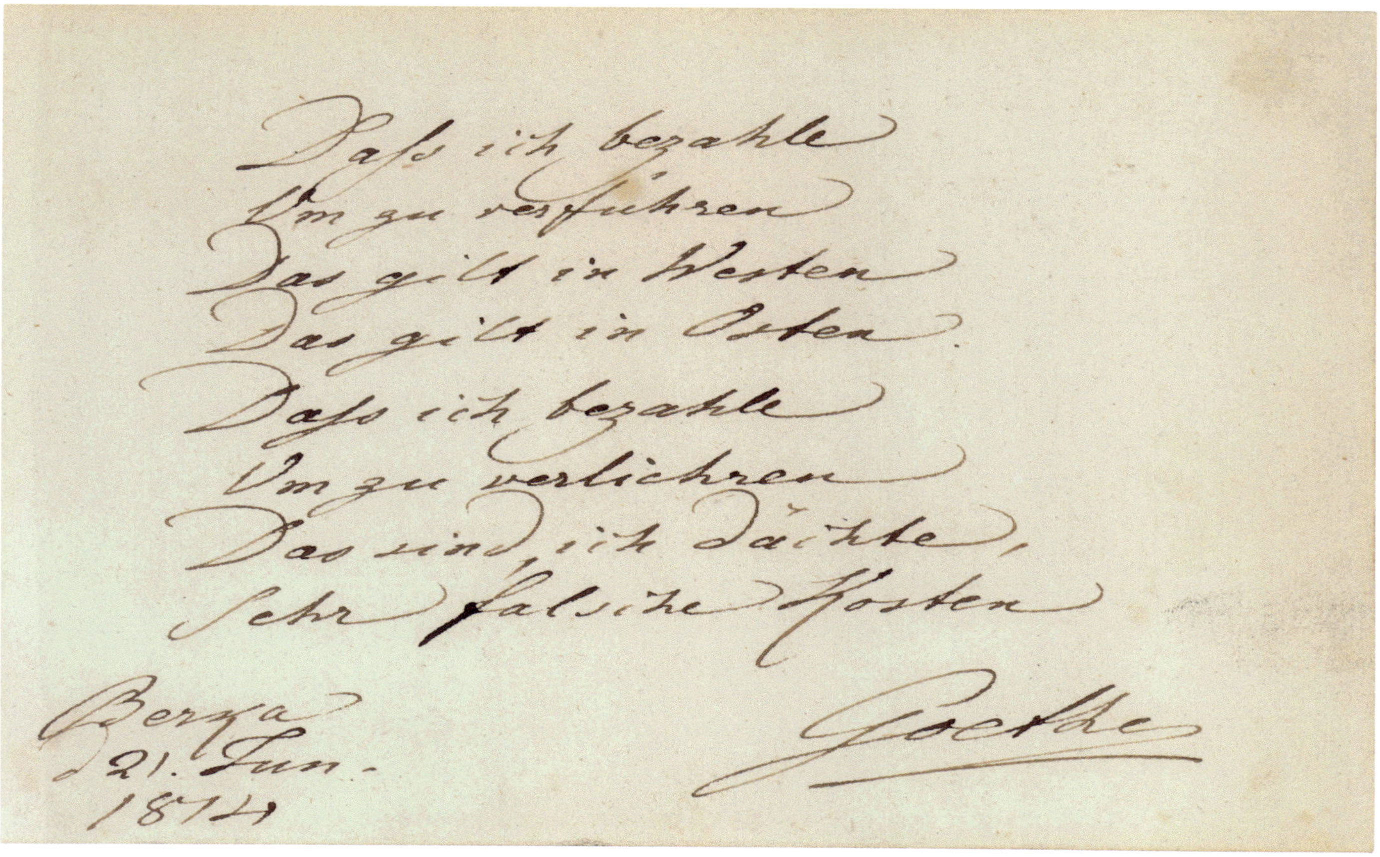

Dass ich bezahle
Um zu verführen
Das gilt in Westen
Das gilt in Osten;
Dass ich bezahle
Um zu verliehren
Das sind, ich dächte,
Sehr falsche Kosten

Berka
d 21. Jun.
1814

Goethe

43 Johann Wolfgang von Goethe
Eigenhändige Reinschrift seines Gedichtes:
»Dass ich bezahle / Um zu verführen […]«
Signiert: »Goethe«
Datiert: »Berka d 21. Jun. 1814«
1 Blatt mit Goldschnitt, 1 S. beschrieben
11,5 x 18,3 cm
Goethe-Museum Düsseldorf

Das Gedicht, das Westen und Osten aufeinander bezieht, ist während Goethes Aufenthalt im thüringischen Kurort Berka entstanden, als er die ersten von Hafis beeinflussten Verse schrieb. Goethe hat es nicht in den *Divan* aufgenommen. Es wurde von seinen Nachlassverwaltern in den Bestand der sogenannten *Zahmen Xenien* eingeordnet.

43 Johann Wolfgang von Goethe
Clean copy of Goethe's poem in his own hand:
"Dass ich bezahle / Um zu verführen …"
(That I pay / To seduce …)
Signed: "Goethe"
Dated: "Berka d 21. Jun. 1814"
1 sheet with gilt edging, 1 page written
11.5 x 18.3 cm
Goethe-Museum Düsseldorf

The poem, which relates to the relationship between East and West, was written during Goethe's stay in the spa town of Berka in Thuringia where he wrote the first verses influenced by Háfiz. Goethe did not include them in the *Divan*. The administrators of Goethe's estate added it into the collection known as the *Zahmen Xenien*.

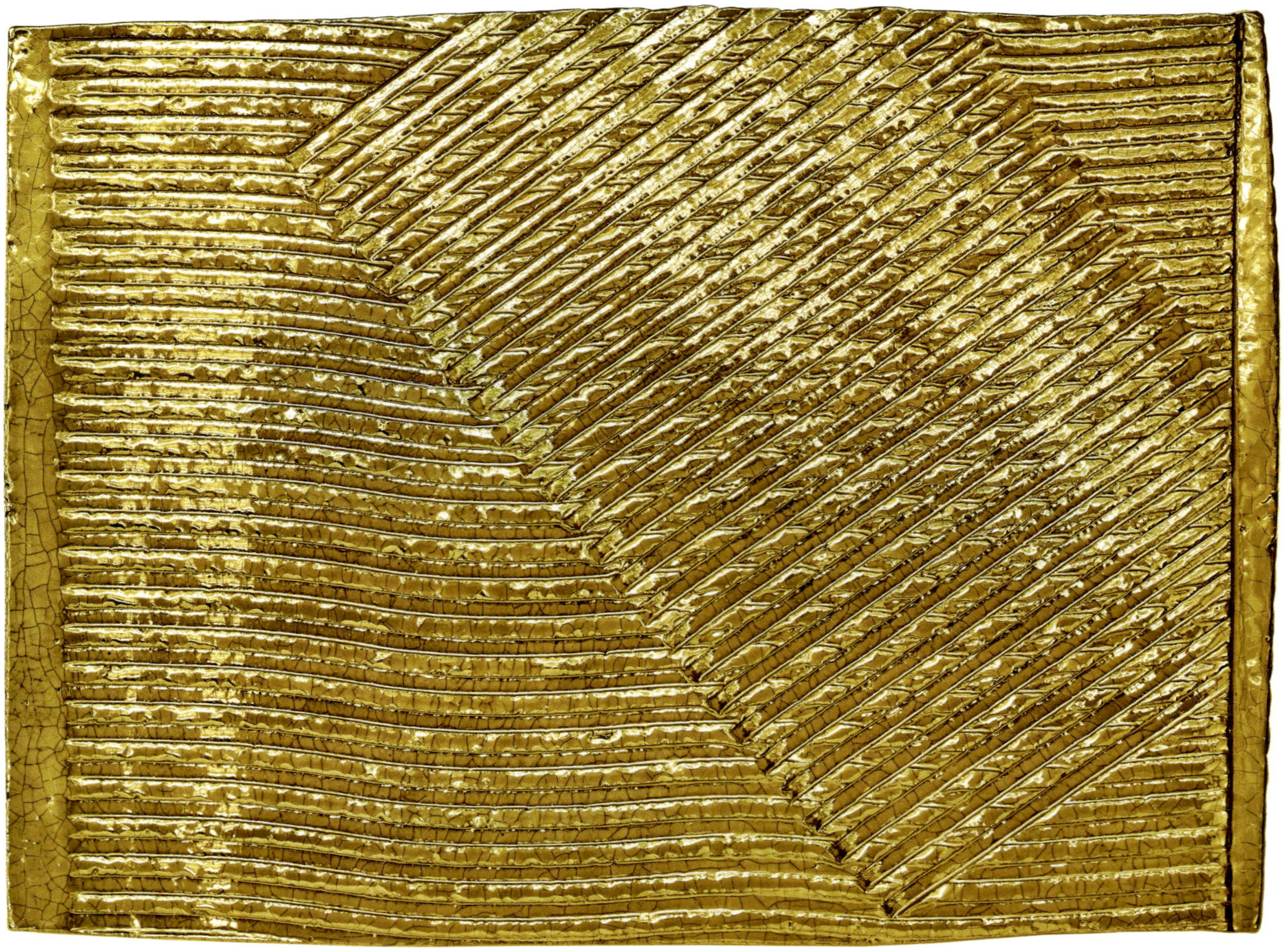

44 Heinz Mack
Ohne Titel
Signiert, datiert: »mack 17«
Keramik, glasiert, Poliergold
37 x 50 x 5 cm

44 Heinz Mack
Untitled
Signed, dated: "mack 17"
Ceramic, glazed, burnished gold
37 x 50 x 5 cm

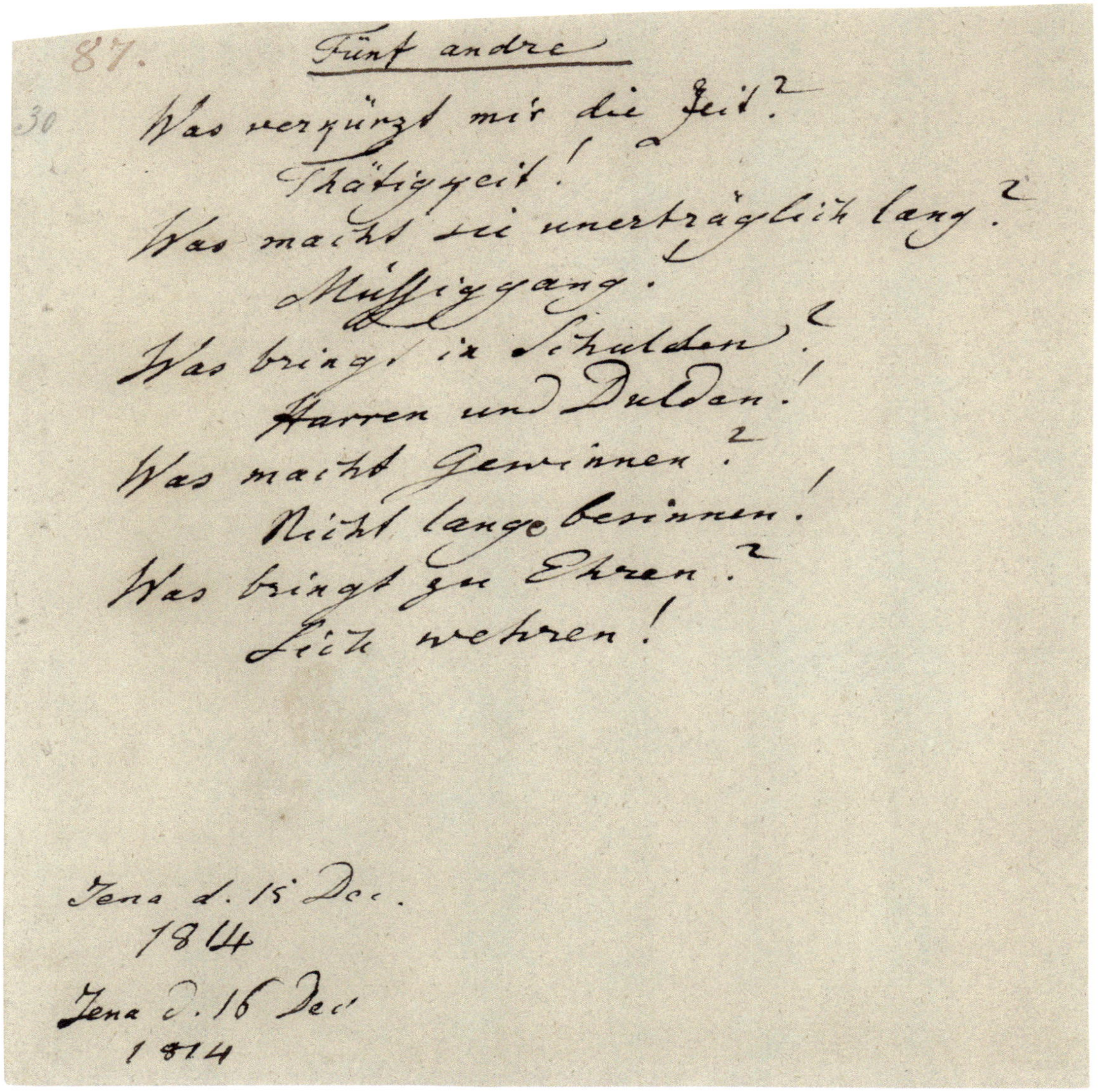

Fünf andre

Was verkürzt mir die Zeit?
Thätigkeit!
Was macht sie unerträglich lang?
Müssiggang.
Was bringt in Schulden?
Harren und Dulden!
Was macht Gewinnen?
Nicht lange besinnen!
Was bringt zu Ehren?
Sich wehren!

Jena d. 15 Dec.
1814
Jena d. 16 Dec
1814

45 Johann Wolfgang von Goethe
Eigenhändige Reinschrift seines Gedichtes:
Fünf andre
Datiert: »Jena d. 15 Dec. / 1814 /
Jena d. 16 Dec / 1814«
1 Blatt, 1 S. beschrieben
19,3–20,2 x 19,1 cm
Goethe-Museum Düsseldorf

Den Spruch dichtete Goethe als ›westliches‹ Gegenstück zu seinem Gedicht *Fünf Dinge,* das einen Tag zuvor entstanden war und zurückging auf eine Spruchweisheit des persischen Mystikers Ferid-eddin Attar (1119/1136–1190/1230) aus seinem *Pend-Nameh* oder *Buch der Ratschläge.* Die beiden im *West-oestlichen Divan* hintereinander abgedruckten Sprüche standen auf demselben Folioblatt, das 1853 von Eckermann zerschnitten wurde (deswegen die doppelte Datierung). Von 1888 bis 1970 galt die vorliegende zweite Hälfte des Blattes als verschollen.

45 Johann Wolfgang von Goethe
Clean copy of Goethe's poem in his own hand:
Fünf andre (Five Others)
Dated: "Jena d. 15 Dec. / 1814 /
Jena d. 16 Dec / 1814"
1 sheet, 1 page written
19.3–20.2 x 19.1 cm
Goethe-Museum Düsseldorf

Goethe wrote the poem as a 'Western' counterpart to his poem *Fünf Dinge* (Five Things), which had been written the day before and was based on a saying by the Persian mystic Ferid-eddin Attar (1119/1136–1190/1230) from his *Pend-Nameh* or *Book of Advice.* The two poems, printed one after the other, in the *West-East Divan* were on the same folio page, which Eckermann cut up in 1853 (hence the double dating). From 1888 to 1970 the second half of the sheet was deemed to have been lost.

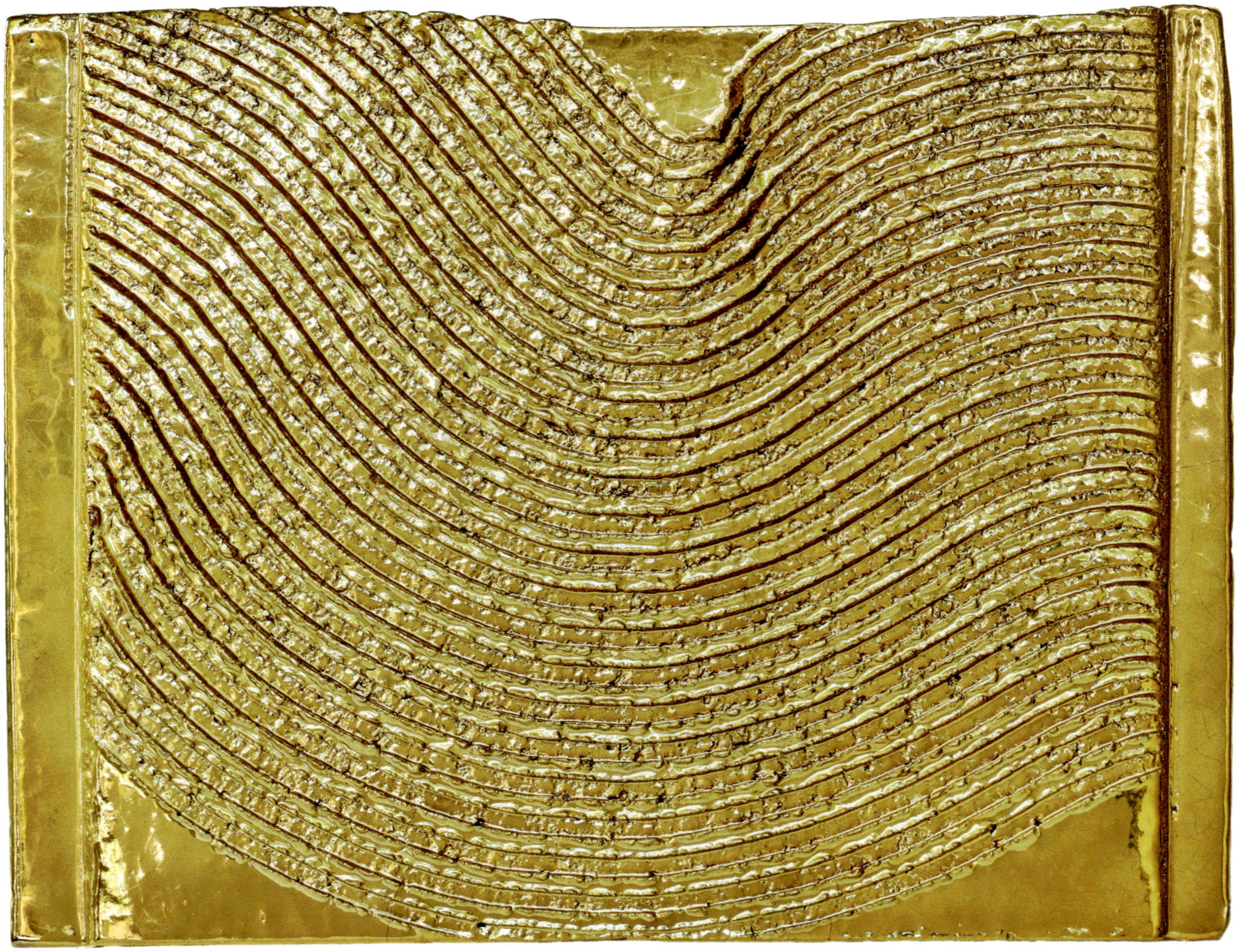

46 Heinz Mack
Ohne Titel
Signiert, datiert: »mack 17«
Keramik, glasiert, Poliergold
38 x 48 x 5 cm

46 Heinz Mack
Untitled
Signed, dated: "mack 17"
Ceramic, glazed, burnished gold
38 x 48 x 5 cm

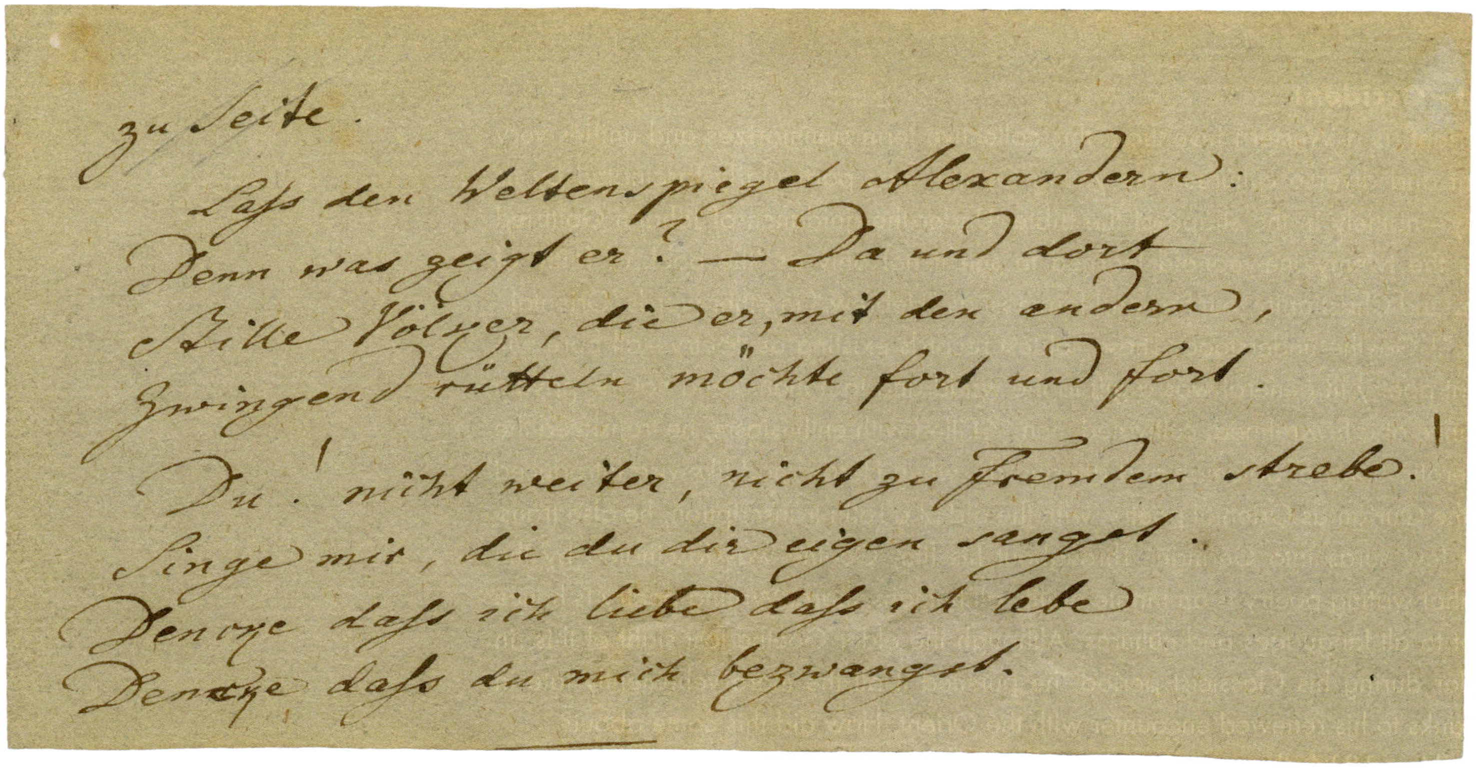
zu Seite.
Lass den Weltenspiegel Alexandern:
Denn was zeigt er? – Da und dort
Stille Völker, die er, mit den andern,
Zwingend rütteln möchte fort und fort.
Du! nicht weiter, nicht zu Fremdem strebe!
Singe mir, die du dir eigen sangst.
Denke dass ich liebe dass ich lebe
Denke dass du mich bezwangst.

47 Johann Wolfgang von Goethe
Eigenhändige Reinschrift seines Gedichtes:
»Lass den Weltenspiegel Alexandern […]«
Vermutlich Sommer 1818
1 Blatt, 1 S. beschrieben
10,2 x 19,5 cm
Goethe-Museum Düsseldorf

Goethe hat das Gedicht 1827 in die erweiterte Ausgabe seines *West-oestlichen Divans* eingerückt. Der orientalischen Sage nach besaß Alexander der Große einen Spiegel, der ihm alles in der Welt Geschehende zeigte. Goethe stellt mit Anknüpfung an Verse des Hafis dem Eroberer den Spiegel des liebenden Herzens entgegen, hier aus der Perspektive der sprechenden Suleika. Hafis hatte gedichtet: »Meiner Freundin Gemüth ist der weltenzeigende Spiegel« (nach der deutschen Übersetzung von Hammer, 1812, Bd. 1, S. 111). Die Handschrift war in ein Exemplar der *Werther*-Jubiläumsausgabe eingeklebt, das Goethe am 8. Dezember 1824 seinem Freund Zelter geschenkt hatte. Beides wurde 1971 vom Goethe-Museum Düsseldorf erworben.

47 Johann Wolfgang von Goethe
Clean copy of Goethe's poem in his own hand:
"Lass den Weltenspiegel Alexandern […]"
(World-mirror leave to Alexander …)
Probably summer 1818
1 sheet, 1 page written
10.2 x 19.5 cm
Goethe-Museum Düsseldorf

The poem was incorporated by Goethe into the extended edition of his *West-East Divan* in 1827. According to the Oriental legend, Alexander the Great possessed a mirror that showed him everything that transpired in the world. With reference to verses of Háfiz, Goethe confronts the conqueror with the mirror of the loving heart, here from the perspective of the speaking Zuleika. The autograph was pasted into a copy of the *Werther* jubilee edition that Goethe had gifted to his friend Zelter on 8 December 1824. Both the autograph and the book were acquired by the Goethe-Museum in 1971.

"I have namely thrown myself—with all my might and ability—toward the Orient ..." Johann Wolfgang von Goethe's 'Oriental' Inspiration

Anke Bosse

Orient—Occident

The 'Orient' is a Western invention: this collective term summarizes and unifies very different and diverse cultures. The young Goethe was particularly fascinated by its diversity—namely in the shape of the Bible. Under the guidance of Johann Gottfried Herder, the twenty-one-year-old learned to see it not only as 'the book of faith' of Judaism and Christianity, but first and foremost as "Hebrew," in other words 'Oriental,' "poetry."[1] Goethe understood: These "oldest records existing as poetry—all bore witness that poetry in general was a gift to the world and to nations, and not the private inheritance of a few refined, cultivated men."[2] Filled with enthusiasm, he translated the highly erotic *Song of Solomon* and afterwards, when Herder had likewise introduced him to the Qur'an as Oriental poetry, with the aid of a Latin transcription, he also translated a few suras into German. Throughout his life, Goethe was fascinated by the notion that writing poetry is an innate ability all humans share. Writing poetry is hence inherent to all languages and cultures. Although the older Goethe lost sight of this, in particular during his Classicist period, he pursued it all the more vehemently late in life—thanks to his renewed encounter with the Orient. How did this come about?

In May 1814, the poet, by now sixty-five years old, received two booklets—the *Diwan* by Muhammad Shams-ad-din, better known by the name of Háfiz—from his publisher, Johann Friedrich Cotta, that he could carry like talismans in his coat pocket and read at any time (ill. p. 356). The Viennese Orientalist Joseph von Hammer was the first to present a complete translation of the *Diwan* from Persian into German, just then published by Cotta. Háfiz was a fourteenth-century Persian poet. To this day, Iranians consider him to be one of their greatest poets, if not the greatest. Háfiz's poems impressed Goethe so vividly that he professed: "I found myself urgently impelled to productive efforts in order to assert my own genius in conflict with this new mighty force. ... [E]verything of kindred sense latent in me started up in emphatic response."[3]

Goethe's basic impulses were thus 'poetic competition' with an equal and a perception that is influenced by what is similar, by what is the own inside the other. Thus he evades irritation through total alterity. For Goethe, an antagonism or opposition of Orient and Occident dissolved itself in similarities. Háfiz's fundamental themes—love, wine, and song—fueled memories of his own lyrical beginnings, thereby simultaneously leading him to experience an exhilarating 'rejuvenation.' "Háfiz, with you, with you alone / I'd vie! Desire and painful moan — / We'll share them both, we twins have grown!" he wrote, concluding his poem *Unbounded* with the lines "My song, your fire's unique to you! You have united old and new."[4] Between May and December 1814, the

1 Johann Wolfgang von Goethe, *Truth and Poetry: From My Own Life,* trans. John Oxenford (London, 1848), p. 352. *Dichtung und Wahrheit,* FA, vol. I 14, p. 445.

2 Ibid. Cf. Katharina Mommsen, *Goethe and the Poets of Arabia,* trans. Michael M. Metzger (Rochester and New York, 2014) and idem, *Goethe und 1001 Nacht* (Frankfurt am Main, 1981).

3 Johann Wolfgang von Goethe, *Annals; or, Day and Year Papers* (London, 1884), pp. 416–17. *Tag- und Jahreshefte* 1815, FA, vol. I 17, pp. 259–60.

4 Johann Wolfgang von Goethe, *West-East Divan,* trans. Martin Bidney (New York, 2010), p. 23. *West-östlicher Divan,* FA, vol. I 3 I, p. 31.

»Ich habe mich nämlich, mit aller Gewalt und allem Vermögen, nach dem Orient geworfen ...«
Die Inspiration ›Orient‹ bei Johann Wolfgang von Goethe

Anke Bosse

Orient – Okzident

Der ›Orient‹ ist eine westliche Erfindung: Unter diesem Sammelbegriff werden sehr unterschiedliche und vielfältige Kulturen vereinheitlichend zusammengefasst. Es ist aber gerade die Vielfalt, die schon den jungen Goethe faszinierte – und zwar in Gestalt der Bibel. Sie lernte der 21-Jährige unter Anleitung Johann Gottfried Herders nicht nur als ›Glaubensbuch‹ des Juden- und Christentums zu sehen, sondern zu allererst als »hebräische« – sprich: ›orientalische‹ – »Dichtkunst«.[1] Goethe erkannte: Diese »ältesten Urkunden als Poesie, gaben das Zeugnis, daß die Dichtkunst überhaupt eine Welt- und Völkergabe sei, nicht ein Privaterbteil einiger feinen, gebildeten Männer«.[2] Begeistert übersetzte er das hoch erotische *Hohelied* und dann, als ihm Herder auch den Koran als orientalische Dichtung nahebrachte, mit Hilfe einer lateinischen Koran-Übertragung auch ein paar Suren ins Deutsche. Dichten als allen Menschen eingeborenes Können, das hat Goethe zeitlebens fasziniert. Dichten als ein somit Sprachen und Kulturen übergreifendes Können, das ist vor allem dem klassizistischen Goethe dann doch aus dem Blick gekommen – um beim alten Goethe umso vehementer in den Fokus zu geraten. Dank einer Wiederbegegnung mit dem ›Orient‹. Wie kam es dazu?

Im Mai 1814 erhielt der nunmehr 65-jährige Dichter von seinem Verleger Johann Friedrich Cotta zwei handliche Bändchen, jederzeit wie Talismane in der Rocktasche griff- und lesebereit bei sich zu führen: den *Diwan von Mohammed Schemsed-din Hafis* (Abb. S. 356). Der Wiener Orientalist Joseph von Hammer hatte den *Diwan* erstmals vollständig vom Persischen ins Deutsche übersetzt, Cotta ihn soeben publiziert. Hafis ist ein persischer Dichter des 14. Jahrhunderts, der noch heute den Iranern als einer ihrer größten, wenn nicht als ihr größter Dichter gilt – und seine Gedichte wirkten so »lebhaft« auf Goethe ein, dass er bekannte: »[...] ich mußte mich dagegen productiv verhalten, weil ich sonst vor der mächtigen Erscheinung nicht hätte bestehen können. [...] Alles was dem Stoff und dem Sinne nach bey mir Ähnliches verwahrt und gehegt worden, that sich hervor [...].«[3]

Goethes Grundimpulse waren also der ›dichterische Wettstreit‹ mit einem Gleichen und eine Wahrnehmung, die vom »Ähnlichen« – dem Eigenen im Anderen – affiziert ist und so einer Irritation durch totale Alterität von vornherein entkommt. Ein Gegenüber oder gar Gegeneinander von Orient und Okzident löste sich für Goethe im Ähnlichen auf. Denn Hafis' Grundthemen Liebe, Wein und Gesang befeuerten die Erinnerung an seine eigenen lyrischen Anfänge – und dadurch erlebte Goethe zugleich eine beglückende ›Verjüngung‹. »Hafis mit dir, mit dir allein / Will ich wetteifern! Lust und Pein / Sey uns den Zwillingen gemein!«, dichtete er – und schloss sein Gedicht *Unbegrenzt* mit den Versen »Nun töne Lied mit eignem Feuer! / Denn du bist älter, du bist neuer.«[4] Euphorisiert dichtete der 65-Jährige zwischen Mai und Dezember 1814 so viele großartige Gedichte wie nie zuvor: 53. Er sah

1 Johann Wolfgang von Goethe, *Dichtung und Wahrheit*, FA, Bd. I 14, S. 445.

2 Ebd. – Vgl. Katharina Mommsen, *Goethe und die arabische Welt*, Frankfurt am Main 1988 und dies., *Goethe und 1001 Nacht*, Frankfurt am Main 1981.

3 Johann Wolfgang von Goethe, *Tag- und Jahreshefte* 1815, FA, Bd. I 17, S. 259 f.

4 Johann Wolfgang von Goethe, *West-östlicher Divan*, FA, Bd. I 3 I, S. 31.

elated sixty-five-year-old wrote more great poems than ever before: fifty-three. He already begins to see them as an ensemble, a 'collection'—that is the translation of the Arabic-Persian word 'dīwān' and the title of the collection of poetry by his 'twin' Háfiz. These 53 poems constitute the nucleus of Goethe's *West-East Divan,* which with a total of 241 poems would ultimately become by far the most extensive ensemble of poems within Goethe's oeuvre. The *West-East Divan* was first published in 1819, two hundred years ago. It was epochal, not only because of the outstanding poems that skillfully oscillate between West and East, but also due to its program, which continues to be relevant to this day: forging links between the Orient and the Occident. The *West-East Divan* shows us that every attentive look into history reveals that these links always existed: Simply 'twins'. This is why Daniel Barenboim, Edward Said, and Bernd Kauffmann named their Israeli-Palestinian orchestra *West-Eastern Divan Orchestra* when it was founded in 1999. The *Divan* poet left a talismanic maxim to the orchestra and to all of those bridge builders among us, a helpful lucky charm:

Wer sich selbst und andre kennt	Who knows himself and others well
Wird auch hier erkennen:	No longer may ignore:
Orient und Occident	Occident and Orient dwell
Sind nicht mehr zu trennen.[5]	Separately no more.[6]

However, the condition of this connection is to know oneself and others—intensely and critically exploring one's self in the other as well as the other in one's self.

Goethe did just that two hundred years ago in the only way possible to him, as travelling was out of the question. He instantly began to extend his enthusiastic poetic competition with Háfiz and proceeded to intensely study more than one hundred books—among them Oriental poetry, travelogues, and scholarly books in German, French, English, Latin, and Italian—with a special focus on Persia and Arabia. He wrote: "I have namely thrown myself—with all my might and ability—toward the Orient … ."[7] His 'literary travels' persuasively confirmed his concept that writing poetry is a skill inherent in all languages and cultures. Goethe never ceased to point out in a (self-)critical manner the degree to which his knowledge of the Orient was imparted and that his experiences had been 'had from paper.' According to him, we are perpetually preconditioned by our language and our culture and hence always remain identifiable due to our "accent."[8] As a visually oriented person and a supporter of sensuous perception, he had to, and wanted to, go beyond what he had acquired through reading.

Ornament and Script

When the *West-East Divan* was first published in 1819, it was preceded by a frontispiece with engraving and title page that Goethe had meticulously supervised himself (ill. p. 358). His intention was to highlight the face-to-face and oscillation between East and West. He therefore sent the draftsman Carl Wilhelm Lieber to Weimar's court library, for which he had arranged the acquisition of an important collection of Oriental

5 Johann Wolfgang von Goethe, *West-östlicher Divan,* FA, vol. I 3 I, p. 614.
6 *West-East Divan* (see note 4), p. 167.
7 Translated from a letter to Christian Heinrich Schlosser, January 23, 1815, WA, vol. IV 25, p. 164.
8 *West-East Divan* (see note 4), p. 176.

sie bereits als ein Ensemble, eine ›Versammlung‹ an – das ist die deutsche Übersetzung von arabisch-persisch ›Dīwān‹ und der Titel der Gedichtsammlung seines ›Zwillings‹ Hafis. Diese 53 Gedichte sind der Nukleus für Goethes *West-östlichen Divan,* der mit schließlich 241 Gedichten das weitaus größte Gedichtensemble des goetheschen Gesamtwerks werden sollte. Der *West-östliche Divan* erschien erstmals 1819, vor 200 Jahren. Er hat Epoche gemacht, nicht nur wegen seiner herausragenden, gekonnt zwischen Westen und Osten oszillierenden Gedichte, sondern auch mit seinem Programm, das weit über ihn hinaus bis heute wirkt: Brücken zu schlagen zwischen Orient und Okzident, die – jeder aufmerksame Blick in die Geschichte zeigt es unumwunden – schon immer miteinander verbunden waren. ›Zwillinge‹ eben. Deshalb haben Daniel Barenboim, Edward Said und Bernd Kauffmann ihr 1999 gegründetes israelisch-palästinensisches Orchester *West-Eastern Divan Orchestra* genannt … Ihm und allen Brückenbauern unter uns hat der *Divan*-Dichter einen talismanischen Spruch, einen hilfreichen Glücksbringer, mit auf den Weg gegeben:

> Wer sich selbst und andre kennt
> Wird auch hier erkennen:
> Orient und Occident
> Sind nicht mehr zu trennen.[5]

Voraussetzung dieser Verbindung aber ist, sich selbst und andere zu kennen – also intensiv und kritisch zu erforschen, das Eigene im Anderen, das Andere im Eigenen kennenzulernen. Genau das hat Goethe vor 200 Jahren getan, auf die ihm mögliche Weise – Reisen kam nicht in Frage. Seinen begeisterten dichterischen Wettstreit mit Hafis erweiterte er punktum und studierte intensiv über hundert Bücher – orientalische Dichtungen, Reisebeschreibungen, Forschungsliteratur und vieles mehr auf Deutsch, Französisch, Englisch, Latein, Italienisch – mit besonderem Fokus auf Persien und Arabien. »Ich habe mich nämlich, mit aller Gewalt und allem Vermögen, nach dem Orient geworfen«[6], schrieb er – und konnte auf seinen ›Lektüre-Reisen‹ seine Vorstellung vom Dichten als ein Sprachen und Kulturen übergreifendes Können überzeugend bestätigt sehen. Wie sehr seine Orient-Kenntnisse aber vermittelt und seine Erfahrungen ›papieren‹ waren, wie sehr wir immer kulturell und sprachlich vorgeprägt sind und an unserem »Accent« erkennbar bleiben, das hat Goethe immer wieder (selbst-)kritisch zum Thema gemacht.[7] Als ›Augenmensch‹ aber, als Verfechter sinnlicher Anschauung musste und wollte er über das Angelesene hinausgehen.

Ornament und Schrift

Deshalb standen dem *West-östlichen Divan,* als er 1819 erstmals erschien, ein Titelkupfer und -blatt voran, die Goethe im Detail betreut hat (Abb. S. 358). Es ging ihm darum, das west-östliche Gegenüber und Oszillieren sinn- und augenfällig zu machen. Daher schickte er den Zeichner Carl Wilhelm Lieber in die Weimarer Hofbibliothek, für die er eine bedeutende Sammlung von orientalischen Handschriften und Büchern hatte anschaffen lassen. Denn »man muß« – so Goethe – »dergleichen Handschriften wenigstens sehen, wenn man sie auch nicht lesen kann, um sich einen Begriff von der orientalischen Poesie und Literatur zu machen«.[8] Die Ornamentik zweier dieser handschriftlich verfassten Bücher hat Lieber zu

5 Ebd., S. 614.
6 Brief an Christian Heinrich Schlosser vom 23. Januar 1815, WA, Bd. IV 25, S. 164.
7 Johann Wolfgang von *Goethe, West-östlicher Divan,* FA, Bd. I 3 I, S. 139.

manuscripts and books. According to Goethe, "one must at least see manuscripts like that, even if we cannot read them, in order to be able to get a notion of Oriental poetry and literature."[9] The ornamentation of two handwritten books inspired Lieber to create a design that Goethe selected as a reference for the *Divan* frontispiece.[10] For the engraving in Arabic script he hired the Jena-based Orientalist Johann Gottfried Ludwig Kosegarten, requesting him to translate "West-East Divan" back into Arabic: "The Eastern Divan by the Western Author." Face to the 'Oriental' frontispiece Goethe placed a Western title page with the title *West-East Divan* in Gothic type. This title with the word "Divan" is in turn borrowed from the Persian-Arabic. The frontispiece and title page thus manifest an East-West face-to-face, a mirror inverted "West-East," reflecting the dialogical approach of a subtle back and forth from East to West, from West to East, which has a programmatic function for the entire *West-East Divan*. In its complexity, Goethe's *Divan* is a clear contrast to the cliché of Orient that began to flourish and to be perpetuated in late-eighteenth-century Europe.[11] Not least because of its abstraction and repetition—typical for Oriental ornamentation—the *Divan* frontispiece inspired Heinz Mack to mirror it in his prints and pictures that were shown in 1999 at Düsseldorf's Goethe-Museum.[12]

Yet what fascinated Goethe much more than Oriental ornamentation was the Arabic script—it is with good reason that it takes center stage in the engraving of the frontispiece. To Goethe this script graphically epitomizes Oriental cultures. He attempted to experience them directly and sensuously and to emulate them in order to gain a "more lively view"[13] of the Orient. In early 1815, Goethe began to copy the mysterious letters from Oriental books. In the fall of 1815, under the guidance of Heinrich Eberhard Paulus, an Orientalist from Heidelberg, he made an attempt at individual Arabic and Persian words in Arabic script, among them the name "Zuleika."[14] What is important is that Goethe never mastered the Arabic language, nor the meanings of the linguistic signs. And this was precisely the basis for his euphoric reaction regarding the purely aesthetic materiality of Arabic letters, in which he suspected elements of sensuous-transcendental character, as Islamic tradition ascribes them to calligraphy: "It won't be long and I shall begin to learn Arabic, at least … I want to practice writing the letters … . There is perhaps no other language that so primordially combines spirit, word, and scripture."[15] The union of the sensuous and the transcendent in the language as conveyed by the Arabic script suggest that Goethe was aware of its 'magical presence' as a manifestation of its 'powerfulness.'[16] This is precisely what the Arabic title of the *West-East Divan* cannot say to those who do not know Arabic, but it can show them.

Ciphers

All writing has always had the task to bridge distance and absence. In the presence of someone, we do not write but speak. However, should one not want a third party to listen in or to read along, a secret code is suggested: for instance, two individuals exchange ciphers that refer exclusively to an agreed-on book. In the summer of 1814, Goethe met Marianne Jung, thirty-five years his junior, who was engaged to be married

9 Translated from a letter to Christian Gottlob von Voigt, January 10, 1815, WA, vol. IV 25, p. 141.
10 Documented in Anke Bosse, "Magische Präsenz – zur Funktion von Schrift und Ornament in Goethes "West-östlichem Divan," *Arcadia. Zeitschrift für Allgemeine und Vergleichende Literaturwissenschaft* 33, no. 2 (1998), pp. 314–36, and idem, *"Meine Schatzkammer füllt sich täglich …" – Die Nachlaßstücke zu Goethes 'West-östlichem Divan.' Dokumentation. Kommentar. Entstehungsgeschichte,* 2 vols. (Göttingen, 1999), pp. 843–44 and pp. 931–32.
11 Cf. Hendrick Birus, "Goethes imaginativer Orientalismus," *Jahrbuch des Freien Deutschen Hochstifts* (1992), pp. 107–28.
12 Heinz Mack, *Buch der Bilder zum West-östlichen Divan von Johann Wolfgang von Goethe* (Düsseldorf, 1999). Cf. illustration on p. 359 in the present catalogue.
13 Translated from a letter to Schlosser (see note 7).
14 Bosse 1999 (see note 10), pp. 607–14.
15 Translated from a letter to Schlosser (see note 7).
16 Bosse 1998 (see note 10).

einem Entwurf inspiriert, den Goethe zur Vorlage für das *Divan*-Titelkupfer bestimmte.[9] Für den Titel in arabischer Schrift hat er den Jenaer Orientalisten Johann Gottfried Ludwig Kosegarten engagiert mit der Bitte, »West-östlicher Divan« ins Arabische zurückzuübersetzen: »Der östliche Diwan des westlichen Verfassers«. Dem ›orientalischen‹ Titelkupfer steht ein westliches Titelblatt gegenüber mit dem Titel *West-östlicher Divan* in ›deutscher‹ Schrift, nämlich in Fraktur. Dieser Titel ist aber seinerseits mit dem Wort »Divan« aus dem Persisch-Arabischen entlehnt. Auf diese Weise veranschaulichen Titelkupfer und -blatt augen- und sinnfällig ein ost-westliches Gegenüber, gegengleich zu »west-östlich«. Titelkupfer und -blatt realisieren das dialogische Verfahren des subtilen Hin und Her von Ost nach West, von West nach Ost, das für den gesamten *West-östlichen Divan* Programmfunktion hat. In dieser Komplexität setzt sich Goethes *Divan* deutlich von der seit Ende des 18. Jahrhunderts in Europa boomenden, Klischees perpetuierenden Orient-Mode ab.[10] Nicht zuletzt hat das *Divan*-Titelkupfer, das in seiner Abstraktheit und Repetition repräsentativ für orientalische Ornamentik ist, Heinz Mack dazu inspiriert, sie in seinen Grafiken und Bildern zu spiegeln, die 1999 im Goethe-Museum Düsseldorf gezeigt wurden.[11]

Doch weitaus mehr noch als von orientalischer Ornamentik war Goethe von der arabischen Schrift begeistert – nicht umsonst steht sie zentral im Titelkupfer. Besonders in ihr verkörperten sich ihm konkret-anschaulich die orientalischen Kulturen. Er versuchte, sie sinnlich-unmittelbar zu erfahren, sie nachzuahmen, um ein »lebendigeres Ansehen«[12] des Orients zu gewinnen. Anfang 1815 begann Goethe, aus orientalistischen Büchern die geheimnisvollen Buchstaben abzumalen, und im Herbst 1815 übte er unter Anleitung des Heidelberger Orientalisten Heinrich Eberhard Paulus einzelne arabische und persische Wörter in arabischer Schrift, darunter auch den Namen »Suleika«.[13] Entscheidend ist, dass Goethe die arabische Sprache nie erlernte, also die Bedeutungen des sprachlichen Zeichens, und dass dies gerade die Voraussetzung dafür war, dass er so euphorisch auf die pure ästhetische Materialität arabischer Buchstaben reagieren und ihren sinnlich-übersinnlichen Charakter erahnen konnte, wie ihn die islamische Tradition der Kalligraphie zuschreibt: »Wenig fehlt, daß ich noch arabisch lerne, wenigstens [...] will ich mich in den Schreibezügen üben [...]. In keiner Sprache ist vielleicht Geist, Wort und Schrift so uranfänglich zusammengekörpert.«[14] Das Ineins von Sinnlichem und Übersinnlichem in der Sprache, vermittelt in der arabischen Schrift, lässt vermuten, dass Goethe sich ihrer ›magischen Präsenz‹ als Manifestation ihrer ›Mächtigkeit‹ bewusst war.[15] Genau dies kann der arabische Titel des *West-östlichen Divans* all jenen, die kein Arabisch können, nicht sagen – aber er kann es ihnen zeigen.

Chiffren

Jede Schrift hat schon immer die Aufgabe, Distanz und Absenz zu überbrücken. Wer ein präsentes Gegenüber hat, schreibt nicht, sondern spricht. Wenn aber kein Dritter mithören und auch nicht mitlesen soll, dann empfiehlt sich die Geheimschrift – wie zum Beispiel der Austausch von Chiffren, die sich auf ein exklusiv zu zweit verabredetes Buch beziehen. Im Sommer 1814 hatte Goethe die 35 Jahre jüngere Marianne Jung kennengelernt, die im Herbst den Frankfurter Bankier von Willemer heiraten sollte. Sie reagierte überaus aufge-

8 Brief an Christian Gottlob von Voigt vom 10. Januar 1815, WA, Bd. IV 25, S. 141.
9 Nachgewiesen in: Anke Bosse, »Magische Präsenz – zur Funktion von Schrift und Ornament in Goethes *West-östlichem Divan*«, in: *Arcadia. Zeitschrift für Allgemeine und vergleichende Literaturwissenschaft* 33 (1998), H. 2, S. 314–336 und dies.: *»Meine Schatzkammer füllt sich täglich ...«. Die Nachlaßstücke zu Goethes »West-östlichem Divan«. Dokumentation. Kommentar. Entstehungsgeschichte,* 2 Bde., Göttingen 1999, S. 841 f. und 931 f.
10 Vgl. Hendrik Birus, »Goethes imaginativer Orientalismus«, in: *Jahrbuch des Freien Deutschen Hochstifts* 1992, S. 107–128.
11 Heinz Mack, *Ein Buch der Bilder zum West-östlichen Divan von Johann Wolfgang v. Goethe,* Mönchengladbach 1999. Vgl. die Abbildung im vorliegenden Katalog S. 359.
12 Brief an Schlosser (wie Anm. 6).
13 Bosse 1999 (wie Anm. 9), S. 607–614.
14 Brief an Schlosser (wie Anm. 6), S. 165.
15 Bosse 1998 (wie Anm. 9).

to Frankfurt-based banker von Willemer in the fall. She reacted very astutely to his 'Orientalizing,' and by the time they met again in the summer and fall of 1815, a love flared up between them, intensifying Goethe's 'rejuvenation,' prompted by Oriental poetry and—even more—by his own poeticizing. Inspired by Háfiz, the poetic celebration of love now unexpectedly corresponded with Goethe's own experience, and vice versa. Virtually like an eruption, he wrote in excess thirty Orientalizing love poems, among them numerous famous poems staging the dialogue between the poet Hatem and his lover, Zuleika, who replies by writing poetry. The fact that poetry and real love intermingled to this degree was due to Marianne: she co-wrote in 'Oriental manner' based on a secret exchange of letters. In September 1815, Goethe sent a cipher letter to her with the heading "Zuleika," written in Arabic script, as he had recently practiced it with Paulus (ill. p. 363).[17] The ciphers refer, how could it be otherwise, to Háfiz's *Diwan,* which Goethe had given to Marianne. Upon deciphering them, they immediately take us to the center of their relationship: "While love is light at first / Difficulties are to ensue." This cipher letter was not simply the beginning of a clandestine love correspondence circumventing Marianne's husband; it also initiated an exchange of poems. Marianne von Willemer confirmed most beautifully that "poetry in general was a gift to the world and to nations, and not the private inheritance of a few refined, cultivated men."[18] She was inspired to compose her own poetry, which Goethe then proceeded to include in his *Divan* as Zuleika poems. She is therefore the only woman in Goethe's life who meets him eye to eye: "What's the meaning of the stirring? / What's the east wind heralding? — / With its wings refreshing, whirring, / Cooling, soothing heart-wounds' sting"[19] (ill. pp. 382–85).

From the East ...

Marianne's poem is closely based on a Háfiz motif when she stages the east wind as a messenger whose news must first be deciphered. Is it cheerful news? A love note? In the dialogues between Hatem and Zuleika in the *Divan,* a steady flow of messages comes from the East—from the Orient—that first have to be deciphered—or remain up in the air as queries, like in the famous poem *Ginkgo Biloba:*

Dieses Baum's Blatt, der von Osten Meinem Garten anvertraut, Giebt geheimen Sinn zu kosten, Wie's den Wissenden erbaut.	Here's a leaf the East, with favor, To my garden would confide — Tree with meanings we may savor, To the wise a vital guide.
Ist es Ein lebendig Wesen? Das sich in sich selbst getrennt, Sind es zwey? Die sich erlesen, Daß man sie als eines kennt.	Do we spy one living being That had split itself in two? It is two things we are seeing That we yet united view?
Solche Frage zu erwiedern Fand ich wohl den rechten Sinn; Fühlst du nicht an meinen Liedern Daß ich Eins und doppelt bin?[20]	To this query quite revealing I have found the right reply: Won't my singing give the feeling That both two and one am I?[21]

17 Bosse 1999 (see note 10), pp. 615–17.
18 *Truth and Poetry* (see note 1), 352 *Dichtung und Wahrheit,* FA, vol. I 14, p. 445.
19 *West-East Divan* (see note 4), p. 111. *West-östlicher Divan,* FA I 3.1, pp. 93–94. Cf. Anke Bosse, "Chiffernbriefe," in Anne Bohnenkamp and Hendrik Birus, eds., *Denn das Leben ist die Liebe ... Marianne von Willemer und Goethe im Spiegel des "West-östlichen Divans"* (Frankfurt am Main, 2014), pp. 98–99.
20 *West-östlicher Divan,* FA, vol. I 3.1, pp. 78–79.
21 *West-East Divan* (see note 4), pp. 92–93.

weckt auf Goethes ›Orientalisieren‹, und spätestens beim Wiedersehen im Sommer und Herbst 1815 flammte zwischen ihnen eine Liebe auf, die die ›Verjüngung‹ Goethes durch orientalische Poesie und eigenes Dichten nun noch steigerte. Die poetische Feier der Liebe, zu der ihn Hafis inspiriert hatte, entsprach nun unverhofft dem eigenen Erleben – und umgekehrt. Geradezu eruptiv entstanden mehr als 30 orientalisierende Liebesgedichte, darunter viele berühmte, die den Dialog zwischen Hatem, dem Dichter, und Suleika, der Geliebten und antwortend Dichtenden, inszenieren. Denn dass sich Poesie und reale Liebe so miteinander verweben konnten, lag daran, dass Marianne ›orientalisierend‹ mitdichtete – gründend auf einer Geheimkorrespondenz. Im September 1815 nämlich sandte Goethe Marianne einen Chiffrenbrief, den er mit »Suleika« überschrieb – in arabischer Schrift, wie er es kurz zuvor mit Paulus geübt hatte (Abb. S. 363).[16] Die Chiffren beziehen sich, wie kann es anders sein, auf Hafis' *Diwan,* den Goethe Marianne geschenkt hatte. Dechiffriert man sie, so treffen schon die ersten ins Zentrum ihrer Beziehung: »Leicht' ist die Lieb' im Anfang / Es folgen aber Schwierigkeiten.« Mit diesem Chiffrenbrief begann nicht nur eine klandestine Liebeskorrespondenz, vorbei am Gatten Willemer. Es hob nun auch ein Gegentausch von Gedichten an. Marianne von Willemer bestätigte nun aufs Schönste, »daß die Dichtkunst überhaupt eine Welt- und Völkergabe« ist, »nicht ein Privaterbteil einiger feinen, gebildeten Männer«[17]: Sie ließ sich zu eigenen Gedichten inspirieren, die Goethe dann in seinen *Divan* als Suleika-Gedichte aufnahm. Damit ist sie die einzige unter den Frauen in Goethes Leben, die ihm von Gleich zu Gleich als Dichterin entgegentritt: »Was bedeutet die Bewegung? / Bringt der Ost mir frohe Kunde? / Seiner Schwingen frische Regung / Kühlt des Herzens tiefe Wunde.«[18] (Abb. S. 382–385.)

Von Osten …

Mariannes Gedicht lehnt sich eng an ein Hafis-Motiv an, indem es den Ostwind als Boten inszeniert, dessen Nachricht aber erst dechiffriert werden muss. Ist es eine frohe Kunde? Eine Liebesnachricht? Von Osten – aus dem Orient – kommen in den Hatem-Suleika-Dialogen des *Divans* immer wieder Botschaften, die erst gedeutet werden müssen – oder als Frage in der Schwebe bleiben. So auch in dem berühmten Gedicht *Ginkgo biloba:*

> Dieses Baum's Blatt, der von Osten
> Meinem Garten anvertraut,
> Giebt geheimen Sinn zu kosten,
> Wie's den Wissenden erbaut.
>
> Ist es Ein lebendig Wesen?
> Das sich in sich selbst getrennt,
> Sind es zwey? Die sich erlesen,
> Daß man sie als eines kennt.
>
> Solche Frage zu erwiedern
> Fand ich wohl den rechten Sinn;
> Fühlst du nicht an meinen Liedern
> Daß ich Eins und doppelt bin?[19]

16 Bosse 1999 (wie Anm. 9), S. 615–617.
17 *Dichtung und Wahrheit,* FA, Bd. I 14, S. 445.
18 Goethe, *West-östlicher Divan* (wie Anm. 3), S. 93 f. Vgl. Anke Bosse, »Chiffernbriefe«, in: *Denn das Leben ist die Liebe … Marianne von Willemer und Goethe im Spiegel des »West-östlichen Divans«,* Hrsg. von Hendrik Birus u. a. Ausst.-Kat. Frankfurter Goethe-Haus/Freies Deutsches Hochstift, Frankfurt am Main 2014, S. 98 f.
19 Goethe, *West-östlicher Divan* (wie Anm. 3), S. 78 f.

The poem's 'vehicle' is the leaf of the East Asian ginkgo tree, which during Goethe's time had long since arrived in the West. He decoratively applied two of these leaves to the clean copy of his poem (ill. p. 41). The cascade of questions in stave two emphasizes that it is unclear whether it is one leaf that splits in two ("in sich selbst getrennt") or two leaves that choose one another ("sich erlesen") to grow together at their stems so that they appear as one leaf. The poem maintains that a "geheimer Sinn" underlies the leaves' mono- or dimorphism that only the "Wissenden" can recognize—an alliance that excludes others. Since this poem is placed amidst the Hatem-Zuleika love dialogues, it is obvious that its "geheimer Sinn" lies in the oneness of two lovers, the brief melding during the sexual act, and the renewed separation into two creatures after the sexual act. They are the "Wissenden." But the third stave steers the interpretation in a poetological direction. Thanks to a rhetorical question, the "du" is virtually urged to recognize in the "Liedern" of the poet-ego its simultaneous oneness and twoness: "Fühlst du nicht an meinen Liedern / Daß ich Eins und doppelt bin?" (Won't my singing give the feeling / That both two and one am I?) This seems even more mysterious at first. It only becomes clear when considering various "songs" instead of just looking at the poem *Ginkgo Biloba* in its beautiful clean copy and positioning the latter within the Hatem-Zuleika dialogues in the *West-East Divan*. Whereas Hatem and Zuleika intertwine in the back and forth of these "songs," in the eye of the reader they separate again after each new "song" with headings for "Hatem" or "Zuleika" as speaker: because the "du" in "Fühlst du nicht an meinen Liedern" addresses us, the readers, directly. Intertwining, separating, intertwining, separating—then occurring in the act of reading.

Light and Fire

The interleaving of East-West motifs in the *West-East Divan* is endless.[22] The present exhibition, *Acts of Light—Mack & Goethe,* is a welcome opportunity to take a brief look at the motif complex of light and fire. Competing with Háfiz, Goethe wrote "My song, your fire's unique to you!"[23] He referred to poetic furor and enthusiasm as extolled since antiquity and at the same time the autonomy of the literary genius as he had celebrated it during his Sturm und Drang years. To Goethe, the pre-Islamic religion of the Parsi, at the center of which stood sunlight and cleansing fire, respect for and responsiveness to nature, was a congenial Oriental counterpart to his pantheism. He not only expounded light as a condition for the play of spectral colors in his theory of colors, he also orchestrated it in his *Divan* poems. We could pursue so many traces of fire and light, yet we are following a solitary trace, when, in the fall of 1815, Hatem-Goethe and Zuleika-Marianne had to separate:[24]

Wie sollt' ich heiter bleiben	How to remain serene,
Entfernt von Tag und Licht?	Far from the day and light?
Nun aber will ich schreiben	Don't want to drink. To dream,
Und trinken mag ich nicht.	Maybe, and try to write …

22 Cf. Christa Dill, *Wörterbuch zu Goethes "West-östlichem Divan"* (Tübingen, 1987).
23 "Unbounded," in *East-West Divan* (see note 4).
23. *West-östlicher Divan,* FA, vol. I 3.1, p. 31.
24 Bosse 1999 (see note 10), pp. 642–46.

›Aufhänger‹ des Gedichts ist das Blatt des ostasiatischen Ginkgo-Baums, den es in der Goethe-Zeit längst gen Westen verschlagen hatte. Zwei dieser Blätter hat Goethe schmückend auf seine Gedichtreinschrift appliziert (Abb. S. 41). Wie die Fragenkaskade der zweiten Strophe deutlich macht, ist unklar, ob es jeweils ein Blatt ist, dass sich aufspaltet (»in sich selbst getrennt«) oder ob es zwei Blätter sind, die »sich erlesen«, sich erwählen, und an der Wurzel so zusammenwachsen, dass sie als ein Blatt erscheinen. Das Gedicht behauptet, dass hinter dieser Ein- oder Zweigestaltigkeit ein »geheimer Sinn« stehe, den nur die »Wissenden« erkennen können – eine Gemeinschaft, die andere ausschließt. Da das Gedicht mitten in die Liebesdialoge zwischen Hatem und Suleika platziert ist, liegt es nahe, den »geheimen Sinn« in der Vereinigung zweier Liebender zu sehen, der kurzen Verschmelzung im Liebesakt und dem Wiederauseinandertreten in zwei Wesen danach. Sie sind die »Wissenden«. Doch die dritte Strophe lenkt diese Deutung in eine poetologische Richtung. Denn mit einer rhetorischen Frage wird das »Du« geradezu gedrängt, an den »Liedern« des Dichter-Ichs dessen gleichzeitige Einheit und Zweiheit zwingend zu erkennen: »Fühlst du nicht an meinen Liedern / Daß ich Eins und doppelt bin?« Das erscheint zunächst einmal noch rätselhafter. Das klärt sich nur, wenn man eben mehrere »Lieder« im Blick hat und das Gedicht *Ginkgo biloba* nicht nur isoliert in schöner Reinschrift liest, sondern in seiner Position innerhalb der Hatem-Suleika-Dialoge im *West-östlichen Divan*. Im Hin und Her dieser »Lieder« verkreuzen sich Hatem und Suleika und treten doch mit jedem neuen »Lied«, über dem »Hatem« oder »Suleika« als Sprecher oder Sprecherin steht, wieder auseinander – im Auge der Leserin, des Lesers. Denn »Fühlst du nicht an meinen Liedern« wendet sich im »du« auch an uns, die Leserin, den Leser. Verkreuzen, Auseinandertreten, Verkreuzen, Auseinandertreten … geschehen dann in unserem Leseakt.

Licht und Feuer

Unendlich sind die ost-westlichen Motiv-Verschränkungen im *West-östlichen Divan*.[20] Die aktuelle Ausstellung *Taten des Lichts – Mack & Goethe* ist ein willkommener Anlass, um den Motivkomplex des Lichts und des Feuers kurz in den Blick zu nehmen. Im Wetteifer mit Hafis hatte Goethe gedichtet »Nun töne Lied mit eignem Feuer!«[21] und damit den poetischen Furor und Enthusiasmus gemeint, wie ihn schon die Antike besang, und zugleich die Eigenständigkeit des dichterischen Genies, wie er sie in seiner Sturm-und-Drang-Zeit feierte. In der vorislamischen Religion der Parsen, in deren Mittelpunkt das Licht der Sonne und das reinigende Feuer, der Respekt vor der und das Eingehen in die Natur standen, fand Goethe ein kongeniales orientalisches Gegenüber zu seinem Pantheismus. Das Licht als Voraussetzung für das Spiel der Spektralfarben hat er nicht nur in seinen Schriften zur Farbenlehre erläutert, sondern auch in *Divan*-Gedichten inszeniert. So vielen Feuer- und Lichtspuren könnten wir nachgehen, doch wir folgen einer einzigen Spur, die entstand, als sich Hatem-Goethe und Suleika-Marianne im Herbst 1815 trennen mussten:[22]

Wie sollt' ich heiter bleiben
Entfernt von Tag und Licht?
Nun aber will ich schreiben
Und trinken mag ich nicht.

20 Vgl. Christa Dill, *Wörterbuch zu Goethes West-östlichem Divan*, Tübingen 1987.
21 Goethe, *West-östlicher Divan* (wie Anm. 3), S. 31.
22 Bosse 1999 (wie Anm. 9), S. 642–646.

Wenn sie mich an sich lockte War Rede nicht im Brauch, Und wie die Zunge stockte So stockt die Feder auch.	When she enthralled my will, Nothing remained to say. But as the tongue was still, Mute is my pen today.
Nur zu! geliebter Schenke, Den Becher fülle still. Ich sage nur: Gedenke! Schon weiß man was ich will.[25]	So — go ahead, my dear, The goblet quickly fill! Keep me in mind, you hear? It's well you know my will.[26]

Goethe's drafts for this poem are kept here at the Goethe-Museum Düsseldorf (ill. pp. 388–89). As in Háfiz's case, "Tag und Licht" stand for the lover. This poem, too, begins with a rhetorical question: "Entfernt" from the lover, the I naturally cannot "heiter bleiben." Writing is introduced as a substitute intended to bridge distance and separation, for which, after all, script was invented. However, the I fails to write because his "Feder" "stockt." The I recalls that being together with the loved one engendered a closeness that made conversation superfluous. How superfluous, then, is it to write... The third stave closely follows Háfiz, who very often set his poems in (wine) taverns as a resting place for the poet and staged his homoerotic closeness to the young innkeeper—a provocation in Islamic Persia that led to all manner of strange reinterpretations. Goethe's poem clearly takes us to a wine tavern, but the young loved "Schenke" is only there to fill the goblet. At least the wine gives the I back the ability to think of his lover, albeit silently, beyond speech and writing. On the other hand, the I turns to us, the readers: "Schon weiß man was ich will." We are "man." We are now supposed to know what the I wants. The lover? The memory of the lover? Writing about the lover? This is left in question and up to us to reflect upon.

Orient—Occident Once More

This suspense that occurs in a *Divan* poem and between *Divan* poems is the program of the *West-East Divan*. The oscillation not only takes place between West and East, East and West, Hatem-Zuleika, Zuleika-Hatem. It is supposed to go on ad infinitum. And there is only one place where it does, and can, take place: in us readers. In Goethe's case, the 'Orient' can therefore not be '*the* Orient.' Hence he has prepared it in us as a space of polyvocal resonance into which he has "woven his own poetry."[27] And each time we read the *West-East Divan*, this continues to have an effect. It is up to us.

25 *West-östlicher Divan*, FA, vol. I 3.1, p. 89.
26 *East-West Divan* (see note 4), pp. 105–06.
27 Translated from *West-östlicher Divan*, FA, vol. I 3.1, p. 549.

Wenn sie mich an sich lockte
War Rede nicht im Brauch,
Und wie die Zunge stockte
So stockt die Feder auch.

Nur zu! geliebter Schenke,
Den Becher fülle still.
Ich sage nur: Gedenke!
Schon weiß man was ich will.[23]

Goethes Entwürfe zu diesem Gedicht liegen hier im Goethe-Museum Düsseldorf (Abb. S. 388 f.). »Tag und Licht« stehen für die Geliebte – wie bei Hafis. Auch dieses Gedicht setzt mit einer rhetorischen Frage ein – denn »entfernt« von der Geliebten kann das Ich natürlich nicht »heiter bleiben«. Das Schreiben wird als Ersatzhandlung eingeführt, die die Entfernung und Trennung überbrücken soll – die Schrift ist ja erfunden worden, um Distanz und Absenz zu überbrücken. Doch die Feder »stockt«, das Schreiben scheitert. Denn das Ich erinnert sich daran, dass das Zusammensein mit der Geliebten eine Nähe erzeugte, die schon das Reden überflüssig machte. Wie überflüssig ist dann erst das Schreiben … Die dritte Strophe lehnt sich eng an Hafis an, der seine Gedichte sehr oft in die Szenerie einer (Wein-)Schenke als Einkehr des Dichters versetzte und dessen homoerotische Nähe zum jugendlichen Schenken inszenierte – eine Provokation im islamisierten Persien, die zu allerlei eigenartigen Umdeutungen führte. In Goethes Gedicht geht es klar in die Schenke, doch der junge »geliebte« Schenke ist nur dazu da, den Becher zu füllen. Der Wein gibt dem Ich immerhin wieder die Fähigkeit, der Geliebten zu gedenken, allerdings stillschweigend, jenseits von Rede und Schrift. Einerseits. Andererseits wendet sich das Ich mit »Schon weiß man was ich will« an uns, die Leserinnen und Leser. Wir sind »man«. Jetzt sollen wir wissen, was das Ich will. Die Geliebte? Die Erinnerung an die Geliebte? Das Dichten über die Geliebte? … Das bleibt in der Schwebe und uns überlassen.

Noch einmal Orient – Okzident

Diese Schwebe, die sich in einem *Divan*-Gedicht und zwischen *Divan*-Gedichten erstellt – sie ist das Programm des *West-östlichen Divans*. Das Oszillieren soll nicht nur zwischen West und Ost, Ost und West, Hatem-Suleika, Suleika-Hatem stattfinden. Es soll unendlich weitergehen. Und es gibt nur einen Ort, an dem es stattfindet und immer stattfinden kann: in uns Leserinnen und Lesern. Deswegen kann bei Goethe der ›Orient‹ nicht ›der Orient‹ sein. Deswegen hat er ihn uns aufbereitet als vielstimmigen Resonanzraum, in den er »sein eignes Poetisches verwebt«[24] hat. Und jedes Mal, wenn wir den *West-östlichen Divan* lesen, wirkt dies weiter. Es liegt an uns.

23 Goethe, *West-östlicher Divan* (wie Anm. 3), S. 89.
24 Goethe, *West-östlicher Divan* (wie Anm. 3), S. 549.

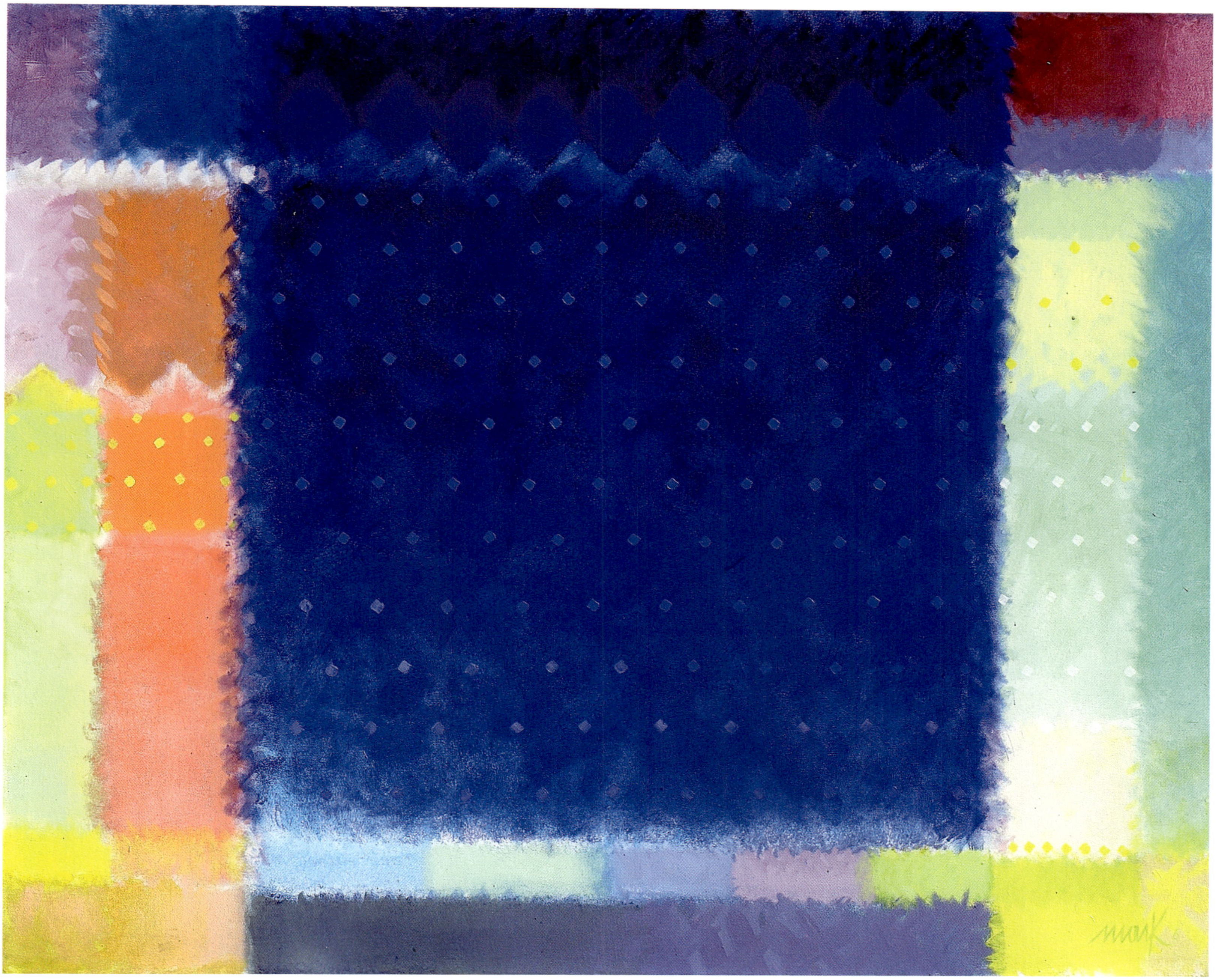

Heinz Mack
La Fiesta (Chromatische Konstellation)
Signiert, datiert: »mack 6«
Acryl auf Leinwand
130 x 160 cm

Heinz Mack
La Fiesta (Chromatic Constellation)
Signed, dated: "mack 6"
Acrylic on canvas
130 x 160 cm

Immersion in this Foreign Beauty
Heinz Mack's Oriental Inspiration

Stephan Geiger

A man walks through the desert. There is no place, no time. Only sun and sand. His tracks destroy the delicate relief that the wind created in the softly flowing landscape. But human tracks are impermanent here. There are no points of reference, no trails, no disruptions, no audience. Only endlessly intensive light and a vast, deep blue, cloudless sky. The man is wearing a silver suit that glistens as it caresses his body in the breeze. We do not know where he came from. Maybe from the future or a distant planet? He seems oddly foreign in this pristine and yet utterly hostile environment. But his steps are firm and determined. He has a goal, an idea, a vision: art far beyond any conventions, outside of galleries and museums, far away, in a different place never before thought of. His goal is this expansive landscape in which light rules, in which the sun alone dictates the rhythm and unleashes a dance of its rays on the reflective surfaces of sublime, indeed of overwhelming beauty. He has set forth to ask this light for a dance. He has come all this way and brought numerous reflecting objects with him for this purpose. Finally, after well over a decade of planning, he has arrived and is part of this intoxicating, indescribable spectacle of light, which, despite all of their technical finesse, the cameras he has brought along are barely capable of capturing (ill. 1).

The man in the silver suit is Heinz Mack, an artist and explorer who dissolves boundaries. In 1968, when he set out to the deserts of North Africa for his *Sahara Project,* he had already substantially influenced European art history for more than ten exciting years.[1] In 1957, he and Otto Piene laid the foundation for ZERO, a group, or rather an idea for a new artistic beginning that would soon grow into an international movement and ultimately unite more than one hundred artists in more than a dozen countries for collaborative exhibition projects. It became a dynamic, self-organized network that extended throughout all of Europe.

ZERO epitomized a new dynamic that can be considered symptomatic of the coming decade, for the years around 1960 mark a period of awakening and experimentation. They stood for a radical recalibration of numerous social and political as well as scientific and artistic standards and norms. Encounters between high and low took place; there was a universal call for freedom and self-determination. Rockets, space travel, and computer were the visionary leitmotifs that inspired and lent wings not only to the ZERO artists. John F. Kennedy gave this vision a voice and a face. And one of the most popular television series of all time would carry into living rooms this spirit of departure from the world, as a hymn of praise to humankind's urge to discover and proclaim the mission "to explore strange new worlds, to seek out new life and new civilizations, to boldly go where no man has gone before."

1 Heinz Mack's *Sahara Project,* which can be considered a precursor of Land Art, has been documented by numerous photographs as well as the film *Tele-Mack,* for which the artist received the Adolf-Grimme Recognition Award in 1970. Sophia Sotke is currently working on her doctoral dissertation entitled "Das Sahara-Projekt von Heinz Mack im internationalen Kontext von ZERO und Land Art, 1957–1976." Her advisor at the University of Cologne is Professor Günter Herzog.

Eintauchen in diese fremde Schönheit
Inspiration Orient bei Heinz Mack

Stephan Geiger

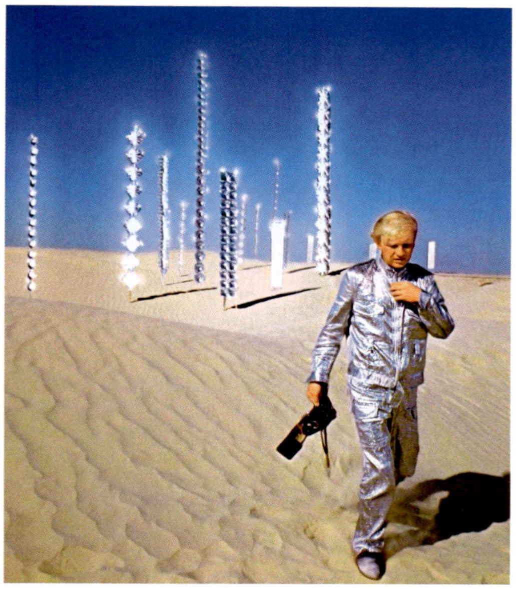

1 Während der Dreharbeiten zum Film *Tele-Mack,* Tunesien 1968

During the filming of *Tele-Mack,* Tunisia 1968

Ein Mann geht durch die Wüste. Kein Ort, keine Zeit. Nur Sonne und Sand. Seine Spur zerstört das zarte Relief, das der Wind in die weich fließende Landschaft gezaubert hat. Doch menschliche Spuren sind hier nicht von Dauer. Es gibt keine Fixpunkte, keine festen Wege, keine Störfaktoren, kein Publikum. Nur endlos intensives Licht und einen Himmel von tiefem, wolkenlos weitem Blau. Der Mann trägt einen silbernen Anzug, der ihn glitzernd umweht, und man kann nicht sagen, woher er kommt. Aus der Zukunft vielleicht, oder von einem fernen Planeten? Er wirkt seltsam fremd in dieser makellos grandiosen und dabei so lebensfeindlichen Umgebung. Doch seine Schritte sind fest und bestimmt. Er hat ein Ziel, eine Idee, eine Vision: eine Kunst weit außerhalb aller Konventionen, außerhalb der Galerien und Museen, weit weg, an einem anderen, nie zuvor gedachten Ort. Sein Ziel ist diese weite Landschaft, in der das Licht regiert, in der die Sonne allein den Rhythmus vorgibt und auf spiegelnden Oberflächen einen Tanz ihrer Strahlen entfesselt, der von erhabener, ja von überwältigender Schönheit ist. Dieses Licht zum Tanz herauszufordern, dazu ist er angetreten, dazu hat er den weiten Weg auf sich genommen und zahlreiche reflektierende Objekte hierhergeschafft. Jetzt endlich, nach gut zehn Jahren Planungsarbeit, ist er angekommen und selbst Teil dieses berauschenden, unbeschreiblichen Lichtschauspiels, das die mitgeführten Kameras mit den Mitteln der Technik nur ansatzweise einzufangen vermögen (Abb. 1).

Der Mann im Silberanzug ist Heinz Mack, Künstler, Entgrenzer, Entdecker. Als er 1968 für sein *Sahara-Projekt* in die Wüsten Nordafrikas aufbricht, hat der Künstler Mack schon über zehn aufregende Jahre hinter sich, in denen er die Kunstgeschichte Europas maßgeblich mitgeprägt hat.[1] 1957 legt er zusammen mit Otto Piene den Grundstein für ZERO, eine Gruppe oder besser: eine Idee des künstlerischen Neubeginns, die schon bald zu einer internationalen Bewegung heranwachsen und schließlich über hundert Künstler in mehr als einem Dutzend Ländern zu gemeinsamen Ausstellungsprojekten vereinen wird. Es entsteht ein dynamisches, sich selbst organisierendes Netzwerk, das sich durch ganz Europa zieht.

Damit verkörpert ZERO eine neue Dynamik, die als überaus symptomatisch für das kommende Jahrzehnt gelten kann. Denn die Jahre um 1960 markieren eine Zeit des großen Aufbruchs und des Experiments. Sie stehen für eine radikale Neukalibrierung zahlreicher gesellschaftlicher und politischer, aber auch wissenschaftlicher und künstlerischer Maßstäbe und Normen. High and Low begegnen sich, Freiheit und Selbstbestimmung werden allgemein eingefordert. Raketen, Raumfahrt und Computertechnik sind visionäre Leitmotive, die nicht nur die ZERO-Künstler inspirieren und beflügeln. John F. Kennedy hat dieser Vision eine Stimme und ein Gesicht gegeben. Und eine der populärsten Fernsehserien aller Zeiten wird den Geist dieses Aufbruchs als Lobeshymne auf den menschlichen Entdeckungsdrang in die Wohnzimmer der Welt tragen und die Mission verkünden: »to explore strange new worlds, to seek out new life and new civilizations, to boldly go where no man has gone before«.

1 Heinz Macks *Sahara-Projekt,* das als ein Vorläufer der Land-Art gelten kann, ist durch zahlreiche Fotografien sowie den Film *Tele-Mack* dokumentiert, für den der Künstler 1970 den Adolf-Grimme-Anerkennungspreis erhielt. Unter dem Titel *Das Sahara-Projekt von Heinz Mack im internationalen Kontext von ZERO und Land-Art, 1957–1976* verfasst Sophia Sotke an der Universität Köln bei Prof. Günter Herzog gerade eine Doktorarbeit über dieses Projekt.

Like few others, Heinz Mack is an artist who advanced the optimistic dissolution of boundaries as well as the creative expansion of art. As early as in the fifties, he recognized that painting and sculpture were in need of material renewal and diversification in order to be able to adequately lend expression to our time, our everyday reality. From that point on he incorporated innovative and modern materials into his creative work such as aluminum, plexiglass, and stainless steel, using their properties with virtuoso ease. He discovered light as one of the guiding themes of his artistic aspiration, making it an integral part of his works. He dispensed with traditional compositional schemes and began to base his creative work primarily on the sequential principle of structure, in which he saw embodied a contemporary expression of our scientific, technological reality. Thus Mack created his first light reliefs and his light-drunken, shimmering rotor that combine reflective surfaces with a realistic element of motion, soon to be celebrated as important works of kinetic art. Yet he did not leave it at these modern diversifications of the material and its means of expression. The young Mack was a restless, creative mind, an artistic free spirit of almost Faustian nature who in 1964 voluntarily gave up his tenured position as a teacher to go to New York as a freelance artist. He is the tirelessly creative spirit who never lingers over just one thing—no matter how beautiful it is (or how successful it is in the art business). Beaten paths or fixed systems of reference are not his thing. His urge to explore and his curiosity soon motivated him to set out for new spaces, new dimensions, and new cultural worlds.

While still a student, Mack's adventurous spirit and his cultural interest took him to North Africa as early as in the fifties. With minimum financial means and under great difficulties, he managed to travel to Morocco for the first time.[2] It was also his first encounter with Islamic art and culture, whereby the primary focus of the young artist was to experience light and nature. He primarily "sought the Orient as a landscape where he can experience his already sharply contoured ideas of the natural force of light."[3] Now his interest was aroused (ill. 2). In the late sixties, when he visited North Africa again as part of his *Sahara Project,* he had a renewed encounter with this foreign and extremely different culture.[4] Although Mack did not take an explicit interest in Islamic culture and its conditions at the time, shaped by a Western aesthetic, the artist was intuitively fascinated by the elegant, natural beauty that speaks to the beholder from the abstract, ornamental patterns of carpets, latticework windows, and mosaics.

Despite the repeated, intense exchanges and mutual enrichment during the eventful history of the East and the West, the Orient, or the Islamic world, developed a genuinely different perception of art than the Western world.[5] Even when dealing with the shared body of thought, the Orient and the Occident have completely different approaches. While Arabic treatises on optics originally influenced the 'invention' of central perspective, this specific cultural technique evolved exclusively in the West.[6] In his book *Florenz und Bagdad—Eine westöstliche Geschichte des Blicks,* the German art historian Hans Belting attempts to explore why there were never any perspectival images of this type in the Arab world.[7] He finds one explanation in the different under-

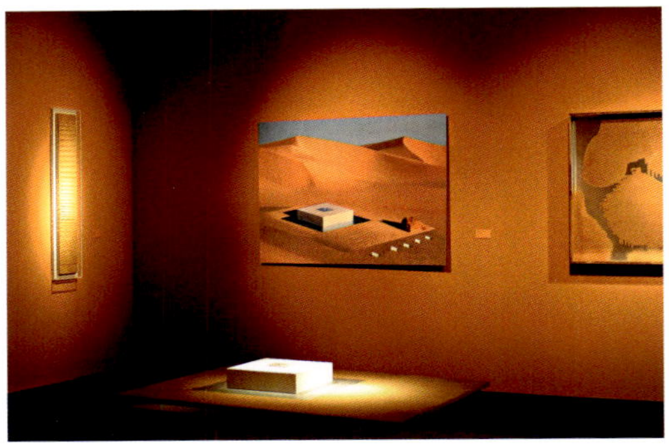

2 Kabinett in der Ausstellung *Mack. Transit zwischen Okzident und Orient* im Museum für Islamische Kunst, Berlin 2006
Foto: Stephan Geiger

Cabinet in the exhibition *Mack. Transit between Occident and Orient* in the Museum für Islamische Kunst, Berlin 2006
Photo: Stephan Geiger

2 Heinz Mack in a conversation with the author on November 5, 2017, in Mönchengladbach.

3 Claus-Peter Haase, "Mack and the Orient: A Cultural Historical Aspect," in *Mack. Transit zwischen Okzident und Orient,* exh. cat. Pergamonmuseum Berlin (Cologne, 2006), p. 25.

4 Mack himself used the following words "When you travel to such countries, you really want to absorb all you can." Heinz Mack in a conversation with the author on November 5, 2017, in Mönchengladbach.

5 Over time, the term 'Orient' underwent multiple transformations. In the English-speaking world, it is a different (more Far Eastern) topographical term. The following text will use 'Orient' within the parameters customary in German, where it includes North Africa as well as the Near East and Pakistan. This is also true for the term 'Islamic Art': it encompasses the same area. We are aware that hence some Far Eastern Muslim countries will remain unconsidered; furthermore, we are unable to take into consideration specific differentiations between 'Arabic' and 'Persian' Art.

6 Hans Belting, *Florenz und Bagdad: Eine westöstliche Geschichte des Blicks* (Munich, 2008), p. 37.

7 Ibid., pp. 16ff.

Heinz Mack ist ein Künstler, der die optimistische Entgrenzung und kreative Erweiterung der Kunst vorangetrieben hat wie nur wenige andere. Schon in den 1950er-Jahren erkannte er, dass Malerei und Plastik einer materiellen Erneuerung und Erweiterung bedürfen, um als adäquater Ausdruck unserer Zeit, unserer Lebenswirklichkeit gelten zu können. Fortan bezieht Heinz Mack neuartige, zeitgemäß moderne Materialien wie Aluminium, Plexiglas und Edelstahl in sein Schaffen ein und nutzt ihre Eigenschaften mit virtuoser Leichtigkeit. Er entdeckt das Licht als Leitthema seines künstlerischen Strebens und macht es zu einem integralen Bestandteil seiner Werke. Er verzichtet auf traditionelle Kompositionsschemata und gründet sein Schaffen nun primär im seriellen Prinzip der Struktur, in dem er einen zeitgemäßen Ausdruck unserer wissenschaftlich-technischen Realität verkörpert sieht. So entstehen Macks erste Lichtreliefs und seine lichttrunken flirrenden Rotoren, die reflektierende Oberflächen mit einem realen Bewegungselement kombinieren und schon bald als wichtige Werke der kinetischen Kunst gefeiert werden. Doch er belässt es nicht bei diesen zeitgemäßen Erweiterungen des Materials und seiner Ausdrucksweise. Der junge Mack ist ein ruhelos Kreativer, ein künstlerischer Freigeist von fast faustischer Natur, der 1964 freiwillig seine Verbeamtung als Lehrer abtritt, um als freier Künstler nach New York zu gehen, ein stetig Schaffender, der nie bei nur einer Sache verweilen mag – und sei sie noch so schön (oder im Kunstbetrieb noch so erfolgreich). Ausgetretene Pfade und fixe Bezugssysteme sind nicht sein Ding. Sein Entdeckerdrang und seine Neugierde lassen ihn schon bald in neue Räume, neue Dimensionen und neue Kulturwelten aufbrechen.

Bereits während seiner Studienzeit in den 1950er Jahren hatten ihn Abenteuerlust und kulturelles Interesse bis nach Nordafrika geführt. Mit minimalen finanziellen Mitteln und unter großen Mühen gelang es Mack damals, durch Marokko zu reisen und erstmals die Erfahrung der Wüste und ihres Lichtes zu machen.[2] In diese Zeit datiert auch seine erste Begegnung mit der islamischen Kunst und Kultur, wobei der Fokus des jungen Künstlers mehr auf dem Licht- und Naturerlebnis lag. Mack hat den Orient zuerst »als Landschaft gesucht, um seine bereits ausgeprägten Vorstellungen von der natürlichen Kraft des Lichts zu erleben«.[3] Doch das Interesse ist geweckt (Abb. 2). Als er dann Ende der 1960er-Jahre für sein *Sahara-Projekt* abermals Nordafrika besucht, kommt es zur erneuten Begegnung mit dieser fremden, so andersartigen Kultur.[4] Auch wenn Mack sich damals noch nicht explizit mit der islamischen Kunst und ihren Voraussetzungen befasst hat, so fasziniert den westlich geprägten Künstler doch intuitiv die elegante, selbstverständliche Schönheit, die aus den abstrakt-ornamentalen Mustern der Teppiche, Fenstergitter und Mosaiken zum Betrachter spricht.

Trotz der Tatsache, dass es in der wechselvollen Geschichte von Ost und West immer wieder einen intensiven Austausch und eine gegenseitige Befruchtung gab, hat der Orient, beziehungsweise die islamische Welt eine genuin andere Auffassung von Kunst entwickelt als der Westen.[5] Und selbst mit dem gemeinsamen Gedankengut gehen Orient und Okzident völlig verschieden um. Obwohl die ›Erfindung‹ der Zentralperspektive ursprünglich von arabischen Optik-Traktaten beeinflusst wurde,[6] hat sich diese spezifische Kulturtechnik ausschließlich im Westen ausgebildet. In seinem Buch *Florenz und Bagdad – Eine westöstliche Geschichte des Blicks* versucht der deutsche Kunsthistoriker Hans Belting zu ergründen,

2 Heinz Mack im Gespräch mit dem Verfasser am 5. November 2017 in Mönchengladbach.

3 Claus-Peter Haase, »Mack und der Orient. Ein kulturhistorischer Aspekt«, in: *Mack. Transit zwischen Okzident und Orient. Faszination und Inspiration der islamischen Kultur. Ein Werk-Aspekt 1950–2006,* hrsg. von Claus-Peter Haase, Ausst.-Kat. Museum für Islamische Kunst, Berlin, Köln 2006, S. 20.

4 Mack selbst hat das in die Worte gefasst: »Wenn man in so ein Land kommt, will man natürlich alles aufnehmen, was aufnehmbar ist«, Heinz Mack im Gespräch mit dem Verfasser am 5. November 2017 in Mönchengladbach.

5 Der Begriff ›Orient‹, der im Laufe der Zeit eine vielfache Wandlung erfuhr und in der angelsächsischen Welt eine ganz andere (mehr fernöstliche) topographische Bestimmung umfasst, wird im Folgenden in seinem für den deutschen Sprachraum üblichen Begriffsumfang auf Nordafrika sowie den Nahen Osten bis nach Pakistan benutzt. Auch der Begriff ›islamische Kunst‹ umfasst in unserem Zusammenhang die Kunstäußerungen dieses Großraums, wohl wissend, dass damit die Kunst einiger fernöstlicher islamischer Länder nicht abgedeckt ist und auch die Unterscheidung zwischen arabischer und persischer Kunst nicht eigens berücksichtigt werden kann.

6 Hans Belting, *Florenz und Bagdad. Eine westöstliche Geschichte des Blicks*. München 2008, S. 37.

standing of 'gaze' and 'window,' of 'inside' and 'outside.' Here, the history of ideas and the cultural history of everyday life directly intertwine. Thus Belting points out that the notion of a picture as an 'open window,' as it became constitutive for European art since Alberti, could not develop in Islamic countries because the window as a transparent opening did not exist. "In the Islamic world, a pierced lattice screen is installed at this threshold; thereby becoming the subject of artistic energy as a latticework window. The screen is permeable, but it is not permeable for the gaze—at least not in principle—but rather only for light."[8]

Transparent lattices and light instead of central perspective and rigid image—this notion is very congenial with the ZERO artist Heinz Mack, who thinks in terms of light kinetics (ill. 3).[9] He has always been fascinated by the specific way in which intense desert light refracts when it hits the narrow lattice openings and causes the interior space to vibrate as dancing spots of light. Moreover, the structures and geometric patterns of these windows with wood latticework, mashrabiyyas, revealed a striking correspondence to those pure, rhythmic structures that had already occupied the avant-garde artist in the ZERO period—a morphological proximity and elective mental affinity that Mack would only gradually become fully aware of (ill. 4). Hence it is hardly surprising that Mack would acquire selected samples of Oriental window lattices and carpets for his own collection, permitting him to lay his eyes on the objects' simple beauty and exquisite elegance in his domestic surroundings as well.

However, for the time being it did not go beyond these highly exhilarating yet selective encounters with Islamic culture, which—after first impressions in the fifties and sixties—continued on a regular basis during later stays in Egypt and Algeria as well as an adventurous north-south expedition through the Ténéré. There was simply insufficient time to delve deeper into this foreign cosmos. The artist's attention was directed elsewhere, binding his energy to diverse large-scale projects, among them participating

8 Ibid., p. 274.

9 The artist Mack has time and again emphatically pointed out that the worldview according to central perspective has permanently lost its constitutive power since Cubism and the development of modern physics and astronomy: "The 20th and even more so the 21st century: We have a concept of space that is astronomically far removed from the space the Renaissance propagated. This notion of space according to central perspective is really over." Heinz Mack in a conversation with the author on September 23, 2011, in Mönchengladbach.

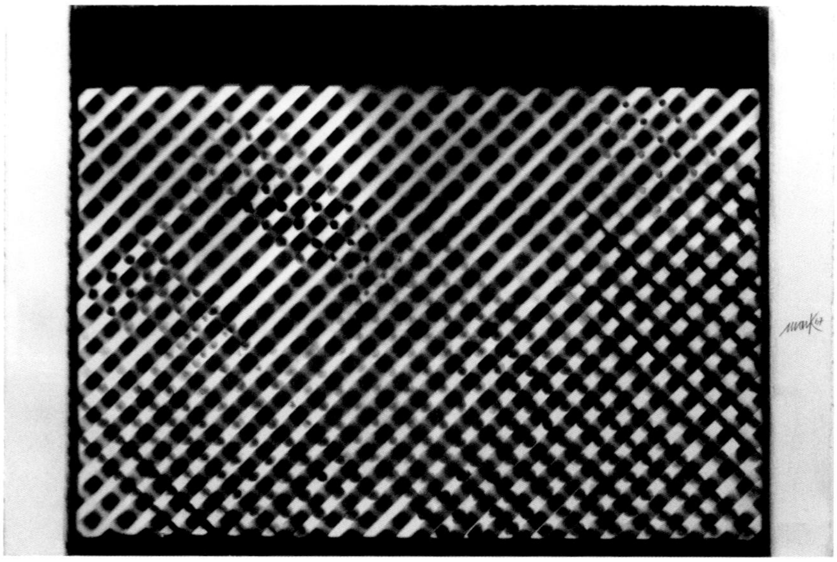

4 Heinz Mack, ohne Titel, 1967
Schwarze Farbe, gesprüht auf Bütten
79,5 x 121 cm

Heinz Mack, untitled, 1967
Black color sprayed on handmade paper
79.5 x 121 cm

warum es in der arabischen Welt das perspektivische Bild in dieser Form nicht gegeben hat.[7] Eine Erklärung dafür findet Belting in einem anderen Verständnis von ›Blick‹ und ›Fenster‹, von ›Innen‹ und ›Außen‹. Geistesgeschichte und Kulturgeschichte des Alltags greifen dabei direkt ineinander. So weist Belting darauf hin, dass sich die Vorstellung vom Bild als ›offenem Fenster‹, wie es seit Alberti für die europäische Kunst konstitutiv wurde, in den islamischen Ländern schon deshalb nicht entwickeln konnte, weil es hier das Fenster als durchsichtige Fensteröffnung gar nicht gab. »In der islamischen Welt wird an dieser Schwelle ein Gitter gebaut, das als Fenstergitter Gegenstand der künstlerischen Energie wurde. Das Gitter ist durchlässig, aber es ist nicht durchlässig für den Blick – zumindest nicht im Prinzip –, sondern für das Licht [...].«[8]

Transparente Gitter und Licht, statt Zentralperspektive und starrem Abbild, diese Vorstellung kommt dem lichtkinetisch denkenden ZERO-Künstler Heinz Mack sehr entgegen (Abb. 3).[9] Die besondere Art und Weise, wie sich das intensive Licht der Wüste an den engen Gitteröffnungen bricht und als tanzende Lichtpunkte den Innenraum zum Vibrieren bringt, hat ihn von Anfang an fasziniert. Zudem entsprachen die Gitterstrukturen und geometrischen Muster dieser ›Maschrabiyya‹ genannten Holzfenster auf geradezu verblüffende Weise jenen reinen, rhythmischen Strukturen, die den Avantgarde-Künstler schon zu ZERO-Zeiten beschäftigt hatten – eine morphologische Nähe und geistige Wahlverwandtschaft, der sich Mack selbst erst nach und nach vollkommen bewusst werden sollte (Abb. 4). So verwundert es nicht, dass der Künstler später sogar ausgewählte Exemplare orientalischer Fenstergitter und Teppiche für sich selbst erwerben wird, um die schlichte Schönheit und die exquisite Eleganz dieser Objekte auch im heimischen Umfeld stets vor Augen zu haben.

Doch zunächst bleibt es für Mack bei diesen zwar höchst beglückenden, doch punktuellen Begegnungen mit der islamischen Kultur, die – nach jenen ersten Eindrücken in den 1950er- und 1960er-Jahren – auch bei späteren Aufenthalten in Ägypten und Algerien sowie einer abenteuerlichen Nord-Süd-Expedition durch die Ténéré-Wüste eine regelmäßige Fortsetzung finden. Für ein tieferes Eindringen in diesen fremden Kosmos fehlt schlichtweg die Zeit. Zahlreiche künstlerische Großprojekte, wie die Teilnahme an der Biennale in Venedig, die Gestaltung des deutschen Pavillons auf der Weltausstellung in Osaka, seine Berufung zum Professor in Japan oder auch die Pläne für eine (nicht realisierte) 70 Meter hohe *Friedens-Stele* vor dem UN-Gebäude in New York, lenken die Aufmerksamkeit des Künstlers in andere Bahnen und binden seine Kräfte.

Die intellektuelle Auseinandersetzung mit dem Orient setzt bei Mack erst viel später ein.[10] Ende der 1990er Jahre entdeckt Heinz Mack den *West-östlichen Divan,* das sprachgewaltige poetische Spätwerk Johann Wolfgang von Goethes, für sich und schafft direkt eine ganze Suite farbkräftiger Pastelle von orientalisch-sinnlicher Finesse, aus der schließlich ein prächtiges Künstlerbuch entsteht (Abb. S. 359). Angeregt durch Goethe, beginnt Mack sich jetzt erstmals ganz intensiv und grundsätzlich mit der Literatur, Kunst und Philosophie des Orients zu beschäftigen. Wie der große Weimarer Dichterfürst, ist auch Mack bereits ein in seiner Welt erfolgreicher und hochgeachteter Künstler, als er tiefer in diese fremde Kultur dringt und zu ihren geistigen Quellen vorstößt.[11] Und wie für Goethe stellt sich auch

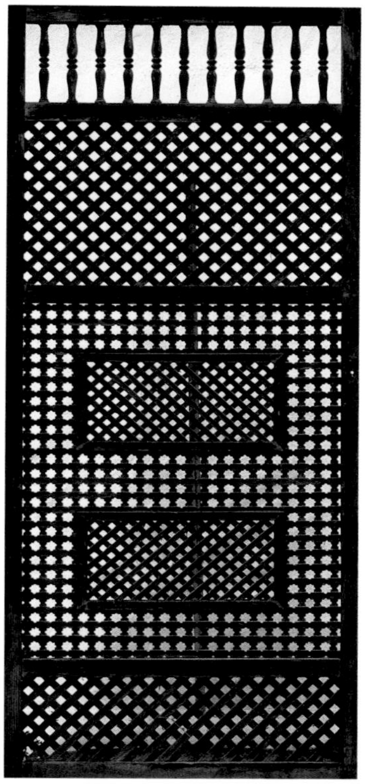

3 Fenstergitter aus Holz
Foto: Heinz Mack

Wooden window grill
Photo: Heinz Mack

7 Ebd., S. 16 ff.
8 Ebd., S. 274.
9 Der Künstler Mack hat immer wieder mit Nachdruck darauf hingewiesen, dass die zentralperspektivische Weltsicht seit dem Kubismus und den Entwicklungen in der modernen Physik und Astronomie ihre konstitutive Kraft endgültig verloren hat: »Das 20. und erst recht das 21. Jahrhundert, wir haben eine Raumvorstellung, die ist astronomisch weit weg von dem Raum, den die Renaissance propagiert hat, dieser zentralperspektivische Raum ist wirklich vorbei«, Heinz Mack im Gespräch mit dem Verfasser am 23. September 2011 in Mönchengladbach.
10 Heinz Mack im Gespräch mit dem Verfasser am 5. November 2017 in Mönchengladbach.
11 Rüdiger Safranski *(Goethe. Kunstwerk des Lebens,* München 2013, S. 546) weist darauf hin, dass Hafis für Goethe zu diesem Zeitpunkt kein Unbekannter war: »Übersetzungen einzelner Gedichte hatte er schon zuvor kennen gelernt« und schon 1773 hatte Goethe sich »mit arabischer und persischer Kultur vertraut gemacht« – eine weitere interessante Parallele zu Mack, der ja auch schon gut vierzig Jahre zuvor der islamischen Kunst staunend begegnet war, aber erst im reifen Alter ihr geistig-ästhetisches Potential entdeckt und diesen Schatz für sich erschließt.

in the Venice Biennale, designing the German Pavilion for the Osaka World's Fair, his appointment as professor in Japan, as well as plans for a (not realized) 200-foot-high *Friedensstele* (Peace Stele) in front of the headquarters of the United Nations in New York.

Mack's intellectual exploration of the Orient came about much later.[10] In the late nineties, he discovered the *West-East Divan,* Johann Wolfgang von Goethe's powerfully eloquent late poetic work, and immediately began to create an entire suite of vibrantly colored pastels of Oriental, sensual finesse, culminating in a magnificent artist's book (ill. p. 359). Inspired by Goethe, Mack began to immerse himself in the literature, art, and philosophy of the Orient. Like the great poet laureate from Weimar, Mack was already a successful and highly respected artist when he began to devote himself to this foreign culture and proceed to discover its intellectual origins.[11] As in Goethe's case, Mack too, realized stimulating and energizing new perspectives. In many instances, he felt more closely connected to traditional Oriental thought than to the prevailing selective, distant art discourse in the West.[12] Of interminable benefit were the writings of al-Ghazālī, the renowned Islamic philosopher, theologian, and mystic whose formative influence on Sufism is of fundamental importance for understanding Islamic art.[13] Al-Ghazālī's theory that "the human being loves perfection, which he finds in beautiful things; he wishes to be perfect himself"[14] aroused Mack's interest, as did the idea that "according to al-Ghazālī, insight as a cohesive whole is only possible through experience."[15] From a philosophical perspective, Islamic art is based on the Aristotelian concept of a separation between form and content, lending it its "autonomous and ultimately worldly character."[16] Most of the works listed under the heading "Islamic art" are far less religious in content than commonly assumed by the West.[17] The fundamental division of good and beautiful and the fact that "beauty in poetry and visual arts are held in high regard as a value per se,"[18] completely unburdened of any content and free of any idealistic, intellectual criticism, corresponds to the aesthetic self-perception of the avant-garde artist Mack. Or, in his own words: "When I have a work of art that impresses me so much, that has so much aura, that totally fascinates me, then at that moment I forget critical thought. All that reaches me is the appearance, the aura of the picture, and to me this is the actual mystery."[19]

Before long, the occasion arose for Mack to immerse himself even more deeply in the aesthetic cosmos of Oriental art. Shortly after the turn of the millennium, he received what was in many respects an extraordinary invitation to present a large-scale solo show of his works at Teheran's Museum of Contemporary Art. Entitled *Elective Affinities,* the exhibition finally opened on October 8, 2001, marking a symbolic opening of the country to the West. It stood under the patronage of the Commissioner of the German Government for Culture and was sponsored by the German Ministry of Foreign Affairs.[20] The presentation was such a tremendous success with the public and sparked so much interest that it had to be extended (ill. 5). Mack had the unique opportunity to speak to students in Teheran about his art, to personally meet leading Iranian intellectuals, and to visit some of the country's most outstanding sites of

10 Heinz Mack in a conversation with the author on November 5, 2017, in Mönchengladbach.

11 Rüdiger Safranski points out that Goethe was aware of Háfiz: "Even before this time he had read individual poems" and by 1773 he "began to familiarize himself with Arabic and Persian culture"—another interesting parallel with Mack, who was surprised when he had encountered Islamic art forty years earlier. Yet it was not until he was a mature man that he began to fathom its intellectual and aesthetic potential, whereupon he proceeded to explore this treasure for himself. Rüdiger Safranski, *Goethe: Kunstwerk des Lebens* (Munich, 2013), p. 546.

12 Heinz Mack in a conversation with the author on November 5, 2017, in Mönchengladbach.

13 Robert Irwin, *Islamische Kunst* (Cologne, 1998), pp. 52–53.

14 Paraphrased by Irwin in ibid., p. 53.

15 Abd-Elṣamad Abd-Elṣamīd Elschazlī, "Einleitung," in Abū-Hāmid Muhammad al-Ghazālī, *Der Erretter aus dem Irrtum,* trans. Abd-Elṣamad Abd-Elṣamīd Elschazlī (Hamburg, 1987), XXV.

16 Doris Behrens-Abouseif, *Schönheit in der arabischen Kultur* (Munich, 1998), p. 142.

17 In this context, Robert Irwin points out that if we were to treat "Islamic art" in the same way we treat "Christian art," such a presentation would be restricted to a "narrow section of specifically religious objects." Irwin 1998 (see note 13), p. 12.

18 Behrens-Abouseif 1998 (see note 16), p. 16.

19 In reference to the mystic al-Ghazālī, Mack adds: "Then I am close to an epiphany." Heinz Mack in a conversation with the author on November 5, 2017, in Mönchengladbach.

20 Starting in 1998, the museum began a careful and tentative dialogue with the West: its new director, Alireza Samiazar, had the government's backing; cf. Dorothée Brill et al., eds., *Die Teheran Moderne: Ein Reader zur Kunst im Iran seit 1960* (Berlin, 2017), p. 40, p. 186.

für Mack plötzlich vieles neu und erfrischend anders dar. In vielen Fragen fühlt er sich dem traditionellen orientalischen Denken näher verbunden als dem selektiv-distanzierten Kunstdiskurs seiner westlichen Gegenwart.[12] Mit nachhaltigem Gewinn liest Mack die Schriften al-Ghazālīs, des großen islamischen Philosophen, Theologen und Mystikers, dessen prägender Einfluss auf den Sufismus für das Verständnis der islamischen Kunst von grundlegender Bedeutung ist.[13] Die von al-Ghazālī vertretene These, »der Mensch liebe die Vollkommenheit, die er in schönen Dingen findet, denn er möchte selbst vollkommen werden«[14], erregte das Interesse von Mack ebenso wie die Vorstellung, dass »Erkenntnis als ein zusammenhängendes Ganzes [...] nach al-Ghazālī nur durch das Erleben möglich« ist.[15] Philosophisch gründet die islamische Kunst auf dem aristotelischen Konzept einer Trennung von Form und Inhalt, die ihr einen »autonomen und in letzter Konsequenz weltlichen Charakter gab«[16]. Die Mehrzahl der unter dem Oberbegriff ›islamische Kunst‹ gefassten Werke ist weit weniger religiös konnotiert, als der Westen sich dies gemeinhin vorstellen kann.[17] Die grundsätzliche Trennung von gut und schön, der Umstand, dass »Schönheit in Dichtung und bildenden Künsten als Wert an sich geschätzt wurde«[18], ganz frei von allem inhaltlichen Ballast und aller idealistisch-intellektueller Kritik, dies deckt sich mit dem ästhetischen Selbstverständnis des Avantgarde-Künstlers Mack. Oder wie Heinz Mack es selbst formuliert: »Wenn ich ein Kunstwerk habe, das mich so beeindruckt, was so viel Ausstrahlung hat, was mich vollkommen fasziniert, dann vergesse ich in diesem Moment das kritische Denken. Ich werde nur noch von der Erscheinung, von der Ausstrahlung des Bildes erreicht, und das ist das eigentliche Mysterium für mich.«[19]

Schon bald ergab sich für Mack die Gelegenheit, noch tiefer in den ästhetischen Kosmos der orientalischen Kunst einzutauchen. Kurz nach der Jahrtausendwende erhielt der Künstler die in vielfacher Hinsicht außergewöhnliche Einladung, eine große Einzelausstellung seiner Werke im Museum of Contemporary Art in Teheran zu zeigen, die schließlich am 8. Oktober 2001 unter dem Titel *Wahlverwandtschaften* eröffnet wurde. Die Ausstellung markierte eine symbolische Öffnung des Landes nach Westen. Sie stand unter der Schirmherrschaft des Beauftragten der Bundesregierung für Kultur und wurde vom Auswärtigen Amt gefördert.[20] Die Präsentation war ein so gewaltiger Publikumserfolg, dass sie aufgrund des großen Interesses sogar verlängert werden musste (Abb. 5). Heinz Mack bot sich dabei die einmalige Gelegenheit, vor Studenten in Teheran über seine Kunst zu sprechen, führende Köpfe des iranischen Geisteslebens persönlich zu treffen und einige der bedeutendsten Kunststätten des Landes zu besuchen. Überwältigt ist der Künstler vor allem von den prächtigen Mosaikgewölben der Moscheen in Isfahan, an denen ihn nicht nur die unglaubliche »handwerkliche Perfektion und Artistik« faszinieren, sondern auch die »enorme Raumsuggestion« und die unvergleichliche »Dynamik des Sehens«, die »dem Blick keine Chance gibt, an einer Stelle zu verweilen, sondern ihn sofort wieder einlädt, weiter zu schauen« (Abb. 6).[21]

Spätestens seit dieser Zeit ist die Auseinandersetzung mit der orientalischen Kunst auch in Macks eigenen Werken unübersehbar. Das lichte Spiel der Farben durchzieht seine Bilder, wie die durch ein Gitter geworfenen Sonnenstrahlen die ornamental geschmückten Räume eines arabischen Palastes. Kleinteilige, abstrakte Strukturen fügen sich zu größeren

12 Heinz Mack im Gespräch mit dem Verfasser am 5. November 2017 in Mönchengladbach.
13 Robert Irwin, *Islamische Kunst,* Köln 1998, S. 52 f.
14 Hier wiedergegeben in der Paraphrase von Irwin, vgl. ebd., S. 53.
15 Abd-Elṣamad Abd-Elṣamīd Elschazlī, »Einleitung«, in: Abū-Hāmid Muhammad al-Ghazālī, *Der Erretter aus dem Irrtum,* hrsg. von Abd-Elṣamad Abd-Elṣamīd Elschazlī, Hamburg 1988, S. XXV.
16 Doris Behrens-Abouseif, *Schönheit in der arabischen Kultur,* München 1998, S. 142.
17 Robert Irwin (wie Anm. 13, S. 12) gibt in diesem Zusammenhang zu bedenken, dass, wenn man das Thema islamische Kunst so behandeln würde, wie es bei der christlichen Kunst gewöhnlich geschieht, dann bliebe eine solche Darstellung »auf einen schmalen Ausschnitt spezifisch sakraler Gegenstände« beschränkt.
18 Behrens-Abouseif 1998 (wie Anm. 16), S. 16.
19 Und mit Blick auf den Mystiker al-Ghazālī fügt Mack noch hinzu: »Dann bin ich fast bei einer Epiphanie«, Heinz Mack im Gespräch mit dem Verfasser am 5. November 2017 in Mönchengladbach.
20 Ab 1998 hatte das Museum unter seinem neuen Direktor Alireza Sami Azar und mit Rückendeckung der Regierung einen vorsichtig tastenden Dialog mit dem Westen begonnen, vgl. *Die Teheran Moderne. Ein Reader zur Kunst im Iran seit 1960,* hrsg. von Dorothée Brill, Joachim Jäger und Gabriel Montua, Berlin 2017, S. 40 und S. 186.
21 Heinz Mack im Gespräch mit dem Verfasser am 5. November 2017 in Mönchengladbach.

art. The artist was overwhelmed in particular by the magnificent mosaic domes of the mosques in Isfahan. Besides their incredible "artisanal perfection and artistry," he was also fascinated by their "insinuation of enormous space" and their incomparable "dynamics of vision," which "gave the gaze no opportunity to linger at any one place but instead immediately invited it to keep on looking" (ill. 6).[21]

From this time on, Mack's examination of Oriental art was unmistakable in his own works. His paintings were infused with the bright play of colors, like the rays of sun falling through a latticed screen into the ornamentally decorated spaces of an Arabian palace. Detailed, abstract structures merged into larger units, evoking the elegant effect of mosaic-embellished domes. In Heinz Mack's new works, classically rigid structures and buoyantly free color elements enter an intimate relationship that is so carefree and unexpectedly beautiful that many Western viewers hardly know what to make of it (ill. 7).

On the other hand, one recognizes the potential of this dialogue between a European avant-garde artist and Oriental art all the more clearly. Berlin's Pergamonmusem honored the seventy-five-year-old artist with a major gesture in 2006: Heinz Mack was invited to use the entire wing of the department of Islamic art—a total of thirteen galleries—to exhibit his art. The show included various small, thematically concentrated rooms and demonstrated the Oriental references in Mack's oeuvre in unprecedented detail and conceptual density. Such an extensive exhibition by a contemporary artist in this special venue remains an unmatched honor to this day, which can only be explained by decades of his remarkable "activity as an ambassador of cultures."[22]

With his interest in Islamic culture, Heinz Mack was for a long time rather isolated within the contemporary art scene. Today, the cultural dialogue between the Islamic and the Western world has become a major issue in the public and in the media; not least because the events of 9/11 and their consequences have caused the sociopolitical topicality of the encounter of these two cultural spheres to manifest itself with new urgency. A number of Islamic states are currently making a deliberate strategic effort toward the values of Western culture, attempting to join them with their own traditions in spectacular large-scale projects. One preliminary highlight in this context is the Louvre Abu Dhabi, which opened in November 2017, with its both technically and aesthetically spectacular architecture. With diffuse light piercing the latticework dome, architect Jean Nouvel takes up exactly those pointed light effects of Islamic windows that Heinz Mack discovered decades ago as one of the distinguishing qualities of Oriental architecture which he then integrated into his own art.

Abu Dhabi has already discovered a formal and intellectual affinity between its own cultural tradition and Heinz Mack's work. As a logical consequence, an entire ensemble of the ZERO artist's monumental light stelae are among the first Western objects acquired for the Guggenheim Museum being planned in Abu Dhabi.[23]

Heinz Mack's two great life themes are light and structure, and the desert's magic light was the first element to link him unswervingly to the Orient. Here, in Islamic culture, the aesthetic, sensual side of art, the striving for beauty, is not taboo per se.

21 Heinz Mack in a conversation with the author on November 5, 2017, in Mönchengladbach.
22 This is the honorary title the exhibition's brochure uses to describe artist Heinz Mack.
23 Mack's stelae were already shown in 2014 in Abu Dhabi in a kind of preview in the exhibition *Seeing Through Light: Selections from The Guggenheim Abu Dhabi Collection*.

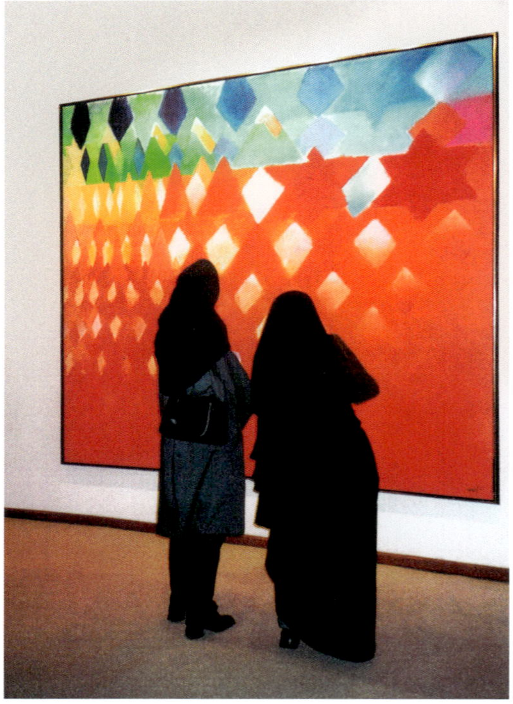

5 In der Mack-Ausstellung im Tehran Museum of Contemporary Art, Teheran 2001

In the Mack exhibition in the Tehran Museum of Contemporary Art, Tehran 2001

6 Mosaikkuppel in Isfahan
Foto: Heinz Mack

Mosaic dome in Isfahan
Photo: Heinz Mack

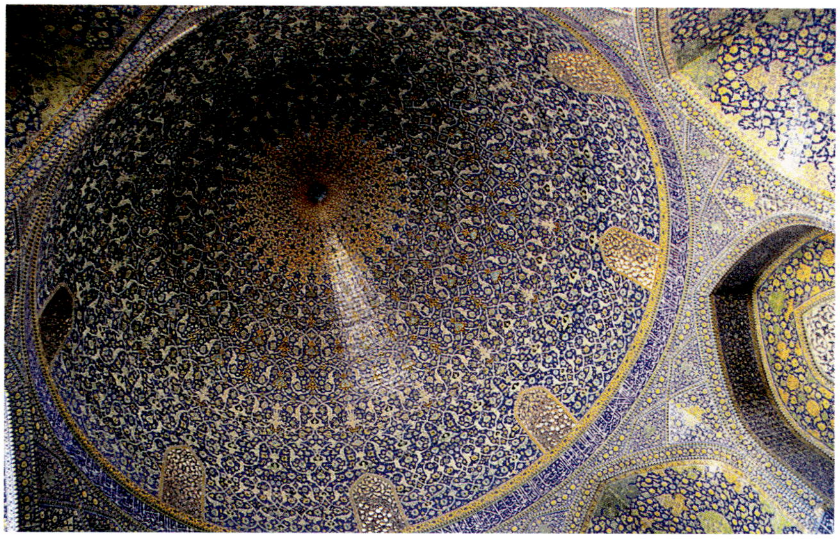

Einheiten, evozieren die elegante Wirkung einer mosaikgeschmückten Kuppel. Klassisch strenge Strukturen und heiter freie Farbelemente gehen in Heinz Macks neuen Werken eine innige Verbindung ein, die so unbekümmert und unvermittelt schön ist, dass viele westliche Kunstbetrachter kaum wissen, wie sie diese einordnen sollen (Abb. 7).

Von anderer Seite aus erkennt man das Potenzial dieses Dialogs eines europäischen Avantgarde-Künstlers mit der Kunst des Orients dafür umso deutlicher. 2006 würdigt das Berliner Pergamonmuseum den 75-jährigen Künstler mit einer großen Geste. Heinz Mack wird eingeladen, den kompletten Flügel der Abteilung für islamische Kunst – insgesamt 13 große Säle – mit seiner Kunst zu bespielen. Die Ausstellung umfasst zahlreiche thematisch konzentrierte Kabinette und zeigt die orientalischen Bezüge im Werk Macks in einer bis dahin nicht gekannten Ausführlichkeit und konzeptionellen Dichte. Eine solch umfangreiche Ausstellung eines zeitgenössischen Künstlers an diesem besonderen Ort ist eine bis heute einzigartige Ehre, die nur durch Macks außergewöhnliche, Jahrzehnte umfassende Tätigkeit als »Botschafter der Kulturen«[22] zu erklären ist.

Lange Zeit stand Heinz Mack mit seinem Interesse für die islamische Kultur innerhalb der zeitgenössischen Kunstszene ziemlich allein. Heute ist der kulturelle Dialog zwischen islamischer und westlicher Welt in der Öffentlichkeit und den Medien ein großes Thema geworden, nicht zuletzt, weil sich durch die Ereignisse und Folgen des 11. September die politisch-gesellschaftliche Brisanz der Begegnung dieser beiden kulturellen Sphären mit einer neuen Dringlichkeit stellt. Dazu betreiben einige islamische Staaten gerade eine sehr bewusste strategische Annäherung an die Werte der westlichen Kultur und versuchen, diese mit ihren eigenen Traditionen in spektakulären Großprojekten zu vereinen. Der dieser Tage eröffnete Louvre Abu Dhabi mit seiner technisch wie ästhetisch aufsehenerregenden Architektur ist hier ein vorläufiger Höhepunkt. Mit der netzartigen Kuppelkonstruktion, die punktuell-diffus vom Licht durchbrochen wird, greift Jean Nouvel dabei auf genau jene Licht-Effekte islamischer Fenstergitter zurück, die Heinz Mack bereits vor Jahrzehnten als herausragende Qualität der orientalischen Architektur für sich und seine Kunst entdeckt hat.

22 Mit diesem Ehrentitel beschreibt der Flyer zur Ausstellung im Pergamonmuseum den Künstler Heinz Mack.

Beauty and pleasure are permitted and positively intertwined. "According to Ghazālī, pleasure is a form of insight … he who cannot feel pleasure is dull and passive."[24] Heinz Mack approves of taking pleasure in sensual phenomena, and he considers the concept of beauty, severely discredited in the contemporary art discourse in the West, to be absolutely essential. For the artist Mack, individual beauty in art, architecture, nature, and everyday life is that sensual manifestation of the highest sophistication and sublime grandeur that he is unwilling to forgo. In a conversation, he cites Camus in this context: "Forsaking beauty and the sensual happiness attached to it exclusively serving misfortune, calls for a nobility I lack," only to add emphatically: "This sentence is of major importance to me."[25]

There are people who open up horizons for us, who dissolve the boundaries of gaze and intellect, who offer us new visuals and thoughts that challenge and broaden our understanding of art and of our human existence. They make us receptive to other cultures and new perspectives, leaving us ever richer than we were before encountering their works. They are wide-awake, open minds full of boundless curiosity and gushing energy and are rather rare in our profane species. Mack and Goethe are such individuals.

24 Behrens-Abouseif 1998 (see note 16), p. 29.
25 Heinz Mack in a conversation with the author on November 5, 2017, in Mönchengladbach; the Camus quote is a passage from *Return to Tipasa*.

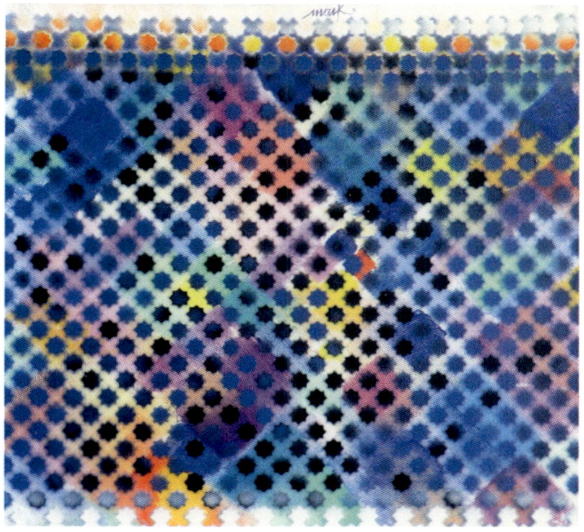

7 Heinz Mack, *Samarkand*, 2005
Acryl auf Leinwand, 83 x 88 cm

Heinz Mack, *Samarkand*, 2005
Acrylic on canvas, 83 x 88 cm

Die formale und geistige Verwandtschaft der Werke Macks mit der eigenen Kulturtradition hat man auch in Abu Dhabi selbst schon erkannt. Und so ist es logisch nur konsequent, dass ein ganzes Ensemble monumentaler Lichtstelen des ZERO-Künstlers zu den ersten westlichen Werken gehörten, die für das geplante Guggenheim Museum in Abu Dhabi angekauft wurden.[23]

Das Licht und die Struktur sind die beiden großen Lebensthemen von Heinz Mack, und das magische Licht der Wüste hat den Künstler als Erstes nachhaltig mit dem Orient verbunden. Hier, in der islamischen Kultur, ist die ästhetisch-sinnliche Seite der Kunst, das Streben nach Schönheit an und für sich kein Tabu. Schönheit und Genuss sind erlaubt und positiv besetzt, »nach Ghazālī ist Genuß eine Form der Erkenntnis […] wer keinen Genuß empfinden kann, ist stumpf und passiv«[24]. Heinz Mack bejaht den Genuss der sinnlichen Erscheinung, wie er überhaupt den im westlichen Kunstdiskurs der Gegenwart stark diskreditierten Begriff der Schönheit für absolut unentbehrlich erachtet. Schönheit in Kunst, Architektur, Natur und Alltag ist für Mack jene sinnliche Manifestation höchster Verfeinerung und sublimer Erhabenheit, auf die er als Künstler und Mensch nicht verzichten will. Im Gespräch zitiert Heinz Mack in diesem Zusammenhang Albert Camus: »Der Verzicht auf die Schönheit und das sinnliche Glück, das damit verbunden ist, die ausschließliche Hingabe an das Unglück erfordert eine Größe, die mir mangelt«, und fügt nachdrücklich hinzu: »Dies ist ein Satz, der für mich von großer Bedeutung ist.«[25]

Es gibt Menschen, die öffnen uns Horizonte, die entgrenzen Blick und Geist, geben uns neues Anschauungs- und Denkmaterial, das unser Kunstverständnis und unser eigenes Menschsein herausfordert und erweitert. Sie machen uns für andere Kulturen und neue Sichtweisen empfänglich und lassen uns immer reicher zurück, als wir vor der Begegnung mit ihren Werken waren. Sie sind hellwache, offene Geister voll grenzenloser Neugier und überschwänglicher Energie. Sie sind in unserer profan gestrickten Spezies ziemlich selten. Mack und Goethe sind solche Menschen.

23 In einer Art Vorschau auf das neue Guggenheim Abu Dhabi wurde Macks Stelen-Ensemble bereits 2014 in der Ausstellung *Seeing Through Light: Selections from the Guggenheim Abu Dhabi Collection* in Abu Dhabi ausgestellt.
24 Behrens-Abouseif 1998 (wie Anm. 16), S. 29.
25 Heinz Mack im Gespräch mit dem Verfasser am 5.11. 2017 in Mönchengladbach; das Camus-Zitat ist eine Passage aus *Heimkehr nach Tipasa*.

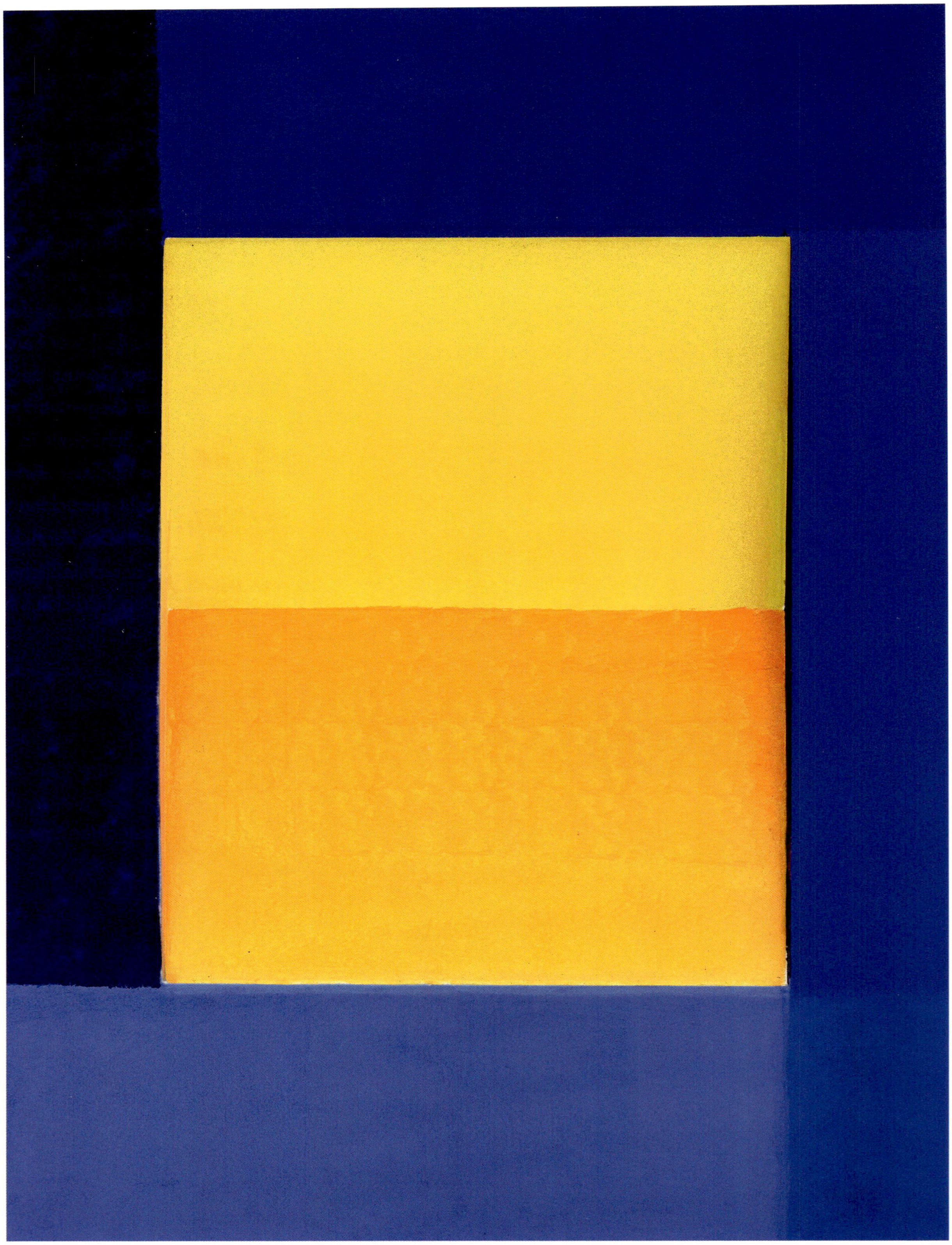

Heinz Mack
Orpheus und Eurydike (2-teiliges Ensemble)
Signiert, datiert: »mack 00«
Acryl auf Holz
160,5 x 119 x 10 cm

Heinz Mack
Orpheus and Eurydike (2-part ensemble)
Signiert, datiert: "mack 00"
Acrylic on wood
160.5 x 119 x 10 cm

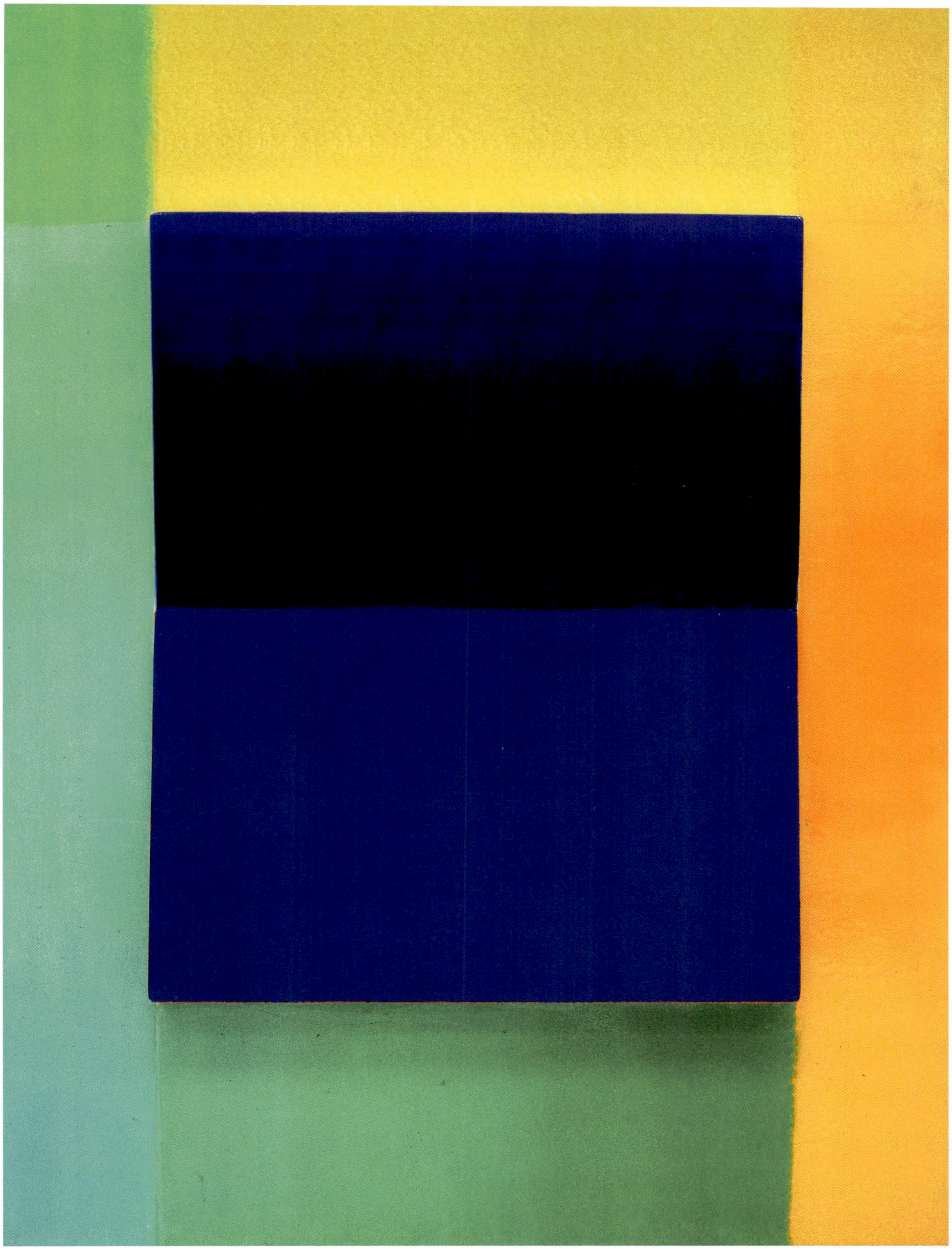

Conversation

Heinz Mack and Veit Loers

VEIT LOERS:
Nowadays, it seems to me that the idea of primary colors in painting is more of an exception. While it has been overused, from a conceptual viewpoint it is still virulent. A look into current conventions indicates something familiar, a topos that refers, almost tongue-in-cheek, to modernity as well as to a pragmatic formula one feels the urge to comment on in an original way. A recent example is the Conceptual artist Philipp Messner, who placed three snow cannons on a lawn near Munich's Alte Pinakothek and proceeded to produce colored snow in the primary colors blue, red, and yellow, calling them super-standard and common printing color (*Clouds,* 2016). Lawrence Weiner is currently showing his project *Wherewithal / Was es braucht* at the Kunsthaus Bregenz. His references in the primaries on the invitation already refer to standards of an idealistic type. Yet this is far removed from Runge, Goethe, and Mondrian. The former utopia is now a past one, one that possesses almost nostalgic traits. What motivated you to deal with the primary colors during the formative ZERO years?

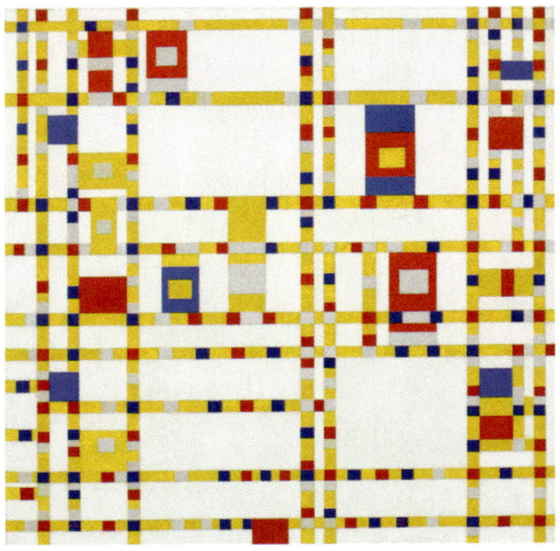

1 Piet Mondrian
Broadway Boogie Woogie, 1942/43
Öl auf Leinwand / oil on canvas
127 x 127 cm
Museum of Modern Art (MoMA), New York
Foto: The Museum of Modern Art / Scala, Florence

HEINZ MACK:
At the 'beginning of the beginning' of the ZERO period, Mondrian's *Boogie Woogie* paintings were still a kind of final reduction of Constructivism and the meaning of composition contained in it. At the same time, these paintings marked a departure into a new structural zone, the open grid. The primary colors in these pictures seemed to be arranged by chance.

What ultimately fascinated us was Yves Klein's ultramarine monochrome, the reduction of all reductions, so to speak, of the multicolors that had dominated Occidental painting since the Renaissance. At the time, we were unaware of Rodshenko's 1921 anticipation of a pure monochrome (presumably Yves Klein was as well).

It was also not until 1957 that we were first introduced to Malevich's Suprematism, when Mr. Sandberg showed his paintings at Amsterdam's Stedelijk Museum.

I was by myself when first making my personal decision—as did Piene—to do without colors. It felt like a confirmation to us when we learned soon thereafter that Castellani and Manzoni had come to the same conclusion at nearly the same time, committing themselves to achromy. I have yet to find out when Fontana created his first picture without colors, calling white the sum of all colors. His *Manifesto blanco* from 1946 was not published in Germany until more than a decade later.

When we presented our *Homage à Fontana* at *documenta III* in 1964, his art was still largely unknown (for example, one of his small paintings was hung in close proximity to a restroom).

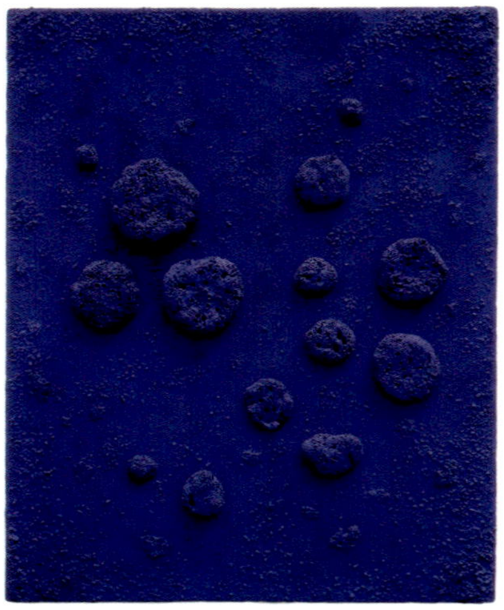

2 Yves Klein
L'accord bleu (RE 10), 1960
198 x 164 x 13,5 cm
Farbe, Schwämme, Kieselsteine auf Holz / paint, sponges and pebbles on wood
Sammlung / Collection Stedelijk Museum Amsterdam
Foto: Stedelijk Museum Amsterdam

Gespräch

Heinz Mack und Veit Loers

VEIT LOERS:
Heutzutage, so scheint mir, ist die Idee der Primärfarben in der Malerei eher eine Ausnahme. Sie war auch entsprechend strapaziert. Konzeptuell ist sie aber immer noch virulent. Ein Blick in heutige Gepflogenheiten verweist auf etwas Bekanntes, einen Topos, der sich fast augenzwinkernd auf die Moderne und eine pragmatische Formel bezieht, die man originell kommentieren will. So hat zum Beispiel unlängst Philipp Messner, ein konzeptueller Künstler, auf eine Wiese bei der Alten Pinakothek in München durch drei Schneekanonen die Grundfarben Blau, Rot, Gelb als Farbschnee realisiert und sie als Superstandard und gängige Druckerfarbe benannt *(Clouds,* 2016). Lawrence Weiner stellt gerade im Kunsthaus Bregenz sein Projekt *Wherewithal / Was es braucht* aus, in dem er schon in der Einladungskarte mit Verweisen in den Primaries Standards ideeller Art benennt. Aber das ist von Runge, Goethe und Mondrian weit entfernt. Die einstige Utopie ist nun eine gewesene, eine, die fast nostalgische Züge besitzt. Was bewegte Sie in der Aufbruchszeit der ZERO-Jahre, sich mit den Primärfarben zu beschäftigen?

HEINZ MACK:
Im ›beginning of the beginning‹ der ZERO-Zeit waren Mondrians Boogie-Woogie-Bilder noch eine Art finale Reduktion des Konstruktivismus und der darin enthaltenen Bedeutung der Komposition; zugleich aber waren diese Bilder ein Aufbruch in die neue Zone des Strukturellen, des offenen Rasters. Die enthaltenen Primärfarben schienen darin vom Zufall geordnet.

Schließlich faszinierte uns das ultramarine Monochrom von Yves Klein, quasi die Reduktion aller Reduktionen der Vielfarben, welche seit der Renaissance die abendländische Malerei beherrscht hatten. Rodtschenkos Antizipation der reinen Monochromie im Jahre 1921 war uns damals unbekannt (wahrscheinlich auch für Yves Klein).

Auch der Suprematismus von Malewitsch wurde uns erst visuell bekannt, als 1957 Herr Sandberg in Amsterdam die Bilder im Stedelijk-Museum zeigte.

Ich habe zuerst alleine – ebenso wie Piene – für mich entschieden, auf die Farben zu verzichten, und wir fühlten uns bestätigt, als wir alsbald erfahren konnten, dass Castellani und Manzoni quasi gleichzeitig diese Entscheidung getroffen hatten und sich zur Achromie bekannten. Unbekannt ist mir bis heute, wann Fontana sein erstes Bild ohne Farben geschaffen und das Weiß als die Summe aller Farben bezeichnet hat. Sein *Manifesto blanco,* 1946 erschienen, wurde ja erst mehr als ein Jahrzehnt später in Deutschland publiziert.

Als wir 1964 auf der *documenta III* die *Hommage à Fontana* präsentierten, war dessen Kunst noch weitgehend unbekannt (so hing ein kleines Bild von ihm in unmittelbarer Nähe einer Toilette).

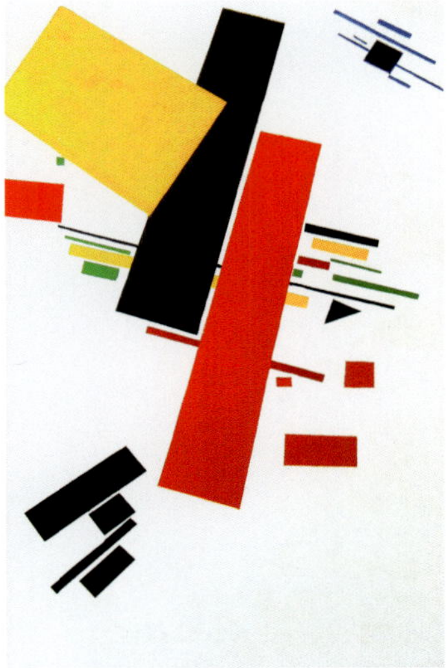

3 Kasimir Malewitsch
Dynamischer Suprematismus Nr. 57 / Dynamic Supre, 1916
Öl auf Leinwand / oil on canvas
102,4 x 66,9 cm

I was first alerted to the primary colors red, yellow, and blue in the late fifties. As a consequence, I produced the first blue, yellow, and red paintings, whose monochrome qualities were also intended to be energized by frequency-like rhythms and colored rows of facets, in my studio at the beginning of the ZERO period. I commented on my attempts in my manifesto *The New Dynamic Structure,* published in 1958.

VEIT LOERS:
You mention Yves Klein's boundless blue as a contemporary witness. It is easy to understand the enthusiasm. This influenced me, and still does. Yet in Klein's case the blue was the dominant part of a triad with a bright purple and gold, slightly shifted primary colors, as it were. My personal belief is that Klein developed this as part of his study of Rosicrucianism. He was extremely fixated on the teachings of Max Heindel, one of Rudolf Steiner's former students. And Steiner himself had absorbed Rosicrucianism—at the time practically obsolete—into his anthropological doctrine. The primary colors originate from this alchemist tradition, which the Rosicrucians maintained. It was by these means—and not solely thanks to Newton and the tradition of physics—that Runge and Goethe learned about them. Mondrian was a follower of Blavatsky's theosophy, which is ultimately the legacy of the Rosicrucians and the Freemasons. The latter incorporated the natural sciences of Paracelsus as pansophy as early as in the seventeenth century. What I really want to say is that this experimental theory of colors—it always saw itself rooted in the cosmos—turned quasi-dogmatic, although, based on its autonomy, it never was. But that always has to be reawakened, as in the case of ZERO, where natural science is the motor, even though with Moholy-Nagy and others the term vibration was in vogue in the twenties.

When I took charge of the exhibition *Red Yellow Blue* from St. Gallen in 1988, I deliberately decided to have it coincide with the first retrospective of Viennese Actionism at Kassel's Fridericianum. There, you can detect white, red, brown, and black. Soil, blood—and black and white as non-colors. While I truly liked the tension, hardly anybody noticed it back then. Thus I believe that we must always strive to remain rebellious. What if we ended up being able to see ultraviolet? Wouldn't that shake everything up?

HEINZ MACK:
As for the dominating part of a triad in the case of Yves Klein, the ultramarine, it looks like a triad with primary colors on equal footing in Rodshenko's three monochrome panel paintings from 1921. None of the colors dominate, and I therefore do not perceive them as sacred expression or dogma. It is impossible to consistently paint monochrome panels throughout one's life, such as Malevich's white or black squares. World famous, these artists are likely to have known this. Does art history know an additional, older anticipation? I was actually fascinated when I learned that the Christian paintings of the Annunciation in the early Renaissance essentially consist of purple, ultramarine (lapis lazuli), and gold. What dominates in them is not alchemy but

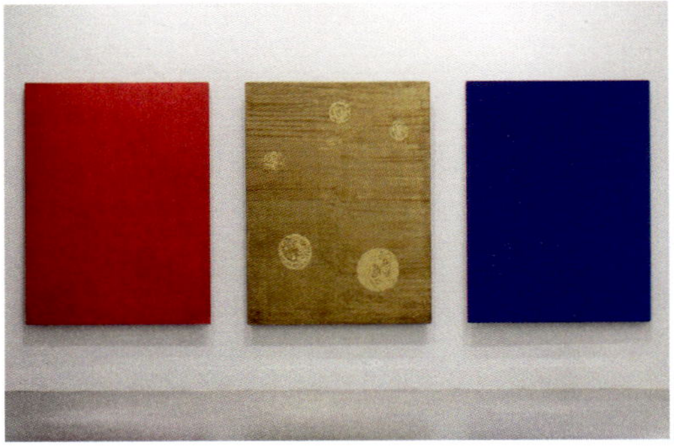

4 Yves Klein
Grand Monopink (MP 16), 1960
Pigment und Kunstharz auf Leinwand auf Holz montiert / Pigment and synthetic resin mounted on canvas on wood
199 x 153 cm

Frémissement (MG 17), 1960
Blattgold auf Tafel / gold leaf on board
199 x 153 cm

Monochrome bleu sans titre (IKB 75), 1960
Pigment und Kunstharz auf Gaze auf Tafel montiert / Pigment and synthetic resin mounted on gauze on board
199 x 153 x 2,5 cm

Louisiana Museum of Modern Art, Humblaek

Foto: Louisiana Museum of Modern Art, Humblaek

Die Primärfarben Rot, Gelb und Blau fanden am Ende der 1950er-Jahre zum ersten Mal mein waches Interesse, und so entstanden zu Beginn der ZERO-Zeit auch in meinem Atelier blaue, gelbe und rote Bilder, deren Monochromie aber durch frequenzartige Rhythmik und farbige Facettenreihen belebt werden sollte. Unter dem Titel *Die neue dynamische Struktur* habe ich 1958 in schriftlicher Form meine Versuche kommentiert.

VEIT LOERS:
Sie erwähnen das grenzenlose Blau von Yves Klein als Zeitzeuge. Man kann sich die Begeisterung vorstellen. Das wirkte und wirkt auch noch auf mich. Aber es war doch bei Klein dominierender Teil einer Trias mit einem hellen Purpur und Gold, das sind sozusagen leicht verschobene Primärfarben. Ich persönlich glaube, dass Klein sie aus seiner Beschäftigung mit dem Rosenkreuzertum entwickelt hat. Er war sehr auf die Lehre von Max Heindel fixiert, einem ehemaligen Schüler von Rudolf Steiner. Und Steiner selbst hatte ja das quasi schon überlebte Rosenkreuzertum in seine anthroposophische Lehre aufgenommen. Die Primärfarben kommen aus dieser alchemistischen Tradition, welche die Rosenkreuzer pflegten. So, und nicht nur durch Newton und die physikalische Tradition, gelangten sie zu Runge und Goethe. Die Theosophie Blavatskys, der Mondrian anhing, ist ja auch mit das Erbe des Rosenkreuzer- und Freimaurertums. Jene hatten schon im 17. Jahrhundert die Naturwissenschaft eines Paracelsus als Pansophia mit aufgenommen. Worauf ich hinaus will: Diese experimentelle Farbenlehre, die sich schon immer im Kosmos verankert sah, wurde quasi dogmatisch, obwohl sie es in ihrer Selbstbestimmung nie war. Aber das muss immer wieder geweckt werden wie bei ZERO, wo die Naturwissenschaft der Motor ist, auch wenn der Begriff der Vibration in den zwanziger Jahren bei Moholy-Nagy und anderen en vogue war.

Die Ausstellung *Rot Gelb Blau,* die ich 1988 aus St. Gallen übernahm, habe ich im Fridericianum Kassel bewusst gleichzeitig mit der ersten Retrospektive des Wiener Aktionismus gezeigt. Da kann man Weiß, Rot, Braun und Schwarz konstatieren. Erde, Blut – Schwarz und Weiss als Nichtfarben. Diese Spannung fand ich schon gut, aber das hat damals kaum jemand bemerkt. So denke ich, müssen wir immer rebellisch bleiben. Was wäre denn, wenn wir Ultraviolett sehen könnten, da käme doch alles ins Wanken, oder nicht?

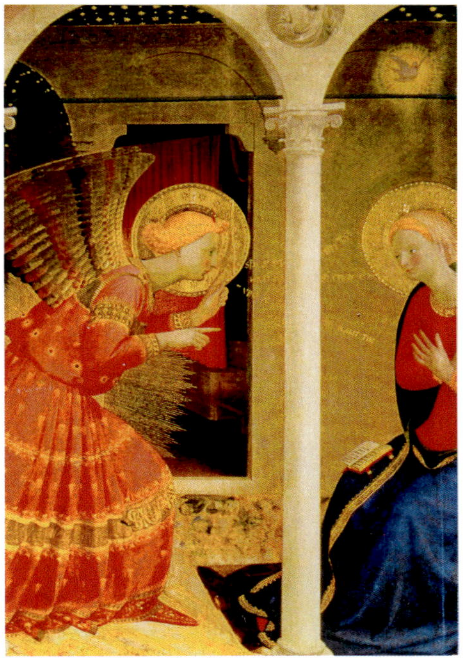

5 Fra Beato Angelico
Die Verkündigung an Maria / The Annunciation, 1432/34
Tempera auf Holz / tempera on wood
180 x 175 cm
Museo Diocesano del Capitolo di Cortona, Cortona

HEINZ MACK:
Was den dominierenden Teil einer Trias bei Yves Klein betrifft, das Ultramarin, erscheint bei Rodtschenkos drei monochromen Tafelbildern von 1921 als Teil einer Trias gleichberechtigter Primärfarben; da dominiert keine Farbe, und ich empfinde sie darum nicht als sakrale Expression oder Dogma. Konsequent monochrom gemalte Farbtafeln, schwarze oder weiße Quadrate bei Malewitsch kann man nicht lebenslänglich malen; diese drei Künstler von kunsthistorischem Weltrang haben das wahrscheinlich geahnt – oder gar gewusst. Kennt die Kunstgeschichte eine weitere, ältere Vorwegnahme? In der Tat faszinierte mich meine frühe Entdeckung und Erkenntnis, dass die christlichen Verkündigungsbilder zu Beginn der Renaissance im Prinzip aus Purpur, Ultramarin (Lapislazuli) und Gold bestehen, bei denen nicht die Alchemie, sondern spirituelle Interessen einer Lichtmetaphysik in der christlichen

the spiritual interests of light metaphysics within the Christian epiphany. Just think of Simone Martini's delightful *Annunciation* in the Uffizi or Fra Angelico's painting in Arezzo; that will help put Yves Klein's triad into perspective!

Gold was the epitome of the sublime in all cultures. Oddly enough, as a non-color it does not appear in the rainbow, a fate it shares with ultramarine purple, whose absence in the color spectrum Goethe regretted. He attributes high dignity to purple, which is attracted by the blue side. Regarding gold, he states that it elevates itself toward pure yellow. Interestingly, neither gold, silver, nor copper appear in any of the numerous color theories. And he continues: "Whoever is acquainted with the prismatic origin of red [Purpur], will not think it paradoxical … that this colour partly actu, partly potentiâ, includes all the other colours."

It appears paradoxical to me that in one instance Goethe calls the color red purple, which he continues vice versa. The Phoenicians already coveted this color; for Christian Romans, it was a symbol of spiritual power. After all: the cardinals hold purple in high esteem to this day. I like painting with ultramarine when it is between manganese blue and a deep violet, wherein the purple receives its equal share, as it is supposed to be contained in the ultramarine. We have good reason to talk about ultramarine purple. It adheres to the color spectrum. Here, too, there is an overabundance of nuances. Adhering to no theory, denying all dogmas, I make my decisions as to which colors are placed into chromatic proximity intuitively, exposing them as much to chance as to the critical discipline of my extended painterly experiences.

It also has to be mentioned that Goethe recognized how only the violet parts of the spectrum appear. He might have been the discoverer of ultraviolet light if he had had access to a fluoride prism in order to have been able to observe fluorescence. Galileo Galilei already achieved this thanks to the luminescence of the barite stone. And here we are back in the arcane world of alchemy, Goethe's 'secret beloved.'

The Kabala appears as alchemy as early as in Arabian Spain and paves the way for the Rosicrucian sects. I was very annoyed by their ceremonial during Yves Klein's funeral. Regarding the ultraviolet rays: they are in fact rays, waves we cannot see. If we were capable of seeing them, then the pigments would be missing!

Dear Veit Loers, ultraviolet utopia is not going to happen for the painter.

VEIT LOERS:

I absolutely agree; painterly practice is fundamentally different from dogmas. Yet, not only the Middle Ages mastered painting according to rules; it continues. Why does Blinky Palermo deal with the primary colors during his sojourn in the United States? Why does Polke work with purple, cobalt, and violet? The triad with yellow certainly has something to do with translucent stained glass, which influenced early panel painting. But beyond all historic developments and color allegories, the human eye is subjected to certain regularities whose physical conditions can be psychologically verified. This inspired Goethe to make a philosophical statement that Hegel could not have formulated more fittingly:

Epiphanie herrschen. Man denke an die wunderbare *Verkündigung* von Simone Martini in den Uffizien, oder Fra Angelicos Bild in Arezzo, dann relativiert sich auch hier die Trias von Yves Klein!

Gold war in allen Kulturen das schlechthin Sublime, welches merkwürdigerweise als Nichtfarbe im Regenbogen nicht vorkommt, ebenso wenig wie der ultramarine Purpur, den Goethe im Farbspektrum vermisste. Dem Purpur spricht er hohe Würde zu, der sich nach der blauen Seite hingezogen sieht; und vom Gold sagt er, dass es sich zum reinen Gelb erhöht. Interessanterweise kommt weder Gold noch Silber oder Kupfer in einer der vielen Farbtheorien vor. Und weiter heißt es: »Wer die prismatische Entstehung des Purpurs kennt, der wird nicht paradox finden [...], daß diese Farbe teils actu, teils potentia alle andern Farben enthalte.«

Paradox erscheint mir, dass Goethe die Farbe Rot einmal Purpur nennt und vice versa damit fortfährt. Begehrt war diese Farbe schon bei den Phöniziern, und für die christlichen Römer war sie ein Symbol geistiger Macht, schließlich schätzen noch heute die Kardinäle den Purpur. Ich male gerne das Ultramarin, wenn es zwischen Manganblau und einem tiefen Violett steht, an dem der Purpur ebenso seinen Anteil hat, wie er im Ultramarin enthalten sein soll; nicht umsonst spricht man vom ultramarinen Purpur. Damit folgt er dem Farbspektrum. Auch hier ist der Reichtum der Nuancen grenzenlos. Keiner Theorie folgend, jedes Dogma verneinend, entscheide ich intuitiv, welche Farben in eine chromatische Nachbarschaft treten, dem Zufall ebenso ausgesetzt wie der kritischen Disziplin meiner langen malerischen Erfahrungen.

Es muss aber auch vermerkt werden, dass Goethe erkannte, wie nur die violetten Teile des Spektrums in Erscheinung treten, und er wäre vielleicht der Entdecker des ultravioletten Lichts geworden, hätte ihm ein Fluoridprisma zur Verfügung gestanden, um die Fluoreszenz beobachten zu können, was schon Galileo Galilei dank des Nachtleuchtens des Schwerspatsteins gelang. Da wäre man schon wieder in der Geheimniswelt der Alchemie – Goethes ›heimliche Geliebte‹.

Schon im arabischen Spanien erscheint die Kabbala als Alchemie und bereitet die Rosenkreuzersekten vor. Bei der Beerdigung von Yves Klein wurde ich durch deren Zeremoniell doch erheblich irritiert. Was die ultravioletten Strahlen betrifft, so sind es eben Strahlungen, Wellen, welche wir nicht sehen können. Wäre es möglich, diese zu sehen, würden die Pigmente fehlen!

Lieber Veit Loers, die ultraviolette Utopie wird für den Maler nicht stattfinden.

VEIT LOERS:
Da gebe ich Ihnen recht, die Malerpraxis ist nochmals was ganz anderes als die Dogmen, aber das Malen nach Regeln beherrschte nicht nur das Mittelalter, sondern es dauert an. Warum beschäftigt sich Blinky Palermo bei seinem Amerika-Aufenthalt mit den Primärfarben, warum arbeitet Polke mit Purpur, Kobalt und Violett? Die Trias mit Gelb hat sicher auch mit der luziden Glasmalerei zu tun, die das frühe Tafelbild beeinflusst hat. Aber jenseits aller historischen Entwicklungen und Farb-Allegorien gibt es für das menschliche Auge bestimmte Gesetzlichkeiten, welche die physikalischen Gegebenheiten psychologisch verifizieren und

"When the distinction of yellow and blue is duly comprehended, and especially the augmentation into red, by means of which the opposite qualities tend towards each other and become united in a third; then, certainly, an especially mysterious interpretation will suggest itself, since a spiritual meaning may be connected with these facts ..."

It seems to me that your manifesto from 1958, *The New Dynamic Structure,* confirms this layer of meaning under the signum of a new physical worldview that the pre-World War II avant-garde had not quite yet adopted for itself. Triangles, color circles, and color stripes: ultimately, we appear to be permanently faced with the same queries and solutions. Although the color pigments—formerly arduously extracted from nature—presently originate from the palette of aniline colors. What drives you, Heinz Mack?

HEINZ MACK:

If I only knew ... The questions that unintentionally accompany me when I paint are more numerous than the answers I try to give. It begins with entirely unexpected ideas containing some type of driving force that evokes the question of whether a discovery is about to reveal itself. Thus the adventure of painting also begins with the question whether something new is to be expected or if somebody else has already made my artistic discovery.

The signum of the physical worldview you refer to is, intended or not, omnipresent; it is now stored in a computer database. Intermediate colors, so-called nuances, sometimes tend to take privilege as primary colors, provided they display a purity previously only attributed to classical primary colors.

It remains a mystery to me why many painters keep maltreating, torturing, mixing, and superimposing colors until they finally lose all of their radiance, no longer breathe, value darkness more than light, and in the end are nothing more than ashes.

Karl Kraus: "Science is spectral analysis, art is light synthesis." An enigmatic, not exactly logical formulation. I do, however, know that if the physical qualities of light edge forward in art, it is bound to lose. Hence when colors are occasionally unkind to me, I continue painting, aware of the risk of failing or winning. This is also a stimulus, inspired by hope, which is the last to perish, and the aspiration that 'bad' colors may transmute into 'good' ones. Goethe's "sensual-moral effect of color" is possibly best understood if translated as sensations and their relationship to the intellect, to the mind.

Just think of the mature Matisse, where all colors look so light—this lightness of being did in fact require an entire working life. In the end, this painter no longer had black pigments on his palette.

And what do you say about Cy Twombly, who, throughout his life, drew much more on his huge canvases than he painted on them. Was he color blind, even when he used blood-red colors in his final pictures? By comparison, Pierre Soulages, denying any

Goethe zu einem philosophischen Satz kommen lassen, den Hegel nicht besser hätte formulieren können:

»Wenn man erst das Auseinandergehen des Gelben und Blauen wird recht gefaßt, besonders aber die Steigerung ins Rote genugsam betrachtet haben, wodurch das Entgegengesetzte sich gegen einander neigt, und sich in einem Dritten vereinigt; dann wird gewiß eine besondere geheimnisvolle Anschauung eintreten, daß man diesen beiden getrennten, einander entgegengesetzten Wesen eine geistige Bedeutung unterlegen könne [...]«.

So scheint mir das von Ihnen verfasste Manifest über *Die neue dynamische Struktur* von 1958 eine Bestätigung in dieser Bedeutungsebene zu sein, unter dem Signum eines neuen physikalischen Weltbildes, das die Avantgarde sich vor dem Zweiten Weltkrieg noch nicht wirklich zu eigen gemacht hatte. Triangeln, Farbkreise und Farbstreifen, am Ende scheint mir, als stünden wir immer vor den gleichen Fragestellungen und Lösungen, auch wenn die einst mühsam der Natur abgerungenen Farbpigmente der Palette der Anilinfarben gewichen sind. Was treibt Sie an, Heinz Mack?

HEINZ MACK:
Wenn ich das wüsste ... Die Fragen, welche mich beim Malen ungewollt begleiten, sind zahlreicher als die Antworten, die ich mir zu geben versuche. Dies fängt schon damit an, dass gänzlich unerwartete Ideen eine Art Antriebsenergie enthalten und die Frage evozieren, ob hier eventuell eine Entdeckung sich anzeigt. Also beginnt das Abenteuer der Malerei auch mit der Frage: Ist etwas Neues zu erwarten, oder ist meine künstlerische Entdeckung schon von anderen gemacht worden?

Das Signum des physikalischen Weltbildes, von dem Sie sprechen, ist – gewollt oder nicht, stets gegenwärtig – nun in der Datenbank der Computer gespeichert. Zwischenfarben, die sogenannten Nuancen, haben manchmal die Neigung, sich als Primärfarben zu privilegieren, vorausgesetzt, dass sie ihrerseits eine Reinheit zeigen, welche man bislang nur den klassischen Primärfarben zuspricht.

Da bleibt es mir unverständlich, warum viele Maler die Farben so lange verletzen, quälen, durcheinandermischen und aufeinanderschichten, bis sie ihre Strahlkraft vollkommen verloren haben, nicht mehr atmen, mehr die Dunkelheit als das Licht schätzen, und zuletzt nur noch Asche sind.

Karl Kraus: »Wissenschaft ist Spektralanalyse, Kunst ist Lichtsynthese« – eine rätselhafte, nicht gerade logische Formulierung. Ich weiß jedoch, dass, wenn in der Kunst die Physik des Lichts sich vordrängt, dann verliert die Kunst. Also: Wenn zuweilen die Farben mir unfreundlich sind, male ich mit dem Risiko weiter, zu scheitern oder zu gewinnen. Dies ist auch ein Antrieb, beseelt von der Hoffnung, dass diese zuletzt stirbt und die ›schlechten‹ Farben sich in ›gute‹ Farben verwandeln. Goethes »sinnlich-sittliche Wirkung der Farbe« versteht man vielleicht am besten, wenn man es übersetzt als Empfindungen und ihren Bezug zum Intellekt, zum Geist.

Denken Sie an den reifen Matisse, da sehen alle Farben so leicht aus; diese Leichtigkeit des Seins hat allerdings ein ganzes Arbeitsleben gefordert. Ein Maler, der zuletzt keine schwarzen Pigmente mehr auf seiner Farbpalette hatte.

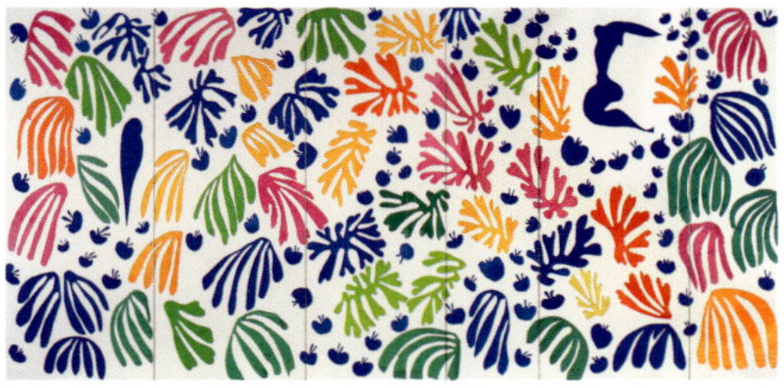

6 Henri Matisse
La perruche et la siren / The Parakeet and the Mermaid, 1952
Gouache auf Papier, geschnitten, geklebt und mit Kohle auf weißem Papier / Gouache on paper, cut, pasted, and charcoal on white paper
337 x 768,5 cm
Sammlung / Collection Stedelijk Museum Amsterdam
Foto: Stedelijk Museum Amsterdam

color, had one alternative left: black light. My black reliefs from the late fifties already anticipated this! Last but not least: Which contemporary painter do you hold in particular esteem, given we assume that colors are the painter's medium?

VEIT LOERS:

If we 'throw light on' Goethe's dictum of moral color and add our accumulated knowledge, then to ask about painters and the effects of their colors is almost paradoxical. Morality does not result in an art canon. Basing his color rules on Goethe, Rudolf Steiner's attempt to dogmatize the canon was unsuccessful. Instead it was always the individual artist who pursued what was not generally valid with experimental means. Matisse's superb color combinations found a plethora of imitators, ranging all the way to kitsch.

Looking back, I have always been interested in painters, whose color nearly slips out of the non-colors black and white, uniting their dual system. Velázquez, Chardin, Manet, Picabia, Guston. Pierre Soulages with his concentration on black, which began in about 1950 with the black-brown of nut stains. It was not until the early eighties that he began to operate with a black system, already sixty at the time.

It takes the viewer, I am actually talking about myself, many years before he recognizes brilliant color situations of painterly mastership and can go beyond simply appreciating what he has read about it. You need to see originals, ideally alongside one another. It was not until I saw your exhibition back then at the Museum Abteiberg Mönchengladbach that the harmonic world of your color system began to present itself in front of my eyes. Thinking of younger painters, I really have to point out Günther Förg, whom you did not particularly like at the time. I guess this was more due to his chaotic appearance than to his painterly results. A young painter who sees Gerhard Richter and Palermo is compelled to construct a different world. While Förg dealt provocatively with color abstraction, he proceeded to produce curious color tensions using the most diverse materials in order to trigger specific emotions. He once told me that he was interested, for instance, in the differences between French and German palettes of color manufacturers. To be quite honest, in Imi Knoebel's case, I am increasingly more interested in his 'quirky' harmonies of color than in his handling of primary colors. Not to forget Albert Oehlen, who in 1985 dedicated his exhibition at the Galerie Ascan Crone to the theory of colors, in particular primary colors, extracting them from their ideality in terms of content.

When you say that you elevate complimentary to primary colors, we reach the phenomenon that we do indeed have Goethe's color circle or Runge's color sphere, but that the deviation constitutes a secret. Is this not exactly what Goethe is striving for in his "moral" color when he talks about "indefinable pleasure"?

HEINZ MACK:

Paik once told a student not to make everything so perfect, because otherwise "God will get angry!"

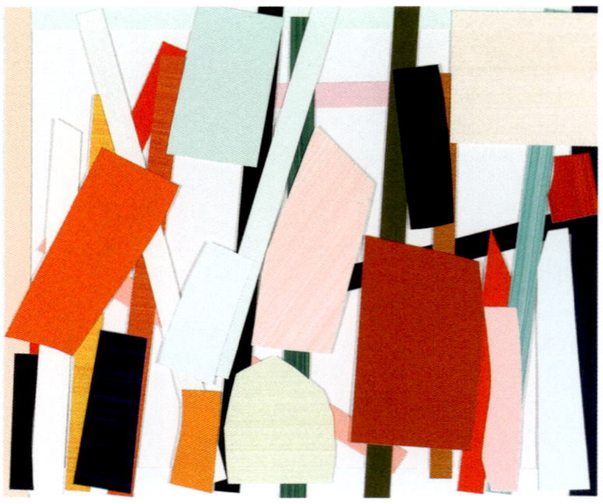

7 Imi Knoebel
Gartenbild 4 / Garden-Image 4, 2013/14
Acryl auf Kunststofffolie / acrylic on plastic film
38 x 46 cm
Privatsammlung / private collection

Und was sagen Sie zum Beispiel über Cy Twombly, der zeitlebens auf den großen Leinwänden weniger gemalt als gezeichnet hat? War er farbenblind, selbst als er in seinen letzten Bildern blutrote Farben benutzte? Pierre Soulages, jede Farbe negierend, hatte vergleichsweise noch eine Alternative: schwarzes Licht. Ende der 1950er-Jahre haben besonders meine schwarzen Reliefs dies bereits vorweggenommen! Last but not least: Welchen Maler unserer Zeit schätzen Sie besonders, wenn wir davon ausgehen, dass es doch die Farben sind, welche das Medium des Malers bedeuten?

VEIT LOERS:
Wenn wir Goethes Maxime der sittlichen Farbe beleuchten und unser angehäuftes Wissen dazunehmen, dann ist Ihre Frage nach den Malern und Ihren Farbwirkungen fast paradox. Aus Sittlichkeit ergibt sich kein Kanon, wie ihn Rudolf Steiner mit seinen Farbregeln nach Goethe vergeblich zu dogmatisieren versuchte, sondern es sind immer wieder einzelne Künstler gewesen, die experimentell etwas nicht allgemein Gültiges verfolgt haben. Die grandiose Farbenkombination von Matisse hat sehr viele Nachahmer gefunden, bis zum Farbkitsch hin.

Mich haben, wenn ich zurückschaue, Maler interessiert, bei denen Farbe quasi aus den Nichtfarben Schwarz und Weiß herausschlüpfte und deren duales System in sich vereinigte: Velázquez, Chardin, Manet, Picabia, Guston. Pierre Soulages mit seiner Konzentration auf das Schwarz, das begann ja um 1950 mit dem Schwarzbraun der Nussbeize. Erst in den frühen 1980er-Jahren operiert er mit einem schwarzen System, da ist er schon 60 Jahre alt.

Der Betrachter, ich rede von mir selbst, braucht auch viele Jahre, um geniale Farbsituationen malerischer Meisterschaft zu erkennen und nicht nur das zu goutieren, was er darüber gelesen hat. Er muss Originale sehen und möglichst einige nebeneinander. Als ich Ihre Ausstellung im Museum Abteiberg Mönchengladbach damals sah, ist mir die Harmoniewelt Ihres Farbensystems erst richtig vor Augen getreten. Aber wenn ich an jüngere Maler denke, dann muss ich doch Günther Förg hervorheben, den Sie damals nicht sonderlich schätzten, jedoch eher seines chaotischen Auftretens wegen als seiner malerischen Ergebnisse. Ein junger Maler, der Gerhard Richter sieht und Palermo, muss sich eine andere Welt konstruieren. Förg ist mit der farbigen Abstraktion provokativ umgegangen, aber hat dann mit den verschiedensten Materialien merkwürdige Farbspannungen erzeugt, die bestimmte Gefühle auslösen. Wie er mir erzählte, interessierte er sich zum Beispiel für die Unterschiede zwischen französischen und deutschen Paletten von Farbenfabrikanten. Bei Imi Knoebel interessierten mich immer mehr die ›schrägen‹ Farbakkorde als sein Umgang mit dem Primären, wenn ich ehrlich bin. Nicht zu vergessen Albert Oehlen, der 1985 seine Ausstellung bei der Galerie Ascan Crone der Farbenlehre widmete, speziell den Primärfarben und sie inhaltlich aus ihrer Idealität herausholte.

Wenn Sie sagen, dass Sie Komplementärfarben zu Primärfarben erheben, dann sind wir bei diesem Phänomen, dass es zwar diesen Goethe-Farbenkreis oder die Runge-Farbenkugel gibt, dass aber ein Geheimnis in der Abweichung besteht. Will Goethe mit seiner »sittlichen« Farbe nicht auf das hinaus, wenn er vom »unaussprechlichen Behagen« spricht?

Deviations in a system are not necessarily mistakes. They mostly hit the artist unexpectedly. Then the question arises of how to deal with it. Luckily, I have the talent to make mistakes, too!

Just think of the phenomenal richness and the diversity of colors whose nuances we can see. This happens within universal nature, hence in the micro- and the macrocosm as well. As always—and here too—scholars attempt to comprehend the underlying principles and laws, whereas the layperson and the artist are the first and the last to be fascinated by beauty, thereby considerably challenging our perceptions and emotions.

The happiness I derive from colors cannot be replaced by anything else. A change of light—it can be warm or cold, clear or opaque, hard or soft, shady or bright—invariably changes the colors. Interestingly, the black-white duality plays a role here as well, wherein the colors appear to be latently hidden. In this regard, I share your interest in the non-colors. I discovered early on that plenty of experience is required before a painter is capable of painting a picture exclusively with the so-called non-colors, which are indeed also light colors. I ought to point out here that for me non-colors are adequate colors. In fact, they have their own privilege within the large color concert.

Black can never be black enough! Just as white can never be too white.

The greatest challenge is if one wants to place white on white. In the late fifties, we managed to convince the gallery owner Alfred Schmela to stage a 'white' exhibition, which attracted a great deal of attention. Numerous artists produced white paintings during the ZERO period—or, like Manzoni, achromatic ones. Thanks to its age, Malevich's white square now has a patina, making the contrast between the white colors increasingly visible. This painting has to be 'painterly' or display an impasto relief supported by the characteristic style of the paint application. Or I paint a cool bluish white on a warm yellow-white background, or vice versa. In the end, you ask the collector to hang the picture on a gray wall so that the light becomes bright and white.

Color and light, light and color, color as light, light as color, color in light, light in the color—this is also a kind of art history.

At times, I also strive to achieve the extreme opposite by painting rows of one hundred preferably clear colors in an additive fashion, and even here I attempt to produce a colorful overall tone. The spectral proportional order—bound to come about intuitively—determines the coexistence and connectedness of the colors. Without it, there would be chaos. Order must repeatedly be sought and found. Here, color theories are but crutches; who would walk with them, let alone dance or float!

It is remarkable that young people obviously have no problem with such an abundance of colors. I wonder what Goethe would have thought in light of a painting with one hundred colors. Yet especially intellectual writers, musicians, painters, philosophers, and even museum directors make lifelong attempts to dress as black as possible. Do they want to protect themselves from colors? Is this, too, a dogma? Black is in fact a beautiful, elegant color, not solely for funerals.

HEINZ MACK:
Paik hat einem Studenten gesagt, er solle nicht alles zu perfekt machen, sonst würde »Gott böse«.

Die Abweichungen in einem System sind nicht notwendigerweise Fehler und treffen den Künstler meistens unerwartet. Dann kommt die Frage auf ihn zu, wie er damit umgehen soll. Glücklicherweise habe ich das Talent, auch Fehler zu machen!

Denken Sie an den phänomenalen Reichtum und die Vielheit der Farben, deren Nuancen wir sehen können, und das geschieht in der Universalnatur, also auch im Mikro- und im Makrokosmos. Wie stets – so auch hier – bemühen sich die Wissenschaftler, die zugrunde liegenden Prinzipien und Gesetze zu erkennen, wogegen der Laie und die Künstler zuerst und zuletzt von der Schönheit fasziniert sind, womit unsere Wahrnehmungen und Empfindungen sehr gefordert werden.

Das Glück, welches mir Farben bereiten, lässt sich durch kein anderes ersetzen. Schon der Wechsel des Lichts, welches warm oder kalt, klar oder trübe, hart oder weich, schattig oder hell sein kann, ändert die Farben. Und interessanterweise spielt auch hier die Schwarz-Weiß-Dualität in der Tat noch mit, in der die Farben latent verborgen zu sein scheinen. In diesem Sinne teile ich Ihr Interesse an den Nichtfarben. Schon früh habe ich erkannt, dass man als Maler sehr umfangreiche Erfahrungen gemacht haben muss, um in der Lage zu sein, allein mit den sogenannten Nichtfarben, die ja auch Lichtfarben sind, ein Bild zu malen. Da darf ich nicht verschweigen, dass Nichtfarben für mich adäquate Farben sind; ja, sie haben ein ihnen eigenes Privileg im großen Farbkonzert.

Schwarz kann gar nicht schwarz genug sein! So wie auch Weiß gar nicht genug weiß sein kann.

Am stärksten wird man gefordert, wenn man Weiß auf Weiß malen will. Ende der 1950er-Jahre ließ sich der Galerist Alfred Schmela von uns überzeugen, eine ›weiße‹ Ausstellung zu machen, die viel Beachtung fand. Nicht wenige Künstler haben in der ZERO-Zeit weiße – oder wie Manzoni achrome – Bilder gemacht. Das weiße Quadrat auf weißem Grund von Malewitsch hat dank seines Alters eine Patina, welche den Kontrast zwischen den Weißfarben sichtbarer macht. Das Malen muss dann ›malerisch‹ sein oder ein pastoses Relief zeigen, unterstützt vom Duktus des Farbauftrags. Oder ich male ein kaltes bläuliches Weiß auf einen warmen gelbweißen Bildgrund, oder umgekehrt. Dann bittet man schließlich den Sammler, das Bild auf eine graue Wand zu hängen, damit es weiß und helles Licht wird.

Farbe und Licht, Licht und Farbe, Farbe als Licht, Licht als Farbe, Farbe im Licht, Licht in der Farbe – das ist auch eine Art Kunstgeschichte.

Das extreme Gegenteil versuche ich zuweilen auch zu erreichen, indem ich einhundert möglichst klare Farben additiv in Reihung male und selbst hier einen farbigen Gesamtklang erstrebe. Das Nebeneinander und Miteinander der Farben wird von einem spektralen Ordnungsverhältnis bestimmt, welches sich intuitiv ergeben muss; ohne dieses würde Chaos herrschen. Die Ordnung muss immer wieder neu gesucht und gefunden werden. Farbtheorien sind da nur Krücken; wer wird damit gehen, geschweige denn tanzen oder schweben?

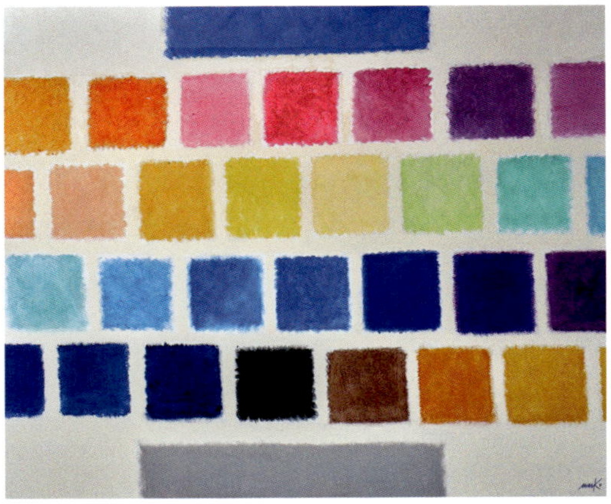

8 Heinz Mack
Ohne Titel *(Chromatische Konstellation)* / Untitled *(Chromatic Constellation)*, 2017
Acryl auf Leinwand / acrylic on canvas
213 x 248 cm

Based on Goethe and Runge as well as Delacroix, in 1922 Paul Klee wrote towards the end of his extremely detailed observations concerning color theory: "There are so many clever people … . The contrapuntal relation between blue, yellow, and red, the fact that they formed a balanced totality, was recognized long ago." Then he defends himself as follows: "Only use the three primary colors blue, yellow, and red, in their most perfect purity. And in their most perfect balance. For they contain all the other colors. Then all the other colors arise by themselves. Such people make a principle of jumping like goats." He continues: "And so I should like to warn you against the impoverishment that comes of taking the low too literally. … Such a misunderstanding might lead you to end up with nothing but gray, on the ground that it … contains all the colors, … even black and white." Then Paul Klee vehemently turns against gray, calling it "one nothing." And Heinz Mack states: The happiness I derive from colors cannot be replaced by anything else!

VEIT LOERS:
Since this is about happiness, how could anyone contradict you? According to your descriptions, the circumstances in which colors appear are bright walls, dark walls, direct light, raking light, as well as the differences between the materials: canvas, paper, wooden panel, metal. There is no room for dogma. And when you mention black and white as non-colors, I immediately think of the respective frames in Mondrian's oeuvre, which are not lines but painted strips, and the white planes are not voids but bright paintings. Apparently, the human condition continues to always require comparisons. This starts with the equilibrium in our brain and ends with a sip of wine that must be placed into a gustatory comparability in order to be appreciated. This is where the problems begin. If you find your equilibrium in a semidry thus sweet wine, your gustatory prerequisites are different from those of someone who prefers dry wine—like myself. Which brings us to analogies pertaining to color. Despite seemingly objective criteria, when it comes to the realm of taste the differences are not solely of an individual nature but entail national and even ethnic facets. Americans grow up with different colors than Germans, and I know precious little about Asian color theory. As is the case with many impressions, our knowledge regarding the influence of the environment and genetics is still severely limited. The only thing that really frightens me are the giant printed colors of international advertisements, which we are unable to escape. Or fashionable colors used to make buildings attractive. I believe that this is where we are as opposed to Goethe's ethics of color. We are in the middle of color manipulation.

Apart from that, in terms of evolution we should accept what has been coming our way for millennia and to which Goethe gave an evolutionary answer with recourse to Plotinus: "Were the eye not of the sun, how could we behold light?" *(Tame Xenias,* 1825). What do you think?

Bemerkenswert ist, dass die jungen Leute mit einer solchen Fülle an Farben offensichtlich gar keine Probleme haben. Ich frage mich, was Goethe gedacht hätte beim Anblick eines Gemäldes mit einhundert Farben. Andererseits kleiden sich besonders intellektuelle Schriftsteller, Musiker oder Maler, Philosophen, aber auch Museumsdirektoren/-innen lebenslang so schwarz und dunkel wie möglich, da sie sich vielleicht vor Farben schützen möchten? Auch ein Dogma? Schwarz ist in der Tat eine schöne, elegante Farbe, nicht nur anlässlich einer Beerdigung.

Ausgehend von Goethe und Runge sowie Delacroix schreibt Paul Klee am Ende seiner denkbar ausführlichen Betrachtungen zur Farbenlehre 1922: »Es gibt sehr viele gescheite Leute [...]. Und so ist auch die Kanonische Bedeutung von Blau Gelb Rot längst erkannt worden, eine Bedeutung mit Bezug auf die Vollständigkeit dieser drei und [...] auf ihr Gleichgewicht.« Dann wehrt er sich dagegen: »[...] nur die drei Primären Blau Gelb Rot in ihrer vollkommensten Reinheit anwenden! und in ihrem vollkommensten Gleichgewicht! Denn sie begreifen alle andern Farben in sich! Alle andern Farben entstehn dann von selber. Das sind Beispiele von Leuten die principielle Bockssprünge machen wollen [...].« Und er sagt ferner: »Ich möchte also warnen vor einer solchen Gesetzlichen Verarmung [...]. Denn sonst könnten wir endlich beim Grau an sich anlangen [...]. [...] In diesem Grau sei alles an Farben enthalten, [...] auch Schwarz und Weiss.« Dann wendet sich Paul Klee heftig gegen das Grau und bezeichnet dies als das Nichts. Und Heinz Mack sagt: Das Glück, welches mir Farben bereiten, lässt sich durch kein anderes ersetzen!

VEIT LOERS:
Wie sollte man Ihnen da widersprechen, wenn es um das Glück geht. Und die Umstände, in denen Farben auftreten, sind so, wie Sie beschreiben, lichte Wand, dunkle Wand, direktes Licht, Streiflicht und die Unterschiede des Trägers, Leinwand, Papier, Holzplatte, Metall; da passt kein Dogma. Und wenn Sie Schwarz und Weiß als Nichtfarben erwähnen, dann denke ich sofort an die entsprechenden Rahmungen bei Mondrian, die keine dicken Linien sind, sondern gemalte Stege, und die weißen Flächen keine Fehlstellen, sondern helle Malerei. Die menschliche Konditionierung bedarf offensichtlich immer des Vergleichs. Das geht schon mit dem Gleichgewicht im Gehirn los und endet mit einem Schluck Wein, den man in eine geschmackliche Vergleichbarkeit setzen muss, damit man ihn goutieren kann. Aber da fangen die Probleme an. Wer sein Gleichgewicht in einem halbtrockenen, sprich lieblichen Wein findet, setzt andere geschmackliche Voraussetzungen als jemand, der trockenen Wein bevorzugt wie ich selbst. Und da sind wir analog bei der Farbe. Trotz scheinbar objektiver Richtlinien sind wir in einem Geschmacksumfeld, das nicht nur individuell, sondern auch national und sogar ethnisch verschieden ist. Amerikaner sind mit anderen Farben groß geworden als Deutsche, und von asiatischer Farbtheorie weiß ich sehr wenig. Wie bei vielen Prägungen verstehen wir noch wenig, was über Umwelt auf uns einwirkt und was genetisch. Das Einzige, was mir Angst bereitet, sind die riesigen geprinteten Farben der internationalen Werbung, der wir nicht entgehen können. Oder Modefarben, mit denen Gebäude attraktiv gemacht werden. Da stehen wir, denke ich, im Gegensatz zu Goethes Farb-Ethik. Da befinden wir uns mitten in einer gesteuerten Farbmanipulation.

HEINZ MACK:
To set the record straight: for me, the colors black and white are equally entitled as pure colors. In Mondrian's late paintings, all colors—including black and white—are truly related to one another in a balanced way.

Goethe's maxim "Were the eye not of the sun ...," anticipated by Plotinus and Pseudo-Dionysius the Areopagite, ingeniously incarnates a sensorial as well as a cognitive status, placing humans way ahead of all other living creatures (who in turn possess other abilities). You are correct to refer to this as "evolutionary." Our ability to see was in fact not—ad hoc et ad nunc—bestowed upon us by a god but has developed in a quasi-self-organized, biological process.

I must cite Goethe once more, whose examining thinking and thinking examination is a type of dialectic that leads to an entity and entelechy. Clearly, for Goethe, sensuous thought was more meaningful than sensuous vision alone. Now we enter the realm of metaphysics, wherein the creative abilities of humankind—according to Goethe, "active and passive modifications"—are emancipated from the dark Middle Ages. Now, humans are responsible for its design. Entering into a secular world, where they are responsible for the condition humaine, humans now replace the Christian creed according to which God created the world. A dynamic process indeed. In it, light acts as enlightenment in the literal sense of the word. This is why I called one of my kinetic sculptures at Düsseldorf's airport *Helios*. Plato already understood that without light eyes would make no sense. In this instance, he is in line with Greek mythology, in which Helios is the god of light.

Our conversation about colors involuntarily approaches philosophy and the metaphysics of light, which Plotinus found particularly fascinating, as did the Persian mystic Ghazālī. For him the Qur'an represents the sun's light and likewise the light-filled transparence of reason. I produced a big, bibliophile book about him with my nonrepresentational, colored pastels. Far ahead of him, in the sense of an end-of-the-world prophecy St. John's Apocalypse elevated mysticism even further. Today, we are forcefully reminded of a possible nuclear inferno that would ultimately blind us. The light's deadly intensity in Hiroshima left no color behind. I said this to Yves Klein, who was in the process of having his anthropomorphic pictures 'painted' with the aid of young nude women. Then the 'imprints' would be traced with the burn marks of flashes of fire.

A philosopher has to understand that the place occupied by the emanation of Christ's light in the Christian notion of Revelation is occupied by artificial light in today's secular world. Even our nighttime metropolises are impressive light carpets or light diadems whose beauty I love to watch from the airplane. The current purpose of light is to make everything in the world visible and controllable. What type of light illuminated the darkness during Goethe's time? In 1921, Lenin stated: "One electrician is worth ten communists." Nowadays, electronic engineering is in a position to present colors in purely virtual ways. After all, within micro- and cosmic research in the natural sciences, the latest development of the scanning electron microscope is just as fasci-

Ansonsten sollten wir evolutiv hinnehmen, was seit Millionen von Jahren auf unsere Körper einströmt und was Goethe in Rückgriff auf Plotin voraussehend evolutiv beantwortet hat: »Wär' nicht das Auge sonnenhaft, die Sonne könnt' es nie erblicken [...]« *(Zahme Xenien,* 1825). Oder wie sehen Sie es?

HEINZ MACK:
Um das richtigzustellen: Für mich sind die Farben Schwarz und Weiß ebenso berechtigt wie die reinen Farben. In Mondrians späten Bildern sind alle Farben – einschließlich Schwarz und Weiß – wirklich gleichgewichtig aufeinander bezogen.

Goethes Maxime »Wär' nicht das Auge sonnenhaft [...]«, von Plotin und vom Pseudo-Dionysios Areopagita vorausgesehen, inkarniert auf geniale Weise einen sensorischen und auch kognitiven Status, mit dem der Mensch allen anderen Lebewesen weit voraus ist (die ihrerseits andere Fähigkeiten haben). Sie bezeichnen das mit Recht als »evolutiv«. Die Fähigkeit, zu sehen, ist ja nicht – ad hoc et ad nunc – uns von einem Gott geschenkt worden, sondern hat sich quasi selbstorganisatorisch in einem biologischen Prozess entwickelt.

Auch hier wäre dann wiederum Goethe zu zitieren, dessen anschauendes Denken und denkendes Anschauen eine Art Dialektik ist und zu einer Entität und Entelechie führt. Für Goethe war das sinnliche Denken also bedeutungsvoller als das sinnliche Sehen allein. Damit begeben wir uns in den Bereich einer Metaphysik, in der die kreativen Fähigkeiten des Menschen – das sind nach Goethe ebenso »Taten und Leiden« – sich vom dunklen Mittelalter emanzipiert haben und der Mensch für seine Gestaltung selbst verantwortlich wird. An die Stelle des christlichen Credos, Gott habe die Welt gemacht, tritt nun der Mensch in einer säkularen Welt und wird für seine ›condition humaine‹ verantwortlich. Das ist wohl ein dynamischer Prozess, in dem das Licht die Funktion einer Aufklärung hat, Aufklärung im wörtlichen Sinne. Darum habe ich eine große kinetische Skulptur, welche im Düsseldorfer Flughafen steht, *Helios* genannt. Platon erkannte bereits, dass ohne Licht die Augen keinen Sinn ergeben würden; da folgt er der griechischen Mythologie, in der Helios der Gott des Lichtes ist.

Unser Gespräch über Farben nähert sich ungewollt der Philosophie und einer Lichtmetaphysik, die besonders Plotin, aber auch den persischen Mystiker al-Ghazālī fasziniert hat, für den der Koran das Licht der Sonne ist und gleichermaßen die lichterfüllte Transparenz der Vernunft. Über ihn habe ich ja ein großes bibliophiles Buch mit meinen gegenstandslosen farbigen Pastellen gemacht. Ihm weit voraus hat die Johannes-Apokalypse die Mystik noch gesteigert im Sinne einer Prophezeiung des Endes der Welt; heute werden wir an die Möglichkeit eines atomaren Infernos gemahnt, in dem wir endgültig geblendet würden. Die tödliche Lichtintensität in Hiroshima hinterließ keine Farben mehr; das sagte ich zu Yves Klein, als er mithilfe unbekleideter Mädchen seine anthropomorphen Bilder ›malen‹ ließ. Dann würden die ›Abdrücke‹ mit den Brandspuren von Feuerstrahlen umzeichnet.

Was man als Philosoph erkennen muss, ist, dass anstelle der christlich gedachten Offenbarung, der Emanation des Lichtes in Christus, heute das Kunstlicht unsere säkulare Welt erhellt. Selbst unsere nächtlichen Metropolen beeindrucken als Lichtteppiche oder Lichtdiademe, deren Schönheit ich vom Flugzeug aus so gerne betrachte. Heute hat das nating as the luminous deep-sea creatures encountered in total darkness at a depth of one thousand meters.

A kind of light mythology developed in ZERO art as well. Its phenomenology was free of all religious claims. After the catastrophic and desolate consequences of the last war, this was a kind of purification. Now, Malevich's white square on white ground was worshipped. Personally, I later bid farewell to doctrines.

The purity, radiance, and luminosity of colors occur thanks to light; and yet we do not know what light is. The obligatory answer of physicists remains entirely enigmatic to me. When he was an older man, Albert Einstein said: "For the rest of my life I will reflect on what is light."

If we can explain miracles we ought to do so; we should not be surprised if we very quickly come up against limits. Colors are a miracle, especially to me. The fact that we are capable of consciously perceiving the world in colors might be cited as a form of proof of God's existence. And here, I once more follow Goethe: "Let man seek nothing behind the phenomena, for they themselves are the theory."

"In our universe, light becomes matter and matter becomes light." (Louis de Broglie). This fundamental definition of natural occurrences could equally be transferred to painting: in painting, light turns into colored matter and colored matter turns into light. The identity of light and color that is made visible in the spectrum is the subject of my painting—it is its sole subject.

Licht die Funktion, alles in der Welt sichtbar und kontrollierbar zu machen. Welches Licht erhellte die Dunkelheit zur Goethe-Zeit? Lenin erklärte 1921: »Ein Elektriker ist zehn Kommunisten wert.« Nun ist die Elektronik in der Lage, die Farben rein virtuell zu präsentieren. Schließlich ist in der Mikro- und Kosmosforschung der Naturwissenschaften die neueste Entwicklung des Rasterelektronenmikroskops ebenso faszinierend wie es die leuchtenden Wesen der Tiefsee in tausend Meter Tiefe in totaler Dunkelheit sind.

In der ZERO-Kunst hatte sich gleichfalls eine Art Lichtmythologie entwickelt, deren Phänomenologie von allen religiösen Ansprüchen sich befreit hatte. Es war eine Art Purifikation nach den katastrophalen und desolaten Folgen des letzten Weltkriegs. Malewitschs weißes Quadrat auf weißem Grund wurde nun angebetet. Ich selbst habe mich von Doktrinen später verabschiedet.

Die Reinheit, Leucht- und Strahlkraft der Farben verdanken wir dem Licht, ohne zu wissen, was Licht ist. Die verbindliche Antwort der Physiker bleibt mir gänzlich unverständlich. Albert Einstein sagte als älterer Mann: »Was das Licht ist, diese Frage wird mich bis an das Ende meines Lebens begleiten.«

Soweit man Wunder erklären kann, sollte man sie erklären, aber sich nicht wundern, wenn man sehr bald an Grenzen steht. Farben sind ein Wunder, besonders für mich. Die Tatsache, dass wir die Welt bewusst farbig wahrnehmen können, kann man eine Art Gottesbeweis nennen. Und da folge ich noch einmal Goethe: »Man suche nur nichts hinter den Phänomenen; sie selbst sind die Lehre.«

»Licht wird in unserem Universum zu Materie, und Materie wird zu Licht.« (Louis de Broglie). Man könnte diese Definition allen elementaren Naturgeschehens auf die Malerei übertragen: Licht wird in der Malerei zu Farbmaterie, und die Farbmaterie wird zu Licht. Die Identität von Licht und Farbe, welche im Spektrum sichtbar wird, ist der Gegenstand meiner Malerei – sie ist ihr einziger Gegenstand.

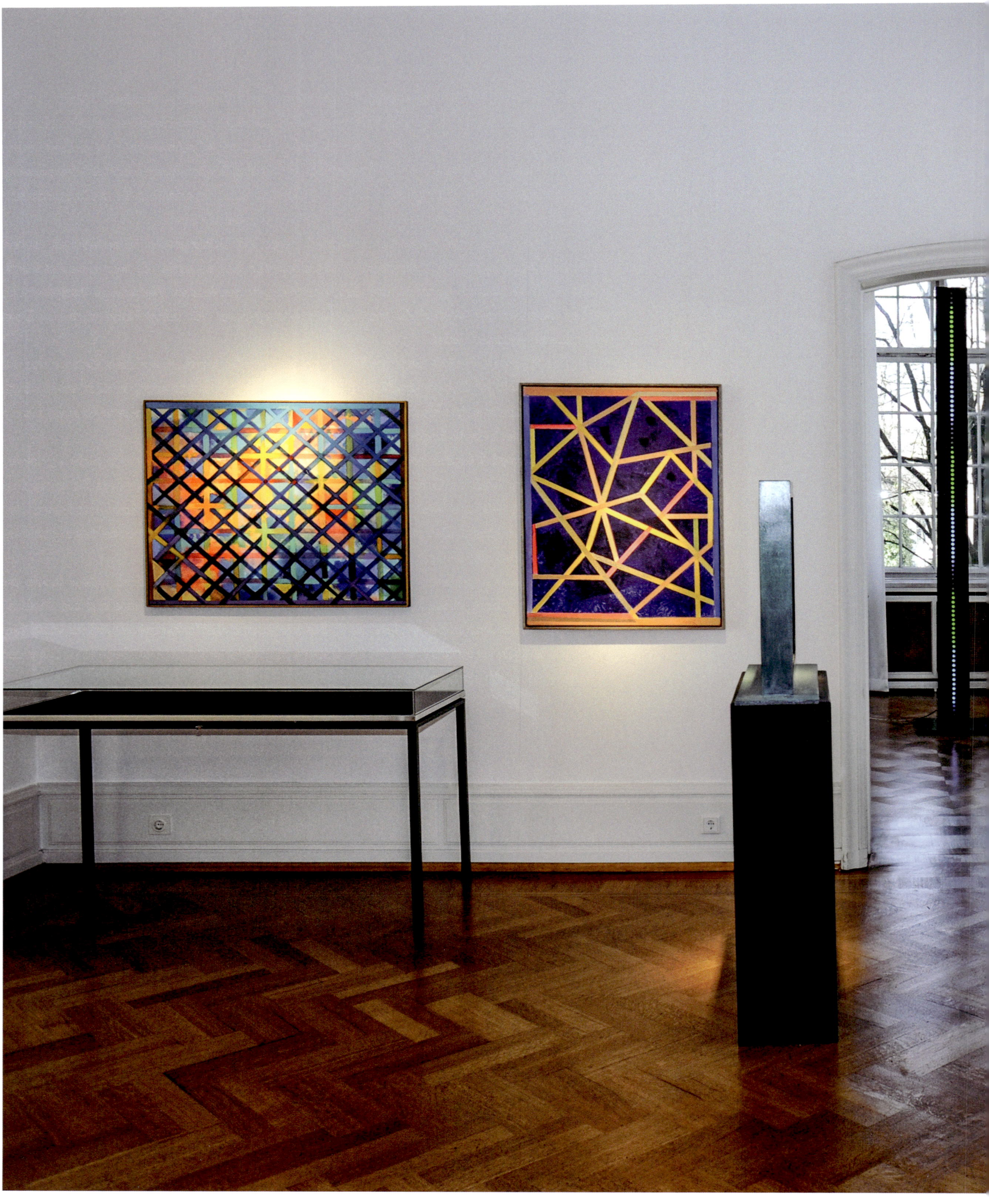

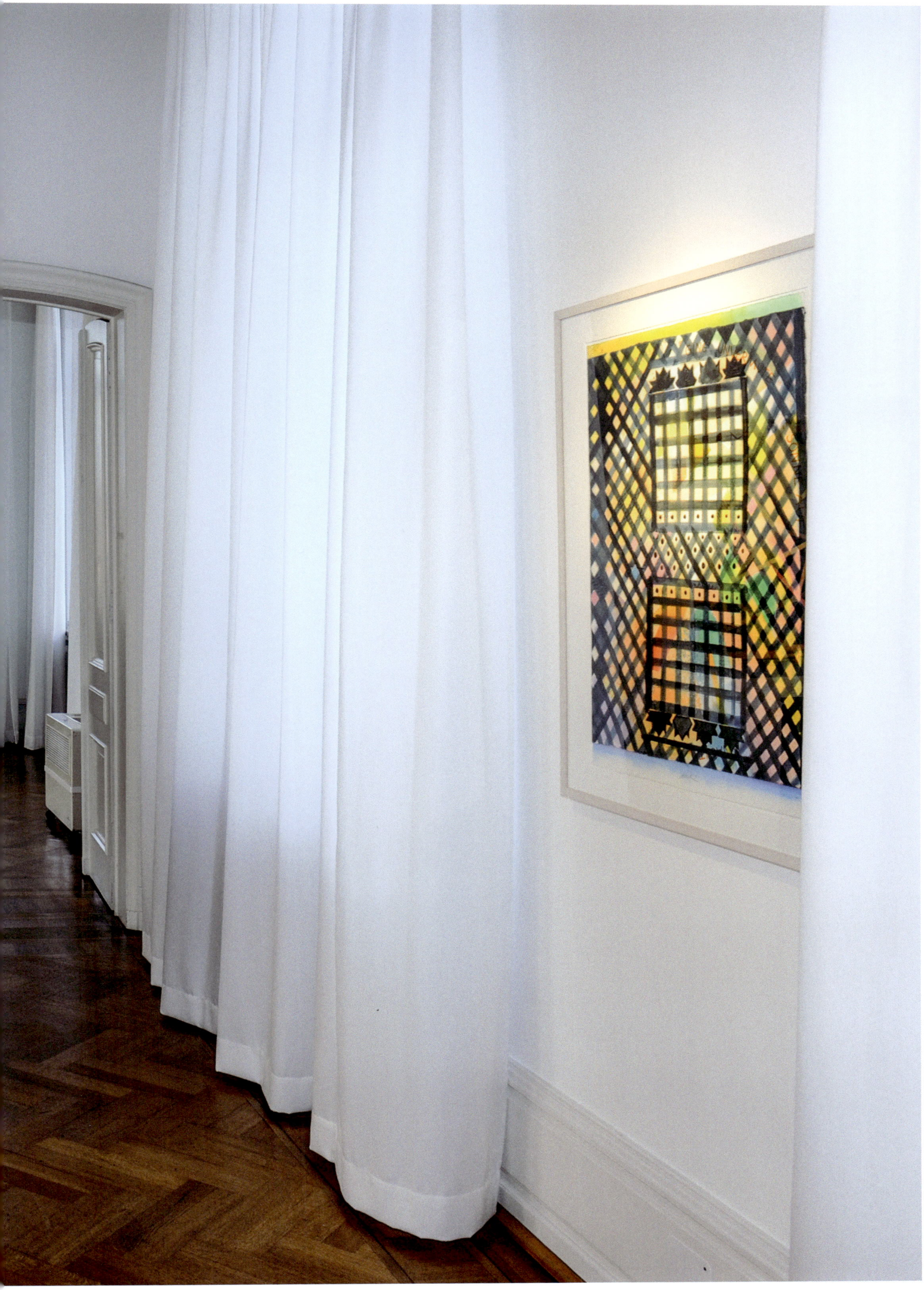

Anhang

Appendix

Johann Joseph Schmeller (1794–1841)
Goethe in seinem Arbeitszimmer
im Wohnhaus am Frauenplan in Weimar,
dem Schreiber John diktierend, 1834
Öl auf Leinwand
66 x 59,5 cm
Klassik Stiftung Weimar, Museen

Johann Joseph Schmeller (1794–1841)
Goethe in the study at his home
on Frauenplan in Weimar,
dictating to his scribe John, 1834
Oil on canvas
66 x 59.5 cm
Klassik Stiftung Weimar, Museen

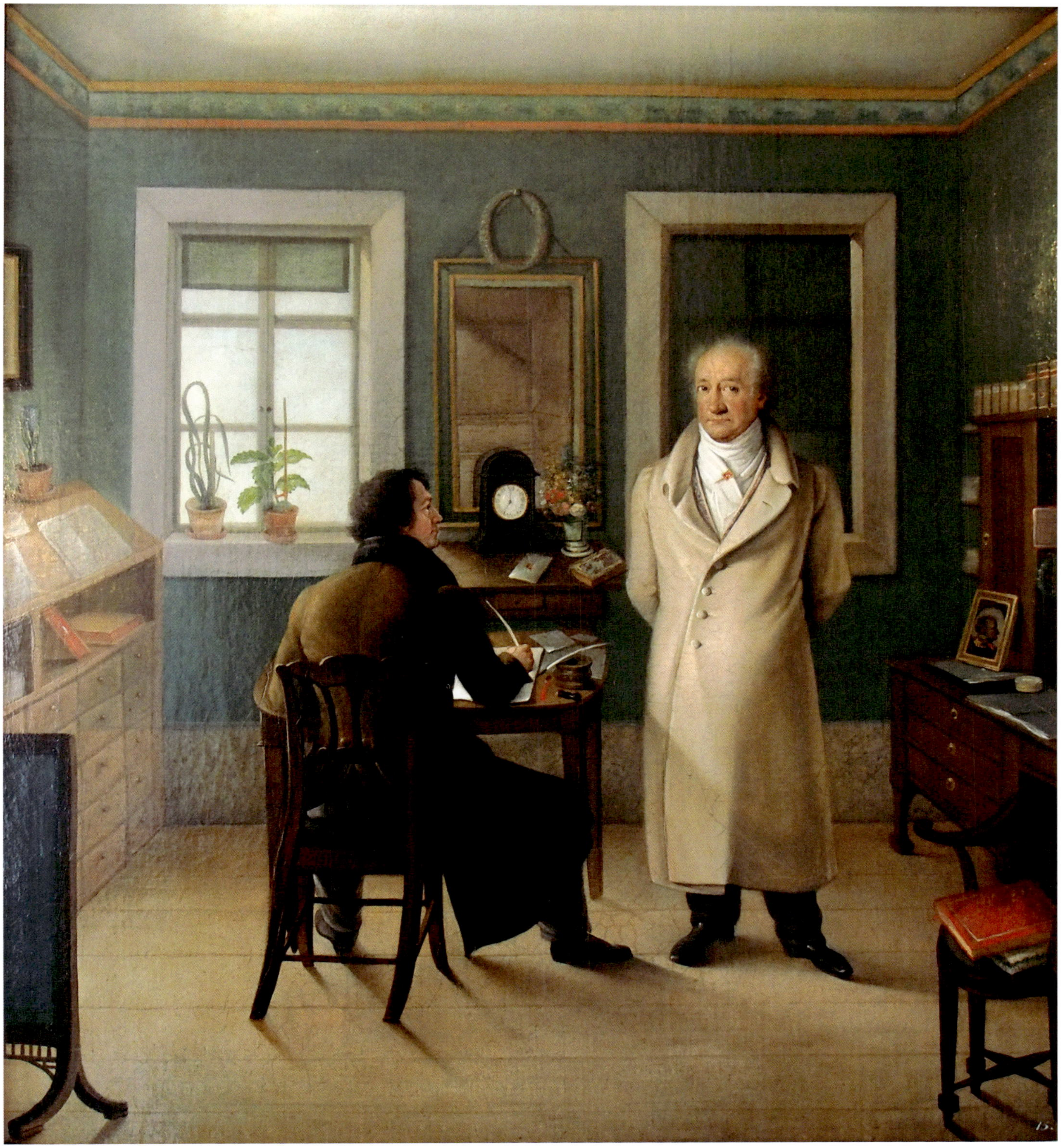

Johann Wolfgang von Goethe

1749
Am 28. August geboren in Frankfurt am Main

1765–1768
Studium der Jurisprudenz in Leipzig

1768/69
Wegen schwerer Krankheit Rückkehr nach Frankfurt

1770/71
Fortsetzung des Studiums in Straßburg
Sturm-und-Drang-Gedichte

1771
Promotion zum Lizentiat der Rechte und Arbeit als Rechtsanwalt in Frankfurt

1774
Besuch bei den Brüdern Jacobi in Pempelfort / Düsseldorf

1775
Ankunft in Weimar auf Einladung des Herzogs Carl August von Sachsen-Weimar-Eisenach

1776
Einzug in das Gartenhaus an der Ilm
Eintritt in den weimarischen Staatsdienst

1777
Entwurf des Sandsteinmonuments *Stein des guten Glücks* aus den Elementarformen Kugel und Würfel für seinen Garten am Stern in Weimar

1779
Beginn meteorologischer Beobachtungen

1784
Entdeckung des menschlichen Zwischenkieferknochens
Studien *Über den Granit*

1785
Beginn botanischer Studien

1786–1788
Aufenthalt in Italien: Kunst- und Zeichenstudien, Konzept der ›Urpflanze‹ und »Spekulationen über Farben«

1790
Versuch die Metamorphose der Pflanzen zu erklären
›Aperçu‹ beim Blick durch ein Prisma

1791/92
Beyträge zur Optik mit Versuchsanleitungen zur Farbwahrnehmung

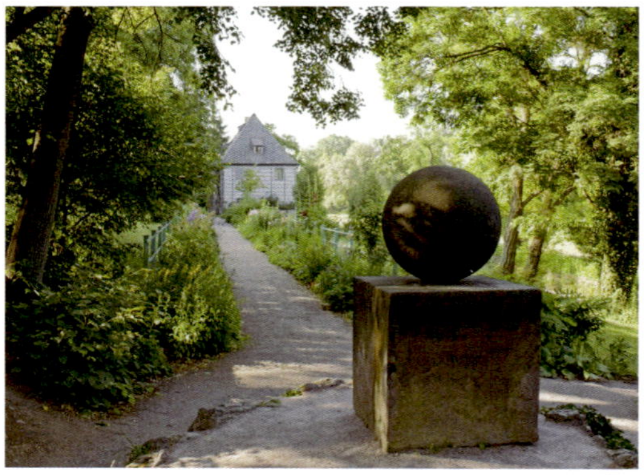

Johann Wolfgang von Goethe
Stein des guten Glücks, s. S. 37

Johann Wolfgang von Goethe
Stone of Good Fortune, see p. 37

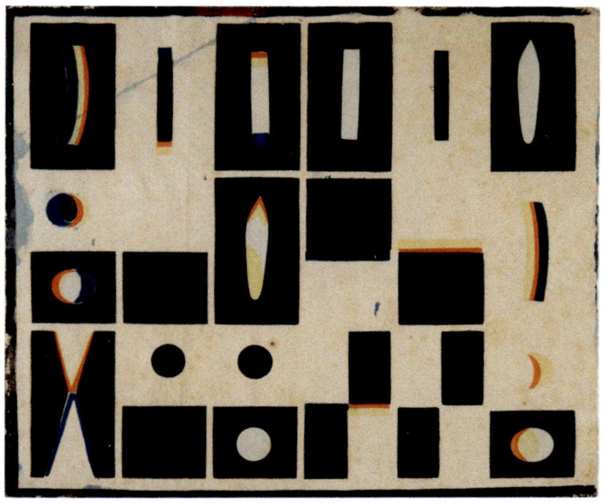

Johann Wolfgang von Goethe
Druckbogen für das ›Optische Kartenspiel‹,
s. S. 201

Johann Wolfgang von Goethe
Print for the 'Optical Card Game',
see p. 201

1792
Auf der Rückreise von der Campagne in Frankreich vier Wochen Aufenthalt in Pempelfort/Düsseldorf bei Friedrich Heinrich Jacobi, wo Goethe die Gesellschaft mit optischen Experimenten unterhielt

1793
Fortgeführte Auseinandersetzung mit Newtons Optik
Ableitung des Farbenkreises aus den prismatischen Farben

1794
Unterredung über die ›Urpflanze‹ mit Schiller

1796
Versuche zur Einwirkung weißen und farbigen Lichtes auf das Wachstum von Pflanzen
Beobachtungen zur Morphologie

1798
Überlegungen zur Harmonie der Farben

1803
Oberaufsicht über die naturwissenschaftlichen Institute der Universität Jena

1808
Faust I

1810
Zur Farbenlehre

1814/15
Lektüre der Gedichtsammlung *Diwan* des persischen Lyrikers Hafis in deutscher Übersetzung
Begegnung mit Marianne von Willemer in Frankfurt
Beginn der Arbeit an dem Gedichtzyklus *West-oestlicher Divan*

1817–1824
Zeitschrift *Zur Naturwissenschaft überhaupt, besonders zur Morphologie*

1819
West-oestlicher Divan

1829–1831
Letzte Forschungen zur Botanik über die Spiraltendenz der Vegetation

1831
Abschluss des *Faust II*

1832
Letzte Mitteilungen zur Farbenlehre in Briefen an Sulpiz Boisserée über den Regenbogen

Johann Wolfgang von Goethe

1749
28th of August born in Frankfurt am Main

1765–68
Study of law in Leipzig

1768–69
Return to Frankfurt due to serious illness

1770–71
Continuation of studies in Strasbourg
Storm and Stress poems

1771
Degree of licentiate in law and lawyer in Frankfurt

1774
Visit to the brothers Jacobi in Pempelfort / Düsseldorf

1775
Arrival in Weimar at the invitation of Duke Carl August of Saxe-Weimar-Eisenach

1776
Move into the garden house on the banks of the river Ilm
Formal entry into the Weimar civil service

1777
Sandstone monument *Stein des guten Glücks* (Stone of Good Fortune), designed by Goethe for his garden at the Stern, using the elementary shapes sphere and cube

1779
Beginning of meteorological observations

1784
Discovery of the intermaxillary bone in humans
Studies *Über den Granit* (On Granite)

1785
Beginning of botanical studies

1786–88
Residence in Italy: drawing and art studies, concept of the 'primordial plant' and "speculations on color"

1790
Versuch die Metamorphose der Pflanzen zu erklären (The Metamorphosis of Plants)
'Aperçu' while looking through a prism

1791–92
Beyträge zur Optik (Contributions to Optics) with instructions on how to conduct experiments on color perception

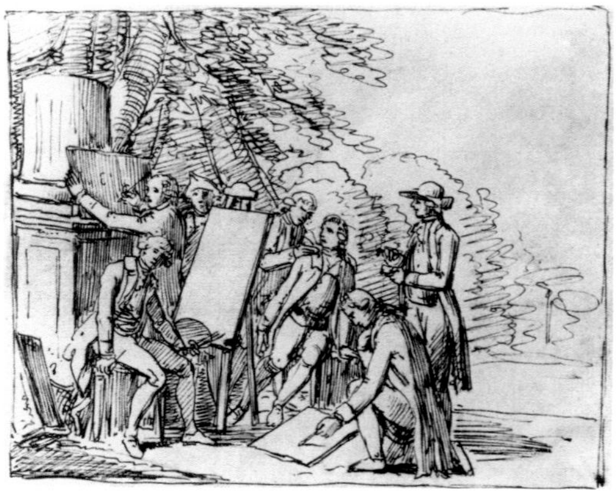

Friedrich Bury (1763–1823)
Goethe und sein römischer Freundeskreis
1786–1788
Tusche, 16,3 x 21 cm
Goethe-Museum Düsseldorf

Friedrich Bury (1763–1823)
Goethe and his Roman Friends, 1786–88
Indian ink, 16.3 x 21 cm
Goethe-Museum Düsseldorf

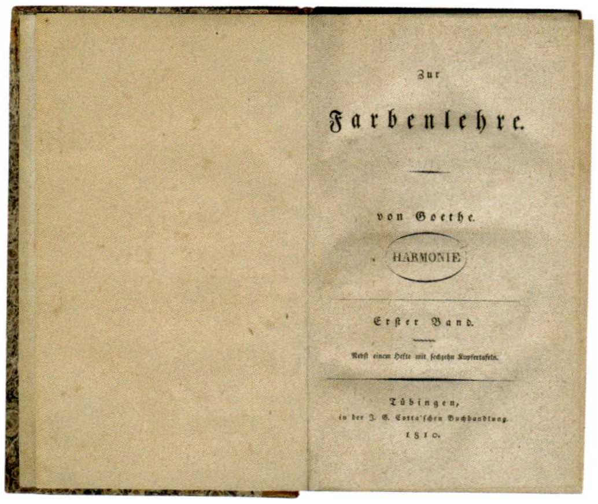

Johann Wolfgang von Goethe
Zur Farbenlehre, s. S. 224 / see p. 224

1792
On the return journey from the campaign in France a four week stay in Pempelfort / Düsseldorf with Friedrich Heinrich Jacobi, where Goethe entertained his friends with optical experiments

1793
Continued contestation with Newton's optics
Derivation of the color wheel from the prismatic colors

1794
Discussion about the 'primordial plant' with Schiller

1796
Experiments on the influence of white and colored light on the growth of plants
Observations on morphology

1798
Considerations about the harmony of colors

1803
Supervision of the scientific institutes of the University of Jena

1808
Faust I

1810
Zur Farbenlehre (Theory of Colours)

1814–15
Reading of the poetry collection *Diwan* by the Persian poet Hafiz in German translation
Encounter with Marianne von Willemer in Frankfurt
Beginning to work on the collection *West-oestlicher Divan* (West-East Divan)

1817–24
Journal *Zur Naturwissenschaft überhaupt, besonders zur Morphologie*
(On Natural Science)

1819
West-oestlicher Divan

1829–31
Last botanical studies on the spiral tendency in vegetation

1831
Completion of *Faust II*

1832
Last notes on the theory of colors in letters to Sulpiz Boisserée concerning the rainbow

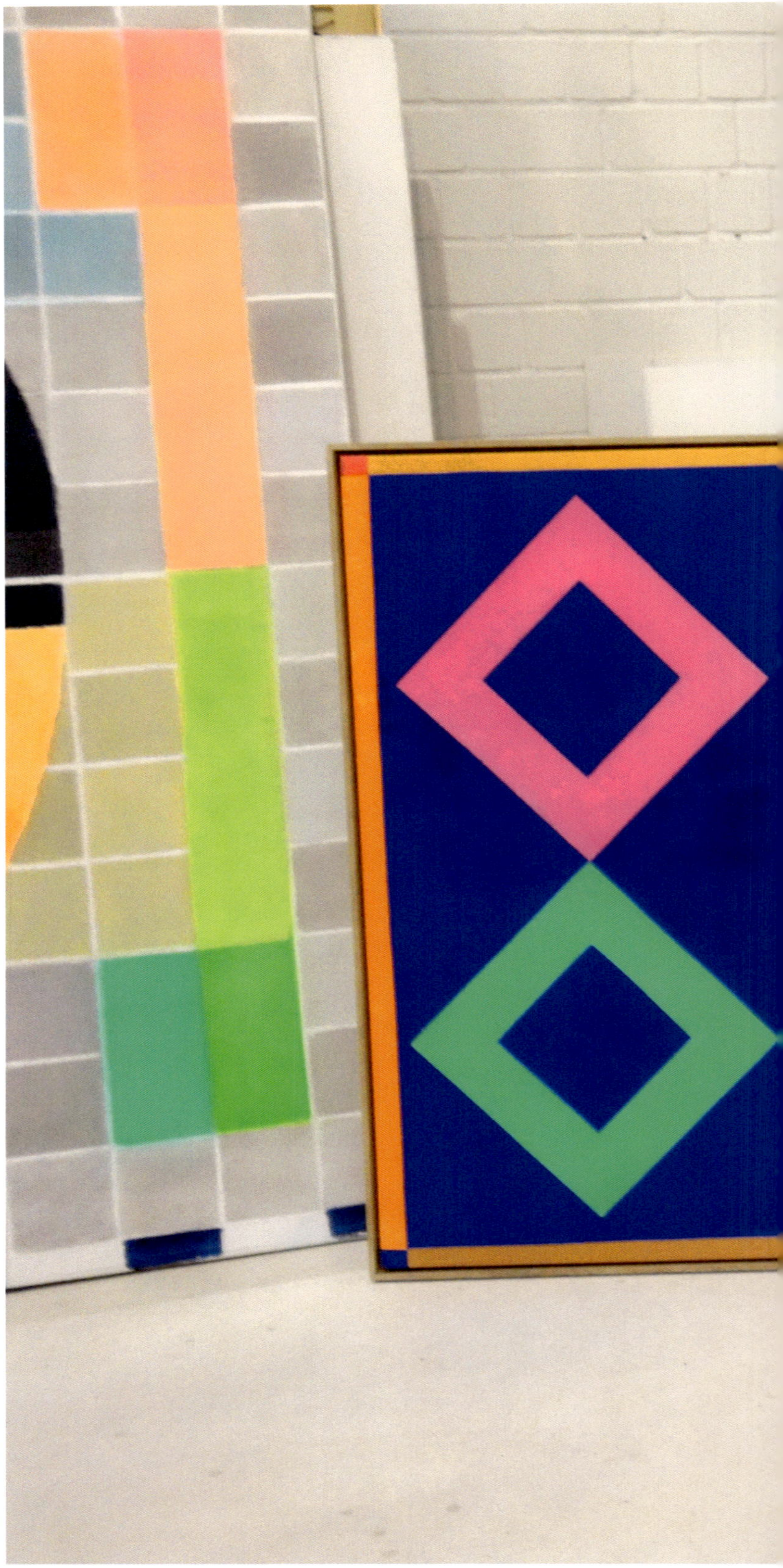

Heinz Mack in seinem Atelier
in Mönchengladbach, 2016
Im Hintergrund:
die *Chromatische Konstellation*
nach einem Experiment zu Goethes
Farbenlehre, s. S. 49

Heinz Mack in his studio
in Möchengladbach, 2016
In the background:
the *Chromatic Constellation*
according to an experiment on
the subject of Goethe's color theory,
see p. 49

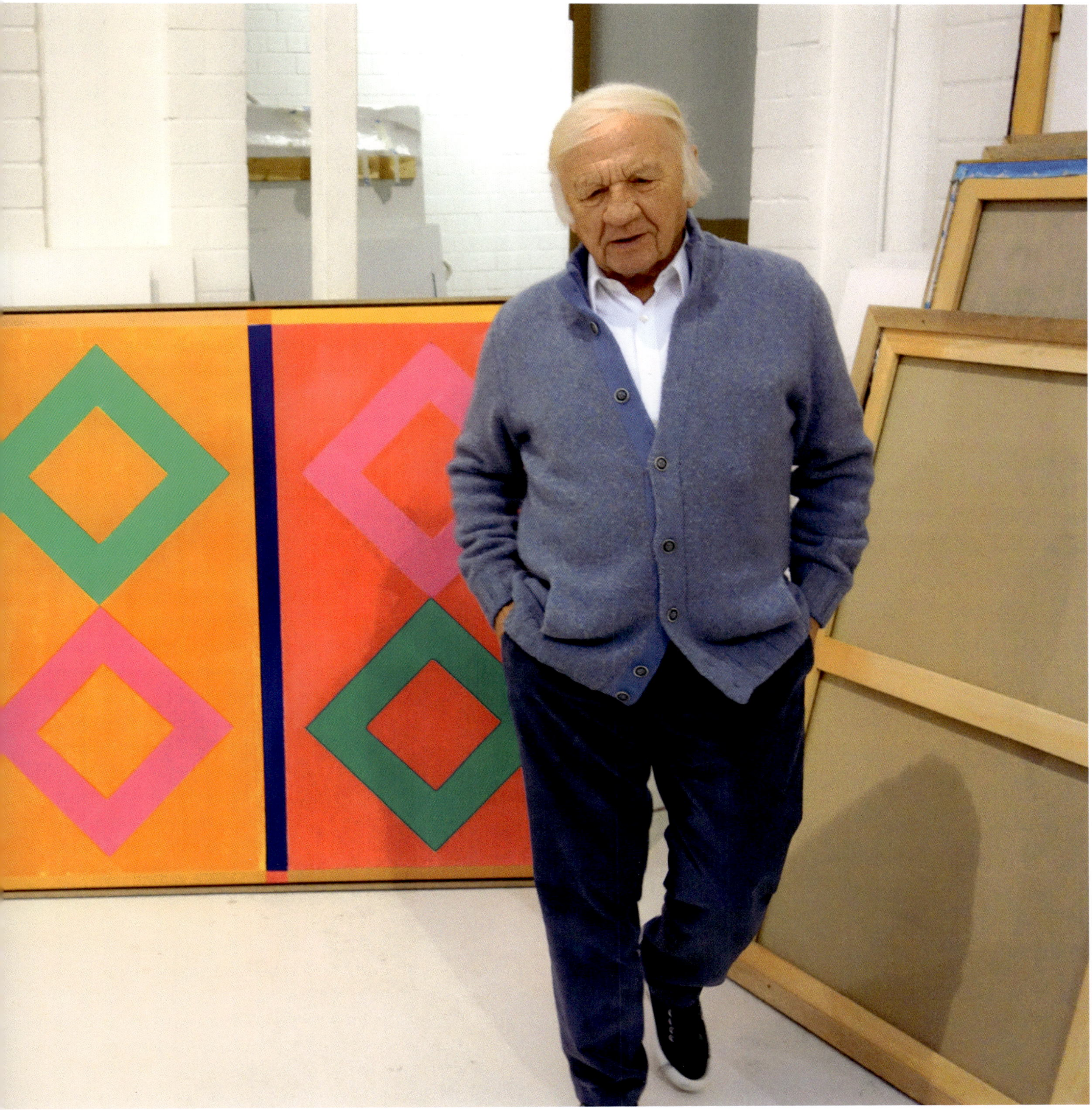

Heinz Mack

1931
Am 8. März geboren in Lollar / Hessen

1950–1953
Studium an der Kunstakademie Düsseldorf mit Abschluss Staatsexamen

1953–1956
Studium der Philosophie an der Universität zu Köln mit Abschluss Staatsexamen

1957
Gründung der Avantgarde-Gruppe ZERO mit Otto Piene

1958
Kunstpreis Krefeld

1959
Teilnahme an der II. Documenta in Kassel

1963
Auszeichnung mit dem Premio Marzotto, Italien

1964
Teilnahme an der Documenta III in Kassel
Pastell *for Mr. Wolfgang v. Goethe* (und ein zweites *for Mr. Newton)*

1965
1. Prix des arts plastiques, Quatrième Biennale de Paris

1970
Adolf-Grimme-Anerkennungspreis für den Film *Tele-Mack*
Professur und Lehrauftrag in Osaka
Ordentliches Mitglied der Akademie der Künste in Berlin
Beteiligung an der Gestaltung des Deutschen Pavillons der 35. Biennale di Venezia

1971
Anerkennungspreis der Film-Biennale Venedig für den Film *Tele-Mack*

1977
Teilnahme an der Documenta 6 in Kassel

1979
1. Preis beim internationalen Wettbewerb *Licht '79,* Eindhoven

1981
3 x 4 Meter großes Licht- bzw. Farbspektrum als *Hommage à Goethe*
anlässlich des 150. Todestages Goethes 1982

1987
Verdienstorden des Landes Nordrhein-Westfalen

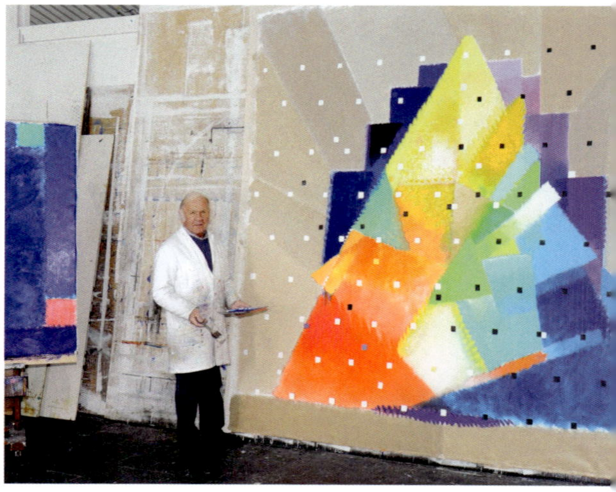

Heinz Mack in seinem Atelier
in Mönchengladbach, 2018

Heinz Mack in his studio
in Mönchengladbach, 2018

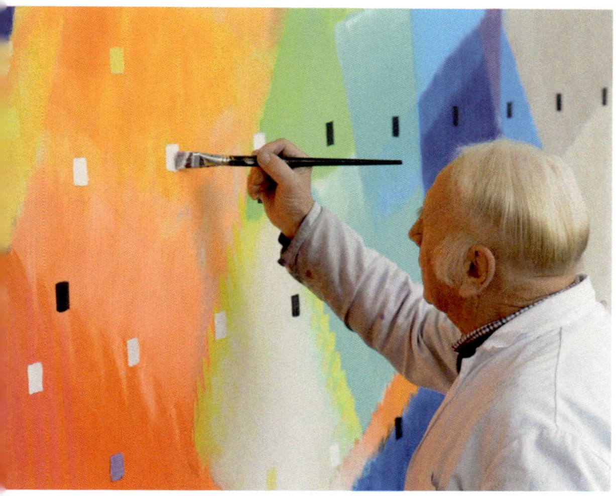

Der Künstler bei der Arbeit, 2018

The artist at work, 2018

1988
Wachskreidezeichnung *Gruß an Goethe*

1991
Zwei Papierarbeiten nach Goethes ›Optischem Kartenspiel‹ von 1791

1991–2011
Chromatische Konstellation nach einem Experiment von Pawlik + Fessler (zu Goethes Farbenlehre)

1992
Großer Kulturpreis der Sparkassen-Kulturstiftung Rheinland
Austritt aus der Akademie der Künste in Berlin

1998
Farb-Oktett Hommage à Goethe (Suite, bestehend aus acht *Chromatischen Konstellationen)*
Umfangreiche Suite von Papierarbeiten zu Goethes *West-oestlichem Divan*

1999
Künstlerbuch *Mack – Ein Buch der Bilder zum West-östlichen Divan von Johann Wolfgang v. Goethe* zum 250. Geburtstag Goethes

2004
Großes Verdienstkreuz der Bundesrepublik Deutschland

2009
Ehrenring der Stadt Mönchengladbach

2011
Großes Verdienstkreuz mit Stern der Bundesrepublik Deutschland

2012
Preis der Kulturstiftung Dortmund

2014–2017
Große ZERO-Ausstellung im Solomon R. Guggenheim Museum in New York, im Martin-Gropius-Bau in Berlin, im Stedelijk Museum in Amsterdam und im Sakip Sabanci Museum in Istanbul
Präsentation des Skulpturen-Ensembles *The Sky Over Nine Columns* auf der Insel San Giorgio Maggiore in Venedig, anschließend vor dem Sakip Sabanci Museum in Istanbul mit Blick auf den Bosporus, in der Ciudad de las Artes y las Ciencias in Valencia und am Ufer des St. Moritzersees

2015/2018
Pastell und Grafik-Edition mit dem aus Goethes Farbenlehre entlehnten Titel *Taten des Lichts*

2016
Jan-Wellem-Ring der Landeshauptstadt Düsseldorf

2017
Ehrenmitglied der Kunstakademie Düsseldorf
Moses Mendelssohn Medaille

Heinz Mack

1931
8th of March born in Lollar / Hessen

1950–53
Study at the Kunstakademie Düsseldorf, state examination

1953–56
Study of philosophy at the University of Cologne, state examination

1957
Foundation of the avant-garde group ZERO with Otto Piene

1958
Art Prize of the City of Krefeld

1959
Participation in II. Documenta in Kassel

1963
Awarding of the Premio Marzotto, Italy

1964
Participation in Documenta III in Kassel
Pastel drawings *for Mr. Wolfgang v. Goethe* (and *for Mr. Newton)*

1965
1. Prix des arts plastiques, Quatrième Biennale de Paris

1970
Adolf Grimme Recognition Award for the movie *Tele-Mack*
Professorship and teaching assignment in Osaka
Full member of the Akademie der Künste in Berlin
Participation in designing the German Pavillon at the 35. Biennale di Venezia

1971
Recognition Award of the Biennale Cinema (Venice International Film Festival) for the movie *Tele-Mack*

1977
Participation in Documenta 6 in Kassel

1979
1. Prize at the international competition *Licht '79,* Eindhoven

1981
Large sized (3 x 4 m) *Spectrum of Light (Spectrum of Color)* entitled *Hommage à Goethe* on the occasion of the 150th anniversary of Goethe's death in 1982

1987
Order of Merit of North Rhine-Westphalia

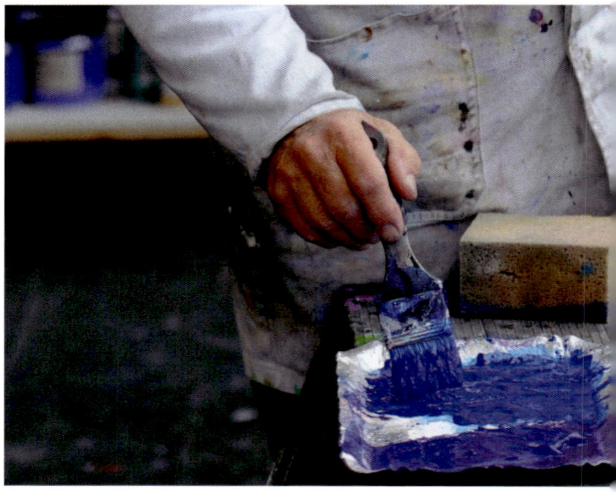

Die Hand des Künstlers, 2018

The artist's hand, 2018

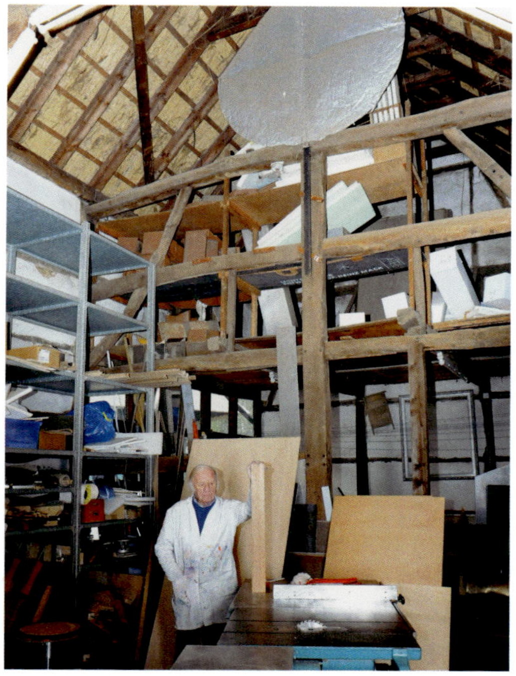

Heinz Mack in seiner Atelier-Werkstatt
in Mönchengladbach, 2018

Heinz Mack in his studio workshop
in Mönchengladbach, 2018

1988
Wax crayon drawing *Gruss an Goethe* (Salute to Goethe)

1991
Two works on paper inspired by Goethe's 'Optical Card Game' of 1791

1991–2011
Chromatic Constellation according to an experiment of Pawlik + Fessler
(after Goethe's Color Theory)

1992
Grand Prize for Culture of the Sparkasse Cultural Foundation of the Rhineland
Resignation from the Akademie der Künste in Berlin

1998
Farb-Oktett Hommage à Goethe (suite of 8 *Chromatic Constellations)*
Extensive suite of paper works inspired by Goethe's *West-East Divan*

1999
Artist's book *Mack—Ein Buch der Bilder zum West-östlichen Divan von Johann Wolfgang v. Goethe,* published on the occasion of Goethe's 250. Birthday

2004
Grand Cross of Merit of the Federal Republic of Germany

2009
Honorary Ring of the City of Mönchengladbach

2011
Grand Cross of Merit with Star of the Federal Republic of Germany

2012
Prize of the Cultural Foundation of the City of Dortmund

2014–17
Major ZERO exhibition at the Solomon R. Guggenheim Museum in New York, also presented at the Martin-Gropius-Bau in Berlin, the Stedelijk Museum in Amsterdam and the Sakip Sabanci Museum in Istanbul
Presentation of the sculpture ensemble *The Sky Over Nine Columns* on the island of San Giorgio Maggiore in Venice, in front of the Sakip Sabanci Museum in Istanbul, at the Ciudad de las Artes y las Ciencias in Valencia and at the shore of the lake in St. Moritz

2015/18
Pastel drawing und graphic edition *Taten des Lichts* (Acts of Light) according to Goethe's *Theory of Colours*

2016
Jan-Wellem-Ring of the Landeshauptstadt Düsseldorf

2017
Honorary Member of the Kunstakademie Düsseldorf
Moses Mendelssohn Medaille

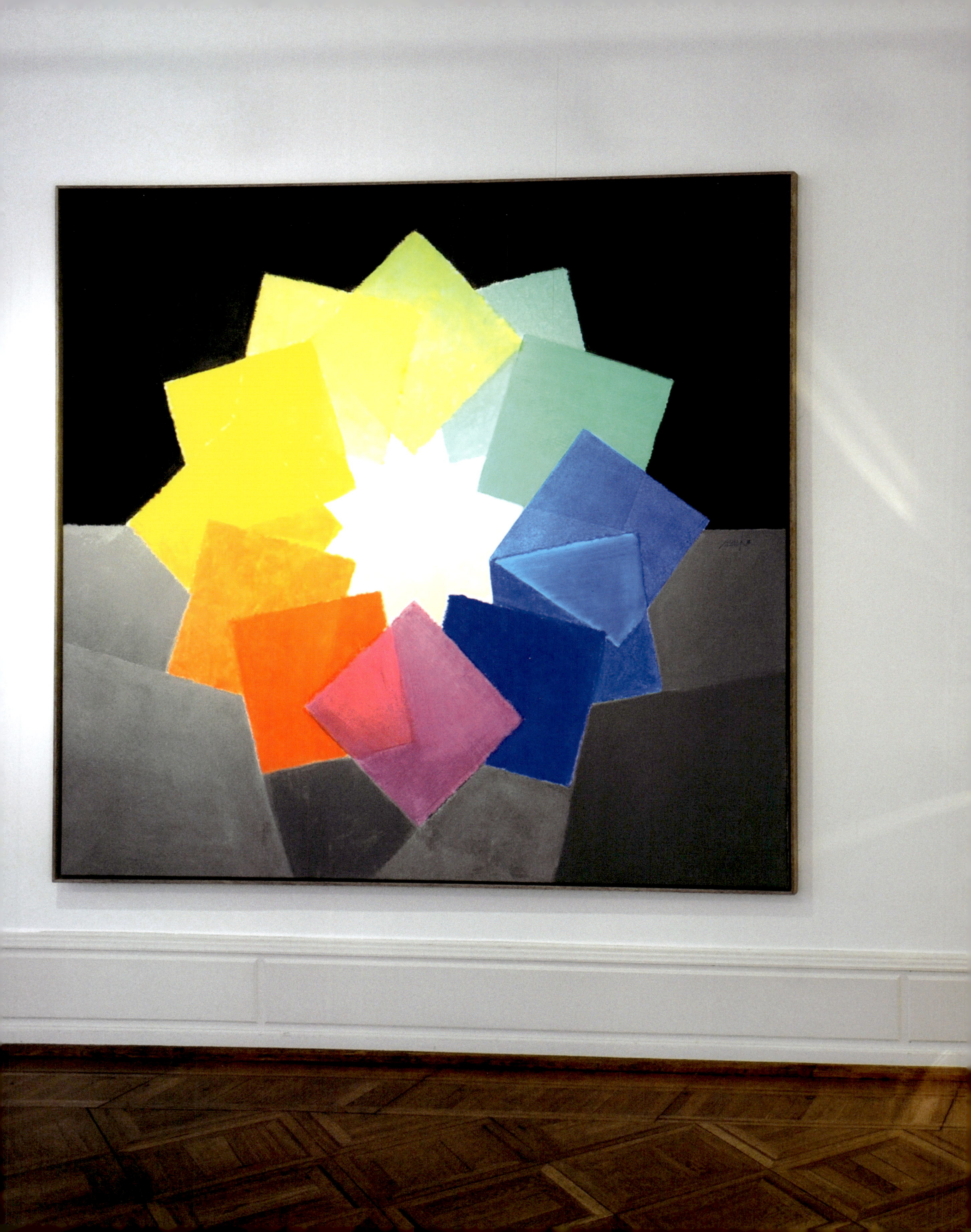

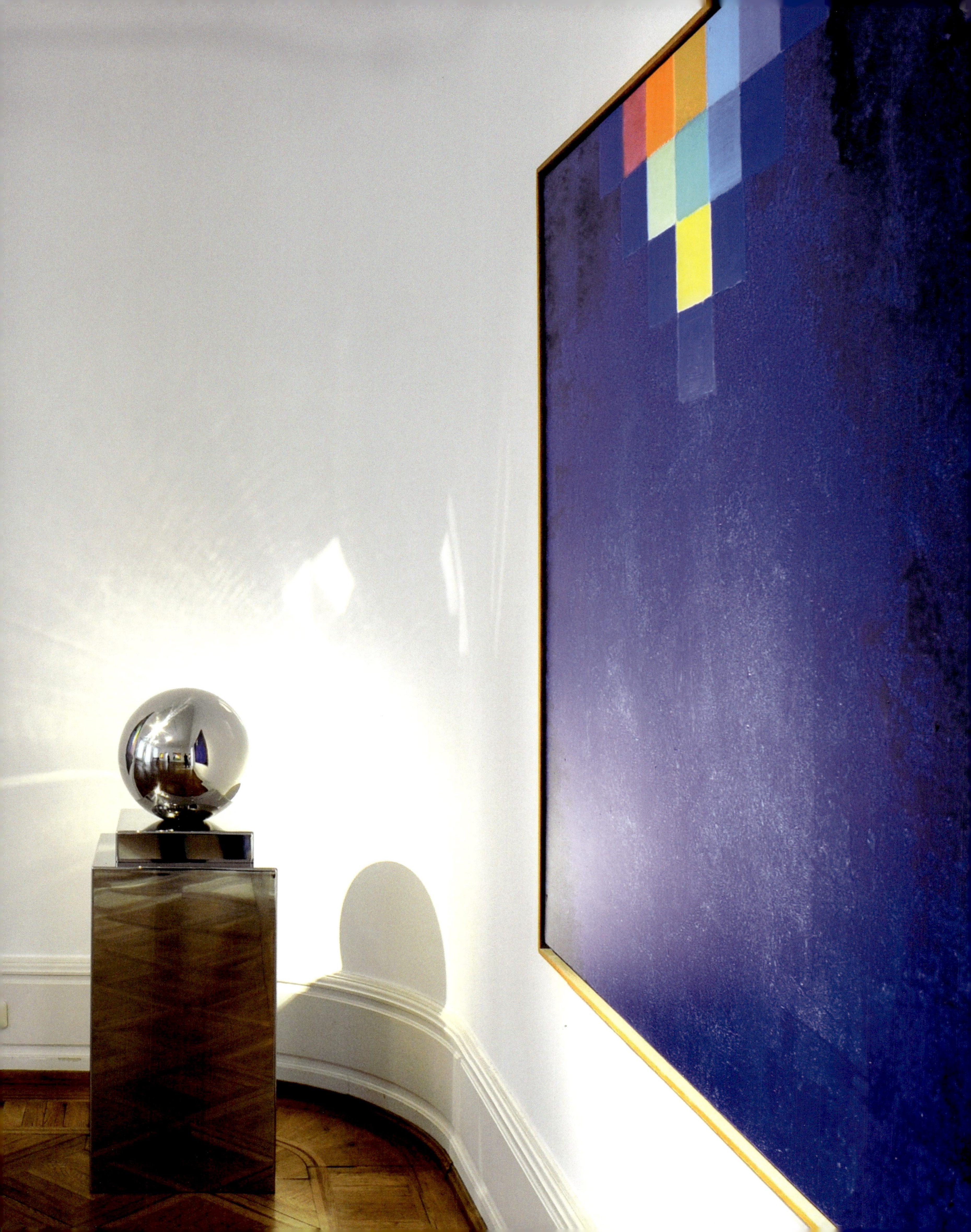

Autoren | Authors

PD Dipl.-Ing. Eckhard Bendin

Studium der Architektur in Weimar; 1970 Mitglied des Verbandes Bildender Künstler bzw. seit 1990 des Sächsischen Künstlerbundes; 1968–1977 Architekt, Bauplastiker und Industriedesigner in Weimar und Erfurt; 1977–1983 Leiter des Büros für architekturbezogene Kunst in Erfurt; 1983–2006 Künstlerischer Oberassistent / Privatdozent für Gestaltungslehre am Institut für Grundlagen der Gestaltung und Darstellung der Fakultät Architektur an der TU Dresden; 1992 Gründer der interdisziplinären Tagungs- und Publikationsreihe *Dresdner Farbenforum*. Seit 2001 Kurator von Ausstellungen zur Geschichte der Farbenlehre; seit 2005 Aufbau und Betreuung der Lehr- und Forschungssammlung Farbenlehre; 2006–2010 Mitglied im Vorstand / Wissenschaftlichen Beirat der Wilhelm-Ostwald-Gesellschaft zu Großbothen; seit 2012 Kuratoriumsmitglied für Farbenlehre im Deutschen Farbenzentrum; 2014–2017 Mitwirkung am BMBF-Verbundforschungsprojekt FARBAKS (Farbe als Akteur und Speicher) – Buchpublikationen (Auswahl): *Zur Farbenlehre. Studien, Modelle, Texte (I), Tafeln (II) und Kreiselscheiben (III)* (2010/11); *Basic Box ›Color Cosmos‹ – 50 Basiselemente zur Farbenlehre* (2014); *Basisexperimente mit Kreiseln* (2014); *Beiträge zur Farbenlehre, Online-Module* (2016); *Farb Wissen I–II–III* (2017); Seit 2014 Herausgabe der *edition bendin* (Beiträge zur Farbe in Wissenschaft, Bildung und Gestaltung).

Studied architecture in Weimar. Since 1970 he has been a member of the Association of Fine Artists and since 1990 the Federation of Saxon Artists. 1968–77: Architect, architectural sculptor, and industrial designer in Weimar and Erfurt. 1977–83: Head of the Office of Applied Architectural Art in Erfurt. 1983–2006: Chief Artistic Assistant / Adjunct Lecturer in Design Theory at the Institute of Foundational Design and Presentation, Faculty of Architecture, at the TU Dresden. 1992: Founded the interdisciplinary convention and publication series *Dresdner Farbenforum*. Since 2001 curator of exhibitions on the history of color theory. Since 2005 responsible for the development and supervision of the teaching and research collection on color theory. 2006–10 Member of the Executive Board / Scientific Advisory Board of the Wilhelm-Ostwald-Gesellschaft of Grossbothen. Since 2012 member of the board of trustees for color theory at the Deutsches Farbenzentrum. 2014–17: Participation in the BMBF joint research project FARBAKS (Colour as agent and knowledge reservoir)—Selected Book Publications: *Zur Farbenlehre. Studien, Modelle, Texte (I), Tafeln (II) und Kreiselscheiben (III)* (2010/11); *Basic Box 'Color Cosmos'—50 Basiselemente zur Farbenlehre* (2014); *Basisexperimente mit Kreiseln* (2014); *Beiträge zur Farbenlehre, Online-Module* (2016); *Farb Wissen I–II–III* (2017). Since 2014 Editor of *edition bendin* (Contributions on colour in science, education and design).

Prof. Dr. Gernot Böhme

Studium der Mathematik, Physik und Philosophie. 1970–1977 Wissenschaftlicher Mitarbeiter des Max-Planck-Instituts zur Erforschung der Lebensbedingungen der wissenschaftlich-technischen Welt, Starnberg; 1977–2002 Professor für Philosophie an der TU Darmstadt; 1997–2001 Sprecher des Graduiertenkollegs Technisierung und Gesellschaft. Seit 2005 Direktor des Instituts für Praxis der Philosophie, Darmstadt. Vorsitzender der Darmstädter Goethe-Gesellschaft. Denkbar-Preis für obliques Denken 2003. – Forschungsschwerpunkte: Klassische Philosophie, besonders Platon und Kant; Wissenschaftsforschung; Theorie der Zeit; Naturphilosophie; Ästhetik; Ethik; Technische Zivilisation; Philosophische Anthropologie; Goethe. – Bücher zur Ästhetik: *Für eine ökologische Naturästhetik* (1989, 2. Aufl. 1993, 3. Aufl. 1999; Übersetzung ins Polnische 2002); *Atmosphäre. Essays zur Neuen Ästhetik* (1995; 3. Aufl. der erweiterten Fassung 2017); *Aisthetik. Vorlesungen über Ästhetik als allgemeine Wahrnehmungslehre* (2001; Übersetzung ins Japanische 2005; Übersetzung ins Italienische 2010); *Atmospheric Architectures. The Aesthetics of Felt Spaces* (2017).

Studied mathematics, physics, and philosophy. 1970–77: Researcher at the Max Planck Institute in Starnberg; researching living conditions in the scientific-technical world. 1977–2002: Professor of Philosophy at the TU Darmstadt. 1997–2001: Spokesman for research training group Technologisation and Society. Since 2005 Director of the Institute for the Practice of Philosophy in Darmstadt. Chairman of the Darmstadt Goethe Society. Winner of the 2003 Denkbar Prize for oblique thought. Research interests: classical philosophy, in particular Plato and Kant; scientific research, theory of time, natural philosophy, aesthetics, ethics, technical civilization, philosophical anthropology, and Goethe.—Books on Aesthetics: *Für eine ökologische Naturästhetik* (1989, 2. ed. 1993, 3. ed. 1999; translated into Polish, 2002); *Atmosphäre. Essays zur Neuen Ästhetik* (1995; 3. ed. of the extended edition 2017); *Aisthetik. Vorlesungen über Ästhetik als allgemeine Wahrnehmungslehre* (2001; translated into Japanese 2005; translated into Italian, 2010); *Atmospheric Architectures. The Aesthetics of Felt Spaces* (2017).

Prof. Dr. Hartmut Böhme

Studium der Germanistik, Theologie, Philosophie und Pädagogik; 1977–1992 Professor für Neuere Deutsche Literaturwissenschaft an der Universität Hamburg; 1993–2012 Professor für Kulturtheorie und Mentalitätsgeschichte an der HU Berlin; Gastprofessuren in den USA, Italien und Japan; Fellow am KWI Essen, IKKM Weimar, IFK Wien. 2000–2002 Dekan der Philosophischen Fakultät III der HU Berlin. Leiter von DFG-Forschungsprojekten; Sprecher des Sonderforschungsbereichs Transformationen der Antike (bis 2012); Meyer-Struckmann-Preis 2006 und Hans-Kilian-Preis 2011. Beirat der Stiftung Bauhaus Dessau 2006–2012. Mitglied im Beirat bzw. Vorstand des Forschungskollegs Morphomata (Köln), der Aby-Warburg-Stiftung, des Neuen Berliner Kunstvereins, des KWI Essen. – Letzte Buchveröffentlichungen: *Der anatomische Akt. Zur Bildgeschichte und Psychohistorie der frühneuzeit-lichen Anatomie* (2012); *Fetishism and Culture. A different Theory of Modernity*

(2014); (mit Bernd Kordaß und Beate Slominski:) *Das Dentale. Faszination des oralen Systems in Wissenschaft und Kultur* (2015); (mit Werner Röcke und U. C. A. Stephan:) *Contingentia. Transformationen des Zufalls* (2015); *Natur und Figur. Goethe im Kontext* (2016); *Aussichten der Natur* (2016).

Studied German language and literature, theology, philosophy, and pedagogy. 1977–92: Professor of German Literary Studies at the University of Hamburg. 1993–2012: Professor of Cultural Theory and the History of Mentalities at HU Berlin; visiting professor in the USA, Italy and Japan. Fellow of KWI Essen, IKKM Weimar and IFK Vienna. 2000–02: Dean of the Faculty of Philosophy at the HU, Berlin. Leader of DFG research projects; until 2012 spokesman of the collaborative research centre Transformations of Antiquity. Meyer-Struckmann Award 2006 and Hans Kilian Award 2011. 2006–12: Advisory board member of the Dessau Bauhaus Foundation. Member of the advisory or management board of the research collegia Morphomata (Cologne), the Aby Warburg Foundation, the Neuer Berliner Kunstverein, and the KWI Essen. Most recent Book Publications: *Der anatomische Akt. Zur Bildgeschichte und Psychohistorie der frühneuzeitlichen Anatomie* (2012); *Fetishism and Culture. A different Theory of Modernity* (2014); (with Bernd Kordass and Beate Slominski:) *Das Dentale. Faszination des oralen Systems in Wissenschaft und Kultur* (2015); (with Werner Röcke and U. C. A. Stephan:) *Contingentia. Transformationen des Zufalls* (2015); *Natur und Figur. Goethe im Kontext* (2016); *Aussichten der Natur* (2016).

Univ.-Prof. Dr. Anke Bosse
Universitätsprofessorin für Neuere deutschsprachige Literatur und Leiterin des Musil-Instituts für Literaturforschung / Kärntner Literaturarchivs an der Alpen-Adria-Universität Klagenfurt. – Studium der Germanistik, Romanistik und Komparatistik in Göttingen, Avignon und München; wissenschaftliche Mitarbeiterin an der LMU München, Assistentin an der Universität Genf; 1997–2015 Professorin, ab 2008 Ordinaria an der Universität Namur. – Buchpublikationen (Auswahl): *»Meine Schatzkammer füllt sich täglich …« – Die Nachlaßstücke zu Goethes ›West-östlichem Divan‹. Dokumentation. Kommentar.* 2 Bde. (1999); *Spuren, Signaturen, Spiegelungen. Zur Goethe-Rezeption in Europa* (hrsg. mit Bernhard Beutler, 2000); *Plurimedialität. Theaterformen der Moderne und der Avantgarden in Europa* (hrsg., 2011). Publikationen und Forschungen zur Editionsphilologie und ›critique génétique‹ sowie zum literarischen Schreiben, zur Literatur der Goethezeit, der Jahrhundertwende (1900) und der Gegenwartsliteratur, zu Intertextualität, Interkulturalität und Intermedialität sowie zur Medialität von Literatur und zu den Digital Humanities.

University Professor of Modern Germanspeaking Literature and Head of the Musil Institute for Literary Research / Carinthian Literary Archives at the University of Klagenfurt. Studied German Studies, Romance Studies and Comparative Literature in Göttingen, Avignon, and Munich. Research Assistant at LMU Munich, Academic Assistant at the University of Geneva. 1997–2015 Professor and since 2008 Chair at the University of Namur. Selected Book Publications: *"Meine Schatzkammer füllt sich täglich …"—Die Nachlassstücke zu*

Goethes 'West-östlichem Divan'. Dokumentation. Kommentar. 2 vol. (1999); *Spuren, Signaturen, Spiegelungen. Zur Goethe-Rezeption in Europa* (pub. with Bernhard Beutler, 2000); *Plurimedialität. Theaterformen der Moderne und der Avantgarden in Europa* (ed., 2011). Publications and Research in Scholarly Editing, 'critique génétique' and Literary Writing Processes, about Literature of the Goethe Period, Literature of the Turn of the Century (1900) and Contemporary Literature, about intertextuality, interculturality and intermediality, about the materiality and mediality of literature and in Digital Humanities.

Prof. Dr. Dr. Christoph Cremer
Studium der Physik an der LMU München. Promotion in Biophysik (Dr. rer. nat.) an der Universität Freiburg. Mehrere Jahre an der University of California; Habilitation an der Medizinischen Fakultät der Universität Freiburg (Dr. med. habil. für Allgemeine Humangenetik und Experimentelle Cytogenetik). Seit 1983 Professor für Angewandte Optik und Informationsverarbeitung an der Universität Heidelberg. 2006–2009 Zweiter Sprecher des Senats der Universität Heidelberg. Seit 2011 Leiter der Arbeitsgruppe Superauflösende Mikroskopie am Institut für Molekulare Biologie, Mainz. Seit 2013 Honorarprofessor (Physik) an der Universität Mainz; seit 2015 Research Associate am Max Planck Institut für Chemie, Mainz. Seit den 1970er-Jahren Entwicklung von lichtoptischen Mikroskopiemethoden für biophysikalische Anwendungen, insbesondere von superauflösenden Verfahren.

Studied physics at LMU Munich and gained a PhD in biophysics (Dr. rer. nat) at the University of Freiburg, where he habilitated in the Faculty of Medicine (Dr. med. habil. for general human genetics and experimental cytogenetics). Several years at the University of California. Since 1983 Professor for Applied Optics and Information Processing at the University of Heidelberg. 2006–09 Second Speaker of Heidelberg University Senate. Since 2011 leader of the working group Superresolution Microscopy at the Institute for Molecular Biology, Mainz. Since 2013 Honorary Professor of Physics at the University of Mainz. Since 2015 Research Associate at the Max Planck Institute for Chemistry, Mainz. Beginning in the 1970s, he has developed methods for biophysical applications of light optical microscopy and in particular for superresolution processes.

Dr. Stephan Geiger
Studium der Kunstgeschichte, Philosophie und Klassischen Archäologie in Bonn. Magisterarbeit über Konrad Fiedlers Konzeption der Kunstgeschichte. Forschungsaufenthalte in New York. Dissertation über die MoMA-Ausstellung *The Art of Assemblage* von 1961. Seit 1996 Kunsthistorischer Leiter der Galerie Geiger in Konstanz sowie Tätigkeit als freier Kurator. Seit 2012 Lehrauftrag an der Universität Konstanz. Autor belletristischer Texte sowie zahlreicher Veröffentlichungen zur Kunst des 20. und 21. Jahrhunderts, unter anderem über Heinz Mack, Christian Megert, Daniel Spoerri, herman de vries und die internationale ZERO-Bewegung.

Studied history of art, philosophy, and classical archeology in Bonn. Master's thesis on Konrad Fiedler's concept of art history. Research residency in New York. PhD thesis about the 1961 MoMA exhibition *The Art of Assemblage*. Since 1996 director of art history at the Gallery Geiger in Konstanz as well as freelance curator. Since 2012 associate lecturer at the University of Konstanz. Author of belletristic texts as well as numerous publications on 20th and 21st century art, including on Heinz Mack, Christian Megert, Daniel Spoerri, herman de vries, and the international ZERO movement.

Prof. Dr. Johannes Grebe-Ellis
Nach einer Ausbildung zum Möbeltischler Studium der Physik und Philosophie in Tübingen. Promotion 2005 über Phänomenologie der optischen Polarisation an der HU Berlin. Mehrjährige Tätigkeit als Physik- und Mathematiklehrer. 2008–2011 Professur für Physikdidaktik an der Leuphana-Universität Lüneburg. Seit 2011 Professor für Physik und ihre Didaktik an der Bergischen Universität Wuppertal. Seit 2015 Leiter des Fachverbands Didaktik der Physik bei der DPG.

After a cabinet maker's apprenticeship studied physics and philosophy in Tübingen. Received a PhD in 2005 from the HU Berlin with a thesis on the phenomenological approach to optical polarization. Worked for several years as a physics and math teacher. 2008–2011: Professor of Phenomenology and Science Education at the Leuphana University of Lüneburg. Since 2011 Professor for Physics and Physics Education at the University of Wuppertal. Since 2015 head of the Division for Physics Education in the German Physical Society.

Dr. Veit Loers
Autor, Kurator und Kunsthistoriker. 1987–1995 Direktor des Fridericianum in Kassel; 1995–2003 Direktor des Museums Abteiberg Mönchengladbach; Kurator der Bundesrepublik Deutschland für die Sammlung zeitgenössischer Kunst. 2010–2012 Leiter des Kunstraums Innsbruck. Kurator von Ausstellungen zu Schlüsselfiguren der Kunst des 20. und 21. Jahrhunderts wie Pierre Soulages, Joseph Beuys, Isa Genzken, Martin Kippenberger, Franz West, Günther Förg, Jeff Koons und jüngeren namhaften Künstlerinnen und Künstlern. 1995 Kurator der Ausstellung *Okkultismus und Avantgarde, 1905–1915* für die Schirn Kunsthalle Frankfurt am Main. Lebt und arbeitet seit 2003 in Italien.

Author, curator, and art historian. 1987–95: Director of the Fridericianum in Kassel. 1995–2003 Director of the Abteiberg Museum, Mönchengladbach. Curator of the Federal Republic of Germany's contemporary art collection. 2010–12: Head of the Kunstraum Innsbruck. Curator of exhibitions on key figures in 20th and 21st century art such as Pierre Soulages, Joseph Beuys, Isa Genzken, Martin Kippenberger, Franz West, Günther Förg, Jeff Koons, and younger well-known artists. 1995: Curator of the exhibition *Occultism and Avantgarde 1905–1915* for the Schirn Kunsthalle, Frankfurt am Main. Since 2003 he has been living and working in Italy.

Dr. Oliver Passon

Studium der Physik, Mathematik, Philosophie und Erziehungswissenschaften an der Bergischen Universität Wuppertal. 2002 Promotion in experimenteller Elementarteilchenphysik am Europäischen Labor für Hochenergiephysik (CERN). 2004–2007 Wissenschaftlicher Mitarbeiter am Forschungszentrum Jülich im Zentralinstitut für Angewandte Mathematik. Danach Lehrer für Physik und Mathematik. Seit 2013 Akademischer Rat in der AG Physik und ihre Didaktik der Universität Wuppertal.

Studied physics, mathematics, philosophy, and educational theory at the University of Wuppertal. 2002 PhD in experimental elementary particle physics at the European High Energy Physics Laboratory (CERN). 2004–07: Research Assistant at the Central Institute of Applied Mathematics's Jülich Research Centre. Thereafter physics and math teacher. Since 2013 Academic Advisor to the Physics and Physics Education Society at the University of Wuppertal.

Dr. Barbara Steingießer

Studium der Germanistik, Philosophie und Kunstgeschichte in Bonn. Parallel dazu: zweiter Magisterstudiengang mit Kunstgeschichte als Hauptfach. 1994 Stipendium der Stiftung Weimarer Klassik. 1994–2003 Mitarbeiterin der historisch-kritischen Schiller-Nationalausgabe. Autorin des Bandes, der die Briefedition der Ausgabe abschließt. Promotion. Seit 2004 freie Autorin, Kuratorin und Kulturjournalistin in Wort und Bild. Zahlreiche Interviews, Texte und Fotos zu Themen der bildenden Kunst, Literatur und Musik im Feuilleton der Rheinischen Post sowie wissenschaftliche Beiträge in Büchern und Fachzeitschriften. Seit 2014 künstlerische Leiterin der von ihr ins Leben gerufenen Konzertreihe *Jazz im Goethe-Museum*. 2015 dort Kuratorin der Kunstausstellung *Summertime*. 2017 Einzelausstellung ihrer fotografischen Musikerporträts im Wilhelm-Fabry-Museum Hilden. 2018 Initiatorin und Kuratorin der Sonderausstellung *Taten des Lichts – Mack & Goethe* im Goethe-Museum Düsseldorf.

Studied German language and literature, philosophy, and history of art in Bonn. Simultaneously studied for a Masters in history of art. 1994: Fellowship of the Stiftung Weimarer Klassik. 1994–2003 worked on the *Schiller National Edition,* the oldest historical-critical edition of Friedrich Schiller's complete works. Author of the volume of letters which colcludes the edition. Awarded a PhD. Since 2004 freelance author, curator and both journalist & photojournalist. Numerous interviews, articles and photos on the fine arts, literature, and music in the Feuilleton section of the Rheinische Post as well as scientific contributions in books and journals. Since 2014 artistic director of the concert series she founded, *Jazz at the Goethe-Museum*. 2015: Curator of the art exhibition *Summertime* at the Goethe-Museum Düsseldorf. 2017: Solo exhibition of her photographic portraits of musicians at the Wilhelm-Fabry-Museum, Hilden. 2018: Initiator and curator of the special exhibition *Acts of Light—Mack & Goethe* at the Goethe-Museum Düsseldorf.

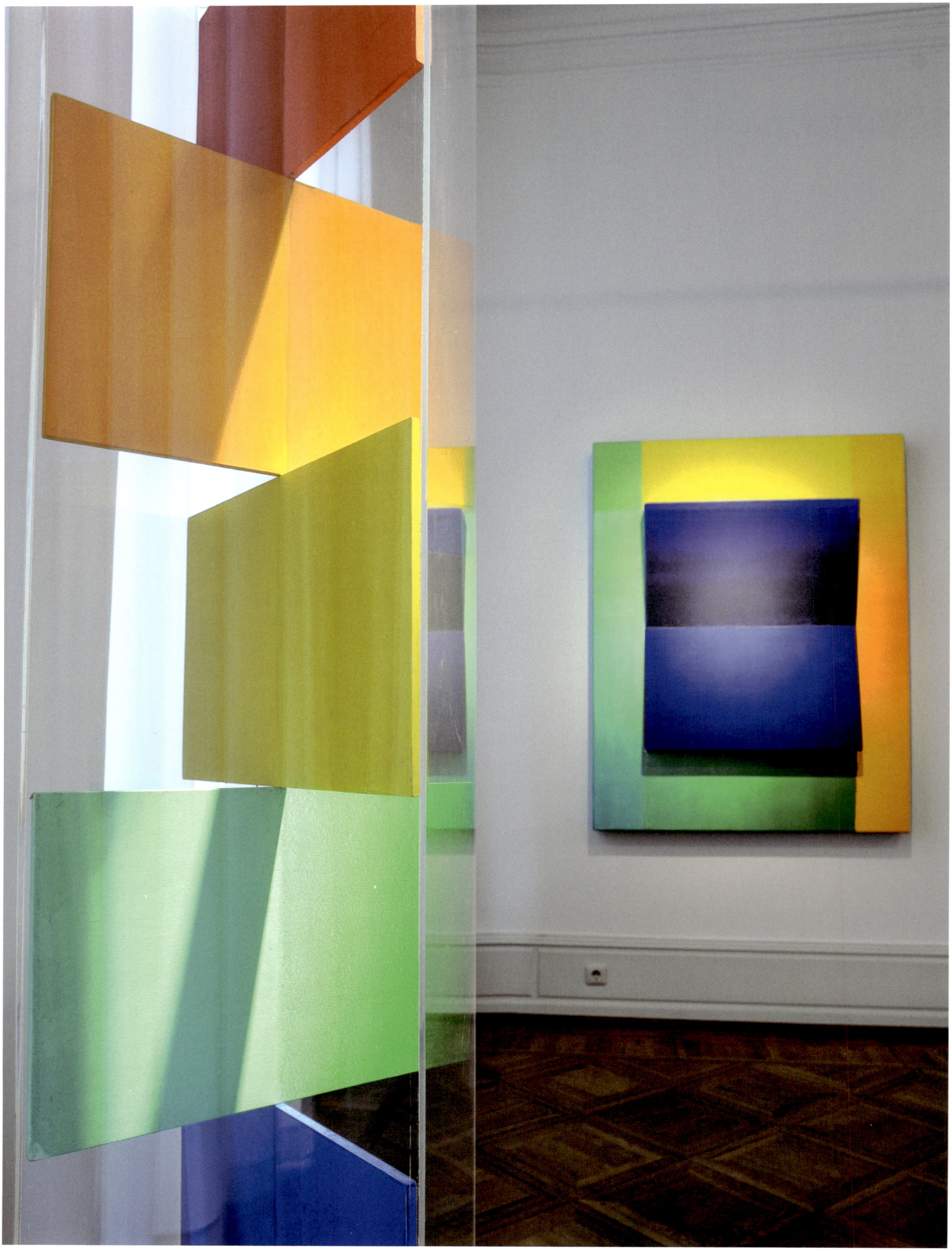

Siglen und Abkürzungen der zitierten Goethe-Ausgaben

Corpus:
Corpus der Goethezeichnungen, hrsg. von den Nationalen Forschungs- und Gedenkstätten der klassischen deutschen Literatur in Weimar, bearb. von Gerhard Femmel u. a., 7 Bde. (in 10), Leipzig 1958–1973.

FA:
Johann Wolfgang Goethe, *Sämtliche Werke.* Briefe, Tagebücher und Gespräche, 40 Bde. (in 45), hrsg. von Friedmar Apel u. a., Frankfurt a. M. und Berlin 1987–2013 [Frankfurter Ausgabe].

GT:
Johann Wolfgang Goethe, *Tagebücher,* historisch-kritische Ausgabe, im Auftrag der Klassik Stiftung Weimar hrsg. von Jochen Golz unter Mitarbeit von Wolfgang Albrecht u. a., ab Bd. 6: im Auftrag der Klassik Stiftung Weimar hrsg. vom Goethe- und Schiller-Archiv, Bd. 1 ff., Stuttgart und Weimar 1998 ff.

HA:
Goethes Werke, Hamburger Ausgabe, 14 Bde., hrsg. von Erich Trunz, 16., durchgesehene Aufl., München 1996.

LA:
Goethe, *Die Schriften zur Naturwissenschaft,* vollständige mit Erläuterungen versehene Ausgabe, im Auftrage der Deutschen Akademie der Naturforscher Leopoldina, begr. von Lothar Wolf und Wilhelm Troll, hrsg. von Wolf von Engelhardt u. a., 21 Bde. (in 31), Weimar 1959 ff. [Leopoldina-Ausgabe].

MA:
Johann Wolfgang Goethe, *Sämtliche Werke* nach Epochen seines Schaffens, Münchner Ausgabe, 21 Bde. (in 33), hrsg. von Karl Richter in Zusammenarbeit mit Herbert G. Göpfert u. a., München 1985–1998.

WA:
Goethes Werke, hrsg. im Auftrage der Großherzogin Sophie von Sachsen, 143 Bde., Weimar 1887–1919, Nachdruck München 1987, Bd. 144–146: Nachträge und Register zur IV. Abt.: Briefe, hrsg. von Paul Raabe, München 1990 [Weimarer Ausgabe].

Nachweis der nicht in den Anmerkungen verzeichneten Zitate

»Bedeutend hab' ich […]«
Johann Wolfgang von Goethe, *Zur Naturwissenschaft. Gebirgs-Gestaltung im Ganzen und Einzelnen* (WA, Bd. II 9, S. [241]–252, hier: S. 246).

»Bei allen ›Lichtfarben‹ […]«
Heinz Mack, »Mein Standort im Reich der Farbe«, in: *Mack. Skulpturen und Malerei,* hrsg. von Harro Lauter, Ausst.-Kat. Galerie Lauter Mannheim, Mönchengladbach 1992, S. 61–65, hier: S. 63.

»Das korrespondiert mit […]«
Heinz Mack, in: Marcus Woeller: »Im Königreich des Lichts«, in: *Welt am Sonntag,* 16. Dezember 2012, S. 60.

»Des echten Künstlers […]«
Johann Wolfgang von Goethe, *Wilhelm Meisters Lehrjahre* (WA, Bd. I 23, S. 125).

»[…] ich als Künstler […]«
Heinz Mack, in: Yvonne Schwarzer, *Das Paradies auf Erden schon zu Lebzeiten betreten. Ein Gespräch mit dem Maler und Bildhauer Heinz Mack (Kunstportrait),* Witten 2005, S. 21–22.

»Jede Farbe also […]«
Johann Wolfgang von Goethe, *Zur Farbenlehre,* Bd. 1, Tübingen 1810 [Faksimile des didaktischen Teils, 2. Aufl., Dortmund 1982], § 583, S. 216 f.

»Meine wiederholten Begegnungen […]«
Karin Adrian von Roques, »Wahaj al Sahara. Im Licht der Wüste«, in: dies. u. a., *Heinz Mack. Wahaj al Sahara. Im Licht der Wüste,* Ausst.-Kat. BFH Fine Art Gallery, Manama, Bahrein, Düsseldorf 2011, S. 12–15, hier: S. 12.

»Mit leisem Gewicht […]«
Johann Wolfgang von Goethe, *Zur Farbenlehre,* Bd. 1, Tübingen 1810 [Faksimile des didaktischen Teils, 2. Aufl., Dortmund 1982], Vorwort, S. XI–XII.

»Schon im vorigen […]«
Johann Wolfgang von Goethe, *Tag- und Jahres-Hefte.* 1815 (WA, Bd. I 36, S. 91).

»So sehr auch […]«
Heinz Mack, »Reflexionen«, in: *Mack. Licht im Schwarz,* hrsg. von Hubertus Schoeller, Ausst.-Kat. Galerie Schoeller, Düsseldorf, Mönchengladbach 2001, S. 16–17, hier: S. 16.

»Wie wir nun […]«
Johann Wolfgang von Goethe, *Beyträge zur Optik,* Bd. 1, Weimar 1791 [Faksimile, Weimar 2007], § 29, S. 17–18.

Die Ausstellung wird ermöglicht durch:

NATIONAL-BANK
Mehr. Wert. Erfahren.

LVR
Qualität für Menschen

KUNST STIFTUNG NRW

AUNDE Group

Hauspartner:

Prof. Otto Beisheim Stiftung

Impressum

Diese Publikation erscheint anlässlich der Ausstellung / This book is published in conjunction with the exhibition
Taten des Lichts – Mack & Goethe

Goethe-Museum Düsseldorf /
Anton-und-Katharina-Kippenberg-Stiftung
4. März bis 30. September 2018 /
4 March to 30 September, 2018

Katalog
Herausgeber / Editor
Barbara Steingießer

Redaktion / Managing editor
Barbara Steingießer

Lektorat / Copyediting
Barbara Steingießer (Deutsch) /
Rebecca van Dyck, Ben Barlow (English)

Exponatbeschreibungen /
Descriptions of the exhibits
Barbara Steingießer, Christof Wingertszahn

Übersetzungen / Translations
Daniel Kletke, Troy Vine, Joseph Russo,
Roswitha Burwick, Frederick Burwick

Grafische Gestaltung / Graphic design
Saskia Helena Kruse, www.rangnamen.de

Schrift / Typeface
Futura

Herstellung / Production
Heidrun Zimmermann, Hatje Cantz

Reproduktionen / Reproductions
Repromayer, Reutlingen

Papier / Paper
heaven 42, 150 g/m²

Druck / Printing
Offsetdruckerei Karl Grammlich GmbH, Pliezhausen

Buchbinderei / Binding
Josef Spinner Großbuchbinderei GmbH, Ottersweier

Erschienen im / Published by
Hatje Cantz Verlag
Mommsenstr. 27
10629 Berlin
Deutschland / Germany
Tel. +49 30 3464678-00
Fax +49 30 3289042-48
www.hatjecantz.com
Ein Unternehmen der Ganske Verlagsgruppe
A Ganske Publishing Group company

Hatje Cantz books are available internationally at selected bookstores. For more information about our distribution partners, please visit our website at www.hatjecantz.com.

ISBN 978-3-7757-4407-2

Printed in Germany

Umschlagabbildung / Cover illustration
Vorderseite / Front
Heinz Mack, ohne Titel – nach einer Vorlage von Goethe, 1991, 76,5 x 111 cm, Pastell auf Bütten

Rückseite / Back
Heinz Mack, ohne Titel – nach einer Vorlage von Goethe, 1991, 111 x 76,5 cm, Pastell auf Bütten

Umschlagentwurf / Cover design
Barbara Steingießer

Vignette auf S. 480 / p. 480:
Heinz Mack
Farbturm, 2018
Edelstahl, Textilmaterial
900 x 104 x 30,5 cm

Heinz Mack
Color Tower, 2018
Stainless steel, fabric
900 x 104 x 30.5 cm

Ausstellung / Exhibition
Goethe-Museum Düsseldorf / Anton-und-Katharina-Kippenberg-Stiftung

Direktor / Director
Christof Wingertszahn

Idee und Konzept / Idea and conception
Barbara Steingießer

Kuratorin / Curator
Barbara Steingießer

Organisation / Organization
Christof Wingertszahn

Vorbereitung / Preparation
Barbara Steingießer, Heinz und / and Ute Mack, Bettina Weiand

Ausstellungsmodell / Exhibition model
Barbara Steingießer

Ausstellungsaufbau / Exhibition installation
Sansoni Art Installation, Team Goethe-Museum

Fotonachweis / Photo Credits
Thomas Höpker: S. / p. 29
Marion Nickig: S. / pp. 37, 61, 268, 458
Arno Rickert: S. / p. 66
Barbara Steingießer: S. / pp. 21, 68, 118 f., 120 f., 168 f., 170 f., 172 f., 194, 206, 211, 218, 219, 223, 238, 239, 240, 247, 305, 454 f., 462 f., 464, 465, 466, 467, 468 f., 476, 480
Archiv Mack / Mack Archive: alle übrigen, Heinz Mack und seine Kunstwerke betreffenden Fotos / all other photos, showing Heinz Mack and his art works
Die Fotos der Leihgaben wurden von den genannten Leihgebern zu Verfügung gestellt / The photographs of the loans were provided by the lenders

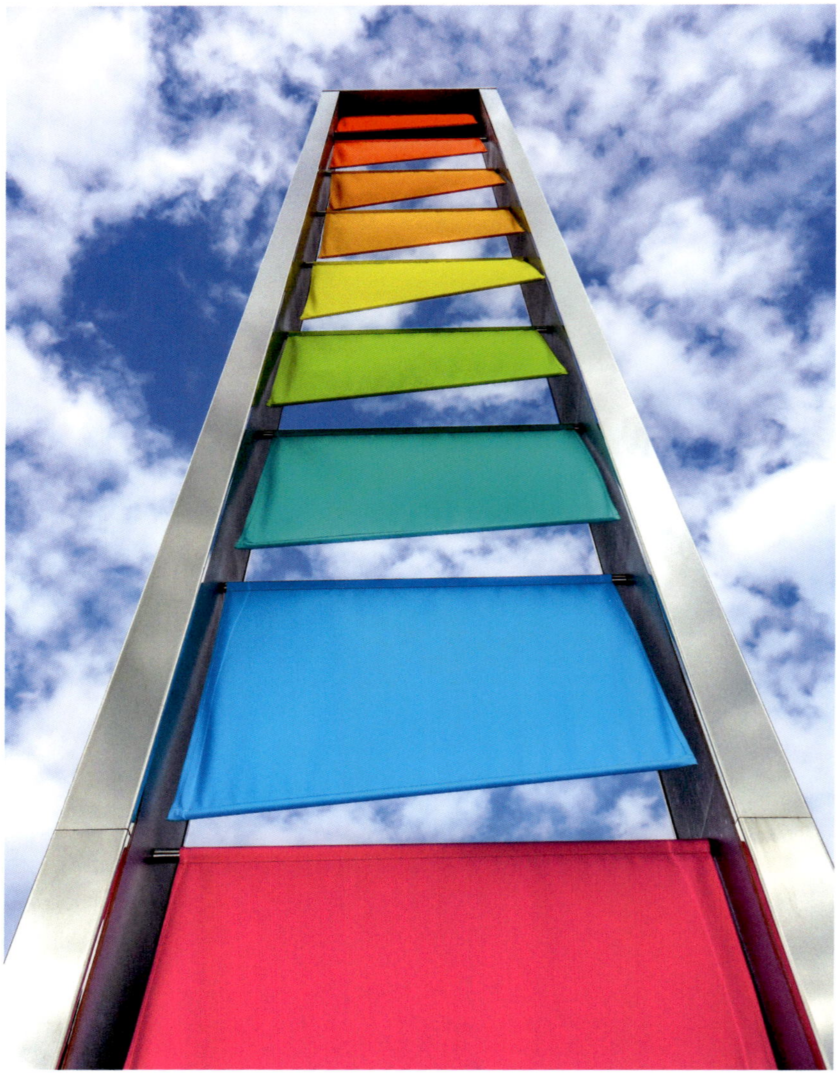